CORPORATE STRATEGY

Third Edition

Richard Lynch

FT Prentice Hall
FINANCIAL TIMES

An imprint of **Pearson Education**
Harlow, England • London • New York • Boston • San Francisco • Toronto • Sydney • Singapore • Hong Kong
Tokyo • Seoul • Taipei • New Delhi • Cape Town • Madrid • Mexico City • Amsterdam • Munich • Paris • Milan

Pearson Education Limited

Edinburgh Gate
Harlow
Essex CM20 2JE

and Associated Companies throughout the world

Visit us on the World Wide Web at:
www.pearsoneduc.com

First published 1997
Third edition published 2003

ISBN 0 273 65854 9

British Library Cataloguing-in-Publication Data
A catalogue record for this book is available from the British Library

10 9 8 7 6 5 4 3 2 1
07 06 05 04 03

Typeset in 9/12 pt Stone Serif by 68
Printed and bound by Rotolito Lombarda, Italy

Ex umbris et imaginibus in veritatem.
From shadows and imagination to the truth.

JOHN HENRY NEWMAN

Contents

List of case studies   xv
About this book   xvii
How to use this book   xxii
Guided tour of this book   xxiv
Acknowledgements   xxvii
Publisher's Acknowledgements   xxx

Part 1 Introduction   1

1 Corporate strategy   4
2 A review of theory and practice   37

Part 2 Analysis of the environment   81

3 Analysing the environment – basics   84
4 Analysing markets and competitors   123
5 Analysing customers   158

Part 3 Analysis of resources   197

6 Analysing resources – basics   200
7 Analysing human resources   249
8 Analysing financial resources   283
9 Analysing operations resources   319

Part 4 The purpose of the organisation   351

10 Purpose shaped by vision, leadership and ethics   354
11 Purpose emerging from knowledge, technology and innovation   386
12 Purpose delivered through mission and objectives   422

Part 5 Developing the strategy   457

13 Developing strategic options: the prescriptive process   460
14 Strategy evaluation and development: the prescriptive process   507
15 Finding the strategic route forward: emergent and
   prescriptive approaches   550
16 Strategy, structure and style   592

Part 6 The implementation process   625

17 Resource allocation, strategic planning and control   628
18 Organisational structure and people issues   663
19 International expansion and globalisation strategies   689
20 The dynamics of strategy development   734
21 Managing strategic change   760
22 Building a cohesive corporate strategy   795

Glossary   817
Indexes   825

Full contents

List of case studies   xv
About this book   xvii
How to use this book   xxii
Guided tour of this book   xxiv
Acknowledgements   xxvii
Publisher's Acknowledgements   xxx

Part 1 Introduction

1 Corporate strategy   4

Introduction   5
Case study 1.1   5
1.1 What is corporate strategy?   6
Case study 1.2   12
1.2 Core areas of corporate strategy   15
1.3 Process, content and context   17
1.4 Process: linking the three core areas   18
1.5 What makes 'good' strategy?   23
1.6 Strategy development in public and
    non-profit organisations   25
1.7 International dimensions in corporate
    strategy   26
Case study 1.3   27
Key reading   32
Summary   33
Questions   34
Strategic project   34
Further reading   35
Notes and references   35

2 A review of theory and practice   37

Introduction   37
Case study 2.1   38
2.1 Historical context of strategy   39
2.2 Prescriptive corporate strategy in practice   43
Case study 2.2   46
Case study 2.3   48
2.3 Emergent corporate strategy in practice   49
Case study 2.4   52
2.4 Prescriptive theories of corporate strategy   53
2.5 Emergent theories of corporate strategy   59
Case study 2.5   66
2.6 Strategy as history – the contributions of
    Penrose and Chandler   68

Case study 2.6   69
Key reading   72
Summary   74
Questions   75
Strategic project   75
Further reading   76
Notes and references   76

Part 2 Analysis of the environment

3 Analysing the environment – basics   84

Introduction   84
Case study 3.1   85
3.1 Exploring the environment   87
3.2 Consideration of the degree of
    turbulence in the environment   90
3.3 Analysing the general environment   92
3.4 Analysing the rate of market growth   94
Case study 3.2   97
Case study 3.3   99
3.5 Key factors for success in an industry   102
3.6 Analysing the competitive industry
    environment – the contribution of Porter   103
3.7 Analysing the co-operative environment   109
3.8 Analysing one or more immediate
    competitors in depth   113
3.9 Analysing the customer and
    market segmentation   115
3.10 Conclusions   116
Case study 3.4   117
Key reading   118
Summary   119
Questions   120
Strategic project   121
Further reading   121
Notes and references   121

4 Analysing markets and competitors   123

Introduction   124
Case study 4.1   124
4.1 Sustainable competitive advantage   125
4.2 Dynamics of competitve advantage   129
Case study 4.2   131

4.3	The intensity of competition in an industry	132
4.4	Aggressive competitive strategies	134
4.5	Analysing an organisation's range of competing products and services	139
4.6	Distributor analysis	145
	Case study 4.3	146
4.7	Analysing the role of government	147
	Case study 4.4	151
4.8	Analysing international competitors	152
	Key reading	153
	Summary	154
	Questions	156
	Strategic project	156
	Further reading	156
	Notes and references	157

5 Analysing customers 158

	Introduction	159
	Case study 5.1	159
5.1	Customers and customer-driven strategy – the contribution of Theodore Levitt	162
5.2	Customer profiling and sustainable competitive advantage	165
5.3	Market segmentation	170
	Case study 5.2	172
5.4	Competitive positioning	174
5.5	Strategy implications: analysing branding and reputation	176
5.6	Strategy implications: communicating with customers and stakeholders	179
5.7	Strategy implications: strategic pricing and value for money	181
5.8	International customer considerations	186
	Case study 5.3	187
	Key reading	191
	Summary	192
	Questions	194
	Strategic project	194
	Further reading	195
	Notes and references	195

Part 3 Analysis of resources

6 Analysing resources – basics 200

	Introduction	200
	Case study 6.1	201

6.1	Prescriptive and emergent approaches to resource issues	203
6.2	Key factors for success in an industry	204
6.3	Analysing the resources of an *individual* organisation	207
	Case study 6.2	210
6.4	Resource analysis and adding value	212
6.5	Adding competitive value: the value chain and the value system – the contribution of Porter	216
6.6	Resource analysis and economic rent – the contribution of David Ricardo	222
6.7	Resource analysis and competitive advantage – the resource-based view	226
6.8	Identifying which resources deliver sustainable competitive advantage	232
6.9	Resource analysis – improving competitive advantage	239
	Case study 6.3	242
	Key reading	244
	Summary	245
	Questions	246
	Strategic project	247
	Further reading	247
	Notes and references	247

7 Analysing human resources 249

	Introduction	250
	Case study 7.1	250
7.1	Human resource analysis and corporate strategy	253
7.2	Human resource audit	255
7.3	Analysis of organisational culture	257
	Case study 7.2	263
7.4	Analysis of strategic change in organisations	265
7.5	Analysis of politics, power and strategic change	270
7.6	International cultural perspectives	272
	Case study 7.3	274
	Case study 7.4	276
	Key reading	279
	Summary	279
	Questions	280
	Strategic project	281
	Further reading	281
	Notes and references	281

8   Analysing financial resources   283

   Introduction   284
   Case study 8.1   284
8.1 Analysing the sources of finance   287
   Case study 8.2   290
8.2 Cost of funds and the optimal capital
   structure   294
8.3 Financial appraisal of strategy
   proposals   296
8.4 Financial management and
   added value: maximising
   shareholder wealth   301
   Case study 8.3   304
8.5 Relationship between financial and
   corporate objectives   306
8.6 International aspects of financial
   resources   308
   Case study 8.4   310
   Key reading   311
   Summary   312
   Questions   313
   Strategic project   314
   Further reading   314
   Appendix I: Heineken NV – extract
   from consolidated accounts   315
   Appendix II: Checklist of the main
   financial ratios   317
   Notes and references   318

9   Analysing operations resources   319

   Introduction   320
   Case study 9.1   320
9.1 Operations and corporate strategy   322
9.2 Analysis of the operations
   environment   323
   Case study 9.2   327
9.3 The role of operations in adding
   value and achieving sustainable
   competitive advantage   331
9.4 Operations activities and
   corporate strategy   334
   Case study 9.3   341
9.5 Service operations strategy   343
   Key reading   346
   Summary   346
   Questions   348
   Strategic project   348
   Further reading   348
   Notes and references   349

Part 4 The purpose of the organisation

**10   Purpose shaped by vision, leadership
   and ethics**   354

   Introduction   355
   Case study 10.1   355
10.1 Shaping the purpose of the organisation   357
10.2 Developing a strategic vision for
   the future   363
   Case study 10.2   365
10.3 Purpose and the role of leadership   367
   Case study 10.3   372
10.4 Purpose shaped by ethical considerations   374
10.5 Corporate governance and the
   purpose of the organisation   377
   Key reading   381
   Summary   382
   Questions   383
   Strategic project   384
   Further reading   384
   Notes and references   384

**11   Purpose emerging from knowledge,
   technology and innovation**   386

   Introduction   387
   Case study 11.1   387
11.1 Knowledge creation and purpose   390
   Case study 11.2   399
11.2 Using technology to develop
   purpose and competitive advantage   400
   Case study 11.3   404
11.3 Innovation and purpose   407
   Case study 11.4   409
11.4 How to innovate: the 'ideas' process   411
   Key reading   416
   Summary   417
   Questions   418
   Strategic project   419
   Further reading   419
   Notes and references   420

**12   Purpose delivered through mission
   and objectives**   422

   Introduction   423
   Case study 12.1   423
12.1 Clarifying the purpose of the organisation   426
12.2 Stakeholder analysis   429
   Case study 12.2   433

12.3 Developing the mission 435
Case study 12.3 439
12.4 Developing the objectives 440
12.5 Purpose in conglomerates – the role of parenting 443
12.6 Quality objectives and corporate strategy 445
12.7 Emergent strategy perspectives 448
12.8 Stakeholder power around the world and its influence on mission and objectives 449
Key reading 451
Summary 451
Questions 453
Strategic project 453
Further reading 453
Notes and references 454

Part 5 Developing the strategy

13 Developing strategic options: the prescriptive process 460
Introduction 460
Case study 13.1 462
13.1 Purpose and the SWOT analysis – the contribution of Andrews 464
13.2 Environment-based options: generic strategies – the contribution of Porter 466
Case study 13.2 470
Case study 13.3 474
13.3 Environment-based strategic options: the market options matrix 477
13.4 Environment-based strategic options: the expansion method matrix 482
Case study 13.4 486
13.5 Resource-based strategic options: the value chain 490
13.6 Resource-based strategic options: the resource-based view 493
13.7 Resource-based strategic options: cost reduction 496
13.8 Resource-based options in some special types of organisation 501
Summary 502
Questions 504
Strategic project 504
Further reading 504
Notes and references 505

14 Strategy evaluation and development: the prescriptive process 507
Introduction 507
Case study 14.1 509
14.1 Prescriptive strategy content: evaluation against six criteria 510
Case study 14.2 516
14.2 Prescriptive strategy content: procedures and techniques 518
14.3 Applying empirical evidence and guidelines 525
Case study 14.3 530
14.4 The classic prescriptive model of corporate strategy: exploring the process 533
14.5 International corporate strategy selection 537
Case study 14.4 538
Summary 543
Questions 545
Strategic project 546
Further reading 546
Appendix 547
Notes and references 547

15 Finding the strategic route forward: emergent and prescriptive approaches 550
Introduction 551
Case study 15.1 552
15.1 The importance of strategy context 553
Case study 15.2 557
15.2 The survival-based strategic route forward 560
15.3 The uncertainty-based strategic route forward 563
Case study 15.3 567
15.4 The negotiation-based strategic route forward 570
15.5 The learning-based strategic route forward 578
15.6 International considerations 582
Case study 15.4 584
Summary 586
Questions 587
Strategic project 588
Further reading 588
Appendix 589
Notes and references 590

16 Strategy, structure and style 592

Introduction 593
Case study 16.1 593
16.1 The basic relationship between strategy and structure 595
16.2 Strategy before structure: Chandler's contribution 597
16.3 Implications of designing structures to fit strategy 598
Case study 16.2 600
16.4 Criticisms: strategy and structure are interlinked 603
16.5 The links between strategy and structure and the concept of strategic fit 610
16.6 The choice of management style and culture 615
Case study 16.3 617
Summary 620
Questions 621
Strategic project 622
Further reading 622
Notes and references 622

Part 6 The implementation process

17 Resource allocation, strategic planning and control 628

Introduction 629
Case study 17.1 630
17.1 The implementation process 631
17.2 Relationship between implementation and the strategy development process 634
Case study 17.2 639
17.3 Objectives, task setting and communicating the strategy 642
17.4 Resource allocation 646
Case study 17.3 648
17.5 Strategic planning 650
17.6 Information, monitoring and control 656
17.7 Implementation of international strategy 658
Key reading 658
Summary 659
Questions 660
Strategic project 660
Further reading 660
Notes and references 661

18 Organisational structure and people issues 663

Introduction 664
Case study 18.1 664
18.1 Building the organisation's structure 666
18.2 Types of organisational structure 671
Case study 18.2 676
18.3 Organisational structures for innovation 677
18.4 Motivation and staffing in strategy implementation 680
18.5 Strategy and structure in international organisations – the role of headquarters 681
Case study 18.3 682
Key reading 685
Summary 686
Questions 687
Strategic project 687
Further reading 687
Notes and references 688

19 International expansion and globalisation strategies 689

Introduction 690
Case study 19.1 691
19.1 International expansion and globalisation: their meaning and importance 692
Case study 19.2 697
19.2 World trade and the international expansion strategies of companies 700
19.3 Influence of institutions involved in international trade 705
Case study 19.3 708
19.4 International and global expansion strategies: the company perspective 711
19.5 International and global expansion strategies: organisation structures 717
19.6 International and global expansion strategies: developing external relationships 721
19.7 Relationships between companies and countries 724
Case study 19.4 726
Key reading 729
Summary 730
Questions 731

Strategic project   732
Further reading   732
Notes and references   732

20 The dynamics of strategy development   734

Introduction   734
Case study 20.1   735
20.1 The dynamics of purpose   737
20.2 The dynamics of resource development   738
20.3 The dynamics of environmental development   743
Case study 20.2   748
20.4 The dynamics of fast-moving markets   750
20.5 The dynamics of slow-moving and mature markets   753
Case study 20.3   754
Key reading   756
Summary   757
Questions   758
Strategic project   759
Notes and references   759

21 Managing strategic change   760

Introduction   760
Case study 21.1   761
21.1 The basic concept of strategic change   763
21.2 Analysing the causes of strategic change   768
Case study 21.2   770
21.3 Prescriptive approaches to managing strategic change   771
Case study 21.3   774

21.4 Emergent approaches to managing change   776
21.5 Developing a strategic change programme   783
Case study 21.4   788
Key reading   790
Summary   791
Questions   793
Strategic project   793
Further reading   794
Notes and references   794

22 Building a cohesive corporate strategy   795

Introduction   796
Case study 22.1   796
22.1 Cohesion in prescriptive and emergent processes   798
22.2 Combining the elements of corporate strategy: the 'Seven S Framework'   800
22.3 Longer-term strategy issues   806
Case study 22.2   809
Key reading   811
Summary   813
Questions   814
Strategic project   814
Further reading   814
Notes and references   814

Glossary   817
Name index   825
Subject index   827

List of case studies

Chapter 1
1.1 Corporate strategy at Hewlett-Packard 5
1.2 Disaster and recovery at IBM: 1 Corporate profit disaster at IBM 12
1.3 Sky-high strategies of Europe's budget airlines 27

Chapter 2
2.1 Attacking a dominant competitor: a joint venture strategy by Nestlé and General Mills 38
2.2 Prescriptive strategic planning at Spillers plc 46
2.3 Prescriptive strategy to rescue Britain's ailing National Health Service 48
2.4 Emergent strategy at Spillers Baking 52
2.5 The rise and fall of Dalgety 66
2.6 Disaster and recovery at IBM: 2 How IBM changed its strategy and revived its fortunes 69

Chapter 3
3.1 Pan-European steel companies merge to cope with the new competitive environment 85
3.2 Different strategies in the ice cream market 97
3.3 Will the steel companies adopt global strategies? 99
3.4 Strategic bargaining to film *The Lord of the Rings* 117

Chapter 4
4.1 Unilever ice cream defends its European market share 124
4.2 Web strategy at Boo.com – To be booed? Or applauded? 131
4.3 Mars ice cream: distribution strategy problems 146
4.4 The call of Africa grows louder 151

Chapter 5
5.1 Will Dyson remain successful? 159
5.2 Two methods of segmenting products in the European ice cream market 172

5.3 Customer strategy at Airbus: competing in the SuperJumbo aircraft segment 187

Chapter 6
6.1 Resource strategy at GSK: negotiating a merger and making it work 201
6.2 How three European companies attempt to utilise their resources 210
6.3 Xbox – the strategic battle for the home entertainment market has just begun 242

Chapter 7
7.1 Royal Dutch/Shell – the sweeping change that failed to materialise 250
7.2 Culture, crisis and power at British Petroleum 263
7.3 Industry groups in Japan, Korea, Hong Kong and Italy 274
7.4 How Xerox Europe shifted its strategy and changed its organisation 276

Chapter 8
8.1 Global expansion: brewing at Heineken NV 284
8.2 The financing of brewers' growth 290
8.3 SCA's financial objectives 304
8.4 Improving shareholder wealth at LucasVarity, Burton and Diageo 310

Chapter 9
9.1 Dell Computers – competitive advantage through low-cost manufacturing 320
9.2 Toyota: taking out costs and adding value 327
9.3 Cost reduction strategy at Bajaj, the India-based motorcycle maker 341

Chapter 10
10.1 DaimlerChrysler: flawed vision or just unlucky? 355
10.2 Leadership in action: Jürgen Schrempp of Daimler-Benz 365

10.3 Negotiation ethics at Portsmouth's
new millennium tower – a double
whammy?   372

Chapter 11
11.1 Developing new knowledge at Nike   387
11.2 Will traditional retail banks survive
the threat of the new technologies –
the Internet and telephone banking?   399
11.3 The problem with innovation at 3M   404
11.4 How Philips exploits its
technology edge   409

Chapter 12
12.1 Ford's new objective: 'Back to basics' 423
12.2 Objectives derailed on the Jubilee
Line Extension   433
12.3 Coca-Cola: Lowering the fizz in
its objectives   439

Chapter 13
13.1 New strategy options at McDonald's   462
13.2 Generic strategy options analysis:
European ice cream   470
13.3 Market-based strategies in global TV:
exciting opportunities in a
fast-expanding market   474
13.4 Building a global media company at
News Corporation   486

Chapter 14
14.1 Nokia – the risk of choosing between
options   509
14.2 Eurofreeze evaluates its strategy
options: 1   516
14.3 Corporate strategic leadership
at Unilever   530
14.4 Eurofreeze evaluates its strategy
options: 2   538

Chapter 15
15.1 How Honda came to dominate two
major motorcycle markets   552
15.2 Europe's leading telecom companies:
overstretched and under threat   557
15.3 How GEC Marconi used game theory
to make an extra US$3 billion   567
15.4 Mobile revolution: Vodafone's struggle
to maintain its success   584

Chapter 16
16.1 How Sony moved out across Asia   593
16.2 How General Motors organised
its future   600
16.3 How ABB empowered its managers
and then reversed the process   617

Chapter 17
17.1 European football: viable strategy badly
implemented? Or does the whole
strategy need a rethink?   630
17.2 Strategic planning at Canon with a
co-operative corporate style   639
17.3 Informal strategic controls at Nestlé 648

Chapter 18
18.1 PepsiCo: Organising to integrate its
acquisitions   664
18.2 Cisco Systems: Benefits of a highly
structured organisation   676
18.3 Ford Motors – Reorganising
back to basics   682

Chapter 19
19.1 Globalisation at Giant Bicycles   691
19.2 International strategy in the
world pulp and paper industry   697
19.3 What strategy now for SCA?   708
19.4 Tate & Lyle plc: globalisation to
sweeten the profit line   726

Chapter 20
20.1 eBay – the auction market that
spans the world   735
20.2 Recorded music on the Internet: only the
beginning of the broadband revolution? 748
20.3 Making an impact in only 100 days   754

Chapter 21
21.1 Shock tactics at BOC   761
21.2 Owens-Corning reveals its
strategies for change   770
21.3 United Biscuits – a shadow of its
former self   774
21.4 StanChart chief swept out by
culture clash   788

Chapter 22
22.1 Next steps for Novartis   796
22.2 Side-effects of age leave Roche reeling 809

About this book

This book explores the fundamental decisions that will guide the future of organisations, and how such matters can be identified, evaluated and implemented. It presents a comprehensive, structured and critical approach to strategic management.

Its underlying theme is the need to consider not only the *rational approach* to strategic decision-making, but also the *creative aspects* of such decisions – an approach that remains unique to this strategy text. The book argues that both of these are essential to enable students and practicing managers to develop successful strategies.

This third edition has been revised in a number of ways: more compact design, yet all the main elements preserved; all cases updated with many that are totally new; revised treatments of the dynamics of competitive advantage, customer-driven strategy, resource-based strategy, the development of mission and objectives, and new approaches to knowledge, innovation and learning. An outline of the main changes appears later in this section.

Objectives

The purpose of the book is to provide a comprehensive, well-structured and interesting treatment of strategic management, covering organisations in both the private and public sectors. The text has been specially designed in a modular format to provide both a summary of the main areas and a more detailed treatment for those wishing to explore issues in more depth.

More specifically, the objectives are:

- *To provide a comprehensive coverage of the main study areas in corporate strategy.* For example, the different functional areas of the organisation and important subject areas such as innovation, knowledge and technology strategy are all explored. The exploration of the strategy contributions from the business functions of marketing, human resources, finance and operations (production) is unique to this text.

- *To present the practical issues and problems of corporate strategy, so that the compromises and constraints of real organisations are considered.* Each chapter contains case studies which both illustrate the principles and raise subjects for group and class discussion. Leadership and ethical issues are also explored.

- *To assist organisations to add value to their assets through the development of successful corporate strategy.* The search for best practice in the context of the organisation's resources and constraints is a constant theme.

- *To explore both the rational and the creative approaches to the development of corporate strategy.* This text takes the view that the classical approaches to rational corporate strategy development need to be complemented by the more recent ideas based on crafting strategy development. Knowledge and innovation are explored.

- *To stimulate critical appraisal of the major theories, particularly with regard to their practical application in organisations.* Many of the leading conceptual approaches are first described and then subjected to critical comment. The aim is to encourage the reader to think carefully about such matters.

- *To outline the international implications of the corporate strategic process.* Many of the cases have an international dimension and most chapters have a separate section exploring international issues. A special chapter on globalisation explores the specific issues raised by this strategic area.

Who should use this book?

The book is intended to provide an introduction to corporate strategy for the many students in this area.

- *Undergraduate students* on Business Studies, modular and other courses will find the subject matter sufficiently structured to provide a route through the subject. No prior knowledge is assumed.
- *MBA students* will find the practical discussions and theoretical background useful. They will also be able to relate these to their own experience.
- *Postgraduate students* on other specialist taught masters' programmes will find that the extensive coverage of theories and, at times, critical comments, together with the background reading, provide a useful input to their thinking.

In addition, the book will appeal to practising middle and senior managers involved in the development of corporate strategy. The case studies and checklists, the structured approach and the comprehensive nature of the text will provide a useful compendium for practical application.

Distinctive features

Two-model structure

For some years, there has been disagreement on the approach to be adopted in studying corporate strategy. The *rational* model – strategy options, selection and implementation – has been criticised by those favouring an approach based on the more *creative* aspects of strategy development. Given the lack of agreement between the approaches, *both* models are used throughout this book. They are *both* treated as contributing to the development of optimal corporate strategy: two sides of the same strategic coin.

Modular structure

The subject can be treated in depth by taking each chapter in sequence. Alternatively, the book has been designed to be used as a complete course through the study of *selected chapters only*. The aim has been to make the subject more accessible at first reading to those requiring such an approach. The precise structure is explained in the section on 'How to use this book'.

Clear chapter structure

Each chapter follows the same format: learning outcomes; short introduction; opening case study; later case studies linked to the theory points in the text; regular summaries of key strategic principles; a key reading, if relevant; chapter summary; review and discussion questions; recommended further reading; a specific project; detailed notes and references. There is also a glossary of terms at the end of the book as an aid to comprehension.

Focused case material

There are around 80 case studies in this book. Each case has been written or adapted to explore strategy issues relevant to its location in the text. Unlike most strategy texts, there are no integrative cases, which are readily available elsewhere. The cases have been especially designed for the larger class sizes and shorter discussion sessions now prevalent in many institutions, so they are shorter and directed at the issues raised in the chapter. All the cases have been updated for the third edition and many new ones added.

Key strategic principles and chapter summaries

To aid learning and comprehension, there are frequent summaries of the main learning points under the heading of *key strategic principles*. In addition, at the end of each chapter there is an integrated summary of the areas explored.

International coverage

There is extensive coverage of international strategic issues throughout the book. For ease of teaching and learning, the international theory has generally been placed towards the end of each chapter, but cases and examples are threaded through the text. In addition, there is a separate chapter on the special issues involved in globalisation strategy.

Selected further readings

Most chapters end with a selected key reading to present another viewpoint or link strategy to another discipline. In addition, each chapter has a list of recommended further readings of items related to the chapter. The purpose is to allow the student to explore the subject matter further and act as a basis for projects, assignments and dissertations.

Strategic project

Each chapter ends with a suggestion for a strategic project. It is based on a theme developed in the chapter and includes a comment on a current strategic issue. The projects are supported by further information available on the Internet.

 A key feature of the text remains the selection of extracts from the *Financial Times*. These extracts are the copyright of the *Financial Times*, which has kindly given permission to reproduce them in this book.

Lecturer's Guide

This is available to those lecturers adopting this textbook. It includes short commentaries on each chapter and comments on the cases, together with OHP masters.

Internet

Visit the *Corporate Strategy* Companion Web site at **www.booksites.net/lynch** to find valuable teacher and learning material including:

For students:

- Study material designed to help you improve your results
- 15–20 MCQs per chapter
- Links to articles on the web and a company directory
- Recommended key readings

For lecturers:

- A secure, password protected site with teaching material
- Case updates
- Suggested lecture formats
- Links to articles for lecturers only
- Suggested answers to seminar questions
- Chapter summaries
- Downloadable OHPs, an Instructor's Manual, and MCQs

Also: This regularly maintained and updated site has biographies of strategy scholars, a syllabus manager, search functions, and email results functions.

New for the third edition

As a result of the helpful feedback on the two earlier editions, this new edition concentrates on a thorough update while maintaining the main structure of the previous edition. The main changes are:

- More compact design, yet keeping all the main elements of the earlier edition. This has meant some judicious editing of the text – for example, the section on financial equations to calculate the cost of capital has been deleted from earlier editions. Our research showed that customers liked the second edition but judged that it was just a little too heavy.
- Many new case studies, especially on well-known international companies.
- New section on innovation and knowledge as a major area of strategy: Chapter 2.
- PEST changed to PESTEL in Chapter 3 to emphasise the importance of the sustainable environment and legal issues in strategy analysis.
- New treatment of the dynamics of competitive advantage and review of the 'dot.com' bubble: Chapter 4.
- Simplified exploration of customer-driven strategy: Chapter 5.
- Revised treatment of the resource-based view: Chapter 6.
- Slightly shortened exploration of human resource, financial and operations strategy analysis: Chapters 7, 8 and 9.
- Restructured treatment of innovation: Chapter 11.
- Revised exploration of Mission and Objectives: Chapter 12.
- Some shortening of the two options-and-choice chapters by reducing coverage of secondary material such as the PIMS data evidence: Chapters 13 and 14. Some later chapters have also received similar treatment. However, Chapter 15 – crucial to the text – has been kept at its original length.

More generally, the opportunity has been taken to present many new cases that reflect the strategic issues of the new millennium. For example, the new airline case in Chapter 1 and the new telecommunications case in Chapter 15 explore important strategic issues that challenge existing strategic theory. At the same time, the strong international perspective of the case studies has been preserved with material from many parts of the world.

About the author

Richard Lynch is Professor of Strategic Management at Middlesex University, London, England. He originally studied at UMIST, Leeds University and the London Business School. He then spent over 20 years in business with well-known companies such as J Walter Thompson, Kraft Jacobs Suchard and Dalgety Spillers in positions in marketing and corporate strategy. During the early 1980s, he was a director of two public companies before setting up his own consultancy company specialising in European and international strategy. In the 1990s he became increasingly involved in Higher Education, eventually taking a full-time position in 1999. He has written four previous books on international marketing and strategy and a number of publications in research journals.

How to use this book

Corporate strategy is all-embracing and covers every aspect of the organisation, so its study can be both lengthy and time consuming. This book has been written to guide the reader through from its early stages of development. It can therefore be read from cover to cover; alternatively, it may be more useful to begin by concentrating on certain key *chapters*, which will provide an overview of the process and show the linkages that exist between the different areas. The areas can then be covered in more depth, if required, by reading the *related chapters*.

Key chapters	Related chapters
Part 1	
Chapter 1	Chapter 2
Part 2	
Chapter 3	Chapters 4 and 5
Part 3	
Chapter 6	Chapters 7, 8 and 9
Part 4	
Chapters 10, 11 and 12	None: all important
Part 5	
Chapters 13, 14 and 15	Chapter 16
Part 6	
Chapters 17 and 21	Chapters 18, 19, 20 and 22

The key chapters might form the basis of a twelve-week modular course. The longer text including the related chapters might form the basis of a two-seminar programme.

Corporate strategy is complicated because there is no final agreement on what exactly should be included in the topic. There are two main strategic approaches worth mastering before venturing too far into the text. They are summarised in Chapter 1 – the *prescriptive* and the *emergent* strategic approaches. Since these approaches are discussed extensively later in the book, they should be studied in Chapter 1 before moving on to other chapters. If you have trouble understanding these two elements, then you might also like to consult the early part of Chapter 2, which investigates them in more detail. Each chapter then follows the same basic format:

- *Learning outcomes and introduction.* This summarises the main areas to be covered in the chapter and is useful as a summary of what to expect from the chapter.
- *Opening case.* This is designed to highlight a key strategy issue in the chapter and to provide an example that will then be explored in the text. It is therefore worth reading and using the case questions to ensure that you have understood the basics of the case. You can return to it once you have read the chapter.

- *Key strategic principles*. Each chapter then explores aspects of the subject and summarises them. These can be used to test your understanding of the text and also for revision purposes later.

- *Comment*. After the outline of a major strategic theory, there may be a section with this heading to explain some of the theoretical or practical difficulties associated with that topic. The opinions contained in such a section are deliberately designed to be controversial. The section is meant to make you think about the topic. If you agree with everything I have written, then I have failed!

- *Later case studies*. These are designed to provide further examples and raise additional strategic issues. It is worth exploring the questions.

- *End of chapter questions*. Some are designed to test your understanding of the material in the chapter. Others are present as possible essay topics and require you to undertake some research using the references and reading from the chapter. Some questions have been developed to encourage you to relate the chapter to your own experience: student societies and outside organisations to which you belong can all be considered using the chapter concepts. You may also be able to relate the chapter to your own work experience or to those of other members of your family or friends. All these will provide valuable insights and help you explore the concepts and reality of corporate strategy.

- *Strategic project*. Each chapter ends with a suggested topic that could form the basis of further research. There is data on the Internet to assist the process and your lecturer or tutor will be provided with details on how to access this.

- *Further reading*. This is designed to help when it comes to essay topics and dissertations. This section tries to keep to references in the major journals and books in order to make the process as accessible as possible.

Guided tour of this book

TWO-MODEL STRUCTURE

Two models of strategic thought are used throughout the book – *prescriptive* and *emergent*. Both are treated as contributing to the development of optimal corporate strategy.

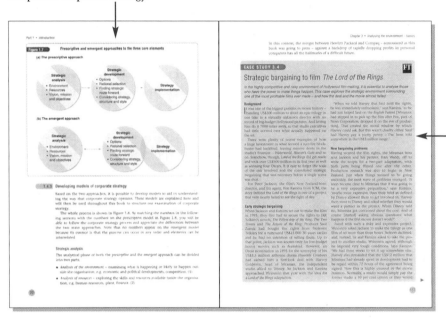

CASE STUDIES

Each chapter contains case studies which illustrate strategic principles and raise subjects for group and class discussion. Over 80 have been included, specially designed for the larger class sizes and shorter discussion sessions in many institutions.

KEY STRATEGIC PRINCIPLES

Frequent summaries are given of the main learning points to aid learning and comprehension.

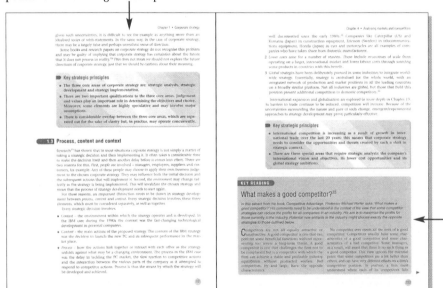

KEY READING

Selected key readings present alternative viewpoints or link strategy to another discipline.

STRATEGIC PROJECT

Each chapter ends with a strategic project based on a theme developed within the chapter.

RECOMMENDED FURTHER READING

Selected readings allow students to explore the subject further and act as a basis for projects, assignments and dissertations.

FURTHER READING

Richard Whittington's *What is Strategy and Does it Matter?* (Routledge, London, 1993) is a lucid, well-structured and thought-provoking book. I have acknowledged some of its interesting research references as this chapter has progressed and it has certainly influenced some elements of the material. Read Chapter 2 of Whittington for an alternative view and structuring of strategy theories and practice.

More recently, two major books of strategy research topics are strongly recommended: Michael Hitt, R. Edward Freeman and Jeffrey S. Harrison, *The Blackwell Handbook of Strategic Management* (Blackwell, Oxford, 2001), Andrew Pettigrew, Howard Thomas, Richard Whittington, *Handbook of Strategy and Management* (Sage, London, 2002).

On strategy as history, classic studies include those by Alfred Chandler, *Strategy and Structure* (MIT Press,

Cambridge, MA, 1962), and his later book *Scale and Scope: Dynamics of Individual Capitalism* (Harvard University Press, Cambridge, MA, 1990). See also Derek Channon's *The Strategy and Structure of British Enterprise* (Harvard University Press, Cambridge, MA, 1973). A more recent study with real insight is Geoffrey Jones' *Evolution of International Business* (Routledge, London, 1996).

J L Moore's *Writers on Strategy and Strategic Management* (Penguin, London, 1992) has a useful survey of some leading writers and theories. Helpful for essay references and revision.

The book by Edith Penrose, *The Theory of the Growth of the Firm*, 3rd edn (Oxford University Press, Oxford, 1993), represents a classic early study of strategy development. Moreover, its precision of language and clarity of thought represent a model for us all to emulate.

A Companion Website accompanies
CORPORATE STRATEGY, 3rd edition **by Richard Lynch**

Visit the *Corporate Strategy* Companion Web Site at
www.booksites.net/lynch to find valuable teaching and
learning material including:

For Students:

- Study material designed to help you improve your results
- For each chapter:
  - An overview including: Learning outcomes and Key concepts
  - 15–20 multiple choice questions to test your understanding
  - Weblinks relating to the case studies from the text
  - Links to related articles on the web
  - Recommended further readings
- A detailed guide to analysing strategy cases, including a spreadsheet to calculate all financial ratios
- Interactive online glossary
- General weblinks relating to Corporate Strategy

For Lecturers:

- A secure, password protected site with teaching material
- A downloadable Instructor's Manual
- Downloadable PowerPoint slides to assist in lecturing
- Biographies of strategy gurus
- A syllabus manager that will build and host a course web page

Also: This site also features a search facility, and email results function.

Acknowledgements

First edition

During the writing of the first edition of this book, the text has benefited enormously from a panel of reviewers set up by Pitman Publishing. They are: Drs Robert Bood, Vakgroep Bedrijfseconomie, Faculty of Economics, Gronigen University; Stuart Bowie, Bristol Business School, University of the West of England; Ms Maria Brouwer, Department of Economics, Amsterdam University; Bruce Lloyd, Head of Strategy, Business School, South Bank University; Professor Bente R Lowendahl, Department of Strategy and Business History, Norwegian School of Management, Sandvika; Richard Morland, Senior Lecturer in Management, Department of Business Management, Brighton University; Dr Martyn Pitt, School of Management, Bath University; Professor Louis Printz, Department of Organisation and Management, Aarhus School of Business, Denmark; Professor Dr Jacob de Smit, Faculteit der Bedrijtskunde, Erasmus University, Rotterdam; and Bill Ramsay, Associate Fellow, Templeton College, Oxford.

In addition, others have also made a significant contribution: Dr Richard Gregson and Richard Cawley, European Business School, London; Professor Colin Haslam, Royal Holloway College, University of London; Dr Carol Vielba and Dr David Edelshain, City University Business School, London; Adrian Haberberg, University of Westminster, London; Professor Kazem Chaharbaghi, University of East London; Laurie Mullins, University of Portsmouth; and Val Lencioni and Dr Dennis Barker, Middlesex University Business School. I am also grateful to Middlesex University for a part-time sabbatical to write sections of the text.

Since becoming involved in higher education, I have lectured at universities in South East England, Singapore and elsewhere. The concepts and cases have benefited from the comments, challenges and contributions of many students over this time period and I am grateful to them all.

To provide real-life examples, I have been able to draw upon material provided by a number of organisations. In particular, I would like to thank Electrolux AB, Stora AB, Ford Motor Company and SKF AB. I am also grateful to the *Financial Times* for permission to adapt a number of articles as case studies for use in the book. Numerous other authors and organisations have also given permission for extracts from their work to be used: these are acknowledged appropriately in the text.

Note that Chapter 14 presents a case study of two companies, Eurofreeze and Refrigor. These are wholly fictional names developed for the purposes of the case study. No link is intended with any real company that might be trading under these or similar names in frozen food or other products. As explained in the case, the data is derived from several real cases and has been disguised to protect confidentiality.

The first edition of this book would never have happened without the major support and encouragement of the editorial team at Pearson Education. Their professionalism, experience and knowledge have been invaluable. My thanks go to Catriona King in the very early days and, later, to the invaluable Stuart Hay, together with Simon Lake and Mark Allin. Elizabeth Tarrant worked magnificently on the editorial process, Colin Reed produced an excellent design and Helen Beltran notably improved the text. Finally, Penelope Woolf provided the bedrock of guidance and support on which all else has rested. My thanks to them all.

This book has a history stretching back over a number of years, including the author's experience in nearly thirty years as a line manager and consultant in industry. To all my many colleagues over the years, I offer my grateful thanks for all the lessons learnt.

Second edition

The second edition owes much to those who contributed to the first edition: they are acknowledged above. In addition, a new panel of reviewers set up by the publishers has commented on the second edition and the text has again benefited considerably from their guidance. They are: Greet Asselburgh, Management Department, RUCA Antwerpen; Peter Berends, Faculty of Economics and Business Administration, University of Maastricht; Andy Crane, Cardiff Business School; Steven Henderson, Southampton Institute; Tom Lawton, Royal Holloway, University of London; Judy Slinn, Oxford Brookes University.

In addition to all those named above across the two editions, others have also made a significant contribution to this edition: the many students who have commented on parts of the text; Professor Harold Rose and the Dean, Professor John Quelch, London Business School; Roger Lazenby, Middlesex University Business School; Gerry Scullion, Ulster University; the participants in the two *Financial Times* Corporate Strategy Workshops in early 1999; the anonymous respondents to the academic questionnaire from the publishers on the first edition; John Meehan and one of his student groups in Liverpool John Moores University. In addition to his comments, John has also taken over responsibility for the web site that operates in conjunction with this text, for which my thanks.

Various companies and organisations have given permission for their material to be used in the text. They are thanked individually in the text.

Importantly, it is right to acknowledge the immense contribution of the publishers, Pearson Education, to the development of this second edition. Their policy of seeking the highest standards in educational publishing has been crucial to this work. Their significant resource commitment to promote and communicate strategic management writing and research has been a vital element in the development of the second edition. In addition to those named above at the time of the first edition, I am particularly grateful to Jane Powell and Beth Barber for these earlier guidance and advice. More recently, Sadie McClelland and Jacqueline Senior have taken over these roles and moved the process forward with considerable skill. I would also like to record my thanks to David Harrison for the desk editing job at Harlow.

Finally, I want to thank two of my nephews: Christian Lynch, who sorted out my computer software, and Stephen Lynch, who sorted out the hardware. Without them and all the others who have contributed to the text, this second edition would never have happened.

Third edition

Once again, Pearson Education set up a panel to comment on the second edition and provide invaluable comments for the third edition. The guidance of the following is much appreciated: John Ball, Swansea Business School; Jack Colford, Oxford Brookes University; Sandy Cripps, East London Business School; Bo Eriksen, University of Southern Denmark; Joyce Falkenberg, Norwegian School of Economics and Business Administration; Moira Fischbacher, University of Glasgow; Simon Harris, University of Stirling, UK; Paul Jackson, Coventry Business School; Tomi Laamanen, Helsinki

University of Technology; Juha Laurila, Helsinki School of Economics; Tim Moran, University of Salford; Robert Morgan, University of Wales, Aberystwyth; Colin M Souster, University of Luton; Barry Witcher, University of East Anglia.

Again, it is right to acknowledge the major contribution of the publishers, Pearson Education, to the development of this third edition. Over the three editions, many Pearson people have contributed with professionalism, enthusiasm and real interest. For the first two editions, I listed all the major Pearson contributors individually. However, there have now been so many over the years that the list has become somewhat unmanageable. May I therefore simply record my thanks collectively to everyone involved.

Publisher's Acknowledgements

We are grateful to the following for permission to reproduce copyright material:

Figure 7.5 from Managing Strategic Change: Strategy, culture and action in *Long Range Planning 25*, Elsevier Science, (Johnson, G.). Figures 1.6, 21.7 and 21.8 from *Managing Change for Competitive Success*, Blackwell, (Pettigrew, A. and Whipp. R., 1991); Table 3.6 from *British Steel Annual Report 1997/98*; Figures 3.4, 6.4, 6.5 and 13.3 from *Competitive Strategy: Techniques for Analyzing Industries and Competitors*, Simon & Schuster (Porter, M.E., 1980), © Michael E. Porter 1980; Figure 4.5 from 'On the description and comparison of economic systems', in Eckstein, A. (ed) *Comparisons of Economic Systems*, University of California Press (Koopman, K. and Montias, J.M.,1971), © The Regents of the University of California; Figure 5.9 courtesy of British Aerospace; Table 6.2 from 'How much does industry matter?' in *Strategic Management Journal*, 18, Summer Special Issue, pp15–30, John Wiley & Sons, Inc. (Rumelt, R.); Figure 6.9 from 'Sustainable Competitive Advantage: towards a dynamic resource-based strategy' in *Management Decision* 37 (1), pp45–50 (Chaharbaghi, K. and Lynch, R. 1999); Table 7.1 from 'Organizational Strategy, Structure and Process' in *Academy of Management Review*, 3, pp546–62 (Miles, R.E., Snow, C.C., Meyer, A.D. and Coleman, H.J., 1978); Figure 7.8 from 'Evolution and Revolution as Organisations grow' in Harvard Business Review, July–August 1972 (Greiner), © The President and Fellows of Harvard College 1972; Figure 11.4 adapted from *Wellsprings of Knowledge*, Harvard Business School Press, (Leonard, D., 1995), © The President and Fellows of Harvard College 1995; Table 8.5 from Strategic Management, Irwin, (Thompson, A. and Strickland, A., 1993), © Richard D. Irwin; Figure 19.3 from *The Competitive Advantage of Nations*, Macmillan, (Porter M.E., 1990); Exhibit 11.2 from *Skandia Annual Report and Accounts 1997*; Exhibit 12.6 courtesy of the Ford Motor Company, 1996, © Ford Motor Company 1996; Figure 12.7 from 'Service productivity: a blasphemous approach' in *Proceedings of the 2nd International Research Seminar in Service Management*, Institut d'Administration des Enterprises (IAE), Université d'Aix-Marseille, France, June 1992 (Gummerson, E., 1992); Figure 13.11 from *Creating and Sustaining Superior Performance*, The Free Press, (Porter, M.E., 1985), © Michael E. Porter 1985; Figure 14.3 reproduced with permission from Arthur D. Little, © Arthur D. Little 1996; Exhibit 19.5 from *Multinational Enterprises and the Global Economy*, Addison Wesley, (Dunning, J.H., 1993); Figure 22.3 from *McKinsey Quarterly*, Summer 1980; Key Reading 'Successful corporate strategy' from Foundations of Corporate Strategy, Oxford University Press, (Kay, J., 1993); Key Reading 'What is Business Strategy' from The Economist, 20 Mar 1993, © The Economist 1993; Key Reading 'Tom Peters: performance artist' from The Economist, 24 September 1994, © The Economist 1994; Key Reading 'What makes a good competitor' from *Competitive Strategy: Techniques for Analyzing Industries and Competitors*, Simon & Schuster (Porter, M.E., 1980), © Michael E. Porter 1980; Exhibit 6.2 adapted from *The Economics of Strategy*, Wiley (Besanko, D., Dranove, D. and Shenley, M., 1996) © John Wiley & Sons, Inc. 1996; Key Reading 'The accounting function and strategy' from *Accounting Theory and Practice*, Pitman, (Glautier, M.W.E. and Underdown, B., 1994); Key Reading 'Manufacturing Strategy' from *Manufacturing Strategy*, Macmillan, (Hill, T., 1993); Key Reading 'Manufacturing Strategy' from *Manufacturing Strategy*, Macmillan, (Hill, T.,

1993); Key Reading 'Balancing the objectives' from *The Practice of Management*, Mercury Books, (Drucker, P., 1961); Key Reading 'The Importance of good structure' from *Management and Organisational Behaviour*, Pitman Publishing, (Mullins, L., 1996); Key Reading 'Globalisation: getting rid of the headquarters mentality' from *The Borderless World*, Collins, (Ohmae, K., 1990), © McKinsey & Co 1990; Key Reading 'Mobilising middle managers' from Rejuvenating the Mature Business, International Thompson Publishing Services Limited, (Baden-Fuller, C. and Stopford, J., 1992), © Charles Baden Fuller and John Stopford 1992; Key Reading 'Entrepreneurship in a dynamic world' from *Strategic Entrepreneurship*, Pitman Publishing, (Wickham, P., 1998).

We are grateful to the Financial Times Limited for permission to reprint the following material:

Case Study 3.4 Strategic Bargaining to film *The Lord of the Rings*, © *Financial Times*, 19 March, 2002; Case Study 4.4 The call of Africa grows louder, © *Financial Times*, 21 August, 2001; Case Study 9.3 Cost reduction strategy at Bajaj, the India-based motorcycle maker, © *Financial Times*, 6 July, 1998; Case Study 10.2 Leadership in action: Jurgen Schrempp of Daimler-Benz, © *Financial Times*, 26 February, 2001; Case Study 11.4 How Phillips exploits its technology edge, © *Financial Times*, 22 March 2001; Case Study 13.1 New strategy options at McDonald's, © *Financial Times*, 3 September, 1998; Case Study 15.4 Mobile revolution: Vodafone's struggle to maintain its success, © *Financial Times*, 26 April, 2002; Case Study 16.1 How Sony moved out across Asia, © *Financial Times*, 15 November, 1995; Case Study 18.2 Cisco Systems: Benefits of a highly structured organisation, © *Financial Times*, 12 April, 1999; Case Study 19.1 Globalisation at Giant Bicycles, © *Financial Times*, 24 October, 1997; Case Study 20.3 Making an impact in only 100 days, © *Financial Times*, 7 July, 1998; Case Study 21.1 Shock tactics at BOC, © *Financial Times*, 29 April, 1999; Case Study 21.2 Owens-Corning reveals its strategies for change, © *Financial Times*, 23 February, 1996; Case Study 22.2 Side-effects of age leave Roche reeling, © *Financial Times*, 1 June, 2001.

In some instances we have been unable to trace the owners of copyright material and we would appreciate any information that would enable us to do so.

Introduction

This part of the book introduces the concept of corporate strategy. Chapter 1 outlines the main elements of the subject and explains its importance and its role in delivering the purpose of the organisation. The two main approaches to the process of corporate strategy are outlined and explored. Chapter 2 gives a fuller review of how corporate strategy has evolved and discusses in greater depth the two main approaches in its development.

Introduction

The *prescriptive* strategic process

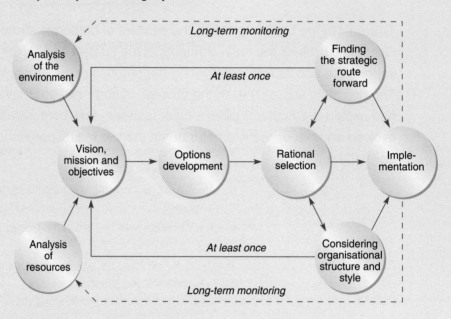

The *emergent* strategic process

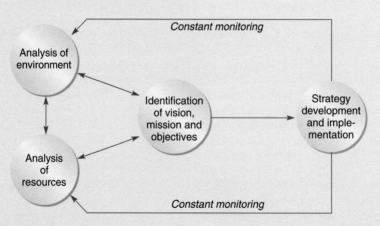

Chapter 1
Corporate strategy

- What is corporate strategy and why is it important?
- What are the core areas of corporate strategy and how do they link together?
- What makes 'good' corporate strategy?
- To what extent is corporate strategy different in public and non-profit organisations?
- What are the international dimensions of corporate strategy?

Chapter 2
A review of theory and practice

- How have current ideas on corporate strategy evolved?
- What are the main approaches to corporate strategy?
- What are the main prescriptive and emergent theories of strategy?
- How does the theory of corporate strategy relate to corporate practice?

Corporate strategy

When you have worked through this chapter, you will be able to:

- define corporate strategy and explain its five special elements;
- explain the core areas of corporate strategy and how they link together;
- distinguish between process, content and context of a corporate strategy;
- identify what makes 'good' corporate strategy;
- describe the extent to which corporate strategy is different in public and non-profit organisations;
- explain the difference between national and international corporate strategy.

Figure 1.1   **Analysing corporate strategy**

What is corporate strategy?

Why is it important?   Core areas

Process, content and context

Prescriptive and emergent approaches

What makes 'good' strategy

Public and non-profit strategy   International strategy

Introduction

Corporate strategy is concerned with an organisation's basic direction for the future: its purpose, its ambitions, its resources and how it interacts with the world in which it operates.

Every aspect of the organisation plays a role in this strategy – its people, its finances, its production methods and its environment (including its customers). In this introductory chapter we examine how these broad areas need to be structured and developed if the organisation is to continue to operate effectively.

Corporate strategy is complicated by the fact that there is considerable disagreement between researchers on the subject and how its elements are linked together. There are two main routes and these are examined in this chapter: the prescriptive process and the emergent process. As a result, two models have been developed to explain the subject. These are shown in the opening diagram to this part of the book (*see* p2).

In exploring corporate strategy, it is useful to begin by examining why it is important and what it contains. A useful distinction can also be drawn between its process, content and context. The two main routes are then examined and the key question explored – what makes 'good' strategy? Finally in this chapter, we examine the special characteristics of public and international strategies – *see* Figure 1.1.

CASE STUDY 1.1

Corporate strategy at Hewlett-Packard[1]

When David Packard died in 1996, he left the bulk of the stake in the company he had founded with his partner, Bill Hewlett, to a charitable foundation. It was worth US$4.4 billion. Yet the two had set out 57 years earlier with only modest ambitions and no strategy for building a world company, let alone US$23 billion bid for a rival.

In 1939 Hewlett and Packard started their company with US$538 cash in a rented garage in Palo Alto, California. By 1996 the company employed 112 000 people in 120 countries and had annual sales of US$38 billion (*see* Figure 1.2). It made computers, printers and a wide range of electronic equipment for use in industry, medicine and science.

The company strategy has always emphasised excellence and innovation, and yet over the years there has been no grand vision of technological breakthrough nor any desire to take great risks. Describing the early days, Hewlett explained with a grin: 'Professors of management are devastated when I say we were successful because we had no plans. We just took on odd jobs.'

Without any doubt, the two partners had some early luck. Their company became an early leader in pocket calculators. They had been doubtful about the product's success but invested because they estimated that they only needed 10 000 unit sales to break even. They went on to sell 100 000 in the first year.

Hewlett was oversimplifying, however, when he said that they had no plans. There were some sound corporate strategies.

- Over the years, the company has built market dominance in computer printers, specialist applications in science and medicine, and a range of joint ventures and alliances with others in the industry.

- Just as importantly, the company has developed its strategy The HP Way, an informal and open management style, introduced early on and practised until recently. A further informal element was added – MBWA: Management by Walking Around – which involved literally wandering casually around anywhere in the operation.

- Profit was not seen as the sole objective. From the early days, employee share options were regularly given to employees.

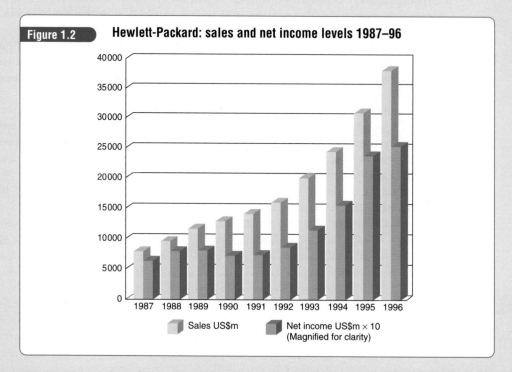

Figure 1.2 Hewlett-Packard: sales and net income levels 1987–96

Sales US$m

Net income US$m × 10
(Magnified for clarity)

In more recent years, the informal style has given way to a more structured, global organisation. Increased size and complexity made the original style difficult to operate. The company also found that it could only secure low-cost operations if there was centralisation of research and development and concentration of manufacturing facilities. In addition, profits were slipping in its main profit lines – personal computers and printers – as competitors drove down prices and market growth dipped.

To recover its former momentum and gain new economies of scale, the new chief executive of HP, Carly Fiorentina, launched a US$23 billion bid for rival computer maker *Compaq* in late 2001. This strategy would drive HP further down the route of a mainstream, volume computer manufacturer and

away from the old HP strategy of informal, innovative and experimental new products. The new strategy carried the significant risk that the cost savings from integrating the two companies would not be achieved and the creative benefits of management informality would be lost.

Case questions

1 *Why did corporate strategy change at HP? Can large corporations be informal and experimental? Or must they always follow strict central direction? Why?*

2 *To what extent does management style also matter in developing corporate strategy?*

1.1 What is corporate strategy?

1.1.1 The essence of corporate strategy

Corporate strategy can be described as the identification of the *purpose* of the organisation and the plans and actions to achieve that purpose.[2] During its early years, Hewlett-Packard's sense of purpose was to provide work for the two partners and their immediate

---

Figure 1.3   **The essence of corporate strategy**

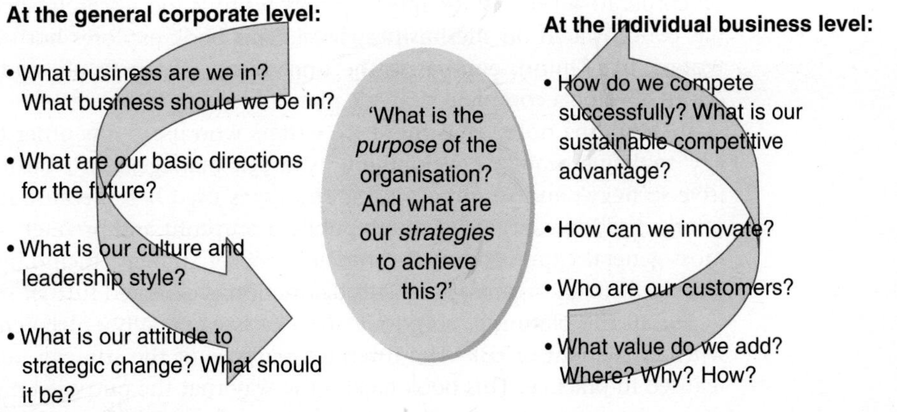

At the general corporate level:

- What business are we in? What business should we be in?

- What are our basic directions for the future?

- What is our culture and leadership style?

- What is our attitude to strategic change? What should it be?

'What is the *purpose* of the organisation? And what are our *strategies* to achieve this?'

At the individual business level:

- How do we compete successfully? What is our sustainable competitive advantage?

- How can we innovate?

- Who are our customers?

- What value do we add? Where? Why? How?

---

employees. In later years, the purpose changed as the company grew larger and it was able to seek new customers and broaden its product range. The purpose became a broader concept that included dividends to independent shareholders beyond its original founders and offering its services to a far wider range of customers.

Corporate strategy consists of two main elements: corporate-level strategy and business-level strategy. Figure 1.3 captures these two important aspects of the topic of Corporate Strategy. Early commentators such as Ansoff[3] and Drucker[4] clearly refer to both these aspects of strategy: mapping out the future directions that need to be adopted against the resources possessed by the organisation.

- *At the general corporate or headquarters level,* basic decisions need to be taken over what business the company is in or should be in. The culture and leadership of the organisation are also important at this broad general level.[5] For example, Hewlett Packard (HP) at the time of writing was negotiating a possible merger with a rival computer manufacturer, Compaq: the basic strategic decision to move further into computer manufacture, rather than expand in peripheral areas, was taken by the corporate headquarters of HP at that time. However, some senior board members of HP were resisting this strategy, so this was a problem connected with the leadership and culture of the organisation. Corporate-level strategy can be seen in the following definition of corporate strategy:

  > Corporate strategy is the pattern of major objectives, purposes or goals and essential policies or plans for achieving those goals, stated in such a way as to define what business the company is in or is to be in and the kind of company it is or is to be.[6]

- *At the business level,* corporate strategy is concerned with competing for customers, generating value from the resources and the underlying principle of the sustainable competitive advantages of those resources over rival companies. For example, HP in the early twenty-first century was investing heavily in new designs for computers and printers that would be faster, cheaper and more reliable than its competitors. Business-level strategy can be seen in the following definition of corporate strategy:

  > The strategy of the firm is the match between its internal capabilities and its external relationships. It describes how it responds to its suppliers, its customers, its competitors and the social and economic environment within which it operates.[7]

However, it has to be said that there is no universally agreed definition of strategy.[8] For example, while some strategy writers, such as Campbell and others,[9] have concentrated on corporate-level activity, most strategy writing and research, such as that by Porter,[10] has concentrated on the business level. This book explores both levels. Equally, some writers, like Quinn, emphasise the uncertainty of the future and suggest that setting out to develop a complete strategic plan may be a fruitless task.[11]

It should be noted that there are writers who use terms other than 'corporate strategy' to define strategy development: 'strategic management', 'business policy', 'competitive strategy', and so on. *Corporate strategy* is used here because it embraces every *type* of organisation – large and small; public, non-profit and privately owned – and it is the most general expression of the *various levels* of strategy, including all the many lower levels within an organisation. This distinction is explored further in Chapter 12.

For all the planning, corporate strategy is essentially entrepreneurial and dynamic, with an element of risk. The intended purpose of the strategy may not necessarily be realised in practice. This book tackles the way that the purpose and the plans or actions of an organisation are developed, the various methods of implementing the plans and how they change over time.

1.1.2 The three main areas of strategy

Examining the actions further at the *business level* of corporate strategy, every organisation has to manage its strategies in three main areas:

1 the organisation's internal *resources*;
2 the external *environment* within which the organisation operates;
3 the organisation's ability to *add value* to what it does.

Corporate strategy can be seen as the linking process between the management of the organisation's internal resources and its external relationships with its customers, suppliers, competitors and the economic and social environment in which it exists.[12]

The organisation develops these relationships from its abilities and resources. Hence, the organisation uses its history, skills, resources, knowledge and various concepts to explore its future actions. Figure 1.4 shows some examples of this process.

Figure 1.4 **Some examples of how corporate strategy links the organisation's resources with its environment**

Resources strategy

The *resources* of an organisation include its human resource skills, the investment and the capital in every part of the organisation. Organisations need to develop corporate strategies to optimise the use of these resources. In particular, it is essential to investigate the *sustainable competitive advantage* that will allow the organisation to survive and prosper against competition. For example, Hewlett-Packard had advantages in the production of computer printers and their associated software that set the standard for the industry. It had also invested heavily in branding its products and distribution systems. All these were part of its resources.

Environmental strategy

In this context *environment* encompasses every aspect external to the organisation itself: not only the economic and political circumstances, which may vary widely around the world, but also competitors, customers and suppliers, who may vary in being aggressive to a greater or lesser degree – customers and competitors are particularly important here. You may care to note that the word 'environment' in strategy does not just mean 'green, preserve the planet' issues, though these are important and are included in the definition.

Organisations therefore need to develop corporate strategies that are best suited to their strengths and weaknesses in relation to the environment in which they operate. For example, Hewlett-Packard faced a highly competitive environment for its printers in relation to Japanese companies such as Canon, Epson and Brother. In addition, the company had to cope with changing levels of economic growth in many markets around the world, which influenced the decisions of its customers to purchase new printers.

Some commentators, such as Ohmae,[13] suggest that a corporate strategy is really only needed when an organisation faces competitors: no competitive threat means there is no need for strategy. This is a rather narrow view of strategy and its environment: even a monopoly without competitors could need a strategy to defend its position. With a general move to privatise the nationalised monopolies around the world, corporate strategy may be required for this reason alone. Equally, charitable foundations compete for funds from donors and sometimes for the volunteers that make the wheels turn. A corporate strategy is no less relevant in this context.

Other commentators, such as Mintzberg,[14] have suggested that the environment is so uncertain, particularly at a global level, that it may be impossible to *plan* a long-term corporate strategy. This may need to be *crafted*, i.e. built up gradually through a learning process involving experimentation. The organisation may be seeking to add value by operating effectively, but the ever-changing environment offers little or no possibility for the management to plan in advance. Such commentators argue that unpredictable environments make the task of devising a realistic corporate strategy more than mere planning. Strategies have to be devised to cope with such difficulties.

Adding value

There is a need to explore further the purpose of corporate strategy beyond the requirements of environmental change and management of resources. In essence, the need is to *add value* to the supplies brought into the organisation. To ensure its long-term survival, an organisation must take the supplies it brings in, add value to these through its operations and then deliver its output to the customer.

For example, Hewlett-Packard takes the supplies it buys in – such as components, energy, skills and capital equipment – and then uses its own resources and expertise to create a product from these supplies – such as a computer or a printer – that has a value which is higher than the combined value of all the supplies which have been used to make the product. It adds value and then passes the product on to its customers.

The purpose of corporate strategy is to bring about the conditions under which the organisation is able to create this vital additional value. Corporate strategy must also ensure that the organisation adapts to changing circumstances so that it can continue to add value in the future. The ways in which value can be added and enhanced are crucial to corporate strategy.

Corporate strategy is both an art and a science. No single strategy will apply in all cases. While most would like to build on their skills, organisations will be influenced by their past experiences and culture, and constrained by their background, resources and environment (just as we are in our own individual lives). Nevertheless, corporate strategy is not without logic, or the application of scientific method and the use of evidence. At the end of the process, however, there is a place for the application of *business judgement,* as in our example, where Hewlett-Packard took a business judgement to go ahead in producing its early design of hand calculators because the break-even was acceptable. Later, it took the business judgement that its best strategy was to acquire a competitor, Compaq, in spite of the doubts of some commentators.

1.1.3 Key elements of strategic decisions

There are five key elements of strategic decisions that are related primarily to the organisation's ability to add value and compete in the market place. To illustrate these elements, examples are given from the highly competitive market for video computer games which was worth around US$20 billion globally in 2002:

1 *Sustainable decisions* that can be maintained over time. For the long-term survival of the organisation, it is important that the strategy is sustainable. There would be little point in Microsoft launching its new Xbox games console if the market disappeared after six months. Up to year 2002, the company had spent millions of dollars developing the product and this would take some years to recover.[15]

2 *Develop processes to deliver the strategy.* Strategy is at least partly about *how* to develop organisations or allow them to evolve towards their chosen purpose. For example, Microsoft began by launching Xbox into the US market in Autumn 2001, followed by Japan in early Spring 2002 and Europe about one month later. But the whole strategic decision of Microsoft to compete in this market had been taken years earlier and then major investments were undertaken to achieve this purpose.

3 *Offer competitive advantage.* A sustainable strategy is more likely if the strategy delivers sustainable competitive advantages over its actual or potential competitors. Corporate strategy usually takes place in a competitive environment. Even monopolistic government organisations need to compete for funds with rival government bodies. Microsoft was much later in entering the global computer games market than its main rivals, Sony and Nintendo. Microsoft therefore needed some special competitive advantages in its new machine to persuade customers of rival products to

change. It was offering what it claimed to be the best video graphics and the ability to play its games on-line. One way of developing competitive advantage is through *innovation* – a constant theme of this book.

4 *Exploit linkages between the organisation and its environment* – links that cannot easily be duplicated and will contribute to superior performance. The strategy has to exploit the many linkages that exist between the organisation and its environment: suppliers, customers, competitors and often the government itself. Such linkages may be contractual and formal, or they may be vague and informal (just because they are not legally binding does not mean they have little importance). In the case of video games machines, Microsoft was able to offer compatibility and connections with its other dominant computer software products: Explorer and Windows XP.

5 *Vision* – the ability to move the organisation forward in a significant way beyond the current environment. This is likely to involve innovative strategies. In the highly competitive video games market, it is vital to have a vision of the future. This may involve the environment but is mainly for the organisation itself: a picture of how video games might look in five to ten years' time will challenge and direct strategic decisions over the intervening period. For Microsoft, its vision of the Xbox would move it from its current involvement primarily with *office* activities like report writing to new, *home entertainment* applications – thus providing a completely new source of revenue. It is highly likely to involve *innovative* solutions to the strategic issues facing the industry.

In the final analysis, corporate strategy is concerned with delivering long-term *added value* to the organisation.

The key reading at the end of this chapter, taken from the work of Professor John Kay, further explores some essential aspects of corporate strategy.

▶ Key strategic principles

Corporate strategy can be considered at two levels in the organisation: the corporate level and the business level.

- **At the corporate level, corporate strategy is the pattern of major objectives, purposes or goals and the essential policies or plans for achieving those goals. It involves a consideration of what business the company is in or should be in.**

- **At the business level, corporate strategy is concerned with the match between the internal capabilities of the organisation and its external relationships with customers, competitors and others outside the organisation.**

- **Strategy is developed by a consideration of the resources of the organisation in relation to its environment, the prime purpose being to add value. The added value is then distributed among the stakeholders.**

- **There are five key elements of strategy, principally related to the need to add value and offer advantages over competitors: sustainability; process; competitive advantage; the exploitation of linkages between the organisation and its environment; vision. Several of these elements may well involve innovative solutions to strategic issues.**

Disaster and recovery at IBM: 1[16]

Corporate profit disaster at IBM

In the early 1990s, the world's largest computer company, International Business Machines (IBM), suffered one of the largest profit disasters in corporate history. Essentially, its problems were rooted in poor corporate strategy. This case study examines how IBM got into such a mess. The case study at the end of Chapter 2 shows how IBM managed to turn itself round.

Over the period 1991–93, IBM (US) suffered a net loss of almost US$16 billion (half the total GDP of the Republic of Ireland). During this period, the company had many of the characteristics of a supposedly good strategy: a dominant market share, excellent employee policies, reliable products (if not the most innovative), close relationships with national governments, responsible local and national community policies, sound finances and extensive modern plant investment around the world. Yet none of these was crucial to its profit problems, which essentially arose from a failure in corporate strategy. This case study examines how this came about: *see* Figure. 1.5. The reasons for the major losses are explored in the sections that follow – clearly the company was continuing to sell its products, but its costs were too high and it was unable to raise its prices because of increased competition.

IBM market domination 1970–85

During the 1970s and early 1980s, IBM became the first-choice computer company for many of the world's leading companies: it had a remarkable global market share – approaching 60 per cent. It constructed its computers to its own proprietary standards so that they were incompatible with other computers but helped to maintain the company's domination of the market.

In essence, IBM offered large, fast and reliable machines that undertook tasks never before operated by machinery: accounting, invoicing and payroll. Above all, choosing IBM meant that risk was low for customers: 'No one ever got fired for buying IBM.' Hence, IBM was the market leader in large *mainframe* computers and earned around 60 per cent of its profits from such machines.

Reflecting its dominance of global computer markets, the IBM culture was relaxed and supremely

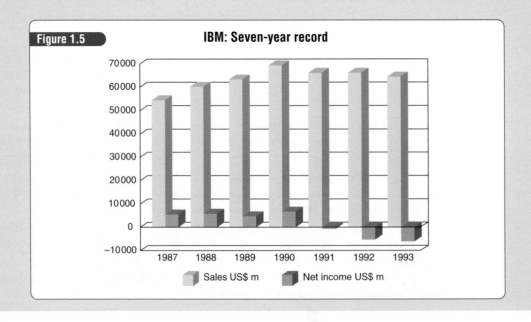

Figure 1.5

IBM: Seven-year record

Sales US$ m | Net income US$ m

(Chart values on vertical axis: 70000, 60000, 50000, 40000, 30000, 20000, 10000, 0, −10000; years on horizontal axis: 1987, 1988, 1989, 1990, 1991, 1992, 1993)

confident of its abilities and resources. Because of its sheer size and global reach, the company was split into a series of national companies, each operating with a great degree of independence. This meant that central management control was limited, with many key strategic decisions being taken at national company level. Often, central management did not even know what was happening in key product groups until the end of the year, when all the figures for the group were added up. For major new market developments, the initiative was often taken by IBM's North American subsidiary. Throughout this period, IBM central HQ was content to rely on the success and profitability of its mainframe computer range and observe the rapid growth of another small but related market in which it had no involvement: the personal computer (PC) market.

Development of the PC market

During the late 1970s and early 1980s, small PCs with names like Osborne, Commodore and Sinclair were developed. Some of these were particularly user-friendly – for example, Apple computers. In these early years, IBM preferred to maintain a lofty technical distance. It took the view that the PC market was small and PCs would never handle the mainframe tasks. Some of these small machines were built around common computer chips and software. Although they did not have the capacity to handle any of the large computational problems of computer mainframes, the PC market was growing fast – over 100 per cent per annum in some years. In the late 1970s, IBM was exploring new growth areas and decided to launch its own small machine onto the market.

The launch of the IBM PC in 1983

Because IBM's existing company structure was large and nationally based and its culture was so slow and blinkered, it chose to set up a totally new subsidiary to manufacture and market its first PC. Moreover, it did not use its own proprietary semiconductor chips and operating software. It acquired them respectively from the medium-sized chip manufacturer Intel (US) and from what was then a small software company called Microsoft (US).

IBM took the view that it was doing Intel and Microsoft and all PC customers a favour by making the IBM designs into the world standard. Indeed, IBM was rather proud of establishing the global benchmark in what was a small specialist market sector, as well as holding the lead in the much larger mainframe market. IBM finally launched its first PC in 1981 without tying either Intel or Microsoft exclusively to itself. The new PC cost US$3000 and, by today's standards, was very small. Although the claim 'IBM-compatible' quickly became a common standard for most PCs, except Apple, these developments had two consequences for IBM:

1 its worldwide PC standard allowed competitors to produce to a standard design for the first time;
2 no restriction was placed by IBM on Intel and Microsoft supplying similar products to other companies.

IBM reasoned that these issues did not matter because it would dominate the small PC market just as it did mainframes. In addition, IBM judged that the small PC would never replace the large mainframe, so it posed no significant threat to its main business. As it turned out, the company was at least partially wrong on both counts.

Technological advance and branding in the later 1980s

Although computer markets were driven by new technology, the key development was IBM's establishment of the common technical design mentioned above. This meant that its rivals at last had a common technical platform to drive down costs. IBM was unable or unwilling to find some way of patenting its design. IBM's strategic mistake was to think that its reputation alone would persuade customers to stay with its PC products. However, its competitors were able to exploit the new common IBM-compatible PC design to produce faster, reliable and cheaper machines than IBM, using the rapid advances in technology that occurred during the 1980s.

IBM and other computer companies continued to spend funds branding their products. However, their suppliers, such as Intel and Microsoft, also began to spend significant sums on advertising. Microsoft's 'Windows' was launched in the late 1980s and Intel's 'Pentium' microchip was launched in 1993. Both were destined to dominate their respective markets.

IBM slips into disaster 1986–93

In the late 1980s, IBM recognised the competitive threat from Microsoft and Intel. It launched its own proprietary software, OS/2 Warp, in 1994 to counteract this. It also negotiated with Apple to set up a new computer chip standard, the Power PC Chip, with the aim of attacking Intel. Although both initiatives had some innovations, they were too little and too late. IBM struggled on with the concepts, but the software made little headway against the established Microsoft and the chip was abandoned in the mid-1990s.

By 1993, IBM's advertising was forced into claiming that its PCs used the Microsoft 'Windows' operating system and its computer chips had 'Intel inside'. The IBM PC was just one of many computers in the small-computer market.

New organisation structure: 1991

Recognising the need for change, the company began to develop a new organisation structure in 1991. Up to this time, the organisation had been centred on two central aspects of the company:

1 *Products*. The company provided the most complete range of products from mainframes to telecommunications networks, from PCs to computer software. Each main product group sold its products independently of other groups.

2 *Country*. The company was the leading provider in most countries, with the ability to provide computer solutions tailored at national level for the particular requirements of each country. Each major country had its own dedicated management responsibilities.

While this provided strong local responsiveness, it meant that global and international company customers were not always well served through country companies and individual product offerings. In a new organisation announced in 1991, the major global industries such as banking, insurance, oil and gas, manufacturing, telecommunications companies and transport were tackled by dedicated teams with a *complete range of products* worldwide: the new structure involved the development of Industry Solution Units (ISUs). Each ISU had its own dedicated management team and was measured not only on sales but also on customer satisfaction. However, the country and the product managers were reluctant to give up control to the ISUs, which often operated internationally across many countries. This resulted in confusion among customers and some internal political battles inside IBM.

Future IBM strategy: 1993 strategic perspective

After the major profit problems of the early 1990s, IBM clearly needed a major shift in strategy. A new chief executive, Mr Lou Gerstner, was recruited from outside the computer industry, but he was faced with a major task. The conventional strategic view in 1993 was that the company was too large. Its true strengths were the series of national IBM companies that had real autonomy and could respond to specific national market conditions, and the wide range of good IBM products. But the local autonomy coupled with the large IBM product range meant that it was difficult to provide industry solutions. Moreover, its central HQ and research facility had difficulty in responding quickly to the rapid market and technological changes that applied across its global markets. The ISUs had been set up to tackle this but did not seem to be working. The most common strategy solution suggested for IBM was therefore to break up the company into a series of smaller and more responsive subsidiaries in different product areas – a PC company, a mainframe company, a printer company and so on.

Case questions

1 *Use the five key elements of strategic decisions (see Section 1.1.3) to evaluate IBM's corporate strategy. What conclusions do you draw for these and added value?*

2 *What are the strengths and weaknesses of IBM? And what are the opportunities and threats that it faces from the competitive environment surrounding the company?*

3 *What strategies would you have adopted in 1993 to turn round the situation at IBM? When you have made your choice, you might like to turn to the end of Chapter 2 and see what the company actually did.*

1.2 Core areas of corporate strategy

The three core areas of corporate strategy are:

1 *Strategic analysis.* The organisation, its mission and objectives have to be examined and analysed. Corporate strategy provides value for the people involved in the organisation – its *stakeholders* – but it is often the senior managers who develop the view of the organisation's overall objectives in the broadest possible terms. They conduct an examination of the *objectives* and the organisation's *relationship with its environment.* They will also analyse the *resources* of the organisation. This is explored in Chapters 3 to 12.

2 *Strategy development.* The strategy options have to be developed and then selected. To be successful, the strategy is likely to be built on the particular skills of the organisation and the special relationships that it has or can develop with those outside – suppliers, customers, distributors and government. For many organisations, this will mean developing advantages over competitors that are sustainable over time. There are usually many options available and one or more will have to be selected. This is covered in Chapters 13 to 16.

3 *Strategy implementation.* The selected options now have to be implemented. There may be major difficulties in terms of motivation, power relationships, government negotiations, company acquisitions and many other matters. A strategy that cannot be implemented is not worth the paper it is written on. This is explored in Chapters 17 to 22.

If a viable corporate strategy is to be developed, each of these three areas should be explored carefully. For the purpose of clarity, it is useful to separate the corporate strategy process into three sequential core areas, as we have done above. It would be wrong, however, to think of the three core areas as being only sequential. While it is not possible to implement something that does not exist, many organisations will have some existing relationships with customers and suppliers that are well developed, and others that have not yet started. Even small, new companies will want to experiment and negotiate. This means that activities in all three areas might well be simultaneous – implementing some ideas while analysing and developing others.

Table 1.1 lists some of the working definitions used in the three core areas of corporate strategy, some of which will already be familiar to you. To clarify the distinction between the terms, the table also includes the example of an ambitious young manager, showing his/her strategy for career progression. However, the example in Table 1.1 highlights two important qualifications to the three core areas:

1 the influence of judgement and values;

2 the high level of speculation involved in major predictions.

The importance of *judgement and values* in arriving at the mission and objectives shows that corporate strategy is not a precise science. For example, in the hypothetical career example in Table 1.1, the person has a clear view on what is important in life if their ambitions are to be achieved; some people would not share these ambitious values. We examine the role of value judgements further in Chapter 12.

Moreover, corporate strategy may be *highly speculative* and *involve major assumptions* as it attempts to predict the future of the organisation. For example, many of the later stages of the career progression in Table 1.1 involve some very difficult projections – on marriage, family and health, for example – that may well not be achieved. Indeed,

Table 1.1 Definition of terms used in the three core areas of strategy[17]

	Definition	*Personal career example*
Mission statement	Defines the business that the organisation is in against the values and expectations of the stakeholders	To become a leading European industrialist
Objectives (or goals)	State more precisely what is to be achieved and when the results are to be accomplished. Often quantified. (Note that there is no statement of how the results are to be attained)	To achieve a directorship on the main board of a significant company by the age of 42
Strategies	The pattern or plan that integrates an organisation's major goals or policies and action sequences into a cohesive whole. Usually deals with the *general principles* for achieving the objectives: why the organisation has chosen this particular route	1 To obtain an MBA from a leading European business school 2 To move into a leading consultancy company as a stepping stone to corporate HQ 3 To obtain a key functional directorship by the age of 35 in the chosen company
Plans (or programmes)	The *specific* actions that then follow from the strategies. They specify the step-by-step sequence of actions to achieve the major objectives	1 To obtain a first-class honours degree this year 2 To take the next two years working in a merchant bank for commercial experience 3 To identify three top business schools by December two years from now 4 To make application to these schools by January of the following year
Controls	The process of monitoring the proposed plans as they proceed and adjusting where necessary. There may well be some modification of the strategies as they proceed	Marriage and children mean some compromise on the first two years above Adjust plans back by three years
Reward	The result of the successful strategy, adding value to the organisation and to the individual	High salary and career satisfaction

given such uncertainties, it is difficult to see the example as anything more than an idealised series of wish-statements. In the same way, in the case of corporate strategy, there may be a largely false and perhaps unrealistic sense of direction.

Some books and research papers on corporate strategy do not recognise this problem and may be guilty of implying that corporate strategy has certainties about the future that it does not possess in reality.[18] This does not mean we should not explore the future directions of corporate strategy, just that we should be cautious about their meaning.

> ### ▶ Key strategic principles
>
> - The three core areas of corporate strategy are: strategic analysis, strategic development and strategy implementation.
> - There are two important qualifications to the three core areas. Judgement and values play an important role in determining the objectives and choice. Moreover, some elements are highly speculative and may involve major assumptions.
> - There is considerable overlap between the three core areas, which are separated out for the sake of clarity but, in practice, may operate concurrently.

1.3 Process, content and context

Research[19] has shown that in most situations corporate strategy is not simply a matter of taking a strategic decision and then implementing it. It often takes a considerable time to make the decision itself and then another delay before it comes into effect. There are two reasons for this. First, *people* are involved – managers, employees, suppliers and customers, for example. Any of these people may choose to apply their own business judgement to the chosen corporate strategy. They may influence both the initial decision and the subsequent actions that will implement it. Second, the *environment* may change radically as the strategy is being implemented. This will invalidate the chosen strategy and mean that the process of strategy development needs to start again.

For these reasons, an important distinction needs to be drawn in strategy development between *process, content* and *context*. Every strategic decision involves these three elements, which must be considered separately, as well as together.

Every strategic decision involves:

- *Context* – the environment within which the strategy operates and is developed. In the IBM case during the 1980s the context was the fast-changing technological development in personal computers.
- *Content* – the main actions of the proposed strategy. The content of the IBM strategy was the decision to launch the new PC and its subsequent performance in the market place.
- *Process* – how the actions link together or interact with each other as the strategy unfolds against what may be a changing environment. The process in the IBM case was the delay in tackling the PC market, the slow reaction to competitive actions and the interaction between the various parts of the company as it attempted to respond to competitor actions. Process is thus the means by which the strategy will be developed and achieved.

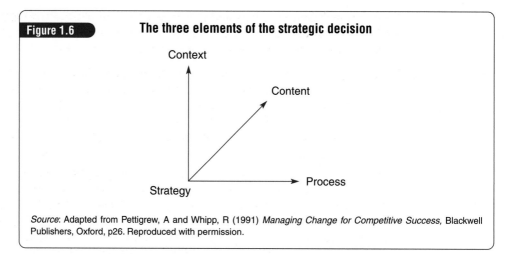

Figure 1.6 **The three elements of the strategic decision**

Source: Adapted from Pettigrew, A and Whipp, R (1991) *Managing Change for Competitive Success*, Blackwell Publishers, Oxford, p26. Reproduced with permission.

These three elements are the axes of the same three-dimensional cube of corporate strategy decision making (*see* Figure 1.6).

In most corporate strategy situations, the *context* and *content* are reasonably clear. It is the way in which strategy is developed and enacted – the *process* – that usually causes the most problems. Processes need investigation and are vague and quixotic because they involve people and rapidly changing environments.

The difficulty is compounded by the problem that, during the implementation period, the process can influence the initial strategic decision. For example, as the process unfolded at IBM, competitive actions forced the organisation to make cutbacks that were not originally identified as part of the strategic content.

At various points throughout this book, the distinction between process, content and context will be useful in clarifying relationships. Much emphasis will be laid on process, which is one of the more difficult parts of strategy.

Key strategic principles

- In corporate strategy development, it is necessary to distinguish between three elements: context, content and process.

- In most corporate strategy situations, the context and content are reasonably clear; it is the process that causes the problem because process may influence the way that people in the organisation develop and implement strategy.

- Process is the way actions link together or interact with each other as the strategy unfolds in the environment, which may itself be changing. It is often one of the more difficult parts of strategy development.

1.4 Process: linking the three core areas

1.4.1 Two different approaches to the process

Until now corporate strategy has been presented as a unified, cohesive subject. It is important at this point to explain and explore a fundamental disagreement which exists among commentators over the way that corporate strategy may be developed. Differing views on the content, process and nature of corporate strategy have arisen because of the breadth and complexity of the subject. For the present, the overall distinctions can be summarised as representing two main approaches to corporate strategy development:

1 *The prescriptive approach.* Some commentators have judged corporate strategy to be essentially a linear and rational process, starting with where-we-are-now and then developing new strategies for the future (*see* Jauch and Glueck[20] and Argenti[21]). A prescriptive corporate strategy is one whose *objective* has been defined in advance and whose *main elements* have been developed before the strategy commences.

2 *The emergent approach.* Other commentators take the view that corporate strategy emerges, adapting to human needs and continuing to develop over time. It is evolving, incremental and continuous, and therefore cannot be easily or usefully summarised in a plan which then requires to be implemented (*see* Mintzberg[22] and Cyert and March[23]). Emergent corporate strategy is a strategy whose *final objective* is unclear and whose *elements* are developed during the course of its life, as the strategy proceeds. The theorists of this approach often argue that long-term prescriptive strategies are of limited value.

In Chapter 2 we examine these important differences in more detail. There are, for example, differences in approach even amongst those who judge that the process is rational and linear. Mintzberg[24] captured the essence of the distinction:

The popular view sees the strategist as a planner or as a visionary; someone sitting on a pedestal dictating brilliant strategies for everyone else to implement. While recognising the importance of thinking ahead and especially of the need for creative vision in this pedantic world, I wish to propose an additional view of the strategist – as a pattern recognizer, a learner if you will – who manages a process in which strategies (and visions) can emerge as well as be deliberately conceived.

It should be noted here that Mintzberg sees merit in *both* approaches. (Both approaches can make a contribution and are not mutually exclusive. In many respects, they can be said to be like the human brain, which has both a rational left side and an emotional right side. Both sides are needed for the brain to function properly.[25]) It can be argued that the same is true in corporate strategy. Reference is therefore made to both the prescriptive and emergent approaches throughout this book. However, it should be understood that these are main headings for a *whole series of approaches* to the process of corporate strategy – explored in more detail in Chapter 2.

1.4.2 Impact on the three core areas

1 *The prescriptive approach* takes the view that the three core areas – strategic analysis, strategic development and strategy implementation – are linked together sequentially. Thus it is possible to use the analysis area to develop a strategy which is then implemented. The corporate strategy is *prescribed* in advance (*see* Figure 1.7(a)).

2 *The emergent approach* takes the view that the three core areas are essentially interrelated. However, it is usual to regard the analysis area as being distinctive and in advance of the other two elements. Because corporate strategy is then developed by an experimental process that involves trial and error, it is not appropriate to make a clear distinction between the strategy development and implementation phases: they are closely linked, one responding to the results obtained by the other. These relationships are shown in Figure 1.7(b).

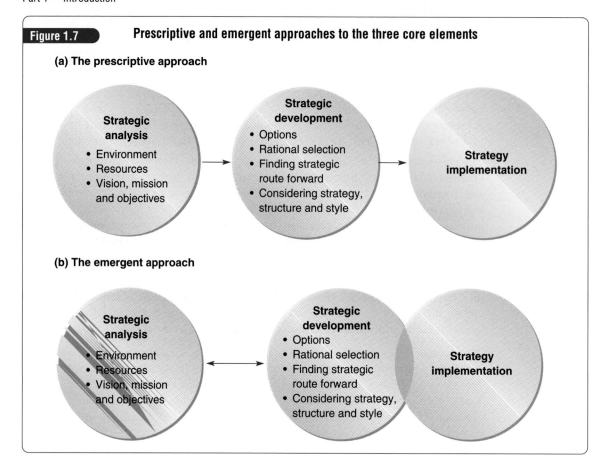

Figure 1.7 **Prescriptive and emergent approaches to the three core elements**

(a) The prescriptive approach

Strategic analysis
- Environment
- Resources
- Vision, mission and objectives

Strategic development
- Options
- Rational selection
- Finding strategic route forward
- Considering strategy, structure and style

Strategy implementation

(b) The emergent approach

Strategic analysis
- Environment
- Resources
- Vision, mission and objectives

Strategic development
- Options
- Rational selection
- Finding strategic route forward
- Considering strategy, structure and style

Strategy implementation

1.4.3 Developing models of corporate strategy

Based on the two approaches, it is possible to develop models to aid in understanding the way that corporate strategy operates. These models are explained here and will then be used throughout this book to structure our examination of corporate strategy.

The whole process is shown in Figure 1.8. By matching the numbers in the following sections with the numbers on the prescriptive model in Figure 1.8, you will be able to follow the corporate strategy process and appreciate the differences between the two main approaches. Note that no numbers appear on the emergent model because its essence is that the process can occur in any order and elements can be interrelated.

Strategic analysis

The analytical phase of both the *prescriptive* and the *emergent* approach can be divided into two parts:

- *Analysis of the environment* – examining what is happening or likely to happen outside the organisation, e.g. economic and political developments, competition. (**1**)
- *Analysis of resources* – exploring the skills and resources available inside the organisation, e.g. human resources, plant, finance. (**2**)

Figure 1.8

The prescriptive and emergent strategic processes

(a) The prescriptive strategic process

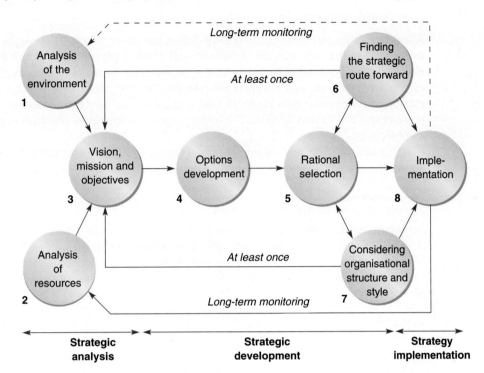

Long-term monitoring

At least once

At least once

Long-term monitoring

| Strategic analysis | Strategic development | Strategy implementation |

(b) The emergent strategic process

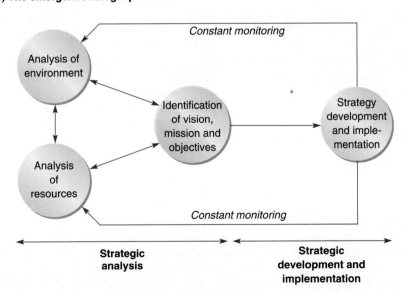

Constant monitoring

Constant monitoring

| Strategic analysis | Strategic development and implementation |

Important: These two models illustrate two extremes of the strategic process. They oversimplify the reality, which is often more complex and interactive. But they are useful in emphasising and thinking about the different facets of the strategic process.

These are followed by a third element:

- *Identification of vision, mission and objectives* – developing and reviewing the strategic direction and the more specific objectives, e.g. the maximisation of profit or return on capital, or in some cases a social service. (**3**)

Some strategists put this third element *before* the other two.[26] They argue that any organisation first sets out its objectives and then analyses how to achieve them. However, this book takes the view that it is necessary to set objectives in the *context* of the environment and competitive resources of the organisation. For example, a manufacturer of straw hats needs to take account of the very limited demand for that product and the limited likelihood of having superior competitive resources *before* setting its objectives.

So vision, mission and objectives are accepted by both prescriptive and emergent approaches but, at this point, the two processes clearly diverge.

Strategy development and implementation

According to the prescriptive approach, the next step is the formal consideration of the options available to achieve the agreed objectives. (**4**) This is followed by a rational selection from the options according to identified criteria, in order to arrive at the prescriptive strategy. (**5**) In most cases, this choice is then subject to two further considerations:

- *Finding the strategic route forward* – taking into account new and emerging information to see how it might impact on the choice, with some adjustment being made if necessary. (**6**)
- *Considering strategy, structure and style* – taking into account the way the organisation is managed and structured, and its style of operation. (**7**)

These may all need to be considered before a final decision is made on which strategy to pursue. It will usually be essential at this point to reconsider the impact of these choices on the basic mission and objectives of the organisation. This is because the strategic choice may have some implications for the mission and objectives, possibly even altering them. For example, it may turn out that the chosen strategy does not meet the objectives; either the strategy or the objectives will need to be changed. Once the strategy has been agreed, it is then implemented. (**8**)

In Figure 1.8(a) the steps in this process can be followed. It should be emphasised, however, that this diagram represents only one description of the approach; there are many different approaches, with strategists unable to agree on the definitive prescriptive route.

Strategy development and implementation – the emergent approach

Essentially, this takes a much more experimental view of the strategy choice and its implementation. It seeks to learn by trial, experimentation and discussion as strategies are developed. There is no final, agreed strategy but rather a series of experimental approaches that are considered by those involved and then developed further. Strategies emerge during a process of crafting and testing.

There is therefore no clear distinction in the emergent approach between the two stages of developing the strategy and its implementation.

Moreover, there is no need to identify a separate stage of discussion inv[...] leadership, culture and organisation, since all these will occur inevitably duri[...] strategy development and implementation phase. Importantly, there is then a stro[...] link back to the earlier analytical phase, enabling changes in the environment and resources to be reflected quickly in the adaptive, learning strategy. This is shown in Figure 1.8(b).

By definition, there can be no single view of a process that emerges within an organisation – each one will be different. Figure 1.8(b) serves to indicate the circulatory nature of the decision-making process according to this approach. There is no definitive emergent route.

▶ Key strategic principles

- There are two main approaches to corporate strategy development: the *prescriptive* approach and the *emergent* approach. Each complements the other, and both are relevant to the strategy process.

- The *prescriptive* approach takes the view that the three core elements are linked together sequentially. The *emergent* approach regards the three core areas as being essentially interrelated.

- The two approaches can be used to develop models for the corporate strategy process. However, it should be recognised that every model is a compromise and may not reflect all the circumstances that exist in reality.

1.5 What makes 'good' strategy?

Given the lack of agreement on a definition of corporate strategy and the difficulty of developing it successfully, it is relevant to explore what makes 'good' corporate strategy. To some, it might appear that there is one obvious answer: 'good' strategy delivers the purpose set out for the strategy in the beginning. However, this begs several important questions:

- Was the purpose itself reasonable? For example, perhaps the purpose was so easy that any old strategy would be successful.

- What do we do when it is difficult to define the purpose clearly, beyond some general objective of survival or growth? Such vagueness may make it difficult to test whether a 'good' strategy has been developed.

- Since the whole purpose of strategy is to explore what we do in the *future*, can we afford to wait until it has been achieved before we test whether it is good?

Essentially, we need some more robust tests of good strategy. These lie in two areas. First, those related to the real world of the organisation and its activities: *application-related.* Second, those that rely on the disciplines associated with the basic principles of *academic rigour*: originality, logical thought and scientific method. It might be argued that academic rigour has no relevance to the real world, but this would be wrong. All organisations should be able to apply these basic principles to the process of strategy development.

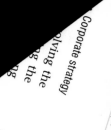
...of good strategy: application-related

...st three tests are available that provide some means of assessing whether a strat-
...s good:

The value-added test. A good strategy will deliver increased value added in the market place. This might show itself in increased profitability, but might also be visible in gains in longer-term measures of business performance such as market share, innovative ability and satisfaction for employees.

2 *The consistency test.* A good strategy will be consistent with the circumstances that surround a business at any point in time. It will take into account its ability to use its resources efficiently, its environment, which may be changing fast or slowly, and its organisational ability to cope with the circumstances of that time.

3 *The competitive advantage test.* For most organisations, a good strategy will increase the sustainable competitive advantage of the organisation. Even those organisations that traditionally may not be seen as competing in the market place – such as charities or government institutions – can be considered as competing for resources. Charities compete with others for new funds, government departments compete with each other for a share of the available government funds.

In practice, such tests can be applied to strategy proposals at any time.

1.5.2 Tests of good strategy: academic rigour

Another five tests might also be employed that relate to the above but are more fundamental to the basic principles of originality, logical thought and scientific method:

1 *The originality test.* The best strategy often derives from doing something totally different. One test that has academic validity is therefore that of originality. However, this needs to be used with considerable caution or it becomes just another excuse for wild and illogical ideas that have no grounding in the topic.

2 *The purpose test.* Even if there are difficulties in defining purpose, it is logical and appropriate to examine whether the strategies that are being proposed make some attempt to address whatever purpose has been identified for the organisation. Such a definition of purpose might be taken to include the aspirations and ambitions of the leaders of the organisation, along with its stakeholders.

3 *The logical consistency test.* Do the recommendations flow in a clear and logical way from the evidence used? And what confidence do we have in the evidence used? Do we trust such evidence – perhaps it is unreliable because it has come from a competitor?

4 *The risk and resources test.* Are the risks and resources associated with the strategies sensible in relation to the organisation? They might be consistent with the overall purpose, but involve such large levels of risk that they are unacceptable. Moreover, they may require resources that are substantially beyond those available to the organisation – not just finance, but perhaps people and skills.

5 *The flexibility test.* Do the proposed strategies lock the organisation into the future regardless of the way the environment and the resources might change? Or do they allow some flexibility depending on the way that competition, the economy, the management and employees and other material factors develop?

While none of these tests are complete in themselves, together they provide a way to explore proposals and the many case studies that appear in this book.

> ### ▶ Key strategic principles
>
> - The lack of agreement on the precise meaning of corporate strategy makes it difficult to identify what is meant by 'good' corporate strategy. If strategy development is to be beneficial, then a careful exploration and definition of the purpose of the task is essential early in the process. Two areas of test are suggested in this search: application-related and academic rigour.
>
> - *Application-related* might be considered as having three major components: value added, consistency with the environment and the delivery of competitive advantage.
>
> - *Academic rigour* can usefully be considered as having five components: originality, relevance to the defined purpose, logical consistency, risks and resources, flexibility.

1.6 Strategy development in public and non-profit organisations

1.6.1 Public organisations

In many countries around the world, the public sector forms the major part of industrial and commercial activity, e.g. telecommunications services in South Africa and the French government controlling shareholdings in its national electricity and gas companies, although some of these have now been privatised.[27] Since such companies often compete internationally with the private sector, many of the same strategy considerations apply to public and to private organisations. The major difference has been the lack in government-owned institutions of the objective to deliver a profit. The European Commission has now taken the view that state subsidies may not be compatible with the Treaty of Rome, and public organisations have come under increasing pressure to apply commercial criteria.[28] In Europe, there are many organisations in the public sector, ranging from electricity supply in some countries to public health bodies in others. Their individual requirements for strategy development will depend on their precise nature. Certainly those that are being privatised will need to consider this area.

Outside Western Europe, many key industries remain in public ownership. However, the trend in most parts of the world is now towards privatising large public companies in the utilities and telecommunications sectors. The arguments in favour of the change of ownership are set out in the *World Bank Report 1994*.[29] The principal impact of privatisation on strategy will depend on the form that privatisation takes. Some companies may still remain monopolies even though they are in the private sector.

The main considerations regarding corporate strategy in public organisations include:

- *Policy and politics.* Some European countries and Asian countries such as India and China are committed to the view that public companies are there to provide a public service. Strategy is therefore directed towards achieving this aim. The political policy of the government will guide strategic development.

- *Monopoly suppliers.* Public authorities are often monopoly suppliers of a service. While they may be under pressure to operate efficiently (however that is defined), they may be unable to spend any surplus profits they generate. Moreover, they will be subject to changes in government policy direction and will lack the consistency of private organisations as a result. The lack of choice for customers will mean the suppliers are not really subject to the market pressures that affect business strategy in the private sector.

● *Bureaucracy and slower rate of change.* Being part of the public sector may affect the management style and values of managers and the workforce, leading specifically to greater bureaucracy and a slower rate of response to outside pressures.

● *Battle for resources from government.* Much of the real strategy in the public sector across Europe is fought over the allocation of resources from central government. Increases in annual budget allocations or cutbacks in funds affect fundamentally the service and level of investment in physical assets available to the public. There is no reason why such considerations should not be subject to strategic scrutiny, but the nature of the evidence and logic may be different.

1.6.2 Non-profit organisations

Both public and private organisations operate in this area: charities, churches, even some educational institutions, for example. Non-profit organisations are usually founded for reasons other than commercial considerations: for instance, bird and animal welfare, disease research, international rescue, poverty alleviation. For these reasons, corporate strategy must first recognise and reflect the values held by such organisations.[30] It also needs to understand the voluntary nature of much of this activity and the varied sources of funds often available.

All of these considerations will have a profound effect on corporate strategy. Decision making may be slower and more uncertain. There may be more lobbying of funding bodies over individual decisions. There may be several conflicting objectives that make strategy difficult to develop. The style and expectations of the organisation need to be built into the strategy process.

▶ Key strategic principles

● **Public organisations are unlikely to have a profit objective. Strategy is therefore governed by broader public policy issues such as politics, monopoly supply, bureaucracy and the battle for resources from the government to fund the activities of the organisation.**

● **Strategy in non-profit organisations needs to reflect the values held by the institutions concerned. Decision making may be slower and more complex.**

● **Within the constraints outlined above, the basic strategic principles can then be applied.**

1.7 International dimensions in corporate strategy

While the principles of corporate strategy can be applied across the world, the international dimensions of strategy do introduce some specific and important considerations.[31]

● *International economies and their impact on trading between nations.* The completion of the Uruguay Round of the General Agreement on Tariffs and Trade in 1994, the enlargement of the EU in the period 2004–2008 and the formation of the North American Free Trade Association in 1994 are all examples of such developments. All may provide opportunities and pose threats for company corporate strategy.

- *International finance, currency and tax.* For example, adverse currency movements alone could severely curtail gains to be made from other aspects of corporate strategy.

- *Economies of scale and production.* Coupled with the lower wage costs available in some countries, these have had a powerful impact on aspects of corporate strategy.

- *Differing cultures, beliefs and management styles around the world.* These are major factors that must form an important part of corporate strategy for international companies. Major strategic problems have arisen where international companies have considered these vital topics too late in the strategy process.

This is not a comprehensive list of major topics, but it does illustrate the specific impact on corporate strategy. Corporate strategy is more complex in international environments, but the same basic principles also apply. International issues are explored at the end of most chapters in this text, with a major review being undertaken in Chapter 19.

▶ Key strategic principles

- The international dimensions of corporate strategy make its development more complicated.

- Among the topics that need careful consideration are: international economies and their impact on world trade; international finance; economies of scale derived from global production; differing cultures and beliefs.

CASE STUDY 1.3

Sky-high strategies of Europe's budget airlines[32]

Between 1993 and 1997, European airline markets were steadily freed from government regulations on competition, pricing and services. Following this deregulation process, the new European budget airlines – like Ryanair (Ireland), Easyjet (UK), Germania (Germany) and Buzz (Netherlands) – presented some serious competition to Europe's leading airlines. This case explores the attack strategies that threaten the very survival of companies like Lufthansa, British Airways and SAS.

'We make money with falling air fares. And we make stinking piles of money with rising air fares ... It's scary' – Michael O'Leary, chief executive of Ryanair in year 2000. None of Europe's largest airlines made any profit in 2001. Two of Europe's leading airlines – Swiss Air and Sabena – went bankrupt, British Airways announced plans to shed 23 per cent of its workforce by the year 2004 and Lufthansa threatened to set up its own budget airline. By contrast and in the same year, Ryanair and Easyjet were making significant profits and ordering new aircraft to expand their European operations. Europe's major air carriers were in major strategic trouble. However, this was not just because of the new budget airlines.

Reasons for the strategic difficulties – high staff costs and poor load factors

Although the budget airlines represented a significant competitive threat to Europe's leading airlines, the problems facing such airlines were more complex than a simple high- versus low-cost strategy. The leading airlines traditionally earned their major profits from their *long-haul* routes – like Amsterdam to New York or London to Singapore. Their *short-haul* routes, i.e. those inside their home countries or within the EU, were rather less profitable. On the long-haul routes, they were able to charge high prices because of special 'open skies' deals that existed between individual EU countries and other nations like the USA. Essentially, country governments in the 1990s signed these deals. They carved up the long-haul markets between countries – like Germany to the USA – between a limited number of airlines and excluded other European and foreign airlines that might offer more competition. In addition, each European country controlled flight access to its major airports and gave preferential treatment to its own national carriers – Air France in France, KLM in the Netherlands and so on – thus reducing competition and raising prices. In 2002, the European Commission challenged these agreements, arguing that they were against the open competition rules of the Treaty of Rome. At the time of writing, this legal challenge was unresolved and 'open skies' policies persisted.

As a result, those airlines with a high proportion of such profitable long-haul routes and destinations – like Lufthansa, British Airways and Air France – were able to earn significant profits and perhaps justify higher numbers of employees. Table 1.2 shows the resulting picture in terms of staff costs in comparison with turnover. Companies like Iberia, SAS and Alitalia had proportionately less long-haul turnover – for example, fewer people wanted to fly from Stockholm to New York than from Frankfurt to New York. Hence, the smaller airlines were unable to benefit to the same extent from such profitable routes. Even so, most European airline companies persisted for many years in maintaining relatively high numbers of staff. Recognising the long-term difficulty with such a strategy, Lufthansa took the strategic decision some years ago to manage with fewer staff. All the other leading airlines had relatively high staff costs and this is reflected in the data in Table 1.2.

Table 1.2 Comparing European airlines – the budget airlines manage with far fewer employees

Airline	Country	Revenue US$ million, year 2000	Number of employees ('000)	Passengers (millions)	Strategic comment
Lufthansa	Germany	14 000	38	41	Withdrew some UK flights 2001 under pressure from budget airlines
British Airways	UK	13 600	63	36	Withdrew part of Gatwick/UK operations as a result of pressure from budget airlines 2002
Air France	France	11 100	56	42	Under threat from Easyjet at Paris/Orly
Swiss Air	Switzerland	9 500	7	15	Bankrupt 2001 – as a result of cost pressures rather than budget airlines
KLM Royal Dutch	Netherlands	6 300	30	16	Competition now opened up Eindhoven – launched own budget airline 2001
SAS	Sweden, Denmark and Norway	5 200	22	23	Real competition from Ryanair and Easyjet to new destinations in Denmark and Sweden – some high domestic prices: see text

Table 1.2 continued

Airline	Country	Revenue US$ million, year 2000	Number of employees ('000)	Passengers (millions)	Strategic comment
Alitalia	Italy	5 000	23	27	New domestic budget competitors plus Go, Easyjet and Ryanair
Iberia	Spain	4 100	27	25	Easyjet and Go offer cheap flights to Spanish destinations
Sabena	Belgium	2 500	8	11	Bankrupt 2001 – as a result of cost pressures rather than budget airlines
Virgin	UK	2 240	7	4	Losses at Virgin Europe are not included in these data – low-cost competition
Austrian Airlines	Austria	1 800	5	4	New competition to Austria from budget airlines 2002
Finnair	Finland	1 600	9	7	Some competition planned
Two selected budget airlines					
Ryanair	Ireland	390	1	6	Just look at the passengers carried for the number of employees
Easyjet	UK	350	1	5	Now vying with Ryanair for leadership of the budget European market

Source: Company Annual Reports and Accounts plus press reports.

In addition to high staff costs, the more recent problem has been 'load factor' – the percentage of seats filled by paying passengers on each aircraft. With a scheduled flight, the aircraft has to keep to a timetable and fly, even if it is half-empty. And two factors reduced passenger numbers dramatically in 2001:

● *Downturn in the world economy* – leading to fewer business-class travellers. These were the real profit earners as they were willing to pay much higher prices than economy class passengers for marginal improvements in flight comfort.

● *Tragic events of September 11* – making people and companies reluctant to undertake unnecessary air travel.

Thus in 2001, long-haul flights were not as profitable as in previous years. In addition, the 'open skies' policy still allowed some competition and all airlines were suffering. The problem here was that no airline had any real competitive advantage over its rivals apart from the 'open skies' deals and the rights to land at some national airports.

Market size, growth and share of the leading European airlines – a controlled strategic environment

At one level, the world airline market is large, with total turnover of over US$600 billion. However, this is misleading strategically because most airlines are concentrated in one geographic continent and because there is little growth, for the reasons outlined above. In the past, this has been compensated by the 'open skies' deals, which meant that many international markets were controlled by small oligopolies of aircraft companies. By co-operating on these leading routes, such airlines were able to hold up their prices and keep out new entrants by government treaty.

Beyond such treaty advantages, no airline company had any significant competitive advantage over its rivals. They were all transporting aircraft seats around the world and competing on offering better in-flight meals, higher quality in-flight entertainment, longer seat-room and so on. The problem with all these supposed 'advantages' was that any company could match another over time and none was really sustainable. Moreover, such advantages were often not possible on routes within Europe because the flights were too short. In addition, the European budget airlines decided that what really mattered to customers was ticket prices.

European airline markets: customers and market segmentation

The European airline market can be broadly divided into two main market segments – business customers and leisure/domestic customers. Roughly 80 per cent of all customers fall into the latter category – they are travelling for holiday or domestic reasons such as study or visiting relations. They are important to fill the aircraft but do not represent the most profitable segment of the airline market. According to Tony O'Leary of Ryanair, 'In this business, it's low cost that wins. Ninety nine per cent of people want the cheapest price. They don't want awards for the inflight magazine or the best coffee. The brand? Who cares? It has to be safe, on time and cheap. It's a bus service, it's transport.'

The other 20 per cent are business customers. They are paid for by their companies and are engaged on business-related activities. It is this latter group that is usually prepared to pay for full-fare tickets and travel in greater comfort. For the airlines, the business customers are therefore the most profitable. There is some recent evidence that business customers are increasingly under pressure from their companies to travel on budget airlines. The main difficulty may be that some budget airports are located far from business destinations: for example, the 'Frankfurt-Hahn' destination of Ryanair from London Stansted is 96 kilometres from the main business centre of Frankfurt.

Perhaps the most important strategic feature of the European airline market is the lack of strong market segments beyond the two above. This makes it difficult to operate dedicated niche strategies that target these segments with special prices, services and related activities. The lack of such segments has made it easier for the budget airlines to attack the leading European companies.

Strategic threat from the budget European airlines

Low-price flights have been available for many years throughout Europe: the holiday charter air companies offered them by taking groups of tourists on holiday using special flights and dedicated aircraft. However, such flights were not available to the general public at scheduled times. This all changed with the *deregulation* of the European airline market in the 1990s. For example, in October 2001 a typical business ticket on a scheduled flight from London Gatwick to Amsterdam cost US$550 on British Airways and US$170 on Easyjet – but see the comment on the availability of tickets later in this section. The difficulty of British Airways and all the other leading European airlines is that they were unable to match the budget airline prices and still make a profit just by cutting out newspapers and coffee. Table 1.2 provides a clue – just compare the number of employees at BA and Easyjet and then look at the number of passengers carried.

Even amongst the budget airlines, low price itself is not a sustainable competitive advantage. However, lower costs than competitors are an advantage – as long as they can be maintained. The difficulty is that such a route to competitive advantage is well known. For example, Ryanair copied this approach from South West Airlines in the US in the late 1980s: 'We went to look at South West. It was like the road to Damascus. This was the way to make Ryanair work' – Michael O'Leary, chief executive of Ryanair.

Table 1.3 lists some of their cost-reduction practices. Nevertheless, it should be acknowledged that the level of service on the European budget airlines may be barely tolerable for some passengers. In addition, some European airports are far from tourist destinations. However, Easyjet and Go both had a deliberate policy of flying to main airports, even if the landing fees are higher. The aim was to attract business travellers. Moreover, the budget airlines often only offer the very low prices on the seats that they have difficulty in filling – just try to book a low-price seat during a main holiday weekend! Perhaps there is not so much competitive advantage on costs over the leading European carriers after all.

Table 1.3 Some examples of how to keep costs down at Europe's budget airlines

Cost reduction strategy	Reason
Rapid turnaround at the airport – maximum of 25 minutes	The aircraft only earns profits when it is flying
Choose airports with low handling charges	Significant savings can be made by avoiding London/Heathrow, Paris/CDG, etc.
No food or newspapers sold or free on the aircraft	Clearing up food and waste paper delays the turnaround time
Few job restrictions – even the pilots may help with baggage	Saves the cost of extra staff
Avoid travel agents and use the Internet for booking	Travel agents charge fees and the Internet can be used to fill seats quickly at the last minute
Operate one type of very modern aircraft – often the latest model Boeing or Airbus	Reduces maintenance costs

Source: Press reports – see references at end of chapter.

Strategic response from Europe's leading airlines up to year 2002: muddled and uncertain

In the face of the significant threat to their European routes, the response of the leading European airlines has been somewhat *inconsistent. For example, British Airways (BA) decided in 1999 to launch its own low-cost airline, called Go. This was duly set up in year 2000. Then in 2001, BA decided that its new strategy was to withdraw from the low-cost end of the market and concentrate on business passengers. The company sold Go to a management buyout in mid-2001. By the end of that year, BA announced a new strategy. It was restructuring its European airlines on low-cost strategic lines, but would not be setting up a separate airline. 'We will not become a no-frills airline, nor will we launch one' – Rodd Eddington, BA's chief executive. Nevertheless, BA would be reducing its fleet costs, reducing levels of service to economy class passengers and assuming the business class passengers would continue to pay full fare.

Lufthansa's response was different but equally defensive. Its immediate strategy was to offer low prices on its own domestic routes and match Germania, its low-cost rival. This prompted a warning to Lufthansa from the German competition office about selling seats below costs. In late 2001, Lufthansa withdrew its services from some UK/German routes where it faced heavy competition. In addition, the airline mounted a legal challenge to Ryanair's German advertising that called on Germans not to let 'Lufthansa strip you down to your underpants'. Ryanair expected 1.5 million German passengers in 2002, rising to 10 million in 2008.

The Dutch airline KLM responded to the budget airline challenge by setting up its own low-cost airline, Buzz. Air France was concerned when its French competitor, Air Lib, collapsed in France, thus releasing some air landing slots at Paris/Orly airport. Easyjet attempted to take all these slots, but has only been awarded a portion of them at the time of writing. SAS, Scandinavian Airlines, set up a series of deals with low-cost rivals Maersk in Denmark and Skyways in Sweden. But these arrangements either broke EU competition rules or were under suspicion of having done so. Thus, they might not stand. Many of Europe's leading airlines have thus far been unable to withstand the strategic challenge of the budget carriers in any substantive way.

In March 2002, a consortium of the leading European airlines launched their own website to sell airline tickets cheaply at the last minute and fill remaining aircraft capacity: it is called opodo and can be viewed at: www.opodo.co.uk. At the time of writing, its benefits remained unproven.

Conclusion

In 2001, Ryanair and Easyjet carried 7.4 million passengers and 7.1 million passengers respectively. At that time, Ryanair was talking of carrying 40 million passengers annually by 2009–10. Easyjet forecast passenger numbers of 30 million by late 2007–8. Other low-cost airlines were also setting ambitious targets. There will be some market growth over this period, but the majority of such passengers can only come from the existing European airline carriers.

Case questions

1 *Why is the development of corporate strategy important for the major European airlines?*

2 *Using the concept of the three major stages of corporate strategy, identify the possible main elements that might appear in a strategic plan for a low-cost airline.*

3 *What sustainable competitive advantages do the main European airlines possess?*

4 *What strategies are needed for the main European airlines to survive?*

KEY READING

Successful corporate strategy[33]

In this extract from his book Foundations of Corporate Success, *Professor John Kay explains the basic nature of corporate strategy and the strategies employed by successful companies.*

The subject of strategy analyses the firm's relationships with its environment, and a business strategy is a scheme for handling these relationships. Such a scheme may be articulated, or implicit, pre-programmed, or emergent. A strategy is a sequence of united events which amounts to a coherent pattern of business behaviour. All firms are part of a rich network of relationships. They must deal with customers and suppliers, with competitors and potential competitors. For many firms, the relationship with the government is also critical to their strategy. The government may buy the firm's products or regulate many of its activities.

These relationships may be *classical* and *contractual* – elaborately articulated in legal documents – or they may be *informal* and *relational*, and enforced primarily by the need the parties have to go on doing business with each other. They are designed to secure outcomes in which all parties win, because in commerce, as in life, relationships are rarely of the type in which one party gains what the other loses. They are designed to deal with the problems of co-operation, of co-ordination, and of differentiation. The unique structure of these relationships, their architecture, is the source of some firms' competitive advantage [*see* Chapter 6 of this book].

If the subject of business strategy focuses on the relationship between the firm and its environment, there are many key management issues which it does not address. Strategy is not principally concerned with employee motivation, or with finance, or with accounting, or with production scheduling and inventory control, although these may influence the firm's strategy and be influenced by it. In the last two decades, the pretensions and prestige of the subject of strategy have been such that strategists have stressed not only the central importance of the issues with which they deal but also the relevance of strategy to all aspects of business behaviour. For the same reasons, everyone involved in business – from the personnel manager to the public relations consultant – has asserted a right to contribute to the strategy process.

But strategy is not simply another word for important. There are many aspects to good management, and to say that strategy and operations management are distinct facets of it is not to disparage either. Yet there is a difference between strategy and these other elements of management practice which illuminates the nature of strategy itself and may partly explain its supposed primacy. In most industries, there are many firms which have their finance and accounting right, their human relations right, their information technology adapted to their needs. For one firm to succeed in these areas does not damage the others. In implementing finance and accounting, human relations, and information technology, it is right and normal, to look to the best practice in other firms.

But strategy is not like that. Honda and BMW did not establish their market positions by meth-ods which built on the best practice of their competitors. For both companies, attempts to match their rivals' strategies failed. BMW's bubble cars were not as well regarded as Innocenti's, and its limousines were inferior to those of Mercedes. Honda was able to sell powerful motor bikes in the US only after its success with quite different products had destroyed its competitors' finances and established its own reputation. Successful strategy is rarely copycat strategy. It is based on doing well what rivals cannot do or cannot do readily, not what they can do or are already doing.

Source: Kay, J (1993) *Foundations of Corporate Success*. Reproduced by permission of Oxford University Press.

Summary

● In this chapter, we have explored the nature of corporate strategy – linking process between the organisation and its environment – which focuses particularly on value added and the sustainable competitive advantages of the organisation and the need to be innovative. Adding value is of particular importance to most organisations, though for non-profit and government organisations this is not necessarily the case.

● There are three core areas of corporate strategy: strategic analysis; strategic development; and strategy implementation. Although the three core areas are often presented as being strictly sequential, they will be simultaneous in some circumstances. There are two important qualifications to the three core areas: the use of judgement and values to derive the strategy and the need to make highly speculative assessments about the future. Unless handled carefully, these may give a false sense of direction about the future.

● In developing corporate strategy, there is a need to distinguish between process, content and context. Process is the method by which the strategies are derived; content is the strategic decisions then made; context is the environment within which the organisation operates and develops its strategies. Process is usually the area that causes the most problems because it is difficult to measure precisely and because it is crucial to strategy development.

● There is a fundamental disagreement between strategists regarding how corporate strategy can be developed. There are two basic routes: the *prescriptive approach* and the *emergent approach*. The prescriptive approach takes the view that the three core areas are linked together sequentially; the emergent approach regards the three core areas as being interrelated. The two approaches have some common elements in the early stages: analysis and the development of a mission for the organisation. Beyond this, they go their separate ways and lead to two different models for the corporate strategy process.

● Because of the difficulties in defining and developing strategy, it is important to explore what is meant by 'good' strategy in a particular context. There are two main areas that can be used to test whether a strategy is good or not. One area relates to its *application* to delivering the purpose of the organisation. The other area relates to the *academic rigour* with which the strategy has been developed.

● In public sector, government-owned organisations, the strategy is usually governed by broader public policy concerns, rather than profits. In non-profit institutions, strategy needs to reflect the values of the particular organisation; the basic strategic principles can then be applied.

● In international terms, the development of corporate strategy is more complex for a number of reasons, including the impact on trade between nations, financial issues, economies of scale in global production and differing cultures and beliefs. All these make international corporate strategy more complex to develop.

QUESTIONS

1 Summarise the main IBM strategies. Take each element of your summary and compare it against the criterion for a successful strategy in Section 1.5. How does each measure up? Did IBM have a 'good' strategy?

2 As a work assignment, analyse the activities of Hewlett-Packard. Investigate in particular how it has had difficulty staying ahead of its competitors. Compare your answer with the five key elements of strategic decisions in Section 1.1.3.

3 In the key reading, Professor Kay makes the comment that motivation of employees is not really part of corporate strategy. Do you agree with this? Give reasons for your views.

4 Take the three core areas of corporate strategy and apply them to a decision with which you have recently been involved. For example, it might be the organisation of a student activity or the purchase of a major item of equipment. Did you analyse the facts, consider the options and make a selection? Does this description oversimplify the process

because, for example, it was necessary to persuade others to spend some money?

5 To what extent do you agree with Professor Mintzberg's description of strategies emerging rather than being prescribed in advance? If you agree with his description, what evidence do you have to support your view? If you disagree, then explain the basis of your rejection.

6 With the three core areas of corporate strategy in mind, identify how the strategy development process might vary for the following types of business: a global company such as IBM; a public service company such as a water provider (which might also be a monopoly); a non-profit organisation such as a student union or society.

7 If corporate strategy is so uncertain and has such a strong element of judgement, is there any point in its formal analysis? What arguments does the chapter use to justify such a process? Using your own value judgement, do you find them convincing?

STRATEGIC PROJECT Corporate strategy in the computer industry

The cases in the chapter have examined aspects of corporate strategy in the global computer industry. You might like to pick up the challenge of investigating this further. For example, you could explore other companies, perhaps Dell Computers, which has come to dominate the PC market, or Apple, which has been marginalised. Why has the PC market become so commoditised? What has happened to sustainable competitive advantage in this market? The references at the end of the Hewlett-Packard and IBM cases will provide a starting point – check them out on the Corporate Strategy website – **www.booksites.net/Lynch**.

FURTHER READING

Professor Kay's book *Foundations of Corporate Success* (Oxford University Press, 1993) is an excellent introduction to the nature of corporate strategy; read the early chapters. In addition, the well-known book of readings and cases by Professors Mintzberg and Quinn, *The Strategy Process* (Prentice Hall, 1991), has a useful selection of material on the nature of corporate strategy; read Chapter 1 in particular. The article by Professor Mintzberg on 'Crafting Strategy' in the *Harvard Business Review* (July–Aug 1987) is also strongly recommended.

NOTES & REFERENCES

1 Case compiled by the author from the following published sources: Packard, D (1995) *The HP Way: How Bill Hewlett and I built our company. Hewlett-Packard Annual Report and Accounts 1994 and 1996; Financial Times*, 21 Jan 1994, p24; 13 June 1994, p27; 28 Sept 1994, p33; 28 Mar 1996, p6; 15 May 1996, p27; 20 July 1999, p24; 16 November 1999, p35; 1 December 2000, p22; 7 December 2000, p32; 9 May 2001, p29; 22 August 2001, p10; 9 January 2002, p28; 31 January 2002, p31.

2 Adapted from Andrews, K (1987) *The Concept of Corporate Strategy*, Irwin, Homewood, IL, Ch2.

3 Ansoff, I (1969) *Corporate Strategy*, Penguin, Harmondsworth, Ch1.

4 Drucker, P (1961) *The Practice of Management*, Mercury, London, Ch6.

5 Leadership is sometimes ignored as part of the topic of strategy, but is actually extremely important. For example, where would Microsoft be without Bill Gates? It might be argued that 'strategy' should stand separately from 'leadership' but this is like trying to separate an orange from its juice.

6 Andrews, K (1971) *The Concept of Corporate Strategy*, Irwin, Homewood, IL, p28.

7 Kay, J (1993) *Foundations of Corporate Success*, Oxford University Press, Oxford, p4.

8 Further definitions are discussed in Quinn, J B (1980) *Strategies for Change: Logical Incrementalism*, Irwin, Homewood, IL, Ch1.

9 Campbell, A, Goold, M and Alexander, M (1995) 'Corporate strategy: the quest for parenting advantage', *Harvard Business Review*, Mar–Apr.

10 Porter, M E (1985) *Competitive Advantage*, The Free Press, Harvard, MA.

11 He argues that strategic decisions are those that determine the overall direction of an enterprise and its ultimate viability in the light of the predictable, the unpredictable and the unknowable changes that may occur in its most important environments. Quinn, J B (1980) Op. cit.

12 Kay, J (1993) Op. cit., Ch1.

13 Ohmae, K (1982) *The Mind of the Strategist*, Penguin, Harmondsworth, p36.

14 Mintzberg, H (1987) 'Crafting strategy', *Harvard Business Review*, July–Aug.

15 Harney, A (2002) 'Microsoft fired up for console wars', *Financial Times*, 7 February 2002, p28.

16 Case compiled by the author from the following published sources: Heller, R (1994) *The Fate of IBM*, Warner Books, London (easy to read and accurate); Carroll, P (1993) *The Unmaking of IBM*, Crown, London (rather one-sided); *Financial Times*: 7 Aug 1990, p14; 5 June 1991, article by Alan Cane; 8 Nov 1991, article by Alan Cane and Louise Kehoe; 5 May 1993, p17; 29 July 1993, p17; 14 Mar 1994, p17; 26 Mar 1994, p8; 28 Mar 1994, p15; *Economist*, 16 Jan 1993, p23; *Business Age*, Apr 1994, p76. Note that this case simplifies the IBM story by emphasising the PC aspects. There are further parts to the story that can be read in the references above.

17 Partly adapted from Quinn, J-B (1991) *Strategies for Change*, Ch 1, and Mintzberg, H and Quinn, J B (1991) *The Strategy Process*, Prentice Hall, Upper Saddle River, NJ.

18 For example, Gilmore, F F and Brandenburg, R G (1962) 'Anatomy of corporate planning', *Harvard Business Review*, 40, Nov–Dec, p61.

19 See, for example, Pettigrew, A and Whipp, R (1991) *Managing Change for Competitive Success*, Blackwell, Oxford. See also Mintzberg, H (1987) Op. cit.

20 Jauch, L R and Glueck, W (1988) *Business Policy and Strategic Management*, McGraw-Hill, New York.

21 Argenti, J (1965) *Corporate Planning*, Allen and Unwin, London.

22 Mintzberg, H (1987) 'Crafting strategy', *Harvard Business Review*, July–Aug, p65.

23 Cyert, R M and March, J (1963) *A Behavioural Theory of the Firm*, Prentice Hall, Upper Saddle River, NJ.

24 Mintzberg, H (1987) Op. cit.

25 This analogy was inspired by Professor Mintzberg's brief comment in his article: Mintzberg, H (1994) 'The fall and rise of strategic planning', *Harvard Business Review*, Jan–Feb, p114.

26 See, for example, Thompson, A A and Strickland, A J (1993) *Strategic Management: Concepts and Cases*, 7th edn, Irwin, Homewood, IL.

27 At the time of writing, the South African government was exploring the possibility of privatising its national telecommunications services carrier, Telekom.

28 For example, the EU Barcelona Summit in 2002 was unable to agree on the complete liberalisation of energy markets across the European Union – in spite of discussing the matter for over 20 years and signing the Treaty of Rome in 1957!

29 International Bank for Reconstruction and Development (1994) *World Development Report 1994*, Oxford University Press, New York. The report surveys this area in thoughtful detail.

30 Whelan, T L and Hunger, J D (1991) *Strategic Management*, 2nd edn, Addison-Wesley, Reading, MA, Ch11.

31 Daniels, J D and Radebaugh, L H (1995) *International Business*, 7th edn, Addison-Wesley, Reading, MA.

32 Case written by author from numerous sources including: *The Economist*, Special Survey, 12 June 1993; Annual Report and Accounts of Ryanair, Easyjet, British Airways, Lufthansa, etc; also from some selected *Financial Times* articles: 8 December 1998; 11 November 2000, pp14, 20; 6 August 2001, p24; 11 August 2001, p11; 23 October 2001, p20; 31 October 2001, p14; 23 November 2001, p25; 23 January 2002, p29; 30 January 2002, p23; 1 February 2001, pp8, 24; 7 February 2002, p24; 8 February 2002, p26; 14 February 2002, p22, 15 February 2002, p26; 20 February 2002, p30.

33 Kay, J (1993) *Foundations of Corporate Success*, Oxford University Press, Oxford.

A review of theory and practice

When you have worked through this chapter, you will be able to:

- outline the historical context of corporate strategy;
- describe and evaluate prescriptive strategic practice;
- describe and evaluate emergent strategic practice;
- identify the main theories associated with prescriptive corporate strategy;
- identify the main theories associated with emergent corporate strategy;
- explain the importance of an organisation's history as a part of its strategy.

Introduction

This chapter provides an overview of corporate strategy theories and practice. Each of the main theories is explored in further detail in later chapters, so it is possible to skip this chapter now and read it later, but you will miss the opportunity to gain an overview of the general theoretical structure of corporate strategy.

To provide a more substantial foundation for corporate strategy development, the prescriptive and emergent approaches of Chapter 1 deserve further exploration. They will benefit from being set against the background of the historical developments that prompted and shaped them.

Even within each route, prescriptive or emergent, there is substantial disagreement among strategists about how corporate strategy can and should be developed. Both routes contain many different interpretations and theories. If the dynamics are to be fully understood, it is important that some of these differences are explored.

Finally, it is argued that corporate strategy can only usefully be understood from a historical perspective. Every organisation's strategy must be seen in the context of its past events, its resources and its experience.

Attacking a dominant competitor: a joint venture strategy by Nestlé and General Mills

Kellogg (US) dominates the world's ready-to-eat breakfast cereal market. In 1989, Nestlé (Switzerland) and General Mills (US) agreed a joint venture to attack the market. The objectives of the new company were to achieve by the year 2000 global sales of US$1 billion and, within this figure, to take a 20 per cent share of the European market. This case examines how this was achieved by the new joint company, Cereal Partners (CP).

Background

In 1997, Kellogg was the breakfast cereal market leader in the US with around 32 per cent share in a market worth US$9 billion at retail selling prices. By 2002, the company was no longer market leader. Its great rival, General Mills (GM), had finally taken over with a share of 33 per cent white Kellogg's share dropped to 30 per cent. GM had achieved this important strategic breakthrough by a series of product launches over a 15-year period in a market that was growing around 2 per cent p.a.

Outside the US, the global market was worth around US$8 to 10 billion and growing in some countries by up to 10 per cent p.a. However, this was from a base of much smaller consumption per head than in the US. Nevertheless, Kellogg still had over 40 per cent market share of the non-US market. It had gained this through a vigorous strategy of international market launches for over 40 years in many markets. Up to 1990, no other company had a significant share internationally, but then along came the new partnership.

Development of Cereal Partners

After several abortive attempts to develop internationally by itself, General Mills (GM) approached Nestlé about a joint venture in 1989. (A joint venture is a separate company, with each parent holding an equal share and contributing according to its resources and skills; the joint venture then has its own management and can develop its own strategy within limits set by the parents.) Nestlé had also been attempting to launch its own breakfast cereal range without much success. Both companies were attracted by the high value added in this branded, heavily advertised consumer market.

GM's proposal to Nestlé was to develop a new 50/50 joint company. GM would contribute its products, technology and manufacturing expertise – for example, it made 'Golden Grahams' and 'Cheerios' in the USA. Nestlé would give its brand name, several underutilised factories and its major strengths in global marketing and distribution – for example, it made 'Nestlé' cream products. Both parties found the deal so attractive that they agreed it in only three weeks. The joint venture was called Cereal Partners (CP) and operated outside North America, where GM remained independent.

Over the next twelve years, CP was launched in 70 countries around the world. Products such as 'Golden Grahams', 'Cheerios' and 'Fibre 1' appeared on grocery supermarket shelves. CP used a mixture of launch strategies, depending on the market circumstances: acquisitions were used in the UK and Poland, new product launches in the rest of Europe, South and Central America and South Africa, and existing Nestlé cereal products were taken over in South-East Asia. To keep Kellogg guessing about its next market moves and to satisfy local taste variations, CP also varied the product range launched in each country. By contrast with Kellogg, CP also agreed to make cereals for supermarket chains, which they would sell as their own brands.

By 2002, CP had largely reached its targets of US$1 billion profitable sales and 20 per cent of European markets. Kellogg was responding aggressively but still losing market share globally and in Europe. CP was beginning to think that its innovative strategies would repeat US experience: it might even replace Kellogg as market leader worldwide.

Case question

Using the description of prescriptive and emergent strategies from Chapter 1 (and Chapter 2 if you need it), decide the following: was CP pursuing a prescriptive strategy, an emergent strategy, or both?

2.1 Historical context of strategy

In Chapter 1, we saw that corporate strategy relates the activities of the organisation to the environment in which it operates. As a result of increasing wealth, changes in industrialisation, shifts in the power balance between nations and many other factors, this environment is constantly changing. Corporate strategy and the prevailing logic supporting it will change as the environment surrounding the organisation changes. Before we examine the theories surrounding corporate strategy, it is therefore appropriate to explore those theories in a historical context.

Until the late nineteenth century, organisations that were not owned by the nation state were too small to be considered as corporations. Small artisan factories driven by crafts may have needed strategies to survive and prosper against competitors, but formal corporate strategy did not exist. Table 2.1 shows how matters have developed since that time.

North America, Europe and Japan were more or less the only areas that had begun to industrialise by the end of the nineteenth century. Countries such as China, India, Korea, Malaysia, Singapore, the Philippines, Saudi Arabia, Iran and Iraq, Nigeria, South Africa were still largely without industry; they supplied commodities and raw materials to world markets but had not yet begun to industrialise.[1] Corporate strategy, which is principally associated with increased industrialisation, was therefore more likely to develop in Europe, North America and Japan than other areas around the world.

2.1.1 Corporate strategy in the early twentieth century

During the early twentieth century, particularly in the US and Europe, managers rather than academics began to explore and define the management task. F W Taylor in the USA and Henri Fayol in France are examples of senior industry figures who started to research and write on such issues.[2] Taylor and Fayol were industrialists rather than academics, holding senior positions in industry for some years. Around the same time, Henry Ford began experimenting to produce goods more cheaply and fulfil growing market demand. In the period 1908–15[3] he developed strategies that we still recognise

---

Exhibit 2.1   **Early strategies still recognised today**

From the period 1908–15: Henry Ford

- Innovative technology
- Replacement of men by machines
- Search for new quality standards
- Constant cost-cutting through factory redesign
- Passing on the cost reductions in the form of reduced prices for the model T car

From the period 1920–35: Alfred Sloan and colleagues

- Car models tailored for specific market niches
- Rapid model changes
- Structured management teams and reporting structures
- Separation of day-to-day management from the task of devising longer-term strategy

---

Table 2.1 **The development of corporate strategy in the twentieth century, showing important environmental influences**

Period	Environment	Strategy and management developments
1900–1910	• Colonial wars • Global trading of commodities	• Beginnings of examination of the management task, e.g. F W Taylor and Henri Fayol
1910–30	• World war and its legacy	• Rise of larger organisations and the consequent need for increased management control
1930s	• Crash: trade barriers erected to protect some countries	• Formal management control mechanisms developed, e.g. budgeting and management accounting, particularly in the US • Early human resource experiments in the US
1940s	• World war and its legacy	• Strong US industry and the birth of formal strategy • Beginnings of organisational theory
1950s	• Sustained economic growth coupled with first European trade and political bloc: European Economic Community	• First real strategy writings in formal series of papers • Organisational theory is applied to management tasks
1960s	• Continued growth until first oil price rise late in the decade	• Corporate strategy techniques are researched • Separate parallel development in organisational research
1970s	• Growth becomes more cyclical with another oil price shock	• Formal corporate strategy techniques adopted • First research writings objecting to same techniques
1980s	• Far East and global developments • Computer data handling develops fast • Beginnings of moves to privatise government institutions	• Major strategic emphasis on competitive aspects of formal corporate strategy • Search continues for new strategy concepts emphasising the human rather than the competitive aspects of the process
1990s	• Telecommunications, global corporations, high growth in the Pacific Rim but currency problems in Japan • Some Asian economies in crisis	• Global concepts of strategy • Greater emphasis on the organisation's own resources rather than competition as the basis for strategy development
2000s	• Global recession	• New emphasis on innovation

today, and included those outlined in Exhibit 2.1. Henry Ford did not believe in major model variations and market segmentation, however, unlike his great rival from the 1920s: General Motors, headed by Alfred P Sloan.[4] Nor did Ford believe in the importance of middle and senior management. He actually sacked many of his senior managers and ultimately left his company in real difficulties when he died.[5] Hence, his rival in the 1920s and beyond, General Motors, was ultimately more successful with other strategies that still exist today (*see* Exhibit 2.1).

After the First World War came the great economic depression of the 1930s. This brought the need for a new order in international currency and, just as importantly, the desire for larger companies to gain economies of scale. However, much of this was confined to North America and competitive strategy itself was still in its infancy.

2.1.2 Corporate strategy in the mid-twentieth century

The Second World War brought its specialist demands for military equipment, coupled with more destruction across much of Europe and Japan; North and South America went largely unscathed. At this time, the Middle East and Far East still remained largely outside the scope of industrial development. This period was hardly the time for corporate strategists to influence events. Yet strategic game theory had its origins in developing more effective British naval tactics when hunting for German U-boats.

The late 1940s probably witnessed the period of the greatest power of North American industry and companies. It was also the real beginning of corporate strategy development and this then continued into the 1950s. It was accompanied by the reconstruction of industry across Europe and the beginnings of the Asian development period, particularly in Japan. Economists like Penrose[6] were beginning to explore how firms grew, and human behaviourists like Cyert and March[7] suggested that rational economic behaviour was an oversimplified way of considering company development.

By the late 1950s, writers such as Ansoff were beginning to develop corporate strategy concepts that would continue into the 1970s. During the 1960s the early concepts of what would later become one of the main approaches to corporate strategy – *prescriptive corporate strategy* – began to take shape. Ansoff[8] argued that there were environmental factors which accelerated the development of corporate strategy. Two trends can be identified:

1 *The accelerated rate of change.* Corporate strategy provided a way of taking advantage of new opportunities.

2 *The greater spread of wealth.* Corporate strategy needed to find ways of identifying the opportunities provided by the spread of increasing wealth, especially in Europe.

It was during this same period that the early research was conducted which subsequently led to the development of the second main approach to corporate strategy, *emergent corporate strategy*, although this really only came to prominence in the 1970s and 1980s.

2.1.3 Corporate strategy into the twenty-first century

The 1970s saw the major oil price rises. They came as a result of the world's increased need for energy and Middle Eastern success in organising an oil price cartel. The business environment was subject to a sudden and largely unpredicted change that caused some corporate strategists to reconsider the value of prediction in corporate strategy.

The 1980s and 1990s have witnessed further environmental developments that are identified briefly in Table 2.1 These trends have had the following effects on corporate strategy:

- *Free market competition.* According to various United Nations and World Bank studies, free market competition has been one element in supporting and encouraging growth in many newly developing countries.[9]
- *Asia–Pacific competition.* Corporate strategy has moved out of being the preserve of North American and European countries. The lower labour costs in the new region have put pressure on Western companies to cut costs or move east. For example, in breakfast cereals, CP has opened factories in Asia to take advantage of low labour costs.
- *Global and local interests.* In addition to economic growth, the world market place has become more complex in cultural and social terms. Markets have become more international, thus making it necessary to balance global interests and local demand variations. For example, in breakfast cereals, CP has adapted its breakfast cereal products to local tastes within its basic worldwide branding.
- *Need to empower and involve employees in strategic decisions.* The higher levels of training and deeper levels of skills of employees mean that they are no longer poorly trained and no longer have difficulty making a contribution to corporate strategy, especially in some Western countries.
- *Greater speed of technical change and rise of new forms of communications.* Technology is changing more quickly and the development of new forms of communication, such as the Internet, have revolutionised strategy.

▶ Key strategic principles

- Corporate strategy responds to the environment existing or developing at that time.
- The early twentieth century was characterised by the increased use of science and technology. This was reflected in greater structuring of management and strategy. Mass production of quality products became possible.
- In the mid-twentieth century, the accelerated rate of technological change and the greater spread of wealth led to new demands for formal strategy development.
- In the late twentieth century, there were five distinct pressures on corporate strategy: free market competition; the importance of the Asia–Pacific economies; global competition; greater knowledge and training of managers and employees; greater speed of technical change and rise of new forms of communication. All five elements in the environment have directed the development of corporate strategy.

2.2 Prescriptive corporate strategy in practice

2.2.1 The basic concept

A prescriptive corporate strategy is one where the *objective* has been defined in advance and the *main elements* have been developed before the strategy commences. However, it should be noted that there are many variations on this basic approach.

- From Chapter 1, prescriptive strategy starts with an analysis of the competitive environment and resources of the organisation.
- This is then followed by a search for an agreed purpose, such as the maximisation of the return on the capital involved in a business (Ansoff, Porter).[10] It should be noted that the objective is not necessarily profit maximisation: for example, in a publicly owned enterprise or social co-operative, the objective could have social service standards as its major aim. One test for prescriptive strategy is to see whether a clearly defined objective has been identified in advance of the commencement of the strategy.
- Against the background of the competitive environment and an agreed purpose, various options are identified to enable the business to achieve the purpose. One option is then selected which is best able to meet the objective.
- The chosen option is implemented by the organisation's managers.

This prescriptive process is shown in Figure 2.1. In summary, the advantages of the prescriptive process are that it assists in providing a complete overview of the organisation, thus allowing a comparison with the objectives of the organisation. In turn, this allows an assessment of the resources of the organisation, especially those that deliver competitive advantage, and the allocation of resources that are scarce. Finally, the prescriptive process lends itself to monitoring the implementation and monitoring of an agreed plan.

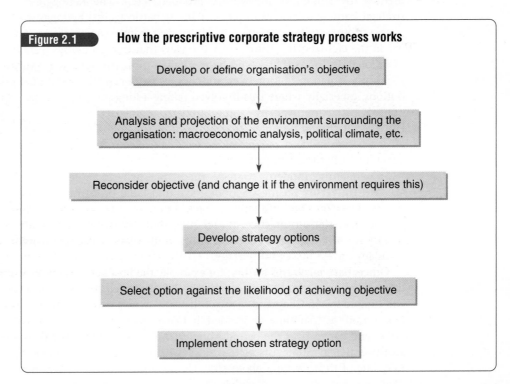

Figure 2.1   **How the prescriptive corporate strategy process works**

Develop or define organisation's objective

Analysis and projection of the environment surrounding the organisation: macroeconomic analysis, political climate, etc.

Reconsider objective (and change it if the environment requires this)

Develop strategy options

Select option against the likelihood of achieving objective

Implement chosen strategy option

> ### ◖◗ Key strategic principles
>
> - Prescriptive strategy begins with an analysis of the competitive environment and the competitive resources of the organisation. In this context, the purpose or objective of the strategy is then identified.
> - The objective may be adjusted if the environment or other circumstances change.
> - To test for prescriptive strategy, it is useful to examine whether a clearly defined, main objective has been identified.
> - The advantages of the prescriptive process include the overview it provides; the comparison with objectives; the summary of the demands made on resources; the picture of the choices to be made; and the ability to monitor what has been agreed.

2.2.2 Foundations of prescriptive strategy

In studies of prescriptive strategy, close parallels have been drawn with what happens in *military strategy*, for example, as seen in the early Chinese military historical writings of Sun Tzu; the writings of the nineteenth-century German strategist, Clausewitz,[11] and those of Captain B H Liddell Hart[12] who wrote about the First World War. All these have been have been quoted by corporate strategists.[13]

Prescriptive business strategy is sometimes seen as being similar to sending the troops (*employees*) into battle (*against competitors*) with a clear plan (*the prescriptive strategic plan*) that has been drawn up by the generals (*directors*) and then has been implemented (by launching innovatory products, etc.). The Kellogg/CP breakfast cereals strategic battle is a good example – CP doing battle against Kelloggs worldwide.

Prescriptive strategic analysis has borrowed from *economic theory*. Adam Smith, writing in the eighteenth century, took the view that human beings were basically capable of rational decisions that would be motivated most strongly by maximising their profits in any situation.[14] Moreover, individuals were capable of rational choice between options, especially where this involved taking a long-term view. Adam Smith has been quoted with approval by some modern strategists, economists and politicians. However, it should be noted that he lived in the eighteenth century and wrote about an era before modern organisations were conceived: for example, he had never seen a factory; only the craftsman's workshop.[15]

Subsequently, modern strategy theorists, such as Professor Michael Porter[16] of Harvard University Business School, have translated profit maximisation and competitive warfare concepts into strategy techniques and structure that have contributed to prescriptive strategic practice. Porter suggested that what really matters is *sustainable competitive advantage* vis à vis competitors in the market place: only by this means can a company have a successful strategy.

Others have taken this further: for example, the Boston Consulting Group used market data to develop a simple, strategic matrix that presented strategic options for analysis (we will explore this in Chapter 3). One of the early writers on corporate strategy was Professor Igor Ansoff, at that time at Vanderbilt University, Tennessee, who wrote a number of books and papers over the period from 1960 to 1990[17] that explored the practice of prescriptive strategy. Strategists such as Andrews,[18] Chakravarthy and Lorange[19] follow in the long line of those writing about strategic planning systems who employ many of these basic concepts. They are still widely used in many organisations around the world.

2.2.3 Criticisms of prescriptive strategy

Despite the advantages claimed for a prescriptive strategy system operating at the centre of organisations, there have been numerous critics of the whole approach. One of the most insightful is Professor Henry Mintzberg of McGill University, Canada. Along with other commentators,[20] Mintzberg has researched decision making at corporate strategy level and suggested that a prescriptive strategy approach is based on a number of dangerous assumptions as to how organisations operate in practice (summarised in Exhibit 2.2).[21] There is significant research to show that these assumptions are not always correct. For example, the market place can change, or employees may not like an agreed strategy – perhaps because it will mean that they lose their jobs – and will find ways to frustrate it. Given this evidence, theories of *emergent strategy* have developed, as an alternative view of the strategy process.

Exhibit 2.2 **Some major difficulties with the prescriptive strategic process**

Mintzberg has identified six major assumptions of the prescriptive process that may be wholly or partially false:

1 *The future can be predicted accurately enough to make rational discussion and choice realistic.* As soon as a competitor or a government does something unexpected, however, the whole process may be invalidated.

2 *It is possible and better to forgo the short-term benefit in order to obtain long-term good.* This may be incorrect: it may not be possible to determine the long-term good and, even if it were, those involved may not be willing to make the sacrifice, such as jobs or investment.

3 *The strategies proposed are, in practice, logical and capable of being managed in the way proposed.* Given the political realities of many companies, there may be many difficulties in practice.

4 *The chief executive has the knowledge and power to choose between options. He/she does not need to persuade anyone, nor compromise on his/her decisions.* This may be extraordinarily naïve in many organisations where the culture and leadership seek discussion as a matter of normal practice.

5 *After careful analysis, strategy decisions can be clearly specified, summarised and presented; they do not require further development, nor do they need to be altered because circumstances outside the company have changed.* This point may have some validity but is not always valid.

6 *Implementation is a separate and distinctive phase that only comes after a strategy has been agreed: for example, a strategy to close a factory merely requires a management decision and then it just happens.* This is extraordinarily simplistic in many complex strategic decisions.

Although highly critical of the formal prescriptive planning process, Mintzberg has modified his views in recent years and accepted that some strategic planning may be beneficial to the organisation.[22]

In conclusion, the period of the 1970s was the era when prescriptive corporate strategic planning was particularly strong. Further strategic competitive concepts, such as generic strategies, would be proposed in the 1980s (*see* Chapter 13), but the basic process of analysis, strategic choice, selection and implementation formed the best practice of many companies. The major UK food company, Spillers, was just one example of prescriptive strategy in action (*see* Case study 2.2). Another recent example of prescriptive strategy is that associated with the turnaround of the ailing public sector health service in the UK (*see* Case study 2.3).

> ### ▶ Key strategic principles
>
> - A prescriptive strategy is a strategy whose objective has been defined in advance and whose main elements have been developed before the strategy commences.
> - The objective may be adjusted if circumstances change significantly.
> - After defining the objective, the process then includes analysis of the environment, the development of strategic options and the choice between them. The chosen strategy is then implemented.
> - Mintzberg identified six assumptions made by the prescriptive process that may prove suspect in practice and invalidate the process.

CASE STUDY 2.2

Prescriptive strategic planning at Spillers plc

Under the guidance of a leading North American consulting company, a strategic corporate planning system was introduced into Spillers plc in 1978–79.[23] The company had a turnover of around £700 million (US$1200 million) and had been largely without any form of central direction up to that time.[24]

Spillers plc consisted of a number of operating companies:

- flour milling and bread baking (Spillers Homepride Flour)
- food coatings (Lucas Food Ingredients)
- meat slaughtering and processing (Meade Lonsdale Group)
- branded petfoods (Winalot)
- restaurant chain (Mario and Franco Italian Restaurants)
- branded canned meats and sauces (Tyne Brand).

The new strategic planning system consisted of an annual plan prepared to a common format by each of the above operating groups. Each plan had to address how it conformed with the Spillers' mission statement and objectives, e.g. on return on capital, market share, capital investment, etc. The plans were gathered together and presented by the operating groups to the Spillers Group Board.

This prescriptive strategy process certainly gave the centre of Spillers a degree of central knowledge and direction that it had never possessed before. It allowed the centre to debate with the senior managers and directors representing the various parts of the group what they judged to be the major strategic issues facing the company. Moreover, for the first time, it gave the company an ability to allocate scarce resources among the competing requests of the operating companies within the group:

- £2 million investment in a new ingredient production line at Lucas Ingredients near Bristol, UK
- £1.5 million investment in a major expansion of the Mario and Franco restaurant chain
- Expansion of Spillers petfood branded products and production facility in Cambridgeshire, UK – estimated cost £3 million capital and a net loss for two years of £2 million in this product group
- £20 million capital requirement spread over three years for a new abattoir at Reading UK. (The existing facility cannot meet the new higher EU standards in the long term, yet it provides over half the profits of the Spillers Meat Group.)

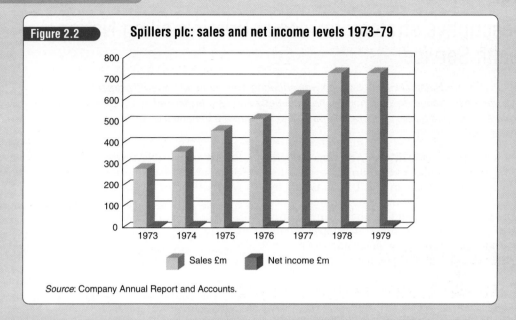

Figure 2.2

Spillers plc: sales and net income levels 1973–79

Sales £m   Net income £m

Source: Company Annual Report and Accounts.

The company did not have the financial resources to meet all the requests. It had to make a selection; techniques such as portfolio matrices [see Chapter 4] were used to analyse and present the results. Even under the new system, however, few strategic options were ever presented by the operating companies to group headquarters: for example, the proposal was for a new abattoir or nothing. Nevertheless, rational choice was considered by the main board. Moreover, beyond the centre, shareholders could now be told about the future plans and direction of the company. Employees were equally interested in the success of their own areas of the group.

Group strategic planning at Spillers had not previously existed. The success of Spillers' operating subsidiaries in obtaining funds up to that point had depended upon which operating company had asked first and who happened to make the most attractive financial case at the time when funds were available. Once prescriptive strategic analysis and rational debate were introduced into this process during 1979, the main board at last had a clear picture of the strategies of each major operating company and their requests for funds to implement these proposals. There had been a few complaints by the operating companies that the estimated system had

been too rigid. Overall, however, the new Spillers system was fairer and less open to individual favouritism.

In practice, for Spillers in 1979 the prescriptive solutions offered by its corporate strategic planning process were too little and too late; the strategic problems that would ultimately lead to its downfall were already evident.

All of this came to an end when Spillers was at the receiving end of a takeover bid by the UK company Dalgety in 1979. Spillers was swallowed up by an audacious acquisition and its strategic plans were used to provide a useful, if static, picture of what had been acquired. Prescriptive strategic planning had its uses for Dalgety, even if this was not quite the purpose originally intended by Spillers.

Case questions

1 *Using Mintzberg's critique of prescriptive processes, what are the main weaknesses of Spillers' proposals?*

2 *Bearing these in mind, was it a worthwhile exercise for Spillers in your judgement?*

CASE STUDY 2.3

Prescriptive strategy to rescue Britain's ailing National Health Service

In 2000, Britain's National Health Service was suffering from years of underinvestment.
There were not enough doctors, nurses, hospital beds and care facilities. The UK government
therefore developed a new prescriptive strategy to turn around the situation over
the years 2001 to 2005.

Following its election in 1997, the new Labour government set about reforming and revitalising the health services in the UK. It began by showing why such reform was required: since 1960, UK health spending had consistently lagged behind that of other developed countries and there were fewer practising doctors in the UK per head of the population than in the rest of the European Union. In addition, there was an increasingly ageing population. There were also more sophisticated and effective medical treatments, but they required higher levels of funding.

The following staged approach was undertaken for health care renewal:

● Background analysis of the health environment and existing UK medical resources: for example, a survey of what UK customers wanted from a health service and what existing medical facilities were available. This highlighted the need for shorter waiting times for treatment.

● Analysis of the views of those involved in delivering the public health services, such as doctors, managers and nurses. Particular attention was paid to their opinions of the difficulties and bottlenecks in the delivery of better health care, e.g. insufficient numbers of nurses.

● Definition of the main criteria for judging health service strategy: *efficiency* and *equity*. For the public sector, it was decided as a matter of policy that any new strategy would be evaluated in terms of whether it provided good value for its cost – 'efficiency' – and whether it was freely available to those who needed it – 'equity'. Such background considerations are especially important in the development of public sector strategy.

● Setting measurable service improvement objectives, such as that all patients should see a doctor within 48 hours by year 2004.

● Consideration of the options available to fund and manage such developments, for example, an examination of the models employed in Germany and France which delivered higher standards but cost more than in the UK.

● Choice between the options and agreement with the UK government over funding the chosen option.

By 2002, Britain's national health service was struggling to achieve its objectives. It had made progress in recruiting extra nurses and doctors but only by taking them from other countries. It had started a major hospital building programme and begun new facilities to train more UK doctors. But patient waiting times were still far too long and there were still many people unable to gain the urgent treatment that they needed.

Case questions

1 *What are the similarities and what are the differences between this approach to strategy and a strategy in a private business?*

2 *Are there any weaknesses in using prescriptive strategy processes to develop strategy in the public sector? You may like to use Exhibit 2.3 on page 51 to assist you.*

2.3 Emergent corporate strategy in practice

2.3.1 The basic concept

Emergent corporate strategy is a strategy whose *final objective* is unclear and whose *elements* are developed during the course of its life, as the strategy proceeds. However, it should be noted that there are many variations on this basic approach.

Deriving in part from the observation that human beings are not always the rational and logical creatures assumed by prescriptive strategy,[25] various commentators have rejected the dispassionate, long-term prescriptive approach. They argue that strategy *emerges*, adapting to human needs and continuing to develop over time. Given this, they argue that there can be only limited meaningful prescriptive strategies and limited value from long-term planning.

Although this approach probably has its roots in the Hawthorn experiments of Elton Mayo in the 1930s,[26] it was not really until the research of Cyert and March in the 1960s[27] and Herbert Simon[28] around the same period that real progress was made. Research into how companies and managers develop corporate strategy in practice has shown that the assumption that strategies are always logical and rational does not take into account the reality of managerial decision making.

● Managers can handle only a limited number of options at any one time – called 'bounded rationality' in the literature.

● They are biased in their interpretation of data.

● They are likely to seek a satisfactory solution rather than maximise the objectives of the organisation.

● Organisations consist of coalitions of people who form power blocs. Decisions and debate rely on negotiations and compromise between these groups, termed political bargaining. Researchers found that the notion of strategy being decided by a separate, central main board does not accord with reality.

● To take decisions, managers rely on a company's culture, politics and routines, rather than on a rational process of analysis and choice. (Who you know and how you present your strategic decision is just as important as the content of the strategy.)

More recently, the research of Pettigrew,[29] Mintzberg,[30] Johnson[31] and others has further developed the *people* areas of strategy. Their empirical research has shown that the development of corporate strategy is more complex than the prescriptive strategists would imply: the people, politics and culture of organisations all need to be taken into account. Strategists such as Argyris[32] and Senge[33] have emphasised the *learning* approach to strategy: encouraging managers to undertake a process of trial and error to devise the optimal strategy.

As a result, according to these researchers, corporate strategy can best be considered as a process whereby the organisation's strategy is derived as a result of trial, repeated experimentation and small steps forward: in this sense, corporate strategy is *emergent* rather than *planned*. Figure 2.3 presents a simplified and diagrammatic view of the emergent process. The process then proceeds as market conditions change, the economy develops, teams of people in the company change, etc. Clearly, such a process is hard to define in advance and therefore difficult to analyse and predict in a clear and structured way. For example, when entering new breakfast cereal markets, Cereal Partners adopted different strategies in accordance with the particular market circumstances.

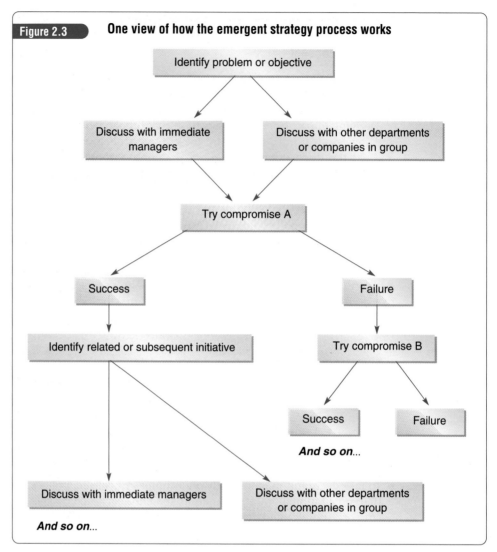

Figure 2.3 — One view of how the emergent strategy process works

If the emergent view of the strategy process is correct, then the implications for corporate strategy are profound:[34][35]

1 Strategies emerge from a confused background and often in a muddled and disorganised way: the resulting strategies themselves may therefore be unclear and not fully resolved.

2 The process is unlikely to reflect reality: options identified will not be comprehensive and the selection process will be flawed.

3 Considering 'implementation' after the rest of the strategy process does not reflect what usually happens.

4 Managers are unlikely to seek the optimal solution: it may not be capable of identification and, in addition, may not be in their personal interests.

5 Working within an organisation's routines and culture will allow the optimal culture to emerge rather than be forced by an artificial planning process.

In summary, the advantages of the emergent strategy process are that it accords with actual practice in many organisations, especially with regard to people issues like motivation. It takes account of the culture and politics of an organisation. In addition, it also allows strategies to experiment and develop as strategic circumstances change, delivering flexibility during the process.

2.3.2 Criticisms of emergent strategy

Those who favour prescriptive strategic approaches have a number of basic concerns about emergent strategy. These are summarised in Exhibit 2.3.[36]

Exhibit 2.3   **Concerns about the emergent strategic process**

1 It is entirely unrealistic to expect board members at corporate level simply to sit back and let operating companies potter along as they wish. The HQ consists of experienced managers who have a *unified* vision of where they wish the group to progress. It may take several steps to arrive at this vision, but the group should make visible progress rather than just muddling along.

2 Resources of the group need to be *allocated* between the demands of competing operating companies; this can only be undertaken at the centre. It therefore demands some central strategic overview.

3 It is entirely correct that there are political groups and individuals that need to be persuaded that a strategy is optimal, but to elevate this process to the level of corporate strategy is to *abdicate responsibility* for the final decisions that need to be taken.

4 In some industries where long time frames are involved for decision making, decisions have to be taken and adhered to or the organisation would become completely muddled: for example, building a new transport infrastructure or telecommunications network may take years to implement. Experimentation may be appropriate in the early years but, beyond this, strategy has to be *fixed* for *lengthy projects*.

5 Although the process of strategy selection and choice has to be tempered by what managers are prepared to accept, this does not make it wrong; rational decision making based on evidence has a greater likelihood of success than hunch and personal whim. Thus the debate should take place but be *conditioned by evidence and logic*.

6 Management control will be *simpler and clearer* where the basis of the actions to be undertaken has been planned in advance.

In practice, many organisations treat the above comments as *limitations* on the prescriptive approach, rather than issues that cannot be overcome. To see how strategy can emerge, refer to Case study 2.4 at the end of this section. The strategy of Spillers plc can be examined from a different, longer-term perspective over the period 1970–80. An *extended time perspective* is essential in order to see how strategic decisions take shape according to the emergent approach. This is explored later in this chapter – *see* Section 2.5.

▶ Key strategic principles

- Emergent corporate strategy is a strategy whose final *objective* is unclear and whose *elements* are developed during the course of its life, as the strategy proceeds.

- The process is one of experimentation to find the most productive route forward.

> ▶ *Key strategic principles continued*
>
> • Emergent strategy does not have a single, final objective; strategy develops over time.
>
> • In fast-developing markets, the time period may be short; in slow-developing markets, it is likely to be longer.
>
> • To test for emergent strategy, it is essential to examine how the strategy has developed in practice over a defined time period.
>
> • The advantages of the process include its consistency with actual practice in organisations; it takes account of people issues such as motivation; it allows experimentation about the strategy to take place; it provides an opportunity to include the culture and politics of the organisation; it delivers flexibility to respond to market changes.
>
> • Six problems have been identified with the emergent strategic process that make it difficult to operate in practice.

CASE STUDY 2.4

Emergent strategy at Spillers Baking

In the face of fierce competition in the UK bread baking industry, Spillers Bakeries tried a series of strategies in the 1960s and 1970s. Their aim was to turn around the ailing business. The strategic trial-and-error process was essentially emergent, rather than prescriptive. This case describes the moves that were made and the eventual disastrous outcome.[37]

Background to the 1970s

Under its major shareholder Garfield Weston, the baking subsidiary company of Associated British Foods (ABF) came to dominate the bread baking market in the UK in the 1950s and 1960s. This was achieved through strategies involving heavy investment in baking plant and the takeover of rival baking companies. At the time, bread was regarded as one of the staple elements of the British diet and was the subject of government price controls. The main rivals of ABF were Ranks Hovis McDougall (RHM) and Spillers; they both struggled to compete against aggressive ABF competition. RHM began investing heavily in new bakeries to achieve similar economies of scale to ABF; Spillers did not have the funds for such investment and needed to seek other strategies.

Spillers' first emergent strategy: *merge with rivals* (1970–74)

By 1970, Spillers was a poor third in the bread baking market. The company decided to build market share by merging its bread-baking interests with those of two smaller rivals, J Lyons and CWS. It formed a new company, Spillers French Baking Ltd. This company then lost £7 million over the period 1970–74.

This was not quite as disastrous as it might appear; Spillers French was purchasing flour for baking from its associated milling company at high prices. Nevertheless, Spillers French was unable to gain a strategic advantage by its attempt to grow larger by merger.

Spillers' second emergent strategy: *invest and consolidate* (1974–76)

The Spillers French group then undertook investment in new plant and marketing; the company invested £5 million in new baking plant around the country. It also attempted a series of marketing initiatives associated with new product launches and bread advertising. These produced some moderately memorable advertising campaigns, but brand loyalty in the bread market was low in the face of strong and sustained price competition.

By contrast with the Spillers investment, ABF and RHM invested £68 million and £62 million respectively in new baking plant over the same period. For both companies, the strategy was to reduce substantially their manufacturing costs below those of Spillers French. Not surprisingly, Spillers French Baking losses continued – £5 million in 1975, £1 million in 1976 and £1 million in 1977. The losses were accompanied by increasing labour militancy in the Spillers French bakeries; workers feared redundancy. The company then tried its third strategy.

Spillers' third emergent strategy: divest (1978–79)

In early 1978, there was a major strike by the bread trade unions at Spillers French Baking. The company lost £9.7 million in that year. New drastic strategies were required. Simply closing the bakeries was not an option: this would have cost £33 million in capital write-downs and £20 million in redundancy payments under the labour laws that existed at that time.

A strategy of divestment that included sale of some of the better bakeries to ABF and RHM, coupled with continuing contracts from ABF and RHM to take flour from Spillers, was therefore negotiated with its two rivals. After difficult discussions, Spillers French managed to sell 13 bakeries to ABF and RHM for £15.5 million and it simply closed the rest. After allowing for the bakery sale, the net cost to Spillers

plc was £22 million with another £7 million to its partners, J Lyons and CWS.

Outcome of emergent strategies: Spillers becomes a takeover target

Having resolved its losses from bread baking, Spillers plc then became much more attractive as a takeover target. In January 1980, the slimmed-down, breadless Spillers was taken over by Dalgety plc. We will return to the fortunes of the new Dalgety plc, including Spillers, later in this chapter. The strategy continued to emerge.

Case questions

1 *The Spillers emergent approach to strategy development required at least a year to elapse between each phase. What might be the reasons for this? Are there any disadvantages in this timing from a strategic perspective?*

2 *Critically evaluate Spillers Bakeries' strategies during the 1970s. Was the company wise to spend nearly ten years pouring funds into such an operation? What would you have done?*

2.4 Prescriptive theories of corporate strategy

Now that corporate strategy has been explored and set in its historical and international context it is possible to turn to the theories that underlie these processes. This section examines prescriptive strategy theories, while emergent strategy theories are explored in Section 2.5. It should be noted, however, that there is some overlap between the two areas. This will be explored further later in this chapter. In broad terms, it is useful to identify four main areas of prescriptive strategy theory:

1 profit-maximising, competition-based theories of strategy;
2 resource-based theories of strategy;
3 game-based theories of strategy;
4 socio-cultural theories of strategy.

2.4.1 Profit-maximising, competition-based theories of strategy

For some companies, *profitability* is the clear goal, and the content of the corporate strategy therefore addresses this objective; over the long term, this is likely to override all other objectives. This profit is delivered by *competing in the marketplace*. Figure 2.4 shows where the emphasis lies within the context of prescriptive strategy.

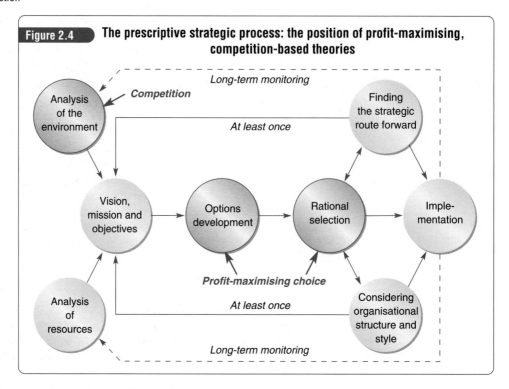

Figure 2.4 The prescriptive strategic process: the position of profit-maximising, competition-based theories

Such concepts derive from the assertion that organisations are rational, logical and driven by the need for profitability. They can be related back to two areas:

1 the eighteenth-century Scottish economist, Adam Smith, and his view that man was rational, logical and motivated by profit;

2 the concepts of military warfare quoted earlier in this chapter that show how the competitive war can be won.

In terms of the development of strategy theory, much of this material only really came together in the 1960s. Igor Ansoff,[38] Alfred Chandler[39] and Alfred Sloan[40] all had an early influence in this area. More recently, writers such as Wheelen and Hunger[41] have laid out the model for rational, analytical and structured development of strategy. During the 1980s, the work of Porter[42] added significantly to this material; he was a dominant influence during this period. Much of his work was based on the study of large companies and the application of economic concepts to strategy, as has been pointed out by Rumelt, Schendel and Teece.[43] The contributions of these researchers will be examined in greater depth later in the book.

In fairness, it should be pointed out that researchers such as Ansoff never saw their work in quite such stark prescriptive terms. For example, an Ansoff 1968 research paper on corporate strategy[44] refers with approval to the emergent strategy work of Cyert and March on human resources strategies, which we explore later in this chapter.

For all these writers, strategy involves formal, analytical processes. It will result in a specific set of documents that are discussed and agreed by the board of directors (or public sector equivalent) of an organisation – a tangible corporate plan for some years ahead. Typically, the plan will include sections predicting the general economic and political situation; analysing competitors, their strengths and weaknesses; considering the resources available to the organisation; and recommending a set of strategies to meet these requirements.

The strategy will primarily (but not exclusively) be driven by the objective of maximising the organisation's profitability in the long term (such profits may particularly accrue to the shareholders). The major argument of the theorists is that the purpose of strategy is to develop sustainable competitive advantage[45] over competitors.

Although these views were broadly endorsed by Kenichi Ohmae,[46] head of the Japanese part of the well-known consulting company, McKinsey, it has been pointed out by Wilks that they remain largely Western and Anglo-American in their orientation.[47] They are primarily concerned with profit and leave only limited room for social, cultural, governmental and other considerations. This view of strategy is therefore unlikely to appeal to countries which demand a higher social content from company plans – for example, within Europe, France, Poland, the Netherlands and Scandinavian countries.

Outside Europe, India has insisted on a strong social content to plans for many years and has only recently come to accept that strong social policies needed tempering by market forces.[48] Japanese companies also have other criteria, as we have already seen. Malaysian and Singaporean companies with their strong relationships with the governments of their respective countries might well also sacrifice profitability to other objectives, such as building market presence or providing extra training for workers.[49] Content for companies in these countries will inevitably be broader.

These nation-state arguments are, however, a matter of degree and do not deny the need to make long-term profits in order to ensure the survival and growth of the enterprise. A more fundamental criticism of profit-maximising theories has been made by Hamel and Prahalad[50] and Kay.[51] They argue that, although competitors are important, the emphasis on competitive comparisons essential to such theories is misleading: it simply shows where organisations are weak. Such theories do not indicate how the company should develop its own resources and skills – the key strategic task in their view. This is explored further in the next section.

Hannan and Freeman[52] argued that markets are so powerful that seeking sustainable competitive advantage for the majority of companies is not realistic; only the largest companies with significant market share can achieve and sustain such advantage. For all the others, complex and detailed strategies are a distraction. Moreover, as soon as all companies have access to Porter's writings on sustainable competitive advantage, Hamel and Prahalad[53] and Kay[54] have argued that the advantage ceases.

From a different perspective, Mintzberg[55] and others have criticised the approach by arguing that this is simply not the way that strategy is or should be developed in practice. Thus human-resource-based theories of strategy would suggest that seeking to maximise performance through a single, static strategic plan is a fallacy. There are no clear long-term mission statements and goals, just a series of short-term horizons to be met and then renewed. Techniques that purport to provide long-term insights may be too simplistic. Using such arguments, Mintzberg in particular has been highly articulate in his criticisms of the formal strategic planning process. However, he has subsequently modified his criticisms and accepted that some strategic planning may be beneficial to the organisation.[56]

2.4.2 Resource-based theories of strategy

Resource-based theories concentrate on the chief resources of the organisation as the principal source of successful corporate strategy. The source of competitive advantage lies in the organisation's resources (*see* Figure 2.5).

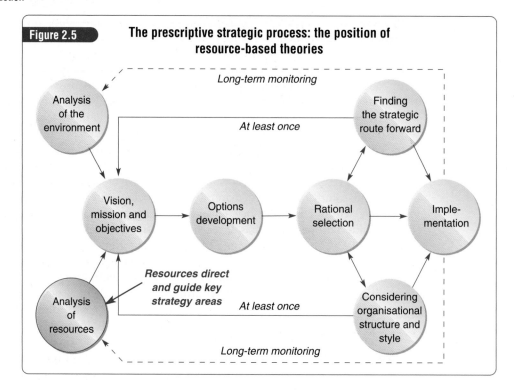

Figure 2.5 — **The prescriptive strategic process: the position of resource-based theories**

Writing in the 1960s, Drucker[57] points out that it is important to '...build on strength...to look for opportunities rather than for problems'. Many basic economic texts have also stressed the importance of resources as the basis for profit development.

One particular aspect of resource-based strategy, emphasised by US and Japanese strategists beginning in the 1960s and 1970s, was operations (manufacturing) strategy and the emphasis on total quality management. Although Henry Ford had developed these areas early in the twentieth century, little emphasis was subsequently given to them. They were probably considered to be too ordinary and insufficiently concerned with overall corporate strategy. (Many strategic texts made no mention of them even in the late 1990s.) Deming, Ishikawa and Taguchi[58] worked on quality issues and Ohno[59] and many others worked on manufacturing strategy issues. Chapter 9 will attempt to redress the balance in this area; some of the major practical advances in corporate strategy during the last 20 years have occurred in this area.

From a different theoretical perspective, resource-based strategy development has emerged as one of the key prescriptive routes of the 1990s. Possibly as a reaction against the strong emphasis on markets and profit maximising of the 1980s (*see* Section 2.4.1 above), researchers began to argue that the organisation's resources were far more important in delivering competitive advantage:

> *The traditional competitive strategy paradigm* [e.g. Porter 1980] *with its focus on product-market positioning, focuses only on the last few hundred yards of what may be a skill-building marathon.*[60]

Wernerfelt,[61] Peteraf,[62] Dierickx and Cool,[63] Kay[64] and others have all explored aspects of what has become known as the *resource-based view* of strategy development. Essentially, although competition is explored, the emphasis in this approach is on the organisation's own resources – its physical resources, such as plant and machinery; its people resources, such as its leadership and skills, and, above all, the ways that such resources interact in organisations. It is this combination of resources that delivers competitive advantage, because such a combination takes years to develop and is therefore difficult for others to copy.

In this context, the resource-based view draws a distinction between the general resources that are available to any organisation, such as accounting skills and basic technology, and those that are special and, perhaps, even unique to the organisation. It argues that it is only those special resources that deliver sustainable competitive advantage. For example, the Nestlé brand name is a unique resource available to Cereal Partners' breakfast cereals – *see* Case study 2.1. The resource-based view is explored in Chapter 6.

An important recent development has been the treatment of the *knowledge* of the organisation as a key resource.[65] It has been argued that the knowledge possessed by an organisation – its procedures, its technical secrets, its contacts with others outside the organisation – will deliver significant competitive advantages to many organisations. Some strategists have gone so far as to suggest that such knowledge is the only resource that will deliver sustainable competitive advantage. While this may be overstated, knowledge is important in strategy development and will be explored in Chapter 11.

2.4.3 Game-based theories of strategy

Game-based theories of strategy focus on an important part of the prescriptive process – the decision making that surrounds the selection of the best strategic option. Instead of treating this as a simple options-and-choice model, game theory attempts to explore the interaction between an organisation and others as the decision is made – the *game* (*see* Figure 2.6). The theoretical background to such an approach is based on mathematical models of options and choice coupled with the theory of chance.[66]

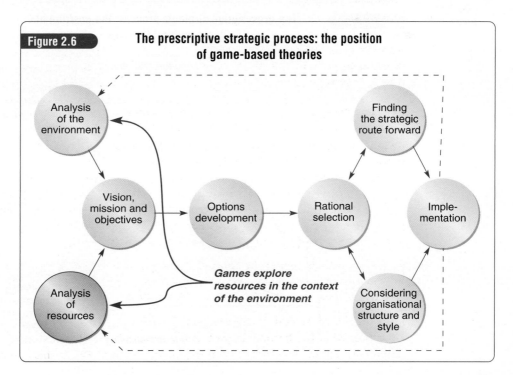

Figure 2.6 The prescriptive strategic process: the position of game-based theories

Game theory begins by recognising that a simple choice of the 'best' strategy will have implications for other companies, such as suppliers and competitors. The consequences for others will be unknown at the time the initial choice is made by the organisation itself. The theory then attempts to model the consequences of such a choice and thereby allow for the choice itself to be modified as the game progresses. Game theory will include not only *competitors*, but also other organisations who might be willing to *co-operate* with the organisation. Such a theory considers that the options-and-choice prescriptive model oversimplifies the options available. It will also involve negotiation with others, anticipation of competitive responses and the search for optimal solutions. Such a process may allow all competitors in the market place to win.

Although game theory has been around since the 1940s, it is only relatively recently that it has been applied to strategy. The reason is that the complex world of strategy decisions is difficult to model adequately using the mathematical theory that lies at the foundation of game theory. In the last few years, strategists have begun to explore some key concepts without necessarily modelling every detail using strict mathematical analysis. The results have been some new insights into the prescriptive strategic process that are explored in Chapters 3 and 15 but it still remains only a partial view of a limited part of the strategic process.

2.4.4 Socio-cultural theories of strategy

Socio-cultural theories seek clearly defined, prescriptive strategies, but they stress the importance of the social and cultural frameworks and beliefs of nations as the starting point for strategy development. Figure 2.7 shows where they fit into the overall model.

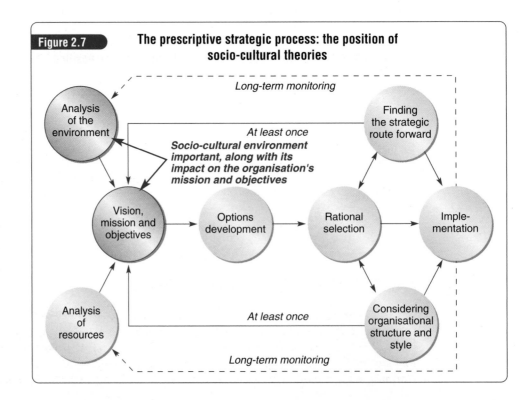

Figure 2.7 The prescriptive strategic process: the position of socio-cultural theories

Such theories have arisen in recent times as a result of the increasing prominence of cultures beyond the Anglo-American mould: the rise of Europe during the 1970s and 1980s and the emergence of Asia–Pacific during the 1980s and 1990s have led to greater awareness of the need for a broader range of parameters and values to measure and drive objectives and other aspects of the organisation.

For example, in countries such as Korea and Japan, the whole structure of society is different from the countries that gave rise to the profit-maximising theories. Both these countries have major structural differences that will influence strategy content – for instance, in the areas of wage costs, industry organisation, relationship with government, and cultural expectations of workers and shareholders. Ultimately, these cultural differences may make the content of strategic plans very different.

Marris,[67] Granovetter[68] and Whittington[69] have all explored aspects of this important, global topic. The essence of their research and arguments is that all companies and their managers are embedded in social and cultural systems that influence their decision making and thus the strategies they develop. Economic activity cannot be separated from the society in which it operates. Networks exist that constrain, direct and influence the strategies for all members, both at the *national* level and the more *local* level of ethnic, religious and other communities in local catchment areas. Prescriptive strategic plans may well be written but they will cover more than profit maximising.

Prescriptive planning may not even be appropriate in some cultures. One of the underlying assumptions of such planning is that companies have the freedom and ability to alter their future. In countries where there is a strong belief in luck and fate, a corporate strategy to alter the direction may be totally inconsistent with such beliefs (*see* Boyacigiller and Adler.[70])

> ### ▶ Key strategic principles
>
> - **Profit-maximising, competition-based theories emphasise the importance of the market place to deliver profits. Strategy should seek sustainable competitive advantage.**
> - **Resource-based theories stress the resources of the organisation in strategic development. Core competencies need to be identified.**
> - **Game-based theories of strategy focus on the options-and-choice stage of the prescriptive model. They explore the commercial realities of competitor reactions and possible counter-moves in the search for an optimal strategy.**
> - **Socio-cultural theories focus on the social and cultural dimensions of the organisation in developing its corporate strategy. They have arisen as a result of greater awareness of cultures beyond the Anglo-American mould. It is possible that in some cultures the profit objective may not even be appropriate.**

2.5 Emergent theories of corporate strategy

When strategies emerge from a situation rather than being prescribed in advance, it is less likely that they will involve a long-term strategic plan. This does not mean that there is no planning but rather that such plans are more flexible, feeling their way forward as issues clarify and the environment surrounding the company changes. Planning is short-term, more reactive to events, possibly even more entrepreneurial.

To understand the background to emergent strategy theory, it is useful to look back to the 1970s. At that time, prescriptive strategies with detailed corporate plans were widely used. Suddenly, oil prices rose sharply as a result of a new, strong Middle East oil price consortium. Many industrial companies around the world were hit badly in an entirely unpredictable way; the prescriptive plans were thrown into confusion. Emergent strategies that relied less on precise predictions about the future were sought. More recently, the economic bubble associated with new Internet companies has also highlighted the uncertainty of the environment. For this reason, some strategists argue that the whole basis of prescriptive strategy is false. They would claim that, even during periods of relative certainty, organisations may be better served by considering strategy as an emergent process.

For our purposes, we can usefully distinguish four sets of emergent strategy theories:

1 survival-based theories of strategy;

2 uncertainty-based theories of strategy;

3 human-resource-based theories of strategy;

4 innovation and knowledge-based theories of strategy.

2.5.1 Survival-based theories of strategy

Survival-based theories of strategy start from Darwin's theory of 'the survival of the fittest'. Such theorists take the view that strategy is primarily decided in the jungle that is the market place. Corporate strategy is about how to survive in an environment which is shifting and changing. There is little point in sophisticated prescriptive solutions: much better to dodge and weave as the market changes, letting the strategy emerge in the process. Figure 2.8 shows where the emphasis is placed by survival-based strategies.

As Section 2.4 explained, profit-maximising, competition-based approaches are concerned with selecting the optimal strategy to maximise the organisation's profitability and then implementing that strategy. Critics have long known that this simple

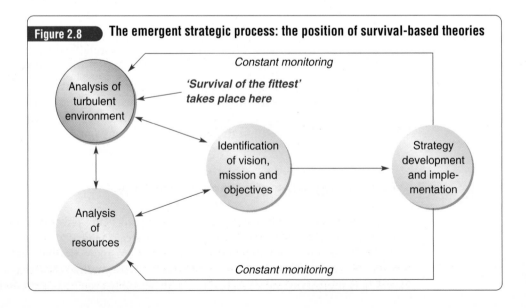

Figure 2.8 The emergent strategic process: the position of survival-based theories

Constant monitoring

Analysis of turbulent environment

'Survival of the fittest' takes place here

Identification of vision, mission and objectives

Strategy development and implementation

Analysis of resources

Constant monitoring

economic model is far from reality. For example, in the late 1930s, Hall and Hitch[71] surveyed companies and showed that they did not set output at the theoretical maximum level, i.e. where marginal cost equals marginal revenue. This was partly because decisions were not necessarily rational and partly because it was unclear what the revenue and cost relationships were anyway.

However, this does not mean that companies just muddle through. The competitive jungle of the market place will ruthlessly weed out the least efficient companies; survival-based strategies are needed in order to prosper in such circumstances. Essentially, according to the survival-based strategy theorists, it is the market place that matters more than a specific strategy; hence, the optimal strategy for survival is to be really efficient. Beyond this, companies can only rely on chance.

To overcome these difficulties, Henderson[72] suggested that what most companies needed to survive in these highly competitive circumstances was differentiation. Products or services that were able to offer some aspect not easily available to competitors would offer some protection. However, other strategists doubt that true differentiation is possible because it takes too long to achieve and the environment changes too quickly. In these circumstances, theorists suggest that survival-based strategies should rely on running really efficient operations that can respond to changes in the environment. As Williamson commented:

Economy is the best strategy.[73]

If the environment matters more than a specific strategy, then survival-based strategists argue that the optimal strategy will be to pursue a number of strategic initiatives at any one time and let the market place select the best.[74] Selection of strategy is therefore incorrect according to this theory. It is better to experiment with many different approaches and see which emerges as the best through natural selection. For example, Whittington[75] points to the example of Sony's Walkman strategy in the 1980s. The company launched 160 different versions in the North American market, never retaining more than about 20 versions at any one time. Ultimately, the market selected the best.

If survival-based theories are correct, then we need to study the organisation's environment carefully (we begin this process in Part 2). In addition to this, we would need to treat the strategy selection process of Chapters 13 and 14 with a great deal of circumspection.

Other strategy writers believe survival-based theories are too pessimistic; there are practical problems in a strategy that only takes small cautious steps and keeps all options open. Major acquisitions, innovative new products, plant investment to improve quality radically would all be the subject of much anxious debate and little action. The bold strategic step would be completely ruled out.[76]

2.5.2 Uncertainty-based theories of strategy

Uncertainty-based theories use mathematical probability concepts to show that corporate strategy development is complex, unstable and subject to major fluctuations, thus making it impossible to undertake any useful prediction in advance. If prediction is impossible, then setting clear objectives for corporate strategy is a useless exercise. Strategy should be allowed to emerge and change with the fluctuations in the environment. Figure 2.9 illustrates where the emphasis lies in such theories.

As a result of the major difficulties in predicting the future environment surrounding the organisation in the 1970s, the development of long-term strategic planning was regarded by some theorists as having little value. Strategic planning could still be used

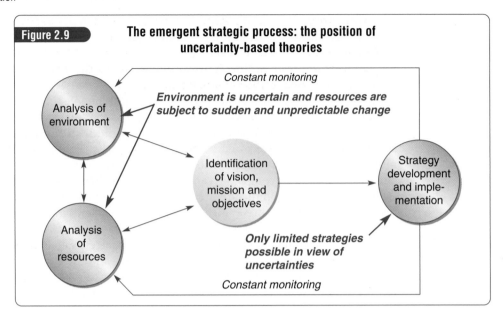

Figure 2.9 — **The emergent strategic process: the position of uncertainty-based theories**

but it had to have much greater flexibility and did not have the absolute certainties of the 1970s. This approach to strategy led not only to survival-based strategies that seek to keep all options open to the last possible opportunity but also to uncertainty-based strategies.

Since the 1960s, chaos theory and mathematical modelling of changing states have been used to map out the consequences of scientific experiments; such procedures were not developed for the business community but for other scientifically oriented topics, as in the mathematical modelling of weather forecasting. Essentially, such techniques were able to demonstrate that, in certain types of uncertain environment, small perturbations in the early stages of a process can lead to major variances in the later stages – not unlike the multiplier effect in macroeconomics. A major implication of such environments – often called *chaotic systems* – is that it is simply not possible to predict sufficiently accurately many years ahead (see Gleick).[77]

One variant of this approach to strategy is provided by the empirical research study conducted by Miller and Friesen.[78] They found that significant corporate strategy occurs in revolutionary ways: there are sudden major shifts in the whole strategy and organisational structure of the company before they reach a new steady state. From a mathematical perspective, it is possible to model such systems and show that they oscillate between steady and turbulent states. Strebel[79] has used a similar argument, pointing particularly to changes in technology that are likely to lead to 'breakpoints' in the development of the organisation.

Business has been identified as such a chaotic system. Stacey[80] has suggested that the environment of many businesses, particularly those in rapidly growing industries such as computers, is inherently unstable. It will never be possible to forecast accurately profits five or ten years into a new project; hence, for example, the apparent accuracy of discounted cash flows and cash projections is largely spurious. It follows that business strategy has to emerge rather than try to aim for the false certainties of the prescriptive approach.

Several writers, such as Miller and Friesen,[81] have also applied the same arguments to the resources of the organisation. They argue that innovation is vital to successful strategy: this can only be achieved in a significant way if the organisation's resources are subjected to revolutionary change, rather than gradual change. Such an approach is likely to have a chaotic, free-wheeling element whose outcome cannot be planned or predicted by strategy in advance.

Some companies would regard this whole approach as being partially true but probably too pessimistic. Although the weather is a chaotic system and cannot be predicted accurately, we do know that the Sahara Desert is hot and dry, Singapore is warmer and more humid than London, and so on. Similarly, it can be argued that there are some certainties about business, even though we are unable to predict accurately. Moreover, organisations (especially large ones) need a basic non-chaotic structure if they are to avoid dissolving into anarchy.

There are patterns of behaviour and trends that may be subject to change but can still be predicted with some accuracy. Business strategy may need to emerge and be adaptable, but it is not necessarily totally random and uncertain. However, strategy does need to identify and estimate risk. (We will return to the problem of risk and risk management in Chapter 14.)

2.5.3 Human-resource-based theories of strategy

These theories of strategy emphasise the *people* element in strategy development and highlight the motivation, the politics and cultures of organisations and the desires of individuals. They have particularly emphasised the difficulties that can arise as new strategies are introduced and confront people with the need for change and uncertainty. Figure 2.10 shows where these theories fit into the emergent process. They involve people and occur wherever human resources are prominent and it is therefore difficult to identify a precise position.

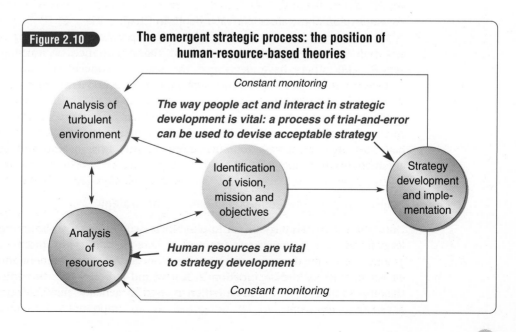

Figure 2.10 The emergent strategic process: the position of human-resource-based theories

Constant monitoring

Analysis of turbulent environment

The way people act and interact in strategic development is vital: a process of trial-and-error can be used to devise acceptable strategy

Identification of vision, mission and objectives

Strategy development and implementation

Analysis of resources

Human resources are vital to strategy development

Constant monitoring

We have already examined the important findings of researchers such as Cyert and March[82] and the work of Herbert Simon[83] – corporate strategy needs to have a human-resource-based dimension. Organisations consist of individuals and groups of people, all of whom may influence or be influenced by strategy; they may make a contribution, acquiesce or even resist the corporate strategy process, but they are certainly affected by it. Nelson and Winter[84] developed this theme further, arguing that the options-and-choice model of the prescriptive process was completely misleading:

> *It is quite inappropriate to conceive of firm behavior in terms of deliberate choice from a broad menu of alternatives that some external observer considers to be 'available' opportunities for the organization.*

The human resource aspects of strategy development will be explored in much greater detail in Chapter 7. However, according to some writers, these matters are not just about peripheral issues of implementation; they are fundamental to the strategy process itself. Nelson and Winter[85] argued that organisations have in reality limited strategic choice. The strategy available is:

> *not broad, but narrow and idiosyncratic; it is built on a firm's routines, and most of the 'choosing' is also accomplished automatically by those routines.*

Strategic logic is restricted by the processes and people already existing in the organisation.

Mintzberg[86] has also developed this theme and argued that strategy thus emerges from an organisation as it adapts continuously to its environment. Implementation is not therefore some separate phase tacked on to the end of the strategy process, but intermingled with corporate strategy as it develops. Quinn[87] has described this gradualist, emergent approach that accepts that it is looking at only a limited number of feasible options as *logical incrementalism*. In the words of Mintzberg's famous phrase:

> *Smart strategies appreciate that they cannot always be smart enough to think through everything in advance.*

We will explore these areas in greater depth in Chapter 15.

More recently, there has been considerable emphasis on the learning aspect of strategy development. Mintzberg emphasised the importance of learning. After him, Senge[88] and others have developed the learning concept, encouraging managers involved in strategy to undertake a process of trial and error to adopt the optimal strategy (*see* Chapter 21).

The main criticisms of the emergent approach to strategy development listed in Section 2.3 apply especially to human-resource-based strategy. Similar comments may have prompted Mintzberg to move more recently towards the modification of his argument outlined above.[89]

2.5.4 Innovation and knowledge-based theories of strategy

During the 1990s, strategy began to place increased emphasis on innovation and knowledge-based strategic processes. Innovation here does not just mean inventing new products or production processes: innovation means the development and exploitation of any resource of the organisation in a new and radical way.[90] In particular, the way that the knowledge of the organisation is used to generate new and radical solutions to strategy has come to be recognised as an important contributor to strategy

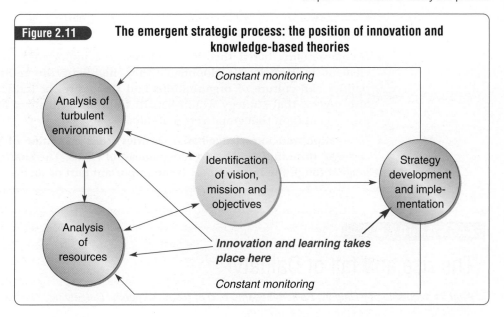

Figure 2.11 The emergent strategic process: the position of innovation and knowledge-based theories

development[91] – 'knowledge' here does not mean data so much as the collective wisdom and understanding of many people in the organisation developed over many years. Figure 2.11 shows where such an approach fits into the emergent strategic process.

The great advantage of such theories is that they begin to tackle the problem that strategy theories are well known and widely available. This means that the traditional and original areas of strategy that might deliver differences are no longer available. However, innovation by its very nature moves forward the traditional thinking of the organisation and thereby delivers the possibility of a new competitive advantage. Case study 2.3 shows that one of the problems faced by Spillers during its independence was that it was involved in a traditional industry – bread baking – with little, if any, thinking 'outside the box'. Radical solutions were needed but were never obtained because of this restricted approach that lacked innovation.

In the process of innovating, one important aspect is that of sharing knowledge and ideas. This has been made much easier in the last ten years as a result of the internet and telecommunications technology. This has now developed into an important topic in strategy with real potential to revolutionise strategic thinking. The rise and fall of some internet businesses around the year 2000 has made no difference to the potential of this important strategic route.

▶ Key strategic principles

- Survival-based theories of strategy are based on the survival of the fittest in the market place. It is difficult to plan strategy actively and possible to survive by differentiation as events unfold.

- Uncertainty-based theories of strategy regard prediction as impossible because of the inherently unstable nature of business and its environment. Strategies must be allowed to react to the changing environment and emerge from the chaos of events. Some would regard this as being a pessimistic view of strategy.

> **Key strategic principles continued**
>
> - Human-resource-based theories emphasise the importance of the people element in strategy development. They highlight the motivation, the politics and culture of organisations and the desires of individuals. They also suggest that strategy would benefit from an element of learning and experimentation that empowers individuals.
>
> - Innovation and knowledge-based theories stress the value of radical new strategic thinking in order to move ahead of rivals. The sharing of knowledge through the Internet may be an important part of such a process.

CASE STUDY 2.5

The rise and fall of Dalgety

After its acquisition by Dalgety, Spillers became part of a new company: Dalgety plc. This case describes the fortunes of Spillers under its new owners.

Dalgety 1980–89: a muddled diversification strategy

During the 1980s, the new group started by consolidating its Spillers acquisition, particularly in agricultural cattle feeds – its *agribusiness*. In addition and after some hesitation, it invested further in the Spillers branded business that it had acquired.

At the same time, Dalgety acquired other companies without any real sense of strategic logic; it made 15 acquisitions in the first six months of 1988 alone in a range of companies. Few of these added anything to the existing parts of the group, such as economies of scale or market share. The purchase reflected the buoyancy and confidence of stock markets at that time. Then came the stock market crash of 1987. It left companies like Dalgety with a ragbag of businesses which had been bought at inflated prices and were difficult to sell.

Overall, Dalgety had done a reasonable job investing in agribusiness, but it had conducted a company acquisition and disposal policy that was, at best, unclear. This perhaps contributed to the sudden departure of the chief executive officer in July 1989.

Dalgety Spillers 1990–97: focus on three core businesses

Dalgety chose to concentrate on what it called its 'three legs', although some might see this as more than three:

1 animal feeds and pig breeding;

2 food ingredients;

3 petfood.

Dalgety claimed that there were real benefits in terms of cost savings between these areas. They came from shared technology and from specialist expertise which also acted as an entry barrier for potential competitors. Sales and net income levels are shown in Figure 2.12.

In practice, pig breeding proved highly profitable because of the special expertise in genetics required. Animal feeds were largely UK-based and thriving. Food ingredients had come from the Spillers acquisition ten years earlier; the strategy was to expand this with some further acquisitions. Petfood was expanded in 1983 by the acquisition of Paragon Petfood from British Petroleum for £42 million[92] and another company in Spain. In 1995, the company purchased all the European petfood business of the Quaker Oats company for £442 million.[93] This strategy stretched the company's finances to the limit and it was forced to sell some of its interests in other product areas: for example, Golden Wonder crisps, snacks, Homepride sauces, flour and baking mixes.

Dalgety Spillers 1996–98: the breakup of Dalgety

Just after acquiring Quaker petfoods, Dalgety faced a real problem: the UK government announced that the cattle disease BSE could be passed on to humans. Millions of cattle were infected, particularly in the UK, and many were therefore slaughtered. The demand for cattle feed dropped and this sent Dalgety's animal feed business into loss. Moreover, the EU banned the export of beef

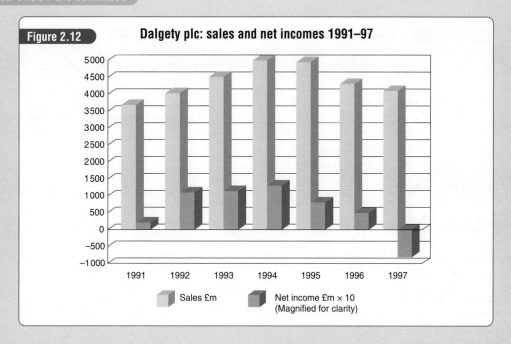

Figure 2.12

Dalgety plc: sales and net incomes 1991–97

Sales £m

Net income £m × 10
(Magnified for clarity)

products from the UK. This was particularly unfortunate for Dalgety because two of its main European petfood plants were located in the UK and beef by-products were used in some petfood products. Such problems could be overcome but they hit profits in the short term.

In addition to all of these external circumstances, Dalgety faced two problems of its own making. One of its petfood factories suffered 'substantial mechanical breakdowns' in 1997. At the same time, the integration of Quaker with Spillers was taking longer to achieve than envisaged, so the expected gains in economies of scale were slower in emerging. Both these events produced severe profit pressures and led to Dalgety declaring a loss after exceptional items in 1997. The solution for the company in 1997 was to replace the Spillers Petfood managing director. The company then undertook a 'fundamental reappraisal' of its strategy but matters did not improve significantly. The 1998 solution was the resignation of the chief executive of the whole Dalgety Group and the sale of its Spillers Petfood Division to Nestlé.

Subsequently, Dalgety sold its North American distribution company in 1997. In the following year, it sold its food ingredients business (largely acquired from Spillers back in 1980) to Kerry Foods

(Ireland) in 1998 and its animal feeds business to a management buy-out. These difficult and dramatic decisions were taken after Mr Ken Hannah was promoted from financial director to chief executive in May 1998. Essentially, he concluded that greater value for Dalgety's shareholders would be gained from the breakup and sale of its individual parts. Most shareholders were highly pleased with Mr Hannah, but others were unimpressed by the strategy of walking away from the business.

By August 1998, Dalgety was largely a global pig breeding business. It had been reduced to a shadow of its former self. Figure 2.13 summarises the rise and fall of Dalgety Spillers.

Case questions

1 *For much of this period, Dalgety concentrated on acquisitions. Is this approach prescriptive or emergent? Within this approach, can you identify any particular strategy route? What does this tell you about the Dalgety strategy?*

2 *During the 1990s, Dalgety decided to concentrate on 'three legs'. What is the main danger that comes from focusing its strategic resources?*

CASE STUDY 2.5 continued

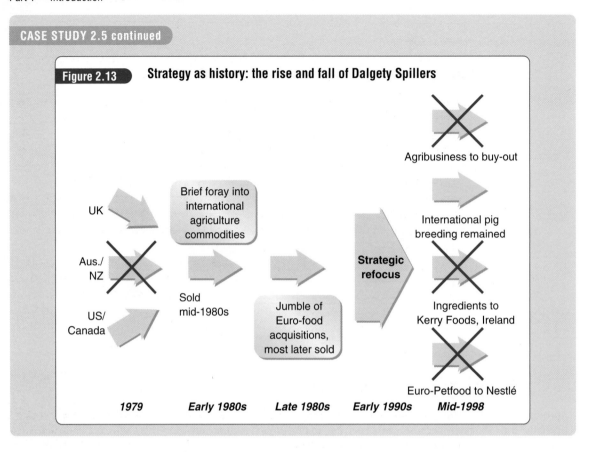

Figure 2.13 Strategy as history: the rise and fall of Dalgety Spillers

UK

Brief foray into international agriculture commodities

Aus./ NZ

Sold mid-1980s

US/ Canada

Jumble of Euro-food acquisitions, most later sold

Strategic refocus

Agribusiness to buy-out

International pig breeding remained

Ingredients to Kerry Foods, Ireland

Euro-Petfood to Nestlé

1979   Early 1980s   Late 1980s   Early 1990s   Mid-1998

2.6 Strategy as history – the contributions of Penrose and Chandler

Back in 1959, before strategy was considered to be a distinct academic subject, the young academic economist Edith Penrose turned traditional economic thinking on its head. She argued that what happened *inside* the firm was just as important as the market place *outside* the firm.[94] Up to this time, it was this latter area that had been the main focus of economics with its consideration of market demand and supply issues. Moreover, in exploring how firms grow, Penrose argued that this was related to a firm's resources, its past history and its evolution over time. Thus the firm's previous history was a key influence on its future development.

In 1962, the US strategist Alfred Chandler published a substantial study of the growth of four great US companies during the early twentieth century:[95] its arguments and language were similar to those of Penrose. Both writers showed that the development of a firm over time is an essential element of understanding strategy. The rise and fall of Dalgety is one example, albeit extreme, of this tracking of company development. To make sense of strategy, it is useful to consider the history of an organisation in three areas:[96]

1 *the processes*: how an organisation has developed its organisational structure, company relationships and leadership, especially in the areas of technology, institutional assets and market assets;

2 *the position*: how the organisation is placed with regard to its competitors, both at present and with regard to the future;

3 *the paths*: how its past history has developed and how its future is envisaged, covering its special resources, innovative ability and knowledge.

In common with us as individuals, organisations are creatures of their history, resources and experience. Strategy needs to consider these if it is to understand how developments should proceed for the future. More specifically, strategy is highly dependent on the leadership, culture and style of those who have come to form the company, especially at a senior level. Some of this will happen by design, but some by chance. In the same way, strategy also needs to be considered in the context of how resources were acquired and market positions obtained.[97] For example, expansion by acquisition brings the history of the acquired company into its new parent. This will include the good and bad aspects of the new resources, the knowledge, experience and organisational culture.

Such an approach provides a means of assessing some aspects of the Dalgety strategy: its lack of understanding of some parts of Spillers, its move into new petfood ventures without the management expertise and its decision to break up the group in 1998 after the arrival of a new chief executive with a strong financial background that was well suited to finding financial solutions to strategic issues.

▶ Key strategic principles

● An organisation's previous history is a key determinant of its future development. Future strategy will be grounded in its past resources developed over time.

● In strategy development, it is useful to consider the history of an organisation in three areas: how its *processes* have developed; how the organisation is *positioned* with regard to competitors; and how its *paths* have developed in the past and are envisaged to continue in the future.

CASE STUDY 2.6

Disaster and recovery at IBM: 2

How IBM changed its strategy and revived its fortunes

After a disastrous period from 1991 to 1993, the world's largest computer company, IBM, managed to revive its fortunes over the following three years. This case examines how this was achieved.

During the three years 1994–97, IBM was able to report a net income after tax of US$18 billion, compared with a loss of over US$16 billion in the previous three years (*see* Case study 1.1). It achieved this remarkable turnaround by adopting radically different strategies on leadership, new investments and cost cutting. It also took advantage of a major new area of customer demand in computers, which IBM was uniquely placed to serve. And it had some luck.

▶

Background

During the 1990s, the computer market continued to grow rapidly, with strong demand for small personal computers (PCs), networked computers and large, mainframe machines. In spite of problems elsewhere, IBM had never lost its dominance of the global mainframe computer market. Nevertheless, it was a stroke of luck for the company that the major development of the Internet happened around this time. It provided a means of boosting IBM's most profitable product area at a time when it was under pressure with its range of small PCs. The IBM case in Chapter 1 explored these issues, so this case picks up the story after that period of major difficulty for the company.

New leadership at IBM: Mr Louis Gerstner

After the former chief executive, John Akers, stepped down in 1993, Louis Gerstner was appointed as his successor. The new man came from the food industry and had a strong reputation for knowing how to cut costs. He knew little about the computer industry but said, at the time, that this was no problem. However, he subsequently admitted that his lack of knowledge had been a disadvantage. Importantly for IBM, this was the first time a leader had been appointed from outside the company, with a clear lesson for those remaining inside.

Mr Gerstner began by spending several months reviewing the situation and talking with IBM customers. He wanted to develop a customer-driven strategy (*see* Chapter 5) and devoted the majority of his time to understanding their views. Over the next year, he and his immediate colleagues then made three major strategic decisions:

1 *IBM would remain one company.* Large customers wanted integrated-technology solutions to their problems and IBM had sustainable competitive advantage in this area. It would therefore not be demerged and the main parts would be retained.

2 *IBM would refocus its strategy around its customers.* Complicated corporate strategy was not needed, rather a simple focus on the needs of customers, their technology requirements and, where appropriate, new R&D and new acquisitions. IBM expected to become closer to its leading customers, perhaps even taking over some functions such as data processing and telecommunications network links that were previously run by its customers.

3 *IBM needed all senior managers to work actively for the new focus and structure.* Mr Gerstner said that some managers had appeared to be blocking strategies that were essential for survival: he called it 'pushback'. He actually removed several senior executives during 1993–94.

IBM had already recognised the need to offer one-stop computer service solutions to its major customers back in 1991; Case study 1.1 described the Industry Solution Units (ISUs) that were set up to tackle this. To build on IBM's strength of being able to offer a one-stop technical solution to many major companies, Mr Gerstner confirmed that ISUs

Table 2.2 The decline of IBM and the growth of Intel and Microsoft (US$ million)

	1991	1992	1993	1994	1995	1996	1997
IBM							
Revenue	64 766	64 523	62 716	64 052	71 940	75 947	78 508
Net profit or (loss)	(598)	(6 865)	(7 987)	3 021	4 178	5 429	6 093
Intel							
Revenue	4 779	5 844	8 782	11 521	16 202	20 847	25 070
Net profit	1 080	1 490	2 295	2 288	3 566	5 157	6 945
Microsoft							
Revenue	1 843	2 759	3 753	4 649	5 937	8 671	11 358
Net profit	650	996	953	1 146	1 453	2 195	3 434

Source: Company accounts.

were to be the main organisational structure, even though their integrated solutions were more suited to IBM's larger customers. Pushback against the ISUs would no longer be tolerated.

The new organisation culture and structure that began to emerge from this new strategic focus was an essential element of IBM's recovery during the subsequent years. New leadership does bring new strategies. As Table 2.2 shows, IBM was able to turn around its fortunes during the latter part of the 1990s. In March 2002, Mr Gerstner retired and was replaced by a new chief executive, Mr Sam Palmisano. Perhaps surprisingly given the previous inward-looking IBM culture, the new leader had been with the company for nearly 30 years. In reality, it is always difficult to recruit a new chief from outside an organisation that is large and complex – Gerstner is on record as saying that he had real difficulty for the first few years. In any event, the strategies introduced over the period 1993–97 had allowed IBM to recover its former dominant position.

New strategies at IBM: 1993–97
In addition to the firm development of ISUs, IBM's recovery from near-disaster came from six main strategies:

1 *New corporate culture* – more lean, more responsive and willing to learn;

2 *Cost cutting.* IBM reduced its workforce by 86 000 to 215 000 in the period 1993–95. The R&D budget was also slashed, especially on the more esoteric products and on some mainframe development. Some of these job losses were accounted for by the sale of companies, rather than outright sackings;

3 *Sale or management buy-out of some peripheral companies* – for example, in hard-disk drives and computer printing peripherals;

4 *Reorganisation of the company away from countries into global product groups.* Economies of scale were delivered by new worldwide product groups working across country boundaries;

5 *Acquisition of companies in fast-growing segments of the computer industry* – for example, IBM acquired the only remaining independent software company of any standing, Lotus Development, for US$3.25 billion cash in 1995;

6 *Investment in the fast-growing segment of computer service outsourcing.* IBM continued to invest in

its own activities to act as a major supplier of computer services to non-computer companies – for example, taking over and running the computing services of a major bank for a contractual fee. This service is called outsourcing. By 2002, IBM had come to dominate this part of the computer industry on a global basis. It had proved a major contributor to the IBM turnaround.

Results of the IBM corporate turnaround
To the present, the results of IBM's new strategies have been successful, with a major recovery in profitability. Although IBM's profits are little better at the time of writing than they were in the mid-1980s, at least the company has been able to stop the rot. It is also well placed with new growth strategies to develop further into the twenty-first century.

Table 2.3 summarises IBM's situation over the years from the early 1980s to the late 1990s. It shows how IBM's objectives changed and the new strategies that were developed to address the new objectives of the company. Both were changed significantly during this lengthy time frame. Although

Table 2.3 How IBM's objectives and strategies shifted over time

Period	Summary objective for company	Examples of strategies to achieve objective
Early to mid-1980s	Grow and maintain market dominance	• Invest in branding • Enhance service • Regular new product initiatives
Late 1980s to early 1990s	Survive competitive threat	• Major cutbacks in costbase • Divest peripheral parts
Mid-1990s onwards	Restart growth	• Acquire new companies • Diversify into software and computer services

Sources for IBM case: See reference 98.

the strategies are presented as static statements at single points in time, they were more fluid and experimental at the time.

Case questions

1 Do you think it was wise of the company to concentrate on ISUs? Consider in your answer the loss of business from smaller companies which did not want integrated solutions.

2 Are there any more general lessons to be drawn for companies from the IBM approach of providing industry solutions? Or is this strategy specific to one very large company in the computer industry?

3 Where would you place the new strategies of IBM – prescriptive or emergent? And within this, which strategic theory represents the most appropriate explanation of the company's development?

KEY READING

What is business strategy?

In this extract from an article from The Economist[99] *we consider the nature of business strategy. Top managers of big firms devote the bulk of their efforts to formulating strategy, though there is remarkably little agreement about what it is…*

No single subject has so dominated the attention of managers, consultants and management theorists as the subject of corporate strategy. For the top managers of big companies, this is perhaps understandable. Served by hordes of underlings, their huge desks uncluttered by the daily minutiae of business, they often consider setting strategy as their most valuable contribution. And it is also understandable that there is a great deal of debate about which strategies work best; business is, after all, complicated and uncertain. More puzzling is the fact that the consultants and theorists jostling to advise businesses cannot even agree on the most basic of all questions: what, precisely, is corporate strategy?

In the January–February 1993 issue of the *Harvard Business Review*, Gary Hamel and C K Prahalad, professors at the London Business School and the University of Michigan, turn much of their recent thinking upside down by asserting that the real function of a company's strategy is not to match its resources with its opportunities, as many businessmen assume, but rather to set goals which 'stretch' a company beyond what most of its managers believe is possible.

The authors cite a number of well-known cases of smaller companies defeating bigger companies with deeper pockets, stronger reputations and larger market shares. Toyota v General Motors, Cable News Network v CBS, British Airways v Pan Am and Sony v RCA are all competitive battles in which most observers would have predicted defeat for the challenger. In all these examples, overwhelming ambition and gritty determination may well have been a vital ingredient in the smaller firm's success. But this is not what most people would call a 'strategy'.

The authors' reduction of strategy to little more than a rallying cry is the apotheosis of a trend away from formal planning at big firms which has been gathering pace for the past 30 years. In a vast outpouring of writing on the subject during this period, management theorists have come up with so many alternative views of what a corporate strategy should contain that they have undermined the entire concept. A growing number of businessmen now question whether thinking consciously about an overall strategy is of any benefit at all to big firms. Grabbing opportunities or coping with blows as they arise may make more sense.

Soon after the Second World War, when a new class of professional managers began to search for ideas about how to run big firms, the original views of strategy were borrowed from the mili-

KEY READING continued

tary. Managers still talk about 'attacking' markets and 'defeating' rivals, but the analogy between generalship and running a firm was quickly abandoned when businessmen realised that slaughtering your opponents and outselling them had little in common.

By the 1960s, corporate strategy had come to mean a complex and meticulously wrought plan based on detailed forecasts of economies and specific markets. That view was endorsed by two celebrated books: Alfred Sloan's *My Years with General Motors*, a memoir by the man who made the car maker the world's biggest industrial enterprise; and Alfred Chandler's *Strategy and Structure*, a history of big, successful American firms in which the Harvard professor argued that their strategies had produced their multi-divisional form.

This approach to strategy fell into disrepute for several reasons. Many people blame it for the over-zealous diversification of the following decade and the creation of poorly performing conglomerates. In the 1970s, the success of Japanese firms, which seemed to eschew detailed planning, cast further doubt on its usefulness. The two sudden oil-price rises of the 1970s also meant that firms found that the reams of statistics and targets, once assembled, sat gathering dust. Occupied with running their operations, few managers at any level of the firm ever bothered to refer again to its handsomely bound corporate strategy.

Then in 1980 came another book: *Competitive Strategy* by Michael Porter, an economist at Harvard Business School. He argued that a firm's profitability was determined by the characteristics of its industry and the firm's position within it, so these should also determine its strategy. Applying the analytical techniques common to industrial economics, Professor Porter said that a firm's primary task was to find niches it could defend from competitors, by becoming the low-cost producer, by differentiating its products in a way which would allow it to command a higher profit margin, or by erecting barriers to the entry of new rivals. Professor Porter's book was an instant hit.

Nevertheless, his ideas have had little impact on how most big firms go about formulating strategy. One reason is that Professor Porter's work is descriptive, not prescriptive. His vast checklists provide little guide to what firms should actually do, or avoid doing. Every firm would like to be in an industry with high barriers to entry, weak rivals and high profits. But few are so lucky.

About the same time as Professor Porter's book appeared, James Quinn, a professor at Dartmouth College's Amos Tuck business school, published the results of a study of how big firms actually went about formulating strategy. He found that they proceeded by trial and error, constantly revising their strategy in the light of new experience. He called this *logical incrementalism*. To a lot of people this sounded suspiciously like 'muddling through' (i.e. no strategy at all), though Professor Quinn vehemently denied this, arguing that there were great benefits to formalising the process.

The most influential strain of theorising about strategy in the 1980s has stressed expanding a firm's skills – a rapid product development, high-quality manufacturing, technological innovation and service – and then finding markets in which to exploit those skills. This is the argument made by Professors Hamel and Prahalad themselves in a 1990 *Harvard Business Review* article.

Despite the changing fashions, decades of theorising have not been entirely useless. How a company views strategy does depend largely on its circumstances. Small firms determined to challenge behemoths may find it helpful to call their aspirations a 'strategy'. Big companies defending a dominant market position may find Professor Porter's industry analysis illuminating. All firms should try to exploit and hone their skills. But there is no single way to approach the future. The next time your boss proudly boasts that he is off to a strategic planning meeting, give him your condolences.

© Copyright *The Economist*, London, 20 Mar 1993. Reproduced with permission.

Questions

1 *Does the writer accurately summarise some of the main theories? What strategy areas, if any, need to be added?*

2 *Does the lack of quoted references invalidate the comments of the writer?*

3 *The writer appears to dismiss many of the major strategy developments of the last 30 years. Do you agree?*

◼ Summary

- Prescriptive and emergent strategies can be contrasted by adapting Mintzberg's analogy:[100]

  Prescriptive strategy is Biblical in its approach: *it appears at a point in time and is governed by a set of rules, fully formulated and ready to implement.*

  Emergent strategy is Darwinian in its approach: *an emerging and changing strategy that survives by adapting as the environment itself changes.*

Given the need for an organisation to have a corporate strategy, much of this chapter has really been about the *process* of achieving this strategy. As has been demonstrated, there is no common agreement on the way this can be done.

- On the one hand, there is the *prescriptive* process, which involves a structured strategic planning system. There is a need to identify objectives, analyse the environment and the resources of the organisation, develop strategy options and select among them. The selected process is then implemented. However, there are writers who caution against having a system that is too rigid and incapable of taking into account the people element in strategy.

- On the other hand, there is the *emergent* process, which does not identify a final objective with specific strategies to achieve this. It relies on developing strategies whose final outcome may not be known. Managers will rely more on trial and error and experimentation to achieve the optimal process.

- In the early part of the twentieth century when industrialisation was proceeding fast, the prescriptive process was the main recommended route. As organisations came to recognise the people element and their importance to strategic development during the middle part of the century, emergent strategies were given greater prominence. In recent years, emphasis has switched between market-based routes and resource-based routes in the development of strategy. Social and cultural issues have also become more important as markets and production have become increasingly global in scale.

- Within the *prescriptive* route, four main groups of strategic theory have been identified:

  1 *the profit-maximising, market-based route* – the market place is vital to profit delivery;

  2 *the resource-based route* – the resources of the organisation are important in developing corporate strategy;

  3 *the game theory route* – concentrating on the way that strategic choice is decided and negotiated with others in the market place;

  4 *the socio-cultural-based route* – focusing on the social and cultural dimensions of the organisation, especially for its international implications.

  Each of these has different perspectives on the development of strategy.

- Within the *emergent* route, four main groups were also distinguished:

  1 *the survival-based route* – emphasising the 'survival of the fittest' in the jungle of the marketplace;

  2 *the uncertainty-based route* – regards prediction as impossible because of the inherently unstable nature of the environment and the need to have innovative processes;

3 *the human-resource-based route* – places the emphasis on people in strategic development. Motivation, politics, culture and the desires of the individual are all important. Strategy may involve an element of experimentation and learning in order to take into account all these factors.

4 *the innovation and knowledge-based route* – stresses the contribution of new ideas and radical ways of thinking and sharing knowledge if an organisation is to outsmart its competitors.

● Strategy development should also be seen in the historical context of the development of the organisation. A firm's previous history is a key influence on its future development. This can usefully be considered under three broad headings: process, competitive position and paths of past and future resource development.

QUESTIONS

1 Is it possible for organisations to follow both prescriptive and emergent strategies or do they need to choose?

2 Examine the criticisms of prescriptive strategies in Section 2.2 and those of emergent strategies in Section 2.3. To what extent, if at all, do you agree with them? Why?

3 Consider the three emergent approaches to strategy outlined in Section 2.5. Which would you judge most closely described the route taken by Spillers in Case study 2.2? What conclusions do you draw from this about the viability of Spillers' approach?

4 What predictions would you make for the environment over the next ten years? What influence will your predictions have on developments in corporate strategy over this period?

5 Take an organisation with which you are familiar. Analyse whether it has been following prescriptive or emergent strategies or both. Within these broad categories, how would you characterise its strategies according to the classifications laid out in Sections 2.4 and 2.5?

6 If you were asked to develop corporate strategy for the following companies, which corporate strategy

theory might you pick as a starting point for your assessment? A large, international car company; an advertising agency with global links; a government institution; a small travel agency with four branches, all in one region of a country.

7 '*When well-managed major organisations make significant changes in strategy, the approaches they use frequently bear little resemblance to the rational–analytical systems so often touted in the planning literature.*' (Professor J B Quinn) Discuss.

8 '*In turbulent environments, the speed at which changes develop is such that firms which use the emerging strategy formation advocated by Mintzberg endanger their own survival. When they arrive on a market with a new product or service, such firms find the market pre-empted by more foresightful competitors who plan their strategic moves in advance.*' (Professor I Ansoff) Explain and critically evaluate this comment.

9 Take an organisation with which you are familiar and explore the extent to which its current strategy is dependent on past events. Use Section 2.6 to structure your answer into processes, position and paths.

STRATEGIC PROJECT   Corporate strategy in the food industry

Several of the cases in the chapter have examined aspects of corporate strategy in the food industry. You will find other cases later in this book. Such companies face real strategic problems because of the increasing power of grocery retailers. They have attempted to hit

back using branding, pricing and even supplying products under the brand name of the retailer, especially in Europe. Consider what further activities the food companies should undertake:

▶

STRATEGIC PROJECT   continued

- Should they merge into larger enterprises?
- Should they move further into supplying the retailer?
- Should they cut down their product range so that they can invest heavily behind a narrower focus (i.e. the Dalgety strategy)?

Examine the French company Danone, which has used a strategic mix of product innovation and acquisitions with some success. Alternatively, explore the UK company Cadbury Schweppes, which has expanded globally with some success.

FURTHER READING

Richard Whittington's *What is Strategy and Does it Matter?* (Routledge, London, 1993) is a lucid, well-structured and thought-provoking book. I have acknowledged some of its interesting research references as this chapter has progressed and it has certainly influenced some elements of the material. Read Chapter 2 of Whittington for an alternative view and structuring of strategy theories and practice.

More recently, two major books of strategy research topics are strongly recommended: Michael Hitt, R. Edward Freeman and Jeffrey S. Harrison, *The Blackwell Handbook of Strategic Management* (Blackwell, Oxford, 2001), Andrew Pettigrew, Howard Thomas, Richard Whittington, *Handbook of Strategy and Management* (Sage, London, 2002).

On strategy as history, classic studies include those by Alfred Chandler, *Strategy and Structure* (MIT Press, Cambridge, MA, 1962), and his later book *Scale and Scope: Dynamics of Individual Capitalism* (Harvard University Press, Cambridge, MA, 1990). See also Derek Channon's *The Strategy and Structure of British Enterprise* (Harvard University Press, Cambridge, MA, 1973). A more recent study with real insight is Geoffrey Jones' *Evolution of International Business* (Routledge, London, 1996).

J L Moore's *Writers on Strategy and Strategic Management* (Penguin, London, 1992) has a useful survey of some leading writers and theories. Helpful for essay references and revision.

The book by Edith Penrose, *The Theory of the Growth of the Firm*, 3rd edn (Oxford University Press, Oxford, 1993), represents a classic early study of strategy development. Moreover, its precision of language and clarity of thought represent a model for us all to emulate.

NOTES & REFERENCES

1 Kennedy, P (1990) *The Rise and Fall of the Great Powers*. Fontana Press, London, Ch5. The historical description of this chapter draws on this well-researched and documented book.

2 Urwick, L (ed) (1956) *The Golden Book of Management*, Newman Neame, London. The book contains brief records of the lives and work of 70 of the early management pioneers, including their publications and a comment on their contribution. The historical material in this chapter draws on this work, which is no longer in print.

3 Williams, K, Haslam, C, Johal, S and Williams, J (1994) *Cars: Analysis, History and Cases*, Berghahn Books, New York, Ch7.

4 Abernathy, W J and Wayne, K (1974) 'Limits of the learning curve', *Harvard Business Review*, Sept–Oct, pp109–19.

5 Drucker, P (1961) *The Practice of Management*, Mercury Books, London, Ch10.

6 Penrose, E (1959) *The Theory of the Growth of the Firm*, Basil Blackwell, Oxford.

7 Cyert, R M and March, J G (1963) *A Behavioural Theory of the Firm*, Prentice-Hall, Englewood Cliffs, NJ.

8 Ansoff, H I (1969) *Business Strategy*, Penguin, Harmondsworth.

9 World Bank (1994) *World Development Report 1994*, Oxford University Press, New York, Ch3.

10 Ansoff, I (1969) Op. cit. Porter, M E (1980) *Competitive Strategy*, The Free Press, Harvard, MA, Introduction.

11 Clausewitz, C von, *On War*, Routledge and Kegan Paul, London, quoted in Kotler, P and Singh, R (1981) 'Marketing warfare', *Journal of Business Strategy*, pp30–41.

12 Liddell Hart, B H (1967) *Strategy*, Praeger, NY, also quoted in reference 4 above.

13 *See*, for example, James, B G (1985) *Business Warfare*, Penguin, Harmondsworth. Also Ries, J and Trout, A (1986) *Marketing Warfare*, McGraw-Hill, Maidenhead.

14 Whittington, R (1993) *What is Strategy – and Does it Matter?*, Routledge, London, p16.

15 Wiles, P J D (1961) *Price, Cost and Output*, Blackwell, Oxford, p78.

16 Porter, M E (1985) *Competitive Advantage*, The Free Press, Harvard, MA.

17 Ansoff, H I (1965) *Corporate Strategy: An Analytical Approach to Business Policy for Growth and Expansion*, McGraw-Hill, New York.

18 Andrews, K (1971) *The Concept of Corporate Strategy*, Irwin, Homewood, IL.

19 Chakravarthy, B and Lorange, P (1991) *Managing the Strategy Process*, Prentice Hall, Upper Saddle River, NJ. The first chapter is usefully summarised in: De Wit, B and Meyer, R (1994) *Strategy: Process, Context and Content*, West Publishing, St Paul, MN.

20 For example, see the following for an extended critique of prescriptive strategy: Stacey, R (1998) *Strategic Management and Organisational Dynamics*, 2nd edn, Pearson Education, London.

21 Mintzberg, H (1990) 'The Design School: reconsidering the basic premises of strategic management', *Strategic Management Journal*, 11, pp176–95.

22 Mintzberg, H (1994) 'The fall and rise of strategic planning', *Harvard Business Review*, Jan–Feb, pp107–14.

23 The evidence in this case comes from personal experience: the author was senior manager at Spillers plc corporate strategy headquarters and acted as liaison manager with the consultancy company.

24 Lester, T (1979) 'Slow grind at Spillers', *Management Today*, Jan, pp59–114.

25 Writing in the 1950s, Herbert Simon was amongst the first to argue that the unreliability and limitations of human decision making made Adam Smith's simple economic assumption that humans would usually take rational decisions somewhat dubious – see reference 28 below.

26 Mayo, E, *Human Problems in Industrial Civilisation*, along with other research on the *Bank Wiring Observation Room*, described in Homans, G (1951) *The Human Group*, Routledge and Kegan Paul, London, ChIII.

27 Cyert, R M and March, J (1963) *A Behavioral Theory of the Firm*, Prentice Hall, Upper Saddle River, NJ.

28 March, J G and Simon, H (1958) *Organisations*, Wiley, New York.

29 Pettigrew, A (1985) *The Awakening Giant: Continuity and Change at ICI*, Blackwell, Oxford.

30 Mintzberg, H (1990) Op. cit.

31 Johnson, G (1986) 'Managing strategic change – the role of strategic formulae', published in: McGee, J and Thomas, H (ed.) (1986) *Strategic Management Research*, Wiley, Chichester, Section 1.4.

32 Argyris, C (1991) 'Teaching smart people how to learn', *Harvard Business Review*, May–June, p99 summarises his many earlier papers.

33 Senge, P M (1990) 'The leader's new work: building learning organisations', *Sloan Management Review*, Fall, pp7–22.

34 Lindblom, C E (1959) 'The Science of Muddling Through', *Public Administrative Review*, 19, pp79–88.

35 Whittington, R (1993) Op. cit. He repeats Weick's true story of the Hungarian troops who were lost in the Alps during the First World War but found a map which they used to reach safety. They then discovered that they were using a map of the Pyrenees. Whittington makes the point that taking *some* action, any action, will constitute strategy in these circumstances, even if the particular choice of strategy is wrong. The issue is not whether the *right* strategic choice has been made and then implemented, but rather whether any choice has been made that will give direction to the people concerned.

36 These comments are taken from a variety of sources: the following is probably the best starting point: Ansoff, I. (1991) Critique of Henry Mintzberg's 'The Design School', *Strategic Management Journal*, 12, pp449–461.

37 Lester, T (1979) Op. cit.

38 Ansoff, I (1965) *Corporate Strategy*, Penguin, Harmondsworth.

39 Chandler, A (1962) *Strategy and Structure*, MIT Press, Cambridge, MA.

40 Sloan, A P (1963) *My Years with General Motors*, Sedgewick & Jackson, London.

41 Wheelen, T and Hunger, D (1992) *Strategic Management and Business Policy*, Addison-Wesley, Reading, MA.

42 Porter, M E (1980) Op. cit. and (1985) Op. cit.

43 Rumelt, R, Schendel, D and Teece, D (1991) 'Strategic management and economics', *Strategic Management Journal*, 12, pp5–29. This contains an extensive and valuable review of this area.

44 Ansoff, I (1968) 'Toward a strategy theory of the firm', in Ansoff, I (ed) (1969) *Business Strategy*, Penguin, Harmondsworth, p39.

45 Porter, M E (1980) Op. cit.

46 Ohmae, K (1983) *The Mind of the Strategist*, Penguin, Harmondsworth.

47 Wilks, S (1990) *The Embodiment of Industrial Culture in Bureaucracy and Management*, quoted in Whittington, R (1993) Op. cit., p160.

48 But problems remain: see Luce, E. (2002) 'Investment in India "riddled with obstacles"' *Financial Times*, 19 March, p14.

49 *See*, for example, the leading article in the *Financial Times Survey on Singapore*, 24 Feb 1995.

50 Hamel, G and Prahalad, C K (1990) 'The core competence of the corporation', *Harvard Business School Review*, May–June. Their 1994 book *Competing for the Future* (Harvard Business School, Baston, M. A) picks up many of the same themes.

51 Kay, J (1993): see 'Key Reading' in Ch1.

52 Hannan, M T and Freeman, J (1988) *Organisational Ecology*, Harvard University Press, Cambridge, MA.

53 Hamel, G and Prahalad, C K (1990) Op. cit.

54 Kay, J (1993) *Foundations of Corporate Success*, Oxford University Press, Oxford.

55 Mintzberg, H (1987) Op. cit.

56 Mintzberg, H (1994) 'The fall and rise of strategic planning', *Harvard Business Review*, Jan–Feb, pp107–14.

57 Drucker, P (1967) Op. cit., Ch9.

58 Slack, N, Chambers, S, Harland, C, Harrison, A and Johnston, R (1995) *Operations Management*, Pitman Publishing, London, p812.

59 Williams, K, Haslam, C Johal, S and Williams, J (1994) Op. cit., Ch7.

60 Hamel, G and Prahalad, C K (1994) *Competing for the Future*, Harvard Business School Press, Boston, MA.

61 Wernerfelt, B (1984) 'A resource-based view of the firm,' *Strategic Management Journal*, 5(2), pp171–80.

62 Peteraf, M A (1993) 'The cornerstones of competitive advantage', *Strategic Management Journal*, 14, pp179–81.

63 Dierickx, I and Cool, K (1989) 'Asset stock accumulation and sustainability of competitive advantage', *Management Science*, 35, pp1540–51.

64 Kay, J (1994) *Foundations of Corporate Success*, Oxford University Press, Oxford.

65 Nonaka, I (1991) 'The knowledge-creating company', *Harvard Business Review*, Nov–Dec.

66 For a useful and accessible review, *see* Dixit, A K and Nalebuff, B J (1991) *Thinking Strategically*, W W Norton, New York. In addition to the references in Chapter 15, it is important to note that writers like Professor Michael Porter also employed game theory in their work without specifically discussing its theoretical background. *See* Chapter 3 for references to Porter.

67 Marris, R (1964) *The Economic Theory of Managerial Capitalism*, Macmillan, London, quoted in Whittington, R (1993) *What is Strategy – and Does it Matter?*, Routledge, London.

68 Granovetter, M (1985) 'Economic action and social culture', *American Journal of Sociology*, 91(3), pp481–510, quoted in Whittington, R (1993) Ibid.

69 Whittington, R (1993) Ibid, p28.

70 Boyacigiller, N and Adler, N (1991) 'The parochial dinosaur: organisation science in a global context', *Journal of Management Studies*, 28(4), pp262–90.

71 Hall, R C and Hitch, C J (1939) 'Price theory and business behaviour', *Oxford Economic Papers*, 2, pp12–45, quoted in Whittington, R (1993) Op. cit.

72 Henderson, B (1989) 'The origin of strategy', *Harvard Business Review*, Nov–Dec, pp139–43.

73 Williamson, O (1991) 'Strategising, economising and economic organisation', *Strategic Management Journal*, 12, pp75–94.

74 Hannan, M T and Freeman, J (1988) Op. cit.

75 Whittington, R (1993) Op. cit., p22.

76 Pascale, R (1990) *Managing on the Edge*, Viking Penguin, London, p114.

77 Gleick, J (1988) *Chaos*, Penguin, London.

78 Miller, D and Friesen, P (1982) 'Structural change and performance: quantum versus piecemeal– incremental approaches', *Academy of Management Journal*, 25, pp867–92.

79 Strebel, P (1992) *Breakpoints*, Harvard Business School Press, Boston, MA. A summary of this argument appears in De Wit, B and Meyer, R (1994) Op. cit., pp390–2.

80 Stacey, R (1993) *Strategic Management and Organisational Dynamics*, Pitman Publishing, London.

81 Miller, D and Friesen, P (1984) *Organisations: A Quantum View*, Prentice Hall, Englewood Cliffs, NJ.

82 Cyert, R and March, J (1963) Op. cit.

83 March, J and Simon, H (1958) Op. cit.

84 Nelson, R and Winter, S (1982) *An Evolutionary Theory of Economic Change*, Harvard University Press, Cambridge, MA, p34.

85 Nelson, R and Winter, S (1982) Ibid.

86 Mintzberg, H (1987) 'Crafting Strategy', *Harvard Business Review*, July–Aug, pp65–75.

87 Quinn, J B (1980) *Strategies for Change: Logical Incrementalism*, Irwin, Burr Ridge, MN.

88 Senge, P M (1990) Op. cit.

89 Mintzberg, H (1994) Op. cit.

90 Major writers in this area include: Kay, J (1994) *Foundations of Corporate Success*, Oxford University Press, Oxford, Chapter 5. Professor Kay also reviews the earlier work of Professor David Teece – see references at the end of chapter 5. For a more recent view, Markides C A (2000) *All the Right Moves*, Harvard Business School Press, Boston, MA.

91 Nonaka, I and Takeuchi, H (1995) *The Knowledge-Creating Company*, Oxford University Press, Oxford. See also Davenport, T H and Prusack, L (1998) *Working Knowledge*, Harvard Business School Press, Harvard, MA.

92 de Jonquieres, G (1993) 'Dalgety buys petfood arm of BP for £42 million', *Financial Times*, 30 Nov, p22.

93 Oram, R (1995) 'Dalgety in £442 million pet food purchase', *Financial Times*, 4 Feb, p20, and Oram, R (1995) 'Dalgety picks an interesting time to sell Golden Wonder', *Financial Times*, 20 Feb 1995, p19.

94 Penrose, E (1959) *The Theory of the Growth of the Firm*, Basil Blackwell, Oxford. Note that a third edition of the text was published in 1993 with a new preface by Professor Penrose: it has a historical perspective that is relevant to strategy development.

95 Chandler, A (1962) *Strategy and Structure*, MIT Press, Cambridge, MA. Chandler later developed this perspective further in his 1990 text: *Scale and Scope: Dynamics of Industrial Capitalism*, Harvard University Press, Cambridge, MA.

96 Developed by the author from the concepts outlined in: Teece, D J, Pisano, G and Shuen, A (1997) 'Dynamic capabilities and strategic management', *Strategic Management Journal*, 18(7), pp509–33.

97 The arguments here are not dissimilar to those used by the human-resource-based strategists outlined in Section 2.5.3. See in particular the views of Nelson and Winter.

98 References for IBM Case: Heller, R (1994) *The Fate of IBM*, Warner Books, London (easy to read and accurate); Carroll, P (1993) *The Unmaking of IBM*, Crown, London (rather one-sided); *Financial Times*, 7 Dec 1990, p14; 5 June 1991, article by Alan Cane; 8 Nov 1991, article by Alan Cane and Louise Kehoe; 5 May 1993, p17; 29 July 1993, p17; 14 Mar 1994, p17; 26 Mar 1994, p8; 28 Mar 1994, p15; 31 May 94, p21; 4 Oct 1994, p16; 10 Oct 1994, p23; 25 Oct 1994, p18; 12 Jan 1995, p22; 5 June 1995, p15; 6 June 1995, p21; 13 June 1995, p 21; 26 June 1995, p15; 29 Sept 1995, p21; 14 Dec 1996, p9; 18 Feb 1997, p4; 22 Nov 1997, p17; 5 Mar 1998, p17; *The Economist*, 16 Jan 1993, p23; 14 Dec 1996, pp102–3; *Business Age*, Apr 1994, p76.

99 *The Economist*, 20 Mar 1993.

100 Mintzberg, H (1990) 'The Design School: Reconsidering the basic premises of strategic management', *Strategic Management Journal*, as adapted by De Wit, R and Meyer, B (1994) Op. cit., p72.

Analysis of the environment

Both the prescriptive and the emergent approaches to corporate strategy consider an organisation's ability to understand its environment – its customers, its suppliers, its competitors, the organisations it co-operates with and the social and economic influences in its operations – to be an important element of the strategy process.

This part of the book begins by examining the basic analytical tools and frameworks used in a study of an organisation's environment and then goes on to tackle particular aspects of this task in more detail, namely the basic market and the organisation's competitors and its customers, co-operators and marketing resources.

Analysis of the environment

The *prescriptive* strategic process

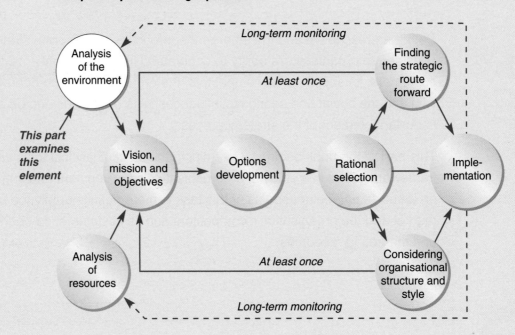

The *emergent* strategic process

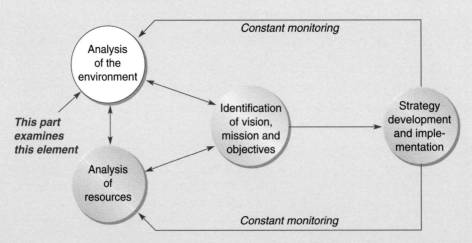

Chapter 3
Analysing the environment – basics

- What is the environment and why is it important?
- What are the main background areas to be analysed?
- What is the strategic significance of market growth?
- How are the more immediate influences on the organisation analysed?
- How do we analyse competitors?
- What is the role of co-operation in environmental analysis?
- How important is the customer?

Chapter 4
Analysing markets and competitors

- Why is sustainable competitive advantage important in strategy?
- How are competitors analysed and competition in the market place analysed?
- How do competitors compete with each other and what is the nature of the competition?
- What is the role of the product portfolio analysis?
- How important are distributors?
- What influence can the government have on the market and corporate strategy?

Chapter 5
Analysing customers

- Why is customer-driven strategy so important?
- How are customers analysed?
- What contribution do reputation and branding make to strategy?
- What is the role of customer communication in strategy development? What is the strategic role of price and value for money?

Chapter 3

Analysing the environment – basics

Learning outcomes

When you have worked through this chapter, you will be able to:

- explain why it is important to study the environment of the organisation;
- outline the main environmental influences on the organisation and relate the degree of change to prescriptive and emergent strategic approaches;
- undertake a PESTEL analysis of the general influences on the organisation;
- understand the implications of market growth and market cyclicality for corporate strategy;
- understand the importance of key factors for success in the environment;
- carry out a Five Forces analysis of the specific influences on the organisation;
- develop a Four Links analysis of the organisation's co-operators;
- undertake a competitor profile and identify the competitor's advantages;
- explore the relationship between the organisation and its customers.

Introduction

In recent years, the term 'the environment' has taken on a rather specialised meaning: it involves 'green' issues and the poisoning of our planet by human activity. These concerns are certainly part of our considerations in this book, but we use the term 'the environment' in a much broader sense to describe everything and everyone outside the organisation. This includes customers, competitors, suppliers, distributors, government and social institutions.

Before examining aspects of the environment in depth in Chapters 4 and 5, it is useful to begin by exploring the seven basic factors in the environment that influence corporate strategy (*see* Figure 3.1). As elements of the environment change, the organisation needs to adjust its corporate strategy accordingly. Prescriptive strategies will want to anticipate how the environment will change in the future in order to meet future needs ahead of competing organisations. Emergent strategies will be content with an understanding of the environment.

| Figure 3.1 | **The seven basic factors influencing the organisation** |

Note: Within an industry, the balance of forces and the interrelationship between the forces can be complex. It is not fully shown above.

CASE STUDY 3.1

Pan-European steel companies merge to cope with the new competitive environment

Until recently, national companies dominated the European steel industry. But the strategic environment has become increasingly competitive, resulting in a series of mergers across the EU. This case explores the pressures to merge.

Government ownership in the 1980s – little competition and loss-making companies

For many years in the latter part of the twentieth century, steel companies were considered to be national assets by national governments: they made the steel that went into a country's defence armaments. In fact, most steel companies were either owned or controlled by their respective national governments across Europe. Then the strategic environment changed in three ways:

1 The threat of war lessened as the old Soviet Union collapsed, so national ownership was no longer so important.

2 It was, at last, recognised that national ownership meant that there was no competitive pressure on steel companies to make a profit – governments and their tax payers simply rescued any steel company making a loss.

3 The advent of the single European market was also a factor: each EU country had signed the Treaty of

Rome and therefore agreed free and fair cross-border competition. This meant no state subsidies. There was considerable pressure to make this happen in the steel industry from the European Commission and some European member states.

Between 1988 and 1998, most European steel companies were sold to the private sector. Big job cuts followed as the companies then began to compete without government subsidy and needed to cut their labour costs. This reduced employment in the European steel industry from 900 000 in the early 1970s to around 300 000 in 1998. At least productivity – measured by tonnes of steel produced per worker – went up as a result. But the newly privatised companies still rarely made any profits.

Small national companies – still subsidised and inefficient

Up to the early 1990s, some governments were still giving significant subsidies to prop up their ailing national steel companies. Not only did this keep inefficient companies alive, but it also made it more difficult for the more efficient private companies to make profits. However, governments across the EU finally agreed in 1994 that such state support would largely end.

Although the major European steel companies were officially encouraged to expand further across European borders, some restrictions were kept in place by governments to protect their national companies. Nevertheless, some of the major steel companies moved out of their national markets through merger, acquisition and the purchase of minority shareholdings. Hoogevens in the Netherlands linked up with several German companies. Arbed in Luxembourg exchanged shares with the major Spanish steel producer, CSI. Usinor, the leading French company, purchased companies in Germany, Spain, Italy and the UK. Some of these were steel manufacturing companies and some were steel distributors – aimed at ensuring that Usinor products were widely available in individual national markets. But none of these moves can explain why substantial losses were still being made by virtually all steel companies in some years. The strategic problems of the steel industry environment remained.

Steel problems: excess production capacity, low-priced imports, aggressive customers and a downturn in the European economy

For many years, there has been excess steel production capacity in Europe – around 20 million tonnes out of a total demand of around 160 to 170 million tonnes. Steel production requires substantial capital investment. Plant typically needs to run at high capacity if such investment is to be profitable. Hence, spare production capacity is always a problem. In years like 1995 and 1999, when there was strong demand to take up such capacity, raise prices and protect volumes, the major European steel companies were able to report significantly increased profits. But this attracted companies from Eastern Europe and Asia to export production to Europe, especially when demand was slack in their home countries. The EU was then forced to place restrictions on the amount of steel that could be imported from such areas but only after the European steel companies had started to make losses again.

There was an additional problem: some of the customers of the steel companies had high bargaining power: companies making cars, like Ford and Volkswagen, and domestic appliances, like Merloni and Electrolux, were heavy users of steel across Europe. They could afford to shop around among the steel companies for the best price and there was little differentiation between the steel companies. A basic bar of carbon steel is much the same from any supplier. The sustainable competitive advantage of the major steel producers was usually associated with the efficiency of their production plant and occasionally with the technology that they possessed to produce specialist steels. For the latter, the steel companies were able to charge higher prices and gain higher margins. However, most steel companies make standard products, where the cost of production was the main point of differentiation.

To add to the pressure, the European economy turned down around the year 2000, resulting in lower demand for steel products across the EU. Steel is produced in blast furnaces that rely on economies of scale and production cannot be easily reduced as demand declines. Taking all these factors, it was not surprising that the steel companies were all showing major losses into the new millennium.

Steel company strategic response: mergers but they remain to be proven

In a further attempt to cut costs, the leading European steel companies have engaged in series of mergers over the last five years – Table 3.1 lists the main activities. Substantial cost reductions were being sought by this means. For example, the merger in early 2002 between France's Usinor, Aceralia of Spain and Arbed of Luxembourg was expected to produce annual savings and sales of US$260m in 2003. By 2006, this was expected to rise to US$610m. However, this would only happen if the three companies shed workers and undertook a major reorganisation of plant capacity. At the time of the announcement of the merger, details of these changes were 'deliberately glossed over'. Entirely understandably, this only made the trade unions increasingly nervous and made the cost savings more unlikely. Equally, investors in the three companies had heard previous claims about cost savings, but the companies were still making major losses.

Table 3.1 Merger strategy at the main European steel companies since 1996

Largest European companies in 1996	Country	Output in 1996 (million tonnes)	Merger activity
British Steel	UK	16	Merged with Hoogevens in 2000
Usinor Sacilor	France	15	Merged with Cockerill Sambre in 1998, then Arbed and CSI in 2002
Riva	Italy	13	Still independent but for how long?
Arbed	Luxembourg	11	See above
Thyssen	Germany	9	Merged with Krupp – see below
Cockerill Sambre	Belgium	6	Acquired by Usinor in 1998
Hoogevens	Netherlands	6	See above
Krupp Hoesch	Germany	5	See above
Huta Katowice	Poland	4	Outside EU until Poland joins, then what?
CSI	Spain	4	See above

Sources: See reference 1.

Case questions

1 *What were the main changes in the strategic environment of the main steel companies? What was their impact on company strategy?*

2 *What were the sustainable competitive advantages of the main steel companies? What implications does this have for the long-term profitability of companies in the industry?*

3 *What does this therefore mean for individual steel company strategy? Is merger strategy the answer?*

3.1 Exploring the environment

3.1.1 Why studying the environment is important

Strategists are agreed that an understanding of the environment is an essential element of the development of corporate strategy. It is important to study the environment surrounding the organisation for three main reasons. First, most organisations compete against others, so a study of the environment will provide information on the nature of competition as a step to developing *sustainable competitive advantage*.[2] Second, most organisations will perceive *opportunities* that might be explored and *threats* that need to be contained.[3] Such opportunities and threats may come not just from competitors but also from government decisions, changes in technology and social developments and many other factors. Third, there are opportunities for networks and other linkages, which lead to sustainable co-operation. Such linkages with others may strengthen an organisation in its environment by providing mutual support.

However, there are three difficulties in determining the connection between the organisation's corporate strategy and its environment.

1 *The prescriptive versus emergent debate.* The first problem arises from the fundamental disagreement about the corporate strategy processes that was explored in Part 1 of this book. Some prescriptive strategists take the view that, in spite of the various uncertainties, the environment can usefully be predicted for many markets. Some (but not all) emergent strategists believe that the environment is so turbulent and chaotic that prediction is likely to be inaccurate and serve no useful purpose. Each of these interpretations implies a quite different status for the same basic topic. This difficulty is explored further in Section 3.2.

2 *The uncertainty.* Whatever view is taken about prediction, all corporate strategists regard the environment as uncertain. New strategies have to be undertaken against a backdrop that cannot be guaranteed and this difficulty must be addressed as corporate strategies are developed. For example, Case 3.1 showed that there was considerable doubt about the cost savings to be achieved from the 2002 three-way steel company merger.

3 *The range of influences.* It is conceivable, at least in theory, that every element of an organisation's environment may influence corporate strategy. One solution to the problem posed by such a wide range of factors might be to produce a list of every element. This would be a strategic mistake, however, because organisations and individuals would find it difficult to develop and manage every item. In corporate strategy, the production of comprehensive lists that include every major eventuality and have no priorities has no value. A better solution is to identify the *key factors for success* in the industry and then to direct the environmental analysis towards these factors. This is considered briefly in this chapter and in more depth in Chapter 6.

3.1.2 The main elements of environmental analysis

To analyse an organisation's environment, while at the same time addressing the three difficulties outlined in Section 3.1.1, certain basic analytical procedures can be undertaken (*see* Table 3.2).

Note that the first two stages in Table 3.2 relate, partly at least, to *all* organisations; the final six stages are mainly concerned with a *specific industry*.

3.1.3 The distinction between proactive and reactive outcomes

When analysing the environment, it is useful to draw a distinction between two types of results from the analysis:

1 *Proactive outcomes.* The environmental analysis will identify positive opportunities or negative threats. The organisation will then develop proactive strategies to exploit or cope with the situation. For example, steel companies might develop cross-border co-operation as a result of new pan-European market opportunities.

2 *Reactive outcomes.* The environmental analysis will highlight important strategic changes over which the organisation has no control but to which, if they happen, it

Table 3.2 Eight basic stages in environmental analysis

Stage	Techniques	Outcome of stage
1 Consideration of the nature of the environment, both for *many* organisations and for the *specific sector* associated with the organisation (*See* Section 3.2)	General considerations: • Change: fast or slow? • Repetitive or surprising future? • Forecastable or unpredictable? • Complex or simple influences on the organisation?	General strategic conclusions: • Is the environment too turbulent to undertake useful predictions? • What are the opportunities and threats for the organisation?
2 Factors affecting *many* organisations (*See* Section 3.3)	PESTEL analysis and scenarios	• Identify key influences • Predict, if possible • Understand interconnections between events
3 Analysis of growth (*See* Section 3.4)	Industry life cycle	• Identify growth stage • Consider implications for strategy • Identify maturity, overproduction and cyclicality issues
4 Factors specific to the industry: what delivers success? (*See* Section 3.5)	Key factors for success analysis	• Identify factors relevant to strategy • Focus strategic analysis and development
5 Factors specific to the competitive balance of power in the industry (*See* Section 3.6)	Five Forces analysis	• Static and descriptive analysis of competitive forces
6 Factors specific to co-operation in the industry (*See* Section 3.7)	Four Links analysis	• Analysis of current and future organisations with whom co-operation is possible • Network analysis
7 Factors specific to immediate competitors (*See* Section 3.8)	Competitor analysis and product portfolio analysis	• Competitor profile • Analysis of relative market strengths
8 Customer analysis (*See* Section 3.9)	Market and segmentation studies	• Strategy targeted at existing and potential customers

will need to be able to react. For example, new EU legislation on mergers and acquisitions might influence strategic activity in the steel industry.

In both cases, the environment will need to be analysed but the strategic implications are very different.

> ◗ **Key strategic principles**
>
> ● Environmental analysis is important because it helps in developing sustainable competitive advantage, identifies opportunities and threats and may provide opportunities for productive co-operation with other organisations.
>
> ● There are three difficulties in studying the environment: the use to which the analysis will be put; uncertainty in the topic; coping with the wide range of environmental influences.
>
> ● Environmental analysis can be used to provide a *proactive* strategy outcome or a *reactive* strategic situation that will need to be monitored.

3.2 Consideration of the degree of turbulence in the environment[4]

Before exploring specific aspects of environmental analysis, it is important to consider the basic conditions surrounding the organisation. Special attention needs to be directed to the nature and strength of the forces driving strategic change – the *dynamics* of the environment. One reason for this consideration is that, if the forces are exceptionally turbulent, they may make it difficult to use some of the analytical techniques – like Porter's 'Five Forces', discussed later in this chapter. Another reason is that the nature of the environment may influence the way that the organisation is structured to cope with such changes.

The environmental forces surrounding the organisation can be assessed according to two main measures:

1 *Changeability* – the degree to which the environment is likely to change. For example, there is low changeability in the liquid milk market and high changeability in the various Internet markets.

2 *Predictability* – the degree with which such changes can be predicted. For example, changes can be predicted with some certainty in the mobile telephone market but remain largely unknown in biogenetics.

These measures can each be subdivided further. Changeability comprises:

● *Complexity* – the degree to which the organisation's environment is affected by factors such as internationalisation and technological, social and political complications.

● *Novelty* – the degree to which the environment presents the organisation with new situations.

Predictability can be further subdivided into:

● *Rate of change* of the environment (from slow to fast).

● *Visibility of the future* in terms of the availability and usefulness of the information used to predict the future.

Using these factors as a basis, it is then possible to build a spectrum that categorises the environment and provides a rating for its *degree of turbulence* (*see* Table 3.3).

When turbulence is low, it may be possible to predict the future with confidence. For example, Usinor and its merger partners might be able to use data on its major customers along with national economic data to predict future demand for its steel products.

Table 3.3 Assessing the dynamics of the environment

	Environmental turbulence	Repetitive	Expanding	Changing	Discontinuous	Surprising
Changeability	Complexity	National	National	Regional Technological	Regional Socio-political	Global Economic
	Familiarity of events	Familiar	Extrapolable		Discontinuous Familiar	Discontinuous Novel
Predictability	Rapidity of change	Slower than response		Comparable to response		Faster than response
	Visibility of future	Recurring	Forecastable	Predictable	Partially predictable	Unpredictable surprises

Turbulence level	Low 1	2	3	4	5 High	

Source: *Implanting Strategic Management* by Ansoff, I and McDonnell, E, © 1990. Reprinted by permission of Prentice Hall, Inc., Upper Saddle River, NJ.

When turbulence is higher, such predictions may have little meaning. The changeability elements influencing the organisation may contain *many* and *complex* items and the *novelty* being introduced into the market place may be high. For example, new services, new suppliers, new ideas, new software and new payment systems were all being launched for the Internet at the same time. Turbulence was high. Predicting the specific outcome of such developments was virtually impossible.

If the level of turbulence is high – called *hypercompetition*[5] by some strategists – and as a result the environment is difficult to study, the analysis recommended in some of the sections that follow may need to be treated with some caution. However, for most fast-growing situations, including the Internet, there is merit in at least attempting to understand the main areas of the environment influencing the organisation. It may not be possible to undertake formal predictions but it will certainly be possible to identify the most important elements.

▶ Key strategic principles

- It is important to begin an analysis of the environment with a general consideration of the degree of turbulence in that environment. If it is high, then this will make prediction difficult and impact on prescriptive approaches to strategy development.

- There are two measures of turbulence: changeability, i.e. the degree to which the environment is likely to change; and predictability, i.e. the degree to which such change can be predicted.

- Each of the two measures can then be further subdivided: changeability can be split into complexity and novelty; predictability can be divided into rate of change and visibility of the future. All these elements can then be used to explore turbulence.

3.3 Analysing the general environment

In any consideration of the factors surrounding the organisation, two techniques can be used to explore the general environment (as opposed to the specific industry or service): these are the PESTEL analysis and scenarios.

3.3.1 PESTEL[6] analysis

It is already clear that there are no simple rules governing an analysis of the organisation. Each analysis needs to be guided by what is relevant for that particular organisation. However, it may be useful to begin the process with a *checklist* – often called a PESTEL analysis – of the Political, Economic, Socio-cultural, Technological, Environment and Legal aspects of the environment. Exhibit 3.1 presents some of the main items that might be considered when undertaking a PESTEL analysis.

Exhibit 3.1   **Checklist for a PESTEL analysis**

Political future

- Political parties and alignments at local, national and European or regional trading-block level
- Legislation, e.g. on taxation and employment law
- Relations between government and the organisation (possibly influencing the preceding items in a major way and forming a part of future corporate strategy)
- Government ownership of industry and attitude to monopolies and competition

Socio-cultural future

- Shifts in values and culture
- Change in lifestyle
- Attitudes to work and leisure
- 'Green' environmental issues
- Education and health
- Demographic changes
- Distribution of income

Economic future

- Total GDP and GDP per head
- Inflation
- Consumer expenditure and disposable income
- Interest rates
- Currency fluctuations and exchange rates
- Investment, by the state, private enterprise and foreign companies
- Cyclicality
- Unemployment
- Energy costs, transport costs, communications costs, raw materials costs

Technological future

- Government and EU investment policy
- Identified new research initiatives
- New patents and products
- Speed of change and adoption of new technology
- Level of expenditure on R&D by organisation's rivals
- Developments in nominally unrelated industries that might be applicable

Environmental future

- 'Green' issues that affect the environment
- Level and type of energy consumed – renewable energy?
- Rubbish, waste and its disposal

Legal future

- Competition law and government policy
- Employment and safety law
- Product safety issues

Like all checklists, a PESTEL analysis is really only as good as the individual or group preparing it. Listing every conceivable item has little value and betrays a lack of serious consideration and logic in the corporate strategy process. Better to have three or four well-thought-out items that are explored and justified with evidence than a lengthy 'laundry list' of items. This is why this book does not recommend simple + and − signs and accompanying short bullet points, although these might provide a useful summary.

To the prescriptive strategists, although the items in a PESTEL analysis rely on *past* events and experience, the analysis can be used as a *forecast of the future*. The past is history and corporate strategy is concerned with future action, but the best evidence about the future *may* derive from what happened in the past. Prescriptive strategists would suggest that it is worth attempting the task because major new investments make this hidden assumption anyway. For example, when Usinor merged with its Spanish and Luxembourg rivals, it was making an assumption that the European market would remain attractive; it might as well *formalise* this through a structured PESTEL analysis, even if the outcome is difficult to predict.

The emergent corporate strategists may well comment that the future is so uncertain that prediction is useless. If this view is held, a PESTEL analysis will fulfil a different role in *interpreting* past events and their interrelationships. In practice, some emergent strategists may give words of caution but still be tempted to predict the future. For example, one prominent emergent strategist, Herbert Simon, wrote a rather rash article in 1960 predicting that, 'We will have the technical ability, by 1985, to run corporations by machine.'[7] The emergent strategists are correct in suggesting that prediction in some fast-moving markets may have little value. Overall, when used wisely, the PESTEL analysis has a role in corporate strategy.

3.3.2 Scenario-based analysis

In the context of a scenario-based analysis, a scenario is a model of a possible future environment for the organisation, whose strategic implications can then be investigated. For example, a scenario might be developed to explore the question: 'What would happen if green environmental concerns forced private cars off the road by the year 2020 and demand for steel in cars collapsed as a result? What impact would this have on European steel companies?'

Scenarios are concerned with peering into the future, not predicting the future. Prediction takes the *current* situation and extrapolates it forward. Scenarios take *different* situations with *alternative* starting points. The aim is not to predict but to explore a set of possibilities; a combination of events is usually gathered together into a scenario and then this combination is explored for its strategic significance. Exhibit 3.2 provides some guidance on the development of scenarios.

Exhibit 3.2   **Some guidance on building scenarios**

- Start from an *unusual viewpoint*. Examples might include the stance of a major competitor, a radical change of government or the outbreak of war.

- Develop a *qualitative description* of a group of possible events or a *narrative* that shows how events will unfold. It is unlikely that this will involve a quantitative projection.

- Explore the *outcomes* of this description or narrative of events by building two or three scenarios of what might happen. It is usually difficult to handle more than three scenarios. Two scenarios often lend themselves to a 'most optimistic outcome' and a 'worst possible outcome'.

▶

Exhibit 3.2 continued

- Include the inevitable *uncertainty* in each scenario and explore the *consequences* of this uncertainty for the organisation concerned – for example, 'What would happen if the most optimistic outcome was achieved?' The PESTEL factors may provide some clues here.

- Test the usefulness of the scenario by the extent to which it leads to *new strategic thinking* rather than merely the continuance of existing strategy.

▶ Key strategic principles

- The PESTEL analysis – the study of Political, Economic, Socio-cultural, Technological, Environmental and Legal factors – provides a useful starting point to any analysis of the general environment surrounding an organisation. It is vital to select among the items from such a generalised list and explore the chosen areas in depth; long lists of items are usually of no use.

- Prescriptive and emergent strategists take different views on the merits of projecting forward the main elements of the PESTEL analysis. The prescriptive approach favours the development of projections because they are often implied in major strategic decisions in any event. Emergent strategists believe the turbulence of the environment makes projections of limited value.

- A scenario is a picture of a possible future environment for the organisation, whose strategic implications can then be investigated. It is less concerned with prediction and more involved with developing different perspectives on the future. The aim is to stimulate new strategic thought about the possible consequences of events, rather than make an accurate prediction of the future.

3.4 Analysing the rate of market growth

The well-known strategic writer, Professor Michael Porter from Harvard University Business School, has described the *industry life cycle* as 'the grandfather of concepts for predicting industry evolution'. The basic hypothesis is that an industry – or a market segment within an industry – goes through four basic phases of development, each of which has implications for corporate strategy. These phases can be loosely described as introduction, growth, maturity and decline and are shown in Figure 3.2.

3.4.1 Industry life cycle

The nature of corporate strategy will change as industries move along the life cycle. In the *introductory* phase, organisations attempt to develop interest in the product. As the industry moves towards *growth,* competitors are attracted by its potential and enter the market: from a strategic perspective, competition increases. As all the available customers are satisfied by the product, growth slows down and the market becomes *mature.* Although growth has slowed, new competitors may still be attracted into the

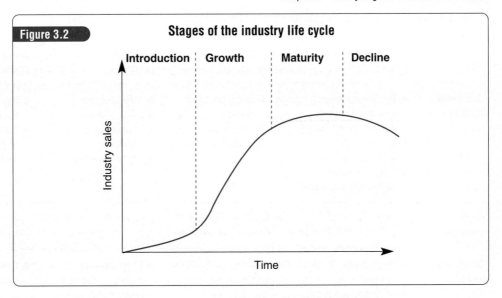

Figure 3.2 **Stages of the industry life cycle**

market: each company then has to compete harder for its market share, which becomes more fragmented – that is, the market share is broken down into smaller parts. Sales enter a period of *decline*.

To explore the strategic implications, it is useful to start by identifying what stage an industry has reached in terms of its development. For each stage in the cycle there are a number of commonly accepted strategies (*see* Table 3.4). In the case of customers, for example, the *introduction* phase will be used to present the product or service to new customers, whereas the *maturity* phase assumes that most customers are aware of the product and little new trial is required.

As in other areas of corporate strategy, there are differing views regarding the choice of appropriate strategies for each phase of the industry life cycle. Table 3.4 represents the *conventional* view of the appropriate strategy for a particular stage in the industry's evolution. In corporate strategy, however, there are often good arguments for doing the *unconventional,* so this list would be seen as a starting point for analysing the dynamics of an industry. The most innovative strategy might well come by doing something different and breaking the mould.

As an example of the conventional view of such an analysis, the industry life cycle suggests that in the *early stages* of an industry's development there may be more opportunities for new and radical R&D. When an industry is more *mature,* rather less investment is needed in R&D.[8] However, the unconventional view argues that it is the mature industry that requires new growth and therefore R&D or some other strategic initiative. In the Usinor case, the company needed to invest in more modern facilities to reduce costs further, showing that, even in the mature phase of a market, heavy investment is often necessary to remain competitive in the market. It is for this reason that the life cycle concept can best be seen as a starting point for growth analysis.

It is important to note in the development of strategy the two consequences of the industry life cycle that can have a significant impact on industries:

1 *Advantages of early entry.* There is substantial empirical evidence that the first company into a new market has the most substantial strategic advantage. For example, Aaker[9] quotes a study of 500 mature industrial businesses showing that pioneer firms

Table 3.4 The industry life cycle and its strategy implications – a conventional view

	Introduction phase	Growth phase	Maturity phase	Decline phase
Customer strategy	• Early customers may experiment with product and will accept some unreliability • Need to explain nature of innovation	• Growing group of customers • Quality and reliability important for growth	• Mass market • Little new trial of product or service • Brand switching	• Know the product well • Select on basis of price rather than innovation
R&D strategy	• High	• Seek extensions before competition	• Low	
Company strategy	• Seek to dominate market • R&D and production particularly important to ensure product quality	• React to competition with marketing expenditure and initiatives	• Expensive to increase market share if not already market leader • Seek cost reductions	• Cost control particularly important
Impact on profitability	• High price, but probably making a loss due to investment in new category	• Profits should emerge here but prices may well decline as competitors enter market	• Profits under pressure from need for continuing investment coupled with continued distributor and competitive pressure	• Price competition and low growth may lead to losses or need to cut costs drastically to maintain profitability
Competitor strategy	• Keen interest in new category • Attempt to replicate new product	• Market entry (if not before) • Attempt to innovate and invest in category	• Competition largely on advertising and quality • Lower product differentiation • Lower product change	• Competition based primarily on price • Some companies may seek to exit the industry

average a market share of 29 per cent, early followers 21 per cent and the late entrants 15 per cent. Although there are clearly risks in early market entry, there may also be long-term advantages that deserve careful consideration in strategic development.

2 *Industry market share fragmentation.* In the early years, markets that are growing fast attract new entrants. This is both natural and inevitable. The consequence as markets reach maturity is that each new company is fighting for market share and the market becomes more fragmented. Again, this has important implications for strategy because it suggests that mature markets need revised strategies – perhaps associated with a segment of the market (*see* Chapter 5).

For strategic purposes, it may be better to examine different *segments* of an industry, rather than the market *as a whole,* as different segments may be at different stages of the industry life cycle and may require different strategies (*see* the European ice cream industry example in Case study 3.2). An industrial example can be taken from the global steel industry where during the same period some specialist steels were still growing strongly whereas standard steel bars were definitely in the mature stage of the life cycle.

CASE STUDY 3.2

Different strategies in the ice cream market

During the 1990s, the European ice cream market underwent significant change: some segments were relatively mature while some were experiencing strong growth. This case study shows how the positions of the main segments can be plotted in terms of the industry evolution (see Figure 3.3) and how strategies vary from one segment to another.

The market can be divided into four distinct segments:

● *The superpremium segment*, typified by Häagen-Dazs, was still in the early stages of its growth at this time. New companies were still entering the segment, e.g. *Ben and Jerry's* from the USA had been acquired by Unilever but had yet to be launched in much of continental Europe. New products were being tried using new methods of carton presentation and new high prices.

● *The premium segment* had developed significantly in 1989 with the introduction of premium-priced *Mars* ice cream. There were few new companies entering the market. The basic product ranges had become established among the leading players; the strategic battle was for distribution and branding.

● *The regular and economy segments* were typified by Unilever's bulk packs, sold under the name

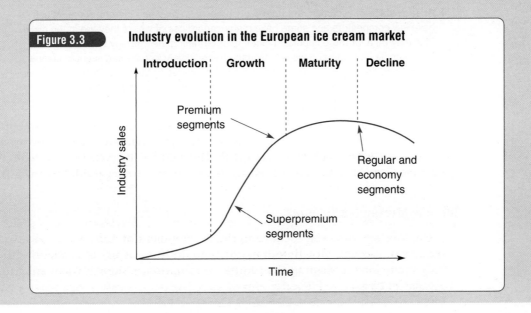

Figure 3.3 — **Industry evolution in the European ice cream market**

Carte d'Or across much of Europe. These had existed for many years but were still growing at around 5 per cent per annum (still regarded as a growth market according to some definitions). The segment also had a large number of other suppliers, not all of whom were national, let alone European. There was keen competition on price and with own-label products from grocery retailers. There was relatively little product innovation.

Case questions

1 What strategies are suggested for each segment of the market from the conventional view of the industry life cycle? (Refer to Table 3.4.)

2 Thinking of strategy as doing the unconventional, how might you modify the strategies identified in question 1?

3.4.2 Comment on the industry life cycle

The concept of the industry life cycle has both supporters and critics. Smallwood[10] and Baker[11] defend its usefulness and offer empirical support for the basic concept. Dhalla and Yuspeh[12] have led the criticisms, some of which certainly have a degree of validity (see Exhibit 3.3).

Exhibit 3.3 Criticisms of the industry life cycle

1 It is *difficult to determine the duration* of some life cycles and to identify the precise stage an industry has reached. For example, the Mars Bar was launched in the 1930s and is certainly not in decline – but is it in the growth or mature phase?

2 Some industries miss stages or *cannot be clearly identified* in their stages, particularly as a result of technological change. For example, has the bicycle reached the mature phase or has it reached a new lease of life as the petrol-driven car pollutes city atmospheres?

3 Companies themselves can instigate change in their products and can, as a result, *alter the shape of the curve.* For example, new life has been brought into the camera industry by the introduction of miniaturisation and, more recently, by the use of electronic storage in place of film.

4 At each stage of evolution, the *nature of competition may be different:* some industries have few competitors and some have many, regardless of where they are in the cycle. This may be a far more important factor in determining the strategy to be pursued. For example, in Chapter 5 we will examine the relatively fragmented vacuum cleaner market and the highly concentrated civil aircraft market: both are relatively mature with corporate strategy being determined not by evolution but by other factors.

There are certainly some difficulties with the industry life cycle approach, but the reason for such an analysis at the corporate strategy level is to identify the *dynamic factors that are shaping the industry's evolution.* The industry life cycle helps us to do this; it will then be possible to compare the organisation's own strategy with this analysis.

Key strategic principles

● The industry life cycle – charting the development of a market from introduction, through growth and maturity to decline – is useful to identify the dynamic factors shaping the industry's evolution, although there are criticisms of its use.

> ● **Key strategic principles continued**
>
> ● It also helps to specify the conventional view of the strategies that are appropriate to each stage of the cycle, even if these are then changed for logical reasons.
>
> ● Aspects of life cycle analysis that are worthy of special consideration include: the advantages of early entry, the fragmentation of market share as markets mature, the incidence of cyclicality and its effect on demand in mature markets.

CASE STUDY 3.3

Will the steel companies adopt global strategies?

Globalisation is an important strategy in some industries, but not yet in steel. This case explores the environmental and other reasons for current strategies in world steel. Is a globalisation strategy the answer to the low levels of profitability in the industry?

Over the past 20 years, the world's 40 largest steel companies have made cumulative losses before tax of US$10 billion, in spite of investing around US$75 billion in new capital equipment. This is hardly impressive, but some companies are now beginning to talk openly of global strategy as a solution to the underlying problems. They suggest that there might be only five major global steel companies by the year 2010.

The current structure of the world steel industry: fragmented, not global

Up to the present time, steel producing companies have had a strong base in one continent – Europe, Asia, North America, etc. – but do not operate in other continents. Globalisation would mean that such regional markets would be replaced by one world market, probably supplied by a few companies with global reach. For example, in the global plastics and aluminium markets, the top ten producers manufacture over 50 per cent of world output. In the world steel market, the top 20 producers only managed to supply 35 per cent of world sales in 2000.

Table 3.5 shows the top steel companies ranked by production, but none are global either in the sense of having sales across all parts of the world or in the sense of having plant to supply markets located strategically around the world. In global steel markets, product ranges, quality and service might be expected to be co-ordinated, with different plants supplying regional variations depending on demand. This is far from the reality at present, but it does not mean that there is no world market for steel.

Global state of the market for world steel: world market demand but at reduced prices and profitability

In a limited sense, there are already well-developed world markets. Steel companies need to maintain high-capacity utilisation in order to deliver consistent profits. If demand falls in one part of the world, producers increase sales elsewhere in order to hold output levels. In this way, steel companies are already selling worldwide. However, it is not global in the sense of one market as the primary driving force but rather a distressed sale after the home market has declined. The world market for steel is therefore inherently low-profit at present for four reasons:

1 Steel is heavy and cheap: for example, standard 'hot rolled' steel sells for only US$200 per tonne. This is similar, weight for weight, to the price of a pot of fruit jam.

2 With such low prices, it is often unprofitable to transport over long distances – globalisation becomes impossible.

3 Steel demand, prices and profitability are linked to national and regional demand – *see* the European steel case.

▶

Table 3.5 World's top steel companies – all sell primarily to their national or regional markets (megatonnes of crude steel)

Company	Country	Estimated 2001 output
Usinor/Arbed/Aceralia	Europe	46
NKK/Kawasaki	Japan	28
Nippon Steel	Japan	27
Posco	Korea	27
Ispat Steel	Loosely based UK	21
Corus	UK/Neth	19
Thyssen Krupp Stahl	Germany	16
Riva	Italy	15
Sail	India	13
US Steel	US	11
Nucor	US	10
Sumitomo Metal	Japan	10
Severstal (Cherepovets)	Russia	9
China Steel	China	9
Bethlehem Steel	US	9
Baoshan	China	9

Source: Author's estimates based on press articles listed at end of chapter.

Table 3.6 Consumption and production by geographic region – Eastern Europe has plenty to sell

World steel consumption 1997	% total	World steel production 1998	% total
Western Europe	20	Western Europe	22
Developing Asia	18	North America	14
North America	18	China	14
China	15	Japan	13
Japan	11	Developing Asia	12
Latin America	6	Former USSR	10
Former USSR	5	Latin America	7
Central Europe	3	Central Europe	4
Others	5	Others	4

Source: British Steel Annual Report 1997/98, pp4 and 6. Reproduced with permission.

world steel prices. This is precisely what happened in 1998 and again in 2001 as some regional economies turned down and national companies exported more steel. Moreover, the main suppliers with excess production capacity are the older and less efficient plants of Eastern Europe – *see* Table 3.6. All this evidence suggests that world steel markets have production overcapacity and depressed prices – not the ideal circumstance for operating globally.

Global customer demand in world steel markets: not yet

In addition to mass markets for some basic steel products, demand for steel can be segmented into many different types. For example:

● thin steel sheet for pressing into beverage cans;

● steel casings for computers and telecommunications equipment;

● specially toughened steel for the high temperatures in combustion engines.

Some of these products will be bought by global companies: Coca-Cola (US) canning, Alcatel

4 Mergers with US companies are expensive: during the 1970s and 1980s, US steel companies reduced employee numbers dramatically but entered into long-term commitments with former employees on pension and health benefits. Any merger would have to assume such high-cost liabilities.

At present, selling on world markets because of poor home demand has the effect of depressing

(France) telecommunications, Honda (Japan) car engines in the case of the products above. However, global customer demand for steel products has not yet emerged. Each of these companies usually buys its steel from companies that are located in the same countries as its production plants, rather than place, or at least negotiate, a global order. Global customer demand for steel is not yet a reality on a large scale, but this does not mean that the situation will remain unchanged for ever.

Global merger and acquisition activity: no clear profit strategy so far

Although it is not easy at present to make a clear case for globalisation, some companies have made modest acquisitions in world regions outside their home base – for example: Arbed/Usinor/Aceralia in Brazil and US Steel in the Czech Republic. In addition, some steel companies have entered into technical agreements to share data outside their home regions. But these represent limited areas of co-operation so far.

More generally, it is possible to identify six major strategies at present – they are shown below. However, it is not clear if any of them were associated with globalisation.

1 *Merge and/or acquire companies* in order to gain geographic expansion and, possibly, some economies of scale. For example, Case study 3.1 outlines the major European moves here.

2 *Cut costs* via reduction in the numbers of workers, the rationalisation of raw material and other suppliers and capital investment in new machinery. For example, Corus reduced its British workforce from 35 000 in 1999 to 22 000 in 2003. The company also reduced its costs by a further US$75 million as a result of negotiations and discussions with its suppliers. Annual capital spending was around US$330m in 2002 and expected to double by 2006.

3 *Investment in research and development* to improve existing products and manufacturing processes. For example, Usinor/Arbed has been co-operating with the German steel producer Krupp/Thyssen to develop a new 'thin strip' casting process which could eliminate part of the production process and thus save substantial costs.

4 *Focus on technically advanced and specialised products that have high value added and higher profitability.* Such new steel products are likely to have higher added value, more unique and beneficial properties and therefore more sustainable competitive advantage. For example, Usinor/Arbed has developed high-quality coated steel for use in car body panelling and lightweight beverage cans for the drinks industry.

5 *Develop close working relationships with major customers* who buy substantial quantities of steel, such as the car manufacturers, through better distribution and specially tailored products. Such a strategy serves to provide higher degrees of service for customers and lock them in to remaining with their existing steel suppliers. For example, Usinor/Arbed has been building new steel service distribution centres throughout Europe and the eastern US. Corus has also been laying more emphasis in this area.

6 *Introduce more employee training and continuous cost reduction programmes* with the aim of permanent cost reduction across the company. For example, Usinor has encouraged the active participation of work groups at each of its sites to find and implement new, more efficient work practices. It should be noted that such a strategy is not necessarily being introduced in all steel companies because it involves quite a change in company culture.

Case questions

1 *What are the benefits of globalisation? Are they likely to be achieved in the steel industry?*

2 *Would companies like Thyssen Krupp Stahl, Usinor and Corus be wise to pursue globalisation, even if they are not doing so at present?*

3 *If globalisation was more likely to be profitable in the future, would you advise companies to begin the process now or wait? If so, why? If not, what environmental conditions would persuade them to change their views?*

Sources: See reference 13.

3.5 Key factors for success in an industry

In a strategic analysis of the environment, there is an immense range of issues that can potentially be explored, creating a problem for most organisations, which have neither the time nor the resources to cope with such an open-ended task. The analysis can be narrowed down by identifying the *key factors for success* in the industry and then using these to *focus the analysis* on particularly important environmental matters.

The key factors for success (KFS) are those resources, skills and attributes of the organisations in the industry that are *essential* to deliver success in the market place. Success often means profitability, but may take on a broader meaning in some public service or non-profit-making organisations.

KFS are common to all the major organisations in the industry and do not differentiate one company from another. For example, in Case study 3.3, the factors mentioned – low labour costs, a range of specialised steel products, etc. – are common to many steel companies. Such factors will vary from one industry to another. For example, by contrast, in the perfume and cosmetics industry the factors will include branding, product distribution and product performance, but they are unlikely to include low labour costs.

When undertaking a strategic analysis of the environment, the identification of the KFS for an industry may provide a useful starting point. For example, the steel KFS item of 'low labour costs' would suggest an environmental analysis of the following areas:

● general wage levels in the country;

● government regulations and attitudes to worker redundancy, because high wage costs could be reduced by sacking employees;

● trade union strength to fight labour force redundancies.

In the steel industry, these elements of the environment would benefit from careful study, whereas, in the cosmetics and perfume industry, they may have some relevance but would be far less important than other areas.

It is therefore important to identify the KFS for a particular industry. Many elements relate not only to the environment but also to the *resources* of organisations in the industry. For example, 'labour costs' will relate to the numbers employed and the level of their wages in individual companies. To identify the KFS in an industry, it is therefore usual to examine *the type of resources* and *the way that they are employed* in the industry and then to use this information to analyse the environment outside the organisation. Hence, KFS require an exploration of the resources and skills of an industry before they can be applied to the environment. Part 3 of this book will explore resources, while the way in which KFS are developed is covered in greater detail in Chapter 6.

Key strategic principles

● Key factors for success (KFS) are the resources, skills and attributes of an organisation that are essential to deliver success in the market place. They are related to the industry and are unlikely to provide differentiation between organisations in the industry.

● KFS can be used to identify elements of the environment that are particularly worth exploring.

> **Key strategic principles continued**
>
> ● KFS are developed from an examination of the type of resources used and the way in which resources are employed in an industry. They need therefore to be developed from an analysis of the organisation's resources.

3.6 Analysing the competitive industry environment – the contribution of Porter

An industry analysis usually begins with a general examination of the forces influencing the organisation. The objective of such a study is to use this to develop the *competitive advantage* of the organisation to enable it to defeat its rival companies. Much of this analysis was structured and presented by Professor Michael Porter of Harvard University Business School.[14] His contribution to our understanding of the competitive environment of the firm has wide implications for many organisations in both the private and public sectors.

This type of analysis is often undertaken using the structure proposed by Porter; his basic model is illustrated in Figure 3.4. This is often called *Porter's Five Forces Model* because he identifies five basic forces that can act on the organisation:

1 the bargaining power of suppliers;

2 the bargaining power of buyers;

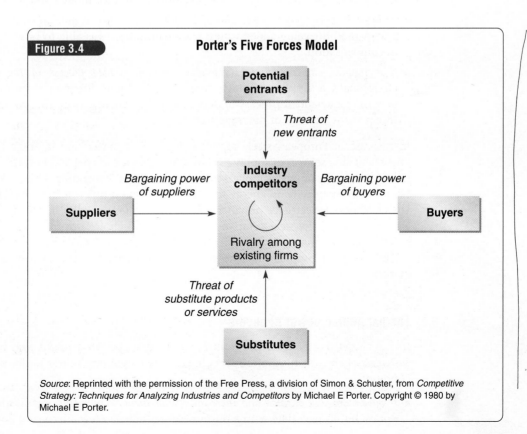

Figure 3.4 — **Porter's Five Forces Model**

Source: Reprinted with the permission of the Free Press, a division of Simon & Schuster, from *Competitive Strategy: Techniques for Analyzing Industries and Competitors* by Michael E Porter. Copyright © 1980 by Michael E Porter.

3 the threat of potential new entrants;

4 the threat of substitutes;

5 the extent of competitive rivalry.

The objective of such an analysis is to investigate how the organisation needs to form its strategy in order to develop opportunities in its environment and protect itself against competition and other threats. Porter himself cautiously described[15] his analysis as being concerned with the 'forces driving industry competition'. However, the general principles can be applied to public service and not-for-profit organisations where they compete for resources, such as government funding or charitable donations.

3.6.1 The bargaining power of suppliers

Virtually every organisation has suppliers of raw materials or services which are used to produce the final goods or services. Porter suggested that suppliers are more powerful under the following conditions:

- *If there are only a few suppliers.* This means that it is difficult to switch from one to another if a supplier starts to exert its power.

- *If there are no substitutes for the supplies they offer.* This is especially the case if the supplies are important for technical reasons – perhaps they form a crucial ingredient in a production process or the service they offer is vital to smooth production.

- *If suppliers' prices form a large part of the total costs of the organisation.* Any increase in price would hit value added unless the organisation was able to raise its own prices in compensation.

- *If a supplier can potentially undertake the value-added process of the organisation.* Occasionally a supplier will have power if it is able to integrate forward and undertake the value-added process undertaken by the organisation; this could pose a real threat to the survival of the organisation.

In the case of European steel, suppliers' bargaining powers are in some respects **low**. There are many sources of supply for raw materials such as coal and iron ore. However, in terms of energy supply, suppliers may have **higher** bargaining power. For example, Usinor will rely heavily on energy to smelt the steel and this will come partially from the French national electricity provider, Electricité de France (EdF). If EdF were to raise its electricity prices, the steel company would have no choice but to accept such changes because EdF is a monopoly supplier. By contrast, in the UK, Corus could bargain with several potential suppliers for the supply of electricity because there is a more open market.

3.6.2 The bargaining power of buyers

In his model, Porter used the term *buyers* to describe what might also be called the *customers* of the organisation. Buyers have more bargaining power under the following conditions:

- *If buyers are concentrated and there are few of them.* When the organisation has little option but to negotiate with a buyer because there are few alternative buyers around, the organisation is clearly in a weak position: national government contracts in defence, health and education are obvious examples where the government can, in theory at least, drive a hard bargain with organisations.

- *If the product from the organisation is undifferentiated.* If an organisation's product is much the same as that from other organisations, the buyer can easily switch from one to another without problems. The buyer is even more likely to make such a shift if the quality of the buyer's product is unaffected by such a change.

- *If backward integration is possible.* As with suppliers above, the buyer's bargaining power is increased if the buyer is able to backward-integrate and take over the role of the organisation.

- *If the selling price from the organisation is unimportant to the total costs of the buyer.*

In the case of European steel, small companies or private buyers are unlikely to have much bargaining power with companies of the size of Usinor or Corus; a letter from an individual to Usinor, threatening to switch from its products to those of Corus or Krupp unless its prices are lowered, is unlikely to have much impact – the threat is **low.** However, if a major steel distributor or steel user, such as an engineering company, were to make such a threat, then it would clearly have to be taken more seriously because of the potential impact on sales. In this latter case, the threat is **high.** Steel companies have reduced this threat by acquiring most of the leading European steel distributors.

3.6.3 The threat of potential new entrants

New entrants come into a market place when the profit margins are attractive and the barriers to entry are low. The allure of high profitability is clear and so the major strategic issue is that of barriers to entry into a market.

Porter argued that there were seven[16] major sources of barriers to entry:

1 *Economies of scale.* Unit costs of production may be reduced as the absolute volume per period is increased. Such cost reductions occur in many industries and present barriers because they mean that any new entrant has to come in on a large scale in order to achieve the low cost levels of those already present: such a scale is risky. We have already examined the computer and steel industries where such cost reductions are vital.

2 *Product differentiation.* Branding, customer knowledge, special levels of service and many other aspects may create barriers by forcing new entrants to spend extra funds or simply take longer to become established in the market. Real barriers to entry can be created in strategic terms by long-established companies in a market (*see* Chapter 6). Retailers such as IKEA with strong branding and specialist product lines and expertise are examples of companies with differentiated products.

3 *Capital requirements.* Entry into some markets may involve major investment in technology, plant, distribution, service outlets and other areas. The ability to raise such finance and the risks associated with such outlays of capital will deter some companies. For example, the high capital cost of investing in a new paper making machine will be covered in Chapter 19.

4 *Switching costs.* When a buyer is satisfied with the existing product or service, it is naturally difficult to switch that buyer to a new entrant. The cost of making the switch would naturally fall to the new entrant and will represent a barrier to entry.

Persuading buyers to switch their purchases of computer software from Microsoft Windows to Apple has an obvious cost and inconvenience to many companies that would need to be overcome. In addition to the costs of persuading customers to switch, organisations should expect that existing companies will retaliate with further actions designed to drive out new entrants. For example, Microsoft has not hesitated to upgrade its products and reduce its prices to retain customers that might otherwise switch.

5 *Access to distribution channels.* It is not enough to produce a quality product; it must be distributed to the customer through channels that may be controlled by companies already in the market. For many years, the leading petrol companies have owned their own retail petrol sites to ensure that they have access to retail customers.

6 *Cost disadvantages independent of scale.* Where an established company knows the market well, has the confidence of major buyers, has invested heavily in infrastructure to service the market and has specialist expertise, it becomes a daunting task for new entrants to gain a foothold in the market. Korean and Malaysian companies are attempting to enter the European car market and face these barriers created by well-entrenched companies such as Ford, Volkswagen and Renault.

7 *Government policy.* For many years, governments have enacted legislation to protect companies and industries: monopolies in telecommunications, health authorities, utilities such as gas and electricity are examples where entry has been difficult if not impossible. The European Commission has been working alongside European governments to remove some but not all such barriers over the last few years.

In the case of the European steel market, it is not easy for small companies to enter the market because there are major economies of scale. For these companies, entry barriers are **high**. However, technology is now beginning to develop that will allow smaller companies to make steel economically so entry barriers may be reduced.

3.6.4 The threat of substitutes

Occasionally, substitutes render a product in an industry redundant. For example, SmithKline Beecham lost sales from its product Tagamet for the treatment of ulcers, due to the introduction of more effective products – first the introduction of Zantac from Glaxo in the 1980s and then, in the 1990s, Losec from the Swedish company Astra. Tagamet is still on sale as an over-the-counter remedy but its major public health sales have largely ceased. More recently, Zantac sales have also suffered, although the difference in performance between that product and Losec has been the subject of dispute between the two companies.

More often, substitutes do not entirely replace existing products but introduce new technology or reduce the costs of producing the same product. Effectively, substitutes may limit the profits in an industry by keeping prices down.

From a strategy viewpoint, the key issues to be analysed are:

● the possible threat of obsolescence;

● the ability of customers to switch to the substitute;

● the costs of providing some extra aspect of the service that will prevent switching;

● the likely reduction in profit margin if prices come down or are held.

In the steel market, there is the possibility of substituting lighter metals such as aluminium for steel, depending on the usage. The threat of substitution may therefore be **high** but this depends on the technology and end-use.

3.6.5 The extent of competitive rivalry

Some markets are more competitive than others. Higher competitive rivalry may occur in the following circumstances.

- *When competitors are roughly of equal size and one competitor decides to gain share over the others,* then rivalry increases significantly and profits fall. In a market with a dominant company, there may be less rivalry because the larger company is often able to stop quickly any move by its smaller competitors. In the European steel industry, companies are roughly of equal size with no company dominating the market – one of the reasons why rivalry is so intense.

- *If a market is growing slowly and a company wishes to gain dominance,* then by definition it must take its sales from its competitors – increasing rivalry.

- *Where fixed costs or the costs of storing finished products in an industry are high,* then companies may attempt to gain market share in order to achieve break-even or higher levels of profitability. Paper making, steel manufacture and car production are all examples of industries where there is a real case for cutting prices to achieve basic sales volumes – thus increasing rivalry.

- *If extra production capacity in an industry comes in large increments,* then companies may be tempted to fill that capacity by reducing prices, at least temporarily. For example, the bulk chemicals industry usually has to build major new plants and cannot simply add small increments of capacity. In the steel industry, it is not possible to half-build a new steel plant: either it is built or not.

- *If it is difficult to differentiate products or services,* then competition is essentially price-based and it is difficult to ensure customer loyalty. Markets in basic pharmaceutical products such as aspirin have become increasingly subject to such pressures. In the steel market, flat-rolled steel from one manufacturer is much the same as that of another, so competition is price-based. However, where specialist steels are made with unique performance characteristics, the products are differentiated on performance and price rivalry is lower.

- *When it is difficult or expensive to exit from an industry* (perhaps due to legislation on redundancy costs or the cost of closing dirty plant), there is likely to be excess production capacity in the industry and increased rivalry. The European steel industry has suffered from problems in this area during the last few years.

- *If entrants have expressed a determination to achieve a strategic stake in that market,* the costs of such an entry would be relatively unimportant when related to the total costs of the company concerned and the long-term advantages of a presence in the market. Japanese car manufacturing in the EU has advantages for Toyota and Nissan beyond the short-term costs of building plant, as EU car markets were opened to full Japanese competition around the year 2000.

In the European steel market, some sectors of the market clearly have intense rivalry – for example, basic steel products competing on price and possibly service. Overall, an analysis would probably conclude that competitive rivalry was **high** in the market place, but would certainly seek to explain the differing reasons in the different segments and draw out the implications for strategy.

3.6.6 Strategy implications from the general industry and competitive analysis

In corporate strategy, it is not enough just to produce an analysis; it is important to consider the implications for the organisation's future strategy. Some issues that might arise from the above include:

- *Is there a case for changing the strategic relationships with suppliers?* Could more be gained by moving into close partnership with selected suppliers rather than regarding them as rivals? The Japanese car industry has sought to obtain much closer co-operation with suppliers and mutual cost reduction as a result.[17] (*See* Chapter 9.)

- *Is there a case for forming a new relationship with large buyers?* Manufacture of own-label products for large customers in the retail industry may be undertaken at lower margins than branded business but has proved a highly successful strategy for some leading European companies.[18] Even Cereal Partners (from Chapter 2) is now engaged in this strategy in order to build volume through its plants.

- *What are the key factors for success that drive an industry and influence its strategic development?* What are the lessons for the future that need to be built into the organisation's corporate strategy? We will return to these questions in Chapter 6.

- *Are there any major technical developments that rivals are working on that could fundamentally alter the nature of the environment?* What is the time span and level of investment for such activity? What action should we take, if any?

3.6.7 Criticisms of the Five Forces Model

Porter's Five Forces Model is a useful early step in analysing the environment, but it has been the subject of some critical comment:

- The analytical framework is essentially *static,* whereas the competitive environment in practice is constantly changing. Forces may move from high to low, or vice versa, rather more rapidly than the model can show.

- It assumes that the organisation's own interests come first; for some charitable institutions and government bodies, this assumption may be incorrect.

- It assumes that buyers (called customers elsewhere in this book) have no greater importance than any other aspect of the micro-environment. Other commentators such as Aaker,[19] Baker[20] and Harvey-Jones[21] would fundamentally disagree on this point: they argue that the customer is more important than other aspects of strategy development and is not to be treated as an equal aspect of such an analysis.

- In general, its starting point is that the environment poses a threat to the organisation – leading to the consideration of suppliers and buyers as threats that need to be tackled. As pointed out above, some companies have found it useful to engage in closer *co-operation* with suppliers; such a strategy may be excluded if they are regarded purely as threats. This is explained more fully in Section 3.7.

- Porter's strategic analysis largely ignores the human resource aspects of strategy: it makes little attempt to recognise, let alone resolve, aspects of the micro-environment that might connect people to their own and other organisations. For example, it considers neither the country cultures, nor the management skills aspects of corporate strategy (see Chapter 7).

- Porter's analysis proceeds on the basis that, once such an analysis has been undertaken, then the organisation can formulate a corporate strategy to handle the results:

prescriptive rather than *emergent*. As we saw in Chapter 2, some commentators would challenge this basic assessment.

In spite of these critical comments, the approach taken in this book is that Porter's model provides a very useful starting point in the analysis of the environment. It has real merit because of the issues it raises in a logical and structured framework. It is therefore recommended as a useful first step in corporate strategy development.

Professor Porter presented his Five Forces Model as an early stage in strategic analysis and development. He followed it with two further analyses: an analysis of *industry evolution* – the extent to which the micro-environment is still growing or has reached maturity[22] – and the study of *strategic groups* within a market. (*See* Chapters 4 and 5.)

> ### ▶ Key strategic principles
>
> - The purpose of industry and competitive strategic analysis is to enable the organisation to develop competitive advantage.
> - Porter's Five Forces Model provides a useful starting point for such an analysis.
> - Suppliers are particularly strong when they can command a price premium for their products and when their delivery schedules or quality can affect the final product.
> - Buyers (or customers) are strong when they have substantial negotiating power or other leverage points associated with price, quality and service.
> - New entrants pose a substantial threat when they are easily able to enter a market and when they are able to compete strongly through lower costs or other means.
> - Substitutes usually pose a threat as a result of a technological or low-cost breakthrough.
> - Competitive rivalry is the essence of such an analysis. It is necessary to build defences against competitive threat.
> - The model has been the subject of some critical comment but it remains a useful starting point for competitive strategic analysis.

3.7 Analysing the co-operative environment

3.7.1 The four links model

As well as competing with rivals, most organisations also co-operate with others, e.g. through informal supply relationships or through formal and legally binding joint ventures. Until recently, such links were rarely analysed in strategy development – the analysis stopped at Porter's Five Forces and some in-depth studies of one or two competitors (*see* Section 3.8). However, it is now becoming increasingly clear that *co-operation* between the organisation and others in its environment is also important:

- it may help in the achievement of sustainable competitive advantage;
- it may produce lower costs;
- it may deliver more sustainable relationships with those outside the organisation.

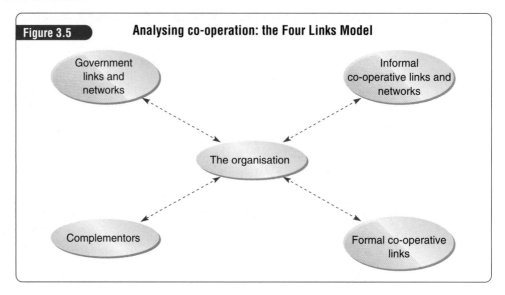

Figure 3.5 **Analysing co-operation: the Four Links Model**

It should be noted that an extreme form of co-operation – collusion between competitors to rig markets – is illegal in most countries and is not explored further here. But there are many other forms of co-operation that are highly beneficial and should form part of any analysis of the environment. For example, European steel companies have formed joint ventures with Brazilian steel companies for the benefit of both parties, and Krupp Thyssen Stahl is co-operating with its energy suppliers to reduce costs. Moreover, all the main European steel companies are co-operating with the government of the EU on policy matters affecting the industry. The co-operative linkages between the organisation and its environment can usefully be explored under four headings:

1 informal co-operative links and networks

2 formal co-operative links

3 complementors

4 government links and networks.

The objective of such an analysis is to establish the strength and nature of the co-operation that exists between the organisation and its environment. It can be conducted through the *Four Links Model – see* Figure 3.5.

3.7.2 Opportunities and threats from informal co-operative links and networks

Informal co-operative links and networks are the occasions when organisations link together for a mutual or common purpose *without* a legally binding contractual relationship. They have long been recognised as providing an important means of understanding the strategy of the firm.[23] By their nature, they may well occur by accident as well as by design. They will include many forms of contact, ranging from formal industry bodies that represent industry matters with other interested parties – for example, the European Confederation of Iron and Steel Industries – to informal contacts that take place when like-minded individuals from a variety of industries meet at a social function – for example, a local Chamber of Commerce meeting.

The analysis will need to assess the opportunities that such links and networks present. Occasionally, there may also be threats from arrangements. In analysing them, it is the **strength or weakness** of the relationship that matters. For example, in some parts of the world such as Japan and Korea, the networks are called *Keiretsu* and *Chaebol* respectively and have provided strong mutual support to those companies that belong to them. In some services such as international banking, it is the strength of the network that provides the competitive advantage for those involved in it and excludes those that are not.[24]

3.7.3 Opportunities and threats from formal co-operative linkages

Formal co-operative linkages can take many business forms but are usually bound together by some form of legal contract. They differ from the networks described above in the higher degree of formality and permanence of the link with the organisation. They are then shown in alliances, joint ventures, joint shareholdings and many other deals that exist to provide competitive advantage and mutual support over many years. Some companies like the UK retailer Marks & Spencer, the Japanese car manufacturer Toyota and the Italian clothing company Benetton have developed such linkages into vital contributors to the uniqueness of their strategies. Suppliers, distributors and other formal co-operators with such companies provide essential products and services at lower prices and higher service levels than those offered to others in the industry. Essentially, formal co-operative linkages develop out of many years of discussion and understanding. They are very difficult for other companies to copy.[25] The **strengths and weaknesses** of such linkages should therefore be measured in terms of their depth, longevity and degree of mutual trust. Although the main interest may come from opportunities offered by such formal linkages, threats may arise from those developed by competitors.

3.7.4 The opportunities and threats presented by complementors

Complementors are those companies whose products add more value to the products of the base organisation than they would derive from their own products by themselves.[26] For example, computer hardware companies are worth little without the software that goes with them – one product *complements* the other. In strategic terms, there may be real benefits from developing new complementor opportunities that enhance both parties and contribute further to the links that exist between them. Typically, complementors come from different industries with different resources and skills that work together to present new and sustainable *joint offerings* to customers. Again, it is the **strengths and weaknesses** of the relationship that need to be analysed. Although the main interest may come from opportunities offered by complementors, threats may arise from the complementor linkages developed by competitors.

3.7.5 Opportunities and threats from government links and networks

Government links and networks concern the relationships that many organisations have with a country's national parliament, regional assemblies and the associated government administrations. In the case of the EU and other international treaties, these clearly extend beyond national boundaries. Such contact may be formal, through business negotiations on investment, legal issues and tax matters. It may also be informal, through representation on government/industry organisations in connection with investment and trade.

Government links and networks can be vital in tax and legal matters, such as the interpretation of competition law. Equally, governments can be important customers of organisations, e.g. in defence equipment and pharmaceuticals. Many organisations have come to devote significant time and effort to developing and cultivating such relationships through lobbying and other related activities. Because of the nature and role of government, it may need to remain relatively remote in its legislative and regulatory dealings with outside organisations. However, it is appropriate to evaluate the degree of co-operation or hostility between government and outside bodies. Thus outside organisations will wish to consider the **opportunities and threats** posed by government activities. These may form a significant part of their corporate strategic development, especially at very senior levels within an organisation.

3.7.6 Comment on Four Links Model: an emergent process

At least in part, such a model may not have the precision and clarity of the Five Forces Model and other competitor analyses: networks come and go, complementors may come to disagree, alliances may fall apart and governments fail to be re-elected. All linkage relationships lack the simplicity of the bargaining power and competitive threat analyses of the Five Forces Model. However, the Four Links Model is essentially concerned with co-operation between organisations (*see* Figure 3.5). This will have many facets that go beyond simple bargaining relationships.

Developing such links is likely to involve, at least in part, an emergent approach to strategy development. Linkages may provide opportunities to experiment and develop new and original strategies. They may allow an unusual move in strategy development that will deliver sustainable competitive advantage. Hence, even though they may be imprecise and lacking in the simplicities of economic logic, such linkages deserve careful analysis.

> ### ▶ Key strategic principles
>
> - In addition to competing against rivals, most organisations also co-operate with other organisations. Such co-operation can deliver sustainable competitive advantage.
> - The main elements that need to be analysed for co-operation are captured in the *Four Links Model*: informal co-operative links and networks, formal co-operative links, complementors and government links and networks.
> - *Informal co-operative links and networks* are the range of contacts that arise from organisations joining together informally for a common purpose. *Formal co-operative linkages* are usually bound by some form of legal contract – examples include alliances and joint ventures. *Complementors* are those companies whose products add more value to the products of the base organisation than they would derive from their own products by themselves. *Government links and networks* concern the relationships that exist between national and international governments and organisations, including those concerning tax, legislation and formal government purchasing.

> **Key strategic principles continued**
>
> ● Such relationships can be measured by the strength of the linkage in the case of the first three. In the case of government, they may be better measured by considering the opportunities and threats posed by the relationship. All such links are often less structured and formalised than those involving competitor analysis but may represent significant areas of long-term competitive advantage.

3.8 Analysing one or more immediate competitors in depth

In any analysis of competitors and their relationship to the organisation, it is useful to analyse some immediate and close competitors: this is often called competitor profiling.

3.8.1 Sustainable competitive advantage and strategic resources

Broad surveys of competitive forces are useful in strategy analysis. But it is normal to select a few companies for more detailed examination. The reason is that the sustainable competitive advantage becomes more precise and meaningful when given a specific comparison. Moreover, some rival companies will have *strategic resources* – those resources that set them apart and make them formidable opponents that need to be identified; for example, well-respected brand names like Coca-Cola and Volkswagen, specialist technologies such as laser printer production at the Japanese company Canon, and unique locations of hotels and restaurants, such as those owned by McDonald's. We return to the topic of strategic resources in Chapter 6.

3.8.2 Competitor profiling

As a starting point, it is useful to undertake competitor profiling – that is, the basic analysis of a leading competitor, covering its objectives, resources, market strength and current strategies.

In many markets, there will be more than one competitor and it will not be possible to analyse them all. It will be necessary to make a choice – usually the one or two that represent the most direct threat. In public service organisations where the competition may be for *resources* rather than for *customers,* the same principle can be adopted, with the choice being made among the agencies competing for funds. In small businesses, the need to understand competitors is just as great although here it may be more difficult to identify which company will pose the most direct threat; a *typical* competitor may be selected in these circumstances. Once the choice has been made, the following aspects of the competitor's organisation need to be explored:

● *Objectives.* If the competitor is seeking sales growth or market share growth, this may involve an aggressive stance in the market place. If the company is seeking profit growth, the company may choose to achieve this by investing in new plant or by some other means that might take time to implement. If this is the case, there will be less of an immediate impact on others in the market place, but new plant may mean lower costs and a longer-term impact on prices. Company annual reports and press statements may be helpful here in defining what the competitor says it wants to do.

These need to be treated with some caution, however, since the company may be bluffing or using some other competitive technique.

- *Resources.* The scale and size of the company's resources are an important indicator of its competitive threat – perhaps it has superior or inferior technology, perhaps overmanning at its plants, perhaps financial problems. Chapter 4 will provide a more detailed checklist in terms of competitive advantage, and Chapter 6 examines resources in more detail.

- *Past record of performance.* Although this may be a poor guide to the future, it is direct evidence that is publicly available through financial statements and stockbrokers' reports.

- *Current products and services.* Many companies buy competing products or services for the sole purpose of tearing them apart. They analyse customers, quality, performance, after-sales service, promotional material and some will even interview former employees – unethical perhaps, but it does happen.

- *Links with other organisations.* Joint members, alliances and other forms of co-operation may deliver significant competitive advantage.

- *Present strategies.* Attitudes to subjects such as innovation, leading customers, finance and investment, human resource management, market share, cost reduction, product range, pricing and branding all deserve investigation. The marketing areas are explored further in Chapters 4 and 5 and resources are examined in Chapters 6 to 9.

Competitor profiling is time-consuming but vital to the development of corporate strategy. Some larger companies employ whole departments whose sole task is to monitor leading competitors. Small businesses also often have an acute awareness of their competitors, although this may be derived more informally at trade meetings, social occasions, exhibitions and so on. In corporate strategy, it is vital to gain a 'feel' for competitors.

3.8.3 Emergent perspectives on competition

One of the main dangers of competitive profiling is that it will be seen as essentially static. In practice, all organisations are changing all the time. Moreover, the competitive profiling process should be regarded as one of discovery and one that never finishes. Emergent perspectives on competitor analysis, which emphasise this changing nature, will deliver useful insights, especially where the environment is changing rapidly. For example, emergent perspectives are *essential* when analysing the Internet competitors – *see* Case study 20.3.

3.8.4 Outcome of competitor profiling

However imprecisely, it is important to draw up a clear statement of the competitive advantages held by a rival organisation. A useful means of summarising this is the SWOT analysis – *see* Section 13.1.

▶ Key strategic principles

- **Competitor profiling is an essential first step in analysing immediate competitors. It will seek to identify the strategic resources of rivals.**
- **More generally, it will explore the objectives, resources, past performance, current products and services, and present strategies of at least one competitor.**

> **Key strategic principles continued**
>
> ● **Competitor profiling should be regarded as an ongoing task. Its emergent nature is particularly important in fast-moving markets.**

3.9 Analysing the customer and market segmentation

Since customers generate the revenues that keep the organisation in existence and deliver its profits, customers are crucial in corporate strategy. In this context it is perhaps surprising that much greater emphasis has been given in some aspects of strategic development to *competition* rather than to the customer.[27] The reason is that the focus of the purchase decision for the customer is a competitive selection between the different products or services on offer. While this is undoubtedly true, it is easy to lose sight of the direct strategic importance of the customer.

There are three useful dimensions to an analysis of the customer:

1 identification of the customer and the market;
2 market segmentation and its strategic implications;
3 the role of customer service and quality.

3.9.1 Identification of the customer and the market

Back in the 1960s, Levitt[28] wrote a famous article that argued that the main reason some organisations were in decline was because they had become too heavily product-oriented, and were not sufficiently customer-oriented. As a result, they defined their customer base too narrowly. To help this process, a useful distinction can be made between:[29]

● *immediate customer base* – for example, those travelling on railways; and
● *wider customer franchise* – for example, those travelling by public transport, including railways, aircraft and buses.

The importance in defining accurately this aspect of the environment lies in developing strategies that identify customers and competitors. Ultimately, if the market environment is incorrectly defined, then competitors may creep up and steal customers without the company realising it until it is too late. Furthermore, it is vital to analyse *future* customers as well as the *current* customer profile (*see* Chapter 5). Moreover, there are some problems associated with Levitt's concept – *see* also Chapter 5.

3.9.2 Market segmentation and its strategic implications

Most markets have now moved beyond *mass marketing* – where one product is sold to all types of customer – *to targeted marketing* – where the seller identifies market segments, selects one or more of these and then develops products or services targeted specially for the segment. Market segmentation is the identification of specific parts of a market and the development of different market offerings that will be attractive to those segments[30] – an important element of any market analysis.

Market segmentation is important for strategy for several reasons:

- *Some segments may be more profitable and attractive than others.* For example, large segments may have low profit margins but their size may make them attractive, even at these levels of profitability.
- *Some segments may have more competition than others.* For example, a specialist segment may have only a limited number of competitors.
- *Some segments may be growing faster and offer more development opportunities than others.*

Porter[31] uses market segmentation to draw a basic distinction between two major generic strategies:

1 *broad target segments* that involve large numbers of customers, e.g. basic flat-rolled steel bars that have wide customer demand; and

2 *narrow target segments* that involve small niches in the market place, e.g. small specialist steel products that are sold for their particular performance characteristics at high prices to a small number of buyers.

In conclusion, careful analysis of segments and their characteristics is therefore important (*see* Chapter 5).

▶ Key strategic principles

- In identifying markets, it is important to identify the customer base sufficiently broadly. A useful distinction can be drawn between the immediate customer base and a wider franchise based on product substitution. It is also important to explore future customers as well as the current customer base.
- Market segmentation is fundamental to the development of corporate strategy: some parts of markets may be more attractive than others. Careful analysis of segments and their characteristics is therefore important.

3.10 Conclusions

Given the amount of analysis that can potentially be undertaken, the question is raised as to whether each aspect of analysis has equal priority. Although there are no absolute rules, it is usually the case that the customer comes first, the immediate competition second and the broader environment surrounding the organisation then follows behind this. In other words, the analytical process may well be arranged in the *reverse order* of this chapter.

In many respects, the real danger in analysing the environment is to limit the process to examining past events and ways of thinking. It is absolutely essential to break out of the current mould and examine alternative routes and ideas. This is particularly likely to be the case if some types of emergent approaches are adopted, because they rely essentially on taking small steps from the current position. As Egan[32] has pointed out:

> *While expedient for conditions of relative environmental stability, [the emergent approach] is likely to be unacceptable in periods of discontinuous change. The rapid demise of Nixdorf Computer and Wang Computer should have sent rapid signals to IBM that more of the same was wholly inappropriate in the rapidly changing computer industry.*

In this context, the merger between Hewlett Packard and Compaq – announced as this book was going to press – against a backdrop of rapidly dropping profits in personal computers has all the hallmarks of a difficult future.

Strategic bargaining to film *The Lord of the Rings*

In the highly competitive and risky environment of Hollywood film-making, it is essential to analyse those who have the power to make things happen. This case explores the strategic environment surrounding one of the most profitable films ever made – and how the deal and the movie almost failed.

Background

It was one of the biggest gambles in movie history – handing US$300 million to shoot an epic trilogy in one take to a virtually unknown director with no record of big-budget Hollywood pictures. And letting him do it 7000 miles away, so that studio executives had little control over what actually happened on the set.

There were plenty of recent examples of how a huge investment in what seemed a sure-fire blockbuster had backfired, leaving massive dents in the studio's finances – *Waterworld*, *Heaven's Gate* and so on. Somehow, though, *Lord of the Rings* did get made and took over US$500 million in its first year as well as winning four Oscars. It is easy to forget the scale of the risk involved and the convoluted strategic bargaining that was necessary before a single scene was shot.

For Peter Jackson, the film's New Zealand-born director, and his agent, Ken Kamins from ICM, the story behind the *Lord of the Rings* is one of a project that very nearly failed to see the light of day.

Early strategic bargaining

When Jackson and Kamins set out to make the film in 1995, they first had to secure the rights to JRR Tolkien's novels, *The Fellowship of the Ring*, *The Two Towers* and *The Return of the King*. Producer Saul Zaentz had bought the rights from Professor Tolkien for a rumoured US$15 000 30 years earlier and he had no intention of selling them. Up to that point, Jackson was known only for low-budget horror movies such as *Braindead*. However, an Oscar nomination in 1995 for the screenplay of his US$3.5 million arthouse drama *Heavenly Creatures* had earned him a first-look deal with Harvey Goldstein, head of Miramax, the independent studio allied to Disney. So Jackson and Kamins approached Weinstein that year with the idea for a *Lord of the Rings* adaptation.

'When we told Harvey that Saul held the rights, he was immediately enthusiastic,' says Kamins, 'as he had just helped Saul on the *English Patient* [Miramax had stepped in to pick up the film after Fox, part of News Corporation, dropped it on the eve of production]. That created the moral window by which Harvey could ask. But this wasn't charity either. Saul had Harvey pay a pretty penny – I've been told somewhere in the US$3 million range.'

New bargaining problems

Having secured the film rights, the Miramax boss sent Jackson and his partner, Fran Walsh, off to write the scripts for a two-part adaptation, with both parts being filmed one after the other. Production research was also to begin in New Zealand. Just when things seemed to be going smoothly, the next wave of problems emerged. 'It soon became clear to Miramax that it was going to be a very expensive proposition,' says Kamins, 'maybe more expensive than their brief as defined by Disney allowed them to get involved in. Harvey then went to Disney and asked whether they would want a partner in the project. When Disney said no, Miramax got concerned about the cost. And of course [started] asking obvious questions: what happens if the first movie doesn't work?'

Faced with such a risky and expensive project, Weinstein asked Jackson to make the trilogy as one film of no more than three hours. Jackson declined, and, instead, he and Kamins asked to take the project to another studio. Weinstein agreed, although he imposed very tough conditions. Says Kamins: 'We had three weeks to set it up somewhere else. Harvey also demanded that the US$12 million that Miramax had already spent in development had to be repaid within 72 hours of the agreement being signed. Now this is highly unusual in the movie business. Normally, a studio would simply pay the former studio a 10 per cent option or they would work out a deal in the budget of the film once the movie got made. Most importantly, he and a partner insisted on 5 per cent of the gross, whether there was one movie, two movies or eight.'

The deal hangs on a knife-edge

With three weeks to find another studio, Jackson and Kamins decided to do two things. While Kamins started submitting the screenplays for the two-part adaptation to every studio in Hollywood, Jackson flew to New Zealand to produce a 35-minute documentary with US$50 000 of his own money. The idea was that, if any of the studios was interested, the documentary would show them where Miramax's US$12 million had gone, and, most importantly, why Jackson was the right director. But Kamins had little success – every studio said no, except two, Polygram and New Line, which was owned by Warner Brothers. Then Polygram pulled out at the last minute: 'So we went to New Line realising that they were the last Popsicle stand in the desert, and them not knowing that,' said Kamins.

But at New Line, they had some luck. Jackson's old friend, Mark Ordesky, turned out to be one of those making the decision. New Line then asked: 'Why are you making two movies? It's three books, so it's three movies.' Negotiations started the next day. Many in the business doubted the sanity of the decision, especially making three rather than two

films. 'But Peter's presentation made it clear that he had an absolutely commanding vision for the film...You would be surprised how, in the movie business, some of these commitments are made on far less sturdy ground.'

By 2002, AOL Time Warner was estimated to have one of the biggest money-spinners in entertainment history on its hands. New Line and its distribution partners had turned *Lord of the Rings* into a worldwide franchise in the *Star Wars* mould, and were exploiting the brand name across a huge range of platforms – DVD, video games, the Internet, merchandise of every sort. The gamble was starting to pay.

Heavily adapted by Richard Lynch from an article by Katja Hofmann in *FT Creative Business*, 19 March 2002, page 10. © *Financial Times* 2002. All rights reserved. Reproduced with permission.

Case questions

1 *Who has the bargaining power in this strategic environment? And who has the co-operating power? Identify and analyse the players.*

2 *What useful strategic concepts, if any, from this chapter can be used in analysing the strategic environment? And what cannot be used? Why?*

3 *If risk and judgement are important in business decisions, can prescriptive strategic analysis be usefully employed?*

The importance of environmental analysis[33]

In this extract from his book, Strategic Management: an introduction, *Ronald Rosen links environmental analysis with its implications for corporate strategy in the organisation.*

An organisation does not exist in a vacuum; it interacts with its environment. A business offers its goods and services in the market place – usually against competition – while the environment provides sources of labour, energy, raw materials, finance, information, etc., over which it has little control.

If the environment were relatively unchanging, an organisation might, after a period of adaptation, settle down to a fairly stable relationship with its customers, suppliers, competitors, channels of distribution and investors. There would be little motivation to make major changes to the objectives or strategy if all parties more or less accepted the status quo. However, this stable state is rare; customers' needs change, a new competitor arises or a superior product is offered, sales decline, shareholders become dissatisfied with the return on their investment, a source of supply dries up or important retail outlets are denied to a manufacturer, a new market opens up. These, or innumerable other, changes in the environment might require a rethink about objectives, strategy, or both.

In other words, changes in strategy or objectives are frequently – although not always – made in response to, or in anticipation of, an environmental change: either reacting to a threat, or taking advantage of an opportunity. These changes may, in turn, provoke a response in the environment which must then be dealt with: for example, reducing prices in order to gain market share may spark off a price war, or launching a new product might trigger competitors to take their new product off the shelf, where it has been awaiting such an eventuality. Conversely, if an organisation responds too late to environmental changes, it runs the risk of failure. Hence, adapting an organisation to its environment is an essential aspect of strategic management.

If the environment were relatively unchanging, the process of strategic management would appear to be fairly simple, largely a matter of keeping an eye on the environment just to make sure that nothing much has changed – or is likely to do so – and concentrating mainly on good housekeeping:

keeping costs under control, maintaining quality and productivity levels by monitoring actual levels of performance against established standards, taking any necessary corrective action to keep on course. In other words, the emphasis would be on the maintenance of existing strategy – keeping the trains clean and running on time – rather than adapting or changing it, although the strategy might still need to be tweaked because of slight changes in the environment or in order to make it more effective.

In a more turbulent environment, the process of strategic management becomes more complex and demanding. Information systems must be sufficiently sensitive to detect change as early as possible in order to analyse the existing, and probable future, situation and to adapt to it in good time. Matching the organisation to its environment may require a more suitable structure, different systems and, in particular, an appropriate organisational culture, all of which are aspects of strategic management.

Source: Rosen, R (1995) *Strategic Management: an Introduction*, Pitman Publishing London.

Summary

In analysing the environment surrounding the organisation, seven main factors were identified.

● *A general consideration of the nature of the environment and, in particular, the degree of turbulence.* When events are particularly uncertain and prone to sudden and significant change, corporate strategy needs to become more flexible and organise its procedures to cope with the situation.

● *A general analysis of the factors that will affect many industries.* This can be undertaken by two procedures: the PESTEL analysis and scenarios. The PESTEL analysis explores political, economic, socio-cultural, technological, environmental and legal influences on the organisation. It is important when undertaking such an analysis to develop a short list of only the most important items, not a long list under every heading. In developing scenarios, it should be recognised that they provide a different view of conceivable future events, rather than predict the future.

● *Growth characteristics* can be explored using the industry life cycle concept. Markets are divided into a series of development stages: introduction, growth, maturity and decline. In addition, the maturity stage may be subject to the cyclical variations associated with general economic or other factors over which the company has little control.

● Different stages of the life cycle demand different corporate strategies. The early stages probably require greater investment in R&D and marketing to develop and explain the product. The later stages should be more profitable on a conventional view of the life cycle. However, there is an argument that takes a more unconventional stance: it suggests that it is during the mature phase that investment should increase in order to restore growth.

● *The identification of key factors for success.* Moving towards an analysis of the environment surrounding the organisation itself, it is useful to establish the key factors for success in the industry (not the organisation). This requires a consideration of the resources of the organisation (*see* Chapter 6).

● *A Five Forces Analysis.* This will involve an examination of buyers, suppliers, new entrants, substitutes and the competition in the industry. The aim is to analyse the balance of power between each force and the organisation in the industry.

● *A Four Links Analysis* of the co-operators of the organisation. This will include a study of the complementors, networks and legal links that the organisation has with its environment. The purpose is to analyse the relative strengths of such links and their ability to enhance the competitive advantages of the organisation.

● *A study of selected direct competitors.* The purpose here is to identify the specific competitive advantages of rival companies and to highlight any strategic resources – unique possessions that will deliver competitive advantage to the rivals. Such a study needs to recognise the fluid and changing nature of competitors and their resources.

● *A study of customers.* The final area of analysis is concerned with actual and potential customers and their importance to the organisation. Segmentation of markets derives from customer analysis and plays an important role in corporate strategy development.

QUESTIONS

1 Using Table 3.3 and your judgement, determine the degree of turbulence in the global steel industry. Give reasons for your views.

2 Undertake a general environmental analysis of an industry of your choice, using both the PESTEL format and scenarios to draw out the major strategic issues.

3 Develop and compare the key factors for success in the following three industries: computer industry (Chapter 1), food industry (Chapter 2) and steel industry (Chapter 3).

4 For the European steel industry, analyse the competitive forces within the industry using the Five Forces Model. Identify also any forms of co-operation in the industry using a Four Links Analysis.

5 Based on your answers to the previous questions, what strategic advice would you offer Usinor/Arbed/Aceralia? Use Section 3.6.6 to assist you.

6 Undertake a life cycle analysis of an industry of your choice. What strategic conclusions would

you draw for organisations in the industry, if any? Comment specifically on the difficulties of this approach.

7 Prepare a full environmental analysis for an industry of your choice and make recommendations on its future corporate strategy.

8 Undertake a customer analysis for your own organisation. What segments can you identify? What role is played by customer service and quality? What strategic conclusions can you draw?

9 Do you agree with the statement that stable environments favour prescriptive approaches to strategy whereas turbulent environments demand emergent strategies? Consider carefully the impact technology may have on a stable environment and the problem of long-term investment, even in turbulent industries.

10 To what extent can competitive analytical techniques be applied to the public sector and charitable institutions?

STRATEGIC PROJECT ▸ **International steel strategy**

This chapter has examined the steel industry. You might like to take this a step further. For example, look at the strategies of Corus to build its low-cost efficient UK operations and its difficulties in making acquisitions in other European countries. In 2002, the company was still highly unprofitable. Why? What strategies has it adopted to recover the situation? Do you believe they will bring success?

FURTHER READING

M E Porter's *Competitive Strategy: Techniques for Analysing Industries and Competitors* (The Free Press, Harvard, MA, 1980) has careful and detailed studies for analysis of the immediate competitive environment.

L Fahey and V K Narayanan's *Microenvironmental Analyses for Strategic Management* (West Publishing, St Paul, MN,

1986) explores the way that the environment influences organisational strategy.

R Rosen's *Strategic Management: an Introduction* (Pitman Publishing, London, 1995) has some useful strategic planning worksheets that will help to structure a study of the environment. However, it is important to treat them as a useful framework rather than a rigid format.

NOTES & REFERENCES

1 References for the European Steel Merger case: Usinor Annual Report and Accounts 1998, pp28, 29 and 30; *Financial Times*, 19 Feb 1997, p30; 7 Jan 1998, p28; 23 April 1999, p32; 3 Jan 2002, p23; 19 February 2002, p26; 20 February 2002, p28. *See* also references at end of Case study 3.3.

2 Porter, M E (1980) *Competitive Advantage*, The Free Press, New York.

3 Andrews, K (1987) *The Concept of Corporate Strategy*, Irwin, Homewood, IL.

4 The early part of this section is based on Ansoff, I and MacDonnell, E (1990) *Implementing Strategic Management*, 2nd edn, Prentice Hall, Englewood Cliffs, NJ.

5 D'Aveni, R (1994) *Hypercompetitive Rivalries*, Free Press, New York.

6 Note: In previous editions of this book, the term 'PEST' analysis has been used. This has now been extended to reflect the increased importance given to environmental and governmental/legal matters.

7 Simon, H 'The corporation: will it be managed by machine?', in Leavitt, H and Pondy, L (eds) (1964) *Readings in Managerial Psychology*, University of Chicago Press, Chicago, pp592–617.

8 Baden-Fuller, C and Stopford, J (1992) *Rejuvenating the Mature Business*, Routledge, Ch2.

9 Aaker, D R (1992) *Strategic Marketing Management*, 3rd edn, Wiley, p236.

10 Smallwood, J E (1973) 'The product life cycle: a key to strategic marketing planning', *MSU Business Topics*, Winter, pp29–35.

11 Baker, M (1993) *Marketing Strategy and Management*, 2nd edn, Macmillan, p100 *et seq.* presents a short

defence and interesting discussion of the main areas.

12 Dallah, N Y and Yuspeh, S (1976) 'Forget the product life cycle concept', *Harvard Business Review*, Jan–Feb, p101 *et seq.*

13 References for global steel case: *Metal Bulletin*, 12 Mar 1998, p17; *Financial Times*, 24 January 1990; 10 Jan 1996, p23; 2 Aug 1996, p7; 15 Nov 1996, p27; 11 Dec 1996, p37; 20 Mar 1997, pp4 and 31; 11 June 1997, p4; 24 July 1997, p30; 30 July 1997, p35; 23 Oct 1997, p4; 13 Nov 1997, p6; 15 Dec 1997, p23; 7 Feb 1998, p17; 9 Mar 1998, p24; 18 Mar 1998, p 43; 22 Apr 1998, p38; 27 May 1998, p27; 28 May 1998, p25; 4 June 1998, p23; 20 February 2001, p19; 16 March 2001, p24; 14 April 2001, p14; 26 November 2001, p12; 17 December 2001, p21; 7 February 2002, p7.

14 Porter, M E (1980) *Competitive Advantage*, The Free Press, New York. Note that Porter's work owes much to the writings of Professor Joel Bain and others in the 1950s on industrial economies. However, it was Porter who gave this earlier material its strategic focus. See also Porter's article, 'How competitive forces shape strategy' (1979) *Harvard Business Review*, Mar–Apr, pp136–45, which is a useful summary of the main points from the early part of his book.

15 Op. cit., p4.

16 Porter actually refers in his book to 'six' areas and then goes on to list seven!

17 Cusumano, M and Takeishi, A (1991) 'Supplier relations and management: a survey of Japanese, Japanese-transplant and US auto plants', *Strategic Management Journal*, 12, pp563–88.

18 Nielsen, A C (1988) *International Food and Drug Store Trends*, Nielsen, Oxford.

19 Aaker, D (1992) *Strategic Marketing Management*, 3rd edn, Wiley, New York.

20 Baker, M (1993) *Marketing Strategy and Management*, 2nd edn, Macmillan, London.

21 Harvey-Jones, J (1991) *Getting it Together*, Heinemann, London, Ch14.

22 Porter (1980) Op. cit., Chs7 and 8.

23 Reve, T (1990) 'The firm as a nexus of internal and external contracts', *The Firm as a Nexus of Treaties*, Aoki, M, Gustafson, M and Williamson, O E (eds), Sage, London. See also Kay, J (1994) *The Foundations of Corporate Success*, Oxford University Press, Oxford, Ch5.

24 Kay, J (1994) Op. cit., p80.

25 Kay, J (1994) Op. cit.: Ch5 on architecture explores this topic in depth.

26 Nalebuff, B J and Brandenburger, A M (1997) *Co-opetition*, HarperCollins Business, London.

27 For example, Porter, M E (1980) *Competitive Strategy*, The Free Press, New York.

28 Levitt, T (1960) 'Marketing myopia', *Harvard Business Review*, Jul–Aug, p45.

29 Davidson, H (1987) *Offensive Marketing*, Penguin, Harmondsworth.

30 Adcock, D, Bradfield, R, Halborg, A and Ross, C (1995) *Marketing: Principles and Practice*, 2nd edn, Pitman Publishing, London, p386.

31 Porter, M E (1980) *Competitive Strategy*, The Free Press, New York, Ch2.

32 Egan, C (1995) *Creating Organisational Advantage*, Butterworth–Heinemann, Oxford, p83.

33 Extracted from Rosen, R (1995) *Strategic Management: an Introduction*, Pitman Publishing, London.

Analysing markets and competitors

When you have worked through this chapter, you will be able to:

- understand the importance of sustainable competitive advantage;
- explain how to move towards dynamic competitive advantage;
- explore the intensity of competition and assess its strategic implications;
- outline the range of aggressive activities undertaken by competitors and assess their strategic significance;
- describe the main elements of product portfolio analysis and comment on its strategic usefulness;
- analyse individual competitors and their influence on strategy;
- explore and assess the importance of distributors;
- explain the role that governments can play in the development of corporate strategy;
- identify the main international strategic competitive issues.

Figure 4.1　　**Market and competitor analysis: the main considerations**

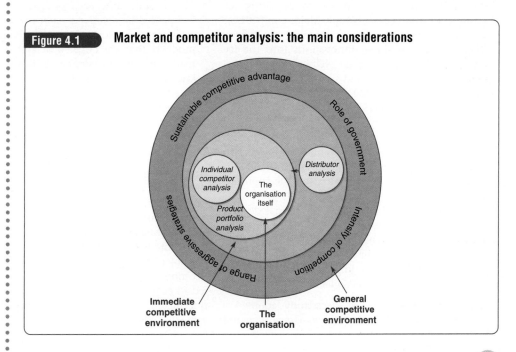

Introduction

A corporate strategy will only succeed in a competitive market place if it is based on a thorough analysis of the organisation's competitors. Any such analysis can usefully begin with a general consideration of the advantages that competitors have in the market place. The intensity of competition and the aggressive strategies that may be employed should then be reviewed in detail.

In addition to these general considerations, it is important to examine three inter-related areas that may affect the *specific* immediate competitive environment of the organisation: strategic groups (i.e. close competitors that can usefully be grouped together), product portfolios and distributors. Government influence on markets and strategy can also usefully be analysed. Market and competitor analysis is summarised in Figure 4.1. This chapter should be read in conjunction with the previous chapter, which explored other aspects of the topic.

CASE STUDY 4.1

Unilever ice cream defends its European market share[1]

With around 40 per cent of the European ice cream market involving sales of US$3 billion, the major multinational company Unilever has much to defend. The company operates across Europe but not under the name of Unilever. It uses a series of local company names and employs strategies which combine both pan-European and national activities.

Unilever has been involved in the European ice cream market for many years. During the 1980s and 1990s, it has faced an increasing threat as its main competitor, Nestlé, began to realise the profitability of ice cream and started acquiring ice cream companies across Europe. Major competition also came from another formidable challenger, Mars, which introduced innovations into the ice cream market by using its well-known branded confectionery products and finding ways of freezing them in the late 1980s – for example, Mars Ice Cream. By the mid-1990s, Nestlé had followed with KitKat Ice Cream. Branded ice cream strategy involved heavy advertising, strong product innovation and major drives to secure distribution in retail freezer cabinets. Unilever had difficulty in responding because it did not possess the appropriate branded food products.

Unilever's strengths lie in its traditional dominance of the ice cream market. It has traditional, well-known brand names. As a result of its long history and extensive resources in many European countries, Unilever can implement a strategy at both a pan-European level and a national level:

● In the 1990s, Unilever successfully adopted a new strategy of developing *pan-European* brand

names – ranging from premium speciality ice creams, like Magnum, to family packs, such as Carte d'Or. In part, this was a reaction to its strategic weakness.

● At the same time each of Unilever's operating companies has a *national name* (see Table 4.1) and each company adds to its range some national products that are targeted at customers in that market alone. This strategy builds on nationally known brand names that would be too costly to extend to other countries (such as Miko in France) and takes account of national taste and price variations that still exist in food products across Europe.

Over the years, the company has developed strong distribution links with retailers, especially the smaller outlets that can only take one freezer cabinet (which in many cases Unilever has supplied free of charge). It used its distribution strength to keep out Mars Ice Cream – *see* Case 4.3 – but is now in dispute with the European Commission, which has objected to this strategy on the grounds of market monopoly. Unilever's large brand share has also led to economies of scale that newer entrants cannot match, preventing them from achieving the same low-cost structure.

Table 4.1 Unilever's operations in the European ice cream market

Country	Main Unilever company	Unilever market share	Competing companies
Germany	Langnese – Iglo	40% (60% of impulse market)	Schoeller Mars Dr Oetker
France	Cogesal Ortiz-Miko (see text)	45%	Gervais/ Nestlé Mars Pilpa
Italy	Algida/ Findus	40%	Italgel/ Nestlé Mars Sammontana
Netherlands/ Belgium	Iglo-Ola	30%	Schoeller Mars Isboerke Artic
Ireland	HB Ice Cream	60%	Nestlé
UK	Birds Eye/ Walls	40%	Nestlé/ Lyons Maid Mars Treats

Probably Unilever's greatest weakness is that the group has no involvement in the confectionery market, unlike Nestlé and Mars. Unilever thus had difficulty in responding to the 1990s' trend to employ confectionery brands in ice cream. (Mars' activities in this area are explored in Case 4.3). In the early 1990s, Unilever made arrangements with national chocolate manufacturers – for example, its UK deal with Cadbury to reproduce Cadbury's Dairy Milk Chocolate in an ice cream as CDM. CDM is largely a national UK brand and cannot be easily presented on a pan-European scale. More recently, the company has developed its own pan-European brands like Magnum. But investing in these new brands has been and continues to be an expensive strategy.

Case questions

1 *What is the source of Unilever's advantages over its competitors?*

2 *What are Unilever's main strengths? Where do its weaknesses lie? What, if anything, would you do about its weaknesses?*

3 *Should Unilever go further in launching truly pan-European products, like those associated with Mars Ice Cream and Nestlé KitKat Ice Cream? How important, if at all, are such products to the overall Unilever strategy?*

4.1 Sustainable competitive advantage

4.1.1 The importance of sustainable competitive advantage

The main reason for analysing competitors is to enable the organisation to develop *competitive advantages* against them, especially advantages that can be *sustained* over time. Sustainable competitive advantage involves every aspect of the way that the organisation competes in the market place – prices, product range, manufacturing quality, service levels and so on. However, some of these factors can easily be imitated: for example, prices can be changed virtually overnight or other companies can make ice cream just like Unilever.

The real benefits come from advantages that competitors cannot easily imitate, not from those that give only temporary relief from the competitive battle. To be *sustainable,* competitive advantage needs to be more deeply embedded in the organisation – its resources, skills, culture and investment over time. Unilever's advantages in ice

Table 4.2 Some possible sustainable competitive advantages in different areas of business

High technology	Services	Small business	Manufacturing market leader
● Technical excellence	● Reputation for quality of service	● Quality	● Low costs
● Reputation for quality	● High quality and training of staff	● Prompt service	● Strong branding
● Customer service	● Customer service	● Personalised service	● Good distribution
● Financial resources	● Well-known name	● Keen prices	● Quality product
● Low-cost manufacturing	● Customer-oriented	● Local availability	● Good value for money

Sources: See reference 5.

cream come from its brand investment, its well-developed distribution service and its sheer size in the market place, which should deliver economies of scale.

More generally, the development of sustainable advantage can take many forms. Such activities may possibly involve seeking something that is possibly *unique* and certainly *different* from the competition, and so it follows that there will be a wide range of possibilities. Table 4.2 presents some possible sources of advantage for certain industries.

For many strategists, the development of sustainable competitive advantage lies at the core of corporate strategy development. Professor Michael Porter wrote persuasively about its importance in the 1980s in two classic strategy texts – *Competitive Strategy* (1980)[2] and *Competitive Advantage* (1985)[3] – which have influenced both academic and industry developments. For example, Stephen South, corporate planning director at Clark Equipment (US), commented:

> The process of strategic management is coming to be defined, in fact, as the management of competitive advantage – that is, a process of identifying, developing and taking advantage of enclaves in which tangible and preservable business advantage can be achieved.[4]

There are other aspects to the development of corporate strategy – for example, those associated with the strategy process and the purpose of an organisation. Hence, the statement may overemphasise the importance of competitive advantage. Nevertheless, it is a vital aspect of corporate strategy development.

4.1.2 Public service and not-for-profit organisations

Most businesses face competitors, so the need for a sustainable advantage to help them compete is evident. It is more questionable, however, whether public service and not-for-profit organisations need sustainable competitive advantages. In one sense, they may not because their services are often provided free to the consumer and without competition – for example, police services, hospitals, charitable institutions and so on.

However, many public services and charities depend for financial support either on government funds or on private donations. Such support is usually not unlimited, and so in this sense such organisations *compete for finance* from potential providers. Developing arguments and evidence to maintain and enhance the funds distributed will be important. Such organisations could usefully consider the decisions that have to be made by the fund providers and the *incremental advantages* that their service provides to the general public and which therefore justify extra funding.

4.1.3 Prescriptive and emergent approaches to sustainable advantage

By definition, if an advantage is to be sustainable, then it cannot be quickly copied by others. It is likely that it will have taken some time, possibly years, for the organisation to have developed the advantage. A prescriptive approach, requiring a sustained period of development, is therefore likely to be required in principle at least. For example, it takes some years to develop and establish a new branded product such as Mars Ice Cream.

Emergent approaches are not excluded, however. The development of sustainable competitive advantage (SCA) may well require a degree of experimentation along with adjustments based on the developments by competitors. For example, the introduction of superpremium ice creams, such as Häagen-Dazs, will benefit from experimenting with new forms of distribution – such as the supply of freezer cabinets in pizza restaurants – in order to overcome the hold that the traditional ice cream suppliers have on more familiar outlets.

Hence, the development of SCA will probably require elements of both prescriptive and emergent strategic approaches. An extension of the emergent perspective on SCA is explored in the next section.

4.1.4 Developing sources of sustainable competitive advantage

In seeking the advantages that competitors cannot easily copy, it is necessary to examine not only the competitors, but also the organisation itself and its resources. Resources are explored in depth in Part 3 of this book, but it is appropriate here to identify some possible sources of advantage as a starting point for later study:

- *Differentiation.* This is the development of unique features or attributes in a product or service that position it to appeal especially to a part of the total market. Branding is an example of this source.

- *Low costs.* The development of low-cost production enables the firm to compete against other companies either on the basis of lower prices or possibly on the basis of the same prices as its competitors but with more services being added. For example, production in some South-East Asian countries may involve lower labour costs that cannot be matched in the West.[6]

- *Niche marketing.* A company may select a small market segment and concentrate all its efforts on achieving advantages in this segment. Such a niche will need to be distinguished by special buyer needs. Fashion items such as those by Yves St Laurent or Dunhill are examples of products that are especially targeted towards specialist niches.

- *High performance or technology.* Special levels of performance or service can be developed that simply cannot be matched by other companies – for example, through patented products or recruitment of especially talented individuals.

The well-known global consulting companies and merchant banks operate in this way.

- *Quality.* Some companies offer a level of quality that others are unable to match. For example, some Japanese cars have, until recently, provided levels of reliability that Western companies have had difficulty in reaching.

- *Service.* Some companies have deliberately sought to provide superior levels of service that others have been unable or unwilling to match. For example, McDonald's set new levels of service in its fast food restaurants that were unmatched by others for many years.

- *Vertical integration.* The backward acquisition of raw material suppliers and/or the forward purchase of distributors may provide advantages that others cannot match. For example, in Chapter 3, the Usinor/Arbed steel company owned some steel distributors.

- *Synergy.* This is the combination of parts of a business such that the sum of them is worth more than the individual parts – that is, $2 + 2 = 5$. This may occur because the parts share fixed overheads, transfer their technology or share the same sales-force, for example. Claims are often made for this approach when an acquisition is made, but this synergy is not necessarily achieved in reality. Nevertheless, it remains a valid area of exploration.

- *Culture, leadership and style of an organisation.* The way that an organisation leads, trains and supports its members may be a source of advantage that others cannot match. It will lead to innovative products, exceptional levels of service, fast responses to new market developments and so on. This area is more difficult to quantify than some of the other areas above, but this only adds to its unique appeal. It is unusual to find such an area listed in strategy texts, but it is a theme of this book.

Some organisations and strategists have become almost obsessed with the first three of these sources of sustainable competitive advantage – Porter's *generic strategies,* as they are often described – and these are discussed under this heading in Chapter 13. This is completely misleading, however, as Professor Porter's books explore all the above areas and more in considerable detail.

It could also be argued that several of the sources in the list involve some form of differentiation. To group these all under differentiation, however, would be to ignore the *specific nature* of the form of advantage and to deny the important individual areas of strategy opened up by such concepts.

More generally, Professor John Kay, the British strategy writer at Oxford University Business School, has argued that competitive advantage is more generally based on the *stability* and *continuity* in relationships between different parts of an organisation.[7] He argues that major advantages are not developed overnight or by some special acquisition or other miraculous strategy. Substantial advantages take many years to develop and involve the whole culture and style of an organisation. To this extent, it may even be misleading to see advantages as being summarised by the short list of items above. However, this does provide a starting point for further analysis.

Ultimately, there is no single route to achieving sustainable competitive advantage. The question that arises is therefore whether it is possible to test whether it has been achieved. Three possible tests for such advantages are shown in Exhibit 4.1.

Exhibit 4.1 **Three tests for sustainable competitive advantage**

The advantage should be:

- *Sufficiently significant to make a difference.* Modest advantages that hold no real benefits to the customer or the organisation are unlikely to be persuasive.

- *Sustainable against environmental change and competitor attack.* The market as a whole may move forward in terms of technology or tastes. Equally, competitors may be able to copy advantages developed by the organisation. In both cases, these advantages are not sustainable.

- *Recognisable and linked to customer benefits.* An advantage needs to be translated from a functional advantage inside the organisation – for example, low costs – into something that the customer will value – for example, low prices. Advantages that cannot be linked in this way may ultimately prove to have no persuasive and competitive edge.

▶ Key strategic principles

- One of the main purposes of analysing competitors is to explore where and how sustainable competitive advantage (SCA) can be generated. The search for SCA will be wide and deep within the organisation.

- Public service and not-for-profit organisations may also wish to explore SCA as they may be in competition for finance from external bodies, such as the government, even if there is no competition for customers.

- SCA will probably require elements of both emergent and prescriptive strategy approaches to strategy development.

- There are numerous sources of SCA. These include: differentiation; low costs; niche marketing; high performance or technology; quality; service; vertical integration; synergy; and the culture, leadership and style of the organisation. Importantly, SCA develops slowly over time; such a list is only the starting point of a more detailed study.

4.2 Dynamics of competitive advantage

Clearly, competitive advantage is unlikely to remain static forever: competitors, technology, managers, customers and many other factors are likely to change over time. Some strategists,[8] particularly those that have studied industries where advanced technology is involved, argue that the static identification of competitive advantage misses an important strategic opportunity. They suggest that competitive advantage should be seen as constantly evolving and that companies should be seeking to make this happen. In other words, competitive advantage is a *dynamic concept* that will provide a constant flow of new opportunities to the organisation.

4.2.1 Dynamic process – structured yet chaotic

According to such strategists, the key issue is for a company to strike a balance between supporting its long-term sustainable advantages and at the same time engaging in the process of constant change and renewal. Such a company will begin by identifying some sustainable competitive advantages that are structured, supported and clear – for example, Intel Corporation supports its 'Pentium' brand name and individual new computer chips as they are launched into the market place. However, at the same time, such a company will also deliberately have some other aspects of its activities that are disorganised and fall essentially outside its existing areas of advantage – for example, Intel Corporation might experiment with some totally new technology or computer software in one of its laboratories that has no obvious relation to its current competitive advantage but would be an interesting point of departure for the company. Thus, the strategy process is both *structured* – advertising the brand name – and *chaotic* – exploring a totally new and unproven technology and, in this sense, dynamic.

4.2.2 Dynamic competitive advantage – some guidelines, not rules

Clearly such a dynamic strategic process has the potential to be both immensely beneficial and also totally unmanageable. Strategists therefore suggest that there should be some guidelines laid down to exploit the real benefits of such an approach. In the words of Brown and Eisenhardt:

> *Successful firms in fiercely competitive and unpredictably shifting industries pursue a competing on the edge strategy. The goal of this strategy is not efficiency or optimality in the usual sense. Rather, the goal is flexibility – that is, adaptation to current change and evolution over time, resilience to setbacks, and the ability to locate constantly changing sources of advantage. Ultimately, it means engaging in continual revolution.*
>
> Brown and Eisenhardt (1998) *Competing on the Edge*,
> Harvard Business School Press, p19

In practice, for such organisations, this means striking a balance between structure and chaos – strong financial control systems are in place, but managers have significant free time to develop their own ideas. Thus the process may be inefficient and have failures. But it will be proactive in the sense of seeking positively after new initiatives and accept that there will inevitably be some failures. The process is often driven by a basic objective that the organisation will derive a significant percentage of its sales from totally new products over time – the 3M case in Chapter 11 will provide more detail.

Fundamentally, the process is guided by the concept of the organisation having a *continuous flow* of competitive advantages rather than a static list. Clearly this is an emergent rather than a prescriptive approach to strategy development.

4.2.3 Critical comment on the concept

There are some obvious flaws in such an approach:

● It may be possible in high-technology industries, but may be difficult to achieve and even irrelevant elsewhere – see Case 4.1, where Unilever's competitive advantage is real but does not depend on a technological advantage.

● There is a real difficulty in managing the difficult boundary between inspired development ideas and total chaos – see Case 4.2, where arguably the company went too far.

● Other important areas of competitive advantage appear to be largely discounted in the quest for benefits. This means that such advantages may be undersupported and thus lost – *see* Case 4.3, where it was important that advertising was maintained for the Mars brand and not dissipated in a search for a totally new area of advantage.

▶ Key strategic principles

- According to some strategists, competitive advantage should be seen as constantly evolving and companies should set out to make this happen, particularly in industries that involve advanced technology. In this sense, competitive advantage is dynamic rather than static.

- The process for developing such competitive advantage is both built around existing strengths – structured – and also exploits new and exciting areas – chaotic.

- The main rule for such a process is to strike a balance between structure and chaos.

- Criticism of the approach has centred on its relevance to more traditional industries outside high technology, on the difficulty of managing the chaotic part of the process and on the possibility of ignoring existing competitive advantages in the pursuit of a new area of advantage.

CASE STUDY 4.2

Web strategy at Boo.com – To be booed? Or applauded?

With the wisdom of hindsight, it is easy to criticise the failed web strategy of the sportswear company Boo.com. This case outlines its brief history and explores whether it was right for investors to take the risk.

Background

In the late 1990s, many senior strategy consultants and well-known companies were enthusiastic about the potential of the worldwide web. It would revolutionise business and alter fundamentally the whole nature of competitive markets and the meaning of sustainable competitive advantage. For example in April 2000, the website of the well-known consultancy company Arthur Anderson made the following claims about the benefits of the web and the related concept of e-business:

eBusiness transforms the business landscape. New companies routinely challenge dominant market players. Unprecedented market efficiencies eliminate middlemen and create increased productivity by more closely matching supply and demand. eBusiness describes the way companies innovate and transform. It mandates rethinking, repositioning and retooling a company's entire value proposition. In a start up company, you basically throw out all assumptions every three weeks.

Thus, it was not only large companies that saw immense possibilities. Small entrepreneurial ventures were being started in every conceivable business area. And substantial funds were available: 'There was a view that raising money to fund a start-up was easy and any monkey could do it.' Venture capital funds were awash with cash and investors were scrambling to invest their money. One of these companies was Boo.com.

Boo.com – the beginnings

In January 1999, a new start-up company called Boo.com was seen as one with great potential. Its strategic purpose was to become the global leader in selling trendy sportswear over the web. Two of its three Swedish founders, Ernst Malmsten – entrepreneur; Kajsa Leander – fashion model; and Patrik Hedelin – investment banker, appeared on the cover of the leading US business magazine *Fortune* with the headline: 'Cool companies '99: 12 start-up companies – will one be the next Yahoo?' Malmsten was the original driving force, having previously founded a successful on-line book store. JP Morgan was the lead bank that helped them bring in some well-known blue-chip lawyers, technology providers and head-hunters.

▶

Boo.com certainly had great ambitions. Its launch in June 1999 would be undertaken simultaneously in 18 countries. Its website was to be truly innovative, multilingual and offering high-class sportswear at premium prices. This last point was quite different from the usual website offer which advertised prices lower than those available in high street shops – for example, Amazon.com in books. In addition, Boo.com was proposing to set up a sales and distribution network in its 18 countries that would allow delivery in just a few days. By any standards, this was very ambitious – even more so for a company whose founders had never managed such a venture previously.

The company recruited some 400 people across its 18 countries. In addition, it spent substantial funds on advertising and software development. The money was spent on shooting television commercials in Los Angeles; spending US$10 000 on clothes at Barneys so that the founders would look good on the cover of *Fortune*; holding smart parties for staff; jetting around the world by Concord or private jet. As a result, the company was spending around US$1 million per week by the year 2000. The company launch was put back five times and US$30 million spent. During this time, it took six months to appoint a chief financial officer and four months to find a good technology director. One investor explained: 'The lack of financial controls was excused because it was considered more important to spend money on promotion. The aim was to stay ahead of the pack.'

In August 1999, Malmsten took all the staff to an expensive lunch in London to announce that a new manager would be creating Project Launch in November 1999. At this time, a Lebanese investment company put in yet another US$15 million. The launch took place in November and pulled in 25 000 web hits – the business objective was 1 million. Sales were around U$4 million over the first six months. By this time, the company had spent over US$100 million on salaries, marketing costs, legal costs, office design costs and software development.

Boo.com goes bust

According to one investor in the company, 'If you looked at Boo in concept as potentially a global company, then spending US$100 million building it was not necessarily a lot of money. We were hoping to build a company worth US$1 billion.' Boo.com mainly sought funds from rich private investors rather than the public. For this reason, the company never made its trading figures public – except one day towards the end of its life when it was forced to reveal the sales figure mentioned above. In March 2000, investors were still debating over whether to put in another US$30 million. In May 2000, investors pulled the plug. The company simply ran out of cash.

Boo.com conclusions

Clearly the company had been too ambitious. It was too lax in financial controls and too unrealistic in wishing to break the rules. But it did attempt to break new ground. It was an important experiment that might have succeeded.

Case sources: See reference 9.

Case questions

1 *What were the competitive advantages of Boo.com, if any?*

2 *Given that many investors in Boo.com were wealthy private individuals, were they right to invest their money? Would you personally invest money in such a company?*

3 *Boo.com claimed to be seizing the initiative and breaking the rules. Under what circumstances, if any, does it make sense to attempt this?*

4.3 The intensity of competition in an industry

Governments will set the basic degree of competitiveness that they wish to see in industries. Having established this, it is useful to start any analysis of competition with Porter's *Five Forces Analysis* (*see* Chapter 3). This will provide a basic starting point in any development of the major factors driving the dynamics of the industry.

In addition to such an analysis, it is possible to examine two further areas:

1 *the degree of concentration of companies in a market* – examined here; and

2 *the range of aggressive strategies of competitors in the market.* (*See* Section 4.4.)

In microeconomic theory, the degree of concentration of companies in a market can be seen as being somewhere between two extremes, each of which will have strategic consequences for companies:

● perfect competition;

● pure monopoly.

In *perfect competition*, there are numerous buyers and sellers, with no single firm able to influence market prices: it is assumed that products are identical in every respect and that the firm accepts the price set by the market. The perfectly competitive firm sets its level of production output to maximise profits. From a strategic viewpoint, this leaves the firm at the mercy of market pressures and is therefore undesirable. It would be much better strategy for the firm to *differentiate* its product, dominate a sector of the market and thus influence that sector's market price – in other words, to gain sustainable competitive advantage.

At the other extreme to perfect competition, there exists the state of *pure monopoly*. In this case, there is no competition and the company has total control over its prices; it erects barriers to entry and maximises profits and value added. It does this at the expense of its customers, but from a corporate strategy viewpoint it might be argued that the corporation has no responsibility to such customers and should seek to maximise profit and value added regardless of their views: strategies would therefore include raising prices to the maximum that the market will bear and setting output accordingly.

In practice, for many companies the environment is neither one of perfect competition nor one of pure monopoly. Corporate strategy needs to deal with a wide range of industrial structures in the middle. For some industries where there are economies of scale, it may actually be more efficient for the state and more profitable for individual companies to have a few large companies in an industry – that is, *an oligopoly*. Corporate strategy in such industries will therefore be directed towards obtaining and sustaining the oligopoly, if this is possible.

Industry structure and market characteristics have a significant impact on corporate strategy. However, the actions that companies take go well beyond the pricing activity often highlighted in microeconomic theory – for example, cost reduction, product differentiation, linkages with other companies through alliances and joint ventures. In the chapters that follow, these areas will be explored further.

The *concentration ratio* is often used to measure the degree to which value added or turnover is concentrated in the hands of a few or a large number of firms in an industry. It is usually defined as the percentage of industry value added or turnover controlled by the largest four, five or eight firms – the C4, C5 or C8 ratio respectively. Typically, C5 averages around 55 per cent in UK manufacturing industries and C4 averages around 34 per cent in US industries. After the ratio has been calculated, two areas of strategic significance can be analysed:

1 The *total number of firms in an industry* may influence their ability to exert buying power over suppliers. If there are few, then buying power may increase as in the case of grocery retailers (*see* Case study 4.3); if there are many, then their buying power will be lower.

2 The *mix of firms making up the industry* will also impact on profitability. If there are a few companies that are roughly equal in size, then there may be some tacit understanding between them to allow profits to grow. As the numbers increase and there is a likelihood of some giants and some smaller companies, then there is a lower possibility of a tacit understanding, so profits will suffer.

Overall, it is likely that corporate strategy will vary with company size and the degree of market competition. Smaller companies, such as small shoe manufacturers, may have to adopt different strategies from larger organisations, such as the large shoe companies that can afford to set up retail chains to sell their products. Highly competitive markets may require different strategies from those with lower degrees of competition. This has profound significance because it suggests that corporate strategy will vary with industry. There may be no single 'corporate strategy' that will suit all industries.

4.4 Aggressive competitive strategies[10]

There is a whole range of aggressive strategies that competitors can undertake. These need to be analysed for two reasons:

1 to understand the strategies competitors may undertake;
2 to assist in planning appropriate counter-measures.

In practitioner literature and even some more academic articles in this area, the language and style are often *militaristic* in tone.[11] For example:

● 'Find a weakness in the leader's strength and attack at that point.'
● 'Strong competitive moves should always be blocked.'

Professor Porter eschews some of the more colourful language but is in no doubt about the importance of this area. Professor Philip Kotler from North Western University, US, has developed the material in his well-known marketing text, *Marketing Management*[12] and has collaborated with Singh to write an influential article on the topic.[13] The analytical process is summarised in Figure 4.2.

4.4.1 Market intelligence

In accordance with the well-known saying 'knowledge is the basis of power', many companies monitor the activities of their competitors constantly. Occasionally, a few may undertake snooping or eavesdropping activities which may be illegal and are probably unethical. Although such behaviour cannot be condoned, it is entirely correct for companies to seek an understanding of their competitors' strategies. There are many entirely legitimate means for investigating this area. For example:

● company annual reports;
● newspaper articles;
● stockbroker analyses;
● exhibitions and trade fairs.

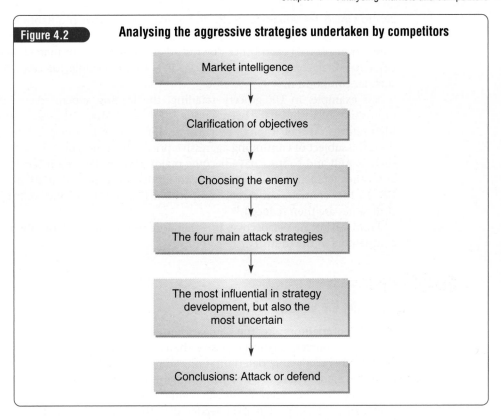

Figure 4.2 Analysing the aggressive strategies undertaken by competitors

4.4.2 Clarification of the objectives of competitors

In military situations, the objective is often the total defeat of the enemy. This is rarely appropriate in corporate strategy for the following reasons:

● It may contravene monopoly legislation, certainly in the EU, the US and many other countries around the world.

● It often becomes increasingly costly to pursue the last remnant of share.

● A weakened opponent that is still in the market may be easier to handle than a new aggressive entrant.

● A defeated opponent may be acquired cheaply in a takeover by a new powerful entrant (*see* Spillers in Chapter 2).

Even military strategists have recognised that the objectives of war may be better served by some form of stalemate or understanding. As Captain B H Liddell-Hart[14] commented:

> *The objective of war is a better state of peace, even if only from your own viewpoint.*

To develop this, it is necessary to understand the competitor's objectives, especially in such areas as market share and sales. Subsequently, the organisation itself will also need to develop its own objectives.

The optimal corporate strategy may define its ideal objective as being a *new market equilibrium* – that is, one that allows all competitors a viable and stable market share accompanied by adequate profits. This may be a more profitable solution than the alternative of continuing aggression, especially if this involves a price war in which competitors outbid each other downwards in the pursuit of market share. Even under strict national competition legislation, it is often possible for companies to develop such an equilibrium.[15]

For example, in UK grocery retailing, the leading supermarkets have engaged in minor price wars but have been willing to settle for shares that allow them all to make high returns on their capital. By contrast, some other European retailing markets have been the subject of continuing aggressive price wars, especially where price discounters – such as Aldi and Netto – have become major players. The result has been that German and other retailers tend to operate with returns on capital that are below those of the UK. In this context, cut-throat competition may serve no one well: the profits of all companies are then reduced.[16]

From a strategic perspective, it is therefore important to clarify the true objectives of competitors in the industry.

4.4.3 Choosing the enemy

Not all competitors are the same: some may be immensely aggressive, with large financial resources, relatively passive shareholders, long-term objectives to take market share and considerable determination. Some well-known Japanese companies provide examples here. These are not the companies to choose to fight, although it may be inevitable that the organisation will compete with them.

Equally, attacking a market leader directly is a high-risk strategy because of the strength of such a competitor, even if the payoff appears to be attractive. Military strategists state that a superiority in people and machinery of 3:1 is needed before launching an attack, if the approach is to be successful. By definition, this is highly unlikely where the market leader is involved.

For these reasons, it may be better to analyse and target competitors of more equal size. Their weaknesses might then form the basis of an aggressive move. They might even be available for takeover.

4.4.4 The four main attack strategies

In any analysis of competitors, it is important to recognise the four main strategies that they may use against each other and any new entrant. It should also be noted that these represent a *checklist of strategy options* for use in Part 5 when it comes to further development of corporate strategy (*see* Chapter 13).

The four main attack strategies are shown in Exhibit 4.2. These are based on three main principles:

1 *the need to concentrate the attack on competition* so that it is overwhelming at that particular point and therefore more likely to be successful;

2 *the element of surprise* so that gains can be made while the competitor is still recovering (perhaps involving rewriting the rules of the game);

3 *the need to consolidate the attack* by continuing to invest for some period (except in the last option which is based on rapid withdrawal and limited losses).

Exhibit 4.2　　　　　**The four main attack strategies**

1 Head-on against the market leader

- Unless resources are sustained, the campaign is unlikely to be successful.
- Attack where the leader is weak.
- Pick a narrow front to open up the campaign.

2 Flanking or market segmentation

- Choose a flank that is relatively undefended.
- Aim to take a significant market share.
- Expect to invest in the flank for some years.
- Pricing and value for money are often distinguishing features of a successful flank.

3 Occupy totally new territory, i.e. where there is no existing product or service

- Innovate if possible.
- Seek market niches.

4 Guerrilla: that is, a rapid sortie to seize a short-term profitable opportunity

- Relies on good information to identify opportunities.
- Fast response needed and rapid withdrawal after success.
- Important not to stand and fight leaders on their own ground but pick new areas.

The principles are derived from those used in military strategy.

- They involve a reliance on brute force to achieve an objective, only when it is useful and achievable.
- They recommend concentrating such force so that it will achieve maximum effect.
- They suggest following up the use of force by longer-term strategies that will secure the position permanently.

For these reasons, the head-on strategy is rarely successful.

It should be emphasised that other strategies are also possible and, for the underdog, may be crucial. They often involve some form of *innovation* in the competitive environment (*see* Section 4.4.5).

4.4.5 Innovatory strategies

There are many forms of innovation but it is useful to identify four for our purposes:

1 rewriting the rules of the game;

2 technological innovation;

3 higher levels of service;

4 co-operation.

Many of these are particularly suited to smaller companies that do not have substantial resources.

Rewriting the rules of the game

In competitive strategy, the existing players in the market will work according to a mutual understanding of how competitors are engaged – the rules of the game. For example, life and household insurance was sold by agents who personally advised their customers on the best product for their circumstances. All the major companies invested vast sums in recruiting and training their people to undertake this task. Ultimately, their heavy investment meant that it was in the interests of such insurance companies not to offer any alternatives. Then along came smaller companies with telephone insurance selling. It changed the rules of the game and sold the product without the same heavy overhead of a large salesforce, so that it was possible to offer much lower prices. The revolution is still taking place in the European insurance industry. Rewriting the rules of the game is important in corporate strategy.

Technological innovation

Especially in the case of new, smaller players, it may be essential to introduce some form of innovation in order to take market share. This does not mean that this is the only way to enter a market and survive, but in certain types of industry it may represent a viable route. For example, the Internet is set to revolutionise the distribution of recorded music – *see* Case study 20.2. Smaller companies will be able to distribute their music more readily.

Higher levels of service

In some industries, technology may not be a dominant feature but service levels may still be important. For example, in the shoe industry, there have been technical advances but some companies have survived because they have offered high levels of personalised service and shoe design. Even in retailing, small shops have been able to survive by staying open for long hours in their local communities.

Co-operation

Formal partnerships or some other form of joint activity have proved useful innovatory strategies in the 1990s. Joint ventures, alliances and other forms of co-operation have been used with success to beat larger rivals (*see* Chapters 3 and 13).

▶ Key strategic principles

- In assessing the aggressive strategies of competitors, it is important to begin by monitoring competitive activity on a regular basis.

- Although total defeat may be appropriate as a military objective, it is rarely relevant in business. A new market equilibrium may be much more profitable, involving stable market shares, no price wars and viable levels of profitability.

- Some competitors may be naturally more aggressive than others and have more substantial resources. If it is possible to choose, then these may be the competitors to avoid.

- Choosing an enemy that can provide a successful outcome is important. Attacking the market leader is not usually wise.

> ▶ *Key strategic principles continued*
>
> ● **The four main attack strategies are: head-on, flanking, occupy totally new territory, and guerrilla.**
>
> ● **Innovatory strategies may prove particularly significant, especially for the underdog. These include rewriting the rules of the game, technological innovation, higher levels of service, and partnerships. (*See* further Chapter 11.)**

4.4.6 Conclusions: attack or defend

In a static market, every company that identifies a market opportunity will present another company with a market problem. Attack strategies therefore invite defensive responses, but they are two sides of the same coin and need to be treated as such in corporate strategy.

The analysis of the range of aggressive strategies open to competitors is a useful starting point in the development of corporate strategy. However, Kay[17] has urged caution in the use of military analogies for two reasons:

1 *It may exaggerate the importance of size and scale.* The use of brute force is supported by the financial resources and market share that can be brought to bear. Kay points out that business success comes from *distinctive capabilities* rather than destroying the enemy. It is therefore important to recognise size and scale as useful but not conclusive devices in strategic terms.

2 *It invites excessive emphasis on leadership, vision and attack.* The generals plotting the strategy are the primary engines for successful military strategy. Kay also points out that many successful companies rely on *teams*, rather than charismatic leaders – a theme that will be explored throughout this book.

In many respects, it is the *prescriptive* view of strategy that is best served by concepts of aggressive attack with plans that are carefully drawn up in advance. The more adaptive approach of *emergent* strategy does not lend itself so readily to such recipes, although the militarists would no doubt recognise the need for adaptation as the battle proceeds. Innovative strategies therefore have an important role.

4.5 Analysing an organisation's range of competing products and services

The majority of companies offer more than one product or service and many serve more than one customer. There are good strategic reasons for this: to be reliant on one product or customer clearly carries immense risks if, for any reason, that product or service should fail or the customer should go elsewhere. Decisions on strategy usually involve a range of products in a range of markets. This is the subject of portfolio analysis and strategy. It was originally suggested by the Boston Consulting Group (BCG) in the 1970s and, as a result, one version of the approach is sometimes called the *BCG matrix* – the matrix described below. Other versions were later developed to overcome weaknesses in the BCG approach – the *directional policy matrix* is also covered below in Section 4.5.3.

When an organisation has a number of products in its portfolio, it is quite likely that they will be in different stages of development: some will be relatively new and some much older. Many organisations will not wish to risk having all their products in the same markets and at the same stages of development. It is useful to have some products with limited growth but producing profits steadily, as well as having others that have real potential but may still be in the early stages of their growth. Indeed, the products that are earning steadily may be used to fund the development of those that will provide the growth and profits in the future.

According to this argument, the key strategy is to produce a *balanced portfolio of products* – some low-risk but dull growth, some higher-risk with future potential and rewards. The results can be measured in both *profit* and *cash* terms. (Cash is used as a measure here because, both in theory and in practice, it is possible for a company to be trading profitably and yet go bankrupt. This is because the company is earning insufficient *cash* as the profits are being reinvested in growth in the business. It is important to understand this distinction.)

4.5.1 The BCG growth–share matrix

This matrix is one means of analysing the balance of an organisation's product portfolio. According to this matrix, two basic factors define a product's strategic stance in the market place:

1 *relative market share* – for each product, the ratio of the share of the organisation's product divided by the share of the market leader;

2 *market growth rate* – for each product, the market growth rate of the product category.

Relative market share is important because, in the competitive battle of the market place, it is advantageous to be larger than rivals: this gives room for manoeuvre, the scale to undertake investment and the ability to command distribution. Some researchers, such as Buzzell and Gale,[18] claim to have found empirical evidence to support these statements. For example, in a survey of major companies, the two researchers found that businesses with over 50 per cent share of their markets enjoy rates of return three times greater than businesses with small market shares. There are other empirical studies that also support this broad conclusion.[19] Jacobsen and Aaker[20] have questioned this relationship. They point out that such a close correlation will also reflect other differences in businesses. High market share companies do not just differ on market share but on other dimensions as well: for example, they may have better management and may have more luck. However, Aaker himself in a more recent work[21] has conceded that portfolios do have their uses, along with their limitations.

Market growth rate is important because markets that are growing rapidly offer more opportunities for sales than lower growth markets. Rapid growth is less likely to involve stealing share from competition and more likely to come from new buyers entering the market. This gives many new opportunities for the right product. There are also difficulties, however, perhaps the chief being that growing markets are often not as profitable as those with low growth. Investment is usually needed to *promote* the rapid growth and this has to be funded out of profits.

Relative market share and market growth rate are combined in the growth–share matrix, as shown in Figure 4.3. It should be noted that the term 'matrix' is misleading. In reality, the diagram does not have four distinct boxes, but rather four areas which merge into one another. The four areas are given distinctive names to signify their strategic significance.

Figure 4.3 **The growth–share matrix – individual products or product groups categorised by market growth and share**

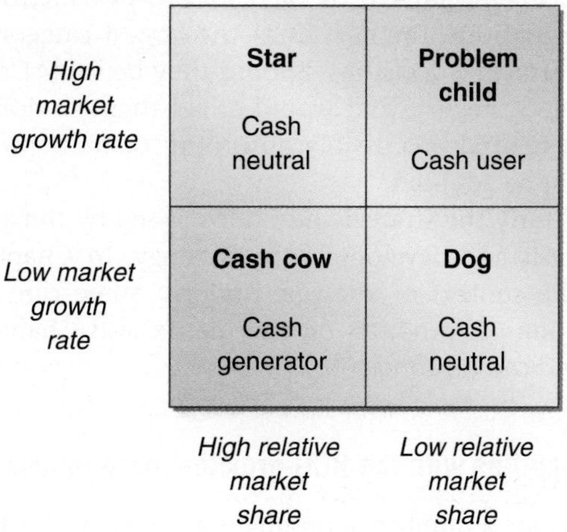

	High relative market share	Low relative market share
High market growth rate	**Star** Cash neutral	**Problem child** Cash user
Low market growth rate	**Cash cow** Cash generator	**Dog** Cash neutral

---

- *Stars*. The upper-left quadrant contains those products with high market shares operating in high-growth markets. The growth rate will mean that they will need heavy investment and will therefore be cash users. However, because they have high market shares, it is assumed that they will have economies of scale and be able to generate large amounts of cash. Overall, it is therefore asserted that they will be cash neutral – an assumption not necessarily supported in practice and not yet fully tested.

- *Cash cows*. The lower-left quadrant shows those product areas that have high market share but exist in low-growth markets. The business is mature and it is assumed that lower levels of investment will be required. On this basis, it is therefore likely that they will be able to generate both cash and profits. Such profits could then be transferred to support the stars. However, there is a real strategic danger here that cash cows become undersupported and begin to lose their market share.[22]

- *Problem children*. The upper-right quadrant contains products with low market shares in high-growth markets. Such products have not yet obtained dominant positions in rapidly growing markets or, possibly, their market shares have become less dominant, as competition has become more aggressive. The market growth means that it is likely that considerable investment will still be required and the low market share will mean that such products will have difficulty generating substantial cash. Hence, on this basis, these products are likely to be cash users.

- *Dogs*. The lower-right quadrant contains those products that have low relative market shares in low-growth businesses. It is assumed that the products will need low investment but that they are unlikely to be major profit earners. Hence, these two elements should balance each other and they should be cash neutral overall. In practice, they *may* actually absorb cash because of the investment required to hold their position. They are often regarded as unattractive for the long term and recommended for disposal.

Overall, the general strategy is to take cash from the *cash cows* to fund *stars* and invest in future new products that do not yet even appear on the matrix. Cash may also be invested selectively in some *problem children* to turn them into *stars*, with the others being milked or even sold to provide funds for elsewhere. Typically in many organisations, the *dogs* form the largest category and often represent the most difficult strategic decisions. Should they be sold? Could they be repositioned in a smaller market category that would allow them to dominate that category? Are they really cash neutral or possibly absorbing cash? If they are cash-absorbers, what strategies might be adopted?

Clearly the strategic questions raised by the approach have a useful function in the analysis and development of strategy. In Chapter 13, we will examine these further in the context of strategic options. Some care needs to be taken in calculating the positions of products on the matrix and Chapter 13 has a worked example to show how it can be done.

4.5.2 Difficulties with the BCG growth–share matrix

There are a number of problems associated with the matrix. The most obvious difficulty is that strategy is defined purely in terms of two simple factors and other issues are ignored. Further problems include:

- *The definition of market growth.* What is high market growth and what is low? Conventionally, this is often set above or below 5 per cent per annum, but there are no rules.

- *The definition of the market.* It is not always clear how the market should be defined. It is always possible to make a product dominate a market by defining the market narrowly enough. For example, do we consider the *entire* European steel market, where Usinor would have a small share, or do we take the *French segment* only, when the Usinor share would be much higher? This could radically alter the conclusions.

- *The definition of relative market share.* What constitutes a high relative share and a low share? Conventionally, the ratio is set at 1.5 (organisation's product to share of market leader's product) but why should this be so?

Hence, although the BCG matrix has the merit of simplicity, it has some significant weaknesses. As a result, other product portfolio approaches have been developed.

4.5.3 Other product portfolio approaches – the directional policy matrix

In order to overcome the obvious limitations of the BCG matrix, other product portfolio approaches have been developed. Essentially, rather than relying on the simplistic (but easily measurable) axes of market growth and market share, the further developments used rather more comprehensive measures of strategic success. In the case of the matrix developed by the well-known management consultants McKinsey, the two matrix axes were market attractiveness and business competitive strength.[23] In the case of strategy planners at the major oil company Royal Dutch/Shell, the matrix axes were called industry attractiveness and business competitive position:[24] Shell called its matrix development the *directional policy matrix* (DPM). Another very similar matrix was developed around the same time by the large US conglomerate General Electric, and called the *strategic business-planning grid*. Most of these matrices have much in common, so our exploration is confined to the DPM.

Figure 4.4	Directional policy matrix

Industry attractiveness

	High	Medium	Low

Strong

Business competitive position *Medium*

Weak

The DPM axes are:

- *Industry attractiveness.* In addition to market growth, this axis includes market size, industry profitability, amount of competition, market concentration, seasonality, cycles of demand, industry profitability. Each of these factors is rated and then combined into a numerical index. The industry attractiveness of each part of a multi-product business can be conveniently classified into high, medium or low.

- *Business competitive position.* In addition to market share, this axis includes the company's relative price competitiveness, its reputation, quality, geographic strengths, customer and market knowledge. Again, the factors are rated and classified into an index shown as strong, average or weak.

The complete matrix can then be plotted: *see* Figure 4.4. It will be evident that, where an organisation has a strong competitive position in an attractive industry, it should invest further. For example, Unilever has continued to invest worldwide in ice cream, with major acquisitions in the US, China and Brazil in recent years. Conversely, where a company has a weak competitive position in an industry with low attractiveness, it should strongly consider divesting itself of such a product area. For example, Unilever divested its Speciality Chemicals Division in 1997, where it was relatively weak compared with other companies and the market was subject to periodic downturns in profitability. Other positions in such matrices suggest other solutions. For example, a strong competitive position in an industry with low attractiveness might imply a strategy of cash generation, since there would be little point in investing further in such an unattractive industry but there would be important cash to be generated from such a strong competitive position. In Unilever's case, such a product group might be its oils and fats business, where it has a strong share in many countries, but the market prospects are not as attractive as in its consumer toiletries business.

All this may seem clear and highly valuable in strategy development. The first problem comes in developing the two axes: for example, exactly how do you develop an index that represents market growth, market size, industry profitability and so on? It can be done, but it is time-consuming and, partly at least, dependent on judgement. This means that it is open to management politics, influence and negotiation rather than the simple rational process of the BCG matrix. Beyond this, there are other problems associated with all product portfolio matrices – *see* Section 4.5.4.

4.5.4 Difficulties with all forms of product portfolio matrices

In spite of their advantages, all such matrices present a number of analytical problems:

● *Dubious recommendations.* Can we really afford to eliminate dogs when they may share common factory overheads with others? Are we in danger of underinvesting in valuable cash cows and diverting the funds into inherently weak problem children? Similar questions can be asked about the DPM.

● *Innovation.* Where do innovative new products fit onto the matrix? Do they have a small share of a tiny market and so deserve to be eliminated before they have even started? What meaning can be given to 'competitive position' in these circumstances?

● *Divesting unwanted product areas.* In many Western countries there may be substantial redundancy costs that make divestment unattractive. Even if there are not, divestment assumes that other companies might be interested in buying such a product range at a fair market price, which may be equally doubtful.

● *The perceived desirability of growth and industry attractiveness.* This assumption is not necessarily appropriate for all businesses. Some may make higher longer-term profits by seeking lower levels of growth.

● *The assumption that competitors will allow the organisation freedom to make its changes.* Competitors can also undertake a product portfolio analysis for both their own and competing products. Competitor reactions may negate the proposed changes in the organisation's portfolio.

Although the development of the product portfolio is useful in raising and exploring strategic issues, it is not a panacea for the development of corporate strategy. To overcome some of the issues raised above, various other formats for the product portfolio have been developed. Aaker[25] has provided a useful recent review of these. In 1977, Day[26] concluded that product portfolios were useful as a starting point in strategic analysis; such a comment still holds today.

🔴 Key strategic principles

● Portfolio analysis provides a means of analysing a company that has a range of products.

● The BCG portfolio analysis is undertaken using only two variables: relative market share and market growth. It is clearly a weakness that other variables are not included.

● The portfolio is then divided into four areas: stars, cash cows, problem children and dogs. These outline categories are then used as the basis for developing a balanced product portfolio. The technique is useful as a starting point only in the analytical process.

● Because of weaknesses in the BCG matrix, other matrices have been developed – for example, the *directional policy matrix* based on industry attractiveness and competitive position. But such dimensions remain vague and unsubstantiated.

4.6 Distributor analysis

An important area of strategy for many organisations is *distribution* or *channel strategy* – covering all the activities that happen beyond the factory gate, such as physical distribution, sales-force activity and customer service actions. To illustrate the strategic importance of distribution in certain markets, we have only to examine pharmaceutical industry strategy: in 1993–94, two US pharmaceutical companies spent over US$10 billion buying US drug distributors because of a fundamental reappraisal of their corporate strategies.[27] European car companies have also invested substantial sums in distribution of their products and regard it as a vital part of overall company strategy.

With regard to distributor analysis, Lynch[28] has suggested that it is useful to distinguish between two types of customer to whom products are distributed:

1 *direct end-users* – who buy and consume the product that is purchased. They do not buy for stock and do not sell to third parties. They often buy in large quantities and usually obtain direct supplies from the manufacturer;

2 *distributors* – who buy a product for stock and then sell it to other customers. They may be agents, stockholders or other trade combinations. What distinguishes this group is that a 'sale' is not really made until they sell out their stock and reorder.

From a corporate strategy perspective, we are concerned not with the detail of such issues, but with the basic issue of how we distribute our product or service to the customer and the costs that are involved. The most striking opportunity in corporate strategy may well be to distribute the product differently. The most difficult problem in some industries has been to obtain any significant distribution for a product at all. Case study 4.3 describes the problems that the well-resourced and skilled company, Mars, had in obtaining distribution for its highly popular ice cream products in the 1990s. Customer demand did not solve the distribution strategy problem.

Areas that the analysis will need to cover include:

● *Direct end-user or distributor objectives.* Many purchasers will be concerned not just with price but also with product quality, levels of service and technical support. At a more fundamental level, it will be important to deliver the levels of profitability or other objectives demanded by the end-user or distributor.

● *Service levels.* Important items under this heading include timetables for delivery but also levels of back-up service, order-taking policies and general after-sales service.

● *Technical and quality specifications.* For many end-users and distributors, specifications are vital. While the detail of such issues is not the subject of general strategy, the principles are important and their internal impact on the organisation will be explored further in Chapters 9 and 11. It should be noted here that international customers may well have more complex requirements than those from the home country.

● *Distributor pricing and discounts.* Competitor information is often just as important in this area as are basic data for the organisation itself.

● *Distributor support.* In many cases, the product or service has not really been 'sold' until the distributor has sold it from the warehouse, supermarket shelf or service centre. Promotional support to help the distributor may be a vital part of the organisation's strategy. In capital goods, design support, commissioning of the new machinery and continued technical advice are often required. The computer software company Microsoft recognised the importance and substantial costs of this when it launched its products Windows 95 and 98 in the late 1990s.

All these areas need careful analysis as part of the strategic development process. There are no strategic 'models' to consider: solid, careful study of the many complex factors and costs involved needs to be set against the sales to be gained. The main general principle to be followed is that of assessing the costs and benefits of each of the distribution options that have been identified.

▶ **Key strategic principles**

- In distribution analysis, it is useful to distinguish between the use of distributors and delivery to direct end-users.
- Objectives for the two groups need to be established because they will have an important effect on the distribution that results.
- Service levels, quality, pricing and discounts and support from the distributor are all issues that then need to be investigated. There are few general models that govern these areas beyond that of an assessment of the costs and benefits that are available from the various options.

CASE STUDY 4.3

Mars ice cream: distribution strategy problems

From the launch of its first product in 1989, Mars has built a European market share, reported as being between 5 per cent and 10 per cent of the total market, with a share of between 10 per cent and 20 per cent of the chocolate ice cream bar segment. Its market penetration has not been without setbacks, however, particularly in the area of distribution.

Mars' share of the European ice cream market has been achieved through the launch of a range of products that largely build on its well-known confectionery products which are pan-European in branding and widely distributed. The ice cream products are all branded exactly the same across Europe and are nearly all produced at one factory in eastern France.

Ice Cream Mars was the first of the product range, followed by others from its confectionery range such as Snickers and Opal Fruits. Its chosen strategy deliberately used high-quality ingredients, such as real cream and real chocolate, the use of significant advertising support across Europe and the establishment of a new premium-price category in the market place. By 1990, Unilever's UK subsidiary was commenting:

Fierce competition brought on by new players like Mars has helped to change the face of impulse ice cream. Ice cream is now coming of age with confectionery values becoming linked more and more with ice cream bars.

European ice cream distribution

In addition to its confectionery branding revolution, Mars has invested considerable effort in freezer distribution as part of its business strategy. Its excellent and long-standing relationships with the grocery trade meant that it had no major difficulty in this sector in obtaining distribution for its multipack items. However, problems have arisen in other sectors of the trade that account for a substantial share of the ice cream market.

Ice cream distribution to retail outlets involves high costs because of the need for frozen storage and vehicle transport. This is made worse by several factors:

- *The low unit cost of the items carried* (particularly impulse ice cream). At only US$1 per item, it is necessary to sell many items to balance out transport costs.

● *The small drop sizes of orders to non-supermarket outlets.* Small shops can only sell limited numbers.

● *The related difficulty of making up economic loads within a sufficiently compact geographic area.*

As a consequence, all ice cream manufacturers have devoted considerable time and expense to ice cream distribution. In the UK, Ireland, the Netherlands, Germany, Denmark, Spain and Greece, Unilever has followed a policy of offering free freezer cabinets to retailers for the *exclusive use* of its products. Large supermarkets and multiple retailers have generally not taken up this offer but many small outlets have done so. In countries where it has some distribution strength, Nestlé has followed the same policy where possible. It has even done this where it was clearly in a weaker marketing position than Unilever.

Mars ice cream distribution strategy

Mars has faced an uphill struggle to gain distribution. Essentially, the company has been denied access to Unilever, Nestlé and Schoeller freezer cabinets in many European markets. Mars formally lodged protests against these practices with the governments of the UK and Ireland and with the European Commission in the case of Germany. Mars argued that freezer exclusivity was anti-competitive and against Articles 85 and 86 of the Treaty of Rome. Its rivals have defended their practices. Essentially, they have said that

it would be a very odd interpretation of the Act to regard as restrictive of competition a refusal on the part of those who had invested in freezers to give a free ride to those who had not . . . The cabinet was a selling tool. It did not dictate winners and losers; success derived from service, brand, quality range and price.

All retailers had the option to install their own freezers.

Mars has been forced to operate schemes either to make loans or sell freezers, depending on the outlet. It has also attempted to negotiate distribution agreements with companies that were in second or third position in various national markets across Europe. In the UK, it had a deal with Lyons Maid before that company was taken over by Nestlé in 1993. In France, it negotiated an arrangement with Ortiz-Miko before it was bought by Unilever in 1994.

From the viewpoint of a retail customer, Mars' strategy is not always attractive because it does not sell dessert ice creams, bulk packs or children's novelty ice creams, for which there is also demand. The retailer thus has to seek alternative suppliers of these items and Mars has to allow them into its cabinets in order that a complete range is stocked.

Overall, it is not surprising that the Mars company said that it had made no profit on its ice cream activities up to the late 1990s. It was unclear whether its chosen strategies would overcome this difficulty in the coming years.

Case questions

1 *How would you summarise the strategies adopted by Mars to launch its ice cream products?*

2 *Do you think that Mars will ever make significant profits from its ice cream operations? Why? How?*

4.7 Analysing the role of government

At government policy level, politics and economics are inextricably linked. Corporate strategy is not concerned with forming such policies but does need to understand the implications of the decisions taken. Governments can stimulate national economies, encourage new research projects, impose new taxes and introduce many other initiatives that affect the organisation and its ability to develop corporate strategy. To analyse these influences, it is useful to identify three areas: the environment of the nation, its system of government and its policies. All these are summarised in the E–S–P paradigm – *see* Figure 4.5.

Figure 4.5 E–S–P paradigm: analysing the role of government

Components
- Human resources
- Natural resources
- Stage of economic development
- Culture and history

Environment (E): background characteristics of a country

Outcomes
- Level and structure of output: agriculture, industry, service
- Attitudes to wealth, work, etc

- Capitalist: laissez-faire
- Socialist: dirigiste
- Mixed

System (S): the country's system of government

- Structure of decision taking
- Role of free markets in allocating resources
- Desire for international commerce
- Nationalisation policy

- Macroeconomic
- Microeconomic
- Education, health, social
- FDI and competition

Policies (P): the main government policies

- Extent and type of government intervention
- Controls exerted
- Performance expected from industry

Source: Adapted from Koopman, K and Montias, J M (1971) 'On the description and comparison of economic systems', in Eckstein, A. (ed) *Comparison of Economic Systems*, University of California Press, Berkeley, CA. Copyright © The Regents of the University of California.

4.7.1 History and momentum in politics – the environment of the nation

Over the last four centuries, politics has been a great driver for industrial growth.[29] Much of this growth has come through a combination of wars, the search for power and the exploitation of resources. Corporate strategy will need to take into account the opportunities and the moral dilemmas that may arise. For example, the problems in China in the early 1990s did not stop major Western companies investing in that country in the years that followed; indeed, some may argue that such wealth creation is a contribution to overcoming the difficulties.

Any corporate strategy that does not take account of the history and momentum of politics is ignoring an essential element of the competitive environment. Looking back from the vantage point of the early twenty-first century, five political trends can be highlighted that are relevant to corporate strategy (*see* Exhibit 4.3).

Exhibit 4.3 Five political trends that have affected corporate strategy

1 *The decline of the centrally directed command economies of Eastern Europe and the move towards democracy and freer markets.* Even the great nation of China is now moving towards a larger element of laissez-faire, market-driven efficiency. This has provided major strategic opportunities for many companies, including those in China itself.

2 *The absence of world wars and the end of the Cold War.* This absence of global conflict has started to shift the balance away from defence industries and towards civilian activities – a development counterbalanced by the concentration of military forces and strongly held religious beliefs in the Middle East.

Exhibit 4.3 continued

3 *The relative weakness of African and South/Central American economies.* This has resulted from their struggle with high inflation, weak currencies, low value-added industries and political instability. The recent changes in countries such as South Africa and Argentina hold out hope for stronger corporate strategic development opportunities in the future.

4 *The rise of international trade, global companies and new trading nations,* such as the 'Tiger' economies of South-East Asia.

5 *The emergence of supportive international finance and economic institutions,* such as the International Monetary Fund (IMF), the World Bank and European Bank for Reconstruction and Development (EBRD). Their research, guidance and influence have had a positive effect on international development.

4.7.2 The role of the state in industrial development – the system of government

In both the EU and the US, there are differing views on the extent to which the state should become involved in industrial development. In France, Italy and Greece, it has long been the tradition that state-owned companies and state intervention are important elements of the national economy. In the UK, Germany and the US, the opposing view has been taken. The approach adopted is essentially a *political* choice made by those in power. The two approaches – often referred to as *laissez-faire* and *dirigiste* – are summarised in Table 4.3. Adam Smith, Karl Marx and many other political commentators have all contributed to the important political debate in this area. Table 4.3 is intended merely to summarise areas that are the most relevant to the development of corporate strategy.

In practice, the distinctions drawn in Table 4.3 are very crude. Some countries offer a *balance* between strong infrastructural support in some areas – for example, education, favoured industries (as in Singapore), investment in roads, power and water – and then couple this with a free-market approach in other areas – for example, privatisation of state monopolies or lower barriers to entry to encourage multinational enterprise (MNE) investment. (MNEs are the large global companies such as Ford, McDonald's and

Table 4.3 Government and industrial policy

Laissez faire: free-market approach	Dirigiste: centrally directed approach
• Low entry barriers	• High entry barriers
• Competition encouraged	• National companies supported against international competition
• Little or no state support for industry	• State ownership of some key industries
• Self-interest leads to wealth creation	• Profit motive benefits the few at the expense of the many
• Belief in laws of supply and demand	• Failure in market mechanism will particularly affect the poor and can only be corrected by state intervention
• High unemployment levels	• Need to correct monopolies controlled by private companies
• Profit motive will provide basis for efficient production and high quality	

Unilever.) Each country will have its own approach so that any corporate environmental analysis will have to be conducted on a country-by-country basis.

At the beginning of the twenty-first century, it might be argued that state intervention is dead: the industrial chaos resulting from the collapse of communism in Eastern Europe certainly highlights the problems. The evidence from Eastern Europe only applies to the totalitarian state, however: it does not follow that all state intervention is useless. State involvement in the 'Tiger' economies of South-East Asia (Singapore, Malaysia, Hong Kong, Thailand, Korea) and selective intervention in Japan, the EU and the US suggest that some governmental policy can be beneficial.[30]

Corporate strategy should therefore anticipate that politics will continue to be a part of the equation. Companies may benefit from policies such as higher state subsidies, better education and international trade incentives, but may be hindered by measures such as new laws restricting competition, new taxes on profits, and limited investment in country infrastructure (e.g. roads, telecommunications).

Hence, corporate strategy needs to be acutely aware of the benefits and problems associated with government policies. It will certainly wish to press for policies that it regards as beneficial during the formation and implementation of strategic decisions. Influencing major political decisions is part of corporate strategy. As long as this is done openly and with integrity, there can be no objection by those with other interests. This means that lobbying of governments by companies, often using professional public relations advisers, is a legitimate part of corporate strategy.

4.7.3 Broader government policy and state institutions – policies of government

In addition to direct state intervention in industry, governments influence companies by a whole variety of other mechanisms:

- *Public expenditure.* In the EU, through the European Commission in Brussels, public expenditure is quite low as a percentage of GDP when compared with the expenditure concentrated at national government level. In the US, public expenditure is higher at federal (central) level in some areas, e.g. defence.

- *Competition policy.* This is strong at EU central level and likely to become stronger; similarly strong in the US at federal level.

- *Taxation policy.* This is weak at EU central level, with taxes largely left to individual nations; in the US, there are clear federal taxes, with further taxes raised at state level.

- *Regional policy.* There is clear EU support for weaker nations and parts of nations with infrastructure investment etc.; in the US, individual states are more likely to fulfil this role but federal support is still important in some industries.

All the above policies can have a major influence on where companies locate and whether they are profitable; in practice, organisations often make considerable efforts to obtain government grants and other forms of support as part of their corporate strategy.

At the international and global level, countries around the world have joined together in essentially politically inspired international institutions, trade agreements and trading blocks (*see* Chapter 19).

4.7.4 Strategic analysis of the national economy

Governments have some direct control over the economy of a country. It is easier for organisations to launch a growth or survival strategy when the national or international economy is showing steady growth with low inflation. Conversely, if economic decline is likely, the company might be well advised to take a more prudent view of strategic expansion. It follows that the *macroeconomic conditions* – that is, economic activity at the general level of the national or international economy – surrounding an organisation are an important element in the development of corporate strategy.

In practice, when exploring corporate strategy, many organisations, both large and small, use their own managers to make economic forecasts, buy in reputable forecasts or simply use published forecast material. The forecasts are usually made on key macroeconomic issues such as:

● gross domestic product (GDP), total and per head of the population;

● growth in GDP;

● retail and consumer price indices;

● trade flows in imports, exports and the balance of payments;

● private sector share of GDP; agricultural share of GDP;

● foreign direct investment (FDI), total and as a percentage of total investment.

Key strategic principles

● Politics has been an important driver of industrial growth. Corporate strategy needs to consider the opportunities and difficulties that derive from such policies.

● Government policies can have a general impact on corporate strategy: some countries have adopted a *laissez-faire*, free-market approach, while others have followed a *dirigiste*, more centrally directed approach to industrial development. Corporate strategy needs to be acutely aware of the benefits and problems of these areas.

● Other areas of government interest, such as public expenditure, competition policy and taxation issues, also need to be analysed. Influencing political decisions in these areas is an important part of corporate strategy.

● Macroeconomic conditions – that is, economic activity at the general level of the national economy – can have a significant impact on corporate strategy, which needs to be explored and assessed.

CASE STUDY 4.4

The call of Africa grows louder[31]

By 2001, mobile telephones outnumbered fixed lines in the continent and presented a major new strategic opportunity.

When Mohamed Ibrahim, the Sudanese chairman of MSI Cellular, first contemplated setting up a mobile telephone company focused on Africa, he was at least partly driven by a desire to give something back to the land that had nurtured him. But his other reason was far less sentimental: he was, and remains, convinced that the world's most marginalised continent offers one of the best opportunities around. Over three years, Dr Ibrahim has backed that belief with a frenzy of activity. When it launched in 1998, MSI Cellular had only one network: Uganda's Celtel. By 2001, it had operations in

11 countries, with another three in preparation, ranging from Egypt to the Democratic Republic of the Congo and (astonishingly, the most profitable) Sierra Leone. From 41 000 GSM customers at the start of 2000, it had 400 000 by mid-2001, as well as 150 000 fixed lines. It is the largest operator in two-thirds of its markets. Such bold growth in a poor, insecure and disease-fraught continent, where political connections often outweigh technical merit and currencies are soft, may raise eyebrows among sceptics. But Dr Ibrahim is convinced that the risks are overstated and the rewards underplayed. His instincts have served him well in the past.

Unlike in the developed world, mobile networks in Africa are often the only means of electronic communication and demand is immense. In 2000, the African market grew by 50 per cent, with penetration reaching 10 per cent in some richer countries such as Gabon. While economies are smaller, the percentage spent on communication is higher: it is estimated that African companies spend 5–15 per cent of their budgets on telecomms compared with 1 per cent in Europe.

MSI's turnover in 2000 was US$58 million and it predicted revenues of US$20 million per month by the end of 2001 – bolstered by Africa's high usage rates ($25–50 a customer per month) and the expansion of pre-paid services (now 90 per cent of business – an important development where revenue collection is difficult). Some analysts are wary of the capital-intensive nature of the business. 'Fourteen children are all feeding to make them grow,' says one consultant: a particular concern in the current telecomms climate. But Dr Ibrahim is unfazed: 'There is money willing to go to Africa,' he asserts, as long as it is backed by credible people. 'African telecomms is no place for opportunists or amateurs. To survive requires a very experienced management team, a successful record and the ability to attract finance.'

Dr Ibrahim boasts that his networks reach operational profit within six months and real profitability within two years. Return on capital is in excess of 30 per cent per annum. 'By any yardstick, these projects are more rewarding than in Europe.' But the next few years could pose some interesting challenges. Although some attractive licences are coming up, analysts say that the initial land-grab phase is coming to an end and a new phase approaches of trying to deepen markets. At the moment, often only the most populated two or three cities of each country are targeted – whether the sector can grow at the same pace further afield remains to be seen. MSI said that it is also looking into value-added services, and is running a wireless Internet pilot in Congo-Brazzaville. The hope is that services like commodity prices, banking and healthcare may prove attractive, thus making the mobile service intrinsically more attractive. At a difficult time for telecomms worldwide, MSI's experience in Africa is highly encouraging. 'We have all suffered from sentiment about telecomms,' says Dr Ibrahim. 'But it can be positive in another way – forcing people for the first time to look at the business case for Africa.'

© Copyright *Financial Times* 2001. Reproduced with permission.

Case questions

1 *How important is the well-placed political contact in gaining telecomms licences? What does this imply for corporate strategy?*

2 *Should MSI Cellular take a prescriptive or emergent approach to strategy? And what reaction should it have to other competitors in Africa?*

4.8 Analysing international competitors

There is significant evidence that growth in world sales has considerably outstripped growth in manufacturing output over the last 20 years – *see* Chapter 19 for details. If this is the case, then it follows that international competition has increased. The key issue is whether international competitors pose similar or increased threats to those from the home country. There is good evidence that they present additional problems in at least three areas:

1 *International ambitions* to deliver world sales volume will certainly pose an additional threat to domestic manufacturers. Global objectives of some companies have been

well documented since the early 1980s.[32] Companies like Caterpillar (US) and Komatsu (Japan) in construction equipment, Ericsson (Sweden) in telecommunications equipment, Honda (Japan) in cars and motorcycles are all examples of companies who have taken share from domestic manufacturers.

2 *Lower costs* arise for a number of reasons. These include economies of scale from operating on a larger, international market and lower labour costs through sourcing some products in countries with this benefit.

3 *Global strategies* have been deliberately pursued in some industries to integrate worldwide strategy. Essentially, strategy is centralised for the whole world, with an integrated network of production and market positions in all the leading countries on a broadly similar platform. Not all industries are global, but those that hold this position present additional competition to domestic competitors.[33]

International expansion and globalisation are explored in more depth in Chapter 19. As barriers to trade continue to be reduced, competition will increase. Because of the uncertainties surrounding the nature and pace of such change, emergent/experimental approaches to strategy development may prove particularly effective.

▶ Key strategic principles

- International competition is increasing as a result of growth in international trade over the last 20 years: this means that corporate strategy needs to consider the opportunities and threats created by such a shift in strategic context.

- There are three special areas that require strategic analysis: the company's international vision and objectives, its lower cost opportunities and its global strategy ambitions.

KEY READING

What makes a good competitor?[35]

In this extract from his book, Competitive Advantage, *Professor Michael Porter asks: 'What makes a good competitor?' His comments need to be understood in the context of his view that some competitor strategies can reduce the profits for all companies in an industry. His aim is to maximise the profits for those currently in the industry. Potential new entrants to the industry might choose exactly the opposite strategies to those outlined below.*

Competitors are not all equally attractive or unattractive. A good competitor is one that can perform some beneficial functions without representing too severe a long-term threat. A good competitor is one that challenges the firm not to be complacent but is a competitor with which the firm can achieve a stable and profitable industry equilibrium without protracted warfare. Bad competitors, by and large, have the opposite characteristics.

No competitor ever meets all the tests of a good competitor. Competitors usually have some characteristics of a good competitor and some characteristics of a bad competitor. Some managers, as a result, will assert that there is no such thing as a good competitor. This view ignores the essential point that some competitors are a lot better than others, and can have very different effects on a firm's competitive position. In practice, a firm must understand where each of its competitors falls on the spectrum from good to bad and behave accordingly.

Tests of a good competitor

A good competitor has a number of characteristics. Since its goals, strategy and capabilities are not static, however, the assessment of whether a competitor is good or bad can change.

Credible and viable. A good competitor has sufficient resources and capabilities to be a motivator to the firm to lower cost or improve differentiation, as well as credible with and acceptable to buyers.

Clear, self-perceived weaknesses. Though credible and viable, a good competitor has clear weaknesses relative to a firm, which are recognised. Ideally, the good competitor believes that its weaknesses will be difficult to change. The competitor need not be weaker everywhere but has some clear weaknesses that will lead it to conclude that it is futile to attempt to gain relative position against a firm in the segments the firm is interested in.

Understands the rules. A good competitor understands and plays by the rules of competition in an industry, and can recognise and read market signals. It aids in market development and promotes the existing technology rather than attempting strategies that involve technological or competitive discontinuities in order to gain position.

Realistic assumptions. A good competitor has realistic assumptions about the industry and its own relative position. It does not overestimate industry growth potential and therefore overbuild capacity, or underinvest in capacity and in so doing provide an opening for newcomers. A good company also does not overrate its capabilities to the point of triggering a battle by attempting to gain share, or shy from retaliating against entrants because it underestimates its strengths.

Knowledge of costs. It knows what its costs are, and sets its prices accordingly. It does not unwittingly cross-subsidise product lines or underestimate overhead.

Moderate exit barriers. A good competitor has exit barriers that are significant enough to make its presence in the industry a viable deterrent to new entrants, but yet not so high as to completely lock it into the industry. High exit barriers create the risk that the competitor will disrupt the industry rather than exit if it encounters strategic difficulty.

Has moderate stakes in the industry. It does not attach high stakes to achieving dominance or unusually high growth in the industry. It views the industry as one where continued participation is desirable and where acceptable profits can be earned, but not one where improving relative position has great strategic or emotional importance.

Has a comparable return-on-investment target. It is less likely to undercut prices or make heavy investments to attack a firm's position.

Has a short time horizon. It does not have so long a time horizon that it will fight a protracted battle to attack a firm's position.

Summary

● *Sustainable competitive advantage* has been placed at the centre of the development of corporate strategy. The real benefits of developing this area derive from those aspects of the organisation that cannot easily be imitated and can be sustained over time. Such advantages can take many forms: differentiation, low costs, niche marketing, high performance or technology, quality, service, vertical integration, synergy and the culture, leadership and style of the organisation.

● For some strategists, competitive advantage may also be *dynamic*. In this sense, it may be seen as constantly evolving and companies should set out to make this happen, particularly in industries that involve advanced technology. In this sense, competitive advantage is continuous and changing rather than static.

● The process for developing such dynamic competitive advantage is both built around existing strengths – structured – and also exploits new and exciting areas – chaotic. The main rule for such a process is to strike a balance between structure and chaos.

● In exploring the intensity of competition in an industry, it is useful to begin by exploring the *degree of concentration* in a market – ranging between the two extremes of perfect competition and pure monopoly. The concentration ratio itself can also be calculated – that is, the percentage of an industry turnover or value added controlled by the largest four, five or eight firms.

● Military language and concepts are often used to describe the *aggressive strategies* of competitors. The four main attack strategies are: head-on, flanking, totally new territory and guerrilla. In addition, *innovatory strategies* may be employed, especially those that rewrite the rules of the game in a market.

● *Product portfolio analysis* plots products or product groups in relation to market characteristics. The *BCG matrix* relates market growth to relative market share for the organisation's main group of products. It identifies four major categories of products: stars, cash cows, dogs and problem children. It permits some consideration of their contribution to the organisation and a comparison with competition. An alternative matrix, the *directional policy matrix,* plots industry attractiveness against industry competitive position. It attempts to overcome some of the weaknesses of the BCG matrix.

● Another area of investigation is that concerning *distributors* – that is, those companies that purchase the product and then resell it to small end-consumers. In some markets, distributors are a vital part of the chain of sale and need to be analysed in detail. Service levels, quality, pricing and discounts and the support from the distributor are subjects for investigation.

● *The role of government* can be seen through its involvement in both political and economic issues. Politics has been an important driver of industrial growth. Corporate strategy needs to consider the opportunities and difficulties that derive from such government influences. Government policies can be broadly classified as *laissez-faire*, free-market, or *dirigiste*, more centrally directed. More specifically, policies on such matters as public expenditure, competition and taxation will all influence organisations and their corporate strategies. Organisations may wish to develop links and influence government policy on relevant aspects of corporate strategy.

● Government policies also influence national economic growth and may affect the market growth of particular sectors. Both these areas need careful study when developing strategy.

● *International competition* has increased over the last 20 years. This has taken many forms but three areas can be usefully highlighted: ambition of some companies for global expansion, low costs through careful sourcing of production, and global strategies to integrate worldwide strategy.

QUESTIONS

1 Consider the two case studies on web-based fashion (4.2) and mobile telephones (4.4) and identify where and how sustainable competitive advantages might be developed in each case.

2 Use the three tests for sustainable competitive advantage (SCA) in Exhibit 4.1 to analyse Mars Ice Cream and other products in the range. What are your conclusions for the Mars company?

3 Take an industry with which you are familiar and estimate its degree of concentration. For example, you might pick the university and college of higher education market in a particular country. What strategic conclusions would you wish to draw from your analysis?

4 Analyse the aggressive strategies undertaken by competitors against Unilever in the European ice cream market. How would you classify their attack strategies?

5 Can you think of any examples of innovatory aggressive strategies? If you are having trouble, then you might like to skim through some of the cases in this book to find those that fit this role. Give reasons for your selection.

6 *Military principles and strategies are not the whole answer to competitive strategy, but they do provide insight into what it takes for a company to succeed in attacking another company or in defending itself against an aggressor.* (Philip Kotler and Ravi Singh)

To what extent do you agree with this statement?

7 Choose an industry familiar to you and identify how it might use the concept of dynamic competitive advantage to develop its strategy. What are the benefits and risks of such an approach?

8 Using the procedures outlined in this chapter, prepare a competitive analysis of the European telecommunications industry over the next five years from the viewpoint of British Telecom. *Or,* if you prefer, take the South-East Asian market or the North American market and prepare the same review from the viewpoint of Singapore Telecom or AT&T respectively. *Or,* if you prefer, you can use your own national telecommunications operator and consider the issues as global competition increases.

9 Bruce Henderson, founder of the Boston Consulting Group, commented:

> *Induce your competitors not to invest in those products, markets and services where you expect to invest most … that is the fundamental rule of strategy.*

Briefly explain this statement and comment on its usefulness.

10 What general conclusions can you draw from the Mars Ice Cream case about the nature and importance of distributor strategy? What lessons does it imply for other companies, if any?

STRATEGIC PROJECT Branded ice cream markets

This chapter has explored the European ice cream market. Take this further by examining the progress Ben & Jerry's ice cream has made into Europe (now acquired by Unilever) and the more recent results of Mars Ice Cream. Several companies in this survey are developing *global* ice cream businesses: find out which ones and assess the likelihood of their success.

FURTHER READING

Professor Porter's two books are the classic texts in this area – *Competitive Strategy* (1980) and *Competitive Advantage* (1985) – both published by The Free Press, New York. They are strongly recommended. In addition, the book by Professor David Aaker, *Strategic Market Management* (Wiley, 1992) has a well-argued exploration of the development of sustainable competitive advantage that merits careful reading.

NOTES & REFERENCES

1 The study of the European ice cream market in this chapter is based on data from published sources. These include: UK Monopolies and Mergers Commission (1994) *Report on the supply in the UK of ice cream for immediate consumption*, Mar, HMSO, London Cmd 2524; *Financial Times*, 19 May 1993, p24; 17 Mar 1994 and 13 Jun 1995, p18; *Dairy Industry International*, May 1994, p33; Aug 1994, p17 and Sep 1994, p19; *Food Manufacture*, June 1994, p24 and July 1994, p28; *Sunday Times*, 7 June 1992, pp1–8.

2 Porter, M E (1980) *Competitive Strategy*, The Free Press, New York.

3 Porter, M E (1985) *Competitive Advantage*, The Free Press, New York.

4 Quoted in Aaker, D (1992) *Strategic Marketing Management*, 3rd edn, Wiley, New York, p182.

5 High technology and services columns developed from Aaker, D (1992) Ibid, p186; others from author.

6 For those obsessed with the generic strategies outlined in Professor Porter's two books, it should be noted that no mention has been made of a company being the lowest cost producer. This book will argue that sustainable advantage may be achieved by having both low costs and other qualities that take the company beyond being merely the lowest cost producer.

7 Kay, J (1993) *Foundations of Corporate Success*, Oxford University Press, Oxford, p367.

8 *See*, for example, Brown, S L and Eisenhardt, K M (1998) *Competing on the Edge*, Harvard Business School Press, Boston, MA and Hamel, G and Prahalad, C K (1994) *Competing For the Future*, Harvard Business School Press, Boston, MA.

9 Case references for Boo.com case: *Economist*, 17 March 2001, p85; *Financial Times*, 19 May 2000, p26 and website of Arthur Andersen. Also the fascinating book by Ernst Malmsten with Erik Portanger and Charles Drazin – *Boo Hoo*, Random House, New York, 2001.

10 This section is based on the work of Professors Porter and Kotler (*see* refs 12 and 13) and on a lecture given by Professor Ken Simmons at the London Business School in 1988.

11 For example, *see* Ries, A and Trout, J (1986) *Marketing Warfare*, McGraw-Hill, New York.

12 Kotler, P (1994) *Marketing Management: Analysis, Planning, Implementation and Control*, 8th edn, Prentice Hall, New York.

13 Kotler, P and Singh, R (1981) 'Marketing warfare in the 1980s', *Journal of Business Strategy*, Winter, pp30–41.

14 Liddell-Hart, B H (1967) *Strategy*, Praeger, New York.

15 Kay, J (1993) Op. cit., pp236–8 provides an interesting discussion of the circumstances under which such an understanding can emerge without contravening monopoly legislation.

16 Lynch, R (1994) *European Business Strategies*, Second Edition, Kogan Page, pp119–21 supplies some evidence here.

17 Kay, J (1994) Op. cit., p364.

18 Buzzell, R D and Gale, B T (1987) *The PIMS Principles*, The Free Press, New York.

19 Aaker, D (1992) Op. cit., pp160–61.

20 Jacobsen, R and Aaker, D (1985) 'Is market share all that it's cracked up to be?', *Journal of Marketing*, Fall, pp11–22. A vigorous debate still continues in the academic press on the benefits of portfolio analysis. For example, a research paper from Armstong and Brodie in the *International Journal in Research in Marketing* (11(1), Jan 1994, pp73 *et seq.*) criticising such matrices produced a strong defence from Professor Robin Wensley in the same journal and a further reply from the two authors.

21 Aaker, D, (1992) Op. cit., p176.

22 *See* McKiernan, P (1992) *Strategies for Growth*, Routledge, London. Ch 1 has an excellent discussion of some of the problems that can arise.

23 Covered in many marketing strategy texts. For example, Kotler P, Armstrong G, Saunders J and Wong V, (1999), *Principles of Marketing*, 2nd European edn, Prentice Hall Europe, pp98–99.

24 Hussey, D E (1978) 'Portfolio analysis: Practical experience with the directional policy matrix', *Long Range Planning*, Aug, pp78–89.

25 Aaker, D (1992) Op. cit., p167 et seq.

26 Day, G S (1977) 'Diagnosing the product portfolio', *Journal of Marketing*, April, pp29–38.

27 Green, D (1995) 'Takeover fever', *Financial Times*, 22 Aug, p12.

28 Lynch, R (1994) Op. cit., Ch22.

29 Kennedy, P (1990) *The Rise and Fall of the Great Powers*, Fontana Press, London, pxvii.

30 World Bank (1994) *World Development Report 1994*, Oxford University Press, New York. Chapter 2 certainly supported selective state support and policies.

31 Case adapted by Richard Lynch from an article by Mark Turner in the *Financial Times*, 21 August 2001, p12. © Financial Times 2001. Article reproduced with permission.

32 Hout, T, Porter, M E and Rudden, E (1982) 'How global companies win out', *Harvard Business Review*, Sep–Oct, p98.

33 Porter, M E (ed) (1986) *Competition in Global Industries*, Harvard Business School Press, MA, Chs3 and 4.

34 Extracted from Porter, M E (1985) Op. cit.

Analysing customers

When you have worked through this chapter, you will be able to:

- outline the main elements of customer-driven strategy and explain its importance;
- identify the relationship between customer profiling and sustainable competitive advantage;
- analyse the strategy implications of market segments;
- position the product or service against competitors;
- explain the strategy implications of branding and reputation;
- outline customer communication and its strategic implications;
- explain the main elements of pricing strategy;
- identify the main international issues in customer strategy.

Figure 5.1　　**Analysing customer strategy: the main elements**

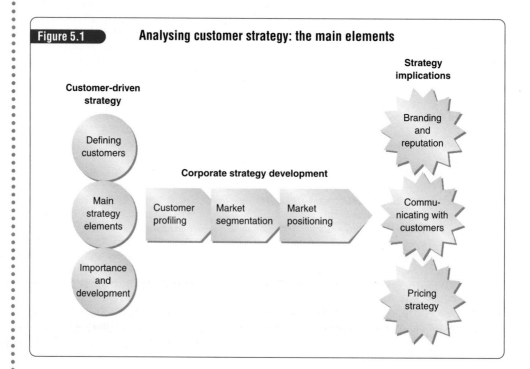

▬ Introduction

Customers are a vital part of corporate strategy development. Ultimately, customers provide either the revenue to generate the wealth of the organisation or the reason for the existence of a public service or charity. Moreover, part of the corporate strategy process will be to persuade customers of the competitive advantages of choosing the organisation's products or services rather than those offered by a rival. For these two reasons, strategy analysis needs to explore its customers with the aim of developing customer-driven strategies.

This chapter considers the process of analysing customers as a part of strategy development. It begins by exploring why strategy should be driven by customers. Customer profiling is then explored in greater depth than the outline in Chapter 3. Market segmentation and competitive positioning are then analysed. The implications for the organisation in several key strategy areas are then investigated: branding and reputation, customer communications and pricing. Finally, the globalisation of markets from a customer perspective is examined. The main process of customer analysis is outlined in Figure 5.1.

CASE STUDY 5.1

Will Dyson remain successful?

By careful customer targeting, James Dyson was highly successful with a new domestic vacuum cleaner in the 1990s. However, his patents were due to expire in 2002. Around the same time, he was launching a new double-drum washing machine with the same customer strategy. Would the company be able to maintain its success?

Following his remarkable success worldwide with the revolutionary Dual Cyclone vacuum cleaner in the 1990s, James Dyson launched his company's Contrarotator washing machine in November 2000. The business strategy for the new machine was similar to that of his vacuum cleaner: high performance, premium-priced and aimed at the top market segment. However, it was unclear whether this strategy would be equally successful. In addition, the floor cleaner faced a new and major competitive threat from existing manufacturers in 2002 as a result of the expiry of patents on the bagless machine.

It would take a strong strategy and considerable determination for Dyson to hold its hard-won success. This case describes the company, its strategy in the European vacuum cleaner market and then its new strategy in the European washing machine market. In the face of these new competitive pressures, it raises the question of whether Dyson will enjoy continued success over the next ten years.

James Dyson and his company

Dyson's background

James Dyson is the founding owner and chief executive of Dyson Appliances Limited – a company based in the Wiltshire countryside in the West of England – with annual sales exceeding £200 million in 1999. It is his leadership, design skills, persistence and imagination that have enabled his company to win against some of the world's leading domestic appliance manufacturers.

In 1978, James Dyson accidentally had the idea of a bagless vacuum floor cleaner while renovating his country home in the West of England. Over the period 1979–84, he made over 5000 prototypes before developing what he called his Dual Cyclone vacuum cleaner, for which he applied for a trade mark and many special patents.

Dyson's new vacuum cleaner

During the years 1982–84, James Dyson visited many of the existing leading manufacturers of

▶

vacuum cleaners and attempted to interest them in licensing his new invention. But he was unsuccessful with the existing manufacturers. A unique feature of his invention was that his new machine did not need to have disposable bags. All existing machines used paper bags that were attached to the machine to collect the waste and were then thrown away when full. Existing machine manufacturers made substantial sales and profits on these disposable bags – over £100 million in the UK alone, according to Dyson – and were therefore reluctant to lose these sales opportunities, even though such a change might be cheaper for their customers.

Dyson's reaction to rejection by the leading manufacturers – launch his own product

James Dyson produced his first prototype vacuum floor cleaner in 1983. Unable to interest any European manufacturer, Dyson went to Japan and found an importer of Western goods that was interested in selling the product. By 1991, it had become so well established that Dyson was able to claim that it had become a status symbol amongst Japanese households.

Encouraged by its Japanese success, James Dyson then decided that he would launch his own company to make the product. He set up his own factory in the West of England and launched his first model, the DC01, in May 1993. By 1995, the machine had become the best-selling vacuum cleaner in the UK. A new improved model, the DC02, was launched in 1995 and production moved to a new, larger factory in the same area to cope with increased demand. During the same year, the company began its overseas expansion, with its own sales and service subsidiaries in Australia and France. In subsequent years, offices were set up in many other European and Asia-Pacific countries to support sales expansion, including Japan itself in 1998. In 2001, fearing that his labour costs were too high, Dyson announced that the manufacture was being transferred to Malaysia, where the cost of labour was lower. However, the design facility, which employed some 800 people, would remain in the UK.

Importantly, the new machines had two other features beyond the innovative new technology. First, Dyson used his art design skills to develop machines that were different in colour combined with the use of plastic materials. His machines were to win design awards across Europe during the

1990s and be lodged in museums as examples of attractive, modern design. Second, Dyson charged a premium price for his product. For example in the UK, premium-performance vacuum cleaners were priced at the time of the Dyson launch at up to £150 each. Cheaper machines were priced at between £50 and £100. Dyson priced the DC01 at £200 and did not hesitate to price higher as he added more features with later models.

By 2000, the annual sales for Dyson products were around U$480 million, including those produced under licence by other manufacturers.

European vacuum cleaner markets – fiercely competitive

Market size, growth and share

The total European market for vacuum cleaners was worth around US$3.8 billion in 1999 and was growing at around 2–3 per cent per annum. Market trends reflect the fact that most vacuum cleaners were bought to satisfy replacement customer demand.

By 1999, Dyson claimed to be market leader in the UK with a share by value of 52 per cent and by volume of 33 per cent. The company also claimed to be market leader across continental Europe with a market share of around 20 per cent by value, reflecting in part at least its later launch into such countries. For example, it was only in January 1998 that the company set up a sales and service office in Germany.

Competition across the EU was fierce. The main competitors were Electrolux (headquartered in Sweden but with manufacturing across the EU) with around 20 per cent of the EU market by value, Hoover (owned by the Italian company Candy) with around 15 per cent of the EU market, and Miele (Germany) with around 7 per cent of the EU market.

Competition – patent protection for Dyson

Although James Dyson had originally attempted to license his product through one of the existing manufacturers, they had rejected his approaches. They were later to regret that decision, given the threat that they faced from the new Dual Cyclone. Once Dyson had become established, its patents provided significant protection against competitors during the 1990s.

After seeing the value of the patents, Hoover attempted to circumvent them with the development, prototyping and launch in year 2000 of its own new machine called the Hoover Triple Vortex. After its launch, Dyson accused Hoover of infringing its patents and brought an action in the UK High Court. Dyson won the action in late 2000, with Hoover being told to withdraw its machine at least until the Dyson patent had expired in June 2001. Electrolux was also considering launching its own bagless product in 2002 once the Dyson patents expired.

European automatic washing machine markets – again fiercely competitive

Market size, growth and share
The total European market for washing machines was worth around US$5.3 billion in 1999 and was growing at around 2–3 per cent each year. Like vacuum cleaners, washing machines were mainly bought to satisfy replacement demand.

Up to November 2000, Dyson was not involved in this market. Competition across the EU was fierce. Electrolux was the market leader in many European markets, with Merloni in second place. The UK market leader was a company called GDA. This was a joint venture with US and UK parents, trading under the well-known brand names Hotpoint and Creda. The company held around 35 per cent of the UK market by both volume and value. It also made own-branded products for some electrical retailers, giving it another 4 per cent share of the market. The position of GDA was much weaker in other European countries.

Dyson launch of its new Contrarotator washing machine in November 2000
It was into this market that Dyson was stepping with its new automatic washing machine. There were three distinct segments in the European automatic washing machine market:

- *Budget-priced segment* – perhaps 35 per cent of the total market by volume and 30 per cent by value.

- *Mid-priced segment* – perhaps 55 per cent of the market by volume and the same by value.

- *Upper-priced segment* – perhaps 10 per cent of the market by volume and 15 per cent by value. It was into this latter segment that the new Dyson machine was launched in November 2000.

Dyson's Contrarotator washing machine was different in that it had two drums as compared

with all other machines, which had one drum. The two drums were constructed one inside the other and rotated in opposite directions to produce a turbulent washing action: Dyson claimed that this was much more like the more efficient hand-washing action that washing machines had replaced. Like his vacuum cleaners, the new Dyson machine was manufactured in strong primary colours and was premium-priced. For example, a typical UK price for the new Dyson machine was around £950 compared with £250–500 for conventional competitors. Clearly, this major launch would stretch the resources of Dyson Appliances to the limit.

Customers of vacuum cleaners and other domestic appliances
Around 85 per cent of EU homes had vacuum cleaners, refrigerators and washing machines. Level of ownership was higher in countries with higher per capita income and a little lower in other countries. Penetration was also lower for other appliances, such as dishwashers, microwave ovens and drying machines. With such a high level of penetration, sales were high across most income groups, with perhaps some skewing in favour of those with highest incomes. For example, vacuum cleaners were owned by over 70 per cent of households, even amongst the lower income groups. Thus sales were prompted mainly by replacement demand and, until the Dyson machine, there was little differentiation beyond branding and the need to gain and hold distribution.

Retail distribution of domestic appliances
This was highly concentrated in most EU countries, with a few leading retail shop chains accounting for most sales.

Case questions

1 *What was the Dyson strategy? What were the main reasons for his success?*

2 *Will he continue to be successful? What changes, if any, does he need to make in his strategy?*

3 *Can other entrepreneurs learn from Dyson? If so, what lessons can be drawn from his example?*

5.1 Customers and customer-driven strategy – the contribution of Theodore Levitt[1]

Customers buy the organisation's products or receive its services and in this way realise the value that the company has added to its activities. Customers are thus vital to corporate strategy development. Indeed, the well-known marketing writer and former Marketing Professor at the Harvard Business School, Theodore Levitt, is on record as saying that: 'The purpose of an enterprise is to create and keep a customer.'

If this is correct, then the prime focus of strategy becomes the development and retention of customers: the *customer-driven* strategy. Levitt wrote clearly and with vision on the topic in the early 1960s and was instrumental in raising the profile of customers in the development of corporate strategy. He would have been delighted by the fact that Dyson chose to deliver a bagless cleaner that provided a new customer benefit.

Nevertheless, Levitt accepted that, as long as customers have a choice, the development of corporate strategy will also need to consider the customer options available from competitors. Customer strategy therefore needs to be linked to competitor strategy. This is crystallised through the sustainable competitive advantages possessed by an organisation. Such advantages will attract customers and keep them, rather than allow them to move to competitors – the customer-driven strategy is designed to build such loyalty and customer satisfaction.[2]

5.1.1 Defining customers and competitors

The first task is to identify who the customers are now and who they might potentially be in the future. This might seem to be abundantly clear to many corporations but nothing is ever obvious in corporate strategy. It was Levitt who pointed out in the 1960s that some large North American companies had made major strategic mistakes by incorrect identification of customers. If customers are not correctly identified, then it is quite possible that companies who are competing for the same customers will be left out of competitive analysis.

In identifying customers, a *broad view* of who they are should be taken initially in corporate strategy. Once this has been considered, a *narrower* view can then be adopted. Levitt[3] gave the example of the US railway industry, which identified its market during the 1950s as being that for *railway transport*. As a result, each company in the industry saw its environment as being largely a matter of competition between the railway companies. This was just around the time when the vast geographical distances in North America, coupled with the increasing cheapness and reliability of air transport, were allowing the new airlines to grow rapidly *at the expense of rail*. The corporate strategies of the railways were directed primarily at each other and ignored the threat of air travel. Levitt argued that the railway companies were not customer-oriented.

The importance of defining customers accurately lies in developing strategies that target them correctly and in ensuring that competitors have been properly identified. Ultimately, if the market environment is incorrectly defined, then competitors may creep up and steal customers without the company realising it until it is too late. However, there is a major difficulty with Levitt's approach. It may be unrealistically broad in its definition of customers. For example, while it is true that railways compete with airlines, buses and cars, it is unclear what practical significance this has: should railways start buying airlines? And car companies?

As an alternative, Professor Peter Doyle of Warwick University has proposed a 'better way' of analysing customers based on three guidelines:[4]

1 *customer segmentation*: the number of segments to be served by the strategy;

2 *customer needs*: the range of needs to be met;

3 *technology*: which technologies to master in the pursuit of customers.

He argues that this will assist in narrowing down the customer definition in a way that is relevant for strategy development.

Comment

Such categorisation may prove useful in some industries, but is largely meaningless in others. The Doyle guidelines are justified with an example from the defence industry, where they work well. It is not at all clear how they might work in the aircraft industry, for example, where there is greater overlap between customer segmentation and customer needs and only one basic technology. In practice, organisations will be forced to use their judgement when identifying customers.

Hence, it is probably better to take a broad view of who the customers might be as a first step; this will ensure that the full range of potential competitors is identified. A narrower view might then be developed of the more immediate customers in order to establish in a manageable way the nature of the competitive advantage that the product or service has over others.

5.1.2 What are the main elements of customer-driven strategy?

As a deliberate part of their corporate strategy, some organisations have set out to become driven by the customer.[5] There are three main strands to this approach to strategy:

1 understanding the customer;

2 responsiveness by the organisation to customer needs;

3 provision of real value for money by the organisation.

The essence of such a strategy is that it goes way beyond the functional areas of the organisation that have traditionally had direct contact with the customer – that is, marketing and sales. The concept is that *everyone* – including, for example, finance and production – becomes involved. Some of the main areas are summarised in Exhibit 5.1.

Exhibit 5.1 **Some examples of customer-driven strategy**

Understanding the customer

● Direct customer contact at many levels

● Widely disseminated research on key customer findings, e.g. on segmentation

● Knowledge of why customers choose the organisation

Responsiveness of the organisation to customer needs

● Regularly receive and act upon customer satisfaction surveys versus competitors

● Responsive to customer complaints and suggestions

● Track key customer data on company image versus competition

---

▶

Exhibit 5.1 continued

Provision of real value for money

- Monitor quality relevant to the positioning of products in the market place
- Conduct comparative surveys of competitive prices and service offerings
- Rewards inside the organisation based on performance with customers

---

5.1.3 Why is customer-driven strategy important?[6]

Essentially, customer-driven strategy is concerned with meeting the needs of the organisation's actual and potential customers and, as a result, delivering the objectives of the organisation, such as profit or service in a public service organisation. The customer-driven concept argues that only by attracting and retaining customers will long-term profits be obtained. To quote Professor Doyle, 'Profit, growth and stability all depend upon management's ability to orientate the organisation to meeting the needs of customers... If a company does not attract and retain customers, it will not have a profitable business for long.'[7]

This view of the organisation is important because it suggests that simple financial measures of profitability will not be enough to ensure the growth and survival of a business: they need to be linked to customer satisfaction and customer loyalty. There is substantial empirical evidence to support this view:

- *Loyal customers are more profitable*: they tend to account for the majority of the sales of most organisations and their loyalty means that they are less sensitive to price increases and may even encourage new customers.

- *Attracting new customers costs organisations more than retaining loyal customers*: the extra cost may be three to five times as much.

- *Retaining existing customers can dramatically increase profits*: some 10 per cent of customers will leave an organisation every year. However, according to one study, increasing customer retention by 5 per cent produced an 85 per cent increase in profits.

Customer-driven strategy can therefore be expected to enhance company profitability and increase customer satisfaction; the latter advantage may be particularly important in public service organisations and is therefore a vital component of strategy.

5.1.4 How can customer-driven strategy be developed and improved?

Both emergent and prescriptive approaches are usually employed in the development and improvement of customer strategy.

An *emergent strategy* approach may be needed in the context of unmet customer needs or more general marketing research in difficult areas. It may also be required to ensure that customer service and quality are *continually* improved. It is likely to employ the innovative conceptual approaches explored in Chapter 11.

A *prescriptive approach* will be required in other contexts, especially where the customer is concerned. If the customer is to be assured of value for money, then it will be necessary to have a clear understanding of the product or service being sold at the price quoted: there can be no sense of trial and error. All this demands the greater clarity and precision of the prescriptive approach.

▶ **Key strategic principles**

● Customers are vital to corporate strategy development. Demand needs to be estimated where possible. A broad view of likely levels of demand may be essential in order to identify possible competitors. However, a narrower definition will lead to identification of the attributes of the product or service that will persuade customers to choose a specific company rather than a rival.

● Some companies have set up customer-driven organisations as a deliberate part of strategy. This is a long-term task rather than a matter of short-term exhortation.

● Customer-driven strategy is important because it delivers the objectives of the organisation and helps increase customer loyalty.

● Both emergent and prescriptive approaches are needed in customer analysis and strategy development.

5.2 5.2 Customer profiling and sustainable competitive advantage

5.2.1 Importance of customer profiling

To continue the strategy development process, it is essential to understand customers and their reasons for choosing particular products and services. Even those customers of public services and charities, who have no choice, may be better served by a deeper understanding of their needs. Moreover, such an analysis will explain why customers buy the products or services of the organisation rather than those of its competitors: it will help to identify the sustainable competitive advantages that the organisation possesses. This means profiling them and their purchase decisions using marketing research, as outlined in Chapter 3. In order to undertake this task, it is important to explore the customer buying decision further through customer profiling.

Customer profiles describe the main characteristics of the customers and how they make their purchase decisions. Exhibit 5.2 provides some examples of typical customer profiles using information that would normally be available in more depth from marketing research. The main features of the different categories are as follows:

● *Domestic customers* buy products or services for themselves or their families. This is called *primary demand*, since demand does not depend on any other group. Primary demand will be influenced mainly by factors from the industry itself. The customers seek immediate satisfaction from their purchases, e.g. eating ice cream. There are a large number of customers, each of whom makes a small purchase, so their individual bargaining power is low. Groups of customers can often be distinguished by some further feature of their lifestyle or consumption, e.g. family consumption of bulk packs of ice cream giving a family segment. Domestic customers can often be persuaded to purchase products by pricing, branded goods and advertising, and by quality and service levels; these elements often form the basis of the sustainable competitive advantage of companies.

● *Large business customers* tend to buy for more rational and economic reasons, e.g. performance measures and cost are taken into consideration in purhasing aircraft from

Exhibit 5.2			Typical customer profiles				
	Domestic consumer	**Large industrial**	**Large private service**	**Not-for-profit charity**	**Public service**	**Small business**	**Strategic implications**
Example	Unilever ice cream	Airbus aircraft	McDonald's restaurants	UNICEF	Health service hospital	Hairdresser or local builder	
Nature of demand	Primary	Derived or joint	Primary	Primary	Primary	Derived or joint	
Selling message	Immediate satisfaction: status can be important	Economic and non-economic needs	Immediate service: quality is part of service	Driven by belief in charity	As private service, but tempered by public service guidelines	As large industrial, but may place greater value on personal service	Major areas of difference may require industry-level strategies
Customer needs	Customers can be grouped into those with similar needs: segmentation	Each customer different	Customers grouped as in domestic	Customers may be grouped but individual service also important	Customers may be grouped but individual service also important	Customers may be grouped but many will be different	Strategies for segments and individual buyers
Purchase motivation	Individual or family	Buy for company	Will partly be driven by location, style	Receive for others and self	Receive for others and self	Local and national service	Major areas of difference may require industry-level strategies
Product	Branding, possibly low technical content	Perhaps technically sophisticated	People providing service are part of product	People providing services are part of product	People providing service are part of product. Also technical content	Possible technical content. Also possibly high and personal service	Technical sophistication in some areas. People as part service in others

Airbus that meet particular travel specifications and criteria. Each business customer may be different, e.g. British Airways and Lufthansa (Germany) will have different requirements. Customers may not usefully be grouped together but often have large enough individual orders to justify the individual attention that they will receive. Demand is often *derived* demand, i.e. it is dependent on the demand from another industry. For example, the demand for aircraft will be derived from the demand for air travel. Derived demand requires the analysis of factors outside the immediate industry. Sustainable competitive advantage for companies in this group is often based on price, service and quality issues.

- *Small business customers* have many of the same characteristics as their larger counterparts. However, the size of their potential orders may not justify the same level of individual attention. Sustainable competitive advantage may be based on the greater levels of service and greater flexibility that a smaller company can offer.

- *Large service customers* often sell products to domestic customers for immediate consumption. Examples of such organisations are retail banks and major hotel chains. Importantly, the *product* includes the person providing the service, the ambience of the buildings and location of the service and the process by which the service is dispensed, e.g. with a friendly smile. Sustainable competitive advantages often relate to price, quality of service and branding.

- *Public service customers* may well exhibit considerable similarities to large service customers. However, commercial considerations may be less important. Sustainable competitive advantage may be less important if the service offered is a monopoly but, increasingly, such organisations have come under pressure to provide enhanced service at lower cost.

- *Not-for-profit charity customers* will also involve service, but may be driven by a stronger sense of beliefs and the need to keep voluntary workers interested. These may guide the charity's strategies towards a more co-operative approach. Sustainable competitive advantage may be inappropriate as a concept except in terms of seeking donations, where branding, focused benefits and value for money may be important.

In considering the strategy implications of typical customer profiles, it should be noted that some areas are specific to the industry and cannot be generalised across all strategic categories. Customer profiling is clearly related to the sustainable competitive advantage of the organisation, because it helps to identify why customers choose one product or service rather than another. For example, the product performance issues of the Dyson vacuum cleaner were clearly vital to choosing that particular model – *see* Case study 5.1. In addition, there are three other areas where customer profiling will support competitive advantage:

- Customer switching costs should be clearer.
- Customer bargaining power will be clarified by such a process.
- Customer co-operation can be identified.

5.2.2 Exploring future needs and breakthrough strategies

Beyond basic customer profiling, strategy is also about identifying future opportunities. To quote Hamel and Prahalad: 'Any company that can do no more than respond to the articulated needs of existing customers will quickly become a laggard.'[8] However, in turbulent markets, the exploration of future needs may be difficult: *see* for example the Hewlett-Packard comment on hand-held calculators in Chapter 1. In this case, strategy will follow an emergent approach and move forward step by step without overexposing the organisation's resources.

It is easier to research reactions to existing products than to elicit responses to the largely unknown. For example, realistic research with passengers on a proposed new

Airbus SuperJumbo in 1996 was difficult. This was because the proposed design involved the unfamiliar and totally new concept of a double-decker aircraft – that is, one with two complete passenger decks, one over the other. Potential customers will always have difficulty getting their minds around such totally novel approaches. Yet customer profiling may be vital in the category of the *revolutionary product* that may deliver the important, new, corporate strategy breakthrough.

Unmet customer needs are difficult to research and require close co-operation between technologists and strategists. Mock-ups, structured marketing research and trial products to test reactions may be beneficial.

5.2.3 The connection between customer profiling and strategy development: the customer/competitor matrix

Because of the infinite variety of customers and competitors, it can be difficult to structure the full strategic implications of customer profiling. However, by making some simple assumptions about the types of customer and competitor, it is possible to explore the strategies that might result. This can be shown in the *customer/competitor matrix*. The purpose of such an analysis is to explore the types of strategy that emerge from customer perceptions and the difficulties of entering or staying in such an industry.

The simplifying assumptions are:

● Customers either all have the same need or all have infinitely varying needs.

● Competitors are differentiated only on the basis of two factors: different economies of scale and product differentiation.

From the areas already explored in the chapter, it will be evident that these are useful but heroic assumptions with all the strengths and weaknesses of such simplicity. The resulting matrix is shown in Figure 5.2 and combines two main elements:

Figure 5.2   Customer/competitor matrix

Customer needs	Competitor advantage	
	Small, so easily imitated	Large, so difficult to imitate
Very varied, so many sources of competitive advantage	Fragmented strategies	Specialised strategies
Largely the same, so few sources of competitive advantage	Stalemate strategies	Volume strategies

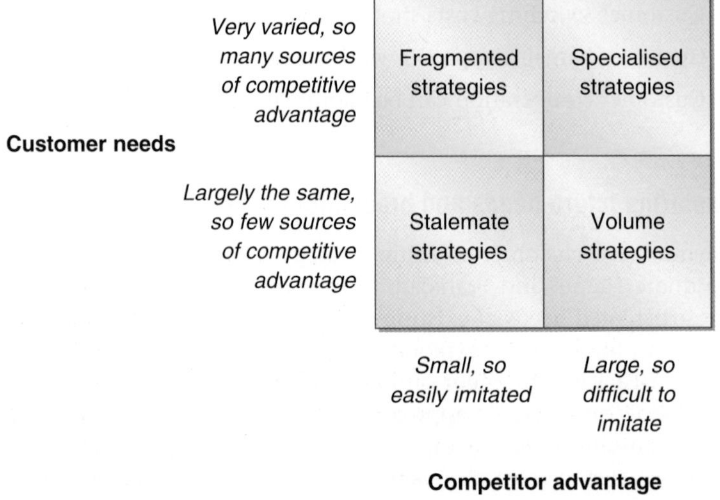

1 Customer needs – providing sources of competitive advantage:

- Some customers have essentially the *same needs* as others, e.g. when purchasing commodities such as sugar, cotton or electricity. The sources of competitive advantage will therefore be limited for such products: minor variations in the price and quality of cotton, for example.

- Some customers have *infinitely varied* needs – for example in hairdressing and strategy consulting, where no two jobs are ever exactly the same. The sources of competitive advantage here are many and varied: type of service, quality of product, length of assignment, etc.

2 Competitor strategies – based on economies of scale and differentiation:

- Some companies will have small competitive advantages because either the scale is low or there is little differentiation possible. For example, coal mining and an average country hotel represent areas where the products are easily imitated.

- Some companies will have large competive advantages because there are economies of scale and the product is well differentiated and difficult to imitate – for example, branded ice cream products at Unilever, and Boeing aircraft.

From the customer/competitor matrix, four types of strategic situation emerge:

1 *Fragmented strategies.* Customer needs are highly varied and provide sources of competitive advantage, but the advantages they deliver are easily imitated. Speciality retailing, hairdressing and other small businesses are examples. Some accountancy companies fall into this category. However, the large, multinational accountancy companies have managed to break out and supply a service that relies on scale to audit their multinational clients: they fit into the specialised strategies below.

2 *Specialised strategies.* There are special or corporate skills, patents and proprietory products that are sold to many different customers who all have varied needs, often on a large scale. Examples are some of the major drug companies with varied endmarkets and strongly patented products, and international consulting companies.

3 *Volume strategies.* These are often based on economies of scale and branding but are sold to customers who basically want standard products with little individual variation. Examples include branded products and some types of basic industrial chemicals. Hospitals are increasingly offering services in this area, such as standard operations and medical checks.

4 *Stalemate strategies.* Here the products are easily imitated and most customer needs are essentially the same. The value added is therefore difficult to raise because customers can easily switch to another supplier. Examples are some staple food products and many commodities.

▶ Key strategic principles

- **Customer profiling will provide a basic understanding of the customer that is crucial to strategy development. Specifically, it will show why customers prefer one product or service rather than another and thus identify the sustainable competitive advantage possessed by the organisation. It may also clarify the organisation's strengths when faced with customers who wish to switch to rival products.**

> ◗ *Key strategic principles continued*
>
> ● Importantly, customers and their future needs may provide the break-through that will deliver a totally new strategic opportunity.
>
> ● The customer/competitor matrix links together two important aspects: the extent to which customers have common needs and the possibilities of achieving competitive advantage in the market place based on differentiation and economies of scale.
>
> ● The matrix identifies four main types of strategic situation: fragmented, specialised, volume and stalemate. The strategic significance of each can then be explored.

5.3 Market segmentation

For many markets, customer analysis needs to move beyond the consideration of basic markets to an analysis of specific parts of a market – *market segmentation* – and to the competitive stance of organisations within the segment – their *market positioning,* which is explored in the next section. The basic sequence for exploring the approach is shown in Figure 5.3. It employs a *prescriptive* approach as a first step in order to explore the elements. In practice, the sequence is likely to be more experimental and, in this sense, *emergent,* because it is often necessary to explore a number of positioning areas: this is also outlined in Figure 5.4.

The three prescriptive stages are:

1 *Identify market segment(s).* Identification of specialist needs of segments will lead to customer profiles of those in the segments.

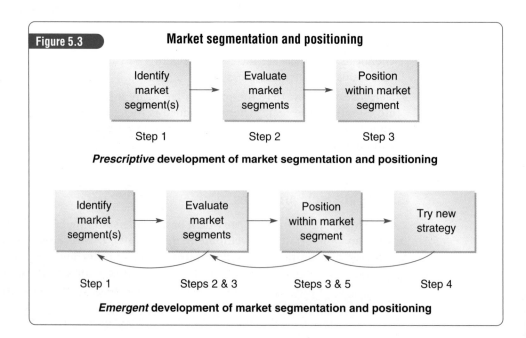

Figure 5.3 **Market segmentation and positioning**

Identify market segment(s) → Evaluate market segments → Position within market segment

Step 1   Step 2   Step 3

Prescriptive **development of market segmentation and positioning**

Identify market segment(s) → Evaluate market segments → Position within market segment → Try new strategy

Step 1   Steps 2 & 3   Steps 3 & 5   Step 4

Emergent **development of market segmentation and positioning**

2 *Evaluate segment(s).* Some segments are likely to be more attractive than others. They need to be identified and targeted.

3 *Position within market segment.* Within the segment, companies will then need to develop a differential advantage over competitors.

In the development of customer strategy, customer analysis will often move rapidly to an examination of market segmentation.[9] Market segmentation may be defined as the identification of specific groups (or segments) of customers who respond differently from other groups to competitive strategies.

The advantages of identifying a market segment include:

- Strength in (and possibly dominance of) a group, even though the overall market is large. It may be more profitable to have a large share of a group than a small share of the main market. Thus competitive advantage may be stronger in a segment than in the broader market.

- Closer matching of customer needs and the organisation's resources through targeting the segment. This will enhance sustainable competitive advantage.

- Concentration of effort on a smaller area, so that the company's resources can be employed more effectively.

Hence, from a strategic viewpoint, the key advantage of market segmentation is probably the ability to dominate a sector of a market and then target benefits that will sustain this position.

For example, Dyson dominated the premium-priced vacuum cleaner segment. Typical bases for segmentation in consumer and industrial markets are listed in Table 5.1. However, markets can be segmented by any criteria that prove helpful and do not necessarily need to conform to this list.

Having established the segments, strategic customer analysis then proceeds to evaluate the *usefulness* of each segment: step 2 in Figure 5.3. It is not enough for a segment

Table 5.1 Typical bases for market segmentation

Consumer products	Industrial products
• Geographic	• Geography
• Demographic (age, sex, education, etc.)	• End-use
• Socio-economic and income	• Customer business
• Ethnic group	• Buying situation
• Benefits sought	• Market served
• Usage rate and brand loyalty	• Value added by customer
• Attitudes	• Source of competitive advantage (price, service, etc.)
• Lifestyle	
• Situation	• Emphasis on R&D and innovation
(where the consumption takes place)	• Professional membership

to be different. There are four important characteristics of any segment if it is to be useful in strategic customer analysis. It must be:

1 *Distinguishable*. Customers must be distinguishable so that they can be isolated in some way.

2 *Relevant to purchasing*. The distinguishing criteria must relate to differences in market demand. For example, they may pay higher prices for higher quality.

3 *Sufficiently large*. If the segment is too small, then it will not justify the resources needed to reach it.

4 *Reachable*. It must be possible to direct the strategy to that segment.

It is also important to assess the future growth prospects of the segment. An example of market segmentation is explored in Case study 5.2.

CASE STUDY 5.2

Two methods of segmenting products in the European ice cream market

Method 1: purchase intention

European ice cream purchases can usefully be segmented into impulse and take-home: the former are bought for immediate consumption, while the latter are usually taken home in bulk for consumption later. Impulse purchases typically take place in small shops such as beach kiosks and newsagents' stores, whereas take-home products are normally bought in grocers' and supermarkets. It would be wrong to draw a rigid distinction between the two segments: bulk packs are purchased by retailers to sell as scoops for impulse demand; impulse items such as chocolate bars are sold in multipacks and may then be consumed on impulse later at home.

In practice, detailed segment data are available for some national markets but no true pan-European study has been published. Best estimates from a variety of sources for some leading European markets are shown in Table 5.2.

Interpreting the data in Table 5.2 is complex since there are several factors at work. In France, eating ice cream is sometimes regarded as a luxury and eating occasions may therefore be taken more seriously, rather than on impulse. In Italy, ice cream is also an expensive item with many luxury ingredients, individual variants and local manufacturers, but it is bought more casually from cafés and gelaterias. In the UK, ice cream has traditionally been manufactured using lower-quality ingredients,

e.g. vegetable oils in place of real cream. During the 1980s, there was substantial growth across Europe in the take-home trade of economy packs and, more recently, more expensive, higher-quality bulk packs. In Germany, ice cream has traditionally been bought on impulse, and more recently there has been substantial growth in the take-home market: in both market segments, expectations have remained high with regard to ingredients and taste.

Within each purchase intention, it is then possible to develop competitive positions for individual or groups of products. For example, the 'take-home' product category will offer competitive positions ranging from the cheap, family category – such as supermarket own brands, to the luxury take-home products – such as Unilever's Carte d'Or. In the same way, impulse products might be positioned for children or grown-ups.

Table 5.2 Customer segmentation in ice cream by purchase intention

Occasion	France	Italy	UK	Germany
Impulse	30%	40%	30%	50%
Take-home	70%	60%	70%	50%

Source: Author's estimates based on various trade articles.

Table 5.3 Customer segmentation by price and quality

Segment	Product and branding	Pricing	Market growth in the mid-1990s
Superpremium	High-quality, exotic flavours, e.g. Häagen-Dazs Mint Chocolate Chip	Very high unit prices: very high value added	Over 15% per annum from a small market base
Premium	Good-quality ingredients with individual, well-known branded names such as Mars and Magnum	Prices set above regular and economy categories but not as high as superpremium: high value added	10% per annum from a larger base than superpremium
Regular	Standard-quality ingredients with branding relying on manufacturer's name rather than individual product, e.g. Walls, Schoeller	Standard prices: adequate value added but large-volume market	Over 5% per annum from a large base
Economy	Manufactured by smaller manufacturers with standard-quality ingredients, possibly for retailers' own brands	Lower price, highly price competitive: low value added but large market	Over 5% per annum from a large base, particularly in some countries such as the UK and Ireland

Source: Author's estimates from trade articles.

Method 2: price and quality

During the 1990s, Europe has seen a marked growth in ice creams using expensive ingredients, high prices and exotic flavours; some customers (but not necessarily all) have become more adventurous in taste, more wealthy and more demanding in terms of quality. There has been a new attempt to redefine customers by *price and quality*. Table 5.3 shows the main areas.

The segments in Table 5.3 need to be treated with some caution: no precise information on the four market segments has been published. The categories probably have too much overlap, with customers buying from several segments, depending on the meal occasion. In spite of the problem of accuracy, the above segments are certainly large enough to justify separate marketing and distribution activity. Many have been targeted accurately through appropriate media: for example, the use of up-market,

young-profile colour magazines to reach potential Häagen-Dazs customers with a sexually suggestive campaign, and the use of TV advertising to present the new Ice Cream Mars branded range to a wider TV audience. Thus some segments have real marketing potential in spite of difficulties in precise definition.

Case questions

1 *What other methods of segmenting the ice cream market are available?*

2 *Using the tests for segmentation, what conclusions do you draw on the usefulness of the two methods above?*

3 *If you were developing a new ice cream product, what segment would you judge to be particularly attractive for a small, new market entrant?*

> ◗ **Key strategic principles**
>
> ● There are three prescriptive stages in developing market segmentation and positioning: identify potential segments, evaluate and select segment(s), and position within segment(s).
>
> ● Market segmentation is the identification of specific groups of customers who respond differently from other groups to competitive strategies. They can be important in strategy development because they provide the opportunity to dominate part of the market.
>
> ● Identification of gaps in segment provision may provide the basis of new strategic opportunities.

5.4 Competitive positioning[10]

Although a useful segment has been identified, this does not in itself resolve the organisation's strategy. The competitive position within the segment then needs to be explored, because only this will show how the organisation will compete within the segment. For example, both the Mars Company (US) and Nestlé (Switzerland) compete in the market for chocolate products. However, the Mars' product Snickers is positioned as a 'meal substitute' – it can be eaten in place of a meal, whereas the Nestlé product KitKat is positioned as a 'snack' – it can be eaten as a break but is not substantial enough to be a substitute for a meal. Competitive positioning is thus the choice of differential advantage that the product or service will possess against its competitors. To develop positioning, it is useful to follow a two-stage process – first identify the segment gaps, second identify positioning within segments.

5.4.1 Identification of segmentation gaps and their competitive positioning implications

From a strategy viewpoint, the most useful strategic analysis often emerges by exploring where there are *gaps* in the segments of an industry: amongst others, Porter[11] and Ohmae[12] recommend this route. The starting point for such work is to map out the current segmentation position and then place companies and their products into the segments: it should then become clear where segments exist that are not served or are poorly served by current products. This is shown in Exhibit 5.3 using the European ice cream case as an example.

5.4.2 Identifying the positioning within the segment[13]

From a strategy perspective, some gaps may be more attractive than others. For example, they may have limited competition or poorly supported products. In addition, some gaps may possess a clear advantage in terms of competitive positioning. Others may not. To explore the development of positioning, we can return to our earlier example of two chocolate countlines from Nestlé and Mars. The full positioning map for the range of such products is shown in Figure 5.4.

The process of developing positioning of chocolate countlines runs as follows:

1 *Perceptual mapping*: in-depth qualitative research on actual and prospective customers on the way that they make their decisions in the market place, e.g strong versus

Exhibit 5.3 **New or underutilised segment gaps: Unilever's presence in the European ice cream market, 1998**

Market basis for possible segmentation

	Buyer type 1	Buyer type 2	Buyer type 3, etc.
Product variety 1			
Product variety 2			
Product variety 3 etc.			

Step 1: Existing segments with Unilever's European presence shown

	Grocery supermarkets	Small grocery stores	Restaurants and takeaways	Newsagents and leisure facilities
Superpremium	✔ market test only			✔ few
Premium	✔	✔		✔ most
Regular	✔			
Economy	✔	✔ some		

Step 2: Some possible new segments *in addition* to the above

	Garages	Temporary facilities at sporting and cultural events	Factory canteens and restaurants: contract catering
Superpremium		✔	
Premium	✔		
Regular			✔
Economy			✔

Note: For the sake of clarity, only Unilever's presence is shown in the above. Moreover, the example is *illustrative only* and may not represent the actual practice of the Unilever subsidiaries in each country. Further segmentation analyses based on criteria such as the geographical country might also produce some useful additional information.

Comment: It will be evident that there are some gaps in the existing coverage of the market. The segmentation criteria outlined in the text above could be used to assess whether it would be worthwhile filling the gaps. One obvious area where Unilever could take action was in the superpremium sector.

weak, cheap versus expensive, modern versus traditional. In the case of chocolate the dimensions of meal/snack and family/individual were established.

2 *Positioning*: brands or products are then placed on the map using the research dimensions. Figure 5.4 presents the existing configuration.

3 *Options development*: take existing and new products and use their existing strengths and weaknesses to devise possible new positions on the map. Figure 5.4 shows some

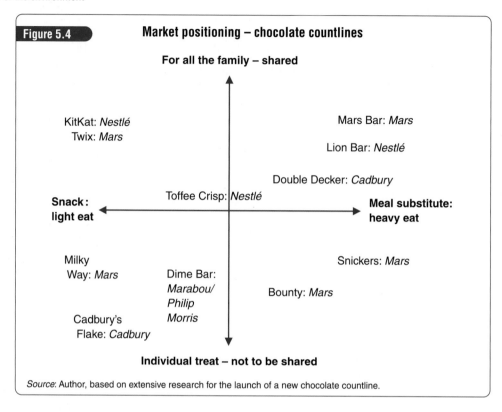

Figure 5.4 Market positioning – chocolate countlines

For all the family – shared

KitKat: *Nestlé*
Twix: *Mars*

Mars Bar: *Mars*

Lion Bar: *Nestlé*

Double Decker: *Cadbury*

Toffee Crisp: *Nestlé*

**Snack:
light eat**

**Meal substitute:
heavy eat**

Milky
Way: *Mars*

Dime Bar:
*Marabou/
Philip
Morris*

Snickers: *Mars*

Bounty: *Mars*

Cadbury's
Flake: *Cadbury*

Individual treat – not to be shared

Source: Author, based on extensive research for the launch of a new chocolate countline.

gaps for some companies and some products that have an unclear position – Toffee Crisp at the time of the research.

4 *Testing*: first with simple statements with customers, then at a later stage in the market place.

It will be evident that this is essentially an emergent rather than a prescriptive process, involving experimentation with actual and potential customers.

Key strategic principles

- Competitive positioning is the choice of differential advantage that the product or service will possess against its competitors.

- The sequence for developing competitive positioning has four main steps: perceptual mapping, positioning, options development and testing. The process is essentially emergent rather than prescriptive.

5.5 Strategy implications: analysing branding and reputation

Undoubtedly, customers will recognise the strength or weakness of an organisation's brands and its overall reputation: they will tend to make the customer more or less loyal. This is equally true for small companies as for large: branding may be limited, but reputation will be a key determinant of sustainable competitive advantage.

It is important to draw a clear distinction between branding and reputation. *Branding is a specific name or symbol used to distinguish a seller's product or service.*[14] Its role is to allow a product or service to charge a higher price than a functionally equivalent non-branded version. In this sense, brands add value to products – for example, the higher price charged for Magnum ice cream over a similar product with no brand name or, more likely for a consumer product, the brand name of a supermarket such as Sainsbury or Carrefour.

Reputation is a broader concept: it is the sum of customer knowledge developed about an organisation over time. This will include branding, where relevant, but will also cover other areas:

- *product performance*: customers will use their experience to form judgements;

- *quality*: customers will expect certain levels, based on pricing, positioning, advertising and built-in performance levels;

- *service*: customers may be offered differing levels of delivery, installation, advice and other forms of customer experience with the organisation;

- *marketing support*: advertising, packaging, promotional activity.

Reputation may be an immediate result of some or all of these areas. In addition, the concept of time is important because reputation will also develop further over time, as well as being influenced by short-term events. The overall relationships are summarised in Figure 5.5 from an *emergent* perspective – the importance of the time relationships makes a prescriptive approach worthless. From a strategic perspective, reputation is important in delivering and maintaining sustainable competitive advantage. For example, the reputation of Boeing was dented in 1998 when it was unable to keep up with demand for its aircraft as a result of manufacturing delays at its factories; this had a clear impact in its competitive battle with Airbus. Reputation also adds value to the organisation and is therefore an important asset.

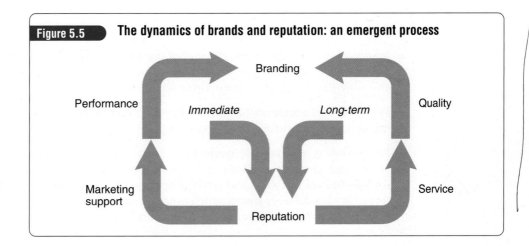

Figure 5.5 **The dynamics of brands and reputation: an emergent process**

Branding

Performance   *Immediate*   *Long-term*   Quality

Marketing support   Service

Reputation

5.5.1 Analysing brands

Given the role and concept of a brand as adding value to a functional product, there are five areas that deserve analysis:[15]

1 Establish the *reputation* of a product (hence the circular nature of Figure 5.5): many have heard of the Disney name.

2 Provide *continuity* in the sense of an assurance that the product will continue to perform as it did in the past: Big Mac is the same everywhere.

3 Reflect a distinctive *formula* that is difficult for others to replicate: Sony's Trinitron television system is patented.

4 Communicate the company's position as an *established incumbent* in the market place: Intel and Microsoft signal their strengths in the computer hardware and software markets.

5 Provide a means for customers to *signal* information about themselves: Nike and Adidas fashion branding in sports shoes and clothing.

Different brands will have varying combinations of the above. From a strategic perspective, the analysis needs to concentrate on the degree of competitive advantage and added value provided by brands. It should be noted that financial measures and techniques have limited, if any, relevance here because they are unable to cope with these vital but vague concepts.

5.5.2 Analysing reputation

Reputation will be won or lost as a result of many activities of the company that go well beyond customer considerations: for example, superior product design and manufacturing techniques have assisted many Japanese car companies to gain a high reputation for quality – *see* Chapter 9. Such areas go well beyond customer analysis because they depend on the resources of the organisation. They are best analysed in this latter context – *see* Chapter 6 on resources.

▶ Key strategic principles

- Branding is a specific name or symbol used to distinguish a product or service from a functional product. It adds value to the basic functional product and provides sustainable competitive advantage.

- There are five elements to brand analysis: reputation, continuity, formula, incumbency and information signalling.

- Reputation is a broader concept than branding. It is the sum of customer knowledge developed about an organisation over time. Reputation will include brands but may also cover other aspects such as quality and service levels. It also delivers sustainable competitive advantage and adds value to basic customer perceptions of the organisation.

5.6 Strategy implications: communicating with customers and stakeholders[16]

Organisations communicate with their customers in order to:

● inform them about their products;

● persuade them to purchase or continue buying products or services;

● establish and secure the sustainable competitive advantages of their product or service.

In communicating with customers, the organisation also sends signals to the world at large: its employees, shareholders, the government and many other bodies. This group, including the customers, is often given the title *stakeholders* in the organisation.

Although the main emphasis of this chapter is on the customer, corporate analysis needs to consider the communications impact not only on customers but also on the *wider group of stakeholders*. This is considered separately below.

5.6.1 Cost-effectiveness in communication

In most situations, personal persuasion is the most effective method of communication because the message can be tailored to the individual customer. However, for many domestic consumer products, it is not cost-effective to call on each customer every time they fancy an ice cream. Mass marketing is required: advertising, branding and promotion.

The key criterion in measuring communication strategy proposals is *cost-effectiveness*, i.e. the cost of obtaining an effective communication with the customer, the effect usually being measured as the sale of the product or service. The difficulty is that it is usually substantially easier to estimate the *cost* of such items as operating a salesforce or telephone service team, or mounting a campaign on television or in the press, than it is to measure the *effects* on sales of such activity. For example, even if the sales go up, it is not always clear that it was the result of the specific communications activity.[17]

There are quantitative measures of the effects of such activity. They work well in some areas such as direct mail, i.e. promotions addressed and posted to individuals. However, they are incomplete in other areas, such as advertising and sponsorship, where there is often a time lag before the impact is fully realised. This means that there is an element of judgement involved in investment decisions in such areas but this does not usually inhibit strategic decisions to invest in brands, advertising and other communications areas.

Some commentators go further. Although communications are important for corporate strategy, advertising is essentially difficult to assess. As Professor John Kay says, 'This leads us to the conclusion that the effectiveness of modern advertising is fundamentally an irrational phenomenon.'[18] He then goes on to defend the role of advertising in building and supporting the *reputation* of the company, but still leaves the impression that it is essentially wayward and unquantifiable. Certainly, it is not easy to assess the effectiveness of advertising, but the empirical research evidence suggests that it can be done. Some other areas of communications *can* be assessed accurately in terms of cost-effectiveness, e.g. direct mail and personal selling.

Communications options available to reach customers

Within the requirement to communicate with customers, there are substantial differences of approach depending on the customer profile. These are shown in Exhibit 5.4.

Essentially, from a corporate strategy perspective, the communications issues are related to the methods of persuading customers to remain with the organisation. They may include:

● *Branding*, i.e. the additional reassurance provided to the customer over the intrinsic value of the assets purchased by the customer. This can be a powerful method of retaining customer loyalty in mass market products.

Exhibit 5.4 **Different customers require different types of communication**

	Domestic consumer	Large industrial	Large private service	Not-for-profit charity	Public service	Small business	Strategic implications
Example	Unilever ice cream	Airbus aircraft	McDonald's restaurants	UNICEF	Health service hospital	Hairdresser or local builder	
Branding and advertising	Yes	Not usually beyond technical press	Yes	Possibly, but doubts about cost-effectiveness	Possible but unlikely	No, except local advertising	Mass market, scatter-gun effect but can be cost-effective
Personal selling	No, except to large distributors	Yes, important	Yes, in the sense of personal service	Unlikely: against the culture	Personal attention but no real selling	Important part of promotion	Targeted and personal but often expensive
Consumer promotions	Yes	Yes, possibly	Yes	Mailing letters important	Not usually	Simple cost-effective methods constantly being tried	Mass market but effect can often be carefully assessed
Technical promotions and exhibitions	No	Yes	No	No	No	Yes	Carefully targeted but some areas difficult to assess
Sponsorship, PR and other third-party events	Yes	Yes	Yes	Yes for fund raising	Possibly	Yes on small scale	One of the most difficult to assess impact, but can be vital

- *Personal selling*, i.e. a personal relationship and individually tailored message for a single customer to purchase the product. Each selling occasion is expensive and can only be justified if the order that is placed is sufficiently large.
- *Technical promotions*, i.e. the use of the technical presentation of data on the product or service to persuade the potential customer of its merits. This may be conducted through research papers, magazines, technical advertising, exhibitions and trade conferences.
- *Consumer promotions*, i.e. devices that promote the product without building any fundamental relationship but may be effective where customer loyalty is low or a new product is being introduced.
- *Public relations and sponsorship*, i.e. the more general activities undertaken by the organisation that will have a customer and other stakeholders. These will include lobbying of governments and other public bodies, as mentioned in Chapter 4. They may also cover a broader range of corporate objectives, such as support for the community and charities, that take them beyond customer communications.

The key to distinguishing between the different communications methods is that they are likely to differ depending on the nature of the customer.

▶ Key strategic principles

- Organisations communicate with their customers in order to inform and persuade them about the merits of their products and services. This will assist in establishing the sustainable competitive advantages of the product.
- Cost-effectiveness is the main criterion when assessing communications proposals. Costs are usually relatively easy to estimate but the effects of some promotional areas may be more difficult to assess.
- Different types of customers will need different forms of communication. Each will operate to communicate and secure the competitive advantages of the organisation.

5.7 Strategy implications: strategic pricing and value for money

In the short term, pricing does not usually form the basis of sustainable competitive advantage because any price changes can be imitated very quickly by competitors. In the longer term, pricing strategy can be a major factor in competitive advantage because it will significantly alter the basis on which companies can compete. Pricing is therefore strategically important for several reasons:

- impact of price changes on profitability;
- positioning of products in the market place: the price can be used to signal more general forms of competitive advantage. There are no cheap Rolls-Royce or Porsche cars;
- value-for-money impression created about the organisation: price needs to be coupled with quality, after-sales service and other aspects of the product.

5.7.1 The pricing decision: the basic considerations

As a starting point for customer analysis, the pricing decision can be considered as a balance of two main factors:

1 *Costs.* Setting the market price below the marginal cost of production will certainly lose the company money.

2 *Competition.* Pitching the market price significantly above competition will result in minimal sales even if there is some product differentiation.

Figure 5.6 shows how these factors can be balanced out to provide some basic considerations in price setting. Beyond this basic structure, the factors that will then influence pricing include:

● price elasticity: the sensitivity of volume to changes in price;

● stage in the product life cycle: the early stages may need some special pricing strategies;

● strategic role of price.

It is this last element that will benefit particularly from further analysis. In some product categories and competitive situations, pricing forms a key part of overall company strategy. For example:

● *Price discounting* – where a company deliberately offers cut-price goods on a permanent basis, e.g. Aldi (Germany and the Netherlands) and Kwiksave (UK) in grocery retailing.

● *Premium pricing* – where a company sets out to price its goods at permanently high prices, e.g. Yves St Laurent, Dunhill and Gucci.

These are basic strategic decisions of the organisation that need careful analysis at an early stage. They will then form part of the *strategic options* considerations of Part 5 of this book.

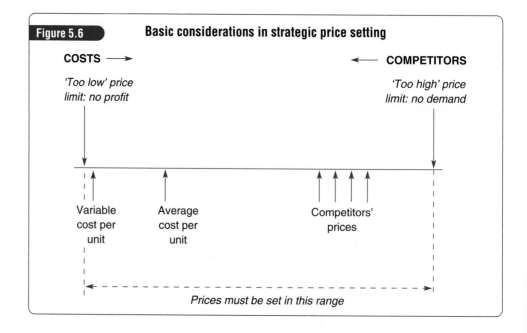

Figure 5.6 **Basic considerations in strategic price setting**

COSTS ⟶   ⟵ COMPETITORS

'Too low' price limit: no profit   *'Too high' price limit: no demand*

Variable cost per unit

Average cost per unit

Competitors' prices

Prices must be set in this range

5.7.2 Value for money

For many customers, other considerations beyond the quoted price also apply, such as quality, availability of stock, product performance, after-sales service, brand value and many other issues. For example, in purchasing aircraft, performance, special financing deals and the currency of purchase may well clinch the deal for a company. For such reasons, *value for money* which includes these broader elements may be a more appropriate method of analysing pricing.

All these items make simple pricing decisions more complex. Determination of costs and prices is not an exact science. Hence there are real issues that need to be resolved in advance of any price negotiations. Exhibit 5.5 outlines the main areas.

Exhibit 5.5	Customer strategy: pricing and value-for-money considerations						
	Domestic consumer	**Large industrial**	**Large private service**	**Not-for-profit charity**	**Public service**	**Small business**	**Strategic implications**
Example	Unilever ice cream	Airbus aircraft	McDonald's restaurants	UNICEF	Health service hospital	Hairdresser or local builder	
Turbulent environment?	Not normally: depends on product	Quite possible	Not normally	No	No	Quite possible	When turbulent, then need for more flexibility and rapid reaction to events
Discounts and special terms?	No	Yes, many	No	Special deals being offered for annual contributions	Heavy negotiating with finance providers	Yes, many	Discounts need more initiative with individual managers, less centralised pricing
Negotiation	No	Yes	No	–	No	Yes	Bargaining power important in negotiation
Strategic role of price	Affects positioning and competition	Technical and complex negotiation	As domestic	Subscriptions used to smooth income across the year	Fixed, but financial providers may need evidence of value for money	Technical and personal negotiation	Can be complex and specific to industry

5.7.3 Target pricing

One major pricing technique that deserves careful analysis because of its strategic significance is *target pricing*. Target pricing sets the price for goods and services primarily on the basis of the competitive position of the company, almost regardless of the costs of producing the goods. Having established the target price, engineers, production workers, marketers, designers, suppliers and others are then given target costs that must be met so that profit targets can be met.

This process contrasts sharply with the traditional practice of *cost-plus pricing*: all the costs are added up, a percentage profit margin is applied and the final price then determined. The two routes to pricing are shown in Figure 5.7.

Target pricing has been used for some years by Japanese car companies to achieve their profit and marketing objectives.[19] It has been highly successful but relies on close co-operation between all elements and the use of innovative ideas at the *design stage* to reduce costs. This aspect is explored further in Chapter 9. The detail of the procedures is not a matter of corporate strategy. However, the principle of target pricing is fundamental as an option for customer strategy analysis.

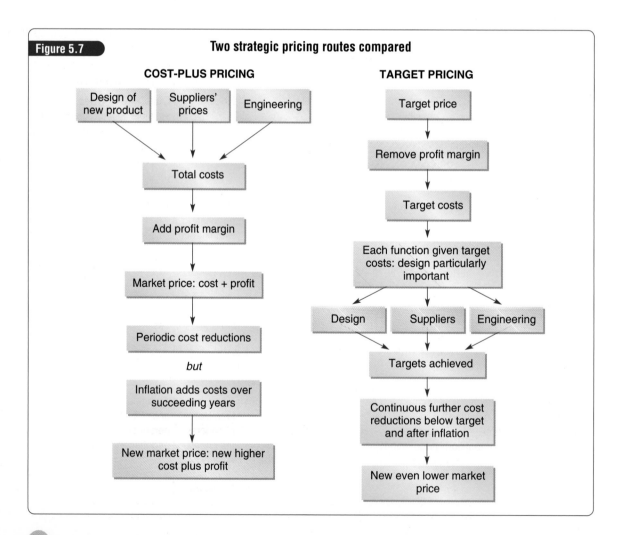

Figure 5.7 **Two strategic pricing routes compared**

Clearly, target pricing can put real pressure on competitors. It has actually been used by Airbus Industrie to compete against Boeing, though it is not entirely clear whether this was intentional or the only way that the company could operate. As Case study 5.3 explains, Airbus is structured as a conglomerate GIE. This means that Airbus has no production facilities of its own but uses those of its shareholders: Dasa, Aerospatiale, BAe and Casa. Airbus therefore has only very limited information on its costs and simply negotiates a price with its customers. It then calculates the *target price* it is prepared to pay its shareholders for their components and tells them. If the aircraft price falls, Airbus drives a harder bargain with its shareholder-suppliers, forcing them to cut costs if they wish to make a profit.[20]

5.7.4 Pricing strategy analysis – the overall process

After analysing the various aspects of price setting, it is useful to consider the overall process; this is shown in Figure 5.8. A *prescriptive* approach is illustrated but it should be noted that a more experimental, *emergent* approach may in fact be used.

In price analysis, there are four main steps in the prescriptive process:

1 *Evaluate competitors' pricing.* The acquistion of competing price lists is an obvious first step. However, it is important to think beyond mere price towards customer perceptions of other factors that have influenced their buying choice, such as quality, performance, service levels. Factoring these matters into pricing will be a matter of judgement.

2 *Establish price objective.* Different products will have different objectives. These might include the following: harvesting mature products with higher prices, driving for growth by lowering prices, signalling quality by selling at a premium and maintaining the existing balance in the industry by matching competitive moves, establishing a new product at a special price. It will be important to analyse what the aim was in the specific circumstances of the organisation.

3 *Consider competitors and the product life cycle.* Within the pricing objective, it is then useful to consider competitors and their possible reactions to the pricing moves that have previously been undertaken. It is also useful to explore the position on the life cycle and its price implications.

4 *Set prices.* Price setting can then be analysed in the context of the customer and value-for-money considerations. This latter comment may include an element of service, design and other matters.

However, it should be noted that this is a highly prescriptive approach to the analytical process of pricing. It therefore needs to be treated with considerable caution because it treats price setting as a formula.

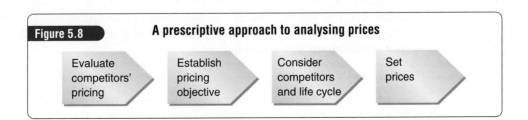

Figure 5.8   **A prescriptive approach to analysing prices**

Evaluate competitors' pricing → Establish pricing objective → Consider competitors and life cycle → Set prices

> ### ◗ Key strategic principles
>
> - In the short term, pricing does not usually form the basis of sustainable competitive advantage because any price changes can be imitated very quickly by competitors. In the longer term, pricing strategy can be a major factor in competitive advantage, because it will significantly alter the basis on which companies can compete.
>
> - Pricing strategy can have strategic significance at three levels: rapid impact on profitability, positioning of the product and value for money.
>
> - The price decision will be determined by a balance of factors under the general headings of costs and competitor analysis.
>
> - Value for money, which includes quality, branding and other factors, represents the broader elements that will determine and condition pricing for many customers.
>
> - It is possible to analyse prices using a four-stage process: evaluation of competitors' pricing; establishing pricing objectives; consideration of competitors and life cycle; the final process of establishing the price. However, this is a highly prescriptive approach and needs to be treated with caution because it treats price setting as a formula.

5.8 International customer considerations

Disney, Benetton, Sony, Heineken and Adidas are all examples of international brands that are instantly recognisable in many countries around the world. Products, tastes and markets are becoming increasingly international. In this sense, customer analysis also needs to become more international in its approach.

Probably the most famous article arguing for an international approach to strategy development was that of Theodore Levitt in 1983, entitled 'The globalisation of markets'.[21] He acknowledged that there were real differences in taste, culture and language around the world but argued that the pressures for globalisation would more than outweigh them. Everyone was developing global tastes: 'Cosmopolitanism is no longer the monopoly of the intellectual and leisured classes; it is becoming the established property and defining characteristic of all sectors everywhere in the world.'

To support his enthusiasm, Levitt quoted the evidence of a washing machine manufacturer who had *not* followed a global approach.[22] He also quotes some brief examples of companies that had successfully internationalised. His main arguments are summarised in Exhibit 5.6. The most significant point in developing international analysis is that it is *far more important to seek the similarities between nations* than to analyse the differences; this remains true at the beginning of the twenty-first century. Levitt also lays great emphasis on international economies of scale to deliver really low prices and thus overcome any differences in taste.

Comment

Levitt's article has certainly been influential. It is written in enthusiastic tones, bordering on the lyrical. However, the quality of evidence is poor, the assertions are inaccurate

Exhibit 5.6 **Levitt's main assertions about the reasons for increased internationalisation**

- Price competition is important and persuasive for customers.
- It is possible to change national tastes if prices are low enough.
- Globalisation will emerge from a standardisation of products and services.
- Tariffs and quotas will not protect national industries against international attack.
- Major economies of scale are possible and will lead to increased international price competition.
- Global branding is meaningful and attractive to customers.

and the argument is open to question at several points. Several years later Douglas and Wind produced a critique that was both accurate and helpful.[23] They emphasised the importance of being sensitive to national (or local) customer variations as well as seeking the benefits of global scale outlined by Levitt. Nevertheless, the central argument that it is better to seek the similarities rather than the differences is still useful today. Chapter 19 explores these matters in more depth.

Key strategic principles

- Many business activities are becoming more international. Customer analysis from an international perspective needs to seek out the similarities rather than the differences between nations. However, it also needs to be sensitive to important national differences.
- There are numerous potential advantages from operating internationally. However, they depend on some assumptions about customers that need careful validation in reality.

CASE STUDY 5.3

Customer strategy at Airbus: competing in the SuperJumbo aircraft segment

During the late 1990s, Europe's leading company in the world civil aircraft market, Airbus Industrie, had to make an important strategic decision: whether to go ahead with a US$8 billion investment in a new SuperJumbo aircraft. The decision was made more difficult because its chief rival, the US company Boeing, had pulled out of a similar project, saying that there was insufficient demand. But, as Airbus knew only too well, customer strategy was more complex than simple estimates of market demand.

Background

Set up in 1975, Airbus Industrie was a special consortium called a Groupement d'Intérêt Economique (GIE). It had an advisory board and its own central management. However, it consisted essentially of the four European aircraft makers, who shared out its work and profits according to their shareholdings. The four were:

187

- Aerospatiale, France: 37.9 per cent share
- Dasa, Germany: 37.9 per cent share. This was part of Daimler-Benz Aerospace
- British Aerospace: 20 per cent share
- Casa, Spain: 4 per cent share.

From nothing in 1975, the company had built its share to around 33 per cent of the world civil aircraft market. In total, Airbus had sold around 2000 aircraft to 140 airline customers worldwide. Its corporate strategy had enabled four medium-sized European manufacturers to compete in the market for large civil aircraft against the US company Boeing, which held around 50 per cent of the market. The US company had consolidated its lead in the market in 1997 when it acquired the world's third-largest civil aircraft company, McDonnell-Douglas, also located in the US.

Airbus sales in 1996 were around US$4.5 billion and in 1997 were US$4.8 billion. There were no profit figures because the company did not declare any profits. Its role was to assemble the parts supplied by its shareholders at cost – the shareholding companies took the profits in the form of the prices they charged to Airbus. Thus Airbus did not even know what profits were being earned by Aerospatiale, DASA, British Aerospace and Casa. Although this arrangement had been developed for good reasons in the past, it carried real disadvantages in the 1990s. Airbus did not know whether it was being overcharged and it could not manage its inputs efficiently. In addition, it had only limited ability and possibly incentive to reduce its costs. As a result, the Airbus partners agreed to change the arrangement around the year 2001 and turn the company into a full commercial enterprise.

These difficulties did not stop Airbus from competing successfully for aircraft, however. Its sustainable competitive advantages lay in its competitive prices, its reliable and modern designs and technology and its aggressive marketing team.

Competitive rivalry

Up to the 1990s, Airbus had been highly successful in taking sales from its great US rival, Boeing. For example, Airbus actually won roughly the same number of sales orders in 1997 as Boeing – 438 for Airbus and 432 for Boeing, according to Airbus figures. However, the US company disputed these figures, claiming that it had actually won 502

orders. Airbus then hit back by questioning the basis on which Boeing had made its estimates. Such a dispute says more about the high intensity of rivalry than about the accuracy of the detailed data. It should be noted that *orders* were often used for comparison because they produced a more inflated picture than the actual deliveries of aircraft. For example, Airbus *delivered* 182 aircraft in 1997 and Boeing 374 aircraft, including those from its newly acquired company McDonnell-Douglas.

Airbus had been particularly successful with its wide-bodied mid-range aircraft, the A330 and the A340. Boeing had responded with its new 777 in 1994–95. But it was in large, long-haul aircraft that Airbus was now seeking to expand, with a new SuperJumbo aircraft design.

Aircraft market segments

Within the civil aircraft market, there were three main segments:

1 single-aisle, short/medium-range aircraft;

2 twin-aisle, short/medium-range aircraft;

3 long-range aircraft.

Airbus and Boeing were competing head-on in the first two sectors, but not in the long-range sector: *see* Figure 5.9. In this latter segment, Boeing had been selling for some years the 747–400 model. This was able to seat 400 people and was used on major intercontinental routes like London to Singapore and Los Angeles to Tokyo. The aircraft was originally designed in the 1960s as a smaller plane and then stretched. This meant that it used older technology, but the development costs of stretching this further were relatively low.

By contrast, Airbus's largest aircraft was the A340, which carried 265 passengers. However, the new A340–600 was expected to carry 380 people when launched in the year 2000. Its technology was newer and included 'fly-by-wire' hydraulics. But the lack of a really large aircraft put Airbus at a disadvantage in two respects:

1 For the world's leading airlines, their long-haul routes were more profitable if they were able to carry the maximum number of passengers in extra-large aircraft, like the 747–400.

2 Some airlines found it more profitable to buy from only one aircraft manufacturer. This saved

CASE STUDY 5.3 continued

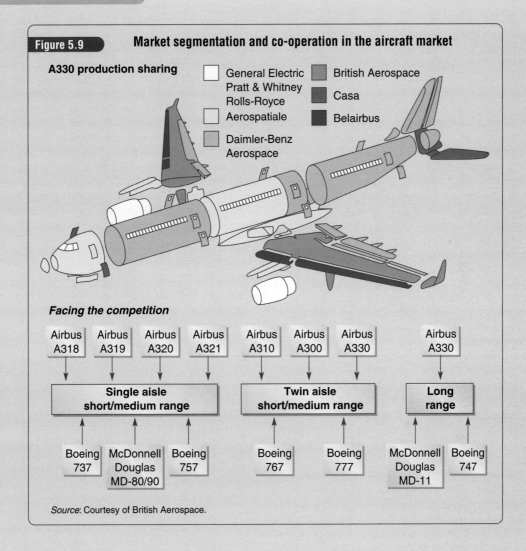

Figure 5.9 **Market segmentation and co-operation in the aircraft market**

Source: Courtesy of British Aerospace.

on spare parts, training and servicing costs. Moreover, the company offering such a deal was also willing to offer special prices to secure a long-term contract on this basis – the so-called 'sole-supplier agreement'.

But such airlines needed the supplier to be able to supply a *complete range* of aircraft, including the largest – only Boeing was able to offer this. It was only as a result of an intervention by the European Commission in 1997 that Boeing was stopped from offering sole-supplier agreements to the world's two largest airlines, American Airlines and Delta. Airbus was given a breathing space with the A340–600 but

needed a SuperJumbo aircraft that would more than match Boeing's 747–400.

SuperJumbo customer strategy at Boeing

In early 1997, Boeing announced that it had conducted a lengthy study of demand for a SuperJumbo aircraft able to carry 500–600 people. It had been considering stretching its 747–400 even further, but there was 'insufficient customer demand' to justify the US$7 billion investment. Its survey of the major airlines showed that only 480 SuperJumbos would be sold over 20 years. Boeing was therefore cancelling further development of the SuperJumbo.

Even the *Financial Times* accepted this estimate, running an editorial headed 'Death of a superJumbo'. The paper argued that the best course for Airbus was to stretch the A340 and drop any ambitions for a totally new large aircraft. What the paper failed to recognise, according to Airbus, was that it was not in Boeing's interest to develop an even larger aircraft at this stage. It had production problems on its entire range and was attempting to integrate its recent acquisition of its US rival, McDonnell-Douglas.

But Boeing's strategy was also more directly competitive. The company had much to gain by rubbishing the market potential of its rival because it was already fulfilling much of the market demand, albeit with the old 747–400. In addition, Boeing also knew that it was planning to launch a stretched version of its 777 that would take up more of the demand from 1999 onwards: its new 777–300 would carry up to 479 passengers with a third less fuel and 40 per cent lower maintainance costs.

According to Jean Pierson, the chief executive of Airbus, in 1997, 'Boeing's strategy is to maintain its monopoly [of the long-haul market] without spending too much money. It's as simple as that, The strategy of Boeing is to say "this is my private garden".' M Pierson continued by saying that, if Airbus was able to prove demand for a SuperJumbo in the next few years, then he had no doubt that Boeing would change its view and rapidly develop its own version.

SuperJumbo strategy at Airbus

In the early 1990s, Airbus co-operated with Boeing on a project called the 'Very Large Commercial Transport' – an attempt to develop jointly a new generation of large aircraft. But Boeing had wanted to think in terms of 600 seats, whereas Airbus wanted a 500-person aircraft. Airbus saw this different perspective as an attempt by Boeing to protect its monopoly of the 400-seat market. By setting up a lengthy project, Boeing was effectively delaying any separate market initiative by Airbus. The joint development failed in 1995 and Airbus was left to develop its own SuperJumbo strategy.

After the failure, Airbus was left with a potential development cost of US$8 billion to develop its own aircraft. At the time, Airbus understood that it would cost Boeing only US$2 billion to stretch its 747–400. Over the next two years, Boeing surveyed its customers, who said that they did not want such an old design. Airlines wanted a totally new aircraft. The development costs of this approach were pub-

licly estimated by Boeing at around US$7 billion. This was considered to be too high and led to Boeing's abandonment of the project in 1997, as described in the previous section. This Boeing announcement had the effect of putting pressure on Airbus to abandon its own SuperJumbo plans, while failing to mention that Boeing was quietly planning to stretch the 777 to meet part of this demand.

But none of this solved the difficulty at Airbus – could it justify spending US$8 billion on the SuperJumbo? It produced a market study saying that the potential demand for a 550-seater SuperJumbo was 1442 aircraft over 20 years. This was rather larger than Boeing's 480 aircraft estimate but Airbus justified its demand projection as follows:

- Based on current projections of airline growth, world aircraft fleets would double from 9400 aircraft in 1997 to 17 100 aircraft in 2016.
- The total number of aircraft seats would increase rather more, from 1.7 million in 1997 to over 4 million in 2016.
- The reason for the proportionately greater increase in seats was that aircraft would need to increase in size. This was related to increasing government opposition in many countries to building new airports. The only way to use existing airports better was to increase the size of the aircraft that were landing at them.

Airbus accepted that the SuperJumbo would only be used on some relatively high-density, long-haul passenger routes. But it pointed out that the existing 747–400 aircraft were already used on flights between only 12 airports worldwide. The company was therefore determined to start designing its new large SuperJumbo. It hoped to start building the first planes early in the next millennium: 'Market studies have confirmed customer interest in a brand new advanced design, rather than a derivative of existing models.'

The outcome in 2002

In 2001, Airbus took the decision to commit by itself to develop the SuperJumbo. It would be called the A380 and would cost around US$10 billion to develop. At the time of writing in early 2002, the company had some 97 firm orders for the aircraft, with significant further interest from other airlines. Boeing announced that it would not develop a similar aircraft, but would move to the next generation with a much faster aircraft – the Sonic Cruiser, which was in the early stages of development.

Case questions

1 What reasons did Boeing give for cancelling its development of the SuperJumbo? Why were these open to another interpretation?

2 What strategic weaknesses did Airbus face in terms of its customer strategy?

3 Is the Airbus strategy driven by customers? Or rather more by a sense of rivalry with Boeing?

4 To what extent do you accept the Airbus demand estimates? What are the implications for customer-driven strategy?

5 Would you support the Airbus decision to proceed with the SuperJumbo?

Sources: See reference 24.

The competitive triangle

The key relationship between the company, its customers and its competitors is explored by Dennis Adcock, Ray Bradfield, Al Halborg and Caroline Ross.

The competitive triangle is inspired by the work of Kenichi Ohmae. It is an excellent way of remembering that customers have choices. From the apex of the triangle customers can assess the different offerings of all companies and their competitors.

Obviously, customers will choose to do business with that company which best matches requirements. Of course, the workings of customers' decision processes are not simple. Nevertheless, the match between the various offerings and particular customers, or groups of customers, should not happen by chance. The role of strategists is to try to influence factors in such a way that their organisations are chosen.

The object of this is to try to gain a sustainable advantage over competitors. Writing in the *Harvard Business Review* on this subject, Pankaj Ghemwat stated:

For outstanding performance, a company has to beat competition. The trouble is that competition has heard the same message.

He summarises three areas of potential advantage from cross-industry findings:

1 *Product innovation.* Competitors secure detailed information on 70 per cent of all new products within a year of their development. Patenting usually fails to deter imitation. On average, imitation costs a third less than innovation and is a third quicker.

2 *Production.* New processes are even harder to protect than new products. Incremental improvements to old processes are vulnerable too. If

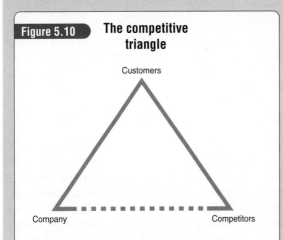

Figure 5.10 The competitive triangle

Customers

Company   Competitors

Source: Adcock, D, Brodfield, R, Halborg, A and Ross, C (1995) *Marketing Principles and Practice*, Pitman Publishing, London.

consultants are to be believed, 60 per cent to 90 per cent of all 'learning' ultimately diffuses to competitors. Production often blurs competitive advantage: recent studies show that unionised workers pocket two-thirds of the potential profits in US manufacturing.

3 *Marketing*. Non-price instruments are usually ascribed more potency than price changes, partly because they are harder to match. Rivals often react to a particular move, however, by adjusting their entire marketing mix. Such reactions tend to be intense; limited data on advertising suggest that the moves and countermoves frequently cancel out.

Nevertheless, Peters still suggests that the goal should be uniqueness. He advises:

Uniqueness most often comes not from a breakthrough idea, but from some accumulation of thousands of tiny enhancements.

In the early days of marketing, it was suggested that organisations looked for one Unique Selling Proposition (USP). In fact, as Peters points out, it is much more complex. Therefore, to achieve competitive advantage a strategist needs to be involved with the total offering, both inside and outside the organisation.

The study of competitors' activities is vital. But it must be closely linked to a study of potential buyers, how those buyers behave and how they are likely to behave in the future. It is necessary for marketers to study both customers and competitors. A focus on one alone is not enough, as it leaves the triangle (Figure 5.10) incomplete. If there is a failure to appreciate the ever-changing competition, then these words of warning are even more relevant:

There are three types of companies. Those who make things happen. Those who watch things happen. And those who wonder what happened.

Summary

● Customers are a vital part of corporate strategy development. Ultimately, customers provide either the revenue to generate the wealth of the organisation or the reason for the existence of a public service or charity. Moreover, part of the corporate strategy process will be to persuade customers of the competitive advantages of choosing the organisation's products or services rather than those offered by a rival. For these two reasons, strategy analysis needs to explore its customers with the aim of developing customer-driven strategies.

● As a starting point, demand needs to be estimated where possible. A broad view of likely levels of demand may be essential in order to identify possible competitors. However, a narrower definition will lead to identification of the attributes of the product or service that will persuade customers to choose a specific company rather than a rival. Some companies have set up customer-driven organisations as a deliberate part of strategy. This is a long-term task rather than a matter of short-term exhortation.

● Customer profiling will provide a basic understanding of the customer that is crucial to strategy development. Specifically, it will show why customers prefer one product or service rather than another and thus identify the sustainable competitive advantage possessed by the organisation. It may also clarify the organisation's strengths when faced with customers who wish to switch to rival products. Importantly, customers and their future needs may provide the breakthrough that will deliver a totally new strategic opportunity.

● The customer/competitor matrix links together two important aspects: the extent to which customers have common needs and the possibilities of achieving competitive advantage in the market place based on differentiation and economies of scale.

The matrix identifies four main types of strategic situation: fragmented, specialised, volume and stalemate. The strategic significance of each can then be explored.

● Market segmentation is the identification of specific groups of customers who respond differently from other groups to competitive strategies. They can be important in strategy development because they provide the opportunity to dominate part of the market.

● There are three prescriptive stages in developing market segmentation and positioning: identify potential segment(s); evaluate and select segment(s); position within segment(s). Identification of gaps in segment provision may provide the basis of new strategic opportunities.

● Competitive positioning is the choice of differential advantage that the product or service will possess against its competitors. Thus the advantages of segmentation in corporate strategy relate to the development of sustainable competitive advantage and to the ability to target products to that segment.

● When considering the implications of customer-driven strategy, there are three main areas: branding and reputation, communicating with customers and pricing strategy.

● Branding is a specific name or symbol used to distinguish a product or service from a functional product. It adds value to the basic functional product and provides sustainable competitive advantage. There are five elements to brand analysis: reputation, continuity, formula, incumbency and information signalling.

● Reputation is the sum of customer knowledge developed about an organisation over time. It will include brands but may also cover other aspects such as quality and service levels. It also delivers sustainable competitive advantage and adds value to basic customer perceptions of the organisation.

● Organisations communicate with their customers in order to inform and persuade them about the merits of their products and services. This will assist in establishing the sustainable competitive advantages of the product. Cost-effectiveness is the main criterion when assessing communications proposals. Costs are usually relatively easy to estimate but the effects of some promotional areas may be more difficult to assess.

● Different types of customers will need different forms of communication. Each will operate to communicate and secure the competitive advantages of the organisation. Communications policy may need an integrated approach across the organisation in the sense of considering other stakeholders as well as customers. It will be essential to examine the activities of competitors in order to identify the issues surrounding competitive advantage. It may also be necessary to consider innovative approaches to communications in order to adopt a fresh approach with customers and develop new areas of advantage.

● In the short term, pricing does not usually form the basis of sustainable competitive advantage because any price changes can be imitated very quickly by competitors. In the longer term, pricing strategy can be a major factor in competitive advantage, because it will significantly alter the basis on which companies can compete.

● Pricing strategy can have strategic significance at three levels: rapid impact on profitability, positioning of the product and value for money. The price decision will be determined by a balance of factors under the general headings of costs and competitor analysis.

● Value for money, which includes quality, branding and other factors, represents the broader elements that will determine and condition pricing for many customers. Target pricing places the main emphasis on competitors' prices and has proved an important element in the success of some companies over the last few years.

● Business is undoubtedly becoming more international. Customer analysis therefore needs to follow this trend. It has been argued that, although there are national differences in taste and culture, it is more important to seek out the similarities than to examine the differences. The greater economies of scale from operating internationally will be reflected in lower prices that will overcome any lingering problems over differences in taste.

QUESTIONS

1 Take the global market for large aircraft and explain the areas of customer analysis you would wish to consider in developing the corporate strategy for Airbus Industrie.

2 To what extent is it worthwhile estimating demand when a market is turbulent? What are the reasons for undertaking the task and what are the problems?

3 On the subject of customer needs, Professor G Hamel and Professor C K Prahalad comment:

   Any company that can do no more than respond to the articulated needs of existing customers will quickly become a laggard.

   Explain briefly the argument that is being used here and then comment on its validity. Are unmet needs so very important for strategy development?

4 Take a market with which you are familiar and explain the differences between immediate competitors and wider competitors. What implications does your distinction have for corporate strategy?

5 Compare and contrast the purchasing behaviour, communications strategy and pricing policies of the following three companies: a branded breakfast cereal manufacturer, a large retail bank and a national charitable institution of your choice.

6 What are the arguments in favour of cost-effectiveness in communicating with the customer? What are the difficulties? In view of your answer, what problems do you foresee in assessing the usefulness of such an approach in communications strategy for Unilever ice cream and for the Airbus Super Jumbo? Are they likely to be cost-effective?

7 Arguably Airbus Industrie over the last few years has followed a strategy of attempting to catch up with Boeing's initiatives. Is this the best approach to aircraft corporate strategy development? Or would Airbus have been better to seek out a new, unmet customer need?

8 What are the likely dangers of target pricing? Is it worthwhile? Are there any circumstances where it could not be used?

9 'A powerful force drives the world toward a converging commonality and that force is technology... the globalisation of markets is at hand.' (Professor Theodore Levitt)
   Discuss the implications for corporate strategy.

10 Identify where the following would fit on the customer/competitor matrix: a large hospital; a major league football team such as Real Madrid, Juventus or Manchester United; the Ford Motor Company; and Airbus Industrie. What are the strategy implications?

STRATEGIC PROJECT The world market for regional aircraft

This chapter has concentrated on the market for international *long-haul* aircraft. There is another market for *regional* aircraft which have between roughly 20 and 70 seats. Many of the same companies are involved, such as Dasa, Aerospatiale, British Aerospace and Casa, along with Alenia (Italy). After growth during the 1980s, the regional aircraft market was unprofitable for many companies during the 1990s. Some companies have lost very large sums of money and Dasa pulled out completely. You might like to investigate the reasons and to explore the corporate strategies necessary for the new millennium.

FURTHER READING

There are two books that explore the subjects of this chapter in much greater detail: Philip Kotler (1994) *Marketing Management*, 8th edn, Prentice Hall, Englewood Cliffs, NJ; and Michael J Baker (1992) *Marketing Strategy and Management*, 2nd edn, Macmillan, London.

NOTES & REFERENCES

1 Levitt, T (1960) 'Marketing myopia', *Harvard Business Review*, July–Aug, pp45–56. One of the classic marketing articles with important implications for strategy.

2 Note that loyalty and customer satisfaction are not necessarily the same thing. Piercy has argued convincingly that loyalty may be superficial and what is more fundamental for strategy development is long-term customer satisfaction: Piercy, N (1997) *Market-Led Strategic Change*, 2nd edn, Butterworth-Heinemann, Oxford, p40.

3 Levitt, T (1960) Op. cit., p45.

4 Doyle, P (1997) *Marketing Management and Strategy*, 2nd edn, Prentice Hall Europe, Hemel Hempstead, p108.

5 Aaker, D (1992) *Strategic Marketing Management*, 3rd edn, Wiley, New York, p213.

6 This section is derived from Doyle, P (1997) Op. cit., Ch2.

7 Doyle, P (1997) Op. cit., p42.

8 Hamel, G and Prahalad, C K (1994) *Competing for the Future*, Harvard Business School Press, Cambridge, MA, p102.

9 Aaker, D (1992) Op. cit., p48.

10 It should be noted that, in theory at least, it is not necessary to segment a market before exploring its competitive positioning. However, it is usual and much easier to select part of a market before undertaking positioning. Many marketing strategy texts do not make this clear.

11 Porter, M E (1985) *Competitive Advantage*, The Free Press, New York, p233.

12 Ohmae, K (1983) *The Mind of the Strategist*, Penguin, Harmondsworth, p103.

13 Probably the best-known text exploring positioning issues in depth is: Hooley, G J and Saunders, J (1999) *Competitive Positioning*, Prentice Hall, Hemel Hempstead.

14 Doyle, P (1997) Op. cit., p166.

15 Kay, J (1994) *Foundations of Corporate Success*, Oxford University Press, Oxford, pp263–4.

16 This whole subject is relatively poorly discussed in corporate strategy literature. Professor J Kay is the only recent strategist to deal in any depth with the issues raised in this chapter: his *Foundations of Corporate Success* has two chapters but they treat the subject from an economics rather than a marketing perspective and are rather simplistic as a result.

17 Baker, M (1992) *Marketing Strategy and Management*, 2nd edn, Macmillan, London, Ch17.

18 Kay, J (1994) Op. cit., p252.

19 Cusumano, M A and Takeishi, A (1991) 'Supplier relations and management: a survey of Japanese, Japanese transplant and US Auto plants', *Strategic Management Journal*, 12, pp56–58.

20 Skapinker, M (1996) 'A struggle to fly to the top', *Financial Times*, 23 Feb, p15.

21 Levitt, T (1983) 'The globalisation of markets', *Harvard Business Review*, May–June, pp92–102.

22 Readers may care to note that some of this evidence is reduced in the shortened version of this article that appears in books such as that by R De Wit and B Meyer (1994) *Strategy: Content, Context and Process*, West Publishing, St Paul, MN. It is a pity that the flimsy nature of the empirical evidence has not been presented in full.

23 Douglas, S and Wind, Y (1987) 'The myth of globalisation', *Columbia Journal of World Business*, Winter. This is also reprinted in De Wit, R and Meyer, B (1994) Op. cit.

24 *See Financial Times*, 13 Sept 1990; 29 Jan 1993, p17; 3 Mar 1993, p19; 11 May 1994, p33; 19 Apr 1995, p17; 23 Feb 1996, p15; 14 Jan 1997, p17; 22 Jan 1997, pp1, 4, 21; 20 Feb 1997, p25; 7 Mar 1997, p6; 18 Apr 1997, p7; 14 Jan 1998, p4; 10 Aug 1998, p9; 3 December 1998, p21; 8 December 1998, p8; 25 February 1999, p38; 17 March 1999, p7; 15 October 1999, p22; 10 December 1999, p20; 23 December 1999, p19; 3 January 2000, p11; 14 March 2000, p3; 28 June 2000, p17; 30 August 2000, p22; 2 November 2000, p28; 20 December 2000, pp12, 24; 8 January 2001, p6; 2 April 2001, p29; 10 April 2001, p15; 27 April 2001, p38; 23 June 2001, p13; 21 September 2001, p33; 5 February 2002, p16; 7 February 2002, p29; Company Annual Reports of British Aerospace, UK; Aerospatiale, France; Boeing, USA.

Analysis of resources

Both the emergent and prescriptive strategy processes regard the organisation's resources as the foundation stone of strategy development.

The resources are the means by which the organisation generates *value*. It is this value that is then distributed to the employees as salaries, to government as taxes, to the shareholders as dividends or retained in the organisation to be reinvested for the future. Resources are also the means by which one organisation distinguishes itself from another. It is this aspect of resources that delivers and maintains *sustainable competitive advantage*. Part 3 introduces the concept of generating value and its fundamental importance to corporate strategy. It also explores how resources can and should generate advantages over the organisation's competitors. The three resources of the organisation – human, financial and operations – are then explored in turn.

Analysis of resources

The *prescriptive* strategic process

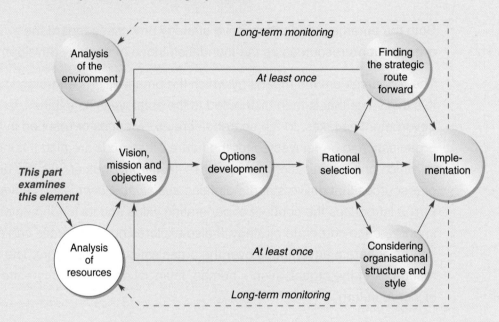

The *emergent* strategic process

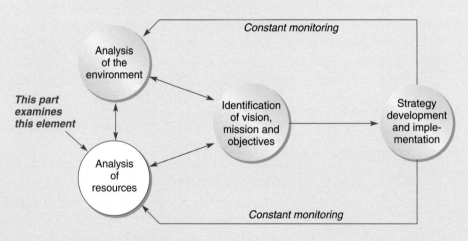

Chapter 6
Analysing resources – basics

- *What key industry factors deliver the objectives of the organisation?*
- *How do resources add value to the organisation?*
- *How can value added be improved?*
- *Which resources are particularly important in adding value and competitive advantage?*
- *What are the main ways that resources deliver competitive advantage?*
- *How can competitive advantage be enhanced?*

Chapter 7
Analysing human resources

- *How do human resources add value? And how do they contribute to sustainable competitive advantage?*
- *What is the organisation's culture? How does it take decisions and develop its strategy?*
- *How does the organisation undertake change?*
- *How does the politics of the organisation affect change?*

Chapter 8
Analysing financial resources

- *How do financial resources add value? And how do they contribute to sustainable competitive advantage?*
- *What are the main sources and the cost of finance?*
- *What are the financial consequences of strategic expansion?*
- *What is the relationship between financial and corporate objectives?*

Chapter 9
Analysing operations resources

- *How do operations resources add value? And how do they contribute to sustainable competitive advantage?*
- *What impact do changes in technology have on corporate strategy?*
- *What areas of operations strategy make a major contribution to corporate strategy?*
- *What are the main elements of operations strategy?*

Analysing resources – basics

When you have worked through this chapter, you will be able to:

- identify the key factors for success in an industry;
- explore the main resources of an organisation and the strategic decision on whether to make or buy;
- explain the concept of value added;
- analyse the value chain and value system of an organisation and comment on their strategic significance;
- outline the concept of economic rent and its relationship with sustainable competitive advantage;
- explain how resources deliver sustainable competitive advantage to the organisation;
- identify and explain the seven main concepts of sustainable competitive advantage;
- explain the roles of different resources in the organisation and relate them to sustainable competitive advantage;
- outline three methods for improving the sustainable competitive advantage of the organisation's resources.

Introduction

Analysing the resources of an organisation involves not only exploring the role and contribution of the main resources, but also developing an understanding of two main issues. First, it is important to explore how resources deliver profits in private companies and provide services in publicly owned organisations. Second, it is essential to identify those resources that enable an organisation to compete and survive against competition. In both cases, such an understanding will form the basis of future strategy development.

As a starting point, it is useful to consider the factors that deliver success in an industry as a whole, covering both the resources and the environment – the key factors for success.

Within the context of the industry, each organisation is then different – perhaps in small ways like a well-established product range, perhaps in major ways like exceptional leadership or a new, patented technology. These differences are important in strategy development, so they need to be analysed carefully for the individual organisation.

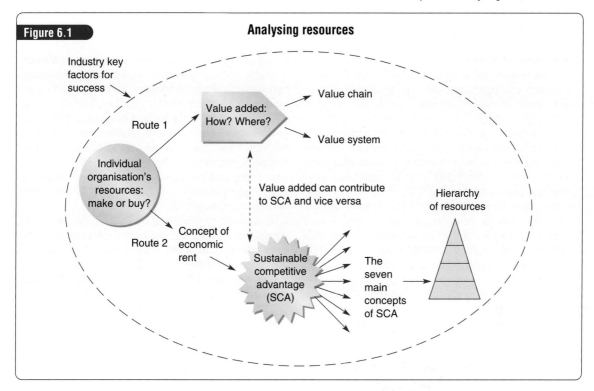

Figure 6.1

Analysing resources

The resource analysis needs to proceed along two parallel and interconnected routes: value added and sustainable competitive advantage. Figure 6.1 identifies the elements involved. The value-added route explores how the organisation takes goods from its suppliers and turns them into finished goods and services that are then sold into the environment: how the organisation adds value to the inputs it receives from its suppliers.

The *competitive advantage* route examines the special resources that enable the organisation to compete: how and why some resources deliver sustainable competitive advantage is crucial to strategy development. This chapter analyses the organisation's resources from both these perspectives and considers how such resources might be improved.

CASE STUDY 6.1

Resource strategy at GSK: negotiating a merger and making it work

In the technically innovative and global market for pharmaceutical products, Glaxo Smith Kline (GSK) is one of the world's largest drug companies – and size can matter in this industry. This case explores the competitive benefits of larger size and how GSK almost failed to develop them.

Background

Over the last 20 years, pharmaceuticals have become increasingly expensive to develop – typically, costing around US$500 million, spread over several years, for one major drug. After develop-

ment, these drugs need to be marketed to customers such as doctors, hospitals and government health services – for example, several thousand specialist sales personnel may be required for such a task in the North American market alone. To support such activities, substantial cash resources are important. In addition, world alliances and other connections between manufacturers can also be highly beneficial: drug companies can use these to support areas where they are both weak geographically and have gaps in their product development programmes.

From the size perspective, it helps to have substantial resources. But this does not explain why even large companies have chosen to become larger over the last five years. For example, the Swedish company Astra merged with the UK company Zeneca and the French company Rhone-Poulenc joined together with part of the German company Hoechst to form Aventis during 1998/99. Over this time, half the world's largest drug companies announced either mergers or takeovers of fellow companies.

Some strategists would argue that if *all* the companies become larger then no drug company has developed any competitive advantage over another. The benefit cannot simply be size alone. It is necessary to examine the *individual* competitive resources of each company to see what size delivers. To explore this, we need to look separately at the two merger candidates in the case in question – Glaxo Wellcome and Smith Kline Beecham.

Competitive resources at Glaxo Wellcome

During the period 1980–95, Glaxo (as it was then called) was highly dependent on its patented drug, Zantac, which is used for treating stomach ulcers. For example, in 1994 this one drug alone accounted for 44 per cent of the company's sales and 50 per cent of its profits. In the early 1990s, Zantac was the biggest single selling drug in the world and its ownership by Glaxo was a major strategic resource.

But this substantial strength faced two threats. First, the patents would begin to expire in 1997 and allow any company to manufacture and market the drug, thus reducing the profit margins that Glaxo was able to charge. Secondly, a new rival drug, Losec, was introduced to health authorities in 1993–94 by the Swedish company Astra Pharmaceuticals. Losec was claimed to be even more effective than Zantac. Glaxo knew the seriousness of such a competitive threat because its own drug, Zantac, had wiped the floor with an earlier rival in the mid-1980s, namely Tagamet, from the pharmaceutical company Smith Kline Beecham.

Faced with these twin threats, Glaxo needed a new resource strategy. Given the time lag in developing new drugs, Glaxo used its existing resource strength – the profitability of Zantac – to acquire two existing drug companies. Wellcome (UK) was bought in 1995 for US$13.5 billion. This delivered a whole new range of patented drugs into the Glaxo portfolio, including the anti-AIDS drug Retrovir and the anti-viral drug Zovirax. In addition, the UK company Affymix was bought for US$533 million. The latter company was developing a range of genetic products whose benefits would be truly revolutionary, if successful.

In addition to acquiring drugs from the two new companies, Glaxo gained other resource benefits from these purchases. The acquisition allowed Glaxo to combine its R&D team with that of Wellcome, saving 1800 jobs and the labour costs associated with this. In addition, 3000 jobs were lost in manufacturing by combining various plants and 2600 jobs were lost in marketing and administration. In total, around US$1 billion cost savings were achieved. But it was not all good news: the patents on the top-selling drug Zovirax were due to expire from 1997 onwards (patents have roughly a ten-year life from first registration).

By 1995, the acquisitions had turned Glaxo Wellcome (as it then became) into the largest pharmaceutical company in the world. It was particularly strong in asthma and anti-viral drugs.

Competitive resources of Smith Kline Beecham

It was the loss of profits from Tagamet mentioned above that forced its makers, the American company Smith Kline, to seek a merger with the UK company Beecham in the late 1980s. Nevertheless, the new company had proceeded to develop many new, patented drugs over the succeeding ten years to the late 1990s. It had also exploited its range of branded medicines sold directly to the general public with higher profit margins than were available on many pharmaceuticals. By 1998, the company was particularly strong in anti-depressants, vaccines, antibiotics and diabetes medicines.

Abortive merger between the two companies in 1998

Glaxo Wellcome explored merging the company with Smith Kline Beecham during 1998. This would have transformed the resource capability of the two companies because they both had different areas of product strength in the drugs market, and the duplication of some facilities and services could have been eliminated. The scale of the proposed merger was substantive: for example, the two companies had combined spending of over US$3 billion on R&D and would have accounted for one-fifth of all the private sector R&D investment in the UK. There would have been considerable scope for short-term cost savings, both in R&D and in production and marketing.

But the merger did not take place. The two companies clashed over two matters: the styles of negotiation and the proposed new management structure. The cultures of the two companies were so different that the merger discussions became difficult – for example, they were so bad that the participants never even had lunch together. In addition, there were differences between the two chief executives and other senior managers over their respective roles in the merged company. The result was that the merger never took place and the substantial resource benefits were never achieved.

Successful merger in 2000/2001

In the face of increased competition and the cost of drug development, the pressure to consolidate remained. What made the difference was that the chief executive of SKB, Jan Leschly, decided to retire early – he was the man with whom some senior executives at Glaxo had absolutely refused to work. In addition, the chief executive of Glaxo, Sir Richard Sykes, decided to step down from his role, while at the same time expressing his regard for a senior manager he had met at SKB, M Jean-Pierre Garnier. Thus the two companies decided to meet

again and agreed a merger with M Garnier as chief executive.

As a result, the combined company was able to employ an enhanced research budget of over US$4 billion in 2002. Annual cost savings of US$750 million had been achieved, but this was slightly short of earlier expectations. It had a sales team in North America alone of over 7500 people. The two product ranges from the two companies complemented each other, with some minor overlap. The company had a global market share of 7.4 per cent. This might appear small but the company dominated some segments of the drug market and was twice the size of its next competitor.

Sources: See reference1.

Case questions

1 *What are the key factors for success in this market? And what are the implications of your answer for large and small drug manufacturers?*

2 *What was the nature of the competitive advantages held by Glaxo Wellcome? And Smith Kline Beecham? Were they sustainable?*

3 *Do cost savings in themselves represent substantive competitive advantage?*

4 *What lesson, if any, on the development of sustainable competitive advantage can be drawn from the case for other companies outside pharmaceuticals?*

6.1 Prescriptive and emergent approaches to resource issues

Both emergent and prescriptive approaches to strategy development regard resources as important. However, their perspectives are very different.

Prescriptive strategists take the view that it is important to use resources efficiently and build on resource strengths. Resources are to some extent regarded as inanimate objects without feeling. Hence it is possible for strategy to manipulate and mould resources in order to provide a more efficient organisation. For example, the GSK merger benefited from significant job cuts and the resultant annual savings of over US$750 million. Prescriptive strategists argue that the company will be stronger as a result.

Although there is not complete agreement among emergent strategists, they would certainly question the certainties of the prescriptive view of resources. For some, doubts centre on the assumption made by prescriptive strategists that change is achievable. Emergent strategists probably lay more stress on the impact of human resources than their prescriptive counterparts. For example, the GSK job cuts were accompanied by considerable uncertainty and worry, which must have affected the ability of those carrying out the changes: some emergent strategists argue that people resources are not just objects but human beings who can help or hinder strategic change.

For other emergent strategists, the environment is changing so fast as a result of forces beyond the control of the organisation that resources need to be flexible and aimed at survival. In this sense, the GSK merger could be regarded as being unwelcome if it produced a larger and less flexible organisation. Yet other emergent strategists question the value of patents to deliver sustainable competitive advantage in the fast-changing drug market.

These differences of views are reflected in the two models used in this book. In the prescriptive model, resources deliver a definite result to the organisation and its future strategies. In the emergent model, the resources and subsequent strategies are much more fluid and interrelated.

This chapter concentrates on the prescriptive approach as it forms the basis of resource analysis for strategy development. This is because it is well developed, with useful insights, and, in addition, even those who doubt its usefulness still need to understand it first.

In Chapter 7 and subsequent chapters, the emergent approach is explored further.

> ### ◗ Key strategic principles
>
> - **Prescriptive approaches regard resources as objects to be moulded for maximum strategic benefit.**
> - **Emergent approaches do not have a consistent theme with regard to resources. However, they tend to value the human element more highly: this is inherently less predictable. They also emphasise the need for a close relationship between the environment and the resources.**
> - **This chapter concentrates on the prescriptive view because it is well developed and has useful strategy insights.**

6.2 Key factors for success in an industry

By now, it will be evident that corporate strategy encompasses the whole organisation. Whether the strategic process is prescriptive or emergent, it needs to consider every part of the organisation and, most importantly, do so with limited resources.

Potentially, this raises a major strategic problem: corporate strategy analysis could be overwhelmed by the size of the task. An analytical process is needed that will examine the many factors that can potentially impact on strategy.

The Japanese strategist Kenichi Ohmae,[2] the former head of the management consultants McKinsey, in Japan, has suggested a way of tackling this matter by identifying *the key factors for success* that are *likely* to deliver the company's objectives. He argued that, when resources of capital, labour and time are scarce, it is important that they should be *concentrated* on the key activities of the business – that is, those most important to the delivery of whatever the organisation regards as 'success'.

This concept of key factors for success is also consistent with Porter's view[3] that there are factors that determine the relative competitive positions of companies within an industry. Moreover, the foundation of Kay's approach[4] is that it is important to concentrate resources on the specific areas of the business that are most likely to prove successful. Amit and Schoemaker[5] provide a more extended theoretical framework for the same topic, but call their treatment 'Strategic Industry Factors'. All the above have said that identifying the key factors is not an easy task.

6.2.1 Identifying the key factors for success in the industry

Key factors concern not only the resources of organisations in the industry but also the *competitive environment* in which organisations operate. There are three principal areas that need to be analysed – Ohmae's *three Cs*.[6]

1 *Customers*. What do customers really want? What are the segments in the market place? Can we direct our strategy towards a group?

2 *Competition*. How can the organisation beat or at least survive against competition? What resources and customers does it have that make it particularly successful? How does the organisation compare on price, quality, etc? Does the organisation have a stronger distributive network than its competitors?

3 *Corporation*. What special resources does the company itself possess and how do they compare with those of competitors? How does the company compare on costs with its rivals? And on technologies? Skills? Organisational ability? Marketing?

Exhibit 6.1 sets out some key questions in more detail. No single area is more important than another. The *competition* and *customer* issues were examined in Chapters 4 and 5 and it is not proposed to repeat this analysis here. The *corporate* factors relate to the *resource* issues which are explored in detail in the remainder of this chapter.

Exhibit 6.1   **Identifying key factors for success in an industry**

Note that key factors for success are directed at *all companies in an industry*, not just the target company for strategy development.

1 Customers

Who are the customers? Who are the potential customers? Are there any special segments? Why do customers buy from us? And from our competitors?

- *Price*. Is the market segmented by high, medium and economy pricing? For example, the market for European ice cream.

- *Service*. Do some customers value service while others simply want to buy the product? For example, top-class fashion retailers versus standard clothing shops.

- *Product or service reliability*. Is product performance crucial to the customer or is reliability useful but not really important? For example, heart pacemakers and pharmaceuticals.

- *Quality*. Some customers will pay higher prices for actual or perceived quality differences. Does this provide a route to success? For example, organic vegetables.

- *Technical specifications*. In some industrial and financial services, technical details will provide major attractions for some customers. Is this relevant in this industry? For example, specialist financial bond dealers.

- *Branding*. How important is branding for the customer? For example, Coca-Cola and Pepsi Cola.

2 Competition

Who are the main competitors? What are the main factors in the market that influence competition? How intense is competition? What is necessary to achieve

▶

market superiority? What resources do competitors possess that we lack and vice versa?

- *Cost comparisons.* Which companies have the lowest costs? Why? For example, Toyota until the mid-1990s.
- *Price comparisons.* Which companies have high prices? For example, Daimler-Benz does not make cheap cars.
- *Quality issues.* Which companies have the highest quality? Why? How? For example, Xerox (US) in the light of fierce competition from Japanese companies such as Canon.
- *Market dominance.* Which companies dominate the market? For example, Nestlé, with the strongest coffee product range in the world and the largest market share.
- *Service.* Are there companies in the industry that offer superior service levels? For example, industrial markets, such as those served by Asea Brown Boveri, which need high levels of service to operate and maintain sophisticated equipment.
- *Distributors.* Which companies have the best distributive network? Lowest costs? Fastest delivery? Competent distributors that really know the product or service? For example, major glass companies such as St Gobain (France) and Pilkington (UK).

3 Corporation

What are our key resources and those of our competitors? What do they deliver to customers? Where are the majority of the industry costs concentrated? A small percentage reduction to a large part of the total costs will deliver more than a large percentage reduction in an area of lower total costs.

- *Low-cost operations.* Are low-cost operations important for ourselves or our competitors? For example, Aldi (Germany) and Tesco (UK) are both low-cost supermarket operators.
- *Economies of scale.* Do these exist in the industry? How important are they? For example, large-scale petroleum chemical refinery operations such as those operated by Royal Dutch/Shell.
- *Labour costs.* Does our industry rely heavily on low labour costs for competitive operations? For example, Philips (Netherlands) has moved its production to Singapore and Malaysia to lower labour costs.
- *Production output levels.* Does our industry need full utilisation of plant capacity? For example, European paper and packaging companies.
- *Quality operations.* Do customers need consistent and reliable quality? How do we compare with others in the industry? For example, McDonald's has applied the same standards around the world in its restaurants.
- *Innovative ability.* Does our industry place a high reliance on our ability to produce a constant stream of new innovations? For example, computer hardware and software companies such as Apple, Epson and Microsoft.
- *Labour/management relations.* Is our industry heavily reliant on good relations? Are there real problems if disputes arise? For example, European large-scale steel production, at companies such as Usinor/Arbed.
- *Technologies and copyright.* Does the industry rely on specialist technologies, especially those that are patented and provide a real competitive advantage? For example, News International (Australia), which has exclusive global control over some forms of decoder cards for satellite television.
- *Skills.* Do organisations in the industry possess exceptional human skills and people? What are such skills? For example, advertising agencies and leading consultancy companies.

6.2.2 Critical comment on the concept

Criticism of the key factors for success has concentrated on four issues:[7]

1 *Identification.* It is difficult to pick out the important factors.

2 *Causality of relationships.* Even though they have been identified, it may not be clear *how* they operate or interact.

3 *Dangers of generalising.* The competitive advantage of a single organisation, by definition, cannot be obtained by seeking what is commonly accepted as bringing success to all organisations in an industry.

4 *Disregard of emergent perspectives.* Success may come from change in an industry, rather than the identification of the current key factors for success.

Beyond these specific criticisms, some strategists have a more general concern about industry analysis (this is explored in the next section). Some of the criticisms can be countered if key factors for success are regarded as *guidelines* for directing strategy development, rather than rigid rules. But the criticisms suggest that key factors for success should be explored with caution. They are only a starting point in strategy analysis – the 'best' strategy may be to reject the key factors and do something completely different!

> ### Key strategic principles
>
> - Identifying the key factors for success shapes the key areas of strategic analysis.
> - Such factors can conveniently be considered under three headings: customers, competition and corporation. By 'corporation' is meant the resources of the organisation.
> - Key factors can be found in any area of the organisation and relate to skills, competitive advantage, competitive resources of an organisation in the industry, special technologies or customer contacts.
> - Four criticisms of key factors have been made: identification, causality of relationships, dangers of generalising, and disregard of emergent perspectives. Caution is therefore needed in their application.

6.3 Analysing the resources of an *individual* organisation

6.3.1 The distinction between industry and *individual* companies in resource analysis

In Part 2, we explored environmental analysis extensively because it is essential for the development of two key strategic concepts: *competitive advantage* and *customer-led strategy*. Both have meaning only in the context of the environment within which the organisation operates. The previous section examined another aspect of environmental analysis: *key factors for success* in the industry. But these studies of the environment are fundamentally incomplete from a strategy perspective.

Organisations seeking competitive advantage over others need to make an offering to customers that is different from and more persuasive than those of its competitors. Therefore resource analysis needs to move beyond factors that apply to the industry as a whole. Each organisation needs to analyse and develop the *individual* resources that will allow it to survive and compete in the environment. For example, GSK is unlikely to survive because it has a powerful marketing and sales team – other companies also have this. GSK needs an effective and well-patented portfolio of its own exclusive drugs. Such products will deliver competitive advantage over others in the industry and high added value in the form of profits, cash and service to its customers.

Although it might seem clear now that industry resource analysis needs to be accompanied by an analysis of the individual organisation, this was not so obvious until recently.[8] For many years in the 1970s, 1980s and 1990s, the main emphasis in strategy development was laid on industry analysis – for example, the work of Porter[9] and others outlined in Chapter 3.[10] However, this stress on industry analysis in turn represented a shift from the 1950s and 1960s, which took a more inclusive approach – the work of Penrose[11] and others outlined at the end of Chapter 2. For our purposes, after analysing the resources of the industry and seeing how organisations add value in the early parts of this chapter, we will explore in the remainder the resources of the individual organisation.

6.3.2 Why does an organisation possess any resources at all? The make-or-buy decision

As a starting point in identifying the strategic role of individual resources, it is useful to explore the reasons for an organisation to possess and use *any* resources beyond the minimum amount needed to stay in existence. Arguably, in an efficient market, there will be outside more specialised suppliers that will be able to sell some activities more cheaply to the organisation than it can make them for itself. For example, GSK does not produce its own advertising campaigns but employs an outside agency. The company also does not manufacture its own cartons, boxes and foil in which to pack its drugs, but buys them in – why? Because it is cheaper to buy from an outside supplier than make them for itself. The company uses the outside 'market' to buy in some goods rather than use its own resources to make them. However, there are also problems with buying in from outside – see Exhibit 6.2 – otherwise all organisations would buy everything and make nothing. Essentially, to resolve the problem of what an organisation should make rather than buy, the costs of using the market must be higher than the benefits.

The make-or-buy decision is part of a broader strategic reappraisal of resources. Over the last 30 years, many organisations have come to redefine the boundaries of their resources – what they *make* is only part of the resources *owned* by the firm. For example, firms also have resources like brand names, which they do not manufacture on a production line but which are important contributors to value added. This profound rethink on the nature and role of resources by writers such as Coase, Penrose and Williamson has led to some important strategic resource decisions.[12]

Companies like Nike Sports (US) and Benetton Clothing (Italy) have achieved strategic success by buying in many of the activities that might previously have been undertaken in-house: both use networks of suppliers and, in the case of Benetton, distributors to make and sell their goods more cheaply. Nike designs and markets its

---

Exhibit 6.2 **Benefits and costs of using the market**

Benefits

- Outside suppliers can achieve economies of scale that in-house departments producing only for their own needs cannot.

- Outside suppliers are subject to the pressures of the market and must be efficient and innovative to survive. Overall corporate success may hide the inefficiencies and lack of innovativeness of in-house departments.

Costs

- Production flows need to be co-ordinated through the value chain of the organisation. This may be compromised when an activity is purchased from an independent market firm rather than performed in-house.

- Private information may be leaked when an activity is performed by an independent market firm – such information may be crucial to the competitive advantage held by the organisation.

- There may be costs of transacting with independent firms that can be avoided by performing the activity in-house.

Source: Adapted from Besanko, D, Dranove, D and Shenley, M (1996), *The Economics of Strategy*, Wiley, New York, p73. © Copyright 1996 John Wiley & Sons, Inc. Reprinted by permission of the publishers.

---

new shoes but has them manufactured by outside suppliers in Asia – *see* Case 11.1. Benetton has a similar arrangement, using a group of local suppliers in northern Italy: this is called *outsourcing* supplies. Although it might appear that Benetton owns the resource of the shop chain that bears the company name, in fact most of the stores are not owned by the company. They are operated under the control of Benetton but owned by others outside the company: this is called *franchising*. The concepts of branded clothing, franchised clothing stores and outsourced supplies formed the basis of Benetton's highly original new strategy in the 1970s. The starting point for such strategy development is an analysis of the resources of the organisation as they exist at present. We undertake this task during the rest of this chapter.

🔊 Key strategic principles

- Key factors for success in an industry represent a starting point for exploring the resources of the individual organisation. But the search for value added and sustainable competitive advantage must move beyond industry solutions. *Individual* resources must be identified for the organisation itself.

- The *make-or-buy decision* concerns the choice that every organisation has of either making its own products or services or buying them from outside. Every organisation needs to reappraise its activities regularly in this area.

How three European companies attempt to utilise their resources

In this case study, three totally different companies are explored to see how each utilises its resources and achieves its corporate objectives. The first two companies operate in the pharmaceutical and national railway service industries respectively; the third is a holding company with a range of activities mainly in construction, public services and television broadcasting.

The three companies under consideration are the UK pharmaceutical company Glaxo (before the merger with Smith Kline Beecham), the Dutch national railway company Nederlandse Spoorwegen, and the French services holding company Bouygues. Each has totally different resources, skills and methods of working, and each is involved in very different environments, including healthcare, transport services and the construction of roads. The purpose of this case is to identify the *key* strategic resources – that is, those that will make a difference to the company's corporate strategy.

Mission and objectives

As a starting point for any strategic analysis, it is important to consider *why* these three organisations are utilising the resources. What are they attempting to achieve? In principle, each is setting out to accomplish its *mission and objectives*. These need to be identified and explored.

Key resource analysis

Each of these companies brings totally different types of resources, skills and methods of operation to the achievement of its objectives. Figure 6.2 has used data taken from recent annual reports and other sources to construct the *cost profiles* for each of the three companies in this case study. The costs of each major item of company expenditure are expressed as a percentage of sales, coupled with profits before tax and interest as a percentage of sales. They are calculated by taking each cost item and dividing it by the sales figure and expressing this as a percentage. The profile demonstrates how each element of *resource* in the company contributes to profit and sales.

Resources for Glaxo

The information for Glaxo is included in the GSK case study at the beginning of this chapter. Case 6.2 considers the situation *prior* to the merger in

2000/2001. There was no substantive change in the balance of resources after the merger, but detailed data were not published at the time to enable the necessary analysis to be undertaken.

Resources for Nederlandse Spoorwegen

- *Increased utilisation of existing railway lines and rolling stock.* The investment in track and trains in most companies is largely complete. The key is to obtain greater usage of what is already present.
- *Marketing, sales and special prices.* These are to encourage customers to use the railways in preference to their competitors: road, air and bus traffic. This is particularly true in the Netherlands with its extensive and well-developed transport infrastructure.
- *High levels of service.* These involve the employees of the company and investment in new equipment on information and signalling to inform customers better of transport network problems.

Most national European railway companies are competing mainly within their national boundaries.[13] Resource analysis therefore needs to concentrate on national transport competitors in the first instance.

With the high fixed investment already made in track, signalling and rolling stock, corporate strategy has relied largely on encouraging *greater utilisation of the existing facilities* – that is, the marketing and sales activities mentioned above.

Another aspect of strategy that is important for most railway companies is *the relationship with government.* During the period from which the data shown in Figure 6.2 were taken, the Dutch railway company was receiving grants from the Netherlands government that amounted to 9 per cent of its total revenue. These were used to subsidise train fares and freight passage so that railways would be used in preference to roads.

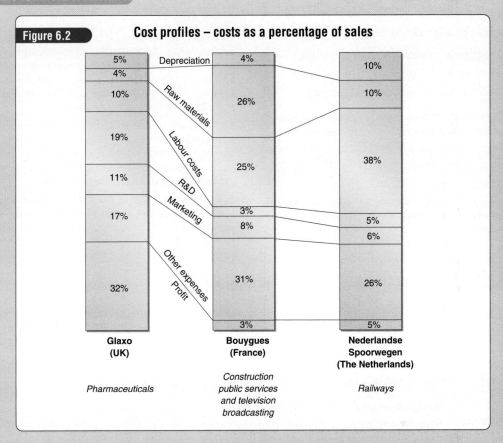

Figure 6.2

Cost profiles – costs as a percentage of sales

Glaxo (UK) — Pharmaceuticals
Bouygues (France) — Construction public services and television broadcasting
Nederlandse Spoorwegen (The Netherlands) — Railways

Categories: Depreciation, Raw materials, Labour costs, R&D, Marketing, Other expenses, Profit

Glaxo values (top to bottom): 5%, 4%, 10%, 19%, 11%, 17%, 32%

Bouygues values (top to bottom): 4%, 26%, 25%, 3%, 8%, 31%, 3%

Nederlandse Spoorwegen values (top to bottom): 10%, 10%, 38%, 5%, 6%, 26%, 5%

Resources for Bouygues

In this case, the resources will be dictated by the precise nature of each of the activities in which the company is engaged. In theory, it will be necessary to analyse each of the hundreds of companies in the group. In practice, three areas of the company accounted for around 92 per cent of sales in 1999:

Building and road construction	63%
Public utilities management	15%
Media – television stations	14%

For the purposes of *strategic analysis*, it is normally acceptable to ignore the remaining collection of areas. This is not a financial audit of the company, simply an overall judgement of the *main thrust* of the company's business. However, in the case of Bouygues, the company has developed a small but fast-growing interest in mobile telecommunications services. This new investment will require substantial capital over the period 1999–2004, even though it

represented only 3 per cent of turnover in 1999. It therefore may deserve comment below. The comment on ignoring the remaining areas of the business would also be invalid if other areas were making huge losses or otherwise represented a significant potential shift in the company. We can identify the reasons involved in the three main areas of business:

1 Building and road construction resources include:
   - raw materials for buildings and roads;
   - labour construction costs coupled with skills and efficiency;
   - design and engineering costs.

2 Public utilities management resources include:
   - quality of services provided;
   - management liaison with government owners;
   - cost control and monitoring skills.

3 Media television station resources – French national channel TF1:

- programme origination and purchasing;
- network management and costing;
- audience monitoring and assessment.

It will be evident that analysing the resources in a diversified holding company is a major task. It has been simplified by concentrating on certain key areas of the business. However, this is a compromise.

Case questions

1 *An examination of the cost profiles of the three companies reveals that research and development (R&D) feature more prominently in Glaxo than in the other two companies. Why is this? What risks, if any, are associated with heavy R&D expenditure? What implications might this have for strategic decisions?*

2 *Marketing and related expenditures are much higher as a proportion of sales in Glaxo than Nederlandse Spoorwegen. What are the reasons for this? Can you make out a strategic case for higher levels of marketing expenditure at the Dutch railway company?*

3 *The case study suggests that holding companies have a more complex task in managing their resources. Do you agree?*

6.4 Resource analysis and adding value

This section explores the value that resources contribute to the organisation. The following two sections consider how value added is related to competitive advantage and how value added can be measured in practice and improved through new strategies.

6.4.1 Adding value – the role of resources in the organisation

The fundamental role of resources in an organisation is to add value. Resources add value by working on the raw materials that enter the factory gate and turning them into a finished product. Added value can be defined as the difference between the market value of output and the cost of inputs. The concept is basically an economic one and is outlined, using Glaxo as an example, in Figure 6.3. For non-profit organisations, the concept of adding value can still be applied. The inputs to the organisation may be similar to those of commercial organisations – electricity, telephones, etc. – and may be very different, particularly voluntary labour which has a zero cost. Equally, the outputs may be difficult to define and measure – service to the community, help for sick people, etc. But the *value added* is real enough, just difficult to quantify. To explore the basic concepts, commercial explanations *only* are examined in this section and the next.

When calculating the value that the company's resources add, it is important to consider three areas of costs: *labour*, *raw materials* and *capital* costs. The first two of these areas are reasonably clear for a company to calculate: the company's management accounts will record these data. Capital costs are more complex. The value of land and buildings, plant and machinery, stocks and work in progress needs to be assessed. *The replacement value* of this capital (not just historic cost depreciation) and the *cost of capital* allowing for an element of risk for the company (*see* Chapter 8), must also be calculated. The detailed calculation is not easy, even when inside information on the organisation concerned is available. Consequently, the value-added calculation is not usually undertaken in detail in strategic analysis. Nevertheless, added value is an important strategic concept. As Kay[14] points out, a commercial

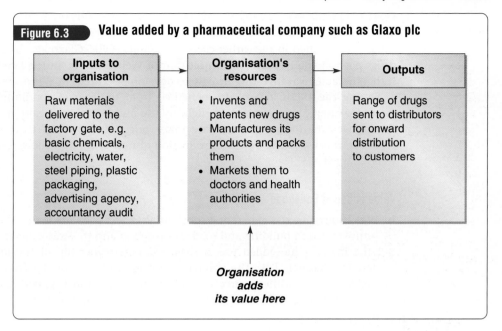

Figure 6.3 Value added by a pharmaceutical company such as Glaxo plc

Inputs to organisation	Organisation's resources	Outputs
Raw materials delivered to the factory gate, e.g. basic chemicals, electricity, water, steel piping, plastic packaging, advertising agency, accountancy audit	• Invents and patents new drugs • Manufactures its products and packs them • Markets them to doctors and health authorities	Range of drugs sent to distributors for onward distribution to customers

Organisation adds its value here

organisation that adds no net value to the inputs it receives from its environment has no long-term reason for existence. Some organisations actually have a *negative* added value: they are not recovering the full costs of their inputs and their survival may be in doubt. In Table 6.1 we return to the three companies of Case study 6.1 and calculate their value added with some interesting strategic consequences. (Data were not available to make direct comparisons for all years but the latest information has been used at the time of writing.)

Value added at Glaxo – prior to the merger in 2000

Clearly, Glaxo adds real value to its inputs. In fact, in a survey quoted by Kay,[16] Glaxo added more value to its inputs than any other large European company between the

Table 6.1 Value added in three large European companies (US$ million)

	Glaxo			Bouygues	Nederlandse Spoorwegen	
	1997	*1994*	*1990**	*1997*	*1997*	*1993*
Sales/outputs	12 791	8 701	5 096	15 164	2 415	2 080
Wages and salaries	2 928	2 000	1 152	3 682	911	1 155
Capital costs	510	978	557	358	173	692
Raw materials	1 685	3 526	1 948	3 441	1 253	1 050
Value added	7 688	2 197	1 439	7 268	78	(817)

* Recalculated from Kay.[15]

Source: Annual reports and accounts calculated by the author.

years 1981 and 1990. During the 1980s, its competitive advantage was chiefly from the anti-ulcer drug Zantac. During the 1990s, this was replaced by a series of other patented drugs – as outlined in the earlier case. In the mid-1990s, Glaxo also benefited from the drugs portfolio delivered by its acquisition of Wellcome plc. In the late 1990s, GSK (as it then became) was investing heavily to develop new drugs.

During the 1980s, Glaxo also benefited from the market conditions that allowed prices for unique drugs to remain high. By the mid-1990s, the health authorities across Europe were beginning to negotiate lower prices for all drugs that they purchased. However, this was offset by the introduction of new drugs that allowed new high prices to be charged.

Value added at Bouygues

In 1997, Bouygues was generating substantial value added. Its main business measured by turnover was in building and road construction and this was generating some value. But the major value added was derived from its ownership of the leading national French TV channel, TF1. The company also held a share of the French mobile telephone market – another source of value added, with much greater growth potential than construction and roads. Wisely, as it turned out, the company never bid for a French third generation mobile licence – *see* Chapter 15.

Value added at Nederlandse Spoorwegen

Nederlandse Spoorwegen had a small, positive value added in 1997, which compared favourably with the negative value added of US$817 million in 1993. The lack of a major positive value added in 1997 is not surprising, given its public service role with a duty to provide low-price travel for its customers.[17] Its costs were just about being fully recovered from its passengers in 1997 as a result of policy changes since 1993.

6.4.2 Value added in not-for-profit organisations

Most of the literature and studies on value added concentrate on commercial organisations, primarily because it was originally developed as a commercial concept. But, in principle, value added can also be applied to not-for-profit organisations.

As outlined earlier, value added may, in practice, be difficult to calculate for not-for-profit organisations. Some of the costs are obvious – photocopying, transport, etc. But some costs may be almost impossible to quantify – for example, the use of voluntary labour. In addition, it may be difficult to put a value on the services delivered, i.e. the *outputs* of the organisation. For example, what value can be assigned to the *outputs* of the Red Cross or Red Crescent global rescue services and what estimate made of the *inputs* of their many voluntary assistants? Yet no one would deny their value to the community.

In general terms, the added value of a not-for-profit organisation is the difference between the service provided and the costs of the inputs, some of which may be voluntary and have zero cost. Because of the difficulty in valuing these elements, some might argue that it is inappropriate to explore the concept of value added in not-for-profit organisations. However, others would suggest that some concept of value, defined to include broader social goals, is relevant to *every* organisation, including those that do not generate profits.

6.4.3 Strategic implications of value added

From the above definition of value added (i.e. outputs minus inputs), it follows that value can be added in an organisation:

● *either* by raising the value of outputs (sales) delivered to the customer;

● *or* by lowering the costs of its inputs (wages and salaries, capital and materials costs) into the company.

Alternatively, both routes could be used simultaneously. Strategies therefore need to address these two areas.

Raising the value of outputs may mean raising the level of sales, either by raising the volume of sales or by raising the unit price. Both these methods are easy to state and more difficult to achieve. Each will involve costs – for example, the cost of advertising to stimulate sales – which need to be set against the gains made. *Lowering the costs of inputs* may require investment – for example, in new machinery to replace workers – at the same time as seeking the cost reduction.

These two strategic routes need to be examined in detail. *Outputs* have already been covered in Part 2; inputs are considered later in this chapter.

A strategic analysis of value added needs to take place at the market or industry level of the organisation, not at a corporate or holding company level. If this analysis were to be undertaken at the general level, the performance of individual parts of the business would be masked. Value added is therefore calculated at the level of individual product groups.

▶ Key strategic principles

● The added value of a commercial organisation is the difference between the market value of its output and the costs of its inputs.

● The value added of a not-for-profit organisation is the difference between the service provided and the costs of the inputs, some of which may be voluntary and have zero cost.

● The market value of its output is typically its sales revenue. The costs of its inputs are the costs of its labour, its materials and its capital costs, including land, plant and machinery and stocks and work in progress.

● All organisations need to ensure that they do not consistently lose value in the long term or they will not survive. For commercial organisations, adding value is essential for their future. For non-profit organisations, adding value may only be a minor part of the reason for their existence, other purposes being centred on social, charitable or other goals.

● In principle, there are only two strategies to raise value added in a commercial organisation: increase the value of its outputs (sales) or lower the value of its inputs (the costs of labour, capital and materials). In practice, this implies detailed analysis of every aspect of sales and costs.

● In companies with more than one product range, added value is best analysed by considering each group separately. Some groups may subsidise others in terms of added value. Not all groups are likely to perform equally.

6.5 Adding competitive value: the value chain and the value system – the contribution of Porter

The concept of value added can be used to develop the organisation's sustainable competitive advantage. There are two main routes – the *value chain* and the *value system*. Much of this approach was developed in the 1980s by Professor Michael Porter of the Harvard Business School.

Every organisation consists of activities that link together to develop the value of the business: purchasing supplies, manufacturing, distribution and marketing of its goods and services. These activities taken together form the *value chain* of the organisation.

When organisations supply, distribute, buy from or compete with each other, they form a broader group of value generation: the *value system*.

The contributions of the value chain and value system to the development of competitive advantage, and the links between the two areas, which may also deliver competitive advantage, are explored in this section.

6.5.1 The value chain

The value chain links the value of the activities of an organisation with its main functional parts. It then attempts to make an assessment of the contribution that each part makes to the overall added value of the business. The concept was used in accounting analysis for some years before Professor Michael Porter[18] suggested that it could be applied to strategic analysis. Essentially, he linked two areas together:

1 the added value that each part of the organisation contributes to the whole organisation; and

2 the contribution to the competitive advantage of the whole organisation that each of these parts might then make.

In a company with more than one product area, he said that the analysis should be conducted at the level of product groups, not at corporate strategy level, as the Bouygues example in Section 6.4. The company is then split into the *primary activities* of production, such as the production process itself, and the *support activities*, such as human resources management, that give the necessary background to the running of the company but cannot be identified with any individual part. The analysis then examines how each part might be considered to contribute towards the generation of value in the company and how this differs from competitors.

Porter's outline process is shown in Figure 6.4. He used the word 'margin' in the diagram to indicate what we defined as *added value* in Section 6.4: 'margin is the difference between the total value and the collective cost of performing the value activities'.[19]

According to Porter, the *primary activities* of the company are:

● *Inbound logistics.* These are the areas concerned with receiving the goods from suppliers, storing them until required by operations, handling and transporting them within the company.

● *Operations.* This is the production area of the company. In some companies, this might be split into further departments – for example, paint spraying, engine assembly, etc., in a car company; reception, room service, restaurant, etc., in a hotel.

● *Outbound logistics.* These distribute the final product to the customer. They would clearly include transport and warehousing but might also include selecting and

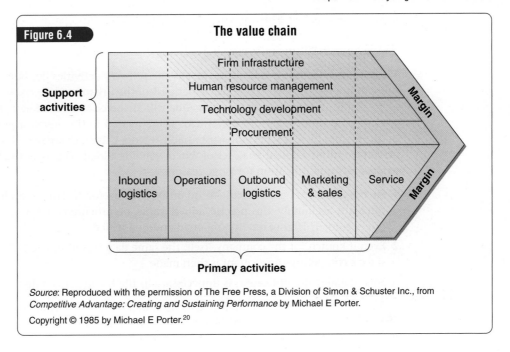

Figure 6.4 **The value chain**

Source: Reproduced with the permission of The Free Press, a Division of Simon & Schuster Inc., from *Competitive Advantage: Creating and Sustaining Performance* by Michael E Porter.
Copyright © 1985 by Michael E Porter.[20]

wrapping combinations of products in a multiproduct company. For a hotel or other service company, this activity would be reconfigured to cover the means of bringing customers to the hotel or service.

- *Marketing and sales.* This function analyses customers' wants and needs and brings to the attention of customers the products or services the company has for sale. Advertising and promotions fall within this area.

- *Service.* Before or after a product or service has been sold, there is often a need for pre-installation or after-sales service. There may also be a requirement for training, answering customer queries, etc.

Each of the above categories will add value to the organisation in its own way. They may undertake this task better or worse than competitors: for example, with higher standards of service, lower production costs, faster and cheaper outbound delivery and so on. By this means, they provide the areas of *competitive advantage* of the organisation.

The *support activities* are:

- *Procurement.* In many companies, there will be a separate department (or group of managers) responsible for purchasing goods and materials that are then used in the operations of the company. The department's function is to obtain the lowest prices and highest quality of goods for the activities of the company, but it is only responsible for purchasing, not for the subsequent production of the goods.

- *Technology development.* This may be an important area for new products in the company. Even in a more mature industry, it will cover the existing technology, training and knowledge that will allow a company to remain efficient.

- *Human resource management.* Recruitment, training, management development and the reward structures are vital elements in all companies.

● *Firm infrastructure.* This includes the background planning and control systems – for example, accounting, etc. – that allow companies to administer and direct their development. It includes corporate strategy.

These support activities add value, just as the primary activities do, but in a way that is more difficult to link with one particular part of the organisation.

In Table 6.1 value added was quantified precisely at Glaxo, Bouygues and Nederlandse Spoorwegen. However, this value related to the *overall* inputs and outputs of the companies. To develop sustainable competitive advantage, it is necessary to undertake more detailed analyses of where value is added. This is normally undertaken *without* any quantification for three reasons:

1 Such assessments are difficult to quantify with accuracy. For example, how do you calculate accurately the precise added value of procurement? Salary costs? Lower prices gained? Higher quality obtained and quantified?

2 Even if known for the company itself, the same data would be needed for competitors, since a competitive assessment is then made.

3 Such detailed quantification is unnecessary in the broad general discussion of strategy.

Value chain analysis is therefore usually undertaken without detailed quantification of the value added. It concentrates on the main areas and makes broad comparisons with competitors on this basis.

Comment

The problem with the value chain in strategic development is that it is designed to explore the *existing* linkages and value-added areas of the business. By definition, it works within the existing structure. Real competitive strategy may require a revolution that moves *outside* the existing structure. Value chains may not be the means to achieve this.

6.5.2 The value system

In addition to the analysis of the company's own value chain, Porter argued that an additional analysis should also be undertaken. Organisations are part of a wider system of adding value involving the supply and distribution value chains and the value chains of customers. This is known as the *value system* and is illustrated in Figure 6.5.

Except in very rare circumstances, every organisation buys in some of its activities: advertising, product packaging design, management consultancy, electricity are all examples of items that are often acquired even by the largest companies. In the same way, many organisations do not distribute their products or services directly to the final consumer: travel agents, wholesalers, retail shops might all be involved in this role.

Competitors may or may not use the same value system: some suppliers and distributors will be better than others in the sense that they offer lower prices, faster service, more reliable products, etc. *Real* competitive advantage may come from using the *best* suppliers or distributors. New competitive advantage may be gained by using a new distribution system or obtaining a new relationship with a supplier. An analysis of this value system may also therefore be required. This will involve a resource analysis that extends beyond the organisation itself.

Value chain and value system analysis can be complex and time consuming for the organisation. This is where the *key factors for success* (see Section 6.2) can be used. If these have been correctly identified, then they will provide the focus for the analysis of

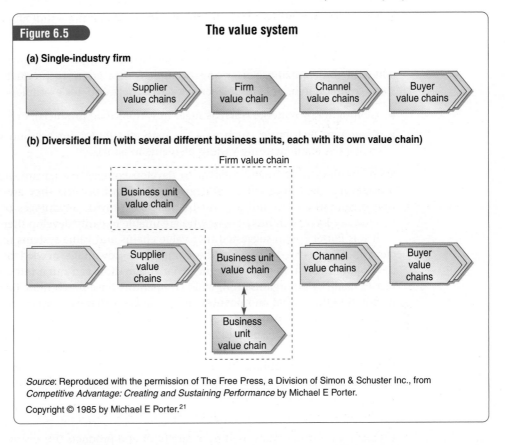

Figure 6.5 — **The value system**

(a) Single-industry firm

Supplier value chains → Firm value chain → Channel value chains → Buyer value chains

(b) Diversified firm (with several different business units, each with its own value chain)

Firm value chain

Business unit value chain

Supplier value chains → Business unit value chain → Channel value chains → Buyer value chains

Business unit value chain

Source: Reproduced with the permission of The Free Press, a Division of Simon & Schuster Inc., from *Competitive Advantage: Creating and Sustaining Performance* by Michael E Porter.

Copyright © 1985 by Michael E Porter.[21]

added value that follows. Key factors may well be those factors that add value to the product or service.

In Section 6.4 we concluded that value added can only be raised by either increasing the outputs (sales) or by lowering the inputs (costs) of a company. Along with the key factors for success, these two value-added options now provide a method of analysing the value-added resources in the company. Such an enquiry will need to examine both the costs and the benefits of any proposed changes.

In the case of Glaxo Smith Kline (GSK), the company might be advised to concentrate its value analysis initially at least on its identified key factors for success: R&D, marketing and product performance. In fact, the company's strategy during the 1990s has been to invest very heavily in research and development. As already explored, GSK acquired the UK pharmaceutical company Wellcome plc for US$13.5 billion in 1995.[22] One of the main reasons for purchasing this company was its strong range of new drugs that would complement the existing Glaxo product portfolio – another way of achieving R&D development.

GSK might also usefully investigate ways of raising the value of key *outputs* and lowering key *costs*. The opening case showed that this is precisely the strategic activity undertaken by the company.

Comment

In common with the value chain, the value system is mainly concerned with the *existing* linkages and may miss totally new strategic opportunities.

6.5.3 Developing competitive advantage linkages between the value chain and value system

Analysis of the value chain and the value system will provide information on value added in the company. For an organisation with a group of products, there may be some common item or common service across the group, for example:

● a common raw material (such as sugar in various food products); or

● a common distributor (such as a car parts distributor for a group with subsidiary companies manufacturing various elements in a car).

Such common items may be *linked* to develop competitive advantage. Such possible linkages may be important to strategic development because they are often *unique* to that organisation. The linkages might therefore provide advantages over competitors who do not have such linkages, or who are unable to easily develop them.

It was Porter[23] who suggested that value chains and value systems may not be sufficient in themselves to provide the competitive advantage needed by companies in developing their strategies. He argued that competitors can often imitate the *individual* moves made by an organisation; what competitors have much more difficulty in doing is imitating the special and possibly unique *linkages* that exist between elements of the value chain and the value systems of the organisation.

In addition to analysing resources for value chains and value systems, therefore, competitive strategy suggests that there is a third element. It is necessary to search for special and possibly unique linkages that either exist or might be developed between elements of the value chain and between value systems associated with the company. Figure 6.6 illustrates this situation.

Examples of such linkages abound:

● Common raw materials used in a variety of end-products: for example, petrochemical feedstocks are used widely to produce various products.

● Common services, such as telecommunications or media buying, where a combined contract could be negotiated at a lower price than a series of individual local deals.

● Linkages between technology development and production to facilitate new production methods that might be used in various parts of a group – for example, direct telecommunications links between large retail store chains such as Marks & Spencer and their suppliers.

● Computer reservation systems that link airlines with travel ticket agents (proving to be so powerful that the European Commission has investigated their effects on airline competition).

● Joint ventures, alliances and partnerships that often rely on different members to the agreement bringing their special areas of expertise to the relationship (*see* Chapter 14).

All the above suggest that linkages that enhance value added may provide significant ways for companies to improve their resources.

Comment

One fundamental problem with the value chain, value system and its linkages is their broad perspective across the *range* of the company's resources. They are sometimes rather vague at identifying the *precise* nature and scope of the advantages such resources possess against competitors. Sustainable competitive advantage is not the

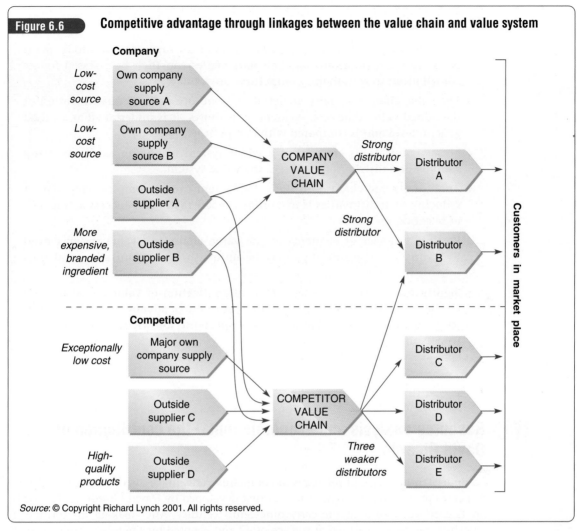

| Figure 6.6 | Competitive advantage through linkages between the value chain and value system |

Source: © Copyright Richard Lynch 2001. All rights reserved.

primary target of the value-added analysis. The remaining sections of this chapter explore more direct ways of tackling this issue.

Another difficulty with value-added analysis is its focus on assets that can be clearly measured. This is a significant weakness because some of the organisation's most valuable assets may be difficult to quantify – such as branding or specialist knowledge. Moreover, some of the organisation's most important assets may be impossible to value, especially human resource assets like leadership and strong team building.

6.5.4 Improving value added

Despite its difficulties, value added is important in strategy development, especially when defined in broad terms rather than by the narrow (outputs minus inputs) definition used in the economic analysis explored in this chapter. The fundamental point remains that, unless organisations add some value to their inputs, their very existence may be in question. For most organisations, this suggests that an important issue is how to impose the value that is added by the organisation's resources. We will pick up this theme in Chapter 13 after exploring resources in more detail.

Key strategic principles

- The value chain breaks down the activities of the organisation into its main parts. The contribution that each part makes can then be assessed for its contribution to sustainable competitive advantage.

- The value chain is usually analysed without any detailed quantification of the added value that each element contributes. It is undertaken at a broad general level and is compared with competitors.

- Most organisations are part of a wider system of adding value involving supplier and distributor channels: the value system.

- Analysing value chains and the value system can be complex. One way of reducing such difficulties is to employ the key factors for success as a means of selecting the items.

- Possible linkages of elements of the value chain and value systems need to be analysed because they may be unique to the organisation and thus provide it with competitive advantage.

- Significant weaknesses in the practical application of value added include a lack of precision in identifying areas of resource advantage and an inability to value clearly major assets like specialist knowledge and company leadership.

6.6 Resource analysis and economic rent – the contribution of David Ricardo

To understand the role of resources in competitive advantage, it is necessary to explore the concept of economic rent. This was first developed by David Ricardo (1772–1823), an English economist of the early nineteenth century. After making his fortune in stockbroking, Ricardo retired at the age of 42 and devoted his life to a consideration of economic and political issues.[24]

6.6.1 The concept of economic rent

Economic rent is defined as any excess that a factor earns over the minimum amount needed to keep that factor in its present use. It was originally explored by Ricardo, who considered the rents earned by landlords from farmland that was used to grow corn. However, it is far more readily understood in the first half of the twenty-first century by examining the vast wages earned by pop stars, famous footballers and highly paid TV newscasters: typically, their annual salaries run to US$500 000 or more. Yet their ability to earn much beyond US$50 000 in other occupations is quite limited, so why pay them US$500 000 when they should be willing to play music, football and read the news for a mere US$50 000? Essentially, because such people are in short and fixed supply. They receive payments greatly in excess of the wages needed to stop them moving to other occupations: this excess of around US$450 000 (500 000 minus 50 000) is called *economic rent*.

6.6.2 Two main types of economic rent

In addition to some *resources* being in short supply, economic rent can also be derived from the market place – in strategic terms, opportunities in the organisation's *environment*. Ricardo never considered this latter form of rent. There are two main types of rent:[25]

1 *Ricardian rents* (after David Ricardo). Such rents derive from the *resources* of the organisation. They are rents generated from resources that possess some real competitive advantage, allowing the company to generate significant additional returns. For example, the advantage derived from a unique geographical location, like that of McDonald's outside the zoo in Berlin, or the possession of a special patent as in the case of the Dyson vacuum cleaner.

2 *Monopoly rents*. Such rents derive from the *markets* in which the organisation operates. They are the rents associated with a company's unique position in the market place that allows it to earn exceptional returns. For example, a government-owned monopoly position in electricity or gas supply might generate exceptional returns. Equally, a privately owned position of market dominance can be built as a result of long and skilled investment in a market – Microsoft's possession of its Windows software with 90 per cent market share is an example here. It is important in this example to note that there is nothing special about Microsoft's resources – other companies have developed similar software but have been unable to dislodge the Microsoft dominance.

There are other forms of economic rent, the most important from a strategic perspective being *Schumpeterian rents*. These are rents that derive from a new and innovatory product or service that allows the organisation to charge considerably above its costs of production. They will often involve risk-taking and entrepreneurial activity – as, for example, at the time of writing, in the case of some forms of digital video disc and digital computer cameras. Such rents are named after the famous US economist Joseph Schumpeter (1883–1950), who wrote extensively on the role of innovation in markets.[26] However, as Schumpeter himself recognised, such a position is inherently unstable because other organisations will enter a market place where high prices are being charged and high profits are being earned. New entrants will clearly need to find their way around any barriers to entry, but the result over time is that this form of rent will either disappear or become a subset of one of the two major types identified above. For example, Xerox (US) held patents on photocopying machinery in the 1960s and 1970s that included innovatory technology and allowed the company to earn exceptional profits. But in the period 1960–85, Canon (Japan) developed an alternative photocopying system that did not rely on the Xerox patents, thus negating the Xerox resource competitive advantage over time.

6.6.3 Implications of economic rent for resource analysis: scarcity and alternative use

Beyond its examination of the environment, the concept of economic rent has two significant implications for resource strategy:

1 *Scarcity of resource*. It identifies this concept and raises the possibility of developing resources that are so scarce that they can earn substantial economic rent.

2 *Alternative use for resources*. The concept explores other and more profitable uses for any resource beyond the one that is currently being pursued. Specifically, it considers the possibility that using the resource for another purpose might produce more rent.

Both these insights have considerable significance for the resource strategy of individual firms. Strategic development of the individual resources of an organisation can, at least in part, be directed at exploring these two issues – scarcity and alternative use. For example, GSK has developed a series of patented drugs that are sufficiently different for the company to charge a price premium – economic rent. Also, British Rail in the 1980s sold parts of the land that it was not using for its rail services to other manufacturing and retailing companies. The company increased its rent from the alternative use of some of its resources. Nederlandse Spoorwegen (Netherlands), discussed earlier in this chapter, might well consider the same strategy.

As far as the productive alternative use of resources is concerned, this is usually treated as an ongoing issue in strategy. In practice, some resources are more flexible than others in terms of alternative use. For example, once a factory has been built, it becomes difficult to make major changes because of its shape, design and layout (*see* Chapter 9). But companies that own their own fleet of transport may well find that they can sell it, invest the money in scarce resources and hire transport from outside companies more cheaply. At present, there is no substantive body of strategic resource theory that explores the alternative use of resources.

The characteristics of scarce resources that will generate high economic rent are explored in Section 6.7.

6.6.4 How does economic rent relate to accounting profit?

Accounting profit is the difference between total revenue and the *explicit* costs of generating this in a given time period – often over one year. Economic rent is different, because it is concerned with the difference between total revenue and the *opportunity cost* of the factors of production. The kernel of the concept of economic rent is that it is not concerned with the accounting profit that will arise from the current strategy, but the extra that might be earned beyond the current profit if the resources were to be used elsewhere. Accounting profit makes no attempt to measure this. More broadly, rent explores strategic concepts related to the organisation's possession and use of resources or its dominance in the market place. Accounting profit does not undertake this task. It is important in any strategic discussion of accounting profit to recognise its significant limitations – many strategies are evaluated in terms of their accounting profits and return on capital, so the problem cannot be dismissed lightly. Exhibit 6.3 compares the two concepts further.

6.6.5 Comment on economic rent

Although economic rent is superior to accounting profit as a strategic concept and is widely used by economists, it has several difficulties:

- It is difficult to estimate because of the conceptual problem of ensuring that *all* alternative uses have been considered and accurately valued.

- It makes the simplistic assumption that every option can always be implemented, without regard for the human resource implications.

- It provides few insights on how to identify new Ricardian or monopoly rent opportunities at the commencement of strategy analysis. It is useful after the event (*ex post*) but is not so useful in advance when strategy is being formulated (*ex ante*).

Thus, its strategic benefits are mainly conceptual: Figure 6.7 provides a post-rationalised example from the world car industry of the strategic relationships between rents and resources.

Exhibit 6.3 **Some differences between economic rent* and accounting profit**

Economic rent*

- Economic concept based on the alternative uses of resources
- Time period unlimited
- Resources assessed for their value on the open market and for their ability to deliver future funds
- Can be associated with specific resources and their ability to deliver unique sources of revenue
- Can also be associated with market dominance and its ability to deliver superior revenue
- Important conceptually but difficult to calculate in practice

Accounting profit

- Accounting concept based purely on artificial definitions of resources, etc.
- Defined time period, e.g. one year
- Quantification of resources based on historical costs rather than broader concept of their current usage
- No realistic possibility of identifying the quality of resources beyond simple numerical values
- Relatively easy to measure and calculate

* *Note*: Sometimes, economic rent is called economic profit. They are the same thing.

Figure 6.7 **Identifying the relationship between rent and resources – the global car industry**

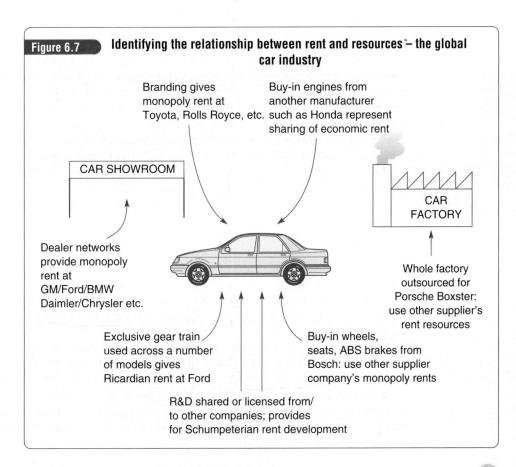

Branding gives monopoly rent at Toyota, Rolls Royce, etc.

Buy-in engines from another manufacturer such as Honda represent sharing of economic rent

CAR SHOWROOM

CAR FACTORY

Dealer networks provide monopoly rent at GM/Ford/BMW Daimler/Chrysler etc.

Whole factory outsourced for Porsche Boxster: use other supplier's rent resources

Exclusive gear train used across a number of models gives Ricardian rent at Ford

Buy-in wheels, seats, ABS brakes from Bosch: use other supplier company's monopoly rents

R&D shared or licensed from/ to other companies; provides for Schumpeterian rent development

▶ **Key strategic principles**

- Economic rent is defined as any excess that a factor earns over the minimum amount needed to keep that factor in its present use.

- There are two main types of rent: *Ricardian* rents derive from the exceptional resources of the organisation and *monopoly* rents derive from the organisation's market position.

- Economic rent is important in strategy analysis because it highlights the scarcity of some resources and the possibility of alternative, more profitable uses for a resource.

- Economic rent is conceptually more relevant to strategic decision making than accounting profit because it is better at highlighting the main issues involved. However, economic rent is more difficult to calculate. Moreover, it oversimplifies some elements of strategy, such as human resource aspects and the strategic process itself.

6.7 Resource analysis and competitive advantage – the resource-based view

If economic rent derives from 'exceptional' resources, i.e. those that have sustainable competitive advantage, then the question arises as to what makes a resource exceptional. Over the years 1984–99, strategy writers have developed a mainly prescriptive answer to this question. It did not happen all at once but emerged from various books and research papers over the period; some of the main contributors are summarised in Exhibit 6.4.[27] Hence, it is not appropriate to attribute the development to one person. The overall title of the approach is the *resource-based view* (RBV) of strategy development. It represents a substantial shift in emphasis towards the *individual* resources of the organisation and away from the market-based view that was emphasised in the 1980s and early 1990s through the work of Professor Michael Porter and others – *see* Chapter 3.

6.7.1 The reasons for the development of the RBV

During the 1980s, strategists like Porter explored and emphasised the need to identify profitable markets and then find competitive advantage by industry solutions in those markets – for example, his 'generic strategies' are explored in Chapter 13. Even while these developments were receiving strong approval from some commentators, disturbing evidence was pointing in a different direction. For example, Rumelt[28] published a study in 1991 of the sources of profits in major US corporations in the 1970s. This suggested that the greatest contributor to overall company profitability was at the *individual company level* rather than at the higher, corporate level or at the level of the industry overall or the cyclicality of the industry. The results are shown in Table 6.2. For this North American sample, they indicate that what matters is the individual business area rather than the industry. Whether this finding is true for other countries and industry samples cannot easily be established. But it did suggest that industry solutions to resources are unlikely to be the main source of profits, thus undermining the Porter approach. In fairness to Professor Porter, he produced similar evidence himself in research published in 1997.[29]

Exhibit 6.4		Some selected contributions to the development of the RBV

Author(s)	Date	Summary
Wernerfelt	1984	Companies were seen as a collection of resources, rather than holding market positions in the development of strategy
Barney	1986, 1991	Competitive market imperfections, market entry barriers and other constraints require differing company resources and the immobility of resources for the development of successful strategy
Rumelt	1987	Importance of resources in strategy development
Dierickx and Cool	1989	Strategic assets are developed internally, not acquired Such assets take time to develop
Schoemaker	1990	Identified factors important in determining useful assets. Some assets not readily tradable for reasons of specialist skills, know-how and reputation
Prahalad and Hamel	1990	Key resources: skills and technologies called core competencies – *see* text
Peteraf	1990	Identified four distinguishing features of resources
Grant	1991	Definition of resources, capabilities and competitive advantage
Connor	1991	Resources long-lived, difficult to imitate
Amit and Schoemaker	1993	Explored processes through which resources are developed, e.g. bounded rationality
Kay	1994	Identified the three most important resources as the firm's ability to innovate, its reputation and its network of relationships inside and outside (architecture) – *see* text
Teece, Pisano and Shuen	1997	Explored the changing nature of resources

Table 6.2 Contributions to the variance of profitability across business units

Source within corporation	Contribution to the total profitability of the corporation
Corporate ownership	0.8%
Industry effects	8.3%
Cyclical effects	7.8%
Business unit specific effects	46.4%
Unexplained factors	36.7%
Total across corporation	100%

Source: See reference 28.

Around the same time, other strategists were puzzled by the different long-term profit performance of companies in the same industry. They argued that, if industry was the main determinant of profits, then all companies in an industry should have similar levels of profitability. But this clearly was not the case. For example, Kellogg (US) had declining profits in its breakfast cereal business while General Mills (US) continued to grow – *see* Chapter 3. Toyota (Japan) and Honda (Japan) made massive strides worldwide in the car industry, often at the expense of General Motors (US), and Ford (US), who were losing profits, even in their home markets – *see* Chapters 9 and 18. Acer (Taiwan) and Dell (US) were growing in personal computers while companies like IBM (US) and Apple (US) were struggling to survive – *see* Chapters 1 and 2. Why did this happen? Industry analysis was certainly not wrong: it was needed to identify sustainable competitive advantage and customer needs. But it was clearly not enough.

The essence of the RBV development is its focus on the *individual* resources of the organisation, rather than the strategies that are common to all companies in an industry. It is important to understand the industry, but organisations should seek their own solutions within that context. Sustainable competitive advantage then comes by striving to exploit the *relevant* resources of the individual organisation when compared with other organisations. Relevance means the identification of resources that are better than those of competitors, persuasive to the customer and available from the range of strengths contained inside the organisation. For example, GSK's strategy on pharmaceutical development should concentrate on drugs that will be more effective than those of the competition, offer genuine benefits to the customer and fit with its existing areas of drug strength in treating asthma, viral drugs, etc. It should not move into an area involving technology that is new to the company but where potential competitors like Johnson & Johnson (US) are already well established, such as surgical equipment and dressings.

Within the context of industry analysis, the starting point for the RBV is a careful exploration of the resources of the organisation – this was explored in Section 6.3. But beyond this *general* analysis it is necessary to identify those attributes that give an individual organisation its *particular* strengths.

6.7.2 The seven elements of resource-based sustainable competitive advantage

Over time, various strategists have explored the advantages that an individual organisation might possess to obtain competitive advantage. There is no agreement amongst them on the precise source of such advantages. For example, Prahalad and Hamel highlighted one key resource,[30] Kay[31] has identified three main areas, Peteraf[32] suggested four areas, and Collis and Montgomery[33] have described five. Certainly, these and other writers have made significant contributions and all are agreed on the importance of individual company resources within an industry. Taking all these views into account, it is useful to identify seven elements that comprise the RBV: *see* Figure 6.8. In addition, it should be noted that several of these elements have *additional* clarifying subordinate aspects – perhaps this is where the disagreement has arisen.

- *Prior or acquired resources.* Value creation is more likely to be successful if it builds on the strengths that are already available to the organisation, rather than starting from scratch in a totally new area. It does not guarantee that the strategy will be successful but it is a major starting point. Moreover, building on existing strengths will exploit any real uniqueness that has been built as a result of the organisation's history and investment over many years – economists call this *path dependency*. It may be very

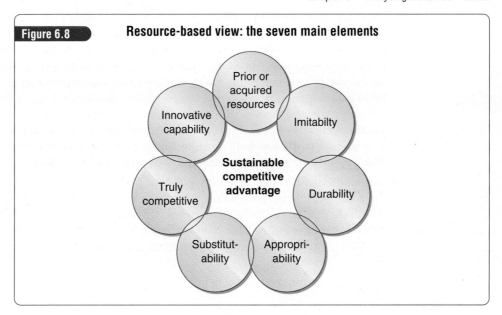

Figure 6.8   **Resource-based view: the seven main elements**

difficult for competitors to develop the same complex resources. We explored this at the end of Chapter 2 in the section on strategy as history. Finally, one other prior strength that is of major importance in the development of future strategy is the existing reputation of the organisation. For example, the UK retailer Marks & Spencer has certain strengths in terms of *reputation* and quality that will form the basis of future strategy.

- *Innovative capability*. Some organisations are better able to innovate than others. Innovation is important because it is particularly likely to deliver a real breakthrough in competitive advantage that others will have difficulty in matching for a lengthy period. Innovation is explored at various points throughout this book, particularly in Chapter 11. For example, the Japanese consumer electronics company Sony has developed a consistent ability to produce new products over many years. We will return to innovation shortly.

- *Being truly competitive*. It is essential that any resource delivers a true advantage over the competition. This comes back partly to the test of *relevance* to customers, competitors and company strengths outlined in Section 6.7.1 above. But it emphasises that identifying the resource as being a real strength is not enough: the resource must be *comparatively* better than the competition. For example, it is not enough to have a 'low-cost, high-quality' factory – it must have low*er* costs and high*er* quality than that of competitors. For example, the US company Microsoft has developed a computer software package and market position that is superior to any other in the world.

- *Substitutability*. Resources are more likely to be competitive if they cannot be substituted. Sometimes unique resources can be replaced by totally new alternatives. This element was explored in Chapter 3 in Porter's Five Forces Model and is equally valid here in the RBV. For example, there is no substitute for the US Walt Disney company's Mickey Mouse character.

- *Appropriability*. Resources must deliver the results of their advantage to the individual company and not be forced to distribute at least part of it to others. Just because a resource has competitive advantage does not necessarily mean that its benefits will come to the owners. They could be forced to give up some profits to others by the bargaining power of the various stakeholders of the organisation – customers, employees, suppliers and so on. We will explore stakeholders in Chapter 12 and bargaining in Chapter 15, in the section on game theory. Another method of maintaining appropriability is through the company patenting its products and processes. Whatever method is used, the company must be able to keep the profits that the resource generates. For example, the Italian company Benetton has organised its business such that it owns both manufacturing and distribution outlets, thus ensuring that it retains the value added that has been generated throughout its value chain.

● *Durability*. Useful resources must have some longevity. There is no point in identifying a competitive resource whose advantage is not sustainable. At some future time, it is likely that all competitive resources will succumb to the fate described earlier in this chapter by Joseph Schumpeter and no longer deliver competitive advantage. But the longer a resource can keep its advantage, the better. Brand names like that owned by the US photographic company Kodak have that durability.

● *Imitability*. Resources must not be easy to imitate if they are to have competitive advantage. Although many resources can eventually be copied, such a process can be delayed by a number of devices:

– *Tangible uniqueness*. Some form of specific differentiation, such as branding or a specific geographic location or patent protection, will delay imitability.

 – *Causal ambiguity*. It may not be obvious to competitors what gives a resource its competitive edge. There may be some complex organisational processes that have taken years to develop that are difficult for outside companies to learn or acquire.

– *Investment deterrence*. When the market has limited or unknown growth prospects and it is difficult to make a small initial investment, a substantial investment by the organisation in the new strategy may well deter competitors from entering the market. This is particularly true where large capital plant or major advertising campaigns are essential to launch products and services.

For example, the Japanese car company Toyota has developed a manufacturing process that has many human resource elements like team working that cannot easily be observed. This has made it difficult for other car companies to copy the superior Toyota practices.

6.7.3 The relationship between the seven elements and the other resources of the organisation – the hierarchy of resources

Although seven RBV elements have been identified, it is unnecessary for an organisation to possess them all before it has competitive advantage over others. In practice, most successful strategies will involve only a few of the above. The precise combination that will deliver competitive advantage is totally dependent on the unique resource structure of each organisation – these can be considered as the *core resources* of the organisation.

One specific area of core resource deserves to be considered particularly carefully: innovative ability. It is very difficult to develop and is more likely to supply an advantage that competitors cannot possess in the short term. It will be in short supply, but any success will transform the competitive advantage of the organisation. Innovative ability can be considered as the *breakthrough resource* of the organisation. This topic is explored further in Chapter 11.

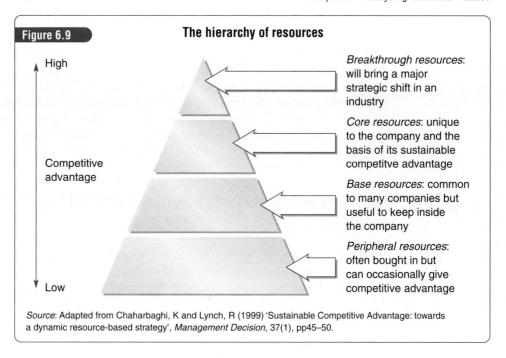

Figure 6.9 **The hierarchy of resources**

High

Competitive advantage

Low

Breakthrough resources: will bring a major strategic shift in an industry

Core resources: unique to the company and the basis of its sustainable competitve advantage

Base resources: common to many companies but useful to keep inside the company

Peripheral resources: often bought in but can occasionally give competitive advantage

Source: Adapted from Chaharbaghi, K and Lynch, R (1999) 'Sustainable Competitive Advantage: towards a dynamic resource-based strategy', *Management Decision*, 37(1), pp45–50.

In addition to the special resources that have been identified as delivering sustainable competitive advantage, most organisations will have other resources that are cheaper and more convenient to own inside rather than purchase outside – perhaps company secretarial skills, information technology and other areas. They may not be unique but are important to the daily operation of the business. It should be noted that even these skills, knowledge and resources may also deliver some competitive advantage to an organisation, but such advantage is unlikely to be as substantive as the seven elements outlined above. They can be considered as the *base resources* of the business.

Finally, for reasons of convenience and history, many organisations also have other resources that they own or buy in as needed. These might include advertising, catering, transport, legal services and so on. They are important for the business and can even deliver competitive advantage – perhaps by the *quality* of the outside knowledge or advice purchased. These can be considered for the most part as the *peripheral resources* of the organisation.

Together the above four areas make up the *hierarchy of resources* of the organisation – *see* Figure 6.9. The distinguishing feature of the levels of the hierarchy is an increased likelihood of sustainable competitive advantage in its higher levels.

Key strategic principles

- The resource-based view (RBV) argues that the individual resources of an organisation provide a stronger basis for strategy development than industry analysis. The reason is that the RBV will identify those resources that are exceptional and have sustainable competitive advantage.

- There are seven elements of resource-based competitive advantage: prior or acquired resources, innovative ability, being truly competitive, substitutability, appropriability, durability and imitability.

> ▶ *Key strategic principles continued*
>
> - It is not necessary for an organisation to possess all of them before it has some competitive advantages. Each organisation will have a unique combination of resources, some of which will involve sustainable competitive advantage (SCA). These resources can be considered as a hierarchy with four areas defined by a decreasing likelihood of possessing SCA: breakthrough resources, core resources, basic resources and peripheral resources.

6.8 Identifying which resources deliver sustainable competitive advantage

We are now in a position to identify those resources of the organisation that are most likely to deliver sustainable competitive advantage (SCA). However , it should be noted that this involves a degree of judgement. Moreover, strategic thinking is still developing in this area. The complete process related to SCA is summarised in Figure 6.10.

6.8.1 Analysing the resources of an individual organisation

In analysing how resources deliver SCA, it is essential to begin by analysing the complete range of resources of the organisation. This is not easy because some resources are difficult to measure or even define in an unambiguous way. For example, the patents of the pharmaceutical company GSK represent resources whose future value cannot simply be determined by examining the company's accounts. The reason is that such assets

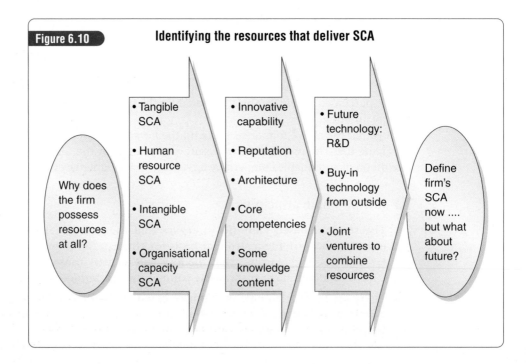

Figure 6.10   **Identifying the resources that deliver SCA**

will decline in value as the patents expire and may not be fully valued in the accounts in any event. Equally, the company's chief executive (Jean-Paul Garnier in 2002) provides an important resource called leadership, which is impossible to quantify but vital to strategy development. In strategy analysis, accounting and management systems data may represent a starting point, but little more.

Essentially, the resources of the organisation are those assets that contribute to the generation of value added. As a starting point, it is useful to divide them into three broad categories:[34]

1 *Tangible resources* – the physical resources of the organisation. Plant and equipment at the German chemical giant Bayer can clearly be identified and valued. The location of McDonald's restaurants on busy highways, rather than obscure secondary roads, is clearly a valuable and tangible resource.

2 *Intangible resources* – those resources that have no physical presence but represent real benefit to the organisation, like brand names, service levels and technology. The Mars Company (US) had a brand name that not only worked in chocolate but was extended into ice cream. The Sharp Corporation (Japan) has a knowledge of flatscreen technology that has allowed the company to develop a strong presence globally in the computer liquid crystal display market.

3 *Organisational capability* – the skills, routines, management and leadership of the organisation. The Toyota Motor Corporation (Japan) has become legendary for low cost, lean manufacturing and also for developing new car models faster than its rivals. We examine this in Chapter 9. Such skills and routines take years to develop and represent an important resource for the organisation.

In practice, such an analysis will concentrate on the main resource areas of the organisation, especially those that deliver added value and competitive advantage. It may well employ the *key factors for success* in an industry as a starting point to make sense of what might otherwise be a time-consuming and unproductive task. An example of the main points of such an analysis is shown in Exhibit 6.5. We will return to these three areas of resource later in the chapter.

6.8.2 The particular importance of three distinctive capabilities: architecture, reputation and innovation

As outlined above, different researchers have approached the issue of the resources that will deliver sustainable competitive advantage in different ways. Two areas in particular deserve further exploration: distinctive capabilities and core competencies. Although they are contained within the framework outlined above, they represent particular areas of interest and insight. They also make the important point that different strategists lay the emphasis on different areas. For example, the distinctive capabilities approach treats 'innovative ability' as being no more important than any other core resources – in contrast to the approach in Section 6.7.3 above. This section explores distinctive capabilities in more depth and the next section examines core competencies.

In the analysis of resources, Professor John Kay argued that the distinctive capabilities of an organisation's resources are particularly important in delivering competitive advantage. *Distinctive capabilities* relate to three possible unique resource areas in an organisation: architecture, reputation and innovative ability.[35] They are complex and not necessarily capable of quantified analysis but they will

---

Exhibit 6.5 **Resource analysis at the worldwide hotel chain Holiday Inns**

	Resource
Tangible	● Physical locations at airports, city centres, holiday destinations, etc. ● Size and facilities of individual hotels: rooms, restaurants, swimming pool, etc.
Intangible	● Brand name of Holiday Inns ● Employees in management, reception, room cleaning, etc.
Organisational capability	● Suppliers of food, telephone services, etc. ● Management training to maintain and improve levels of service ● Management organisation and leadership ● Organisational routines that allow each hotel to run smoothly and efficiently

---

undoubtedly contribute to the distinctive development of a company's strategy. He introduced and explored them by explaining that an organisation has a series of contracts and more informal relationships:

● with its employees inside the organisation;

● with its suppliers, distributors and customers outside in the environment and

● possibly between a group of collaborating firms inside and outside the immediate industry.

The relationships have been built over time. Some are formal and some informal. They are similar to, but more extended than, the linkages explored in the value system of Section 6.5.2 above. They provide the organisation with three major ways for their resources to be distinctive from competitors':

1 *Architecture*. This is the network of relationships and contracts both within and around the firm. Its importance lies in its ability to create knowledge and routines, to respond to market changes and to exchange information both inside and outside the organisation. Long-term relationships with other organisations can lead to real strategy benefits that competitors cannot replicate. Examples include:

● the contacts between major construction companies such as Bouygues and government departments which place substantial contracts;

● negotiations between rail companies such as Nederlandse Spoorwegen and trade unions on new working practices to introduce new technologies and reduce costs;

- corporate negotiation between pharmaceutical companies such as GSK and Merck and governments on new drug price structures.

2 *Reputation*. This allows an organisation to communicate favourable information about itself to its customers. It is particularly concerned with long-term relationships and takes lengthy periods to build. Once gained, it provides a real distinctiveness that rivals cannot match. Examples include:

- Reputation for good-quality work, delivered on time and to budget. Construction companies can gain immensely over time as they perform consistently in this area.

- Reputation for a quality service that is usually punctual and reliable. Railway companies can gain or lose in this area, particularly when they are competing for business against alternative forms of public transport such as buses.

3 *Innovative ability*. Some organisations find it easier to innovate than others because of their structures, culture, procedures and rewards. They may even innovate and then fail to take advantage of this against competitors. This is a highly important area of strategy that deserves careful study. It is therefore explored more fully in Chapter 11.

Comment

The above areas of resource will apply to a greater or lesser extent to most organisations. In themselves, they are important but uncontroversial.

All three areas usually require years of development. The first two are easier to define than they are to develop in terms of options: the *method* by which architecture and reputation are to be improved begs numerous questions about their nature that are difficult to explore. There is a tendency towards worthy, but largely meaningless, wish-fulfilment statements about the desirability of improving them. Kay offers no clear exposition in this area. The third element, innovation, will be explored in Chapter 11.

The real point is how they are understood and used to gain competitive advantage. Resource analysis in these areas needs to take into account the changes that can occur over time and the need to explore not only the area itself but how it can be developed further. This is where the alternative viewpoint of the seven elements of the RBV can make a contribution.

6.8.3 The particular importance of core competencies

In a related area of study, Hamel and Prahalad have explored the area of core skills and competencies.[36] They define core competencies as a group of production skills and technologies that enable an organisation to provide a particular benefit to customers. Core competencies underlie the leadership that companies have built or wish to acquire over their competitors.

Core skills are a fundamental resource of the organisation. The two authors describe the example of Sharp (Japan) and Toshiba (Japan), both of which identified *flat-screen electronic technology* as an opportunity area that they expected to see grow in the future. Both companies invested hundreds of millions of dollars in developing their technology and skills in the market for flat screens that would then be used in miniature televisions, portable computers, digital watches, electronic video recorders and other areas. Importantly, this investment was made *before* it was possible to build a product-specific business case that would justify this level of investment. Core competencies form the basis of core products which, in turn form the basis of the business areas of the company.

Core competencies cover an integration of skills, knowledge and technology. This combination can then lead to competitive advantage. The analysis of such areas is derived from a study of its components in an individual organisation. A skills analysis needs to be conducted at a level that is detailed enough to reveal useful strategic insights but not so detailed that it is unmanageable. The two authors suggest that if only three or four skills are identified this may be too broad, but if 40 or 50 are identified this may be too detailed. They suggest there are three areas that distinguish the major core competencies:

1 *Customer value.* Competencies must make a real impact on how the customer perceives the organisation and its products or services.

2 *Competitor differentiation.* This must be competitively unique. If the whole industry has the skill, then it is not core unless the organisation's skills in the area are really special.

3 *Extendable.* Core skills need to be capable of providing the basis of products or services that go beyond those currently available. The skill needs to be removed from the particular product group in which it currently rests. The organisation needs to imagine how it might be exploited in the whole area of its operations.

Importantly, core competencies are a vital *prerequisite* for the competitive battle that then takes place for market share: the development of key resources has to come before and not during market place activity. It should be noted that Hamel and Prahalad couple core competencies with the organisation's *vision of the future* – this is explained and explored in Chapter 12.

Examples of core skills will include:

- *GSK* – not just its ownership of its drug patents, but also the whole range of skills and contacts that the company has in the pharmaceutical market place with customers, distributors and health authorities.

- *Nederlandse Spoorwegen* will have core skills related to its operation of a rail network. But, more importantly from a competitive viewpoint, it will have skills in customer handling, timetabling, service scheduling and so on, as against those related to buses and aircraft.

- *Bouygues* has core skills in road building that relate to road design and construction. But many companies will have such skills. Its real competencies will relate to its ability to gain large contracts and manage such assignments once agreed. It will need to deliver on time to an agreed standard and within the agreed budget.

Comment

David Sainsbury, the chairman of the leading UK retailer, has said that he believes that the ideas contained in the above have real merit.[37] But he also comments that:

- Core skills may be easier to apply to larger rather than smaller companies, which may not have the depth of management talent. Certainly, the examples on core skills quoted in the text are all from large companies.

- The ideas have been most thoroughly developed for electronics and related markets. The concepts may need to be adapted for others, e.g. medium-sized engineering companies.

Beyond these comments, one of the practical problems with core competencies is that the developers never really offer any clear checklist of points for their development – they are all rather vague. Ten guidelines that explore resource-based competencies and capabilities are offered in Exhibit 13.3.

More fundamentally, core competencies ignore other areas highlighted by the RBV as contributing to resource analysis and development. Competitive advantage may be just as well served by a strong brand, an exclusive patent or a superior geographical location. These and other resources have little or no connection with core competencies.

6.8.4 Knowledge management as the main source of competitive advantage?

In recent years, some strategists have taken the view that the knowledge management of the organisation represents the main source of competitive advantage.[38] They argue that the retention, exploitation and sharing of knowledge are extremely important in the ability of companies to stay ahead of their rivals. In particular, the way in which knowledge is managed and disseminated throughout the organisation represents an important advantage, especially in international companies.[39]

By knowledge is meant the accumulation over time of the skills, routines and capabilities that shape the organisation's ability to survive and compete in markets. In addition, as Leonard points out, 'Knowledge reservoirs in organisations are not static pools but wellsprings, constantly replenished with streams of new ideas and constituting an ever-flowing source of corporate renewal.'[40] We will explore the role of knowledge in the context of innovation in Chapter 11.

Comment

Clearly, it is conceivable that, in some types of organisation, knowledge is extremely important – for example, consulting companies, some accountancy and legal practices. But to raise the role of knowledge to be the prime source of advantage for *all* organisations may be to exaggerate its importance. For example, GSK has relied on its patented drugs and McDonald's has employed branding of the Big Mac to deliver competitive advantage that is sustainable. Neither of these has any substantive connection with knowledge.

6.8.5 Resource-based view and SMEs

Although it might at first appear that the RBV is particularly suited to large companies with vast resources, it is also relevant for small and medium-size enterprises (SMEs). Such organisations tend to have a smaller number of resources but they can also be more flexible and entrepreneurial. Typically, organisations of this size often develop strategies that might include:

- higher levels of personal service;
- specialist expertise;
- design skills;
- regional knowledge;
- bespoke solutions.

All of these can be contained within the seven elements of the RBV. They suggest that core resources at SMEs need to be carefully developed to reflect these strategies – perhaps extra people, extra training, the use of local knowledge and so on. Some areas of the RBV may be difficult to develop in the early years, such as *tangible uniqueness* and *investment deterrence*. Microsoft was once an SME but now it has the ability to develop some of these more capital-intensive resource areas. In principle, the elements therefore provide useful guidance for SMEs.

6.8.6 Comment on the RBV

Although the RBV represents greater clarity in strategy development, it still harbours a number of important weaknesses:

- It is still just a list of factors to consider – there is no guiding logic between the elements. Probably there never will be because, by definition, such logic might imply an industry solution.

- Beyond the concept of innovation (and this is not present in many explorations of the RBV), there is little guidance on how resources develop and change over time. The dynamics of resource development are an important element in strategy and the RBV adds little insight to this.[41] We will explore this in Chapter 20.

- There is a complete lack of consideration of the human element in resource development. We will explore this in Chapter 7.

- Some recent critical comment suggests that the whole concept is a case of tautology.[42]

- There is little or no emphasis on emergent approaches to resource development and almost no recognition of the process aspects of strategy development. The simple assumption that each element just needs to be defined and then it will happen automatically is a gross oversimplification of the reality of strategy development.

Finally, some proponents of various aspects of the RBV hold exaggerated views of its role as the solution to most strategic issues. It is clearly an advance but it is no substitute for the comprehensive development of every aspect of strategy analysis.

▶ Key strategic principles

- In identifying the SCA of an organisation, it is important to begin by analysing the complete range of resources of the organisation: tangible, intangible and organisational capility. Such resources go beyond the usual definitions of accounting and finance concepts into areas like the value of patents and leadership.

- Because of the potentially extensive nature of such an analysis, it should concentrate in practice on those areas that relate to the key factors for success in an industry and those that deliver value added.

- There is no general agreement on what constitutes the best single approach to the development of SCA. Two approaches have proved useful – *distinctive capabilities* from Kay and *core competencies* from Hamel and Prahalad.

- Distinctive capabilities identify three possible unique resource areas in an organisation: architecture, reputation and innovative ability.

- Core competencies are a group of production skills technologies that enable an organisation to provide a particular benefit to customers.

- The RBV has a number of weaknesses: it is simply a list of possible factors to consider; it ignores many aspects of human resource issues and it partially ignores the process aspects of strategy development.

6.9 Resource analysis – improving competitive advantage

After analysing resources, organisations often find that they have few assets that are *truly* competitive. This is quite normal since most organisations will consist of a range of resources, many being similar to those of competitors, with just a few being exceptional. In this context, the long lists of 'core competencies' seen in some analyses suggest that the compiler has not been sufficiently rigorous rather than that the company is multitalented.[43] Regardless of the length of the list, the identification of the truly competitive resources based only on the analysis undertaken so far in this chapter may be misleading. The reason is that the approach so far has been largely static:

● the analysis of value added represents the picture at a point in time;

● the identification of the seven elements of RBV is usually based on current resources.

Although a static approach is useful, a resource analysis at a point in time is a distortion of reality. An organisation's capabilities will change over time, its competitors will invest in new assets and so on. For example, assets will be constantly consumed in an oil company and they will have a limited life in a fast-changing computer business. The real role of resource analysis is to act as the first step in improving resources.

Any enhancement of value added and competitive advantage will come about through a course of action over time. This is a strategic *process* with all that this implies in terms of the human resources of the organisation, its change of culture and its leadership. The process may be *emergent* as well as *prescriptive*. For example, it may involve experimental, trial-and-error approaches to resource development (emergent) just as much as the strict application of RBV analysis (prescriptive). Our main exploration of the ways of improving our resources must await a more detailed look at resources and a clarification of the purpose of the organisation in Chapters 7–12. But it is convenient and relevant to consider three elements now:

1 benchmarking;

2 exploiting existing resources – leveraging;

3 upgrading resources;

6.9.1 Benchmarking

One approach to the task of assessing the comparative performance of parts of an organisation is *benchmarking* – the comparison of practice with other organisations in order to identify areas for improvement. Such practice does not necessarily have to be with another organisation in the same industry. The comparison simply has to be with another whose practices are recognised as leading the field in that particular aspect of the task or function.

For example, the Ford Motor Company (US) might wish to test the competitiveness of its supplier relationships. It might then identify a world leader in supplier relationships, such as the well-known UK retailer Marks & Spencer. Ford might then approach the retailer directly or indirectly through consultants or an industry association. Ford will ask to compare its performance against that of Marks & Spencer in this specific functional area. The differences in performance between Ford and the retailer in its chosen activity are then analysed to form the basis of improving the resource at Ford. The results are then used in the sequence shown in Exhibit 6.6.

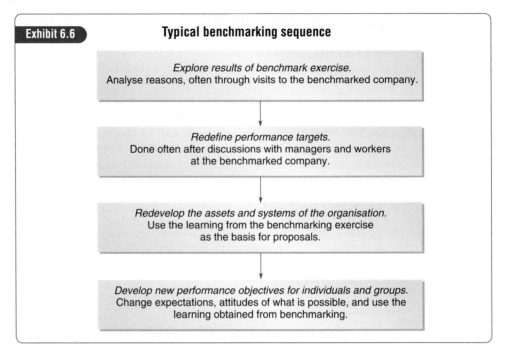

Exhibit 6.6 **Typical benchmarking sequence**

Explore results of benchmark exercise.
Analyse reasons, often through visits to the benchmarked company.

Redefine performance targets.
Done often after discussions with managers and workers
at the benchmarked company.

Redevelop the assets and systems of the organisation.
Use the learning from the benchmarking exercise
as the basis for proposals.

Develop new performance objectives for individuals and groups.
Change expectations, attitudes of what is possible, and use the
learning obtained from benchmarking.

6.9.2 Exploiting existing resources – leveraging

In any organisation, it is essential to exploit its existing resources to the full – this is sometimes called *leveraging resources*.[44] For example, for many years after Walt Disney died, his film company continued to make good films but made no attempt to exploit the many characters in any other medium. It took the arrival of Michael Eisner at the head of Disney in the 1980s to exploit the Disney resources and move the company into hotels, brand merchandising and publishing. More generally, existing resources can be exploited in five areas:

1 *Concentration* – focusing resources on the key objectives of the organisation and targeting, in particular, those that will have the largest influence on value added

2 *Conservation* – using every part of the resource, perhaps recycling where possible, with the aim of exploiting every aspect available to the organisation

3 *Accumulation* – digging deep into the resources of the organisation to discover every scrap of accumulated knowledge and skill, coupled with the acquisition of outside skills and experience, where appropriate

4 *Complementarity* – analysing resources from the perspective of blending new elements together, such as marketing and operations, and supporting stronger elements so that they do not suffer from weaknesses elsewhere in the organisation

5 *Recovery* – ensuring that resources generate cash quickly where possible, thus achieving the full benefit of new and existing resources sooner rather than later

These are all prescriptive routes towards exploiting existing resources and deserve careful study. A classic example in strategy development has been the way that News Corporation (Australia) used its existing strength in UK newspapers in the early 1990s to support and enhance its development of its new satellite television channels: they were heavily promoted in its leading UK newspapers the *Sun* and *The Times* – *see* Chapter 13.

6.9.3　Upgrading resources

Unfortunately, the results of a competitive analysis may show that an organisation has little or no competitive advantage, although it continues to add some value to its inputs. This situation is common in some industries, such as those involved with commodity products where there is little differentiation between products beyond the price – for example, agricultural products, mining and metals. There are three main ways to respond:

1 *Add new resources to support an existing product or service area.* Some organisations have tried to brand their commodities – for example, Intel Corporation with 'Intel Inside' and its Pentium computer chip. A programme of product development would also be relevant here.

2 *Enhance directly the resources that are threatened by competition.* This could be done by buying new, more cost-efficient machinery or negotiating a new joint venture – for example, the 1998 merger that formed DaimlerChrysler has transformed (potentially, at least) the resources of two medium-sized car companies to create a global player.

3 *Add complementary resources that will take the organisation beyond its current competition.* Sometimes the industry will remain unattractive and it may be better to develop resources that will eventually allow the organisation to move beyond its current competitors – for example, some farmers have moved into the leisure industry, setting up golf courses, accommodation and similar activities and thus moving out of reliance on agricultural pricing and into other areas with higher profit margins.

Upgrading resources raises the whole issue of how an organisation moves forward over time with regard to the resources at its disposal, the purpose of the organisation and the moves made by its competitors. Importantly, it relies on a strategic vision of where the organisation is headed – perhaps more of the same, perhaps moving into new areas. This requires a careful exploration of the purpose of the organisation – *see* Part 4.

> ## ▶ Key strategic principles
>
> - There are at least three ways to improve sustainable competitive advantage: benchmarking, exploiting existing resources and upgrading resources.
>
> - *Benchmarking* is a comparison of practice with another organisation considered to display best practice in its field of operation. The aim of benchmarking is to identify areas of improvement in the resources of the organisation.
>
> - *Exploiting existing resources – leveraging.* There are five main methods for undertaking this task. They are: concentration, conservation, accumulation, complementarity and recovery.
>
> - *Upgrading resources.* There are three main methods: developing new resources, enhancing those threatened by competitors and adding complementary resources.

CASE STUDY 6.3

Xbox – the strategic battle for the home entertainment market has just begun

Microsoft's launch of its Xbox games console through 2001 into 2002 is only the beginning of a new strategic thrust. It is using its competitive resources to take a share of the market for home computer video gaming machines. In addition, it aims to establish itself as a leading player in the broader market of home entertainment. But it faces formidable opponents in two Japanese companies, Sony Corporation and Nintendo.

Background – the early years

There is nothing new in the home video game machine battle. The Californian firm Atari was the early leader back in the 1980s. However, it had no proprietary software or hardware – competitors could copy its machines and software games developers had unrestricted access to its games. As in the case of the IBM personal computer – *see* Chapter 1 – this was not a recipe for success.

Then along came the Japanese company Nintendo and it had learnt some important strategic lessons about competitive resources. First, it used a branded character called Mario. Second, it sold the games consoles at low prices and made its profits from its exclusive software games. Third, it made sure that the games consoles were unique and could not work with other games. Finally, it restricted the number of software houses that it licensed to develop its games, thus ensuring that it had some control over the quality of the games.

Game wars hot up in the 1980s and 1990s

Such success attracted another Japanese company, Sega. This company picked up some of the best ideas from Nintendo; for example, it developed its own branded character, Sonic the Hedgehog. In addition, it launched a more advanced machine and stole market share from Nintendo in a rapidly expanding market. By the early 1990s, Sega had become market leader with around 50 per cent market share. Then Sony entered the market in the mid-1990s.

Sony gains market leadership in the late 1990s

Sony used its competitive resources well. As a result of its involvement in films, it had the use of branded characters from its entertainment business. In addition, it used its financial resources to acquire a software development company and its expertise in consumer electronics to develop a new generation of games machines based on CD-ROMS.

In 1998, Sega responded with its Dreamcast machine, which had superior graphics. Sony then hit back with Playstation, which had even better graphics and was much faster than the Sega machine. Meanwhile, Nintendo was holding its own with Gameboy.

In 2001, Sega decided to throw in the towel on games machines – it had not made a profit for six years. Sony had invested US$500 million in Playstation and its successor, Playstation 2. It was reaping the rewards, with market leadership of around 80 per cent in a global market worth around US$20 billion per annum. Sony's games machine profits were the biggest contributor to its total business over this time. Then along came Microsoft in 2000.

Microsoft enters the home entertainment battle

Microsoft has been the market leader in personal computer software with its Windows system since the early 1980s. It has so dominated the global market that it has been the subject of anti-trust legal action in its home country, the US, which, at the time of writing, remained unresolved. Microsoft would not deny that it dominated this market worldwide. But the Windows system was largely employed for home *work* rather than home *entertainment*.

Market opportunity 2001–2006

If you are an aggressive company like Microsoft, you can see an obvious opportunity to expand into entertainment – especially when the video-games console market is worth around US$20 billion and projected to grow at over 20 per cent per annum up to 2005. Thus BIll Gates launched the new Microsoft games machine, the Xbox, in the US in late 2001 and in Japan and Europe in early 2002. Importantly, the new machine was in some respects more like a dedicated home computer, thus illustrating how the

Table 6.3 The rival products

Games machine	Maker	Price	Facilities	Number of games available
Xbox – launched US Autumn 2001, Japan and Europe early 2002	Microsoft	UK price £299 subsequently reduced to £200	DVD ROM, 8GB hard drive, Ethernet port and broadband	20 games at launch
GameCube – launched May 2002 but compatible with GameBoy (launched 1998)	Nintendo	UK price £160–170 subsequently reduced to £140	Optional 56k modem, links with GameBoy Cannot play CDs or DVDs	At least 20 games at launch plus compatible with previous games
PlayStation 2 – launched November 2000	Sony	UK price £199	DVD ROM, optional hard drive, optional broadband	Many games

personal computer and the games machine may converge technically over the next few years. Arguably, this might threaten the Microsoft dominance of home PCs in the long term. Certainly, it also provided an opportunity for Microsoft to tackle a new and potentially lucrative market in the short term.

In the first years, Microsoft was not aiming to beat Sony's market share. Its machine was technically more sophisticated but was initially priced higher – *see* Table 6.3. Sony's Playstation 2 largely matched the Xbox performance. The Nintendo GameCube was simpler technically, but significantly cheaper. Both Sony and Nintendo had a wider range of software games in the early years than Microsoft. However, Microsoft claimed to have built into its new machine the technical ability for gamers to use the much faster broadband telecommunications system so that fast games could be played between homes. But, since broadband was only in 4 per cent of homes at the time of launch, this was not expected to be a major competitive advantage in the early years.

In its first year, Microsoft was aiming to sell around 4–6 million machines, with sales of an estimated 25 million machines over the five-year life of the model to 2006. This can be compared with Nintendo, which also expected to sell around 25–30 million machines over the same five-year period,

and Sony with 90–110 million over the period. The lengthy time period was important as typical launch costs of US$300–500 million would not be recovered for several years – rather like a car manufacturer recovering the costs of developing a new model.

By 2006, it was expected that a new generation of machines would be launched. Microsoft was not expecting to be market leader with its first launch. But the market was sufficiently dynamic for anything to be possible over time. Perhaps the company would come to dominate home entertainment as it did the home office?

Sources: See reference 45.

Case questions

1 *What conclusions do you draw about the competitive advantages of Microsoft? Are its advantages sustainable over time?*

2 *What core competencies does Nintendo possess? Is it capable of leveraging them further? If so, how?*

3 *How does Sony score on Kay's three areas of distinctive capabilities? What conclusions can be drawn on future resource development?*

4 *What is the strategic significance, if any, of the efforts of games machine makers to establish their own special technical standards? What are the risks of such strategies?*

Defining strategy in an uncertain world[46]

The chapter has taken a largely prescriptive approach to resource analysis. In part, at least, it has relied on a quantified view of added value and a formulaic approach to sustainable competitive advantage. In this extract from his book Strategic Management and Organisational Dynamics, *Professor Ralph Stacey explains how an emergent strategic perspective might take the view that the whole procedure is largely worthless.*

When we try to use measures of performance, benchmarks, and associated analytical techniques to select acceptable strategies for the future, we face the problem of forecasting. Using financial measures in a future-oriented way requires forecasts of what will happen to an organisation's cash flows and profit levels over long periods into the future. While everyone recognises the great difficulty of doing this, most continue to believe that it is possible to forecast accurately enough to justify using the criterion of financial acceptability. Under what conditions will this belief be justified?

It is possible to predict the performance outcome of a sequence of actions if, and only if, there are clear-cut connections between causes and effects. Only when this is true can we say that, in principle at least, if we pursue action A in circumstance B it will lead to performance C. We may still have great difficulty in forecasting because we may not be sure whether circumstance B will actually occur or not and we may not accurately know the quantitative relationship between A and C. But we will be able to make some kind of forecast with some probability of success. However, if a sequence of actions is being generated in a system in which the relationships between cause and effect are lost in the minute detail of what happens, then it becomes impossible in principle even to predict, let alone forecast, specific outcomes.

To summarise then, the prescription to select a strategy well in advance of acting that satisfies the criterion of acceptable financial performance makes the following unquestioned assumptions:

- Organisations are systems that are driven by laws producing predictable long-term futures. Although it is difficult to identify what those laws are, and it is also difficult to use them to make accurate forecasts, it is nevertheless possible to do so in principle. Progress therefore lies in gathering data and researching the laws and the techniques of forecasting.

- Those laws establish clear-cut links between cause and effect, between an action and an outcome.

- Organisations are successful when they are close to a state of stable equilibrium, i.e. when their behaviour regularly repeats its past.

- The dynamics of successful organisations are therefore those of stability, regularity and predictability where any tensions or contradictions have been resolved.

The most widely accepted view of the cause of organisational success today is based on a particular set of assumptions about the nature of organisational dynamics. These assumptions indicate that success is achieved when an organisation gets close to a position of stable equilibrium. Here the organisation produces regular patterns of behaviour over time; it displays internal harmony and external adaption to its environment. According to this view organisations can reach success by selecting strategies that are acceptable, feasible and suitable. Successful organisations stick to one of a number of configurations. Because of the assumptions of the dynamic, it is assumed to be possible to predict the long-term outcomes of strategies to some extent, even if that extent is only a qualitative vision. Successful strategies can therefore be selected in advance and systems put in place to deliver success. Leaders choose future strategies and are in control of the organisation and plan its future direction.

Recent studies, however, are increasingly raising question marks over this widely accepted view. The differences centre around what we are assuming about the dynamic.

Looking at the pattern of development of successful companies over a period, we find that they make incremental adjustments much of the time, but occasionally they experience crises that provoke revolutions or sudden jumps to new configurations. The idea here is that creativity is closely related to

KEY READING continued

destruction; that instability is required to shatter existing paradigms, thus making way for the new.

Some of the latest work on strategic management is pointing away from equating success with a movement to stable equilibrium. It seems to be pointing to success as having to do with being away from equilibrium and [instead being] in a state of contradiction and instability. It seems to be doing so in the context of feedback systems that show self-reinforcing and amplifying behaviour,

generating virtuous and vicious circles. It seems to be behaviour characterised by qualitative patterns that are irregular. And development over time for this far-from-equilibrium, amplifying feedback system occurs through paradigm-shattering crises and revolution that produces newly negotiated paradigms and configurations.

Source: Stacey, R D (1993) *Strategic Management and Organisational Behaviour*, 1st edn, Pitman Publishing, London.

Summary

● For both prescriptive and emergent strategists, the resources of the organisation are an important element in strategy. Prescriptive approaches emphasise the need to build on strengths, whereas the emergent view favours flexibility and harnessing the more unpredictable human element. This chapter has concentrated on the prescriptive view.

● In seeking to understand the key factors for success in an industry, the three 'Cs' can be used as a basis for analysis: customers, competitors and company. The purpose of such an approach is to identify those strategic factors that are common to most companies in an industry and are essential to delivering the objectives of such companies. The key factors for success can be used to focus on other areas of strategy development.

● One basic resource decision facing every organisation is whether to make or buy, i.e. whether to make its own products or buy them from outside in the market place. Every organisation needs to reappraise its activities regularly in this area. The decision will be based not only on simple cost considerations but also on broader aspects related to the maintenance of sustainable competitive advantage.

● Resources are difficult to measure because many of them are intangible and cannot easily be captured in numerical data. It is important to go beyond accounting and management information systems in the measurement process.

● Resources add value to the organisation. They take the inputs from suppliers and transform them into finished goods or services. The value added is the difference between the market value of outputs of an organisation and the costs of its inputs. It is possible to calculate this accurately for an overall company but very difficult to do so for individual parts of the company. When used in developing competitive advantage for the individual parts of the company, the concept is therefore often left unquantified.

● In order to develop sustainable competitive advantage, it is necessary to consider the various parts of the organisation and the value that each part adds, where this takes place and how the contribution is made. The value chain undertakes this task. It identifies where value is added in different parts of the organisation and where the organisation may have competitive advantage.

● It may also be necessary to consider the *value system*, i.e. the way that the organisation is linked with other parts of a wider system of adding value involving suppliers, customers and distributors. Unique linkages between elements of the value system may also provide competitive advantage.

● Economic rent is defined as any excess that a factor earns over the minimum amount needed to keep that factor in its present use. Economic rent is important in strategy because it highlights the scarcity of some resources and the possibility of alternative, more profitable uses for a resource.

● In searching for sustainable competitive advantage, the resource-based view (RBV) argues that the individual resources of an organisation provide a stronger basis for strategy development than industry analysis. The reason is that RBV will identify those resources that are exceptional and deliver competitive advantage.

● There are seven elements that may be associated with resource-based competitive advantage: prior or acquired resources; innovative ability; being truly competitive; substitutability; appropriability; durability, and imitability. It is not necessary for an organisation to possess them all before it has some competitive advantages: each organisation will have some unique combination of resources, some of which will deliver sustainable competitive advantage.

● To begin identifying the truly competitive resources, there are three main areas of resource analysis that need to be undertaken – tangible: the physical resources; intangible: resources that have no physical presence but have real benefit; organisational capability: the skills, routines and management leadership of the organisation. Because of the extensive nature of such analysis, it should concentrate on those areas that are more likely to deliver value added and match with the key factors for success in an industry.

● There is no general agreement on what constitutes the best single approach to the development of sustainable competitive advantage. Two approaches have proved useful: distinctive capability (architecture, reputation and innovation) and core competencies.

● There are at least three ways to improve competitive advantage: benchmarking, improving existing resources and upgrading resources.

QUESTIONS

1 Using your judgement, determine the key factors for success in the following industries: pharmaceuticals, fast food restaurants, charities helping homeless people, travel companies offering package tours.

2 Outline the value chain for an organisation you know. Explain the implications of your study for competitive advantage.

3 Take the value added and other data for Glaxo and outline the value chain for the company. Develop the value system within which the company operates. What strategy conclusions can you draw?

4 How do the seven elements of the resource-based view contribute to corporate strategy? What are their limitations?

5 Using the evidence from the case studies on IBM in Chapters 1 and 2, identify the main elements of IBM's competitive advantage. Use the seven elements of RBV to classify your answer and the hierarchy of resources to explain the relationship with the other resources possessed by the company.

6 Take an organisation with which you are familiar and identify its distinctive capabilities, using the key guidelines to assist the process. Compare the organisation with its competitors and comment on the strategy implications.

7 Identify the core competencies of pharmaceutical companies in general and GSK in particular. What do your observations mean for corporate strategy development at GSK?

8 Can core competencies be bought in as a short-term strategic solution or do they have to be developed over the long term? Use an example to support your answer.

9 Could Microsoft's Xbox (see Case 6.3) use any of the three main ways to improve its competitive advantage? Which methods might be used? Why?

10 How would you rate human resources in relation to other aspects of resources in the development of corporate strategy? Do you think the value chain adequately captures your answer?

11 The writer in the Key Reading passage argues that successful new strategy comes from crisis, provoking revolutions and new configurations. Can this view be reconciled with those outlining a more analytical approach, as described in this chapter? Do you agree or disagree with the writer? Give reasons.

STRATEGIC PROJECT **The global pharmaceutical industry**

This chapter has examined the pharmaceutical industry. You might like to explore this global industry further – for example, the strategies that have been adopted by the large US and European companies. For instance, why did Merck refuse to engage in takeovers for a long time and why did Pfizer spend large sums on such activities?

FURTHER READING

For key factors for success: Ohmae, K (1983) *The Mind of the Strategist*, Penguin, Harmondsworth.

For the value chain and value system: Porter, M E (1985) *Competitive Advantage*, The Free Press, New York.

For core competencies: Hamel, G and Prahalad, C K (1994) *Competing for the Future*, Harvard Business School Press, Boston, MA.

For distinctive capabilities: Kay, J (1994) *Foundations of Corporate Success*, Oxford University Press, Oxford.

A useful summary of the resource-based view: Collis, D and Montgomery, C (1995) 'Competing on resources', *Harvard Business Review*, July–August, pp118–28.

NOTES & REFERENCES

1 *Financial Times*, 7 Dec 1993, p22; 16 July 1994, p10; 24 Jan 1995, p17; 27 Jan 1995; 9 Mar 1995, p33; 24 Mar 1995, p27; 24 Apr 1995, p11; 8 Sept 1995, p15; 9 Nov 1995, p25; 27 November 1995, pIV of Biotechnology Supplement; 17 June 1998, p25; 28 July 1998, p24; 14 April 1999, p14; 20 July 1999, p23; 17 January 2000, p18; 22 January 2000, p15; 16 February 2000, p25; 20 April 2000, p28; 23 February 2001, p26; Glaxo Wellcome Annual Report and Accounts 1997, pp2, 3, 8, 9, 86 and 87.

2 Ohmae, K (1983) *The Mind of the Strategist*, Penguin, Harmondsworth, Ch3.

3 Porter, M E (1985) *Competitive Advantage*, The Free Press, New York, Ch7.

4 Kay, J (1993) *Foundations of Corporate Success*, Oxford University Press, Oxford, Chs5 to 8.

5 Amit, R and Schoemaker, P (1993) 'Strategic assets and organizational rent', *Strategic Management Journal*, 14, pp33–46.

6 Ohmae, K (1983) Op. cit., p96.

7 Ghemawat, P (1991) *Commitment*, The Free Press, New York.

8 Some early articles on this shift in position include: Wernerfelt, B (1984) 'A resource-based view of the firm', *Strategic Management Journal*, Sept–Oct, p171; Barney J B (1986) 'Strategic factor markets: Expectations, luck and business strategy', *Management Science*, Oct, p1231; Rumelt, R 'Theory, strategy and entrepreneurship', in Teece, D J (ed) (1987), *The Competitive Challenge: Strategies for Industrial Innovation and Renewal*, Ballinger, Reading, MA.

9 Porter, M E (1980) *Competitive Strategy: Techniques for Analyzing Industries and Competitors*, The Free Press, New York. But note that this was based on earlier work, particularly that of Bain, J (1956) *Barriers to New Competition: Their Character and Consequences in Manfucturing Industries*, Harvard University Press, Cambridge, MA.

10 In particular, many marketing strategy texts make no mention of individual resource analysis. From this perspective, they should all be read with caution. However, many definitions of marketing have long recognised the importance of resources – one used at several universities in the UK makes explicit reference to the resources of the organisation.

11 For example: Penrose, E (1959) *The Theory of the Growth of the Firm*, Basil Blackwell, Oxford; Ansoff, I (1965) *Corporate Strategy*, McGraw-Hill, NY.

12 *See* the pioneering work of Coase, R (1937) 'The nature of the firm', *Economica*, 4, pp386–405. Also Penrose, E (1959) Op. cit., and Williamson, O (1975) *Markets and Hierarchies*, The Free Press, New York.

13 Lynch, R (1994) *European Business Strategies*, 2nd edn, Kogan Page, London, p43.

14 Kay, J (1993) Op. cit., p24.

15 Kay, J (1993) Ibid, p24.

16 Kay, J (1993) Ibid, p28.

17 Kay, J (1993) Ibid, discusses this further in Ch12.

18 Porter, M E (1985) Op. cit., Ch2.

19 Porter, M E (1985) Ibid, p38.

20 Porter, M E (1985) Ibid.

21 Porter, M E (1985) Ibid.

22 Cookson, C and Luesby, J (1995) 'Glaxo Wellcome giant changes the drug mixture', *Financial Times*, 9 Mar, p33.

23 Porter, M E (1985) Op. cit., Chs9, 10 and 11.

24 Ricardo, D (1817) *Principles of Political Economy and Taxation*, J Murray, London. More detail on the origin of economic rent is contained in the following: Lipsey, R G and Chrystal, A (1995) *Positive Economics*, 8th edn, Oxford University Press, Oxford.

25 For a consideration of rent and its strategic implications, *see*: Mahoney, J and Pandian, J (1992) 'The resource-based view within the conversation of strategic management', *Strategic Management Journal*, 13, pp363–80. This gives a useful overall view. *See* also Schoemaker, P (1990), 'Strategy, complexity and economic rent', *Management Science*, 36, Oct, pp1178–92.

26 Schumpeter, J (1934) *The Theory of Economic Development*, Harvard University Press, Harvard, MA.

27 Many of these research papers are referenced elsewhere in this text. The remainder are: Dierickx, I and Cool, K (1989) 'Asset stock accumulation and sustainability of competitive advantage', *Management Science*, 35, pp1504–11; Connor, K (1991) 'A historical comparison of resource-based theory and five schools of thought within industrial organisation economics: Do we have a new theory of the firm', *Journal of Management*, 17(1), pp121–54; Amit, R and Schoemaker, P (1993) 'Strategic assets and organizational rent', *Strategic Management Journal*, 14, pp33–46; Grant, R (1991) 'The resource-based theory of competitive advantage: implications for strategy formulation', *California Management Review*, 33, pp114–22.

28 Rumelt, R (1991) 'How much does industry matter?', *Strategic Management Journal*, Mar, pp64–75.

29 McGahan, A and Porter, M E (1997) 'How much does industry matter, really?' *Strategic Management Journal*, 18, Summer Special Issue, pp15–30.

30 Prahalad, C and Hamel, G (1990) 'The core competence of the corporation', *Harvard Business Review*, May–June, pp 79–91.

31 Kay, J (1994) Op. cit.

32 Peteraf, M (1993) 'The cornerstones of competitive advantage: a resource-based view', *Strategic Management Journal*, 14, pp179–91.

33 Collis, D and Montgomery, C (1995) 'Competing on resources: strategy in the 1990', *Harvard Business Review*, July–Aug, pp119–128.

34 Collis, D and Montgomery, C (1995) Ibid., pp118–128.

35 Kay, J (1993) Op. cit., Chs5, 6 and 7.

36 Hamel, G and Prahalad, H K (1994) *Competing for the Future*, Harvard Business School Press, Boston, MA, Chs9 and 10.

37 Sainsbury, D (1994) 'Be a better builder', *Financial Times*, 2 Sept, p11.

38 Roos, J (1997) *Financial Times Mastering Management*, Pitman, London, Module 20.

39 Roos, J (1998) *Financial Times Mastering Global Business*, Pitman, London, Part 5, pp14–15.

40 Leonard, D (1998) *Wellsprings of Knowledge*, Harvard Business School Press, Boston, MA, p3.

41 *See* also Chaharbaghi, K and Lynch, R (1999) 'Sustainable competitive advantage: towards a dynamic resource-based strategy', *Management Decision*, 37(1), pp45–50.

42 Priem, R L and Butler, J E (2001) 'Is the resource-based view a useful perspective for strategic management research?', *Academy of Management Review*, 26, 1, pp22–40 and Lynch, R (2000) 'Resource-based view: paradigm or checklist?' *International Journal of Technology*, 3, 4, pp550–561.

43 Collis, D and Montgomery, C (1995) Op. cit., p123, emphasise that lengthy lists of core competencies have sometimes become just a 'feelgood' factor.

44 Hamel, G and Prahalad, C K (1994) Op. cit., Ch7.

45 References for Xbox case: Brandenburger, A M and Nalebuff, B J (1997) *Co-opetition*, Harper-Collins, London; *The Economist*, 19 May 2001, p83; *Guardian Newspaper* 12 March 2002, p21; *Financial Times*, 14 October 1999, p31; 19 January 2000, p28; 28 August 2000, p9; 6 September 2000, p3; 25 January 2001, pp23, 29; 26 January 2001, p24; 1 February 2001, p32; 18 May 2001, p11; 19 May 2001, p12; 23 May 2001, p36; 7 July 2001, p14; 21 September 2001, p34; 6 October 2001, p18; 8 January 2002, p30; 7 February 2002, p28.

46 Stacey, R (1993) *Strategic Management and Organisational Dynamics*, 1st edn, Pitman Publishing, London, pp85–7 and 113–15. © R D Stacey. Reproduced with permission.

Analysing human resources

When you have worked through this chapter, you will be able to:

- conduct a human resource audit of an organisation and explore the strategic implications;

- outline the strategic issues involved in organisational culture and analyse the culture of the organisation;

- understand the impact of strategic change on strategy development;

- comment on the impact of downsizing and business process re-engineering in the context of human resources;

- analyse the political network of an organisation and assess its strategic implications;

- explain the strategic management implications of four major types of human resource approaches to strategy development;

- appraise the impact of international culture on strategy development.

Figure 7.1   **The relationship between resources, culture, change and power**

■ Introduction

For many organisations, people are a vital resource. Their strategic significance extends beyond the resource context, however, because strategy development often involves change and some people may resist change to such an extent that it becomes impossible to implement the planned strategy. Human resource analysis is therefore essential during the development of corporate strategy and cannot simply be left as a task to be undertaken after the strategy has been agreed.

One possible starting point for the analysis is an *audit* of the human resources of the organisation – the people, their skills, backgrounds and relationships with each other. An assessment of the *culture* of the organisation is also required – the style and learned ways that govern and shape the organisation's people relationships. *Strategic change* is analysed and its forces are explained (although covered in greater detail in Chapter 21). Finally, *power and politics* may guide and direct the organisation in its strategy development and therefore need careful assessment. The relationship between these subjects is circular – that is, no single area is dominant and all are interrelated – and is shown in Figure 7.1.

CASE STUDY 7.1

Royal Dutch/Shell – the sweeping change that failed to materialise

In a bid to improve growth and profitability, the world's largest oil company Royal Dutch/Shell announced a radical reorganisation in 1995 that would sweep 'barons out of fiefdoms'. Some years later, the company's problems were worse and the barons – the managing directors of its national companies – were still there. This case explores what went wrong and its strategic consequences.

Background

Royal Dutch/Shell is one of the world's great oil companies. It is based on a merger in 1907 between the UK company Shell Transport and the Dutch oil company Royal Dutch. Over the years, the combined enterprise grew, becoming the largest oil company in the world in 1998, measured by turnover. However, leadership was lost in 1999 – as we shall see later.

Unlike other oil companies which had become more centralised, the delicate balance between the UK and Dutch interests was still preserved up to 1998. There was no overall holding company but two owners of all the subsidiaries: Royal Dutch owned 60 per cent of each subsidiary and Shell owned the other 40 per cent. This arrangement had originally been negotiated when the group was founded. There was no strong central core, nor any combined board of directors. The nearest that the company came to full co-ordination was a central management forum called 'The Conference'. This was a meeting of the management boards of the two operating companies but it had no legal existence.

Although managers and employees referred to themselves as members of Royal Dutch/Shell, they were in fact members of one of its various subsidiaries. This meant that all decision making was slow, laborious and careful – not necessarily a bad thing in an industry where time horizons for oil investment are typically 30 years. 'There is a committee culture,' said Mr Enst van Mouvik-Boekman, one of the senior human resource managers in the company. The co-operative style extended around the world to the company's interests in North America, Australasia and many other areas. The company had been much admired over the years for 'breeding the right corporate types and fostering a co-operative atmosphere'. But by 1998 the structure 'has become part of the problem – reducing accountability, blurring responsibility and increasing costs', commented stockbrokers BT Alex Brown.

Proposed strategy and organisational changes in 1995

One result of the company's consultative style was that it had no chief executive to take final decisions. There was a 'Committee of Managing Directors' but its decisions were achieved by consensus and its chairman was simply the 'first amongst equals'. Decisions on capital expenditure were often decidedly odd. The national companies were legal entities and demanded a share of the capital budget, regardless of whether they could make the best strategic case. Until recently, the collegiate style of the Committee of Managing Directors had limited powers to resist such demands.

In practical terms, this meant that key strategic decisions either took lengthy periods to emerge or were taken lower down in the organisation by the powerful national companies that made up the Royal Dutch/Shell empire, namely the barons

referred to above. It also meant that there were large numbers of staff in London and Rotterdam whose job it was to co-ordinate the national policies associated with the regional barons. For many years, this had served the company well. However, by the mid-1990s, the company's return on capital was stuck below 10 per cent and was set to decline further.

The 1995 reorganisation was supposed to 'sweep away' such a decision-making structure and its consequences in terms of poor investment decisions based on national company interests rather than the global good of Royal Dutch/Shell. The national companies would report to a series of global operating companies and some 1170 co-ordinating jobs would go at the centre. The aim was to save costs and focus decisions on the regional and global decision making. Figure 7.2 shows the change that was to be undertaken from 1995 onwards.

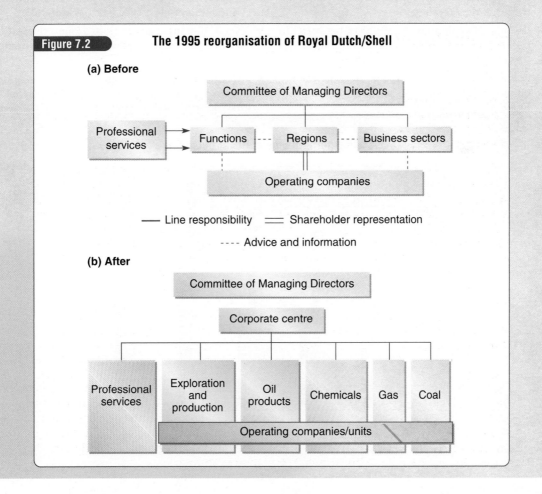

Figure 7.2 The 1995 reorganisation of Royal Dutch/Shell

But the reorganisation quickly ran out of steam. Although some 900 staff jobs were cut, there was considerable resistance to the proposed changes. The consultation culture of the company led to 'laborious' negotiations with staff, especially in the Netherlands. Moreover, the barons were still in power through their membership of the new business committees and the company's profitability was declining – *see* Figure 7.3. Much more drastic strategic change was required, according to many outside observers.

The 1998/99 strategic reorganisation

By the late 1990s, it was much more difficult for all oil companies to make profits than earlier in the decade for four main reasons.

1 Higher environmental standards meant that capital investment in oil refineries was much higher than in earlier decades.

2 Oil prices had declined from US$15 per barrel in the early 1990s to around US$10 in the late 1990s because supply worldwide outstripped demand.

3 Political uncertainty was higher in some leading oil-producing countries such as Russia and Indonesia.

4 Rival companies like Esso (US), BP (UK) and Total (France) were acquiring or merging with rivals in order to gain further economies of scale: Exxon had acquired Mobil; BP had acquired Amoco, Atlantic Richfield and Castrol-Burmah; Total had merged with Fina and then with Elf. The subsequent success of these moves made Royal Dutch/Shell look weak strategically.

Royal Dutch/Shell realised that new and more drastic strategies were required, so it announced the following:

● Closure of its national company headquarters in the UK, Germany, France and the Netherlands

● Write-off of US$4.5 billion assets

● Sale of underperforming subsidiaries, especially 40 per cent of its chemicals business

● Cutbacks in annual capital investment from US$15 billion to US$11 billion per annum

● Several substantial acquisitions around the world that had been made earlier in the 1990s would be put up for sale

● The Chairman of the Committee of Managing Directors would be given new powers to take final decisions on capital expenditure. It was

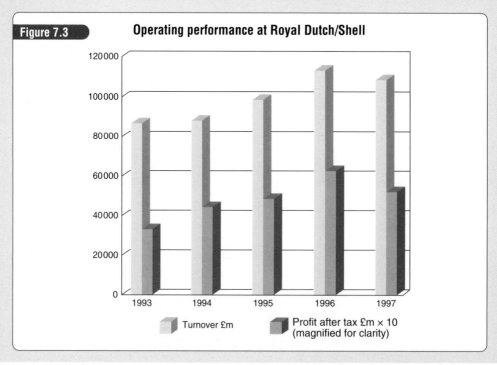

Figure 7.3 **Operating performance at Royal Dutch/Shell**

Turnover £m

Profit after tax £m × 10 (magnified for clarity)

expected that, over time, his position would 'emerge' as that of a dominant chief executive.

The annual cost savings from this reorganisation were projected by Royal Dutch/Shell as being US$2.5 billion by year 2001. 'I am absolutely clear that our group's reputation with investors is on the line', said the Chairman of the Committee, Mr (later Sir) Mark Moody-Stuart. He also used a phrase that in the past has been rarely heard at senior executive levels in Royal Dutch/Shell: he stressed the importance of 'executive accountability' when commenting on the 1998 reorganisation. He also said that the company had immense financial strength and flexibility to withstand further falls in the price of oil, even below US$10 per barrel.

Case questions

1 *Why was the failure of the 1995 reorganisation so predictable?*

2 *Do you think that the management changes of the late 1990s will be any more successful? Why?*

3 *What lessons, if any, can we draw about the human resource aspects of strategy analysis from this case?*

7.1 Human resource analysis and corporate strategy

7.1.1 Prescriptive and emergent approaches

Human-resource-based analysis emphasises the *emergent* approach to corporate strategy. People are not machines: they respond to leadership, enthusiasm and shared decision making. Emergent strategy is more in tune with these issues because it encourages consensus and experimentation. Prescriptive stategy, with its emphasis on the rational solution, is less flexible and amenable to this stance.

Some prescriptive strategists have taken the view that human resources should be considered *only after the basic strategy has been derived*. Their view is based on two areas of evidence and thinking:

1 Alfred Chandler's highly influential research text, *Strategy and Structure*.[1] This book analysed strategy development at four leading US companies during the early twentieth century. Among its many conclusions, it said that it was necessary to formulate the strategy of the company *before* considering how the company should be organised to implement the strategy.

2 The focus on *important* strategy issues might be diluted by the consideration of other matters, such as human resource issues. For example, Porter's two books on *Competitive Strategy*[2] and *Competitive Advantage* certainly include human resource issues but lay the emphasis on competitive strategy development.

In fact, the Chandler text does not preclude the discussion of leadership and human resources in the formulation of strategy. On the contrary, it accurately describes their role in strategy development in some situations.[3] Moreover, Porter's concept of competitive strategy is consistent with the comparative analysis of human resources in an organisation as compared with those of its competitors. Nevertheless, the fact remains that some prescriptive strategists only consider human resource issues *after* the formulation of strategy.[4]

However, human resources need to be considered *during* the strategic resource analysis phase for four related reasons:

1 People-related strategies may form an integral part of the new strategy – for example, a change in the organisation's way of conducting its business. The purpose of such

a change might be to achieve greater responsiveness and efficiency from people within the company, as at Royal Dutch/Shell.

2 The increased technological skills required by, and the knowledge-based complexities of, many commercial processes have meant that an analysis of the existing human resources is essential for an accurate assessment of the options that are available.

3 Research and writings on organisational change and culture[5] have emphasised the importance of values and cultures in the *development* of organisational structure. These cannot simply be added on afterwards.

4 The resource-based view of strategy development (*see* Chapter 6) clearly identifies the role of the *network* of people in an organisation and their *relationships* with each other as a key element of strategy.

7.1.2 Sustainable competitive advantage

For most organisations, people are a vital resource. There are some industries where people are not just important but are the *key factor* for successful performance. For example:

- *Advertising and creative development*, where innovation through people is a crucial element in success.
- *Leisure and tourism*, where a company has a direct, intangible interface that relies on individual employees to give interest and enjoyment to customers.
- *Management consultancy and the advertising industry*, where client relationships are vital to successful outcomes.
- *Hospitals and the medical profession*, where people and personal relationships are essential to the delivery of quality services.

Even in organisations where there are other key factors for success, such as oil resources at Royal Dutch/Shell, human resources clearly play a major part in the process. The smooth-running Shell man or woman is an essential feature of the company and close management co-ordination around the world is crucial to key strategic decisions.

In this context, the ability of people in some organisations to be more *adaptable to changes* in the environment is a real skill. It may even be a source of competitive advantage in fast-moving markets.[6] Arie De Geus, the former head of planning at Royal Dutch/Shell, has said:

> *The ability to learn faster than your competitors may be the only sustainable competitive advantage.*[7]

Such skills are essentially people-related and the strategic approach is emergent.

7.1.3 Strategic change

The recognition that the threat posed to people by strategic change can be a significant barrier to the development of corporate strategy has come in the last 30 years. They fear that they may lose their jobs or their status: the Royal Dutch/Shell reorganisation in 1995, which threatened over 1000 jobs, took longer to implement and resulted in fewer cost savings than originally envisaged because of such fears.

To quote Whittington, writing about corporations in crisis:[8]

History is littered with managers apparently unable to adapt to new and threatening circumstances, and suffering the penalty of dismissal.

Even when companies are not in crisis, some writers take the view that the ability of people in the organisation to cope with change is a vital element in the development of strategy. This issue is explored later in this chapter and further in Chapter 21.

> ### Key strategic principles
>
> - Human-resource-based analysis emphasises the emergent approach to strategic development. It is essential to consider human resources during the development of corporate strategy because of the need to explore people-related strategies at an early stage.
> - People are a vital competitive resource in most organisations. The adaptability of people in the organisation may be a source of real competitive advantage in fast-moving markets.
> - The analysis of strategic change needs to be explored and built into the development of corporate strategy.

7.2 Human resource audit

7.2.1 Audit

In undertaking the human resource audit of an organisation, it is important to give careful thought to a basic list of important areas in the business. Exhibit 7.1 shows a suggested list.[9] The main principles are:

- to obtain some basic information on the people and policies involved in the organisation;
- to explore in detail the role and contribution of the human resource management function in the development of corporate strategy.

7.2.2 Strategic implications

The difficulty is to move beyond a list to something of strategic significance. Three factors need to be added:

1 analysis of the list in Exhibit 7.1 using the *key factors for success*;

2 comparative data for a *leading competitor* or, in the case of a smaller company, several competitors of comparable size; and

3 consideration of the ownership shareholding and stakeholders of the organisation – *see* Chapter 12.

Using these additional factors, it should be possible to develop a human resource analysis that is rather more focused on the *key strategic issues* related to the company. Equally, it should be possible to define and explore the role of human resources in the development of *competitive advantage*. The development of such advantages is likely to derive both from:

- *Issues common to all organisations in the industry* – for example, levels of service expected in all organisations, such as the frequency of oil deliveries by Shell to an industrial customer.
- *Factors that are unique to the organisation itself* – for example, aspects of the service that only the organisation itself can provide, such as rapid local back-up by Shell.

Exhibit 7.1   **Human resource audit**

People in the organisation

- Employee numbers and turnover
- Organisation structure
- Structures for controlling the organisation
- Use of special teams, e.g. for innovation or cost reduction
- Level of skills and capabilities required
- Morale and rewards
- Employee and industrial relations
- Selection, training and development
- Staffing levels
- Capital investment/employee
- Role of quality and personal service in delivering the products or services of the organisation
- Role of professional advice in delivering the product or service

Role and contribution of human resource strategy

- Relationship with corporate strategy
- Key characteristics of human resource strategy
- Consistency of human resource strategy across an organisation with several divisions
- The responsiveness of human resource strategy to changes in business strategy and the environment
- The role of human resource strategy in leading change in the organisation
- The monitoring and review of human resource strategy
- The time frame for the operation of human resource strategy

---

▶ Key strategic principles

- The human resource audit will have two main elements: people in the organisation and the role and contribution of human resources to the development of corporate strategy.
- The development of sustainable competitive advantage will derive both from issues common to all organisations in the industry and to factors that are unique to the organisation itself.

> ▶ *Key strategic principles continued*
>
> ● A basic analysis of human resources can be constructed for the company. However, from a strategy viewpoint, it would be more valuable if this were filtered using key factors for success, competitive comparisons and, if appropriate, international considerations.

7.3 Analysis of organisational culture

7.3.1 The elements of organisational culture

Every organisation has a culture – its set of beliefs, values and learned ways of managing – and this is reflected in its structures, systems and approach to the development of corporate strategy. Its culture derives from its past, its present, its current people, technology and physical resources and from the aims, objectives and values of those who work in the organisation.

Because each organisation has a different combination of the above, each will have a culture that is unique. Analysis is important because culture influences every aspect of the organisation and has an impact on its performance.[10] Specifically, it is the filter and shaper through which the leaders, managers and workers develop and implement their strategies. For these reasons, it will be one of the factors that influences the development of corporate strategy.

In spite of its importance, there is a significant problem in analysing culture. The difficulty is the lack of agreement amongst leading writers on its nature, structure and influence. As a starting point, this book explores the matter from a strategic perspective only and is therefore selective in its approach to this issue.[11]

The main elements of organisational culture are set out in Figure 7.4.

7.3.2 Environmental influences on organisational culture

Outside the organisation itself, there will be a whole series of influences on the organisational culture of the organisation.

People

We are concerned here with the impact on the organisation of people in the environment: such people will include customers and suppliers, along with government and professional advisors. The main areas are:

● *Age profile.* As the population grows older, so tastes change and recruitment changes.

● *Socio-economic group.* As people become richer, their needs and aspirations increase. Strategy will need to reflect these differences.

● *Male and female roles.* In some Western-based societies, females have not only extended their working lives but are asserting their right to equal status with males. In other societies, this has not happened. Strategy will need to be sensitive to such variations and be devised accordingly.

● *Language and communication.* Variations within and between countries represent real differences that need to be accommodated in strategy, both to control strategy better and to motivate those involved in the strategy process better.

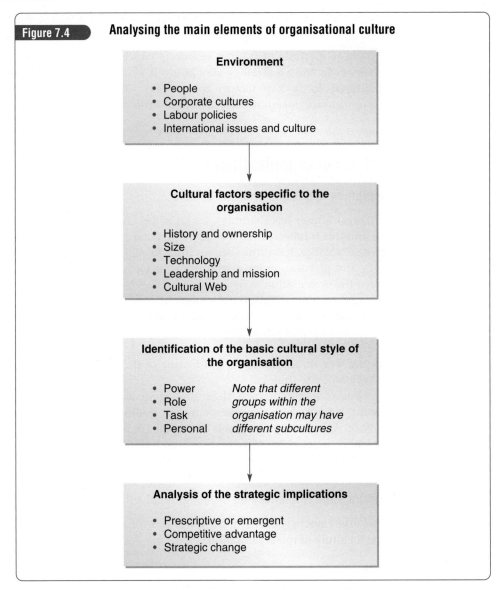

Figure 7.4   **Analysing the main elements of organisational culture**

Environment

- People
- Corporate cultures
- Labour policies
- International issues and culture

Cultural factors specific to the organisation

- History and ownership
- Size
- Technology
- Leadership and mission
- Cultural Web

Identification of the basic cultural style of the organisation

- Power
- Role
- Task
- Personal

Note that different groups within the organisation may have different subcultures

Analysis of the strategic implications

- Prescriptive or emergent
- Competitive advantage
- Strategic change

- *Religion and beliefs*. Strongly held beliefs must be respected and reflected in strategy development.
- *Government policy*. Policy on education, training, social welfare provisions, health and pensions provisions will have a significant influence on people development inside the organisation.

Corporate cultures[12]

The corporate cultural environment covers the *links* that the organisation has with *other similar organisations*. The connections may be both formal and informal in nature. The reasons for such links are varied but may stem from an aspect of national cultures: group goals matter more than the individual in some societies, such as those in Japan and Korea. They may also arise from the common interests that organisations share, such as petitioning governments for grants, laws and favourable economic status. There is also a tendency in many countries for like-minded companies to group together for reasons of history, common shareholdings, common customers, common enemies and so on.

Labour and employment policies

In some industrialised countries, trade unionism forms part of the environment that needs to be considered. However, the influence of organised labour has been declining over the last few years with union membership declining around the world.[13]

International issues

International cultures may have a significant impact on corporate culture (*see* Section 7.6).

7.3.3 Cultural factors specific to the organisation

To understand the culture of an organisation, it is useful to consider the factors that have influenced its development.

History and ownership

A young company may have been founded by one individual or a small group who will continue to influence its development for some years. Centralised ownership will clearly concentrate power and therefore will concentrate influence and style. Family firms and owner-dominated firms will have clearly recognisable cultures.

Size

As firms expand, they may lose the tight ownership and control and therefore allow others to influence their style and culture. Even if ownership remains tight, larger companies are more difficult to control from the centre.

Technology

This will influence the culture of the company but its effects are not always predictable.[14] Those technologies that require economies of scale or involve high cost and expensive machinery usually require a formal and well-structured culture for success: examples might include large-scale chemical production or beer brewing. Conversely, in fast-changing technologies, such as those in telecommunications, a more flexible culture may be required.

Leadership and mission

Individuals and their values will reflect and change the culture of the organisation over time, especially the chief executive and immediate colleagues. These issues are vital to the organisation (*see* Chapters 10 and 12).

Cultural Web

The Cultural Web is a useful method of bringing together the basic elements that are helpful in analysing the culture of an organisation (*see* Figure 7.5).

The main elements are:

● *Stories*. What do people talk about in the organisation? What matters in the organisation? What constitutes success or failure?

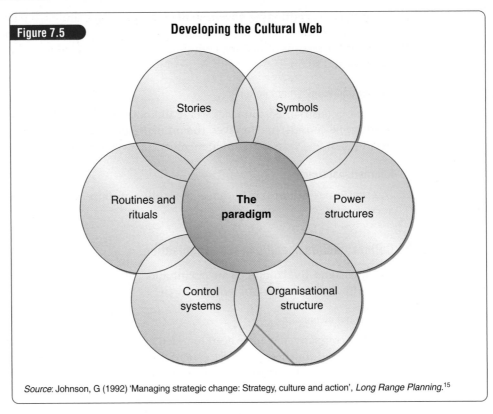

Figure 7.5 **Developing the Cultural Web**

Stories

Symbols

Routines and rituals

The paradigm

Power structures

Control systems

Organisational structure

Source: Johnson, G (1992) 'Managing strategic change: Strategy, culture and action', *Long Range Planning*.[15]

- *Routines*. What are the normal ways of doing things? What are the procedures (not always written down)?
- *Rituals*. Beyond the normal routine, what does the organisation highlight? For example, long service? Sales achievement? Innovation? Quality standards? How does it highlight and possibly reward such rituals?
- *Symbols*. What are the symbols of office? Office size? Company car size? Separate restaurants for different levels of managers and workers? Or the absence of these? How do employees travel: first, business or tourist class?
- *Control systems*. Bureaucratic? Well-documented? Oriented towards performance? Formal or informal? Haphazard? (*See* Part 6.)
- *Organisational structure*. Who reports to whom in the organisation on a formal basis and who has an informal relationship?
- *Power structures*. Who makes the decisions? Who influences the decisions? How? When? (*See* Section 7.3.4.)

The Cultural Web can usefully distinguish also between what is done *officially* in an organisation, such as press releases and post-project evaluation, and what is done *unofficially*, such as grapevine stories, office parties, e-mail messages and so on.

The paradigm not only links the elements but may also tend to *preserve* them as 'the way we do things here'. It summarises the culture of the organisation. Chapter 12 contains a worked example of the Cultural Web.

7.3.4 Identification of the basic cultural style of the organisation

Although each organisation has its own unique culture, Handy[16] has used the work of Harrison to suggest that there are four main types.

The power culture

The organisation revolves around and is dominated by one individual or a small group. *Examples*: small building companies; formerly, some newspapers with dominant proprietors. *Strategic change*: fast or slow depending on the management style of the leader.

The role culture

This organisation relies on committees, structures, logic and analysis. There is a small group of senior managers who make the final decisions, but they rely on procedures, systems and clearly defined rules of communication. *Examples*: civil service, retail banks. *Strategic change*: likely to be slow and methodical.

The task culture

The organisation is geared to tackling identified projects or tasks. Work is undertaken in teams that are flexible and tackle identified issues. The teams may be multidisciplinary and adaptable to each situation. *Examples*: advertising agencies, consultancies. *Strategic change*: will depend on the circumstances but may be fast where this is needed.

The personal culture

The individual works and exists purely for him/herself. The organisation is tolerated as the way to structure and order the environment for certain useful purposes, but the prime area of interest is the individual. *Examples*: co-operatives, communes and also individual professionals such as architects or engineers working as lone people in larger organisations such as health authorities. *Strategic change*: can be instant, where the individual decides that it is in his/her interests to make such a move.

In examining the four main types of organisational culture, there are three important qualifications:

1 *Organisations change over time*. The entrepreneur, represented by the *power culture*, may mature into a larger and more traditional business. The bureaucracy, personified by the *role culture*, may move towards the more flexible structure of the *task culture*. Hence, an analysis may need to be reassessed after some years.

2 *Several types of culture usually exist in the same organisation*. There may be small task-teams concentrating on developing new business or solving a specific problem and, in the same organisation, a more bureaucratic set-up handling large-volume production in a more formal structure and style. Corporate strategy may even need to consider whether different parts of the organisation should develop *different* cultures – for example, a team culture for a radical new venture, a personal culture for the specialist expertise required for a new computer network.

3 *Different cultures may predominate, depending on the headquarters and ownership of the company*. Hofstede's research[17] indicates that national culture will also have an influence and will interact with the above basic type (see Section 7.6).

For these reasons, strategic cultural analysis needs to be approached with caution. Nevertheless, there are many organisations, both large and small, where the mood, style and tone are clear enough as soon as you walk through the door. There is one prevailing culture that permeates the way in which business is done in that organisation. The implications for competitive advantage and strategic change follow from this.

7.3.5 Conclusions on organisational culture

Exhibit 7.2 lists ten guidelines for analysing cultural issues within an organisation. Both Brown[18] and Handy[19] have provided longer questionnaires than are shown in Exhibit 7.2. From a strategy viewpoint, they are useful but the danger with such an analysis is that it becomes another descriptive list of possible factors. The analytical process needs to be undertaken with reference to possible areas of strategic interest. For example, it is *interesting* to know that the organisation's culture is risk averse, but it is much more *relevant* to set this against a new corporate strategy that requires a higher degree of risk taking than was previously the case. Hence, Exhibit 7.2 also provides some possible criteria to test for relevance. This is sometimes referred to as *testing for strategic fit* with the current strategy.

Exhibit 7.2 **Ten guidelines for analysing organisation culture and its strategy implications**

1 How old is the organisation? Does it exist in a stable or fast-changing environment?

2 Who owns it? Shareholding structure? Small company owner-proprietor? Government shareholding? Large public company? What are the core beliefs of the leadership?

3 How is it organised? Central board? Divisions? Clear decision-making structure from the top? Are structures formal or informal? Is competition encouraged between people in the company or does the organisation regard collaboration as being more important?

4 How are results judged? Sympathetically? Rigorously? What elements are monitored? Is the emphasis on looking back to past events or forwards to future strategy?

5 How are decisions made? Individually? Collectively and by consensus? How is power distributed throughout the organisation? Who can stop change? And who can encourage it?

6 What qualities make a good boss? And a good subordinate?

7 How are people rewarded? Remuneration? Fear? Loyalty? Satisfaction in a job well done?

8 How are groups and individuals controlled? Personal or impersonal controls? Enthusiasm and interest? Or abstract rules and regulations?

9 How does the organisation cope with change? Easily or with difficulty?

10 Do people typically work in teams or as individuals? What does the company prefer?

Overall: Is the *whole* organisation being analysed or just a *part*?

Tests for strategic relevance might include:

● *Risk*. Does the organisation wish to change its level of risk?

● *Rewards*. What reward and job satisfaction?

● *Change*. High or low degree of change needed?

● *Cost reduction*. Is the organisation seeking major cost reductions?

● *Competitive advantage*. Are significant new advantages likely or will they be needed?

▶ Key strategic principles

- Organisational culture is the set of beliefs, values and learned ways of managing that govern organisational behaviour. Each organisation has a culture that is unique.

- Culture influences performance and corporate strategy. It is the filter and shaper through which strategy is developed and implemented.

- Factors within the organisation influencing culture include: history and ownership, size, technology, leadership and mission, along with the Cultural Web of the organisation.

- The Cultural Web provides a method of summarising some of the cultural influences within an organisation: stories, routines and rituals, symbols, power structures, organisation structure, control systems.

- Factors external to the organisation influencing culture include: people, national cultures, corporate cultural environment, labour and employment policies.

- There are four main types of culture: power, role, task and personal. Their importance for corporate strategy lies particularly in their ability to encourage or cope with the *strategic change* that is likely to be needed with specific strategic initiatives and to deliver *competitive advantage*. Some types are better able to cope and manage strategic change than others.

- Guidelines can be developed for analysing organisational culture. For the purposes of strategy development, such an analysis needs to be assessed against the strategy in areas such as attitudes to risk, change, reward, cost reduction and competitive advantage.

CASE STUDY 7.2

Culture, crisis and power at British Petroleum[20]

In early 1990, Bob Horton, the new Chairman of British Petroleum, announced major changes in the management organisation, processes and culture of Europe's second-largest oil company. Over the next two years, the implementation process brought him into open conflict with fellow board members. Horton was ousted in a boardroom coup in June 1992.

After gaining something of a reputation as an 'axeman' at BP Chemicals and BP Oil in North America, Horton was appointed deputy chairman at British Petroleum (BP) in 1989. Horton had inherited a company with some major business problems. Principally, BP had incurred major debts when it purchased back a block of its shares from the Kuwait Investment Office in 1987. By 1992, it had a 100 per cent gearing ratio and US$16 billion of debts (*see* Chapter 8). The world economic markets were also depressed so oil consumption was weak.

The company certainly knew Horton's management style well. He called BP's first group management conference in March 1989 and identified major problems with BP's structures, systems and management: they were overbureaucratic, sluggish and committee-driven. His intention was to revise the structure and achieve a new 'tight–loose' structure in the phrase of the strategy book, *In Search of Excellence*. The new form would be leaner, have more delegated powers and be able to respond faster to the market place.

Rather than asking his main board colleagues to mastermind the changes he had outlined, Horton recruited from within BP a team of seven 35- to 40-year-old mid-ranking executives to take a fundamental look at the whole corporation. From March to December 1989 the team interviewed all the senior management and employed outside advisers to help develop recommendations for streamlining BP. The team also sent questionnaires to one in six BP employees, seeking their views on the company. Two-thirds (4000) responded. Their opinions made dismal reading and confirmed all the team's worst fears.

During Autumn 1989, the team met weekly with Horton to put together proposals for the new slimmed-down BP. They identified a series of problems in the organisation: for example, no shared vision, poor communications and little trust.

At the same time, Horton's project team leader, David Pascall, was feeding some of this message to other main board members on an informal basis. The aim of this process had been to fire them up for the major review meeting with Horton scheduled for December 1989. This meeting duly took place outside London and in great secrecy, with all the managing directors (MDs) attending. In general, the meeting accepted the changes that were needed in culture and style. Some proposals went through quite quickly, such as the need to give the MDs more authority over capital spending limits. Others led to more lengthy debate – for example, whether the head office central planning and control functions should be cut as drastically as proposed. This was only finally settled after the meeting.

There was only one open revolt at the meeting over an appeal by Horton for BP to work its managers less hard. Various senior MDs had supported the view, but Horton's deputy chairman designate, David Simon, then disagreed: 'I wouldn't overdo the chances of the system changing.' Two other MDs supported this view, so Horton backed off. More importantly, one MD on leaving the meeting was heard to comment that the MDs themselves were having a meeting the following day without Horton; his opinion was that the proposals might be overturned at that session. In fact they were not, but the comment epitomised the resentment shown by many senior managers.

Over the next two years, Horton, who was now chairman, moved to put in train his changes in the programme, which had been named *Project 1990*. Over US$30 million was spent on workshops, communications and training programmes. There

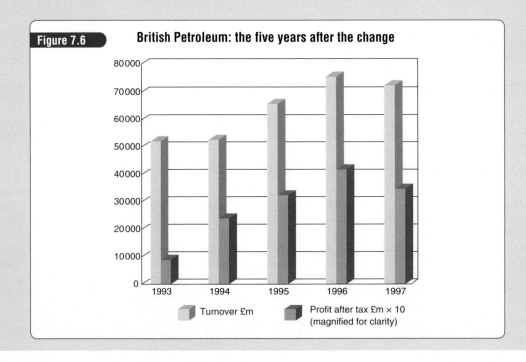

Figure 7.6 | **British Petroleum: the five years after the change**

Turnover £m

Profit after tax £m × 10 (magnified for clarity)

was to be a transformed view of human resource management in the company. There was a major drive to change the culture to one of 'ownership' of problems by individuals rather than committees.

Horton had come to BP headquarters with a reputation as a straight-talking manager. His attitude was that there would be many managers, especially those over 40, who might well obstruct his attempt to introduce a new culture at BP. He was quite open that he was not prepared to let such people get in the way of strategic and cultural reforms which he regarded as essential. He even went on record to the press to say that the biggest mistake he had made when reorganising BP Chemicals some years previously was 'to allow some guys to stay in place whom I should have got rid of on day three'. He understood that not all managers would find this acceptable but felt that it was sometimes necessary to take difficult decisions. That was the function of senior management.

Slowly, the resentment began to build during 1990 and 1991. 'Culture change teams' were introduced to bring about the new era. The baronies were attacked, revised job descriptions were introduced and job cuts were achieved. It was inevitable that some managers would be feeling discomfort. Satirical stories began to circulate in the company about Horton himself: one likened him to Napoleon. He was described as autocratic and quick-tempered by a senior colleague. Horton him-

self became increasingly restive about the pace of change, but judged that what he was doing was for the benefit of BP.

Finally, his board turned on him in June 1992. His deputy, David Simon, took over as MD. Simon was reported to represent the more traditional BP culture. An outside chairman was also brought in, Lord Ashburton, a City merchant banker. The culture change programme continued and some 6000 people left the company during 1992 and 1993. However, BP had decided that Bob Horton was part of the problem rather than the source of the solution.

After Horton's departure, the company immediately cut its dividend as it struggled to reduce debts. The company also drastically cut its debt with a programme of asset disposals and job cuts.

Case questions

1 *What was the significance for Horton of involving 35- to 40-year-old managers? And his fellow board members? What impact did this have on BP strategy?*

2 *What is your assessment of the cultural changes that took place in the period 1990–92 against the cultural change models outlined in the chapter?*

3 *Should other companies follow Horton's approach to strategic change? Or should they adopt a different approach? If so, what?*

7.4 Analysis of strategic change in organisations

Although some organisations may continue successfully with their current strategies, many will need to change. Any change brings uncertainty and some organisations and individuals are better able to cope with this than others. Some may even resist proposed new strategies and put at risk the new proposals. Strategic change can usefully be explored as the three interrelated topics shown in Figure 7.7.

7.4.1 Types of organisation and their ability to cope with strategic change – the contribution of Miles and Snow

Given the uncertainties that usually come with strategic change, organisations need to be analysed in advance for their ability to cope with this process. If they are likely to have difficulty, then there may be an argument for adjusting the proposed strategy to reflect this situation. There is no overall agreement on an analytical procedure for examining the link between organisation and strategic change. Commentators have proposed various ways of analysing the process.

Figure 7.7 **The analysis of strategic change in organisations**

Miles and Snow[21] proposed four main strategic types of organisation which can be analysed for their ability to cope with change:

1 *Defender organisations* produce products or services with the objective of obtaining market leadership. They may achieve their objectives by concentrating on a market niche through specialisation and cost reductions. The market may be mature and stable. The organisation is able to cope with sudden strategic change but would be more comfortable with steady strategic change.

2 *Prospector organisations* are involved in growing markets where they actively seek new opportunities through innovation. They are typically flexible and decentralised in their approach to the market and able to respond quickly to change. Their objectives are to seek new opportunities. Strategic change is no problem for such companies.

3 *Analyser organisations* seek to expand but also to protect what they already have. They may wait for others to innovate and delay while others prove new market opportunities before they enter. Large and small organisations can take this route, using mass production to reduce costs but also relying on some areas such as marketing to be more responsive and provide flexibility where required. Strategic change would need careful analysis and evaluation before it could be adopted.

4 *Reactor organisations* are those that respond inappropriately to competitors and to the more general environment. They rarely, if ever, take the initiative and, in a sense, may have no strategy: they always react to other strategies. Even if they have a strategy, it is entirely inappropriate to the environment and hence the resulting reactor organisation is bound to be inadequate. Strategic change will therefore be a problem.

In conclusion, the *prospector organisation* is probably the best able to cope with strategic change. The ability to cope is built into the culture, organisation and management style. Some markets are changing faster than previously, especially with new technologies and new international competition. The ability to cope and even enjoy change is a major competitive advantage.

Table 7.1 Four strategic types and their approaches to strategy

	Strategic environment	Strategic approach	Resource strategy	Simplified process approach
Defender	Stable	Protect market share Hold current position	Efficient production Tight control Centralised Manage via rules	Prescriptive
Analyser	Slow change	Hold market share but with some innovation Seek market opportunities but protect existing areas	Efficient production but some flexibility in new areas Tight control in existing areas but lower control in new products	Prescriptive
Prospector	Growing, even, dynamic	Find new opportunities Exploit and take risks	Flexible production Innovate with decentraised control	Emergent
Reactor	Growing or slow	Responding only to others Often late and inadequate	Muddled, centralised Slow	Prescriptive

Source: Adapted from Miles, R E, Snow C C, Meyer A D and Coleman, H J (1978) 'Organizational Strategy, Structure and Process', *Academy of Management Review*, 3, pp546–62.

For strategy purposes, it will be essential to analyse the various parts of an organisation against their ability to cope with change. The above classification may oversimplify the real situation and needs to be treated with some caution. Nevertheless, it does provide real guidance on strategic change – *see* Table 7.1.

7.4.2 Phase of organisational growth

Whatever organisational classification is used in the analytical process, some changes may be more rapid and more dramatic than others. It is probably the case that the more intense the debate, the more difficult the change process and the more problems there are with the strategy. It is appropriate therefore to examine the *type of change* that might be expected. Greiner[22] identified two major determinants to clarify this process:

1 *The age of the organisation*. Young organisations are typically full of ideas, creative, perhaps a little chaotic but actively seeking change. As they grow older and achieve success, there is more to defend and more to co-ordinate.

2 *The size of the organisation.* Small organisations may be closer to the market place and have simpler administration. As the organisation becomes larger and acquires more people, it sets up systems and procedures to cope.

Greiner's five phases of growth are shown in Figure 7.8.[23] They are not meant to be taken literally – organisations can overcome their problems – but they are helpful in identifying the main issues to be met and the types of strategic change that may be needed.

Particular types of organisation will experience particular pressures for change.

● *Small business.* As a small business expands, the owner-proprietor begins to lose control because s/he can no longer keep in contact with everyone personally. Moreover, the administration becomes more complex. Hence, it may become increasingly difficult to take rapid decisions and respond to changes in the environment. One strategic solution is to remain small and refuse to grow. Another solution is to sell out to a new group.

● *Large organisations that were formerly in government ownership.* Having previously relied on government funds, the organisation now needs to engage in marketing and other related business areas. However, it is large and has little experience of business pressures and culture. It is used to the bureaucracy that is demanded of government systems. Strategic change needs to be seen as a shift in *culture* just as much as new business-oriented *strategies*.

● *Not-for-profit institutions.* For an organisation which relies on public donations and voluntary help, there is an increasing problem as it grows older and expands in size. It needs to set up systems to manage its finances and services while at the same time

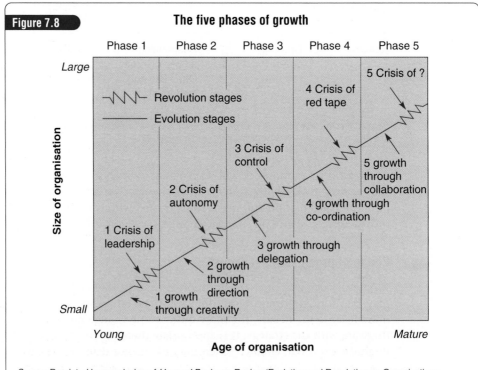

Figure 7.8 — **The five phases of growth**

Source: Reprinted by permission of *Harvard Business Review*. 'Evolution and Revolution as Organisations grow' by Greiner, July–August 1972. Copyright © 1972 by the President and Fellows of Harvard College; all rights reserved.

keeping the personal touch and enthusiasm of its individual helpers. Change will present real problems.

● *Medium-sized business.* With expansion, it may no longer be possible to control every aspect of strategy from the centre. There will be a need for greater autonomy and delegation. Some managers are better able to delegate than others. The change strategy may involve not only new strategies but *new managers* recruited into the organisation.

7.4.3 Strategic pressures driving organisational change

As corporate strategy is analysed and developed, there are two main strategic pressures that may drive organisational change:

1 internal – desire for increased profitability, growth or some other objective, such as quality or innovation;

2 external – competitive pressures or other environmental change.

Such pressures need to be assessed for each organisation. For example, the pressures in both oil company cases in this chapter built up during the 1990s and led to major change around the time of the millennium – major reorganisation at Royal Dutch/Shell and acquisition at BP.

Exhibit 7.3 **Examples of two strategic techniques to drive organisational change**

Delayering

Traditionally, big companies believed that one manager could only control a certain number of people – the *span of control* – often between seven and ten. Several layers of management were therefore needed to allow one senior person to control several hundred lower down in the organisation. With the new computer and telecommunications control systems, there is now a view that managers can control 30 people. This reduces the need to have so many managerial layers and thus opens the way for companies to cut costs – for example, the process undertaken by Shell to reduce its headquarters workforce by 1170 employees.

To work properly, delayering needs to be undertaken with careful planning: this means examining the paperwork and bureaucracy that often accumulate in large companies and cutting these down at the same time. It also needs to be done radically once rather than in piecemeal fashion, because of the impact on morale every time cuts are made.

Business process re-engineering[24]

This is the process of using modern computer technology to simplify radically the organisation's handling of administrative tasks. This may accompany delayering but is a different process. It is more likely to occur in the lower levels of the company, rather than at managerial level. It is likely to involve combining departments such as customer handling, complaints, stock ordering, stock delivery and control. Typically, there will be a dismantling of demarcation between departments and a radical reduction in the number of employees. The human resource aspects of such a strategy are obvious. (*See* Case study 7.2.)

Two specific strategies driving organisational change in the 1990s include *delayering*, which involves removing layers of management and administration, and *business process re-engineering*, which involves replacing people in administrative tasks by technology. Exhibit 7.3 explains the elements of these two techniques for driving change.

Strategic change will lead inevitably to organisational change. The starting point is careful *analysis* of the current situation. The subject of *managing* strategic change is explored in Chapter 21.

> ### ▶ Key strategic principles
>
> - Given the uncertainty that usually comes with strategic change, organisations need to be analysed for their ability to cope with this process.
> - There are no agreed procedures for such an analysis but they usually involve categorising organisations into specific strategic types: four have been identified. The ability of each type to cope with change is then assessed.
> - As strategies are developed in organisations, they may grow in size and certainly in age. In consequence, the nature of the strategic problems changes. Five stages of growth have been identified: creativity, direction, delegation, co-ordination and collaboration.
> - Change also needs to be assessed against the pressures that are on the organisation. These will be both internal and external. Strategies such as delayering and business process re-engineering are specific modern examples of such influences.

7.5 Analysis of politics, power and strategic change

When writing about his life in politics, the British politician Lord Butler called his book *The Art of the Possible*. Although certain changes in national life might be *desirable*, he argued that they were not always *possible*, given the electorate and the environment of that time. In politics, he believed that people needed to be persuaded and this was an art, not an exact science. Business and not-for-profit organisations also involve people. The early twentieth-century view of management pioneers such as F W Taylor and Henry Ford was that there was one best way to achieve results and organisations were machines that could be directed to these ends. Views are now more sophisticated, especially where strategic change is concerned.

In organisations, there will be individuals and groups who are likely to have an interest in any strategic change. There may be pressure groups, rivalries, power barons and brokers, influencers, arguments, winners and losers. Some dispute may be disinterested and rational and some may be governed by strongly held views and interests. All these areas form the *politics* of the organisation. Strategic change cannot be separated from such issues.

Strategy too is about 'the art of the possible'. An analysis of the organisation's political situation is important in the early stages of strategic development. It may be highly desirable to alter radically a company's structure, but the cost in terms of management time may be too high in some circumstances, even with an imposed solution. Case study 7.2 explored the difficulties that faced the new chairman of BP over the period

1990–92 as he attempted to achieve radical change and impose his preferred solutions on the organisation.

7.5.1 What are the main components of politics in organisations?

Taking an emergent strategy perspective, Handy points out[25] that it is wishful thinking to attempt to 'manage change' in the sense that it is possible not only to know where the organisation is heading but also to instruct everyone to take the same route. It is much more realistic and rewarding to 'cultivate change', suggesting that a positive attitude to change, coupled with learning and persuasion, is more likely to be productive.

There is nothing wrong with healthy competition between groups and individuals in an organisation. It can stretch performance and help groups to become more cohesive. It also helps to sort out the best. The difficulty arises when it gives rise to conflict and political manoeuvring. There are two principal reasons for organisational conflict:

1 *Differing goals and ideologies.* For example, different groups or individuals within an organisation may have different goals, make different value judgements, be given different and conflicting objectives, etc. There may also be a lack of clarity in the goals and objectives. It should be possible in the context of strategic change to ensure that conflict and confusion over goals is minimised.

2 *Threats to territory.* For example, some groups or individuals may feel threatened by others doing the same jobs, become jealous of other roles, be given instructions that cut across other responsibilities, etc. It is in this area that the greatest strategic difficulty is likely to arise. If savings are to be made or improved performance to be obtained, then it may be necessary to accept the conflict here.

Addressing the strategic change issue, Mintzberg[26] suggests that there are benefits from competition in organisations. It can be a force for achieving change. In this sense, politics is an inevitable consequence of strategic change and needs to be accepted and channelled for the best results.

7.5.2 How can strategic change be analysed in a political context?

It is important to clarify right at the start the organisation's objectives and the implications for individual parts of the organisation. If it is true that conflict arises as a result of confusion over objectives, then it follows that these need to be fully explored before other matters are raised.

In addition, five areas would benefit from analysis at this early stage:

1 *The extent to which the organisation has developed a culture of adaptation or experiment.* Such an approach will help when it comes to implementing agreed strategies later.

2 *The identification of major power groups or individuals,* whose influence and support is essential for any major strategic change.

3 *The desirability or necessity of consultation rather than confrontation,* as the strategic analytical process continues.

4 *The role and traditions of leadership in the organisation* and the extent to which this may enhance the success and overcome problems associated with strategic change.

5 *The nature and scope of the external pressures on the organisation.*

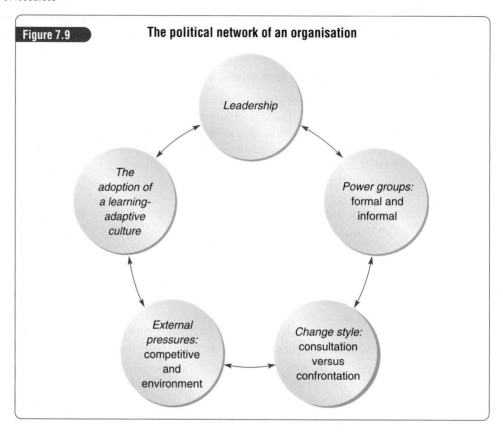

Figure 7.9 **The political network of an organisation**

These are the subjects that need to be analysed in the context of strategic change. They are interconnected as a network of relationships (*see* Figure 7.9). Once the main outline of strategies has been agreed, it will be necessary to return to the politics of strategic change again. We will do so in Chapter 21.

Key strategic principles

- Strategic change needs to take into account what is possible in terms of change, rather than what is desirable.
- Competition is healthy in organisations, except when it degenerates into unhealthy conflict and political manoeuvring.
- During the analysis phase of strategic development, there are political issues that can usefully be explored. In analysing the political network, it is necessary to survey power groups, leadership, the change style of the organisation, the adoption of a learning-adaptive culture and the nature of the external pressures.

7.6 International cultural perspectives

In one sense, *national culture* is just one of the organisational culture issues explored in Section 7.3. However, from a strategy viewpoint, it is important enough to be highlighted on its own. The reason is that some corporate strategies may be desirable in theory but extremely difficult to implement in practice, once national culture is considered. It would therefore be better to identify any national culture problems in the analysis phase and develop a different and more acceptable strategy.

There is no single agreed definition of national culture, but for our purposes we will use that of Hofstede:[27]

> *The collective programming of the mind which distinguishes the members of one human group from another ... Culture, in this sense, includes systems of values; and values are among the building blocks of culture.*

National culture governs much of the way in which society operates, and so it needs to be taken into account in deriving corporate strategy. Asking members of a company to undertake tasks that they do not understand, or find unacceptable to their culture and beliefs, will lead to a failed strategy. Kluckhohn and Strodtbeck[28] defined six basic cultural orientations and these are listed in Table 7.2.

National culture governs both the style and content of the way business is done internationally. To a large extent, the basics are learnt in the early years of life, before individuals ever encounter the business world. As people then move into different companies, they encounter aspects of culture which their previous cultural expectations allow them to cope with easily or with varying degrees of difficulty.

Table 7.2 Six basic national cultural orientations

Orientation	Range of variations
What is the nature of people?	• Optimistic or pessimistic in expectations about people? • Believing in people basically being good or evil or a mixture? • Suspicious or trusting of others?
What is the person's relationship to nature?	• Does s/he want to dominate and exploit nature or remain fatalistic about nature and what the future holds?
What is the person's relationship to other people?	• Individual or collective? • Does personal achievement matter or is the group's goal more important?
What is the modality of human activity?	• Are tangible reward and achievement important as a way of life? • Or are we born to a certain path with merit being rewarded in after-life or a future reincarnation?
What is the temporal focus of human activity?	• Is the future, present or past to be the focus of activity? • Can we plan and control society? • Or should we primarily look back to past events to guide the future?
What is the conception of space?	• Private, mixed or public? • Do meetings and events take place behind closed doors? Is it easy to visit colleagues without an invitation? • Or do most activities take place in public or semi-public areas?

Probably the most comprehensive study undertaken of the importance of different national cultural groups was that undertaken by Hofstede.[29] Over a number of years, he

---

CASE STUDY 7.3

Industry groups in Japan, Korea, Hong Kong and Italy

Companies often coalesce into informal industry groupings within a country. These can have a substantial influence on the strategy of group members, ranging from support in time of trouble to mutual benefits and co-operation on new strategic initiatives. Occasionally, such co-operation may be in danger of breaching anti-monopoly legislation.

For examples of such groupings, we can look at the Far East and Europe. In Japan, such groupings are called *Keiretsu* and in Korea *Chaebol*. (It should be noted that they are not quite the same in the two societies but they fulfil similar roles. The *Keiretsu* are more informal, while the *Chaebol* are effectively conglomerates.) From a strategy viewpoint, the links between the companies in the *Keiretsu* or *Chaebol* can be mutually supportive of new business initiatives. They can be used to help in difficult times and also to secure business deals that might otherwise prove difficult. The regular meetings of senior managers from such groupings can also be a source of useful business information. Competitors need to understand such groupings and to anticipate their mutual support in any negotiations.

Mitsubishi and Mitsui are examples of *Keiretsu* in Japan: they had 25 and 22 companies respectively in 1993 in their organisational orbit. The top six *Keiretsu* controlled 38 per cent of Japan's market capitalisation, 16 per cent of sales and 17 per cent of listed company profits in 1993.[31] In the same way, the three leading Korean *Chaebol* controlled over US$15 billion sales in 1993. Samsung, Hyundai and Lucky-Goldstar were the three biggest with sales of US$5.6, 4.6 and 3.5 billion respectively.[32] However, the Korean situation was not to last.

In spite of the Asian economic crisis of 1997–99 and the more general difficulties in the Japanese economy after this time, the *Keiretsu* groupings proved remarkably resilient. However, the Fuyo *Keiretsu*, which includes the Fuji Bank and Nissan cars, was under pressure in Japan.[33] The Ssanyong

Chaebol was being broken up in Korea. Most of the remaining Korean groups have subsequently disintegrated under political and economic pressure. However, a few Korean groups grew stronger as a result of acquiring weakened outside competitors.[34]

Such links are not confined to these two countries: networking has long been an important characteristic of Chinese families. The Riady family connections through their Lippo Group of companies in China, Hong Kong, the US and Indonesia are an example of a group that has now grown to a capitalised value of around US$2.5 billion.[35]

This should not be seen as a purely Eastern phenomenon. The Agnelli family in Italy have extensive interests that go well beyond Fiat cars into chemicals, aerospace and banking.[36] The Seagram family in the US in 1995 completed their purchase of MCA for US$2 billion. In 1998, the same family bought another entertainment group, Polygram, for around US$8 billion. They then sold all their media interests to the French company Vivendi in 2001. In both cases, there is a web of companies that have interconnections that extend across the corporate environment. They add to the complexity of the analysis of corporate strategy.

Case questions

1 *Compared with the other cultural areas outlined in this chapter, how important do you believe corporate cultures are for the companies above?*

2 *What are the main features of such a culture in terms of their influence and control over individual companies?*

3 *Can you identify a corporate culture close to your own organisation? For example, how about the student union? Or a trade association to which the company belongs? What are its chief distinguishing features? How does it influence the strategy of its members, if at all?*

surveyed 116 000 employees at IBM in 50 countries and three regions (note the specialist nature of the sample). He grouped the data he obtained against four, and later five, dimensions which were largely independent of each other.

1 *Power distance* – the extent to which those who were poorest in a society were willing to accept their position. Countries such as Panama, Malaysia and Venezuela emerged as being those where such acceptance was common. Israel, Denmark, Ireland and Sweden were countries where such inequalities were less acceptable.

2 *Individualism/collectivism* – the extent to which societies are collections of individuals or are bound together in a cohesive whole. The US, UK, Australia and the Netherlands were among the more individual, with South American countries such as Guatemala, Panama and Columbia being typical of those who were more collectivist.

3 *Masculinity versus femininity* – the extent to which a country is placed on a spectrum from masculine to feminine. In *male* cultures, there is a sharp distinction between the role the two sexes play in society and at work: males are expected to emphasise the importance of work, power and wealth. In *female* cultures, there is more equality between the two, with achievements being measured in terms of the environment and human contacts. Japan, Austria and Italy were typical masculine cultures and Sweden, the Netherlands and Finland typical feminine cultures.

4 *Uncertainty avoidance* – the extent to which members of a culture feel threatened by the unknown. Where uncertainty avoidance is *weak*, people are willing to embrace uncertainty and ambiguous situations: precision and punctuality for meetings were useful but not essential. In *strong* uncertainty avoidance countries, people need certainty, planning and order. Strong country cultures include Japan, Portugal, Greece and Belgium. Weak countries covered Singapore, Denmark, Jamaica and Hong Kong.

5 *Confucian versus dynamism* – Hofstede later added this category to those above. He discovered that different cultures have different time horizons – long-termism versus short-termism – which were also linked with the Confucian concept of 'virtue' versus the more Western concept of 'truth'. Thus *long-termism* emphasises the importance of taking a long view and adapting traditions to a modern context, while stressing perseverance. *Short-termism* seeks not only the short-term view but also the importance of status, social obligations and quick results. China, Hong Kong and South Korea typify the former, whereas the US, Nigeria, Canada and the UK were typical of the latter.

For a critique of the Hofstede research, *see* Meade.[30]

Such cultural variation will also be reflected in the corporate group cultures of various countries. These are explored in Case study 7.3.

From a national strategy perspective, the implications may be significant:

● For organisations engaged primarily in one national market, it will have some relevance if people from a number of cultural backgrounds are employed. For example, in South Africa, there are white and black communities with quite different cultural backgrounds working together.

● For organisations with a range of national companies in different countries, possibly across Europe, Africa or South-East Asia, the implications are equally important. There will be a need to devise a strategy that takes account of not only central HQ issues but also local cultures and styles, values and expectations. For example, a mission statement or a timetable for strategic change may need to reflect national cultural values and sense of urgency.

- For global companies, the cultural issue is more likely to be how to bring together the many cultures that exist. This may involve special integration programmes to break down cultural barriers.

Beyond these national-specific cultural issues, Olie[37] has pointed out that some management theories may be *culture-specific* – in other words, they may not 'work' outside the national culture in which they were invented. As an example, we might take Peters and Waterman's loose–tight principle:[38]

> Organisations that live by the loose–tight principle are on the one hand rigidly controlled, yet at the same time allow (indeed, insist on) autonomy, entrepreneurship and innovation from the rank and file.

This may operate well in the US but not in other cultures such as Korea, where there is a stronger need for certainty and collectivism. This is an important point that needs to be considered throughout this text.

▶ Key strategic principles

- National culture is defined as the collective programming of the mind which distinguishes the members of one human group from another.
- National culture governs both the style and content of the way business is done internationally. It may therefore influence corporate strategy.
- Hofstede developed five dimensions that help to define and describe national cultures: power distance, individualism/collectivism, masculinity versus femininity, uncertainty avoidance, Confucian versus dynamic.
- The evidence from these national characteristics would suggest that they can have a profound effect on the human aspects of corporate strategy. They need to be taken into account during the development of strategy, not later.
- It may even be the case that *national* culture will influence some aspects of *organisational* culture.

CASE STUDY 7.4

How Xerox Europe shifted its strategy and changed its organisation[39]

During the 1990s, Xerox Europe has reduced the size of its workforce, reorganised its operating companies and introduced a new organisation and culture to the company. This case study examines the shift in its strategy and structure.

Background

For 30 years, the US company Xerox has been engaged in a major global battle with its Japanese rivals, especially Canon and Ricoh. From dominance of the photocopying market in the 1960s, Xerox's market share has slowly been reduced. Its sales have risen but not as fast as the market has grown. It has been the Japanese companies that have made all the running in terms of new products, higher quality, ease of use and maintenance-free equipment.

Outside the Americas, Xerox has managed its operations in Europe, Africa and parts of Asia through Xerox Europe, a UK-based company in which it had a controlling share interest and total management control. In 1997, Xerox Europe had sales of around US$5.5 billion. This case study examines the shift in strategy and organisation at Xerox Europe during the 1990s.

Markets, competitors and customers

When Japanese companies decided to enter international photocopying markets in the 1960s, they had to find a way to overcome the dominance of Xerox. They chose to open up a new market segment: copiers for medium and small businesses that needed little maintenance and no regular service support. Xerox had a policy of always leasing its machines and then providing service engineers to maintain them: this was attractive to large companies with heavy printing demands, but smaller companies rapidly found the Japanese offerings more acceptable.

By the 1990s, Xerox had lost market share of the overall market, but still continued to maintain its market leadership in the high-end segment. Its competitive strengths still lay in its ability to provide a high level of service to customers. This was an area that the Japanese companies had never really attempted to match because of the high set-up costs and difficulty in obtaining minimum levels of business to make profits.

Xerox had made several attempts to break into the lower end of the market. However, its strengths and cost structures were still largely geared to large company customers. In 1993, its European subsidiary, Xerox Europe, undertook a survey of its customers' photocopying requirements: it found that they were spending 8 per cent of their turnover creating and managing documents, including creating and developing printed material, photocopying it, and filing and recording the results. This compared with 3 per cent of turnover spent on information technology. Moreover, up to 60 per cent of their customers' time was regularly spent on various activities associated with documentation.

Shift of mission statement and strategy

Given the time spent by its customers and its own strengths in servicing large customers, Xerox Europe decided during the early 1990s to shift the emphasis of its mission statement and basic business strategy. It changed from servicing photocopying to becoming The Document Company. This implied higher degrees of service for all the document requirements of its customers, not just the photocopying part. The strategy shifted from simple photocopying towards offering a wider range of services and products to cater for the *document management* needs of

Figure 7.10 — Xerox Europe: eleven-year record

its customers. Naturally, it continued to offer photocopying to those customers who preferred this.

Xerox Europe commented that it would take time for customers to see the benefits of its broader range. It noted that its rivals soon picked up the same theme: 'document management' and the 'document solution' were soon appearing. However, it was convinced that its strategy was sound: it was built on its core skills and based on service. When done well, a service competitive advantage is immensely difficult for competitors to match because service is localised. However, quality of service is vital.

New strategy initiatives

Between 1992 and 1994, Xerox Europe reorganised the company and introduced new strategies that it claimed would strengthen its profitability. There were four main areas:

Customer business units

Up to the mid-1990s, the operation of customer services was based on national boundaries. However, the company found that, whatever the economic environment, it was the smaller countries that always performed better – Austria, Portugal, Switzerland, Belgium. Xerox Europe investigated and discovered that the ideal company size for customers was around 400 employees, corresponding to the size in the smaller countries. Hence, all the larger countries were split in 1992–93 into smaller units, including the major markets of France and Germany. Country and regional managers became Customer Business Unit (CBU) managers.

Devolved power

The CBU changes were accompanied by a devolution of power and decision making to individual CBUs, including profit and loss responsibility. Managers could then make a whole range of decisions as to how the unit operated. The effect on profitability in some cases was highly beneficial. For example, in Italy the country was divided into three CBUs. After years of consistent losses, revenues increased 25 per cent and profitability was in sight.

Re-engineering processes

Xerox Europe has set out to re-engineer some of its major processes with the aim of a 20 per cent reduction in costs. Re-engineering is the detailed examination of every process to see how costs are built up and hence where costs can be saved. It is

usually beneficial to approach the processes with a radical and open mind. For example, Xerox Europe does not define its processes by functional areas such as marketing, sales, services, but by the way the customer orders are picked up and processed through the company. The four areas for re-engineering were:

1 *market to collection* – the organisation of the sales force and business development;

2 *invoice to collection* – customer payments, including debt collection;

3 *integrated supply chain* – all areas from purchases through to deliveries;

4 *service quality* – including product maintenance.

By concentrating on these areas, the company was able to make major cost savings: percentage inventory to revenue reduced from 15 per cent to 12 per cent with 10 per cent the aim, for example. Such savings were part of a continuing process that was still operating in the year 2002.

Benchmarking

Xerox Europe set up an international team to explore how it was that a business unit in one country was more successful than other units in selling the same product range. The team took the top-performing units as a *benchmark* for the others. It then set out to strip down the performance of the marketing function in this unit in a very detailed way. The group drew up a list of ten key benchmarking practices which it circulated to all CBUs.

Conclusion: team players and innovators but what was the impact on profit?

With such strategies, the process was continuous and the strategy emphasised group development:

Xerox people are team players. Teams that achieve a 'black belt' in teamwork earn the title 'X Team' – a group of innovative people who deliver results and whose best practices are shared across organizational lines. It is the highest level of team recognition in Xerox.

Annual Company Report 1997

Unfortunately, all the efforts had only limited impact on the Xerox profits. The company made a series of strategic mistakes with regard to the markets in which it wished to expand. For example, it decided to take on Hewlett-Packard by developing and launching a new range of computer printers in 1998 – the range was withdrawn in 2001. By 2002, it was in major trouble and its very survival was in doubt.

Case questions

1 *How would you summarise the strategies adopted by Xerox Europe in the face of strong Japanese competition? Do you think they will be successful?*

2 *The company argued that there were real benefits from moving to CBUs: what were they? Is it possible that the company has lost out on central control and economies of scale as a result of these moves? Do you think CBUs will still be around in five years' time?*

3 *Xerox Europe laid great emphasis in its strategy initiatives on re-engineering and benchmarking: what organisational, morale and human resource problems might arise as a result?*

4 *Given the failure of Xerox ultimately to improve its profitability, can other campanies learn anything at all from the Xerox Europe experience? Would other companies need to adopt the Xerox culture and strategic approach if they wished to emulate the limited success that was achieved?*

KEY READING

Organisational culture, strategy and performance[40]

In this extract from his book Organisational Culture, *Dr Andrew Brown comments on the process of strategy development*

While it is tempting to think of strategy as a dependent variable determined and constrained by the culture in which it develops, such a view is not sustainable. Strategy does not merely reflect or externalise culture, but influences and modifies it. An organisation's strategy makes visible its culture, expressing it in much the same way that speech creates meanings in language. This is an important point.

It is vital to remember that organisational strategy is not just a reflection of organisational culture. The formulation of strategy is generally influenced by a wide variety of non-cultural environmental factors such as the activities of competitors, customers and suppliers. Certainly the resulting trends, activities and events will be interpreted through the perception filter of culture, but this fact does not make a new technological breakthrough or a reduction in the number of supplier companies any less real. This means that it is impossible to accurately predict an organisation's strategy from knowledge of its culture alone. It also means that when we observe an organisation it is possible for its strategy to appear not to match its culture because of the influence of external exigencies.

If it is true that as a general rule strategy gives voice to culture, then in analysing the relationship between any particular culture and strategy we should expect to find a number of coughs, splutters and hiccups that distort the pattern.

Source: Brown, A (1995) *Organisational Culture*, Pitman Publishing, London.

◼ Summary

● The analysis of human resources is important for strategy development for two reasons. People are a vital resource. In addition, strategy development often involves change and some people may resist it. There are four areas to explore in the analysis of this area: resource audit, organisational culture, strategic change and its implications in terms of the power and politics of the organisation.

● Human-resource-based analysis emphasises the emergent approach to corporate strategy. Sustainable competitive advantage will often depend on human resources. In fast-moving markets, the adaptability of people inside the organisation becomes a special and important skill. Coping with strategic change is a vital element in the development of corporate strategy.

● The human resource audit will have two main elements: *people* in the organisation and the *contribution* of human resources to the development of corporate strategy. A basic analysis will reflect these two areas but also needs to consider key factors for success, competitive comparisons and possibly international issues.

● Culture is the set of beliefs, values and learned ways of managing the organisation. Each organisation has a culture that is unique. In analysing culture, there are four main areas: environment, cultural factors specific to the organisation, the basic cultural type of the organisation and the strategic implications.

● Factors within the organisation influencing culture include: history and ownership, size, technology and leadership. These can be coupled with the Cultural Web of the organisation to provide a method of summarising the main cultural influences. The Cultural Web includes stories, routines and rituals, symbols, power structures, organisation structure and control systems.

● The four main types of culture are power, role, task and personal. Their importance for corporate strategy lies in the ability of each type to cope with strategic change and to deliver competitive advantage.

● Analysis of strategic change needs to consider three areas: the type of organisation, the phase of organisation growth and the strategic pressures for organisational change. Four types of organisation have been identified, with each having a different response to strategic change. The age and size of an organisation will provide information on its phase of growth. The strategic pressures for organisational change need careful assessment. They may include such concepts as delayering – the reduction of the number of reporting layers in an organisation – and business process re-engineering – the use of new technology to reduce the administrative task and reduce costs.

● Strategic change needs to take into account what is possible in terms of change in the organisation, rather than what is theoretically desirable. Political issues in the organisation therefore need to be carefully explored – the political network.

● Four distinctive types of strategic decision makers have been identified: defender, analyser, prospector and reactor. Each is associated with a different approach to strategic decision making. In particular, the four approaches show different attitudes to risk and to the style of managing the business.

● International cultures may have a profound impact on corporate strategy. They may even make some strategy proposals very difficult to implement.

QUESTIONS

1 Use Exhibit 7.1 to audit the human resources of an organisation with which you are familiar. What conclusions can you draw with respect to corporate strategy?

2 You have been retained by a well-known fast-food restaurant chain to advise it on corporate strategy. You are aware that human resources are important in this work. What considerations would you wish to explore initially? How would you approach this task?

3 Analyse the culture of British Petroleum over the period of Case study 7.2. Compare it with the Royal Dutch/Shell culture.

4 *'There is no robust, generalisable evidence that business process re-engineering has made any significant impact on business performance.'* (Professor Colin Egan)[41]

If you were a senior manager at Xerox Europe, what would you make of this?

5 What are the general environmental influences on the culture of higher education at present? What are the strategic implications for institutions involved in this area?

6 Develop the Cultural Web for Xerox Europe from Case study 7.4 and identify the basic cultural style of the company. Give reasons for your views.

7 Use the criteria from Exhibit 7.2 to characterise the culture of the following four organisations: a multinational car company; a small, new computer software company; a recently privatised national telecommunications company (such as British Telecom or Deutsche Telekom); a local police station.

8 Analyse the strategic change implications of an organisation of your choice. Use the typology of Section 7.4 to explore the *type* of organisation, the *phase* of organisational growth, and the *pressure* for strategic change.

9 *'An organisation's strategy makes visible its culture, expressing it in much the same way that speech creates meaning in language.'* (Dr Andrew Brown)

How important is culture to strategy development when compared with other aspects of the analytical process?

10 Is *delayering* feasible in every national culture? Use Hofstede's analysis of culture to explain your answer.

STRATEGIC PROJECT **International oil companies**

This chapter has explored companies in the oil industry mainly from a human resource angle. You might like to take a broader look at strategy in the oil industry. During the late 1990s, there have been some substantial mergers such as BP (UK) and Amoco (US) and Exxon (US – also known as Esso in some countries) with Mobil (US). What are the human resource implications of such strategies?

FURTHER READING

For a well-developed exposition of culture: Brown, A (1995) *Organisational Culture*, Pitman Publishing, London.

For some excellent and provocative reading on the relationship between human resources and strategy: Egan, C (1995) *Creating Organisational Advantage*, Butterworth-Heinemann, Oxford.

For a well-developed survey of the international aspects of human resource management: Harzing, Anne-Wil and Van Ruysseveldt, J (eds) (1995) *International Human Resource Management*, Sage, London, with the Open University of the Netherlands.

Daniels, J and Radebaugh, L (1995) *International Business – Environments and Operations*, Addison-Wesley, Reading, MA, Ch 3. Useful for the general environment surrounding business and organisations.

NOTES & REFERENCES

1 Chandler, A (1962) *Strategy and Structure: Chapters in the History of the Industrial Enterprise*, MIT Press, Cambridge, MA, p14.

2 Porter M E (1980) *Competitive Strategy* and (1985) *Competitive Advantage*, The Free Press, New York.

3 Chandler, A (1962) Op. cit. *See*, for example, the roles of Durant, Du Pont and Sloan in Ch3 on General Motors.

4 There are several well-known strategic management texts that take this approach.

5 Handy, C (1989) *The Age of Unreason*, Business Books, London; Handy, C (1991) *The Gods of Management*, Business Books, London; Tyson, S (1995) *Human Resource Strategy*, Pitman Publishing, London, Chs4, 5 and 6; Brown, A (1995) *Organisational Culture*, Pitman Publishing, London, p198.

6 Pettigrew, A and Whipp, R (1991) *Managing Change for Competitive Success*, Blackwell, Oxford.

7 De Geus, A (1988) 'Planning as learning', *Harvard Business Review*, Mar–Apr, p71.

8 Whittington, R (1993) *What is Strategy and does it Matter?* Routledge, London, p122.

9 This exhibit has been derived from Tyson, S (1995) *Human Resource Strategy*, Pitman Publishing, London, pp171–4 and Rosen, R (1995) *Strategic Management: an Introduction*, Pitman Publishing, London, p166.

10 Brown, A (1995) *Organisational Culture*, Pitman Publishing, London, p198.

11 Brown, A (1998) *Organisational Culture*, 2nd edn, Financial Times/Pitman Publishing, London.

12 This subject area does not seem to have been the subject of any major research study. It is included because of the practical experience of many companies.

13 International Labour Office (1993) *World Labour Report*, Geneva.

14 Handy, C (1993) *Understanding Organisations*, 4th edn, Penguin, Harmondsworth, pp193–4.

15 Johnson, G (1992) 'Managing strategic change: strategy, culture and action', *Long Range Planning*, 25, pp28–36.

16 Handy, C (1993) Op. cit., p183. Handy uses the work of Harrison, R (1972) 'How to describe your organisation', *Harvard Business Review*, Sep–Oct. Handy uses Greek gods to typify the four cultural types: they make an interesting read, but mean rather less to those of us who studied *The Aeneid*.

17 Hofstede, G (1980) *Culture's Consequences: International Differences in Work-related Values*, Sage, Beverly Hills, CA.

18 Brown, A (1995) Op. cit., pp62–5.

19 Handy, C (1993) Op. cit., pp210–16.

20 References for BP Case: *Financial Times*, 23 Mar 1990; 25 Mar 1990, p20; 10 May 1991; 26 June 1992, pp1, 18, 19; 28 June 1993, p17; 15 Mar 1995, p29.

21 Miles, R E and Snow, C C (1978) *Organisational Strategy, Structure and Process*, McGraw-Hill, New York. See also Miles, R, Snow, C, Meyer, A and Coleman (1978) 'A strategy typology of organisations', *Academy of Management Review*, July, and reprinted in

De Wit, R and Meyer, R (1994) *Strategy: Content, Context and Process*, West Publishing, St Paul, MN. There is clearly some overlap here with the classification developed by Handy on types of culture. It is hardly surprising that the two areas are consistent; it would be alarming if they were not.

22 Greiner, L (1972) 'Evolution and revolution as organisations grow', *Harvard Business Review*, July–Aug.

23 *Source*: Greiner, L (1972) Ibid, p265.

24 Readers may care to note that there is a useful critique of this strategy in Egan, C (1995) *Creating Organisational Advantage*, Butterworth-Heinemann, Oxford, pp109–11.

25 Handy, C (1993) Op. cit., p292.

26 Mintzberg, H (1991) 'The effective organisation: forces and forms', *Sloan Management Review*, Winter.

27 Hofstede, G (1980) Op. cit.

28 Kluckhohn, C and Strodtbeck, F (1961) *Variations in Value Orientations*, Peterson, New York, quoted in Meade, R (1994) *International Management Cross Cultural Dimensions*, Blackwell, Oxford, p50.

29 Hofstede, G (1991) *Cultures and Organisations, Software of the Mind*, McGraw-Hill, Maidenhead, and *Images of Europe: Valedictory Address* given at the University of Limberg, 1993.

30 Meade, R (1994) Op. cit., pp73–6.

31 *Financial Times* (1994) 30 Nov, p15.

32 *Financial Times* (1994) 16 Sept, p26.

33 *Financial Times* (1998) 28 Oct, p24.

34 *Financial Times* (1998) 23 Nov, p23.

35 *Financial Times* (1993) 14 Apr, p30.

36 Friedman, A (1988) *Agnelli and the Italian Network of Power*, Mandarin, London.

37 Olie, R (1995) 'The culture factor in personnel and organisation policies', Ch6 in Harzing, A and Van Ruysseveldt (1995) *International Human Resource Management*, Sage, London, in association with Open University, Netherlands.

38 Peters, T and Waterman, R (1982) *In Search of Excellence*, Harper and Row, New York, p318.

39 References for Rank Xerox Case: *Financial Times*, 24 Sep 1991; 25 Aug 1992, p5; 13 Jan 1995, p19; 13 Feb 1995, p19; 28 Apr 1995, two-page advertisement; Lynch, R (1994) *European Business Strategies*, 2nd edn, Kogan Page, London, p87; Xerox *USA Annual Report 1992*.

40 Extracted from Brown, A (1995) Op. cit., p182. © Andrew Brown.

41 Egan, C (1995) Op. cit., p109.

Analysing financial resources

When you have worked through this chapter, you will be able to:

- identify the sources of funds available to an organisation;

- carry out an analysis of an organisation's current financial resources;

- assess an organisation's potential for further funding and the costs and risks involved;

- identify and quantify the financial benefits of strategies and their cash flow implications;

- understand the role and importance of shareholder value-added concepts;

- understand the impact on the organisation of greater international activity;

- appreciate the importance of balancing the organisation's financial objectives with its other corporate objectives.

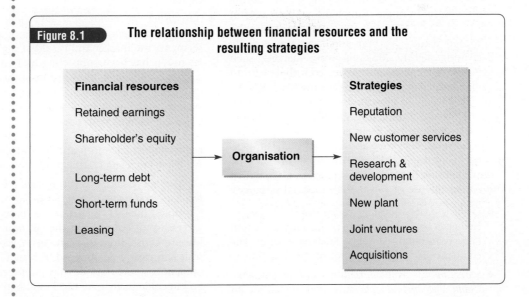

Figure 8.1 — **The relationship between financial resources and the resulting strategies**

Financial resources		Strategies
Retained earnings		Reputation
Shareholder's equity		New customer services
	Organisation	Research & development
Long-term debt		New plant
Short-term funds		Joint ventures
Leasing		Acquisitions

◼ Introduction

Many corporate strategies involve the organisation's financial resources: investment in the organisation's activities now will be rewarded by profits or other benefits later. This chapter explores the *relationship* between the financial resources that are available for corporate strategy – their sources, costs and the risks involved – and the returns that may be achieved (*see* Figure 8.1).

Financial analysis deals primarily with the precision of numbers, and therefore tends to be prescriptive rather than emergent in its approach. However, leading financiers are well aware that in practice there is an element of judgement to the subject. This chapter considers both approaches and then goes on to explore the importance of maintaining the fine balance between the financial objectives of the organisation and those objectives involving more general issues, such as the public good, better pay and job satisfaction. The implications for those organisations engaged in international trade are also considered.

CASE STUDY 8.1

Global expansion: brewing at Heineken NV

As Heineken and other leading European brewers expand internationally, the financial implications of this process need careful and consistent analysis.

Heineken claims to be the world's third-largest company brewing beer and lager. Table 8.1 shows its sales against those of leading global competitors.

Heineken sales experienced strong growth during the 1990s, for example rising almost 11 per cent in Europe between 1996 and 1997, at a time when the European market for beer and lager was actually decreasing slightly. Major growing markets, such as China, Indonesia and Japan, contributed to an 11 per cent rise in sales to Asia over the same period – an extremely high growth rate for a beverage product.[1] However, some of this growth occurred before the downturn of the Asian economies in 1998. US and European sales were also showing some growth.

The company achieved this level of sales by implementing the following strategies, all of which involved the use of substantial financial resources:

- *Carrying out company acquisitions in Europe.* Heineken bought breweries, particularly in Eastern Europe, including Slovakia, Bulgaria, Poland. The company also bought control of Interbrew Italia.

- *Setting up new plants in countries such as Indonesia, China, Vietnam and Malaysia.* A typical plant might cost US$5 million. Local partners will develop some plant but still need a major capital injection

from Heineken. It should be noted that there are some cost savings from economies of scale in brewing plant,[2] but larger plants need more capital.

- *Advertising, promoting and distributing the new premium speciality beers.* This product group segments the market and is sold at higher prices. Heineken has been supporting its Heineken and Amstel brands with sponsorship of the Heineken Cup in European rugby and various tennis events such as the Davis Cup, US and Australian Open events. A typical major sponsorship deal might cost US$1 million per event. There are cost economies of scale in branding and sponsorship, but these are related to the funds invested.

- *Carrying out research and development into new plant processes and product and packaging innovations.* Examples include the new ice beers and the successful introduction in the UK of a version of Murphy's Irish Stout in a can. Again, economies of scale can clearly be obtained. Research and development costs are not normally published by brewers but could easily total US$5 million per year.

- *Developing joint ventures and licensing* in countries such as the UK, Greece, Brazil, Bulgaria and China

Table 8.1 Annual sales of the world's leading brewers in 2000

Company	Home country	World beer sales (million hectolitres)	Comment
Anheuser Busch	US	158	Sales chiefly in US under Budweiser brand, but major global strategy now under way
Interbrew	Belgium	76	Owns Stella Artois (Belgium), Labatts (Canada), Beck's (Germany), Whitbread (UK) – series of takeovers in 1990s
Heineken	Netherlands	74	Real strengths in some European markets, with growth being sought from Asia-Pacific and Africa
South African Breweries	South Africa	56	Series of Eastern European and other acquisitions during 1990s
Ambev	Brazil	56	Dominates South America's largest market with two brands
Miller Brewing	US	54	Subsidiary of tobacco giant Philip Morris (US)
Carlsberg	Denmark	47	Limited representation in some countries
Scottish & Newcastle	UK	36	Acquired Kronenbourg from Danone in 2001
Asahi	Japan	35	Made acquisitions in late 1990s
Kirin	Japan	33	Japan's leading brewer, mainly in that country but with a stake in Lion Brewery (New Zealand)

Source: Author, from trade estimates and company annual reports.

Table 8.2 Market share in home country of some of Europe's leading brewers

Company	Home country	Market share in home country
Heineken	Netherlands	50%
Carlsberg	Denmark	70% including Tuborg
Guinness	Ireland (for beer and stout)	60% but note that home market small
Kronenbourg	France	50% of French market and 30% of Spanish market
Interbrew	Belgium	60%
Bass	UK	21% in highly competitive market
Binding Brauerei	Germany	8% in the fragmented German beer market

Source: Trade estimates.

▶

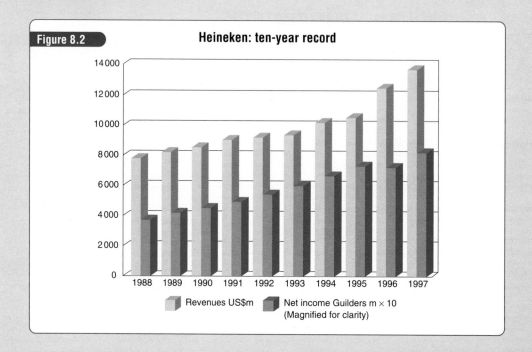

Figure 8.2

Heineken: ten-year record

Revenues US$m

Net income Guilders m × 10 (Magnified for clarity)

to share the costs of distribution with other partners. It is not possible to estimate typical costs since these will depend on the size of the joint venture or other deal, but significant funds are usually involved.

None of the above could be carried out without extra capital to finance them. Moreover, it should be noted that, even if none of the above activities had taken place, there might still have been a need for increased financial resources, due to the 11 per cent increase in Heineken's sales in 1997 compared with 1996 (13 512 million guilders versus 12 189 million guilders). When sales increase, there is often a need to extend the company's credit terms to new customers: extra finance is required for this purpose alone. Sales can be increased without an attendant rise in credit, but this cannot be assumed.

According to Heineken, the strategic consequence for the leading companies in the brewing industry worldwide of the high market growth, economies of scale and significant investment has been an increased concentration of market share.[3] However, it may also be significant that, before global expansion, the major global brewers already had high market shares in their home countries (*see* Table 8.2). High home market share may provide a useful *cash cow* strategy (*see* Chapter 5) from which to launch an expansion programme.

Case questions

1 *Using the following information:*
   - *one company acquired every three years at typically US$50 million*
   - *one new Far Eastern plant per annum*
   - *ten events sponsored per annum for the new speciality beers*
   - *research and development costs as stated in the case*
   - *joint ventures and licences cost US$10 million per annum*

   estimate the order-of-magnitude finance required by Heineken for new strategies in a typical year.

2 *Compare this with the Heineken balance sheet and profit and loss statement located at the end of this chapter. You will need to convert the financial data to US$, using 2.01 N Fl = 1 US$.*

3 *Does Heineken have any problems financing such strategies?*

8.1 Analysing the sources of finance

Company ownership varies greatly around the world. In some countries, such as the UK and US, there is a strong tradition of private share ownership with public share quotation. In other countries, such as Germany, Italy and Spain, rather more companies may be at least part owned by banks, private trusts, families and government institutions. As a starting point, we ignore these differences and simply identify the main *sources of finance* for strategic development or retrenchment. As an example, Figure 8.3 shows the sources of finance used by Heineken in 1997.

8.1.1 Sources of finance

Retained profits

Instead of distributing profits as share dividends to the shareholders, these are retained and invested in new ventures. Although full evidence is not available,[4] this probably represents the most common source of finance for the organisation's strategies. However, strategies that demand a bold, new step – like a major acquisition – may need totally new sources of finance.

- *Advantages*. The company does not have to ask any outside group or individual. There are no issue costs involved in raising the funds and the company does not

---

Figure 8.3 — **Sources of finance at Heineken (1997)**

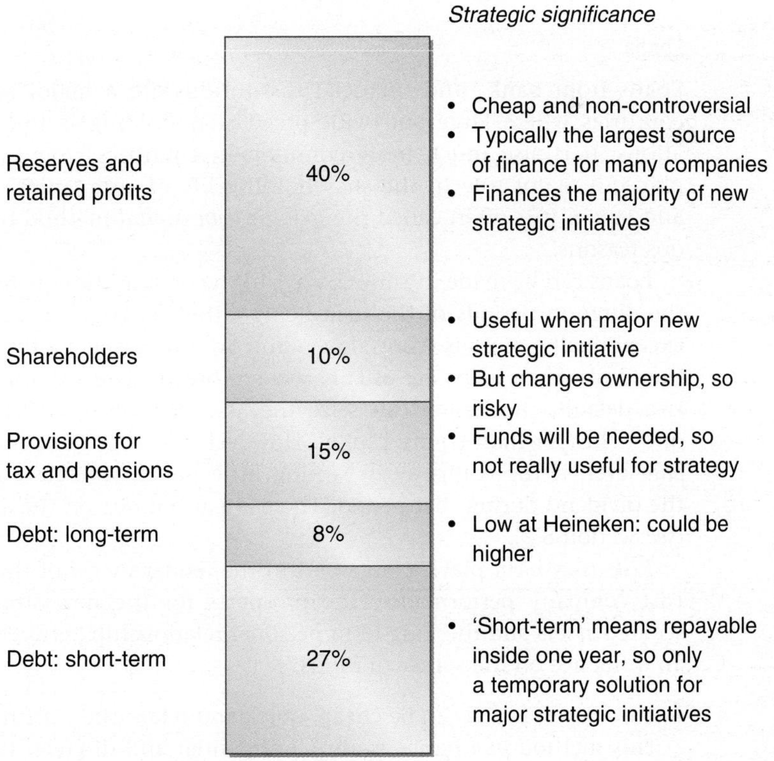

Strategic significance

Source	%	Strategic significance
Reserves and retained profits	40%	• Cheap and non-controversial • Typically the largest source of finance for many companies • Finances the majority of new strategic initiatives
Shareholders	10%	• Useful when major new strategic initiative • But changes ownership, so risky
Provisions for tax and pensions	15%	• Funds will be needed, so not really useful for strategy
Debt: long-term	8%	• Low at Heineken: could be higher
Debt: short-term	27%	• 'Short-term' means repayable inside one year, so only a temporary solution for major strategic initiatives

---

need to reveal its plans to outsiders such as banks in order to gain agreement. It is essentially non-controversial.

● *Disadvantages*. Profits that are retained and not distributed to shareholders represent dividends foregone to the owners. Owners may demand a regular dividend from the company. The company needs to be generating adequate profits, so this route is not suitable for those in financial difficulties.

Share issues

Share issues are frequently called the *equity capital* method of raising funds because they involve the 'equity' or shareholding of a company. It is often possible to seek further funds from existing shareholders through a *rights issue* – that is, the right to purchase new shares is issued to current shareholders in proportion to their existing voting rights in the company – although the success of such an issue clearly depends on how enthusiastic existing shareholders are about the company's prospects.

● *Advantages*. This method is useful when a large tranche of new capital is needed – for example, for an acquisition. Unlike a bank loan (*see* below), there is no automatic commitment to pay interest, nor repay the capital: dividends are paid only if the new funds earn profits. It rewards those shareholders who have stayed with the company.

● *Disadvantages*. It can clearly change the shareholding structure and allow predators to enter. Any share issue will have significant administrative costs, such as the cost of underwriting the issue.

Loans

Loans from banks and financial institutions are a major source of funds in those countries where large and widespread shareholding is not a part of normal operations. It is also much more common in countries where banks have traditionally played a major role in the shareholding life of companies – for example, Germany and Japan. It is often called the *loan* or *debt capital* method of raising funds, for obvious reasons.

Loans can be made in various ways to the organisation, with the rates of interest and the duration periods of the loan being either fixed or varied. Larger loans may carry exceptionally onerous terms, depending on how desperate the organisation is to obtain the funds. Such loans are usually secured on the assets of the organisation so, if there is a default, the lender can seize the asset. Because of this security, loan capital is often cheaper than equity capital. However, it carries the penalty that interest *must be paid* even if the company is earning little profit, whereas equity capital could forgo the dividend during that period. There are also limits on the amount of debt financing (*see* Section 8.2).

Risk assessment plays a large part in the lender's view of the loan and the company. Past company performance, the prospects for the new strategy, the quality of the secured assets and the long-term personal relationship between the parties will all have an influence on the source of funds.

● *Advantages*. Loans can be cheap, quick and retain the existing shareholding structure. This method of finance is also confidential and discreet. It may be essential where widespread public shareholding is not available.

- *Disadvantages.* This method can be painful, intrusive and involve increased risk for the company. The date of repayment and the need to pay interest in most circumstances can be a major burden if the strategy begins to show signs of weakness.

Leasing

Leasing from specialist companies can be important in those countries where there are tax advantages and the company does not need to own the assets. The other advantage to the organisation taking out the lease is that it does not have to find the capital.

- *Advantages.* Leasing is clear, quick and perhaps tax-efficient. It is also a method for increasing the organisation's return on capital, because leasing reduces the capital employed by the organisation.

- *Disadvantages.* This method has limited scope and there is no ownership at the end of the period.

A reduction in short-term debt

An organisation can reduce its short-term debt by introducing one of the following measures:

- *Paying creditors more slowly.* Taking longer to pay means that such funds are kept in the company for a longer period and are therefore available for investment.

- *Reducing stocks.* An organisation's *stock turn* – its ratio of turnover divided by stock – is a measure of its ability to operate with lower stocks. A lower level of funds invested in stocks will increase the organisation's ability to raise funds for use elsewhere.

- *Insisting on more prompt payment by debtors.*

- *Advantages.* This method has many of the advantages of retained profits in the sense that it involves the more efficient use of the organisation's existing funds.

- *Disadvantages.* This method may be difficult for the organisation to achieve if it is already operating reasonably efficiently. There may need to be significant expenditure to achieve the saving – for example, a new computer system to control stocks will mean investment in the new system along with the subsequent stock reduction.

Sale of assets

Sale of some existing company assets to finance expansion elsewhere has proved to be a major strategy for some companies in the 1990s. The route clearly has merit when resources are limited and spread too thinly. Following from the logic of the *resource-based view* (*see* Chapter 6), it will be evident that this approach may have real benefits for some companies.

- *Advantages.* This method of finance is simple, clear, concentrates on core strengths, and clearly involves no dilution in shareholding interests.

- *Disadvantages.* This method is drastic, no going back, and forces choice when not essential. The sale of assets may have to be undertaken at less than their full value, depending on the timing of the sale.

Other methods

For large and global companies, there is an increasingly sophisticated and complex range of financial mechanisms for raising finances.

CASE STUDY 8.2

The financing of brewers' growth

With extensive business activity taking place in the brewing industry, this case study examines the sources from which the brewing companies have financed their expansion.

Heineken's expansion of recent years was funded from the following sources:

- *Shareholders.* Heineken is a family-controlled company and so issuing new shares would dilute the family's control over the firm and be unacceptable. Heineken made four *bonus share issues* in 1986, 1989, 1992 and 1995. These simply split existing shares into smaller amounts and made no attempt to raise fresh capital. By definition, bonus shares are issued in proportion to existing shareholdings and have no impact on the family interests.

- *Retained profits.* Heineken has used this method more than any other to expand. Because it is family-controlled, it does not have the same pressures to pay a dividend each year. It is therefore able to ignore any outside pressures, so long as the family members themselves continue to agree.

- *Increased long-term debt.* Heineken has not used this method of financing in any significant way. Danone/Kronenbourg, on the other hand, has used loans from banks or other lending institutions extensively to expand its worldwide interests.

- *Short-term funds.* If brewery companies can negotiate it, there is nothing to stop them paying their creditors more slowly and insisting that those who owe them money pay faster. For example, Heineken increased its stock turn by nearly 40 per cent over the period 1990–94.

Table 8.3 shows how Heineken raised its funds up to 1997. For comparison, two other leading European brewers are also shown. (It is important to point out that the companies do not have the same year end, and figures have been translated into a common currency (US$) at rates that may not be those used by the individual companies themselves. All this makes comparison only approximate.) An additional item in the table – *Provisions for tax, pensions, etc.* – relates to the need for companies to set aside funds that are owed to the government as tax and to their former employees as pensions. Because of the special pur-

pose of such funds, they should not be used for financing the business and are therefore excluded from the above list of the sources of funds.

In terms of sources of finance, the financial resources of the three brewers shown in Table 8.3 need to be considered in the context of the *objectives* and *values* of the companies concerned.

Heineken is a family-controlled company with little desire to raise funds from outside shareholders or the debt from banks. If this has meant that it has grown more slowly, then the company has been willing to accept this as the price of family control.

Carlsberg is controlled by a Danish trust. Typically, such organisations do not have great ambitions for the future. However, Carlsberg has become more

Table 8.3 Sources of capital in some of Europe's leading brewers

Source of funds	Heineken	Danone/ Kronenbourg*	Carlsberg
Reserves and retained earnings	40%	25%	31%
Shareholders	10%	24%	10%
Provisions for tax, pensions, etc.	5%	6%	14%
Debt: long-term	8%	22%	10%
Debt: short-term	27%	23%	35%
Total	100%	100%	100%
Total capital	US$5 595 m	US$16 415 m	US$3 666 m

Source: Company annual reports.

* Note that capital is used for non-beer trading, which is the majority of total turnover at Danone/Kronenbourg. In 2001, Kronenbourg was sold by Danone to the UK company Scottish and Newcastle breweries.

expansionist in recent years and has raised some debt on a long-term basis.

Danone/Kronenbourg has its shares quoted on European stock exchanges and has wide share ownership. It has followed a vigorous and imaginative strategy of expansion over the last ten years, with a mix of acquisitions, divestment and internally generated growth activities. Its product range includes not only Kronenbourg beer, but also Danone dairy products (in which it is world leader), biscuits, glass containers, mineral waters and grocery products. All these areas have benefited from its ability to raise substantial finance, especially from the banks through long-term debt financing.

Case questions

1 *If you were Heineken, would you raise more finance through long-term debt and expand faster?*

2 *If you were Carlsberg, what arguments would you wish to consider about how you raised new finance? From whom would you seek advice?*

3 *If you were Danone/Kronenbourg and had observed the increased segmentation in the beer market and global trends, what strategy would you follow to extend the company's beer sales beyond France? Where would you go? Why? What factors would you consider in the financing of any such expansion?*

▶ Key strategic principles

- There are six main sources of finance for strategic activities. Each has its merits and problems.

- *Retained profits*: the most common method of funding new strategy.

- *Equity finance*, i.e. the issuance of new shares to either existing or new shareholders, is one clear route but it has numerous disadvantages associated with the costs of issue and the possible loss of control in the company.

- *Long-term debt finance* is simpler and cheaper, but there are limits to the amount and major difficulties if the company defaults on paying the interest charges.

- *Leasing (renting) of plant and machinery* has some specialist uses and attractions: it can have tax benefits and lower costs. However, the equipment remains the property of the lessor at the end of the period.

- *Savings from reductions in short-term debt* can be a substantial source of funds to a company, but these can usually be made only once.

- *The sale of some existing assets* to fund development elsewhere is useful but drastic.

8.1.2 Constraints on sources of finance

After reviewing the main sources of finance for an organisation, we now need to consider two important constraints on the ability of the organisation to act:

1 difficulties with debt financing; and

2 difficulties with the dividend payout policy on equity shareholdings.

Difficulties with debt financing

As we saw in Section 8.1.1, debt financing means that the organisation agrees to pay interest on the debt it acquires. The rate of interest is usually fixed and has two constraints:

1 If there is a drop in profits, payment of interest *takes priority* over payment of dividends to shareholders.

2 The interest *must be paid*, regardless of how profits might fluctuate. (Clearly, if the company goes into loss then the interest cannot be paid and the company is technically bankrupt.)

It is, therefore, the *shareholders* who bear the risk of profit fluctuation, not the *debt lenders*, such as the banks. As a result, because the shareholders are bearing this greater risk, they look for a higher return on their funds than the debt lenders. Debt financing is therefore usually cheaper than equity financing and as a result some companies prefer a proportion of debt capital.

In spite of its lower cost in relation to equity financing, however, companies restrict their level of debt financing because, when debt capital is present, it causes any fluctuation in profits at the organisation to be reflected *disproportionately* in retained profits and dividends. Debt interest takes priority in payments from the organisation's profits. It is a simple mathematical task to show that the remainder, available as retained profits and dividends to shareholders, is bound to fluctuate more widely than if there had been no debt finance. Since retained earnings may well fund strategy, any fluctuation as a result of higher gearing – that is, the proportion of debt finance to total shareholders' funds (*see* Exhibit 8.1) – will impact disproportionately on corporate strategy.

Exhibit 8.1   **The gearing ratio**

Most companies begin life with financing by shareholders – *equity financing*. They then generate some profits and retain part of those profits in the company, paying the rest out as dividends, tax, etc. The *total shareholders' funds* that then exist in the company are the original equity finance plus the retained profits.

At some stage in its life, the company may acquire significant amounts of long-term debt – *debt financing*. The ratio of debt finance to total shareholders' funds is called the *gearing ratio* of the company – often called *gearing* for short – and is usually expressed in percentage terms. For example, if a company with US$10 million of shareholder's funds raises US$5 million of debt finance, it has a gearing ratio of

$$\text{Gearing ratio} = \frac{\text{Debt finance}}{\text{Total shareholders' funds}} = \frac{\text{US\$5 million}}{\text{US\$10 million}} \times 100 = 50\%$$

Thus any company *with* debt is more exposed to fluctuations in dividends than one *without* debt – the higher the gearing, the more the exposure. Although debt finance is cheaper, there is therefore a limit to the amount of debt that a company can usually accept. Typically, companies with strong growth strategies and widespread public share ownership (such as Danone in Case study 8.2) will have a gearing ratio of 50 per cent. When the gearing of a company reaches 100 per cent, banks and other lenders become nervous because the company is so reliant on a steady, non-fluctuating stream of profits. It is for this reason that some companies are reluctant to *gear up* their company – that is, raise the proportion of debt to equity. Heineken is an example of a company with low gearing at 13 per cent.

Table 8.4 Heineken NV profits and dividends per share (guilders)

	1997	1996	1995*	1994	1993	1992*	1991	1990	1989*	1988
Net profit per share	15.13	13.06	13.24	12.03	10.34	9.22	8.17	7.29	6.49	5.80
Dividend per share	3.50	3.50	3.50	2.80	2.80	2.80	2.24	2.24	2.24	1.79

* Plus bonus shares of 6.25 guilders value and cash payment of 0.69 guilders per share in these three years.
Source: Annual Report and Accounts.

However, lower gearing means that fewer funds are available for growth strategies. Although Heineken does not seem to have suffered excessively from lower gearing, it has been unable to grow at the same rate as Danone over the last ten years. Earnings per share almost tripled at Danone over the ten years between 1984 and 1993 (FF18.4 to FF50.96 per share), whereas they doubled at Heineken over a roughly comparable period from 1985 to 1994 (54.8 to 108.5 guilders per share). These considerations reflect the risks over gearing that the company is willing to take and the value the company puts on growth as part of its objectives.

Difficulties with the dividend payout policy on equity shareholdings

In addition to constraints arising from gearing, it is also necessary to consider the *dividend payout policy* of the company on its ordinary shares. The higher the dividend, the lower the profit retained in the company and the more difficult it becomes to fund new strategies. In theory,[5] there is a balance to be struck between maximising the dividend payout and retaining profit for the company. In practice, companies usually prefer to keep the dividend payout *steadily and gently rising*. It is a reward for loyalty and is often reflected back in shareholder confidence and a stable share price. Moreover, retained profits are not lost to the shareholders but should themselves contribute to the capital appreciation of the shares. The data for Heineken in Table 8.4 show that dividends have not tracked profit, but have gone up in three stages.

The implication of a stable dividend policy for retained earnings is clear: if dividends are steady, then any fluctuation in profits must be taken up by *retained earnings*. The reasons are just the same as those for debt capital interest above. Since it is retained earnings that fund corporate strategy, it is the *strategy area* that suffers disproportionately if there are major variations in profitability.

Overall, the choice between the funding methods for strategy will depend on a balance of the factors outlined above along with one other consideration – the cost of each route to the company – which we examine in Section 8.2.

▶ Key strategic principles

- There are three main constraints on debt financing:
  1 the need to fund the interest payments regardless of profit fluctuations;
  2 the company with debt is more exposed to profit fluctuation than the one without;
  3 the reluctance of banks to offer finance that would gear companies above 100%.

▶

- **The main constraint on equity financing is the need in many companies to establish a steady increase in dividend payouts, regardless of profit variations.**
- **As a result of the debt and equity payout constraints, fluctuations in profits impact disproportionately on the funding needed for strategic change.**

8.2 Cost of funds and the optimal capital structure

In order to assess alternative sources of capital, we need to start by considering their costs to the company. There are two principal sources of funds to the company: equity and debt. We will examine each of these separately and look at the problems, mainly in estimating the costs of equity capital. We then consider the factors surrounding the optimal combination of the two different sources and why calculating the cost of funds is important.[6]

8.2.1 Costing equity capital using the Capital Asset Pricing Model

It may seem slightly surprising to view *equity capital*, which includes the company's retained profits and its original share capital, as having a *cost*. The cost comes in the organisation's refusal to distribute profits to its shareholders, who could, in theory, have invested this money in shares in other companies. They might even have purchased a government bond in their home country. (Such bonds usually pay interest that is *guaranteed* and *virtually risk-free*, unless the state itself goes bankrupt. Naturally, the rate of interest on government bonds is lower than would be expected from commercial organisations that carry greater risks of failure.)

In both theory[7] and practice, it is often the case that the organisation invests part of its own funds *outside* the organisation, rather than in its own corporate strategies. Indeed, for reasons of high market risk and low profitability in an industry, companies occasionally find that their proposed new strategies are so unattractive that they actually invest some of their funds outside the company.[8] Investing in corporate strategies *inside* the organisation therefore has a *financial cost* associated with it. As a *minimum*, this cost would be the interest that might have been obtained from the alternative investment of the same funds *outside* the organisation. However, this still does not estimate the *actual* cost of the capital inside the company, only this *minimum* threshold.

The *Capital Asset Pricing Model*[9] is an attempt to estimate the actual cost of equity capital inside the company. The detail of the model is beyond the scope of this book. However, in essence, the model suggests that the cost of equity for a company is equal to the *risk-free cost of equity* plus a factor calculated as the average cost of equity in the *market* multiplied by a beta factor for the *company* concerned.

8.2.2 Cost of equity capital using risk-free rates of interest

Where there is no widespread share ownership, a much simpler alternative to the Capital Asset Pricing Model has been used to estimate the cost of equity capital. It begins by estimating the value of the risk-free bond rate. This should be readily available in most countries. It then adds several percentage points to this rate to take into account the risks of dealing with shares where the returns are not guaranteed.

The difficulty with this method comes in estimating the additional rate of interest. It is usually derived from an examination of rates of return available on commercial bonds, other shares if available and other types of commercial contract. There are no clear rules and the method relies on judgement, but it does have the merits of simplicity and flexibility. With these problems, some will question whether it is important to calculate the cost of capital. We return to this issue once we have considered long-term debt capital.

8.2.3 Cost of long-term debt capital

The cost of debt capital is rather more straightforward. For existing funds, it is simply *the weighted average of the interest costs* of the individual loans already made to the company, after deducting the tax.

8.2.4 The weighted average cost of capital

The *weighted average cost of capital* (WACC) is simply the combination of the two costs for equity and debt above – the cost of equity capital and the cost of long-term debt capital – weighted in proportion to their part in the overall capital of the company. In practice, it is the average cost of raising additional funds for the company since the two elements are largely valued on the basis of their current and future interest rates. Hence, WACC is defined by the following formula:

$$\text{WACC} = \frac{(\text{cost of long-term debt}) \times (\text{long-term debt})}{(\text{total company capital})} + \frac{(\text{cost of equity}) \times (\text{equity})}{(\text{total company capital})}$$

8.2.5 The optimal capital structure

The overall aim of an analysis of the cost of capital will be to arrive at the optimal balance between equity and debt capital. In undertaking this task, it will be evident that each organisation has a unique set of circumstances that need to be taken into account. Financial strategy will wish to take the mathematical formulae shown above and adjust them for other factors that are more difficult to quantify. Factors that need to be considered include:

- the risk involved in the organisation's future strategies;
- company attitudes to risk (e.g. entrepreneurs might relish the risk whereas multinationals might be more dubious);
- the risk in the industry (some markets have greater uncertainty than others);
- competitors' costs of capital and capital structures (others may have good ideas, access to their own unique sources of funds, different attitudes to risk, etc.);
- possible trends in interest rates and factors that might substantially alter these, such as national economic performance.

Some of these considerations cannot easily be quantified but will have an important influence on the final choice of funding route. Having taken these considerations into account, it is now possible to address the questions:

- Can the organisations raise *more funds*?
- If so, *from what source* and *at what cost?*

- How does the cost of new funds *compare* with the cost of existing funds?
- What are the *risks involved* in tapping the new sources of funds?

The many sources of finance were discussed in Section 8.1, retained profits, equity and debt capital being the most common.

8.2.6 The importance of calculating the cost of funds

With all the complexities and uncertainties already mentioned, we may ask whether it is really necessary to calculate the cost of funds. Knowing the cost of funds is important for two reasons:

1 All the stakeholders need to be reassured that their efforts are worthwhile. There is no point in undertaking years of effort and investment if the financial resources could earn more in a lower-risk fund outside the organisation. The only rational way of approaching this is to start, however crudely, by estimating the cost of the funds being used inside the enterprise.

2 More specifically, the cost of funds is the starting point for the analysis of new strategies. If the return on the new proposals does not even match the cost of the funds that are required to undertake this task, then such projects should not be pursued. We consider this further in Section 8.3.

▶ Key strategic principles

- The cost of equity capital can be calculated using the Capital Asset Pricing Model but it only really works where there is wide public shareholding.
- An alternative method starts with the cost of risk-free government bonds and then adds a factor for the risk of owning shares.
- The cost of long-term debt is calculated from the weighted average of the individual loans made to the company.
- For the company overall, the combined cost of debt and equity is called the weighted average cost of capital (WACC). It combines equity and debt in proportion to their use in the company.
- The optimal capital structure for a company will also involve the assessment of risks, in addition to the costs estimated above.
- Calculating the cost of capital matters because it reassures the stakeholders that their efforts are worthwhile and because it provides a benchmark for assessing the profitability of future strategies.

8.3 Financial appraisal of strategy proposals

When an organisation undertakes a new strategy, this essentially means that funds are invested today for benefits that will accrue in the future. In this section, we explore the *general concepts* of financial resource appraisal in relation to that initial investment (some of the more detailed aspects of this process are covered in Chapter 14, Section 14.2.4). Because of its implications for the survival of the organisation, we separate out the analysis of cash flow from more general financial analysis. In the next section, we explore recent developments that connect finance with the strategic concept of value added.

8.3.1 General concepts of strategic financial appraisal

Prescriptive strategists have a very clear view of financial appraisal for strategic decisions. They take the investment to be made and predict the financial returns in the future. They use forecasts of demand, resources, inflation and likely tax regimes in the country or countries in which the investment is being made. The whole process is often built using a computer spreadsheet and has a precision and consistency that is a model of rational decision making. To this is then added some more judgemental evaluation of:

- the *risks* involved;
- the *financial exposure*, if the project were to fail;
- the *opportunity cost* of the strategy; that is, the benefits that would arise if the funds were used for an alternative investment.

It was probably Joel Dean[10] in 1954 who introduced the concept of *discounting* future funds into financial analysis. He argued that the practice in government bonds of treating earnings several years away as worth less than money today should be extended to company analysis. He also pointed out that the *time pattern* of future flows must also be appraised – that is, the fact that future funds do not always accrue evenly over time but may be bunched. Hence, it was important to predict accurately the expected future cash flows and reduce them by a discounting factor based on the *cost of capital* of the company. In the 1960s, Merrett and Sykes[11] were among several writers who wrote persuasively in the UK and across Europe on this approach. For the last 30 years, *discounted cash flow* (DCF) techniques have been widely employed to reduce the future value of strategies to their present value (*see* Figure 8.4).

More recently, among others, Grant[12] has argued that for international investment decision making it is essential to follow discounted cash flow procedures. Competitive pressure for excellence on a global basis is so intense that every strategy needs to be ruthlessly appraised for its contribution to long-term profit maximisation. Although there are some difficulties over the projection of future cash flows in uncertain fast-moving environments, it is essential to ensure that the post-tax rate of return for the strategy exceeds the company's cost of capital. These techniques are widely used in many institutions.

There are three difficulties with this approach.

Accurate prediction

There can be little doubt that, if markets are fast moving, then there are real difficulties in predicting future cash flows accurately. Even markets with steady growth will have real uncertainties as technology changes, government policies alter, social values and awareness evolve, wars occur and so on. This is the most difficult problem to overcome with discounted cash flow techniques.

By 1982, Hayes and Garvin[13] were pointing out that firms often coped with such uncertainties by setting tougher criteria. The net result of the need for accurate prediction, coupled with the increased uncertainty, was that many US companies were seeking extraordinarily high rates of return on strategic investments. Many investments were then mistakenly rejected because they did not meet these demanding criteria.

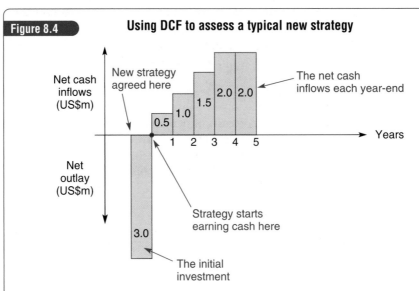

Figure 8.4 — **Using DCF to assess a typical new strategy**

Cost of capital: Project needs to earn a minimum 10%
so use 10% discount factor and discount tables

DCF calculation

End of year	Discount factor	×	Cash inflow		Present value (US$m)
1	0.9091	×	0.5	=	0.455
2	0.8264	×	1.0	=	0.826
3	0.7153	×	1.5	=	1.073
4	0.6831	×	2.0	=	1.366
5	0.6208	×	2.0	=	1.242
	Present value of cash inflows				4.962
	Less: net outlay initially				3.000
	Net present value				US$ 1.962 million

Source: Adapted from Glautier, MWE and Underdown, B (1994) – see reference 32.

Note: In recent years, new techniques that claim to be better than DCF have been introduced. See Luerhman, T (1997) 'Using APV: A Better Tool for Valuing Operations', *Harvard Business Review*, May–June, p145. DCF is used in this book because of its wide acceptance, but this may change over time.

Arbitrariness of investment assumptions

Hayes and Garvin also pointed out[14] that investment decisions rely on three rather arbitrary assumptions:

- *The profitability of the project.* Arbitrary estimates are sometimes used regarding the funds that will be needed to undertake the strategy.
- *The deterioration of the assets employed.* Estimates that may be relevant for accounting and tax purposes may be arbitrary as far as the real life of the assets is concerned.
- *The external investment opportunities.* It may be somewhat arbitrary to assume that government bonds, alternative stocks and other investment possibilities are available.

Moreover, unless care is taken, *new* investments are treated on the same basis as the replacement of *existing* businesses.[15] This is highly dubious because new business is likely to be less well known and therefore have a higher degree of risk than existing business. This could perhaps be reflected in the calculation by using two different interest rates for new and existing business in the DCF calculations. However, the *choice* of the two interest rates will depend on individual judgement and be largely arbitrary.

Incorrect application of techniques

Even in those Western countries that strongly favour the DCF approach, there has been evidence that DCF techniques are incorrectly used or even ignored. Marsh *et al*[16] showed in their survey of three UK companies that strategic decisions often ignored the formal guidelines laid down in their financial manuals. Whittington[17] describes other research that supports the contention that there are widespread problems in the use of DCF techniques in some UK companies. For example, one UK manufacturer adopted a segmentation strategy and proceeded to make the financial investment *before* the financial calculations had even been undertaken. According to these researchers, the idealised techniques described above do not accord with the reality of use.

The implications of these difficulties for strategy are explored in Section 8.3.3.

8.3.2 Basic cash flow analysis

Profit projections of the future strategy are the basis for DCF calculations. However, *profit* differs from *cash* in at least four ways:[18]

1 timing differences between when cash is paid or received and when transactions appear on the profit and loss (P&L) statement;
2 the effect of depreciation;
3 accounting transactions which are recorded on the balance sheet but do not go through the P&L account;
4 changes in working capital requirements.

Although there may be some debate over the use of financial appraisal techniques such as DCF, there can be no doubt that a basic cash flow analysis – that is, an analysis that does *not* involve discounting the future cash flows – of every strategic decision is essential. As Ellis and Williams[19] point out, without cash a business cannot survive. It is usually possible to adjust sales, costs and profits so that they fit whatever financial appraisal technique is being used and produce an acceptable return on capital, but 'creating *cash* is virtually impossible'. It is therefore vital to undertake some form of cash flow analysis for new strategies, however difficult the projections.

In strategic investment appraisal, the difficulties with cash flow usually arise in two areas:

1 in the initial period, where the project is likely to be a cash user rather than a cash generator; and
2 with projects that have a long payback, where there may be a major cash requirement some years into the venture before it starts to earn major revenues.

Cash flow analysis is particularly important in periods of uncertainty such as national economic decline or rapid currency fluctuation. The additional pressures from such events can worsen an already tight cash situation and cause real problems. Hence, in addition to conducting a normal cash flow analysis, it is usual to undertake a *sensitivity* or *worst-case analysis* for such events – that is, a cash flow analysis of the worst possible combination of events for that particular strategy.

8.3.3 Impact on corporate strategy

Whatever the problems, prescriptive strategists take the view that there is merit in conducting a thorough financial appraisal of the financial results against the costs of capital. It may be that some companies are incompetent in their approach but this does not invalidate the technique. Certainly, there are also genuine problems in projecting future profits and cash in some projects, as the Channel Tunnel financial appraisal proved. However, there is no alternative.

Emergent strategists take the view that there are real uncertainties in the whole process: it is so difficult to predict the future that there is little point in trying. Moreover, there is evidence to support the view that corporate strategy decision making is not the rational process assumed by analytical formulae.

From the narrow viewpoint of strategic analysis, it is evident that there is little compromise between these views. This book takes the approach that there is merit in both arguments but that, ultimately, it is better to undertake some analysis, however flawed. What really matters is that the corporate strategy appraisal is undertaken with *imagination* and *vision, in addition to* the narrower financial criteria that have been explored in this chapter. We will explore this further in Chapters 10 and 11.

Moreover, judgement does play an important role in determining the sales, costs and profits on the one hand, and the risks and attractions, on the other, of a major new strategic initiative. This means that accurate projections are unlikely and some decisions will be wrong. For many companies, there is a need to accept the uncertainties that real life analysis will bring, while taking the positive decisions demanded of the highly original strategies that bring real competitive advantage.

> ### ◗ Key strategic principles
>
> - Strategic expansion is often analysed using discounting techniques to reduce future projected profits back to their value in today's monetary terms.
> - Several difficulties have been identified with this approach. Probably the most substantial is the difficulty of producing accurate projections of future profitability.
> - DCF is not to be confused with basic cash flow analysis, which is not discounted but projects net cash flows during the life of the project. Cash flow analysis is essential for project assessment in order to identify and avoid bankruptcy.
> - Overall, while there are certain difficulties involved in the techniques, it is probably better to undertake these analyses rather than ignore them.

8.4 Financial management and added value: maximising shareholder wealth[20]

One of the main purposes of strategy is to add value to the inputs of the organisation. In recent years, financial management has taken added value and combined it with the concepts explored earlier in this chapter to emphasise one purpose for the organisation – the maximisation of shareholder wealth. This section explores this approach and its consequences for financial analysis and corporate strategy. Because most shareholdings occur in business situations, the topic inevitably concentrates on *commercial business perspectives* and makes little or no reference to not-for-profit organisations.

8.4.1 Shareholder wealth and value added – the contribution of Alfred Rapaport

In his influential text on shareholder value Rapaport[21] argued, in the late 1980s, that the purpose of a business was essentially to increase the wealth of its owners – that is, its shareholders. All the activities of a business therefore need to be managed towards this approach to adding value:

> Business strategies should be judged by the economic returns they generate for shareholders, as measured by dividends plus the increase in the company's share price ... The shareholder value approach estimates the economic value of an investment (e.g. the shares of the company, strategies, mergers and acquisitions, capital expenditures) by discounting forecasted cash flows by the cost of capital. These cash flows, in turn, serve as the foundations for shareholder returns from dividends and share-price appreciation.

Rapaport goes on to quote a financial journalist: 'Any management – no matter how powerful and independent – that flouts the financial objective of maximizing share value does so at its own peril.'

If the sole objective of a business is to increase the wealth of its owners, then all other activities must be judged against this criterion. Attempts to grow the business, provide service to the community, invest in environmentally friendly policies, deliver extra customer service and so on are implicitly rejected unless they also increase shareholder wealth. The clear merit of this approach is that it provides for simplicity in the analysis of strategy proposals. Such a theme was picked up enthusiastically by some members of the financial community in the 1990s – for example, the well-respected Lex Column in the *Financial Times*: 'Buybacks, demergers and the like are expressions of a single philosophy – shareholder value. The notion that companies should be run in the interest of shareholders, for long considered a weird Anglo-Saxon concept, is [now] taking root in Continental Europe.'[22]

Comment

We are entitled to view with suspicion such simplicities and certainties when they are applied to the real world. Full discussion of this important topic is pursued in Part 4 on the purpose of the organisation. However, others such as employees and government will also have an interest in the way that the business develops. To quote Charles Handy:[23]

> The idea of a corporation as the property of the current holders of its shares is confusing because it does not make clear where the power lies. As such, the notion is an affront to natural justice because it gives inadequate recognition to the people who work in the corporation and who are, increasingly, its principal assets. To talk of owning other people, as shareholders implicitly do, might be considered immoral.

Essentially, the importance of shareholders depends on the *values* of the organisation, the *power* of the stakeholders in the organisation, amongst whom will be the shareholders, and the other *external pressures* that impinge on every organisation. Nevertheless, the elevation of shareholder wealth represents an important pressure on many organisations today. For example, shareholders have been known to call successfully for the dismissal of senior executives whose strategies have turned out to be poor.

8.4.2 Calculating shareholder value added[24]

Shareholder value added (SVA) is the difference between the return on capital and the cost of capital, multiplied by the investment made by the shareholders in the business. For example, referring back to the earlier case studies in this chapter and to the Appendix on Heineken, we can estimate the 1997 return on capital at around 27 per cent, the cost of capital at around 9 per cent and the capital invested in the business at US$5595 million: this gives an SVA in 1997 of US$1007 million (0.27 minus 0.09, multiplied by 5595). Measurement consists of estimating each of these three items. Three questions can be asked that will clarify the analysis:

1 What investment has been made by shareholders in the business?

2 What rate of return is currently being earned by such investment?

3 Is this sufficient to cover the cost of capital? What is the excess return over the cost of capital?

The excess return over the cost of capital can be multiplied by the investment to obtain the SVA. From the previous sections of this chapter, it should be possible to answer the three questions in outline. However, in practice, more detailed adjustments need to be undertaken. The consultants Stern Stewart of New York, who are leading exponents of this approach, claim that anything up to 164 changes may be required to the basic company accounts. They call their version of the concept *economic value added* and have successfully used it in the first two of the three companies described in Case study 8.4.

To illustrate the difficulties in calculating SVA, we can consider the expenditures that companies make on research and development and marketing. By accounting convention, both these items are normally written off to the profit and loss account of the company in the year in which they are incurred. However, SVA argues that investment in these two items contributes to the *future value* of the business. These expenditure items should therefore be added to the balance sheet as assets and depreciated (amortised) over the years that the company will benefit from such investment, which is rather longer than the one year required by accounting convention. In the same way, by accounting convention, goodwill on acquisitions is normally written off to the profit and loss account. In SVA, it is returned both to profits and expressed as an asset, thus raising both profitability and also the invested capital.

The SVA adjustments raise a number of important issues. For example, over what period should marketing investment in a brand such as Heineken or Guinness be depreciated – since the brands were developed in the early nineteenth century or merely over the last ten years? And how far back should goodwill be adjusted – the last five years, or ten years, or when? The answers to these questions will depend on individual judgement, meaning that different analysts will arrive at different results in their calculations.[25]

In addition to the three questions above on calculating SVA, an additional question also arises. Using the concept of *economic rent* – see Chapter 6 – could the business increase its rate of return by redirecting the capital currently invested in the business towards other activities? Although redirecting the capital that is currently invested is more speculative and problematic, it can be usefully explored from a strategic perspective. Perhaps part of a business could be worth more if it was sold or simply closed down in the face of mounting losses. For example, Guinness (now part of Diageo) between 1991 and 1997 invested around US$1400 million in acquiring and developing the Spanish brewing company Cruzcampo. Yet its investment was still only earning US$30 million annual profits in 1997 – a rate of return of just 0.2 per cent.[26] Perhaps not surprisingly, the company sold its Spanish subsidiary to Heineken in a bidding auction in 2000.

8.4.3 Future strategy and SVA: estimating risk

From a strategic perspective, the concept of SVA needs to be directed towards the returns from *future strategy*, rather than past events. This means that the rate of return for each proposed strategy needs to be estimated and assessed against the current and future cost of capital. But compared with the SVA calculation described above, there is one major difficulty: the problem of risk. Future strategy is not certain, unlike the balance sheet analysis of past events outlined in the previous section. Clearly, when Guinness invested in Cruzcampo in 1991, it was not projecting profit levels as low as those achieved, otherwise it would not have acquired the company. There is a strong element of judgement involved in assessing the degree of risk, which adds to the difficulties in estimating SVA.

8.4.4 Problems with SVA

There are seven problems with this approach to financial analysis:

1 *It uses accounting data from organisations.* Such data were often never designed to provide information on the current replacement value of assets, merely historic costs. Moreover, it ignores the strategic question of whether the company would replace the asset in any event.

2 *It totally ignores many of the company's best assets.* For example, its human resources, its networks, reputation and innovative ability – *see* Chapters 6 and 7 – never appear in the company accounts but are crucial to future strategic strength.

3 *It relies on an accurate measure of the cost of capital.* Professor Paul Marsh of the London Business School has pointed out that such estimates are at best within 3 percentage points either way.[27]

4 *It takes a defined time period for measurement – usually one year.* Measuring SVA over such a period privileges the short term over the full period of benefit from such an activity. Longer-term projects like basic R&D, brand building and telecommunications infrastructure are all disadvantaged.

5 *It is difficult to apply at the business unit level.* Although it may be calculated for a group of companies, it is more difficult to calculate for individual business units that *share costs*, benefit from *shared facilities* and so on. This matters because many strategic decisions cannot be taken at group level.

6 *It involves estimates of many key items – see* Section 8.4.2.

7 *It involves estimating the risk associated with future strategies – See* Section 8.4.3.

Comment

None of this would matter if companies were simply using SVA as a guide to future strategies. But it is being used to incentivise managers – see Case study 8.4. There is a real danger that SVA short-termism, based on inadequate accounting data, will distort the fundamental strategic decisions that need to be taken by the organisation. To quote the principle in English law, *Caveat emptor!* (Let the buyer beware!)

▶ Key strategic principles

- One view of the prime purpose of a company is to increase the wealth of its owners/shareholders: this is often called the shareholder value added (SVA) approach.

- SVA is the difference between the return on capital and the cost of capital, multiplied by the investment made in the business.

- For use in strategy analysis, the SVA concept needs to be directed at estimating the profits from future strategic initiatives. The difficulty is that the future involves risk and therefore uncertain returns.

- There are seven problems with the SVA approach: use of accounting data; it ignores the company's best assets; it relies on an accurate measure of the cost of capital; it takes a defined time period; it is difficult to apply at the individual business level; it involves the use of judgement, and risk assessment is problematic.

CASE STUDY 8.3

SCA's financial objectives[28]

This case study explores the relationship between group and financial objectives at the Swedish paper and packaging company, Svenska Cellulosa (SCA)

Extract from SCA 1992 Report and Accounts	Comment
'The SCA Group's financial targets combine growth with financial balance. As a result of the divestment of the Energy business group, the capital structure changed substantially, reducing financial risk.'	*A good example of the need to balance different business and financial requirements.*
'Visible shareholders' equity almost doubled, at the same time as net debt decreased significantly. The objective is to sustain this enforced capital structure. Therefore, a certain downward adjustment of the return requirement on shareholders' equity is justified, from the current 15 per cent to 13 per cent.'	*The company decreased its gearing substantially and reduced its reliance on heavy debt finance. Such a major change would reduce the risk to shareholders and allow a reduction in shareholder return targets.*
'Profitability is the overriding guideline. Accordingly, expressed as return on shareholders' equity after tax, the requirement is 13 per cent, calculated as an average over an economic cycle.'	*The company has chosen to define profitability in terms of its shareholders only. Other stakeholders are ignored. It has calculated this over the whole cycle because of the cyclicality of the iron and steel industry (see Case study 3.3). It means that in some years profitability needs to be above this level and in other years will be below it.*

'This is based on yield on a risk-free, long-term investment in the European money market and a 3 per cent risk premium for share investments.'

The calculation of 13 per cent is clearly explained with a reference to R_i. Instead of trying to calculate R_m, the company simply added 3 per cent to R_i for the risk involved in shares on a stock exchange. The company does not explain why it chose 3 per cent.

'Considering the current tax situation, interest and equity/assets ratio, this requires a consolidated return on capital employed of slightly less than 15 per cent.' 'The [15 per cent] requirement varies between the business groups.'

From the 13 per cent shareholder return, the company has then calculated the amount that it needs to earn on its assets to deliver this figure – that is, just below 15 per cent. Some markets are inherently more profitable than others, and so the company varies the 15 per cent for different business groups within the overall portfolio of its products. Some will be above 15 per cent and some below in order to average at 15 per cent overall.

'Individual operations within each business group are managed on the basis of the return required on its operating assets, as differentiated, taking into account local inflation rates and the age structure of the assets.'

Within each business group, further distinctions are then made for each operating asset. Where country inflation is high, this will inflate the profit figure, so the target is also set higher – a good example of country management. The comment on age structure is unclear. Old assets may perform worse and be less profitable. However, they may have been largely depreciated, in which case they would easily achieve the return on capital targets.

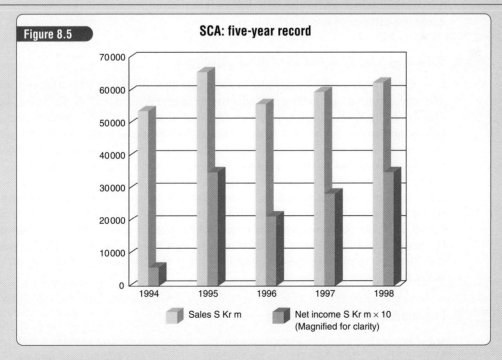

Figure 8.5

SCA: five-year record

Source: SCA Annual Report and Accounts 1992.

CASE STUDY 8.3 continued

Case questions

1 *What were the main financial objectives of SCA in the early 1990s?*

2 *How do the financial objectives relate to the WACC? And to the return on capital required for strategy proposals?*

3 *If some workers are more profitable than others, why might the company maintain its involvement in less profitable areas? What are the implications for the financial objectives and for setting corporate objectives?*

8.5 Relationship between financial and corporate objectives

Without adequate financial performance, the survival of all commercial organisations would be put at risk. The same is also at least partially true of the many not-for-profit organisations that need to survive, if only to provide the services they offer. Much of this chapter has considered the analysis of financial resources against the background of maximising profits, retaining part of those profits, delivering attractive earnings per share, paying steadily increasing dividends and similar objectives. It has been argued that a basic criterion against which to judge strategy is the opportunity cost of capital.

All these matters have been judged in terms of the shareholder returns. For example, in Case study 8.3, SCA states that its main guideline is the profit delivered to shareholders, as represented by shareholder's equity after tax. Equally, the Capital Asset Pricing Model is essentially a quantification based on the primacy of shareholder interests. There are two reasons for suggesting that this view is oversimplistic and incomplete:

1 long-term *versus* short-term objectives; and

2 the importance of key stakeholders.

8.5.1 Balancing long-term and short-term objectives

It is perfectly possible to maximise shareholder profits after tax by stopping research and development, cancelling all advertising and promotional expenditure, and by implementing such policies as a run-down of stocks and zero maintenance of the factory and so on. *In the short term*, profits and shareholder equity would rise substantially. *In the long term*, the organisation would die, which is clearly undesirable. The strategic issue is how to strike a *balance* between the short term and long term.

There is a subsidiary problem with the short-term approach to objectives. As soon as there are unfavourable variations in the external environment, the short-term view would suggest that longer-term investment should be cut back and the short term protected. For example, economic downturn might mean a major strategic capital project being delayed, even though its benefits were significant. Corporate strategy needs to consider how to manage the organisation so that this balance is not thrown off course at the first sign of difficulty.

8.5.2 Importance of key stakeholders

Some key stakeholders in a business – such as management and workers – seek rewards from the firm other than the maximisation of profit – job satisfaction and rewards, for example. A variety of research sources suggests that reasonable rather than maximum profits may be a more accurate reflection of their views. This is reflected in the Ford Motor Company mission and objectives statement (*see* Exhibit 12.6) which refers to its mission as 'allowing us to prosper as a business and to provide a reasonable return for our stockholders, the owners of the business'. The implication for financial evaluation is that there is a need to explore what 'reasonable' profit means and then to assess the organisation's financial resources in that context.

This does not mean that organisations should not raise new funds and explore the means of achieving this as cheaply as possible. It is perfectly rational to explore th cost of the capital that has been raised or is being sought. It is always desirable for the benefits of a strategy to be greater than the cost of capital, however calculated. It is nevertheless important for the benefits to be seen in a broader context than simply the maximisation of profit.

8.5.3 Distinction between strategic and financial objectives

It is important for a distinction to be drawn between an organisation's financial and strategic objectives. The starting point is to recognise the need to invest in the long-term future of the business and to establish the legitimate interests of other stakeholders in the business. Both of these aspects then need to be reflected in the organisation's objectives, which make up the organisation's broad strategies for the future. Essentially, this will lead to *strategic* rather than *financial* objectives. The distinction is shown in Table 8.5.

There can be little doubt that strategic objectives are essential for the long-term development of strategy.

Table 8.5 Financial and strategic objectives[29]

Financial objectives	Strategic objectives
● Faster revenue growth	● Bigger market share
● Faster earnings growth	● Higher, more secure industry rank
● Higher dividends	● Higher product quality
● Wider profit margins	● Lower costs relative to key competitors
● Higher returns on invested capital	● Broader or more attractive product line
● Stronger bond and credit ratings	● Stronger reputation with customers
● Bigger cash flows	● Superior customer service
● A rising stock price	● Recognition as a leader in technology and/or product innovation
● Recognition as a 'blue chip' company	● Increased ability to compete in international markets
● A more diversified revenue base	● Expanded growth opportunities
● Stable earnings during recessionary periods	● Higher salaries and other employee benefits

Source: Thompson A and Strickland A, *Strategic Management*, 9th edn.

© Richard D Irwin, a Times Mirror Higher Education Group, Inc. Company, Burr Ridge, IL, USA, p31. Adapted with permission of the publisher.

> ### ▶ Key strategic principles
>
> - To define objectives purely in terms of the organisation's short-term financial profitability would be oversimplistic and incomplete.
> - There are two principal reasons for this. First, it is often possible to sacrifice long-term profits to boost the short term at the expense of the survival of the organisation. Second, such an approach ignores the interests of other stakeholders in the organisation, such as employees.
> - Hence, a distinction needs to be drawn between strategic and financial objectives.

8.6 International aspects of financial resources

In examining international financial resources, there are many similarities with the techniques outlined in Sections 8.1 to 8.5. This section will therefore concentrate on the differences. There are five main areas to be considered:

1 capital structure of overseas holdings;

2 international fund remittances;

3 risk management, including currency;

4 taxation considerations;

5 cost of capital variations across countries.

8.6.1 Capital structure of overseas holdings

In principle, the same mixture of equity, debt and other forms of finance is available in overseas companies as in the home country. Retained earnings are often the main method of financing overseas subsidiaries, but debt capital can also sometimes be high.[30] Special considerations that might be applied to overseas companies include:

- Where the company is located in a country with widely fluctuating exchange rates, there is a case for using as much *local* debt finance as possible. This allows the company to avoid the uncertainties of using its own funds.
- Special grants and investment loans from sources such as the EU and World Bank may make a substantial difference to strategy profitability.

8.6.2 International fund remittances

Paying funds to and obtaining dividends from foreign subsidiaries will almost certainly need careful thought. For example, some years ago a South American government had a policy that allowed only limited repatriation of company profits back to Europe from activities in that country. There was no point in evaluating the cost of capital without taking this into account. One way round the problem was to seek payment from foreign subsidiaries for other services beyond dividends on shares – for example, royalties on the use of brand names, patents, management services, goods supplied from the home country and so on. Naturally, these other payments were all agreed with the government authorities of the country concerned, but they did make the financial resource evaluation task more complex and hence the strategic analysis more difficult.

8.6.3 Risk management

When companies are forced to rely on payments from countries with weak currencies, they always face the risk that their earnings will decline from the projections made at the time when the strategy was devised. There are a number of mechanisms for reducing such risks, but none is without its problems. Essentially, they all amount to some form of insurance and have a cost that needs to be built into the analysis of financial resources. Judging by some major corporate disasters of the last few years, probably the most important area of risk is that of *currency management.*

8.6.4 Taxation considerations

Among the many matters to be evaluated, there are the issues of:

- the choice of the country in which to take any profits earned;
- the possibility of moving funds to countries that have no corporation tax;
- the complexities of different national tax systems on profits.

Even within the EU, there has been no real harmonisation of the important tax rates, nor is there likely to be in the near future.[31] Tax matters make the evaluation of financial resources for overseas companies sufficiently complex to require specialist advice and consultation.

8.6.5 Cost of capital variations across countries

For reasons associated with levels of inflation, currency and national resources, different countries have differing costs of capital. In practice, this important issue can be explored both within large companies and, using outside financial advisers, with smaller companies. The important point from a strategy perspective is to know that this is a question that must be properly investigated.

> ### ▶ Key strategic principles
>
> - When international operations are involved, financial resource analysis becomes more complex.
> - The capital structure of equity and debt is broadly similar, but sending funds to and obtaining dividends from overseas companies is more difficult because of barriers to trade, country differences on tax and economies' growth and currency uncertainties.
> - Probably the greatest single area of risk in many overseas operations is currency fluctuation.
> - Taxation and cost of capital are both subjects that require in-depth and possibly specialist financial analysis.
> - For a variety of reasons, the cost of capital will vary between countries. This means that the financial analysis of strategic projects will need to be conducted on an individual country basis.

> ### CASE STUDY 8.4

Improving shareholder wealth at LucasVarity, Burton and Diageo

Some companies focus on the financial objective of increasing shareholder wealth as the major corporate objective. This case exposes this financial approach to strategy development at three companies – LucasVarity, Burton and Diageo.

LucasVarity

This company is one of the world's leading suppliers of car parts to companies like Ford (US) and Toyota (Japan). Its profits have been under the same pressure as those of the leading car companies, so its strategies sought major cost reductions during the 1990s.

As part of an earlier effort to drive down costs and increase shareholder wealth, LucasVarity adopted economic value added (EVA) techniques in 1997. How did this work in practice? John Grant was the finance director of the company at this time:

LucasVarity starts by working out what kind of return shareholders implicitly expect on their investment, as reflected in the share price. The company then works out what rate of improvement is needed over the next 10 years to meet those expectations. That is, having set a figure for EVA in year one, it fixes the rate at which EVA must rise in succeeding years. It then uses that figure to set the incentives for staff. When we have agreed the group target we move to allocate it for our seven divisions, with a little for the corporate centre. We aim to push it down absolutely as far as we can.

In the first year of the plan, starting in February 1998, the aim was to cover the whole management population which at that time had an incentive plan – around 2000 people. But Grant also pointed to Varity's Perkins engine subsidiary, where the system applied to the entire 4000 workforce, down to the shop floor. Ideally, he said, this should be applied in time to the whole group.

The bonus system itself was straightforward. Suppose an EVA target was set for year 1 at US$15 million. If the manager met it exactly, he/she would be paid a 'normative' bonus. If the result was US$30 million, the bonus was doubled. But – an important qualification – not all the bonus would be paid out in year 1. Half was retained for payment in the following year; and if the manager missed that year's target, a corresponding amount of the money was forfeited. This was a safeguard against managers

massaging the first year's figures – say, by running down inventories – in ways that would show up in year 2.

Burton

This company owns several leading chains of retail shops in the UK. Its activities cover men's and women's clothing, with high street shops like Burtons and Principles, but also a major chain of city centre department stores trading as Debenhams. The company has been under fierce competition from newer chains, grocery supermarkets and other forms of retailing. Its sales are also dependent on increased optimism in the national economy. The company introduced EVA approaches in 1997. It applied its incentive scheme at the level of area store managers or, in the case of the big department stores, at the individual store level.

Andrew Higginson, the finance director of Burton comments:

It's the underlying philosophy which is the key thing. Three years ago, before introducing EVA, we paid bonuses on sales. Then we moved to profit. Now we're looking for something which more accurately reflects the shareholder's position in a capital-intensive business.

One of the boldest changes, he said, was to increase the value of the group's properties in line with freeholds: to impute the full cost to the manager running the store.

In philosophical terms, you're trying to get people to recognise the real value of capital. All companies assess the value of a project before they spend the money, but very few make people accountable afterwards. Here, you have to live with the consequences of your spending decisions, since you carry them forward as part of your capital.

Diageo

Diageo is the name given to the largest company selling spirits in the world. It was formed in 1997 by the merger of two UK-based companies, Grand Metropolitan and Guinness. Its spirits brands include J&B Scotch whisky, Smirnoff vodka, José Cuervo tequila and Bailey's liqueur. It also owns the Guinness beer brands, Pillsbury packaged foods business and the Burger King Fast Food franchise. Sales only grew 1 per cent in the year after the merger, as a result of decline in emerging markets, such as Asia, and maturity in its other markets. The company is also under pressure for some of its products from strong competitors, such as McDonald's, and from the bargaining power of grocery retailers. This has particularly reduced the profits on some of its grocery brands like Old El Paso Mexican foods.

Shareholder value-added schemes were introduced in 1997 as a means of focusing leading managers on increasing the shareholder wealth of the business. 'Managing for value', as it is called, helped during 1998 to redirect investment from low-margin brands towards the most profitable, and to focus on the most promising markets. However, John McGrath, the group's pugnacious chief executive, admitted that it would take time for top-line growth to come through as managers translated their targets into detailed strategies. Mr McGrath wanted to double shareholder value at the group by the end of 2002. 'Incrementalism is no longer good enough. We have set our people very aggressive targets that will force them to explore every possibility.'

If they succeeded, they would be well rewarded: the pay of more than 1200 managers was linked to shareholder value added targets. And a handful of senior executives stood to gain shares worth up to 150 per cent of their annual salary – more for those based in the US – if total shareholder return over the three years to the end of 2002 was in the top half of a group of 20 global companies.

Mr McGrath was convinced that these incentives would dramatically change behaviour. 'The divisions are beginning to talk to each other much more, particularly brewing and spirits. We are stretching people's imaginations to achieve these aggressive targets.'

Source: Adapted by Richard Lynch from two articles in the *Financial Times*, 7 Oct 1997, p12, by Tony Jackson, and 17 Dec 1998, p31, by John Willman. © Copyright *Financial Times*, 1997. Used with permission.

Case questions

1 *What strategies are likely to be adopted at each of the three companies as a result of the application of such a strongly financial approach to strategy development?*

2 *Are there any dangers in such an approach? (See main text for comment)*

3 *Would you pursue this approach to strategy development if you were a senior manager at these companies? Would you be attracted by this approach if you were a senior manager at a totally different company?*

The accounting function and strategy[32]

In this extract from their book Accounting Theory and Practice, *Professors M Glautier and B Underdown comment on the relationship between the accounting function, finance and the development of corporate strategy.*

Given that long-range planning is concerned with the totality of the enterprise's strategy in every sphere of action, it is evident that the information that is needed goes much beyond that which normally is defined as accounting information.

In the final analysis, cash flows into and out of a business enterprise are the most fundamental events upon which accounting measures are based. Management and investors, in particular, are very concerned with the cash flows generated by corporate assets. These cash flows are not only central to the problem of corporate survival, but they are essential to the attainment of corporate objectives. The size, timing and risks inherent in estimating future cash flows are critical aspects of this process.

The recognition of the importance of future cash flows has led many writers to define the objective of business corporations in terms of maximising corporate wealth, defined as the present value of the future stream of net cash flows to be earned by corporate assets. This objective is also expressed as the maximisation of shareholders' wealth, since they are deemed by law to be the owners of the enterprise.

There is general agreement that the return on capital employed (ROCE) is the most important performance measurement for long-range planning and for setting long-range profit targets. It is a common practice to compute the ROCE for each year covered by the long-range plan in order to show whether planned increases in annual profits will keep pace with annual increases in assets. This analysis also indicates the effectiveness with which management will be required to use corporate assets.

The accountant's task is not to attempt the impossible by deciding what should be the maximum possible long-range profit on the basis of assumed long-range resources for planning purposes: his/her job is to quantify the size of the profit which is required as the profit objective. The required profit as a planning goal is never a theoretical ideal, such as the 'maximum long-term profit' or 'the maximum long-term return to shareholders', but represents rather the outcome of discussion as to what is a possible and desirable target for the time-span considered. As a guide to selecting the profit target, one of the most influential factors is the minimum rate of return expected by investors and creditors. A satisfactory profit ensures that debt and dividend payments may be made, thereby reducing the risks attached to investing in the firm.

Source: Glautier, M W E and Underdown, B (1994) *Accounting Theory and Practice*, 5th edn, Pitman Publishing, London Ch28.

Summary

● Organisations need to finance their existing and proposed new strategies. There are six main sources of funds for such activities, each with its own merits and problems. *Retained profits* are the first source of finance for most organisations, probably the largest and cheapest source of funds. *Equity finance* – that is, the issuance of new shares to either existing or new shareholders – is another way of raising funds. *Long-term debt finance* is simpler and cheaper than equity but there are limits to the amount that can be raised. There are also major constraints on debt finance. These relate to the need to pay interest on the debt regardless of the profit fluctuations in the business.

● Other sources of finance include *leasing* (renting) plant and machinery, *savings* from reductions in short-term debt and the *sale of existing assets*. They all have their advantages and problems.

● All capital raised by the organisation has a cost associated with it. Calculating the cost matters because it reassures the stakeholders that their efforts are worthwhile and because it provides a benchmark for assessing the profitability of future strategies.

● The cost of equity capital can be calculated using the Capital Asset Pricing Model, but it really only works where there is wide public shareholding. The cost of debt is calculated from the weighted average of the individual loans to the company. For the company overall, the combined cost of debt and equity is called the weighted average cost of capital (WACC).

● When assessing new strategic proposals, it is normal to undertake a financial appraisal. Discounting techniques are often used as part of this in Western companies. They reduce future net cash flows back to their value in today's terms. Several difficulties have been identified with this approach. Probably the most substantial is the problem of producing accurate projections of future profitability.

● Basic cash flow analysis is also undertaken. It should not be confused with the discounting techniques above. Analysing cash flow is essential to ensure that the company avoids bankruptcy.

● One view of the prime purpose of a company is to increase the wealth of its owners/ shareholders. This is often called the *shareholder value added* (SVA) approach. SVA is the difference between the return on capital and the cost of capital, multiplied by the investment made in the business. From a strategic perspective, SVA has a number of difficulties, including that of estimating the uncertain future returns from new strategy initiatives.

● To define objectives purely in terms of the organisation's short-term financial profitability would be oversimplistic and incomplete. A distinction needs to be drawn between strategic and financial objectives.

● When international operations are involved, financial resource analysis becomes more complex. Probably the greatest source of risk for many companies is currency fluctuation. Taxation and the cost of capital are both subjects that require in-depth and possibly specialist financial analysis.

QUESTIONS

1 You have been commissioned to comment upon a proposal to invest US$100 million in a new mobile telephone service. The company already operates such a facility but it has seen opportunities for expansion into new geographical areas. Competition is strong and the market is growing around 12 per cent per annum. The company currently has gearing of around 90 per cent and a WACC of 12 per cent. The new funds would double the total already invested in the company. What would you advise?

2 Use Section 8.1 to analyse the financial resources of an organisation with which you are familiar. Comment particularly on the strategic implications.

3 Explain the constraints on sources of finance likely to be experienced by Heineken, Carlsberg and Danone. To what extent can these constraints be overcome?

4 'Marketers and finance people seldom see eye to eye. The marketers say, "This product will open up a whole new market segment." Finance people respond, "It's a bad investment. The discounted rate of return is only 8%." Why are they so often in *opposition*?' (Professors Patrick Barwise, Paul Marsh and Robin Wensley)

How would *you* approach this issue?

5 Investigate the cost of capital for an organisation of your choice. How would you calculate it? With what result? What are the implications for the development of corporate strategy?

6 Compare the shareholding structures of the brewery companies named in the chapter and comment on the financial and strategic implications.

7 There appears to be a conflict in companies between financial and strategic objectives. Do you agree? How can any such conflict be resolved?

8 'Capital investment represents an act of faith, a belief that the future will be as promising as the present, together with a commitment to making the future happen.' (Professor Robert Hayes)

Discuss the implications for financial and strategic appraisal of new corporate strategies.

9 Why has SVA grown in importance over the last ten years? What implications does this have for corporate strategy?

STRATEGIC PROJECT International brewing strategy

This chapter has examined the brewing industry. Develop this study further. For example, explore the international expansion of the world's biggest brewer, Anheuser-Busch, outside its US home base. The company has been building its Budweiser brand through the slow strategies of establishing alliances and joint ventures. Does it perhaps need to take a bolder approach and make a major acquisition? What are the financial and strategic implications?

FURTHER READING

For a general survey of financial issues: Glautier, M W E and Underdown, B (1997) *Accounting Theory and Practice*, 6th edn, Pitman Publishing, London.

For a critical look at DCF techniques: Hayes, R (1982) 'Managing as if tomorrow mattered', *Harvard Business Review*, May–June.

For the link between finance and strategy: Barwise, P, Marsh, P and Wensley, R (1989) 'Must finance and strategy clash?' *Harvard Business Review*, Sep–Oct.

For a discussion of cost of capital and financial issues: Watson, D and Head, T (1998) *Corporate Finance: Principles and Practice*, Financial Times Management, London, Chs8 and 9 – an admirably clear text. Arnold, G (1998) *Corporate Financial Management*, Financial Times Management, London, Chs15 and 16, is also admirably clear.

Appendix I

Heineken NV

Extract from the consolidated accounts for the year ended 31 December 1997 (million guilders)

Balance sheet

	1997	1996
Assets		
Fixed assets		
Tangible fixed assets	5 653	5 503
Financial fixed assets	945	838
	6 598	6 341
Current assets		
Stocks	1 026	985
Accounts receivable	1 761	1 699
Securities	112	225
Cash at bank and in hand	1 759	1 403
	4 658	4 312
Total assets	11 256	10 653
Liabilities		
Group funds		
Shareholders' equity	5 103	4 514
Minority interests	401	410
	5 504	4 924
Investment facilities		
equalization account	100	100
Provisions	1 694	1 618
Debts		
Long-term debts	908	792
Current liabilities	3 050	3 219
	3 958	4 011
Total liabilities	11 256	10 653

▶

Profit and loss statement

	1997	1996
Net turnover	13 512	12 189
Raw materials	7 442	6 756
Excise duties	1 849	1 621
Personnel costs	2 274	2 174
Depreciation	744	626
Total operating expenditure	12 309	11 177
Trading profit	1 203	1 012
Earnings of non-consolidated participants	63	67
Interest	−27	−26
Profit on ordinary activities before taxation	1239	1053
Taxation	−456	−368
Group profit on ordinary activities after taxation	783	685
Minority interests	−22	−29
Net profit on ordinary activities	761	656
Dividends	176	176
Retained profit	585	480

Shareholder data (guilders per share)

	1997	1996
Net profit	15.18	13.06
Dividend	3.50	3.50
Shareholders' equity	101.71	89.97

Appendix II

Checklist of the main financial ratios

Note: It is important to obtain comparative data for competitors and to analyse the trends over several years. It is also valuable, where possible, to make comparisons with the norms across an industry.

Liquidity – measures the ability to survive and avoid default

$$\text{Current ratio} = \frac{\text{Current assets}}{\text{Current liabilities}}$$

$$\text{Acid test} = \frac{\text{Current assets} - \text{Stocks}}{\text{Current liabilities}}$$

Gearing – examines the financial strength and the different forms of finance

$$\text{Gearing} = \frac{\text{Long-term borrowing}}{\text{Capital and reserves}}$$

$$\text{Interest cover} = \frac{\text{Earnings before interest and tax (EBIT)}}{\text{Interest}}$$

Profitability

$$\text{Profit margin} = \frac{\text{EBIT}}{\text{Sales}}$$

$$\text{Return on capital employed} = \frac{\text{EBIT}}{\text{Capital employed}}$$

Investor ratios – measures the earnings available to those who own the company

Usually uses profit after tax and interest, i.e. *net profit*.

$$\text{Net profit margin} = \frac{\text{Net profit}}{\text{Sales}}$$

$$\text{Earnings per share} = \frac{\text{Net profit margin}}{\text{Number of shares}}$$

$$\text{P/E ratio} = \frac{\text{Price per share}}{\text{Number of shares}}$$

$$\text{Earnings yield} = \frac{\text{Earnings per share}}{\text{Price per share}}$$

$$\text{Dividend per share} = \frac{\text{Dividends}}{\text{Number of shares}}$$

Trading activity

$$\text{Stock cover} = \frac{\text{Cost of sales}}{\text{Stock}}$$

$$\text{Debtor days} = \frac{\text{Debtors} \times 365}{\text{Sales}}$$

$$\text{Creditor days} = \frac{\text{Other creditors} \times 365}{\text{Sales}}$$

$$\text{Fixed asset turnover} = \frac{\text{Sales}}{\text{Fixed assets}}$$

NOTES & REFERENCES

1 *Heineken Annual Report* (1997), p32.
2 Groupe MAC (1988) *Cost of Non-Europe Volume 1*, OOPEC, Luxembourg, p431.
3 *Heineken Annual Report* (1997) Op. cit.
4 There is evidence for the UK which showed that in 1990 it accounted for around 50 per cent of the total source of funds: *Annual Abstract of Statistics*, HMSO, London, 1993. Such data do not appear to have been researched for a broader range of countries. However, sampling of company accounts would appear to confirm this at least for Europe and the US.
5 Gitman, L J (1982) *Principles of Managerial Finance*, 3rd edn, Harper and Row, NY.
6 This section makes no attempt to explore the Modigliani/Miller argument that there is no difference between the cost of equity and the cost of debt. It is beyond the scope of this text. For a full and admirably clear exposition, *see* Watson, D and Head, T (1998) *Corporate Finance: Principles and Practice*, Financial Times Management, London, Ch8.
7 Franks, J R and Broyles, J E (1979) *Modern Managerial Finance*, Wiley, Chichester, Ch2.
8 For example, the UK company General Electric has held large cash balances for many years rather than invest these in company projects.
9 Franks, J R and Broyles, J E B (1979) Op. cit., pp106 *et seq.*
10 Dean, J (1954) 'Measuring the productivity of capital', *Harvard Business Review*, Jan–Feb, p21.
11 Merrett, A J and Sykes, A (1966) *Capital Budgeting and Company Finance*, Longman, Harlow.
12 Grant, R M (1991) *Contemporary Strategy Analysis*, Blackwell, Oxford.
13 Hayes, W and Garvin, J (1982) 'Managing as if tomorrow mattered', *Harvard Business Review*, May–June, p71.
14 Hayes, W and Garvin, J (1982) Ibid, p75.
15 Hayes, W and Garvin, J (1982) Ibid, p76.
16 Marsh, P, Barwise, P, Thomas, K and Wensley, R (1989) *Managing Strategic Investment Decisions in Large Diversified Companies*, London Business School Centre for Business Strategy, London.
17 Whittington, R (1993) *What is Strategy and Does it Matter?*, Routledge, London, pp64–5. The comments in this reference include a much more extensive discussion of the problems than is possible in this text.
18 Ellis, J and Williams, D (1993) *Corporate Strategy and Financial Analysis*, Pitman Publishing, London, p172.
19 Ellis, J and Williams, D (1993) Ibid, p168.
20 This section has benefited from Chapters 15 and 16 of Glen Arnold's book *Corporate Financial Management*, Financial Times Management, London, 1998.
21 Rapaport, A (1986) *Creating Shareholder Value: The new Standard for Business Performance*, The Free Press, New York, Ch1. An extract from the opening chapter of this book is also contained in De Wit, R and Meyer, R (1998) *Strategy: Process, Content and Context*, 2nd edn, International Thompson Business Press, London.
22 Lex Column, *Financial Times*, 28–29 Dec 1996.
23 Handy, C (1997) 'The citizen corporation', *Harvard Business Review*, Sept–Oct, pp26–28.
24 For a review of SVA techniques as used in economic value added (EVA), *see* Young, D (1997) 'Economic value: A primer for European managers', *European Management Journal*, 15, Aug, pp335–43.
25 Arnold, G (1998) Op. cit., pp704–5.
26 Oram, R (1997) *Financial Times*, 4 Feb, p25.
27 Quoted in the *Financial Times*, 7 Oct 1997, p12.
28 Extracts from 1992 Report and Accounts.
29 Adapted from Thompson, A and Strickland, A (1993) *Strategic Management*, 9th edn, Irwin, Homewood, IL, p31.
30 Brooke, M Z (1992) *International Management*, 2nd edn, Stanley Thornes, Cheltenham, Ch8.
31 *See* Citron, R (1991) *Getting into Europe*, Kogan Page, London, for a more detailed discussion of this area.
32 Extracted from Glautier, M W E and Underdown, B (1994) *Accounting Theory and Practice*, 5th edn, Pitman Publishing, London, Ch28.

Analysing operations resources

Learning outcomes

When you have worked through this chapter, you will be able to:

- assess the contribution of operations strategy to the corporate strategy process;
- identify the competitive advantage and value-added contributions that the operations function makes to the organisation;
- analyse the operations environment for relevant trends, especially major changes in technology;
- identify how and where operations strategies contribute to value added;
- analyse operations in organisations for the specific areas that are most likely to impact on corporate strategy;
- understand the importance of the main elements of operations strategy;
- explore the differences that exist between operations in manufacturing and in service industries.

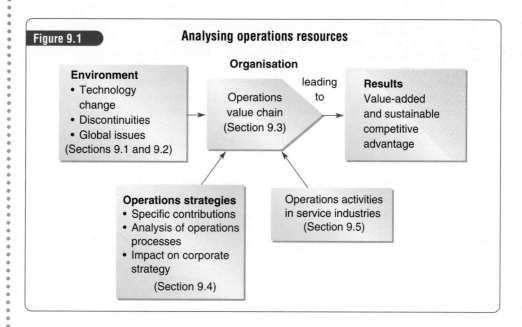

Figure 9.1 **Analysing operations resources**

Environment
- Technology change
- Discontinuities
- Global issues
(Sections 9.1 and 9.2)

Organisation
Operations value chain
(Section 9.3)

leading to

Results
Value-added and sustainable competitive advantage

Operations strategies
- Specific contributions
- Analysis of operations processes
- Impact on corporate strategy
(Section 9.4)

Operations activities in service industries
(Section 9.5)

▬ Introduction

Operations management covers all manufacturing processes in an organisation and includes raw material sourcing, purchasing, production and manufacturing, distribution and logistics – in other words, the contribution of the production function to the organisation's ability to add value to its goods or services. Importantly, human resource aspects of the function are just as significant as machinery. In many corporate strategy texts, operations management barely rates a mention, and yet it has delivered real benefits to organisations in both the commercial and public sectors over the last 25 years.

There are four main topics in this chapter: the environmental forces that have been a powerful influence on operations development; the contribution of operations to value and sustainable competitive advantage; operations activities and corporate strategy; and the application of operations concepts to the service industry (*see* Figure 9.1).

CASE STUDY 9.1

Dell Computers – competitive advantage through low-cost manufacturing

When Michael Dell first thought of selling computers-by-mail in his student room at Texas University in 1987, he could hardly have foreseen the consequences. Today, Dell Computers is one of the market leaders in the worldwide personal computer (PC) market. Dell itself had sales in 2001 of around US$30 billion and was the most profitable company in the PC industry. And Michael Dell, still aged only 37, was the eighteenth richest person in the US. The company's main competitive advantage is that it has lower manufacturing costs than its competitors – this case describes the main elements.

Dell history

Michael Dell was 19 when he first had the idea of using mail order to cut the costs of selling PCs – no distributor profit margins, no inventory held to meet future customer demand, one centralised customer supply-base per country or region. Within two years, he had launched into Europe. 'We had 22 journalists turn up [for the launch] and 21 said it was a horrible idea,' says Mr Dell. 'It wouldn't work. It was an American concept. I've been underestimated, rejected, describe it any which way you want, but every time we opened new offices round the world, people said it wouldn't work.'

Perhaps journalists do have a point with regard to customer demand. Even today, some 70 per cent of European PCs are bought through shops and other distributors. Only 30 per cent are bought through mail order, though the percentage is higher in the US, where over half are sold by this method. Yet PCs bought by mail order have lower prices than shop PCs. And, at least in the case of Dell, the lower price comes from Dell's lower manufacturing costs.

Dell's competitive advantage

Dell's advantage is much deeper than the costs it saves by selling via mail order: some rivals, like

Gateway Computers, also sell using this method. What sets Dell Computers apart is its manufacturing system. Most of its leading rivals, like Compaq, Hewlett-Packard and IBM, have their PCs made for them in low-cost labour in countries like Taiwan. Dell makes virtually all its own PCs in-house, thus retaining all the manufacturing profits. And Dell claims to have the lowest manufacturing costs in the world.

How does it achieve such low costs? By borrowing manufacturing concepts from the car industry and applying them rigorously, with strict monitoring of results.

The Dell value chain

Unlike competitors who may have four *weeks'* stock of component supplies, Dell has only two *hours'* supply. It uses just-in-time delivery to call off components from stocks held locally to its massive Round Rock factory in Texas: the cost of these stocks is borne by its suppliers, not by Dell. It uses similar systems at its main European factory in Limerick, Ireland.

Parts come into the factory to fulfil actual customer orders – no PCs are made for stock, so there is no cost of holding stock. The detail of each customer order – RAM size, hard disc storage,

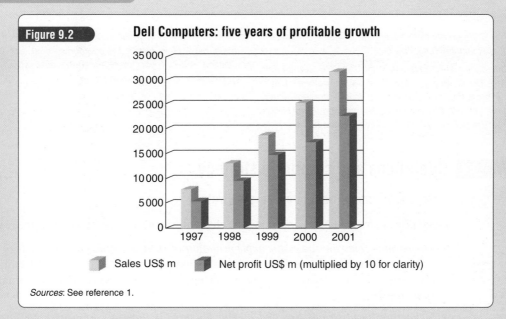

Figure 9.2

Dell Computers: five years of profitable growth

Sales US$ m   Net profit US$ m (multiplied by 10 for clarity)

Sources: See reference 1.

CD-format, etc. – is turned into a white bar code label. Each label is then scanned and the relevant parts selected automatically and placed in a box. Workers then assemble the parts, often using clips to fix them rather than screws because clips are faster. In many cases, the parts are colour-coded with the PC frame to make it easier to see where and how to fit them. This *attention to detail* is essential to produce efficient, quality products.

PCs are then individually boxed, addressed and shipped immediately to customers, who can then be billed. There is direct telephone and computer tracking between the placing of the customer order and the factory floor – all the way through to final delivery.

Dell monitoring

Importantly, such a system lends itself to very detailed and constant monitoring of order-taking, supplier delivery, factory production, customer delivery and so on. This highly analytical approach means that *every* worker has detailed targets. These will include sales and profit targets for senior managers, quality and production targets for factory floor workers, order-taking for sales personnel. Every quarter, every employee is assessed against profit, cost, quality and productivity targets.

This means first that Dell knows where it stands in relation to its annual plan. But it also allows Dell to lay off workers rapidly if demand falls – for example, 6 000 workers were sacked after the IT

spending slowdown in year 2001. It also means that if suppliers, like Intel Corporation, lower the price of computer chips then Dell can lower its PC prices quickly and announce them over the Internet. Dell takes over 50 per cent of its orders from the Internet in the US and finds that customers compare prices before making decisions.

Dell's competitive advantage – the results

In 2001, Dell reported its operating expenses at 10.2 per cent of sales. This can be compared with 18.3 per cent at Compaq and 20.6 per cent at Hewlett-Packard. Essentially, Dell operates a *lean manufacturing system* – *see* Section 9.4.7. It concentrates on standardised technologies for high volume production. It does not focus on product innovation. John Mendica, Dell's vice president of client products, formerly worked for Apple Computers. 'At Apple, demand is created through innovative products. At Dell, our innovation is around the business [production] model.'

During 2001, the PC market declined in the US by 9 per cent. However, Dell's sales rose by 10 per cent, its US market share gaining 5 per cent and its worldwide market share 2 per cent. Essentially, it was able to cut its prices because it had a lower manufacturing cost base than its rivals. Thus Dell was able to deliver better value for money to its customers and profits for its shareholders (*see* Figure 9.2).

CASE STUDY 9.1 continued

Case questions

1 *What is the competitive advantage of Dell Computers? Is it sustainable? If so, how?*

2 *What competitive advantages do rival PC companies have? Could they go down the same route as Dell? Why have they avoided this up to the present time? Would you advise companies like Compaq and HP to follow the Dell route? What are the problems, if any?*

3 *In what way is new technology a risk to Dell? Is it the main risk? How can it be overcome, if at all? [See Section 9.2.2 if you want to know more about the significance of this question.]*

9.1 Operations and corporate strategy

9.1.1 Why operations matters to corporate strategy

Operations management is an important element of corporate strategy for three reasons:

1 *The rewards from the successful implementation of such strategies can be very high* – for example, *see* Case study 9.1 on Dell and its gains in terms of market leadership and Case study 9.2 on Toyota and the resulting delivery of US$1.5 billion annually to that company.

2 *Major investment in physical and human resources is necessary to achieve the identified results* – for example, *see* the large investments needed in production plant in European steel companies described in Chapter 3.

3 *Fundamental changes in both people and machines need to be addressed by every company* – for example, *see* the Ford Motor Company's new shift strategy described in Chapter 12. The Dell Computer case also shows the importance of major changes in these areas if improvement is to be obtained.

As Hill comments,[2] operations strategy has two major contributions to make to corporate strategy:

1 It aims to provide manufacturing and related processes that will give the organisation competitive advantage over competition.

2 It supplies co-ordinated support for products so that they will win sales orders in a competitive market place.

As a result, operations resource analysis is important to strategic development because it can lead to *competitive advantage* in areas such as:

● *adaptable production* to make products that are more precisely tailored to individual customer requirements – *see* Case study 6.2;

● *lower costs* than competitors for the same product performance – *see* Case study 9.1;

● *product quality* that is superior to that of the competition – *see* Case study 9.2;

● *enhanced services and delivery* associated with the product that is superior to rivals – *see* Case study 6.2.

For small companies in particular, operations strategies have sometimes provided a means to tackle larger, more established competitors. Small companies often lack size, market position and proprietary technology. But they can benefit from greater flexibility and operational knowledge gained over time.[3]

9.1.2 Prescriptive and emergent approaches

Traditionally, the operations function has seen itself as using machines to undertake tasks as efficiently as possible. Professionally, it has an engineering and science background and has viewed its tasks as essentially oriented towards the same goal. Its management roots go back to Taylor, Gantt, the Gilbreths and Knoeppel – all pioneers in the field of 'scientific management'.[4] In keeping with these traditions, operations management has often been *prescriptive* in its solutions to strategy issues.

The one-sidedness of this approach has been recognised for many years. In 1945 a number of psychologists formed a group to redress the balance – the Tavistock Institute in London and the Socio-Technical Round Table in the US, for example.[5] The *emergent* strategy approaches of team working and empowerment, as described in the Toyota case study, were pioneered during that period. At the same time, similar Japanese developments were being initiated by people such as Ohno (*see* Case study 9.2) and others. In a similar way German and French social reconstruction was also being initiated that took the same broader view of the nature of work and its social role.

Corporate strategy needs to take both this broader emergent perspective and the important prescriptive approaches. All the topics in this chapter therefore need to be explored from both emergent and prescriptive perspectives.

> ### ▶ Key strategic principles
>
> - **Operations needs to be considered as part of corporate strategy because of the sustainable competitive advantage it brings, the major investments that may be required and the fundamental changes that may be needed.**
> - **Traditionally, operations has taken a prescriptive approach to strategy issues. It is becoming increasingly recognised that emergent perspectives are also required.**

9.2 Analysis of the operations environment

Over the last 30 years, there have been many fundamental changes in the environment surrounding operations at the strategic level. Although factors are specific to the organisation itself, three general trends deserve investigation:

1 technological environment;

2 discontinuities in technology;

3 global activity and cost reductions.

9.2.1 Technological environment

Owing to the impact of technology, the world has changed more dramatically over the last 150 years than it did in the previous 2000 years.[6] Arguably, the pace is increasing: this will have an even greater effect on the corporate environment. Hill[7] identifies five factors that have allowed Far Eastern countries, particularly Japan, to move ahead of the West, although it should be noted that Germany and France are perhaps less guilty than the others of lagging behind. More recently, there have been setbacks in Asian economic development. But the five strategic opportunities listed below and seized by Asian economies remain substantial in countries like Singapore and Taiwan:

1 the increased pace of technological change;

2 the failure to appreciate the impact of increased world manufacturing capacity. In some markets, there is now substantial excess capacity, which impacts particularly during a downward trade cycle. Shipbuilding is an example. Competition is inevitably keener;

3 lack of willingness to invest in research and development in some countries;

4 top management lack of experience in manufacturing;

5 the production manager's obsession with short-term output, rather than the longer-term strategic viewpoint.

In analysing technological change, the pervasiveness of electronics and the rapid pace of electronic development have led to shorter life cycles in some industries, particularly industrial markets.[8] In addition, better communications have meant that any technological advance is now shared much more quickly around the world, so that it is difficult to sustain technological advantage without patents. At the same time, research and development is becoming more expensive. Analysis of technology will need to examine both the life cycle of the organisation's major products and, at a more fundamental level, the technological resources available to the company.

When the Swiss pharmaceutical company Roche lost its exclusive patents to the tranquilliser Valium in the 1960s, it faced the real problem of how to generate the same profitability from new drug sources. It invested heavily in research for many years and achieved some success. The real breakthrough in technology, however, was its acquisition of 60 per cent of the shares in the US biotechnology company Genentech in 1990 for US$2 billion. This was a company with sales of US$500 million and hardly any profit, but its acquisition opened up a window of new technology opportunity for Roche.

However, not all organisations are at the cutting edge of technological development: many parts of the poorer nations and many markets in richer nations rely on more mundane activities for the production of their goods. For example, technology is unlikely to be the main strategy in some of the more traditional parts of the food industry. While some markets may see rapid technological change, others are better seen as being more mature. Technology strategies need to be seen in the context of industry life cycles (*see* Chapter 3).

9.2.2 Discontinuities in technology

Many students will be aware of the powerful, portable personal computers that have coloured liquid-crystal displays and are used to undertake complex calculations. These are likely to be battery-driven and cost upwards of US$1000. Compare them with the 'calculating aids' that have been available over the last 40 years:

1950s Slide rules and logarithm tables

1960s Mechanical calculating machines, each with a turning lever that was cranked around to undertake the calculations

1970s Large, simple electronic calculators with an electronically lit display

1980s The first liquid-crystal displays, but the calculations were still simple.

What is striking is not just the change of technology but the drastic implications for those businesses still producing the older versions of the above equipment – for example, the slide rule manufacturers. These companies changed or went out of business many years ago because of a discrete change in the technology – a *discontinuity*.

For shareholders, managers and employees, the impact of a discontinuity on an organisation is significant. It may be caused by anything from a change in fashion to a radically new technology. Essentially, it is a change in the organisation's environment that makes a radical difference to its strategy. One of the more likely reasons for this in the 1990s is a change in technology and its consequent impact on manufacturing.

Owing to its radical nature, it is often not possible to predict such a change. It is therefore important not to predict, but rather to develop, a strategy that needs to be followed once a discontinuity has occurred. According to Strebel,[9] there are two distinct phases after such an event has taken place:

1 *Development phase*. Competitors attempt to develop the value of the product, its functionality, uses and benefits. The phase is often characterised by product innovation, new technologies, new suppliers and new entrants. At the *end* of this phase, an industry standard of performance is developed. Strebel points to the example of the IBM personal computer which set a standard in that market. Case 9.1 showed that it is not IBM that has benefited from this standard but Dell Computers.

2 *Consolidation or cost reduction phase*. Having established an industry standard, competition then moves on to produce this at increasingly lower costs. For example, in personal computers, Dell Computers has successfully reduced the cost of personal computer components *once the standard was set*. The phase will typically include price wars and similar products. The bargaining power may shift from manufacturers to distributors. Dell has maintained its bargaining power by setting up its *own distribution system* – its computer-by-mail-order operations.

At a later stage, Strebel suggests that there may well be another phase that links back towards development again, as technology makes another breakthrough. The cycle may then repeat itself with periods of *divergence* (the development phase) followed by periods of *convergence* (the consolidation or cost reduction phase). It is important for organisations to understand what phase of the industry development they are engaged in and develop appropriate operations and other strategies. Naturally, there will be many that will attempt to analyse or, at least, be sensitive to discontinuities as they begin to occur.

9.2.3 Global activity and cost reductions

During the 1970s and 1980s, the Italian sportswear company Fila slowly transferred its production from Italy to a range of subcontract manufacturers in the Far East, in countries such as China and Indonesia. Its workforce in Italy declined from 2500 employees in the 1950s, through 1800 in the 1960s to around 250 in the mid-1990s. In 1994, a further 670 employees, spread worldwide, were working on design, distribution, marketing and liaising with their manufacturing operations.

The reason for this shift was that it was the only way for Fila to survive. By 1994, it was around eight times more expensive to produce the goods in Italy than in China. The company faced low-priced competition using low-cost labour and could only respond by moving its own operation onto a global basis.

To take another example from the textile trade, Great Future Textiles Ltd of Taipei was described by the World Bank[10] as an important supplier to Modern Fashions GmbH in Düsseldorf, Germany. Fashions are designed in Taipei, but are made up in a factory near Bangkok, Thailand. The factory imports cloth from Rajasthan, India, cotton from Texas, US, and yarn from Java, Indonesia. The finished product is air-freighted directly from Bangkok to Düsseldorf. This system is operated to take advantage of the *comparative advantages* of the various nations involved and the low barriers to trade that exist in the world textile industry.

In practice, the world is beginning to return to the policies of free trade of the early twentieth century.[11]

There are two main implications for operations strategy:

1 *World trade barriers have been reduced.* These will come down further as the 1993 GATT Uruguay Round of tariff cuts is implemented into the new millennium.

2 *World manufacturing has become more complex.* Some companies now source products in one country and market in another.

More generally, markets around the world have been subject to slower growth and to the attack of new industrial competitor nations, such as Singapore and Malaysia. This has led to pressure on costs, fragmentation in market share, rapid copying of competitors' products and increasing globalisation of market demand. Customers have also become more demanding, especially in terms of quality and value for money. The implication is that production machinery has needed to be more flexible and workers have either been forced to adapt or face the possibility that their company will not survive. Western manufacturers have had to reduce costs and increase quality to remain competitive.

In the consumer electronics market, the two factors identified above have both been at work. Japanese companies such as Sony and Matsushita dominate the world industry. Key components are made in Japan but much of the basic assembly now takes place in the Asian 'Tiger' economies – Singapore, Malaysia, Thailand, Korea and Hong Kong.[12] Components and parts are imported into such countries, assembled using low-cost labour and exported again. This is done inside the countries, using free-trade zones which do not attract import and export tariffs and controls. As the Japanese yen increased in value against world currencies in the 1980s, such manufacturing strategies became even more important. If the companies had kept their production in Japan, their products would probably have been priced out of world markets. Even at the beginning of the twenty-first century, such differences remain.

The implications for the operations of companies all around the world need to be carefully explored. Importantly, it does not automatically follow that all production should be shifted to low-labour-cost countries. Higher-labour-cost countries may have other advantages in terms of higher productivity through better training and knowledge that can offset their labour cost disadvantages. However, such skills are most likely to be best used in the more sophisticated manufacturing operations. In turn, these are likely to be those with higher value added that can support higher labour costs.

Moreover, global activities are only possible for some goods and for services. Other important conditions might include:

● high value-added consumer products that can support the transport costs;
● long shelf-life items that will not perish during transport;
● industrial goods with a high-labour-cost content.

Other considerations apply to *service products*, such as consultancy, restaurants and hotels. If these services require various forms of direct and ongoing contact with the customer, then they are often wholly unsuited to production on the other side of the globe, although they may still be part of a *global services network*.

When considering global manufacturing, operations strategy will need to consider where the balance of cost, services, feasibility and skill is likely to rest over the coming years.

> ### ▶ Key strategic principles
>
> - Particularly in the area of operations, new technology can shape future strategy. The pace of change is growing. There are other environmental difficulties facing some companies, especially a lack of awareness of the implications of new manufacturing capacity and the impact of new production techniques.
>
> - Discontinuities, i.e. major changes in technology and markets, can have a substantial impact on strategy. By definition, they are difficult to predict, so organisations should sensitise themselves to the environment in these circumstances. Typically, after a discontinuity, industries go through two phases: divergence, which is a development phase, then convergence, which is a cost reduction or consolidation phase.
>
> - The lowering of trade barriers around the world and the movement of some company production to low-labour-cost countries have had a significant impact on operations strategy in some industries. However, not all industries are affected by such trends.

CASE STUDY 9.2

Toyota: taking out costs and adding value

Over the last 30 years, Toyota Motor Corporation has become one of the top four global car companies, alongside General Motors (US), Daimler Chrysler (Germany/US) and Ford (US). Its rise centres on twin strategies related to operations and marketing. This case study concentrates mainly on its operations successes but also touches briefly on marketing, since the two areas are interlinked. The Toyota operations strategies have been copied around the world, though rarely with the same success.

Background

In the year to end-June 2001, Toyota sold over 5 million vehicles around the world.[13] The company had only started car production in the 1930s. Even in the early 1950s, it was still only averaging 18 000 vehicles per annum.[14] The increase in production and sales between 1950 and 2000 was, by any standards, remarkable – Figure 9.3 shows recent data. Toyota's strategic problem was that it was a tiny company competing against large competitors. The only way that it could survive was by finding new, flexible production methods that could be used by smaller companies. 'The Toyota Production System originated as a means of achieving mass production efficiencies with small production volumes' (Toyota Annual Report and Accounts 1998).

Many of the production successes between 1950 and 1980 have been accredited to the Toyota Production System and its chief engineer during that time, Taiichi Ohno. He started experimenting to improve production in the late 1940s, but it took many years to develop the systems described below, such as *kaizen* and *kanban*, and to have them widely adopted across the company. Even in the 1990s, experimentation and change were still taking place to improve production. Indeed, such change was by definition an *integral* part of the process of achieving production improvements: it was called 'continual improvement'[15] or *kaizen* in Japanese.

During the same period of time, Toyota operated a separate marketing company that essentially sold Toyota production. It was headed by Shotaro

▶

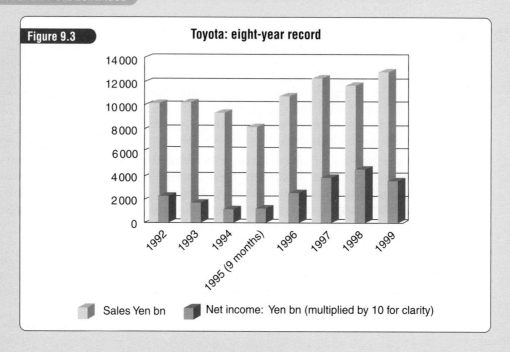

Figure 9.3 Toyota: eight-year record

Sales Yen bn   Net income: Yen bn (multiplied by 10 for clarity)

Kimaya, who had trained in US marketing methods after the Second World War. He is credited with many marketing innovations in the company during the 1960s and 1970s. They slowly propelled Toyota to market leadership in Japan with over 40 per cent of the market. Among other initiatives, he set up dealer networks, cheap car finance for customers and a strong, dedicated salesforce. He also developed Toyota exports so that by the 1970s around 40 per cent of all production was being sold outside Japan, especially in the US.[16]

Operations initiatives at Toyota between 1950 and 1980
During this period, Toyota introduced a whole series of operations initiatives that assisted car and truck production – essentially a repetitive, mass-manufacturing process. The new procedures were designed to achieve three main objectives:

1 to reduce costs;

2 to increase quality;

3 to control the production process more tightly, thus reducing the inputs needed and making the company more responsive to market demand.

The first two objectives had an immediate impact on added value in the plant; the last had an indirect influence on added value. To achieve these objectives, Toyota had a number of key operations strategies:

● *Design.* More costs can be taken out at the design phase of operations than at any other stage. For example, Toyota has consistently used research and development to undertake such tasks as combining components together so that they can be produced by one process rather than two.

● *Kaizen.* This means 'continuous improvement' across every aspect of production. Toyota's engineers invented this approach to operations strategy.[17] It is reflected in Toyota's attention to detail, which is legendary.[18] The result of one stage in *Kaizen* is shown in Figure 9.4.

● *Kanban system.* This was originally a system of coloured cards on the factory floor that were associated with the amount of stock available for production. These were used to signal when stock needed to be replenished and provided a simple but extremely effective visual system both to tell operatives when to reorder and to keep stocks controlled and low up to that time.

● *Layout.* Instead of long, linear layouts for production lines, cellular layout arrangements of plant

Figure 9.4 — **Axle-stand production line at a car accessory factory**

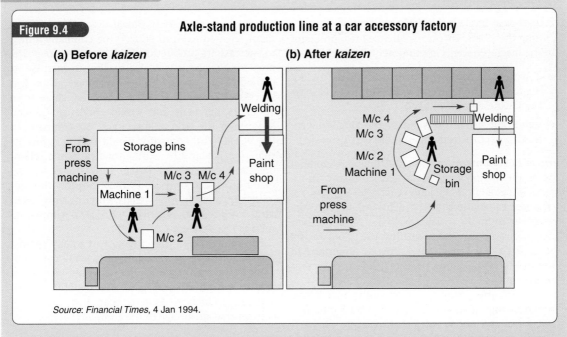

Source: Financial Times, 4 Jan 1994.

machinery were designed. They allowed workers to operate a number of machines and allowed them to work in teams to provide support and back-up more effectively. The teams had to be flexible in their willingness to operate any machinery in the layout and needed to be highly trained to complete the varied range of tasks. Some other Japanese companies, such as Nissan, have had difficulty in achieving the same results,[19] probably because of the sophistication needed to operate this system.

- *Supplier relationships.* Close co-operation was obtained and maintained with a small group of leading suppliers to Toyota. It was used to work jointly on cost reduction schemes and seek higher quality from bought-in components. This was particularly important in the value-added process at Toyota because the company had a higher proportion of bought-in items from suppliers than its main international rivals. This arrangement applied to other companies in Japan but was extended when Toyota opened its plants overseas – for example, in 1993 at Burnasten in the UK.[20]

- *Just-in-time systems.* Toyota pioneered the arrival of stock from suppliers using methods which involve close contacts with suppliers. When stocks in the factory run low, they are replaced by stocks from suppliers very rapidly using computer linkages and daily or even more frequent deliveries – *just in time for production*. The clear advantage to companies such as Toyota is that their capital investment in stock is permanently kept lower than otherwise. The company is not unique in the use of such systems.

Each of these developments was equally important at Toyota. All contributed to the general improvement in the production efficiency of the company.

By the early 1980s, the Toyota Production System was being described and recommended for introduction into Western companies.[21] Japanese rivals such as Nissan and Honda also attempted to introduce the same or similar schemes. During the 1990s, the Toyota plant at Takaoda was compared as a model of production with the worst North American plant.[22] Toyota was used as a pointer to the changes required in the US. However, there are cultural and industry structure problems that make complete adoption of the Toyota system difficult: for example, team working and flexibility may be closer to the Japanese model of society than to Western cultures.[23] Toyota itself saw the techniques it had developed as being a set of evolving production strategies with no single ideal solution: *kaizen* meant what it said.[24]

Production at Toyota in the 1990s and beyond

During the 1990s, Toyota experienced real problems in the macroeconomic environment. They were:

- downturn in worldwide demand for cars, including for the first time ever a drop in demand in its key Japanese home market;
- significant rise in the value of the Japanese yen, making exports from Japan more expensive.

These developments prompted a major reappraisal of its production methods at the company and a redoubling of efforts to achieve new, lower costs. All Japanese car manufacturers including Toyota were forced to shift in a major way the focus of their operations strategy from quality and rapid model changes to cost reductions.[25] Toyota responded to the pressures by setting up a major cost reduction programme.

By 1994, the company was claiming that it had found savings at an annual rate of US$1.5 billion.[26] But it was still not satisfied. For example, in 2001, Toyota announced a totally new programme called 'Construction of Cost Competitiveness for the 21st Century' or *CCC21*, for short. The relentless drive for improvement would be renewed. The company was looking again at every aspect of design, manufacturing, procurement and fixed costs. This was expected to lead to better utilisation rates for manufacturing equipment and less 'expenditure on human resources'. But this will not necessarily mean sacking workers, which is against the Toyota tradition. It may mean that some of the workers on temporary contracts will not have their contracts renewed, but the company was keen to avoid even this, if possible.

Some would question how Toyota could have been so efficient during the 1980s if it was still able to generate such massive savings in the 1990s. Toyota has always had problems transferring its production system beyond its factories to other areas of the value chain. It had some success with its immediate suppliers but struggled both with raw material suppliers and with the marketing/selling end of the value chain.[27] These difficulties were then compounded as the Toyota Production System was subjected to the pressures of worldwide demand, the implications for production at its factories and a slump in Japanese domestic demand in the late 1990s. Nevertheless, personal and team motivation remain an important of the Toyota system.

According to the *2010 Global Vision* Toyota document released in April 2002,[28] the company aimed to increase its production by 50 per cent over the next nine years. It was also seeking to increase its market share by the same percentage. If it was successful, it would increase its market share from 10 to 15 per cent and would challenge General Motors for the title of the largest car company in the world. The company would seek to grow its share, particularly in North America, while retaining its dominance in Japan. It was also seeking major growth in India and China, possibly through joint ventures. It was already entering into technical cooperation alliances with rival companies such as PSA Peugeot Citroën.[29]

The one strategy that Toyota was totally against was acquisition or takeover of a rival car company.[30] The reason was simple: it would be impossible to introduce and gain the benefits of the Toyota Production System that was the main competitive advantage of the company.

Case questions

1 *Using the definition of corporate strategy in Chapter 1, identify which of the operations strategies undertaken by Toyota (kaizen, kanban, design, etc.) have a corporate strategy perspective and which are mainly the concern of operations management alone.*

2 *Examining the Toyota Production System overall, to what extent do you judge this to be critical to the company's strategic success? If you believe it to be critical, then how does this fit with strategy theories that lay stress on the market aspects of corporate strategy, such as Porter's Five Forces Model? If you believe operations to be relatively unimportant, then how do you explain the remarkable success of Toyota globally since the 1950s?*

3 *Some commentators argue that it is relatively easy for market leaders such as Toyota to undertake the investment in machinery and training programmes to achieve strategic success but more difficult for smaller organisations. Do small companies have anything to learn from Toyota? If so, what?*

4 *The case describes how Toyota remains ambitious to take global market leadership by 2010. Do you believe that the company will really overtake Ford and Daimler Chrysler by this time?*

9.3 The role of operations in adding value and achieving sustainable competitive advantage

9.3.1 Value added, competitive advantage and operations strategy

Operations strategy has two major structural constraints:

1 Operations resources take time to plan and build: for example, many factories take years.

2 Once installed, they are difficult and expensive to change: for example, bulldozing the completed factory is not an easy option.

Moreover, resource analysis in the operations area is *complex* because it often involves the bulk of the organisation's assets and employees.

Ideally, operations strategy really needs to be split into a series of separate, but inter-linked, analyses. Each of these would cover the different parts of the operations process and would be different for each organisation. Porter's *value chain* from Chapter 6 can be used as a starting point for such studies (*see* Case 9.1 and Figure 9.5). Importantly, much of this is *not* corporate strategy, in the sense that the detailed day-to-day operations are outside the definition of corporate strategy. Nevertheless, corporate strategy will set the *focus*, *agenda* and *priorities* in these areas – for example, on issues such as which customers take priority, how quality is improved, the relationships between subsidiaries of the same company. The strategies are then translated into decisions that are subsequently followed in detail by the managers concerned.

When dealing with strategy in such tangible areas as building a new factory or producing an existing product, corporate strategy might be primarily *prescriptive* rather than *emergent* in its approach: after all, the factory or product is a physical entity. In practice, the corporate strategy of operations resources has elements of *both*.

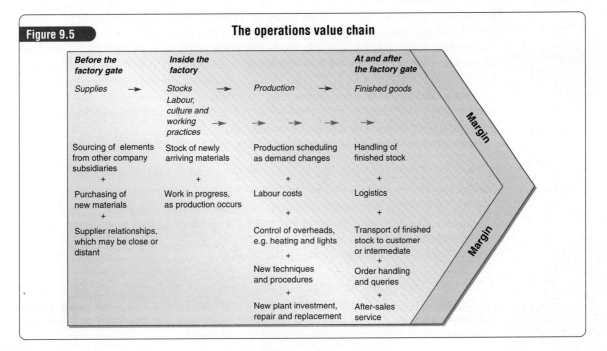

Figure 9.5 **The operations value chain**

Before the factory gate	Inside the factory		At and after the factory gate
Supplies →	Stocks → Labour, culture and working practices →	Production →	Finished goods
Sourcing of elements from other company subsidiaries	Stock of newly arriving materials	Production scheduling as demand changes	Handling of finished stock
+	+	+	+
Purchasing of new materials	Work in progress, as production occurs	Labour costs	Logistics
+		+	+
Supplier relationships, which may be close or distant		Control of overheads, e.g. heating and lights	Transport of finished stock to customer or intermediate
		+	+
		New techniques and procedures	Order handling and queries
		+	+
		New plant investment, repair and replacement	After-sales service

Margin

- After the strategic decision has been taken to build a new factory, the actual building process will typically be lengthy. The decision to embark on this process can only be based on assumptions and predictions about the future. Moreover, in existing factories, sales estimates are often required in advance of the sales order actually being taken, so that production can be scheduled smoothly and at the lowest costs. This is essentially *prescriptive* in its strategic approach.

- However, after the new factory has been built and certainly in existing sites, many aspects of the production process rely heavily on worker attitudes, culture and motivation. Typically, change is undertaken in small steps. Some companies even refer to this process as 'continuous improvement' with no specified final end-point. This is essentially *emergent* in its strategic direction.

9.3.2 Operations' contributions to value and competitive advantage

These can be grouped into six areas:

1 market adaptability;

2 winning against competition;

3 adding value through enhanced performance or service;

4 achieving low costs in manufacture;

5 delivering human resource objectives;

6 the link between manufacturing and marketing.

The additional task of improving quality and dependability will be explored in Chapter 12.

Market adaptability

Where a repetitive product such as a car or food product is being made by mass production, there is usually a need to match production of an individual type, brand, model, colour, etc., with consumer demand. Otherwise, significant costs may be incurred in holding finished stock. *Production needs adapt to market demand.* This is an important part of the production/marketing interface and is well described in the literature (*see*, for example, Hill[31] and Wild[32]). However, the detailed planning that is necessary does not take place at the level of corporate planning. It is a day-to-day or week-to-week task, depending on the length of time it takes to produce variations in the products and on the nature of the customers.

There are two corporate strategy aspects of market adaptability:

1 *The extent to which an organisation will wish to respond to individual customer needs.* In essence, this will depend on two balancing factors:
   - the size of the customer's individual order – whether it is sufficiently large to justify the time and costs of producing a product that is specialised to that customer; and
   - the capacity and adaptability of the production machinery to reduce the costs involved.

2 *The contribution that market adaptability might make to beating competition.* Some customers may find the option of customised production highly attractive. Companies, like Toyota, that have been able to achieve this possess highly valuable resources that deliver sustainable competitive advantage.

Winning against competition

The development of manufacturing strategy to win orders against competition is an important aspect of operations resource analysis. Hill[33] explains that this process may be market-led but manufacturing has a major role in two areas: contributing to the debate and delivering the successful products that beat competitors. The resource-based view recognises the importance of operations resources in this task.

Adding value through enhanced performance or service

We explored this in Chapter 6. Many of the operations areas are directly concerned with adding value to the supplies that are brought into the company. Although the detail of such matters does not come within corporate strategy, the basic arrangements made by the organisation are at the centre of the strategy process.

Value can be added to a product not just by physical production but also by the performance or the quality of the service that is related to the product. Technology can also contribute to product added value by providing new opportunities and variations from competition. The resource-based view lays special emphasis on the uniqueness of operations' core resources.

Achieving low costs in manufacture

As the Toyota case showed, many of the strategies in the operations area have the basic objective of achieving low costs. For the sake of clarity, it is important to distinguish here between the *objective* of cutting costs – for example, in order to raise profits at Toyota – and the *strategy* by which this is achieved – for example, by redeploying labour in the Toyota plant. The resource-based view supports this approach but lays greater emphasis on finding ways of doing this that are owned by the company and not easily available to competitors.

Delivering human resources objectives

This objective is naturally a part of the human resource analysis of the company. In addition, it appears here for two reasons:

1 the large number of people often employed in the operations function;
2 the crucial need, in many instances, to obtain the co-operation of such people in order to deliver the other objectives.

The resource-based view also highlights this area for its contribution to the special *knowledge and skills* often possessed by those working in the company. These may form the basis of competitive advantage, as well as providing job satisfaction.

The link between manufacturing and marketing

From the above factors, it will be evident that successful operations strategy demands that there is a strong link between these two functional areas. Hill[34] lists five steps to achieving this:

Step 1   Define corporate objectives.
Step 2   Determine marketing strategies to meet these objectives.
Step 3   Assess how different products win orders against competitors.
Step 4   Establish the most appropriate mode to manufacture these sets of products – *process choice*.
Step 5   Provide the manufacturing infrastructure required to support production.

It is essential to see the steps as *sequential*, but also *interactive*, with feedback loops connecting the first three in particular.[35]

> ## ▶ Key strategic principles
>
> ● Operations faces two structural constraints: the length of time to build new resources and the difficulty of altering them once they are installed. For these reasons, it is useful to apply the value chain concept to the process and analyse every element individually.
>
> ● It is essential to clarify the purposes to be served by operations and technologies strategies, because they are complex and may need to be prioritised.
>
> ● Market adaptability, winning against competition, added value through enhanced performance or service, cutting the costs of manufacture, improved quality and human resource objectives are the main elements that need to be considered. Many of these will contribute to the sustainable competitive advantage of the organisation, according to the resource-based view.
>
> ● The five steps that enable marketing and manufacturing strategy to link together are a vital part of the development of operations analysis. They will determine the manufacturing processes and infrastructure required for the corporate strategy.

9.4 Operations activities and corporate strategy

In examining this area from a corporate strategy perspective, the difficulty is the large number of possible strategies that are available. There are dangers for the analytical process from:

● becoming immersed in the detail that is important to those undertaking the strategy but largely irrelevant to the corporate strategist;

● failing to identify those strategies that will have a *real* impact on the future direction of the business, as against those that are useful but not crucial.

Corporate strategy really needs to confine itself to an awareness of the areas to be probed and a sense of priority regarding the areas that will deliver the organisation's objectives. A strong analysis will start by considering this matter rather than plunging into long lists of specific strategies. As guidance, the criteria shown in Table 9.1 are suggested. With these words of caution, we can now turn to consider the areas that may need to be analysed in more detail. We tackle this under several headings that broadly follow the way that value is added during the manufacturing process and link with basic texts in this area:[36]

● Make or buy?

● Supplier relationships

● Manufacturing strategy

● Product design prior to manufacture

● Factory layout and processes

● Logistics and transport

Table 9.1 Criteria for the relevance of manufacturing strategy to corporate strategy

Strategic area	Issues to be explored
Organisation objectives	Possible impact? Some strategies may be more important than others
Added value	To what extent does the strategy add significant value?
'What if?' questions	Explore what would happen if certain conditions were changed and assess the impact on objectives, e.g. what would happen if we were able to reduce supply prices by 10 per cent? Would this have a substantial impact or not make much difference?
Key factors for success	In Chapter 6, we explored this area. They may well guide the selection of the most appropriate manufacturing strategies
Human resource implications	Operations strategy often involves change in working practices, responsibilities and reporting relationships. Some strategies may be difficult to operate unless these human factors are explored against the organisation's human resource objectives

- Lean thinking
- Human resource implications
- International manufacturing
- Conclusions

9.4.1 Make or buy?

Instead of buying products from suppliers, some manufacturers will choose to make the products themselves. The strategic decision on the best route to take is complex but can be summarised as:

Make, when:

- the company has specialised needs;
- it needs to have a really secure source of supply; or
- the cost of supply is a high part of the total costs.

Buy, when:

- the company wants to maintain flexibility in its sources of supply;
- the company has only limited skills and resources in the supplier's area.

The decision is clearly related to *vertical integration* of the organisation back into its suppliers. However, in the case of such integration, the company would actively market the products that formerly came from its supplier, as against merely supplying its own factories.

Analysis will clearly need to examine not just the costs of each alternative make-or-buy decision but also the skills, resources needed and broader strategic direction of the company. It will also look at what competitors do and explore the reasons for any differences.

9.4.2 Supplier relationships

Two different and opposing trends[37] can be observed in the strategies adopted by manufacturing companies:

1 *Closer relationships with suppliers.* As used by Toyota, this will involve sharing technical and development information in order to lower the cost of the finished product. It implies closer co-operation over many years, often with a small number of key suppliers. Inevitably, some of the value added is passed from the manufacturer to the supplier. However, it can help to drive down costs overall and raise quality.

2 *More distant relationships with suppliers.* This will involve aggressive negotiating to obtain the lowest possible price for an agreed specification. For example, Saab Cars (part-owned by General Motors) actually telephoned its suppliers of car mirrors twice a day for two weeks requesting lower quotes before deciding.[38] In this case, supplier relationships are at arm's length and obtain the lowest prices. However, there may be only limited involvement in the development process and the contributions to quality improvement are strictly defined rather than a joint ideas process. This supplier system is used by General Motors and Volkswagen, Germany (who recruited the GM purchasing director in 1994).

As described in Section 9.2.3, there is also increasing *globalisation* in the sourcing of supplies. This makes the purchasing task more complex and demanding.

9.4.3 Manufacturing strategy

To analyse this area, it is useful to examine the six basic areas of manufacturing strategy. In addition to the make-or-buy decision above, there are five other key areas:[39]

1 *Factory location and size.* Most organisations start with an existing configuration, from one site to several. For example, Ford Motors has a number of plants in several different European countries; each has different products and capacities and many are linked together in the production chain.

2 *Processes.* Each factory will have certain types of equipment and procedures for making products, dealing with variations in demand and so on. For example, Toyota makes different models at different plants; each plant has different production equipment relevant to the models at that location. Each factory has links with sales to vary demand accordingly.

3 *Production capacity.* From a strategic perspective, the capacity of the plant to meet customer demand is an important consideration. Clearly, in the long term this will change as markets grow and decline. In addition, there are short-term plant capacity scheduling issues which are largely outside the interest of corporate strategy. For example, Chapter 3 explored the strategic implications of excess production capacity in the European steel industry.

4 *Manufacturing infrastructure.* Planning and control of stocks, quality, work-in-progress inventories and the flow of goods are vital to factories. The overall principles by which this is done are part of corporate strategy but the detail is not. For example, Case study 9.1 on Dell showed how the company introduced the principles and then allowed the factory floor to follow them up.

5 *Links with other functions.* Manufacturing has started to move towards production that meets *precise* customer demand through *flexible manufacturing*. This is only

possible from close links with sales. The *range of the products* that are manufactured will also depend on such links. In both cases, there are often economies of scale from manufacturing a limited range in large quantities, but this may not match market demand. With new modern flexible equipment and telecommunications links, a new strategy may be to introduce shorter production runs and rapid changeover to other products. For older plant and some manufacturing processes, a *compromise* is needed and this is a strategic decision. For example, the prime objective of a factory which regularly produces six months' supply of some confectionery lines, such as Hazelnut Brittle, is to reduce the cost of its production, rather than the cost of its finished goods stock and the fresh quality of its finished product.

Overall, Skinner[40] comments that:

- It is not necessary to be the lowest-cost producer – quality and service being more important for some customers – but this implies an understanding of competitors and how they compete on costs, quality and service.

- Factories need to *compromise* regarding a number of variables. For example, the flexible, low-volume product with frequent model changes needs to be balanced by the lower costs of large-volume production runs and the stockholding that may result. Another example is the need for investment to increase plant capacity against the need to house it in a new building because existing ones are full.

- Simple repetitive tasks in mass manufacturing are more likely to lead factories down the cost experience curve (*see* Chapter 13).

9.4.4 Product design prior to manufacturing

In some cases, up to 70 per cent of the cost of manufacturing a product is determined at the design stage – that is, before the product ever reaches the factory.[41] The reason is that it is at the design stage that major savings can be made on components, plant and procedures. It is more difficult to make them once products have reached the factory floor because of the inflexibility of installed machinery and the high cost of changing over time.

Design procedures might include analysing the product for the *number of parts* it contains: the smaller the number, the quicker it will be to assemble. Procedures might also cover *methods of assembling the product*. For example, by careful design, it may be possible to put the product together without using a machine to grip or hold the product (commonly called a *jig*). The advantage of such a procedure is that any variation in the product might otherwise involve resetting the jig, which takes unproductive time and adds no value to the product. Clearly, the detail of such procedures is not part of corporate strategy but the *principle* of careful and adequate expenditure on design is vital.

In addition, efficiency in the design procedures themselves has become an important element in the process. It can take years to design some products with all the consequent costs involved. If time can be saved, this reduces the cost of the process. For example, Renault Cars (France) announced a new design and development facility in 1995 costing US$1.22 billion.[42] The aim was to reduce design time from 58 months to 38 months for a new car launch in the year 2000. The facility's current cost per car was between US$1 and 5 billion, depending on the model: this would be reduced by US$200 million per model simply by producing each design more quickly.

Again, analysis of this topic needs a study of *competition*. For example, Renault may have invested a large absolute amount in design but comparison with the amounts invested by other car companies would:

● show whether it would improve the French company's competitive position; or

● simply mean that Renault was catching up with others, especially some Japanese car companies.

9.4.5 Factory layout and procedures

Within an existing factory installation, it is possible to make substantial cost savings and other improvements by changes in the factory layout. For example, Case study 9.2 showed how changes in factory procedures at Toyota could have a dramatic effect on production costs.

9.4.6 Logistics and transport

Once the product is ready to leave the factory, there are further decisions on two areas:

1 *Logistics* – where to hold the finished product, in what quantity and with what delivery schedule to customers.

2 *Transport* – what product to send, in what economic delivery quantity, by what transport method and from what location.

Essentially, these decisions involve a balance between the customers, who might like small amounts of the product frequently, and the costs involved in such lengthy and detailed procedures. According to Christopher,[43] there are five basic elements to balance in the analytical process:

1 *Facility decisions*. These involve deciding where warehouses and factories are to be located. Clearly, this is a long-term issue.

2 *Inventory decisions*. Stockholding has a cost but may be necessary to provide adequate customer service.

3 *Communications decisions*. Information is essential to deliver the correct goods to the customer. Thus, ordering, processing and invoicing goods all form part of the essential information. A system for handling normal customer queries and complaints is also needed.

4 *Utilisation decisions*. Pallets, containers and other means of transporting the goods need to be resolved.

5 *Transport decisions*. The method of transport, ownership, leasing or hiring of vehicles all need resolution; the choice of road, rail, ship and air may all be key decisions.

As Lynch comments,[44] the balance of these issues will vary with the type of industry, as well as with the customer. It will also depend on competitors and the level of service that they are offering. Industry distribution costs for the above have been published and provide a basis for comparison for national and international expansion.

9.4.7 Lean Thinking[45]

Deriving many of its principles from studies of car companies like Toyota, *Lean Thinking* has become a well-established part of operations strategy. The underlying

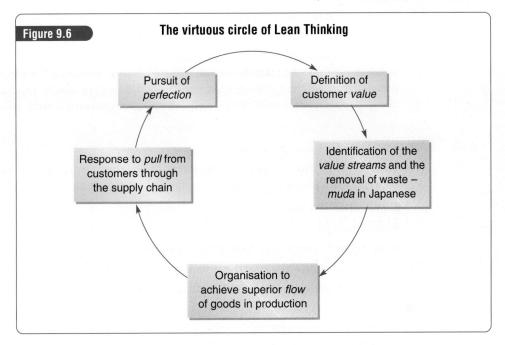

Figure 9.6 — **The virtuous circle of Lean Thinking**

concept is one of *value*, as perceived by the customer and defined by the performance of the product. Competitive advantage derives from the application by managers of the five Lean Thinking principles (*see* Figure 9.6) which will deliver superior value to customers and superior profits to companies. The word 'lean' is used to emphasise the rational concentration on the essentials and the trimming of all waste in the development of operations strategy. The concepts of value and the value chain were explored in Chapter 6, but need to be reconsidered here from the perspective of the value delivered to the *customer*. The other concepts are explored elsewhere in this chapter.

9.4.8 Human resource implications

When the Norwegian engineering company Kvaerner acquired the Govan shipyard in Scotland in 1988, it needed to boost productivity dramatically.[46] Part of the change came through the investment of US$52 million in the yard by the new owners. However, just as important, the company introduced new procedures for working that involved many of the concepts described above. They involved:

- devolved responsibility;
- frequent progress reports to management on progress;
- improved internal communications;
- changed staff attitudes;
- shared responsibility and commitment;
- joint management and workers' committee to monitor progress.

In each of the cases, there was a significant human resource element that needed to be analysed during the formative phase of the corporate strategy process. The impact on workers, their attitudes and the degree of co-operation required are all important elements to be estimated in assessing the feasibility of strategy. Specifically, worker participation is a key element in many aspects of manufacturing strategy.

9.4.9 International manufacturing

Manufacturing strategies have been developed that cover *regions* of the world, such as the North American Free Trade Area, Association of South-East Asian Nations and the European Union. As an example of pan-regional activity, the *European single market* was designed to help deliver economies of scale, reduce excess production capacity, integrate operations across the EU and deliver significant cost savings to companies.

9.4.10 Conclusions

There are some broader lessons to be learned from the research. The increased standard-isation has allowed some companies to tackle such problems as:

- overcapacity in production;
- stock reduction;
- critical production mass from fewer locations;
- more efficient transport and logistics operations;
- better planning, processes and procedures.

To summarise operations strategy, there are ten guidelines for analysing the operations and technology manufacturing strategies of organisations. These are shown in Exhibit 9.1.

Exhibit 9.1

Ten guidelines for analysing operations and technology manufacturing strategy

1 Does the company buy or make all its supplies? How do competitors handle this decision?

2 What relationship does the company have with its suppliers? Distant or close? Why?

3 Where is value added in the production process? What stage of the production process is really important? How does this compare with competition?

4 What is the role of technology? High? Low? What investment normally takes place in R & D? How does this compare with competition?

5 How does at least one competitor organise its production? What factories? Stock levels? Age of factories, plant and machinery? Investment programmes? Comparative costs?

6 How is production organised in our own factories? What factories and departments? What machines and workflow? How old are the machines and what is their capacity? What costs of production? How do the organisation, its machinery and costs compare with competition?

7 How are stocks organised and controlled? Before, during and after production? How does competition organise this area?

8 What is the style of operation? Centre-dominated? Workplace and co-operative?

9 How are links organised with other departments? Are they good or poor?

10 Is there organised labour? And what is its role and style? Co-operation or conflict?

🔴 Key strategic principles

- Before starting on a detailed analysis of manufacturing strategy, it is useful to establish what areas are particularly important. Six tests can be employed to assist this process but it is essentially a question of judgement.

> ▶ *Key strategic principles continued*
>
> ● Whether a company makes or buys in its products will depend on the balance between the costs and benefits of the two routes. It is useful to explore what competitors do in this area.
>
> ● Supplier relationships can be close or distant. This will depend on the company's basic management style and culture. There are no conclusive reasons for choosing one approach.
>
> ● Manufacturing strategy is complex and depends on a number of interrelated factors: factory location, size, production capacity and infrastructure. In addition, links with other functions such as sales are important in determining both efficiencies and customer service. Comparison with competition is an important element in the analysis.
>
> ● With many products, greater cost savings are achieved during the design stage of the process than during the subsequent procedures. Expenditure in this area usually has a clear positive payback. Competitor expenditure and effort in this area needs also to be analysed.
>
> ● Factory layout and procedures need to be governed by attention to detail and co-operation with the workforce. Coupled with specific techniques, the corporate strategy interest lies mainly in initiating the task rather than in the detail that follows.
>
> ● Logistics and transport need careful planning, both to reduce costs and to provide adequate service to customers. The level of service that competitors offer will be a factor in deciding the optimal configuration.
>
> ● The human resource implications of all the above need to be considered during the analysis phase of corporate strategy, not later.

CASE STUDY 9.3

Cost reduction strategy at Bajaj, the India-based motorcycle maker

Bajaj Motor is India's biggest scooter and motorcycle manufacturer, yet it faces intense competition from some of the world's leading scooter and motorcyle manufacturers. This case explores how it was using supplier strategies originally developed by General Motors (US) to reduce its costs and remain competitive.

In 1998, Bajaj Motor – India's biggest scooter and motorcycle manufacturer – was struggling to shake off a strong challenge from Honda, Suzuki and Piaggio in its home market. The family-owned company, which lacks the technological resources of its competitors, had to compensate by watching its expenses. 'We must remain the lowest cost producer in the world,' says Rahul Bajaj, the chairman.

But no matter how hard Bajaj tries to control costs and improve productivity at its plants near Pune, in West India, the incrememental savings are a sliver of the sale price of its bikes. This is because most of the costs are incurred before the components enter Bajaj's factory gates. 'In-house costs make up about 10 to 12 per cent of the sales price,' says Sangiv Bajaj, Rahul Bajaj's younger son and general manager of corporate finance. Advertising and distribution costs account for a further 3 to 4 per cent. By contrast, 'about 65 per cent of the sales price comes from costs outside our direct control'. This can rise to 75 per

▶

cent for new models. Bajaj has recently realised that further big cost savings are more likely to come from its suppliers than from the manufacturing process.

GM-style supplier management

Sangiv Bajaj is heading an effort to introduce US-style supply chain management, using General Motors as a model. It is a task for which he is well suited. A trained engineer, he went into the finance department because his elder brother, Rajiv, had already been groomed to take over the core manufacturing responsibilities. 'I am in the wrong job,' he jokes. But in this instance, engineering expertise helps him to understand where costs can be trimmed.

Bajaj, which produces 1.3 million vehicles a year, has about 900 direct tier-1 suppliers. According to the GM model, it should have 80. Many of them are small, low-technology, family-run businesses with poor productivity and slack quality control.

'We need to identify who the good vendors are, reduce the number of vendors and give them a bigger share of the pie,' says Sangiv Bajaj. Then, he adds, the company will try to negotiate lower prices for higher volumes. As in the case of GM, Bajaj hopes to work with its suppliers to improve 'quality and reliability'. The company aims to help its chosen suppliers invest in new equipment and improve productivity over the long term, bearing in mind 'our future requirements'.

Bajaj has followed GM principles by dividing its suppliers into different categories: those that own specialist knowledge and provide it in the form of proprietary items such as headlamps; those that provide model design parts on the basis of knowledge passed on by Bajaj; those that provide basic nuts and bolts hardware; and non-core product suppliers.

It has also set out four issues to be looked at with its suppliers: the 'make-or-buy' decisions that determine which products a customer buys, issues pertinent to each component sector, a vendor rating system, and a vendor integration programme to introduce quality control systems used by Bajaj to its suppliers.

Difficulties with applying US-style strategy

But this is where the similarity with GM ends. 'You can't use textbook theories,' says Sangiv Bajaj. 'In India you have to consider questions like labour and power supply.' Unlike GM, Bajaj cannot afford to rely on only one supplier for a particular part because its operations would be paralysed if that supplier's workers went on strike – a common occurrence in India's highly unionised manufacturing industry. Similarly, having just one supplier would be risky because its output could be disrupted by power shortages, another regular occurrence. It makes sense to have suppliers in different areas, since simultaneous power failures are less likely.

Bajaj also has to wrestle with problems such as India's poor road system, which affects distribution and makes location important. Few Indian suppliers could shoulder the responsibilities GM puts on its US suppliers. There are also issues that relate specifically to components. 'Two of our three suppliers of shock absorbers are subsidiaries of competitors,' says Sangiv Bajaj. 'Long term this is questionable.' The company may opt to build up a third supplier in a relationship of 'interdependence'.

Rationalising the supply chain will take several years. When it is completed, Bajaj will still have far more suppliers than the GM model suggests it should. Sangiv Bajaj talks of '200, 300 or 400', though he says the company will decide the final figure 'from the bottom up'.

Bajaj hopes this will produce costs savings and quality improvements that will help compete against world-class products in an increasingly discerning market. It remains to be seen whether this will be enough. Bajaj will also have to match Honda and its other rivals in design, engine technology and marketing. But better management of its suppliers, while not guaranteeing success, is likely to be a necessary requirement for it.

This case has been adapted from Krishna, G (1998), 'India's scooter giant seeks US style kickstart', *Financial Times*, 6 July, p15. © *Financial Times* 1998. Used with permission.

Case questions

1 *What are the main problems facing Bajaj Motor? To what extent are they related to operations issues?*

2 *Is it possible or even realistic to employ US-style operations strategies in a country where the suppliers present rather different problems from those experienced in the US?*

3 *Can you think of any other options to assist Bajaj develop its strategy beyond supply chain issues? What are the problems and opportunities with such options?*

4 *What lessons can companies draw from the experience of Bajaj on the application of the strategic issues outlined in this chapter?*

9.5 Service operations strategy

A survey of research published in the area of operations strategy[47] seemed to show that most of the research has concentrated on *manufacturing* strategy – that is, strategy concerned with making products in factories – and yet, in 1989, *services* such as telecommunications, travel and banking accounted for almost 50 per cent of the gross domestic product of Japan and the EU and 54 per cent in the US.[48] Moreover, the services sector continued to grow faster than manufacturing.

From an operations strategy perspective, the difficulty is that services have a number of major differences from products. For example:

- *Retail banking counter services* depend heavily on the performance of the employees behind the counter at the time of the service. The employees are part of the product.
- *Rail commuter services* cannot be stored as finished goods in a warehouse.

Service operations involve people and immediate responses that need special consideration when it comes to operations strategy development.

9.5.1 Services and products compared

Although there are differences in *nature* between products and services, it is important to keep this in perspective, since there are likely to be service elements in the supply of most products. The service content might range from a pre-sales personalised training course to an after-sales maintenance contract. From the extensive research on services marketing, five main differences between services and products have been identified and these are outlined in Table 9.2.[49] In addition to the five distinguishing features at the point of service, there will also be various *tangible* elements that are clearly product-oriented. For example, telephone lines, hotel beds, hospital reception areas and advertising agency studios are physical areas that are part of the service. These areas are part of the operation. They can be quantified and be the subject of a normal manufacturing-type analysis – for example, a stock analysis.

9.5.2 The value chain in operations services

It is now possible to examine how the value chain will change for services operations (*see* Figure 9.7). Many of the early operations aspects do not change radically. For example, there is still a need to obtain raw materials and also likely to be a requirement for after-sales service, albeit of a different kind. In truth, many service businesses rely heavily on *repeat business*, in just the same way as many products. This directs the operations task closer to that of products than might otherwise be the case.

9.5.3 Implications for the analysis of service operations strategy

With the growing importance of service industries, the detail of their operations strategy needs careful analysis. It will be evident that many of the early aspects of the analysis are not significantly different from manufacturing: at least the same elements apply in principle. Where services differ is in *the direct customer interface*. It is here that operations need to be redefined.

Table 9.2 The five main differences between services and products

Distinguishing features at the point of service	Description	Example	Impact on operations strategic analysis
Intangibility	● Cannot be seen or tasted like a product	● Bank counter service ● Airline booking	● More difficult to define but important for setting standards. Hence, difficult to analyse
Inseparability	● Cannot be separated from the person of the seller ● Consuming and selling may be undertaken at virtually the same time	● Telephone selling of car insurance ● McDonald's 'Big Mac'	● High reliance on the people delivering the service ● Need for careful selection and training
Heterogeneity	● Difficult to standardise service output ● Reliant on human element	● Hospital in-patient care ● Reception welcome at Holiday Inns Hotel	● Decision on whether it is necessary, desirable or even possible to standardise service
Perishability	● Services cannot be stored	● Empty hotel room ● Telephone call not made	● Concept of stock may be irrelevant ● Strategy needs to address issue of immediate utilisation of service
Ownership	● Customer may not own what is being consumed	● Cinema, night club, football stadium	● No physical need for logistics and transport

From a competitive strategy perspective, we should also note that service has become an increasingly strong element in manufacturing strategy. This is not a new idea. As Levitt[50] observed in 1972:

> There is no such thing as service industries. There are only industries whose service components are greater or less than those of other industries. Everybody is in service.

This has important implications for corporate strategy for three reasons:

1 Operations needs to consider carefully the service requirements of its customers. If the service is to run smoothly, there needs to be a direct link connecting production to the customer. Such an arrangement has to be part of the organisation's strategy.

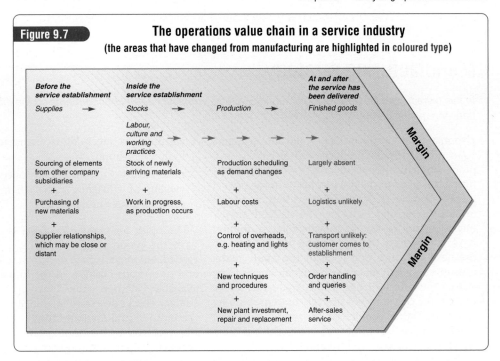

Figure 9.7 **The operations value chain in a service industry**
(the areas that have changed from manufacturing are highlighted in coloured type)

2 One way of enhancing sustainable competitive advantage might be to strengthen the service element associated with a product – for example, more comprehensive after-sales and follow-up.

3 In those markets that have become increasingly global, one defence strategy is to offer higher levels of service. The reason is that, almost by definition, services are difficult to offer from a distance. They are best delivered locally. The cost and local knowledge required to set up and maintain such services will benefit the national operator against the global organisation.

Overall, the whole approach to service is likely to need an increased reliance on human resources and investment in training and education if it is to be successful.

Key strategic principles

● The people element and the need for immediate responses mean that services need special consideration from operations.

● There are five main points of difference between products and services that have implications for operations analysis: intangibility, inseparability, heterogeneity, perishability, ownership.

● Nevertheless, there are many points of similarity along the value chain for both products and services, so many of the same basic principles apply to both areas.

● Even in manufacturing strategy, services have become an increasingly strong element in the overall mix. They may provide a means to support and enhance competitive advantage.

Manufacturing strategy

In this extract from his book Manufacturing Strategy, *Professor Terry Hill comments on the interface between manufacturing strategy and corporate strategy.*

Companies invest in processes and infrastructure in order to make products and sell them at a profit. Consequently, the degree to which manufacturing is aligned to the product needs in the market place will make a significant contribution to the overall success of a business. The size and fundamental nature of the manufacturing contribution is such, however, that the wrong fit will lead to the business being well wide of the mark. Many executives are still unaware that what appear to be routine manufacturing decisions frequently come to limit the corporation's strategic options, binding it with facilities, equipment, personnel and basic controls and policies to a non-competitive posture which may take years to turn around.

The reason for this is that companies, having invested inappropriately in process and infrastructure, cannot afford to reinvest to put things right. The financial implications, systems development, training requirements and the time it would take to make the changes would leave it, at best, seriously disadvantaged.

In the past, manufacturing's role in terms of its corporate contribution has been perceived by the company as a whole as being the provider of requests. The corporate strategy debate has stopped short of discussing the implications of decisions in terms of manufacturing. And this has been based on two incorrect assumptions, that:

1 within a given technology, manufacturing is able to do everything;

2 manufacturing's contribution concerns the achievement of efficiency, rather than the effective support of the business needs.

The result for many companies is that not only have the profit margins they once enjoyed been eroded, but also the base on which to build a sound and prosperous business in the future is no longer available. Without the frequent manufacturing strategy checks necessary to evaluate the fit between the business and manufacturing's ability to provide the necessary order-winning criteria of its various products, then the absence of these essential insights leaves a business vulnerable and exposed.

In times of increased world competition, being left behind can be sudden and fatal. In many cases, averting the end is the only option left. Turning the business around, however, will only be achieved by switching from an operational to a strategic mode, and one which will require a corporate review of the marketing and manufacturing perspectives involved in the alternatives to be considered and the financial implications of the proposals involved.

Source: Extracted from Hill, T (1993) *Manufacturing Strategy*, 2nd edn, Macmillan, London, pp25, 56–7. Reproduced with permission of Palgrave Macmillan.

Summary

● Operations includes raw materials sourcing, purchasing, production and manufacturing, distribution and logistics. Its coverage of the organisation's resources is therefore wide and comprehensive. Its importance in the strategic process is in delivering sustainable competitive advantage and in providing co-ordinated support for products – that is, every aspect of order handling, delivery and service to the customer – so that sales orders can be won by the organisation.

● There are two major constraints on operations:

  1 they take time to plan and build; and
  2 once installed, they are expensive to change.

These constraints mean that great care needs to be taken in arriving at the optimal strategy. The analytical process that accompanies such considerations will need to examine *where* and *how value is added* in the operations process from raw materials arriving at the factory gate through to finished goods being shipped to the final customer.

● It is evident from any analysis of the operations environment that the pace of technological change has clearly increased. Major changes in technology, often called *discontinuities*, also deserve careful analysis, as does global activity, particularly where it is aimed at cost reduction through the use of low-cost labour.

● Value added is an important part of the analytical process. It is likely to occur in the following areas:

1 adapting products to meet customer needs;
2 delivering better products than competitors;
3 adding value through enhanced performance or quality;
4 cutting the costs of manufacture.

The methods of achieving operations strategy involve both human resource considerations and the link between manufacturing and marketing. Such approaches are major contributors to the sustainable competitive advantage of the organisation.

● In any detailed analysis of operations strategies, part of the problem is the size and complexity of the resources under consideration. Tests can be applied to identify the major factors affecting the achievement of corporate objectives, adding value and the critical success factors identified for an industry. In addition to these basic procedures, operations strategy needs to examine nine strategy areas:

1 make-or-buy decisions
2 supplier relationships
3 manufacturing strategy
4 product design prior to manufacture
5 factory layout and procedures
6 logistics and transport
7 Lean Thinking
8 human resources implications
9 international manufacturing.

When analysing organisations involved primarily in services, such as banking or travel, some special considerations apply. Services are different in five areas: intangibility, inseparability, heterogeneity, perishability and ownership. However, they still cover areas that have much in common with manufacturing – for example, raw materials, supplier relationships, stocks and work in progress.

● In practice, service has become an increasingly strong element in manufacturing strategy. Service usually needs to be delivered locally, and as a result this has provided some protection against increased globalisation of manufacturing. More generally, service is heavily reliant on human resources and investment in training and education.

QUESTIONS

1 Operations strategy has made major contributions to corporate profitability over the last 20 years, yet has not always featured in some descriptions of corporate strategy. What are the reasons given in the chapter for this? Do you think that they are likely to continue to apply over the next few years?

2 Hill contends that manufacturing strategy needs to be led by changes in customer demand. If this is the case, how is it possible to develop products that are revolutionary in their technology and essentially unknown to the customer?

3 The chapter argues that the low-cost-labour strategies of some developing countries can be offset by more sophisticated operations strategies in Western countries. If you were managing a Western company, what type of manufacturing would you seek to keep in the West and what would you move to a developing country?

4 In Section 9.4, the comment is made that some detailed operations decisions are more likely to be outside the scope of corporate strategy. For each *element* of Section 9.4, explain the extent to which corporate strategy is involved and the extent to which it is not.

5 Analyse the world car industry for the contribution that operations strategy has made to the corporate strategies of companies in these industries. Comment also on the future potential of operations strategy in these industries. Use the references at the end of this chapter to assist the process.

6 Operations strategy has become more international over the last 20 years. Do you think this trend will be reflected in services? What are the problems in the services area?

7 Apply the ten guidelines for analysing operations to an organisation of your choice. What are the implications of your analysis for corporate strategy?

8 *'Design is a strategic activity whether by intention or default.'* (Daniel Whitney) Discuss.

STRATEGIC PROJECT International engineering companies

This chapter has taken several examples of international computer and car companies and shown how they have used operations to improve their overall strategic capability: Dell and Toyota are examples. You might like to take this further. For example, what new production procedures have been introduced at the Japanese car company Nissan after the French company Renault began to take a controlling interest? What happened to profitability? Has it picked up as a result? The book's website will provide some suitable references here.

FURTHER READING

Slack, N, Chambers, S, Harland, C, Harrison, A and Johnston, R (1998) *Operations Management*, 2nd edn, Pitman Publishing, London, is a comprehensive text, clearly written and presented. This book explores manufacturing issues in further detail.

Hill, T (1993) *Manufacturing strategy*, 2nd edn, Macmillan, Basingstoke. This is a clear, basic text that is well referenced and directed at exploring corporate strategy issues.

For an exploration of the future of manufacturing strategy in the car industry, read: Special Report – Car Manufacturing, *The Economist*, 23 February 2002, pp99–101, which contains many useful insights and is clearly written.

Harrison, M (1993) *Operations Management Strategy*, Pitman Publishing, London. This is thoughtful and has useful academic references.

Whitney, D (1988) 'Manufacturing by design', *Harvard Business Review*, July–Aug. This explores some of the areas outlined in the chapter, especially concentrating on the strategic implications of design and technology.

Womack, J P and Jones, D T (1996) *Lean Thinking*, Simon & Schuster, New York. This is an excellent text on exploring the strategic shift required in operations (much better than the earlier text involving these authors, *The Machine that Changed the World*). If you read this, then you should also consider reading the critical appraisal of the approach: Piercy, N F and Morgan, N A (1997) 'The impact of Lean Thinking and the Lean Enterprise on marketing', *Journal of Marketing Management*, 7, Oct, pp679–94.

NOTES & REFERENCES

1 Sources for Dell Computer Case 9.1: *Dell Computer Company Annual Report and Accounts 1999–2001; Financial Times*, 16 February 2001, p13; 2 April 2002, p22.

2 Hill, T (1993) *Manufacturing Strategy*, 2nd edn, Macmillan, Basingstoke, p18.

3 Hayes, R H and Upton, D (1998) 'Operations-based strategy', *California Management Review*, 40(4), pp8–25. This article provides further extensive examples, particularly of smaller companies that have been successful.

4 Urwick, L (1956) *The Golden Book of Management*, Newman Neame, London.

5 Mumford, E (1996) 'Restructuring: values, visions, viability', *Financial Times*, 9 Apr, p12. A really interesting article on the history of this subject.

6 Kennedy, P (1989) *The Rise and Fall of the Great Powers*, Fontana, London, p259.

7 Hill, T (1993) Op. cit., Ch1.

8 Lorenz, C (1991) 'Competition intensifies in the fast track', *Financial Times*, 28 June.

9 Strebel, P (1992) *Breakpoints*, Harvard Business School Press, Boston, MA, Chs1 and 2.

10 World Bank Report (1991), *Trade and Industry Logistics in Developing Countries*, H J Peter.

11 Kennedy, P (1989) Op. cit., p535.

12 Wong Poh Kam (1991) *ASEAN and the EC*, ASEAN Economic Research Unit, Singapore, pp170 *et seq.*

13 Three useful articles here from Tim Burt and David Ibison on *Toyota, Parts 1, 2 and 3: Financial Times*, 12 December 2001, p16, 13 December 2001, p13 and 14 December 2001, p15.

14 Williams, K, Haslam, C, Johal, S and Williams, J (1994) *Cars: Analysis, History and Cases*, Berghahn, Providence, RI, p108. *See also* the graphic account of the early Toyota years in Womack, J P and Jones, D T (1996) *Lean Thinking*, Simon & Schuster, New York, Ch10. Riveting story, well told.

15 Toyota (1994) *Annual Report and Accounts*, p11 (English language version).

16 Williams, K *et al* (1994) Op. cit., p118.

17 Gourlay, J (1994) 'Back to basics on the factory floor', *Financial Times*, 4 Jan, p7.

18 Griffiths, J (1993) 'Driving out the old regime', *Financial Times*, 20 Aug, p8.

19 Williams, K *et al* (1994) Op. cit., p115.

20 Griffiths, J (1995) '£200m Toyota expansion may create 3,000 jobs', *Financial Times*, 17 Mar, p9.

21 Hartley, J (1981) *The Management of Vehicle Production*, Butterworth, London.

22 Womack, J, Jones, D and Roos, D (1990) *The Machine that Changed the World*, Rawson Associates, New York.

23 Williams, K *et al* (1994) Op. cit., p115.

24 Sobek, D K, Liker, J K and Ward, A K (1998) 'Another look at how Toyota integrates product development', *Harvard Business Review*, July–Aug, pp36–50. A good description of the importance of management and human resource strengths that make Toyota so difficult for other companies to copy.

25 Butler, S (1992) 'Driven back to basics', *Financial Times*, 16 July, p16.

26 Toyota (1994) *Annual Report and Accounts*, p1 (English language version).

27 Womack, J P and Jones, D T (1996) Op. cit., p241.

28 Ibison, D (2002), 'Toyota plans to challenge US dominance', *Financial Times*, 2 April, p24.

29 Burt, T. and Ibison, D (2001) 'PSA welcomes Toyota as latest co-driver', *Financial Times*, 9 July, p29.

30 Burt, T (2001) 'A pace-setter gears up for growth', *Financial Times*, 24 September, p15. Interview with Toyota company chairman, Hiroshi Okuda.

31 Hill, T (1991) *Production and Operations Management*, 2nd edn, Prentice Hall, Hemel Hempstead.

32 Wild, R (1984) *Production and Operations Management*, 3rd edn, Holt, Reinhart and Winston, New York.

33 Hill, T (1993) Op. cit., Ch2.

34 Hill, T (1993) Op. cit., p36. (*See also* pp55 and 56 for further clarification of these matters.)

35 *See also* Hill, T and Westbrook, R (1997) 'The strategic development of manufacturing: market analysis for investment priorities', *European Management Journal*, 15(3), pp296–302.

36 Hill, T (1991) Op. cit.

37 *See*, for example, Cusumano, M and Takeishi, A (1991) 'Supplier relations and management; a survey of Japanese, Japanese-transplant and US auto plants', *Strategic Management Journal*, 12, pp563–88. Also Macduff, J P and Helper, S (1997) 'Creating lean suppliers: diffusing lean production throughout the supply chain', *California Management Review*, 39(4) pp118–51.

38 Marsh, P (1995) 'Car mirror rivalry turns cut-throat', *Financial Times*, 14 June, p10.

39 Hill, T (1991) Op. cit.

40 Skinner, W (1974) 'The focused factory', *Harvard Business Review*, May–June.

41 Whitney, D (1988) 'Manufacturing by design', *Harvard Business Review*, July–Aug, p83.

42 Ridding, J (1995) 'Renault unveils plant to speed launches', *Financial Times*, 17 Feb, p24.

43 Christopher, M (1992) *Logistics and Supply Chain Management*, Pitman, London. (*See* also Christopher, M (1993) 'Logistics and competitive strategy', *European Management Journal*, June, pp258–61.)

44 Lynch, R (1992) *European Marketing*, Kogan Page, London, p214.

45 Womack, J P and Jones, D T (1996) *Lean Thinking*, Simon & Schuster, New York. This section largely derives from this text. But note that most of the examples come from slowly growing markets – prescriptive approaches. An excellent critique of the 'Lean Thinking' approach is contained in Piercy, N F and Morgan, N A (1997) referenced in the Further Reading section above.

46 Carnegy, H (1995) 'Time to chart a different course', *Financial Times*, 7 Aug, p9.

47 Adam, E A and Swamidass, P M (1989) 'Assessing operations management from the strategic perspective', reprinted as Ch19 in Voss, C (1992) *Manufacturing Strategy – Process and Content*, Chapman and Hall, London.

48 *See* 'Can Europe compete?', *Financial Times*, 1 Mar 1994, p14.

49 *See*, for example, Cowell, D (1984) *The Marketing of Services*, Heinemann Professional, Oxford, Ch2.

50 Levitt, T (1972) 'Production line approach to service', *Harvard Business Review*, Sep–Oct, pp41–52.

The purpose of the organisation

It is impossible to develop corporate strategy without first establishing the general direction of the organisation. Building on the analyses of the organisation's environment and resources, this part of the book now explores the purpose of the organisation. It explores purpose from three perspectives: how purpose is shaped by vision, leadership and ethics; how purpose emerges from knowledge, technology and innovation; and how purpose is delivered through the organisation's mission and objectives.

The mission and objectives of the organisation are developed in the context of the organisation's stakeholders. In a prescriptive approach, they are likely to be defined in general terms for some years to come. In an emergent approach and in turbulent markets, they will be more fluid and contingent upon unfolding events.

The purpose of the organisation

The *prescriptive* strategic process

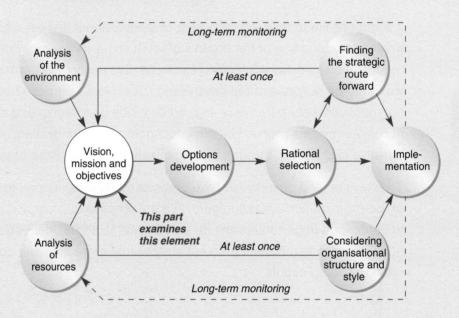

The *emergent* strategic process

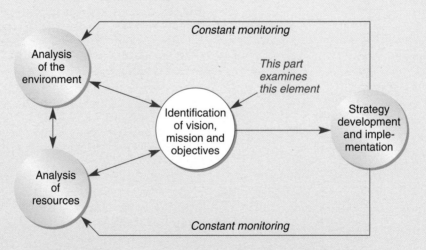

Chapter 10

Purpose shaped by vision, leadership and ethics

- *How is purpose shaped by the organisation?*
- *What vision does the organisation have for its future? What does this mean for purpose?*
- *How does leadership shape purpose?*
- *What are the organisation's views on ethical issues? How will they affect purpose?*
- *What is the relationship between purpose and the corporate governance of the organisation?*

Chapter 11

Purpose emerging from knowledge, technology and innovation

- *What knowledge does the organisation possess? How can it create and share new knowledge? What will be the impact on the organisation's purpose?*
- *What are the strategic implications of new technologies?*
- *Can innovation contribute to the organisation's purpose? If so, how?*

Chapter 12

Purpose delivered by mission and objectives

- *What is the purpose of the organisation?*
- *Who are the stakeholders in the organisation and what do they want from it?*
- *What is the organisation's mission?*
- *What are the objectives of the organisation?*
- *How is purpose defined and developed in conglomerates? Does purpose need to be focused?*
- *What is the organisation's policy on quality?*

Chapter 10

Purpose shaped by vision, leadership and ethics

Learning outcomes

When you have worked through this chapter, you will be able to:

- outline the main considerations in the development of purpose;
- explore the organisation's vision for the future and its strategic implications;
- explain the contribution of leadership to the development of corporate strategy;
- identify the three main approaches to leadership analysis and explain why the contingency approach is the most useful from a corporate strategy perspective;
- identify the main areas of the ethical considerations that surround the organisation;
- outline the chief areas of corporate governance that will influence corporate strategy and decision making at the centre of the organisation;
- show how all these areas shape the purpose of the organisation.

Figure 10.1   **The purpose of the organisation: shaped by vision, leadership and ethics**

▬ Introduction

In developing the purpose of the organisation, there is a need to stand back and consider why the organisation exists, who it is meant to serve and how its value added should be generated and distributed. In addition, it is important to take the process beyond the current horizons and explore future opportunities and challenges. Some may conclude that the future is too turbulent to predict and therefore the result is worthless. However, in many strategic situations, this will not be the case, even in turbulent markets. The purpose of the organisation and its vision for the future will set the boundaries and stretch the organisation as it develops its mission and objectives.

There are two additional areas that will help shape the purpose of the organisation and deserve early examination in its development. These are: the leadership of the organisation and the ethical policies that it will pursue. Ethics covers not only the general conduct of the organisation but also the specific activities of its senior managers – called the corporate governance of the organisation. These are considered in this chapter before we return to the issues of value added and competitive advantage and examine their relationships with purpose. These areas are shown in Figure 10.1.

CASE STUDY 10.1

DaimlerChrysler: flawed vision or just unlucky?

In 1998, the Daimler-Benz takeover of the Chrysler car company was presented as the beginning of a new, truly global car operation. By the beginning of 2002, DaimlerChrysler had become loss-making after exceptional items. The global vision of the Daimler chairman, Jürgen Schrempp, had turned distinctly cloudy. Was his vision fundamentally flawed? Or was he just unlucky?

Daimler-Benz: focus on cars and trucks

When Jürgen Schrempp took over as chairman of Daimler-Benz in 1995, the German group lacked focus strategically. It had the benefit of the well-regarded and highly profitable Daimler-Benz car and truck range. However, it also contained a loss-making aircraft manufacturing subsidiary, Fokker, and numerous other subsidiaries making everything from traffic lights to freezer cabinets: many of these units also had low profitability. Mr Schrempp rescued the group by focusing on the car and truck business and selling the rest. But his vision went further than merely developing a profitable German transport manufacturing operation. He wanted to build a global car and truck company. After considering various possibilities (including the acquisition of the car company Nissan), Mr Schrempp did the deal in 1998 that would in his words 'change the face of the industry forever'. Daimler-Benz bought the company that was third in the American market, Chrysler, for US$38 billion.

Takeover of Chrysler: the euphoria of 1998

During the 1990s, the former chairman of Chrysler, Bob Eaton, and his team turned the company from being the sick man of the US car industry into one of its most profitable companies. This was done by focusing on niche markets, like those for sports utility vehicles and minivans, and avoiding the low-profit mass car manufacture of its rivals, General Motors and Ford. The result was that the company was highly valued on the US stock exchange when Daimler-Benz began negotiations in 1998. Chrysler was eventually sold for US$38 billion – arguably, the company did a good deal by selling at what turned out to be the peak of Chrysler's profitability to date.

Daimler-Benz was very happy with the price of its North American purchase. The chairman, Jürgen Schrempp, commented: 'We'll have the size, profitability and the reach to take on everyone.' Initially, after its purchase, the deal was presented as a merger between equals. For nearly a year,

▶

Chrysler was largely left to manage itself in the North American market. Daimler pursued its global ambitions by buying 34 per cent of the Japanese car company Mitsubishi and taking a 10 per cent stake in the Korean car company Hyundai. Daimler also acquired further companies to support its truck interests in North America and elsewhere.

Downturn in 2000: the group in trouble

Unfortunately, although the German Daimler operation remained highly profitable, the acquisitions started to go wrong. Chrysler was forced to lower its prices to clear old models; new sports utility and minivans were launched by rival companies; new Chrysler models were slow to appear and expensive to launch. At the same time, Daimler-Benz realised that the benefits of globalisation – greater economies of scale, shared research and development costs – could not be achieved if Chrysler was allowed to operate completely on its own. Integration was needed. In addition, the company culture of the German parent – technocratic, planned and precise – was at odds with the Chrysler culture – free wheeling, opportunistic and informal.

The 'merger between equals' rapidly became a straight takeover. Eaton and other senior colleagues left the company and Daimler-Benz put in its own top management team. The German company was determined to combine operations, cut costs and return to high profits.

Economic downturn in 2001

But still things did not improve. The American economy turned down, so people delayed car purchases. The German economy itself was also in trouble, though the Daimler-Benz brand in Germany remained profitable and helped to keep the business afloat – see Figure 10.2. However, the losses deepened at Chrysler and dramatic new measures were needed. After careful study by the new German senior management team, it was announced that Chrysler would seek to cut its supplier costs by 15 per cent, it would close six plants and cut its workforce by 26 000. Dieter Zetsche, the new German boss at Chrysler, explained: 'We are not starting from a favourable position. The strategy of this company was based on growing overall market share and charging high revenues per car through content per vehicle.

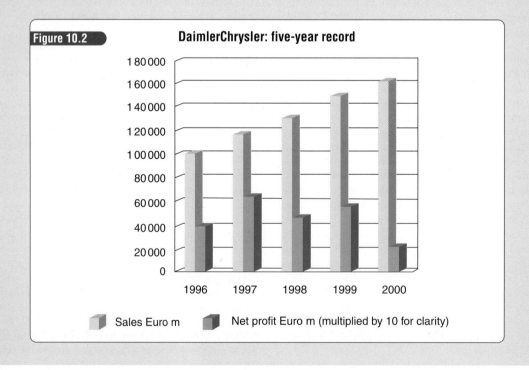

Figure 10.2 DaimlerChrysler: five-year record

That allowed for pretty aggressive cost increases in fixed and variable costs. If you put that in a situation where markets are shrinking and where pricing developments are negative, you find a tremendous mismatch between the internal and external environments.' However, the company could hardly be blamed for the downturn in the North American economy that had brought about such difficult economic conditions. Its Japanese operations were also showing a loss, partly at least because of the poor Japanese economy. Again, this was arguably not the fault of the company.

Difficulties remained in 2002

By 2002, Daimler-Benz was still in trouble. The problems were so bad that the company was forced to declare a loss after taking into account exceptional items. It had to reduce its dividend for the first time for many years and said that it would take much longer to turn around its North American and other operations.

The global vision had become clouded, at least temporarily: 'The first year almost was tremendous hype. We were the heroes,' explained Mr Schrempp. 'This was a spectacular deal, we were lifted to the heights where we didn't belong. Then came reality day, that is what we are experiencing.'

Sources: See reference 1.

Case questions

1 *What was the vision of Daimler-Benz when it took over Chrysler? What were the benefits? To what extent were such benefits consistent with the manner in which Chrysler was initially managed?*

2 *To what extent, if at all, should the vision of an organisation take account of external factors – such as national economic conditions?*

3 *To what extent should an organisation's vision be truly challenging, as was clearly the case with Daimler-Benz?*

10.1 Shaping the purpose of the organisation

In Chapter 1, the topic of corporate strategy was defined in the context of the purpose of the organisation – strategy is only a means to an end, that end being the purpose of the organisation. It follows that it is impossible to develop strategy if the organisation's purpose remains unclear. It is perhaps surprising therefore that there has been so little exploration of purpose in the strategy literature; purpose is often simplified to 'profit maximisation' by writers such as Professor Michael Porter[2] or 'survival' by Professor Oliver Williamson[3] or some other simplifying assumption. The reason for such a reduction in the definition is that purpose is *complex and multifaceted*, involving not only profit and survival but also the motivations of the people involved and the relationship of the organisation with society and the community. Moreover, purpose will be *unique* to each organisation. Yet, however complex and singular, the general principles underlying the development of purpose need to be understood and clarified if the subsequent development of strategy is to be meaningful.

For many writers,[4] purpose is explored or defined solely in terms of business organisations, with profit featuring somewhere in its definition. But many other not-for-profit organisations, such as government institutions, charities and public services, also generate value-adding activities that have a clear purpose and need strategies to attain that purpose. An exploration of purpose therefore needs to be broad enough to include such bodies.

Whether private company or public body, every organisation needs to develop its purpose and develop a common understanding of the main elements. The potential complexity of this approach is usually overcome by identifying and concentrating on the essentials for that organisation. Such a process takes time and is best described as a process of *shaping* the purpose of the organisation. There are five main areas to be considered:

1 What is our area of activity – and what should it be?

2 What kind of organisation do we wish to be?

3 What is the relative importance of shareholders and stakeholders?

4 Do we want to grow the organisation?

5 What is our relationship with our immediate environment and with society in general?

However, such questions are somewhat *prescriptive* in their approach: they assume that clear answers can be given and that the actions that might follow are within the power of those people shaping the purpose of the organisation.[5] Neither of these assumptions is necessarily correct. For example, it may be difficult and unwise to define too clearly the area of activity because it may preclude opportunistic alternatives. Moreover, decisions on the type of organisation, growth and society depend on external forces, like governments and economic growth, that are not within the control of those asking the questions. *Emergent* approaches will also be needed if the organisation is to develop its purpose successfully. However, as a starting point in the development of purpose, it is useful to explore the questions.

10.1.1 What is our area of activity – and what should it be?

Fundamental to purpose is an examination of the area of activity that is undertaken – the business in which a company is engaged or the service offered by a non-profit organisation. This is fundamental to the definition of corporate strategy explored in Chapter 1.

With all the certainty of hindsight, we can conclude that Jürgen Schrempp was probably right to concentrate the purpose of Daimler-Benz on cars and trucks. Many other successful companies, like Micosoft and Intel, also focus purpose on a narrow business. But the Daimler-Benz related purpose of building a global company over a short time scale using acquisition may have been too challenging. In contrast to a concentrated purpose, some companies have successfully adopted broad roles for purpose: for example, the US conglomerate General Electric is involved in a range of industries from electric turbines to television broadcasting. The first issue in purpose is therefore one of *focus* – should we concentrate the purpose or allow it to range broadly? From an examination of the evidence on the profitability of focused versus diversified organisations,[6] there is no clear answer to this question – purpose can be broad or narrow. However, smaller companies will probably benefit from focus or they risk possessing insufficient competitive advantage in one area as a result of becoming merely competent in a number of areas. More generally, purpose needs to be narrow enough to be actionable and broad enough to allow scope for development.

Excluding start-up organisations, the strategy writer Professor Peter Drucker explored the issue of the area of activity from a different perspective. He recommended that the area of activity is examined by a consideration of *customers*.[7] He argued that it was the organisation's customers that defined the nature of the organisation and therefore shaped the breadth of its purpose.

More recently, strategists would add to his answer by suggesting that the *competitive resources* of an organisation will also define its purpose.[8] For example, the car manufacturing plant and skill resource at Daimler-Benz would make it difficult for the company to define its purpose as being engaged in fast-food restaurants. The resource-based view – *see* Chapter 6 – certainly suggests that the chosen area of activity should be related to the competitive advantage of the organisation. In practice, there needs to be a *balance* between customers and resources.

Neither of these customer/resource considerations explores where the organisation *should* locate its activities. Purpose is about the future direction of the organisation just as much as the present. All organisations have the opportunity to redefine and redirect their activities in the future. This may be particularly important if their survival is threatened in the present or if they see unique and attractive opportunities that would require a redefinition of purpose.

10.1.2 What kind of organisation do we wish to be?

Given the amount of time and effort that individuals devote to organisations, it is arguable that the purpose of the organisation is, at least in part, to provide living space for those engaged in its activities. All organisations have some choice to develop in two related areas:

1 culture and style – their *organisational culture*;

2 challenges to be posed to the members of the organisation.

For example, some may choose to be hard-nosed and competitive, while others may choose to be caring, considerate and co-operative. It should be acknowledged that complete freedom of choice in organisational culture is unlikely for two reasons: it is highly dependent on the previous history of the organisation and, in most cases, can only be changed slowly.[9] Nevertheless, it would be equally misleading to suggest that organisations are unable to make any change in their culture and it is therefore appropriate to explore this matter in the context of purpose.

To some extent, the kind of organisation will be dictated by the environment in which it operates:[10] for example, a fast-moving, buccaneering market like mobile telephones may not be well served by an organisation that chooses to be staid and sober in its purpose and culture. However, there are other aspects of choice in relation to purpose and culture that deserve consideration. The four types of organisational culture explored in Chapter 7 – power, role, task and personal – are to some extent matters of choice by the organisation.[11] The purpose of the organisation might therefore range from the *personal satisfaction* provided to someone involved in charity work to the *group goals* involved in meeting a challenging new product launch.

In addition to culture, organisational purpose may also be defined in terms of the *challenge* that purpose should pose to the organisation's members.[12] This approach will have an additional impact on the working style of the organisation.

> *No organisation can depend on genius; the supply is scarce and always unpredictable. But it is the test of an organisation that it can make ordinary human beings perform better than they are capable of, that it brings out whatever strength there is in its members and uses it to make all the other members perform more and better.*

Clearly, organisations have a choice here to offer no challenge. But some strategists would argue that those organisations which offer a challenge are more successful because they 'make common people do uncommon things', to paraphrase Lord Beveridge.

10.1.3 What is the relative importance of shareholders and stakeholders?[13]

For some companies, the purpose of the organisation is ultimately to advance the interests of its owners, usually the shareholders. Typically, this means that purpose is defined in terms of increasing the wealth of the shareholders. One example is the SVA concept explored in Chapter 8. Other ways of pursuing increased shareholder wealth include encouraging higher share prices and larger dividends in the short term and, for those strategies concerned with the longer term, they may also include some measure of long-term profit growth. This approach to purpose is called the *shareholder perspective* on purpose.

With such an approach to purpose, the problem is often the separation between ownership by the shareholders and control of the enterprise by its senior managers. Since the 1930s, it has been recognised that, as companies grow larger, two trends emerge.[14] Shareholdings become more widespread and diffuse, so giving individual shareholders less power. At the same time, managers gain control over a larger range of assets and acquire increasingly large remuneration and power. Thus purpose, according to this view, tends to drift from a clear focus on owners, who have lost the power to influence events, towards the senior management, who may pursue other interests as long as they keep the shareholders happy with steady increases in dividends and a generally rising share price.

Another wholly different view of purpose views the ownership of the organisation merely as one input to its continued existence.[15] On this view, shareholders supply the financial capital to which is added the managerial expertise of the organisation's senior managers, the labour input of other workers, the expertise and skills of its suppliers and so on. In this sense, the organisation is a joint venture between a number of its participants, each of whom has a stake in the purpose of the organisation. This is called the *stakeholder perspective* on purpose.

Clearly, the shareholder and stakeholder perspectives have considerable potential for conflict. For example, shareholders' higher dividends might need to come at the expense of paying managers and workers lower salaries. This matter is explored further in Chapter 12 in the context of the specific proposals on purpose summarised in the mission and objectives of the organisation.

10.1.4 Do we want to grow the organisation?

Some writers have argued that organisations need to see growth as at least part of their purpose. For example, the management guru Tom Peters argued that 'A firm is never static – it is either growing or stagnating,'[16] and the strategy writers Gertz and Baptista claimed that 'No company ever shrank to greatness.'[17] For some people, such phrases are vapid sloganising, but there is an established tradition in economic writing that assumes that organisations will wish to grow. For example, the well-respected work of the economist Edith Penrose – *see* Chapter 2 – is based on the assumption that firms will wish to grow.[18] Yet organisations may have a choice on growth and not all organisations will wish to grow – they may be perfectly satisfied to continue on their present course. The decision on growth is an important one but entirely dependent on the organisation and its environment – the choice is not automatic.

10.1.5 What is our relationship with the immediate environment and with society in general?

Purpose cannot be set without some consideration of the environment within which the organisation operates. This can conveniently be considered from the twin perspectives of the immediate environment and the wider context of society in general, though there may in practice be other approaches.

In the immediate environment, the main problems affecting purpose are likely to be general turbulence and strong competitive activity. There may be occasions when the environment is so chaotic or competition so powerful that survival is the only sensible purpose. All other aspects of purpose will need to be subordinated to this. It may even be that survival is not possible, in which case an orderly exit should be the purpose.

In the wider environment of society in general, there may be some need to define purpose in the context of the pressures and demands of that society. For example, government policy may dictate an adjustment in purpose. Equally, society may put pressure on a company to alter its purpose, such as the campaign to have responsible environmental 'green' policies written into the purpose of organisations.

More generally, from the perspective of the environment within which the organisation operates, some strategists argue that all organisations will adapt their purpose to reflect the values and pressures of such societies. The socio-cultural theories of strategy stress the contingent nature of every aspect of strategy development, starting with purpose – *see* Chapter 2.

10.1.6 Conclusions: the Purpose–Process–Outcome (P–P–O) Paradigm

With so many divergent views and little coherent thread, what are we to make of purpose? How can it be developed? As mentioned earlier, one response has been to simplify purpose down to a single, leading role such as:

1 growth; or

2 survival; or

3 profit maximisation.

In the development of strategy theory, such definitions play an important role in clarifying the logic of the strategies that should then be followed. However, they inevitably oversimplify the development of purpose, as the above sections have demonstrated. The purpose of the organisation is multidimensional and not just a simple matter of defining a single specific purpose, such as the three areas listed above. Morgan best captures the fullness of purpose in his comments on the different ways of exploring organisations: 'There can be no single theory or metaphor that gives an all-purpose point of view and there can be no one "correct theory" for structuring everything we do.'[19] It follows that a simple definition of purpose may fail to capture the full range of roles of the organisation.

In spite of this, most organisations have found some simplified definition of their purpose to be helpful because it provides a method of communicating the basis of the organisation's values and a forum for focusing on its future direction. Given this stance, three general guidelines on purpose can be developed:

1 *The importance of value added*: every organisation, including those in the public and not-for-profit sectors, needs to consider where and how it adds value to its inputs.[20] [21]

2 *The balance between shaping and being shaped by the environment*: some organisations may choose to shape the environment in which they operate, as well as passively coping with changes in the environment.[22]

3 *The changing nature of purpose over time – the P–P–O Paradigm*: the organisational *purpose* will be delivered by the *process* of strategy development. This will then provide an *outcome* (often as a profit or a service) that will then feed back into purpose

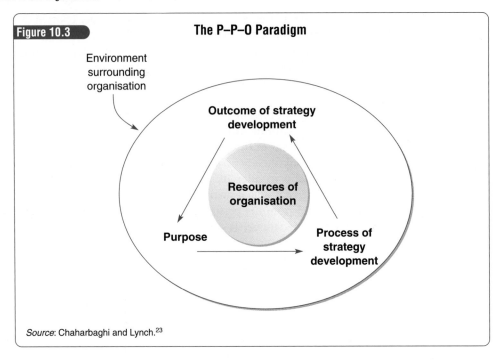

Figure 10.3 **The P–P–O Paradigm**

Environment surrounding organisation

Outcome of strategy development

Resources of organisation

Purpose

Process of strategy development

Source: Chaharbaghi and Lynch.[23]

at a later stage. These three elements make up the P(urpose)–P(rocess)–O(utcome) Paradigm – *see* Figure 10.3.

Comment

One final cautionary note on purpose is essential in relation to this section. The whole concept of purpose above is built on the assumption that it is useful and desirable to develop a clearly defined purpose for the organisation. Chapter 11 will explore the important strategic areas of knowledge, technology and innovation, where it may be better to leave some aspects of purpose much more open and flexible.

▶ Key strategic principles

- Fundamental to the exploration of purpose is the definition of the organisation's activities. It needs to be narrow enough to be actionable and broad enough to allow scope for development. It will develop from a consideration of the organisation's customers and its competitive resources.

- Organisations have some opportunity to influence the type of organisation that they wish to be. This will be reflected and defined in the organisation's culture. However, culture is confined by its past and is difficult to change, so this will restrict the choices available in the context of purpose.

- Different stakeholders – shareholders, employees, etc. – will have different perspectives on the purpose of the organisation. These need to be recognised and explored in the context of purpose.

> ▶ *Key strategic principles continued*
>
> - **Purpose will also be defined by any specific desire to grow the organisation and by an exploration of the demands of the environment in which the organisation exists.**
>
> - **Organisations are multidimensional and unlikely to have a single purpose. However, for reasons of focusing on specific objectives and communicating with those in the organisation, a simplified definition of purpose is often developed.**
>
> - **The P–P–O Paradigm captures the developing relationship between the future purpose of the organisation and its past performance. It does this by highlighting three consecutive elements – P(urpose), P(rocess) and O(utcome) – in the context of the organisation's resources and its environment.**

10.2 Developing a strategic vision for the future

In developing the purpose of the organisation, there is a need to develop a vision of the future of the organisation. Vision can be defined as 'a mental image of a possible and desirable future state of the organisation'.[24] There are five reasons to develop a strategic vision:

1 Most organisations will compete for business and resources. They will have ambitions that go well beyond the immediate future and *purpose needs to explore this vision*. Even not-for-profit organisations or those in the public sector usually need to compete for charitable or government funds and often desire to increase the range of services that they offer; such organisations will also benefit from a picture of where they expect to be in the future.

2 The organisation's *mission and objectives may be stimulated* in a positive way by the strategic options that are available from a new vision.

3 There may be major strategic opportunities from exploring new development areas that go *beyond the existing market boundaries and organisational resources*.[25] These require a vision that deserves careful exploration and development.

4 Simple market and resource projections for the next few years will miss the opportunities opened up by a whole new range of possibilities, such as new information technologies, biogenetics, environmental issues, new materials and lifestyle changes. Virtually every organisation will feel the impact of these significant developments. *Extrapolating the current picture is unlikely to be sufficient*.[26]

5 Vision provides a desirable *challenge* for both senior and junior managers.

Vision is therefore a backdrop for the development of the purpose and strategy of the organisation.

To be clear, vision is not the same as purpose: vision is the *future* picture, with purpose being the more immediate and broader role and tasks that the organisation chooses to define based on the current situation. However, it may be that the vision will lead to the purpose: for example, the Daimler-Benz vision of a global car company led directly to its acquisitions of Chrysler and its minority shares in Mitsubishi and Hyundai.

Vision may also lead to a change in purpose. For example, a small grocery store competing against a new hypermarket might see its *vision* as being increased competition from a newly opened hypermarket. It might then change its purpose to that of moving from that geographical area, rather than be driven out by the larger store in two years' time.

Hamel and Prahalad[27] have suggested five criteria for judging the relevance and appropriateness of a vision statement. These are shown in Table 10.1. They are important because it would be all too easy to develop some wild and worthy vision that bore no relationship to the organisation, its resources and the likely market and competitive developments. Daimler-Benz was in this category during the period 1995–2000.

The important action points that arise from the investigation of vision are connected with:

- *special resources*: do we have the technology and skills to meet this vision?
- *market opportunities*: what will this mean for market development? How can we take the opportunities as they arise?

It is also necessary to consider *how* the vision of the organisation is to be developed. It is likely that this will be guided by the chief executive officer. To quote Warren Bennis and Burt Nanus in their well-known text on leadership:

> *To choose a direction, a leader must first have developed a mental image of a possible and desirable future state of the organisation…The critical point is that a vision articulates a view of a realistic, credible, attractive future for the organisation, a condition that is better in some important ways than what now exists.[28]*

However, other strategists would argue that this should not be a task just for the leader but should involve many in the organisation. There is a strong case for using multi-functional teams that are brought together to investigate an area of the business. However, the precise format will depend on the prevailing culture of the organisation – *see* Chapter 12 for a further exploration of this important area.

Table 10.1 Five criteria for judging the organisation's investigation of its vision

Criterion	Indicative area to be investigated
Foresight	What imagination and real vision is shown? Over what time frame?
Breadth	How broad is the vision of the changes likely to take place in the industry? And of the forces that will lead to the changes?
Uniqueness	Is there an element of uniqueness about the future? Will it cause our competitors to be surprised?
Consensus	Is there some consensus within the organisation about the future? If not, there may be a problem if too many different visions are pursued at once
Actionability	Have the implications for current activity been considered? Is there basic agreement on the immediate steps required? Have the necessary core competencies and future market opportunities been identified?

Comment

Although the idea of vision is widely accepted as a useful addition to the general development of purpose, there is a problem. Vision has little meaning unless it can be successfully communicated to those working in the organisation, since these are the people that will have to realise it. The usual assumption is that such vision will be widely welcomed throughout the organisation. However, Hunt has questioned this and suggested that there will be groups of workers associated with many companies that do not have this degree of commitment.[29] He cites part-time workers, contracted suppliers and other flexible workers who may not feel committed to such a vision. 'This raises the question about the value of attempting to establish shared visions and values amongst different contributors. It highlights the fallacy of many human resources policies and practices based on some average employee.' As an example, Royal Dutch/Shell – *see* Chapter 7 – shows the difficulties that can arise from a senior management vision of a global company and a middle management view which was rather different.

◗ Key strategic principles

- When developing purpose, there is a need to develop a vision of the future within which the organisation will operate. The main reason is to ensure that every opportunity is examined.

- Vision is not the same as the organisation's purpose, though the two may be related.

- There are five criteria that may assist in developing the organisation's vision: foresight, breadth, uniqueness, consensus and actionability.

CASE STUDY 10.2

Leadership in action: Jürgen Schrempp of Daimler-Benz

In 1995, Mr Jürgen Schrempp became the new chairman of the famous German car and truck company. He took over at a difficult time and steered the company towards building a global car and truck company. This case describes his leadership style and strategic decisions over the difficult period to 2001. Commenting on his leadership style, the Financial Times *described him as 'a corporate animal driven by an insatiable appetite for power'.*

In spite of the difficulties up to 2001 – *see* Case 10.1 – Jürgen Schrempp was still upbeat in 2001: 'DaimlerChrysler is on the way up and I have no doubt that what we have in mind will bring us to a new plateau. All the pillars are in place.'

Sitting on the 11th floor of the DaimlerChrysler Stuttgart headquarters, the chairman insists that he will not be deflected from his mission. 'We have done basically all the acquisitions we need and the divestments; we are 90 per cent automotive,' he says.

'Now the concentration is to have the right people and to have the right execution of our strategy.'

That grand perspective seems a long way from Mr Schrempp's humble origins at Daimler, where he began work as an apprentice mechanic at his local Mercedes dealership. In the intervening 40 years, the engineering graduate has emerged as the most powerful industrialist in Germany, with a global reputation as a turnaround expert. That record was honed in South Africa and the US,

Jürgen Schrempp of Daimler-Benz

where he ran Mercedes' car operations and Euclid's heavy truck business, respectively. It culminated in a brutal overhaul of Daimler's European aerospace activities in the mid-1990s.

His attempt to repeat the exercise at Chrysler has won him few friends at the US carmaker. His reputation at the company's Auburn Hills headquarters has been scarred by a management exodus. Two successive Chrysler presidents, Tom Skallkamp and Jim Holden, have been fired. And the group has actioned six plant closures and 26 000 job losses. But Mr Schrempp is ready to defend his action. 'I deal with criticism by facing the music. I go to see the people,' he says. ' I listen and often go away with additional input, and sometimes think maybe we should address this or that point.'

In the end, however, he usually gets his way. In 1995 he wrested control of Daimler Benz from Edzard Reuter, his previous boss, and set about refashioning the business from a diversified industrial group into a focused automotive business. He also engineered the departure of other executives, including Helmut Werner, former head of Mercedes car and truck businesses. 'Over the last five years, there have been a lot of management changes, notably more on the German side than the US. The job of the chief executive is to analyse, find weaknesses and to decide on change.'

His detractors argue that he has abandoned German-style social contracts in favour of US business values. Claiming DaimlerChrysler attaches more importance to its share price than workers' rights, they point to his dismemberment of Fokker, the Dutch aircraft maker, in the mid-1990s and the closure of Dornier factories in Germany.

He maintains that these are not 'lonesome decisions' but part of a long process, fully endorsed by the supervisory board and its labour representatives. In spite of his reputation as a tough cost-cutter, Mr Schrempp is said to be passionate about union representation in the supervisory board. He insists that restructuring is easier with union-management consensus, and his not about to abandon co-determination at DaimlerChrysler. He says his record in South Africa, where he challenged apartheid policies, shows his commitment to corporate citizenship. He is still attached to the country and serves as South Africa's honorary consul general to Germany. To unwind, he likes to return to South Africa where he owns a game farm. 'I like the bush, I relax extremely well in the bush,' he says.

Not that the man described by friends as 'stateless, not rootless' gets a lot of time to watch game. 'I know what my priorities are at the moment. I so much believe in what we're doing and I put all my life and heart into proving the point.' As on most other matters, Mr Schrempp details those priorities at breakneck speed. Indeed, he is in such a rush that he has pulled on the wrong jacket as he runs between offices. Aides say his speed at work owes much to a personal fitness regime. Hotels on his itinerary are chosen according to gym facilities, with time reserved three or four times a week for hard exercise.

The DaimlerChrysler chairman also hints that fitness proves a useful antidote to his habit of living life to the full. 'I believe that where there's a healthy body there's a healthy brain,' he says. 'I like my wine; I like to live. But I have to do it in a disciplined way. I have weaknesses, as everybody knows. But I try to get people around me who have strengths where I have weaknesses.' What these weaknesses are he does not make clear. But a lack of willpower is not one of them. If a company could be driven to greater profits and shareholder value by force of personality, DaimlerChrysler would be one of the world's highest performing carmakers.

CASE STUDY 10.2 continued

Overall, the effort to transform the company and build the global base is led by a group chairman who is reluctant to slow down. 'Sometimes friends ask: "Can you sustain that?" You can only do that if your life is in balance. I have a very happy private life,' he says. 'But there are people saying, "Shift one gear back" but there is no way – right or wrong – and I stand on the accelerator pedal to do it.'

Case adapted by Richard Lynch from an article by Tim Burt, *Financial Times*, 26 February 2001, p12. Copyright *Financial Times*. Used with permission.

Case questions

1 *How would you characterise the leadership style of Mr Schrempp?*

2 *To what extent has the purpose of the company changed under the chairmanship of Mr Schrempp? How important was leadership here?*

3 *Are there any dangers in leaders dominating their organisations? What are they? How might they affect the development of strategy? How should strong leaders cope with such dangers?*

10.3 Purpose and the role of leadership

As the case study on Jürgen Schrempp of Daimler-Benz demonstrates, leadership will have a significant influence on the purpose of the organisation. However, the basic argument of this section is that the precise relationships between leadership and purpose are complex and depend on the specific circumstances. This means that it is difficult to provide prescriptive general principles on the relationship between the two topics. Two ways are suggested in this section. One relies on the notion that leadership needs to avoid lasting conflict with subordinates. The other suggests that specific styles of leadership are likely to be associated with specific approaches to the development of purpose. Finally, it is suggested that the most successful leadership needs not just to define purpose in a cold, abstract manner but also to communicate trust, enthusiasm and commitment to the organisation.

10.3.1 Understanding the influence of leadership

Jürgen Schrempp of Daimler-Benz, François Michelin of Michelin Rubber, Bill Gates of Microsoft, Akio Morita of Sony, Gianni Agnelli of Fiat are all examples of leaders who have guided and shaped the direction of their companies. *Leadership* is defined as 'influence, that is the art or process of influencing people so that they will strive willingly and enthusiastically toward the achievement of the group's mission'.[30]

The organisation's purpose and strategy do not just drop out of a process of discussion, but may be actively directed by an individual with strategic vision.

Visionary leadership inspires the impossible: fiction becomes truth.[31]

Leadership is a vital ingredient in developing the purpose and strategy of organisations. The potential that leaders have for influencing the overall direction of the company is arguably considerable. There is substantial anecdotal evidence to support this observation, though it is important to be aware of the hagiography (sainthood) that sometimes surrounds leaders – for example, the description of Jürgen Schrempp in Case study 10.1 portrays him in a generally favourable, if dominant, way. Nevertheless, in drawing up purpose and related strategy, it would be wise to consider carefully the personality, role and power of the leading person or group in the organisation.

Given the evident power that leaders may have in developing the company's mission and strategy, it is important to note some areas of caution based on research:

- Leaders should to some extent *reflect* their followers[32] and may need to be good team players in some company cultures if they are to effect change or they will not be followed.
- Vision can be eccentric, obsessed and not always logical.[33]
- It is certainly possible to exaggerate the importance of individuals when they are leading large and diverse groups that have strong company–political instincts.[34]

Certainly, these latter features are important in the modern, complex consideration of corporate strategy. Companies such as Philip Morris (US), Royal Dutch/Shell (UK/Netherlands) and Toyota (Japan) may all be more comfortable with a corporate leader who is inclined to be evolutionary rather than revolutionary. To this extent, we may be suspicious of the hero worship of management saviours who have ridden with vision and purpose to the rescue of failing businesses. The same variations can be found in small business, not-for-profit and government organisations. In every case, leadership can have a profound effect on purpose.

10.3.2 Analysing leadership in the context of purpose

In order to understand the way that purpose and strategy interrelate with leadership, it is useful to analyse the leadership role. However, in spite of extensive study reaching back to the 1950s, there is no general agreement on leadership analysis.[35] There are three main approaches:

1 *Trait theories*. These argue that certain types of individual can be identified who will provide leadership in virtually any situation. According to the research that has been done, such individuals will be intelligent, self-assured, able to see beyond the immediate issues and come from higher socio-economic groups. In recent times, such theories have been discredited because the evidence to support them is inconsistent and clearly incomplete in its explanation of leadership. *Purpose* here would be decided largely by the individual leader.

2 *Style theories*. These suggest that individuals can be identified who possess a general style of leadership that is appropriate to the organisation. For example, two contrasting styles would be the authoritarian and the democratic: the former imposes the leader's will from the centre and the latter allows free debate before developing a solution. According to the research, this has some validity, but leadership is much more complex than the simplicities of style. For example, it needs to take into account the varied relationships between leaders and subordinates, the politics of decision making and the culture of the organisation. Such theories have therefore been downplayed in recent years. *Purpose* here would be defined by the leadership style.

3 *Contingency theories*. These explore the concept that leaders should be promoted or recruited according to the needs of the organisation at a particular point in time. The choice is *contingent* on the strategic issues facing the organisation at that time and leaders need to be changed as the situation itself changes. Thus the leader needs to be seen in relation to the group whom s/he will lead and the nature of the task to be undertaken. For example, recovery-from-disaster strategies will require a different type of leader from the steady development type of strategy. There is some evidence to support this approach but it is still anecdotal and oversimplifies the leadership task. *Purpose* here would clearly depend on the strategic situation.

Figure 10.4 An example of the best-fit approach to leadership analysis

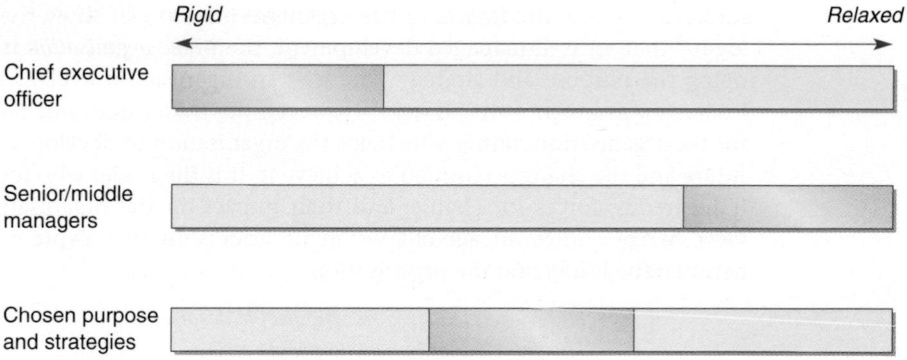

- **Chief executive officer** prefers a structured style, possibly even dominant.
- **Senior/middle** managers like to be given more personal initiative and responsibility.
- **Chosen strategies** are tightly defined in some areas, but allow some managerial initiative.
- **Conclusion:** In the above case, the three areas do not 'fit' – change and compromise are needed. Purpose here may not be achieved with such contrasting styles and disagreements.

From a strategic perspective, the contingency theory approach holds the most promise for two reasons. It is the one that best captures both the leader and the relationship with others in the organisation, and it also identifies clearly the importance of the strategic situation as being relevant to the analysis of leadership.

Within contingency theory, there is one approach that is particularly used: it is called the *best-fit* analytical approach. This is essentially based on the notion that leaders, subordinates and strategies must reach some compromise if they are to be successfully carried forward. There may be some difference of views but, ultimately, purpose will best be developed by some agreement between them. This is useful in corporate strategy because it allows each situation to be treated differently and it identifies three key analytical elements:

1 the chief executive officer or leader;

2 the senior/middle managers who carry out the tasks; and

3 the nature of the purpose and strategies that will be undertaken.

Each of these is then plotted on a common scale, ranging from rigid (or heavily structured) to relaxed (or supportive and flexible). The best fit is then sought between these three elements. An example is shown in Figure 10.4. The result is inevitably vague but may prove useful in identifying the balance of style and its influence on people, strategies and purpose.

10.3.3 Leadership style and its relationship with the development of purpose

Leadership style can vary from the *shared vision* approach of Senge to the *dominance* of individuals like the first Henry Ford or Margaret Thatcher in the UK in the late 1980s. Each style will influence the way that purpose is developed and the content that results.

Shared vision approach

Senge had a useful perspective on the relationship between the organisation and its leadership.[36] It is the *leaders* of the organisation who can show the way. However, he argued that, in well-managed development, the *whole organisation* is involved in developing the purpose and strategy. The way an organisation evolves is a function of its leadership as much as its strategy. However, the leader does not dominate and decide for the organisation; rather s/he helps the organisation to develop a *shared purpose* of its future and the changes required to achieve it. It is the leader who focuses on the underlying trends, forces for change and their impact on the organisation. To explain his view, Senge quotes an age-old vision of leadership that expresses this relationship between the leader and the organisation:

> *The wicked leader is he who people despise.*
> *The good leader is he who people revere*
> *The great leader is he who the people say, 'We did it ourselves.'*

Lao Tsu

Thus, purpose here is developed by co-operation, discussion and broad agreement. The outcome may be slow, complicated and a compromise but it is likely to be well understood by everyone and to generate strong commitment from those involved in developing it.

Dominance approach

The words of Lao Tsu read well, but they may not be appropriate in some strategic situations. If a company is in crisis, then it may need strong and firm central leadership to enable it to survive. When a company is in the early stages of development, with a new vision about its future, it may also benefit from a strong, entrepreneurial leader with a quite different style and approach to the purpose.

In this case, purpose is developed mainly by the choice of the leader and, possibly, the immediate subordinates. It will be largely imposed on others in the organisation and will not engender the same degree of commitment.

Contrasting the two basic approaches: other styles of leadership

The leadership system that best describes the management style of the leader needs to be taken into account in devising the purpose and strategy. Where the leader is dominant then s/he will be involved early. Where the leader is more consultative then early involvement will be on a more participative basis. In addition, the style of the leader will be conditioned by the style and culture of the organisation and the development of purpose and strategy will also need to take this into account in devising its procedures.

In order to explore the main elements, the above discussion has relied on two basic leadership styles in the exploration of purpose. Other styles can be identified – some are shown at the end of Chapter 16 in Exhibit 16.6.

Choice of leadership style

Leaders and their organisations will wish to consider how they should be led. The choice of leadership style will ultimately depend on a number of factors that go beyond the personality and personal wishes of the individual. Some factors that will influence leadership style are shown in Exhibit 10.1.[37]

> **Exhibit 10.1** **Factors influencing the leadership style of organisations**
>
> - Personality and skills of leader
> - Size of company
> - Degree of geographical dispersion
> - Stability of organisation's environment
> - Current management style of the organisation's culture
> - Organisation's current profitability and its desire and need for change

10.3.4 The importance of trust, enthusiasm and commitment – the contribution of Bennis and Nanus

In developing the purpose of the organisation, it is important to recognise that such a process will affect many parts of the organisation in terms of its impact. Thus, if leadership is to be successful, it cannot be regarded as just a cold and abstract analytical statement. The leader needs to generate trust, enthusiasm and commitment amongst key members of the organisation for the chosen purpose.

Amongst the most widely read writers on leadership in relation to the tasks of the organisation are Warren Bennis and Burt Nanus. These two US authors researched leadership amongst US organisations in the 1980s. They included failure as well as success and wrote a highly successful book full of short anecdotes and pithy conclusions on leadership and especially its people aspects.[38]

With regard to purpose only, their conclusions on successful leadership suggest that:

- Leaders need to generate and sustain *trust* in the strategy process and the general integrity of the organisation while developing its purpose.

- Leaders will deliver a more robust statement of purpose if they have generated and used the *intellectual capital* of the many people involved in the organisation. This means that leaders have tapped the knowledge, interest and experience of those below them in the organisation.

- Leaders need to demonstrate a *passion and determination* to seek out and then achieve the purpose that has been identified by the process.

As was clearly demonstrated with Mr Jürgen Schrempp in Case study 10.1, leadership is not just a matter of identifying purpose in a cold and abstract manner. Leadership needs to demonstrate commitment, develop understanding and fire enthusiasm for the purpose if it is to be successful. Readers are also referred to the reading at the end of this chapter which describes the approach of Mr Andy Grove, the highly successful leader of Intel, the US computer chip manufacturer. He also needed to go beyond the cold, clinical definition of purpose to redirect his company's purpose at several crucial points during the 1990s.

10.3.5 Prescriptive and emergent approaches to leadership

Airport bookshops are full of leadership texts that claim to identify good leaders and the characteristics that are essential to fulfil such a role. These are usually prescriptive approaches to the leadership task and imply that all good leaders have particular attributes. But such books need to be treated with caution if contingent theories are correct, because such theories suggest that leadership depends on the strategic circumstances of the organisation. There is no one best way.

There is an additional reason for caution. The act of identifying leadership as a prime mover in the development of strategy reduces the role of other elements that are important. For example, team building and family ownership of the company can be equally important factors in certain types of organisation.

▶ Key strategic principles

- Leaders can have a profound influence on mission and objectives. They may be particularly important in moving the organisation forward to new challenges. However, in large and complex organisations their role is more likely to be evolutionary rather than revolutionary.

- There is no agreement on how to analyse leadership. Contingency theories are probably the most useful approach. They state that the choice and style of leadership is *contingent* on the strategic issues facing the organisation at that point in time.

- Within the context of contingency theory, the best-fit analytical approach can be used. It is useful in strategy because it allows each situation to be treated differently.

- Leadership style can vary from shared vision to dominance. The style needs to be modified to suit the strategic situation, with other styles being possible depending on the organisation and its environment.

- With regard to purpose, leaders need to generate trust in the strategic process. They need to draw upon the intellectual capital of the organisation and to demonstrate passion and determination.

- In some circumstances, leadership may be better served by allowing the purpose to emerge from the group working on a strategic task, rather than be imposed by the leader from the centre.

CASE STUDY 10.3

Negotiation ethics at Portsmouth's new millennium tower – a double whammy?

Twice in the last few years, the centrepiece of the £90 million (US$140 million) Portsmouth Harbour Renaissance Scheme – its 170-metre-high millennium tower – has come close to being scrapped. First, in 1998, the original developers secured a profitable, related development and then withdrew from the tower. Then, halfway through building the tower in 2002, the new construction company claimed that the design needed expensive modifications and stopped work until extra funds were agreed. This case explores the business ethics involved in the 'Tower Fiasco', as the local newspaper called it.

Background

For the last few hundred years, Portsmouth harbour on the southern coast of England has been a prime base for Britain's Royal Navy. But with a reduction in the use of naval power during the 1990s, the naval facilities were reduced drastically. The local councils on both sides of the harbour were forced to seek alternative work for the local economy. Fortunately, the harbour also had a unique collection of historic ships and museums – HMS *Victory*, *Mary Rose*, HMS *Warrior*, Alliance submarine – and these formed the basis of a new tourist industry. But there were still acres of former naval land that could form the basis of new commercial development. Then along came the Millennium Commission.

The Portsmouth Harbour Renaissance Scheme

To celebrate the new millennium, the UK government's Millennium Commission offered major national lottery grants in the mid-1990s for key millennium projects. A combined bid by Portsmouth, Gosport, Hampshire County Council and interested local businesses put in a successful bid for £40 million funding grant. The condition on this grant was that it would be coupled with commercial development of around another £55 million to complete the work. The grant would provide new infrastructure and open up the areas round the harbour with new promenades and leisure facilities. The accompanying leisure developments would include yachting harbours, housing, retail shops and restaurants. Together, they would transform the face of the harbour, with the centrepiece being a new millennium tower at the harbour entrance. On the Portsmouth side of the harbour, this new development would cover 30 acres (12 hectares) and be called Gunwharf Quays.

Successful negotiations in 1997, followed by the first whammy

In a competitive bidding process, a consortium that included the well-known UK building developers, the Berkeley Group, produced the most attractive plans for Gunwharf Quays – including housing and retail shopping. It was awarded the outline contract in late 1997. Negotiations for the development were led by the political leader of Portsmouth City Council, Leo Madden, and its permanent chief

executive, Nick Gurney. In early 1998, they signed a deal to give the go-ahead for the development, expecting the millennium tower contract to follow shortly. Thus the Berkeley Group had secured a highly attractive development contract for 30 acres of land, on which it began construction during 1998. Local press reports complimented the company on its sensitive handling of various aspects of the architectural design during this time.

However, negotiations about the tower contract dragged on into the summer of 1998. Finally, the Berkeley Group said that it would only put £3 million into any tower development, not the £10 million that had been understood. Although the initial brief had clearly stated the need for visitors, Berkeley claimed that it had always wanted to erect a non-accessible tower, just as a harbour feature.

At a meeting with the city council in July 1998, Berkeley said: 'New proposals put forward . . . were for a different tower involving major leisure attractions and therefore special operating skills. Accordingly, Berkeley was not willing to build the tower or operate it.' The company also pointed out that the latest estimate on the number of visitors to the tower was only around 350 000, compared with the planned 700 000, thus making the project commercially unattractive. The statement concluded that the Berkeley Group and the council 'continue to be apart on too many issues and to see matters from a different perspective'. However, the construction group offered £3 million as a contribution to any tower development though it would not take part in its construction or management. They were able to take this stand because no tower contract had been signed.

Furious local reaction to the reduced involvement

Local reaction was furious. The local daily newspaper, *The News*, Portsmouth, was particularly critical of the way that the matter had been handled. Under the

Picture source: Courtesy of *The News*, Portsmouth.

heading, 'Oversight has cost the city dearly', it commented:

It beggars belief that the Berkeley Group was allowed to get its hands on the prized land at Gunwharf on Portsmouth's seafront without being signed up to all the conditions. It can now build 30 acres of money-spinning shops, houses and leisure business – and apparently walk away from its full commitment to the harbour tower... Cynics might say that Berkeley was prepared to go along with the idea until past the point of no return and then cut its risks on huge profits. Only the naïve might not suspect money-makers of wanting to lick off the cream for themselves.

The following day, the paper added:

If the developer signs anything now, it will still have escaped a £7 million cost. What it says about the integrity of its bosses is clear enough. The company can obviously not be trusted, either in Portsmouth or in Gosport where it is also the chosen waterfront developer.

No further response from the Berkeley Group was published to this broadside from the local paper. But the group could undoubtedly argue that it had a duty to its shareholders. It was entitled to take a conservative view of visitor numbers. Moreover, it had no brief to protect the leaders of the local council from their own incompetence – that was why the council employed professional advisers and had a permanent chief executive. The Gunwharf Quays development opened in 2001 and was visited by over 6 million people in its first year – twice the original estimate. But the tower development was still under discussion with new builders.

The second whammy in 2002

After much further negotiation, construction of the tower was begun in late 2001 using new builders,

Mowlem Construction. Because it was hoped to open the tower at Easter 2003, building started without a full contract being signed – just a 'letter of intent'. However, this was considered quite normal on large construction projects in the building industry. Then, after spending £5.6 million (US$8.4 m), the builders said in April 2002 that the tower could not be built for the original estimate: they needed an extra £2.75 million. The builders knew this meant that, if the tower was scrapped, the £5.6 million received so far by the City Council from the Millennium Commission would need to be repaid in full by the taxpayers of the City of Portsmouth.

One option open to the Council was to sue the builders, but this was a lengthy and uncertain process that would delay the tower even further. Thus the Council was caught for a second time – sue the builders, pay the extra money to the builders or repay an even larger sum to the Commission. At the time of writing, negotiations were still continuing between the City Council and the builders. Work was suspended on building the tower and there was much talk of the ethics of negotiation once again: 'Not a penny more' was the initial stance taken by the local newspaper.

Case questions

1 *What are the main ethical issues here? Or was this just a matter of 'business negotiation' with no underlying ethical issues?*

2 *Who do you think behaved ethically? The Berkeley Group, Mowlem or the local council? Or all three?*

3 *How does your answer shape purpose at Portsmouth City Council?*

10.4 Purpose shaped by ethical considerations

By ethical considerations are meant the standards and conduct that an organisation sets itself in its dealings within the organisation and outside with its environment. Such issues concern not only commercial organisations like the Berkeley Group but also not-for-profit organisations like Portsmouth City Council – *see* Case study 10.3 above.

In the new millennium, both businesses and not-for-profit organisations can wield significant power both inside and outside their organisations. Most therefore now accept that some form of ethical standards should govern and guide their activities. There are plenty of examples of the significance of such issues: for example, the *Exxon Valdez*; disposal of a Royal Dutch/Shell North Sea oil platform; the international ivory trade; the case of the American company Enron.[39] There is no one appropriate time to introduce such standards but it is appropriate to consider them in the development of the organisation's purpose.

10.4.1 Ethical conduct: basic issues[40]

To study ethical issues is to try to identify what is morally correct behaviour for the organisation. There are four main reasons for considering the ethical conduct of organisations:

1 In every society, such considerations are sometimes *inescapable*, e.g. legal limits on conduct.[41]

2 They may be *important* to conduct in that society, e.g. respect for 'green issues' in the environment that go beyond legal limits.[42]

3 A consideration of ethics is part of the *professionalisation* of business, e.g. the treatment of workers and ethnic groups.[43]

4 The *self-interest* of organisations is often best served by developing attitudes to ethical issues before they become acute, e.g. bad publicity as a result of accusations of incorrect behaviour.

Exhibit 10.2 shows some examples of the type of issues that can readily arise. Any one of these would justify the exploration of ethical conduct. They raise three basic areas that need to be explored in the context of purpose and strategy development:

1 the extent of ethical considerations;

2 the cost of such considerations;

3 the recipient of the responsibility.

Exhibit 10.2	**Some examples of ethical issues that might impact on purpose**

- *Espionage.* How does a company find out about competition? Where does reasonable enquiry finish and aggressive search for additional data commence? Perhaps anything goes?

- *Tyrannical regimes.* Does a company sell weapons or even life-saving equipment to a country that is run by regimes retaining power by unjustified use of force and human rights abuses? After all, the argument might be that lives might be saved in that country and jobs could be preserved in the selling company.

- *Bribery and corruption.* Should all organisations refuse to engage in such activity in every circumstance? Jobs may be saved and contracts won for only limited sums to a small number of people. On the other hand, the organisation itself would not wish to be on the receiving end of such conduct so why should it encourage it in others? Moreover, perhaps it is profoundly unacceptable in society?

- *Telling half-truths and operating misleading negotiating tactics.* If such practices are unacceptable in general society, are they also unacceptable in business negotiations? Or does business operate by a different set of rules?

In more detail:

Extent. Beyond the legal minimum, to what extent does the organisation wish to consider the ethical issues that could arise in its conduct of its business? Does it wish to be involved in every area or lay down some basic principles and then leave parts or individuals to conduct themselves appropriately?

Cost. Some actions will have a cost to the organisation. Many of the real conflicts arise here because if they were without cost then they would be easily undertaken. There are no abstract rules but each organisation will need to consider this area.

Recipient. Is it considered that the organisation has a responsibility to the state? To the local community? To individuals? To special interest groups? These matters will need careful consideration in the light of the particular circumstances of the organisation.

Beyond these matters, ethical considerations may influence corporate strategy at a number of levels – these are shown in Exhibit 10.3. The values of the organisation will then need to be reflected in its purpose and possibly its mission statement; even the *absence* of values in the mission is itself a statement about the organisation and its view about its role in society. Such matters may well reflect the role that the organisation sees itself playing in society, if any, and the responsibilities that flow from this.

Exhibit 10.3   **Ethical considerations and corporate strategy**

- *The national and international level* – the role of the organisation in society and the country. Political, economic and social issues such as those explored in Chapter 3 will impact here: *laissez-faire* versus *dirigiste*, the role and power of trade blocks and closer economic union. The organisation is entitled to have a view on these matters and seek to influence society, if it so desires.

- *The corporate level* – ethical and corporate issues over which the organisation has some direct control. Such matters as the preservation of the environment, contributions to political parties, representations to the country's legislative parliament are all examples of direct corporate activities that need to be resolved.

- *The individual manager and employee level* – standards of behaviour which organisations will wish to set for individual managers and workers. Some of these matters may not be strategic in nature in the sense that they are unlikely to affect the future direction of the organisation overall but rather the future of individuals. However, there may well be some general policies on, for example, *religious, ethnic and equality issues* that involve both the individual and fundamental matters relating to the direction of the organisation. These general matters of policy deserve to be treated at the highest possible level and therefore come within the ambit of corporate strategy.

10.4.2 Ethical issues: shareholder and stakeholder perspectives[44]

It should be noted that not all commercial organisations believe that they have a role beyond their own business. They take the view that society is perfectly capable of looking after itself and the prime responsibility of the enterprise is to care for its shareholders. Such a view would probably mean that the company's purpose is unlikely to include any explicit comment on business ethics. It should be emphasised that this does *not* mean that such a company would behave unethically: simply that there is no need to reflect this in its purpose and its responsibilities are essentially limited to the interests of the company. Essentially, this is related to the *shareholder perspective* explored earlier in the chapter.

There are other companies which take the view that it is in the long-term benefit of both the company and the shareholders for the company to play a role in society beyond the minimum described by law. Sponsorship of outside initiatives, welfare provisions for workers, strong ethical beliefs and standards may all follow from such a view and be reflected in comments *associated with* the purpose and possibly the mission statement. This is the *stakeholder perspective* explored earlier in the chapter.

Beyond this again, there are organisations that exist primarily or wholly for their social functions in society, e.g. those engaged in providing social services. Clearly, for these latter groups, it will be vital to specify the relationship with society. This group may well wish to include some statement of its beliefs and values in its overall purpose and also in its mission statement.

As an example of how business can both work within the community and at the same time focus on its more obvious commercial concerns, the UK charity Business in the Community provides a useful model. Essentially, it allows those businesses which believe that they should have a role in the community to *channel their efforts* while at the same time focusing on what they do commercially. No doubt similar organisations exist in other countries, ranging from Chambers of Commerce to some specific industry initiatives.

> ### ▶ Key strategic principles
>
> - By business ethics is meant the standards and conduct that an organisation sets itself in its dealings within the organisation and outside with its environment. These need to be reflected in the mission statement.
> - There are three prime considerations in developing business ethics: the extent of ethical considerations, their cost and the recipient of the responsibility.
> - There are numerous differences between organisations over what should be covered under ethics, reflecting fundamentally different approaches to doing business.

10.5 Corporate governance and the purpose of the organisation

In association with the general ethical issues explored above, there is the more specific matter of corporate governance, which has ethical and other implications related to the mission and objectives of the organisation. Corporate governance relates primarily to the selection and conduct of the senior officers of the organisation and their relationships with the owners, employees and others who have an interest in the organisation (often called the 'stakeholders'). Its relationship with strategy arises as a result of the opportunities given to senior managers to influence the future direction of the organisation.

The senior officers are usually the directors of the organisation. However, they may also include senior representatives of workers and senior outside advisers with no daily responsibility for strategy development. In some European countries such as Germany, Sweden and the Netherlands, this latter group would constitute a supervisory board that oversaw the work of the directors.

Many public bodies will also have corporate governance structures. These are likely to cover the major issues of the not-for-profit sector, including the monitoring of the quality of public services and the value-for-money obtained by taxpayers and charity givers.

For some organisations, corporate governance goes beyond selecting and reviewing the conduct of the senior officers. It will also include a review and approval process for the main corporate strategies that have been developed by the officers. Typically, such a procedure might take place on an annual basis. In addition, to quote the corporate governance statement of the major international oil company British Petroleum,[45] there may be additional monitoring during the year to test 'the confidence in or risks to the achievement of the performance objectives and the observance of the strategy and policies'.

10.5.1 The power of corporate governance

The importance of corporate governance lies in the *power* that is given to the senior officers to run the affairs of the organisation. In recent times, this power has not always been used in the best interests of the shareholders, employees or society in general. Examples of the abuse of this power abound, but are illustrated by a consideration of the UK company magnate Robert Maxwell. This man was chairman of a major international publishing and media group in the late twentieth century. By all accounts, he was corrupt yet continued to operate with impunity for some years; the situation was only discovered after he died in a boating accident in 1993.

More recent governance incidents may not be so extreme. They have often related to the pay and other privileges that board members have awarded themselves to the detriment of others inside and outside the organisation – for example, the 'fat cat' company directors of the UK gas and electricity companies who gave themselves large share options at the time of privatisation and ended up with vast fortunes at the expense of the nation.

As a result of these and other matters, professional bodies (especially those in the accounting profession) have set up standards to govern the ethical and professional conduct of the senior officers of organisations. Several commissions on such standards have also produced reports: for example, the Cadbury, the Greenbury and the Hampel Committees in the UK, the Vienot report in France and the Dutch Governance Commission. Some of the detail of the resulting standards need not concern us here, but the principles are important and will influence the objectives and conduct of the organisation. These views on the purpose of the organisation will then influence its strategies.

10.5.2 Governance and information flows

The problem with so much power concentrated into the central management of the organisation is that it needs to be used with responsibility. This difficulty is made worse if poor-quality information about the organisation's performance is given to other stakeholders in the organisation – wrong-doing will go unchecked as long as it remains unknown or unreported. Thus one of the key aspects of corporate governance is that of information and its availability – good-quality information will encourage responsible conduct.

It might be thought that the easy way to ensure governance would be to ensure that information is freely available on all the main activities of the organisation. The difficulty here is that some information will be commercially sensitive, so cannot easily be sent outside the organisation or even circulated fully inside it. However, the danger of not circulating the full information is that it can be used as an excuse to hide what is going on by those who do not wish to reveal it.

Exhibit 10.4   **Typical information available to different stakeholders in a company**

Stakeholder	Information regularly obtained	Comment
Shareholders	Annual report and accounts	Limited to what the organisation wants its shareholders to know
Investment analysts, e.g. in stock-broking companies; also journalists	Regular updates of progress, sometimes face-to-face meetings	Better informed but still possible for the organisation to mislead
Main company board	Relatively full information but possible to mislead; legal obligation to be properly informed and to inform	Full disclosure of all issues is assisted by the character and independence of any non-executive directors
Senior managers	Detailed information in some areas but rely on managers to bring issues to their notice – remember Nick Leeson of Barings Bank	Likely to be without the full picture available to the main board; can be the 'whistleblower' on unethical, illegal or improper conduct but may also engage in such conduct
Managers	Some information but often incomplete	Can sometimes be the 'whistleblower' but under considerable pressure to conform to company rules
Employees	Usually only limited information unless the workers have representatives on a supervising board	New EU directives make senior representation more likely and offer some protection here

---

The starting point in resolving such a conflict is to identify the normal flows of information that exist between the organisation and those inside and outside it. Exhibit 10.4 lists some of the typical flows of information that will be regularly available to different stakeholder groups. Ultimately, stakeholders are often reliant on independent professional advisers to inspect the information on a confidential basis – as accountants do in an annual audit – to confirm responsible conduct.

Another important check can be provided if some of the main board members have semi-independent status, i.e. their main responsibilities and experience rest elsewhere. They are usually associated with organisations that have no commercial or other interest whatsoever in the organisation but have sufficient senior experience to comment on its affairs. These people are usually called *non-executive directors*, meaning that they have no day-to-day management responsibility for the operation of the organisation. In recent years, the appointment of these independent directors has been seen as a means of ensuring that the conduct of the organisation is beyond reproach. The danger of such a system is that the choice of who to appoint to non-executive positions remains with the company being monitored. However, if non-executives are of sufficient prominence in their own fields, then other stakeholders can have confidence in their independence of judgement.

10.5.3 Governance and corporate conduct

Beyond the matter of information availability, corporate governance is more a matter of the principles for conducting the organisation's affairs than of hard and fast rules. It is concerned with ensuring that the value added generated by the assets of the organisation is distributed equitably among the stakeholders. The principal officers of the organisation bear prime responsibility for this task under the supervision of the main or supervisory board. Importantly, corporate governance often insists on a separation between the chairman and the chief executive of the organisation:

- *Chairman.* The most senior person in the organisation but without day-to-day responsibility for its operation. The chairman often concentrates relations *outside* the organisation, such as those with banks, government and shareholders.
- *Chief executive.* The most senior manager with responsibility for day-to-day operations, including the preparation and implementation of strategy. All directors, apart from the non-executive directors, would report to this person. The chief executive often concentrates on relations *within* the organisation.

Some organisations combine the two roles. Others have different structures to ensure compliance, or no structures and policies at all. Such a separation may be too elaborate

---

Exhibit 10.5　　**Corporate governance at British Petroleum: the principal committees of its board of directors**

Membership of each committee includes a number of non-executive directors, who have no day-to-day responsibility for the development and execution of the affairs and strategies of the organisation. However, they will have relevant outside experience and knowledge of other similar organisations so that they can ask difficult but appropriate questions.

Committee	Responsibility
Chairman's Committee	Reviews the structure and effectiveness of the group's organisation and the overall performance of the group chief executive
Audit Committee	Reviews the application and effectiveness of the policies and processes of the group on matters of internal financial policy, control and risk
Ethics and Environment Committee	Reviews policies and processes which bear upon the group's reputation and its community, customer, employee, health, safety, environmental and other relationships
Remuneration Committee	Determines on behalf of the board the terms of engagement and remuneration of the group chief executive and managing directors
Nominations Committee	Recommends to the board candidates for appointment as directors and proposes the directors to retire by rotation at the annual general meeting

Source: BP Annual Report and Accounts, 1997.

for small companies. The main way of monitoring the corporate governance task is typically through a series of committees that have responsibility for specific areas of the organisation – an example is shown in Exhibit 10.5. Many of these committees will have decision-making influence in areas that are directly related to corporate strategy – for example, those responsible for the effectiveness of the organisation and for considering attitudes to business risk.

▶ Key strategic principles

- Corporate governance relates primarily to the selection and conduct of the senior officers of the organisation. It is also concerned about their relationships with the owners, employees and other stakeholders of the organisation.

- The importance of corporate governance lies in the power that it gives the senior officers to run the affairs of the organisation. The problem with power is that it needs to be used responsibly.

- One check on the responsible conduct of the organisation is the information relayed to all the stakeholders – good-quality information will encourage responsible conduct. The problem is that such information may be commercially sensitive. Confidential independent advisers, such as accountants in an audit, may be the means of keeping check on corporate conduct.

- Another way of checking on the conduct of the company is by the appointment of non-executive directors who have no other commercial connection with the company.

- Beyond the matter of information availability, corporate governance is more a matter of the principles of conduct than simple rules. The main aim is to ensure that the value generated by the assets of the organisation is distributed equitably amongst the stakeholders.

KEY READING

In this extract from his book The Leadership Gene, *Professor Cyril Levicki identifies some of the major strategic decisions that will involve the leader of the organisation.*

Many apparently short-term decisions can have longer-term potential consequences. The leader's expertise should be to know which they are and focus on the ones with the most profound strategic long-term effects. For example, all culture change decisions are likely to have long-term effects. They can cause profound corporate scar tissue. So although decisions to change the culture can be easily taken and look like a one- or two-year process, it is rare that the culture can be changed, in medium and large organisations, in less than five to ten years. Sometimes there may not be enough time to change the culture before the organisation dies.

Decisions about product and service quality are usually strategically important. For example, at L'Oreal, one of the world's leading beauty products manufacturers, a decision to change a single line of the hair style on the picture of the model on their Elnett Hair lacquer (a world leading brand) goes to the main board in Paris for approval. L'Oreal has become one of the leading suppliers of hair and body preparations in the world. They maintain their position by being obsessively focused about the detail of their key products and brands.

Drastic changes in human resource policies can reverberate for decades. In the early 1980s, when John Harvey-Jones was in the chair at ICI, he

▶

decided to change the ICI human resource policy of 'jobs for life'. He wanted to declare the first £1 billion profit year in the history of the business. He achieved that goal, in part, by making thousands of people redundant. This was the first time ever in the history of ICI that such a level of profit had been reached. One cannot judge, even now, whether it was right to change the guarantee that ICI offered a 'job for life'. There should be no doubt, however, that the amazing loyalty and dedication to ICI that the workers felt before he took action was changed for ever.

Long-term decisions with strategic import involve anything to do with new markets, international expansion, developing new skills and core competencies or investing a large percentage of the organisation's capital resources (therefore locking up the firm's wealth flow for many years). In fact, anything that the analysts, Wall Street, the London Stock Exchange, stock-brokers and investors regard as changing the nature of the company should be considered a long-term decision with strategic import. These are the really substantive decisions of which the average leader will take only five or six in his whole career. If he takes more than this it will be either because he is running a global corporation with divisions around the world, or because he is taking too many decisions! Such decisions require much preparation and careful thought. They require the input of multiple sources of data. They are also typical of the kind of decision the success of which may be impossible to judge until many years after the leader has drawn his final success bonus and departed.

Source: Levicki C (1998) *The Leadership Gene*, Extracted from pp130–2, Financial Times Pitman Publishing, London.

Summary

- The definition of the organisation's activities is fundamental to the exploration of its purpose. It needs to be narrow enough to be actionable and broad enough to allow scope for development. In addition, organisations also have some opportunity to influence the type of organisation that they wish to be. This will be reflected and defined in the organisation's culture. However, culture is confined by its past and is difficult to change, so this will restrict the choices available in the context of purpose.

- Different stakeholders – shareholders, employees, etc. – will have different perspectives on the purpose of the organisation. These need to be recognised and explored in the context of purpose. Purpose will also be defined by any specific desire to grow the organisation and by an exploration of the demands of environment in which the organisation exists. Although organisations are multidimensional and unlikely to have a single purpose, a simplified definition of purpose is often developed. The reasons are that it allows the organisation to focus on specific objectives and communicate the definition to those within it.

- The P–P–O Paradigm captures the developing relationship between the future purpose of the organisation and its past performance. It does this by highlighting three consecutive elements – P(urpose), P(rocess) and O(utcome) – in the context of the organisation's resources and its environment.

- When developing purpose, there is a need to develop a vision of the future within which the organisation will operate. The main reason is to ensure that every opportunity is examined. Vision is not the same as the organisation's purpose, though the two may be related. There are five criteria that may assist in developing the organisation's vision: foresight, breadth, uniqueness, consensus and actionability.

● Leaders can have a profound influence on the organisation's purpose, especially through the development of its mission and objectives. Leaders may be particularly important in moving the organisation forward to new challenges. However, in large and complex organisations their role is likely to be evolutionary rather than revolutionary.

● Because leadership is so important, it is necessary to analyse it. However, there is no agreement on the analytical process. Contingency theories are probably the most useful approach. They state that the choice and style of leadership are *contingent* on the strategic issues facing the organisation at that point in time. Within the context of contingency theory, the best-fit analytical approach can be used. It is useful in strategy because it allows each situation to be treated differently.

● Leadership style can vary from shared vision to dominance. The style needs to be modified to suit the strategic situation, with other styles being possible depending on the organisation itself and its environment. With regard to purpose, leaders need to generate trust in the strategic process. They need to draw upon the intellectual capital of the organisation and to demonstrate passion and determination. In some circumstances, leadership may be better served by allowing the purpose to emerge from the group working on a strategic task, rather than be imposed by the leader from the centre.

● By business ethics is meant the standards and conduct that an organisation sets itself in its dealings within the organisation and outside with its environment. These need to be reflected in the mission statement. There are three prime considerations in developing business ethics: the extent of ethical considerations, their cost, and the recipient of the responsibility. There are numerous differences between organisations over what should be covered under ethics, reflecting fundamentally different approaches to doing business.

● Corporate governance relates primarily to the selection and conduct of the senior officers of the organisation. It is also concerned about their relationships with the owners, employees and other stakeholders of the organisation. The importance of corporate governance lies in the power that it gives the senior officers to run the affairs of the organisation. The problem with power is that it needs to be used responsibly.

● One check on the responsible conduct of the organisation is the information relayed to all the stakeholders – good-quality information will encourage responsible conduct. The problem is that such information may be commercially sensitive. Confidential independent advisers, such as accountants in an audit, may be the means of keeping check on corporate conduct. Another way of checking on the conduct of the company is by the appointment of non-executive directors who have no other commercial connection with the company.

● Beyond the matter of information availability, corporate governance is more a matter of the principles of conduct than simple rules. The main aim is to ensure that the value generated by the assets of the organisation is distributed equitably amongst the stakeholders.

QUESTIONS

1 Take an organisation with which you are familiar and attempt to define its purpose: how has this been influenced by the factors outlined in Section 10.1, including its environment, resources, culture and stakeholders? How has the purpose changed over time? Why have these changes occurred?

2 Examining Daimler-Benz around 1990, the company claimed that its vision of the future was that of an 'integrated technology group'. Use the classification developed by Hamel and Prahalad to evaluate this vision critically (*see* Section 10.2).

▶

QUESTIONS continued

3 Can *organisations* have vision or is it the *managers* inside the organisation who have the vision? What are the implications of your answer for the development of strategy, especially in terms of communication within the organisation?

4 In what strategic circumstances should a leader be dominant? And in what circumstances should a leader work with a shared vision? Give examples to support your views and show how other factors can also influence leadership style.

5 Do companies always need to behave ethically, regardless of the costs?

6 Should 'green' environmental issues form part of the ethics of a business? How, if at all, will your answer impact on the strategy of the business?

7 How is corporate governance related to corporate strategy? What systems, if any, does DaimlerChrysler need to put in place to ensure compliance with corporate governance issues?

8 Take an organisation with which you are familiar and assess the information that it supplies to its stakeholders in terms of corporate governance issues. Is it doing a good job by its own standards and by the likely standards of its stakeholders?

9 Can the concept of purpose and competitive advantage be applied to the whole of Daimler-Benz? Compare your answers with the statements in the text from the company and comment on any differences.

STRATEGIC PROJECT   Daimler-Benz

As described in this chapter, Daimler-Benz merged with the US car company Chrysler. The purpose was to build a truly global car company and obtain the supposed advantages that will arise from this. Perhaps using Chapter 19 on globalisation, you might like to explore this further? Note that it can be explored not just from an economic perspective but also from a cultural/management viewpoint. For example, Jürgen Schrempp largely replaced the Chrysler senior management with German directors. In addition, considerable investment in new equipment and models was being made to turn around Chrysler with specific promises on profitability by Mr Schrempp for the years 2003 and 2004. There is updated material on our website.

FURTHER READING

On purpose: read Drucker, P. (1961) *Practice of Management*, Mercury, London.

On vision: Tregoe, B B *et al.* (1989) *Vision in Action*, Simon & Schuster, London. *See also* Hamel, G and Prahalad, C K (1994) *Competing for the Future*, Harvard Business School Press, Boston, MA. Both books are at the practical end of the subject.

On leadership: Bennis, W and Nanus, B (1997) *Leaders: Strategies for Taking Charge*, HarperCollins, New York. A readable text with some useful insights.

On ethical issues: a good basic text is Chryssides, G D and Kaler, J H (1993) *An Introduction to Business Ethics*, International Thomson Business Press, London.

NOTES & REFERENCES

1 References for Daimler-Benz: *Economist* 27 Apr 1991, p87; 26 June 1993, p77; *Financial Times* 7 Apr 1993, p26; 23 Sept 1993, p24; 1 Dec 1993, p49; 16 Dec 1993, p21; 20 Dec 1993, p13; 21 Dec 1993, p3; 11 July 1995, p24; 8 Aug 1995, p13; 20 Dec 1995, p25; 18 Jan 1996, p27; 14 Feb 1996, p23; 7 Mar 1996, p28; 12 Apr 1996, p23; 4 May 1999, p26; 10 October 2000, p24; 30 October 2000, p26; 24 January 2001, p37; 21 February 2001, p30; 27 February 2001, p20; 8 February 2002, p28.

2 Porter, M E (1980) *Competitive Strategy*, The Free Press, New York.

3 Williamson, O (1991) 'Strategizing, economizing and economic organization', *Strategic Management Journal*, 12, pp75–94.

4 For example, *see* Drucker, P (1961) *Practice of Management*, Mercury, London, p5.

5 The comments of one of the anonymous reviewers of the 2nd edition are acknowledged in this section of the text.

6 Whittington, R (1991) *What is Strategy and Does it Matter?*, Routledge, London, p99.

7 Drucker, P (1961) Op. cit., Ch6.

8 For example, see Prahalad, C K and Hamel, G (1990) 'The core competence of the corporation', *Harvard Business Review*, May–June, pp79–91.

9 Handy, C (1993) *Understanding Organisations*, 4th edn, Penguin, Harmondsworth, Ch4.

10 Lawrence, P R and Lorsch, J W (1967) *Organisation and Environment*, Harvard University Press, Cambridge, MA.

11 Handy, C (1993) Op. cit., Ch4.

12 Drucker, P (1961) Op. cit., Ch13.

13 For an extended exploration of this area, *see* De Wit, B and Meyer, R (1998) *Strategy: Process, Context and Content*, 2nd edn, International Thompson, London, Part V, pp805–86. But note that the purpose of the organisation is a much broader concept than that explored in this text.

14 Berle, A A and Means, G (1932) *The Modern Corporation and Private Property*, Macmillan, New York.

15 Handy, C (1993) Op. cit., Ch4.

16 Peters, T (1987) *Thriving on Chaos*, Pan Books, London.

17 Gertz, D and Baptista, J P (1995) *Grow to be Great*, The Free Press, New York.

18 Penrose, E (1959) *The Theory of the Growth of the Firm*, Oxford University Press, Oxford.

19 Morgan, G (1998) *Images of Organization*, Sage, Thousand Oaks, CA, p10.

20 Drucker, P (1961) Op. cit., p5.

21 Kay, J (1994) *The Foundations of Corporate Success*, Oxford University Press, Oxford, Ch2.

22 Drucker, P (1961) Op. cit., p9. He was thinking of the work that started with Adam Smith, David Ricardo, Alfred Marshall and others.

23 Chaharbaghi, K and Lynch, R (1997) 'Sustainable Business Growth: Origins, Conditions and Process', *University of East London Research Paper*.

24 Bennis, W and Nanus, B (1997) *Leaders: Strategies for Taking Charge*, HarperCollins, New York, p82.

25 Hamel, G and Prahalad, C K (1994) *Competing for the Future*, Harvard Business School Press, Boston, MA, p31.

26 Hamel, G and Prahalad, C K (1994) Ibid, p29.

27 Hamel, G and Prahalad, C K (1994) Ibid, p122.

28 Bennis, W and Nanus, B (1985) *Leaders: the Strategies for Taking Charge*, Harper and Row, New York.

29 Hunt, J (1998) 'Questions of commitment', *Financial Times*, 20 May, p18.

30 Weihrich, H and Koontz, H (1993) *Management: Global Perspective*, 10th edn, McGraw-Hill, New York, p490.

31 Westley, F and Mintzberg, H (1989) 'Visionary leadership and strategic management', *Strategic Management Journal*, 10, pp17–32.

32 Homans, G (1965) *The Human Group*, Routledge and Kegan Paul, London. Chapter 7 on the 'Norton Street Gang' is illuminating and reflects research by Whyte in 1943.

33 Whittington, R (1991) Op. cit., pp47–9.

34 Miles, R E and Snow, C C (1978) *Organisation Strategy, Structure and Process*, McGraw-Hill, New York.

35 Handy, C (1993) Ibid, Ch4. This whole section has benefited from this excellent text.

36 Senge, P (1990) 'The leader's new work: building learning organisations', *Sloan Management Review*, Fall. Reprinted in De Wit, R and Meyer, R (1994) *Strategy: Process, Content, Context*, West Publishing, St Paul, MN, pp132–41.

37 Developed from the work of Bourgeois, L J and Brodwin, D (1983) 'Putting your strategy into action', *Strategic Management Planning*, Mar/May. The complete paper is reprinted in De Wit, B and Meyer, R (1998) *Strategy: Process, Content and Context*, 2nd edn, International Thompson Business Press, London, pp682–90.

38 Bennis, W and Nanus, B (1997) Op. cit.

39 Useful survey of Enron ethics: Chaffin, J and Fidler, S (2002) *Financial Times*, 9 April, p30.

40 This section has benefited from Chryssides, G D and Kaler, J H (1993) *An Introduction to Business Ethics*, International Thomson Business Press, London.

41 Dickson, T (1995) 'The twelve corporate commandments', *Financial Times*, 11 Oct, p18.

42 *Financial Times* (1998) *Visions of Ethical Business*, Volume 1, October. Various authors.

43 Dickson, T (1994) 'The search for universal ethics', *Financial Times*, 22 July, p11.

44 For a fuller discussion, *see* Chryssides, G D and Kaler, J H (1993) Op. cit., Ch5. *See* also Badaracco, J L and Webb, A (1995) 'Business ethics: a view from the trenches', *California Management Review*, 37, Winter, pp8–29, and reply in *California Management Review*, 39 Spring 1997, Letter to the Editor, p135. *See* also Reich, R B (1998) 'The new meaning of corporate social responsibility', *California Management Review*, 40, Winter, pp8–17.

45 British Petroleum (1997) *Annual Report and Accounts*.

Chapter 11

Purpose emerging from knowledge, technology and innovation

Learning outcomes

When you have worked through this chapter, you will be able to:

- define and explore the implications of tacit and explicit knowledge;
- explain how purpose emerges from knowledge creation;
- examine the implications of developments in technology for the organisation's purpose and strategy;
- identify the main innovation processes relevant to purpose;
- show how purpose changes with innovation;
- explain why an organisation's purpose may sometimes be emergent rather than prescriptive.

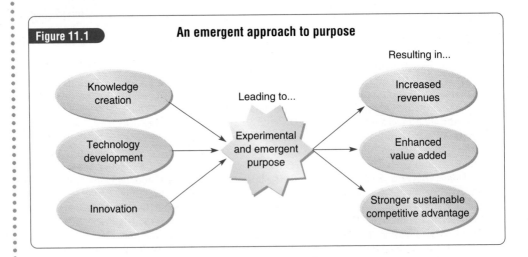

Figure 11.1   **An emergent approach to purpose**

■ Introduction

Chapter 10 concentrated on shaping purpose in a defined and explicit way. Essentially, it adopted a *prescriptive* approach. Typically, many organisations seek to define purpose in such terms – for example, they might develop a defined code of ethical conduct, a target for earnings per share, a specific increase in the return on capital employed, a gain in market share and so on. One of the consequences of shaping purpose explicitly in this way is that it will exclude, by definition, alternative purposes and strategies whose outcomes are unknown and non-specific or whose outcomes are predicted to fail to meet the defined prescriptive criteria. The danger of such approaches is that they may exclude purposes and strategies that may be more rewarding in the long term and deserve some early exploration as part of strategy development. The objective of this chapter is to redress the balance.

In open-ended investigations, purpose might be allowed to be more experimental and developed from the process itself – an *emergent* approach to purpose. The issue is how to set about this task. There are many routes, three of which are explored in this chapter: knowledge creation, technology development and innovation. Ultimately, all three processes need to be related back to the organisation, especially their ability to contribute to value added and to sustainable competitive advantage. These two areas are useful criteria for this more open-ended approach to the development of purpose – *see* Figure 11.1.

CASE STUDY 11.1

Developing new knowledge at Nike

When Phil Knight founded Nike with US$500 in 1964, he would have had little credibility if he had defined his purpose as being to build the world's largest sportswear company. Yet this is what the company had become by 2001. This case examines the foundations of the company's growth, especially the knowledge developed and retained within the company over the years.

Early learning years: the 1960s and 1970s

Back in 1958, Phil Knight was a middle-distance runner in the University of Oregon's track team. He complained on a number of occasions to his coach, Bill Bowerman, about the lack of any really good US running shoes. But he continued to study accountancy, eventually graduating and moving to teaching in his home town of Portland, Oregon. Then in 1964, he and Bowerman each put up US$500 to found the Nike shoe company, named after the Greek goddess of victory.

To start the company, Knight used his athletics contacts to sell running shoes from a station wagon at track and field events. He bought the shoes from Japan but always felt that there was potential for a US-designed shoe. By the early 1970s, Knight was working on his new design ideas. At the time he was exploring these, demand for Nike shoes was sufficient for him to consider developing his own shoe manufacture. However, he was concerned to use Japanese experience of shoe production. In 1972, he placed his first contract in Japan to begin shoe manufacture to a Nike all-American design.

Over the next couple of years, the yen moved up against the dollar and Japanese labour costs continued to rise. This made Japanese shoe production more expensive. In addition, Nike itself was gaining more experience of international manufacture and making more contacts with overseas shoe manufacturers. In order to cut production costs, Nike switched its operations in 1975 from Japan to two newly industrialised nations, Korea and Taiwan, whose wage costs were exceptionally low at that time. Nike's costs came down dramatically, allowing the company more scope for funding further product development and marketing.

▶

In sourcing production internationally from low-wage countries, Nike's approach to shoe manufacture was revolutionary for its time. The company realised that sports shoe manufacture required substantial labour input, so labour costs were potentially high and justified manufacture in countries where workers were paid much lower wages. However, there were real risks in manufacturing overseas because the greater geographical distance and different national cultures made it more difficult to control production and quality. Thus the company only switched contracts for large-scale production when it could be sure that a new manufacturing contractor was able to meet its quality standards. In this context, the company had to learn how to handle overseas production, how to brief manufacturers on new designs and models, and how to set and maintain quality standards.

The decade of difficulty and renewal: the 1980s

By the early 1980s, Nike was profitable and continuing to develop its role as a specialist US sports shoe manufacturer with no production facilities in its home country. Then along came competition in the form of a new sports shoe manufacturer, Reebok. From a start-up company in 1981, Reebok went into battle against Nike under its founder and chief executive, Paul Fireman. Reebok launched a strong and well-designed range of sports shoes with great success. By the mid-1980s, Reebok had equalled Nike's annual sales in a fierce competitive battle. In 1987, Reebok was clear market leader with sales of US$991 million and a market share of 30 per cent, compared with Nike sales of US$597 million and a share of 18 per cent.

To hit back against Reebok, Nike then began to invest considerable sums on developing new and innovative sports shoe designs. The most successful of these was begun in the late 1980s, the Nike Air shoe. 'It was an intuitively simple technology to understand,' said John Horan, publisher of Sports Goods Intelligence, a US industry newsletter. 'It's obvious to consumers that if you put an airbag under the foot, it will cushion it.' But it was not until 1990 that the Nike Air shoe was launched and began to deliver success for Nike. Thus the 1980s were both the decade of difficulty and the time for renewal. Nike had learned about the heat of competition and the need for innovation and continual R&D in its shoe designs.

The new heights of the 1990s

Coupling the new Nike Air shoe with advertising featuring Michael Jordan was a touch of marketing inspiration. The US basketball star, top of his chosen sport, was signed up to promote the new product in a multimillion-dollar deal that added a new dimension to sports sponsorship. The marketing campaign developed links between Nike and Jordan's athletic ability and image. Reebok hit back with its own design, the Reebok Pump shoe, but it was forced to use Shaquille O'Neal, a major basketball star but second to Michael Jordan. Thus around the turn of the decade, Nike's market share rose from 25 per cent in 1989 to 28 per cent in 1990 while Reebok's share dropped from 24 per cent to 21 per cent.

Building on this success, Nike realised that such promotion provided powerful support for the brand. Over the next few years, this was enhanced by the heavy funds Nike was prepared to invest. For example, in 1995 Nike invested almost US$1 billion in sports marketing, compared with Reebok's spending at around US$400 million.

In addition, Nike began sports sponsorship deals. These included the golf star Tiger Woods and, for a previously unheard-of sum, the whole Brazilian football team. By signing a ten-year deal in 1996 worth between US$200 and 400 million, Nike broke new ground in football sponsorship. But it was not just the amount of money invested at Nike. The brand and the message were also important. During the 1980s and 1990s, the company had come to understand its target market well – young, cool and competitive teenagers. The 'swoosh' logo was highlighted on all its goods to help brand the product and the main message, 'just do it', was developed to express the individuality of the target group. The accompanying slogan of 'winning your own way' captured the aggression, competition and individual success epitomised by the sports stars who were signed up. However, Nike was criticised for its use of cheap labour in some countries and was forced to take steps to deal with this. The company's approach to this matter still rankles with some members of the target group to this day.

The new millennium

Throughout the 1990s, Nike continued to develop rapidly in two further, related activities. It had been

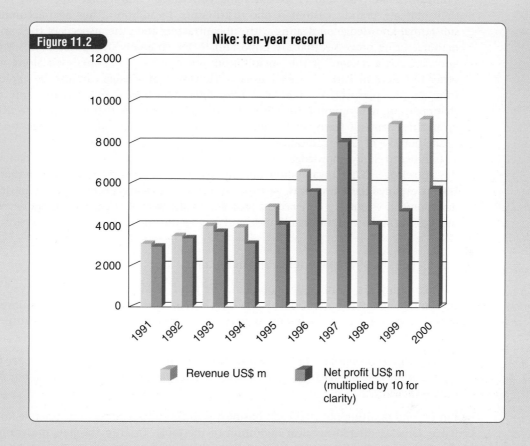

Figure 11.2

Nike: ten-year record

Revenue US$ m

Net profit US$ m (multiplied by 10 for clarity)

expanding its international sales for some time and these continued to grow rapidly. In addition, it was developing the Nike brand into non-shoe areas such as clothing and sports equipment. By the year 2000, Nike was the biggest sports goods manufacturer in the world. However, the Asian economic downturn in the late 1990s hit the company hard and there was also heavy overstocking of its products in the US retail trade that hit the company in 2000 and onwards. Profits were well down and painful job cuts were necessary, but the company was still optimistic about the future. Phil Knight had become the chairman and Mr Tom Clarke had taken over as chief executive. Mr Clarke was quite clear:

You grow a lot, then you need a period when things aren't booming to ask what works and what doesn't . . . Remember, we're a fairly self-critical bunch. We're running the company for the longterm, not to keep people happy for the next couple of quarters.

Although Nike was not to be diverted from its prime purpose of remaining the world's largest sports goods company, it was hard to forget the modest start – selling from the back of a station wagon in 1964.

Source: See reference 1.

Case questions

1 *What knowledge has Nike acquired over the years? Use the definitions of knowledge contained in this chapter to help you move beyond the obvious.*

2 *What other resources beyond knowledge does the company possess that offer clear sustainable competitive advantage?*

3 *From a consideration of this case, what conclusions can you draw on the emergent purpose of Nike in relation to its knowledge?*

11.1 Knowledge creation and purpose

Companies like Nike and Reebok develop considerable knowledge over time about their markets, brands, customers and distributors. In addition, they also accumulate substantial knowledge on dealing with subcontractors and other aspects of the various manufacturing processes that are important to the company's purpose. In this sense, knowledge is a *resource* of the organisation and deserves to be analysed along with other resources in Part 3 – *see* Chapter 6. However, knowledge can also be explored from another perspective – that of *creating future knowledge* – and it is this approach that opens up new opportunities. It is this second perspective that we will concentrate on in this chapter. Clearly, such a viewpoint could have a considerable impact on the future purpose of the organisation.[2]

In order to clarify knowledge creation, it is helpful to begin by exploring the nature of the knowledge of an organisation and by assessing its existing knowledge resources. Having explored these two areas, we can then move on to consider the issue of knowledge development, essentially an *emergent* process. Finally, we can relate knowledge development to the purpose of the organisation and explore the implications of this approach.

11.1.1 Knowledge: its strategic origins and definition

For many years in strategy development, the topic of knowledge never received any substantive or explicit attention.[3] Some early writers on strategy recognised its importance but only Drucker made any significant attempt to explore its significance. He wrote in 1964:

> *Knowledge is the business fully as much as the customer is the business. Physical goods or services are only the vehicle for the exchange of customer purchasing – power against business knowledge.*[4]

But beyond pointing out that each business is likely to have areas of distinctive knowledge, Drucker offered no clear definition of the topic. Even in the new millennium, there is no widely agreed definition of the main aspects of knowledge from a strategic perspective. But if we are to use knowledge in strategy development then we need to be able to recognise it, so some form of definition is important. For our purposes, we will adopt the definition of knowledge proposed by Davenport and Prusack:[5]

> *Knowledge is a fluid mix of framed experience, values, contextual information and expert insight that provides a framework for evaluating and incorporating new experiences and information. It originates and is applied in the minds of knowers. In organisations, it often becomes embedded not only in documents or repositories but also in organisational routines, processes, practices and norms.*[6]

The keys to this lengthy but helpful definition lie in such words as 'fluid mix... embedded... practices'. The most useful knowledge in many organisations is often the most difficult to understand, codify and replicate. Just as it is difficult to pin down a simple definition of knowledge, it is also problematic to identify the knowledge of an organisation. Importantly, the above definition also tells us what knowledge is not:

● Knowledge is not just *data* – a set of discrete, observable facts about events, e.g. the market share data on Nike quoted in the earlier case. The weakness with such data is that it only describes a small part of what happened at Nike and gives little idea of what made the company so successful.

- Knowledge is not just *information* – the information message, often in a document or some other form of communication, certainly has meaning but it has little depth. And knowledge requires depth from a strategy perspective. For example, it is useful to know that Nike's positioning was summarised in the phrase 'just do it'. But the meaningful part is to understand why such wording was chosen and how it was developed.

More generally, Nike's experience of dealing with its customers and suppliers cannot be usefully summarised in statistical data and information, although this might form part of a broader whole. Nike's knowledge will have two main parts:

1 a range of manufacturing contracts, procedures and practices built up over time – the 'routines and processes' part of its knowledge;

2 a whole series of working experiences, personal friendships and other activities also developed over time that are much more difficult to summarise – the 'framed experiences, values' part of the definition above.

Because it is difficult to define knowledge, most organisations have taken a broad view on what should be included. This has the disadvantage of possible information overload but avoids pre-judging what will be important for individuals in developing new areas of purpose.

Whatever view is taken of knowledge, the information age will certainly mean that it will be central to corporate strategy. Knowledge will go well beyond basic market share, financial data and management accounting information and involve people and unquantifiable assets. To paraphrase Professor Gary Hamel,[7] Madonna may have been the material girl but what sets her apart are her immaterial assets – her knowledge-based copyrights, recording deals, television and film contracts and so on. In addition, her reputation, her life and her relationship with her audience will also represent important assets. Many of these items are less easy to measure, but represent the real wealth and knowledge at the centre of the global information environment. They are Madonna's sustainable competitive advantage.

11.1.2 Knowledge: the distinction between tacit and explicit knowledge

With hindsight, some knowledge assets are clear enough. But the company itself may be unclear on what knowlege is needed for future product developments. Moreover, some knowledge – called *explicit knowledge* – may be clearer than other, rather more vague but equally valuable, knowledge – called *tacit knowledge*.

This useful distinction between two types of knowledge was first drawn by Nonaka and Takeuchi.[8] They researched the experiences of the Japanese domestic appliance company Matsushita Electric in 1985. The company was attempting to develop a new home bread-baking machine. For months, dough was analysed and X-rayed and prototype machines were built. But none produced a decent loaf. They were all undercooked, burnt, unevenly cooked or simply dried out. Finally, a software developer, Ikuko Tanaka, proposed a practical solution: find the best bread maker in the local town and watch how bread was made. She discovered that it was made in a distinctive way, involving stretching and kneading the dough. After a year of study and experimentation, Matsushita was able to launch its bread-making machine, which made good bread and achieved high sales. Nonaka and Takeuchi drew two specific conclusions on the nature of knowledge from this and other studies:[9]

1 Some knowledge is difficult to specify. It is fuzzy, often complex and unrecorded; they called this *tacit* knowledge.

2 After such knowledge has been carefully analysed, it is often possible to define it more precisely; they called this *explicit* knowledge.

All organisations have tacit and explicit knowledge, including Nike. It is the tacit knowledge that often delivers the sustainable competitive advantage because it is this part that competitors have trouble in replicating. For example, the managing director of one of Toyota's car manufacturing plants in the US never had any doubts about inviting competitors to tour his plant. He knew that they would never discover the real secrets of the Toyota Production System because much of the knowledge was tacit and impossible to observe on one quick visit.

However, explicit knowledge may also provide sustainable competitive advantage – for example, a company's patents will be recorded for other companies to examine but remain exclusively owned by the originating company. Although both types may contribute to the sustainable competitive advantage of the organisation, tacit knowledge may be particularly important because it is less easy for competitors to comprehend and therefore copy. Exhibit 11.1 shows examples of tacit and explicit knowledge in a company.

Exhibit 11.1 **Examples of tacit and explicit knowledge in a company**

Tacit knowledge

- Practical and unwritten procedures for unblocking production stoppages
- Informal networks and procedures for sales order processing
- Multifunctional team working on new projects that rely on informal contacts
- Experience of what has worked in practice in branding development over a number of years
- Specific company treatments of some detailed aspects of management accounting

Explicit knowledge

- Costing procedures codified in company accounting manuals
- New product development through formal company review procedures
- Company patents and legal contracts
- A company's written history of its past events and experiences, successes and failures – often very limited
- Training schemes and apprenticeship programmes that develop and teach best practice

---

Importantly, the description of the interrelationship between tacit and explicit knowledge shows that one can lead to the other. Thus a mechanism is provided for emergent strategy development.

11.1.3 Knowledge audit and management

If knowledge creation is important for purpose, the question arises as to whether it is possible to draw up an inventory of existing knowledge and renewal capacity as a starting point for future development. In the phrase of the Swedish insurance company Skandia, can we assess the *intellectual capital* of an organisation? It is this company that has provided a lead in this area. In the early 1990s, it argued that many of the accounting laws and rules developed after the Second World War were outmoded because they did not measure a company's intellectual assets, only its physical assets such as land, plant and raw materials.

Skandia defined the intellectual capital of its operations as its:

future earnings capacity from a deeper, broader and more human perspective than that described in [its financial reports]. It comprises employees as well as customers, business relations, organisational structures and the power of renewal in organisations. Visualising and interpreting these contexts can provide better insight into future development at an earlier stage.[10]

The company then divided the basic concept of intellectual capital into a number of components, each of which contributes to the creation of market value. It pointed out that in traditional economics only one of these aspects is measured – the financial capital – but, in reality, there are many other contributors to a company's future profits summarised in its intellectual capital. These elements are shown in Exhibit 11.2.

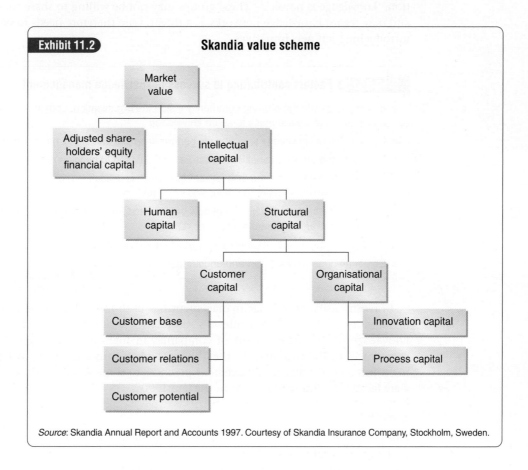

| Exhibit 11.2 | Skandia value scheme |

Source: Skandia Annual Report and Accounts 1997. Courtesy of Skandia Insurance Company, Stockholm, Sweden.

Intellectual capital has two main components: *human capital*, which is similar to the tacit knowledge outlined in the previous section, and *structural capital*, which is similar to the explicit knowledge also covered. Structural capital can then be divided into two further elements related to the *customer capital* and the *organisational capital* of a company. The organisational capital includes information systems, databases, information technology solutions and other related knowledge areas. The company has then developed a method of exploring the implications of this knowledge valuation exercise that lays particular emphasis on the future value of knowledge.

Over the last few years, similar approaches to knowledge assessment and its transferral around the organisation have been adopted in varying ways by many other organisations.[11] Rather than concentrating on the calculation of the total sum of knowledge in an organisation – the intellectual capital approach – such efforts have focused on the gathering and sharing of knowledge around an organisation – the *knowledge management* approach. But they cover similar areas.

Particularly in service and consultancy organisations, knowledge management has come to be regarded as the prime source of competitive advantage. Hence, the collection and dissemination of knowledge around the organisation has become a top strategic priority. Assessments have been made of the factors that are most likely to contribute to the success of knowledge management.[12] These are shown in Exhibit 11.3. The first point is particularly important because, for some groups in an organisation, 'knowledge is power'.[13] These groups may not be willing to share such knowledge and may regard knowledge networks as a threat. Care therefore needs to be taken when introducing such new initiatives.

Exhibit 11.3 **Factors contributing to success in knowledge management**

- Building a knowledge-sharing community inside the organisation, both in technical terms and in terms of a willingness to share knowledge
- Contribution of knowledge to economic performance and value, e.g. profits and cost savings
- Technical and organisational infrastructures, which need to be wide-ranging to succeed
- The need to gather both the tacit knowledge, which is difficult to record, and the explicit knowledge, which is easier to record and circulate
- Clarity on the background history of how the knowledge was derived, its context in relation to other areas and the learning that has resulted
- Recognition that many channels are needed for knowledge gathering and transfer
- Senior management support and encouragement

In recent years, knowledge management has been used to share best practice across organisations. For example, Unilever's subsidiaries in South America had considerable knowledge of the management of companies in high-inflation economies, after the experiences in the continent in the 1980s. The company used its knowledge management intranet to transfer management practices to some Asian subsidiaries when they were faced with similar problems in the late 1990s.

Comment

From a strategic perspective, knowledge management has become important. However, no single concept or process has yet been devised that will capture all the main elements.[14] The audit and its implications remain to be fully developed. Moreover, in spite of the enthusiastic reception for auditing knowledge, it has three disadvantages in strategy development:

1 The approach may lend itself to what can be easily audited and circulated – *explicit* knowledge – rather than the *tacit* knowledge that will also deliver competitive advantage but remains, by definition, less easily defined and audited.

2 An audit makes little attempt to distinguish between what is merely interesting and what is vital to strategy and purpose. Companies run the risk of being swamped by the irrelevant in the name of knowledge management.

3 The knowledge audit is backward-looking while strategy development is forward-looking. Its value may therefore be somewhat limited.

11.1.4 The knowledge creation process

Knowledge creation can be considered as the development and circulation of new knowledge within the organisation. Although the knowledge audit helps to define the starting point, its role is essentially static. Creation arguably requires a more dynamic approach and offers a new strategic opportunity. The full mechanisms for knowledge creation remain to be resolved but some key elements can be distinguished:

● organisational learning mechanisms;

● knowledge creation and acquisition processes;

● knowledge transfer processes.

Organisational learning mechanisms – the contributions of Argyris and Garvin

The creation of new knowledge in an organisation needs to start from the basis of its existing knowledge. *Learning* may be seen as the process of expanding the knowledge of the organisation. It involves a *loop* of activity consisting of acquiring new knowledge, checking this against reality and then storing the result – for example, reading the room temperature on a thermostat, checking the room temperature to ensure comfort and adjusting the thermostat if required. The learning process may involve study, tuition and practical experience. In the complex world of business and not-for-profit organisations, learning will involve all three mechanisms and thus become complex.

For organisations, learning has a further degree of difficulty because periodically it needs to embrace a fundamental review of the organisation's purpose and objectives. This will involve the managers of the organisation asking difficult questions and will place demands on them that go beyond mere data gathering and checking against reality. It was Professor Chris Argyris of Harvard Business School who first coined the term *double-loop learning* to explain this extra complexity. In addition to the first learning loop described in the paragraph above, there is a second learning loop which questions the whole mechanism served by the first loop. To take the example from the previous paragraph, he likened it to checking whether a thermostat was really needed and whether a completely different temperature control mechanism would produce better and cheaper results.[15] It is this fundamental reappraisal that is important to corporate strategy and to the acquisition of totally new knowledge by organisations – *see* Figure 11.3.

Given such difficulty, it is not surprising that there is no agreed definition of the learning organisation. Most people accept that organisations learn over time and that increased knowledge will deliver increased performance, but the processes beyond this are open to dispute. Some argue that organisations must change the way that they behave for true learning to occur, whereas others argue that simply acquiring new ways of thinking is sufficient. Recognising these difficulties, Professor Daniel Garvin, also from Harvard University Business School, has provided the following definition:[16]

> *A learning organisation is an organisation skilled at creating, acquiring and transferring knowledge, and at modifying its behaviour to reflect new knowledge and insights.*

It is the second part of this definition, 'and modifying its behaviour', that constitutes the second learning loop. The mechanisms identified by this definition – knowledge creation, acquisition, transferral and modification – are explored in the paragraphs that follow. Importantly, the latter point that organisations will only show that they have learnt when they have modified and changed their past behaviour is one that will be picked up under the topic of strategic change in Chapters 15, 16, 20 and 21 in this text.

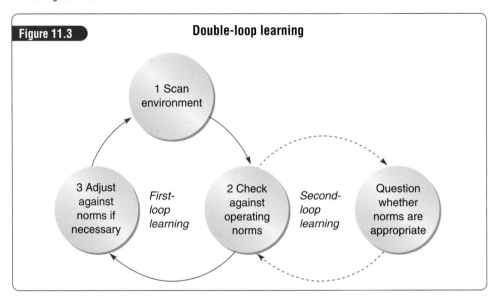

Figure 11.3 — Double-loop learning

Knowledge creation and acquisition processes

As a starting point in the exploration of knowledge creation, it is useful to return to the concepts of tacit and explicit knowledge and to explore the mechanisms by which organisations develop from one to the other. Because tacit knowledge is personal and context-specific, i.e. it can only be used for a defined task, it is difficult to communicate to others. But knowledge creation requires some form of sharing of the knowledge, however difficult the process. This will take place through words and phrases that are then 'crystallised into explicit concepts'.[17] This process of *externalising* the tacit knowledge is an important step in knowledge creation.

Beyond this process, Davenport and Prusak recommend six mechanisms that will assist in knowledge creation.[18] They are:

1 *Acquisition.* New knowledge does not necessarily come from inside the organisation. British Petroleum is reported by Davenport and Prusak to award a 'Thief of the Year' award to the employee who has 'stolen' the best ideas in applications development from other companies.

2 *Rental.* Knowledge can also be rented or leased in the sense that it can be sponsored and developed by an outside institution such as a university or a consultant. It is important in this case for the sponsoring organisation to retain the ownership of its use.

3 *Dedicated resources.* Typically in many organisations, special groups or task forces are set up with the objective of generating new knowledge in a specific area. For example, a task force might be used by Nike to develop new areas of sponsorship.

4 *Fusion.* For certain complex problems, some organisations bring together people from different functional backgrounds and with differing personalities. They are *fused* together in the sense of forcing interaction in order to develop totally new approaches to a task. For example, the Matsushita bread machine required bakers, engineers and software developers. This is a well-proven method of knowledge development.[19]

5 *Adaptation.* Many external pressures will force organisations to adapt to new realities or they will not survive. Case study 11.2 later in this chapter describes the new knowledge that will be needed in the banking market if traditional banks are to survive.

6 *Networks*. Formal and informal communities of knowledge sharing exist in many organisations. Such networks of knowledge are now being supplemented by such electronic mechanisms as the intranet, a formal computer network inside an organisation for the exchange of knowledge. For example, Heineken set up a new company-wide intranet site in 1998 under the heading 'Knowledge is Power'.[20]

Knowledge transfer processes

New knowledge is unlikely to deliver its full potential if it remains with the originators in an organisation – it needs to be transferred to others. This is not a simple task because such a process involves people and groups. People may not understand each other, may feel threatened by new developments and may be unwilling to tolerate the mistakes or ambiguity that will surely occur during the process of transferral. In addition, groups of people may judge themselves to be the main owners of certain types of knowledge and also judge that their status will be lowered if such knowledge is shared.[21] These matters need to be addressed if the knowledge transfer process is to be successful. They may involve changes in the culture of the organisation, which cannot be achieved quickly.

Beyond these difficulties, there are some mechanisms that will assist in the transfer of knowledge. The 3M company is a well-known and successful exponent of them. The reader is therefore referred to the description of these mechanisms in Case study 11.3 later in the chapter.

11.1.5 Knowledge and purpose

If new knowledge is significant in its impact, then it may well change the purpose of the organisation, perhaps providing the opportunity for global market leadership, as happened at Nike, perhaps threatening the survival of a business, as occurred with the mechanical calculator companies described in Chapter 9, which were overwhelmed by the new electronic machines.

The important point here is that the purpose of the business will only be changed *after* the new knowledge has been developed and made explicit. In this sense, a new definition of purpose *emerges* from the new acquisition of knowledge and cannot be easily defined in advance. This has not stopped companies attempting to define purpose in advance of a specific breakthrough in their knowledge: Hewlett-Packard (US), 3M (US) and Glaxo Wellcome (UK) are examples. But the attempt is usually made to focus minds and energy inside the company, rather than anything more explicit. It follows that the success rate is mixed – just look at the poor growth in the 3M case study later in this chapter from a company that has consistently set innovative growth targets and then struggled to meet them.

Within this caution about the emergent nature of purpose, it is possible to be more explicit about the way that knowledge management will contribute to the purpose of the organisation. This book has argued that, fundamentally, the purpose of an organisation is to *add value* and that this is assisted by the development of *sustainable competitive advantage*. It is therefore appropriate to explore how knowledge contributes to these two areas. Knowledge is essentially a resource of the organisation, so these two issues can be explored by considering the *resource-based view* of the organisation, outlined in Chapter 6. Teece has argued that knowledge can contribute to competitive advantage through two related mechanisms:[22]

1 *Replicabililty*. As outlined above, knowledge is often only useful when it is transferred and replicated in other parts of an organisation. This is particularly difficult where

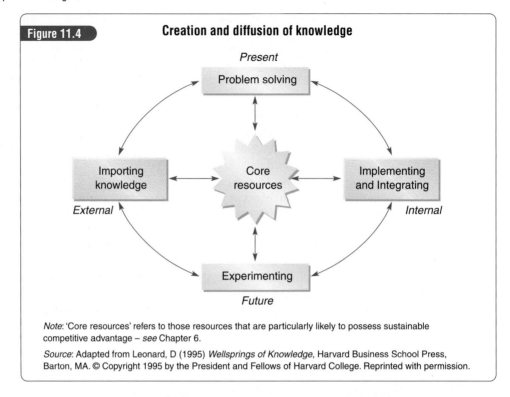

Figure 11.4 **Creation and diffusion of knowledge**

Present

Problem solving

Importing knowledge

External

Core resources

Implementing and Integrating

Internal

Experimenting

Future

Note: 'Core resources' refers to those resources that are particularly likely to possess sustainable competitive advantage – *see* Chapter 6.

Source: Adapted from Leonard, D (1995) *Wellsprings of Knowledge*, Harvard Business School Press, Barton, MA. © Copyright 1995 by the President and Fellows of Harvard College. Reprinted with permission.

tacit knowledge is the main asset. Even where knowledge is explicit, organisations may have difficulty in replicating it where such knowledge is complex, relies on local cultures and faces other impediments.

2 *Imitability*. This simply means the ability of competitors to replicate the knowledge of the first organisation. If replication is difficult for the original owner, then it will surely be more difficult for competitors. However, when knowledge becomes explicit and published, then it is more likely to be imitated. This is particularly possible where an organisation has failed to defend its knowledge through the acquisition of intellectual property rights, such as patenting.

Finally, knowledge adds value through a circular mechanism that will impact on purpose at various stages of development. This is best seen in Dorothy Leonard-Barton's model of the creation and diffusion of knowledge – *see* Figure 11.4. This makes a clear distinction between the current and future tasks of an organisation: *in the present*, the organisation can problem solve, whereas *in the future* it can experiment without being clear about the outcome. The model also separates two mechanisms for the acquisition of knowledge: *internally* through discussion, implementation and integrating mechanisms, and *externally* through the knowledge acquisition.

Key strategic principles

- The knowledge of an organisation is hard to define precisely. Essentially, it is a constantly changing mixture of experience, values, contextual information and expert insight. Importantly, knowledge is not just data and information.

▶ *Key strategic principles continued*

- The distinction between explicit and tacit knowledge is important. Explicit knowledge is recorded and structured. Tacit knowledge is fuzzy and difficult to set out. Both types may contribute to the sustainable competitive advantage of the organisation, but tacit knowledge may be particularly important because it is less easy for competitors to comprehend and therefore copy.

- An organisation's knowledge can be audited but the process is easier with explicit than tacit knowledge. The audit might form the basis of strategy development but suffers from several disadvantages.

- Knowledge creation – the development and circulation of new knowledge – offers a dynamic strategic opportunity. There are three mechanisms: organisational learning, knowledge creation and acquisition, and knowledge transfer.

- If new knowledge is significant in its impact on the organisation, then it may well change the purpose of the organisation. Importantly, the purpose will only change after new knowledge has been developed. In this sense, the purpose of the organisation *emerges* from knowledge creation.

CASE STUDY 11.2

Will traditional retail banks survive the threat of the new technologies – the Internet and telephone banking?

In the new millennium, retail banks around the world are under two related strategic threats from a totally new technology: banking on the Internet and banking by telephone. This case study examines this competitive problem. Some adaptation is clearly required, but perhaps the threat is exaggerated? Or will traditional retail banks largely disappear?[23]

Back in 1994, Bill Gates, the chief executive of Microsoft (US), upset the banking community by deriding them for being 'dinosaurs' and claiming that his company could 'bypass them'. Subsequently, he explained that what he meant was that banking software systems were old-fashioned, rather than the whole banking infrastructure. But the jibe hit home, with some banks reconsidering how they handled customer transactions. This has become particularly acute as computer usage has grown, telephone messaging has become cheaper and more reliable, and the Internet World Wide Web network has shown explosive growth.

Traditionally, retail banks asked their customers to come into their marble-clad banking halls to receive their cheque books, pay in their cash and negotiate their loans with their friendly but often rather distant bank managers. Now such transactions are increasingly being done on the telephone to call operators at central locations or on the Internet without human intervention. There are still some security problems but these will be overcome. The pace of modern life, the lower loyalty of newer customers and the increased competition from many new lenders are beginning to transform the nature of banking transactions. To what extent should banks therefore embrace the new technologies? The easy decision would mean moving onto the World Wide Web. The much more difficult problem would be whether to close many branches and provide a service mainly through the web and through telephone banking.

Some suggest that there is no fundamental strategic issue. Essentially, they argue that telephone and

▶

Internet banking will shortly be offered by all the major banks, so there will be no competitive advantage in it. Moreover, bank branches are still important for paying in cash, raising loans and many other more complex transactions that require the personal touch. Finally, they point out that the real benefit for customers would only come if they changed their account, and this is a long and tedious procedure that deters many people.

Others argue that the revolution is coming. New customers are computer literate, the Internet provides the possibility of a 'financial supermarket' of choice for a wide range of financial services and a one-stop shop. Moreover, the rapid acceptance of the new services shows that there is substantial customer demand. Professor Gary Hamel has dismissed traditional retail banks as 'mausoleums-in-

the-making' and suggested that they will largely disappear within ten years. For *new* providers of financial services, there would be a clear case for using the new technology. But for the *existing* retail banks, their substantial investment in a branch network makes the strategic decision more difficult.

Case questions

1 *What strategy would you recommend if you were managing a large retail banking network?*

2 *Can you think of other industries and markets that might also be affected by the new technology of telephone service and the Internet? What are the strategy implications?*

11.2 Using technology to develop purpose and competitive advantage

11.2.1 Technology and competitive advantage[24]

Given the pace of change over the last 20 years, technology has come to play an important role in the development of sustainable competitive advantage. Even in mature industries, not-for-profit organisations and small businesses, it is technology that has on occasions added the extra element to differentiate the organisation. For these reasons, technology strategy deserves careful investigation.

New technology developments are just as likely to alter the vision and purpose of the organisation as any other area. They can extend and enhance the existing position of the company. However, it should be noted that this will take time and resources – there may be no short-term impact on strategy. There are two main phases to this task:

Phase 1 Survey of existing technologies

Phase 2 Development of technology strategy

This phase has four elements:

Phase 1 Survey of existing technologies

1 *An organisation-wide survey of existing technologies.* This should examine areas in detail rather than making broad generalisations, as this ensures that no opportunities are missed. The result will be an audit of which technologies are used and where in the organisation they are used. The *audit* data are then classified into three areas:

- *base technologies* that are common to many companies;
- *core technologies* that are exclusive to the organisation itself, possibly delivering real competitive advantage;
- *peripheral technologies* that are useful but not central to the organisation.

Figure 11.5	**Technology/product portfolio matrix**	
New products	Possible growth opportunities in new areas	Embryonic, new stars
Mature products	Cash cows	New possible opportunities and, importantly, competitive threats
	Mature technologies	*New technologies*

2 *An examination of related areas inside the organisation.* For example, patents and intellectual property may form the basis of important areas of competitive advantage. Some companies have special skills that have never been patented but come from years of experience and training; these may also present real advantages over competitors.

3 *A technology scan external to the organisation.* This will identify opportunities that are available for later consideration.

4 *A technology/product portfolio.* A matrix can be constructed relating products and technologies (*see* Figure 11.5).

Phase 2 Development of technology strategy

To develop technology strategy, it is important to take one technology at a time or risk muddle and confusion. It may also be important to develop both the technology and the *operations* (manufacturing) processes at the same time because the two areas are interrelated and because lead times need to be shortened.

The technology development initiative then needs to be analysed in two ways:

1 the technological developments of the organisation compared with those of competitors; and

2 the costs of further development compared with the time that this will take. (There is always a trade-off here.)

In addition to these two tasks, it is important to consider the possibilities of *acquiring* new technology – possibly through company acquisition, joint ventures or the purchase of a licence to use technology, probably from a company outside the home market.

Two final issues then need to be considered:

1 *the speed of imitation.* It is important to estimate how quickly any technology development could be imitated by competitors;

2 *issues of globalisation.* It may be possible to exploit the new area on a worldwide scale and thus alter the attractiveness of the business proposition.

The above procedure may be too elaborate for some small companies and for not-for-profit organisations. However, small companies often gain their initial advantage from a technology edge. Larger companies may fail to consider the benefits of a clear drive on technology development, especially when they are operating in mature industries. The area has considerable potential strategic importance.

Technology developments are probably prescriptive in their overall approach in the sense that there needs to be a definite objective. However, they may be emergent in their detailed processes and by the nature of the experimental process.

11.2.2 Information technology and its implications for corporate strategy

Whether it needs to make a profit or not, every organisation needs information to survive. It needs data to monitor its progress and inform its members of the present status. Information and the way it is gathered can also make a contribution to competitive advantage. The provision of effective information systems is therefore an important part of the corporate strategic task.

Global information environment

With the active encouragement of the many companies involved, it is evident that the computer industry, telecommunications operators and media companies are now converging in terms of the services they offer:

- Computers come supplied with CDs, sound and fax cards and a link to the Internet.
- Telecommunications are able to transmit film and home shopping to the domestic TV screen.
- Media companies are linking commercially with consumer electronics companies.

We are in the middle of what has been called the third industrial revolution – *the information age*. Moreover, the information is global, not just local or national. For example, a major UK company now has a permanent *three-way* telecommunications link between its engineering design teams in the US, UK and India. The communications use the specialist engineering knowledge of the US team, the skills but low labour costs of their Indian colleagues, and the overall co-ordination and marketing skills of the UK headquarters. Such activity was simply not possible some years ago.

Other information examples include:

- The development of global treasury links, as multinationals and banks transfer overnight funds around the world to obtain the most favourable currency deals and interest rates.
- Major cost savings across Europe as warehouses no longer have to be sited in each country. As trade barriers have come down, operating one centre to service several countries has led to major reductions in inventory with no loss of service to the customer.
- Higher service levels using mobile telephone systems to contact salesforce and delivery vehicles, internationally as well as nationally.
- New production techniques, such as just-in-time, that require much closer co-operation between supplier and customer, relying heavily on communications technology.

New information technology has thus opened up the possibility of *greater strategic control* in companies. It has allowed corporations to be better informed and to monitor events more closely. At the same time, it has allowed subsidiaries to have greater strategic freedom, within defined parameters. One commentator has even argued that the greater spread of information will actually make it more difficult for the centre to control events because the subsidiaries may know so much and can communicate with each other, bypassing the centre.

Information resource analysis and competitive advantage

In Chapter 6, we explored Professor John Kay's view that the *architecture* of an organisation – that is, its network of formal and informal relationships – links the business together and helps to drive it forward.[25] He argued that this was one of the four distinctive areas that helped shape corporate strategy. Information resources and capabilities are a key part of an organisation's architecture.[26] Specifically, the *way* that information is gathered and the *substance* of that information will have a profound effect on architecture. Analysis of information therefore needs to address these two topics.

The involvement of less easily measurable assets, such as people, time and the immaterial assets mentioned above, means that the full cost of the information resource is difficult to determine. However, it usually amounts to a substantial investment and represents a significant part of the organisation's architecture. In this sense, information is a substantial asset for the organisation seeking to develop competitive advantage.

According to this view of strategy, competitive advantage can be developed from an organisation's information resources by what is essentially a prescriptive process. Specifically, information technology (IT) may influence competition in three ways:[27]

1 *Change of industry structure.* Porter's Five Forces Model explores the forces that influence industry strategy. Fast and accurate information can alter the *balance* of the forces, particularly where an industry needs a high information content. For example, those banks that were first into the Internet may alter the balance of power in their favour by exploiting the cost benefits of the Internet – *see* Case 11.2.

2 *Creation of competitive advantage.* Faster information and the lower costs of acquiring data will provide advantage to those companies that update their information systems more quickly and use it more effectively. For example, the introduction of insurance by telephone as against personal selling has delivered major cost savings to some companies, like Direct Line in the UK, and has revolutionised the insurance industry.

3 Ability to reach new customers. With the creation of the Internet and the development of new forms of telecommunications between individual homes and the supplier, there are real opportunities to conduct shopping and other services from an increased number of locations. Examples include home shopping, which is beginning to develop, especially for those who are housebound, and home banking on a 24-hour basis in some countries.

Comment

With regard to all the above, it is important to note that all such competitive advantages last only for a limited period of time – for example, traditional banks and insurance companies have begun telephone selling, where required. It is conceivable that technology advantages are not sustainable unless they involve some form of patent.

▶ Key strategic principles

- An internal and external scan of technologies is vital to corporate strategy development. It may alter the purpose of the organisation over time.

- Technologies should be classified into base, core and peripheral. Base areas are common to many companies. Peripheral areas are not mainstream to the organisation. The core areas are most likely to deliver competitive advantage, along with patenting and special skills.

> ▶ *Key strategic principles continued*
>
> ● Each technology should be assessed separately against competition along with the costs of further development against the time taken.
>
> ● The speed of imitation and possible global exploitation also deserve examination.
>
> ● New information technology (IT) has opened up the possibility of greater strategic control in organisations.
>
> ● The information that is collected will go well beyond basic market share, financial data and management accounting information, involving people and unquantifiable assets.
>
> ● Analysis of information needs to explore the way that it is gathered and the substance of the information.
>
> ● IT may influence the competitive situation in three ways: a change in the balance of power in industries, the creation of competitive advantage in some companies and the ability to reach new customers. But such benefits may be only temporary.

CASE STUDY 11.3

The problem with innovation at 3M

Ever since the US multinational 3M invented 'Scotch tape' and 'Post-it notes' in the mid-twentieth century, the company has been held up as an example of innovative growth. The company has developed structures and strategies to promote and nurture innovation. Yet 3M has a problem because innovation has not delivered significant growth in either total sales or profits in recent years. This case examines its famed innovation processes and the possible reasons behind the slowdown.

Early years

To give the company its full title is to reveal its early origins. The Minnesota Mining and Manufacturing Company – commonly known as 3M – started when a group of investors bought a mine in 1902 that was understood to contain the valuable and highly abrasive mineral corundum. When they discovered that only low-grade minerals were present, they decided to branch out into other products that would be more profitable. This approach typifies some of the spirit of the present company, which has made its purpose to seek out high profitability from a wide range of products.

Wide product range in the year 2000

By 2000, the 3M turnover was US$16.7 billion and its wide product range included Scotch tape (clear adhesive tape), scrub sponges, tooth-filling materials, microflex electrical circuits and replacement

Table 11.1 3M turnover in 2000 (US$ million)

Industrial	3 525
Transportation, graphics and safety	3 518
Health care	3 135
Consumer and office	2 848
Electro and communications	2 467
Speciality material	1 197
Corporate	34
Total company	16 724

Source: 3M Annual Report and Accounts.

CFC chemicals. Table 11.1 shows the broad product areas in which the company was involved.

The reasons for this breadth of product range relate to the development style and investment criteria of the company:

- Does a proposed new product deliver high profit margins?
- Does a proposed new product provide innovative growth opportunities?

Importantly, there is no requirement for the product range to stay within the basic core resources of the company – the strategic concept of the resource-based view seems to have been implicitly rejected. New products can come from anywhere. Some outsiders regarded the company as a conglomerate, which is rather unfashionable in the context of 'core competencies' – *see* Chapter 6. However, 3M's chief executive stoutly defends its range of 50 000 products: 'A very large part of what this company does has sticky stuff on it. Whether you talk about Post-it notes, or office tape, or bonding tape for industry, they're clearly sticky,' said Mr Desi DeSimone. 'The knowledge we have [allows us] to make those [basic products] valuable.'

3M's innovative process: two examples

The company is famed for its innovative processes. Its year 2000 Annual Report comments: 'In 2000, the company experienced one of the highest levels of innovation in our history, generating US$5.6bn – nearly 35 per cent of total sales – from products introduced in the past four years, with over US$1.2bn of sales coming from products introduced in 2000.' Innovation is at the essence of its business strategy and this is stimulated and supported throughout the organisation.

To illustrate the 3M approach to innovation, it is useful to consider two famous 3M examples – Scotch tape and Post-it notes. These two major products came about as a result of the company's support for the personal initiatives of two of its managers, Dick Drew and Art Fry. Mr Drew developed the former product and Mr Fry invented the latter. The way that these developments happened is important in exploring innovation at 3M.

Dick Drew was a 3M sandpaper salesman who had customers in the automobile industry. He noticed one day that they were having difficulty painting two-tone cars: it was difficult to stop the paint spreading from one area to the other. He had an idea for a sticky tape that would protect and separate the areas. He approached his company, which at that time did not make sticky tape, and was allowed to work on the project over the ensu-

ing months. At one stage, he had so little success that he was told by the president of his division at 3M to stop work on the project, but after some persuasion, he was allowed to continue. The product was eventually perfected and was used five years later as the basis of Scotch tape, which became market leader in North America.

Art Fry sang in his local church choir and needed some markers for his hymn book that would not fall out. He had the idea of taking a peelable adhesive that had been developed some years earlier at the 3M Research Laboratories and spreading it on the markers. It worked well and he asked if he could develop the product commercially. He was given permission and, after some persistence, developed a manufacturing process. But the marketing team was discouraging, pointing out that customer research suggested that a weak adhesive would not sell. Mr Fry then decided to make some markers anyway and distributed them to colleagues to try in the company. The result was a highly successful product, which became known as Post-it notes.

3M's innovative company culture

The stories above are important because they illustrate the style of 3M: 'Pursue your dream with freedom'. Employees today can spend up to 15 per cent of their total time developing their own ideas. They are given extensive support, especially from their superiors, who act as coaches and mentors, rather than judges and leaders. Failure is accepted without criticism as part of the process and there is an obsession right across the company with new ideas that have no boundaries. Regular meetings and knowledge fairs are held to allow researchers to exchange ideas. The company on-line knowledge base is extensive and widely used. The whole company culture is supportive of new ideas. This style of innovation management has led to 3M being held up as a classic example of the best practice in the area. The company has often been in the top ten of *Fortune* magazine's most admired US companies.

Slower recent growth

For all the innovation practices at 3M, the company has failed to maintain its growth rate: sales growth in 1994–95 was around 11 per cent per annum. By year 2000, this had dropped to 6 per cent per annum and profits were, at best, flat – *see* Figure 11.6. Part of the reason for the slower growth was the Asian crisis of the late 1990s:

▶

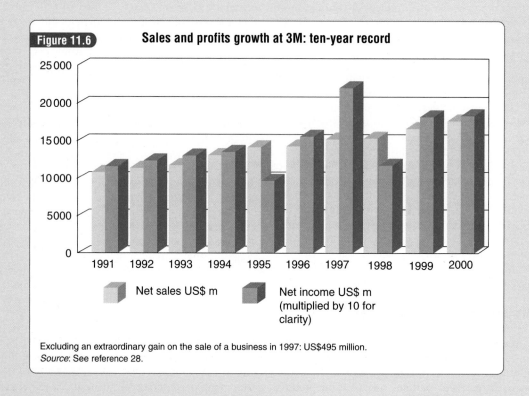

Figure 11.6 Sales and profits growth at 3M: ten-year record

Net sales US$ m

Net income US$ m (multiplied by 10 for clarity)

Excluding an extraordinary gain on the sale of a business in 1997: US$495 million.
Source: See reference 28.

around 25 per cent of the company's sales were in this region and its profit margins were also under pressure here. This was then followed by a slow-down in its home country economy – the US – which accounted for 45 per cent of turnover.

In addition, the company had another target associated with innovation that was proving difficult. The company had an objective that each division should generate at least 25 per cent of its annual sales from products that were not around five years earlier. Although it has achieved this specific target in recent years, *total* sales and profits were not growing as fast as this objective might imply. For example, 3M's net income grew by only 3.4 per cent per annum between 1996 and 2000 before allowing for inflation. There are various possible explanations and it is not clear which is correct. They include:

- the possible failure of 3M to support traditional products that might have some remaining life;
- the possibility that 3M's new products had lower profit margins, especially after launch support costs were included;

- the possibility that 3M innovative culture with regard to new products failed to focus on cost saving strategies.

However, the company was working hard to recover the situation and was optimistic that it would return to growth as the millennium progressed.

Case questions

1 *What are the main elements of the innovative process at 3M? Is it possible and desirable for other companies to emulate them?*

2 *Given its lack of success with innovation, should 3M continue to pursue this strategy? What other strategies are available to the company to increase profits? Should 3M try some of these?*

3 *To what extent, if at all, does innovation matter in setting the purpose of an organisation?*

11.3 Innovation and purpose

The analytical process described in the earlier parts of this book brings with it three potential dangers:

1 *Backward looking*. Inevitably, historical data form the starting point for future action. However, whether the strategy intends to build on past success or to fight its way out of problems, it cannot rely just on the past. There needs to be a determined attempt to move forward.

2 *Sterility*. Too much analysis may stifle creativity. New ideas, new approaches to old problems, may be weakened by overemphasis on analysis and data collection.[29]

3 *False sense of security*. Because they have already happened, events in the past can be viewed with some certainty. However, it would be wrong to see the future in the same way. Whatever is predicted stands a high probability of being at least partially incorrect.[30]

Innovation is an important antidote to these real problems. In corporate strategy, we need to move beyond the obvious and comfortable into the new and interesting. The 3M example in Case 11.3 shows how a company has attempted to use innovation to achieve its stated organisational purpose – substantial profit growth.

11.3.1 The strategic role of innovation

By definition, innovation moves products, markets and production processes beyond their current boundaries and capabilities. Innovation is the generation and exploitation of new ideas. It also provides organisations with the ammunition to move ahead of the competition. Hence, innovation can deliver three priceless assets to corporate strategy:

1 substantial future growth;

2 competitive advantage;

3 ability to leapfrog major competition, even dominant competitors.

However, none of the three above areas will automatically deliver future profitability to innovating companies – *see* Figure 11.7. Consider the cases of Canon (Japan) and EMI (UK). Both companies developed major new innovations during the 1970s.

● *Canon* set out to compete with and beat Xerox (US) in world photocopying markets. It developed a series of new processes that did not infringe the Xerox patents yet produced products that turned Canon into one of the world's leading photocopying and printing companies. By the mid-1990s, it had a larger market share than Xerox.[31]

● *EMI* was so badly wounded by its foray into medical electronics that its scanner business had to be sold off at a knock-down price. This happened despite the fact that its product was truly innovative and was the first in the market place by a significant period.[32]

Innovation is not without risk. Yet, if it is successful, the payoff is significant. There are two principal sources of innovation to be examined, neither of which is sufficient in itself:

● customer needs analysis – *market pull*

● technology development analysis – *technology push*.

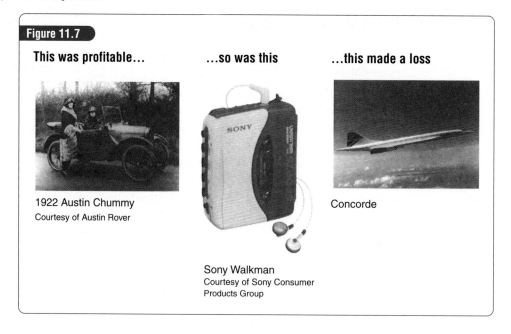

Figure 11.7

This was profitable...   **...so was this**   **...this made a loss**

1922 Austin Chummy
Courtesy of Austin Rover

Sony Walkman
Courtesy of Sony Consumer
Products Group

Concorde

11.3.2 Customer needs analysis: market pull

Baker[33] suggests that innovation occurs when companies identify new market opportunities or a segment of an existing market that has been neglected. Essentially, it is important to develop such opportunities in terms of the *customer need served* in broad general terms – for example, transport, convenience – rather than by examining current products and how they meet demand. For example, Canon photocopiers were innovatory in meeting the general demand for photocopying rather than the needs of the existing customer base, which was biased towards large companies. The company developed new machines requiring little maintenance or repair which were sold to a much broader range of customers – the medium-sized and small businesses. This process is known as *market pull* – *see* Figure 11.8.

As Whittington points out,[34] the importance of market pull in successful innovation has been well validated by research. It relies on identifying a market need that needs to

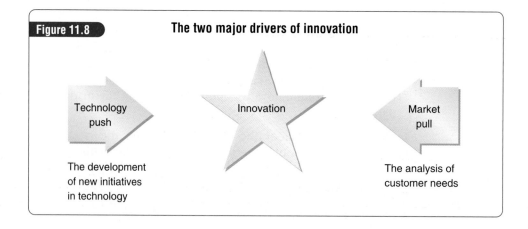

Figure 11.8   **The two major drivers of innovation**

Technology push

Innovation

Market pull

The development
of new initiatives
in technology

The analysis of
customer needs

be satisfied by a technological advance – essentially a *prescriptive* approach to corporate strategy. It is used in research and development of some new pharmaceuticals, consumer electronics and other areas of technology that are market-driven.

However, prescriptive approaches to the study of market demand carry the danger that customers are often constrained in their vision by their current experience and knowledge. More experienced approaches to market need may also be worthwhile.

11.3.3 Technology development analysis: technology push

Market pull procedures do not fully describe the way that many real innovations happen, however.[35] Innovation may be born out of developments at small companies, often in a two-way process with their customers, who may be larger companies. Alternatively, innovations may start as narrow solutions to particular problems. For example, Thomas Watson, President of IBM, said that a new calculator built by his company in 1947 (the Selective Sequence Electronic Calculator) would be able to solve many of the world's major scientific problems but had no commercial applications. It proved to be one of the first IBM computers.

Successful technology often takes time to diffuse through to other industries. It follows that, in addition to monitoring customer needs, an innovatory company should also survey other industries for their technology developments and assess their relevance to its own – essentially an emergent approach to corporate strategy. This process is sometimes known as *technology push* – *see* Figure 11.8.

Case 11.4 describes how technology push works at the Dutch electronics company Philips. Importantly, it shows that how the company is organised and how it handles the human side of technology are just as important as the new product derived from technology push.

> ## Key strategic principles
>
> - Innovation contributes growth, competitive advantage and the possibility of leapfrogging major competition.
>
> - However, innovation can be risky and can result in major company losses.
>
> - There are two major drivers for innovation: customer needs analysis (often called *market pull*) and technology development analysis (often called *technology push*).

CASE STUDY 11.4

How Philips exploits its technology edge

The Dutch-based electronics giant, Philips, has a poor record of turning its scientific brilliance into revenues and profits. This case explores how the company is changing.

Background – global from its Dutch base

Philips has over 250 000 employees and US$36 billion sales in year 2000. These covered lighting, consumer electronics, small domestic appliances, semiconductor components, medical technology, optical storage and displays. The company has its headquarters in Eindhoven, Holland, but is a truly global company in terms of both production and sales.

Table 11.2 Philips' inventions

1926	Pentode radio tube
1934	High-pressure mercury lamp
1968	Charge-coupled devices for sensing
1968	Spiral groove bearings for mechanical engineering
1972	Video long-play systems
1976	Nickel-metal-hydride batteries
1980	Modulation systems for compact discs
1980s	Low-frequency lasers for telecommunications
1995	High-speed transistors for cell phones
1997	Plastic semiconductors

Philips has around 1 500 'creative' research staff, mainly scientists in 13 laboratories, who are funded by a research budget of US$250 million. It owns 65 000 patents and claims an illustrious list of inventions – *see* Table 11.2. About two-fifths of its researchers are based in Eindhoven. But there are others in the UK, France, Germany, Taiwan and China. In addition, the company spends about six times its research budget on product development – primarily in the company's six product divisions.

Research record – inventive but not yet sufficiently exploitative

In spite of its record of invention, many observers think that Philips has failed to make the most of its research in fields such as medical equipment, home video recorders and disc-drive technology. One technology consultant says that the company has not done enough to link its researchers with outsiders, preventing it from making the most of good ideas. 'The company's research establishment has been inward-looking and arrogant,' he says. While not necessarily accepting the direct criticism, Philips' worldwide head of research, Mr Ad Huijser, recognises that there has been a problem. He has set himself the task of increasing the rate at which Philips' scientific ideas turn into profits. 'When a venture capitalist invests in new ideas, he wants to make a return,' says Mr Huijser. 'We must try to develop the same mindset.'

Organising the links for invention

In such a large company, managing the research effort is a complex task. Yet it is vital if the benefits of new inventions are to be exploited commercially. Linking the company's scientists to the six divisions of the company is one aspect of Mr Huisjer's approach. This is partly accomplished by making the divisions pay for the research: two-thirds of the research bill is covered by contracts that they have instituted. The divisions pay for directed research areas such as software, materials, integrated circuit design, electronic storage and communications technologies. The other third of the money is accounted for by 'blue sky' research authorised by Philips' research staff. An essential part of the link between product divisions and scientists is the chief technology officers who work in each division. Their job is to scout for new technologies, devised either in Philips or outside, that could help commercial efforts.

In a second part of Mr Huisjer's efforts to institute 'market pull' Philips has recruited ten business development officers. They are based in the company's worldwide research laboratories and their role is to provide a critical view of the ideas coming from the research. They may also suggest ways to commercialise them. These people, says Mr Huisjer, tend to have more of a business background than the research scientists. 'They provide a different perspective. They set targets for the ideas being pursued inside laboratories and a timetable for potential commercialisation.'

The business development officers also provide a potential conduit between Philips' research staff and other businesses with which the company might want to form a partnership to commercialise particular ideas. According to Mr Huisjer, such links are growing and now number several dozen. Mr Huisjer says that Philips has to be 'more alive' to the idea that sometimes other companies are in a better position to take on its scientific ideas than Philips itself.

The third Huisjer initiative consists of attempts to quantify the output of Philips' reseach employees. This is controversial, because measurement of the results from research involves difficult questions of what constitutes success. Even so, many think such efforts worthwhile as part of the interest in getting away from valuing research solely in terms of how much has been spent. Mr Huisjer treads carefully, looking at factors such as licensing income, patent registrations and publication of scientific papers. More unusually, every year he asks Philips' product divisions how much of their revenues in the previous 12 months has come from new scientific ideas devised by research staff. The exercise is imperfect and subjective, Mr Huisjer admits, and for this reason the results are never published.

A more radical solution

For all Mr Huisjer's efforts, Philips' critics could claim the company still has some way to go. According to this view, his ideas merely add bureaucracy to the systems already in place to govern – and sometimes cramp – the way the company exploits its science. More radical suggestions – such as dissolving Philips' research establishments and leaving research to be done either at arm's length in external organisations or directly under the control of the product divisions – seem unlikely to be taken up by the company's senior executives, who have built up a reputation over the years for conservatism. Mr Huisjer believes that his moderate efforts are paying off. The company is progressing towards the goal of making the

research effort sharper. 'We are better structured and there is less waste,' he says. 'I believe we are at least as good as other companies around the world.'

Adapted by Richard Lynch from an article by Peter Marsh, *Financial Times*, 22 March 2001, p12. Copyright *Financial Times*. Used with permission.

Case questions

1 *What three methods has the company introduced to exploit its research base? How successful has it been so far?*

2 *How does Philips attempt to employ what it calls 'market pull'? Is this really market pull, as defined in the chapter, or is it, in reality, 'technology push' with a more commercial bias?*

3 *What are the problems, if any, with seeking links with other companies when attempting to exploit technology innovation?*

4 *Given the difficulties of quantifying research output, would you look for a more radical solution as suggested by some in the case? What are the benefits and problems of such an approach?*

11.4 How to innovate: the 'ideas' process

11.4.1 The phases of innovation

Innovation often occurs through a diffusion process.[36] It may well be adopted slowly at first, then the pace quickens until finally there are just a few late-adopters left to take up the process. Diffusion thus follows the S-shaped curve shown in Figure 11.9.

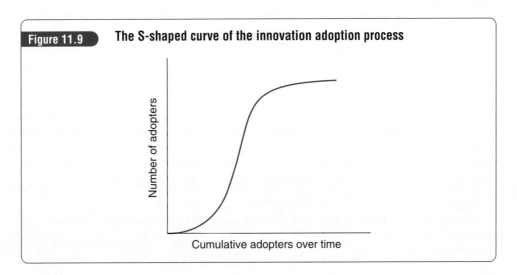

Figure 11.9 The S-shaped curve of the innovation adoption process

Number of adopters

Cumulative adopters over time

Sometimes the early pioneering companies fail to make profits because there are still few purchasers and large sums have been invested in developing the process. It is at this stage that business failures like that of the EMI scanner occur. The real profits are made during the rising part of the curve when there is major demand, pricing is still high to reflect the genuine innovation or costs have been dramatically reduced as a result of a technological breakthrough.

In some respects, corporate strategy may therefore be better served by those who are 'fast seconds' into the market place: the curve is still rising and the original innovator has still not come to dominate the market. For example, the anti-ulcer drug Zantac (Glaxo Wellcome, UK) was second into the market after Tagamet (SmithKline Beecham, UK/US) yet came to dominate the market eventually and make a substantial contribution to Glaxo profitability. The inventions at Philips – *see* Table 11.2 – also support the point that being first does not necessarily deliver profit.

This finding is supported by the research of Mansfield,[37] who tracked innovations over a 30-year period. He estimated that on average those who were second into a market could make a new product for two-thirds of the cost and time of the original innovating company. The strategic problem is how to identify correctly and react quickly to the truly new innovation – not an easy task. Utterback[38] has identified three phases in individual innovation that may help in this identification process:

1 *Fluid phase*. In the early days of an innovation, the market is in a state of flux. The products are not standardised. There are often very few small-scale producers and the manufacturing equipment is general-purpose and small-scale. Competition is limited, with heavy reliance on further product development initiatives. Innovation comes from new product development.

2 *Transitional phase*. After a period, demand has risen sufficiently to justify dedicated production machinery. At least one product design has established itself to deliver volume sales. More competitors have entered the market but the rate of entry is beginning to decline as a dominant design emerges and some companies adopt this and get ahead of competition. The competitive threat is likely to come, for the first time, from producers with lower costs and higher quality. Innovation is more likely to come from developments in the manufacturing process.

3 *Specific phase*. Over time, innovation slows down and becomes small and incremented. A few large-scale manufacturers dominate the market. They produce their goods on a relatively large scale, using specialist and dedicated machinery. Competition is more likely to be based on price and branding, until a new and genuine innovation is again developed.

We return to the dynamics of innovation in Chapter 20. For now, we should note that the above description is based on two basic assumptions and empirical observations:

1 that economies of scale and scope are possible in an industry and remain the chief means of reducing costs;

2 that custom demand can be satisfied by standardised products.

These may not be true in all industries – *see* the customer/competitor matrix in Chapter 5 and flexible manufacturing in Chapter 9.

11.4.2 The routes to delivering innovation

Given its value to the organisation, the real issue is how to deliver innovation.

For the original innovators, the payoff can be substantial with the right product. Professor James Quinn[39] of Dartmouth College, US, investigated the innovation process of a variety of companies and concluded that large companies need to behave like small entrepreneurial ventures to be truly successful. He suggested that innovatory companies should ideally follow the process he called 'controlled chaos' (*see* Exhibit 11.4) – not an easy task.

Quinn believed strongly in the *emergent process* for innovation strategy. Writing around the same time, Fred Gluck[40] of the consulting company McKinsey took largely the opposite view. He argued that the really innovatory achievements needed a '*big bang*' approach. They need masses of information, a decision-making process that can discern patterns in these undigested data and the functional skills to implement the decisions once they were made. He urged the larger corporations, to which he was addressing his remarks, to become more sensitive to major environmental changes and to create a better climate to explore *big bang* ideas.

Exhibit 11.4 **The controlled chaos approach to generating innovation**

- *Atmosphere and vision* – with chief executives providing support, leadership and projecting clear, long-term ambitions for their company
- *Small, flat organisation* – not bureaucratic, but flexible
- *Small teams of innovators* – multidisciplinary groups of idea makers
- *Competitive selection process* – with innovatory ideas selected from a range in the company, and encouragement and support, not penalties, for the losing team
- *Interactive learning* – random, even chaotic, consideration of ideas from many sources and from a range of industries

---

This conflict of views as to the best way forward for innovation would appear to be equally true for Japanese researchers. One study[41] describing Japanese practice was based on a survey of products in eight major companies including Honda, NEC, Epson and Canon. It found that the process was informal, multifunctional and involved excess information over that initially identified to solve the problem. The conclusion was that the most successful innovation processes often involved redundant information that interacted through chance, even chaotic, processes to produce the innovatory result. By contrast, another study[42] of Japanese innovation processes concluded that a more analytical approach can also be employed in some circumstances.

The overall conclusion is probably that there is no one route to innovation: both prescriptive and emergent approaches have been successfully used. There are, however, seven general guidelines that might be used to encourage the innovation process.[43]

1 *Question the present business strategies and market definitions.* Once the present strategy has been defined, there is a clear case for questioning every aspect of it. There are bound to be areas that would benefit from new definitions and approaches. A real problem for many organisations is that they live with their existing preconceptions for many years and have real problems raising their sights to new perspectives.

For example, the market and its customers might be redefined either more broadly or more narrowly. This might lead to a redefinition of the competitors and the threats and opportunities that arise. In turn, this might suggest new insights into areas where the organisation has a competitive advantage – some real leverage over others in the market. The Walt Disney Corporation redefined its market in the 1970s as one of providing pleasure using themed characters such as Mickey Mouse and Donald Duck: it used these ideas to develop another way of delivering such entertainment with the first of its Disney theme parks in Anaheim, California.

2 *Consider carefully the purpose served by the current products or services.* Exploring carefully the purpose served by the current offerings may lead to ideas about the future. It may be possible to reach the same end by new and more rewarding means. While some piano manufacturers were unable to compete for the attention of youngsters against the attractions of computer games such as Nintendo and Sega, Yamaha had other ideas. It redefined its piano as a keyboard and added new designs, sizes and technology to provide as much fun as a game.

3 *Explore external timing and market opportunities.* There are often strategic windows of opportunity that may provide real benefits if they can be tackled. Resources then need to be concentrated on such areas to ensure progress is quick, but the rewards are significant. Timing is vital, however. For example, Asea Brown Boveri (Switzerland/Sweden) and Deutsche Babcock (Germany) have seized opportunities to develop products in the area of environmental control engineering over the last few years, building on the new concerns of some governments, especially those in northern Europe and the US.

4 *Seek out competitors' weaknesses.* Most organisations have areas in which they are weak. These might provide opportunities for others to expand. However, such an approach does invite competitive retaliation and so needs to be considered carefully. For example, Microsoft has dominated world markets for computer software for years with its Windows system. The company did not notice that Netscape Communications had quietly developed software for the Internet 'browser' market and by 1995 had come to dominate this segment. Microsoft was then involved in some expensive joint deals to recover the situation in this area.

5 *Deliver new and better value for money.* Companies sometimes become locked into assumptions about the possibilities of further reductions in costs and improvements in quality. However, design and technology development is moving at such a pace in some markets that new opportunities have arisen. For example, all the Japanese car manufacturers were able to make real share gains in the 1970s and 1980s not only by competitive prices but also by offering superior quality and performance standards.

6 *Search wide and far.* Examining areas such as lifestyles, technology, regulatory regimes and demographics can generate significant opportunities. For example, Motorola (US) and Nokia (Finland) have both benefited from the rise of the mobile telephone, having developed expertise in this market over the last ten years. In the same way, Sharp (Japan) was the leading company in the launch of pocket computer organisers because it recognised trends to busier and more complex lives that needed to be managed.

7 *Seek to challenge conventional wisdom.* Acceptance of the current market and resource status is unlikely to lead to major new developments. There is a need to challenge every aspect of what is believed to be the generally held view in markets. This might include a challenge to areas such as *key factors for success*, perhaps by finding a totally new method of delivering a product or service. Some managers are better at the challenge process than others and need to be encouraged and supported as they engage in this task. For example, as late as the 1980s it was considered impossible for personal car insurance to be sold over the telephone: it was far too complicated and customers would not accept it. This has proved to be totally false. By the mid-1990s,

telephone selling had become the dominant mode of selling in several of Europe's largest markets. As a result, the new companies such as Direct Line (now a subsidiary of the Royal Bank of Scotland) have taken over market leadership in the UK.

It will be evident that there is no one piece of conventional strategic theory that will prompt innovative developments, but the strategic payoff from such processes can be substantial.

11.4.3 International perspectives on innovation

International country comparisons on innovation pose significant problems. This is because innovation is dependent on the *product group*: for example, innovation is likely to be higher in biotechnology and lower in food products because of the state of technological development in these two categories. Different countries have different strengths in different product groups (*see* Chapter 19 for an exploration of this area). Hence, it is difficult to make generalisations about countries without assessing the product groups with which they are involved.

Nevertheless, the reasons why the pace of innovation seemed to be higher in some countries than in others were explored in the 1980s.[44] Three interrelated groups of factors were identified:

1 factors that influence *inputs* to the innovation process, such as the quality of the country's scientific community, especially its educational institutions;

2 factors that influence *demand*, such as receptive and interested customers;

3 an *industrial structure* that favours intense competition to stimulate growth and provides some method for companies to spread the cost and results of scientific research, such as through a government agency.

These conclusions are similar to those of Porter when exploring the competitive advantage of nations (*see* Chapter 19).

The role of government may also be important. In France, the UK and the US, it was 'top down', directed at specific industries, such as defence, and with specific measurable objectives. In other countries such as Sweden, Switzerland and Germany, government acted in a more 'diffusion-oriented' way. It responded to market signals and provided education and training and set industry standards that raised quality and diffused technology.

In terms of competitive advantage, over the centuries nations have come to rely less on the possession of raw material wealth, which can be bought through international trade. They also place less emphasis on being close to markets, since transport costs have come down dramatically. Countries now rely heavily on scientific skills, not only to invent products but also to manufacture those that have been developed. In turn, such developments require a highly skilled workforce and investment by the state in education. In seeking sources of innovation, organisations will wish to consider the role that the state has played and is continuing to play in investing in its future workpeople. Countries such as Singapore and Malaysia have recognised the importance of investment in education to provide the structural basis for the innovatory process.

11.4.4 How purpose can emerge from innovation

If the purpose of the organisation is defined in terms mainly of survival, then it can be argued that such a purpose is present in most organisations in advance of any process of innovation. In this sense, purpose cannot be said to emerge from innovation but, rather, to precede it. However, if the purpose of the organisation is defined in some broader way to include, for example, the delivery of additional value, quality or service, then innovation can take on a very different role.

Given the right circumstances and people, innovation can occur anywhere in an organisation. It is not confined to corporate technologists or marketing managers. Innovation can thus provide new opportunities to move beyond the current position in an industry. But until the full extent and implications of an innovation have been explored, its true potential cannot meaningfully be assessed. In this sense, the new purpose that will be presented by a radical innovation – such as some aspect of bioengineering or the Internet – cannot be defined in advance but must be left to *emerge* as the innovation proceeds. Corporate strategy may be better served if at least some part of it is free from the strait-jacket of a tightly defined purpose.

▶ Key strategic principles

- The innovation process is complex and risky – early innovation pioneers did not always gain the full financial benefit from their work.

- Innovation development often follows an S-shaped curve, with the real profit being made during the growth phase, after the initial development.

- There are three phases in industrial innovation: fluid, transitional and specific. Change from the first to the second phase occurs when a product design becomes dominant. Change from the second to the third phase occurs through large-scale production.

- The innovation process can be *emergent*, with ideas freely generated from many sources. It can also be *prescriptive*, with a more analytical and directed approach to the task.

- The seven guidelines offered on innovation to start this process do not claim to be comprehensive. They have as their central theme the need to challenge conventional understanding and wisdom.

- International perspectives in innovation suggest that a strong national education structure is useful.

- If the purpose of the organisation includes an element of growth, then it may be better to allow such a purpose to *emerge* from an innovative opportunity, whose full potential cannot be known in advance.

KEY READING

Technology, innovation and corporate strategy[45]

Technology can revolutionise corporate strategy. In this extract from their book The Corporate Environment, *Huw Morris and Brian Willey explore the factors that cause technological change and its impact on society and business.*

An important question for policy makers in government and business is: what causes technological change? The answer to this question has important implications for the research and development strategies pursued by different countries and companies. New inventions and discoveries offer people the opportunity of better standards of health and education. They also provide the physical basis for an expansion of the wealth of nations and their citizens.

Conventionally, the opinions of scientific and economic historians about the causes of technological change could be divided into roughly two groups. One group of writers believed that the role of scientists and engineers engaged in pure research was central. The breakthroughs made by these specialists, they argued, produced the technological push for the development of new products, processes and organisational forms. By contrast, another group tended to highlight the role of customers and financial backers who, they suggested, provided the demand for new ways of doing things. This approach emphasised the power of the market place and the importance of the final consumer, who, they maintained, provided the demand pull which inspired new approaches.

In recent years, this polarisation of the debate between advocates of the technological-push theory and believers in market pull has been superseded by more complex explanations which combine elements of each approach. Freeman (1987)[46] provides a good example of this approach with his distinction between four forms of innovation:

● Incremental innovations

● Radical innovations

● Changes of technology system

● Technology revolutions.

Incremental innovations

Incremental innovations happen continuously in any industry or service activity. They arise as a consequence of engineers, managers and workers making suggestions to improve the goods or services being produced.

Radical innovations

Radical innovations occur irregularly and often as a result of deliberate research and development activity by companies, universities or government laboratories. The causes of these developments are difficult to ascertain. Radical innovations often provide the stimulus for the development of new markets and industries.

Changes of technology system

In this case a number of related innovations appear simultaneously and they can provoke fundamental changes in the corporate structure and composition of specific industries. Comprising a combination of incremental and radical innovation, these developments can give rise to the emergence of new industrial sectors as well as rapid and turbulent restructuring or decline within established industries.

A recent example of this type of technological change is provided by the development of multimedia forms of entertainment which combine digital communication with established television and computer technologies.

Technology revolutions

In these circumstances changes to technology are so substantial and far-reaching that they have the capacity to change the way in which people think and behave within an entire economy. These revolutions happen relatively infrequently and take many years to affect everyone; however, when they occur, they necessitate changes in the knowledge, skills and systems of working for entire populations.

A number of writers have suggested that technological revolutions occur in cycles or waves. These waves, it is argued, provide the impetus for economic growth as people find ways of exploiting these technologies.

Source: Morris, H and Willey, B (1996) *The Corporate Environment*, Pitman Publishing, London.

Summary

● The knowledge of the organisation can be used to deliver and maintain sustainable competitive advantage. Knowledge is hard to define precisely but can be considered as a constantly changing mixture of experience, values, contextual information and expert insight. It will be evident that such areas might well be exclusive to the organisation and provide distinctiveness from competition.

● Knowledge needs to be divided between its tacit and explicit forms. Explicit knowledge is recorded and structured. Tacit knowledge is fuzzy and difficult to set out. Both can lead to competitive advantage but tacit knowledge may be particularly important because it is less easy for competitors to comprehend and copy. An organisation's knowledge can be audited as the basis for strategy development, but the audit has several disadvantages.

● Knowledge creation – the development and circulation of new knowledge – offers a dynamic strategic opportunity. There are three mechanisms: organisational learning, knowledge creation and acquisition, and knowledge transfer.

● If new knowledge is significant in its impact on the organisation, then it may well change the purpose of the organisation. Importantly, the purpose will only change after new knowledge has been developed. In this sense, the purpose of the organisation *emerges* from knowledge creation.

● An internal and external scan of *technologies* is vital to the development of corporate strategy. It may alter the purpose of the organisation over time. Technologies need to be classified into base, core and peripheral. It is the core area that is most likely to deliver sustainable competitive advantage. Each technology then needs to be assessed against its competitors and for time and costs of development estimated.

● *New information technology* (IT) has opened up the possibility of greater strategic control in organisations. The control that can be exercised needs to go beyond basic financial data into people aspects of the organisation. At the same time, IT may present new opportunities to develop sustainable competitive advantage, but they are likely to be short-lived unless backed by patents.

● *Innovation* contributes growth, competitive advantage and the possibility of leapfrogging competition. However, it can also be risky and result in major losses to the organisation. There are two major drivers for innovation: customer needs analysis (market pull) and technology development analysis (technology push). The innovation process can be both prescriptive and emergent.

● There are three phases in industrial innovation: fluid, transitional and specific. Change from the first to the second phase occurs when a product design becomes dominant. Change from the second to the third phase occurs through large-scale production. The first of these is primarily concerned with product innovation. The second and third phases are more likely to be associated with manufacturing process innovation.

● If the purpose of the organisation includes an element of growth, then it may be better to allow such a purpose to *emerge* from an innovative opportunity, whose full potential cannot be known in advance.

QUESTIONS

1 Take an organisation with which you are familiar and identify its areas of explicit tacit knowledge. To what extent, if at all, does the process assist in identifying the sustainable competitive advantage of the company?

2 In what ways might a company like Nike use a 'knowledge audit' as part of its strategy development process? What are the problems with this approach? Would you recommend it?

3 'In an economy where the only certainty is uncertainty, one sure source of lasting competitive advantage is knowledge.' (Ikijuro Nonaka) Do you agree with Professor Nonaka about the unique importance of knowledge?

4 Take an organisation with which you are familiar and classify its technologies into basic, core and peripheral. What conclusions can you draw on sustainable competitive advantage for the organisation's strategy?

5 With the introduction of the World Wide Web, it has been argued that this: *'will give consumers increased access to a vast selection of goods but will cause a restructuring and redistribution of prof- its amongst stakeholders along the [value] chain'* (Robert Benjamin and Rolf Wigand). Discuss the strategic implications of this comment from the viewpoint of (a) a major retailer and (b) a small to medium-sized supplier of local building services.

6 Do you think that the increased use of IT will affect all organisations equally? Will some remain rela- tively unaffected apart from the introduction of a few computers and a link to the Internet? What are the strategic implications of your answer?

7 Identify some recent innovations and classify them into market pull and technology push. Explain how each innovation has been delivered into the market, using the S-shaped curve to show the process.

8 Quinn argues that large companies need to behave like small entrepreneurial ventures to be truly inno- vative. Gluck suggests that major innovations only come from a 'big-bang' push that needs major resources. Can these two views of the innovative process be reconciled? (*See* references 39 and 41.)

9 *'Innovate or fall behind: the competitive imperative for virtually all businesses today is that simple.'* (Professors Dorothy Leonard and Susan Straus) Is this true? Is innovation fundamental to all business strategy?

STRATEGIC PROJECT 3M

Given the company's reputation for innovative growth, you might like to track its recent progress. For example, has it overcome its difficulties in Asia and the US? You might also like to consider whether 3M would be better concentrating its innovation on a smaller range of initiatives or seeking other strategic initiatives that rely less on innovation – like cutting costs. Also, can companies like 3M continue to set specific business objectives for the results of innovation? Or is the whole process largely dependent on luck with the results emerging over time?

FURTHER READING

On knowledge: Davenport, Thomas and Prusack, Lawrence (1998) *Working Knowledge*, Harvard Business School Press, Boston, MA, is comprehensive and insightful. Nonaka, I and Takeuchi, H (1995) *The Knowledge-Creating Company*, Oxford University Press, Oxford, is one of the leading texts. Leonard, Dorothy (1995) *Wellsprings of Knowledge*, Harvard Business School Press, Boston, MA, is also about innovation.

On technology and corporate strategy: Contractor, F-J and Narayanan, V K (1990) 'Technology development in the multinational firm', *R&D Management*, Basil Blackwell, Oxford, republished in Root, F R and Visudtibhan (eds) (1992) *International Strategic Management*, Taylor and Francis, London, pp163–83, is well developed, thoughtful and comprehensive.

On IT and corporate strategy: Porter, M E and Millar, V E (1985) 'How information gives you a competitive advan- tage', *Harvard Business Review*, July–Aug. *See* also Benjamin, R and Wigand, R (1995) 'Electronic markets and virtual value chains on the information superhigh- way', *Sloan Management Review*, Winter, p62.

On innovation: Tidd, Joe, Bessant, John and Pavitt, Keith (1997) *Managing Innovation*, John Wiley, Chichester, is comprehensive, with a useful academic foundation. Trott, Paul (1998) *Innovation Management & New Product Development*, Financial Times Management, London, is also a useful and insightful text, including knowledge. Utterback, James (1996) *Mastering the Dynamics of Innovation*, Harvard Business School Press, Boston, MA, is an excellent text with strong empirical research base.

NOTES & REFERENCES

1 References for the Nike case: *Financial Times*, 15 July 1996, p9; 15 Dec 1996, p9; 22 Dec 1996, p18; 2 Apr 1997, p22; 11 Oct 1997, p17; 17 Jan 1998, p6; 16 July 1998; Seth, A (1998) *Marketing Business*, Feb.

2 Nonaka, I (1991) 'The knowledge-creating company', *Harvard Business Review*, Nov–Dec.

3 Nonaka, I and Takeuchi, H (1995) *The Knowledge-Creating Company*, Oxford University Press, Oxford, Ch1. This chapter traces the development of knowledge as a topic area and clearly demonstrates that it was tangential to strategy development for many strategy writers. It should also be noted that many strategy texts make no significant reference to the subject even to the present time.

4 Drucker, P (1964) *Managing for Results*, William Heinemann, London, Ch6.

5 Davenport, T H and Prusack, L (1998) *Working Knowledge: How Organizations Manage What They Know*, Harvard Business School Press, Boston, MA, pp2, 3.

6 Davenport, T H and Prusack, L (1998) Ibid, p5.

7 Hamel, G (1995) Foreword, *FT Handbook of Management*, Financial Times, London. *See* also his article in *Financial Times*, 5 June 1995, p9, for an abridged version of the article (highly entertaining phraseology but somewhat confused argument).

8 Nonaka, I and Takeuchi, H (1995) Op. cit., pp109–11.

9 Nonaka, I and Takeuchi, H (1995) Op. cit., p27.

10 Skandia, Annual Report and Accounts 1997, p62. *See* also Edvinsson, L (1997) 'Developing intellectual capital at Skandia', *Long Range Planning*, 30(3), pp366–73. Mr Edvinsson has made a significant contribution in this area at Skandia.

11 For example, *see* Davenport, T H and Prusack, L (1998) Op. cit., pxv.

12 Davenport, T H, De Long, D W and Beers, M C (1998) 'Successful knowledge management projects', *California Management Review*, 39(2), pp43–57. *See* also Norman, R and Ramirez, R (1993) 'From value chain to value constellation', *Harvard Business Review*, July–Aug, p65 (which explores knowledge and elements of key resources). Chan, Kim W and Maurborgue, R (1997) 'Fair process: managing in the knowledge economy', *Harvard Business Review*, July–Aug, p65 (which explores the impact on employees). Evans, P B and Wurster, T S (1997) 'Strategy and the new economics of information', *Harvard Business Review*, Sept–Oct, p70 (which discusses the Internet).

13 This is actually the headline in the 1998 Annual Report and Accounts of Heineken NV (*see* Chapter 8) introducing its new knowledge management world network. It is not clear whether the company was aware of the political significance of this phrase and its impact on some groups within the company.

14 Boshyk, Y (1999) 'Beyond knowledge managment', *Financial Times Mastering Information Management*, 8 Feb, pp12–13.

15 Argyris, C (1977) 'Double loop learning in organisations', *Harvard Business Review*, Sept–Oct.

16 Garvin, D (1993) 'Building a learning organization', *Harvard Business Review*, July–Aug. The precision and care of its wording make this article particularly valuable.

17 Nonaka, I and Takeuchi, H (1995) Op. cit., p86.

18 Davenport, T H and Prusack, L (1998) Op. cit., Ch3.

19 For example, *see* case studies quoted in Davenport and Prusak, and Nonaka and Takeuchi above. But also *see* researchers like Kanter R (Changemasters) and Quinn explored in Chapter 16.

20 Heineken Annual Report and Accounts 1998.

21 For an extended discussion of this important area, *see* Davenport, T H and Prusak, L (1998) Op. cit., Ch5. The author (RL) will never forget the months of negotiation with his fellow finance director on one such knowledge issue.

22 Teece, D (1998) 'Capturing value from knowledge assets', *California Management Review*, 40(3), pp55–79.

23 References for the Internet retail banking case study: *Financial Times*, 2 Oct 1996, Information Technology Supplement, p1; 15 Oct 1996, p18; 14 Mar 1997, p21; 30 Apr 1997, p27; 15 Sept 1997, p15; 7 Apr 1998, p29; 9 Apr 1998, p32; 15 Apr 1998, p19.

24 This section has benefited from Contractor, F J and Narayanan, V K (1990) 'Technology development in the multinational firm', *R&D Management*, Basil Blackwell, Oxford, republished in Root, F R and Visudtibhan (eds) (1992) *International Strategic Management*, Taylor and Francis, London, pp163–83. Well developed, thoughtful and comprehensive.

25 Kay, J (1994) *Foundations of Corporate Success*, Oxford University Press, Oxford, Ch5.

26 Farbey, B, Targett, D and Land, F (1994) 'The great IT benefit hunt', *European Management Journal*, 12, Sept, p270.

27 Porter, M E and Millar, V E (1985) 'How information gives you a competitive advantage', *Harvard Business Review*, July–Aug. *See* also Benjamin, R and Wigand, R (1995) 'Electronic markets and virtual value chains on the information superhighway', *Sloan Management Review*, Winter, p62.

28 Sources for the 3M case study: Annual Report and Accounts 1997 and 2000; Takeuchi, I and Nonaka, H (1995) Op. cit., pp135–40; Davenport, T H and Prusak, L (1998) Op. cit., pp104–6; *Financial Times*, 7 Sept 1998, p14.

29 Hamel, G and Prahalad, C K (1994) *Competing for the Future* Harvard Business School Press, Harvard, MA, p274.

30 Stacey, R (1993) *Strategic Management and Organisation Dynamics*, Pitman Publishing, London, p115.

31 Harvard Business School (1983) *Canon (B)*, Case 9–384–151 plus note on world photocopying industry.

32 Harvard Business School (1984) *EMI and the CT Scanner (A) and (B)*, Case 383–194 and the *Economist Survey on Innovation*, 11 Jan 1992, p21.

33 Baker, M (1992) *Marketing Strategy and Management*, 2nd edn, Macmillan, London, p28.

34 Whittington, R (1993) *What is Strategy and Does it Matter?*, Routledge, London, p82.

35 *The Economist* (1992) Loc. cit., p21.

36 Baker, M (1992) Op. cit., p110, and *The Economist* (1992) Loc. cit., p22.

37 *The Economist* (1992) Loc. cit., p22.

38 Utterback, J M (1996) *Mastering the Dynamics of Innovation*, Harvard Business School Press, Boston, MA, pp94–5.

39 Quinn, J B (1985) 'Managing innovation: controlled chaos', *Harvard Business Review*, May–June, p73.

40 Gluck, F (1985) 'Eight big makers of innovation', *McKinsey Quarterly*, Winter, p49.

41 Nonaka, I (1990) 'Redundant, overlapping organisations: a Japanese approach to managing the innovation process', *California Management Review*, Spring, p27.

42 Kawaii, T (1992) 'Generating innovation through strategic action programmes', *Long Range Planning*, 25, June, p42.

43 Developed principally from two sources: Hamel, G and Prahalad, C K (1994) Ibid, Ch4, and Day, G S (1987) *Strategic Marketing Planning*, West Publishing, St Paul, MN, Ch6.

44 Ergas, S, quoted in *The Economist* (1992) Survey on Innovation, 11 Jan, p23.

45 Morris, H and Willey, B (1996) *The Corporate Environment: A Guide for Human Resource Managers*, Pitman Publishing, London, pp136–8.

46 Freeman, C (1987) 'The case for technological determinism' in Finnegan, R, Salaman, G and Thompson, K (eds) (1987) *Information Technology: Social Issues. A Reader*, Hodder and Stoughton, Sevenoaks/Open University.

Chapter 12

Purpose delivered through mission and objectives

Learning outcomes

When you have worked through this chapter, you will be able to:

- define the main factors that form the purpose of the organisation;
- identify the main stakeholders and conduct a stakeholder power analysis;
- understand the role that organisational culture plays in establishing the mission and objectives;
- develop a mission statement for the organisation;
- develop the objectives consistent with this mission statement;
- explain how purpose can be defined for conglomerates;
- understand and develop the organisation's policy on strategic quality issues.

Figure 12.1   **The process from purpose to mission and objectives**

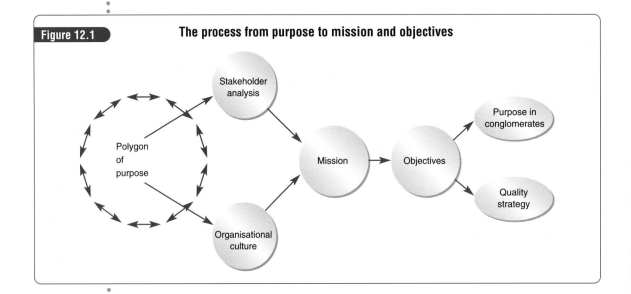

■ Introduction

Having explored the main issues surrounding the purpose of the organisation, it is now time to define the purpose more precisely. This chapter begins by drawing the various elements together in the polygon of purpose. It stresses the need to take into account several important sets of interests – the stakeholders (shareholders, employees, etc.) in the organisation, the corporate governance (the way senior managers behave) and the culture of the organisation. But the focus of the chapter is on the development of the *mission and objectives* of the organisation. Such a definition is crucial to the development of the strategy that follows later. As part of this definition, the particular problems posed by conglomerates and by the issue of quality are explored. The process is shown in Figure 12.1.

CASE STUDY 12.1

Ford's new objective: 'Back to basics'

Ford, the world's second-largest car company, challenged its competitors in 1994 when it announced a new global company objective. By 1999, it was adjusting this objective as it came to face new realities in the world car market. By 2001, it had sacked its chief executive and gone back to the basic business of delivering profits in its volume car business. This case examines how and why Ford shifted its objectives over time.

Ford's international operations

Ford was founded in the US around the turn of the twentieth century. After rapid and innovatory development in its home country, the company's founder, Henry Ford, set up the first overseas factory in the UK in the late 1920s. Seventy years later, the company had major production facilities in the UK, Germany, Belgium and Spain. But these operations were part of a European Division that worked semi-independently of its US headquarters. In addition, Ford had manufacturing and marketing operations in South America, India and Australasia that were also operated partly independently of the US. There was some central co-ordination but production and models were still largely confined to a particular continent. The reasons were the need to meet local customer demand in terms of style, price-points and performance.

'Ford 2000' – the global project announced in 1994

For many years, Ford had been attracted by the idea of a 'global' car. There were three good reasons for thinking that globalisation would deliver major benefits:

1 Major economies of scale and scope were expected in production.

2 Global manufacturers were able to negotiate global sourcing of car components, which would also deliver substantial additional cost savings.

3 Research and development on new models had become substantial, typically US$8 billion. Spreading this cost across more production would bring down the cost per vehicle and also save duplication costs.

But this would require massive reorganisation and co-ordination across a company as large as Ford, so it was not a project to embark upon lightly. In 1994, the company therefore launched a totally new project called 'Ford 2000'. Its objective was to develop a fully integrated global company by the year 2000. It was expected that there would be annual cost savings of between US$2 and 3 billion by the end of the decade and that this would present a serious challenge to Ford's competitors, like General Motors (US) and Toyota (Japan). The Ford plan was put into operation in early 1995 and involved integrating all its operations into one company. Core engineering and production were simplified in order to achieve considerable savings. New models were designed around a reduced number of platforms that would also save funds. Mr Jacques Nasser was put in charge of Ford's global

▶

automotive operations to see through the changes. He was so successful at killing off unprofitable vehicles, cutting costs and pressing suppliers and dealers for lower costs that he became known as 'Jack the Knife'. But substantial savings were made and Mr Nasser was promoted to chief executive officer in 1999.

'Ford 1999' – Global niche strategy

Mr Nasser then went on to oversee a major change in strategy in the company – the global niche strategy. He argued that there was a shift in car demand across the world towards *niche* car markets – 4-wheel drive off-road vehicles, people carriers, small luxury town cars, sports cars, etc. Moreover, such vehicles had higher profit margins than the traditional Ford business of volume cars – like the Mondeo and Ka. 'What you're seeing are niche cultures', explained Mr Nasser. Customers want more than a metal box that stops and starts and

looks just like the neighbour's car. For Ford, the new trend in customer variable demand is 'a marvellous business opportunity'.

To meet such demand variations, the company also embarked on at least five further ventures that would not even use the Ford brand name:

1 *Acquisition and development of Jaguar Cars.* Ford had bought the luxury company in the late 1980s and then spent billions of dollars developing new models, refitting factories and other activities. It kept the marque separate from its Ford 2000 project in order to emphasise the special niche. By the late 1990s Jaguar had launched a series of models that were well received by the press and were attacking a market niche in which Ford had previously hardly any representation, namely the luxury segment of Mercedes-Benz, Rolls-Royce and Toyota's Lexus.

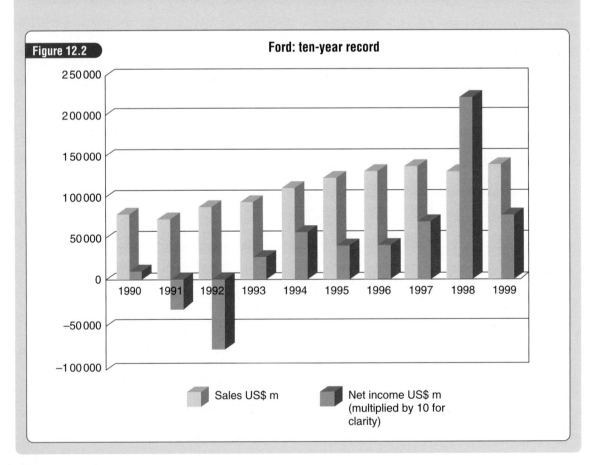

Figure 12.2

Ford: ten-year record

Sales US$ m

Net income US$ m (multiplied by 10 for clarity)

2 *Development of the Lincoln.* Ford had some representation in the luxury segment in the US only under the Lincoln name. Another development under consideration was to introduce some of the leading Lincoln models to other parts of the world.

3 *Acquisition of Volvo Cars.* This Swedish company was acquired by Ford in 1999 for US$6.5 billion in order to increase its representation in the upper market segments, where it had previously been only partially successful. Again, this would tackle new market niches where its rivals were stronger – for example, BMW and Mercedes-Benz. But, in this case, it would also deliver major cost savings in purchasing and logistics.

4 *Acquisition of Land-Rover.* The British 4-wheel drive company was also bought by Ford in 1995 and used to develop its interests in this specialist car area. As with the other purchases above, Ford invested substantial new investment in people and machinery to modernise existing plant and develop new models over a number of years.

5 *Acquisition of KwikFit and consolidation of control of Hertz.* The tyre, battery and exhaust-fitting company, KwikFit, was bought by Ford in the late 1990s for US$1 billion in order to offer customers a complete range of services. The company's link with the car rental company Hertz was also extended to take control of that company.

Exhibit 12.1

Ford company culture as it started to go 'Back to Basics' in 2001: analysing its cultural web[1]

Stories. Too early for clear development but the new chief executive, Bill Ford, was inexperienced and therefore supported by a chief operating officer from Europe, who was well known – Sir Nick Scheele. The story of the actual sacking of the former chief officer, Mr Nasser, was told in vivid detail around the company. Just a week before his sacking, stories were circulating that Mr Nasser was laughing off his reported demise: 'It would be like someone saying you're about to be moved, and you know nothing about it.'

Routines. New routines were introduced to turn around the business – special meetings were called for all senior executives at the company's head offices. They were totally non-routine to emphasise the seriousness of the situation.

Rituals. The announcement of the departure of Mr Nasser was announced at a special employee meeting. Mr Ford's announcement 'received a standing ovation from cheering and whooping employees at Ford headquarters'.

Symbols. The meeting rooms – called 'energy rooms' – to devise the new back-to-basics Ford strategy were not designed to be comfortable. Executives summoned to such meetings were told to make only brief presentations and given a simple agenda – 'Tell us how you are going to cut costs.'

Organisation. A totally new team was set up to develop a revised cost-cutting strategy between November 2001 and the announcement of the new strategy in January 2002. This would be followed by thousands of job losses, the closure of four US car plants, the sale of non-core activities like KwikFit.

Control. Some new controls were introduced but the Ford system already had substantial systems for the monitoring of performance.

Rewards. Given the nature of the crisis, the 'reward' was to keep your job. At the time of Mr Nasser's departure, 20 top managers 'decided to retire' or were re-assigned to other jobs or were replaced.

Power. A major power battle took place in the run-up to the sacking of Mr Nasser. This was then followed by a period of stability that would see power concentrated such that the proposed changes could be made over the following three years to 2004–05.

'Ford 2001' – 'Back to Basics' strategy

Overall, the five-pronged global-niche strategy outlined above was expected to increase Ford's unit sales from 250 000 in 1998 to 750 000 in year 2000. Moreover, such sales would carry higher profit margins than those of its volume car range. However, such a strategy took longer to emerge over the period 1999–2001. In addition, the strategy took Ford's strategic focus away from its major activity of making profitable volume cars. In addition, Ford suffered a major drain on profits as it coped with the Firestone tyre debacle: some Ford cars fitted with Firestone tyres were involved in accidents that were blamed on the tyres and both Ford and Firestone were sued for damages. Ford also became engaged in a price war on a number of its basic volume models and its cost base was too high to respond and still make a profit. Then came the tragic events of September 11 and the economic downturn in the US.

The result was a profit disaster in 2001 – *see* Figure 12.2. Although Mr Nasser had not been solely responsible for the strategy, he paid the price and was asked to leave suddenly in late 2001. "The board had reached a conclusion and, in reaching that conclusion, the sooner we told Jac [Nasser] the better," said Sir Nick Scheele, the former chairman of Ford Europe and new chief operating officer. "What we need is to get back to basics. We have had a terrible year for a variety of unrelated circumstances, but we have to move on." The Ford family – still important minority shareholders in the Ford company – had become increasingly disenchanted with the strategy, which was simply not delivering the company's objectives. Mr Bill Ford, grandson of the founder Henry Ford, took over as chairman and chief executive of Ford. He then began an immediate drive to cut costs very substantially across every part of the Ford company. Clearly this had a significant impact on the organisational culture and morale of the company around that time – the *cultural web* of the Ford company around that time is shown in Exhibit 12.1.

Sources: See reference 2.

Case questions

1 *What were the main arguments in favour of the various Ford strategies over the last ten years?*

2 *Why do organisations like Ford set objectives, such as the need to cut costs?*

3 *Is it acceptable for organisations to change their objectives before they are fully achieved?*

12.1 Clarifying the purpose of the organisation

Clarifying the organisation's purpose is crucial to strategy development – it is difficult to develop strategies to achieve a purpose that remains unclear. The problem is that there is no simple formula that can be applied to define the purpose of an organisation. Moreover, as the Ford globalisation case demonstrates, there may be proposals for a change to the purpose at some point before the original one has been achieved. This chapter is concerned with the task of clarifying the purpose and developing the mission and objectives of the organisation that arise from purpose. This task is an essential prelude to the strategy development of the rest of this book.

As a starting point, it is important to bring together the influences on purpose explored in Chapters 10 and 11. In addition, several other factors will influence purpose, especially those relating to the underlying ambitions of the organisation and those linked with the timing of new strategy initiatives – the latter may be particularly important when the underlying environment is changing significantly. The stakeholder

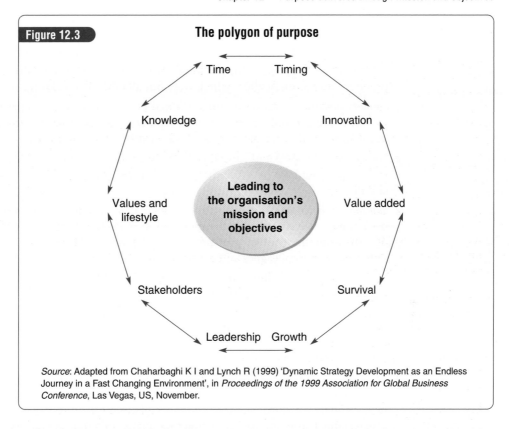

Figure 12.3

The polygon of purpose

Time — Timing

Knowledge — Innovation

Values and lifestyle — **Leading to the organisation's mission and objectives** — Value added

Stakeholders — Survival

Leadership — Growth

Source: Adapted from Chaharbaghi K I and Lynch R (1999) 'Dynamic Strategy Development as an Endless Journey in a Fast Changing Environment', in *Proceedings of the 1999 Association for Global Business Conference*, Las Vegas, US, November.

dimension mentioned below was explored briefly in Chapter 10 and is further covered in the next section of this chapter.

To bring all the elements together, it is possible to construct the *polygon of purpose* shown in Figure 12.3.[3] Polygon means a many-sided figure with no obvious dominant side. This is precisely the situation with the development of purpose, where there are a number of factors, none of which is usually crucial. The main elements of the polygon are shown below with examples from the Ford objectives case:

● *Time dimension* – long- and short-term perspectives will have a substantive impact on the purpose.[4] Ford's niche market strategy was a five-year programme but it also had annual profit targets which were not met.

● *Timing* – when to begin or end a new period of change. This will in turn depend on such issues as the cyclicality and the static or dynamic nature of the environmental forces.[5] After Ford launched its programme, North American and Asian economies turned down. With the benefit of hindsight, it is apparent that Ford's timing was wrong.

● *Innovation* – the generation and exploitation of new ideas. These may have a profound impact on the purpose of the organisation – *see* Chapter 10. Ford looked on the nature and extent of its earlier globalisation strategy as being in advance of any other car company and therefore innovatory.

● *Value-added dimension* – for every organisation, it is axiomatic that some value needs to be added for the organisation to continue to exist.[6] Value here does not necessarily mean economic rent. It could mean service or some other concept associated with other aspects of purpose. For business organisations, it means *profits* and related issues. Ford forgot that value added has a short-term time dimension.

- *Survival dimension* – the desire to survive. This is particularly important in some environments, perhaps all in the long term.[7] Ford's existence was threatened by the problems that arose in 2001, which were not all of its own making.

- *Growth dimension* – the desire for sustained growth. This will not apply to all organisations, but certainly needs to be considered as an objective for some.[8] By its acquisitions and other policies, Ford was clearly intending to grow its business.

- *Leadership* – the style and substance of the way the organisation is led. The impact of this on purpose may be substantial – *see* Chapter 10.[9] Alex Trotman, Jacques Nasser and Bill Ford were crucial to the Ford strategy.

- *Stakeholder dimension* – definition and delivery of value added to the various interested parties, especially those with the most power.[10] The Ford sacking of Mr Nasser came directly from shareholder pressure for radical change. However, it should also be noted that some colleagues and employees were also in favour of his departure.[11]

- *Values and lifestyle* – different organisations will hold different principles on what is important about the quality of life and the way that their activities should be conducted – *see* Chapter 10.[12] Ethics and corporate governance will form part of the considerations here – *see* Chapter 10. Ford's values are reflected in the way that it approached the business of integration and people issues. They are expressed in the Ford mission statement later in this chapter.

- *Knowledge* – the constantly changing mixture of experience, values, contextual information and expert insight – *see* Chapter 10. Knowledge has the ability to create new elements of purpose. At Ford, the globalisation project was accompanied by a determined attempt to bring together many different managers from different continents, both in person and over the Ford intranet; the foreign travel was quite exhausting and disruptive for those involved.

The polygon is useful as one way of summarising the nature of purpose. But it is not conclusive and other factors not covered in the list may be more important for some organisations – for example, aspects of service delivery in the public services and power and wealth creation for some entrepreneurs. It is for this reason that it has been called a many-sided polygon rather than the ten-sided polygon that is actually drawn in Figure 12.3.

> ### ▶ Key strategic principles
>
> - It is essential to clarify the purpose of the organisation at the outset of strategy development. Many different aspects are potentially involved. In most cases, no single element is dominant.
>
> - The polygon of purpose is one way of drawing the elements together. Although ten specific elements can be identified in the polygon, other elements may be more important and some of those highlighted may have little relevance in particular organisations.
>
> - The ten identified elements are: time dimension, timing, innovation, value added (including profitability), survival, growth, leadership, stakeholders, values and lifestyle, and knowledge.

12.2 Stakeholder analysis

12.2.1 Identifying the stakeholders

An organisation's mission and objectives need to be developed bearing in mind two sets of interests:

1 the interests of those who have to carry them out – for example, the managers and employees; and

2 the interests of those who have a stake in the outcome – for example, the shareholders, government, customers, suppliers and other interested parties.

Together these groups form the *stakeholders* – the individuals and groups who have an interest in the organisation and may therefore wish to influence its purpose, mission and objectives.

Given this situation, it is perhaps not surprising that the organisation's mission is not formulated overnight. It can take months of debate and consultation within the organisation. When its implications are clearly set out for the directors, managers and employees, they may not necessarily accept the mission without question: there may be objections as it is realised that individuals will have to work harder, undertake new tasks, or face the prospect of leaving the company. The individuals and groups affected may want to debate the matter further. Such individuals and groups have a *stakeholding* in the organisation and therefore wish to influence its mission.

This concept of stakeholding extends *beyond* those working in the organisation. Shareholders in a public company, banks which have loaned the organisation money, governments concerned about employment, investment and trade may also have legitimate stakeholdings in the company. Customers and suppliers will also have an interest in the organisation. They may be informal, such as government involvement in a private company, or formal, such as through a shareholding in the company. All can be expected to be interested in and possibly wish to influence the future direction of the organisation. It is not necessary to have a *shareholding* in order to have a *stakeholding*.

12.2.2 Conflict of interest amongst stakeholders

The key issue with regard to stakeholders is that the organisation needs to take them into account in formulating its mission and objectives. If it does not, they may object and cause real problems for the organisation: for example, major shareholders may sell their shares and key employees may leave.

The difficulty is that their interests may be in conflict. For example, workers may want more pay at the expense of profits and dividends for the shareholders. There are other areas where interests may also conflict. Some of these are summarised in Table 12.1. Consequently, the organisation will need to resolve which stakeholders have priority: *stakeholder power* needs to be analysed.

Importantly in many organisations, it is no longer the case that the shareholders who own the organisation automatically have absolute power. Ever since the 1930s, there has been evidence of an increasing gap between shareholders and senior managers in large companies. Berle and Means[13] surveyed top management in the US and produced evidence that there was an increasing gap between senior managers and shareholders. In about half of the 2000 US companies studied, 'ownership' had become separated from 'control'. Stakeholder *managers* did not necessarily have the same interests as stakeholder *shareholders*.

Table 12.1 **Stakeholders and their expectations**

Stakeholder	Expectations	
	Primary	Secondary
Owners	Financial return	Added value
Employees	Pay	Work satisfaction, training
Customers	Supply of goods and services	Quality
Creditors	Creditworthiness	Payment on time
Suppliers	Payment	Long-term relationships
Community	Safety and security	Contribution to community
Government	Compliance	Improved competitiveness

Source: Adapted from Cannon, T (1994) *Corporate Responsibility*, Pitman Publishing, London.

Managers may be more interested in size than profits: as companies grow, they are more protected from takeover and can afford to offer larger and more prestigious rewards to their leading managers.[14] By contrast, owners are more likely to be concerned with maximising profits and seeking only moderate growth. Unless managers in large organisations are threatened by takeover or incentivised financially, they may take a broader view of the purpose of the organisation than shareholders:[15] [16] [17] for example, shareholder dividends may be less important to senior managers than power and prestige. Because shareholding is fragmented in large companies, such managers have considerable power.

12.2.3 Analysing and applying stakeholder power

From a corporate strategy viewpoint, the major issue is to identify the influence of *stakeholder power* on the direction of the organisation, typically its mission and objectives. Importantly, this can be positive as well as negative – many organisations will welcome the contributions of and discussions with those who have power. Ford shareholders ultimately used their power in 2001 to force a change in leadership at the company – *see* Case 12.1.

Some of the major possible stakeholders are shown in Figure 12.4. The analysis of their relative power is likely to vary country by country. In addition, there is likely to be variation by industry: the volume car industry may well have a different profile from a more fragmented industry such as the textile garment industry with its smaller companies and family shareholdings. It is difficult to generalise but the checklist in Exhibit 12.2 may provide a useful guide on analysis for a particular organisation.

However welcome contributions may be to the development process, the fact remains that there are likely to be conflicts of interest. Those with the most power therefore need to be considered most carefully. A *stakeholder power study* needs to be undertaken. This is shown in Exhibit 12.3.

As part of the analysis of stakeholder power, some explicit investigation needs to be undertaken of the *sanctions* available against specific stakeholder groups. These might be used to ensure that, where conflict exists between stakeholder groups,

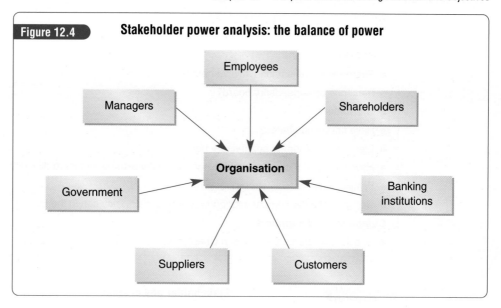

Figure 12.4 **Stakeholder power analysis: the balance of power**

some resolution is achieved. Such an analysis may be the beginning of a *bargaining process* between the various groups. This is likely to involve compromise, depending on the power of groups of stakeholders and their willingness to agree. However, it may also involve the use of sanctions to bring pressure to bear on particularly difficult groups. Such a negotiation process can involve the game theory outlined in Chapter 15.

Exhibit 12.2 **Checklist for the analysis of stakeholder power**

Managers

- Large or small company? Relative remuneration versus employees?
- Power of middle managers to support or disrupt any chosen purpose?
- Style of company on hiring and firing?
- Company profitability versus that of the industry?

Employees

- Trade union legislation?
- Presence of workers' representation on supervisory board?
- Widespread presence and acceptance across company?
- Presence of workers' co-operative?
- National traditions on unionisation and influence?

Government

- *Laissez-faire* or *dirigiste*?
- Shareholding and ownership policy beyond national institutions?
- Support for favoured industries? Encourages registration of shares in companies?
- Favours world trade or protectionist?

▶

Exhibit 12.2 continued

Banking institutions

- Shareholding or just loan involvement?
- Presence on supervisory board?

Shareholders

- Have full voting shares?
- Elect management to supervisory board?
- Have blocking or cross-shareholdings that make external pressure difficult?
- Family influence (still) strong?
- Can they sue the company for poor performance? (They can in the US.)

Customers and suppliers

- *See* the Five Forces Analysis in Chapter 3.

Exhibit 12.3   **Stakeholder power study**

There are six major steps:

1 Identify the major stakeholders.

2 Establish their interests and claims on the organisation, especially as new strategy initiatives are developed.

3 Determine the degree of power that each group holds through its ability to force or influence change as new strategies are developed.

4 Development of mission, objectives and strategy, possibly prioritised to minimise power clashes.

5 Consider how to divert trouble before it starts, possibly by negotiating with key groups.

6 Identify the sanctions available and, if necessary, apply them to ensure that the purpose is formulated and any compromise reached.

▶ Key strategic principles

- Stakeholders are the individuals and groups who have an interest in the organisation. Consequently, they may wish to influence its mission and objectives.

- The key issue with regard to stakeholders is that the organisation needs to take them into account in formulating its mission and objectives.

- The difficulty is that stakeholder interests may conflict. Consequently, the organisation will need to resolve which stakeholders have priority: *stakeholder power* needs to be analysed. Where conflict exists, negotiations are undertaken to reach a compromise. Sanctions may form part of this process.

- A stakeholder power study covers six stages: identification of stakeholders; establishment of their interests and claims; estimation of their degree of power; prioritised mission development; negotiation with key groups; sanctions application where relevant.

Objectives derailed on the Jubilee Line Extension

In 1993, London Transport accepted the twin objectives of opening the 10-mile (16-km) extension to its Jubilee Underground Line on time and on budget. The whole project seemed at the time to be challenging but feasible. If only the organisation had known the problems that would follow, it might have been more cautious before agreeing the objectives. This case explores the issue of setting and managing objectives in the public sector.

Background

For over 50 years, London Transport had been considering extending its underground rail network to south-east London. In the early 1980s, this was given added impetus by plans to turn part of the area into a major new office development called Canary Wharf. In addition, there were also plans to regenerate the neighbouring domestic area, which had become run-down with the decline in business using London's River Thames over many years.

The basic aim of the proposed new service was to provide workers and home dwellers with commuter, shopping and entertainment links to the major facilities in central London. After detailed study, it was estimated that the cost of the new Jubilee Line Extension (JLE) would be £1.8 billion (US$2.7 billion) and it would involve state-of-the-art trains, signalling and station design. Given a start date in 1993, the objective was to offer a full service in spring 1998. Neither of these twin objectives – related to time and to cost – was ultimately to be achieved.

Early enthusiasm for the JLE

In the 1980s, such was the enthusiasm for the Canary Wharf office scheme and the related regeneration of homes in London's Docklands that government funding was generous. A new road – the Limehouse Extension – was built to connect the area with the existing road network at a greater cost per mile than any other road development in the UK. Planning permissions were quickly given for a US investment company owned by a Texan, G. Ware Travelstead, to start knocking down buildings and preparing the area. The company also secured promises from the government of improved transport links with central London.

However, the economics of the construction were such that the US development company eventually pulled out in the mid-1980s. It was replaced by a Canadian company called Olympia and York, under the management of the Reichman brothers.

It was this company that promised a major contribution to the construction costs of the JLE – some £400 million. But then Olympia and York went into receivership as a result of the company being overstretched in its construction developments around the world. Consequently, the company was totally unable to honour its commitment to assist the JLE, which had still not been started. But this did not stop the government proceeding with the underground development in the hope that Canary Wharf would still be built.

JLE over time and beyond budget

In late 1993, London Transport accepted the objectives – cost £1.8 billion and completion by spring 1998 – and placed the first contracts for the JLE. An added, later complication was that the government decided in 1996 to site its key celebration of the year 2000 at Greenwich, using the JLE to transport 60 per cent of visitors to the site. This added extra pressure for the successful completion of the project in 1998 or early 1999. London Transport was still confident that it would hit its objectives, even if they had slipped slightly. This was overoptimistic given that it was already hitting a whole series of problems, some of which might have been foreseen and some of which were still unknown.

Certainly, the technology of boring tunnels and laying track inside them was well tried. The task of planning and operating the largest single construction contract in Western Europe should also have been manageable, if demanding. The task of tunnelling under some of London's most historic buildings without allowing them to move was carefully engineered and planned successfully. Even the unforeseen problems – such as the threat of a tunnel collapse necessitating a different construction method – did not delay the project more than six months.

But by early 1999, the JLE was still not complete and it was considerably over budget. The project management was taken away from London

Exhibit 12.4   **Some problems on building the Jubilee Line Extension**

Problem	Consequences
Construction contracts underpriced: firms were so keen to gain the work that they deliberately underestimated their bids – not unusual in some large public works	● Original cost estimates were unrealistically low ● Construction firms renegotiated for their inevitable cost overruns, which delayed construction
State-of-the-art signalling was difficult to install and test: the contractor gave reassurances, but the new technology had never been tested elsewhere on the Underground	● Signalling delayed, track electrics uncertain ● Major doubts over number of trains that could be operated once the signalling was installed
Technical difficulties in tunnelling: London's soil proved very wet and difficult for tunnelling	● Some delays in completing certain sections ● Higher costs
New Austrian tunnel method chosen for some sections proved to be too risky: the project reverted to traditional tunnelling methods	● Six months' delay ● Higher costs
Electricians' strike: asked for higher bonuses in return for higher productivity	● More delay ● Higher costs
Political meddling: pressure increased for rapid completion to meet millennium celebration deadline	● Project uncertainty ● Extra pressure on senior management

Transport by the government and handed over to the Canadian engineering consultants Bechtel. The project was expected to cost £3.0 billion and to be completed by October 1999 – some 18 months late and 66 per cent over budget. Some of the well-documented problems are listed in Exhibit 12.4.

JLE management responsibility

After so many difficulties and a clear failure to meet deadlines and budgets, it was likely that the project team and its leader would be forced to take the blame. Mr Hugh Doherty, the project leader at London Transport, was forced to step down in September 1998 at the same time as Bechtel took over the project. Even after careful study, the new contractors offered no guarantee that the project would be completed on time and to its revised, higher budget – this was one company that was not going to be caught out by the uncertainties that still remained.

Sources: See reference18.

The *Corporate Strategy* website contains an article that provides more detail on aspects of this development.

Case questions

1 *Should the original managers also have been more cautious and resisted the pressure on timing and budgets from their political paymasters?*

2 *Was it wise to choose such challenging new technical signalling systems? Or should it be the role of publicly funded bodies to move technology forward?*

3 *Were there any failures in management that went beyond the difficulties in managing a large and uncertain contract?*

4 *How would you have cast the objectives for this project? Challenging or conservative?*

5 *What lessons, if any, can public service organisations learn from the London Transport experience?*

12.3 Developing the mission

The *mission* of an organisation outlines the broad directions that it should and will follow and briefly summarises the reasoning and values that lie behind it. Such a mission needs to be defined in the context of the purpose explored earlier. The *objectives* are then a more specific commitment consistent with the mission over a specified time period. They may be quantified, but this may be inappropriate in some circumstances.

As explored in Chapter 1, the strategies that will achieve the objectives then follow from this. The mission and objectives define the whole strategic process and are therefore important in the development of corporate strategy.

12.3.1 Prescriptive approach to mission development

Under prescriptive theories of strategy, the organisation will set out its mission and objectives for the next few years. It then develops strategies consistent with the mission and aimed at achieving the objectives – for example, Ford's global ambitions fit here.

The analysis of the environment and resources is used to develop the mission and objectives of the organisation. A prescriptive *mission statement* is then developed, setting out the organisation's purpose over a period of time. Several examples are given later in the chapter.

12.3.2 Emergent approaches to mission development

In contrast to the prescriptive approach, some emergent strategists argue that it is a contradiction in terms to couple the concept of purposeful planning with the idea of a strategy emerging in the organisation. They would argue that, by definition, purposes do not emerge.

For other emergent strategists – the *uncertainty-based* strategy theorists of Chapter 2 – the whole idea of purpose for an organisation is largely incomprehensible. For example, they would argue that Ford's global ambitions outlined at the beginning of the chapter are a waste of time; too many chance events may blow the company off its chosen route. They would reject those parts of this chapter concerning mission and objectives. They would probably accept the stakeholder and cultural sections of the chapter but would see them as supporting their view that the uncertainties they introduce only make it more difficult to set out clearly an organisation's purpose.

For yet other emergent strategists – the *survival-based* theorists and the *human-resource-based* theorists of Chapter 2 – the situation is less clear. Certainly, they would have doubts about a mission that was developed without consideration of the external forces and without careful discussion between the interested parties in the organisation. But they would not reject the concept of purpose completely – they would accept it with reservations. Ford's global ambitions would probably meet their criteria for acceptance since they were developed out of Ford's views on the way that external forces were moving and were discussed among senior managers before being introduced.

Some emergent strategists would want the complexity of the interests of the *stakeholders* in the business to become part of the purpose – that is, the interests not only of the shareholders but also of the senior managers and the employees, who all have a share in the success of the organisation. They would be impressed by Ford's attempts to communicate the global purpose to all employees and, as we will see, to take account of employee-stakeholders in the Ford mission statement.

As we saw in Section 12.2, stakeholders may well have conflicting interests – for example, shareholders' desire for profits versus the employees' desire for continued employment even when it may not be profitable. The organisation's purpose for the human resource theorist may thus need to be tempered by *compromise* between the various interested parties.

12.3.3 What is a mission statement?

The mission statement outlines the broad directions that the organisation will follow and briefly summarises the reasoning and values that lie behind it. The purpose of the mission statement is to *communicate* to all the stakeholders inside and outside the organisation what the company stands for and where it is headed. It therefore needs to be expressed in a language and with a commitment that all of those involved can understand and feel relevant to their own circumstances.[19] Importantly, mission statements must reflect the areas of purpose developed above and in previous chapters.

Amongst strategists, there is some dispute over the definition of a mission statement.[20] [21] There is really no agreed definition. There has been a high degree of interest by companies and other practitioners but relatively limited definition and research of a more academic nature. In addition, some researchers have questioned the lengthy nature and content of such statements: some [22] [23] have even suggested that companies should concentrate on short and concise statements of their 'strategic intent'.

There are considerable differences of view on the form, purpose and content of such statements. At the same time, many leading companies in Europe and North America have developed and quoted their mission statements in their annual reports and accounts. Even if there is no agreed definition, companies still find the process of developing their mission statement useful.

12.3.4 How to formulate a mission statement

Because no two organisations are exactly the same in terms of ownership, resources or environmental circumstances, the mission statement is specific to each organisation. Essentially, there are five elements:

1 Consideration of the *nature* of the organisation's business. Typical questions include: 'What business are we in? What business *should* we be in?'

2 The responses need to be considered from the *customer* perspective, rather than the organisation itself: 'We are in the business of developing books that will inform and educate our readers about strategy', *rather than* 'We are in the business of developing textbooks on strategic issues.'

3 The mission needs to reflect the basic *values and beliefs* of the organisation:[24] 'We believe it is important to respect the environment and offer employment that is free from any prejudices associated with culture, race or religion.'

4 Where possible, the mission needs to reflect the element of the *sustainable competitive advantage*:[25] 'It is our aim to be a leader in this field.' This may not be possible in a diversified holding company. It may also be more appropriate to adjust this to reflect *distinctiveness* in an organisation which has no direct competitors, e.g. a charity.

5 The mission needs to summarise the *main reasons* for its choice of approach: 'We are a team. We must treat each other with trust and respect' is a good example from the Ford mission statement.

All the above will rely on *business judgement*, which is imprecise and difficult to define by its very nature. Business judgements are usually made by senior managers in the company.

Because a mission statement needs to be communicated as well as to summarise the organisation's purposes, it needs to be worded carefully. It needs to be written in language that is commonly understood. Some criteria for judging the results of attempting to draft a mission statement are shown in Exhibit 12.5.[26]

Exhibit 12.5   **Some criteria for judging mission statements**

Mission statements should:

- be specific enough to have an impact upon the behaviour of individuals throughout the business;

- reflect the distinctive advantages of the organisation and be based upon an objective recognition of its strengths and weaknesses;

- be realistic and attainable;

- be flexible enough to take account of shifts in the environment.

The need for precision and care is an important part of the analysis and development of mission statements. As an example of a complete mission statement, Exhibit 12.6 returns to the Ford Motor Company of the opening case in this chapter and gives the material circulated within the company on this matter.

Exhibit 12.6   **Ford Motor Company**

Company mission, values and guiding principles

MISSION

Ford Motor Company is a worldwide leader in automotive and financial products and services. Our mission is to improve continually our products and services to meet our customers' needs, allowing us to prosper as a business and to provide a reasonable return for our stockholders, the owners of our business.

VALUES

How we accomplish our mission is as important as the mission itself. Fundamental to success for the Company are these basic values:

▶ **People** – Our people are the source of our strength. They provide our corporate intelligence and determine our reputation and vitality. Involvement and teamwork are our core human values.

▶ **Products** – Our products are the end result of our efforts, and they should be the best in serving customers worldwide. As our products are viewed, so are we viewed.

▶ **Profits** – Profits are the ultimate measure of how efficiently we provide customers with the best products for their needs. Profits are required to survive and grow.

Exhibit 12.6 continued

GUIDING PRINCIPLES

▶ **Quality Comes First** – To achieve customer satisfaction, the quality of our products and services must be our number one priority.

▶ **Customers are the Focus of Everything We Do** – Our work must be done with our customers in mind, providing better products and services than our competition.

▶ **Continuous Improvement is Essential to Our Success** – We must strive for excellence in everything we do: in our products, in their safety and value – and in our services, our human relations, our competitiveness, and our profitability.

▶ **Employee Involvement is Our Way of Life** – We are a team. We must treat each other with trust and respect.

▶ **Dealers and Suppliers are our Partners** – The Company must maintain mutually beneficial relationships with dealers, suppliers and our other business associates.

▶ **Integrity is Never Compromised** – The conduct of our Company worldwide must be pursued in a manner that is socially responsible and commands respect for its integrity and for its positive contributions to society. Our doors are open to men and women alike without discrimination and without regard to ethnic origin or personal beliefs.

Source: Copyright © Ford Motor Company 1996. Reprinted with permission.

Key strategic principles

- The *mission* of an organisation outlines the broad directions that it should and will follow and briefly summarises the reasoning and values that lie behind it.

- The *objectives* are then a more specific commitment consistent with the mission over a specified time period. They may be quantified, but this may be inappropriate in some circumstances.

- Prescriptive approaches emphasise the need to set out a mission and objectives for the next few years for the organisation.

- Some emergent approaches doubt the usefulness of a mission and objectives because the future is so uncertain. Other emergent approaches accept the need for a mission and objectives but place great emphasis on the need to include the managers and employees in their development.

- The purpose of the mission statement is to *communicate* to all the stakeholders inside and outside the organisation what the company stands for and where it is headed.

- There are five elements in formulating a mission statement: nature of the organisation; customer perspective; values and beliefs; competitive advantage or distinctiveness; main reasons for the approach.

- Mission statements rely on business judgement but criteria can be developed to assess the results.

CASE STUDY 12.3

Coca-Cola: Lowering the fizz in its objectives

Coca-Cola, the world's largest soft drinks company, reduced its key earnings objective in 2002. This case examines the reasons for the downgrade and questions whether the company has gone far enough.

Objective setting at Coca-Cola

For most companies in relatively mature markets like soft drinks, the starting point in setting the future objective of the company is what has happened in the past. Coca-Cola achieved annual growth in its earnings for shareholders of between 15 and 20 per cent in the years 1991 to 1997 – see Figure 12.5. There then followed three years of sharply declining earnings before a rebound in 2001. For this reason, the company's chief executive, Mr Douglas Daft, has set what he regards as a more realistic objective for the next few years of 11 to 12 per cent per annum earnings growth. Yet, there are at least four reasons to question whether even this lower objective will be achieved.

Soft drink market growth

The first problem is the low growth in the market. Carbonated soft drink markets grew by only 2 per cent by volume worldwide during 2001. Coca Cola dominates this market, from which it derives 87 per cent of its total sales. If the market is growing so slowly and the company is heavily reliant on the market, it is difficult to see how the company can outpace market growth without other measures.

Coca-Cola and its bottling companies

The second problem is the way that Coca-Cola earns its profits. The company does not just sell products in the market place. It works around the world through local bottling companies, some of which it owns and some of which it does not. Essentially, the company makes part of its profits by charging its local bottlers for the concentrates and syrups supplied from its headquarters – the bottlers add carbonated water, bottle and distribute the finished product. During the 1990s, Coca-Cola was reported to be buying up small bottling companies around the world and then selling them at a higher price to larger regional bottling companies, putting the profits from the sale into the Coca-Cola profit line.[27] The company was also charging ever-higher prices for its concentrates, again taking the profits.

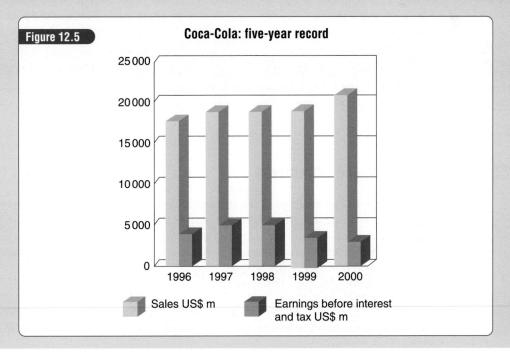

Figure 12.5

Coca-Cola: five-year record

- Sales US$ m
- Earnings before interest and tax US$ m

Part 4 • The purpose of the organisation

CASE STUDY 3.1 continued

Such strategies did not necessarily result in losses at its bottling companies or higher prices for bottles of Coke. The reason is that the consolidation from smaller to larger regional bottlers produced economies of scale that cut costs. But Coca-Cola has now recognised that this process could not continue indefinitely and that it must share more of its profits with the bottlers, some of which were owned by the company anyway. For this reason, it reduced its earnings growth objective for the latest period.

New product development

The third reason for doubt about the earnings growth objective relates to the successful introduction of new products. Coca-Cola's record here is disappointing. Its great rival, Pepsi Cola, has a significantly smaller market share in most countries than Coke. But it has a good, possibly even superior, record on new product introductions – Pepsi was first to launch a diet cola and first to introduce cola with a lemon twist in 2001. Coke beat Pepsi to the launch of cherry Coke but this was back in 1985 and the variety still only accounts for 3 per cent of the volume generated by classic Coke. In addition, customers, employees and bottlers still remember the major protests generated when Coca-Cola attempted to replace classic Coke with a more modern version in the early 1990s and eventually had to bring back the original variety.

Earnings growth through acquisition

The fourth problem is the reluctance of the company to make acquisitions that might enhance earnings growth. Coca-Cola bought the Schweppes mixer drink brand from Cadbury Schweppes (UK) in some parts of the world in 1999 and it has made a series of bottling plant acquisitions in recent years. Yet the Coca-Cola board failed to support the recommendation of its chief executive, Mr Daft, to acquire the Quaker Oats company in 2001. The attraction of the purchase was the Quaker sports drink brand called Gatorade. This would have moved Coca-Cola firmly into a new market segment in which it is currently unrepresented and which is growing fast. However, the board felt that the price of US$16 billion was too high. Quaker was bought by Pepsi Cola in 2001.

Conclusion

The above are all the down-side arguments against a revised earnings growth objective of 11–12 per cent per annum over the next three years. But there are other ways of achieving such growth – for example, cutting production, administrative and marketing costs. However, a better solution might be to lower the earnings growth target.

© Copyright Richard Lynch 2003. All rights reserved. This case was written by Richard Lynch from published information only.

Sources: See reference 27.

Case questions

1 *What is your view of the earnings growth objective? Is it set too high? If you would lower it, what figure would you pick? You should read the next section about challenging but achievable objectives in arriving at your conclusion.*

2 *How should organisations set objectives? Past experience? Current market performance? Challenging objectives? Or what?*

12.4 Developing the objectives

Objectives take the generalities of the mission statement and turn them into more *specific* commitments: usually, this will cover *what* is to be done and *when* the objective is to be completed. Objectives may include a *quantified* objective – for example, a specific increase in market share or an improvement in some measure of product quality. But the objective will not necessarily be quantified.

The purposes of objectives therefore are:

● to focus the management task on a specific outcome;

● to provide a means of assessing whether that outcome has been achieved after the event.

440

12.4.1 Different kinds of objectives

In the 1960s and 1970s, several writers were keen to make the objectives quantified and thus measurable.[28] It is now generally recognised that some objectives cannot easily be quantified, e.g. those associated with business ethics and employee job satisfaction, yet they may represent extremely important parts of the activities of companies.

Nevertheless, a company that has a mission but no quantified objectives at all would be in danger of engaging in meaningless jargon. As we saw in Chapter 8, it is usual for companies to set objectives in two types of areas, the first of which is likely to be quantified and the second only partially:

1 *financial objectives*, e.g. earnings per share, return on shareholders' funds, cash flow.

2 *strategic objectives*; e.g. market share increase (quantified); higher product quality (quantified); greater customer satisfaction (partially quantified); employee job satisfaction (supported by research survey but not necessarily quantified).

None of the areas above is necessarily more important than any other. Individual organisations will devise their own lists depending on their stakeholders, culture, leadership, mission and future direction.

12.4.2 Conflict between objectives

There are some objectives that ensure the *survival* of the organisation, e.g. adequate cash flow, basic financial performance. These need to come early in the process. But for many organisations, survival is not really the main issue for the future: for example, the two organisations in this chapter, Ford and London Transport, are not about to disappear tomorrow. A major issue for these organisations concerns *development and growth* – for example, the Ford statement contains the phrase 'survive and grow'.

Development and growth take time and require investment funds. Money invested in growth is not available for distribution now to shareholders. Growth objectives are therefore potentially in conflict with the short-term requirement to provide returns to shareholders, the owners of the company. Taking money out of the business today will not provide the investment for the future. Objectives therefore need to reach a *compromise* between the short and long term. It is for this reason that the Ford statement refers to providing a '*reasonable* return for our stockholders, the owners of our business'. This comment will then be translated into a numerical objective in terms of a dividend payout at Ford that reflects the need to invest as well as satisfy the shareholders.

Where a *competitive environment* exists, as in the global car industry, it is particularly important to recognise that any funds distributed now make it much more difficult to maintain performance against competitors in the future. For any organisation that needs to distribute the value that it adds, there will always be a potential conflict between the short and long term.

12.4.3 Implications of shareholder structure

The conflict between the long and short term becomes even more acute in some national markets where *shareholder power* is particularly demanding. The North American and UK stock markets have a reputation for *short-termism*:[29] that is, companies need to maintain their dividend record or face the threat of being acquired. Other European, Japanese and South-East Asian companies have had less pressure here because their shares are often held by governments and banking institutions, which have been able to take a longer-term view. For example, German car companies such as Volkswagen and Mercedes-Benz have had large share interests held by leading German banks. By contrast, Ford and General Motors have had their shares largely held on the open stock exchanges of Europe and North America. Thus the US companies have faced more acute shareholder pressures than the German companies. These priorities are bound to be reflected in how the objectives for the company are devised initially and monitored later.

12.4.4 Challenging but achievable objectives

When developing objectives, one of the real issues that arises is just how *challenging* the objectives should be. Do we merely set objectives that are easy to achieve so that we can then show real success beyond this? Or do we set objectives that are more challenging but still achievable? If we set the latter, to what extent are these open to negotiation with those who will be responsible for delivering them? Do we need a contract? And a reward?

These are difficult questions to resolve and will depend on the culture and style of the organisation and its senior managers, along with the nature of the organisation's mission and its competition, if any. Some will set demanding objectives and assess performance accordingly; others will discuss and agree (rather than set) a balance between demanding and easy objectives. In spite of Peter Drucker's optimism that this might be done more scientifically by the late 1990s,[30] this aspect of objective setting still requires great business judgement.

12.4.5 Developing objectives in larger organisations

In larger organisations and those with scarce resources, the situation may be more complicated. Very often such organisations are split up by the type of business: in the Ford example at the beginning of the chapter, there were five groups, each responsible for a different car model range. Such groups are often called *divisions* or *strategic business units* (SBUs): each may be so large that it has its own CEO and functional managers. In these circumstances, the corporate objectives need to be examined by each of the SBUs. In addition, the corporation may not have unlimited funds and will need to allocate those that it has. Where an SBU has received less than the funds it requested, it may be inappropriate for the headquarters to set an objective as demanding as it might otherwise have been.

For these reasons, corporate objectives will not necessarily translate into the same objective for each SBU. For example:

● There may be limited financial resources which are *rationed* between the SBUs, so it would not be realistic to expect them all to perform against the group objectives.

● Some divisions may be in rapidly growing markets that will need substantial funds but will deliver well above any standardised group-wide objective; other divisions may be in decline and struggle to perform against any averaged corporate objective regardless of the resources they are given.

In larger organisations, a distinction needs to be drawn between what the overall corporation will achieve and what each of the divisions will be expected to achieve. The *corporate objectives will need to be translated into divisional or SBU objectives*. The divisional objectives will also be subordinate to the corporate objectives – *see* Figure 12.6.

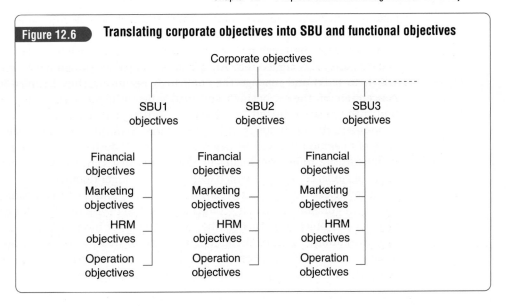

Figure 12.6 Translating corporate objectives into SBU and functional objectives

▶ Key strategic principles

- Objectives take the generalities of the mission statement and turn them into more *specific* commitments: usually, this will cover *what* is to be done and *when* the objective is to be completed.

- Different kinds of objectives are possible. Some will be quantified and some not.

- There may be conflict between objectives, particularly between the long- and short-term interests of the organisation.

- Shareholding structures will impact on objectives. UK and US companies are under greater pressure for short-term performance.

- Objectives need to be challenging but achievable.

- In larger organisations and those with scarce resources, the objectives may need to be adjusted to take into account the circumstances and trading situation of different parts of the organisation.

12.5 Purpose in conglomerates – the role of parenting

Some companies have major subsidiaries engaged in a number of quite different markets with totally different resources and different modes of operation: for example, 3M in Chapter 11 is involved in a whole series of industries from medicine to office products. Such companies are called *conglomerates*.

Over the last 30 years, opinion on the strategic purpose in conglomerates has changed quite markedly. It used to be said that being involved in a series of unrelated industries meant that the risks of overall failure were lower because the upswing in one market, such as medicine, would counterbalance any downswing in another market, such as office products.[31] In addition, it was also argued that basic technological linkages between companies meant that they could provide mutual technical support – *see* the Daimler-Benz case in Chapter 10 for an example of this approach.

Some recent thinking on strategic purpose in conglomerates has tended to emphasise *strategic focus*. It is argued that any group of companies should have a clear core around which to build and manage the company's resources. Thus Daimler-Benz decided to concentrate on the car business and shed some of its other areas such as traffic control and medium-sized aircraft manufacture. Although this has increased the company's exposure to the car industry, it has been more than offset by the greater resources and scale of operation that can be devoted to the car industry. One of the reasons that such arguments are more convincing in the twenty-first century is the increased size and scope of global companies, which demand much larger resources.

Nevertheless, such evidence is not conclusive and some companies still strongly believe in conglomerates. The companies need to devise methods for developing their mission and objectives. Each of the subsidiaries may have little or no trading connection with another part of the group, and each of them will have its own resources. In addition, the whole enterprise will have a corporate headquarters. It is this special resource, the *parent* of the subsidiaries, that is being explored here.

12.5.1 Corporate strategy and parenting

In some texts,[32] the words 'corporate strategy' refer *exclusively* to strategies pursued by such a corporate headquarters. In this book, the term 'corporate strategy' has been used more freely, as explained in Chapter 1. *Parenting* is another term covering the same general areas. It means the special strategies pursued by the headquarters of the diversified group. The parenting resource of corporate headquarters can offer:

- *corporate functions and services* such as international treasury management and central human resource management;
- *corporate development initiatives*, such as centralised R&D and new acquisitions;
- *additional finance for growth or problem areas*, on the principle of the product portfolio outline in Chapter 3;
- *development of formal linkages between businesses* such as the transfer of technology or core competencies between subsidiaries.

For example, at News Corporation the film library of Twentieth Century-Fox is available to its TV stations in both the US and the UK, even though they are operating totally independent schedules and are completely independent companies. In addition, the centre is the major provider of funds for the main growth areas such as its Far Eastern satellite ventures and the new, exclusive sports channels and contracts.

Clearly, such parenting resources are formidable if carefully developed. Each group will have its own combination of resources, depending on its mix of businesses and the relevant strategic issues. However, corporate headquarters have a cost. The purpose of parenting is to add value to the subsidiaries that are served, otherwise the parental cost cannot be justified.[33] Subsidiaries need to perform better with the parent than they would independently.

12.5.2 Parenting characteristics

To perform better with the parent requires that the parenting resource itself, the corporate headquarters, comes under careful scrutiny. It is not enough for the headquarters to provide a few add-on services, as might be the case at Daimler-Benz – *see* Case study 10.1. It means understanding the core skills of the parent itself; these are called the *parenting characteristics* of the headquarters.[34]

The parent needs two attributes:

1 an understanding of or familiarity with the *key factors for success* relevant for all of the diverse industries in which each of its subsidiaries is engaged;

2 an ability to *contribute something extra* beyond the subsidiaries that it manages. These might be from any of the four areas listed earlier in this section, e.g. R&D, finance.

Some parents do not understand the key factors for success. In the case of Daimler-Benz, it was almost impossible for the chairman, Edzard Reuter, to understand the key factors in such a wide range of industries. Some parents are unable to contribute much extra to the subsidiaries. Daimler-Benz had little to offer here, whereas the new, more focused headquarters of the merged DaimlerChrysler operation – *see* Case study 10.2 – were able to offer a range of resources that would be relevant to its subsidiaries. The reason was that the new headquarters were more tightly focused on a narrow range of transport (car, lorry, possibly aircraft) activities.

▶ Key strategic principles

- Parenting concerns the corporate headquarters of a group of subsidiaries, whose areas of business may be unrelated to each other. Such a business still needs to define its purpose and develop its mission and objectives. This may be difficult where the activities are widely spread.

- The role of the parent is to add value to the subsidiaries that are associated with the organisation, otherwise the cost of running a corporate headquarters cannot be justified.

- The parenting resource of the corporate headquarters can make offerings in four areas: corporate functions; corporate development initiatives; additional finance for growth or problem areas; the development of formal linkages between parts of the group.

- Parents need two special attributes to operate effectively: an understanding of the key factors for success in the diverse industries of their subsidiaries and an ability to make a special contribution.

12.6 Quality objectives and corporate strategy

Over the last 30 years, organisations have increasingly highlighted quality as a fundamental part of their purpose. The reason is that it increases the value added of the organisation. In addition, it often provides the sustainable competitive advantage that competitiors have real difficulty in matching. Equally, some competitors may have started to emphasise their quality and force their competitors into a catch-up strategy. For example, Japanese car companies have forced their US and European competitors to develop major quality performance objectives over the last ten years. Essentially, in order to stress its importance, quality has become part of the purpose and objectives of many leading companies, rather than being relegated to a lesser strategic role.

Quality is important for most organisations but needs to be defined in the context of customer expectations about the product, its price and other issues. For example, quality does not mean the same thing to Rolls-Royce or Mercedes as it does to a market trader. Although both should attempt to deliver quality to their customers as part of their overall strategy, not all quality issues are strategic. Quality needs to form part of the defined objectives of most organisations. It therefore needs to be tackled early in strategy development.

Total quality management (*TQM*) is the modern approach to the management of the whole organisation that emphasises the role of quality in meeting the needs and expectations of its customers.[35] It is essential to operate this as part of the corporate objectives and strategy of the organisation. Not every organisation operates TQM, although virtually all have some form of *quality control*, i.e. the regular inspection of goods and services to ensure that they meet minimum standards. Quality control is involved with day-to-day detail and is *not* strategic in its approach.

TQM is strategic for three reasons:

1 the TQM emphasis on the *whole* organisation;

2 the TQM requirement for active support from *senior* management;

3 the significant contribution that TQM can make to competitive advantage.

Quality procedures in general and TQM in particular can be considered as having an influence on corporate objectives, such as profitability, by a series of interconnected routes. These are shown in Figure 12.7 and backed by empirical research. The PIMS database of 3000 companies showed a strong correlation between quality and profitability – *see* Chapter 14.[36]

TQM has a strategic role because of the success of some companies in developing quality and reliability as competitive weapons in the international market place. Thus quality itself has become a sustainable competitive advantage. Although quality was first conceived in the US in the mid-1950s, it was Japanese interest and persistence that really developed this area during the period between 1955 and 1985. Pioneers worked mainly in Japan and included Deming, Juran, Ishikawa, Taguchi and Crosby.[37]

After the proven success of Japanese companies in slowly and painfully developing new procedures over 30 years,[38] TQM was picked up by Western companies. This does not mean that Western companies had no quality procedures prior to this time – they simply used more limited and different methods. With the benefit of hindsight, some would argue that such Western procedures were less successful but this has not been conclusively proved. Many Western companies do not operate TQM procedures at the present time but do place significant and successful emphasis on quality control. The detail of this area is beyond the scope of this book and is not strategic as such.[39] However, there are two aspects that have strategic relevance:

1 *Differences in management approach.* A TQM business is more co-operative, less Taylorist in its style.

2 *Results in terms of customer relationships with the organisation.* A TQM business is likely to have a deeper, more quality-based relationship with its customers.

Both of these might possibly form the basis of competitive advantage. However, TQM is not without its costs and difficulties. Japanese companies such as Honda, Nissan, Toyota and Matsushita have been working on TQM for over 35 years. Among the earlier Western companies to adopt the approach are Motorola (US) and Texas Instruments (US), which began operating TQM procedures in the early 1980s.[40] One of the real problems found by all the companies, including the Japanese ones, is that the benefits take time to

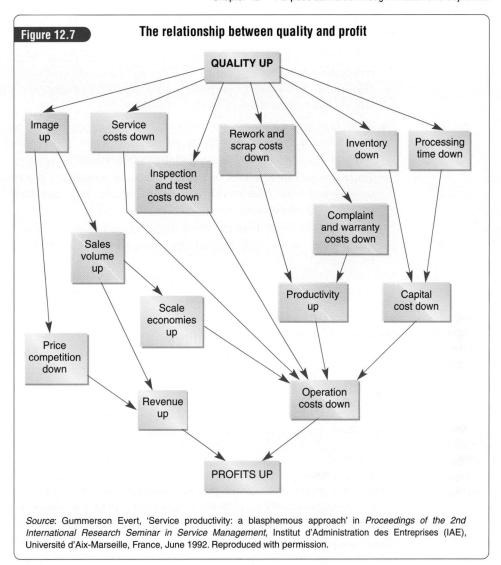

Figure 12.7 — **The relationship between quality and profit**

Source: Gummerson Evert, 'Service productivity: a blasphemous approach' in *Proceedings of the 2nd International Research Seminar in Service Management*, Institut d'Administration des Entreprises (IAE), Université d'Aix-Marseille, France, June 1992. Reproduced with permission.

emerge but the costs are only too obvious from an early stage. In some cases, benefits emerge quickly as early procedures tighten and then the rest come slowly over a period of years. To this extent, TQM is probably best seen as an *emergent* rather than a *prescriptive* process, in spite of the clear decision needed to undertake the task at the outset.

Key strategic principles

- Quality is vital for most organisations and will form part of their strategic purpose and objectives. It delivers value added and may contribute to sustainable competitive advantage. Total quality management (TQM) is the modern strategic approach to quality delivery. It is not the same as quality control.

> ▶ *Key strategic principles continued*
>
> - TQM is an approach to the management of the whole organisation that emphasises the role of quality in meeting the needs and expectations of its customers. Not every organisation operates TQM procedures, though virtually all have some form of quality control.
>
> - TQM lays the emphasis on workers being responsible for quality, rather than using a separate quality department. It aims to 'get things right first time' rather than have defects that are corrected later.
>
> - There are real differences in the approach to managing TQM-based organisations and their relationships with customers. They may form the basis of competitive advantage.
>
> - Although there are benefits from TQM, there are many costs. It frequently takes years for the full benefits to emerge but the costs are often obvious from an early stage.

12.7 Emergent strategy perspectives

In the latter part of this chapter, we have been exploring mission and objectives from the viewpoint of the *prescriptive* corporate strategist. This has been done because it is occasionally easier to explore aspects of a topic without all the qualifications that might apply in practice. Specifically, the work of Professor J B Quinn on 'logical incrementalism'[41] has been ignored up to this point.

Quinn began his seminal 1978 paper with a quote from an interview he undertook:

When I was younger, I always conceived of a room where all these [strategic] concepts were worked out for the whole company. Later I didn't find any such room . . . The strategy [of the company] may not even exist in the mind of one man. I certainly don't know where it is written down. It is simply transmitted in the series of decisions made.

Quinn went on to comment that, when well-managed major organisations make significant changes in strategy, the approaches they use frequently bear little resemblance to the rational-analytical systems so often touted in the planning literature. He was reacting (with justification, in my view) to the formalised planning systems that were being recommended in the 1970s: strategy was seen almost to be a mathematical formula rather than the craft it actually is. An important issue is whether his comments should still be applied to some of the processes described during this chapter, especially in the later sections.

Stakeholder analysis and company culture analysis would probably not cause a problem. Business ethics might also be acceptable. However, Quinn might have difficulty with the mission statement. It was for this reason that Campbell and Yeung commented on the need to see a mission statement not just as a statement of purpose but also as expressing the *values of the organisation*. Nevertheless, the practice of producing mission statements might cause Quinn some concern. But, as we have seen, they are extensively used by companies in the early twenty-first century. Translating these into objectives involves such an element of business judgement that Quinn might judge that his original research was still valid.

▶ Key strategic principles

- There is a danger in being too rational in the development of mission and objectives.
- Mission statements need to reflect the *values* of the organisation as well as a statement of its purpose.

12.8 Stakeholder power around the world and its influence on mission and objectives

From the earlier discussion of stakeholders, it will be evident that they have a substantial influence on the mission and objectives of an organisation. However, the roles and power of owners, shareholders, financing banks and worker-owners will differ around the world as a result of different ownership structures, national government policies and other matters. In particular, *shareholding structures* can vary significantly. Thus the mission and objectives may also change and this needs to be considered in international strategy development.

Much of the shareholder research appears to have been conducted in an Anglo-American context. In the UK and North America, stock markets have been described as demanding short-term results from quoted companies. Shares are widely held and many larger companies have *public share quotations*. This does not imply that shareholders always put direct pressure on senior company managers, but company shares can always be sold as a means of applying pressure. Privatisation has largely taken place so that most companies are influenced only indirectly by governments. Some unions are still powerful in the US in certain industries, but in the UK unions lost their substantial power base through the Thatcher labour law reforms of the 1980s.

Owner–stakeholder interests across other parts of Europe are not necessarily the same. Specifically, *large commercial banks* have much larger shareholdings in major companies in Germany,[42] France,[43] Italy[44] and Spain.[45] For example, in Germany, the large German banks have traditionally held large share blocks in leading German companies: Deutsche Bank in 1994 owned 28 per cent of Daimler-Benz, 10 per cent of Allianz and 25 per cent of Karstadt – Germany's largest car, insurance and department store chain respectively. Such banks will certainly be interested in the long-term profitability of their investments but do not have the short-term profit horizons of the Anglo-American model. The banks can afford to wait for years because each shareholding is only a small part of their total portfolio and because they are able to spread the risk. Banking power has usually been benign and supportive.

Across Europe, it is not just a question of bank shareholding. For example, it was estimated in 1991 that only seven of the top 200 companies listed in Milan had over half their shares in public hands.[46] There has been some resistance to the widespread ownership of shares in Germany. In France, the state has been the traditional owner of companies, some of which were privatised in the 1980s, with more in the mid-1990s.

We must also not forget the strong tradition in some European countries of *worker co-operatives* and other mutual and non-profit organisations, where the workers and others own the shares of the enterprise. These are shown in Exhibit 12.7. In these organisations, power will be distributed differently. There will be more worker involvement, open discussion and employee representation on senior company councils.

Exhibit 12.7 **Worker co-operatives and similar forms of power**

They are particularly strong in the following:[47]

- Co-operative banks
- Production co-operatives such as farmers' agricultural organisations, including for example the largest milk producer in the EU, the Dutch company Campina MelkUnie[48]
- Consumer co-operatives such as retail and wholesale shops, including the CWS in the UK and Migros in Switzerland[49]
- Social pharmacies where legislation permits
- Social tourism organisations: for example, in France they represent 12 per cent of the overall tourist activity of the country[50]
- Housing and social accommodation co-operatives

In addition to all the above, there is also a range of *mutual* companies whose shares are essentially owned by their members. The UK has a particularly strong tradition in this area. These include, for example, some of the larger insurance companies in Europe. In all these cases, it would be quite correct to envisage co-operative organisations having a rather broader perspective on the purposes of the organisation.

Moving beyond Europe, Japanese share ownership is widespread but the structure of industry is different, with strong groupings and interlocking shares of companies.[51] Hostile takeovers are almost unheard of: the Japanese word for takeover is the same as that for hijack and indicates the same degree of enthusiasm. The threat of hostile shareholder activity is muted. Union membership is low and has been in decline,[52] so stakeholder power from this source is also not high. Government involvement in industry development has traditionally been high in certain industries.[53] Power relationships are therefore more complex. The same considerations apply in other Asian countries such as Korea, Malaysia and Singapore.

Although the same depth of research has not been conducted on employee influence on the mission of the organisation, the history of twentieth-century labour relations would suggest that there have periodically been conflicts in some Western countries (but not all) between managers and workers. Stakeholder interests may not be the same.

Around the world, it is not at all clear how the balance of stakeholder interests will develop. What is certainly evident is the need to conduct a thorough analysis of stakeholders early in the process of developing corporate strategy.

▶ Key strategic principles

- In developing mission statements, recognition needs to be given to the different power of shareholders in different countries around the world. There are greater pressures on companies in the UK and US for short-term results.

- Mutual and non-profit co-operatives will approach power issues in the development of mission statements in a different way from other more commercial institutions.

KEY READING

Balancing the objectives

In this extract from his book The Practice of Management, *Peter Drucker considers the importance of balancing objectives.*

In addition to balancing the immediate and the long-range future, management also has to balance the objectives. What is more important: an expansion in markets and sales volume, or a higher rate of return? How much time, effort and energy should be expended on improving manufacturing productivity? Would the same amount of effort or money bring greater returns if invested in new product design?

There are few things that distinguish competent from incompetent management quite as sharply as the performance in balancing objectives. Yet, there is no formula for doing the job. Each business requires its own balance – and it may require a different balance at different times. The only thing that can be said is that balancing objectives is not a mechanical job, is not achieved by 'budgeting'. The budget is the document in which balance decisions find final expression; but the decisions themselves require judgement; and the judgement will be sound only if it is based on sound analysis of the business. The ability of a management to stay within its budget is often considered a test of management skill. But the effort to arrive at the budget that best harmonises the divergent needs of the business is a much more important test of management's ability. The late Nicholas Dreystadt, head of Cadillac and one of the wisest managers I have ever met, said to me once: 'Any fool can learn to stay within his budget. But I have seen only a handful of managers in my life who can draw up a budget that is worth staying within.'

Objectives in the key areas are the 'instrument panel' necessary to pilot the business enterprise. Without them management flies by the 'seat of its pants' – without landmarks to steer by, without maps and without having flown the route before. However, an instrument panel is no better than the pilot's ability to read and interpret it. In the case of management, this means ability to anticipate the future. Objectives that are based on completely wrong anticipations may actually be worse than no objectives at all.

Source: Drucker, P (1961) *The Practice of Management*, Mercury Books, London. Reprinted by permission of Butterworth Heinemann Publishers, a division of Reed Educational & Professional Publishing Ltd.

Summary

- The purpose of the organisation needs to be clarified at the outset of strategy development. Many different aspects are potentially involved. In most cases, no single element is usually dominant.

- The polygon of purpose is one way of drawing the elements together. Although ten specific elements can be identified in the polygon, other elements may be more important and some of those highlighted may have little relevance in particular organisations. The ten identified elements are: time dimension, timing, innovation, value added (including profitability), survival, growth, leadership, stakeholders, values and lifestyle, and knowledge.

- The mission of an organisation outlines the broad directions that it should and will follow and briefly summarises the reasoning and values that lie behind it. The objectives are then a more specific commitment consistent with the mission over a specified time period. They may be quantified, but this may be inappropriate in some circumstances. Prescriptive approaches emphasise the need to set out a mission and objectives for the next few years for the organisation. Both mission and objectives must be connected with the defined purpose of the organisation.

● Some emergent approaches doubt the usefulness of a mission and objectives because the future is so uncertain. Other emergent approaches accept the need for a mission and objectives but place great emphasis on the need to include the managers and employees in their development.

● Stakeholders are the individuals and groups who have an interest in the organisation. Consequently, they may wish to influence its mission and objectives. The key issue with regard to stakeholders is that the organisation needs to take them into account in formulating its mission and objectives.

● The difficulty is that stakeholder interests may conflict. Consequently, the organisation will need to resolve which stakeholders have priority. Stakeholder power needs to be analysed. Stakeholder power analysis covers five stages: identification of stakeholders; establishment of their interests and claims; estimation of their degree of power; prioritised mission development; negotiation with key groups.

● The purpose of the mission statement is to communicate to all the stakeholders inside and outside the organisation what the company stands for and where it is headed.

● There are five elements in formulating a mission statement: nature of the organisation; customer perspective; values and beliefs; competitive advantage or distinctiveness; main reasons for the approach. Mission statements rely on business judgement but criteria can be developed to assess the results.

● Objectives take the generalities of the mission statement and turn them into more specific commitments. Usually, this will cover what is to be done and when the objective is to be completed. Different kinds of objectives are possible. Some will be quantified and some not. There may be conflict between objectives, particularly between the long- and short-term interests of the organisation. Shareholding structures will impact on objectives. UK and US companies are under greater pressure for short-term performance. Objectives need to be challenging but achievable.

● There is a danger in being too rational in the development of mission and objectives. Mission statements need to reflect the values of the organisation as well as a statement of its purpose.

● Parenting concerns the corporate headquarters of a group of subsidiaries, whose areas of business may be unrelated to each other. Such a business still needs to define its purpose and develop its mission and objectives. This may be difficult where the activities are widely spread. The role of the parent is to add value to the subsidiaries that are associated with the organisation, otherwise the cost of running corporate headquarters cannot be justified.

● The parenting resource of the corporate headquarters can make offerings in four areas: corporate functions; corporate development initiatives; additional finance for growth or problem areas; the development of formal linkages between parts of the group. Parents need two special attributes to operate effectively: an understanding of the key factors for success in the diverse industries of their subsidiaries and an ability to make a special contribution.

● Quality is vital for most organisations and will form part of their strategic purpose and objectives. It delivers value added and may contribute to sustainable competitive advantage. Total quality management (TQM) is the modern strategic approach to quality delivery. Not every organisation operates TQM procedures, but every organisation needs to place quality high in priority with regard to corporate strategy. Although there are benefits from TQM, there are many costs. It often takes years for the full benefits to emerge but the costs are often obvious from an early stage.

QUESTIONS

1 Considering the Ford case at the beginning of the chapter, is 'back-to-basics' an objective or a strategy to achieve an objective?

2 Critically evaluate the form and content of the Ford mission and values in this chapter against its back-to-basics approach.

3 In developing mission statements, the chapter suggests that this should be conducted from a customer viewpoint. Do you agree with this? What are the difficulties of this approach?

4 Choose two organisations with which you are familiar, one from the commercial sector (perhaps from work or from your place of study) and one voluntary body (perhaps from a hobby, sport or society to which you belong). Analyse their leadership and culture and show how these relate to their objectives.

5 Do small companies really need mission statements and objectives? What might be the problems of setting these in small companies? Do smaller companies like Bajaj Motorcycles in Chapter 9 need a mission and objectives?

6 What are the benefits and problems of short-termism, i.e. the concentration on delivering short-term objectives such as immediate shareholder dividends? How might this affect the development of the mission and objectives of an organisation?

7 Take an organisation with which you are familiar and suggest some areas where it has both quantified and unquantified objectives. Is it important that some are unquantified?

8 'Good corporate parents constantly search for ways in which they can improve the performance of their businesses.' (Michael Goold)

   Is it wise for corporate parents to interfere in the strategies of multidiversified companies?

9 Take an organisation with which you are familiar and assess the importance of quality in the organisation's strategy. How is quality defined? How is it monitored? Are competitors also monitored? In your view, is the process useful?

10 If emergent approaches to corporate strategy have any significance, then why do companies insist on defining and sticking rigidly to prescriptive corporate objectives?

STRATEGIC PROJECT   Mission statements

Search out the mission statements and objectives of some large companies from their annual reports and accounts. Critically evaluate the content of such statements.

FURTHER READING

On mission statements: Andrew Campbell and Sally Yeung (1991) 'Creating a sense of mission', *Long Range Planning*, Aug.

On parenting strategy: Campbell A, Goold M and Alexander, M (1995) 'Corporate strategy: the quest for parenting advantage', *Harvard Business Review*, Mar–Apr. *See* also their book: *Corporate-level Strategy: Creating Value in the Multibusiness Company*, Wiley, New York, 1994. Michael Goold has also written a useful article: Goold, M (1996) 'Parenting strategies for the mature business', *Long Range Planning*, June, p359.

On quality and TQM, read the chapters in Slack, N, Chambers, S, Harland, C, Harrison, A and Johnson, R, *Operations Management*, Pitman Publishing, London, 1995. A good starting point.

NOTES & REFERENCES

1 Based on Tim Burt, 'Jac the knife falls foul of family pressures', *Financial Times*, 29 November 2001, and other articles in the same paper on 17 Feb 1992, p14; 29 Mar 1994, p30; 11 Apr 1994, p20; 23 Apr 1994, p11; 4 Oct 1994, pVII; 2 Dec 1994, p17; 6 Jan 1995, p17; 23 Jan 1995, p10.

2 Some other sources for the Ford globalisation strategy are: *Financial Times*, 22 Apr 1994 (reprinted in the first edition of this text); 16 Nov 1998, p12; 29 Jan 1999, p1; 3 Mar 1999, p14 (interesting article by Professor John Kay on globalisation in the car industry); 9 Mar 1999, p25.

3 A fuller discussion of this depiction of purpose is contained in Chaharbaghi, K and Lynch, R (1999) 'Dynamic Strategy Development as an Endless Journey in a Fast Changing Environment', *Proceedings of the 1999 Association for Global Business Conference*, Las Vegas, US, November.

4 Stalk Jr, G and Hout, T (1990) *Competing Against Time: How Time Based Competition is Reshaping Global Markets*, The Free Press, New York.

5 Grinyer, P, Mayes, D and McKiernan, P (1988) *Sharpenders: the Secrets of Unleashing Corporate Potential*, Blackwell, Oxford.

6 Kay, J (1994) *Foundations of Corporate Success*, Oxford University Press, Oxford.

7 Williamson, O (1991) 'Strategizing, economizing and economic organization', *Strategic Management Journal*, 12, pp75–94.

8 Penrose, E T (1959) *The Theory of the Growth of the Firm*, Basil Blackwell, Oxford.

9 Harrison, J and Caron, H (1993) *Strategic Management of Organizations and Stakeholders: Concepts*, West Publishing, St Paul, MN.

10 Berle, A A and Means, G (1932) *The Modern Corporation and Private Property*, Macmillan, New York; Rappaport, A (1986) *Creating Shareholder Value: the New Standard for Business Performance*, The Free Press, New York; Kay, J (1994) Op. cit.

11 Burt, T. (2001) 'Jac the knife falls foul of family pressures', *Financial Times*, 29 November, p32.

12 Bennis, W and Nanus, B. (1997) *Leaders: Strategies for Taking Charge*, Harper and Row, New York.

13 Berle, A A and Means, G C (1967) *The Modern Corporation and Private Property*, Harvest, New York (originally published in 1932).

14 Marris, R (1964) *The Economic Theory of Managerial Capitalism*, Macmillan, London.

15 Holl, P (1977) 'Control type and the market for corporate control in large US corporations', *Journal of Industrial Economics*, 25, pp259–73.

16 Lawriwsky, M L (1984) *Corporate Structure and Performance*, Croom Helm, London.

17 Whittington, R (1993) *What is Strategy and Does it Matter?* Routledge, London.

18 References for the Jubilee Line Extension case: numerous press reports in London's local paper, *The Standard*, and in the *Financial Times* – *see* specifically a useful summary article on 23 Feb 1999, p10.

19 Christopher, M, Majaro, S and McDonald, M (1989) *Strategy: a Guide for Senior Executives*, Wildwood House, Aldershot, Ch1.

20 Campbell, A and Yeung, S (1991) 'Mission statements: selling corporate values to employees', *Long Range Planning*, 24(3).

21 Hooley, G, Cox, A and Adams, A (1991) 'Our five year mission to boldly go where no man has been before', *Proceedings, Marketing Education Group Annual Conference*, Cardiff, pp559–577.

22 Prahalad, C and Doz, Y (1987) *The Multinational Mission*, The Free Press, New York.

23 Hamel, G and Prahalad, C (1989) 'Strategic intent', *Harvard Business Review*, May–June, pp79–91.

24 Campbell, A and Yeung, S (1991) Op. cit.

25 Christopher, M *et al* (1989) Op. cit.

26 Adapted from Christopher, M *et al* (1989) Op. cit., p8.

27 Tomkins, R. (2002) Added spice, *Financial Times*, 5 April, p16 and Hope, K (2002) 'A worldwide bottling empire looks to Athens', *Financial Times*, 19 April, p13. The first article quotes a financial analyst, Andrew Conway of Crédit Suisse First Boston, who describes this approach to profit taking. The second article quotes company managers from one of the company's leading bottlers, showing how profits are generated partly from the acquisition and rationalisation of bottling companies. Other references: Coca Cola Annual Report and Accounts 2001; Tomkins R and Liu B (2001) *Financial Times*, 15 March, p20; Daft, D (2000) *Financial Times*, 27 March, p20.

28 Ansoff, I (1968) *Corporate Strategy*, Penguin, Harmondsworth, p44.

29 There are many papers on this controversial topic: *see*, for example, Williams, K, Williams, J and Haslam, C (1995) 'The hollowing out of British manufacturing and its implications for policy', *Economy and Society*, 19(4).

30 Drucker, P (1961) *The Practice of Management*, Mercury Books, London, p54.

31 *See*, for example, Heller, R (1967) 'The legend of Litton', *Management Today*, Oct, pp60–7. But note that the claim is made in the article that subsidiaries were interconnected. It was only later that this proved to be overstated and Litton was broken up.

32 *See*, for example, Porter, M E (1987) 'From competitive advantage to corporate strategy', *Harvard Business Review*, May–June.

33 Goold, M (1996) 'Parenting strategies for the mature business', *Long Range Planning*, June, p359.

34 Campbell, A, Goold, M and Alexander, M (1995) 'Corporate strategy: the quest for parenting advantage', *Harvard Business Review*, Mar–Apr.

35 Slack, N, Chambers, S, Harland C, Harrison, A and Johnston, R (1995) *Operations Management*, Pitman Publishing, London, p684.

36 Buzzell, R D and Gale, B T (1987) *The PIMS Principles*, The Free Press, New York, Ch6.

37 Slack, N *et al.* (1995) Op. cit., pp812–14.

38 *The Economist*, (1992) 'The cracks in quality', 18 Apr, p85.

39 Slack, N *et al.* (1995) Op. cit., p824

40 *The Economist* (1992) Loc. cit., p86.

41 Quinn, J B (1978) 'Strategic change: logical incrementalism', *Sloan Management Review*, Fall.

42 For example, in Germany Deutsche Bank has major shareholdings in some of Germany's leading companies: Simonian, *Financial Times*, 27 Oct 1989; *The Economist*, 30 Nov 1991, p81; Waller, 'German group's reluctant to list', *Financial Times*, 21 Feb 1994, p21, takes this into Germany's family-owned *Mittelstand*, the middle-rank private companies; Waller, 'Resisting the bait of equity ownership', *Financial Times*, 14 July 1994, p27, takes this further.

43 For example, banks such as Indo-Suez and Crédit Lyonnais have been much criticised for their extensive, relatively non-productive shareholdings in French companies during 1995.

44 For example, *see* the labyrinthine bank shareholdings controlled by Italy's largest merchant bank, Mediobanca, and described in Friedman, A (1988) *Agnelli and the Network of Power*, Mandarin, London.

45 For example, *see* Bruce, P (1991) 'Climate control in corporate Spain', *Financial Times*, 16 July.

46 *The Economist* (1991) 30 Nov, p81.

47 Panorama of EC Industry 1991–92, *Cooperative, Mutual and Non-profit Organisations in the EC*, Luxembourg: OPOCE, pp121–41. Note that, because they were not members of the EU at the time, Sweden and Finland, which have some very large cooperative organisations, are not included in this survey.

48 *See* Lynch, R (1994) *European Business Strategies*, 2nd edn, Kogan Page, London, p62.

49 Lynch, R (1994) Ibid, pp119, 120.

50 Panorama of EC Industry 1991–92, Loc. cit., p129.

51 Tasker, P (1987) *Inside Japan*, Penguin, London, p307.

52 Jetro, (1990) *Nippon 1990: Business Facts and Figures*, p131.

53 Tasker, P (1987) Op. cit., p68.

Developing the strategy

Having explored and defined the purpose of the organisation, it is now possible to develop the strategy. With no single process agreed by all strategists, in this part of the book we first introduce the *prescriptive* approach to the development process – the generation of a number of strategic *options*, followed by a *rational selection* between them, using agreed strategic criteria – and then in later chapters we apply the *emergent* approach to adjust the basic recommendations.

The routes suggested by the prescriptive approach may need to be re-examined. Some strategists may choose to introduce the emergent approach at an earlier stage.

Finally, the organisation structure and the style of the company are explored as these elements may have an important influence on the strategy, possibly even entailing a further reworking of it. It should be noted, however, that some strategy writers regard the structure as something to be resolved *after* the strategy has been agreed and would therefore not include a consideration of the organisation structure at this stage in the development process. For the reasons explained in Chapter 16, this book takes the view that it is better to consider strategy, structure and style together.

Note: There are no separate key readings in this part of the book because the treatment of corporate strategy includes the main elements of such topics.

Developing the strategy

The *prescriptive* strategic process

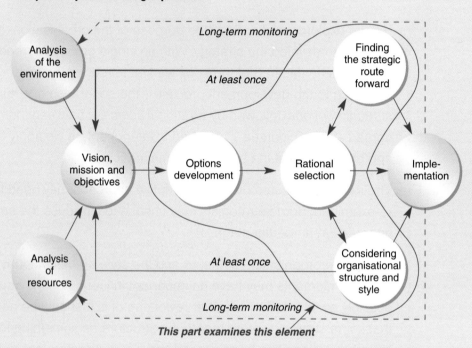

Using the *emergent* strategic process

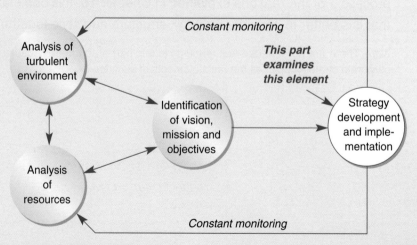

Chapter 13
Developing strategic options: the prescriptive process

- *What are the main environment-based opportunities available to the organisation?*
- *What are the main resource-based opportunities available to the organisation?*
- *What strategy options arise from these opportunities?*

Chapter 14
Strategy evaluation and development: the prescriptive process

- *Which options are consistent with the purpose of the organisation?*
- *Which options are particularly suitable for the environmental and resource conditions facing the organisation?*
- *Which options make a valid assumption about the future?*
- *Which options are feasible?*
- *Which options contain acceptable business risk?*
- *Which options are attractive to stakeholders?*

Chapter 15
Finding the strategic route forward: emergent and prescriptive approaches

- *How do emergent strategic considerations alter the decisions?*
- *What are the main features of alternative strategic approaches?*
- *What are the consequences for the chosen strategies?*

Chapter 16
Strategy, structure and style

- *What organisation structures and styles are appropriate for the chosen strategies?*
- *Do the chosen strategies need to be altered as a result?*

Chapter 13

Developing strategic options: the prescriptive process

Introduction

In many prescriptive approaches to strategy development, it is usual to define the purpose of the organisation and then develop a range of *strategy options* that might achieve that purpose.[1] After developing the options, a selection is made between them. This chapter is concerned with the options development part of this sequence. The following two chapters then explore the issue of strategy selection and related matters.

In Parts 2 and 3 of this text we analysed the organisation's environment and its resources. Before embarking on an exploration of the strategic options that emerge from this study, it is useful to summarise the situation. One approach is to produce an analysis of the organisation's strengths and weaknesses and explore the opportunities and threats that connect it with the environment – this is often called a SWOT analysis. In addition, such an analysis might be supported by a consideration of such issues as vision, innovation and technology outlined in Part 4. As a result of these considerations, the strategic options will then focus on *achieving the mission and objectives* agreed as a result of Part 4. In addition to the SWOT analysis, most organisations would also draw up a summary of the main elements of the organisation's purpose as a starting point for options development.

To develop the strategic options, both rational and more imaginative processes can be used. Inevitably, because of the difficulty of modelling imagination, strategic research papers and books tend to concentrate on the more rational aspects, which are easier to outline, structure and study. Thus this chapter concentrates on the more rational approaches, but it acknowledges the importance of the creative process in options generation – *see* Figure 13.1.

The options development process begins by exploring the *competitive environment* through three rational strategic routes: generic strategies, market options and expansion methods. It then turns to the organisation's *own resources* and explores another three rational areas: the value chain, the resource-based view and cost-cutting options. Importantly, it should be noted that there are considerable *cross-linkages* between these two routes: for example, the market environment considers the resources of competitors and the company's own resources need to be considered in the context of its competitors.

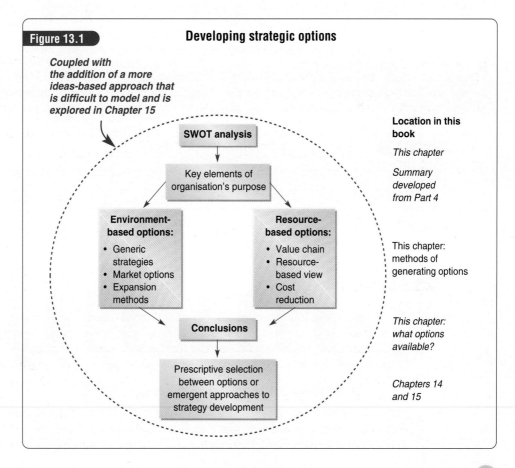

Figure 13.1 | **Developing strategic options**

Coupled with the addition of a more ideas-based approach that is difficult to model and is explored in Chapter 15

SWOT analysis

Key elements of organisation's purpose

Environment-based options:
• Generic strategies
• Market options
• Expansion methods

Resource-based options:
• Value chain
• Resource-based view
• Cost reduction

Conclusions

Prescriptive selection between options or emergent approaches to strategy development

Location in this book

This chapter

Summary developed from Part 4

This chapter: methods of generating options

This chapter: what options available?

Chapters 14 and 15

In theory, there is a very large number of options available to any organisation, probably more than it can cope with. Because of this problem, some final comments are therefore offered on how to reduce these to a more manageable size. The structure of the chapter is summarised in Figure 13.1.

CASE STUDY 13.1

New strategy options at McDonald's

Just before the new millennium, the world's biggest fast food chain appeared to have lost its way. Under a new chief executive, it was attempting to recover the vitality it displayed in the 1960s. After pioneering the concept of fast, totally standardised recipes and globally branded service, McDonald's was now seeking new areas of competitive advantage and growth.

Early innovation, recent problems

When the company began with Mr Ray Croc opening the first restaurant in 1955, no one had heard of the Big Mac or Chicken McNuggets. Just as importantly, the concept of operating a restaurant where all the recipes, cooking times and serving conditions were decided centrally was totally new. McDonalds's eventually developed its three 'Hamburger Universities' in the UK, Germany and the US to ensure that all employees would produce and serve its products in exactly the same way – very difficult in a service business where localised, on-site activity is part of the product.

In the early years, the company was unique, but by the year 2000 McDonald's no longer had sustainable competitive advantage from its basic fast food range. Other companies like Burger King were catching up and offering new competition. McDonald's still had its leading brand names and Golden Arches symbol, its well-sited locations and its well-trained staff. But the competition also had developed its own brand names and good sites. Moreover, competitors were claiming that customers preferred the rival products when tested blind against those of McDonald's.

None of this meant that McDonald's had stopped growing. Its worldwide turnover based on its 18 000 restaurants was still increasing (*see* Figure 13.2) as it continued to open new restaurants in countries outside North America. But the underlying trend amongst its existing operations was much slower and this was the strategic problem.

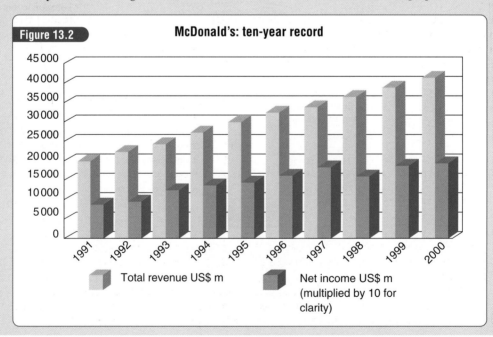

Figure 13.2 McDonald's: ten-year record

Total revenue US$ m

Net income US$ m (multiplied by 10 for clarity)

Strategic problems at McDonald's

For many years, McDonald's scarcely seemed to need new products. The company had something akin to a 'fry-it-and-they-will-come' mentality, increasing sales and profits by the simple expedient of opening ever-larger numbers of restaurants. But by 1996 things had started to go wrong. In the US, still its most important market, profits barely changed in the years 1996–2000. The US accounted for 40–45 per cent of operating profits, yet sales growth had slowed to the point where it was no longer keeping up with the pace of restaurant openings, so sales per store fell, hitting profits. Alarmingly, McDonald's also found itself losing market share to Burger King and Wendy's, its two biggest rivals, and some poor marketing campaigns did nothing to reverse the slide.

New strategy: new products

For many strategists, the world's biggest fast food chain needed to rethink its approach if it was to generate new growth. 'What we need to do is get back to our roots, which is to drive the growth of this business through innovation,' said Jack Greenberg, the new chief executive appointed in 1998, whose mission was to buff up the Golden Arches.

This did not mean the end of the venerable Big Mac, which remained McDonald's best-selling sandwich, but it did mean that big changes were looming as Mr Greenberg carried out his vow to 'reinvent' fast food. For example, in 1998 no fewer than eight new products were test marketed in the US. They included the Big Xtra, a burger with lettuce and tomato; a range of breakfast bagel sandwiches, one example containing steak, egg and cheese; and fried strips of chicken breast, called Chicken Selects. 'If they don't make the national menu, that's not a failure,' Mr Greenberg said.

New strategy: new leadership and organisation

Given the lack of growth, something had to happen and, at last, it did. In May 1998, McDonald's announced that Mr Greenberg, who had been given the task of turning around the US business only 18 months earlier, would take over as chief executive of the entire company, only the fourth in its 43-year history. In some ways, Mr Greenberg, aged 55 at the time, seemed an unlikely choice for the job. An affable ex-accountant, he had joined McDonald's as chief financial officer 16 years earlier, and, until becoming head of the US business in 1996, had little operational experience.

Still, in his short time with the US operation, he had already made big changes. He decentralised the business, splitting it into five regional divisions with a degree of autonomy; brought in new managers from outside; announced a plan to change the kitchen equipment in all the US restaurants; and started testing new menu items.

New strategy: new production processes

Mr Greenberg explained that the new, computerised kitchen equipment was the key to product innovation in fast food because it allowed employees to make food to order instead of cooking items in batches and leaving them under a hot lamp until bought. Under the old system, employees could not make many different items because of the risk that some would remain unsold for more than the maximum permitted ten minutes. Under the 'made-for-you' system, any number of items could be offered because they were prepared individually for each customer.

And this, Mr Greenberg said, was just the start: 'If you are going to grow the business in the US, you need to test the elasticity of the McDonald's brand, and our belief is that the way we do that is through food and food innovation.' Big changes will not take place overnight because that would alienate McDonald's customers, but within five years McDonald's could be offering 'almost anything people will eat', provided it is consistent with McDonald's mode of operation.

New strategy: new food tastes, even a new chain?

Mr Greenberg was reluctant to be more specific, perhaps because neither he nor anyone else could yet be sure what 'reinventing' fast food meant. But in a notable decision in 1998, McDonald's took a minority stake in Chipotle Mexican Grill, a chain of upmarket Mexican fast food restaurants based in Denver, Colorado. Could Mexican food be the way ahead? Mr Greenberg said that he did not think McDonald's would ever serve Mexican burritos, but that did not mean it might not serve a Big Xtra 'with salsa and oaxaca cheese and whatever else sounds Mexican'. In a later development, McDonalds acquired a London-based sandwich shop chain, but this was not successful and it was sold again.

bilities,' he says. 'You don't
sell food that has a Mexican
ntriguingly, Mr Greenberg
at, if Chipotle Mexican Grill
ufficient potential, or any
merged, McDonald's would
consider building it up into an entirely new restaurant chain operating independently of the original burger business.

'Ninety-nine per cent of our effort is on building the business under the Golden Arches,' he said. 'But given our competencies and our resources, I think we owe it to our shareholders to experiment with other concepts, maybe at different price points, and see if we can find another global brand.'

Case questions

1 *What are the competitive advantages of the McDonald's group? Which, if any, are sustainable over time?*

2 *Why and how did McDonald's competitive position change in the late 1990s? How has the company chosen to tackle the problem? Do you think that it will be successful?*

3 *Can companies in service industries, like restaurants and banking, gain and retain competitive advantage simply by offering new products? Or do they need to rethink other aspects of their strategy? If so, which aspects?*

13.1 Purpose and the SWOT analysis – the contribution of Andrews

As a starting point for the development of strategic options, Professor Kenneth Andrews first identified the importance of connecting the organisation's mission and objectives with its strategic options and subsequent activities. 'The interdependence of purposes, policies, and organised action is crucial to the particularity of an individual strategy and its opportunity to identify competitive advantage.'[2] He went on to argue persuasively that the rational analysis of the possibilities open to organisations was an essential part of strategy development. A SWOT analysis of the organisation – its Strengths, Weaknesses, Opportunities and Threats – is a useful way of summarising the current status of the organisation. This approach follows from the distinction drawn by Andrews between two aspects of the organisation:

1 strengths and weaknesses – explored in the *resource-based* analysis of Part 3 of this book;

2 opportunities and threats – explored in the *environment-based* analysis of Part 2 of this book.

Each analysis will be unique to the organisation for which it is being devised, but some general pointers and issues can be drawn up. These are indicated in Table 13.1 which provides a checklist of some possible factors.

In devising a SWOT analysis, there are several factors that will enhance the quality of the material:

● Keep it brief – pages of analysis are usually not required.

● Relate strengths and weaknesses, wherever possible, to industry key factors for success.

● Strengths and weaknesses should also be stated in competitive terms, if possible. It is reassuring to be 'good' at something, but it is more relevant to be 'better than the competition'.

● Statements should be specific and avoid blandness – there is little point in stating ideas that everyone believes in.

Table 13.1 Some possible factors in a SWOT analysis

Internal

Strengths	*Weaknesses*
● Market dominance	● Share weakness
● Core strengths	● Few core strengths and low on key skills
● Economies of scale	● Old plant with higher costs than competition
● Low-cost position	● Weak finances and poor cash flow
● Leadership and management skills	● Management skills and leadership lacking
● Financial and cash resource	● Poor record on innovation and new ideas
● Manufacturing ability and age of equipment	● Weak organisation with poor architecture
● Innovation processes and results	● Low quality and reputation
● Architecture network	● Products not differentiated and dependent on few products
● Reputation	
● Differentiated products	
● Product or service quality	

External

Opportunities	*Threats*
● New markets and segments	● New market entrants
● New products	● Increased competition
● Diversification opportunities	● Increased pressure from customers and suppliers
● Market growth	● Substitutes
● Competitor weakness	● Low market growth
● Strategic space	● Economic cycle downturn
● Demographic and social change	● Technological threat
● Change in political or economic environment	● Change in political or economic environment
● New takeover or partnership opportunities	● Demographic change
● Economic upturn	● New international barriers to trade
● International growth	

Note: See text for dangers of lists and bullet points!

● Analysis should distinguish between where the company *wishes to be* and where it is *now*. The gap should be realistic.

● It is important to be realistic about the strengths and weaknesses of one's own and competitive organisations.

Probably the biggest mistake that is commonly made in SWOT analysis is to assume that it is certain to be 'correct' because it contains every conceivable issue and is truly comprehensive. Nothing could be further from the truth. This merely demonstrates a paucity of real thought and a lack of strategic judgement about what is really important for that organisation.

Another common error is to provide a long list of points but little logic, argument and evidence. A short list with each point well argued is more likely to be convincing. Arguably, Table 13.1 with its bullet points and lack of any explanation is thoroughly misleading on this point. Whittington has a useful summary of some more general criticisms of SWOT analysis.[3]

13.2 Environment-based options: generic strategies – the contribution of Porter

We begin our exploration of environment-based options by considering the *generic strategies* first outlined by Professor Michael Porter of Harvard Business School. Porter's contribution was based on earlier work in industrial economics, exploring how firms compete.[4] Porter made the bold claim that there were only three fundamental strategies that any business could undertake – that is why he called them *generic*. During the 1980s, they were regarded as being at the forefront of strategic thinking. Arguably, they still have a contribution to make in the new century in the development of strategic options. However, strategists concentrating on the resource-based view now regard generic strategies as being largely historic. We return to a consideration of their merits at the end of this section.

Generic strategies were first outlined in two books from Professor Porter, *Competitive Strategy*[5] in 1980 and *Competitive Advantage*[6] in 1985. The second book contained a small modification of the concept. The original version is explored here. After exploring the basic elements, a case example is considered and some comments on their theoretical validity and practical usefulness are offered. Professor Porter confined his books to business situations and did not explore not-for-profit organisations.

13.2.1 The three generic competitive strategies: the three options

Professor Porter argued that there were three basic, i.e. *generic*, strategies open to any business:

1 cost leadership

2 differentiation

3 focus.

According to the theory, every business needs to choose one of these in order to compete in the market place and gain sustainable competitive advantage. Each of these three strategic options represents an area that every business and many not-for-profit organisations can usefully explore. The three options can be explained by considering two aspects of the competitive environment:

1 *The source of competitive advantage.* There are fundamentally only two sources of competitive advantage. These are *differentiation* of products from competitors and *low costs*. We explore these two areas below.

2 *The competitive scope of the target customers.* It is possible to target the organisation's products as a *broad target* covering most of the market place or pick a *narrow target* and focus on a niche within the market.

Porter then brought these two elements together in the well-known diagram shown as Figure 13.3.

In his second book, Porter modified the concept to split the niche sector into:

● niche differentiation

● niche low-cost leadership.

The figure is sometimes shown in this modified form.

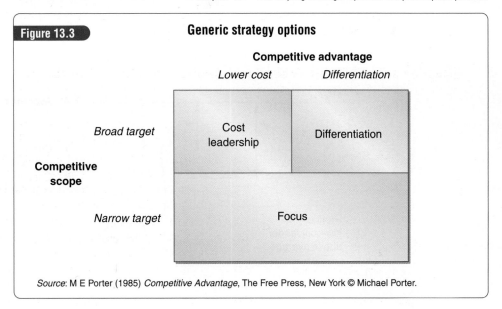

Figure 13.3   **Generic strategy options**

Source: M E Porter (1985) *Competitive Advantage*, The Free Press, New York © Michael Porter.

13.2.2   Low-cost leadership

The low-cost leader in an industry has built and maintains plant, equipment, labour costs and working practices that deliver the lowest costs in that industry.

Later in this chapter, we will explore a number of options that organisations can follow for reducing costs – *see* Section 13.7. The essential point is that the firm with the lowest costs has a clear and possibly sustainable competitive advantage. However, in order to cut costs, a low-cost producer must find and exploit *all* the sources of cost advantage. Low-cost producers typically sell a standard, or no-frills, product and place considerable strategic emphasis on reaping scale or absolute cost advantages from all sources. In practice, low-cost leaders achieve their position by shaving costs off every element of the value chain – the strategy comes from attention to detail. McDonald's Restaurants achieves its low costs through standardised products, centralised buying of supplies for a whole country and so on.

The profit advantage gained from low-cost leadership derives from the assertion that low-cost leaders should be able to sell their products in the market place at around the average price of the market – *see* line A–A in Figure 13.4. If such products are not perceived as comparable or their performance is not acceptable to buyers, a cost leader will be forced to discount prices below competition in order to gain sales.

Compared with the low-cost leader, competitors will have higher costs – *see* line Y–Y in the figure. After successful completion of this strategy option, the costs of the lowest-cost producer will be lower by definition than those of other competitors – *see* line X–X in Figure 13.4. This will deliver *above-average profits* to the low-cost leader.

To follow this strategy option, an organisation will place the emphasis on cost reduction at every point in its processes. It should be noted that *cost leadership does not necessarily imply a low price*: the company could charge an average price and reinvest the extra profits generated. Referring back to Chapter 5, an example of cost leadership in the European ice cream market would be Unilever's product range across Europe. The company enjoys the advantage of the substantial cost benefits of being market leader in a high fixed cost industry.

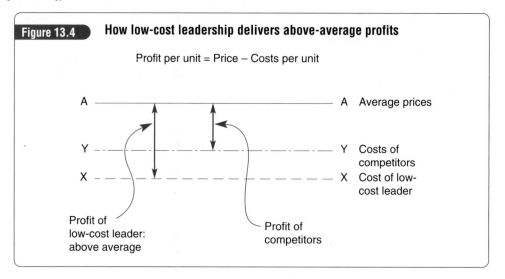

Figure 13.4 **How low-cost leadership delivers above-average profits**

Profit per unit = Price – Costs per unit

A — — Average prices

Y — — Costs of competitors

X — — Cost of low-cost leader

Profit of low-cost leader: above average

Profit of competitors

13.2.3 Differentiation

Differentiation occurs when the products of an organisation meet the needs of some customers in the market place better than others. When the organisation is able to differentiate its products, it is able to charge a price that is higher than the average price in the market place.

Underlying differentiation is the concept of *market segmentation*, which was explored in Chapter 5 – the identification of specific groups who respond differently from other groups to competitive strategies. Essentially, they will pay more for a differentiated product that is targeted towards them. Examples of differentiation include better levels of service, more luxurious materials and better performance. McDonald's is differentiated by its brand name and its 'Big Mac' and 'Ronald McDonald' products and imagery. Another example can be taken from the European ice cream industry. The Mars Ice Cream range is clearly differentiated by its branding and its consequent ability to charge a premium price.

In order to differentiate a product, Porter argued that it is necessary for the producer to incur *extra costs*, for example, to advertise a brand and thus differentiate it. The differentiated product costs will therefore be higher than those of competitors – *see* line Z–Z in Figure 13.5. The producer of the differentiated product then derives an advantage from its pricing: with its uniquely differentiated product it is able to charge a premium price, i.e. one that is higher than its competitors – *see* line B–B in Figure 13.5.

There are two problems associated with differentiation strategies:

1 It is difficult to estimate whether the extra costs incurred in differentiation can be recovered from the customer by charging a higher price.

2 The successful differentiation may attract competitors to copy the differentiated product and enter the market segment. There are often costs associated with being first into a market, so there may be additional cost advantages from moving in second – for example, other companies have followed McDonald's and Mars Ice Cream.

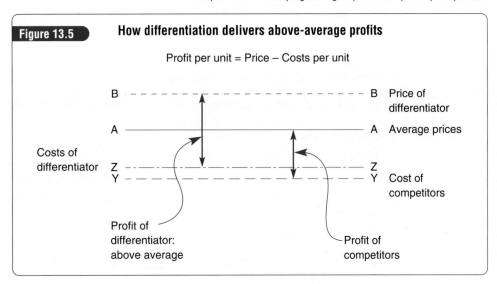

Figure 13.5 **How differentiation delivers above-average profits**

Profit per unit = Price − Costs per unit

Neither of the above problems is insurmountable but they do weaken the attractiveness of this option.

13.2.4 Focus strategy (sometimes called niche strategy)

Sometimes, according to Porter, neither a low-cost leadership strategy nor a differentiation strategy is possible for an organisation across the broad range of the market. For example, the costs of achieving low-cost leadership may require substantial funds which are not available. Equally, the costs of differentiation, while serving the mass market of customers, may be too high: if the differentiation involves quality, it may not be credible to offer high-quality and cheap products under the same brand name, so a new brand name has to be developed and supported. For these and related reasons, it may be better to adopt a *focus* strategy.

A focus strategy occurs when the organisation focuses on a specific niche in the market place and develops its competitive advantage by offering products especially developed for that niche.

Hence the focused strategy selects a segment or group of segments in the industry and tailors its strategy to serve them to the *exclusion* of others. By optimising its strategy for the targets, the focuser seeks to achieve a competitive advantage in its target segments, even though it does not possess a competitive advantage overall. In a later development of his theory, Porter argued that the company may undertake this process either by using a cost leadership approach or by differentiation:

- In a *cost focus* approach a firm seeks a cost advantage in its target segment only.
- In a *differentiation focus* approach a firm seeks differentiation in its target segment only.

The essence of focus is the exploitation of a narrow target's differences from the balance of the industry.

By targeting a small, specialised group of buyers it should be possible to earn higher than average profits, either by charging a premium price for exceptional quality or by a cheap and cheerful low-price product. For the European ice cream market, examples would be:

- *differentiation focus* – superpremium ice cream segment;
- *cost focus* – economy ice cream segment.

In the global car market, Rolls-Royce and Ferrari are clearly niche players – they have only a minute percentage of the market worldwide. Their niche is premium product and premium price.

There are some problems with the focus strategy, as follows:

- By definition, the niche is small and may not be large enough to justify attention.
- Cost focus may be difficult if economies of scale are important in an industry such as the car industry.
- The niche is clearly specialist in nature and may disappear over time.

None of these problems is insurmountable. Many small and medium-sized companies have found that this is the most useful strategic area to explore.

13.2.5 The danger of being stuck in the middle

Professor Porter concluded his analysis of what he termed the main generic strategies by suggesting that there are real dangers for the firm that engages in each generic strategy but fails to achieve any of them – *it is stuck in the middle.* A firm in this position

> *will compete at a disadvantage because the cost leader, differentiators, or focuser will be better positioned to compete in any segment ... Such a firm will be much less profitable than rivals achieving one of the generic strategies.*

Several commentators, such as Kay,[7] Stopford and Baden-Fuller[8] and Miller[9] now reject this aspect of the analysis. They point to several empirical examples of successful firms that have adopted more than one generic strategy: for example, Toyota cars and Benetton clothing manufacturing and shops, both of which are differentiated yet have low costs.

CASE STUDY 13.2

Generic strategy options analysis: European ice cream

It is useful to explore some of the benefits and problems of options that have been developed from generic strategies. To undertake this, we can use the data from Chapter 6 to analyse the possible strategy options in this industry in the mid-1990s. The generic strategies are set out in Figure 13.6.

Although the market is still growing, it is relatively easy to position the basic companies in the European ice cream market. The position of a company such as Nestlé is highlighted because it is neither the low-cost leader, nor does it have

a strong range of existing ice cream brands that will allow a premium price to be charged. Nevertheless, the direction in which the company appears to be moving can be identified from the matrix.

Case questions

1 *If you were Nestlé in the European ice cream market, what strategy options would you pursue?*

Figure 13.6   **Generic strategies in European ice cream**

Competitive advantage

Lower cost   Differentiation

	Lower cost	Differentiation
Broad target	**Cost leadership** Unilever	**Differentiation** • Mars ice cream • Nestlé?
Narrow target	**Cost focus** Economy ice cream made by small, local ice cream companies with low overheads	**Differentiation focus** Superpremium, e.g. Häagen-Dazs

Competitive scope

2 *If you were Häagen-Dazs and someone recommended a low-cost option, what would your reaction be?*

3 *Are there any weaknesses in using Porter's generic strategies to generate market-based options in the* *European ice cream market? Make sure that you have read and understood the text before answering this question.*

13.2.6 Comment on Porter's generic strategies

Hendry[10] and others have set out the problems of the logic and the empirical evidence associated with generic strategies that limit its absolute value. We can summarise them as follows:

Low-cost leadership

- If the option is to seek low-cost leadership, then how can more than one company be *the* low-cost leader? It may be a contradiction in terms to have an *option* of low-cost leadership.

- Competitors also have the option to reduce their costs in the long term, so how can one company hope to maintain its competitive advantage without risk?

- Low-cost leadership should be associated with cutting costs per unit of production. However, there are limitations to the usefulness of this concept, which are described in Section 13.7. They will also apply here.

- Low-cost leadership assumes that technology is relatively predictable, if changing. Radical change can so alter the cost positions of actual and potential competitors that the concept may have only limited relevance in fast-changing, high-technology markets.

- Cost reductions only lead to competitive advantage when *customers* are able to make comparisons. This means that the low-cost leader must also lead *price* reductions or competitors will be able to catch up, even if this takes some years and is at lower profit margins. But permanent price reductions by the cost leader may have a damaging impact on the market positioning of its product or service that will limit its usefulness.

Differentiation

- Differentiated products are assumed to be higher priced. This is probably too simplistic. The form of differentiation may not lend itself to higher prices.
- The company may have the objective of increasing its market share, in which case it may use differentiation for this purpose and match the lower prices of competitors.
- Porter discusses differentiation as if the *form* this will take in any market will be immediately obvious. The real problem for strategy options is not to identify the *need* for differentiation but to work out what *form* this should take that will be attractive to the customer. Generic strategy options throw no light on this issue whatsoever. They simply make the dubious assumption that once differentiation has been decided then it is obvious how the product should be differentiated.

Competitive scope

- The distinction between broad and narrow targets is sometimes unclear. Are they distinguished by size of market? Or by customer type? If the distinction between them is unclear then what benefit is served by the distinction?
- For many companies, it is certainly useful to recognise that it would be more productive to pursue a niche strategy, away from the broad markets of the market leaders. That is the easy part of the logic. The difficult part is to identify *which* niche is likely to prove worthwhile. Generic strategies provide no useful guidance on this at all.
- As markets fragment and product life cycles become shorter, the concept of broad targets may become increasingly redundant.

Stuck in the middle

- As was pointed out above, there is now useful empirical evidence that some companies do pursue differentiation *and* low-cost strategies at the same time. They use their low costs to provide greater differentiation and then reinvest the profits to lower their costs even further. Companies such as Benetton (Italy), Toyota (Japan) and BMW (Germany) have been cited as examples.

Resource-based view

- In Chapter 6, we explored the arguments supporting this view of strategic analysis. They also apply to strategy options and suggest that options based on the uniqueness of the *company* rather than the characteristics of the *industry* are likely to prove more useful in developing competitive strategy. We return to these issues later in this chapter, but comment now that the resource-based view does undermine much of Porter's approach.

Fast-moving markets

- In dynamic markets such as those driven by new Internet technology, the application of generic strategies will almost certainly miss major new market opportunities. They cannot be identified by the generic strategies approach.

Conclusions

Faced with this veritable onslaught on generic strategies, it might be thought that Professor Porter would gracefully concede that there might be some weaknesses in the concept. However, he hit back in 1996 by drawing a distinction between basic strategy and what he called 'operational effectiveness' – the former concerned the key strategic decisions facing any organisation while the latter are more concerned with such issues as TQM, outsourcing, re-engineering and the like.[11] He did not concede any ground but rather extended his approach to explore how companies might use *market positioning* within the concept of generic strategies – this topic was explored in Chapter 5.

Given these criticisms, it might be concluded that the concept of generic strategies has no merit. However, as long as it is treated only as part of a broader analysis, it can be a useful tool for generating basic *options* in strategic analysis. It forces exploration of two important aspects of corporate strategy: the role of *cost reduction* and the use of *differentiated products* in relation to customers and competitors. But it is only a starting point in the development of such options. When the market is growing fast, it may provide no useful routes at all. More generally, the whole approach takes a highly *prescriptive* view of strategic action. We will leave our consideration of this issue until Chapter 15.

▶ Key strategic principles

- Generic strategies are a means of generating basic strategy options in an organisation. They are based on seeking competitive advantage in the market place.

- There are three main generic options: cost leadership, differentiation and focus.

- Cost leadership aims to place the organisation amongst the lowest-cost producers in the market. It does not necessarily mean having low prices. Higher than average profits come from charging average prices.

- Differentiation is aimed at developing and targeting a product against a major market segment. Because the product is especially developed, it should be possible to add a small premium to the average price. Differentiation has a cost but this should be more than compensated for in the higher price charged.

- Focus involves targeting a small segment of the market. It may operate by using a low-cost focus or differentiated focus approach.

- According to the theory, it is important to select between the options and not to be 'stuck in the middle'. Some influential strategists have produced evidence that has cast doubt on this point.

- There have been numerous criticisms of the approach based on logic and empirical evidence of actual industry practice. Undoubtedly these comments have validity, but generic strategies still represent a useful starting point in developing strategy options.

Market-based strategies in global TV: exciting opportunities in a fast-expanding market

Over the last ten years, global television has become a major source of business opportunity. This case explores how such opportunities have arisen and been exploited by some of the leading companies. It also outlines some further market possibilities for both national and global companies in the new millennium. To illustrate some points, it uses the example of the Australian-based global media company News Corporation, which has been particularly successful. The company is explored more fully in Case study 13.4.

Industry-based change: technology and politics bring new opportunities

Until recently, newspapers have been highly competitive in many countries of the world, but TV has not. Because of technical limitations on the numbers of TV channels that could be broadcast and the deep influence of TV on its audience, TV companies were often controlled by the state or a small number of commercial interests. However, by the late 1990s, the global media market was growing rapidly. Major new profit opportunities came from two new sources: technology and politics.

- *Technology* – via new satellite channels and the greater availability of cable TV broadcasting. At the beginning of the twenty-first century, technology will be augmented by the advent of digital broadcasting, the essential effect here being to allow many more TV channels to appear on-air.

- *Politics* – through national governments either privatising government-owned channels or simply allowing new, private, commercial TV channels to broadcast.

The two main profit streams of global media: production and broadcasting

Media companies can generate revenue and profits in TV in two main ways: TV production and network broadcasting.

- *TV production* – the manufacture of programmes for broadcast. Creative ideas, popular stars and strong entertainment values can deliver competitive advantage. TV production facilities, such as studios, can be hired and are relatively inexpensive. Production costs can range from cheap game shows to expensive TV drama. Revenue then comes from the sale of such programmes to the TV broadcasters.

- *Network broadcasting*. Traditionally, this has involved competition between a limited number of companies broadcasting across the airwaves. In recent years, new forms of transmission using cable and satellite and new technology are extending dramatically the number of channels available. But the capital cost of such developments is high, especially for cabling to homes. Revenues are then derived from advertising or from subscription revenues to the cable (or satellite) channel or both.

Many companies are engaged in both production and broadcasting. However, there is also a large number of independent production companies because the barriers to entry are much lower than for broadcasting. The costs of setting up a production company to make TV programmes might typically be US$1 million, but these are much smaller than the costs of developing a broadcasting station – typically US$10 to 100 million. Strategically, the broadcasters have the greater bargaining power because they control access to large numbers of viewers, whose only bargaining power is to turn off the TV.

International TV markets: still not truly global

Although some programmes are regularly broadcast around the world – ranging from *Star Trek* to World Cup football – both customer tastes and the various competitors vary from one continent to another. In many respects, there is no single global market. In terms of size, three main areas are currently important:

1 the US

2 Europe

3 Asia–Pacific.

However, it should also be recognised that other important and sizable markets exist, such as those in the Middle East and South Africa.

The US: market fragmentation produces new industry linkages

In the US, TV broadcasts by the three main traditional channels – ABC, NBC and CBS – are available free across the airwaves – the programmes are paid for by advertising. In strategic terms, the battle between these channels has become fiercer as a new national network station has been developed, namely Fox TV from News Corporation, which is described in Case study 13.4. The traditional networks have also been fighting increased *market fragmentation* of their audience. This has derived mainly from the cable and satellite channels, which have grown in power, offering live sport, new films and specialist music to their subscribers, who traditionally watched one of the three national channels.

To fight this competition, strong links have developed between the main traditional network broadcasters and six leading film companies – see Table 13.2. The sustainable competitive advantage is strong when a company owns exclusive rights to popular films, such as the James Bond series or Disney cartoons. Essentially, all the main network broadcasters were acquired by film or other companies during the 1990s.

To pursue the battle further, some of the main film companies have also acquired the other enemy: cable and satellite channels. Warner Brothers, Disney, Twentieth Century-Fox and Paramount had all bought into the new method of accessing media. Table 13.2 outlines some of the linkages.

Competition in European network broadcasting: cable and satellite represent the major threat

In Europe, the dominant broadcasters for many years have been the limited number of national broadcasters, such as the BBC and ITV (UK), TF1 and Antenne 2 (France), ZDF and NDR (Germany), RAI (Italy). There have not been the same links between TV production and film companies because film is largely dominated by the major US studios. Much of the production has therefore been undertaken by the broadcasters, though there has been a recent trend to employ independent TV production companies.

In addition to the national European broadcasters, the 1990s have seen the rise of a series of cable channels, mostly based on subscription. Some of these rely purely on cable delivery, but some use satellite direct broadcast into people's homes with a set-top box decoder.

Table 13.2 Leading film and television companies in the USA

Holding company	Film company	Television: broadcast, cable and satellite
Time Warner	Warner Brothers	Turner Broadcasting; Cable News Network: extensive cable service
Vivendi Universal	MCA/Universal Studios	Linked to French pay-TV channel and other US cable channels
Walt Disney	Disney	ABC national TV network
News Corporation	Twentieth Century-Fox	Fox national TV network; also owns a major stake in BSkyB (UK)
Sony	Sony	None, but sells programmes and films to broadcasters
Viacom	Paramount	MTV, Nickelodeon, extensive cable network
Westinghouse		CBS national broadcast TV network plus extensive cable network; also largest radio network in USA
General Electric		NBC national broadcast TV network

Source: Author from various studies.

Asian and Far Eastern markets: national broadcasters threatened by satellite channels

In Asia and Far Eastern markets, the dominant broadcasters are still the national TV networks – satellite and cable are still in the early stages of development. However, satellite transmission does have real potential for growth because it is cheaper to put up one satellite for a large geographic area, rather than build an extensive network of small transmitters each serving a small geographic area. This principle has been used extensively in India by the national TV broadcaster Doordarshan, for example. However, in many parts of Asia the traditional broadcasters still hold the majority of the audience: Hong Kong TV, Malaysian TV and Singapore TV are examples of such dominance.

Some of the new satellite owners are local companies, such as those operating in the Philippines. However, News Corporation has also been active, with new satellite channels planned or launched in Hong Kong (Star TV), Japan (JSkyB) and India (ISkyB). Such new channels have not always been welcomed by the relevant national governments and local rival media channels. For example, the Chinese government was still cautious about Star TV, but had agreed to News Corporation broadcasts in southern China. The company was pursuing the opportunity because of the very large potential audience in the area.

TV business strategies: the choice between software and hardware and the need for innovation and negotiation skills

There is some disagreement between the leading companies about the most effective business strategies for the 1990s. Viacom (US) believes the best approach is through 'software', i.e. the purchase of exclusive rights to films, TV programmes and books. Other companies such as News Corporation and Disney have spent at least part of their efforts on 'hardware', i.e. the devices that deliver the TV signal to the final customer through ownership of TV stations in some countries, satellite or cable channels. Both these routes can produce high barriers to entry in terms of the substantial investment required.

Other strategies in the TV market include:

- delivery of *attractive programmes* such as live and exclusive TV sport or recent films;
- *restrictive access*, meaning that the viewer has no choice but to buy into the network. This is undertaken by supply via cable or an encrypted TV signal that takes a special box to decode;
- *outright acquisition of old films*, delivering unique competitive advantage here;
- *heavy investment in new cable and satellite channels* – for example, cable companies are investing around US$10 billion in the US and a similar amount in the UK;
- *company acquisitions and joint ventures* – for example, Disney acquired the ABC TV network and other assets for US$19 billion;
- *cross-promotion deals* across the different media, e.g. from book to film or video to satellite.

Because the necessary investment often amounts to billions of dollars, companies may not have the resources to pursue *both* strategies and need to make a choice. More generally, it will be evident that the fast-moving environment has required two strategies above all others:

1 *innovation* – seizing opportunities in film and sports deals, new channels, new technologies, etc.

2 *negotiation skills* – many of the new strategies needed deals to be struck with governments, competitors, sports bodies, technology companies, etc.

Key factors for success in TV: how to build sustainable competitive advantage and value added

Because there is some disagreement on corporate strategy across the industry, the key factors cannot be identified with certainty. However, it is likely that on a global basis they would include the following:

- highly creative and innovative people to create programme content;
- strong financial base in order to fund the high market growth. However, it has recently emerged that some deals, e.g. the Vivendi purchase of Universal from Seagram and the Time Life merger with America On Line, may have overpaid;
- real strengths in selected markets in terms of market share, at least in some market segments. This might be built using sports contracts, media contracts, a strong film library and even total control over subscribers to their channels;
- means of overcoming barriers to entry – either access to programmes or channels of distribution;
- commercial acumen and deal-making skills.

Sources: See reference 12.

Case questions

1 *Do Porter's generic strategies provide any useful insights in structuring the strategic opportunities in global TV? Think carefully about the criticisms before you answer this question.*

2 *If you were developing strategy options for a small company, what strategy options would you consider? What problems might you encounter?*

3 *What strategy options would you consider if you were given the task of developing a truly global TV network? Would it be profitable?*

4 *What lessons, if any, can be drawn from the global TV market on the broad task of developing strategic options?*

13.3 Environment-based strategic options: the market options matrix

The market options matrix presents the product and market choices open to the organisation. The distinction is drawn between *markets*, which are defined as customers, and *products*, which are defined as the items sold to customers. Thus, for example, one customer could buy several different products, depending on need.

The market options matrix examines the options available to the organisation from a broader strategic perspective than the simple market/product matrix (called in some texts the *Ansoff matrix*). Thus the market options matrix not only considers the possibility of launching new products and moving into new markets, but explores the possibility of *withdrawing* from markets and moving into *unrelated* markets. Nevertheless, the format is based on product/market options. It is shown in Figure 13.7.

Each of the strategic options is now considered in turn.

13.3.1 Withdrawal

It may seem perverse to begin the consideration of market options with the possible strategy of withdrawing from them. But strategy must always consider the unpredictable if it is to develop competitive advantage. There are a number of circumstances where this option may have merit, for example:

● *Product life cycle in decline phase with little possibility of retrenchment.* In the context of global TV, the time will come in the next 20 years when digital TV channels will take over from analogue broadcasts and all the old products will simply be scrapped.

● *Overextension of product range which can only be resolved by withdrawing some products.* In television, some of the many channels now being offered may have such small audiences that they do not justify even the minimal expense of keeping them operating.

● *Holding company sales of subsidiaries.* Such companies often see their subsidiary companies, perhaps in diverse industries, as being little more than assets to be bought and sold if the price is attractive. US TV companies regularly sell local TV stations and withdraw from that market for reasons associated with finance, ability to link with other stations, change of corporate objectives, etc.

● *Raise funds for investment elsewhere.* Organisations may be able to *sell* the asset they are planning to withdraw from the market. Even without a sale, the working capital

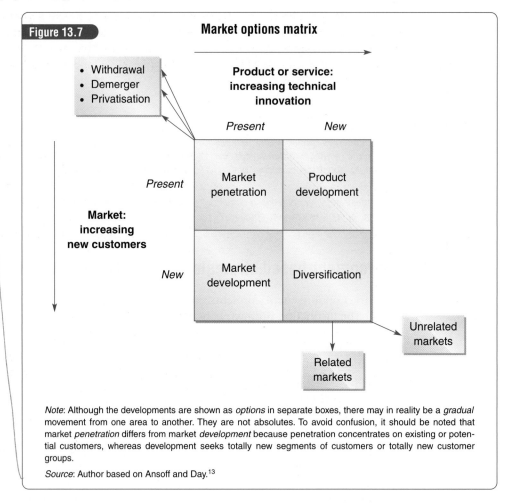

Figure 13.7 **Market options matrix**

Product or service: increasing technical innovation

- Withdrawal
- Demerger
- Privatisation

	Present	*New*
Present	Market penetration	Product development
New	Market development	Diversification

Market: increasing new customers

Unrelated markets

Related markets

Note: Although the developments are shown as *options* in separate boxes, there may in reality be a *gradual* movement from one area to another. They are not absolutes. To avoid confusion, it should be noted that market *penetration* differs from market *development* because penetration concentrates on existing or potential customers, whereas development seeks totally new segments of customers or totally new customer groups.

Source: Author based on Ansoff and Day.[13]

and management time devoted to the asset might be redeployed to other more productive uses. Government-owned companies faced with restrictions on outside funds might regard withdrawal and sale as a useful strategy here.

13.3.2 Demerger

In a sense, this is a form of withdrawal from the market, but it has a rather specialist meaning with some attractive implications. For some companies whose shares are openly traded on the stock exchange, the value of the *underlying assets* may be rather larger than the value implied by the *share price*. For example, the UK-based chemical company ICI was split into two companies in 1993 by issuing two sets of shares to its existing shareholders. The shares of the two companies were then separately traded on the London Stock Exchange at a greater value than when they had been combined. The reason was that part of the company's product range was in basic and specialist chemicals. A separate part was in agrochemicals and pharmaceuticals, the latter being highly attractive to stockholders. ICI was *demerged*, with the first part keeping the name ICI and the second part taking the name Zeneca. Subsequently, other chemical companies – such as the major German chemical company Hoechst – have followed a similar strategy.

This strategy has been used increasingly to realise the underlying asset values in publicly quoted companies. It also has the benefit that companies with totally unrelated market activities allow each part to focus on its own activities without competing for scarce resources. It has the disadvantage that it may destroy the benefits of size, cross-trading and uniqueness of a larger company.

13.3.3 Privatisation

In many countries around the world, there has been a trend to privatise government-owned companies – that is, to sell the company's shares into private ownership. This has become a major option for some institutions. For example, many national telecommunications companies have now been privatised, except in the US where they have always been in the private sector. The results in terms of management style, public accountability, ownership and strategy changes have been substantial. The changes in the product range, levels of service and public perceptions have also been significant.

13.3.4 Market penetration in the existing market

Without moving outside the organisation's current range of products or services, it may be possible to attract customers from directly competing products by penetrating the market. Market penetration strategy should begin[14] with *existing* customers. A direct attack on *competing* customers invites retaliation that can nullify the initial gains and erode the company's profit margins. Retaining an existing customer is usually cheaper, especially in consumer goods markets. Car companies such as Toyota and BMW make great efforts to retain customers when they change cars.

If a direct attack is to be mounted on a competitor in order to penetrate the market, it is likely to be more effective[15] if a *combination* of activities is mounted – for example, an improvement in product quality and levels of service along with promotional activity. Clearly, this is likely to be more expensive in the short term but should have benefits in the long run in terms of increased market share. News Corporation satellite operations regularly combine new TV channels with advertising and special deals on decoders as part of its strategy to penetrate the market.

Market penetration may be easier if the market is *growing*. The reason is that existing customer loyalties may be less secure and new customers entering the market may still be searching for the most acceptable product. The most attractive strategy in these circumstances will vary with the company's market share position:

● Existing companies with *low relative market share* in a growing market have little to lose from aggressively attacking the market or a segment of it. For example, the smaller Burger King (Grand Metropolitan, UK) has attacked McDonald's hard over the last few years with some success.

● Existing companies with a *high relative market share* in a growing market have potentially an attractive position which might be lost. Predatory price cutting is a strategy sometimes employed to keep out the smaller new entrants. It will work well and move the company down the experience curve, as long as it has the production capacity. This strategy has been employed by Intel to launch new-generation computer chips and hold off the smaller new entrants such as Cyrix and AMD (all US companies).

13.3.5 Market development using existing products

For this strategic route, the organisation moves beyond its immediate customer focus into attracting new customers for its existing product range. It may seek new *segments* of the market, new *geographical areas* or new *uses* for its products or services that will bring in new customers.

Expansion to bring totally new customers to the company for its existing products could easily involve some slight repackaging and then promotion to a new market segment. It will often involve selling the same product in new international markets – there are many examples of such a strategy throughout this book. Using core competencies and a little ingenuity, it may be possible to find new uses for existing products. For example, the pharmaceutical company Glaxo (UK) has sought to develop the markets for its anti-ulcer drug Zantac as markets have matured in Western Europe and North America. Thus it has marketed the product to an increasing range of countries and it has also developed a lower-strength version to be sold without prescription as a stomach remedy in place of antacid remedies.

We explore the methods by which organisations can undertake such expansion in the next section.

13.3.6 Product development for the existing market

We refer here to significant new product developments, not a minor variation on an existing product. There are a number of reasons that might justify such a strategy:[16]

- to utilise excess production capacity;
- to counter competitive entry;
- to exploit new technology;
- to maintain the company's stance as a product innovator;
- to protect overall market share.

Understanding the reason is key to selecting the route that product development will then follow. Probably the area with the most potential is that associated with innovation: it may represent a threat to an existing product line or an opportunity to take market share from competition. Sometimes product development strategies do not always fall neatly into an existing market. They often move the company into markets and towards customers that are not currently being served. This is part of the natural growth of many organisations.

13.3.7 Diversification: related markets

When an organisation diversifies, it moves out of its current products and markets into new areas. Clearly, this will involve a step into the unknown and will carry a higher degree of business risk. However, the organisation may minimise this risk if it moves into related markets. (*Related* here means a market that has some existing connection with its existing value chain.) It is usual to distinguish three types of relationship based on the value chain of Chapter 6:

1 *Forward integration.* A manufacturer becomes involved in the activities of the organisation's *outputs* such as distribution, transport, logistics – for example, the purchase of glass distributors by Europe's two leading glass manufacturers, St Gobain (France) and Pilkington (UK).[17]

2 *Backward integration*. The organisation extends its activities to those of its *inputs* such as its suppliers of raw materials, plant and machinery – for example, the purchase by the oil company Elf (France) of oil drilling interests in the North Sea.[18]

3 *Horizontal integration*. The organisation moves into areas immediately related to its existing activities because either they compete or they are complementary – for example, the acquisition by BMW (Germany) of the UK car company Rover in 1994.

News Corporation has engaged in forward integration by purchasing cable and satellite channels to deliver TV programmes directly to customers. It has integrated backwards into film production companies. It has undertaken horizontal integration by extending the range of its activities from newspapers to books, TV and electronic media.

Synergy is the main reason given for such activities.[19] It means essentially that the whole is worth more than the sum of the parts: the value to be generated from owning and controlling more of the value chain is greater because the various elements support each other. This concept is relatively easy to understand but rather more difficult to analyse precisely. This means that it is difficult to assess its specific contribution to corporate strategy. It is related to the concept of *linkages* in the value chain that were explored in Chapter 6 and is probably best assessed using these concepts.

13.3.8 Diversification: unrelated markets

When an organisation moves into unrelated markets, it runs the risk of operating in areas where its detailed knowledge of the key factors for success is limited. Essentially, it acts as if it were a *holding company*. Some companies have operated such a strategy with success, probably the best known being Hanson plc (UK, but with strong interests in the US) and General Electric (US). The logic of such an expansion is unlikely to be market-related, by definition, since the target market has no connection with the organisation's current areas of interest. This does not mean that the strategy is without merit for two reasons:

1 There could be other connections in finance with the existing business that would justify such expansion.

2 There may be no connection but the diversification could still be operated successfully if the holding company managed such a venture using tight but clear financial controls.

Clearly, such strategies are directly related to the discussion on strategic parenting in Chapter 12. However, it should be pointed out that unrelated diversification is not popular at present: it flies against the evidence and logic of the resource-based view.

Comment

The market options matrix is a useful way of structuring the options available. However, it does not in itself provide many useful indicators of which option to choose in what circumstances. Thus its value lies in *structuring* the problem rather than *solving it*. The main strategic insights come from the possibilities that it raises to challenge current thinking by opening up the debate.

Such routes may involve the expenditure of some funds on new product development, research, advertising and related matters. Hence, the options are more likely to be favoured by those organisations with significant financial resources. Many of the options are more likely to be considered by profitable companies, rather than those attempting to recover from substantial losses. However, by disposing of some assets, market-based options may actually raise funds and provide greater freedom of action for those remaining in the organisation. Typically, these might include the sale of parts of companies.

The market options matrix may be more appropriate in the commercial, non-government-owned sector because state companies are usually set up to fill a specific role with little room for development beyond this definition.

> ### ▶ Key strategic principles
>
> - By examining the market place and the products available, it is possible to structure options that organisations may be able to adopt: the overall structure is called the *market options matrix*.
>
> - Options include moving to new customers and new products. As these are developed further, they may involve the organisation in diversifying away from its original markets.
>
> - Synergy is the main reason behind diversification into related markets, the whole being more than the sum of the parts. This concept is associated with linkages in the value chain.
>
> - The market options matrix is a method of generating options but provides no guidance on choosing between them. The main strategic insights come from the possibilities that it raises to challenge the current thinking by opening up the debate.

13.4 Environment-based strategic options: the expansion method matrix

The expansion method matrix explores in a structured way the methods by which environment-based options might be achieved. By examining the organisation's internal and external expansion opportunities and its geographical spread of activity, it is possible to structure the various methods that are available.

In addition to exploring the routes to develop strategy options, it is also important to explore the methods by which these can be achieved. For example, launching a new product could be done using an existing company or an acquisition, merger or joint venture with another firm. As companies have moved outside their home countries, the methods used for such development have also increased. We have already seen how News Corporation has used a variety of contractual arrangements in different countries in the world to develop its global presence. The full list of options is set out in Figure 13.8.

13.4.1 Acquisitions

Probably the most important reason for this method of market expansion is that associated with the particular assets of the company: brands, market share, core competencies and special technologies may all represent reasons for purchase. News Corporation acquired its encryption technology by buying a company in 1990. The obvious disadvantage is that, if a company really has an asset, there may be a substantial premium to

Figure 13.8	Expansion method matrix

Company

	Inside	Outside
Home country	• Internal development	• Merger • Acquisition • Joint venture • Alliance • Franchise
Geographical location **International**	• Exporting • Overseas office • Overseas manufacture • Multinational operation • Global operation	• Merger • Acquisition • Joint venture • Alliance • Franchise • Turnkey • Licensing

Note: All the above methods must add value to the organisation if they are to justify their costs.

pay over the asset value of the company. For example, Nestlé paid double the value at which the shares of Rowntree had previously been quoted on the stock exchange when it bought the chocolate company in 1989.

Acquisitions may also be made for competitive reasons. In a static market, it may be expensive and slow to enter by building from the beginning. For example, in the slow-growing coffee market, Philip Morris/Kraft General Foods has made a series of company purchases to add to its Maxwell House brand: Café Hag and Jacobs Coffee. In fast-growing markets, acquisitions may be the means to acquire presence more rapidly. For example, the purchase of the Biogen Company by Roche (Switzerland) moved the Swiss company from its traditional drugs into the totally new area of biomedical sciences at a stroke.

13.4.2 Mergers

Mergers are similar to acquisitions in the sense of two companies combining. However, mergers usually arise because neither company has the scale to acquire the other on its own. This has the potential benefit of being more friendly but requires special handling if the benefits are to be realised. In other respects, it is similar to an acquisition in terms of the main strategic issues.

13.4.3 Joint ventures and alliances

A *joint venture* is the formation of a company whose shares are owned jointly by two parent companies. It usually shares some of the assets and skills of both parents. Cereal Partners Inc. is a 50/50 joint venture between Nestlé and General Mills (US) whose purpose is to attack Kellogg's Breakfast Cereals around the world except in North America – *see* the case in Chapter 2.

An *alliance* is some form of weaker contractual agreement or even minority share-holding between two parent companies. It usually falls short of the formation of a separate subsidiary. Several of the European telecommunications companies have built alliances as the basis for international expansion.

13.4.4 Franchise

A franchise is a form of licensing agreement in which the contractor provides the licensee with a pre-formed package of activity. It may include a brand name, technical service expertise and some advertising assistance. Payment is usually a percentage of turnover. McDonald's Restaurants are among the best-known franchises.

The main advantages and disadvantages of the various methods of market expansion are summarised in Table 13.3.

13.4.5 International options

In spite of the publicity on some occasions across Europe, acquisitions are relatively infrequent outside the UK and North America.[20] They are also used sparingly in many countries of South-East Asia and in Japan. There are two main reasons: shares are more openly traded in Anglo-Saxon countries than in parts of Europe and Asia, where bank and government holdings are more important; and there is a stronger tradition in some countries of interlocking shareholdings that makes outright acquisition difficult, if not impossible.

Beyond this basic issue, the greater degree of global trading has made options that might have applied in a few Western countries now available around the world. There are two that have some importance for overseas operations:

1 *Turnkey*. A contractor who has total responsibility for building and possibly commissioning large-scale plant. Payment can take many forms.

2 *Licensing*. Technology or other assets are provided under licence from the home country. Payment is usually by royalty or some other percentage of turnover arrangement.

More generally, overseas expansion for many companies may take the form of the following sequence:[21]

● *Exporting* as a possible first expansion step.

● *An overseas office* may then be set up to provide a permanent presence.

● *Overseas manufacture* can take place but this clearly increases the risk and exposure to international risks such as currency.

● *Multinational operations* may be set up to provide major international activity.

● *Global operations* may be introduced. The distinction from multinational operations lies in the degree of international commitment and, importantly, in the ability to source production and raw materials from the most favourable location anywhere in the world.

Table 13.3 Methods of expansion: advantages and disadvantages

Advantages	*Disadvantages*
Acquisition	
● Can be relatively fast	● Premium paid: expensive
● May reduce competition from a rival, although such a move usually has to be sanctioned by government competition authorities	● High risk if wrong company targeted
	● Best targets may have already been acquired
● Cost savings from economies of scale or savings in shared overheads	● Not always easy to dispose of unwanted parts of company
● Maintenance of company exclusivity in technical expertise	● Human relations problems that can arise *after* the acquisition: probably the cause of more failures than any other
● Extend to new geographical area	
● Buy market size and share	● Problems of clash of national cultures particularly where target 'foreign'
● Financial reasons associated with purchase of undervalued assets that may then be resold	
Joint venture	
● Builds scale quickly	● Control lost to some extent
● Obtains special expertise quickly	● Works best where both parties contribute something different to the mix
● Cheaper than acquisition	
● Can be used where outright acquisition not feasible	● Can be difficult to manage because of need to share and because parent companies may interfere
● Can be used where similar product available	● Share profits with partner
Alliance	
● Can build close contacts with partner	● Slow and plodding approach
● Uses joint expertise and commitment	● Needs constant work to keep relationship sound
● Allows potential partners to learn about each other	● Partners may only have a limited joint commitment to make alliance a success
● Locks out other competitors	● Unlikely to build economies of scale
Franchise	
● Lower investment than outright purchase	● Depends on quality of franchise
● Some of basic testing of business proposition undertaken by franchise holder: lower risk	● Part of profits paid over to franchise holder
	● Risk that business built and franchise withdrawn
● Exclusive territory usually granted	

Source: Adapted from Lynch, R (1994) *European Business Strategies*, 2nd edn, Kogan Page, London. © Richard Lynch 2000. All rights reserved.

There are various risks and opportunities associated with all the above operations. Probably the most important of these is currency variation – that is, the difficulty of trading in currencies that are volatile and may cause significant and unexpected losses.

Comment

The expansion method matrix suffers from the same disadvantage as the previous matrix. That is, it is useful at structuring the options but offers only limited guidance on choosing between them.

> ### ▶ Key strategic principles
>
> ● The *expansion method matrix* explores in a structured way the methods by which market options might be achieved. By examining the organisation's internal and external expansion opportunities and its geographical spread of activity, it is possible to structure the various methods that are available.
>
> ● Within the home country, the four main methods of expansion are: acquisition, joint venture, alliance and franchise. Each has its advantages and problems.
>
> ● Beyond the home country, there are additional means of international expansion, including exporting, setting up overseas offices and undertaking full manufacturing. The most important risk associated with international expansion is probably currency fluctuation.

CASE STUDY 13.4

Building a global media company at News Corporation

From a small Australian/UK newspaper operation, News Corporation has been built into a global force in media over the last 20 years. This case outlines the strategies that have proved so successful, including those that challenge the conventional 'strategic options' approaches.

Company background: newspapers developed by risk taking and innovation

Over the last 20 years, News Corporation has been shaped by its chairman and chief executive, Rupert Murdoch. He had the reputation as a young man of being something of a rebel. However, he was born into a wealthy family and inherited his father's chain of newspapers in Australia at the age of 21. He then used these as the starting point for his ambitions.

Murdoch radically repositioned his Australian newspapers by taking some downmarket and others upmarket. Building on this success, he moved from Australia to the UK and acquired control of a similar range there during the 1960s and 1970s. The newspapers included the brash and breezy *Sun* and the prestigious *The Times*. Murdoch had the reputation of being aggressive, plain speaking and a good judge of managers. He knew what he wanted and controlled the main elements of his company with clarity and vision. He did not hesitate to plan and pick a fight with the UK print trade unions in the 1970s in order to break their power over the industry – he won and added to his reputation for ruthless efficiency. His companies were prepared to take risks and innovate in order to advance strategic-

ally, but they were still small by international standards and had no significant TV interests.

News Corporation: innovation in TV nearly brought down the company

In the 1980s, News Corporation was one of the earliest companies to see the potential for satellite broadcasting. By a series of bold moves in the UK, it launched a TV service 18 months ahead of the official government-sponsored rival. The early days were difficult, with the new venture being a major drain on cash across the group. At one stage in 1990, the whole News Corporation group was within hours of bankruptcy. Eventually, Murdoch's own and the rival channel were merged to form British Sky Broadcasting (BSkyB), in which News Corporation held 50 per cent share (subsequently reduced to 35 per cent). When BSkyB was floated on the stock exchange in 1994, it had a valuation of US$8.7 billion.

In the late 1980s, Murdoch also identified the US as having major TV potential. His company acquired the film company Twentieth Century-Fox in 1985. He then made a typically bold move and announced that he was going to build a fourth national US TV channel to rival the existing three

CASE STUDY 13.4 continued

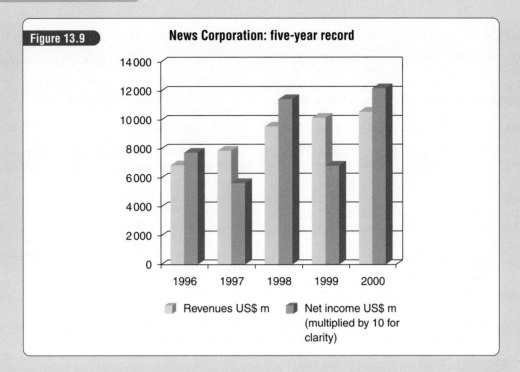

Figure 13.9

News Corporation: five-year record

Revenues US$ m

Net income US$ m
(multiplied by 10 for clarity)

networks, ABC, CBS and NBC. He used the Fox Studios as a base for four years of expansion by buying or setting up cable, satellite and terrestrial broadcast stations across the US. When it was pointed out to him that only US citizens could own TV stations in the US, he renounced his Australian nationality and became a US citizen. The whole TV strategy had never been undertaken before and was highly innovative.

During the 1990s, News Corporation began building TV networks in the Far East. The company acquired Star TV in Hong Kong as a basis for expansion into China. It also acquired TV channels on several Far Eastern satellites in order to broadcast over much of Asia. By year 2000, News Corporation had built an international media group with a strong record of growth in both revenue and net profit – *see* Figure 13.9.

News Corporation: competition is fierce and well financed

In the rapidly changing global media market, it is difficult to keep track of competitors and their particular strengths. In every area of its operations, News Corporation faces aggressive rivals. This is

partly because it is competing against North American companies where this is part of the culture. It has also arisen because of the world opportunities that leading companies have identified over the next five years: they all judge that now is the time to establish their positions and many have access to substantial funds. Major US and European companies like Viacom (US), Disney (US), Bertelsmann (Germany) and Mediaset (Italy) have put considerable competitive obstacles in the expansion path of News Corporation.

News Corporation: its future vision and core resources

The key to understanding the News Corporation TV strategy is its vision of the future: 'Our evolution from primarily a newspaper publisher to an electronic media powerhouse' sums up the company's intentions. It also envisaged only four or five leading global TV companies by the end of the decade and News Corporation would be one of them.

Over the fifteen years to 2000, the company had enhanced its core resources in the development and management of global TV operations. Specifically, these have included:

◀

- entertainment and news-gathering skills coupled with TV production knowledge;
- an adequate library of entertainment programmes, though it was weaker in the Far East and Latin America and Africa. It was not really comparable to the library of the very large US companies such as Disney, Viacom (Paramount Films) and Time Warner (Warner Brothers Films);
- management skills to produce programmes on time and to budget;
- a range of satellite and cable channels for global coverage;
- the ability to negotiate useful deals with other broadcasters and owners of attractive media opportunities such as sport;
- skill in identifying revolutionary and imaginative new media opportunities;
- satellite encryption technology (explained below).

News Corporation was the first company to identify satellite encryption technology as an important aspect of business strategy. The TV signal from its satellite channels is scrambled on broadcast and then decoded using a special machine and smart card in the individual home. Smart cards are purchased from News Corporation on a monthly or annual subscription. The company owns the exclusive world rights to the technology. By 1995 in developed world markets such as the UK and the US, News Corporation was receiving about five times more revenue from subscription to the smart cards than it was from advertising on its channels. However, News Corporation's encryption itself is not exclusive as a route to sustainable competitive advantage. Other forms of encryption exist. In addition, cable companies have a similar ability to control the signal that is delivered to individual homes. They do not need encryption but simply disconnect homes that do not pay.

News Corporation: corporate strategies are opportunistic, innovative and deal making

From a standing start in the mid-1980s, News Corporation has built one of the world's largest television networks. Many of its strategies are *negotiation-based* and derive from the rapid growth in world electronic media. In some respects, News Corporation's main strategy has been opportunistic.

It has seized the market and technical opportunities that have emerged over the last few years. For example:

- the acquisition of Star TV was clearly dependent on the Chinese owners being willing to sell;
- the encryption technology relied on the availability of this technical development at that time.

News Corporation has also attempted to negotiate an interest in the major media around the world. In addition to the examples already discussed, another deal was attempted with the German TV companies controlled by the Kirch Gruppe. By 2002, the German group was in liquidation and News Corporation had lost over US$800 million on this deal – the company accepted that risks had to be taken if new deals were to be obtained.

News Corporation has itself identified four basic strategies underlying these emerging business opportunities:

1 *Vertical integration* from film making through to delivery of the electronic signal to the final customer. Thus it acquired the film company, Twentieth Century-Fox, as well as having an interest in the satellite broadcaster BSkyB.

2 *Content creation*, not only through creative skills but also by negotiating exclusive new sports deals that buy up the media rights to world sporting events. For example, the company's deals for Southern Hemisphere Rugby, exclusive live coverage of Premier League football in the UK, and the US TV rights to American Football were all dramatic ways to build a new, loyal audience. They delivered real sustainable competitive advantage to the company while the contract lasted.

3 *Globalisation* to give world coverage of electronic media. This is particularly important for news and sports events. It is less important for entertainment, which is more culture-specific. For example, News Corporation announced in late 1995 that it would use its UK-based TV news channel to develop a world news network to rival CNN. There are competitive risks from such a strategy – *see* below.

4 *Convergence* of newspapers, books and TV so that they all support each other and promote each others' interests. For example, the cross-promotion of News Corporation's TV channels in the company's

newspapers, which had a much wider audience in the early days, was an important contributor to their success.

In practice, News Corporation has also chosen to add two more strategies that are important in delivering competitive advantage:

1 *Low programming costs*. Nearly all the News Corporation channels use relatively cheap pro-grammes, such as quiz shows and old US soaps, outside the large sports deals. They simply do not produce the same range of new drama programmes, documentaries and comedies as their national rivals.

2 *Alliances and joint ventures*. To extend its global network, the company has entered into a number of deals with companies in individual countries or regions of the world – *see* Figure 13.10.

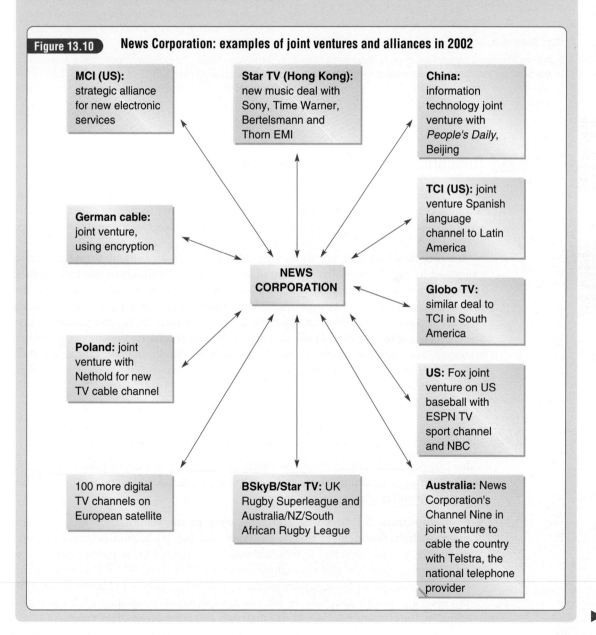

Figure 13.10 **News Corporation: examples of joint ventures and alliances in 2002**

MCI (US): strategic alliance for new electronic services

Star TV (Hong Kong): new music deal with Sony, Time Warner, Bertelsmann and Thorn EMI

China: information technology joint venture with *People's Daily*, Beijing

German cable: joint venture, using encryption

TCI (US): joint venture Spanish language channel to Latin America

NEWS CORPORATION

Globo TV: similar deal to TCI in South America

Poland: joint venture with Nethold for new TV cable channel

US: Fox joint venture on US baseball with ESPN TV sport channel and NBC

100 more digital TV channels on European satellite

BSkyB/Star TV: UK Rugby Superleague and Australia/NZ/South African Rugby League

Australia: News Corporation's Channel Nine in joint venture to cable the country with Telstra, the national telephone provider

Finally, it should be noted that Murdoch himself did not believe in economies of scale in the industry: 'There may be diminishing returns to being bigger.' But this had not stopped his rivals growing.

Source: See reference 22.

Case questions

1 *Among the media companies, there is disagreement on the best route forward for corporate strategy: the soft-* ware route versus the hardware route. Where does News Corporation stand in this debate? Do you judge that News Corporation has chosen the most successful long-term strategies?

2 *How and where does News Corporation add value to its services? And where does it obtain its competitive advantage? What strategies has it adopted on barriers to entry?*

3 *In such a fast-changing market, is it possible to follow the prescriptive approach of options development and selection? Would News Corporation perhaps be better advised to have a general vision and then grab business opportunities as they arise?*

4 *Why has News Corporation been so successful? Where does it go from here?*

13.5 Resource-based strategic options: the value chain[23]

From Penrose[24] to Hamel and Prahalad[25] the development of strategy options based on resource considerations is reasonably well established. This section is concerned only with the *value chain*. The following two sections explore two other resource-based options.

Resource-based options are those that arise from the analysis of the organisation examined in Part 2. There was a period in the 1970s and 1980s when the focus shifted to environment-based opportunities (these were explored earlier in this chapter), but the resource-based approach has now regained its deserved role as a means of generating options. It is particularly relevant when market opportunities are limited, either because the market is only growing slowly or because the organisation itself has very limited resources. For example, public sector organisations with limitations placed on their resources by government may find that resource-based options provide more scope than environment-based opportunities.

13.5.1 Identifying sources of value added: upstream and downstream

Value can be added early in the value chain, i.e. *upstream*, and later in the value chain, i.e. *downstream*. Examining where and how value can be added by the resources of the organisation will generate strategic options.

● *Upstream* – those activities that add value early in the value chain. Such activities might include procurement of raw materials and the production processes. To add value here, it is useful to buy in bulk and make few changes to the production process, thus keeping costs low and throughput constant. This is assisted if the organisation produces *standardised* items. Upstream value is added by low-cost efficient production processes and process innovations, such as those described in Chapter 11. Value is also added by the efficient purchase of raw materials and other forms of procurement.

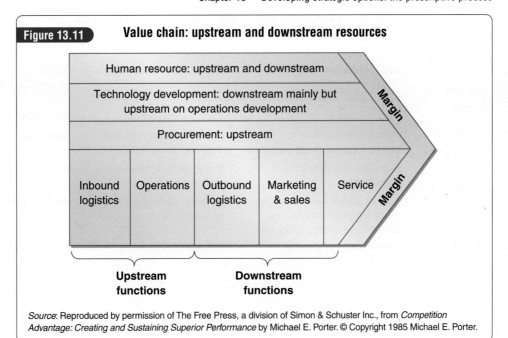

Figure 13.11 Value chain: upstream and downstream resources

Source: Reproduced by permission of The Free Press, a division of Simon & Schuster Inc., from *Competition Advantage: Creating and Sustaining Superior Performance* by Michael E. Porter. © Copyright 1985 Michael E. Porter.

● *Downstream* – those activities that add value later in the value chain. These activities may rely on *differentiated* products for which higher prices can be charged. Such product variations may mean stopping the production line and making changes, which incurs extra costs. The resources may also involve elements of advertising or specialised services to promote the differentiated items. Downstream value is also added by research and development, patenting, advertising and market positioning.

The value chain can itself be associated with upstream and downstream activities – see Figure 13.11.

Many organisations are, of course, involved in adding value both upstream and downstream. For example, News Corporation would clearly have resources in the downstream part because its magazines and books are targeted at specific groups of customers. However, it would also use largely undifferentiated newspaper and printing inks to produce its products which would be located upstream.

Nevertheless, some organisations are *primarily* located either upstream or downstream. Some examples for different industries engaged in one main business are shown in Table 13.4.

13.5.2 Resource implications of upstream and downstream value added

Using the concept of upstream and downstream value added, it is possible to develop resource options. For example, if *standard* products are required, then economies of scale may be possible. Other resource options that might produce standardised products more cheaply will also deserve investigation – the upstream activities of Exhibit 13.1.

Table 13.4 The location of the main source of value added in different single-product industries

Main resources	Examples of industries	Location: primarily upstream or downstream?
Raw material extraction	Coal, oil, iron ore	Upstream
Primary manufacture to produce standardised output	Paper and pulp, iron and steel, basic chemicals	Upstream
Fabrication of primary manufacture	Paper cartons, steel piping, simple plastics	Upstream
Further added value through more complex manufacture, patents and special processes	Branded packaging, cars, specialist plastic products	Downstream
Marketing and advertising	Branded products	Downstream

For *differentiated* products that are carefully targeted at niche markets, it will be necessary to promote them carefully with resources based on downstream activity. The resource options more likely to be associated with downstream activities are also shown in Exhibit 13.1.

Exhibit 13.1   Possible resource options associated with upstream and downstream activities

Upstream resource options might include:

- Increased standardisation of products
- Investment to lower the costs of production
- Operations innovation to lower the costs of production or improve the quality
- Capital investments that add value
- Seeking many customers from a wide range of industries that require a common product without variation.

Downstream resource options might include:

- Varied products targeted at particular market segments
- R&D and product innovation to add more value
- Advertising investment and branding
- New increased services to add value.

▶ Key strategic principles

- Resource options can be developed by considering the value chain of the organisation. This is particularly important because the chain will help to identify competitive advantage.
- Value can be added early in the value chain, *upstream*, or later in the value chain, *downstream*. Examining where and how value can be added will generate strategic resource options.

> **Key strategic principles continued**
>
> - Upstream activities add value by processing raw materials into standardised products. Resource options concentrate on lower costs.
> - Downstream activities use intermediate products to manufacture differentiated items targeted at specific customer needs. Resource options focus on R&D and marketing areas.

13.6 Resource-based strategic options: the resource-based view

As explored in Chapter 6, resource-based strategies need to consider the opportunities presented by the resource-based view. The identification of those resources that are particularly important in delivering sustainable competitive advantage will represent an important starting point in the development of strategic options – for example, the brands of the organisation, its special and unique locations, its patents and its technologies. New resources might also be licensed from other companies or obtained through acquisition.[26]

13.6.1 Finding resource-based options: architecture, reputation and innovation

Essentially the resource-based view argues that organisations need some form of *distinctiveness* over competitors. In seeking out options, one method would be to test our resources against the criteria of architecture, reputation and innovation.[27] This would focus the process in terms of both current resources and those needed for the future. For example, using these three concepts, we can specify the ways in which News Corporation has been developing in this area:

- The network of relationships and contracts both within and around the organisation: the *architecture*. News Corporation has built a range of companies that are all focused in the areas of news, sport and entertainment. They make the company quite distinctive from Disney or Time Warner. This is clearly an asset that the company has developed.
- The favourable impression that News Corporation has generated with its customers: *reputation*. Again, News Corporation has developed a clear image in this area, based on its newspapers in particular. Its aggressive, open and iconoclastic style has set it apart from its rivals. This is clearly an asset of the organisation.
- The organisation's capacity to develop new products or services: *innovation*. Several examples of the innovative ability of News Corporation are recorded in Case study 13.3. This may well cover core competencies as well as resource assets at the company.

13.6.2 Finding resource-based options – core competencies

Core competencies are defined as a group of skills and technologies that enable an organisation to provide a particular benefit to customers.[28] We explored them in Chapter 6 and can use them again here to guide the development of strategy options. Options that do not address core competencies are less likely to contribute to strategy than those that do. This suggests that a careful exploration of core competencies in the context of strategy development is desirable. (Readers are referred to the earlier chapter for an exploration of this area.)

One way of generating options based on core competencies is to consider them as a *hierarchy of competencies*, starting with low-level individual skills and rising through the organisation to higher-level combined knowledge and skills. The basic assumption behind such an approach is that some competencies are formed from the integration of more specialised competencies.[29] Exhibit 13.2 shows the basic hierarchy of competencies, which might be used to identify and structure new areas.

13.6.3 Strategic options based on the resource-based view

Beyond the two areas outlined above, there are no detailed structures to conduct such an examination because every organisation is different. It will be necessary to survey each of the functional areas of the organisation for their resources. The aim of such an exercise is to explore those areas for their contribution to value added and competitive advantage.

The checklist presented in Exhibit 13.3 has been prepared to assist the search for key resource options. However, such a list is not without its strategic dangers – readers are referred to the comments on SWOT analysis at the beginning of the chapter for a discussion. Moreover, a mechanistic combination of resources would miss the important issue that unique resources may derive from the *tacit knowledge* of the organisation. Such knowledge is unlikely to be discovered by a checklist.[30]

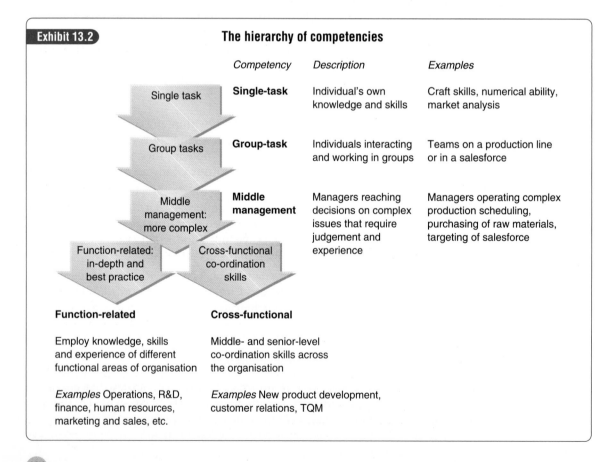

Exhibit 13.2   **The hierarchy of competencies**

	Competency	Description	Examples
Single task	**Single-task**	Individual's own knowledge and skills	Craft skills, numerical ability, market analysis
Group tasks	**Group-task**	Individuals interacting and working in groups	Teams on a production line or in a salesforce
Middle management: more complex	**Middle management**	Managers reaching decisions on complex issues that require judgement and experience	Managers operating complex production scheduling, purchasing of raw materials, targeting of salesforce
Function-related: in-depth and best practice	Cross-functional co-ordination skills		

Function-related

Employ knowledge, skills and experience of different functional areas of organisation

Examples Operations, R&D, finance, human resources, marketing and sales, etc.

Cross-functional

Middle- and senior-level co-ordination skills across the organisation

Examples New product development, customer relations, TQM

Exhibit 13.3 **Ten guidelines for the options based on the resource-based view**

1 What *technology* do we have? Is it exclusive? Is it at least as good as the competition? Is it better?

2 What *links* are there between the products that we manufacture or services that we operate? What common ground is there?

3 How do we generate *value added*? Is there anything different from our competitors? Looking at the main areas, what skills are involved in adding value?

4 What *people skills* do we have? How important is their contribution to our competencies? How vital are they to our resources? Are there any key workers? How difficult would they be to replace? Do we have any special values? What is our geographical spread?

5 What *financial resources* do we have? Are they sufficient to fulfil our vision? What is our profit record (or financial record in not-for-profit organisations)? Is the record sufficiently good to raise new funds? Do we have new funding arrangements, tax issues or currency matters?

6 How do our *customers* benefit from our competencies and resources? What real benefits do they obtain? Are we known for our quality? Our technical performance against competition? Our good value for money (*not* low cost)?

7 What *other skills* do we have related to our customers? What are the core skills? Are they unique to our organisation or do many other companies have them? How might they change?

8 What *new resources*, *skills and competencies* do we need to acquire over the next few years? How do they relate to our vision?

9 How is the *environment* changing? What impact will this have on current and future core skills and resources?

10 What are our *competitors* undertaking in the area of resources, skills and competencies?

Note: Caution is required in using this checklist – *see* text.

▶ Key strategic principles

- The resource-based view argues that it is important to identify and develop the key resources of the organisation, i.e. those that deliver value added and sustainable competitive advantage.

- Some resource areas are more likely to be important in developing options than others; those relating to architecture, reputation and innovation may represent one useful starting point.

- Core competencies explore options deriving from such areas as the basic skills, knowledge and technology of the organisation. They may also represent a way of structuring new strategic options in an organisation. A hierarchy of competencies can be built to explore the potential for new options.

- Because such resources are unique to each organisation, it is not possible to develop a general formula that will generate new options. However, a general checklist of some key areas can be developed, though caution is required in using it.

13.7 Resource-based strategic options: cost reduction

Strategic options are not only concerned with expansion into new resource capabilities and core competencies. The organisation may also need to consider cutting back its current operations in order to reduce costs. Given the increasingly global nature of competition in some markets, it is quite possible that low-wage-settlement countries such as Thailand, Malaysia and the Philippines will provide real competition. This will mean that companies are unable to survive in Western countries unless they can cut costs drastically (e.g. *see* the Fila example in Section 9.2.3). Cost reduction strategy options therefore need to be considered. The main routes to cost reduction are:

1 *Designing in cost reduction.* In some industries, large cost reductions come not from activity in the production plant, but *before* the product ever reaches the factory. By carefully designing the product – for instance, so that it has fewer parts or is simpler to manufacture – real reductions in costs can be achieved.

2 *Supplier relationships.* If a supplier is willing and able to maintain quality and reduce costs, then the organisation will achieve a cost reduction.

3 *Economies of scale and scope.* For a large plant, unit costs may fall as the size of the plant increases. It may also be possible for different products to share some functional costs.

4 *The experience curve.* As a company becomes more experienced at production, it may be able to reduce its costs.

5 *Capacity utilisation.* Where plant has a high fixed cost, there may be cost reductions to be obtained by running production as close to capacity as possible.

The first two areas deserve detailed consideration and are explored under the subject of operations (production) in Chapter 9. They are headlined here because it is important to have a comprehensive view of the options available and these two areas can be major contributors to the process. The discussion here is therefore confined to the last three areas.

13.7.1 Economies of scale and scope

When it is possible to perform an operation more efficiently or differently at large volumes, then the increased efficiency may result in lower costs. Economies of scale can lead to lower costs – for example in major petrochemical plants and in pulp and paper production.

Economies of scale need to be distinguished from capacity utilisation of plant. In the latter case, costs fall as the plant reaches capacity but would not fall any further if an even larger plant were to be built. With economies of scale, the larger plant would lead to a further cost reduction.

Economies of scope occur when cost savings are available as a result of providing two distinct products from the same company compared with providing them from separate companies. An example might be those products that share the same retail outlets and can be delivered by the same transport.

Economies of scale are also available in areas outside production. They may occur in areas such as:

● *Research and development.* On some occasions, only a large-scale operation can justify special services or items of testing equipment.

- *Marketing.* Really large companies are able to aggregate separate advertising budgets into one massive fund and negotiate extra media discounts that are simply not available to smaller companies.

- *Distribution.* Loads can be grouped and selected to maximise the use of carrying capacity on transport vehicles travelling between fixed destinations.

In the analysis of resources, economies of scale are a relevant area for analysis. It is important to make an assessment for at least one leading competitor if possible. Factors to search for will include not only size of plant, but also age and efficiency of equipment.

Although writers such as Porter[31] are clear about the basic benefits of economies of scale and scope, real doubts have been expressed about the true reductions in costs to be derived from them – *see* for example, Kay.[32] The doubts centre on the argument that larger plant will have lower costs. When Henry Ford built his massive new Baton Rouge car plant in the 1930s, he was driven by this view. In practice, he encountered a number of problems.[33] They included:

- *Machine-related issues* – the increased complexity and inflexibility of very large plant

- *Human-related issues* – the increasingly depersonalised and mechanistic nature of work in such plant, which made it less attractive or interesting for workers to perform to their best ability.

Although there were other management problems associated with the relative failure of this plant, some of the major reasons lay in the above areas. In the 1990s, large-scale steel plant was held up as providing lower costs, but new technologies have now allowed much smaller-scale operations to make the same profits.

Moreover, the competitive advantage of large plant is lost if the market breaks into segments that are better served by higher-cost plants that produce variations on the basic item which more directly meet customers' needs. Car markets and consumer electronics markets are examples where, respectively, four-wheel-drive vehicles and specialist hi-fi systems are not the cheapest in terms of production but meet real customer demand.

The conclusion has to be that economies of scale have their place but are only part of a broader drive for competitive advantage.

13.7.2 Using the experience curve effect

In the 1960s, a large number of unrelated industries were surveyed in terms of their costs and the cumulative production *ever achieved.* (Note that this is cumulative production ever achieved, not just in one year.) It was shown that an empirical relationship could be drawn between a cost reduction and cumulative output. Moreover, this relationship appeared to hold over a number of industries from insurance to steel production. It appeared to show dramatic reductions in costs: typically, costs fall by 15 per cent every time overall output doubles. It is shown in Figure 13.12. The relationship was explained by suggesting that, in addition to economies of scale, there were other cost savings to be gained – for example through:

- technical progress;
- greater learning about the processes;
- greater skills from having undertaken the process over time.

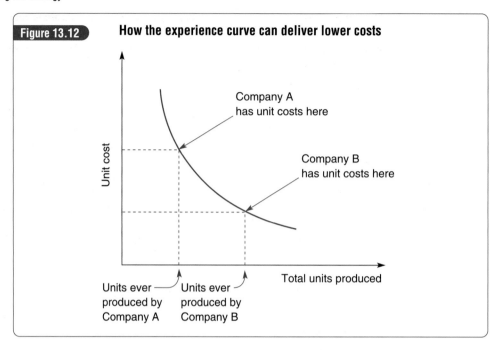

Figure 13.12 **How the experience curve can deliver lower costs**

The cost experience concept can be seen at both the *company* level and the *industry* level.

- At the company level, the market leader will, by definition, have produced cumulatively more product than any other company. The leader should have the lowest costs and other companies should be at a disadvantage.

- At the industry level, costs should fall as the industry overall produces more. Every company should benefit from knowledge that is circulated within its industries.

When comparisons are drawn across different and unrelated industries, the similarities in the cost-curve relationship are remarkable for industries as far apart as aircraft manufacture and chicken broiler production. But there are few, if any, broad lessons for corporate strategy. As Kay points out,[34] the only similarity between aircraft and chickens is that they both have wings. There may be an *apparent relationship* in that the cost-curves look similar, but the *causes* are entirely different. Hence, the strategy implications are entirely different. Aircraft production is essentially global – *see* Case study 5.3. Chicken production relies largely on national markets and requires somewhat less sophisticated technology and totally different forms of investment from aircraft manufacture and assembly. It is essential to consider the concept of experience curves *within an industry* only.

Even within an industry, there are ways of overcoming experience curve effects, the most obvious being by new technology. Another way would be to entice an employee of a more experienced company to join the organisation. As Abernathy and Wayne[35] point out, there are real limits to the benefits of the experience curve:

- Market demand in market segments for a special product change or variation cannot easily be met: to achieve scale, production flexibility may have to be sacrificed.

- Technical innovation can overtake learning in a more fundamental way: a new invention may radically alter the cost profile of an existing operation.

● Demand needs to double for every significant proportionate cost reduction. In markets where growth is still present but slowing down, this is only possible if an ever-larger market share is obtained. As market share becomes larger, this becomes progressively more difficult and expensive to achieve. In a static market where a company already has 51 per cent market share, this becomes logically impossible.

Within a defined market, the experience curve may suggest a significant route to cost reduction, but it is not always a key source of cost advantage.

13.7.3 Capacity utilisation

In the European iron and steel industry discussed in Chapter 3, we saw an example of the cost benefits to be gained by full utilisation of plant capacity. But we also saw how companies cut their prices as they scrambled to fill their plant, thus reducing their profit margins. High-capacity utilisation is useful but relies on competitors allowing such activity to take place, which may weaken its effect.

13.7.4 Structured process to achieve cost reduction options

We explored the basic issue of cost reduction above. However, Ohmae has suggested a model which structures this process in a logical and cross-functional way. It deserves to be examined for its implications in this area, and is shown in Figure 13.13. Overall, the model does not pretend to be comprehensive but rather to show the options that are possible, their logical flow and the interconnections between the various elements. For example, News Corporation over the last five years has emphasised the need to cut costs in order to remain competitive. It has introduced various programmes to achieve this.

▶ Key strategic principles

● There are *at least* six routes to cost reduction: design, supplier relationships, economies of scale and scope, the experience curve, capacity utilisation and synergistic effects.

● Economies of scale and scope are generally seen to reduce costs and raise value added, but the lack of production flexibility and the depersonalised nature of the work may be significant drawbacks.

● The experience curve suggests that significant reductions in costs are achieved as companies and the whole industry produce more product. The cost reductions relate to the cumulative production ever achieved, not just in one year.

● Experience curve cost reductions arise from a whole series of sources. They need to be sought and do not just happen automatically.

● Comparisons of experience curves across industries have little meaning, if any, in terms of the strategy lessons to be drawn.

● Utilising existing plant capacity is an important consideration in cost reduction.

● In exploring cost-cutting options, it is possible to develop a model which examines this in a structured and cross-functional way.

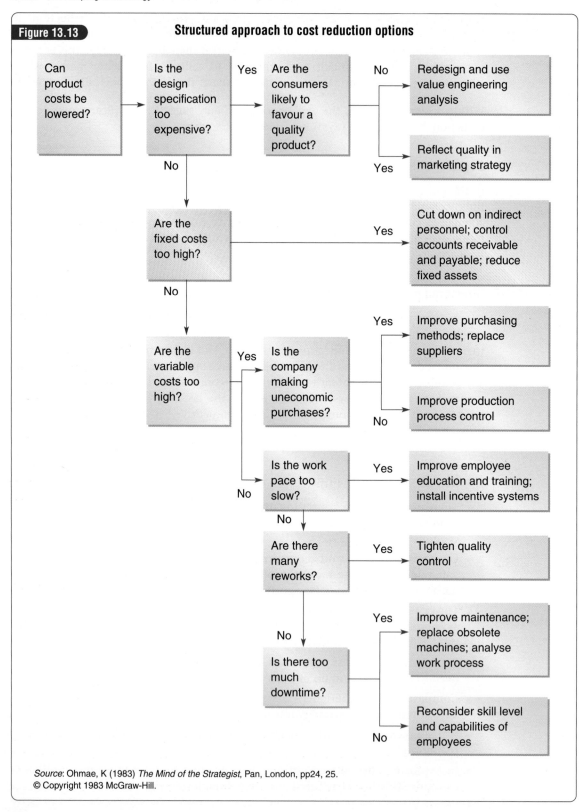

Figure 13.13   **Structured approach to cost reduction options**

Source: Ohmae, K (1983) *The Mind of the Strategist*, Pan, London, pp24, 25.
© Copyright 1983 McGraw-Hill.

13.8 Resource-based options in some special types of organisation

In addition to a consideration of general resource options, some specific types of organisation present special opportunities and problems in terms of managing resources. It is useful to identify two situations:

1 small businesses

2 not-for-profit organisations.

13.8.1 Small business resources

By definition, small businesses are unlikely to contain the range of resources available to the larger companies. There will be fewer people, more limited finance and so on. The strategic issue is how to manage this special resource situation. There are three main methods:

1 *Employ outside advisers such as consultants.* This can be expensive but is probably appropriate where particular specialist skills are needed. Outside resources are hired temporarily.

2 *Concentrate resources on particular tasks that are more likely to yield added value and competitive advantage.* The problem here is that other areas of the organisation are inevitably neglected. Correct choice of the selected area is therefore vital. For these reasons, resources are often concentrated on a segment or niche of the market that is likely to bring long-term benefit. The limited resources are focused.

3 *Offer superior service.* This can be an area where smaller companies can win against larger competitors. By being unencumbered by the slow decision making of large companies, smaller organisations can react faster and more flexibly to customers. This may even justify slightly higher prices than the larger competitors. Resource strategies here may involve extra training and possibly even the hiring of extra service staff in some cases.

13.8.2 Resources in not-for-profit organisations

These vary from the small charitable organisation to large government-funded institutions. They need to be considered separately.

Charitable organisations

These have two unique areas of resource:

1 *Beliefs.* These drive the organisation forward in terms of the charitable purpose. This means that everyone is likely to be highly motivated. It is a real resource in terms of extra work that people are prepared to undertake on occasions.

2 *Voluntary workers.* These people can put exceptional effort into the enterprise and undertake major tasks. However, because of the voluntary nature, such a resource needs to be handled with care. People can become demotivated. Some need to be given a greater degree of freedom than would be appropriate in a commercial organisation.

Government-funded institutions

These often have highly professional resources but may be strongly bureaucratic. The culture of such organisations needs to be taken into account in devising resource options. Resources may be large and unwieldy and slow to respond to outside events.

▶ Key strategic principles

- Some specific types of organisation present special opportunities and problems in the management of resources.

- Small businesses are unlikely to contain the range of resources of larger enterprises. However, this problem can be overcome by employing outside advisers and concentrating resources. More flexible service may provide a real competitive advantage.

- Charitable organisations benefit from exceptional resources: the beliefs that drive the society and the use of voluntary workers. However, they may need to give such people extra freedom to keep them motivated.

- Government institutions have highly professional resources but may be bureaucratic in their approach. Resources may be unwieldy and slow to respond to events.

▬ Summary

- In the prescriptive strategy process, the development of strategic options is an important part of the strategic process. Essentially, it explores the issue of what options are available to the organisation to meet its defined purpose. Although rational techniques are usually employed to develop the options, there is a need in practice to consider generating creative options from many sources. This chapter has concentrated on the more rational techniques because they are more suited to analysis and development.

- There are two main routes to options development: market-based and resource-based approaches. These correspond to the analytical structure of the earlier part of the text. Within the market-based approach, there are three main routes: generic strategies, market options and expansion methods. Each of these can usefully be considered in turn.

- According to Professor Michael Porter, there are only three fundamental strategic options available to any organisation – he called them generic strategies. The three options are:

  1 *cost leadership*, which aims to place the organisation amongst the lowest-cost producers in the market;

  2 *differentiation*, which is aimed at developing and targeting a product that is different in some significant way from its competitors in the market place;

  3 *focus*, which involves targeting a small segment of the market. It may operate by using a low-cost focus or differentiated focus approach.

According to the theory, it is important to select between the options and not to be 'stuck in the middle'. Some influential strategists have produced evidence that has cast doubt on this point. There have been numerous criticisms of the approach based on logic and empirical evidence of actual industry practice. Undoubtedly, these comments have validity, but generic strategies may represent a useful starting point in developing strategy options.

● By examining the market place and the products available, it is possible to structure options that may be possible for organisations to adopt: the overall structure is called the *market options matrix*. The matrix represents a method of generating options but provides no guidance on choosing between them. The main strategic insights come from the possibilities that it raises to challenge the current thinking by opening up the debate.

● The *expansion method matrix* explores in a structured way the methods by which market options might be achieved. By examining the organisation's internal and external expansion opportunities and its geographical spread of activity, it is possible to structure the various methods that are available.

● In addition to the market-based options, there is a range of options based on the resources of the organisation. There are three main approaches to the development of such options: the value chain, the resource-based view and cost reduction. Each of these approaches may be useful in options development.

  1 Value can be added early in the value chain, *upstream*, or later in the value chain, *downstream*. Upstream activities add value by processing raw materials into standardised products. Downstream strategies concentrate on differentiated products, targeted towards specific market segments.

  2 The resource-based view argues that each organisation is unique in terms of its resources. This means that there can be no formula that will identify the strategic options. However, the criteria developed by Kay – architecture, reputation and innovation – may provide some guidance. In addition, Hamel and Prahalad's core competencies may also provide some strategic options. A hierarchy of competencies may be developed to identify and develop new competencies in the organisation.

  3 Cost reduction options also deserve to be explored. Opportunities exist in many organisations to reduce the costs incurred by the resources of the organisation. There are five main opportunity areas for cost reduction: designing in cost reductions, supplier relationships, economies of scale and scope, the experience curve and capacity utilisation.

● Some specific types of organisation need special consideration in the development of options:

  1 *Small businesses* are unlikely to contain the range of resources of larger enterprises. However, this problem can be overcome by employing outside advisers and concentrating resources. More flexible service may provide a real competitive advantage.

  2 *Charitable organisations* benefit from exceptional resources: the beliefs that drive the society and the use of voluntary workers. However, they may need to give such people extra freedom to keep them motivated.

  3 *Government institutions* have highly professional resources but may be bureaucratic in their approach. Resources may be unwieldy and slow to respond to events.

QUESTIONS

1 Do small firms have anything useful to learn from a consideration of the options available from generic strategies?

2 Plot the position of News Corporation on the generic strategies matrix. What conclusions, if any, can you draw from this about future strategies for the company? (Note the hint in the 'if any' phrase.)

3 'Generic strategies are a fallacy. The best firms are striving all the time to reconcile opposites.' (Professors Charles Baden-Fuller and John Stopford)
   Discuss.

4 Take an organisation with which you are familiar, such as a small voluntary group, and consider the possibilities of expansion: apply the market options matrix and expansion method matrix to your choice. What conclusions can you draw about future expansion strategy?

5 'A recurring theme to criticisms of strategic planning practice is the pedestrian quality of the strategic options that are considered.' (Professor George Day)

   By what methods might this legitimate concern be overcome, if at all?

6 Choose an organisation with which you are familiar and identify the upstream and downstream parts of the value chain for that organisation. Which is the most important for that organisation or do they contribute equally?

7 Identify the probable key competitive resources of the following: a charity like UNICEF; a major consumer electronics company; a holiday travel tour operator; a multinational fast-moving consumer goods company.

8 'During the 1990s, top executives will be judged on their ability to identify, cultivate and exploit the core competencies that make growth possible.' (Professors Gary Hamel and C K Prahalad)
   Discuss – is this still relevant in the twenty-first century? Was it appropriate in the last century?

9 If key competitive resources are important, can they be acquired in the space of a few months or do they take years to develop? What are the implications of your response for the development of competitive advantage?

10 Take a small student society or charitable institution with which you are familiar. What strategic options based on its resources does it have for development?

11 It has been argued in this chapter that small businesses can develop competitive advantage over larger companies by offering higher degrees of service. What are the possible problems with this approach?

STRATEGIC PROJECT Media companies

This chapter has examined global media and News Corporation. There have been major strategic opportunities during the 1990s for such organisations – for example, the battle to supply new satellite TV channels in France and Germany. You might like to explore these areas further. There are updated references on the Internet at http://www.booksites.net/lynch

FURTHER READING

The two books that need to be read on environment-based options are Porter, M E (1980) *Competitive Strategy*, The Free Press, New York, and Porter, M E (1985) *Competitive Advantage*, The Free Press, New York. It should be noted that they also provide a much broader view of strategy than this single topic.

The market options matrix and expansion method matrix are covered in many marketing texts in a more limited form. Professor George Day's book is probably the best at providing a breadth of viewpoint beyond the marketing function: Day, G S (1984) *Strategic Marketing Planning*, West Publishing, St Paul, MN.

On distinctive capabilities, the book by Professor John Kay represents an important, well-referenced text on the topic: Kay, J (1993) *Foundations of Corporate Success*, Oxford University Press, Oxford.

On core competencies, you should read Hamel, G and Prahalad, C K (1994) *Competing for the Future*, Harvard Business School Press, Boston, MA. *See* also by the same authors, 'The core competence of the corporation', *Harvard Business Review*, May–June, 1990.

NOTES & REFERENCES

1 Many of the popular texts take this approach.

2 Andrews, K (1987) *The Concept of Corporate Strategy*, Irwin, Homewood, IL.

3 Whittington, R (1993) *What is Strategy and Does it Matter?*, Routledge, London, pp73–4.

4 Bain, J (1956) *Barriers to New Competition: Their Character and Consequences in Manufacturing Industries*, Harvard University Press, Cambridge, MA.

5 Porter, M E (1980) *Competitive Strategy*, The Free Press, New York.

6 Porter, M E (1985) *Competitive Advantage*, The Free Press, New York.

7 Kay, J (1993) *Foundations of Corporate Success*, Oxford University Press, Oxford, Ch1.

8 Stopford, J and Baden-Fuller, C (1992) *Rejuvenating the Mature Business*, Routledge, London.

9 Miller, D (1992) 'The generic strategy trap', *Journal of Business Strategy*, 13(1), pp37–42.

10 Hendry, J (1990) 'The problem with Porter's generic strategies', *European Management Journal*, Dec, pp443–50.

11 Porter, M E (1996) 'What is strategy?', *Harvard Business Review*, Nov–Dec, pp61–78.

12 References for Case study 13.3: *Financial Times*, 16 Feb 1994, p32; 20 Feb 1995, p16; 28 Mar 1995, p21; 21 Apr 1995, p27; 1 Aug 1995, p17; 3 Aug 1995, p19; 31 Aug 1995, p11; *Sunday Times (UK)*, 6 Aug 1995, p2.3; News Corporation Annual Report and Accounts for 1995 and 1997. The direct quote comes from the 1995 document.

13 Ansoff, I (1989) *Corporate Strategy*, rev edn, Penguin, Harmondsworth. The matrix also uses concepts outlined by Day, G S (1987) *Strategic Market Planning*, West Publishing, St Paul, MN.

14 Day, G S (1987) Ibid, p104.

15 Buzzell, R and Wiersema, F (1981) 'Successful share-building strategies', *Harvard Business Review*, Jan–Feb, pp135–44.

16 Kuczmarski, T and Silver, S (1982) 'Strategy: the key to successful product development', *Management Review*, July, pp26–40.

17 Lynch, R (1994) *European Business Strategies*, 2nd edn, Kogan Page, London, p208.

18 Lynch, R (1993) *Cases in European Marketing*, Kogan Page, London, p31.

19 Synergy is explored in Ansoff, I (1989) Op. cit., Ch1, p22.

20 Kay, J (1993) Op. cit., p146.

21 More information on international expansion is available in Lynch, R (1992) *European Marketing*, Kogan Page, London, Ch8.

22 References for Case study 13.4: *Financial Times*, 4 Sept 1993, p6; 5 Mar 1994, p11; 3 Aug 1994, p22; 10 Aug 1994, p14; 6 Jan 1995, p15; 24 Jan 1995, p23; 13 Feb 1995, p3; 14 Feb 1995, p25; 3 Apr 1995, p13; 7 Apr 1995, p1; 11 Apr 1995, p17; 27 May 1995, p8; 14 June 1995, p1; 18 June 1995, p9; 27 July 1995, p25; 2 Aug 1995, p15; 19 Aug 1995, p17; 30 Aug 1995, p15; 8 Nov 1995, p33; 30 Nov 1995, p8.

23 This section has benefited from the paper by Galbraith, J R (1983) 'Strategy and organisational planning', *Human Resource Management*, Spring–Summer, republished in Mintzberg, H and Quinn, J (1991) *The Strategy Process*, Prentice Hall, Englewood Cliffs, NJ, pp315–24. Galbraith's concept has been applied to the value chain, although he did not use this terminology.

24 Penrose, E (1959) *The Theory of the Growth of the Firm*, Oxford University Press, Oxford.

25 Hamel, G and Prahalad, C K (1994) *Competing For the Future*, Harvard Business School Press, Boston, MA, Ch1.

26 Stalk, G, Evans, P and Shulman, L (1992) 'Competing on capabilities', *Harvard Business Review*, April–May. Hamel and Prahalad make no reference to this paper and its criticism of core competencies in their book published in 1994. However, their letter to the *Harvard Business Review* in 1996 stated that they could see no essential difference between core competencies and core capabilities.

27 Kay, J (1993) Op. cit., p64.

28 Hamel, G and Prahalad, C K (1994) Op. cit., p221 and Ch10 that follows.

29 Grant, R M (1998) *Contemporary Strategy Analysis*, 3rd edn, Blackwell, Oxford, pp122–3. I am grateful to one of the reviewers of the second edition for suggesting this approach to options generation.

30 I am grateful to one of the reviewers of the second edition for making these important points.

31 Porter, M (1985) Op. cit., Ch3.

32 Kay, J (1993) Op. cit., pp170–5. It is difficult to convey fully the interesting data that Kay brings to this discussion in summary format in the text.

33 Abernathy, W and Wayne, K (1974) 'Limits of the learning curve', *Harvard Business Review*, Sept–Oct, p108.

34 Kay, J (1993) Op. cit., p116, where he reproduces the two charts.

35 Abernathy, W and Wayne, K (1974) Op. cit., p128.

Chapter 14

Strategy evaluation and development: the prescriptive process

Learning outcomes

After working through this chapter, you will be able to:

- distinguish between the content and the process of the prescriptive approach;

- identify the six main criteria that might typically be used to evaluate the content of strategic options;

- outline the main prescriptive procedures and techniques used in selecting between strategy options;

- undertake an evaluation of strategic options in order to select the most appropriate option;

- apply empirical evidence and guidelines to the various options in order to assist the selection procedure;

- describe the main elements of the classic prescriptive process for developing corporate strategy;

- comment on the weaknesses in the classic process and suggest how these might be overcome.

Introduction

After identifying the options available, classical prescriptive corporate strategy has always argued that the next strategy task is to select between them.[1] The selection procedure is the subject of this chapter. It follows on from the options development process explored in Chapter 13.

Strategy selection involves two aspects that should be clearly distinguished: content and process.

- By *content* is meant the actual strategy that is finally selected to meet the objectives of the organisation. Content is about *what* is in the plan.

- By *process* is meant identifying the managers and others who will contribute to the task and outlining the way in which they will communicate and discuss with each other to make the selection decision. Process explores such questions as *who* develops the plan, *how* they undertake the task and *where* they are located in the organisation.

The first part of the chapter is about content and the second about process.

To select strategy content, the chapter begins by exploring in Section 14.1 the main criteria that might be used. It then identifies in Section 14.2 the main procedures and techniques that might be employed in selection. Finally, to assist the process, it also outlines in Section 14.3 some general guidelines and empirical evidence that might suggest which options would work best.

To identify the strategy process, the classic prescriptive route is described in Section 14.4 and the main contributors and their responsibilities are identified. Finally, some international issues are explored in Section 14.5. In the next chapter, some alternative processes are presented and their implications examined.

In addition to the cases throughout the chapter, there is a longer case study at the end which sets out the various options available to a company and invites the reader to select one of them (or perhaps even reject all of them) using the techniques explored in the chapter. The structure of the chapter is shown in Figure 14.1.

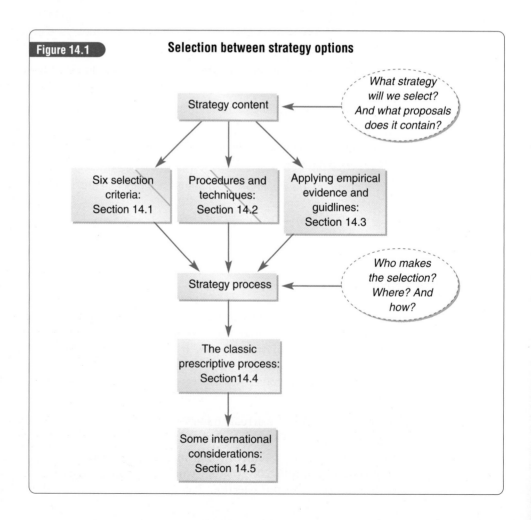

Figure 14.1 **Selection between strategy options**

Nokia – the risk of choosing between options

The Finnish company Nokia has undergone a major transformation in its strategy over the last few years, selling off or closing down various subsidiaries and concentrating on mobile telephones. This case explores the criteria used by Nokia to choose its options and the high-risk strategic consequences of its choice.

Background

In the late 1980s, Nokia was involved in a wide range of businesses. For example, it made televisions and other consumer electronics and claimed to be 'third in Europe'. It had a thriving business in industrial cables and machinery. The company also had a wide range of other goods from forestry logging to tyre making. It had been expanding fast since the 1960s and was beginning to struggle under the vast range of goods that it sold. Sadly, the group's chief executive at that time, Kari Kairamo, was so overwhelmed that he committed suicide. It is rare that strategic pressures are so intense but the impact on management of strategy evaluation and development is an important factor in generating stress.

The early 1990s

In 1991 and 1992, Nokia lost FM482 million (US$120 million) on its major business activities. The company had to find new strategies to remedy this situation. It had already cut out some of its activities but was still left with its telephone business, an unprofitable TV and video manufacturing business and a strong industrial cables business. After careful consideration, it chose to develop two existing divisions: mobile telephone and telecommunications equipment (switches and exchanges). Subsequently, it realised that it would need to concentrate even further so it focused exclusively on the mobile market.

There were four criteria to justify this strategic choice:

1 It was judged that the mobile telephone market had great worldwide growth potential and was growing fast.

2 Nokia already had profitable businesses in this area.

3 Deregulation and privatisation of telecommunications markets around the world were providing specific opportunities.

4 Rapid technological change – especially the new pan-European GSM mobile system – provided the opportunity to alter fundamentally the balance between competitors.

Clearly, all the above judgements carried significant risk. In addition, the company's strategic choice was limited by constraints on its resources. The heavy losses of the group overall were a severe financial constraint. In addition, it was not able to afford the same level of expenditure on research and development as its two major rivals, Motorola (US) and Ericsson (Sweden). Moreover, although it had the in-house skills and experience of working with national deregulated telecommunications operators through competing in Nordic markets in the 1970s and 1980s, it would need many more employees if it was to develop the market opportunities. However, by selling off its other interests and concentrating on mobile telephones it was able to overcome the difficulties.

Benefits and problems of strategic choice

In fact, Nokia was highly successful in its expansion, as the results of the company show over the period to 2000 – *see* Figure 14.2. But concentrating the company on one product group was subsequently to have a downside.

By the year 2000, the company had developed a range of mobile telephones that were both attractive to look at and innovative in their use of the new digital technology that was becoming available. The result was that by 2000 Nokia was world leader in mobile telephone manufacture, with 35 per cent global share. But, having concentrated its resources into mobile telephones, it then had to cope with a major downturn in the world market 2000–2002 which occurred for two main reasons. First, the market became saturated in some parts of the world – for example, 72 per cent of people in the EU had mobile telephones. In addition, the telephone service providers were delaying the introduction of the next generation of mobile telephone licenses – see Case 15.2 – for reasons of technical feasibility and lack of funds. The result was that all the mobile telephone manufacturers, including

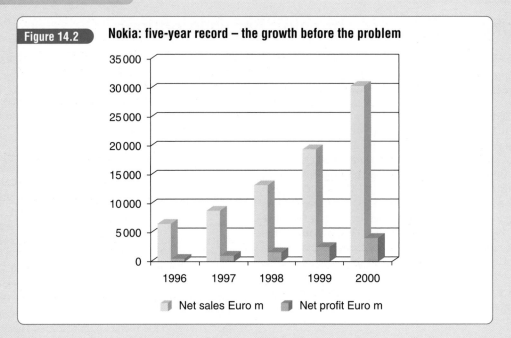

Figure 14.2 Nokia: five-year record – the growth before the problem

Net sales Euro m   Net profit Euro m

Nokia, were hit by falling profits in 2001–2002, but were hoping that demand would pick up as the new 3G services were offered from 2003 onwards. Strategy selection can also lead to problems.

Sources: See reference 2.

Case questions

1 *Why did Nokia select only one area for development? What is the strategic risk involved in selecting one area out of four?*

2 *What was the significance of the introduction of the new GSM system for Nokia's chosen strategy? Do companies always need such a development to ensure strategic success?*

14.1 Prescriptive strategy content: evaluation against six criteria

Prescriptive strategy has taken the approach that a rational and fact-based analysis of the options will deliver the strategy that is most likely to be successful: logic and evidence are paramount in choosing between the options. The content of strategy options therefore needs to be evaluated for their contribution to the organisation. We need to be able to understand in a structured way such comments as, 'Plausible...but not very likely'.[3] We need *evaluation criteria*.

In practice, each organisation will have its own criteria – for example, those for Nokia were outlined in the case above. However, and as a starting point, we can identify six main criteria[4] that can be used in evaluating strategy options: consistency, suitability, validity, feasibility, business risk, stakeholder attractiveness. This section examines each of these.

14.1.1 Criterion 1: consistency, especially with the mission and objectives

If the main purpose of the organisation is to add value, then the way that this is defined for the purposes of corporate strategy is through the organisation's mission and objective – Chapter 12 explored this in detail. In a non-profit-making organisation, the prime purpose may be better defined in terms of some form of service. Whatever the purpose of the organisation, a prime test of any option has to be its consistency with such a reason for its existence.

In a business context, this is likely to be the mission and its ability to deliver the agreed objectives of the organisation. If an option does not meet these criteria, there is a strong case for:

- either changing the mission and objectives, if they are too difficult or inappropriate;
- or rejecting the option.

If the mission and objectives have been carefully considered, then the rejection option is the most likely course. For example, the US telecommunications company WorldCom/MCI has a minimum required rate of return on investment of 15 per cent.[5] This means that strategy options that do not deliver at this level of profitability *in the long term* are rejected by the company. The qualification on the long term relates to the fact that there may well be a period in the early years of a new option when the project will lose money, but it must still justify itself at the identified level of profitability over a longer period.

14.1.2 Criterion 2: suitability

In addition, some options may be more suitable for the organisation than others: how well does each option match the environment and resources and how well does it deliver competitive advantage?

The environment can be explored from the mixture of opportunities to be taken and threats to be avoided. Competitive advantage can be built on the organisation's strengths, especially its core competencies, and may try to rectify weaknesses that exist.

The SWOT analysis at the beginning of Chapter 13 summarises the main elements that have been identified here. Strategy options can also be examined for their consistency with the elements of the SWOT analysis. For example, Nokia mobile telephones have strengths in marketing to the main telecommunications distributors across Europe. A new option that ignored these strengths and pursued a policy of new mobile outlets, such as grocery supermarkets, would need careful study and possibly (but not necessarily) rejection. In fact, this option has been picked up with vigour because it represented a way for Nokia to extend its market penetration.

14.1.3 Criterion 3: validity

Most options will involve some form of *assumptions* about the future. These need to be tested to ensure that they are valid and reasonable, i.e. that they are logically sound and conform with the available research evidence.

In addition, many options will use *business information* that may be well grounded in background material or, alternatively, doubtful in its nature. For example, some of the information that Nokia has about its competitors is soundly based, e.g. the market share data, but some is likely to be rather more open to question, e.g. information on the future plans and intentions of Motorola.

For both the above, it will be necessary to test the validity of the assumptions and information in each option. In practice, there is some overlap between suitability and validity. Because of the element of judgement in such issues, this is done under the general heading of applying business judgements and guidelines.

14.1.4 Criterion 4: feasibility of options

Although options may be consistent with the mission and objectives, there may be other difficulties that limit the likelihood of success. An option may, in practice, lack feasibility in three areas:

1 culture, skills and resources *internal* to the organisation;

2 competitive reaction and other matters *external* to the organisation;

3 *lack of commitment* from managers and employees.

Constraints internal to the organisation

As we explored in Chapters 7, 8 and 9, an organisation might not have the culture, skills or resources to carry out the options. For example, there might be a culture in the organisation that is able to cope with gradual change but not the radical and sudden changes required by a proposed strategy option. For example, the difficulties experienced by the highly centralised company Metal Box (UK) when it merged with the decentralised company Carnaud (France) were largely in this area and caused the group major problems.[6]

Equally, an organisation may lack the necessary technical skills for a strategic option. It may not be possible for a variety of reasons to acquire them by recruiting staff.

Exhibit 14.1   **Ten-point checklist on internal feasibility**

1 Capital investment required: do we have the funds?

2 Projection of cumulative profits: is it sufficiently profitable?

3 Working capital requirements: do we have enough working capital?

4 Tax liabilities and dividend payments: what are the implications, especially on timing?

5 Number of employees and, in the case of redundancy, any costs associated with this: what are the national laws on sacking people and what are the costs?

6 New technical skills, new plant and costs of closure of old plant: do we have the skills? Do we need to recruit or hire temporarily some specialists?

7 New products and how they are to be developed: are we confident that we have the portfolio of fully tested new products on which so much depends? Are they real breakthrough products or merely a catch-up on our competition?

8 Amount and timing of marketing investment and expertise required: do we have the funds? When will they be required? Do we have the specialist expertise such as advertising and promotions agency teams to deliver our strategies?

9 The possibility of acquisition, merger or joint venture with other companies and the implications: have we fully explored other options that would bring their own benefits and problems?

10 Communication of ideas to all those involved: how will this be done? Will we gain the *commitment* of the managers and employees affected?

In addition, some organisations have insufficient finance for an option to succeed. For example, the French computer company Groupe Bull had real problems financing its strategic development during the mid-1990s as it struggled to survive after a series of overambitious strategy initiatives earlier in the decade.[7]

Exhibit 14.1 summarises some of the main internal feasibility issues.

Constraints external to the organisation

Outside the organisation, there are four main constraints that may make a strategic option lack feasibility: customer acceptance, competitive reaction, supplier acceptance and any approvals from government or another regulatory body.

In Chapter 5, we observed that customers need to find a new strategy attractive. In addition, competitors who are affected by a strategy option may react and make it difficult to achieve. For example, the US software company Microsoft has around 90 per cent of the world market for personal computer software with its Windows operating system. It has been accused by competitors of deliberately pre-announcing some of its products to stall sales of new, competing software products.[8] The likelihood of competitive response is an area that must be assessed.

There may also be other constraints outside the organisation that make strategy options difficult if not impossible. For example, Nokia above had to consider carefully the implications of the reduction in government control over telecommunications markets. This was not only an opportunity but also a problem because governments were still sensitive over their national interests in this area.

The questions that might probe this area are summarised in Exhibit 14.2.

Exhibit 14.2   **Four-point checklist on external feasibility**

1 How will our *customers* respond to the strategies we are proposing?

2 How will our *competitors react*? Do we have the necessary resources to respond?

3 Do we have the necessary support from our *suppliers*?

4 Do we need government or regulatory approval? How likely is this?

Lack of commitment from managers and employees

If important members of the organisation are not committed to the strategy, it is unlikely to be successfully implemented. For example, the major US toy retailer Toys 'R' Us had major problems implementing its business strategy in Sweden during 1995 because the local managers and employees considered it to be inconsistent with the Swedish approach to labour relations.[9]

This constraint may arise because some organisations make a clear distinction between strategy development by senior managers and day-to-day management by more junior managers.[10] Hence in such organisations, junior managers and employees are unlikely to have been involved in the strategy development process: in essence, they have the results communicated to them and they may not feel *committed* to its implications.

Some strategic decisions may need to be made by a senior management centralised group – for example, the Nokia decision to divest some companies. In spite of Nokia's commitment to an open Finnish culture, the key decisions on the new strategy were taken by a group of *senior* managers. The more junior managers and employees were not really consulted. Since the proposals included divesting part of Nokia, this is not really surprising.

14.1.5 Criterion 5: business risk

Most worthwhile strategies are likely to carry some degree of risk. Such areas need to be carefully assessed. Ultimately, the risks involved may be unacceptable to the organisation.

There are countless examples in corporate strategy of organisations taking risks and then struggling to sort out the difficulties. For example, Germany's largest industrial company, Daimler-Benz, took considerable risks with its expansion strategy during the 1980s and 90s (*see* Chapter 10). In 1998, the company chose to merge with the US car company Chrysler, involving significant risk if the benefits were to be achieved.[11]

It is easy to see business risk only as a major strategic constraint. The Japanese strategist Kenichi Ohmae comments that this may stop a company from breaking out of the existing situation.[12] Yet some degree of business risk is likely in most worthwhile strategy development. The important aspects are:

- to make an explicit *assessment* of the risks;
- to explore the *contingencies* that will lessen the difficulties if things go wrong;
- to decide whether the *risks are acceptable* to the organisation.

There is no single method of assessing risk in the organisation, but there are a number of techniques that may assist the process. Two are explored below – financial risk and sensitivity analysis – and other techniques are examined in Sections 14.2.4 and 14.2.5.

Financial risk analysis[13]

For most strategy proposals in both the private and public sectors, it is important to undertake some form of analysis of the financial risks involved in strategy options. There are a number of types of analysis that can be undertaken:

- *Cash flow analysis*. This analysis is essential. An organisation can report decent levels of profitability at the same time as going bankrupt through a lack of cash. Each option needs to be assessed for its impact on cash flow in the organisation.
- *Break-even analysis*. This is often a useful approach: it calculates the volume sales of the business required to recover the initial investment in the business. The important point about such a result is to explore whether this volume is reasonable or not – *see* Exhibit 14.4. Break-even analysis at Eurofreeze on the main options, discussed later in the chapter, would be useful.
- *Company borrowing requirements*. The impact of some strategies may severely affect the funds needed from financial institutions and shareholders. This area was explored in Chapter 8 and represents a real area of risk for strategy analysis.
- *Financial ratio analysis*. Liquidity, asset management, stockholding and similar checks on companies can be usefully undertaken. It might be argued that they are not needed since the company should know in detail about these areas. But what about key suppliers? And key customers? The knock-on effects of bankruptcy in one of these, when the company itself is stretched financially, deserve consideration (*see* Chapter 8).

For international activities, there is one other area that is also important: *currency analysis*. A major shift in currencies can wipe out the profitability of an overseas strategy option overnight (or, more optimistically, increase it). A number of major companies have discovered the impact of this over the last few years. Specialist help may be required.

Sensitivity analysis

This is a most useful form of analysis and would be regarded as part of the basic strategy proposals in many organisations. Essentially, it explores the 'What if?' questions for their impact on the strategy under investigation. The basic assumptions behind each option, e.g. economic growth, pricing, currency fluctuation, raw material prices, etc., are varied and the impact is measured on return on capital employed, cash and other company objectives. The key factors for success may be used to identify the major points that need to be considered.

The sensitivity of each these factors, as they are moved up or down by arbitrary variations, is then assessed in order to determine which are crucial. Those variations that turn out to be particularly sensitive can then be re-examined carefully before the strategy is accepted. They can also be monitored after it has been put into operation.

For example, the key assumptions of the Nokia mobile telephone expansion might be tested by examining what would happen if they varied:

- What impact would there be if Nokia carried on without the new rate of investment? This is quite specific and the result could be used to assess the strategy.

- What impact would there be if Nokia only limited cost savings as a result of its new plans? Perhaps only another 10 per cent cost savings instead of the 20 per cent assumed in the plan? Again a specific calculation could be undertaken to test the sensitivity of this change.

- What impact would there be if Nokia lost its market leadership? Perhaps the simplest calculation would be to assume that the three main companies – Nokia, Motorola and Ericsson – ended up with equal shares and the result was recalculated. The sensitivity to share variation could then be assessed.

Clearly, the results of all sensitivity analyses can provide those selecting the strategies with a useful estimate of the risks involved.

14.1.6 Criterion 6: attractiveness to stakeholders

As we explored in Chapter 12, every organisation has its stakeholders, such as the shareholders, employees and management. They will all be interested in the strategic options that the organisation has under consideration because they may be affected by them. But stakeholder interests and perspectives may not always be the same. For example, an option might increase the *shareholders'* wealth but also mean a reduction in *employees* in the organisation. Hence, stakeholders may not find all the strategic options equally attractive.

One way of resolving this issue is to *prioritise* the stakeholders' interests – for example, by putting the shareholders' interests first and raising dividends, cutting costs and possibly even sacking some workers. Some writers and companies would have no hesitation in pursuing this route. However, it may be oversimplistic for corporate strategy.

▶ **Key strategic principles**

- Evaluating strategy options relies on criteria for the selection process. There are six main criteria: consistency, especially with the organisation's mission and objectives, suitability, validity, feasibility, business risk and attractiveness to stakeholders.

- Consistency with the purpose of the organisation is a prime test for evaluating and selecting strategies.

- Suitability of the strategy for the environment within which the organisation operates is clearly important.

- Validity of the projections and data used in developing the option must be tested.

- In examining whether an option is feasible, there are three main areas to explore: first those that are internal to the organisation, which are mainly those that arise from a lack of resources; second, those external to the organisation, such as customer acceptance and customer reaction; finally, special consideration needs to be given to employee and manager acceptance and commitment.

- The risks that a strategy option may bring to an organisation also need to be assessed because they may be unacceptably high. Such risks can be assessed under two broad headings: financial risk and sensitivity analysis.

- Stakeholders also need to be assessed for their reactions to major strategy initiatives. It may be necessary to prioritise the interests of stakeholders: shareholders may or may not come first. Stakeholder reactions need to be assessed under five headings, each of which is related to the prime interests of the stakeholder group in question.

CASE STUDY 14.2

Eurofreeze evaluates its strategy options: 1

With sales in 1999 of US$1.05 billion, Eurofreeze is one of Europe's larger frozen food companies. However, it was being squeezed between two major competitive forces: its larger rival Refrigor, and the grocery supermarket own-brands which were becoming increasingly powerful across Europe. The time had come for a complete strategic rethink at Eurofreeze: the company was part of a large multinational and group headquarters had turned up the heat.

This case begins the process by exploring the objectives, the environment and the resources of the company. At the end of the chapter, there is a follow-up case that examines the options identified by Eurofreeze.

Mission and objectives

As a starting point for the exploration of its options, Eurofreeze decided to re-examine its mission and objectives. It decided that it still wished to remain strong in European frozen food and therefore defined its mission as: 'To be a leading producer of frozen food products in the European Union.' This mission was based on its core strengths, its competitive position as the second largest in the EU, and the way it envisaged freezing technology would retain its position in preserving food over the next five years. Within this context, it then reviewed its current profitability, shareholder performance and market share position and defined its objectives over the next five years as being:

- to raise its return on capital from the current level of 12 per cent by 0.5 per cent per annum with the aim of reaching 15 per cent after six years;
- to raise its contribution to its earnings per share at a similar rate over time, but allow for some lag as it reinvested in the immediate future;
- to hold its overall market share but to move from low-value-added items (like frozen vegetables) to higher-value-added (like prepared pizza dishes).

To understand fully the implications of these demanding objectives, it was necessary for Eurofreeze to explore the background to the frozen food market and the competitive trends that were operating.

Frozen food products and added value
The first products to be frozen commercially were vegetables and fish in the 1940s. For many years, the higher food quality resulting from the freezing process allowed such products to be sold at premium prices to the competition from cans, glass jars and other forms of preserved fruit. But by the year 2000, freezing was old technology – there was no sustainable competitive advantage in this as such. Specifically, this meant that products like frozen vegetables and frozen meat, whether carrying a nationally recognised brand or not, had little value added to them before arriving in the shops.

Thus, the major supermarkets negotiated their own branded versions of many basic products and obtained keen prices from suppliers such as Eurofreeze. By the mid-1990s, the profit margins on basic vegetables and other commodities were very low: added value was minimal.

Over the same period, household incomes had risen across Europe, home freezers were more widespread, and tastes had become more international. For example, people across Europe had come to know and like a wider range of fresh recipe dishes and international products, everything from Quattro Stagioni Pizza to Double Layer Chocolate Gateaux. Such products had much higher added value. They were sold as branded items, usually under a name that had been well established over the years: Birds Eye, Dr Oetker, Heinz Weight Watchers and Findus were examples of the brand names that had become

familiar in this context. The brand name was used across all products from the company so that it supported the strong, well-advertised products along with the weaker ones – a group branding policy.

Key factors for success
The following factors were considered to be critical to success in the industry:

- experienced and talented buyers to negotiate price and quality on low-value-added items;
- fast and efficient freezing processes coupled with good freezer storage and distribution;
- excellent relationships with the main supermarket chains;
- strong and consistent group branding;
- vigorous and innovative new product development programmes.

Eurofreeze core resources
As a result of its history and present market position, the company had core competencies in the following areas:

- purchase of raw materials such as vegetables, including the buying function;
- freezer technology;
- recipe development for new frozen dishes;
- frozen food distribution;
- supermarket negotiating and service;
- developing branded food products (it had a well-known brand name across Europe).

Within these areas, its key resource advantages over its leading rival were its brand names, its European market leadership in branded meat and fish products, and its corporate parent, which was one of the world's leading fast-moving consumer goods companies, with extensive financial resources.

The competition
During the 1980s and 1990s, companies such as Eurofreeze sought new strategies to avoid the low-priced competition – the own-branded supermarket sales of vegetables and other low-value-added items had become a real problem. Profit pressures were such that Eurofreeze was even considering phasing out its range of branded vegetables.

517

In addition, many large grocery chains wanted *only one* market-leading frozen brand to put alongside their own brands. In this context, Eurofreeze faced a specific problem: in some European product categories, it was not the market leader. Eurofreeze was second in its markets to its major rival, Refrigor.

Refrigor had invested heavily in frozen food brands, manufacturing and grocery distribution over the last few years at a rate in excess of Eurofreeze. However, the company had been rather less profitable. It had much the same grocery customers as Eurofreeze. Both competitors offered a full range of frozen branded food products and, at the same time, supplied own-label versions to the leading grocery chains.

In total, Eurofreeze faced four competitive threats, the first two below being particularly strong:

1 The market leader, Refrigor, the low-cost leader.

2 In many supermarkets such as Sainsbury (UK) and Albert Heijn (part of Ahold, the Netherlands), increasing freezer space was given to supermarket chains' own-branded products at the expense of the manufacturer's branded product.

3 In other supermarkets with strong cut-price positioning, such as Aldi and Netto, the same freezer space was used for local or regional branded products that had no national advertising or promotional support but were low-priced.

4 In some specific product lines, such as French fries or gateaux, specialised companies such as McCain (US) and Sara Lee (US), respectively, sold branded products that had a significant share of that particular market segment.

Overall, the market was becoming volume-driven and highly competitive in many sectors. It was also becoming increasingly difficult to afford the investment in advertising and promotions to support branded lines.

© Copyright Richard Lynch 2003. The case is based on real companies which have been disguised to protect confidentiality. Market share and financial data have also been changed.

Case questions

1 *What is your assessment of the mission and objectives of Eurofreeze? How do they stack up against the pressures of the highly competitive market? Are they too demanding?*

2 *Should the objectives be expanded? What about branded and non-branded items, for example? Clearer on the competitive threat? Further reference to financial objectives such as the precise relationship with headquarters? Specific reference to other matters such as ecological issues and employee job satisfaction? If your answer is yes to any of these questions, then what considerations should Eurofreeze take into account in making its decision? If your answer is no, then what are the implications for strategy selection?*

3 *What are the possible implications of the customer and competitive trends on the development of strategy options for Eurofreeze? You may wish to undertake some of the analyses contained in Chapter 13 in preparing your answer.*

14.2 Prescriptive strategy content: procedures and techniques

In examining the many criteria that can be employed, it is sometimes useful to consider whether some criteria are more important than others. It is possible that no useful prioritisation can be undertaken in this case.

14.2.1 Criteria in commercial organisations

For most organisations, the criteria will be prioritised by the mission and objectives. Within these, the following three questions represent the areas that may need exploration:

1 Is each strategy option consistent with the mission of the organisation? How well does it deliver the objectives? For example, at Eurofreeze how does each option meet the stated desire for a return on capital of 15 per cent and rising? How does each option contribute to the shift to higher-value-added products?

2 Does each option build on the *strengths* of the organisation? Does it exploit the *opportunities* that have been identified? And the *core resources* of the organisation? Thus at Eurofreeze, it should be possible to test the option for its usefulness in contributing to freezer technology or to supermarket opportunities. If it is not consistent with these issues, then there *may* be a case for rejecting it. However, it should be noted that rejection is not automatic.

3 Does each option avoid, or even overcome, the weaknesses of the organisation? And does it do the same for the threats that have been identified? At Eurofreeze, an option that involved development of its basic vegetable business would move the company further into this weak area and would invite rejection.

Question 3 has *lower priority* than questions 1 and 2.[14] It is much more important to deliver the organisation's mission and objectives and to build on its strengths than to worry about its weaknesses. However, there will be occasions when the weaknesses cannot be ignored and strategy options need to consider these.

It would be a great mistake to consider only those criteria that can be put into numbers. For example, many organisations will have guidelines related to *customer quality and satisfaction*; others will include *service to the broader community*. These may not be easy to quantify but are no less important in spite of this. All of them need to be reflected in the criteria for selection of strategy options. Such matters simply underline the importance of carefully defining the purpose of the organisation.

14.2.2 Criteria in not-for-profit organisations

Great care needs to be taken in such organisations that any quantified criteria do not come to dominate the selection between strategies when such selection measures are inappropriate. All not-for-profit organisations will need to create added value. However, beyond this, the criteria may need to reflect strongly the important aspects of the service or the value to the community appropriate to the mission.

Criteria in not-for-profit organisations also need to take into account the different decision-making processes and beliefs that motivate many such organisations. The reliance on voluntary support, the strong sense of mission and belief in the work of the organisation, and the style of the organisation may not lend themselves to a simple choice between a series of options.

Not-for-profit organisations may involve high loyalty to a mission, which is often clear, but the organisation may be decentralised, with local decision making.

Exhibit 14.3	Comparison of possible criteria in commercial and not-for-profit organisations
Commercial organisation	*Not-for-profit organisation*
• Quantified	• Qualitative
• Unchanging	• Variable
• Consistent	• Conflicting
• Unified	• Complex
• Operational	• Ambiguous
• Clear	• Non-operational
• Measurable	• Non-measurable

Exhibit 14.4   **Ten steps towards an initial strategy evaluation**

1 Screen out any *early no-hopers* that are highly unlikely to meet the objectives.

2 Estimate the *sales* of each of the remaining options based on market share, pricing, promotional support and competitive reactions.

3 Estimate the *costs* of each of the remaining options.

4 Estimate the *capital and other funds* necessary to undertake each option.

5 Calculate the *return on capital employed* for each option.

6 Calculate the *break-even* of each option.

7 Calculate the *net cash flow* effects of each option.

8 Evaluate whether the *projected sales levels* imply exceptional levels of market share or unusually low costs. Are these reasonable? Real strategic weaknesses can emerge here.

9 Assess the likely *competitive response* and its possible impact on each strategy option.

10 Assess the *risks* associated with each option.

If this is the case, then a centralised evaluation of options is difficult. A comparison of the objectives with commercial organisations is shown in Exhibit 14.3. The evaluation of strategy options in not-for-profit organisations may be more diffuse and open-ended.

14.2.3 Taking the first steps in selection

Before exploring the problems associated with strategic options, it is usual to make some initial selection of one or more options. To some extent, the initial evaluation will depend on the type of organisation. In commercial circumstances, the selection might start with the *profitability* of the venture. In a not-for-profit situation, other factors, such as the ability to *deliver the service*, might be more important. These are the reasons that make careful exploration of the mission and objectives so important. Sometimes, it is useful to eliminate the obvious strategic options that have no hope of long-term success. The steps that might be involved in the initial evaluation are summarised in Exhibit 14.4.

14.2.4 Evaluation techniques: financial[15]

Having removed any options that have no hope of meeting the basic evaluation criteria, the next step is to undertake a financial evaluation of the remaining options. As a first step, most evaluations of strategic options in commercial organisations attempt to analyse the profit against the capital employed. In this case, it is important to note that extra capital will be needed in most organisations[16] *as soon as sales rise*, not just when new buildings or plant are bought. This arises because of the need to fund new debtors and pay for the extra stocks required for the new business activity. There are at least five main financial techniques:

1 return on capital employed (ROCE);

2 net cash flow;

3 payback period;

4 discounted cash flow (DCF);

5 break-even.

There are some important words of caution to note in the use of any financial evaluation of strategic options. These are summarised in Exhibit 14.5 at the end of this section.

Return on capital employed (ROCE)

This is a measure of the profitability of a strategic option. It is defined as the ratio of profits to be earned divided by the capital invested in the new strategy. Profits are usually calculated *before* any tax that might be charged, because tax matters go beyond the assessment of individual strategy options.

This ratio is commonly used to assess strategies. The expected operating profit is assessed after the strategy has been in operation for an agreed number of years, usually defined before tax and interest. It is divided by the capital employed in the option, which is commonly averaged across a year, given the tendency of capital to vary during the course of a year.

One of the major difficulties is defining the *incremental* capital used purely for that strategy. It is easy where a new piece of plant has been installed, but more difficult where the strategy involves using existing plant or a service where the capital involved cannot be easily distinguished from more general trading.

For ongoing business investments, companies often have *hurdle rates* for ROCE: if they do not earn at these rates then there is serious discussion about abandoning that strategy. Such rates are usually set in relation to the company's *cost of capital*: if capital is cheap, then a lower rate can be set. Readers are referred to Chapter 8 for a more detailed exploration of this area.

Net cash flow[17]

The net cash flow is the profit *before* depreciation less the periodic investment in working capital that is required to undertake the project. The importance of this calculation of cash flow lies in the ability of a negative cash flow to bankrupt a company. It is perfectly possible to deliver significant profits in the distant future, so that the return on capital looks good. However, there may be major negative outflows of cash in the short term, with the implication that the firm will go bust – the company may be unable to pay its current bills while waiting for its distant profits. An approximation of the net cash flow calculation is obtained by regarding it as the sum of pretax profits from the new strategy option, plus depreciation, less the capital to be invested in the new strategy.

Payback period

Payback period is used where there is a significant and specific capital investment required in the option. In the early years of the option, capital is invested in it. As the company earns profits from the venture, it recovers the capital that has been invested. Payback is the time it takes to recover the initial capital investment and is usually measured in years. The cash flows in payback are not discounted but are simply added and subtracted equally, whatever year they occur.

Typically, payback on a capital project in the car industry will be around three to five years. This is because of the large amounts of capital involved (often into US$ billions) and the competitive nature of the industry, which makes profit margins low. In consumer goods, the period may be shorter, not because markets are any less competitive but because the profit margins on some items are higher, e.g. in fashion clothing and cosmetics. By contrast, the payback period may be 20–60 years for some highly capital-intensive items such as telecommunications infrastructure and roads.

Discounted cash flow (DCF)

DCF is now used extensively for the assessment of strategic options. Essentially, DCF takes account of the fact that cash in five years' time is worth less than cash today, unlike payback above. It begins by assessing the net cash flow for each year of the life of the option, as in payback above. The cash is usually assessed after subtracting the taxation to be paid to the government. Each annual cash amount is then discounted back to the present using the organisation's *cost of capital* (discussed in Chapter 8). It is probably negative in the early years as capital is expended and then positive as the option increases its sales. There are discounting tables or computer spreadsheet programs that make this process relatively easy. The net present value (NPV) is the sum in today's values of all the future DCFs. Case study 14.4 shows the procedure for some Eurofreeze options – the analysis is typical of that undertaken by many organisations when exploring the consequences of strategic options.

Break-even analysis[18]

Break-even is defined as the point at which the total costs of undertaking the new strategy are equal to the total revenue. It is often restated as the number of units of a product that need to be sold before the product has covered all its fixed costs.

Break-even analysis is directed at the break-even point, i.e. that point where fixed and variable costs equal total revenue. It is based on a number of assumptions that make its use in practice rather crude in strategy options analysis:

- Costs can easily be split into fixed and variable elements.

- Fixed costs are constant.

- Variable costs and revenue are linear in their relationship with volume over the range used in the analysis.

Exhibit 14.5　　　**Caution on the use of financial criteria**

Following on from the discussion in Chapter 8, there are some clear difficulties with these methods of appraisal of strategic options:

- The cost of capital is a vital element in two of the calculations above. The difficulties associated with its calculation were explored in Chapter 8. It is especially difficult to estimate where investment takes place over a lengthy period.

- There are real problems in estimating the future sales accurately up to ten years away, which is a typical period in many DCF calculations, even in consumer goods companies. However, direct costs can usually be estimated satisfactorily. The projections are therefore doubtful. Payback may be better here.

- With shorter product life cycles and greater product obsolescence in some product categories such as computers, the DCF process may rely on an overextended time span. Payback may again be better here and this is the justification used by some Japanese companies for using this approach.

- Comment was made above on the difficulty of isolating incremental from ongoing capital. This applies not only to ROCE calculations but to all such appraisals.

- Because of the emphasis on cash generated in the project itself, the appraisal tends to concentrate on the quantified financial benefits and may ignore some of the broader strategic benefits that are more difficult to quantify – for example, synergies and value chain linkages.

- ROCE is by definition an accounting calculation that looks back at a project's past rather than forward to its future potential. It may therefore not be suitable for strategic use.

- Variable costs vary proportionately with sales, within given limits.
- It is possible to predict the volume of sales at various prices.

In spite of these problems, break-even has the great merit of being easily understandable and therefore communicable across an organisation. Used with caution, it can therefore be a useful tool in strategy options analysis.

14.2.5 Evaluation techniques: shareholder value added (SVA)[19]

In Chapter 8, we undertook a more detailed review of the above topic. This section presents a brief reprise, with readers being referred back to the earlier chapter for the more detailed examination. Although many Western companies continue to use DCF techniques in their evaluation of strategies,[20] they became conscious in the 1980s of the difficulties of ignoring the broader strategic benefits. There were also two other developments:

1 Professor Michael Porter's work emphasising the value chain and its relevance in strategy development – *see* Chapter 6.

2 Other writers[21] began to doubt the wisdom of seeking a steady increase in earnings per share as a measure of shareholder wealth. Such wealth can be measured in terms of a company's share price. It was shown empirically that share price was more closely correlated with long-term cash generation in a business than it was with earnings per share.

Taking the goal of a public company as being to maximise shareholder value, the concept of shareholder value added (SVA) was developed from DCF techniques and these difficulties. Its purpose is to develop corporate strategy, 'maximising the long-term cashflow of each SBU [strategic business unit]'.[22] Thus SVA evaluation differs in the following areas from the profitability approaches above:

- SVA takes the concept of cash flow but applies it to the complete business rather than to individual strategy options.
- It takes into account the cost of capital of the company and measures shareholder return against this benchmark.
- It lays particular emphasis on the critical factors for success in that business, defining them as being those that are particularly important in generating cash or value added. It calls these critical factors *value or cost drivers*. Such critical factors may bear some relationship to the key factors for success in an industry explored in Chapter 6. However, the value or cost drivers are different in that they relate to the *individual* business, not the *industry*.
- It supports the interrelationship of value or cost drivers in the development of cash generation. In this sense, it differs from the simpler DCF view that an option can be analysed by itself.

Comment

Although SVA represents an advance on some simpler DCF techniques, it still relies on a prescriptive view of strategy projections – a projection of future profit over an extended period of time is required. Moreover, it makes the crucial assumption that maximising shareholder value is the prime objective of strategy development. This may be true in UK and US companies but does not necessarily apply in some other leading industrialised countries. Other criticisms of this prescriptive approach were covered in Chapter 8.

14.2.6 Evaluation techniques: cost/benefit analysis[23]

Ever since cost/benefit analysis was used to assess the justification for building London Underground's Victoria Line in the 1960s, this has been an appraisal method favoured when the benefits go beyond simple financial benefits: for example, they might include lower levels of pollution or greater use of recycled materials. It is regularly used in public service investment decisions. It attempts to quantify a much broader range of benefits than sales, profits and costs.

When the benefits of some forms of public service go beyond simple financial appraisal, cost/benefit analysis may be used. It may be especially valuable where the project delivers value to users who are not directly investing their own funds. Thus, for example, in the analysis of the new Victoria Line on the London Underground, it attempted to assess:

- the faster and more convenient travel to be enjoyed by passengers on the London Underground;
- the ability of road transport to move more freely because roads were less congested.

As well as the benefits, there may also be social costs that need to be assessed. In the case of Underground transport, these might include building subsidence or inconvenience while the line is being built.

The key point in cost/benefit analysis is that all such broader benefits and costs are still assessed in monetary terms. Much of the research in this area is concerned with the quantification of such benefits and the costs that may be associated with them. The direct investment costs are usually rather easier to determine and form another element in the equation.

The difficult part of such a cost/benefit analysis is usually where to place the limit on the possible benefits and costs. For example, it might be argued that easier travel would mean that there would be less atmospheric pollution, more healthy people and therefore a need to quantify the health benefits. There might also be benefits in terms of a more stress-free life style that need to be quantified, and so on. In spite of this difficulty and the more general problem of quantifying the intangible, cost/benefit analysis does serve a useful function in the appraisal of public projects and strategy initiatives.

▶ Key strategic principles

- In making an initial selection of the best option, it is important to clarify the basis on which this is to be done. Evaluation against the mission and objectives is important but needs to be rigorous and precise if it is to provide real benefit. Non-quantified objectives may be just as important for some organisations.

- Additional criteria for evaluation include the ability to build on the strengths and core competencies of the organisation and avoid its weaknesses. Generally in evaluation, strengths are more important than weaknesses, but occasionally a weakness cannot be ignored.

- Different parts of an organisation, such as the HQ, the strategic business unit (SBU) and those involved in individual projects, will have different perspectives on the evaluation process. There is a need to recognise this in selection.

> **Key strategic principles continued**

- In not-for-profit organisations, the criteria need to reflect the broader aspects of their service or contribution to the community. They also need to take into account the different decision-making processes and beliefs that motivate many such organisations. This may make the evaluation of strategy options more diffuse and open-ended.

- To undertake the initial evaluation in commercial organisations, it may be worth eliminating any options that have little chance of success. It is then usual to calculate initially for each option the profitability, break-even and net cash flow.

- Beyond this, ten steps can be undertaken to make an initial evaluation. From a *strategic* perspective, it is particularly useful to examine whether the projected sales levels of each option imply *exceptional* levels of market share or low costs in order to achieve their targets. If these occur, then it may imply that the option has real weaknesses.

- Evaluation usually employs common and agreed criteria across the organisation, such as contribution to value added and profitability. The strengths and weaknesses of these criteria need to be understood.

- The shareholder value approach (SVA) takes a broader perspective on evaluation than that provided by the specific project. It seeks to determine the benefit of such developments in the context of the whole SBU in which the project rests. However, it still relies on the assumption that shareholders are always the prime beneficiaries.

- Cost/benefit analysis has been successfully employed in public sector evaluation, where it is important to assess broader and less quantifiable benefits. The main difficulty is where to place the limit on such benefits and costs.

14.3 Applying empirical evidence and guidelines

In addition to the logic of strategy development covered in the previous section, there is also empirical evidence of strategies adopted by other organisations in the past that have succeeded or failed. Such evidence also provides guidance that can be used to select the optimal strategy from the options available. We will consider this under three headings:

1 Generic industry environments;

2 Evidence on the link between profitability and three key strategic issues;

3 Mergers and acquisitions.

14.3.1 Generic industry environments[24]

Some strategies have been shown through logical thought to provide a higher chance of success than others. Such insights may aid the selection of strategy options. Exploration and understanding of the main concepts is called the study of *generic strategy environments*.[25] Essentially, it is proposed that strategies can be selected on the basis of their ability to cope with particular market and competitive circumstances. One of the best-known examples of this general approach is the *ADL matrix*. The well-known management consultants Arthur D Little (ADL) developed the matrix during the 1970s. It relies on matching an organisation's own strength or weakness in a market with the life cycle phase of that market. Specifically, it focuses on:

- *stage of industry maturity* – from a young and fast-growing market through to a mature and declining market;
- *competitive position* – from a company that is dominant and able to control the industry through to one that is weak and barely able to survive.

It would be wrong to oversimplify the strategies that can be adopted depending on a company's competitive position in the above. As a starting point, the matrix shown in Figure 14.3 was developed in order to illustrate some of the choices that might be made. For example, if a company was in a *strong* position in a *mature* market, then the strategic logic of the matrix would suggest that it:

- sought cost leadership *or*
- renewed its focus strategy *or*
- differentiated itself from competition

while at the same time growing with the industry.

Hence, if other strategy options for this market and competitive combination were presented and they did not conform with one of the above proposals, there would be a case for rejecting them. However, it will be evident from the Nokia case that such analyses can be flawed where major technological change and marketing initiatives are introduced.

14.3.2 Profitability and three key strategic issues[26]

According to some research evidence, profitability in commercial organisations is linked to three key strategic issues:

1 the role of quality as part of strategic decision making;
2 the importance of market share and marketing expenditure as a contributor to strategy development;
3 the capital investment required for new strategic initiatives.

The evidence in this area comes from the Strategic Planning Institute (SPI), located in the US. For the last 20 years, the SPI has been gathering data on about 3000 companies (some 600 of which are located in Europe). The information collected covers three major areas:

1 the *results* of strategies undertaken (profits, market share, etc.);
2 the *inputs* by the company to this activity (plant investment, finance, productivity, etc.);
3 the *industry conditions* within which the company operates (market growth, customer power, innovation, etc.).

The data are often described as the *PIMS Databank* (PIMS is short for **P**rofit **I**mpact of **M**arket **S**trategy), which is unique in the extent of its empirical database on corporate strategy coupled with its inputs and outputs. It collects data and calculates statistical correlations between various elements; whether such relationships have any real meaning has been the subject of fierce academic debate.[27] This book takes the view that it

| Figure 14.3 | **Evaluation using the life cycle portfolio matrix** |

Maturity / Competitive position	*Embryonic*	*Growing*	*Mature*	*Ageing*
Clear leader	**Hold position** Attempt to improve market penetration *Invest slightly faster than market dictates*	**Hold position** Defend market share *Invest to sustain growth rate (and pre-empt potential competitors)*	**Hold position** Grow with industry *Reinvest as necessary*	**Hold position** *Reinvest as necessary*
Strong	**Attempt to improve market penetration** *Invest as fast as market dictates*	**Attempt to improve market penetration** *Invest to increase growth rate (and improve position)*	**Hold position** Grow with industry *Reinvest as necessary*	**Hold position** *Reinvest as necessary or reinvest minimum*
Favourable	**Attempt to improve position selectively** Penetrate market generally or selectively *Invest selectively*	**Attempt to improve position** Penetrate market selectively *Invest selectively to improve position*	**Maintain position** Find niche and attempt to protect it *Make minimum and/or selective reinvestment*	**Harvest, withdraw in phases, or abandon** *Reinvest minimum necessary or disinvest*
Defensible	**Attempt to improve position selectively** *Invest (very) selectively*	**Find niche and protect it** *Invest selectively*	**Find niche or withdraw in phases** *Reinvest minimum necessary or disinvest*	**Withdraw in phases or abandon** *Disinvest or divest*
Weak	**Improve position or withdraw** *Invest or divest*	**Turn around or abandon** *Invest or disinvest*	**Turn around or withdraw in phases** *Invest selectively or disinvest*	**Abandon position** *Divest*

Note: The boxes indicate suggested strategies depending on life cycle and share position held by the company. They can be used both to stimulate options and to *evaluate proposed options* to ensure that they are consistent with the company's strategic position.
Source: Reproduced with permission from Arthur D Little. © Copyright Arthur D Little 1996.

has made a useful contribution to empirical strategy research. The overall results have been published and a few of the key findings are explored below. In addition to its general work, the results are also fed back to contributing companies on a detailed and more confidential basis for them to assess their performance and draw relevant conclusions. From the results of these extensive studies, three key factors emerge – namely: quality, market share and marketing spend, and capital investment.

Quality

In the long run and according to the PIMS Databank, the most important single factor affecting a business unit's performance is the quality of its products and services, relative to those of its competitors. Strategy options that seek to raise quality are more likely to be successful than those that do not. This supports much of the activity described in Chapter 12 in this area on the subject of TQM, etc. Strategy options that consider quality in relation to the price charged are more likely to have a greater chance of success.

Market share and marketing expenditure[28]

In Chapters 3 and 5, we explored the strategic importance of a company having significant power in the market place. This is usually measured using market share and will be related, at least in part, to the marketing expenditure by the company on the product or service. PIMS monitors market share and has shown a strong correlation with return on investment. It also monitors marketing expenditure, where the results depend on whether the company already has a high or low marketing share.

The PIMS evidence suggests that there is a correlation between high levels of marketing activity and market share.[29] For those companies that already have a high share, there is merit in maintaining their levels of expenditure. For those companies with low market share, the correlation implies that it may not be the best strategy to spend funds on marketing activity to increase market share. Strategy options that attempt to buy market share with additional marketing activity may result in low return on investment.

However, it should be noted that the evidence is circular in the sense that, if high-share firms have higher profits, then they have more funds to invest in cost-saving devices, higher quality and more marketing activity. This will, in turn, raise their market share and profitability even further. Moreover, such evidence may be of little strategic help to the majority of companies that do not have a high share: what can they possibly do to catch up? It may be prohibitively expensive to invest in marketing and plant economies. However, Japanese car and electronics companies were in much that position in the 1960s, but have developed to become a major force in the world car industry. Innovation and the mistakes of the market leaders provide clues on the strategies needed.

Capital investment[30]

In the context of the operations strategies reviewed in Chapter 9, it might be argued that it will usually be worthwhile to invest in extra mechanisation to improve productivity and thus return on investment. The PIMS Databank suggests that this does not necessarily follow. Companies that have *high* levels of capital investment as a percentage of their sales tend also to have *lower* profitability. The higher productivity gained from such capital investment may not completely offset the damage.

There are several reasons for this: capital-intensive plant usually needs to be run at high production capacity to make profits, as the European steel industry case demonstrated in Chapter 3. Such production requirements need steady or increasing sales to deliver the profits and, as we have seen, this may be a dubious assumption. There may even be a temptation to keep production running at capacity by offering special deals to customers, stealing sales from competitors and so on, all of which will reduce profitability. By contrast, direct labour is more flexible and can be switched around when demand fluctuates. Moreover, if the company decides to leave the industry, the investment in fixed capital may make it more difficult, as we also saw in the European steel industry case in Chapter 3. Such companies may be tempted to reduce prices in order to survive, which will in turn reduce the profitability of all companies in the industry, even those that have invested in the latest capital-intensive equipment.

Strategy options that rely on heavy capital expenditure to generate profits need to be examined carefully. In some industries, there may be no choice. But there is no automatic likelihood that such expenditure will always deliver higher profitability.

14.3.5 Mergers and acquisitions[31]

Mergers and acquisitions often form part of the strategy options that are expected to transform company performance. Chapter 13 summarised the main reasons for seeking these routes, particularly as a means of entry into new markets. However, it should be stated that these activities are mainly confined to the UK and the US. They are less common in the rest of Europe and the Far East. Although there are clear reasons for seeking mergers and acquisitions, the empirical evidence on their performance suggests that they add little value to the companies undertaking the activity.

Given the amount of energy and publicity expended, this conclusion may be regarded as somewhat disappointing. Professor John Kay has gathered together the main evidence, which is summarised in Table 14.1. Essentially, it shows that, when pre- and post-merger profitability is compared, even the most optimistic interpretation of the results concluded: 'No consistent pattern of either improved or deteriorated profitability can therefore be claimed across the seven countries. Mergers would appear to result in a slight improvement here, a worsening there.'[32]

Table 14.1 The performance of mergers

Method of evaluation	Major studies	Conclusions
1 Subjective opinions of company personnel	Hunt *et al.* (1987)	Around half were successful
2 Whether acquired business is retained in the long term	Ravenscraft and Scherer (1987)	More divested than retained
3 Comparison of overall profitability before and after the merger	Meeks (1977), Mueller *et al.* (1980), Ravenscraft *et al.* (1990), Scherer (1987)	Nil to negative effect
4 Effect on stock market valuation	Franks and Harris (1986), Franks, Harris and Mayer (1988)	Positive initial impact

Source: Compiled by Professor John Kay, *see* reference 31. Note – there is a summary of more recent evidence by Professors Michael Hitt, R Duane Ireland and Jeffrey S Harrison in Chapter 12 of Hitt, M A, Freeman, R E and Harrison, J S (2001) *Handbook of Strategic Management*, Blackwell Business, Oxford.

None of the evidence suggests that it is impossible for mergers or acquisitions to succeed in adding value. What the evidence does suggest is that many do not and the main reason would appear to be overoptimistic and vague objectives rather than some deeper inherent flaw.[33] Generally, they are more likely to be successful where the partners are of similar size. In addition, cost cutting and asset downsizing may not be the most effective ways of improving performance. It may be more useful to consider ways of transferring competencies and exploiting revenue synergies.[34] Beyond this, such options have no proven record of success in terms of delivering value.

▶ Key strategic principles

- Business judgement needs to be applied to selection because no one can be certain about the outcomes of strategy proposals.

- Generic industry environments have been analysed to provide some guidance on strategy evaluation. They are based on two broad categories: the *stage of industry maturity* and the *competitive position* of the organisation involved. After identifying where the organisation fits on these two parameters, simple choices then suggest themselves.

- Beyond this general work, further guidance on appropriate strategies has been developed for specific types of industry situation: fragmented industries, emerging industries, mature markets, declining markets have all been identified.

- Empirical evidence based on the PIMS Databank also exists on the connection between strategic actions and the results in terms of profitability and other criteria.

- According to PIMS, high quality and strong market share can make a positive contribution to profitability. High capital intensity is less likely to have a positive impact. Some researchers doubt the cause and effect relationships here.

- Acquisitions and mergers have also been studied for their impact on profitability. The evidence is, at best, mixed and, at worst, suggests that many are unsuccessful.

CASE STUDY 14.3

Corporate strategic leadership at Unilever

As one of the world's largest food and consumer goods companies, Unilever operates in over 100 countries and across more than 14 major product groups ranging from ice cream to personal fragrances. Yet its corporate strategic leadership comes from a central executive committee of only seven directors and its strategies are essentially prescriptive. How and why this works is the subject of this case.

Unilever in the new millennium

Unilever has some areas of significant market strength: it is the world's largest maker of ice cream products, tea beverages, margarine and cooking oils and some soap products. Its major competitors worldwide include Procter & Gamble (US) and Nestlé (Switzerland). They are both equally dominant in related product areas, with Unilever often in second position. Although Unilever has been trading successfully over the

CASE STUDY 14.3 continued

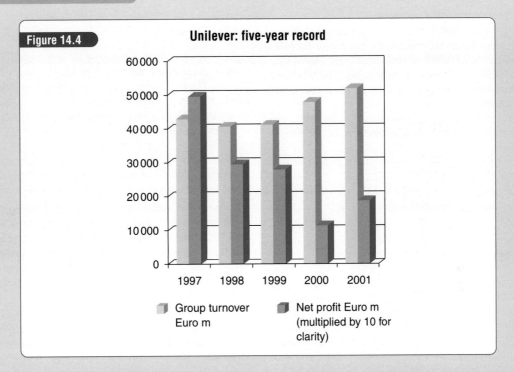

Figure 14.4

Unilever: five-year record

Group turnover Euro m

Net profit Euro m (multiplied by 10 for clarity)

last few years – *see* Figure 14.4 – it has been operating in relatively mature markets that have been subject to economic downturn. As a result, the Executive Committee decided in the late 1990s to weed out underperforming areas and focus on strengths. To understand the circumstances leading to such prescriptive strategic solutions, it is useful to begin by exploring Unilever's history.

Background – strategy as history

Unilever began as a merger between the British soap and detergent manufacturer Lever Brothers and the group of Dutch margarine and food oil companies Van Den Bergh and Jurgens, after the First World War. Both parents already had extensive international activities which they sought to consolidate and extend through the new joint company. But the national sensitivities were such that the new company had some special characteristics that still affect the way that Unilever operates in the twenty-first century: it has two worldwide headquarters and two chairpersons – specifically, in 2000 Antony Burgmanns (Dutch) and Niall Fitzgerald (Irish/UK). Especially in the 1970s and 1980s, it also had a strong tradition of international co-operation and

human resource development between the semi-autonomous national companies that made up the group.

In the early years, the various national companies were allowed to manage their own affairs. In the 1960s, global 'co-ordination' was introduced at the joint headquarters in product areas like detergents. But national companies were still allowed to keep their own national brands, strategies and manufacturing facilities. Thus, for example, Unilever's detergent activities across Europe in the period 1965–90 were a patchwork of national brands – Persil in the UK, Skip in France and Portugal, Omo in the Netherlands, Austria and parts of Africa – each with its own production operation. By contrast, its rival Procter & Gamble (P&G) was developing a more focused pan-European branding and manufacturing operation under the brand name Ariel. Profit margins at P&G were consequently significantly higher than at Unilever. However, there was more co-ordination in some newer Unilever product areas – for example, Dove skin care, Liptons Tea and ice cream products like Cornetto and Magnum were encouraged to develop worldwide.

Unilever's prescriptive approach

In the late 1990s, the relative independence of Unilever's national companies gave way to much greater international co-ordination and global strategy, at least in some product areas. The Executive Committee drove such a change from the centre with two major initiatives.

In 1997, Unilever announced a new organisational structure that had several specific objectives:

● to clarify worldwide management responsibilities and stimulate growth;

● to inject some new life into a company whose culture had become worthy but dull;

● to increase product co-ordination with a view to stimulating greater responsibility and innovation across the group.

In 1999, it coupled this reorganisation with a new, bold strategy: the 'Path to Growth.' This would concentrate the company's resources on its 400 leading brands. It would either sell off or slowly run down its other 1200 brands. Marketing, research and personnel were focused on its leading power brands. The objective was to achieve annual sales growth of 6 per cent by 2004 and to boost profit margins from 11 to 15 per cent. Major costs savings would result from simplifying operations and reducing suppliers – over US$1 billion per annum.

Subsequently, and in spite of approving a mission statement that was both bland and boring ('Our purpose at Unilever is to meet the everyday needs of people everywhere'), the small Executive Committee at the centre took some bold strategic decisions:

● It sold the speciality chemicals division for US$4.6 billion.

● It divested a range of peripheral activities such as NordSee Restaurants in Germany and John West fish products in the UK, Mazola cooking oil in the US, and a range of European soups: Batchelors in the UK, Royco and Lesieur in France and Heisse Tasse in Germany.

● It bought new ice cream companies in Brazil, the US, Mexico and China – including the US super-premium ice cream company Ben & Jerry for US$125 million.

● It acquired the major slimming foods company, Slim Fast, for US$2.3 billion and the global food company, Bestfoods, that owned Hellman's

Mayonnaise and Knorr Soups and Sauces for US$20 billion.

Equally, it decided to reorganise its entire operation to give more emphasis to key product groups and brands. Globalisation, even with local variations, meant that each national company could no longer go entirely its own way. The group's new structure included the following:

● Business product groups would now have more power. National companies would continue but the business groups would be pre-eminent.

● Some seven starred product groups were identified with significant international growth potential for the first time: laundry, ice cream, yellow fats, personal wash, tea-based beverages, prestige products, skin care. These were considered to have real growth potential and would receive priority investment accordingly.

● Another three categories were also identified as established world products: hair care, oral hygiene, deodorants. However, these did not have quite the growth potential of the categories above and would receive investment accordingly.

● Innovation officers were appointed for each company.

● Unilever would work on a time horizon of eight to ten years for its basic category planning.

At the time of writing, the company was part-way through these developments. Major sales and profit improvements had been obtained, but there were residual difficulties – smaller low-growth brands could not just be ignored. Bold prescriptive strategies also have risks.

Sources: See reference 35.

Case questions

1 *In what way is the Unilever strategic planning process prescriptive?*

2 *To what extent is Unilever's strategic decision-making process a result of its history?*

3 *Given the size of the operation, would you make any changes to Unilever's strategic decision-making process?*

14.4 The classic prescriptive model of corporate strategy: exploring the process

Having made our choice of the *content* of a strategic plan, we now turn our attention to the related issue of who will make the choice and how it will be made – the strategic *process*. Clearly, in practice the two topics of process and content will be interlinked, but it is useful to separate them in our exploration here. The aim of this section is not merely to describe the process but also to evaluate its usefulness because it is important to be aware of such issues. We consider the matter under three headings:

1 The prescriptive process of corporate strategy

2 Some problems with the prescriptive process

3 Solutions within the prescriptive process to its problems.

14.4.1 The prescriptive process of corporate strategy

In describing their version of the classic prescriptive model, Wheelen and Hunger[36] state that the process of corporate strategy involves five major elements:

1 *environmental scanning* – the external opportunities and threats of the SWOT analysis;

2 *internal scanning* – the strengths and weaknesses of the SWOT analysis;

3 *strategy formulation* – mission, objectives, strategies and policies;

4 *strategy implementation* – including programmes, budgets and other procedures;

5 *evaluation and control* – to ensure that the strategic process remains on its predicted path.

For example, at Unilever the company is constantly scanning its major competitors such as Procter & Gamble (US) and Nestlé (Switzerland) – environmental scanning. It is also examining its own resources – internal scanning. It then considers its business objectives and develops new strategies such as its investment in global ice cream markets – strategy formulation. It then implements such strategies by building or acquiring ice cream companies as described in Case study 14.3 – strategy implementation. After it has begun its strategies, it will monitor their profits to ensure that they meet group strategic objectives and it will then take corrective action if necessary – evaluation and control.

Some commentators on the classical model, such as Jauch and Glueck,[37] put the mission and objectives before environmental scanning. This book puts the objectives after the environmental and internal scanning for the reasons given in Chapter 1. However, in practice, the process is circular, with no firm rule at this point. Table 14.2 sets out a typical sequence for the classical model with, in this case, the objectives first.[38]

Just as important as the precise sequence of events in the process is *who* undertakes them. This becomes particularly acute when the organisation consists of a group of industries that are possibly unrelated. In these circumstances, it is likely that there will be a corporate centre that might undertake some tasks and strategic business units (SBUs) that will undertake others. But who does what tasks? There is no single answer to this question. For example, Unilever's approach described in Case study 14.3 is unique to the opportunities, history and products of that company.

Table 14.2 The prescriptive model of the corporate strategy process

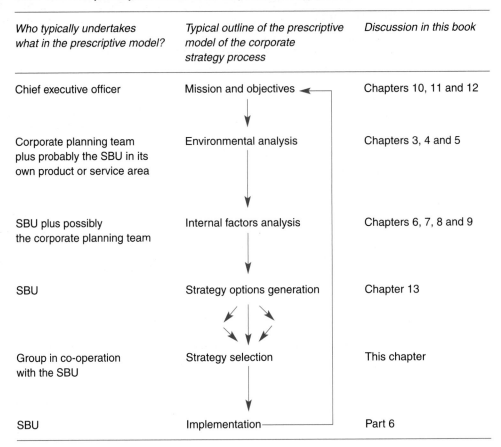

Who typically undertakes what in the prescriptive model?	Typical outline of the prescriptive model of the corporate strategy process	Discussion in this book
Chief executive officer	Mission and objectives	Chapters 10, 11 and 12
Corporate planning team plus probably the SBU in its own product or service area	Environmental analysis	Chapters 3, 4 and 5
SBU plus possibly the corporate planning team	Internal factors analysis	Chapters 6, 7, 8 and 9
SBU	Strategy options generation	Chapter 13
Group in co-operation with the SBU	Strategy selection	This chapter
SBU	Implementation	Part 6

Note: The process is largely linear but with feedback mechanisms at various points to ensure that the objectives, analysis and strategies are all consistent with each other. This is shown by the directions of the arrows, whose significance will become clearer when we examine alternative processes in Chapter 15.

Although there are dangers in generalising, several commentators have identified which groups are particularly likely to be involved at each stage.[39] In a large multinational like Unilever, the group's SWOT analysis is usually undertaken at the corporate level and it is also the corporation that defines the overall mission and objectives. The reason is that only the corporation can have the overview needed to direct the main strategic thrusts and the resources to fund them. The results are then passed down for the strategy *option* process to be developed by the SBUs. In the case of Unilever, some SBUs would be given specially favoured treatment – such as ice cream and tea-based beverages – while others would have a tougher evaluative regime. The strategy *selection* might then be undertaken at corporate headquarters, in consultation with the SBU and in the context of the available funds that the group has at its disposal. The SBU then implements the agreed strategies.

The process is therefore usually driven by corporate headquarters, on the basis that it is the only part of the organisation to have a complete picture of all aspects. However, individual businesses are often given considerable freedom within the guidelines to develop their strategy, as is the case at Unilever.

Such a relationship between the headquarters and the SBUs has been in operation at General Motors (US) since the 1920s when Alfred Sloan was brought in from one of the subsidiaries to rescue and reorganise what became one of the world's largest companies. He was one of the early strategy pioneers to propose such a process. His work is recorded in his own writing[40] and that of Alfred Chandler.[41] As well as examining General Motors, Chandler also conducted a historical survey of three other large companies in the early twentieth century to discover what made US industry so powerful.

> *Strategic plans can be formulated from below, but normally the implementation of such proposals requires the resources which only the general office [i.e. the corporate HQ] can provide. Within the broad policy lines laid down by that office and with the resources it allocates, the executives at the lower levels carry out tactical [i.e. day-to-day, non-strategic] decisions.*

However, it should be pointed out that, in the late twentieth century, more strategy decision-making freedom was given to the subsidiaries than described by Chandler. Although many companies around the world have adopted the classical prescriptive process, there are a number of well-documented problems with this approach. We now explore them.

14.4.2 Some problems with the prescriptive process

There are a number of assumptions or simplifications in the prescriptive process that may not be valid in reality. We summarise four here but should note that other difficulties have been identified.

1 *Environment.* It is assumed that this is predictable, so that a clear direction can be used to develop the opportunities and threats to the organisation. There have been numerous instances of major variations in the environment that make this difficult to sustain.

2 *Clear planning procedure.* The major strategic decisions are initiated by this procedure that, once set in motion, can arrive at a clear and simple decision point: the strategy selection. In many companies, planning procedures are complicated by the need to persuade managers to undertake specific strategies. They may be reluctant for a variety of reasons, from a loss of power to a personality clash.

3 *Top-down procedures.* These procedures from corporate HQ to the SBUs represent the most efficient method of developing new and innovative strategies. It is assumed that they can cope with the environment and gain commitment from the managers who will implement them. Many research studies have shown that managers find such a process demotivating. By contrast, the Japanese Honda case, with its frequent consultation and dialogue, may be far more effective.

4 *Culture.* The culture of organisations will allow the classical model to operate. Culture here has two meanings: the style, beliefs and practices of the *organisation itself* and, more broadly, the culture of the *country* in which the organisation operates. Both of these are assumed to be consistent with the top-down classical model. In practice, some cultures are clearly more suited to a dominant top-down approach than others. The ABB case at the end of Chapter 16 provides an example of how the company's culture was actually changed.

Hence, all the above assumptions have been shown to have significant flaws.

Marx[42] quotes the chairman of the giant US corporation General Electric, Mr Jack Welch, on the problems encountered in strategic planning in the 1960s using the classical process:

> *Our planning system was dynamite when we first put it in. The thinking was fresh, the form mattered little – the format got no points. It was idea-oriented. We then hired a head of planning and he hired two vice-presidents and then he hired a planner, and the books got thicker and the printing got more sophisticated, and the covers got harder and the drawings got better. The meetings kept getting larger. Nobody can say anything with 16 or 18 people there.*

Welch became increasingly concerned about the whole planning process in General Electric and moved to change it. Mr Welch was concerned about three areas:

1 the *bureaucracy* that may breed under classical strategy processes;

2 the *judgement* required to make choices, which may not be as rational as the simple options and choice selection process suggests;

3 the need to encourage a *culture of ideas* rather than a top-down approach as in the classical strategy process.

14.4.3 Solutions to problems within the prescriptive process

To explore the solutions available within the prescriptive process, it is useful to do a careful survey of the difficulties encountered. One such survey in the early 1980s observed that the prescriptive model had become excessively rational, bureaucratic and formalised.[43] There are a number of ways to overcome these problems. They involve a more open strategic planning culture with less emphasis on quantification of data. Stress can also be laid on two aspects of the actual process:

1 exploring the *assumptions* on which the strategy is based with the proposers of the strategy. When such assumptions are incorrect, the whole strategy is open to doubt;

2 during the strategy review sessions, requesting a simple *verbal summary* of the main proposals. If this cannot be done, then the proposals themselves may be suspect.

The whole process and system by which a strategy is developed should also be re-examined periodically in companies: this is a *planning process audit*. The aim would be to remove the impediments that creep in over time. It was just such an audit that led Unilever to rethink its strategy decision-making processes during 1996–97. The company felt the need to redefine its direction, highlight key business areas and clarify the procedures that linked them together. It is notable that it also coincided with the appointment of a new co-chairman, Niall Fitzgerald. Two specific aims were to gain greater individual ownership of strategic decisions and more emphasis on innovation.

14.4.4 Conclusion

Overall, it will be evident that prescriptive strategists are aware of the problems that the process causes. They may attempt to overcome them by revising the process and renewing it. They may try to undertake this by more radical measures to change the culture of the company. But there are still residual problems and some strategists favour more radical solutions than the prescriptive process, as we will see in Chapter 15.

Key strategic principles

- The prescriptive model of the strategic *process* is largely linear. It has feedback mechanisms at various points to ensure that objectives, options and strategy choice are consistent with each other.

- Problems with the prescriptive approach cover four main areas: environment unpredictability, planning procedures, top-down approaches driven by the centre, and the culture of the organisation that will allow the model to operate.

- Specific criticisms include the need for more dialogue, a greater flow of ideas and more adaptation to the environment.

- It may be possible to solve these problems within the prescriptive process but some strategists take a more critical view.

14.5 International corporate strategy selection[44]

Strategy selection across international boundaries is more complex because additional factors such as currency, national cultures, tariff barriers and other matters need to be considered. These aspects have been explored in previous chapters.

Probably the single most important aspect from a selection perspective is to clarify the *objectives* for international expansion. The reason is that these will provide the direction for the development and selection of the relevant international activities. In practice, there are many variations. Exhibit 14.6 contains some examples of possible links between international objectives and strategic choice.

Exhibit 14.6 **Two examples of the connection between international objectives and strategy selection**

Example 1

Objective: international expansion because the home market is mature

Key factors for success: include economies of scale

Implication: retain home-based production to obtain increased economies of scale

Strategy choice: select low-cost strategy based on production economies of scale from home-base factory and then export production

Example: BMW car production is still based largely in Germany, but sales are international

Example 2

Objective: international expansion because trade barriers are high

Key factors for success: need to obtain distribution inside the barrier, as well as economies of scale in production

Implication: need to set up manufacturing operation inside trade barrier

Strategy choice: select country that represents a useful entry point behind the trade barriers, but also allows good communications with the home country

Example: Nissan and Toyota cars have set up operations in the UK and Spain behind the trade barriers represented by the EU

The difficulty in international strategy is that the linkage between objectives and strategy selection may be more complex than simple business logic. The presence of international subsidiaries, each with its own culture, history and resources, may make this more difficult. Such companies may have conflicting views on objectives, strategy options and the practicality of their implementation. The writer clearly remembers having an international food launch – a powdered orange drink made up with water and called Apeel in the UK and Tang in the rest of Europe – imposed on a UK subsidiary by corporate headquarters in the US. But it was part of a 'Europe-wide strategy' and was therefore deemed to apply everywhere. It was only after it had generated substantial losses that the group headquarters was able to accept that the strategic choice was incorrect.[45] There are dangers therefore in the centre imposing its strategic choice on subsidiaries outside the home country. Further discussion on strategy choice, particularly in a global context, is contained in Chapter 20.

▶ Key strategic principles

- International strategy selection is more complex. The starting point is clarity on the objectives and reasons for international expansion.

- Conflicting views on objectives, resources and cultures may exist between different international subsidiaries of an organisation. Such differences may make it more difficult to make strategic choices. There are dangers in the centre imposing its choice on subsidiaries.

CASE STUDY 14.4

Eurofreeze evaluates its strategy options: 2

After developing its mission and objectives, Eurofreeze began to examine the strategy options that were available and the important strategic decisions that would follow. Importantly, the case presents the strategic options in the form used by many companies to reach strategic decisions.

Future strategy options for Eurofreeze

The company was now considering a number of strategy options. It had undertaken the basic analysis using a cost of capital of 9 per cent. To help analyse the options, it gathered basic market data for its own products and those of its main competitor, Refrigor. The information covered all its main European markets and is shown in Table 14.3. Within the product groups, there was little useful additional information: product sales data were available on individual items, but varied so much by country and by store chain that there was little to be gained from analysing the data.

Refrigor was market leader in vegetables and fruit. Eurofreeze was market leader in branded meat and fish dishes, with Refrigor second. Neither company was market leader in savoury dishes (including pizza) or gateaux. (McCain was leader in savoury dishes, with a 30 per cent share, and Sara Lee in gateaux, with a 25 per cent share.)

The company undertook a portfolio analysis in 2003. This is shown as Figure 14.5. The calculation of the relative market shares for this analysis is shown in the Appendix at the end of the chapter.

Eurofreeze then proceeded to consider each of the options that were available to it. The results are outlined below. (There could be some further combination of options but it was felt that the following reflected the main routes available to the company.)

Table 14.3 Market data on the European frozen products market 1999

	Eurofreeze		Refrigor		Market growth of product category	
	Sales (US$ m)	Market share of product category (%)	Sales (US$ m)	Market share of product category (%)	2003	2012
Branded vegetables and fruit	400	10	800	20	+ 2%	–
Private label vegetables and fruit	200	5	300	7.5	+ 2%	–
Branded meat and fish	300	30	200	20	+ 4%	+ 6%
Private label meat and fish	150	15	100	10	+ 4%	+ 6%
Branded savoury dishes including pizza	30	6	80	16	+ 7%	+ 5%
Private label savoury dishes including pizza	none	–	40	8	+ 7%	+ 5%
Branded cakes and gateaux	25	12	25	12	+ 8%	+ 6%
Private label cakes and gateaux	none	–	20	9.6	+ 8%	+ 6%

Eurofreeze options

The strategic options available to Eurofreeze are summarised in Table 14.4; their financial implications are then explored in the following text.

Option 1

Stop supplying all basic frozen products including its branded and own brand (i.e. with the retailer's private brand name) vegetables. Dropping this range would

mean that the overhead contribution made by carrying these products would no longer be available to the group. The financial implications are shown in Table 14.5.

Option 2

Cancel its current branded range of basic frozen food products such as vegetables, but continue to manufacture own brand versions. This would keep some overhead contri-

Figure 14.5 **The European frozen foods market: portfolio matrices for Eurofreeze and Refrigor**

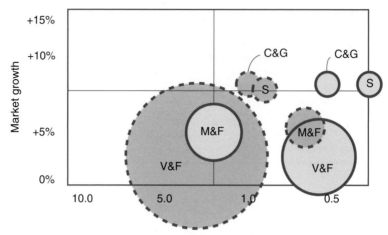

Diameter of circle proportionate to size of sales for each company in that product category.

Eurofreeze

Refrigor

V&F = Vegetables and Fruit
S = Savoury
C&G = Cakes and Gateaux
M&F = Meat and Fish

Table 14.4 Summary of the Eurofreeze strategy options

Option	Implication for sales
1 Stop selling branded and own label vegetables and fruit	Sales decline US$400 million in Year 1, US$200 million in Year 2
2 Stop selling branded vegetables and fruit but continue own label	Sales decline US$400 million in Year 1
3 Extend specialist branded food ranges, e.g. pizza and gateaux	Sales gain US$50 million each year
4 Major cutback of range in first two years, then rebuild specialist areas from Year 4 onwards	Sales decline US$205 million in Year 1, US$300 million in Years 2 and 3 Sales gain US$50 million in Year 4, US$100 million in each year from Year 5 onwards
5 Become lowest cost producer through major investment	Build sales by at least US$100 million per annum

CASE STUDY 14.4 continued

Table 14.5 Financial projection for Option 1 (US$ million)

| | Current Projected on option | | | | | | | | | | | Option 1 |
	2003	2004	2005	2006	2007	2008	2009	2010	2011	2012	2013	NPV*
Sales	600	200	–	–	–	–	–	–	–	–	–	–
Incremental profit impact	24	(5)	(8)	(8)	(8)	(8)	(8)	(8)	(8)	(8)	(8)	(48.6)**
Capital impact: working capital	–	10***	20***	–	–	–	–	–	–	–	–	26.0****
Capital impact: fixed capital	–	–	–	–	–	–	–	–	–	–	–	–

Note: Current position shows the situation for the option only. All other sales and profits operate as previously.
* NPV = Net Present Value at 9% cost of capital 2003 = (5) × 0.917 + (8) × 0.842 + (8) × 0.772 + etc.
** Net effect of lower sales and some lower overheads, but freezer transport and warehousing would still be needed for other products.
*** Working capital no longer required to support sales.
**** US$26 million working capital released from lower sales when discounted back to base year 2003.

Table 14.6 Financial projection for Option 2 (US$ million)

| | Current Projected on option | | | | | | | | | | | Option 2 |
	2003	2004	2005	2006	2007	2008	2009	2010	2011	2012	2013	NPV*
Sales	600	200	200	200	200	200	200	200	200	200	200	–
Incremental profit impact*	24	(5)	(6)	(6)	(6)	(6)	(6)	(6)	(6)	(6)	(6)	(37.6)
Capital impact: working capital	–	8**	12**	–	–	–	–	–	–	–	–	17.4
Capital impact: fixed capital	–	–	–	–	–	–	–	–	–	–	–	–

Note: Current position shows the situation for the option only. All other sales and profits operate as previously.
* Highly efficient to deliver own label to few supermarkets with no branded advertising. However, this is offset by the need to continue to deliver branded savoury, meat and fish dishes to all outlets.
** Reduction in working capital proportionately larger on smaller outlets: US$17.4 million released.

bution but would have very low added value. At the same time, the company would keep and slowly extend its range of higher-added-value branded items. (*See* financial implications in Table 14.6.)

Option 3
Drive hard to redevelop and substantially extend some specialist branded ranges; for example, its *range of frozen cakes and gateaux and its market-leader range of meat and fish products*. This would take time and resources but would produce higher added value. It would keep its broader range of branded products, including its low-value-added items, as long as they made a contribution to overheads. (*See* financial implications in Table 14.7.)

CASE STUDY 14.4 continued

Option 4

Become a specialist producer. This would be done by dropping almost all of its low-added-value basic range, closing a number of freezer factories, contracting out its freezer distribution, investing heavily in specialist menu ranges, advertising these ranges only. Clearly this is a more radical solution, but would emulate the success of several US companies across Europe, such as McCain and Sara Lee. (*See* Table 14.8 for financial implications.)

Option 5

Becoming the lowest-cost producer. This would be done by building on existing sales to all major customers: major investment in new factories, new warehouses and new transport networks would be needed. This would be coupled with major (and largely unknown) manufacturing innovation, all with the aim of reducing costs, so that they would move below those of its competitor, Refrigor. Although this option was available in theory, it

Table 14.7 Financial projection for Option 3 (US$ million)

	Current	Projected on option										Option 3
	2003	2004	2005	2006	2007	2008	2009	2010	2011	2012	2013	NPV*
Sales	1105	1150	1200	1250	1300	1350	1400	1450	1500	1550	1600	–
Incremental profit impact*	80	(5)	(5)	4	6	8	10	12	14	14	14	35.7
Capital impact: working capital	–	(2.5)**	(2.5)	(2.5)	(2.5)	(2.5)	(2.5)	(2.5)	(2.5)	(2.5)	(2.5)	(16.0)
Capital impact: fixed capital***	–	–	(5)	–	(10)	–	–	–	–	–	–	(11.3)

Note: In this option, the current column considers total sales and profits because they will all be affected by the option.
* Net effect of increase in sales less the branded expenditure needed to achieve this.
** Steadily increasing sales so extra working capital required.
*** Some new capital investment required in plant and equipment to handle extra sales.

Table 14.8 Financial projection for Option 4 (US$ million)

	Current	Projected on option										Option 4
	2003	2004	2005	2006	2007	2008	2009	2010	2011	2012	2013	NPV*
Sales	1105	900	600	600	650	700	800	850	900	1000	1200	–
Incremental profit impact*	80	(50)	(100)	(40)	(20)	10	30	100	225	250	300	258.7
Capital impact: working capital	–	10	30	–	(2.5)	(2.5)	(5)	(2.5)	(2.5)	(5)	(10)	19.0
Capital impact: fixed capital**	–	(50)	(100)	(50)	–	(50)	–	–	–	–	–	(201.1)

Note: In this option, the current column considers total sales and profits because they will all be affected by the option.
* Quite difficult to calculate the profit impact with certainty: need to explore detailed projections for each major product area but not presented above for reasons of space.
** Need to provide for factory closure costs and, in year 2008, for factory reinvestment.

Table 14.9 Financial projection for Option 5 (US$ million)

	Current Projected on option											Option 5
	2003	2004	2005	2006	2007	2008	2009	2010	2011	2012	2013	NPV*
Sales	1105	1400	1500	1600	1800	2000	2200	2400	2600	2800	3000	–
Incremental profit impact*	80	5	5	10	12	20	30	40	50	60	70	160.0
Capital impact: working capital	–	(15)	(5)	(5)	(10)	(10)	(10)	(10)	(10)	(10)	(10)	(60.7)
Capital impact: fixed capital**	–	(100)	(300)	(150)	(50)	(50)	–	(200)	–	(200)	–	(729.4)

Note: In this option, the current column considers total sales and profits because they will all be affected by the option.
  * Profit attempts to take into account the increased move to build higher-value-added products less the extra advertising and promotional costs to support these, especially in the early years.
 ** Substantial investment in new factories and other facilities will be required.

was based on three assumptions that carried some risk:

1 Refrigor would slow down its current rate of investment and allow itself to be overtaken.

2 Major cost savings of the order of 20 per cent below existing costs were still available in the industry.

3 Market leadership could be gained through a low-cost route.

For this option, it was recognised that it would also be necessary to provide substantial extra advertising and promotional support to sustain and build the brands. Overall, this was the option with the highest investment. (*See* Table 14.9.)

confidentiality. Market share and financial data have also been changed.

Case questions

1 *What are the relative merits and problems of each option?*

2 *In what way does the use of the portfolio matrix help the strategic debate? And in what way might it mislead the strategic decisions?*

3 *Consider what other strategic analytical tools, if any, might provide useful insights into the strategic choice debate: you might wish to consider a PESTEL analysis, a Five Forces Analysis, generic strategies, a market options matrix, value chain, innovations checklist (in Chapter 11).*

4 *Which option, if any, would you recommend to Eurofreeze? Give reasons for your choice and explain the strengths and weaknesses of your choice.*

Summary

• In evaluating strategic options, it is useful to distinguish between the content of the option (What strategy will we select?) and the process by which the selection will be undertaken (How will we undertake the selection task?).

In considering strategy content, the chapter provides an overview of the classic prescriptive evaluation approach. Such an approach relies on developing criteria as a starting point for selection. These need to be developed bearing in mind the nature of the organisation: for example, commercial and non-profit-making organisations will clearly require different criteria.

- There are six main criteria usually employed in commercial organisations: consistency (especially with the organisation's mission and objectives), suitability, validity, feasibility, business risk, attractiveness to stakeholders.

1 Consistency with the purpose of the organisation is a prime test for evaluating and selecting strategies.

2 Suitability of the strategy for the environment within which the organisation operates is clearly important.

3 Validity of the projections and data used in developing the option must be tested.

4 Feasibility will depend on two factors: constraints internal to the organisation, such as technical skills and finance; constraints external to the organisation, such as the response of competitors.

5 Business risk also needs to be assessed because it may be unacceptable to the organisation.

6 Attractiveness to stakeholders such as shareholders and employees is important: some options may be more attractive to some stakeholders than others.

- There may be international variations in evaluation criteria, depending on national differences in the roles and values of stakeholders and governments.

- In making an initial selection of the best option, it is important to clarify the basis on which this is to be done. Evaluation against the mission and objectives is important but needs to be rigorous and precise if it is to provide real benefit.

- Financial criteria can also be used as the basis of selection. The shareholder value approach takes a broader perspective on evaluation than that provided by the specific project. It seeks to determine the benefit of such developments in the context of the whole company against the cost of the company's capital. Major weaknesses are that it still relies on the assumption that shareholders are always the prime beneficiaries. In addition, it makes the dubious prescriptive assumption that revenue and profit streams can be forecast with accuracy some years into the future.

- Cost/benefit analysis has been successfully employed in public sector evaluation, where it is important to assess broader and less quantifiable benefits. The main difficulty is where to place the limit on such benefits and costs.

- Beyond the issues of criteria to aid strategy selection, business judgement is important. General empirical evidence is available through a number of routes. The ADL matrix summarises some broad decision-making parameters. It is based on two broad categories: the stage of industry maturity and the competitive position of the organisation involved. After the position of the organisation on these two parameters has been identified, simple choices then suggest themselves.

- Empirical evidence based on the PIMS Databank also exists on the connection between strategic actions and the results in terms of profitability and other criteria. According to PIMS, high quality and strong market share can make a positive contribution to profitability. High capital intensity is less likely to have a positive impact. Some researchers doubt the cause and effect relationships here. Acquisitions and mergers have also been studied for their impact on profitability. The evidence is, at best, mixed and, at worst, suggests that many are unsuccessful.

● International strategy selection is more complex. The starting point is clarity on the objectives and reasons for international expansion. The difficulty in international strategy is to find some basic pattern and logic for such developments in order to facilitate their selection. There may be some conflict between corporate headquarters and the individual international operating companies as a result of different competitive pressures, differing customer tastes and different cultures.

● After exploring the likely *content* of the selected strategy above, it is important to consider the *process* by which the selection is undertaken. The prescriptive model of the strategic process is largely linear. It has feedback mechanisms at various points to ensure that objectives, options and strategy choice are consistent with each other.

● Problems with the prescriptive approach cover four main areas: environment unpredictability; planning procedures; top-down approaches driven by the centre; and the culture of the organisation that will allow the model to operate. In addition, there are some specific criticisms which include the need for more dialogue, a greater flow of ideas and more adaptation to the environment. It may be possible to solve these problems within the prescriptive process model but some strategists take a more critical view.

QUESTIONS

1 Using Section 14.1, what criteria would you consider were particularly important if you were evaluating strategy options in the following organisations: a small chain of petrol stations; a large multinational developing a global strategy; a government telecommunications company that was about to be privatised; a student career planning service?

2 If you were developing strategy for a small company with 50 employees and a turnover of around US$5 million, would you use all the selection criteria outlined in Section 14.1 or would you select only some for this purpose? Give reasons for your answer and, if only choosing some, explain which you would pick.

3 Japanese companies have tended to favour payback criteria while US/UK companies have been more inclined to use DCF criteria in evaluating strategic options. What are the merits of the two approaches? Can you suggest any reasons why one might be preferred to another?

4 'Discounting techniques rest on rather arbitrary assumptions about profitability, asset deterioration and external investment opportunities.' (Professor Robert Hay)

Explain the implications of this comment for strategy evaluation and comment on its application in strategy selection.

5 What are the dangers, if any, of using quantified and precise evaluation criteria in strategy selection?

6 'Strategy evaluation is an attempt to look beyond the obvious facts regarding the short-term health of a business and appraise instead those more fundamental factors and trends that govern success in the chosen field of endeavour.' (Professor Richard Rumelt)

Discuss.

7 A well-known German company is primarily engaged in supplying motor components such as car radios and gear boxes to car companies in the EU, such as Ford and Toyota. It is considering acquiring a medium-sized US company as the basis for its first expansion outside Europe. What would you advise in this relatively mature and fiercely competitive industry?

8 With regard to new, fast-growing markets such as that for mobile telephones, the ADL matrix would suggest that weak and dominant companies face quite different strategic opportunities and problems. Is this really true when the market is changing so rapidly?

9 'Merger and acquisition is the most common means of entry into new markets.' (Professor John Kay)

What is the evidence of success from such ventures? What are the strategic implications of your answer for organisations considering this option?

10 'Most firms rarely engage in explicit formal strategy evaluation...rather, it is a continuing process that is difficult to separate from normal planning, reporting and control.' (Professor Richard Rumelt)

Discuss the implications for the evaluation criteria explored in this chapter.

STRATEGIC PROJECT

The world mobile telephone equipment industry is led by three major companies – Nokia (Finland), Ericsson (Sweden) and Motorola (US). All such companies now face major strategic problems as demand for new mobile telephones has become saturated for existing models and the new 3G technology has yet to have an impact. You might like to consider the prescriptive options-and-choice process in such companies: how can they survive and grow in such an uncertain market? What is the role of innovation and strategic alliances? What are the implications for the prescriptive strategic process that has been explored in this chapter?

FURTHER READING

On criteria for selection, *see* Day, G S (1987) *Strategic Market Planning*, West Publishing, St Paul, MN; Tiles, S (1963) 'How to evaluate business strategy', *Harvard Business Review*, July–Aug, pp111–22; Rumelt, R (1980) 'The evaluation of business strategy', originally published in Glueck, W F, *Business Policy and Strategic Management*, McGraw-Hill, New York, but republished in two more recent texts: De Wit, Bob and Meyer, R (1994) *Strategy: Process, Content and Context*, West Publishing, St Paul, MN; Mintzberg, H and Quinn, J B (1991) *The Strategy Process*, Prentice Hall, New York.

On financial evaluation, Glautier, M W E and Underdown, B (1994) *Accounting Theory and Practice*, 5th edn, Pitman Publishing, London, is a useful summary of the main areas. *See* also Arnold, G (1998) *Corporate Financial Management*, Financial Times Pitman Publishing, London, which provides an excellent review of the topic.

For a rational view on the use and abuse of investment criteria: Hay, R (1982) 'Managing as if tomorrow mattered', *Harvard Business Review*, May–June, pp72–9.

Feasibility is explored along with other criteria in Professor Richard Rumelt's article on 'The evaluation of business strategy' mentioned above.

Appendix

Calculation of relative market shares for portfolio analysis in association with Case study 14.4

For Eurofreeze

Vegetables and fruit: $(10\% + 5\%) \div (20\% + 7.5\%) = 0.54$

(Note that these could be redefined as separate branded and private product categories. Given the low added value from both routes, this has not been undertaken here. There are no clear rules.)

Meat and fish: $(30\% + 15\%) \div (20\% + 10\%) = 1.5$

Savoury dishes: $6\% \div 30\% = 0.2$

(Note that McCain is market leader in this category and it is this share that has been used.)

Cakes and gateaux: $12\% \div 25\% = 0.48$

(Note that Sara Lee is market leader in this category and it is this share that has been used.)

For Refrigor

Vegetables and fruit: $(20\% + 7.5\%) \div (10\% + 15\%) = 1.1$

Meat and fish: $(20\% + 10\%) \div (30\% + 15\%) = 0.67$

Savoury dishes: $(18\% + 6\%) \div 30\% = 0.8$

Cakes and gateaux: $(12\% + 9.6\%) \div 25\% = 0.86$

NOTES & REFERENCES

1 *See*, for example, Gilmore, F and Brandenburg, R (1962) 'Anatomy of corporate planning', *Harvard Business Review*, Nov–Dec, pp61–9.

2 Carnegy, H (1995) 'Scared of growing fat and lazy,' *Financial Times*, 10 July, p11. *See also Financial Times*, 30 Oct 1998, p18; 24 March 1999, p12; 9 July 1999, p21; 31 July 2000, p28; 8 December 2000, p16; 13 March 2001, p32; 29 May 2001, p29; 14 June 2001, p18; 20 June 2001, p13; 22 June 2001, p13; 20 November 2001, p29; 7 December 2001, p32; Nokia Annual Report and Accounts 1997 and 2000. For earlier data and comment on Nokia see Lynch, R (1994) *European Business Strategies*, 2nd edn, Kogan Page, London, p151.

3 Used with some effect to dismiss options by the late Professor 'Mac' MacIntosh in 1967 in London Business School MBA lectures and case discussions.

4 Different commentators have employed other criteria. Those used here have been developed from Day, G S (1987) *Strategic Market Planning*, West Publishing, St Paul, MN; Tiles, S (1963) 'How to evaluate business strategy', *Harvard Business Review*, July–Aug, pp111–22; Rumelt, R (1980) 'The evaluation of business strategy', originally published in Glueck, W F, *Business Policy and Strategic Management*, McGraw-Hill, New York, and republished in two more recent texts: De Wit, Bob and Meyes, R (1994) *Strategy: Process, Content and Context*, West Publishing, St Paul, MN; Mintzberg, H and Quinn, JB (1991) *The Strategy Process*, Prentice Hall, New York.

5 *Financial Times* (1995) 'Strategic choice at MCI', 2 Nov, p17.

6 *See* Lynch, R (1993) *Cases in European Marketing*, Kogan Page, London, Ch16.

7 *See Financial Times*, 15 Apr 1995, p9; 13 Oct 1994, p2; 1 Mar 1994, p29; and Lynch, R (1994) Op. cit., p84. Groupe Bull is a company with some real strategic problems that would make an interesting strategy project.

8 Kehoe, L (1995) 'Restrictive practice claims put Microsoft back in firing line', *Financial Times*, 6 Feb, p6.

9 Carnegy, H (1995) 'Bitter Swedish dispute to end,' *Financial Times*, 3 Aug, p2.

10 *See* Chapter 2 for details.

11 Munchau, W and Norman, P (1995) 'Planes, trains and automobiles,' *Financial Times*, 7 Nov, p19.

12 Ohmae, K (1982) *The Mind of the Strategist*, Penguin, Harmondsworth, p86.

13 For a more detailed treatment of this topic, *see* Arnold, G (1998) *Corporate Financial Management*, Financial Times Management, London, Chs2–6.

14 This is consistent with the emphasis on core competencies in Chapter 13.

15 Further detailed exploration of the techniques outlined in this chapter is contained in the recommended reading at the end of the chapter: namely, Glautier and Underdown (Pitman) and Arnold (Financial Times Management).

16 The main exceptions are the large grocery multiple retailers which sell for cash to the general public and buy on credit from the manufacturers. Retailers have relied on their suppliers to fund increased sales for many years, but they do need careful stock control procedures to handle the situation.

17 *See* Arnold, G (1998) *Corporate Financial Management*, Financial Times Pitman Publishing, London, Ch3.

18 This section is based on the example in Chapter 31 of Glautier, M W E and Underdown, B (1994) *Accounting Theory and Practice*, 5th edn, Pitman Publishing, London, p540.

19 This was essentially proposed by Rappaport, A (1983) *Creating Shareholder Value*, The Free Press, New York. *See* also Rappaport, A (1992) 'CEO and strategists: forging a common framework', *Harvard Business Review*, May–June, p84. A clear and careful discussion of this area is also contained in Ellis, J and Williams, D (1993) *Corporate Strategy and Financial Analysis*, Pitman Publishing, London, Ch10.

20 It is not true of some Japanese companies according to the work of Williams, K, Haslam, C and Williams, J (1991) 'Management accounting: the Western problematic against the Japanese application', *9th Annual Conference of Labour Progress, University of Manchester Institute of Science and Technology*. The authors examined car and electronics companies only and made no claim to have extended their research to the *whole* of Japanese industry. Professor Toyohiro Kono also comments that 'DCF is not used very often' in his interesting survey of Japanese practice, which is more broadly based: Kono, T (1992) *Long Range Planning of Japanese Corporations*, de Gruyter, Berlin, pp277, 281.

21 Rappaport, A, quoted above, and Woolridge, G (1988) 'Competitive decline and corporate restructuring: Is a myopic stock market to blame?', *Continental Bank Journal of Applied Corporate Finance*, Spring, pp26–36, quoted in Ellis, J and Williams, D (1993) Op. cit.

22 Quoted from the UK chemist retailer Boots plc definition of strategy: Buckley, N (1994) 'Divide and thrive at Boots,' *Financial Times*, 4 July, p12.

23 *See*, for example, Rowe, A, Mason, A and Dickel, K (1985) *Strategic Management and Business Policy*, 2nd edn, Addison-Wesley, New York.

24 This section is based on Porter, M E (1990) *Competitive Strategy*, The Free Press, New York, Chs9 to 13. The comments on leaders and followers also draw on Kotler, P (1994) *Marketing Management*, 8th edn, Prentice Hall International, Englewood Cliffs, NJ, Ch15.

25 Porter, M E (1990) Op. cit., p191.

26 This section relies heavily on Buzzell, R and Gale, B T (1987) *The PIMS Principles*, The Free Press, New York, and other researchers who are individually acknowledged below.

27 Described in Buzzell, R and Gale, B T (1987) Ibid.

28 Described in Buzzell, R and Gale, B T (1987) Ibid.

29 PIMS (1991) 'Marketing: in pursuit of the perfect mix', *Marketing Magazine, London*, 31 Oct.

30 Described in Buzzell, R and Gale, B T (1987) Op. cit.

31 This section relies essentially on the work and data in Kay, J (1993) *The Foundations of Corporate Success*, Oxford University Press, Oxford, Ch10.

32 Mueller, D (1980) 'The determinants and effects of merger: an international comparison', Oelschlager, Gunn and Hain quoted in Kay (1993) Op. cit.

33 Ghemawat, P and Ghadar, F (2000) 'The dubious logic of global mega-mergers', *Harvard Business Review*, July–August.

34 Capron, L (1999) 'The long-term performance of horizontal acquisitions', *Strategic Management Journal*, November, 20, pp987–1018.

35 References for the Unilever case: Unilever 1997 and 2001 Annual Report and Accounts. *Financial Times*, 10 June 1997, p26; 1 July 1997, p27; 27 Sept 1997, p19; 3 Oct 1997, p24; 23 Dec 1997, p9; 6 Jan 1998, p18; 11 Feb 1998, p28; 12 Mar 1998, p1; 15 Mar 1998, p22; 17 Mar 1998, p25; 22 Apr 1998, p10; 28 Apr 1998, p14; 15 May 1998, p15; 4 June 1998, p15; 10 July 1998, p33; 19 Jan 1999, p32; 24 Feb 1999, p31; 22 September 1999, p25; 24 September 1999, p27; 25 November 1999, p25; 11 December 1999, p15; 23 February 2000, p27; 30 May 2000, p29; 30 October 2000, p28; 22 January 2001, p1; 30 January 2001, p27; 9 February 2001, p24; 27 April 2002, p13.

36 Wheelen, T and Hunger, D (1992) *Strategic Management and Business Policy*, 4th edn, Addison-Wesley, Reading, MA.

37 Jauch, L R and Glueck, W F (1988) *Business Policy and Strategic Management*, 5th edn, McGraw-Hill, New York.

38 The prescriptive model presented in this chapter is shown in a number of texts in one format or another. In addition to references 2 and 3 above, similar versions of the model are also to be found in the well-known text by Thompson, A and Strickland, A (1993) *Strategic Management*, 7th edn, Irwin, Homewood, IL. The leading and well-respected European text is that by Johnson, G and Scholes, K (2002) Op. cit., and is also essentially built around the options-and-choice model of prescriptive strategy with implementation of the agreed strategic choice.

39 *See*, for example, Andrews, K (1987) *The Concept of Corporate Strategy*, Irwin, Homewood, IL; also

Chakravarthy, B and Lorange, P (1991) *Managing the Strategy Process*, Prentice Hall, Englewood Cliffs, NJ.

40 Sloan, A P (1963) *My Years with General Motors*, Sedgewick and Jackson, London.

41 Chandler, A (1962) *Strategy and Structure*, MIT Press, Cambridge, MA.

42 Marx, T (1991) 'Removing obstacles to effective strategic planning', *Long Range Planning*, 24 Aug. This research paper is reprinted in the book by De Wit and Meyer recommended in the further reading at the end of the chapter.

43 Lenz, R T and Lyles, M (1985) 'Paralysis by analysis: Is your planning system becoming too rational?', *Long Range Planning*, 18 Aug. This is also reprinted in De Wit and Meyer recommended at the end of this chapter.

44 This section is based on Porter, M E (1990) Op. cit., Ch13; Thompson, A and Strickland, A (1993) Op. cit., pp136–7; Lynch, R (1994) Op. cit.

45 Such a record did not stop the US president moving several years later to a well-known pharmaceutical company, where he made a real contribution to its international development.

Chapter 15

Finding the strategic route forward: emergent and prescriptive approaches

Learning outcomes

When you have worked through this chapter, you will be able to:

- understand the importance of context in the development of strategy;
- explain four approaches to strategy development that go beyond the classic prescriptive approach;
- identify the relevance of a survival-based route forward in the context of the circumstances of the organisation;
- outline the importance of the uncertainty-based route forward and comment on its relevance, depending on the organisation's context;
- explain the three main elements of the negotiation-based route forward and comment on their significance to the strategic route forward, depending on context;
- outline the main elements of game theory and comment critically on its usefulness;
- decide the extent to which a learning-based strategy is needed as part of an organisation's strategy process;
- assess the implications for the strategy process where an organisation operates internationally.

Introduction

Although the classic prescriptive model is probably the most widely used approach in strategy development, its simplifying assumptions have long been recognised. In this chapter, we explore alternative approaches to strategy development. Some alternative routes are still prescriptive, but the majority have an emergent aspect.

In Chapter 14, we distinguished between the *content* (What?) of strategy development and the *process* (Why? Who? How?). In this chapter, we add a third element that helps to move beyond the simplifying assumptions of the classic prescriptive approach: the *context* within which strategy is developed.

Context means the circumstances surrounding and explaining the way that strategy operates and develops. For classic prescriptive strategy, context is assumed to involve slow, steady circumstances which are easy to predict.[1] However, this may be an over-simplification of real strategic situations: for example, context may contain periods of upheaval and rapid growth. Context is therefore developed further in the opening section of this chapter to explore some of the realities and uncertainties of real situations. Four routes forward for strategy development are identified; each of them relies on different contexts and implies alternative strategic approaches. All of them include this more complex view of context but also consider other aspects of the strategic process and content. The four routes forward are shown in Figure 15.1.

Amongst the four routes, the chapter argues that the learning-based approach can usefully be added to the classic prescriptive approach developed in Chapter 14 in order to find the strategic route forward for all organisations. The other routes may also be useful depending on the context within which the strategy is being developed.

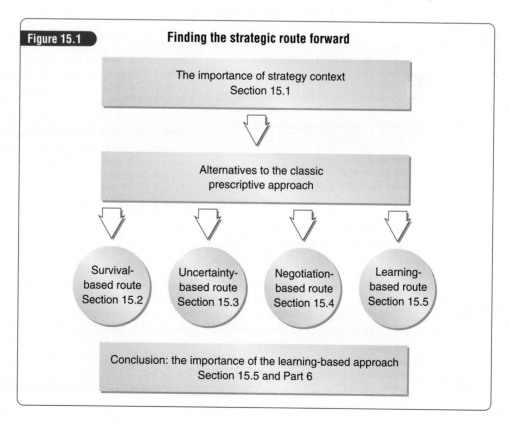

Figure 15.1   **Finding the strategic route forward**

The importance of strategy context
Section 15.1

Alternatives to the classic prescriptive approach

| Survival-based route Section 15.2 | Uncertainty-based route Section 15.3 | Negotiation-based route Section 15.4 | Learning-based route Section 15.5 |

Conclusion: the importance of the learning-based approach
Section 15.5 and Part 6

CASE STUDY 15.1

How Honda came to dominate two major motorcycle markets

This case study describes how Honda Motorcycles achieved its dominant market share of the US and UK markets. Although the strategic approach was originally seen as prescriptive, it was shown that, in reality, the strategies were much more emergent in their development.

During the period 1960–80, Honda Motorcycles (Japan) came to dominate motorcycle markets in the US and UK. Professor Richard Pascale has researched and described two perspectives on the process that Honda used to develop its strategies over this period.[2] They resulted in Honda moving from zero market share to domination of the US and UK markets, leaving the home-based industries with only small, niche-based market shares.

Professor Pascale first examined a study undertaken by Boston Consulting Group for the UK motorcycle industry in 1975 on the strategic reasons for the success of Honda. Two key factors for the success of Honda were identified:

1 an advantage in terms of Honda's economies of scale in technology, distribution and manufacturing;

2 the loss to other companies of market share and profitability as a result of the Honda attack.

The diagnosis appeared to be an example of the classical model and its prescriptive solutions in action.

Professor Pascale then interviewed the Honda executives who had actually launched the motorcycles in the US and subsequently in the UK. He discovered that Honda's strategy had at first been a failure and that it was as a result of sheer desperation that they had stumbled on the strategy that proved so successful. The executives at Honda had a full range of motorcycles that could be imported into the US. They ranged from small scooters to very large machines. All were more reliable and had higher performance than equivalent US competitors.

Honda US initially tried to compete head-on against the US main competition by using their large machines. However, Japanese motorbikes lacked credibility in the US market against the well-known US brands, even though the Honda bikes were better. The launch programme was unsuccessful. By chance, Honda then tried to sell some small scooters into the US market purely for local transport. They

were immediately successful and provided the platform for Honda to launch its attack on the main motorbike market several years later.

If corporate strategists had listened to the consulting company, they might have concluded that a major strategic initiative had been undertaken by Honda, based on careful strategic analysis and evaluation of options. But the reality was more haphazard and opportunistic, especially in the early days of the programme.

In conclusion, Pascale commented that Japanese managers at Honda and elsewhere did not use the term *strategy* to outline a *prescriptive* strategic plan. They were more inclined to see the process as providing an emerging process of trial and error, with the strategy evolving from experimentation as the process unfolded. According to his findings, Japanese companies were unlikely to develop a single strategy that was set to guide the company unerringly forward into the future.

In the Honda case, the strategy was developed from the managers in the market experimenting to find the most effective strategy. As each success was obtained, the Honda managers reported this back to Japan, with their ideas and suggestions for the next phase. There was frequent dialogue between Japan and the individual markets, with consensus being far more important to the emergence of the final strategy. Professor Pascale concluded that strategy needed to be redefined as:

All the things necessary for the successful functioning of an organisation as an adaptive mechanism.

It should be noted, however, that during the 1980s Professor Toyohiro Kono repeatedly surveyed strategic planning in Japanese companies.[3] His conclusions suggested that, in large Japanese companies at least, there is rather more strategic planning than was observed by Professor Pascale. Other examples also exist that suggest that Japanese companies have now adopted some aspects of the prescriptive process, although there is still a strong element of

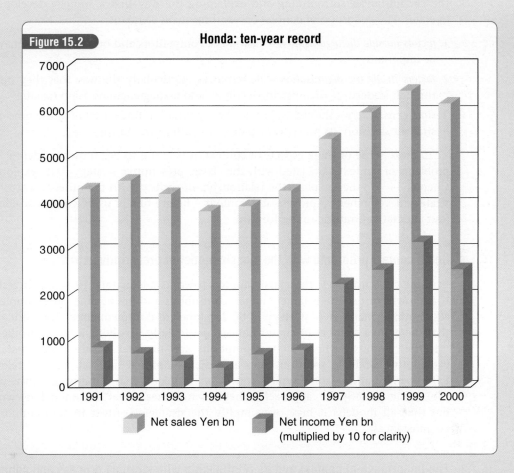

Figure 15.2

Honda: ten-year record

Net sales Yen bn

Net income Yen bn (multiplied by 10 for clarity)

experimentation and consensus in deriving the final plans.

Case question

Does prescriptive strategy need to be modified or would it be better, as Pascale suggests, to redefine the strategic process completely?

15.1 The importance of strategy context

As the Honda case demonstrates, the company's success in the US motorcycle market was the result of three interrelated strategic factors:

1 *strategy content* – Honda's use of small machines as an entry point, followed by its launch of the larger machines;

2 *strategy process* – the way this strategy was developed by a combination of luck, product performance and management persistence in the face of initial difficulties;

3 *strategy context* – the historical dominance of the US manufacturers initially led to the failure of Honda's prescriptive entry strategy, but the industry's relative weakness in the small market provided an opening for Honda.

Although all three elements are important in strategy development, this section of the book concentrates on context (Chapter 14 explored the other two).[4] Context means the circumstances surrounding and explaining the way that a strategy develops and operates. The definition of context covers three main elements:

1 *factors outside the organisation* – customers, competitors and other areas that may also be important;

2 *factors inside the organisation* – its resources, particularly the way that they interact through leadership, organisational culture and management decision making;

3 *strategy as history* – the situation that the organisation finds itself in at the time of the strategic decision: its procedures, pathways, culture and history.

To make sense of these aspects of context, it is useful to begin by considering some problems of context associated with the classic prescriptive strategy route explored in Chapter 14. We then explore the relationship of context with the other two aspects of strategy development – process and content – before finally using context to identify four alternative strategic routes forward.

15.1.1 Some context problems with the classic model of prescriptive strategy

In some circumstances, the classic approach works adequately. However, it assumes that growth or decline is largely linear, continuous and predictable. Such simplifying assumptions enable new strategy to be developed and implemented. The difficulty is that there are a number of circumstances, particularly involving a more turbulent or uncertain context, where such assumptions are incorrect. In these circumstances, prescriptive strategic solutions are, at best, suboptimal and, at worst, irrelevant. Exhibit 15.1 outlines some typical contextual problems that can arise from the use of the classic prescriptive approach. They do not mean that the model is 'wrong', but (like all models) it may oversimplify the strategic context in some important circumstances.

15.1.2 The importance of context and its relationship with strategy process and content

Strategy context is important because it suggests that those alternatives to classic prescriptive strategy that include a fuller treatment of context may work better. There are two main reasons:[5]

1 *The external context.* This may be particularly uncertain – for example, Internet banking may revolutionise the retail banking industry in ways that remain essentially unknown at the time of writing. This makes the prescriptive route, which relies on predicting the environment, largely meaningless.

2 *The internal context.* The organisation's resources and decision making are undoubtedly more complex than the simple options and choice of the classic prescriptive strategy model – for example, organisational politics, formal and informal networks, styles of leadership and many other issues all undermine the assumptions of the classic approach.

The *context* in which the strategy is developed may thus influence the *process* of strategy development. For example, an uncertain context may make a simple decision-making process irrelevant. As a result, the *content* of the strategy may therefore differ from that suggested by classic prescriptive strategy. For example, it will be difficult to

Exhibit 15.1   **How context can weaken classic prescriptive strategy**

Typical outline	Some assumptions and characteristics of classic prescriptive strategy	Some resulting problems of context
Mission and objectives	● Objectives can and should be identified in advance	● Objectives may need to be more flexible in fast-moving markets
Environmental analysis	● Environment sufficiently predictable	● Technology, war and economic disaster may make this assumption meaningless
Resource analysis	● Resources can be clearly identified and developed	● Tacit knowledge needs to be seen in the company context in which it was developed (*see* Chapter 11) ● The context of a leadership change may fundamentally alter resources (*see* Chapter 10)
Strategy options generation	● It is only necessary to identify options once ● It is possible to identify options clearly	● May want to keep options open where the context is unclear ● Competitor reactions may be unknown, context will alter
Strategy options selection	● Only one option can be chosen ● It is possible to make a clear choice between options	● Why choose only one option? Surely this depends on the context of the time, resources, etc.
Implementation	● Implementation only needs to be considered at this late stage in strategic development	● Context may make this highly dubious (*see* opening sections of Part 6 and Chapter 17)

decide the content of a strategy if the context within which it is being developed remains uncertain. It is this *combination* of context, process and content that will guide us in the search for alternative approaches to strategy development.

15.1.3 Alternative approaches to strategy development

Corporate strategy is not rocket science – combining context, process and content involves judgement that may go beyond the simple logic of classic prescriptive strategy. There is no well-tried and generally agreed scientific formula for finding the strategic route forward. As a consequence, there are many alternative approaches to strategy development.

Some approaches still have a strong prescriptive element, while others are more emergent in their exploration of strategic issues. The difficulty is how to explore the many alternative ways forward that have been suggested by strategy writers. This book has chosen four main routes for reasons of contrast and because each provides an insight into strategy development:[6]

1 *Survival-based*. This route puts heavy emphasis on organisations being able to survive in a hostile and highly competitive context. It does this through an *emergent* process, seeking out opportunities in strategy content as they occur.

2 *Chaos-based*. This route also emphasises the importance of context, treating the environment as uncertain and the processes as opportunistic and transformational. The process is therefore *emergent*.

3 *Negotiation-based*. This route has three aspects. One concentrates on the human resource aspects of strategy decision making. Another explores the external networks that exist between the organisation and its environment. The third examines how to reach optimal strategic decisions by treating them as a competitive game that involves negotiation between the main players. All three depend on the precise context and involve a complex process with both *prescriptive* and *emergent* elements.

4 *Learning-based*. This route lays heavy emphasis on the context and the process derived from the existing knowledge and experience of the organisation. This essentially involves learning from the past and from the contributions of those involved at present. Thus both the historical context and the current process will influence strategy content – the process is, essentially, *emergent*.

This book places special emphasis on the last of the four above. The reason is that most organisations will benefit from its insights on the strategy process. However, all four (and more not covered in this text) have their place in finding the most appropriate strategic route forward for the organisation.

▶ Key strategic principles

- In developing strategy, it is important to distinguish three distinct elements: the contents of the strategy, the process by which it has been derived and the context in which it has been developed.

- In the classic prescriptive model, context is assumed to be largely linear and predictable. This is not always the case, particularly when the context is turbulent and uncertain. Alternative approaches to strategy development may therefore be required.

- The context, process and content of a strategy are interconnected and it is this combination that is important in strategy development.

- There are a number of alternatives to the classic prescriptive approach to strategy development. Four are explored in the remainder of this chapter, but others may also be relevant.

> ### CASE STUDY 15.2

Europe's leading telecom companies: overstretched and under threat

As a result of paying too much for acquisitions, all Europe's leading telecommunication companies were overstretched financially in 2002. In addition, they were under a competitive threat from new technologies that could potentially undermine their future profitability. This case traces the strategies that produced this muddle.

Privatisation in the 1980s and 1990s – the old telcos still dominated their national markets

Up to the 1990s, most European countries had one monopoly supplier of telephone services (called a 'telco' for short), often owned by the government. Even in the UK, where British Telecom had been privatised in 1984, the company still dominated services, with around 90 per cent market share. Then, during the 1990s, European governments decided to privatise their leading telcos. However, each national operator continued to dominate its national market, thus delivering high profits, good cash flow, stable business and often a steady programme of equipment and service modernisation – for example, investment in new digital telephone exchange equipment.

Starting in 1992, the European Union began to take an interest with the liberalisation of *data* telephone services – the transmission of data along telephone lines. This was followed in 1998 by the liberalisation of *voice* telephone services. This was meant to open up European markets to some real competition. In practice, Europe was still a closed shop, with each national company attempting to keep rival telcos out of its markets. The more ambitious companies like British Telecom (BT) were forced to seek expansion elsewhere, especially the US. At various times in the 1980s and 1990s in North America, BT acquired a mobile telephone company, a telecommunications equipment company and an alliance with a major US telecoms operator – MCI. But all of this failed to deliver any real profit and in 2000 BT was still reliant for 90 per cent of its profits from its UK operations. Only in Scandinavia was there some successful co-operation between the national telcos and that was in the area of mobile telephones. Even here, the proposed merger of two telcos did not materialise, with national interests being dominant.

The expansion of mobile telephone services – a new competitive threat

During the 1990s, a new competitive threat to the national telcos emerged: mobile telephone licences were awarded to small rival companies that often had no previous experience of telecommunications. For example in Germany, a new licence was awarded to the German engineering company, Mannesmann. At the same time, a licence was also awarded to the main German telco, Deutsche Telekom, but there was at last some competition. Importantly, although mobile call prices were initially high, customers liked mobile telephones. They were no longer tied to a fixed telephone line; mobiles were convenient, trendy and useful in an emergency. By 2002, the European Commission estimated that mobile telephone services made up 38 per cent of the Euro telecomms market, up from 23 per cent in 1998. In Portugal, Finland, Austria and Spain, mobile services generated more revenue than fixed lines.

Potentially, this was a major competitive threat to the former national telcos which had invested billions over the years in their fixed line systems. The customer base formed from such network connections constituted one of the principal areas of sustainable competitive advantage for such companies and it was being undermined by the new mobile operators. The competitive threat was even greater because, unlike fixed lines, mobile services had the potential for extra cost savings through economies of scale in procurement, engineering and branding.

The national telcos solved the competitive threat in almost every European country by setting up their own mobile services. The only exception was the UK, where the government realised the importance of encouraging competition in order to reduce telephone call prices and refused to allow BT to own such a service outright until the late 1990s.

▶

By 2002, the former national telcos had taken a grip of their national mobile markets, with market shares of over 60 per cent. In addition, the leading European telcos were well placed to dominate the pan-European mobile services market outside their home territories: they achieved this strong strategic position by a series of acquisitions that are discussed in the next section. Table 15.1 shows the leading pan-European market shares – the only non-national European operator was the UK-based company Vodafone, which had also built its market position largely by acquisition – *see* Case 15.4.

The consequence of unbridled acquisition – massive debt

The eight leading European telcos expanded across Europe by a series of acquisitions of their rivals over the years 1998 to 2001. For example, France Telecom bought Orange in the UK, British Telecom acquired Viag in Germany and so on. The consequence of this major buying spree was that the leading eight European telcos borrowed between them US$ 800 billion over the years 1998–2002. Such a level of debt was unsustainable. Some com-

Table 15.2 Levels of net debt in leading European telecommunications companies – US$ billion

Company	2000	2001	2002
France Telecom	54	55	57
Deutsche Telekom	50	56	57
Telefónica	24	26	23
British Telecom	42	23	23
Telecom Italia	18	22	21
KPN – Holland	20	15	14

Source: See references.

Note: In practice, the levels of indebtedness above need to be compared with the stock exchange valuations of the equity of the listed companies. Equity valuations vary, but at the time of compiling the above data debt was significantly higher than equity.

panies like British Telecom were rapidly forced to sell some of their assets to reduce their debts during 2001–2002. As Table 15.2 shows, other European telcos were not so quick to shed their debt. At the time of writing, such companies remained severely handicapped in terms of their ability to expand further as a result of their high debt levels.

Part of the reason that the companies paid such high prices for shares was that European stock exchanges gave inflated values to European telco shares during this period – a stock market 'bubble' – and that the European telcos had optimistic views of their future prospects. In some cases, the problem was compounded because companies only acquired minority shareholdings in the target companies – what British Telecom once called a 'family of alliances'. This meant that the acquirer was unable to benefit from a controlling interest that might have delivered economies of scale.

In addition to acquisition, there was another reason for the high levels of debt – the need to bid for the new '3G' mobile telecoms licences.

Table 15.1 Pan-European market shares of the six leading mobile telephone operators

Company	Home country	Pan-European market share (%)
Vodafone	UK	24
France Telecom – Orange	France	12
British Telecom – now a separate company called MMO2	UK	12
Telecom Italia – TIM	Italy	10
Deutsche Telekom	Germany	8
Telefónica	Spain	6

Source: McKinsey analysis – *See* references.

Bidding for '3G' licences – piling on the debt

Ever seeking new ways of raising money, European governments decided in the late 1990s that the new frequencies needed for a new generation of mobile telephone services should be auctioned to the highest bidder. The third generation mobile services – '3G' for short – would deliver full web-casts and moving pictures so callers could see each other on their mobile telephones. They would require a new generation of mobile telephones, new transmitters and other equipment, along with technology, which was totally untested when the auctions took place during the period around year 2000. Each country had its auction and each national operator, along with some new telephone companies, was encouraged to bid. Most of the auctions, except in France, were structured with secret bidding such that the European telcos felt the need to outbid each other. The result was to raise the price of the new 3G licences to the extent that US$79 billion was raised by the auctions in the UK and Germany alone. The total cost across Europe was over US$100 billion – note that this is smaller than the cost of acquisitions outlined earlier. But it was a significant contributor to the debt mountains of the leading European telcos. In addition to this cost, there was then the need to develop, install and maintain the new equipment that would operate the 3G network. One estimate of the roll-out costs for Germany, Italy and the UK alone was an additional US$36 billion. This would be spread over the years 2001 to 2005 as the new 3G services were launched.

At the time when all these debts were being incurred, there was no substantial evidence that customers actually wanted 3G services. Thus the above investment had a degree of risk and experimentation that would challenge some strategists.

Market growth prospects – maturing except in mobile and data services

After growing at around 20 per cent per annum in the late 1990s, it is likely that overall industry revenue growth will slow down. It is predicted to barely exceed growth in gross domestic product over the next few years. Thus, the national European telcos are engaged in a relatively mature industry with very high levels of debt. This means that their future strategies need to take into account the lower growth prospects:

1 cost cutting to reduce staff costs where possible;

2 marketing to exploit the well-known brand names;

3 exploitation of new 3G technology – in practice, some older technology is also available.

Competition increasing – including mobile and cable operators

The fundamental difficulty is that the sustainable competitive advantages of the existing national telcos are being undermined by the new mobile and other services. In former years, the national telcos had a monopoly of the final access to individual households through the fixed line that delivered the telephone signal – the so-called 'local loop'. This meant that such a telco was able to exclude competitors either by refusing to carry their signals or, more likely in practice, making it excessively expensive or inconvenient. However, not only can mobile operators overcome this problem, but the national telcos now face new competition from television cable operators that are able to carry telephone signals as well. In addition, many cable operators are able to deliver faster Internet connections than traditional telcos and therefore pose a real threat in terms of data services.

Competition – the opportunity of 'broadband' and other technology

Given that the national telcos still control the local loop, one strategy that has become increasingly attractive for such operators is to develop the new technology of broadband digital services. Data transmission is vital to the development of the Internet and the World Wide Web. Such data can only be transmitted slowly with the traditional local loop: *see* Table 15.3 for an example. Germany's national telco, Deutsche Telekom, introduced a new broadband service in 2000 and by attractive pricing and good marketing it had signed up 2 million subscribers by 2002. The next largest European supplier was British Telecom with 50,000 subscribers: BT announced a rapid extension of its service in this area during 2002. This would

Table 15.3 The benefit of broadband technology

Home–telco link	Time taken
Traditional 56 Kbps modem – the type linked to many home computers in 2002	over 30 minutes
Digital ISDN line with 128 Kpbs link	10 minutes
ADSL 'broadband' technology	10 seconds

need significant finance but at least BT was able to support the increased debt.

The strategic difficulty here is that telecommunications technology is changing all the time. This means that innovating through broadband might shortly be overtaken by some new technical system. At the same time, all such technologies are expensive to install and commit the telcos away from alternative future developments.

Source: See reference 7.

Case questions

1 *Given the lower levels of market growth coupled with the grip of the existing telcos on their national markets,* *what are the advantages and problems with adopting the classic prescriptive strategy process to develop strategies in this market?*

2 *Some strategists argue that it is useless to predict what will happen, given that technology is uncertain. What would be the consequences, if any, of following this advice in the European telecommunications market and not making any predictions? What implications does your answer have for a prescriptive strategy process that is built on the need to make predictions?*

3 *Can smaller companies attempting to find opportunities in this market also employ the prescriptive process? Or would they be better to use a process that is more radical and innovative to structure their approach? If so, do you have any suggestions on the process that might be employed?*

15.2 The survival-based strategic route forward

As the European mobile telephone market has grown, competition has increased. Companies have entered each other's markets on a limited basis and made the necessary investments. Markets have shown reasonable growth rates but are now beginning to mature. Hence, the sales increases from such growth are unlikely to satisfy the objectives of the major companies. Moreover, in spite of high levels of debt finance, some European telecom companies still wish to expand. One important conclusion that some strategists have therefore drawn about the European telephone industry is that by the year 2010 only five major global companies will remain. The rest will have been swallowed up in a shakeout of the industry. The contrast with the relative stability of the state monopoly companies of the 1980s and early 1990s is striking. Survival-based strategy processes provide one explanation of the likely outcome after liberalisation.

15.2.1 The nature of survival-based strategies

Essentially, the survival-based process begins with the concept of *natural selection* first introduced in the nineteenth century by Charles Darwin to explain the development and survival of living creatures. He argued that survival was a constant battle against the environment. The species most likely to survive were those best suited and adapted to their surroundings. On this basis, adaptation to the environment is the main strategy that needs to be developed in a business context. Those that fail to change quickly enough will be the ones that select themselves for extinction.[8] The fittest companies survive because they are selected on the basis of the demand for their goods or services and the profits that they make.[9]

In the survival-based process there are two mechanisms in operation:

1 adaptation to the environment;

2 selection among those present for survival.

Using these two processes, together with principles and concepts from sociology, researchers have analysed the way that some industrial companies have developed.[10] They noted that, of the top 500 companies listed in *Fortune* magazine in 1955, only 268 were still listed in 1975: 46 per cent had disappeared, merged or otherwise declined over the 20-year period. They suggested that *adaptation to the environment* was the preferred mechanism for change in many companies because it was less painful than selection. This was influenced by a built-in inertia with regard to change in many industrial situations (*see* Exhibit 15.2).

Exhibit 15.2   **Examples of inertia towards change in company environments**

Internal inertia

● Existing investment in plant and machinery

● Previous experience and history of the company

For example, in European telephone companies the existing bureaucracy, which had been built up during many years in government ownership, was very difficult to shift.

External inertia

● Barriers to entry and exit from an industry

● Difficulty and cost of acquiring information on how the environment itself might be changing

For example, European telephone companies' existing investment in exchanges and telephone equipment, coupled with external government restrictions that would prevent new companies entering until 1998, had created an inertia towards change within the industry.

Most strategy literature takes an *adaptive* perspective as its starting point in developing strategy options. Importantly, some survival-based strategists argue that this may not be sufficient. It may be necessary to add a *selection* perspective. There may come a time, precisely because of the inertia in the industry, when some organisations do not or cannot adapt quickly enough to the changes in the environment, and will not survive against the powerful forces ranged against them. Nevertheless, there may be an element of chance in selecting precisely who will disappear. For example, some European telephone companies may adapt to the changed environment of the late 1990s, while others will change too slowly, and the pressures on them will be so great that they will not survive in their present form and will have to amalgamate with more efficient or luckier enterprises.

From a strategy *selection* perspective, the industry environment is the main determining factor of strategy development and survival. There is only a limited amount that individual companies can do in the time available before changes arrive. The only companies for which this may not apply are those that already have substantial market power and can influence the way their markets develop. However, even these may be overtaken by events – for example, in the case of European telecommunications, the advent of new communications technologies such as 3G mobile or the World Wide Web.

15.2.2 Consequences for the corporate strategy process

On this basis, corporate strategy has a limited ability, if any, to influence the environment. Moreover, an organisation may not be able to adapt quickly enough to change. In addition, the techniques recommended by the prescriptive process will be so well publicised that they will provide no competitive advantage to individual companies. As a result, and for those companies without real market power, Williamson[11] has recommended that the best strategy is to develop the most cost-effective operation possible, which he calls *economising*. He distinguishes this from new strategic moves beyond basic cost-effectiveness, which he calls *strategising*.

> *I aver that, as between economizing and strategizing, economizing is much the more fundamental ... A strategizing effort will only prevail if a program is burdened by significant cost excesses in production, distribution or organisation. All the clever ploys and positioning, aye, all the king's horses and all the king's men, will rarely save a project that is seriously flawed in first-order economizing respects.[12]*

What, therefore, can be done? Table 15.4 summarises the main strategies that can be undertaken if this view of the strategy process is correct. It is clearly important to be cautious. It will also be necessary to seek clues from the environment on possible change and what is needed to survive. Finally, it will be useful to generate plenty of options so that whatever happens in the environment can be accommodated by the organisation.

Table 15.4 The survival-based strategy process compared with the prescriptive process

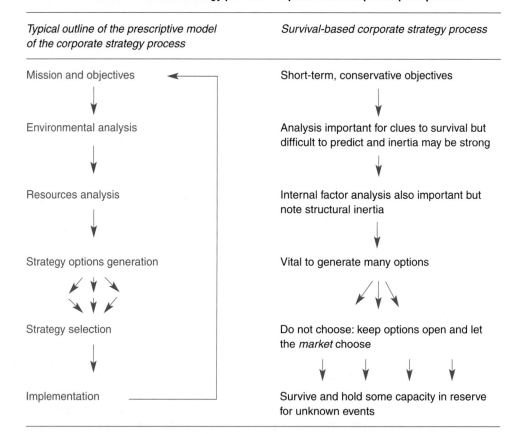

Typical outline of the prescriptive model of the corporate strategy process	*Survival-based corporate strategy process*
Mission and objectives	Short-term, conservative objectives
Environmental analysis	Analysis important for clues to survival but difficult to predict and inertia may be strong
Resources analysis	Internal factor analysis also important but note structural inertia
Strategy options generation	Vital to generate many options
Strategy selection	Do not choose: keep options open and let the *market* choose
Implementation	Survive and hold some capacity in reserve for unknown events

Overall, if this view of the strategy process is correct, then the organisation is severely restricted in its strategies. Arguably, the way in which the European telephone companies have been building alliances and cross-shareholdings suggests that they cannot see the way ahead clearly and have chosen these mutually supportive strategies as the best protection.

Comment

This is a pessimistic view of the role of corporate strategy and the ability of organisations to shape their destiny. It rejects the insights offered by the prescriptive process but offers little alternative. It is useful in rapidly changing and turbulent environments, but offers only limited solutions in other circumstances.

▶ Key strategic principles

- Survival-based strategies emphasise the importance of adapting strategies to meet changes in the environment. The ultimate objective is survival itself.
- The approach adopted is to develop options for use as the environment changes. Options that seek low costs are particularly useful.
- Beyond taking the precaution of developing strategic options, there is little that the individual organisation can do. There is an element of chance in whether it will survive or not.

15.3 The uncertainty-based strategic route forward

According to uncertainty-based strategists, Europe's telephone companies are wasting their time developing corporate strategies to cope with the events of the new millennium. They would argue that the environment is too uncertain and the outcomes largely unknown. Even striving for survival-based efficiency is useless. To understand the reasoning behind this, we need to examine the origins and thinking behind this approach.

15.3.1 Rationale

The key to understanding this route forward is its assumption about the purposes of most organisations: success will come from the ability of an organisation to survive by *innovating* and *transforming* itself.[13] Uncertainty-based strategists argue that it is not enough for most organisations simply to co-exist with others. In today's rapidly changing world, renewal and transformation towards new directions are key tasks for corporate strategy. To paraphrase the title of the strategy director at the mobile telephone company Orange, strategy is at least partially about 'imagineering and futurology' in an unknown world.[14]

Given this definition of success, the strategic process by which this is achieved will inevitably involve uncertainty. However, uncertainty can be modelled mathematically and its consequences set out in the science of *chaos theory*[15] – a system of modelling originally applied to scientific processes such as flow of liquid through a tube and subsequently to weather forecasting. The theory demonstrates that, in certain types of uncertain environment, *small* changes in the early stages of a process can lead to *major* variances in the later stages. This is not unlike the multiplier effect in macroeconomics.

In the classic strategy process, there is a mechanism of cause and effect that controls the dynamics of change. *Feedback* arises from an initial strategic decision, but goes *beyond* such a decision by multiplying its effects. *Uncertainty* is the unknown result of a strategic decision which may be affected by chance events along with those that are more predictable.

An example will help to clarify the concept. When the price of an item such as a telephone call is raised relative to competing products, the sales of the item are predicted to fall. According to uncertainty-based theory, this simple process may not represent the *full* outcome of events. The *feedback mechanism* suggests that the rise in telephone prices may not only affect sales but may also feed back into a lower level of loading at the telephone exchange. This may in turn influence the ability of the company to recover overheads from the exchange. Thus, the exchange loading, overheads and overall profitability may all be influenced by the one pricing decision. As soon as these items are affected adversely, there may be some attempt to recover profitability by a *further* price increase, i.e. the initial problem has fed back on itself. This will have a deleterious effect on the organisation, and so is usually referred to as *negative feedback*.

Conversely, in the above example, a reduction in price might have the opposite effect. It might cause profitability to rise more than the initial move in pricing, as a result of other consequences in the organisation. This is called *positive feedback*.

Uncertainty theory then adds another possibility. It can be proved mathematically that, where positive and negative feedback mechanisms operate, the system can *flip* between the positive and negative states. Importantly, it is not possible to predict in advance which of these three outcomes – that is, positive, negative or flip – will occur. The long-term consequences are therefore unknown and cannot be foreseen.

15.3.2 Consequences for the corporate strategy process

Uncertainty-based strategists argue that there is little to be gained by predicting the future, because virtually all strategy is composed of feedback mechanisms and involves uncertainty; therefore the outcome cannot be predicted. If the future is unknown, the effects of long-term strategic actions will also be unknown and the classical prescriptive process has little meaning.

This does not mean that uncertainty-based strategists believe that nothing can be done. They take the view, however, that actions should be much shorter-term in nature. Organisations must be able to learn and adapt to changed circumstances. Thus workers and managers in organisations are capable of assessing the results of their actions – in the example above, the effects of raising or lowering the price of telephone calls. They are also capable of learning to adapt to the consequences. More generally, for strategy purposes, they are capable of experimenting and innovating in the organisation and assessing the results of their work.

The implications of such theories are profound for corporate strategy. The majority of organisations need to innovate in order to survive and they exist in the increasingly turbulent world of the early twenty-first century, and yet uncertainty-based strategists would suggest that it is not possible to predict how innovation will succeed in the long term. According to these strategists, however, new ideas and new directions are necessary to survival and growth and should be pursued using the learning mechanisms mentioned above in order to refine and adapt strategies to a rapidly changing environment.

As an example of uncertainty-based strategy in action, you might like to consider the consequences of the launch of Sky television by News Corporation in 1990 and its later dominance of digital television broadcasting in the UK – *see* Case study 13.4. Such an outcome was clearly impossible to predict at the time of the launch. According to the uncertainty-based theorists, corporate strategy based on, for example, a prescriptive approach would have been largely irrelevant in these circumstances.

For the uncertainty-based strategist, long-term strategy is a contradiction in terms. The only possible objectives are short-term, possibly with a strong innovative content.[16] There is no point in undertaking environmental analysis because it is essentially unpredictable, but it is useful to understand the organisation's resources in order to assess their contribution to the innovative process. As for strategy options and selection, this has no relevance to the strategy process that actually occurs. What is important is the way the company is organised to learn and respond to its changing environment: loose, informal networks of managers are required, rather than rigid functional divisions. Exhibit 15.3 presents some of the implications suggested by Stacey.[17]

Exhibit 15.3   **Some practical implications of uncertainty for the corporate strategy process**

Basic objectives: develop new strategic directions and innovate.

Eight actions consistent with the uncertainty-based approach are:

1 Loosen control – let things happen.

2 Reconfigure power in groups to make them less competitive and more co-operative.

3 Allow groups to develop and set their own challenges, objectives and processes.

4 Encourage new organisational cultures in order to develop new perspectives.

5 Set open challenges ('Develop a new initiative in …') rather than defined objectives ('Your job is to double our profits in …').

6 Expose the business to demanding and challenging situations.

7 Spend time and resources developing the learning skills of groups in the organisation.

8 Develop time and space for managers to experiment.

Overall, there is no clear flow process, unlike in prescriptive strategy – only constant monitoring of the environment in order to take advantage of opportunities that occur. Table 15.5 makes a comparison between the prescriptive and uncertainty-based processes.

Comment

The approach may be useful when market conditions are turbulent, but it has few insights into some of the areas of strategic decision making, such as the short-term pressure to deliver profits or service. However, the approach is still in its early stages of development.

Table 15.5 Comparison of the uncertainty-based strategic route with the prescriptive process

Typical outline of the prescriptive model of the corporate strategy process	Uncertainty-based strategy process	Flow process
Mission and objectives	Short-term only: possibly some strategic intent with innovation as a stated aim	?
Environmental analysis	Unpredictable: waste of time	
Resources analysis	Important to be aware of internal factors but the analysis will not have the predictive thrust of the prescriptive approach	No clear flow process ?
Strategy options generation	Options generation is irrelevant since the outcomes are unknown and unpredictable	Chaotic only with constant monitoring of the environment
Strategy selection	Strategy selection is also irrelevant but spontaneous small groups and learning mechanisms might be involved in short-term selection	?
Implementation	Informal, destabilising networks are useful. It may also be worth holding some resources in reserve because of the unknown	Flexible response from informal groups depending on the opportunities that emerge

▶ Key strategic principles

- Renewal and transformation are vital aspects of strategy. Inevitably, they will involve uncertainty. Such uncertainty can be modelled mathematically. However, the long-term consequences are unknown and cannot be foreseen or usefully predicted.

- Uncertainty-based approaches therefore involve taking small steps forward. Management needs to learn from such actions and adapt accordingly.

- Because of the uncertainty about the future, strategy options and selection between them using the prescriptive approach are therefore irrelevant.

CASE STUDY 15.3

How GEC Marconi used game theory to make an extra US$3 billion

In a series of negotiations in late 1998, the UK company GEC Marconi sold its defence interests for US$12 billion – some US$3 billion more than they had been valued several months earlier. This case explains how it used strategic game theory to help structure the deal.

Background – worldwide consolidation in defence industries

With the end of the Cold War in the early 1990s, many world governments were keen to reduce their defence spending. Moreover, the cost of developing new defence weapons was continuing to rise. The result of falling sales and rising costs was pressure on the world's leading defence companies to merge and share the costs of development and production. The first merger moves came in the US, with a shake-out in the mid-1990s that produced three big players: Lockheed Martin, Boeing and Raytheon. Table 15.6 shows the contracts that the leading companies had with the US goverment in 1997. It should be noted that most companies also had civil (non-defence) contracts which are not listed in the table.

European defence industry: political background

Although some European companies had defence sales in the US, their largest sales were in Europe and

Table 15.6 Top US defence contractors in 1997 (value of contracts with the US Department of Defense, US$ billion)

Contractor	Value of contracts
Lockheed Martin	12.4
Boeing	10.9
Raytheon	6.5
Northrop Grumman	4.1
GEC	2.2
General Dynamics	2.1
United Technologies	1.9
Litton Industries	1.8
Science Applications	1.1
ITT	0.9

Source: Government Executive Magazine.

outside North America. All defence companies need to make sales outside their home markets because national territories provide insufficient revenue. The main customers are national governments so the tendency in Europe has been for combinations of such governments to commission new equipment: for example, the new European fighter aircraft involves the governments of the UK, Germany, Italy and Spain. France has had a long tradition of independent manufacture and sale and Sweden has also remained outside the usual consortia.

In the late 1990s, the three major European governments of Germany, France and the UK were keen to see consolidation in the European defence industry. There were three main reasons:

1 The US defence consolidation meant that US companies were well ahead of Europe in terms of the potential cost savings and rationalisation that were possible.

2 The European governments were determined as a matter of policy to ensure that their European defences were supplied by European-manufactured equipment. The alternative was that they would be reliant on the US which was strategically much weaker. This meant that it was vital to secure a continued defence manufacturing base in Europe.

3 Defence manufacture in Europe continued to employ large numbers of workers – roughly 1 million across the EU. It was important to preserve these jobs.

However, it should be noted that there was some cross-Atlantic defence co-operation. For example, GEC itself was able to acquire the US defence company Tracor in 1998 for US$1.4 billion and become the fifth-largest contractor to the US government. Equally, the main US companies all had some manufacturing facilities in Europe, even though some were for civil rather than military use.

In 1997, Germany, France and the UK began to put pressure on their respective companies to combine. However, apart from the French government, they did not own the companies so their direct negotiating power was limited.

European defence industry: company perspectives

Naturally, the defence companies themselves could also see the case for consolidation. From their perspective, the issue was not whether this should be done, but how. During the course of 1997–98, a series of discussions and negotiations were undertaken amongst the leading players. Virtually any combination was possible but some companies

Table 15.7 The main companies in the European defence industry

British Aerospace	UK
GEC Marconi	UK
Deutsche Aerospace: Dasa	Germany
Aerospatiale	France
Dassault	France
Thomson-CSF	France
Matra (subsidiary of Lagardère)	France
Casa	Spain
Alenia	Italy
Agusta	Italy
Saab	Sweden

already had minority stakes or strong technical links with others – useful but not conclusive. The main players are shown in Table 15.7. However, there were three companies that would have to be involved if the final concept of a consolidated European defence company was to be achieved: British Aerospace, Dasa and Aerospatiale.

British Aerospace, Dasa and Aerospatiale: core companies in any European defence consolidation?

These three companies already co-operated on the European Airbus – *see* Case study 5.3 – and were thus used to working together. The aerospace activities of each were roughly of equal size in terms of turnover and numbers employed – *see* Table 15.8. But they each had very different ownership structures which made combination difficult. British Aerospace had been privatised many years earlier and its shares were widely held. Dasa was still a subsidiary of the German/US DaimlerChrysler car company and it had no separate share quotation at all. Aerospatiale was majority owned by the French government but being prepared for privatisation so that it could form part of a larger European company. The main effect of such ownership variations was to complicate any negotiations and therefore slow them down.

Nevertheless, British Aerospace had entered into detailed discussions with Dasa during 1998. There was a strong willingness to combine the two companies and agreement had been reached on many issues, including the combined company split

Table 15.8 Three main players in European consolidation

Daimler-Benz Aerospace (Dasa): Germany	Aerospatiale: France	British Aerospace: UK
Ownership: 100% DaimlerChrysler by parent	Ownership: French government 48%, Lagardère 30%, private shareholders the rest	Ownership: private, quoted on London Stock Market. The best profit record of the three leading players
Sales 1997: US$7.7 billion	Sales 1997: US$11.6 billion	Sales 1997: US$12.8 billion
Number of employees: 43 500	Number of employees: 56 000	Number of employees: 43 000
Partner in Airbus and Eurofighter. Also produces other military and civil aircraft, space systems, satellites and electronic systems.	Partner in Airbus but no pan-European defence interests. Also produces satellites, missiles, space systems. Owns 46% of Dassault, which produces Mirage and Rafaele fighter aircraft.	Partner in Airbus and Eurofighter. Also produces other military and civil aircraft, missiles, electronic systems, munitions; 36% share in Saab, Sweden. Also links with Alenia, Italy.

of 60 per cent to British Aerospace and 40 per cent to Dasa. By December 1998, the main sticking point was the problem that such an ownership split would have given effective control to Dasa: the fragmented shareholdings in British Aerospace would have meant that Dasa was the largest single shareholder.

However, operating in parallel with this unresolved battle was a related strategy from GEC Marconi – and this company had its own objective.

GEC Marconi: UK

When George Simpson took over as the chief executive of the GEC Group in 1996, he decided that it needed to have greater worldwide market share in a limited number of ventures. Up to that time, the company had been involved in a whole range of ventures, some of which were profitable, but they were all rather disparate. For example, it was involved in the manufacture of petrol vending machines, computer printers and power generation equipment. It also owned the large defence electronics company GEC Marconi. Simpson and his colleagues decided that the group needed more focus so it disposed of its shareholdings in some companies and concentrated on others, such as those producing telecommunications equipment.

Initially, the group decided to develop GEC Marconi. In 1998, as part of this strategy, it acquired the US defence company Tracor for US$1.4 billion. This made it one of the largest defence contractors in the US (*see* Table 15.6) and raised its ambitions for further developments. It began discussions with the French defence electronics company Thomson-CSF but the acquisition was blocked by the French government. As it cast around for further growth in the worldwide defence market, it made a fundamental strategic decision: either it would grow larger or it would exit the industry with a good price for its company. By mid-1998, it was again in discussions with Thomson-CSF but it had also opened up negotiations with British Aerospace, Northrop Grumman and Lockheed.

At least, it *said* that it was in discussion with these companies but there may have been an element of bargaining in this signal to the market. The purpose of such announcements would have been to make the real targets, British Aerospace and Thomson-CSF, more anxious to complete a deal. In fact, by late 1998, the GEC Group was using game

theory to operate a special strategy called Project Superbowl. The object was to sort out GEC Marconi. It knew that its subsidiary was valued at US$9 billion and entered into discussion with this as the minimum price. From these negotiations, it became clear that British Aerospace and Dasa were close to doing a deal. The GEC Group realised that this would substantially weaken its negotiating position because GEC Marconi would then become a much smaller player in a larger pool. Thus George Simpson decided to sell GEC Marconi to the highest bidder while the company still had real negotiating power. It gave the story to the *Financial Times* which ran the headline:

> BAE given ultimatum over Marconi: GEC sets end-of-week deadline for bid as other companies signal interest in defence electronics arm.

After further discussion, GEC Marconi was sold to British Aerospace for US$12 billion five days later in January 1999.

British Aerospace: also a game player

What the GEC Group did not know was that British Aerospace was also using strategic game theory to plot its moves in the consolidation battle. It had worked out that by combining with GEC Marconi it was able to ensure that it had a dominant interest in any further consolidation that would then take place. Moreover, it expected any subsequent moves towards consolidation to be more limited as a result. For these reasons, it was willing to pay rather more than the initial valuation of GEC Marconi – US$3 billion more, to be precise.

Outcomes – not always predicted by game theory!

After the deal was agreed, European governments were not very happy because the solution was a purely UK affair. However, British Aerospace took the view that this problem could be sorted out later. Its market position was enhanced by its new acquisition, even after paying an extra US$3 billion.

After divesting its defence interests, GEC was renamed Marconi. It went on to acquire a whole series of telecommunications equipment companies during 2000 and 2001 – just before the market for telecommunications equipment went into steep decline. By mid-2002, GEC had used up its extra US$3 billion and was in deep trouble – both

▶

the chairman, George Simpson, and all his senior colleagues were forced to resign.

Source: See reference 18.

Case questions

1 *What are the strengths and weaknesses of using game theory to plot this strategic battle?*

2 *To what extent were other negotiations involved that went beyond game theory? Were these significant?*

3 *What lessons can we draw from the case on the usefulness of game theory in strategy development?*

15.4 The negotiation-based strategic route forward

Even after British Aerospace completed its acquisition of GEC Marconi (*see* Case study 15.3), it is important from a strategy perspective to see this as only the beginning of a new phase in European defence industry consolidation. Further developments will involve *negotiation* inside British Aerospace and between that company and others involved in the defence industry. The purpose of such negotiations will be to extract the full added value from the takeover and any others that subsequently occur, while at the same time developing the sustainable competitive advantage of the enlarged company. However, the strategic context suggests that it is likely that there will be a need for increased global consolidation in defence industries. Thus the takeover process at British Aerospace needs to include at least three areas of negotiation:

1 *Inside the newly enlarged British Aerospace* – with groups of workers and managers in particular functions. They may see their interests threatened or enhanced by the new larger parent and react accordingly. This is the human-resource-based element of negotiation strategy discussed below.

2 *Outside the merged British Aerospace/Marconi* – with customers, suppliers and competitors. They will see the balance of competitive advantage altered in the industry with new threats and opportunities for added value. This is the *network-based* element of negotiation strategy discussed below.

3 *Outside the merged British Aerospace with other defence companies* – through a totally new phase of consolidation between those involved in the industry. This might entail British Aerospace combining its resources in the long term with Dasa and Aerospatiale. It might even consider merging its interests with one or more of the US independent defence companies such as Grumman or Northrop. The discussions that might take place are explored in the *game-based* element of negotiation strategy discussed below.

The need to develop strategy through negotiation-based routes involves considerations both inside and outside the organisation. The theoretical background can be considered in terms of three main conceptual areas:

1 *human resource strategy*, which attempts to structure the negotiation between people needed for strategic decisions and mainly inside organisations;

2 *network-based strategy*, which explores the degree of co-operation and competition present in related organisations and industries;

3 *game theory strategy*, which examines the way that the actual strategic negotiations are conducted and suggests some guidelines for taking optimal strategic decisions.

These three elements are explored separately in the sections that follow. However, they are in fact aspects of the same negotiation-based strategic route forward. Each area makes the simplifying assumption that the other two areas do not exist: strategy writers usually concentrate on one strategic approach and make no reference to other aspects of the task. Importantly, each of the three areas above arises from a separate academic tradition – respectively, human resources, microeconomics and economic mathematical modelling – so it is difficult to bring them together.

15.4.1 Rationale: human resource strategy

Back in the 1960s, research showed the importance of coalitions and groups in organisations.[19] They may have some interests that are the same as those stated by the organisation but other interests will not necessarily coincide. Typically, groups and individuals negotiate with each other inside a company and arrive at a compromise on important issues, including aspects of corporate strategy. For example, in the acquisition of the UK mobile telephone company Orange by France Telecom in 2000, this was only achieved after compromises on the nature, power and status of the managers employed in the acquisition. The key point is that it may be difficult for senior management simply to define the precise combined strategy in advance because of the need for some form of negotiation. This process may involve 'policy side payments' between the various interested groups and is undertaken in exchange for agreement to the strategy: 'If we support you on this then will you support us in our negotiations?' Moss Kanter[20] provides graphic detail of how departments negotiate with each other in US companies. From a prescriptive strategy perspective, the negotiation process means that simple objectives such as profit maximisation are subject to the reality of the politics of the organisation.

Over the period 1960–80, the UK chemical company ICI needed to change its strategies to cope with an environment which had changed radically. However, the company was large and bureaucratic, with a range of experienced and intelligent senior managers and groups who had vested interests in the current strategies. For example, some faced the loss of their jobs if the new strategy proposals were implemented. Pettigrew researched the long human resource process that was required to obtain the changes:[21]

> *This kind of process management also necessitated patience and perseverance; waiting for people to retire to exploit any policy vacuum so created; introducing known sympathisers as replacements for known sceptics or opponents; using succession occasions to combine portfolios and responsibilities and integrate thought and action in an otherwise previously factious and deadlocked area of change; backing off and waiting, or moving the pressure point for change into another area when continuing downright opposition might have endangered the success of the whole exercise.*

The point here is that, according to such strategists, this is not something added on to strategy after it has been formulated but is part of the strategy itself. As stated in Chapter 7, Section 7.5, *strategy is the art of the possible*. Thus rational decisions on markets, finance or products are deeply influenced by the social and political texture of the firm. Corporate strategy is not a simple unemotional process but is, in fact, interpreted by managers and groups of workers according to their own frames of reference, their particular motivations and information.[22] The *limits* to managerial action are just as important to strategic decisions as the ability to choose any strategy option. In case this might be regarded as only a UK phenomenon, it is worth pointing to the difficulties companies in Germany, such as Daimler-Benz and Volkswagen, had during the late 1990s in restructuring their workforces against low-cost EU and global competition.

15.4.2 Rationale: network-based strategy

Network-based strategy refers to the value-adding relationships that organisations develop *inside* their own organisation and *outside* it with other organisations. For example, European telecommunications companies have their own telephone exchange resources and employees that generate profits. In addition, they compete with each other in some national European telephone markets while, at the same time, developing co-operative linkages with other telephone companies in global markets. It is this complex web of internal and external activities that constitutes the network and delivers added value to the organisation.

From a strategic perspective, the issue is how to optimise the value added from such internal and external activities. As a starting point, we can refer to the two principles explored in Chapter 6:

1 *The benefits of owning and managing resources, rather than buying them in from outside.*[23] This can be used to identify the important relationships that organisations have both inside and outside their own organisation.

2 *The value chain and value linkages.*[24] The chain provides a picture of networks inside the organisation and the linkages do the same for the outside relationships.

In order to develop network-based strategy, these general principles need to be used to map out the networks that exist in and with every organisation. A largely prescriptive approach to this task is shown in Exhibit 15.4.

Exhibit 15.4   **How networks can add value to the organisation**

From *internal networks*, value added can be increased by:

- economies of scale and scope;
- development of superior, even unique, knowledge and technologies;
- investment in customer service, marketing and reputation;
- skills, knowledge and expertise in cash handling, financial transactions and other financial instruments.

From *external networks*, value added can be increased by:

- cost-effective logistics, stock handling and other outside transport facilities;
- superior purchasing from suppliers;
- skilled external sourcing of new technical developments, licensing of new technologies and other technical advances;
- strong and stable relationships with government and other influential organisations.

Note that these are only examples of the many networks that exist in and between organisations.

As a result of optimising value added, network-based strategic approaches also influence sustainable competitive advantage. For example, at the European telephone companies, those with superior value-added activities, based on an attractive combination of keen prices and high-quality service, are also likely to be able to compete strongly with competitors: high profits are likely to be associated with sustainable competitive advantage. However, such a combination of price and service will probably also derive, at least in part, from the valuable co-operative linkages that such superior companies have with others.

In more general economic terms, the 'invisible hand' of market competition should drive companies to greater efficiency in the use of their internal resources. At the same time, the 'visible hand' of co-operative linkages will generate real, and perhaps unique, external networks and value for organisations. In a sense, networks rely both on invisible and visible guidance in the generation and maintenance of relationships – a relationship more like a 'continuous handshake' than an intermittent hand clasp.[25]

Thus in network-based strategy, value is added and competitive advantage is developed by the precise *combination* of competition and co-operation that organisations have with others. As a result, organisations will construct a unique network of relationships both inside and outside their own organisation. For example, over time salespeople may strike up relationships with customers, purchasing managers with suppliers and so on. Long-term relationships with outsiders may be a crucial element of the company's strategy, as those in the aerospace, defence, telecommunications equipment and other industries negotiating with government will quickly confirm.

Negotiation is a vital strategic aspect of such relationships and the process becomes effectively one of the key determinants of success. Thus, for example, in the case of mobile telephones, governments may well be involved in the purchase or specification of such items. More generally, direct government control may be achieved by access to preferential credit, joint ownership, a threat to call in new suppliers, the allocation of R&D contracts and assistance in export sales.[26] Developing corporate strategy without negotiating with a government may be an expensive luxury. The bargaining power that each side has in such negotiations will depend on the maturity of the market and the technology involved.

In many respects, therefore, the organisation can be seen as a *network of treaties* both outside and inside the company.[27] Moreover, if such agreements are important for the development of strategy, then it follows that it is important to understand the dynamics of these networks in order to develop optimal strategy.[28] Because of the sheer complexity of this task, it may be better to use critical success factors to focus attention on the important areas of the process (*see* Chapter 3).

Comment

Some strategists argue that what matters is not the *combination* of competitive and co-operative networks but the *primacy* of one or the other:

- either competitive relationships are paramount: 'The essence of strategy formulation is coping with competition', according to Professor Michael Porter;[29]
- or co-operative networks represent the main scope for strategic development: 'The realisation is growing that cooperative behaviour is at the root of many success stories in today's management', to quote J Carlos Jarillo.[30]

Such a choice is profoundly misleading.[31] All organisations both compete and co-operate and there is no 'strategic paradox' between these two that needs to be resolved. The only issue is the *balance* between the two. This will depend on the context within which the strategy is being developed. For example, in the European telephone companies in the late 1990s, *competition* was the main driving force. It was increasing inside countries like the UK and Germany, though co-operation was also important in providing international telephone networks. By contrast, in the European defence industry in the late 1990s, increased *co-operation* was being developed on a pan-European basis in order to allow European companies to compete more successfully in the global market place against the big US defence companies.

15.4.3 Rationale: game-based strategy

In the negotiation process, the successful acquisition of a large contract, such as the takeover of GEC Marconi by British Aerospace, may be crucial to the profitability or even the survival of the organisation. This has increasingly become the case in the former public sector as more industries, such as the telephone companies, have been privatised. During the 1940s, mathematical models were first developed to handle in a structured way the commercial decisions that are involved: they are known under the general title of *game theory*.[32] Game-based theory is concerned with the immediate negotiation and its related strategy: it says little or nothing about the implementation stages that follow once the negotiation has been concluded. Game theory has two clear advantages for strategy development:

1 It clarifies the *nature of the negotiation*, identifying the players, setting out their options, identifying the outcomes of each option and the sequence of events that need to take place.

2 It can predict the *optimal outcomes of some games*, particularly by permitting the manipulation of the payoffs to the players. It does this by providing insights into the nature of the relationships that exist between players, including the identification of the competitors and co-operators.[33]

Game theory attempts to predict competitor reactions in the negotiating situation. The circumstances may be regarded as being similar to a game of chess, where anticipation of the opponent's moves is an important aspect of the challenge. Much of game theory has been modelled mathematically, with the rules specifying how the scarce resources of the company can be employed and what benefits will be obtained by particular moves or a combination of moves – the benefits are often called *payoffs*.[34]

● In a *zero-sum game*, there is ultimately no payoff because the gains of one member are negated by the losses of another.

● In a *co-operative game*, the benefits may add up to a positive payoff for all.

● In a *negative-sum game*, the actions of each party undermine both themselves and their opponents.

Although game theory has provided a useful basis for structuring negotiations and the consequences of each move, it has proved difficult to model strategic options and decisions which are often highly complex and interrelated. Probably the most interesting strategic insights provided by game theory are in the likely outcomes of various stages of the negotiation process. For example, when British Aerospace was negotiating the restructuring of the European defence industry, it used game theory to show that it was useful to acquire GEC Marconi for two reasons:

1 The increased size gave it much greater influence on the final shape of the pan-European consolidation game.

2 The acquisition reduced the number of options available in the industry, thus lowering the number of moves that it would take to achieve the consolidation required.

Given these advantages, the issue is how to make use of game theory to analyse and conduct competitive strategic games. There are six essential steps in what is essentially a prescriptive process; these are shown in Exhibit 15.5.

Exhibit 15.5

Game theory: six steps to playing strategic games in the European defence industry

Step 1

Identify the players. It is important to identify the potential as well as the actual players in any game. The main players are listed in the European defence industry case, but the Americans are excluded (perhaps unwisely).

Step 2

Analyse their strengths and weaknesses. Include potential links to outside influencers and complementors – see Chapter 3. For the European defence industry, some pointers are given in Case study 15.3 but more information would be needed in practice.

Step 3

Establish the extent to which the game will be played with sequential or simultaneous moves. In practice, most games are played with both. The significance of this analysis lies in its consequences for the way that the game will develop:

● Sequential moves mean that one of the players acts and then another responds, e.g. a game of golf or serving in tennis.

● Simultaneous moves mean that the players act without knowing what action the others are taking at the same time, e.g. a swimming tournament.

In the European defence industry, there were some simultaneous negotiations taking place – for example, between Dasa, British Aerospace and GEC Marconi. But once the British Aerospace bid for GEC Marconi had been tabled, the others backed off and it became sequential.

The next step depends on whether simultaneous or sequential moves represent the main way forward.

Step 4A: Sequential moves only

For sequential moves, plot out the consequences of each move – often called a game tree – and choose the best outcome. Then reason backwards from this on the best way to achieve this outcome.

At the time of writing on the European defence industry, the immediate best outcome for British Aerospace had been established. However, other companies would be plotting their next moves – for example, Dasa was signalling that it was willing to consider combining with a US company, but this may have been bluff.

Step 4B: Simultaneous moves only

For simultaneous moves, plot out all the possible outcomes in the form of a table – often called a payoff table – and then undertake the following in order:

1 Identify any *dominant* strategy, i.e. one that is clearly better than the competition. If one can be found, play it.

2 If no dominant strategy can be found, identify any *dominated* strategy, i.e. one that is clearly worse than the competition. If it can be identified, eliminate it from further analysis.

3 If there is no dominant or dominated strategy, seek other outcomes – often called a *Nash Equilibrium* – that represent each player's best judgement of its own interests. Essentially, here, each player understands the strategies of the opponent but cannot improve on his or her own position by making an alternative choice.

In the case of British Aerospace, the dominant strategy was clearly to become larger than its competitors. By this means, it was able to improve its negotiating position in subsequent negotiation moves. The best move for Aerospatiale might then be to become equally large through a merger with one of its French rivals such as Thompson-CSF or Dassault. Notice here that the best move for one company might not be the best for another.

Step 5

Consider how to signal moves to the other players. The best play may not be an open bidding process against an opponent because this invites an aggressive direct response which may be expensive. Even in simultaneous games, a better outcome may be possible if players are not presented with simple stark choices – many supposedly impossible games can be solved by allowing the players to signal to each other.

In the European defence industry at the time of writing, many signals were being made to other players. Companies were expressing their willingness to consider further consolidation, but on their own terms.

Step 6

Begin playing. It is vital to reassess the status of the game and its outcomes because the essence of the game is that it will alter as it progresses.

The *Appendix* at the end of this chapter provides some more detail.

More generally, the mechanics and logical decision-making aspects of game theory are well represented in the various theoretical descriptions. But they say little about other vital aspects of most strategic negotiations. The leadership of the teams involved, the personalities and cultures of their members, the ambitions and the history of the players are not covered at all. The strategic context in which negotiations are taking place can lead to consequences that go well beyond the mathematics of game theory. For example, in the European defence industry case, the various personalities of the leading chief executives and their other responsibilities influenced the outcome of the game: George Simpson was determined to sort out the GEC Group that he had inherited while Jürgen Schrempp at Daimler was preoccupied with the massive merger with Chrysler.

To capture some of these practical complexities of negotiation, the *negotiation checklist* at the end of the chapter has been constructed. Readers may care to note that it can be used not only for acquisitions but for many other negotiation situations, including personal strategies. There are four aspects of game theory in the checklist that are worth highlighting here:

1 *Viewpoint of the game.* It is important to assess the game not just from one player's perspective of the outcome. It is essential to gauge what rivals expect to take out of the game and possibly make some attempt to accommodate this.

2 *Rewrite the rules of the game.* The outcome of some games can be altered by totally rewriting the way that the game is played, even part-way through the game. In this sense, game theory is not like chess or football. This can provide a real opportunity.

3 *Reassessment of the game.* It is usually worth reconsidering whether a game is worth pursuing part of the way through the game. Some negotiations can simply be a waste of time and resources.

4 *Reassurance about the final outcome.* In any game, even where there are multiple winners, it is worth remembering that people are involved. Players need to be reassured after the outcome that it was the best that could be achieved.

Comment

There are three main problems with game theory in negotiation-based strategy:[35]

1 The mathematical complexity makes the analytical results useful but limited. Moreover, it assumes that a dynamic and interacting environment can be modelled by a series of static equilibria. This is a dangerously simple approximation of reality.

2 Many of its conclusions, especially about Nash equilibria, are ambiguous and based on a narrow view of context. For example, game theory largely excludes all psychological insight. Game theory has so far proved incapable of handling the many complexities of real business situations.

3 Importantly, game theory focuses on a small fraction of the strategic process. For example, it provides no insight whatsoever into the development of the competitive resources of the organisation, nor any useful guidance on the massive task of implementing whatever has been negotiated.

15.4.4 Consequences of all these aspects for corporate strategy

Essentially, nothing is fixed and everything is open to negotiation. Therefore, objectives may need to be revised and selection may be compromised by the need to persuade groups to adopt a particular route. In a sense, the implementation process itself is now part of the selection process and part of the strategy.

Table 15.9 illustrates the major implications of such a negotiation-based route forward. It should be noted that the timetable for any strategic change may need to be lengthened to accommodate this process. It is not possible to show this adequately in the table.

Comment

There can be little doubt that politics and negotiations are a part of many organisations, both large and small. However, there is still a need to drive the strategy process forward. This is where *leadership* is probably vital. Negotiation-based strategies are unlikely to represent a complete route in themselves, but need to take place alongside prescriptive and learning-based strategy processes.

Table 15.9 Comparison of the negotiation-based process with the prescriptive process

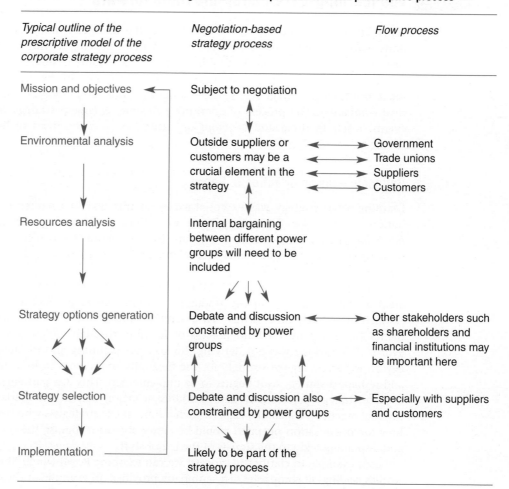

Typical outline of the prescriptive model of the corporate strategy process	Negotiation-based strategy process	Flow process
Mission and objectives	Subject to negotiation	
Environmental analysis	Outside suppliers or customers may be a crucial element in the strategy	Government Trade unions Suppliers Customers
Resources analysis	Internal bargaining between different power groups will need to be included	
Strategy options generation	Debate and discussion constrained by power groups	Other stakeholders such as shareholders and financial institutions may be important here
Strategy selection	Debate and discussion also constrained by power groups	Especially with suppliers and customers
Implementation	Likely to be part of the strategy process	

> ▶ **Key strategic principles**
>
> - Negotiation-based strategies emphasise the need to persuade colleagues and outside stakeholders. Coalitions and groups play an important part in strategy development.
>
> - Such a strategic approach also needs to be seen in the context of negotiations with powerful customers and suppliers where bargaining and trade-offs will take place.
>
> - Game theory attempts to predict the outcomes of customer reactions or, in some cases, to show how the outcome of negotiations may well produce a suboptimal solution unless both sides of the negotiations realise the consequences of their actions.
>
> - Game theory has some value in negotiations but suffers from three difficulties: mathematical complexity; ambiguous conclusions; being only one small part of the strategy process.

15.5 The learning-based strategic route forward

When there is considerable uncertainty, as in the European mobile telecommunications market, it may not be possible or prudent to develop a strategy that is firmly fixed for some years ahead. It may be better to have some basic business objectives, possibly even a vision of the future (*see* Chapter 10), but also be prepared to experiment and react to market events. These might include the launch or disappearance of rival companies. The process of adopting a flexible, emergent strategy that monitors events, reacts to them and develops opportunities is at the heart of learning-based strategies.

15.5.1 Rationale – the contribution of Senge

Learning-based strategy was explored earlier in this text in Chapter 11. The contribution of Professor Peter Senge was to extend the learning concept from the *individual* as a learning unit to the group. To understand this contribution, we begin by reviewing the main elements of the emergent strategy process and the theory of learning.

In a persuasive article in 1987, Mintzberg argued that the rational analysis of such areas as markets and company resources was unlikely to produce effective strategy. A much more likely process was that of *crafting strategy* where 'formulation and implementation merge into a fluid process of learning through which creative strategies evolve'.[36] Mintzberg was not denying the need for planning and formulation of strategy. However, he argued strongly for the flexibility that comes from learning to shape and reshape a strategy as it begins to be implemented. This was particularly important because strategy occasionally had to address a major shift in the market place or in internal practice – a *quantum leap*. At such a time, those strategists who had really *learnt* how the organisation operated would be better able to recognise the need for change and respond quickly to the signals of the major shift.

As an example to clarify the process, we can examine Royal Dutch/Shell, one of the world's leading oil companies. The company provided an example of the quantum leap and the learning process during the 1980s.[37] In 1984, oil was priced around US$28 per barrel. Against this background, the company's central planning department developed a speculative scenario based on the price dropping to US$16 per barrel. Purely as an exercise, they urged senior management to speculate on the consequences of such a radical price drop. Some senior managers felt it was unlikely but were willing to enter into the spirit of the exercise. The consequences were explored well enough so that, when the price actually dropped to US$10 per barrel in 1987, the company was well prepared.

One of Royal Dutch/Shell's leading planners later concluded:

> *Institutional learning is the process whereby management teams change their shared mental models of their company, their markets and their competitors. For this reason, we think of planning as learning and of corporate planning as institutional learning.*

The key words here are *change their shared mental models* and the process of *learning*. Most companies explore strategic issues not just as individuals but also as a management team or group that meets together. It is this *group* that develops assumptions about the company and its environment: these need to be made explicit and shared. These may then need to be changed, depending on the circumstances – for example, a quantum leap as mentioned above.

Back in the 1970s, Professor Christopher Argyris of the Harvard Business School developed the concept of *double-loop learning* that was to prove highly influential in learning approaches to strategy development.[38] Essentially, it involved not only learning by comparison with accepted standards but also questioning the standards themselves (Section 11.1.4 has a fuller explanation). In 1990, Peter Senge, Professor of Organisational Systems and Learning at the Massachusetts Institute of Technology, employed the learning principles but added to them significantly by using operations research feedback mechanisms and by suggesting that the most powerful learning was by *groups or teams*, not individuals. He applied the group learning concept to strategy development, referring to:

> *[t]he Learning Organization...where people continually expand their capacity to create the results they truly desire, where new and expansive patterns of thinking are nurtured, where collective aspiration is set free and where people are continually learning how to learn together.*[39]

Senge argued that such knowledge was best acquired by setting interesting and challenging targets and by encouraging group interaction. These ideas move strategy generation on from simply searching for simple, prescriptive solutions. A key point of Senge's text was that strategy development involved the knowledge creation process, which was best undertaken by groups. The aim was to develop a new 'mental model' of an issue through the group dynamic.

There are a number of well-recognised mechanisms for developing and sharing mental models as part of the learning process.[40] Probably the best known of these are the five learning disciplines of Peter Senge.[41] They are crafted to help organisations and individuals learn. However, *learning* here does not mean memory work or even merely coping with a changing environment. Learning has a more positive and proactive meaning: *active creativity* to develop new strategies and opportunities. The five learning disciplines developed to achieve this are summarised in Exhibit 15.6.

Exhibit 15.6   **The five learning disciplines**

1 *Personal mastery* – not only developing personal goals but also creating the organisational environment that encourages groups to develop goals and purposes

2 *Mental models* – reflecting and speculating upon the pictures that managers and workers have of the world and seeing how these influence actions and decisions

3 *Shared vision* – building commitment in the group to achieve its aims by exploring and agreeing what these aims are

4 *Team learning* – using the group's normal skills to develop intelligence and ability beyond individuals' normal abilities

5 *Systems thinking* – a method of thinking about, describing and understanding the major forces that influence the group

Source: Based on the writings of Peter Senge.

To survive in today's turbulent business climate, it has been argued that strategy must include mechanisms that transfer learning from the individual to the group.[42] There are then three advantages from the learning process for the group and for the whole organisation:

1 It will provide fresh ideas and insights into the organisation's performance through a commitment to knowledge.

2 Adaptation through renewal will be promoted so organisations do not stultify and wither.

3 It will promote an openness to the outside world so that it can respond to events – for example, the quantum change of an oil price shock or the rapid developments in the European mobile telephone market.

It is often the well-educated, highly committed senior professional in an organisation who has the most difficulty with this process.[43] Such an individual may misunderstand the meaning of the word 'learning' and interpret it too narrowly as being purely about problem solving. It may also not be understood that the *process* of learning is about more than just instructions from the teacher or the senior management. The implications for corporate strategy are that learning is a two-way process and is more open-ended than prescriptive strategy would suggest.

15.5.2 Consequences for the corporate strategy process

In the learning process, the concept of 'top-down' management handing semi-finished objectives to the more junior managers and employees clearly carries no meaning. Generative learning needs to have a greater element of co-operation and discussion. Nevertheless, the analytical element of the process can proceed, though perhaps more openly and with more people involved. This will inevitably slow it down but it may be a small price to pay for the greater commitment achieved and the alternative insights on strategy from group members. Strategy options and selection are still conceivable but the process may be more complex and multilayered than the prescriptive route. However, it is clearly possible that the implementation phase may actually be faster because people will be better informed and more committed to strategies that they themselves have helped to form.[44]

Table 15.10 outlines the main elements of the learning-based process. The key point is that the learning process itself is part of the strategy, not something added after the strategy has been developed. This means that the fully developed strategy only emerges over time.

Comment

The learning-based route has real value in the development of corporate strategy. However, it has to be said that it is sometimes vague and non-operational in its proposals, beyond the need to consult everyone. Moreover, there is still a need in some circumstances for senior managers to take decisions *without* consultation (*see* Case study 14.1 on Nokia and Case study 16.3 on Asea Brown Boveri). More generally, *how* and *when* organisations should adopt the learning-based approach has been the basis for fully justified criticism of this route forward.[45] In spite of these weaknesses, the route does not preclude the use of the prescriptive process. It will be explored further in later chapters of this book.

Table 15.10 Comparison of the learning-based process with the prescriptive process

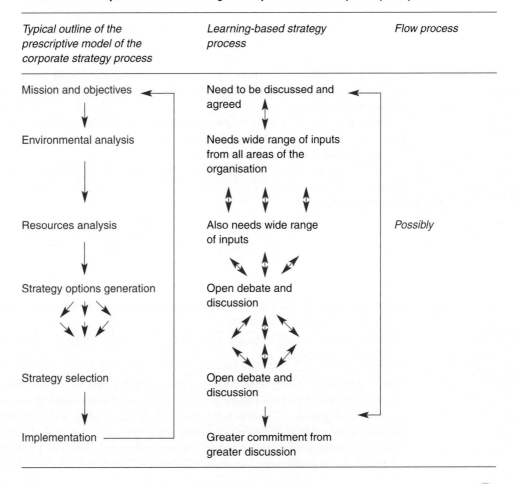

Typical outline of the prescriptive model of the corporate strategy process	Learning-based strategy process	Flow process
Mission and objectives	Need to be discussed and agreed	
Environmental analysis	Needs wide range of inputs from all areas of the organisation	
Resources analysis	Also needs wide range of inputs	*Possibly*
Strategy options generation	Open debate and discussion	
Strategy selection	Open debate and discussion	
Implementation	Greater commitment from greater discussion	

▶ **Key strategic principles**

- Learning-based strategy emphasises the importance of flexibility in developing unique strategies. It suggests that group dynamics are more important than individuals in developing new, experimental strategies.

- Learning is not concerned with memory work, but with active creativity in developing new strategic opportunities. There are five principles to group learning: personal mastery, group mental models, share vision, team learning and systems thinking.

- It has real value as a concept but is vague and lacks operational guidance in practice.

15.6 International considerations

Differences around the world in cultures, social values and economic traditions mean it is possible that some strategy processes may be difficult, if not impossible, to introduce and manage in certain countries. For example, the learning process of Section 15.5 requires a relaxed and open relationship between superior and subordinate that is available in some northern European countries but much more rare in Malaysia and India.[46] Some writers have promoted the idea of the *borderless world* and the *global corporation*. Undoubtedly, in terms of common customer tastes and sourcing of production, there are real commonalities, but in terms of the strategy process, which is more detailed and requires more commitment, real differences still exist.[47]

International considerations may impact on the strategy process during every stage. However, they do not influence the process in a single, consistent fashion. Thus there is no 'international strategy process'.

15.6.1 Stakeholders

As we have seen, stakeholders and their relative power vary throughout the world: shareholders, employees, managers, financial institutions, governments and other interested groups. Importantly, their ability to influence the strategy process will also vary:

- In some areas of the Far East and Africa, government influence will be important in guiding strategy development.

- In the UK and North America, shareholders are often given the first consideration in developing strategy.

These differences have arisen for historic, cultural and economic reasons. In each country, different sets of values, expectations and beliefs will influence the strategic process: companies may not hold the simple economic, rational views that have been used to guide strategic processes in some Western countries. The influences may be more complex and embedded in culture and social values.[48] Explicit awareness of stakeholders' expectations is an important part of the strategic process.

15.6.2 Mission and objectives

Strategic goals and processes are likely to reflect the social systems of the country in which the strategy is developed. Thus, the missions and objectives of companies need to be seen in the context of their countries of origin. However, it should be recognised that even within countries there will be major variations in ambitions, ideas and values. The importance of socio-cultural elements should, therefore, not be overemphasised. As Whittington commented: 'Societies are too complex and people too individualistic to expect bland uniformity.'[49]

15.6.3 Environment

In one sense, the international environment is the same for all companies: they will all be subject to the same trends in economic growth as they compete in world markets, the same major shifts in political power and the same social changes and technological developments. However, because the *base country* of the stakeholders may differ, their responses to and expectations of environmental changes may give rise to major variations in strategy. For example, the mid-1990s saw a significant rise of the Japanese yen against the US dollar: the impact of this environmental change on the world car industry is entirely different, depending on the base country of the stakeholders. Japanese car companies have suffered and US car companies benefited.[50]

15.6.4 Options and choice

The whole concept of the rational choice between options may be Western, even Anglo-American, in its cultural and social background. For example, some cultures place more emphasis on preordained fate as an important element of life, including business matters. If events are decided by fate, then this may significantly influence the options and choice process.[51]

Options and choice also require some basic agreement on the *method* and *criteria* by which they will be discussed and judged. These are also culture-specific, as one researcher has described:[52]

- *Anglo-Saxon* style is comfortable with open debate about different perspectives, and sees compromise as the best outcome from disagreement.

- *Teutons and Gauls* both like to debate but prefer to undertake this with those from the same intellectual and social backgrounds. This makes for less antagonism but for a more limited exposure to different expectations. Teutons then seek rigour in the debate before the elegance of the theories, whereas the Gauls take the reverse viewpoint, preferring the aesthetic nature of the argument itself rather than the conclusion.

- *Japanese* do not debate, partly because they have no tradition and partly because of a desire not to upset the social relationships that have already been established.

It is perhaps not surprising that there are problems when it comes to operating strategic decision-making processes across international boundaries.

> **Key strategic principles**

- International considerations may impact on the strategy process during every stage. The ability of stakeholders to influence the process will vary from country to country for historical, political and cultural reasons.

- The mission and objectives are likely to be rooted in the social and cultural systems of the country in which the strategy is developed. The environment may also be important to another aspect of strategy development: the *home country* of an organisation will influence the way in which its international strategy is developed and managed.

- Options and choice in the selection process will be governed by the culture and social systems of the people involved in the process.

> **CASE STUDY 15.4**

Mobile revolution: Vodafone's struggle to maintain its success

The company that dominated the mobile phone industry in the late 1990s was under pressure in the new millennium. Investors were sceptical about whether data services would restore its previous high growth.

Vodafone, the British mobile telephone group that became one of the world's most valuable companies in the technology boom of the 1990s, had a miserable year in the year ended March 2002. As faith in the sector has sagged – see Case 15.2 – the promise of rapid growth has faded. In the year to 2000, it grew its subscriber base by 425 per cent over the previous year. This dropped to 46 per cent in the year ended 2001 and 26 per cent in the year ended 2002. Much of this increase came as a result of a series of spectacular acquisitions, but these were largely over by 2002. Its previous record of high revenue growth – *See* Figure 15.3 – was in danger.

Investors feared that there was limited potential for subscriber growth, as most Europeans already have a mobile phone. There were also growing concerns that third-generation mobile services will take time to materialise, forcing operators such as Vodafone to trim their revenue forecasts. The company's shares were also hit by worries that it could be forced to write down some of its acquisitions – notably its US$150 billion purchase of the German company Mannesmann, which was made near the peak of market share values.

Future revenue growth – uncertain after past successes

'Write-downs will have a symbolic impact but the real worry is future revenues,' says one Vodafone shareholder. 'The concern is about where future revenues are coming from. The jury is still out on this one, which is causing many shareholders to assume the worst.' For several years up to 2002, Sir Christopher Gent, the mobile operator's chief executive, could do no wrong. Institution investors' faith in him was encouraged by the fact that he always kept his promises. Under his stewardship, Vodafone never issued a profits warning.

This strong support gave Sir Christopher a virtual carte blanche to pursue an aggressive acquisition strategy to build Vodafone into the world's biggest mobile operator. Having bought Airtouch of the US in 1999, he turned his sights to Mannesmann, launching the world's largest ever hostile takeover. But in 2002, support was beginning to wane. Some shareholders were beginning to question whether the factors needed to drive future growth at the mobile operator were still within Sir Christopher's control.

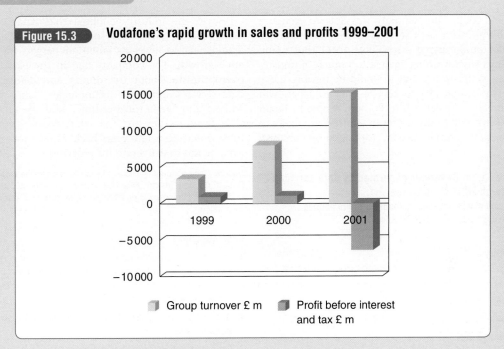

Figure 15.3 **Vodafone's rapid growth in sales and profits 1999–2001**

Group turnover £ m   Profit before interest and tax £ m

The chief concern was that Vodafone could no longer rely on subscriber growth to drive up future revenues. Throughout Vodafone's key markets across Europe, mobile phone penetration was over 70 per cent and dangerously close to effective saturation. That meant the company had to persuade its existing customers to use their phones more if it was to stand a chance of delivering revenue growth. This was a hard strategy to follow because, like all big mobile operators, Vodafone had been following a four-year losing battle to stem revenue declines in the average spend of its mobile customers. Voice calls on mobile were still rising, but increased competition was driving down the cost of such calls, leading to overall declines in revenues from voice calls.

There were also regulatory pressures on pricing. The European Commission was examining the cost of mobile calls made outside the user's home country and the UK Competition Commission was investigating 'termination charges' – the cost of calls between different mobile networks. As a result, voice revenues were expected to remain flat at best in the coming years. This was a particular problem for Vodafone because its size made it hard for it to expand market share. In most of its markets, Vodafone was the number one or number two.

New growth – heavy reliance on new data services

As a result of the above problems, Vodafone was pinning virtually all of its growth hopes on new data services. A new form of text messaging service was launched in late 2002 across many of its markets, allowing users to send electronic pictures between handsets. This was done with existing networks but its main hopes for the years after this rested on the so-called third-generation (3G) data services.

Third-generation technology will allow users to send and receive moving pictures. Vodafone placed a big bet on 3G, having spent a total of US$22 billion on 3G licences in various markets. But there were technical problems over developing the mobile telephones to use such services. Some other mobile operators expected such services to be delayed until 2004 or 2005. This meant that Sir Christopher's aim of achieving between 20 and 25 per cent of revenues from data by 2004 look particularly challenging.

To counteract this caution, Vodafone pointed sceptics to its experience in Japan, where data use had taken off in a dramatic way. Its Japanese subsidiary, J-Phone, had launched a handset with built-in camera in 2001 and had already persuaded one third of its 12 million subscribers to switch

CASE STUDY 15.4 continued

by mid-2002. The company was able to charge a higher price for such services as well as encourage greater phone usage – see Table 15.11. But many analysts were warning against too much optimism. 'Japan is illustrative but it would be terribly naïve to assume that the success of data in Japan will be directly translated into Europe. People in Japan don't just talk in lifts or trains, so they are likely to use data in a different way,' explained one analyst.

Table 15.11 Revenues generated by data services in March 2002 at Vodafone
(per cent of total revenue by country – the remaining percentage was generated by voice)

Country	Text messages (%)	Wireless Internet (%)
Vodafone UK	12.3	1.1
Vodafone Germany	14.5	0.7
Vodafone Italy	9.5	0.3
J-Phone Japan	6.6	13.2

Source: Vodafone.

Few in the industry doubted that data would boost revenue growth. But some said that Vodafone would have to lower its ambitious targets for revenue growth. The company had in the past been overoptimistic about the timing and delivery of data services and other technologies. 'Chris Gent will certainly get a tougher time,' said one analyst. 'The revenues are just not what people thought they would be a few years back. Now, more than ever, he has to deliver on his promises.'

Source: Case adapted by Richard Lynch from an article written by Robert Budden in the *Financial Times*, 26 April 2002, p18. © Copyright *Financial Times* 2002. All rights reserved. Used with permission.

Case questions

1 *In order to generate new growth, which, if any, of the four strategic routes described in this chapter would you employ? You can also consider the use of classic prescriptive strategy if you wish.*

2 *Are there any routes that you would definitely not employ? Why?*

3 *Do large acquisitions that produce some market consolidation represent a well-chosen strategic route in markets where the technology remains uncertain and still to be fully developed?*

▬ Summary

● This chapter first explored the importance of strategic *context* in the development of strategy. In the prescriptive model of strategy development, context is assumed to be linear and predictable, whereas, in reality, it may be turbulent and uncertain. Because of this difficulty, alternatives to the prescriptive process have been developed. The chapter then examined four models out of the many that are available. Particular emphasis was given to the *learning-based strategy* approach as one that has a contribution to make in conjunction with prescriptive approaches.

● *Survival-based* strategies emphasise the importance of adapting strategies to meet changes in the environment. The ultimate objective is survival itself. The approach adopted is to develop options for use as the environment changes. Options that seek low costs are particularly useful. Beyond taking the precaution of developing options, there is little that the individual company can do. There is an element of chance in whether the company will survive.

● *The uncertainty-based approach* concentrates on the difficult and turbulent environment that now surrounds the development of corporate strategy. Renewal and transformation are vital aspects of such strategy. Inevitably, they will involve uncertainty. Such uncertainty can be modelled mathematically. However, the long-term consequences are unknown and cannot be foreseen or usefully predicted. Uncertainty approaches therefore involve taking small steps forward. Management needs to learn from such actions and adapt accordingly. Because of the uncertainty about the future, it is argued that the prescriptive approach of looking at strategy options and selecting between them is irrelevant.

● *Negotiation-based strategies* emphasise the need to persuade colleagues and outside stakeholders to take a particular course of action. Coalitions and groups play an important part in strategy development. Such a strategic approach also needs to be seen in the context of negotiations with powerful customers and suppliers where bargaining and trade-offs will take place. Game theory attempts to predict the outcomes of customer reactions or, in some cases, to show how the outcome of negotiations may well produce a suboptimal solution unless both sides of the negotiations realise the consequences of their actions.

● *Learning-based strategy* emphasises the importance of flexibility in developing unique strategies. It suggests that group dynamics are more important than individuals in developing new, experimental strategies. Learning is not concerned with memory work, but with active creativity in developing new strategic opportunities. There are five principles to group learning: personal mastery, group mental models, share vision, team learning and systems thinking. It has real value as a concept, but in practice is vague and lacks operational guidance.

● *International considerations* may impact on the strategy process at every stage. The ability of stakeholders to influence the process will vary from country to country for historical, political and cultural reasons. The mission and objectives are likely to be rooted in the social and cultural systems of the country in which the strategy is developed. The environment may be important in another aspect of strategy development: the home country of an organisation will influence the way in which the international strategy is developed and managed. Options and choice in the selection process will be governed by the culture and social systems of the people involved in the process.

QUESTIONS

1 Professor Charles Handy has described recent technological breakthroughs in global development as *discontinuous*. He commented: '*Discontinuous change required discontinuous upside-down thinking to deal with it, even if thinkers and thought appear absurd at first sight.*' Can discontinuities be handled by the prescriptive process or is an emergent process required? If so, which one?

2 Why does context matter in strategy development? What are the main elements of context in the case of European telecommunications? How do they influence strategy development?

3 Take an organisation with which you are familiar and consider to what extent it plans ahead. How does it undertake this task? Is it reasonably effective or is the whole process largely a waste of time? To what extent does any planning process rely on 'people' issues and negotiation? What model from this chapter does the process most closely follow, if any?

4 Is it possible for the prescriptive strategy process to be creative?

5 Some have argued that the survival-based strategic route is overpessimistic in its approach. Do you agree?

6 For organisations, such as the telecommunications companies, involved in lengthy investment decisions that take many years to implement, the uncertainty-based route forward with its very short time-horizons appears to have little to offer. Can this strategic route provide any useful guidance to such companies?

▶

QUESTIONS continued

7 Why is negotiation important in corporate strategy? Why is it not better to have a strong leader who will simply impose his/her will on the organisation?

8 The learning-based strategic route emphasises creativity in strategy development. Why is this important and how might it be achieved?

9 '*Management theories are judged, among managers at least, by the demonstrable results that they deliver,*' comments Professor Colin Egan. Apply this comment to the strategic routes described in this chapter and outline your conclusions.

10 If you were advising Honda Motorcycles about its strategies in the 1990s, what strategic approach or combination of approaches would you adopt? Give reasons for your views.

STRATEGIC PROJECT

This chapter has examined some of the developments taking place in telecommunications strategy around the world. There is expected to be a revolution in this area over the next ten years, with some winners and losers. For example, it is doubtful that all the European telcos in Case 15.2 will survive. But which ones will disappear? How do you predict that this will happen? You might like to consider the strategies for survival and growth in this exciting area.

FURTHER READING

For a comparative review of strategic approaches, the book by Dr Richard Whittington remains one of the best: Whittington, R (1993) *What is Strategy – and Does it Matter?*, Routledge, London.

For a discussion of survival-based approaches, *see* Rumelt, R, Schendel, D and Teece, D (1991) 'Strategic management and economics', *Strategic Management Journal*, 12, pp5–29. This is a very useful general review and would provide a good link for those who have already studied economics.

For a description of the uncertainty-based approach, *see* Stacey, R (1996) *Strategic Management and Organisational Dynamics*, 2nd edn, Pitman Publishing, London.

For a useful discussion of learning approaches, *see* Senge, P (1990) *The Fifth Discipline: the Art and Practice of the Learning Organisation*, Century Business, London. For a critical examination of learning, Professor Colin Egan's book is strongly recommended: Egan, C (1995) *Creating Organisational Advantage*, Butterworth–Heinemann, Oxford.

For an exploration of game theory, *see* Dixit, A and Nalebuff, B (1991) *Thinking Strategically*, W W Norton, New York. *See* also Nalebuff, B and Brandenburger, A M (1997) *Co-opetition*, HarperCollins Business, London.

Appendix

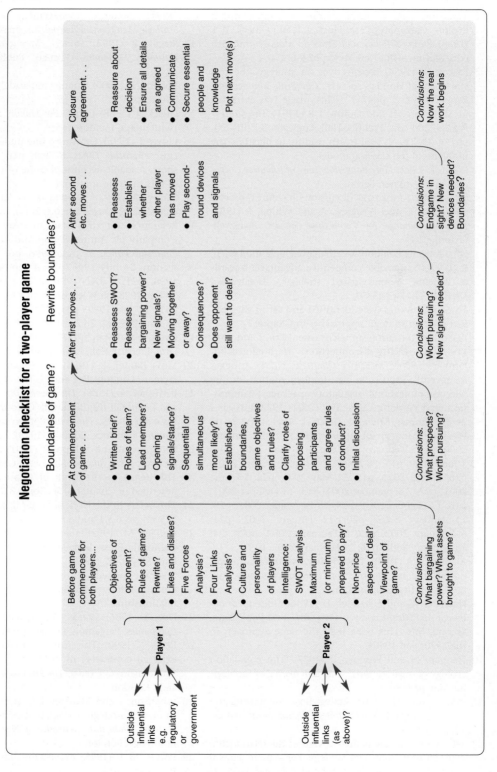

Negotiation checklist for a two-player game

Player 1

Outside influential links e.g. regulatory or government

Before game commences for both players...

- Objectives of opponent?
- Rules of game? Rewrite?
- Likes and dislikes?
- Five Forces Analysis?
- Four Links Analysis?
- Culture and personality of players
- Intelligence: SWOT analysis
- Maximum (or minimum) prepared to pay?
- Non-price aspects of deal?
- Viewpoint of game?

Conclusions: What bargaining power? What assets brought to game?

Player 2

Outside influential links (as above)?

Boundaries of game?

At commencement of game. . .

- Written brief?
- Roles of team?
- Lead members?
- Opening signals/stance?
- Sequential or simultaneous more likely?
- Established boundaries, game objectives and rules?
- Clarify roles of opposing participants and agree rules of conduct?
- Initial discussion

Conclusions: What prospects? Worth pursuing?

After first moves. . .

- Reassess SWOT?
- Reassess bargaining power?
- New signals?
- Moving together or away?
- Consequences?
- Does opponent still want to deal?

Conclusions: Worth pursuing? New signals needed?

Rewrite boundaries?

After second etc. moves. . .

- Reassess
- Establish whether other player has moved
- Play second-round devices and signals

Conclusions: Endgame in sight? New devices needed? Boundaries?

Closure agreement. . .

- Reassure about decision
- Ensure all details are agreed
- Communicate
- Secure essential people and knowledge
- Plot next move(s)

Conclusions: Now the real work begins

NOTES & REFERENCES

1 Thus, for example, classic prescriptive strategy might explore 'Gap analysis': *see* Jauch, L R and Glueck, W F (1988) *Business Policy and Strategic Management*, 5th edn, McGraw-Hill, New York, pp24–6.

2 Pascale, R (1984) 'Perspectives on strategy: the real story behind Honda's success', *California Management Review XXVI*, 3, pp47–72. This article was extracted in Mintzberg, H and Quinn, J B (1991) *The Strategy Process*, 2nd edn, Prentice Hall, Englewood Cliffs, NJ, pp114–23. This is well worth reading to illustrate the problems of the classical model.

3 Kono, T (1992) *Long Range Planning of Japanese Corporations*, de Gruyter, Berlin.

4 *See* Chapter 1 for a basic discussion on context, process and content. Also Pettigrew, A and Whipp, R (1993) *Managing Change for Competitive Success*, Blackwell, Oxford, Ch1.

5 For a fuller exploration, *see* Chaharbaghi, K and Lynch, R (1999), 'Sustainable competitive advantage: towards a dynamic resource-based strategy', *Management Decision*, 37(1), pp45–50.

6 These four routes were identified and set in the context of other strategic approaches in Chapter 2.

7 References for European telcos case: Isern, J and Rios, M I (2002) 'Facing disconnection – Hard choices for Europe's telcos', *McKinsey Quarterly*, No 1; Annexes to Seventh Report on the implementation of the telecommunications regulatory package, Commission Staff Working Paper, SEC (2001) 1922 Brussels – 26 November; *Financial Times*: 1 August 1998, p5 Weekend Money; 24 April 1999, p21; 27 January 2000, p1; 3 February 2000, p24; 1 May 2000, p11; 3 June 2000, p15; 28 March 2001, p23; 3 April 2001, p26; 2 May 2001, p15; 11 May 2001, p22; 13 June 2001, p27; 7 September 2001, p13; 13 October 2001, p16; 17 October 2001, p23; 18 December 2001, p23; 11 January 2002, p20; 12 January 2002, p11; 6 February 2002, p19; 8 February 2002, pp20, 24; 13 February 2002, p16; 23 February 2002, p19.

8 Alchian, A A (1950) 'Uncertainty, evolution and economic theory', *Journal of Political Economy*, 58, pp211–21, first proposed this.

9 Hofer, C W and Schendel, D (1986) *Strategy Formulation: Analytical Concepts*, 11th edn, West Publishing, St Paul, MN. This book used the same approach in the 1970s and 1980s.

10 Hannan, M and Freeman, J (1977) 'The population ecology of organisations', *American Journal of Sociology*, 82, Mar, pp929–64.

11 Williamson, O E (1991) 'Strategizing, economizing and economic organisation', *Strategic Management Journal*, 12, pp75–94.

12 This represents one particular view of the relationship between economics and strategy. For a more general discussion, see Rumelt, R, Schendel, D and Teece, D (1991) 'Strategic management and economics', *Strategic Management Journal*, 12, pp5–29.

13 Stacey, R (1993) *Strategic Management and Organisational Dynamics*, Pitman Publishing, London, p211.

14 Roberts, D (2000) 'Orange renegade', *Financial Times*, 3 June, p15.

15 Gleick, J (1988) *Chaos: the Making of a New Science*, Heinemann, London.

16 Lloyd, T (1995) 'Drawing a line under corporate strategy', *Financial Times*, 8 Sept, p10. This provides a short, readable account of some of the consequences of this strategic approach.

17 Stacey, R (1993) 'Strategy as order emerging from chaos', *Long Range Planning*, 26(1), pp10–17.

18 References for GEC Marconi case: General Electric Company plc Annual Report and Accounts for 1998; *Financial Times*, 27 June 1998, p6, Weekend Money section; 24 July 1998, p21; 4 Sept 1998, p11; 5 Dec 1998, p21; 9 Dec 1998, p26; 10 Dec 1998, p15; 19 Dec 1998, p6 Weekend Money section; 14 Jan 1999, p31; 19 Jan 1999, pp1, 25, 27; 21 Jan 1999, p21; 23 Jan 1999, p2; 26 Feb 1999, p19.

19 Cyert, R and March, J (1963) *A Behavioral Theory of the Firm*, Prentice Hall, Englewood Cliffs, NJ.

20 Moss Kanter, R (1983) *The Change Masters,* Unwin Hyman, London. The book is full of examples.

21 Pettigrew A (1985) *The Awakening Giant: Continuity and Change at ICI*, Blackwell, Oxford, p458. Note also his earlier book, *The Politics of Organisational Decision Making*, Tavistock, London (1973).

22 Pettigrew, A and Whipp, R (1991) *Managing Change for Competitive Success*, Blackwell, Oxford, p30.

23 This refers to the work of Coase and Williamson described in Chapter 6, Section 6.3.2.

24 This refers to the work of Porter described in Chapter 6, Sections 6.5.1 and 6.5.2.

25 Gerlach M (1992) *Alliance Capitalism*, University of California Press, Berkeley, CA. Quoted in De Wit, R and Meyer, R (1998) *Strategy: Process, Content and Context*, 2nd edn, International Thomson Business Press, London, p512. But note my rephrasing of this relationship.

26 Doz, Y (1986) *Strategic Management in Multinational Companies*, Pergamon, Oxford, pp95, 96.

27 Reve, T (1990) 'The firm as a nexus of internal and external contracts', in Aoki, M, Gustafsson, M and Williamson, O E (eds), *The Firm as a Nexus of Treaties*, Sage, London.

28 Johanson, J and Mattson, L-G (1992) 'Network positions and strategic action', in Axelsson, B and Easton, G (eds), *Industrial Networks: a New View of Reality*, Routledge, London.

29 Porter, M E (1985) *Competitive Advantage*, The Free Press, New York.

30 Jarillo, J C (1988) 'On strategic networks', *Strategic Management Journal*, June–July.

31 This choice is presented as the prime focus of the 'debate' in De Wit, R and Meyer, R (1998) Op. cit., Ch7.

32 Useful introductory texts include: Nalebuff, B and Brandenburger, A M (1997) *Co-opetition*, HarperCollins Business, London; Schelling, T C (1980) *The Strategy of Conflict*, 2nd edn, Harvard University Press, Cambridge, MA; also the text by Dixit and Nalebuff referenced below.

33 Nalebuff, B and Brandenburger, A M (1997) Op. cit., Ch2.

34 Dixit, A and Nalebuff, B (1991) *Thinking Strategically: the Competitive Edge in Business, Politics and Everyday Life*, W W Norton, New York.

35 Amongst the critical comments on game theory, it is worth consulting: Camerer, C F (1991) 'Does strategy research need game theory?', *Strategic Management Journal*, 12, Winter, pp137–52. Postrel, S (1991) 'Burning your britches behind you', *Strategic Management Journal*, Special Issue, 12, Winter, pp153–5. *See* also Fisher, F M (1989) 'The games economists play: a noncooperative view', *RAND Journal of Economics*, 20, pp113–24.

36 Mintzberg, H (1987) 'Crafting strategy', *Harvard Business Review*, July–Aug.

37 De Geus, A (1988) 'Planning as learning', *Harvard Business Review*, Mar–Apr, p70.

38 Argyris, C (1977) 'Double loop learning in organizations', *Harvard Business Review*, May–June, pp99–109.

39 Senge, P (1990) *The Fifth Discipline: The Art and Practice of the Learning Organisation*, Century Business, London, Ch1.

40 *See The Economist* (1995) 'The knowledge', 11 Nov, p107.

41 Senge, P (1990) 'The leader's new work: Building learning organisations', *Sloan Management Review*, Fall, and Senge, P (1990) *The Fifth Discipline*.

42 Quinn, S, Mills, D and Friesen, B (1992) 'The learning organisation', *European Management Journal*, 10 June, p146.

43 Argyris, C (1991) 'Teaching smart people how to learn', *Harvard Business Review*, May–June, p99.

44 Burgoyne, J, Pedler, M and Boydell, T (1994) *Towards the Learning Company*, McGraw-Hill, Maidenhead.

45 Jones, A and Hendry, C (1994) 'The learning organisation: adult learning and organisational transformation', *British Journal of Management*, pp153–62. *See* also a thoughtful critique of the learning approach in Egan, C (1995) *Creating Organisational Advantage*, Butterworth–Heinemann, Ch5.

46 *See* the Hofstede research and the *power/distance* data in the last section of Chapter 7 of this book.

47 Hu, Y S (1992) 'Global or stateless firms with international operations', *California Management Review*, Winter, pp115–26.

48 Granovetter, M (1985) 'Economic action and social culture: the problem of embeddedness', *American Journal of Sociology*, 91(3), pp481–510.

49 Whittington, R (1993) *What is Strategy – and Does it Matter?*, Routledge, London, p37.

50 *Financial Times* (1995) 'Hollowing out in Japan', 28 Mar, p21; Nakanoto, M (1995) 'Knocked off the road again', *Financial Times*, 20 Apr, p25.

51 Kluckhohn, C and Strodtbeck, F (1961) *Variations in Value Orientations*, Peterson, New York.

52 Furnham, A (1995) 'The case for cultural diversity', *Financial Times*, 8 Dec, p11. The author was Professor of Psychology at University College, London, at the time the article was written.

Strategy, structure and style

Learning outcomes

After you have worked through this chapter, you will be able to:

● understand the historical background to the development of organisational structures to match chosen strategies;

● evaluate critically the arguments that strategy and structure have a more complex relationship than that suggested by the early strategists;

● assess the benefits and problems associated with the newer, learning-based organisational structures;

● explore how strategy and structure are interrelated;

● understand the concept of strategic fit;

● evaluate the importance of changing an organisation's management style at the same time as changing its strategy.

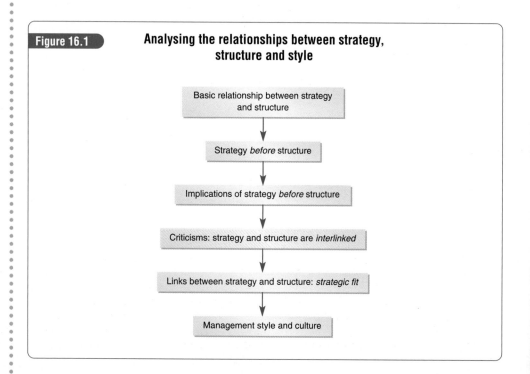

Figure 16.1 Analysing the relationships between strategy, structure and style

Introduction

A major debate has been taking place over the last 30 years regarding the relationship between the strategy and the structure of the organisation. In the past, it was considered that the strategy was decided first and the structure then followed. Some researchers have questioned this approach and taken the view that strategy and structure are interrelated. In this chapter we examine this important debate.

Since the 1980s, there has been another important strategic debate concerning the organisation's ability to change its style and culture. Such a change could have a profound impact on the organisation's development and choice of strategic options – for example, a more risk-taking style may well produce strategic options different from those of a more conservative style.

In this chapter we examine these important debates, and Figure 16.1 shows the overall structure of the chapter.

CASE STUDY 16.1

How Sony moved out across Asia[1]

Over a period of 20 years, Sony has developed its trading and manufacturing across the continent of Asia. This case examines the reasoning which lay behind its development strategy and the implications of the organisational links that have been formed.

Market progress

In the late 1990s, Sony, the Japanese consumer electronics group, planned to make more than 1 million mobile telephones a year at an industrial plant near Beijing airport in China. The US$29 million joint venture was Sony's first on the mainland of China. It was typical of a great wave of Japanese investment flooding over many of its industrial neighbours, in particular focusing on China.

The potential political and financial risks of investing in China were significant but Sony, like others, could no longer afford to be overcautious about entering a market of more than 1 billion people. Moreover, the Chinese market for consumer electronics was growing at 20 per cent per year. As Mr Kenji Tamiya, Sony's senior managing director, explained, East Asia, including China, was a 'gold-mine for existing products'.

Sony's experience in East Asia is a good illustration of the Japanese investment trends in the region – *see* Figure 16.2. The first cautious steps into local assembly used mainly imported components for export to third countries. There followed ever-larger investment now using higher proportions of locally made components and selling into the local market as well as to other Asian countries, the US and, increasingly, back to Japan.

The history of the company

Sony first entered the market in East Asia in April 1967 almost by chance, when the acquisition of another Japanese company happened to include a radio and telephone production unit in Taiwan. Its second step into the region – a television tuner factory in South Korea – also came as the result of a company acquisition in 1973. Then followed a nine-year gap, during which Sony made no further investments in the region, focusing instead on the home market. That was understandable, in a period when the domestic market in Japan was experiencing unprecedented growth.

In 1984 Sony opened a radio, Walkman and telephone plant in Malaysia – the company's first greenfield site in Asia. This was followed the same year by a video-cassette recorder factory in Taiwan (*see* Figure 16.3). It was not until after the 1985 Plaza Accord, when the world's leading economies agreed to co-operate to devalue an overvalued US dollar, that the turning point came. That year the yen touched Y263 to the dollar, but has since moved to around Y100 to the dollar, in the process rendering large areas of Japanese domestic manufacturing uncompetitive.

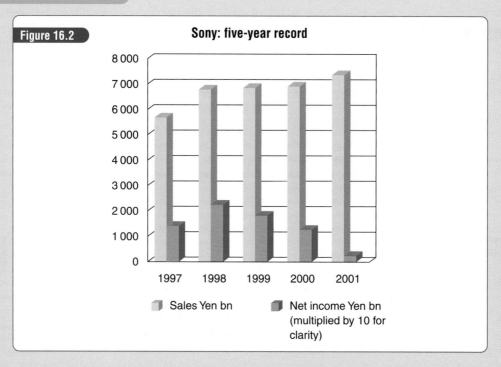

Figure 16.2 Sony: five-year record

Sony's move into Asia

Like many other Japanese companies, Sony took the option to move its production offshore in search of cheaper costs and easier exchange rates. 'We just had to do it, to keep our products competitively priced,' explained Mr Toshiyuki Takinaga, the general manager for consumer and audiovisual products. By the end of the 1980s, eight more Sony plants were in operation in Singapore, Malaysia and Thailand. These have subsequently been joined by another five – in Indonesia, Singapore, China, Vietnam and India. By the 1990s, some 25 000 of Sony's employees were in Asia, out of 135 000 employees worldwide, although most of the company's technical and production development was still conducted in Japan.

The Plaza Accord and the need to compensate for the high yen dictated the timing of Sony's Asian expansion. However, this was only part of the underlying rationale. Mr Tamiya explained: 'We were not only seeking inexpensive labour. We had a clear vision at that time that making investments would raise the purchasing power in Asian countries so that they would become more important markets for Asian products.'As workers gained higher wages, they would spend a portion on electronic goods.

Sony planning

Sony's planners were also guided by the company philosophy of keeping its sales split – supported by local production – in proportions roughly equal to the breakdown of the world consumer electronics market. Thus one-fifth of Sony's sales were in Asia, compared with a one-quarter share of the market in Europe and a one-quarter share in North America. Mr Tamiya aimed to keep the balance about the same for the foreseeable future. However, Asian economic dynamism was such that he believed that, while maintaining the balance, the area could double its world share of Sony's existing products to between 40 and 50 per cent in the next ten years.

Asian economic downturn

Subsequently, many Asian economies suffered a severe downturn in the late 1990s. The US economy continued to be buoyant but European economies also slowed down. The result was that Sony's expectations about the sales potential of Asia remained unfulfilled. The company needed to devote more effort to its US and European operations if it was to

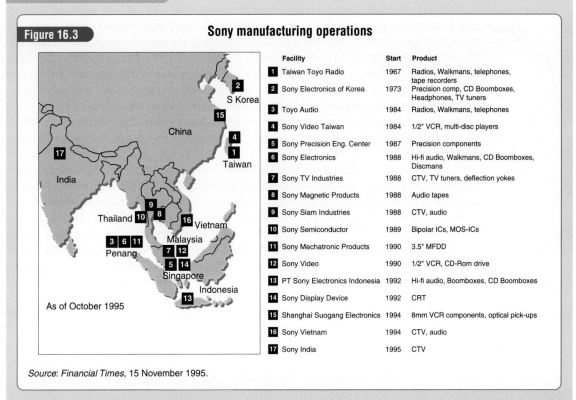

Figure 16.3

Sony manufacturing operations

	Facility	Start	Product
1	Taiwan Toyo Radio	1967	Radios, Walkmans, telephones, tape recorders
2	Sony Electronics of Korea	1973	Precision comp, CD Boomboxes, Headphones, TV tuners
3	Toyo Audio	1984	Radios, Walkmans, telephones
4	Sony Video Taiwan	1984	1/2" VCR, multi-disc players
5	Sony Precision Eng. Center	1987	Precision components
6	Sony Electronics	1988	Hi-fi audio, Walkmans, CD Boomboxes, Discmans
7	Sony TV Industries	1988	CTV, TV tuners, deflection yokes
8	Sony Magnetic Products	1988	Audio tapes
9	Sony Siam Industries	1988	CTV, audio
10	Sony Semiconductor	1989	Bipolar ICs, MOS-ICs
11	Sony Mechatronic Products	1990	3.5" MFDD
12	Sony Video	1990	1/2" VCR, CD-Rom drive
13	PT Sony Electronics Indonesia	1992	Hi-fi audio, Boomboxes, CD Boomboxes
14	Sony Display Device	1992	CRT
15	Shanghai Suogang Electronics	1994	8mm VCR components, optical pick-ups
16	Sony Vietnam	1994	CTV, audio
17	Sony India	1995	CTV

Source: *Financial Times*, 15 November 1995.

renew growth. Moreover, Sony's most profitable operations were computer games, films and television, which were centred on the US rather than Asia. Traditional consumer electronics goods – like TVs and CD players – were facing heavy competition, lower prices and poor profitability.

Source: Adapted and updated by Richard Lynch from an article originally in the *Financial Times*, 15 Nov 1995. © Copyright *Financial Times* 1995.

Case questions

1 *What were the main reasons for Sony's expansion into East Asia?*

2 *How should Sony set up structures to manage such a range of manufacturing and market opportunities?*

3 *Given the Asian economic turnaround in years 2000/2001, what does this mean for Sony's Asian operations, if anything?*

16.1 The basic relationship between strategy and structure

From a *prescriptive* strategy perspective, the purpose of an organisational structure is to allocate the work and administrative mechanisms that are necessary to control and integrate the strategies of an organisation.[2] Thus work is allocated to functions, such as finance and marketing, and recombined in divisions or departments, with power being distributed accordingly. Such a definition is consistent with other, broader definitions of structure taken from an organisational theory perspective.[3] Importantly, in this definition the strategy is developed first and only then is the organisational structure defined. For the prescriptive strategist, organisational structure is a matter of how the strategy is *implemented*: it does not influence the strategy itself. For example, Sony would define its strategy for moving into Asia and only consider the necessary structure after it had made the opening moves.

From an *emergent* strategy perspective, however, the relationship between strategy and structure is more complex. The organisation itself may restrict or enhance the strategies that are proposed. The existing organisational structure may even make certain strategies highly unlikely. For example, an informal, free-flowing structure might be better able to generate new strategic initiatives than a bureaucratic structure. In the case of Sony, for instance, the move into Asia through joint ventures could require different structures from those required where the company had wholly owned subsidiaries.

Figure 16.4 illustrates the differing prescriptive and emergent perspectives. It should be noted, however, that the two options oversimplify the many combinations that exist in practice.

Organisational structure therefore deserves careful consideration. In Chapter 7 we began the exploration of the organisation's culture and power structures. We now examine different types of organisational structure and how they relate to strategy.

From at least the 1960s[4] the *prescriptive* approach was employed. It was recommended that the formulation of strategy was studied *before* the development of the organisational structure to implement that strategy. There was empirical evidence to support this approach from the strategist Alfred Chandler and others.[5] In the 1970s, the economist Oliver Williamson explored the role of the centre as companies become larger and strategies more diverse.[6] Both Chandler and Williamson took the view that the organisation's strategy came first and structure second. These are not the only two approaches to organisational structure, however.

Since the 1960s, some strategists and organisational theorists have looked further at the evidence of how strategy is best developed. They have concluded that there are two problems with the concept of putting strategy before structure:[7]

1 There is an artificial distinction between the *content* of strategy and the *process* by which that strategy is implemented.

2 It is incorrect to describe the relationship between strategy and structure as being one-way only. They have argued that it is possible that a different organisational *structure* may actually lead to a different corporate *strategy*.

On these arguments, strategy and structure are more closely interrelated. Therefore structure needs to be considered while strategy is still being developed. For this reason,

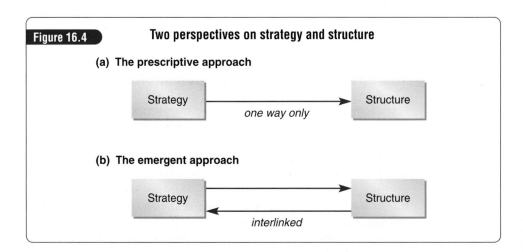

Figure 16.4 **Two perspectives on strategy and structure**

(a) The prescriptive approach

Strategy — one way only → Structure

(b) The emergent approach

Strategy ⇄ Structure
interlinked

the relationship between these two elements is explored in Part 5 of this text, i.e. while strategy is still under development and before it is 'implemented', as explored in Part 6.

◗ Key strategic principles

- For the prescriptive strategist, strategy is developed first and then the organisational structure is defined afterwards. Structure is a matter of how strategy is implemented and does not influence the strategy itself.

- For the emergent strategist, the relationship is more complex. The organisation itself may restrict or enhance the proposed strategies.

- Two well-known writers, Alfred Chandler and Oliver Williamson, took the view that strategy came first and structure second.

- Other strategists and theorists have argued that strategy and structure are more closely interrelated and structure needs to be considered while strategy is being developed.

16.2 Strategy before structure: Chandler's contribution

To understand the logic behind this prescriptive approach to the development of organisational structures, it is helpful to look at the historical background. Prior to the early 1960s, the US strategist Alfred Chandler Jr studied how some leading US corporations had developed their strategies in the first half of the twentieth century.[8] He then drew some major conclusions from this empirical evidence, the foremost one being that the organisation first needed to develop its strategy and, after this, to devise the organisation structure that delivered that strategy.

Chandler noted how, during the late nineteenth and early twentieth century, US companies moved from craft industry production to mass production: their strategies changed fundamentally. Craftsmen had previously made individual items using their skills, knowledge and judgement. Steam power and electricity had already made manufacturing easier but, in many cases, it was still undertaken on a piece-by-piece basis. There were limited economies of scale. Then came the age of standardised products coupled with simplified engineering techniques. Machinery was developed that gave much lower costs and allowed customer prices to drop. Instead of such products only being available to the few who were rich, mass markets developed. This led to further economies of scale that reduced prices even further. Strategy changed fundamentally for such companies.

The classic example of such change took place under the guiding genius of Henry Ford with his development of the Model T car. Between 1909 and 1916, the price of the car dropped from US$850 to US$360 and the number of cars shipped rose from 14 000 per annum to 506 000 per annum.[9] New strategies and organisational structures were needed in every aspect of the company during this period.

Chandler studied a number of North American companies during the first half of the twentieth century, including Ford's rival, General Motors. He did not study Ford itself. He concluded that as companies grew in size and complexity they needed what he called a *general office* to handle the main planning and co-ordinating work of the various functions of a business, including the marketing, operations, finance and human resources (discussed in Parts 2 and 3 of this book). The general office was concerned with the long-term health of the enterprise: *it devised the company's strategy.*

Once the strategy was formulated, the general office then *implemented* it by designing a suitable organisational structure and allocating resources such as finance, equipment and people to the various parts of the organisation.

Chandler drew a clear distinction between *devising* a strategy and *implementing* it. He defined strategy as:

> [t]he determination of the basic long-term goals and objectives of an enterprise, and the adoption of courses of action and the allocation of resources necessary for carrying out these goals.[10]

The task of developing the strategy took place at the centre of the organisation. The job of implementing it then fell to the various functional areas.

Chandler's research suggested that, once a strategy had been developed, it was necessary to consider the structure needed to carry it out. A new strategy might require extra resources, or new personnel or equipment which would alter the work of the enterprise, making a new organisational structure necessary: 'The design of the organisation through which the enterprise is administered', to quote Chandler.

The principle that strategy came before organisational structure was formed, therefore, by considering the industrial developments of the early twentieth century.[11] Whether such considerations are still relevant as we move into the new millennium will be considered in Section 16.5 of this chapter.

▶ Key strategic principles

- Chandler contended that it was first necessary to develop the strategy. After this task was completed, the organisation was devised to deliver that strategy.

- His conclusion was based on his study of the way that North American businesses were formed and organised in the early part of the twentieth century. He only studied businesses that had developed from small enterprises into larger, more diversified structures.

16.3 Implications of designing structures to fit strategy[12]

At this stage it is useful to consider some basic implications of structure following from strategy, although the detailed design of organisational structures will be explored in Chapter 18. Once the organisation's strategy had been decided, Chandler recommended that there were four main questions to be explored in developing its structure:

1 What work needs to be undertaken to implement the strategy?

2 Who should undertake this work?

3 Is any of the work interrelated?

4 Are there limits to the size of the organisation?

In the early to mid-twentieth century, managers answered these questions by specifying the *formalised relationships* between employees, managers and directors in an organisation. They were supported by such early writers as F W Taylor and Henri Fayol and by later strategists, including Alfred Sloan, and Frank and Lilian Gilbreth. Many modern strategy texts also follow this approach, employing the following principles:[13]

- formal structures;
- clear responsibilities;

- identified lines of reporting;
- a *central directorate* whose strategy decisions are handed down to employees.

As we saw in Chapter 15, such concepts have been increasingly questioned in more recent years by strategists such as Senge and Mintzberg. However, in terms of clarity of purpose, formalised relationships do have real merit and may be particularly appropriate to certain companies and cultures. Moreover, even if some modification is required, they do present a clear approach to the development of organisational structure.

Beyond these general design issues, Chandler identified four key parameters for strategy growth that would influence organisational structure:

1 expansion of volume;

2 geographical dispersion;

3 vertical integration (adding value by absorbing the tasks of the supplier or customer);

4 product diversification.

He argued that, as any of the four changes occurred, new organisational structures were needed to handle them. Two principal consequences of this approach required to be explored.

1 *Increased bureaucracy.* During the early twentieth century, some leading organisations grew substantially in size and required more complex organisational structures – for example, the growth of General Motors (US) as described in Case study 16.2. These larger units were often associated with increased bureaucracy but they were not necessarily less efficient. Research evidence suggests that larger companies performed better when they had more, rather than less, bureaucracy. However, larger companies were also often associated with lower job satisfaction, higher absenteeism and higher staff turnover.[14]

2 *Increased decentralisation.* As an organisation becomes more diverse in its products or markets, there is a greater likelihood that it will need to reorganise its structures. Specifically, more complex forms of organisational structure may be necessary because the centre becomes increasingly isolated from the place where decisions are needed and can best be made. Separate divisions within the organisation may need to be set up and some power delegated to them. When an organisation changes from being a one-product company to including these more complex elements, it may need to move from *centralisation* to *decentralisation*.

In designing organisational structures, one important issue is the extent to which decision making is taken from the centre of the organisation and passed to subsidiaries or divisions.[15] There are no simple solutions to the *balance* that may need to be struck. According to many strategists, this should only be explored once the basic strategy has been agreed. There are no simple rules to decide where the balance needs to be struck.

▶ Key strategic principles

- According to the early strategists, formal structures, clear responsibilities, identified lines of reporting and, for strategy development, a central directorate are all important elements of organisational design. They are undertaken after the basic strategy has been agreed.

▶

> *Key strategic principles continued*
>
> ● As organisations become larger and more complex, it may be necessary to form divisions and decentralise some power by delegating it to them.
>
> ● The centralisation versus decentralisation issue may be particularly important in designing the organisation's structure. According to many strategists, this should only be undertaken once the basic strategy has been decided. There are no simple rules to define where the balance needs to be struck between centralisation and decentralisation.

CASE STUDY 16.2

How General Motors organised its future

General Motors Corporation (US) is the world's largest manufacturer of cars and trucks. This case study examines the strategies and the organisational structures used by the company to gain and maintain its dominance of its chosen businesses. It contrasts the strategies and structures of 1924 with those of 2000.

General Motors gained market leadership from Ford in the 1920s and maintained this position for the remainder of the century, in spite of what some strategists would regard as major strategic errors. The company has also grown in other directions but remains primarily a vehicle manufacturer.

General Motors (GM) in 1924[16]

After the near-collapse of GM around 1920, René Du Pont appointed a young manager with ideas to restructure the company: Alfred Sloan. The company was then reorganised by Sloan along the lines of what today we would recognise as the principles of *market segmentation*, e.g. Cadillac in the low-volume, high-price segment; Chevrolet in the high-volume, low-price segment. Each operation was set up as a separate division with its own marketing, finance and operations management structure. Specifically, the new organisation ensured that the divisions did not compete against each other in the market place. The organisation structure is shown in Figure 16.5.

To ensure that there was adequate co-ordination across the divisions on engineering, manufacturing and especially distribution, interdivisional committees were also established. It was found that such co-operation worked more smoothly when the groups did not compete. Nevertheless, where products were sold between divisions (e.g. accessories), the goods were valued at the prices existing in the *market place*. This ensured that it was always possible to evaluate the performance of divisions, especially those parts and accessories groups supplying several divisions across GM.

In devising the new structure, special emphasis was laid on statistical and financial controls. These were considered essential for the monitoring of divisional performance by the central executive committee. The lack of such controls had been one of the reasons why the company had major problems around 1920. Advisory staff were also introduced to help co-ordinate and plan the provision of expert advice which was offered across the group.

It was the executive committee that made all the major entrepreneurial and strategic decisions for the group. This consisted of the chairman, chief executive and heads of the leading divisions. It was given time, space and commitment to examine the broad strategic direction of the company. Strategic control was vested in the centre, with day-to-day operations firmly decentralised to the individual operating companies. This was a totally new policy for its time. The management principles developed for this type of organisation have been adopted subsequently by many companies around the world as they have grown in size and complexity.

Between 1924 and 1928, GM's new structure served the company well:

● Its market share rose from 18.8 per cent to 43.3 per cent. Sales in 1928 were US$276 million.

● Production more than doubled from 1.5 million cars per annum to around 4 million per annum.

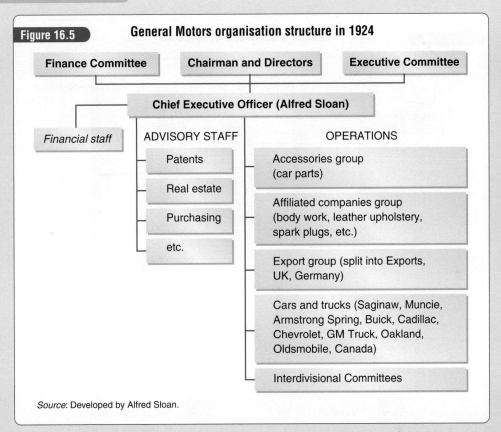

Figure 16.5 **General Motors organisation structure in 1924**

Source: Developed by Alfred Sloan.

GM was helped by major problems at its chief rival, Ford Motor Company. Ford completely closed down for 18 months during the period in order to reorganise and rebuild. However, even when Ford returned, GM maintained its market leadership, which it continued to hold in North America in the 1990s.

General Motors in 2000[17]

By 2000, the company had grown from its base in cars and trucks into other areas. Total sales were US$184 billion, of which US$148 billion was in cars and trucks. The outline organisational structure at this time is shown in Figure 16.7.

During the 1980s, the company had expanded into two important new areas as a result of decisions taken by the then chief executive and his immediate colleagues. EDS and Hughes (*see* Figure 16.7) were acquired in 1984 and 1985 for US$2.55 billion and US$2.7 billion respectively, when GM decided that it needed to diversify out of cars. The purchases were funded with car profits earned between 1979 and 1985 when the North US car market had been protected from Japanese competition. Rather than using this period to lower its car production costs, GM moved outside the industry. At the same time, Japanese car manufacturers were reported to have lower production costs (by US$2000 per car) coupled with higher quality than most US cars. Subsequently, EDS was sold.

Although the company was the world's largest producer of cars and trucks, it was heavily reliant on the massive North American market for nearly 80 per cent of its sales and was working on the low sales margin of just 0.7 per cent in its North American operations. Both its two leading rivals, Ford and Toyota, had lower production costs. GM's international operations had clearly developed substantially since the early 1920s, but it still displayed the strategic insularity that has led some US companies to downgrade the importance of international expansion and involvement.

From an organisational viewpoint, its North American operations were still substantially the same in 2000, compared with 1924, even if they

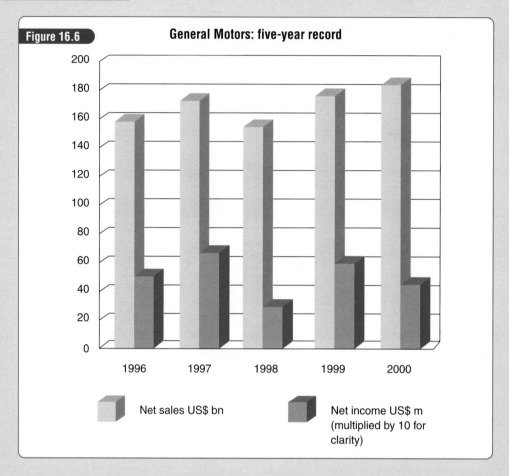

Figure 16.6 General Motors: five-year record

Net sales US$ bn

Net income US$ m (multiplied by 10 for clarity)

were rather larger. The main differences lay in the increased activities overseas and the totally new business activities acquired during the 1980s. GM was also building a global purchasing operation for all its car and truck interests and moving into related areas such as diesel engines. More fundamentally, it had grown so large that it had no choice but to operate company divisions at a distance from each other. It was now a vast, major enterprise that was attempting to introduce new quality standards, lean manufacturing techniques and greater manufacturing flexibility (*see* Chapter 9 for descriptions of these areas) across its North American and international operations. However, its whole strategy was geared towards catching up with the Japanese car producers who had become like-for-like more efficient, possessed lower costs and produced some more reliable products than GM. Even the advantage to GM of the rising

Japanese yen had diminished as the Japanese car companies continued to open up car manufacturing in the US.

Global competition, overcapacity in a cyclical car market (*see* Chapter 3) and widely diversified operations had radically altered some aspects of GM's strategy in 2000 compared with 76 years earlier. It had become a major world company, but many of its problems were the result of its own strategic mistakes.

Case questions

1 *Since the 1920s, the organisation structure of GM does not appear to have changed fundamentally: separate divisions still report to the centre. So what has changed about the company and its environment?*

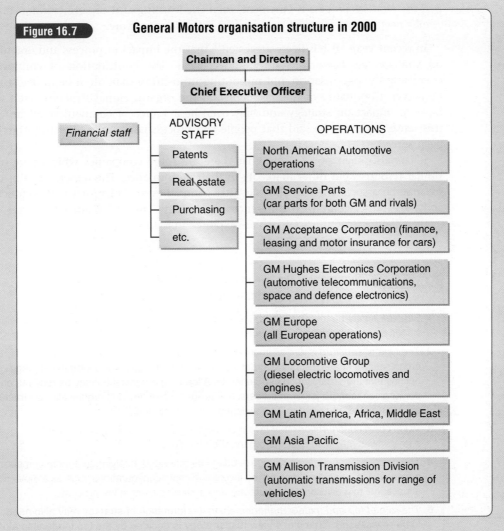

Figure 16.7 **General Motors organisation structure in 2000**

What implications, if any, might this have for a change in the relationship between the centre and the divisions?

2 When a company grows as large as GM, what problems would you envisage in operating a divisional structure?

3 Are the learning strategy concepts of Senge relevant to GM's strategy and structure? (See Chapter 15 and Section 16.4.2 for guidance.)

4 Can strategy 'emerge' in such a large company? If so, why, where and how?

16.4 Criticisms: strategy and structure are interlinked

According to some modern strategists, strategy and structure are interlinked. It may not be optimal for an organisation to develop its structure *after* it has developed its strategy. The relationship is more complex in two respects:

1 Strategy and the structure associated with it may need to develop *at the same time* in an experimental way: as the strategy develops, so does the structure. The organisation *learns to adapt* to its changing environment.

2 If the strategy process is emergent, then the learning and experimentation involved may need a *more open and less formal* organisation structure.

In recent years, it has been suggested[18] that the impact of process and organisation on strategy has been constantly underplayed. The contribution of employees in energising the organisation and promoting innovation may often be underestimated. Moreover, the quality of management and the organisational structure itself will all have an impact on strategy and may even be a source of competitive advantage. In this sense, it cannot be said that people and process issues arise after the strategy has been agreed.

It has also been pointed out that there are some companies which have broadly similar resources but differ markedly in their performance. The reasons for this disparity may be associated with the way that companies are organised and conduct their activities, rather than with differences in strategy. The five main weaknesses of the strategy before structure approach are explored in Exhibit 16.1.

Exhibit 16.1 **Summary of the five main criticisms of the strategy-first, structure-afterwards process**

1 Structures may be too *rigid, hierarchical and bureaucratic* to cope with the newer social values and rapidly changing environments of the 1990s.

2 *The type of structure* is just as important as the business area in developing the organisation's strategy. It is the structure that will restrict, guide and form the strategy options that the organisation can generate. A learning organisation may be required and power given to more junior managers. In this sense, strategy and organisational structure are interrelated and need to be developed at the same time.

3 *Value chain configurations* that favour cost cutting or, alternatively, new market opportunities may also alter the organisation required.

4 *The complexity of strategic change* needs to be managed, implying that more complex organisational considerations will be involved. Simple configurations such as a move from a functional to a divisional structure are only a starting point in the process.

5 *The role of top and middle management* in the formation of strategy may also need to be reassessed: Chandler's view that strategy is decided by the top leadership alone has been challenged. Particularly for new, innovative strategies, middle management and the organisation's culture and structure may be important. The work of the leader in empowering middle management may require a new approach – the collegiate style of leadership.

16.4.1 Changes in the business environment and social values

To explain the movement from functional to divisional structures, we examined how corporations in the early twentieth century set up the first multidivisional organisations. Since that time, the environment has changed substantially.[19] The workplace itself, the relationships between workers and managers, and the skills of employees have all altered substantially. Old organisational structures embedded in past understandings may therefore be suspect. Exhibit 16.2 summarises how the environment has changed.

Exhibit 16.2	A comparison of the early- and late-twentieth-century business environments

Early-twentieth century	*Late-twentieth century*
• Uneducated workers, typically just moved from agricultural work into the cities	• Better educated, computer-literate, skilled
• Knowledge of simple engineering and technology	• Complex, computer-driven, large-scale
• The new science of management recognised simple cause-and-effect relationships	• Multifaceted and complex nature of management now partially understood
• Growing, newly industrialising markets and suppliers	• Mix of some mature, cyclical markets and some high-growth, new-technology markets and suppliers
• Sharp distinctions between management and workers	• Greater overlap between management and workers in some industrialised countries

---

16.4.2 The learning organisation, empowerment and organisational structure

According to Senge and others, the strategy processes of the late twentieth century need to be adaptive and involve *learning* throughout the organisation, not just top management (*see* Chapter 15). Learning must be matched by the appropriate organisational structure. It needs to be more responsive to the changing environment, adaptable and open to initiatives from middle and junior management. More junior managers need to be given more power – *empowerment*.

Importantly, Senge draws an important distinction between two types of learning, only one of which arises from the environmental changes outlined in Exhibit 16.2. These are:

1 *adaptive learning* – understanding changes *outside in the environment* and adapting to these;

2 *generative learning* – creating and exploring new strategy areas for positive expansion *within the organisation itself*.

Both types of learning will come from experimentation, discussion and feedback within the organisation. Rigid, formal, hierarchical organisations are unlikely to provide this. New, more fluid structures are needed, according to Senge. It is interesting to note that, in the high-growth economies of Japan in the 1970s and 1980s and in South-East Asia in the 1990s, one of the major distinguishing features has been participation in the planning process, coupled with flexibility and adaptability, rather than rigid, formal plans.[20] [21]

Using similar evidence, the management guru Tom Peters[22] suggests that leaders and organisations need to be more adaptive if they are to have a greater probability of developing sustainable competitive advantage. If the organisational structure has been successfully developed to produce a flexible, adaptive organisation then it will be able to deliver what he has called the three main outcomes of strategy:

1 total customer satisfaction;

2 innovation;

3 total commitment by all its members to provide service and quality.

Given these three prime outcomes, Peters argues that they will only arise if the organisation is flexible. Such a structure is more important than any specific strategy. Hence, structure comes *before* strategy. It is the process itself that will deliver the successful strategy, rather than some predefined strategy handed down from top management.

A specific example of the link between organisation structure and strategy concerns the generation of the strategy options outlined in Chapter 13. Kanter[23] has argued that the way the company is organised is crucial to this task. Such a structure must come *before* the strategy options are explored in order to ensure that the most innovative options are developed: top management is unlikely to be able to generate these by itself.

Case study 16.3 on ASEA Brown Boveri describes a modern attempt to introduce the strategies of learning and empowerment into a large company. Importantly, the case also shows that such approaches can have major weaknesses. The implementation aspects of learning are explored in Chapter 21, Section 21.4.

16.4.3 Value chain implications for organisational structure

In Chapter 13, we examined Galbraith's view[24] that the value chain could be divided into two broad categories:

1 upstream components involving incoming logistics, purchasing and production;
2 downstream components covering marketing, service and R&D.

According to this basic division, typical strategies to add value might be:

● *upstream*: cost reduction strategies, mass production strategies for unsegmented markets;

● *downstream*: marketing, branding, innovation, often in segmented markets.

Although this two-way separation oversimplifies the complexities of strategy development, it does contain a useful and workable distinction. From a strategy viewpoint, the organisation required for upstream activities, according to the Galbraith definition, is very different from that required further downstream:

● *Upstream organisation structure*. A tightly controlled, centralised structure to achieve such strategies as economies of scale. Profits may be made by operating few plants that are centrally controlled and organised.

● *Downstream organisation structure*. Looser control and a more decentralised structure capable of responding to differentiated market initiatives. Profits are made by small, locally flexible plants with management responsibility only loosely co-ordinated at the centre.

The above separation into two areas is an oversimplification of reality. For example, some recent advances in manufacturing processes have been designed to deliver greater product variety while maintaining low production costs. Equally, some differentiated marketing has been seeking underlying economies of scale from range-branding in order to make marketing more cost-effective. However, for many companies involved in mass production of goods and services, it is quite likely that the upstream parts will tend to be more centralised and the downstream to be more decentralised. To this extent, the strategy and the organisation structure associated with it are at least partially interrelated: some strategies *demand* some structures. One does not come after the other, as outlined by Chandler.

16.4.4 Managing the complexity of strategic change

Much of the prescriptive approach is built around the notion that it is possible to choose precisely what strategies need to be introduced. The issue then becomes one of building the organisation and plans to achieve the chosen strategy. From empirical research, Professor J B Quinn[25] has suggested that this grossly oversimplifies the process in many cases:

- Simple strategic solutions may be unavailable, especially where the proposed changes are complex or controversial.
- The organisation structure may be unable to cope with the 'obvious' solution for reasons of its culture, the people involved or the political pressures.
- Organisational awareness and commitment may need to be built up over time, making it impossible to introduce an immediate radical change.
- Managers may need to participate in the change process, to learn about the proposed changes and to contribute specialist expertise in order to develop the strategic change required.

Quinn suggests that strategic change may need to proceed *incrementally*, i.e. in small stages. He called the process *logical incrementalism*. The clear implication is that it may not be possible to define the final organisation structure, which may also need to evolve as the strategy moves forward incrementally. He suggests a multistage process for senior executives involved in strategy development: this is shown in Exhibit 16.3. Importantly, he recognises the importance of informal organisation structures in achieving agreement to strategy shifts (*see* Chapter 7). If the argument is correct, it will be evident that any idea of a single, final organisation structure is dubious.

Comment

The description of the process certainly accords with the evidence of other researchers. Formal organisation structures are important for day-to-day responsibilities and work, but are only part of the strategy process when it comes to implementing complex and controversial strategic change. The validity of the above description relies on the extent to which radical change is required. Quinn's assumption that change needs to be radical enables him to conclude that the final organisational structure may have to emerge at the end of this period.

16.4.5 Coping with changing strategies and organisations: the new collegiate leadership style

To cope with the uncertainties of strategy development, those who lead the organisation have a key role in guiding, controlling, initiating and employing considered value judgements to move the strategy process forward.[27] The work of leadership is crucial in the development of strategy and the optimal organisational framework. The *authoritarian* leader will continue to decide strategy and then define the organisation to achieve this. However, for leaders who have a different, more collegiate style,[28] strategy and organisation have more complex interrelationships.
In the words of Peter Senge:[29]

> *The old days when a Henry Ford, Alfred Sloan or Tom Watson [the founder of IBM] learned for the organisation are gone. In an increasingly dynamic, interdependent and unpredictable world, it is simply no longer possible for anyone to 'figure it all out at the top'. The old*

Exhibit 16.3 Quinn's logical incremental strategy process and its organisational implications[26]

Strategic stage	Organisational implications
1 Sensing the need for change	Use informal networks in organisation
2 Clarify strategy areas and narrow options	Consult more widely, possibly using more formal structures
3 Use change symbols to signal possible change	Communicate with many who cannot be directly consulted: use formal structure
4 Create waiting period to allow options discussion and newer options to become familiar	Encourage discussion of concerns among interested groups: use formal and informal organisational structures
5 Clarify general direction of new strategy but experiment and seek partial solutions rather than a firm commitment to one direction	General discussion without alienation, if possible, among senior managers. Use formal senior management structure
6 Broaden the basis of support for the new direction	Set up committees, project groups and study teams outside the formal existing structures. Careful selection of team members and agenda is essential
7 Consolidate progress	Initiate special projects to explore and consolidate the general direction: use more junior managers and relevant team members from the existing organisation
8 Build consensus *before* focusing on new objectives and associated strategies	Use informal networks through the organisation. Identify and manage those people who are key influencers on the future strategic direction

Over time, possibly years

Strategic stage	Organisational implications
9 Balance consensus with the need to avoid the rigidity that might arise from overcommitment to the now successful strategy	Introduce new members to provide further stimulus, new ideas and new questions
10 New organisation	*Reorganise the organisation's formal structure to consolidate the changes: at last!*

model 'the top thinks and the local acts' must now give way to integrative thinking and acting at all levels. While the challenge is great, so is the potential payoff.

If these comments are accurate, then it is possible that the structures of the early twentieth century are no longer appropriate. There may need to be a process of discussion *before* strategies and structures are finalised.

According to Senge,[30] there are three key dimensions to the role of the more collegiate leader in strategic change:

1 *Creative tension.* The tension that exists as a new leader moves to close the gap between his/her vision of the future and the current position of the organisation.

2 *New leadership role.* The former role of the authoritarian decision-maker may be too simplistic for the new millennium. The new role will involve:

  ● building the core values and purpose of the organisation;

  ● allowing strategy to emerge (see Mintzberg, Handy and others, Chapter 15);

  ● putting in place processes that allow an organisation to develop and renew itself;

  ● motivating, inspiring and coaching others in the organisation;

  ● adopting the role of custodian or steward of the organisation's people and its purpose.

3 *New skills.* None of the above will be achieved unless new skills are developed and employed, both by the leader and others in the organisation. The four main skill areas are:

  ● building a shared vision so that members of the organisation are committed to its future purpose;

  ● challenging deeply held assumptions without causing individuals to become overly defensive, so that new ideas can surface;

  ● identifying the key interrelationships and the factors critical to the success of the organisation (*see* Chapter 6);

  ● distinguishing the complex but unimportant details from the dynamic and important events that really shape strategy in the organisation.

The new role and skills imply more flexible relationships between the leader and the organisation. Such changes will include not only the organisational relationships but also the strategies associated with them: it is not possible to be a 'listening' leader while at the same time holding fixed, preconceived views on the strategic consequences. Hence, it follows that strategy, structure and leadership have more complex interrelationships. Naturally, the authoritarian leader can define the organisation structure that will implement his/her chosen strategies but, for other leadership styles, the position is more complicated.

Comment

Although the above values and comments may appear more in tune with some of the management thinking of the new millennium, caution is required in three areas:

1 It is not easy or necessarily appropriate to move quickly from a more authoritarian structure to a more collegiate organisation. Informing middle managers that they now have greater freedom may simply make older-style managers perplexed: they may have little experience, knowledge or skills in the new areas. It is too easy to underestimate the changes required in the *attitudes* and *skills base* to operate such an

approach. Such changes involve both the leader and all the members of the organisation learning new roles and relationships over time.

2 According to Hofstede (*see* Chapter 7), some national cultures need greater certainty and dominance from their leaders. Learning and adaptive cultural solutions may not be appropriate in these circumstances. The problems may outweigh the benefits.

3 The resource-based view of strategy development was just beginning to consider the implications for organisational structures. This remained to be fully developed.[31]

▶ Key strategic principles

● According to some modern strategists, Chandler's concept of strategy first and then structure to deliver it may oversimplify the situation. There have been five major criticisms.

● Changes in the business environment and social values of the late twentieth century suggest that others beyond top management may need to contribute to strategy. This is called empowerment of the middle and junior ranks of managers. This can best take place before the final organisation structure is finalised.

● New processes for developing strategy are adaptive and involve learning mechanisms. They also need open, fluid structures that may not be best served by simple functional structures.

● The two broad parts of the value chain, upstream and downstream, suggest two broad organisation routes, one more rigid and centralised than the other. The implication is that strategy and organisation structure are more interrelated than previously suggested.

● When strategic change is radical, it may not be possible to define clearly the final organisation structure. It may be necessary to let the structure emerge as strategy changes and develops.

● Leadership style and content are key determinants of strategy, especially where they involve a more collegiate and less authoritarian approach. In these circumstances, new skills and roles will certainly alter the balance between organisation and the related strategy.

16.5 The links between strategy and structure and the concept of strategic fit

To provide an overview of the ongoing debate between prescriptive and emergent strategists regarding the relationship between strategy and structure, it is useful to examine the approach of the strategist Professor Henry Mintzberg to the links between strategy and structure. He is certainly of the opinion that the two are interlinked, but he provides a thoughtful and useful starting point for exploring the *nature* of the relationship.

Additionally, the concept of the *strategic fit* between strategy and structure (as described by the US strategists Galbraith and Kazanjian) does not claim to be conclusive, but it does provide another way of examining the relationship between the two areas.

16.5.1 The Mintzberg theory of the links between strategy and structure

Mintzberg[32] has provided a methodology for this task. There are two essential elements:

1 the six parts of every organisation;

2 the six basic co-ordinating methods that link them together.

We shall examine these two elements separately and then draw them together to explore the links with strategy.

The six parts of every organisation

Mintzberg refers to these parts of every organisation that have to be connected together, because between them they add value to the organisation (*see* Figure 16.8). The six parts are:

1 *operating core,* where production takes place or services are provided, e.g. factory floor, restaurant, hospital ward;

2 *strategic apex,* where the overall management of the organisation is undertaken, e.g. chief executive and board of directors;

3 *middle line,* containing the managers that exist between the apex and the core;

4 *technostructure,* consisting of those staff who design the processes that monitor and control the operating processes, e.g. engineers, accountants, computer specialists;

5 *support staff,* who directly provide internal services to the operating core, e.g. secretarial, transport, canteen, laundry;

6 *ideology* – the beliefs or culture that drive the organisation. This category is clearly less tangible than the others.

The above areas need to be co-ordinated in order for value to be added by the organisation.

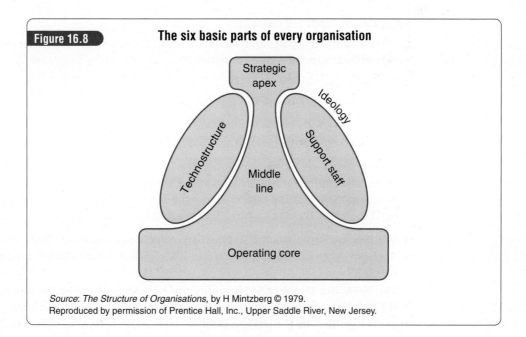

Figure 16.8   **The six basic parts of every organisation**

Source: *The Structure of Organisations,* by H Mintzberg © 1979.
Reproduced by permission of Prentice Hall, Inc., Upper Saddle River, New Jersey.

Six co-ordinating methods

There are six co-ordinating methods that can be employed to link the six parts of the organisation together.

1 *Mutual adjustment* may be carried out, using informal communications. This type of direct discussion is typical in small organisations, where people actually work closely together. It is also used in some complex circumstances to explore difficult strategies, e.g. understanding of the research and development implications of strategic issues.

2 *Direct supervision* may be implemented from the strategic apex to the middle line and operating core.

3 *Standardisation of work processes* may be used to define the way that work is done. For example, factory engineers may be involved in detailed specifications to map out an engineering process and effectively standardise it. Vehicle assembly and quality procedures in car factories are examples of such standardised processes.

4 *Standardisation of outputs* may be employed so that what comes out of a factory or service is predictable. For example, detailed specifications are used at McDonald's to ensure that the Big Mac burger is the same product wherever it is produced in the world: ingredients, cooking times, cooking temperatures, etc., are all carefully defined. Note that such procedures may involve the use of the standardised processes mentioned above as well as standardised *outputs*.

5 *Standardisation of skills* involves the standardisation of the workers' skills (including knowledge in this definition), rather than the process or the output. Professional services in medicine or consultancy are examples in this area. They are assisted by the fact that some skills are common and shared.

6 *Standardisation of norms* may also be introduced to ensure that workers share the same common beliefs. This may be important in voluntary organisations or those that are driven by strong social or religious convictions.

Combination of parts and methods

Using the above six parts and methods, Mintzberg then developed six major types of organisational structures that combine:

- the environment;
- the internal characteristics of the organisation (age, size, etc.);
- the key part of the organisation in delivering its objectives; and
- the key co-ordinating mechanism that binds it together.

He then gave each of these combinations a name that would characterise its main features. The configurations are shown in Exhibit 16.4.

The importance of the matrix lies in the light it throws on the types of *organisation* needed to deliver types of *strategy*. Two examples will make the point:

1 *The machine organisation* is typified by work standardisation. Such an organisation may not wish to seek higher-value-added work in small market segments because this would not be consistent with its current resources and work methods.

2 *The innovative organisation* is typified by mutual adjustments between members of the organisation rather than standardisation of work, skills or output. An organisation structured in this way is unlikely to be able to start turning out standardised

items, unless it changes radically, invests in totally new resou...
skills.

On this basis, when an organisation's structure is defined in broade... merely its reporting structure, then such a structure will guide the strateg... open to the organisation. To this extent, *strategy is linked to structure*.

It should be noted that most organisations will rarely match Mintzberg's six conf... rations precisely. However, they do provide guidelines that link the earlier characteristic... with their strategy and structure implications. Moreover, they could be used to show the implications of what might happen as the organisation changes – for example, becoming larger, with a more complex product range.

Exhibit 16.4	Mintzberg's configuration of organisations and the way they operate			
Mintzberg's strategic configurations	Background: see Part 2 of this book		Structures and linkages		Example
	Environmental analysis	Resource analysis	Key part of organisation	Key co-ordinating mechanism	
Entrepreneurial organisation	Simple/dynamic	Small, young Duplication of jobs	Strategic apex: the boss or owner	Direct supervision	Small computer service company
Machine organisation	High growth or cyclical	Older, large Defined tasks, techno-structure	Techno-structure	Standardisation of work	Computer assembly or car plant
Professional organisation	Stable, complex, closed to outsiders	Professional control by managers	Operating core	Standardisation of skills	Management consultancy or hospital
Divisionalised structure	Diverse	Old and large Strong links possible Standard criteria for resource allocation	Middle line	Standardisation of outputs	Fast-moving consumer goods group
Innovative organisation*	Complex and dynamic	Often young, complex work, experts involved	Support staff	Mutual adjustment	Advertising agency
Missionary organisation	Simple, static	Ideologically driven co-operative Small groups within total	Ideology	Standardisation of norms	Charity or social work

* Note that innovative organisation is called an *adhocracy* in some texts and versions of the above.

Source: Mintzberg, H, 'The Structuring of Organisations' in *The Strategy Process: Concepts and Contexts* 3/E by Mintzberg, H and Quinn, J B, © 1991, pp330–50. Adapted by permission of Prentice-Hall Inc, Upper Saddle River, New Jersey.

...igurations clearly oversimplify the possible organisational combina-
...number of more fundamental criticisms of the approach:

...gued that Mintzberg's version of the *divisionalised structure* is so vague
...ed in value: there may be a number of other different configurations
...ide the divisionalised configuration. In a sense, it is not discriminatory
...lude a number of the other categories, each in its own division.

...be said that some companies do not just standardise one variable as
...as work or processes, but standardise several and that the distinctions
...rg draws between them may not reflect reality. In these cases, there is no
single key co-ordination mechanism.

- There may be connections between the innovative and entrepreneurial organisation types: the way some entrepreneurial companies grow may involve a strategy of innovation.

- Chapter 9 showed how manufacturing innovation has made some real contributions to strategy over the last few years. However, in Mintzberg's categorisation, manufacturing is probably a *machine* rather than an *innovative* organisation.

- This book takes the view that *all* companies need to include innovation as part of all their strategies. To confine it to one configuration is dubious at best.

Overall, Mintzberg's configurations provide some useful guidelines on organisation structure and its relationship with strategy, but they need to be treated with caution.

16.5.2 The concept of strategic fit between strategy and structure

Having examined the relationships that exist between strategy and structure, there is a need to ensure that these two elements are consistent with each other. For an organisation to be economically effective, there needs to be a matching process between the organisation's strategy and its structure: this is the concept of *strategic fit*.[33]

In essence, organisations need to adopt an internally consistent set of practices in order to undertake the proposed strategy effectively. It should be said that such practices will involve more than the organisation's structure. They will also cover such areas as:

- the strategic planning process (see Chapter 17);
- recruitment and training (see Chapter 18);
- reward systems for employees and managers (see Chapter 18);
- the work to be undertaken (see Chapter 18);
- the information systems and processes (see Chapter 17).

This means that issues of strategic fit may not be fully resolved by considering only strategy and structure. It may be necessary to revisit strategy, even when the implementation process is formally under consideration (*see* Chapter 17).

There is strong empirical evidence, however, whether it is from Chandler or Senge, that there does need to be a degree of strategic fit between the strategy and the organisation structure.

Although the environment is changing all the time, organisations may only change slowly and not keep pace with the outside. It follows that it is unlikely that there will be a perfect fit between the organisation's strategy and its structure. There is some evidence that a minimal degree of fit is needed for an organisation to survive.[34] It has also been suggested that, if the fit is close early on in the strategic development process, then higher economic performance may result. However, as the environment changes, the strategic fit will also change. We return to the consequences for organisation structure in Chapter 18.

> ▶ **Key strategic principles**
>
> - In designing organisational structure, it is important to consider the complex links that exist between the structure and strategy. Mintzberg has provided a process for this.
>
> - There are six parts to every organisation and six methods by which they can be co-ordinated. These can then be combined to produce six main types of organisational strategy and structure. They can be linked with typical key elements of the environment and others mechanisms.
>
> - By this process, the organisation's strategy and its likely structure can be interrelated. In this sense, strategy is linked to structure.
>
> - Most organisations do not match the six different configurations precisely, but they do provide guidelines that link strategy to structure.
>
> - At a broader level, the choice between strategies and organisational structures will be determined by the strategic fit between the two areas, i.e. the congruence between an organisation and its structure.

16.6 The choice of management style and culture

16.6.1 Background

Although this chapter has explored the main discussions that have taken place over the last few years on the relationship between strategy and structure, there has been another equally vigorous debate about management style and culture, spanning both practitioner books and academic journals. Early writers included Professor Peter Drucker, who started writing in the 1950s but was still producing books of interest in the 1990s.[35] In the 1980s, Peters and Waterman wrote their influential book *In Search of Excellence*, though Tom Peters has subsequently repudiated some of the guidance.[36] The writings of Charles Handy also represent a significant contribution.[37] Most are a good read but they also present research on how to operate companies, especially from the viewpoint of culture and style.

16.6.2 Culture, style and the relationship with strategy

Although every organisation is the result of its history, products and people, it periodically has the chance to renew itself. In other words, it is able to change its management culture and style. Inevitably, this will have an impact on strategy both in obvious ways, such as the attitude to risk taking, and in more subtle ways, such as the ability of the company to innovate.

To some extent, an organisation will evolve in response to its continually changing environment. Furthermore, the leadership and top management at any point in time will clearly influence the organisation's culture and style. Nevertheless, organisations can also make the deliberate choice to change their culture and style as part of a major shift in strategy. The issues are therefore:

- Should the organisation change its culture and style?
- If so, in what way should the company change these?

It should be noted that this is not just an issue of implementation *after* the strategy has been chosen, but a fundamental choice available as part of the process.

Most of the writers and researchers quoted earlier in this section would argue that a shift in culture and style is essential if a fundamental change in strategy is proposed. They would support this view for three reasons:

1 Fundamental strategic change needs to impact on people in the organisation as well as on decision making. People issues are essentially summarised in culture and style.

2 Leadership is usually important for major changes in strategy. This is likely to encompass some shift in style and, occasionally, a change of leader.

3 Such a shift in culture and style is a *powerful symbol* of the related change in strategy.

16.6.3 The content of the new culture and style

As a starting point in exploring this area, the reader is referred back to the discussion of culture in Chapter 7. In addition, the final decision will clearly be related to the proposed strategic changes. There will also need to be a degree of *strategic fit* between the strategy and the style, just as there was between strategy and structure earlier in the chapter.

More generally, Hart has suggested a range of styles from which the choice can be made: they vary from the autocratic to the collegiate and are shown in Exhibit 16.5. The content of each style can be matched to how the organisation sees itself developing over the period of the strategy.

Importantly, it should be noted that culture and style do not change overnight: it is often possible to introduce a new strategy more quickly than bring about a related change in style. Culture and style take time to develop so the strategic fit may need some adjustment. Hence, the process of introducing a new style needs careful thought.

▶ Key strategic principles

- **Every organisation has the choice of changing its culture and style when it changes its strategy.**
- **In many cases, a change of style is essential when a fundamental change of strategy is proposed.**
- **The content of the culture and style depends on the strategies proposed. There needs to be a degree of strategic fit between the two areas. Importantly, culture and style take time to change and may move more slowly than the proposed strategy.**

Exhibit 16.5		Strategy and style options			
Descriptors	Command	Symbolic	Rational	Transactive	Generative
Style	**Imperial** Strategy driven by leader or small top team	**Cultural** Strategy driven by mission and a vision of the future	**Analytical** Strategy driven by formal structure and planning systems	**Procedural** Strategy driven by internal process and mutual adjustment	**Organic** Strategy driven by the initiatives of those empowered in the organisation
Role of top management	**Commander** Provide direction	**Coach** Motivate and inspire	**Boss** Evaluate and control	**Facilitator** Empower and enable	**Sponsor** Endorse and sponsor
Role of organisational members	**Soldier** Obey orders	**Player** Respond to challenge	**Subordinate** Follow the system	**Participant** Learn and improve	**Entrepreneur** Experiment and take risks

Source: Adapted from Hart, S (1992) 'An integrative framework for strategy-making processes', *Academy of Management Review*, Vol 17, pp327–51. Also reprinted in Hart, S and Banbury, C (1994) 'How strategy-making processes can make a difference', *Strategic Management Journal*, Vol 15, pp251–69.

CASE STUDY 16.3

How ABB empowered its managers and then reversed the process[38]

When the world's largest electrical engineering company, ASEA Brown Boveri (ABB), was formed in 1987, one of its earliest strategic decisions was to reorganise and move power from the centre to its operating companies: empowerment. This case study explores the reasoning and consequences of this major shift in approach and the reasons why it was reversed in 2001.

Rise and fall of ABB

With 2001 revenue of over US$23.7 billion and 157 000 employees around the world, ABB is one of the world's largest traditional electrical engineering companies. Its products include electrical power transmission and distribution, building technologies and automation. It operates in global markets and competes against such major companies as General Electric (US), Westinghouse (US), Siemens (Germany) and GEC Alsthom (UK/France) as well as with the major Japanese groups Mitsui and Mitsubishi.

After success in building its turnover during the 1990s, ABB's sales and profits were down by the time

of the millennium: it actually made a loss in 2001 – *see* Figure 16.9. The reasons for this decline included fierce competition and a weak world economy. However, the company's costs were also higher than those of its competitors: some commentators judged that its whole organisation structure needed simplifying and further costs taking out.

Company history

ABB was formed in 1987 from the engineering interests of the Swedish company ASEA and the Swiss engineering company Brown Boveri. Over the period 1988 to 1990, the company was completely

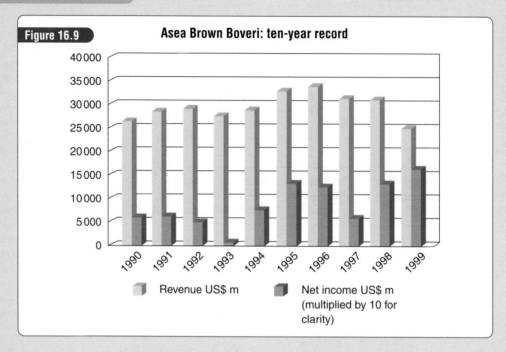

Figure 16.9

Asea Brown Boveri: ten-year record

Revenue US$ m

Net income US$ m (multiplied by 10 for clarity)

reorganised by its new chairman, Percy Barnevik. The central HQ in Switzerland was reduced to a total of 150 people, with a matrix management structure introduced worldwide. The company was split into 1300 smaller companies and around 5000 profit centres, functioning as far as possible as independent operations. Several layers of middle management were stripped out and directors from the central HQ moved into regional co-ordinating companies.

At the same time, the company engaged in a major programme of acquisitions that grew the order intake of ABB from US$16 billion to US$25 billion over two years. Major companies were purchased in the US, Spain, Italy, the UK, France, Spain and Germany. All the negotiations for these major decisions were handled centrally by ABB. A period of consolidation then followed from 1991 to 1993.

Company strategy to empower management

Under the direction of its chief executive, Percy Barnevik, ABB pursued its bold initiative of breaking up the company into 1300 smaller units, each with profit responsibility. The company became something of a case study for business schools

during this period. The moves were essentially aimed at empowering managers to move closer to their customers and at giving them the incentives to act as smaller and more entrepreneurial units. Even research and development was decentralised, with the new operating companies controlling 90 per cent of the group's US$2.3 billion budget. However, central finance and cash management were excluded from the decentralisation process and then used to monitor the performance of the empowered companies across the world.

Barnevik considered that the greatest strategic challenge in running a group of this size was motivating middle and lower managers and shifting entrenched corporate values. As he explained, previously managers had been happy to coast along with 2 per cent gross margins when a 5 per cent margin was possible with more commitment.

By 1991, the company was able to show that empowerment had become the norm for many managers. However, it was still necessary to reinforce the message: 'Now the problem is that they get too happy when they see profit doubled; they think 4 per cent margin is fantastic, and you have to tell them that American competitors can make 10 per cent.' Central management therefore continued to devote much of its time to 'indoctrinating' managers.

Inevitably there were problems. Goran Lindahl, one of ABB's top-level executive team, was given the key role of identifying areas where ABB managers had become complacent or allowed their units to drift. He was given the power 'to shake things up to create an environment of learning'. Five other problems emerged over the next few years:

● The small, empowered units of ABB were not well adapted to handling the big global companies who wanted one centralised negotiating and decision-making unit.

● It was difficult to find sufficient trained, experienced managers in Eastern Europe and Asia.

● There were strains on central staff from the need to manage a complex, decentralised global operation.

● Extra costs were incurred in duplicating management positions in a large number of small companies.

● Small companies were not always able to gain the economies of scale that would be available to larger, more centralised organisations.

New leadership and new organisation structure – 1997

In 1997, Percy Barnevik gave up his position of chief executive. His successor was Goran Lindahl. Their leadership styles were quite different: Barnevik was eloquent, conceptual and led from the front, whereas Lindahl was more down-to-earth, consensual and interested in detail. Nevertheless, Barnevik stayed on as non-executive chairman.

In 1998, Lindahl announced two major strategic moves. First, he accelerated the shift to using Asian labour. Another 10 000 jobs would be lost in Europe and the US and be replaced by the same number of jobs in Asia. The cost for shareholders was estimated at US$1 billion. Second, he scrapped the group's matrix organisational structure and brought in some new, younger executives to the group's managing board. This was later followed by the sale of two unprofitable divisions – power generation and transport – over the next eighteen months.

Then, in 2000, Lindahl suddenly gave up his job. His explanation was that he believed ABB should be led by someone who understands how to exploit the IT revolution and he was not that person. It is fair to say that his sudden departure halfway through his expected term caused some shock among outside observers.

New leadership and new organisation structure – 2000

The new chief executive, Jorgen Centermann, lost no time in completely restructuring ABB. He developed an organisation with four worldwide customer segments, coupled with two backup product segments. He cut the number of subsidiaries form over 1000 to 400, thus having the effect of undoing the 'empowerment' strategy of the early 1990s. He gave three reasons:

1 the need to focus more on its main large, global customers;

2 the need to cut costs, especially those associated with the duplication of management essential to decentralisation;

3 the need to exploit the power of the Internet.

In addition, he appointed two new main board directors, one with responsibility for 'corporate processes' and the other for 'corporate transmission'. These were both associated with his desire to turn ABB into an 'agile, knowledge-based company' and to develop 'brain power' as a corporate motto.

Case questions

1 *How important to the strategy of empowerment is a sophisticated financial control system? And how vital is the central monitoring (e.g. Lindahl)? What does this mean for empowerment?*

2 *If the world is becoming increasingly global, do you think that ABB's unit empowerment ever stood any chance of success?*

3 *To what extent, if at all, can large, global companies empower local managers? What are the implications for strategy development – centralised or decentralised?*

Summary

● For the *prescriptive* strategist, the strategy is developed first and then the organisational structure is defined afterwards. Thus, organisational structure is a matter of how the strategy is implemented and does not influence the strategy itself.

● However, from an *emergent* strategy perspective, the relationship between strategy and structure is more complex. The organisation itself may restrict or enhance the proposed strategies and may even make the implementation of certain strategies highly unlikely.

● The strategist Alfred Chandler contended that it was first necessary to develop the strategy. After this task was completed, the organisational structure was then devised to deliver that strategy. His conclusion was based on his study of the way in which US businesses were formed and organised in the early part of the twentieth century. However, he only studied businesses that had developed from small enterprises into larger, more diversified structures.

● According to the early strategists, formal structures, clear responsibilities, identified lines of reporting and a central directorate for strategy development are all important elements of organisational design. They are undertaken after the basic strategy has been agreed. As organisations become larger and more complex, it may be necessary to form divisions and decentralise some power to them.

● The *centralisation* versus *decentralisation* issue may be particularly important in designing the organisation's structure. According to many strategists, this should only be undertaken once the basic strategy has been decided. There are no simple rules to define where the *balance* needs to be struck between centralisation and decentralisation.

● According to some modern strategists, Chandler's concept – strategy first and then structure to deliver it – may oversimplify the situation. There have been five major criticisms. Changes in the business environment and social values of the late twentieth century suggest that people other than top management may need to contribute to strategy. This is called *empowerment* of the middle and junior ranks of managers. This can best take place before the organisational structure is finalised.

● New processes for developing strategy are adaptive and involve learning mechanisms. They also need open, fluid structures that may not be best served by a simple functional organisation.

● The two broad parts of the value chain, *upstream* and *downstream*, suggest two broad organisation routes, one more rigid and centralised than the other. The implication is that strategy and organisation structure are more interrelated than was previously suggested.

● When strategic change is radical, it may not be possible to define clearly the final organisation structure. It may be necessary to let the structure emerge as strategy changes and develops. Leadership style and content are also key determinants of strategy, especially where they involve a more collegiate and less authoritarian approach. In these circumstances, new skills and roles will certainly alter the balance between the organisation and the related strategy.

● In exploring strategy and structure, it is useful to examine the links between the two elements, starting with the basic *design* of organisational structures. This will be governed by four main criteria: simplicity, the least-cost solution, motivation of those involved, and the existing organisation culture.

- In designing organisation structure, it is also important to consider the *complex links* that exist between the structure and strategy. Mintzberg has provided a process to understand this. There are six parts to every organisation and six methods by which they can be co-ordinated.

- The parts and methods can be combined to produce six main types of organisational strategy and structure. They can be linked with typical key elements of the environment and other mechanisms. By this process, the organisation's strategy and its likely structure can be interrelated. In this sense, strategy is linked to structure. Most organisations do not match the six different configurations precisely, but these do provide guidelines that link strategy to structure.

- The choice between strategies and organisational structures will more broadly be determined by the *strategic fit* between the two areas, i.e. the congruence between an organisation and its structure.

- Every organisation has the choice of changing its *culture* and *style* when it changes its strategy. In many cases, a change of style is essential when a fundamental change of strategy is proposed. The content of the culture and style depends on the proposed strategies. There needs to be a degree of strategic fit between the two areas. Importantly, culture and style take time to change and may move *more slowly* than the proposed strategy.

QUESTIONS

1 Is Alfred Chandler's view of the relationship between strategy and structure correct? Give reasons for your views.

2 Should the Sony Corporation be centralised or decentralised in its manufacturing operations?

3 How should strategy and structure be developed in the following organisations?

  (a) A large multinational involved in several different but interconnected product fields

  (b) A major local government department with a heavy administrative workload

  (c) A small manufacturing business with 25 employees

  (d) A small self-governing trust that administers a charitable foundation

4 Examine each of the criticisms of the strategy-first structure-afterwards argument. To what extent is each valid?

5 Does the comparison in the GM case study between the business environments of the early and late twentieth century exaggerate the differences between the two periods? What are the implications of your view for the organisational structures and strategy?

6 'Strategy deals with the unknowable, not the uncertain … Hence logic dictates that one proceed flexibly and experimentally from broad concepts toward specific commitments, making the latter concrete as late as possible.' (Professor J B Quinn)

Discuss the implications for the design of organisational structure.

7 What problems might there be with the new collegiate leadership style? Consider your answer both in terms of its introduction and its appropriateness for organisations.

8 Are the critical comments on Mintzberg's six strategic configurations outlined in Section 16.5 accurate and valid? What are the implications of your response?

9 Take an organisation with which you are familiar and characterise its management style according to the strategy and style options set out in Exhibit 16.5. What are the implications for the way that strategy is likely to be developed?

STRATEGIC PROJECT

ABB is a traditional electrical engineering company that has needed to adapt to the new millennium. It has chosen to decentralise and then to become more centralised. It has also elected to focus on the Internet and knowledge-based strategy. What have been the strategies of its competitors – their names are listed in the case study? To what extent might ABB learn from them? Do they have higher profit margins than ABB? What are the organisation structures and styles of competitors? Does knowledge-based strategy really matter or are other areas of greater importance in a global environment?

FURTHER READING

J R Galbraith and R K Kazanjian (1986) *Strategy Implementation*, 2nd edn, West Publishing, St Paul, MN. An excellent book for its clarity of thought, research evidence and precision of argument. It has contributed significantly to the development of this chapter. It is a pity that it appears to be out of print. Highly recommended.

Professor Dan Schendel (1994) 'Introduction to competitive organisational behaviour: toward an organisationally-based theory of competitive advantage,' *Strategic Management Journal*, 15, pp1–4. This whole issue has an interesting review of the way in which

strategy and organisational theory have developed since the 1960s.

Alfred Chandler (1987) *Strategy and Structure: Chapters in the History of the American Industrial Enterprise*, MIT Press, Cambridge, MA. Still a classic text.

Professor D Pugh (1984) *Organisation Theory*, Penguin, London. This book brings together various papers, including those of other influential theorists of the early twentieth century such as F W Taylor and H Fayol.

Professor R M Kanter (1983) *The Change Masters*, Unwin, London. This is a well-researched, thoughtful and provocative book on innovation.

NOTES & REFERENCES

1 This case is adapted from an article by William Dawkins (1995) 'Japan in Asia Supplement', *Financial Times*, 15 Nov, pVI.

2 Galbraith, J R and Kazanjian, R K (1986) *Strategy Implementation*, 2nd edn, West Publishing, St Paul, MN, p6.

3 Mullins, L (1996) *Management and Organisational Behaviour*, 4th edn, Pitman Publishing, London, Ch10.

4 Schendel, D (1994) 'Introduction to competitive organisational behaviour: toward an organisationally-based theory of competitive advantage', *Strategic Management Journal*, 15, pp1–4. This whole issue has an interesting review of the way in which strategy and organisational theory have developed since the 1960s.

5 Chandler, A (1987) *Strategy and Structure: Chapters in the History of the American Industrial Enterprise*, MIT Press, Cambridge, MA.

6 Williamson, O (1975) *Markets and Hierarchies*, The Free Press, New York.

7 Schendel, D (1994) Op. cit.

8 Chandler, A (1987) Op. cit., pp8–14.

9 Williams, K, Haslam, C, Williams, J and Johal, S (1994) *Cars*, Berghahn Books, Providence, RI, p98.

10 Chandler, A (1987) Op. cit., pp13–14.

11 Pugh, D (1984) *Organisation Theory*, Penguin, London. This book brings together various papers, including those of other influential theorists of the early twentieth century such as Taylor and Fayol.

12 Mullins, L (1996) Op. cit. Chapter 10 has a good general description of the principles of organisational design. However, the Mullins text treats such matters in a more general context than the specific requirements of strategy.

13 For example, *see* Thompson, A and Strickland, A (1993) *Strategic Management*, 7th edn, Irwin, Homewood, IL, and Johnson, G and Scholes, K (1993) *Exploring Corporate Strategy*, 3rd edn, Prentice-Hall, London.

14 Mullins, L (1996) Op. cit., Ch10.

15 Mullins, L (1996) Op. cit., pp344–5.

16 Chandler, A (1987) Op. cit. This section is based on parts of Ch3.

17 *Sources*: General Motors Corporation, *Annual Report and Accounts 1994*; Done, K (1994) 'Upbeat sounds in Motown', *Financial Times*, 19 Jan, p19; *The Economist* (1992) 'Survey of the car industry', *Supplement*, 17 Oct; 'General Motors Case B', Mintzberg, H and Quinn, J B (1991) *The Strategy Process*, Prentice Hall, New York, pp978–93.

18 Prahalad, C K and Hamel, G (1994) 'Strategy: the search for new paradigms', *Strategic Management Journal*, Summer Special Issue, p11.

19 This section has been adapted from the ideas of Kanter, R M (1983) *The Change Masters*, Unwin, London, pp42–3 and pp398–9. This is a well-researched, thoughtful and provocative book.

20 Pucik, V and Hatvany, N (1983) 'Management practices in Japan and their impact on business strategy', *Advances in Strategic Management*, 1, JAI Press Inc, pp103–31. Reprinted in Mintzberg, H and Quinn, J B (1991) Op. cit.

21 World Bank (1994) *World Development Report 1994*, Oxford University Press, New York, pp76–9.

22 Peters, T (1984) 'Strategy follows the structure: developing distinctive skills', *California Management Review*, Spring. Reprinted in Mintzberg, H and Quinn, J B (1991) Op. cit.

23 Kanter, R M (1983) Op. cit. See references at the end of Ch15.

24 Galbraith, J R (1983) 'Strategy and Organisational Planning', *Human Resource Management*, Spring–Summer. Galbraith's ideas have been re-expressed in 'value chain' terminology for the purposes of this book. He used the term 'industry chain'.

25 Quinn, J B (1980) 'Managing strategic change', *Sloan Management Review*, Summer. Reprinted in Mintzberg, H and Quinn, J B (1991) Op. cit. and De Wit, B and Meyer, R (1994) *Strategy: Process, Content and Context*, West Publishing, St Paul, MN.

26 *Source*: Lynch, R, based on reference 25.

27 These comments arise directly from the writings of Quinn quoted above. They are also consistent with the conclusions of Chandler earlier in the century.

28 *See* Hart, S and Banbury, C (1994) 'How strategy making processes can make a difference', *Strategic Management Journal*, 15, p254 and Ch17.

29 Senge, P (1990) 'The leader's new work: building learning organisations', *Sloan Management Review*, Fall. Reprinted in De Wit, B and Meyer, R (1994) pp132–41.

30 Senge, P (1990) Op. cit.

31 Moingeon, B, Ramanantsoa, B, Métais, E and Orton, J D (1998) 'Another look at strategy–structure relationships: the resource-based view', *European Management Journal*, 16(3), June, pp297–305.

32 *See* also Mintzberg, H (1991) 'The structuring of organisations', pp330–50 in Mintzberg, H and Quinn, J B (1991) Op. cit.

33 Galbraith, J R and Kazanjian, R K (1986) Op. cit., Ch7.

34 Galbraith, J R and Kazanjian, R K (1986) Op. cit., p113.

35 Examples: Drucker, P (1961) *The Practice of Management*, Heinemann/Mercury, London, and (1967) *Managing for Results*, Pan Books, London.

36 Peters, T (1992) *Liberation Management*, Macmillan, London.

37 Handy, C (1989) *The Age of Unreason*, Business Books, London, and (1991) *The Gods of Management*, Business Books, London.

38 ABB Case study references: Ghoshal, S and Bartlett, C (1995) 'Changing the role of top management: beyond structure to process', *Harvard Business Review*, Jan–Feb; *Financial Times*, 15 Nov 1989; 21 Mar 1990, p27; 5 Apr, 1991, p11; 15 Nov 1991; 20 Aug 1993, p15; 25 Aug 1993, p19; 15 Mar 1994, p32; 12 Aug 1994, p17; 18 Aug 1994, p18; 13 Aug 1998, p27; 24 Aug 1998, p8; 24 March 1999, p26; 1 March 2000, p28; 26 October 2000, p28; 30 October 2000, p16; 12 January 2001, p24 (Lex) and p29; 18 January 2001, p13; 25 April 2001, p24 (Lex); 25 July 2001, p28; 19 September 2001, p30; 25 October 2001, p28; 22 November 2001, p22 (Lex) and p28; 23 November 2001, p28; 31 January 2002, p30; 14 February 2002, p30; 21 February 2002, p29; *ABB Annual Report and Accounts*, 1993, 1994 and 2001; video interview with Percy Barnevik on Tom Peter's 1993 video film: *Crazy Times Call for Crazy Organisations*. *See* also reference 36 above and the interview with Mr Barnevik.

The implementation process

This part of the book addresses implementation – the process by which the organisation's chosen strategies are put into operation. It may involve planning new activities, developing an organisational structure to undertake them and considering how to persuade stakeholders that their best interests will be served by undertaking the strategy.

However, empirical research has shown that the implementation process itself may influence the organisation's strategy. In other words, the distinction between the implementation process and the strategy choice may be overstated. Nevertheless, many organisations consider planning and control separately from the generation of strategy, while also recognising the interaction between the two. These issues are fully explored in the following chapters.

The implementation process

The *prescriptive* strategic process

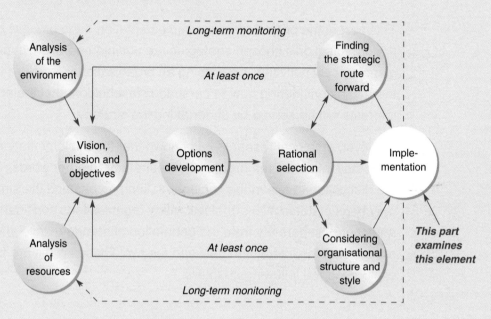

The *emergent* strategic process

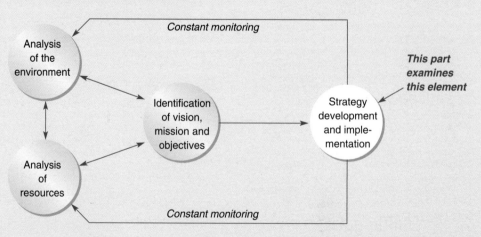

Chapter 17

Resource allocation, strategic planning and control

- What is the process of implementation?
- How are tasks and objectives set?
- How are resources allocated?
- How is strategic planning conducted and what is its influence on strategy?
- How is strategy controlled?
- What is the role of information processing and systems?

Chapter 18

Organisational structure and people issues

- What are the main principles involved in designing an organisation's structure to implement its strategy?
- What special considerations apply when seeking innovatory strategies?
- How are managers selected and motivated to implement strategies?

Chapter 19

International expansion and globalisation strategies

- What is meant by international expansion and globalisation? How are they implemented?
- What are the main theories involved and how do they relate to individual countries and companies?
- What are the benefits and problems of company globalisation strategy?

Chapter 20

The dynamics of strategy development

- What is the relationship between an organisation's changing purpose and the dynamics of its strategy?
- How do the various elements of strategy interact?
- What are the implications of strategy dynamics for implementation?

Chapter 21

Managing strategic change

- Why do people resist strategic change?
- What are the main principles involved in strategic change?
- How can we devise a programme to manage such change?

Chapter 22

Building a cohesive corporate strategy

- How can the various elements of strategy be brought together?
- How are relationships changing between stakeholders?
- How is strategic management changing?

Chapter 17

Resource allocation, strategic planning and control

Learning outcomes

When you have worked through this chapter, you will be able to:

- outline the nature and limitations of the implementation process;
- identify the interrelationships between strategy and implementation;
- understand the way that the objectives, tasks and timing are implemented;
- describe how resources are allocated between parts of the organisation;
- explore how strategic planning can be conducted and critically evaluate its merits;
- outline the main elements of control and monitoring, and investigate their importance for corporate strategy implementation.

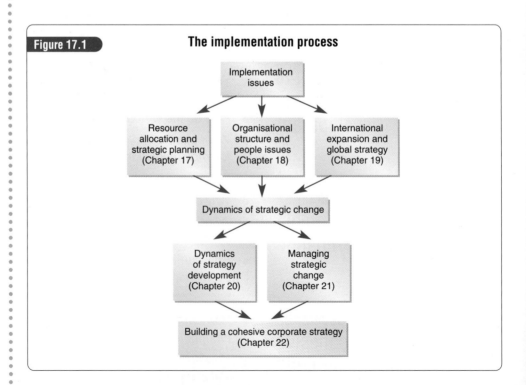

Figure 17.1 **The implementation process**

Introduction

By whatever method strategies are selected, there will come a time when every organisation will need to put its strategies into practice, i.e. to implement them. This chapter explores the basic steps involved in this process and the possible links between strategy development and implementation.

As the prime aim in implementing strategy is to deliver the mission and objectives of the organisation, this chapter discusses these and considers especially the implications for the tasks to be undertaken by individuals and the allocation of the necessary resources. Detailed strategic plans are often developed, especially where there are elements of experimentation or uncertainty in the chosen strategies. As the strategies are implemented, they clearly need to be monitored and controlled. The way in which these activities are linked together is shown in Figure 17.1.

Importantly, the process of implementation relies on *human resources* to carry out these tasks. Changes in strategy may necessitate reorganisation. Individuals and groups may need to experiment and to learn about new areas. They need to be organised, given incentives and may possibly even require to be recruited. These areas are explored in Chapter 18.

International strategy development is more complex to plan and more time-consuming to implement. Because of the implementation issues, we tackle this as a separate topic in Chapter 19. However, it should be said that some organisations might wish to consider international strategy earlier.

Strategy implementation usually involves change. In fact, both the organisation and its environment are constantly changing. Most of this part of the book (Part 6) makes the simplifying assumption that such changes can be ignored for a limited period while the chosen strategies are implement. However, Chapters 20 and 21 are an attempt to redress the balance.

Chapter 20 explores the dynamics of change on the purpose, resources and environment of the organisation. In particular, it examines the way that the dynamics interact with the concept of implementation itself.

Chapter 21 concentrates on the *people aspects* of change, such as change in responsibilities, work practices and the balance of power. *Strategic change* can be either a major opportunity or a significant threat to the people in the organisation and therefore to the implementation of strategy itself. To some extent, change can be managed positively to achieve the desired implementation.

Chapter 22 then briefly explores some areas of modern strategic activity that form part of the implementation process and contribute also to current strategic debate. In particular, it attempts to draw together the various strands of strategy development and implementation.

European football: viable strategy badly implemented? Or does the whole strategy need a rethink?[1]

Many of Europe's leading football clubs are in financial trouble as a result of changes in the way that football strategy has developed over the last 20 years. Yet the money pouring into the leading football clubs has rocketed over the same time. This case explores the strategic issues.

There are real difficulties across European football: for example, the famous Italian club Lazio, the 2002 European Championship Spanish club Real Madrid and the top English club Leeds United have all reported significant losses in recent years. Beyond the leading clubs, the situation is far worse – at the time of writing, some 30–40 English League football clubs have either gone into administration or are threatened with immediate trouble.

What is the basic strategic problem?

Even wealthy football clubs, like Manchester United, have to watch their profits carefully. But from a strategy perspective, they cannot survive by themselves – they need other clubs to make up a league to play against. Moreover, such a league must inevitably have winners and losers if the game is to be interesting. This means that clubs will go through periods when they achieve success and then periods when success may be more elusive. During the losing periods, strategic game theory can be used to show that this is likely to have financial consequences.

If this is correct then it follows that football clubs will always face strategic uncertainty. But does it mean that the losing clubs will always make losses and can never recover the situation? For example, the English League club Bradford City was relegated from the Premiership in 2001. In the following football year 2001/02, Bradford lost revenue from television and other sources amounting to around US$45 million and simply could not cut its costs fast enough. Its alternative strategy was to fund the loss from its bank for one year, hope that it would gain promotion in the season ending in 2002 and then pull in the funds again. In practice, it ended up filing for administration in May 2002 and, at the time of writing, this proud club could totally disappear. There will be other clubs in later years facing the same difficulty.

Is this endemic to football strategy across Europe at the present time? Or just a feature of a few foolish clubs who have not realised that any strategy needs to be implemented carefully? To explore this question, it is useful to explore the way that football clubs generate and use their funds.

Where does football money come from and where does it go?

Across Europe's main football leagues, the sources of funds will vary, depending on whether the club has a rich patron, the fame of the club and its loyal fan base, the extent of television deals and the size of the league – the Belgian league is inevitably smaller than the Bundesliga or UK Premiership and therefore generates less funds. It will also depend on club ownership – Manchester United is a public company with shareholders and able to raise funds from them; Real Madrid is a mutual company owned by its 50,000 fans and therefore not able to raise funds in the same way. However, there are broadly five main sources of funds:

1 *Gate money*: typically, this makes up 10–15 per cent of a club's total income.

2 *Transfer fees*: these could be anything between 10–40 per cent of total income. Some of the smaller clubs have survived by selling players. Even large clubs can benefit: Italy's Juventus sold Zinedine Zidane for US$70 million in 2001 to Real Madrid and Filippo Inzaghi to AC Milan for US$25 million. (And then the money was promptly spent on Pavel Nedved from Lazio, Lilian Thuram from Parma and Gianluigi Buffon from Parma.)

3 *Television rights*: typically, these could account for up to 40 per cent of total income for some leading clubs but much less for the smaller clubs. For example, BSkyB spent US$1.8 billion buying the rights to three years of live games in the English Premiership – shared equally between the clubs that survive each year. The Italian Serie A television rights for three years cost around US$450 million in 2001. It is widely believed that such television payments across Europe will be lower in the future.

4 *Merchandising and sponsorship*: typically, this could be worth around 10–20 per cent of total income for many clubs. Clearly, the most famous clubs are able to negotiate much larger deals.

5 *Wealthy owners*: these could be responsible for anything from zero to 80 per cent of total income. For example, the Agnelli family (who control Fiat cars) have ploughed well in excess of US$100 million into Juventus over the years and Mohamed Al Fayed (who owns the London department store Harrods) has invested some US$90 million into the English league club Fulham in recent years.

Where is the money spent? Apart from administration and management, there are obvious costs like football training and medical fees, hotel accommodation costs and travel costs. Some funds are also taken by the national and European leagues to invest and develop the game. But the majority of the funds go in players' wages – for instance, David Beckham's 2002 contract will pay him nearly US$7 million per year for three years. With a typical squad of some 40 players, the leading clubs can easily spend most – perhaps all – of their income in this area. It might be argued that Beckham and his colleagues are overpaid, but his wages can be justified by the concept of economic rent – *see* Chapter 6.

Case question

Is this a problem of the correct strategy – finances and costs essentially sound but the implementation – players' wages and so on – needing some adjustment? Or does the strategy itself need to be changed in the face of fundamental problems across Europe?

Note: The book's website has some further articles that provide more background.

17.1 The implementation process

17.1.1 Basic elements of the implementation process

Whether the organisation faces the strategic problems of European football or the opportunities of new technologies such as the Internet, it will have to draw up plans to pursue its strategies. Essentially, these need to address the following questions:

● What activities need to be undertaken in order to achieve the agreed objectives?

● What is the timescale for the implementation of these plans?

● How will progress be monitored and controlled?

To turn general strategies into specific implementation plans involves four basic elements:[2]

1 Identification of general strategic objectives – specifying the general results expected from the strategy initiatives;

2 *Formulation of specific plans* – taking the general objectives and turning them into specific tasks and deadlines (these are often cross-functional);

3 *Resource allocation and budgeting* – indicating how the plans are to be paid for (this quantifies the plans and permits integration across functions);

4 Monitoring and control procedures – ensuring that the objectives are being met, that only the agreed resources are spent and that budgets are adhered to. Importantly, monitoring also takes place against the projections on which the strategies are based – for example, national economic change and competitive activity.

The relationship between these activities is shown in Figure 17.2.

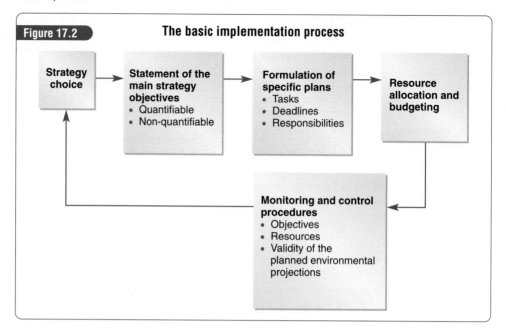

Figure 17.2   **The basic implementation process**

17.1.2   Types of basic implementation programme

Implementation programmes will vary according to the nature of the strategic problems which the organisation faces. These problems will range from the extreme and urgent need for change, such as at a bankrupt European football club, to the more ongoing strategic development processes of Canon or Nestlé (described in the case studies later in this chapter). The two essential causes of variation in implementation programmes are:[3]

1 the degree of uncertainty in predicting changes in the environment;

2 the size of the strategic change required.

In response to these issues, several types of basic implementation programme can be carried out. At one extreme, there is the *comprehensive implementation programme* for fundamental changes in strategic direction. At the other extreme, there is the *incremental implementation programme*, where implementation is characterised by small changes and short time spans within the general direction implied by the strategy. Both these approaches have their difficulties, so a compromise may be chosen in practice: the *selective implementation programme*.

● *Comprehensive implementation programmes* are employed when the organisation has made a clear-cut, major change in strategic direction, such as crisis faced by bankrupt European football clubs at the beginning of this chapter. Other reasons might include a new competitive or new technological opportunity. Implementation then becomes a matter of driving through the new strategies, regardless of changes in the environment and the reactions of those affected. Close co-ordination across the organisation is usually essential for success.

● *Incremental implementation programmes* may be used where there are conditions of great uncertainty – for example, rapidly changing markets or the unknown results of R&D. As a result, timetables, tasks and even objectives are all likely to change, depending on the outcome of current activities. Important strategic areas may be left deliberately unclear until the outcome of current events has been established.[4] Essentially, the uncertainty is handled by a flexible strategic approach.

- *Selective implementation programmes* may be used where neither of the above represents the optimal way forward. Comprehensive programmes involving radical change may require such fundamental changes that they encounter substantial resistance, such as negative reactions from fans to the collapse of their favourite European football club. Incremental programmes may be inappropriate when it is necessary to make a significant change that needs the impetus generated by a single, large step. Selective programmes represent the compromise required: a major programme developed in selective areas only.

Readers will recognise that the above two extremes are related to the prescriptive and emergent strategic approaches explored throughout this book.

To determine the type of implementation programme required, the following three criteria can be employed:

1 Are clear and substantial advantages to be delivered in a specific area, e.g. investment in a new drug that will provide competitive advantage?

2 Are there large increments that cannot be subdivided, e.g. a new factory with long lead times for construction?

3 Is it important to protect some future step that may be required but cannot be fully justified on the basis of current evidence, e.g. an investment in a new distribution facility that will be needed if development programmes proceed according to plan?

For many organisations, it is useful to draw a basic distinction between:[5]

- *ongoing, existing activities* with higher certainty and more predictable strategic change, barring a major cataclysm;
- *new activities* with higher uncertainty and possibly major strategic change.

17.1.3 Implementation in small and medium-sized businesses

The basic elements of the implementation process – the identification of general strategic objectives; the formulation of specific plans; resource allocation and budgeting; monitoring and control procedures – are equally applicable to smaller organisations. All organisations need to specify the tasks to be undertaken and monitor progress. Moreover, choosing the correct type of implementation programme – comprehensive, incremental or selective – according to the nature of the problem and the particular environment of the organisation is also important to small and medium-sized businesses. Indeed, any small or medium-sized business that attempts to obtain finance for a new venture will be asked to supply the essential information outlined above. Banks and other lending institutions no longer rely on vague promises and good intentions.

Key strategic principles

- **Implementation covers the activities required for an organisation to put its strategies into practice. There are several basic elements to this process: general objectives, specific plans and the necessary finances, coupled with a monitoring and control system to ensure compliance.**

> ▶ *Key strategic principles continued*
>
> - **Within the implementation process, it is useful to draw a distinction between different types of implementation. There are three major approaches: comprehensive, incremental and selective.**
> - **Implementation in small and medium-sized businesses may be less elaborate but needs to follow the same general principles.**

17.2 Relationship between implementation and the strategy development process

Although many strategy researchers and writers have fully supported implementation as a separate stage after strategy choice,[6] over the last 20 years others have expressed significant and well-founded doubts. Their concerns have been based on empirical research into the way that strategy actually develops.

In the light of this research, it is important to view the basic implementation process as a series of steps over time, with complex learning and feedback mechanisms between implementation and strategy. This does not mean that Section 17.1 on basic implementation is incorrect; it does mean that implementation needs to be seen as a process over time that may well alter strategy. Consequently, it may even alter the organisation's vision and purpose.

The main areas of research that contributed to this alternative view of the implementation process were:

- the empirical research of Pettigrew and Whipp;
- the concepts of bounded rationality and minimum intervention;
- the Balanced ScoreCard of Kaplan and Norton;
- the work of other emergent theorists, such as Quinn and Senge.

17.2.1 The empirical research of Pettigrew and Whipp

In a series of research studies between 1985 and 1990, the UK-based researchers Pettigrew and Whipp analysed how strategic change occurred in four sectors of UK industry.[7] Their evidence did not extend beyond the UK but their conclusions are likely to be applicable to other geographic areas. They suggested that strategic change can most usefully be seen as a *continuous* process, rather than one with distinct stages such as the formulation of strategy and then its implementation. In this sense, they argued that strategy was not a linear movement with discrete stages but an experimental, iterative process where the outcomes of each stage were uncertain. A first small step might be actioned and then the strategy itself adjusted, depending on the outcome of the actions.

Comment

The empirical evidence to support this view is significant. The description of the continuous process is similar to, but not necessarily the same as, the incremental implementation programme described in Section 17.1.2. According to this interpretation, strategy implementation at bankrupt European football clubs outlined in Case study 17.1 might have been better served by a series of separate smaller actions, conducted on an experimental basis, rather than one major restructuring announcement. Chapter 21 will explore further the research of Pettigrew and Whipp.

17.2.2 Bounded rationality and minimum intervention

In exploring how managers develop their implementation plans, the strategists Hrebiniak and Joyce[8] have suggested that the implementation process is governed by two principles: bounded rationality and minimum intervention.

● *Bounded rationality* derives from the work of researchers Cyert and March (see Chapters 2 and 7). They showed that managers in practice have difficulty in considering every conceivable option. They therefore reduce their logical choices to a more limited 'bounded' choice. Arguing in a similar way, Hrebiniak and Joyce suggest that implementation is also likely to be limited: managers will act in a rational way but will reduce the overall task to a series of small steps in order to make it more manageable. Thus the strategic goals and implementation are likely to be split into a series of smaller tasks that can be more easily handled but may not be optimal.

In addition, the authors suggest that *individuals* will make rational decisions but will include in this process their *personal* goals which are not necessarily the same as those of the organisation itself. Implementation needs to ensure that there is consistency between personal and organisational goals.

● *Minimum intervention* has been summarised by the authors as follows:

> *In implementing strategy, managers should change only what is necessary and sufficient to produce an enduring solution to the strategic problem being addressed.*

Practising managers might recognise this principle as the rather more basic sentence: 'If it ain't broke, don't fix it.' The implication here is that implementation may be constrained by the need to consider the impact on the strategy itself.

Comment

Both approaches represent useful, if somewhat simple, guidance on strategy implementation. They suggest that implementation, strategy and goals are interrelated, which needs to be taken into account in the development of implementation plans.

17.2.3 The Balanced Scorecard: the contribution of Kaplan and Norton

During the course of researching and implementing strategy at a number of US corporations in the early 1990s, Professor Robert Kaplan of the Harvard Business School and David Norton of the international strategy consultants Renaissance Solutions developed the Balanced Scorecard. 'The scorecard is not a way of formulating strategy. It is a way of understanding and checking what you have to do throughout the organisation to make your strategy work.'[9]

The Balanced Scorecard arose from their perceptions about two significant deficiencies in the implementation of many corporate strategic plans:

1 *Measurement gap.* Although most companies measure performance ratios, quality and productivity, these are mainly focused on historical figures – for example, 'How are we doing, compared with last year?' The two authors discovered that such measures may have little to do with future success. In addition, although such ratios were important, they did not measure other important aspects of future strategy, especially those that

were more difficult to quantify. For example, future strategy might stress the importance of customer satisfaction and loyalty, employee commitment and organisational learning, but none of these might be measured.

2 *Strategy gap between general plans and managerial actions.* The authors claimed that many companies began major new strategic initiatives but that these often had little impact on the organisation. The reason was that the strategic plans were often not translated into measures that managers and employees could understand and use in their daily work.

Kaplan and Norton were particularly keen to move beyond the normal financial ratio data such as return on capital employed and earnings per share. They claimed that these are essentially functional measures and that what really matters in strategy implementation is the process: 'Processes have replaced (or are replacing) departments and functions.'[10] They identified three main types of process that are important:

1 *management* – how the leader runs the organisation, how decisions are made and how they are implemented;

2 *business* – how products are designed, orders fulfilled, customer satisfaction achieved and so on;

3 *work* – how work is operationalised, purchased, stored, manufactured and so on.

They argued that these are the activities that implement the agreed strategies but they are not the same as return on capital, market share and growth data and the other measures that often summarise the outcome of a corporate strategy.

Kaplan and Norton developed the Balanced Scorecard to overcome these problems.[11] The Balanced Scorecard combines quantitative and qualitative measures of the selected strategy. It acknowledges the different expectations of the various stakeholders and it attempts to link scorecard performance measures to the chosen strategy. There are four key principles behind the scorecard:

1 *translating the vision* through clarifying and gaining consensus;

2 *communicating and linking* by setting goals and establishing rewards for success;

3 *business planning* to align objectives, allocate resources and establish milestones;

4 *feedback and learning* to review the subsequent performance against the plan.

While recognising that every strategy is unique, they then identified four strategy perspectives that need to appear on every scorecard. These are summarised in Exhibit 17.1. The four areas are:

1 *Financial perspective.* This translates the purpose of the organisation into action through clarifying precisely what is wanted and gaining commitment to it. For example, if the survival of the business is important, then cash flow features prominently on the scorecard.

2 *Customer perspective.* Purpose needs to be seen in the context of customer-oriented strategy. This should include not only market share data but also areas explored in Chapter 5, such as customer retention, customer profitability measures and customer satisfaction. For example, if the strategy highlights the introducton of a new product, then the scorecard might go beyond sales and share data to explore the extent of customer satisfaction and repeat business.

3 *Internal perspective.* This concerns internal performance measures related to productivity, capital investment against cost savings achieved, labour productivity improvements

and other factors that will indicate the way that the organisation was undertaking the strategy inside the company. This might also involve setting internal strategy targets and establishing milestones for the implementation of the strategy. For example, the development of a new Internet site will involve not only the customer satisfaction mentioned above but also registration of the web page, design of the site, maintenance of the site – all of these elements might be specified and targeted with dates and costs.

4 *Innovation and learning perspective*. This provides feedback and learning through strategy reviews and sharing comments on the outcome of events. It has the effect of highlighting the importance of communicating and linking people with the purpose through education, goal setting and rewards for achieving the required performance. For example, the achievement of a market share objective might be accompanied by a review of what was done well and what could be improved next time.

Comment

Some of these areas represent nothing new: educating, obtaining feedback, setting targets and milestones have been known for many years. Moreover, as Norton himself has acknowledged, the danger of the scorecard is that it lays strong emphasis on what is measurable, which is not necessarily what is important strategically, rather than on gaining commitment and action. Moreover, the scorecard may lead to too much measurement in larger companies, turning the whole process into a bureaucratic nightmare. However, the scorecard does represent a useful attempt in two major areas:

1 translating the abstract vision of strategic purpose into practical and useful action areas;

2 moving the strategy beyond a few overly simple measures such as earnings per share and return on capital employed.

Exhibit 17.1 **Balanced Scorecard: summary of strategy perspectives**

Strategy perspective	*Example*	*Example of scorecard measure*
Financial perspective	Shareholders' views of performance	• Return on capital • Economic value added • Sales growth • Cost reduction
Customer perspective	Customer satisfaction	• Customer satisfaction • Customer retention • Acquisition of new customers
Internal perspective	Assess quality of people and processes	• Training and development • Job turnover • Product quality • Stock turnover
Future perspective	Examine how an organisation learns and grows	• Employee satisfaction • Employee retention • Employee profitability

17.2.4 Further emergent approaches to implementation

In Chapter 15, the work of Quinn, Senge and others on the strategy process was examined. They suggest quite clearly that implementation needs to be considered not just as a single event with fixed and rigid plans but rather as a series of implementation activities whose outcome will shape and guide the strategy. The full strategy will not be 'known' in advance but will 'emerge' out of the implementation.

This work has been complemented by that of Pettigrew and Whipp[12] who concluded that there were three interlinking aspects to strategic change:

1 *Analytical aspects.* Implementation must involve many aspects of the organisation. These are the areas that have been emphasised in various strategic models and frameworks and are explored in Parts 2 and 3 of the book.

2 *Educational aspects.* 'The new knowledge and insights into a given strategy that arise from its implementation have to be captured, retained and diffused within the organisation' (Pettigrew and Whipp). Thus implementation cannot be regarded as immutable and unchanging. The organisation will learn about its strategies as it implements them.

3 *Political aspects.* 'The very prospect of change confronts established positions. Both formulation and implementation inevitably raise questions of power within the organisation. Left unattended, such forces can provide obstacles to change . . . Indeed, in the case of Jaguar [Cars] in the 1970s, ultimately such forces can wreak havoc' (Pettigrew and Whipp).

Comment

Educational and political aspects (examined further in Chapter 21) are important elements of the implementation process and again suggest that implementation and strategy formulation are interlinked. The three emergent perspectives that ask for implementation are summarised in Exhibit 17.2.

Exhibit 17.2

Three emergent perspectives on the implementation process

1 Implementation must involve many parts of the organisation.

2 Implementation needs to be seen as an ongoing activity rather than one major event with a finite outcome.

3 Implementation needs to be flexible and responsive to outside and internal pressures.

▶ Key strategic principles

- According to Pettigrew and Whipp, implementation is best seen as a continuous process, rather than one that simply occurs after the formulation of the strategy.

- Hrebiniak and Joyce placed boundaries on implementation in terms of the ability of managers to consider every choice rationally and to evaluate the impact of implementation on strategy itself.

- Emergent approaches to strategy imply that implementation needs to be considered not just as a single event but rather as a series of activities, the outcome of which may to some extent shape the strategy.

▶ *Key strategic principles continued*

- The Balanced Scorecard was developed as a method of translating abstract strategy into specific areas of company action to help strategy to work. The Balanced Scorecard combines quantitative and qualitative measures of the selected strategy. It acknowledges the different expectations of the various stakeholders and it attempts to link scorecard performance measures to the chosen strategy.

- There are four key principles behind the scorecard: *translating the vision* through clarifying and gaining consensus; *communicating and linking* by setting goals and establishing rewards for success; *business planning* to align objectives, allocate resources and establish milestones; *feedback and learning* to review the subsequent performance against the plan.

- The four strategy perspectives that appear on every scorecard are: financial, customer, internal, future.

- The main benefits lie in the focus of the scorecard on turning strategy into implementation and the development of objectives that go beyond simple financial measures.

CASE STUDY 17.2

Strategic planning at Canon with a co-operative corporate style

Since 1957, the Japanese company Canon has operated strategic planning. However, it has not been a rigid, inflexible process imposed by top management. Instead, it has been a free-flowing, open approach driven by the strategic vision of Canon's senior and other managers. This vision covered the values of the company, the market position it expected to hold over many years and the resources needed to develop and sustain it. The strategies and their implementation have proved highly successful. This case study examines the planning process in more detail.

Canon's sales have grown from Y4.2 billion in 1950 to Y2907 billion in 2001 (US$22 billion). The company has developed a strong market share in its leading products: for example, 70 per cent of the world laser beam printer engine market, 40 per cent of the world bubble jet printer market, second only to Hewlett-Packard. Overall, it has a strong global base in its major product areas: photocopiers, computer peripherals, computer and fax equipment, cameras, video recorders and optical products. Its ten-year record is shown in Figure 17.3.

As an example of its strategic vision, Canon identified the world photocopying market back in the 1960s as an area for growth. Xerox Corporation (US) had been the world leader since the 1950s, with its exclusive, patented technology. However,

this did not stop Canon declaring its intention in 1967 of taking 30 per cent of the world market by the 1980s and its vision 'to catch Xerox through technological differentiation'. Through the 1960s and 1970s, it went about this by developing technology that was totally different from the Xerox patents and pursuing the small photocopier market niche, which remained poorly served by Xerox. Today, Canon is world market leader and has developed its core competencies out of photocopiers into laser printers, digital scanners, colour bubble jet printing, digitised optical images and other areas. It will be noted that printing was only one of Canon's areas of competence by the 1990s (*see* Table 17.1).

Strategic planning at Canon, however, is not just a matter of vision and the identification of core

CASE STUDY 17.2 continued

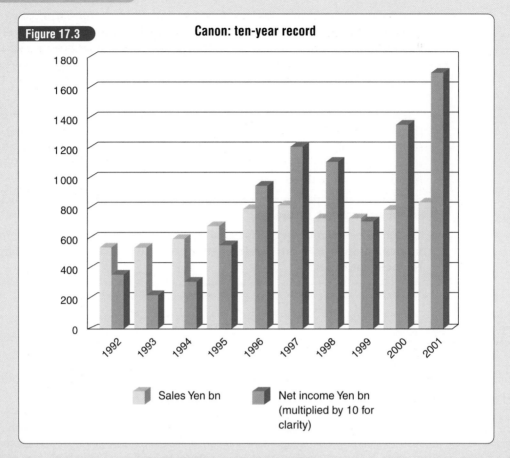

Figure 17.3 Canon: ten-year record

Legend: Sales Yen bn; Net income Yen bn (multiplied by 10 for clarity)

Table 17.1 Canon's core competencies and product development

	1950s	1960s	1970s	1980s	1990s
Core competencies	• Optical • Precision mechanical	• Electronics • Fine optical	• Printing • Materials technology • Communications	• As 1970s but more advanced	• Biotechnology • Energy saving
Additional new products	• Still camera • Movie camera • Lenses	• Reflex camera • Calculators	• Copier • Laser printer • Word processing • Fax	• Office automation • Video recorders • Computers	• Audio visual • Energy saving • Information systems • Medical equipment

competencies. Exhibit 17.3 outlines the strategic planning process at Canon. It is driven initially by the centre and its strong belief in customer satis-faction. Typical of large Japanese companies, the centre has also defined its main growth plan under the headline 'Excellent Global Corporation Plan'.

Some Western companies might find this title vague and lacking in commercial directness, However, the detail from Canon is clear with its focus on 'gaining and maintaining top market shares. At Canon, top share and profitable operations must go hand in hand.' In other words, there is no question of driving for market share at the expense of profits.

Exhibit 17.3 **The process of strategic planning at Canon**

Activity	Content		Examples in 2001
Basic assumptions, analysis and projections *(prepared by the centre, but after open discussion)*	• Canon's strengths and weaknesses • Opportunities and threats • Business philosophy and beliefs		• Customer satisfaction • Cost reduction • Competitive products
Long-range strategy: six years *(decided by centre but with input and discussion from divisions)*		• Vision • Long-term objectives • Key strategic projects	• Beat Xerox • World class • Develop Asian markets • TV broadcasting equipment • Colour personal copiers • Power-saving laser printers
Medium-range strategy: three years *(started by divisions and then consolidated at HQ)*	• Canon itself: resources cultures, etc. • Environment: general outlook; competition; scenarios if major shift in assumptions • Basic assumptions and projections • Resource allocation • Goals and policies • Contingency • Timetables		• Specific quantified goals developed • Resources include capital projects, human resources and the key strategic projects
Short-term plan: one year *(developed by the divisions)*	• Budgeting: financial goals are stressed • Build on the medium-range plan		

Such elements appear regularly in strategic planning in Japanese companies and are employed in order to shape the approach to strategy development in its early stages. They appear in the basic analysis along with the assumptions and projections about the future (as explored in Parts 2 and 3 of this book). In developing its long-range plan, Canon has to be directed and constrained by the distinctive features of its business. It is these characteristics that determine the nature of the strategic planning process at the company:

● *Highly automated manufacturing plant* that takes years to design, install and bring to full efficiency. Planning therefore needs to be developed over a number of years, not just the short term. It also needs to take into account the possibility that new designs will need further work and detailed co-operation from all those working to install them.

● *High-technology products* that take years to develop and perfect, including the possibility of some failures. Planning will again need to be experimental but will also need to be open and not involve criticism of failure to implement a new, experimental product.

● *Synergy and core competencies* that provide linkages across a number of product areas. These take time and resources and rely on strong co-operation across different divisions. Planning will act as co-ordinator and will also direct the divisions towards the areas that have been identified: it is likely to be centralised.

Although the centre sets the long-term strategy, the product divisions begin the *medium-range planning*

within the constraints set by the centre. Considerable emphasis is placed on scenarios and contingency planning so that Canon is not caught out by an unexpected event, such as a sudden rise in the value of the yen. These plans are then consolidated by the centre.

For the short-term plan, financial objectives take greater precedence. They are usually prepared as budgets which are derived from the medium-term plan. Each division prepares its budget and these are then consolidated by the centre. From this amalgamation, the corporate HQ then prepares short-term plans on personnel, capital investments and cash flow. The data are also used to build the balance sheet and profit and loss account.

Although this might appear bureaucratic and unwieldy, Canon actually operates the process in an open, friendly and challenging fashion. Employees are encouraged to debate the issues, to take risks and to present new ideas. Strategy planning is regarded as an opportunity and a challenge, rather than a chore driven by hide-bound company rules.

Source: See reference 13.

Case questions

1 *What are the main problems of large companies such as Canon in managing the strategic planning process?*

2 *How has Canon succeeded in remaining innovative? Could it do even better? If so, how?*

17.3 Objectives, task setting and communicating the strategy

It is important to set out and agree clear guidelines with those individuals who will implement the strategies: typically, this process of task setting and communications will cover what is to be done, by what time and with what resources. This is a significant implementation issue and involves five basic questions, which are summarised in Exhibit 17.4.

Exhibit 17.4   **Task setting and communications: the basic questions**

1 Who developed the strategies that are now being implemented?

2 Who will implement the strategies?

3 What objectives and tasks will they need to accomplish?

4 How can objectives and tasks be handled in fast-changing environments?

5 How will the implementation process be communicated and co-ordinated?

In reality, the answers to these questions will depend primarily on the way that the strategies have been developed. In this sense, the strategy development phase and the strategy implementation phase are interconnected.

17.3.1 Who developed the strategies that are now being implemented?

In the past, some strategy writers have taken the view that the strategies in large corporations will be largely developed at the centre:

> Most of the people in the corporate centre who are crucial to successful strategy implementation probably had little, if anything, to do with the development of the corporate strategy.[14]

If this is the case, then the implementation process is very different from one where there has been a lengthy debate and agreement on the strategies. In this latter case, managers will know that they are likely to be responsible for implementing something that was discussed with them some weeks or months earlier. For example, if strategies have been produced using the procedures described in the Canon Case study 17.2, then most managers will be clear on who will be doing what because they will have been closely involved in developing them. Ignorance will be higher and commitment to the new strategy will be lower among those managers who have had no involvement in developing the strategy.

It is important therefore to address the question of who developed the strategy, rather than simply the question of who will implement it. For example, was it just a central team or was there full consultation? The response to this question will shape the implementation process.

17.3.2 Who will implement the strategies?

This question is important because it will define who is responsible for implementing a specific strategy. It is difficult to review progress at a later stage if no one is accountable for the way the strategy is being carried out. In many small companies, it is possible that a number of managers will be involved in the strategy development process because of the small size. The question needs more elaboration as organisations grow in size.

One important issue here is who makes the decision: is it the centre telling the managers or is the matter open for discussion and negotiation? Generally, this book takes the view that discussion is preferable because it is more motivating and rewarding all round. However, it may occasionally be necessary to instruct those involved.

17.3.3 What objectives and tasks will they need to undertake?

In Chapter 12, we examined the concept of the hierarchy of objectives – corporate, divisional and functional – cascading down from the top of the organisation. The main objectives and activities for implementation can also be considered as following a similar process. The overall corporate objectives need to be translated into objectives for each of the main areas of the business and then these objectives need to be reinterpreted into the tasks and action programmes that then need to be undertaken in order to achieve them.

Figure 17.4 gives an example in a functional company of how the overall objective is reinterpreted in this way. The corporate objectives are translated into functional objectives that are each designed to make a contribution to the whole. This is not necessarily a simple task and may require several iterations before a satisfactory result is achieved. The marketing, operations and other tasks are then defined from the functional objectives. These are then broken down into plans: timetables, resources to achieve the objectives and other matters. Deadlines are usually set to indicate the date for completion of a particular task, as are *milestones* – interim indicators of progress so

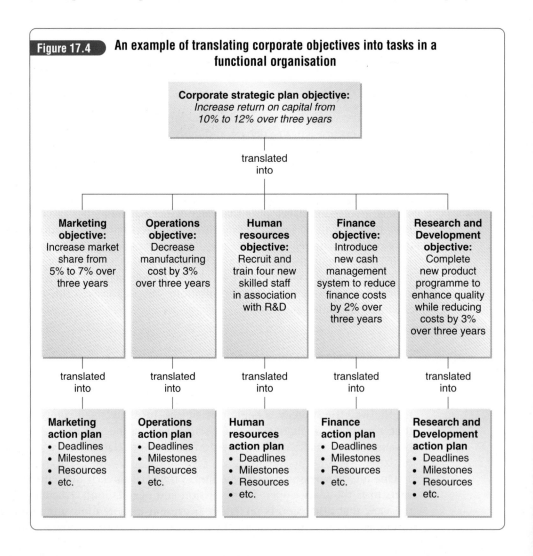

Figure 17.4 An example of translating corporate objectives into tasks in a functional organisation

Corporate strategic plan objective:
Increase return on capital from 10% to 12% over three years

translated into

Marketing objective:	Operations objective:	Human resources objective:	Finance objective:	Research and Development objective:
Increase market share from 5% to 7% over three years	Decrease manufacturing cost by 3% over three years	Recruit and train four new skilled staff in association with R&D	Introduce new cash management system to reduce finance costs by 2% over three years	Complete new product programme to enhance quality while reducing costs by 3% over three years

translated into

Marketing action plan	Operations action plan	Human resources action plan	Finance action plan	Research and Development action plan
• Deadlines • Milestones • Resources • etc.	• Deadlines • Milestones • Resources • etc.	• Deadlines • Milestones • Resources • etc.	• Deadlines • Milestones • Resources • etc.	• Deadlines • Milestones • Resources • etc.

that those monitoring events can review implementation while there is still time to take remedial action.

In practice, the definition of objectives, tasks and plans may be simpler in smaller companies and more complicated in larger companies. For example, at Canon three sets of objectives and plans are prepared: on six-year, three-year and one-year time-horizons. They do not all have the same degree of detail but they are all fully co-ordinated across the company.

17.3.4 How can objectives and tasks be handled in fast-changing environments?

When environments are changing fast, it may be exceptionally difficult to specify satis-factory objectives and tasks: by the time they have been agreed and communicated, the environment may have changed. As changes occur, the objectives may rapidly become impossible or straightforward, depending on the nature of the changes. In this situa-tion, it makes little sense to adhere to objectives developed for earlier situations. Three guidelines can be applied:

1 flexibility in objectives and tasks within an agreed general vision;
2 empowerment of those closest to the environment changes, so that they can respond quickly;
3 careful and close monitoring by the centre of those reacting to events.

The purpose of such surveillance is to ensure that actions taken do not expose the centre itself to unnecessary strategic or financial risk. This is vital if the organisation wishes to avoid the fate of companies such as Barings Bank in 1995, which crashed with debts of over US$1.5 billion, partly as a result of inadequate controls in such a rapidly changing environment.

17.3.5 How will the implementation process be communicated and co-ordinated?

In small organisations, it may be unnecessary, overcomplex or inappropriate to engage in the elaborate communication of agreed strategies. People who have explored the strategic tasks together during the formulation of the strategy and meet each other on a regular basis may not need lengthy communication during implementation. However, in larger enterprises, it is likely to be essential for four reasons:

1 to ensure that everyone has understood;
2 to allow any confusion or ambiguity to be resolved;
3 to communicate clearly the judgements, assumptions, contingencies and possibly the choices made during the strategy decision phase;[15]
4 to ensure that the organisation is properly co-ordinated.

This last point deserves particularly careful thought and action because co-ordination involves two major strategic areas: value chain linkages and synergy.

In Chapter 6, the value chain was introduced and its ability to deliver *unique linkages* across the organisation was discussed. The purpose of such linkages is to develop com-petitive advantage because they are unlikely to be capable of exact replication by other companies whose history, competencies and resources will be marginally different. Such linkages will be meaningless at the implementation stage if careful co-ordination is lacking.

> ### ▶ Key strategic principles
>
> - When setting objectives and tasks, the first question to be established is that of who developed the strategy that is now to be implemented. The answer to this question will influence the implementation process.
> - Individual objectives and tasks follow from the agreed overall objectives. It may be necessary to experiment to find the optimal combination of events.
> - In fast-changing environments, it may not be possible or desirable to have rigid objectives because they may be made redundant by outside events.
> - Communication and co-ordination are vital to satisfactory implementation. These are especially important to ensure understanding of the plan and its underlying assumptions.

17.4 Resource allocation

Most strategies need resources to be allocated to them if they are to be implemented successfully. This section explores the basic processes and examines some special circumstances that may affect the allocation of resources.[16]

17.4.1 The resource allocation process

In large, diversified companies, the centre plays a major role in allocating the resources among the various strategies proposed by its operating companies or divisions.[17] In smaller companies, the same mechanism will also operate, although on a more informal basis: product groups, areas of the business or functional areas may still bid for funds to support their strategic proposals.

There are three criteria which can be used when allocating resources.

1 *The contribution of the proposed resources towards the fulfilment of the organisation's mission and objectives.* At the centre of the organisation, the resource allocation task is to steer resources away from areas that are poor at delivering the organisation's objectives and towards those that are good. Readers will recognise this description as being similar to that employed when considering the movement of funds in the BCG *product portfolio matrix* in Chapter 4: in that case, cash was diverted from cash cows towards stars and so on. The principle is similar here but relies on centrally available funds rather than the diversion of funds.

2 *Its support of key strategies.* In many cases, the problem with resource allocation is that the requests for funds usually exceed the funds that are normally available. Thus there needs to be some further selection mechanism beyond the delivery of the organisation's mission and objectives. This second criterion relates to two aspects of resource analysis covered in Chapter 6:

- *the support of core competencies,* where possible, in order to develop and enhance competitive advantage;
- *the enhancement of the value chain,* where possible, in order to assist particularly those activities that also support competitive advantage.

Although both of these should underpin the organisation's objectives in the long term, they can usefully be treated as additional criteria when resources are allocated.

3 *The level of risk associated with a specific proposal.* Clearly, if the risk is higher, there is a lower likelihood that the strategy will be successful. Some organisations will be more comfortable with accepting higher levels of risk than others so the criterion in this case needs to be considered in relation to the risk-acceptance level of the organisation.

17.4.2 Special circumstances surrounding the allocation of resources

Special circumstances may cause an organisation to amend the criteria for the allocation of resources. Still based on the common principle of *bargaining* for the centre's funds, some organisations will consider the following:

- *When major strategic changes are unlikely.* In this situation, resources may be allocated on the basis of a *formula*, e.g. marketing funds might be allocated as a percentage of sales based on past history and experience. The major difficulty with such an approach is its arbitrary nature. It may, however, be a useful shortcut.

- *When major strategic changes are predicted.* In this situation, additional resources may be required either to drive the strategic process or to respond to an expected competitive initiative. In both cases, *special negotiation* with the centre is required rather than the adherence to dogmatic criteria.

- *When resources are shared between divisions.* In this situation, the centre may seek to enhance its role beyond that of resource allocation. It may need to establish the degree of collaboration and, where the areas disagree, *impose* a solution. The logical and motivational problems associated with such an approach are evident.

17.4.3 Caution regarding the resource allocation process

Hamel and Prahalad have reservations about the whole resource allocation process.[18] They view it as offering the wrong mental approach to the strategy task, arguing that it is more concerned with dividing up the existing resources than with using the resources more effectively and strategically.

> *If top management devotes more effort to assessing the strategic feasibility of projects in its resource allocation role than it does to the task of multiplying resource effectiveness, its value added will be modest indeed.*

They make an important cautionary point.

▶ Key strategic principles

- **The resource allocation process is used to provide the necessary funds for proposed strategies. In circumstances of limited resources, the centre is usually responsible for allocating funds using various decision criteria.**

- **Criteria for allocation include the delivery of the organisation's mission and objectives, its support of key strategies such as core competencies and its risk-taking profile. Some special circumstances such as unusual changes in the environment may support other resource allocation criteria.**

- **There is a risk that the resource allocation process will ignore the need to use resources more effectively and strategically.**

Informal strategic controls at Nestlé[19]

Because of the diversity of its product portfolio, Nestlé has chosen in the past to devolve strategy to its main operating areas and control them informally from the centre. This case study describes the strategic planning procedures, but also shows how they are becoming more centralised as the company attempts to improve its performance and operational efficiency.

With sales of over US$70 billion, Nestlé (Switzerland) is the world's largest food and consumer goods company. Its main product areas include coffee (Nescafé), milk and baby foods, confectionery and frozen foods. It operates globally through a series of geographical zones and a set of product *strategic business units* (SBUs). For example, zone 1 is Europe and there is an SBU for the confectionery and ice cream product area operating on a worldwide basis.

Because of the wide variation in the SBUs in its portfolio, Nestlé has chosen to give *strategic* control

of its operations to the individual SBUs. Each SBU has a full range of functional expertise in its business area: marketing, production, research and so on. However, *operational* decisions rest with the zones and below them the national companies. In the past, the role of the centre has been to co-ordinate and to allocate resources and this continues to the present with some modifications, described later in the case. The Nestlé structure for strategic planning, budgets and reporting is shown in Figure 17.6. The centre begins the process by issuing instructions to the SBUs for the next planning

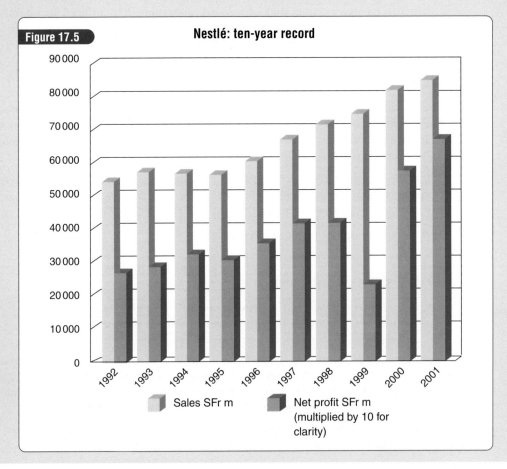

Figure 17.5

Nestlé: ten-year record

Sales SFr m

Net profit SFr m (multiplied by 10 for clarity)

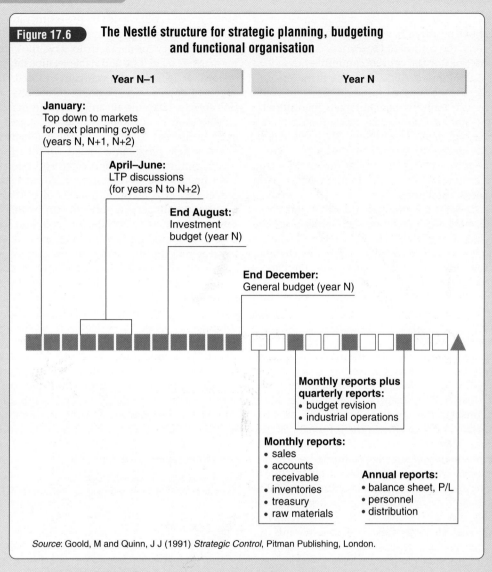

Figure 17.6

The Nestlé structure for strategic planning, budgeting and functional organisation

Source: Goold, M and Quinn, J J (1991) *Strategic Control*, Pitman Publishing, London.

cycle. The SBUs then work on their three-year long-term plans (called LTPs). Every SBU prepares an LTP each year but some are merely updates from previous years. In order to promote strategic discussion with the centre, the LTPs are then circulated. They will include such areas as brand positioning, market share and competitive activity, pricing, capital proposals and new product development. However, as from 2000, the centre has initiated an additional layer of co-ordination and control on an experimental basis that will take some five years to be fully implemented.

Because the company operates in relatively mature markets, it is able to operate a system of checks and balances with more lengthy debate between the centre and the SBUs than might be appropriate where markets are changing fast and quick decisions are required. Hence, following the LTP preparation early in the year, discussions are held on content in the period from April to June between the SBUs, zones and the centre. The Nestlé executive committee has to give its approval. Later in the year, there is an investment and revenue budget review. The strategies and activities can be

▶

changed at this point if the market situation or competitive positions have altered significantly.

However, the controls and balances do not simply take the form of the official committees described above but are more subtle. A Nestlé manager commented on the control procedures: 'You could achieve your monthly budget targets by disturbing the strategy; for example, by repositioning brands or chang[ing] media expenditure. But if you did so, it would quickly be noticed by the product group director at the centre. This would not be through a formal report, but through informal contacts with the country in question.'

In a similar way, although the SBUs and zones are separated in decision-making terms from the centre, most are located in the same geographical location – at Nestlé's HQ in Vevey, Switzerland. Here is a senior manager talking about the chocolate strategy group, which was at one time located in York, England. 'I got increasingly sucked into Vevey because of the need to talk to the various zone managers, and to all the corporate functions and services . . . I don't believe in electronic communication: face-to-face discussions are vital, especially in a group the size of Nestlé.' This principle of direct informal contact is encouraged, even if it means that some managers have extensive travel commitments. The aims are to produce an integrated team and to maintain the informal communications that provide the real checks and balances to the Nestlé style of strategic planning.

Nestlé believes that such informal approaches to planning and monitoring by the centre are useful in guiding and developing corporate strategy. They are probably just as effective as the formal reporting against strategic objectives. Financial rewards for achieving strategic targets are not an important aspect of the strategic process. Peer pressures, promotion and personal competitiveness are greater incentives in ensuring that strategies are delivered. A longer-term view is taken of management per-

formance and competence by the centre rather than specific achievement against targets. This is reflected in the tendency for managers to serve the company for many years in long and stable relationships.

However in 2000, the company realised that its devolved approach to planning meant that it was not able to take full advantage of the benefits of globalisation – economies of scale, shared R&D expenditure and so on. Hence, the company introduced a new programme called GLOBE. The aim was 'to improve the performance and operational efficiency of our businesses worldwide. In the process, we will revisit all aspects of our business practices to shape new ways to run Nestlé.' Thus the company was introducing common coding around the world for items such as raw and packaging materials, finished goods and customers.

The aim of GLOBE was to consolidate information, leveraging the company's size, and to communicate better across the world. There would also be an exchange of best practice and data: common information systems would be developed to achieve this. The whole project was expected to cost US$1.9 billion and, by 2006, deliver cumulative savings of the same magnitude. It would be introduced progressively throughout the company, starting with Switzerland, part of South America and Malaysia/Singapore. Clearly, the new project represented a shift from the informal controls of the current system, even though the new system would not replace that approach.

Case questions

1 *What characterises the Nestlé style of strategic planning? To what extent is this a function of its large size? Its product range? Its geographical spread?*

2 *What, if any, are the dangers of informal strategic controls such as those operating at Nestlé?*

17.5 Strategic planning

17.5.1 What is strategic planning?

The purpose of strategic planning is to use a *formal planning system* for the development and implementation of the strategies related to the mission and objectives of the organisation. Importantly, strategic planning is no substitute for strategic thinking; it

merely for...
will *integrate* t...
tion of each stag...

Professor George...
be an isolated event t...
ongoing activity that resp...
of the calendar. To ensure...
process must come from man...
formulating the strategy and ens...
strategies, objectives and action plan...

Many companies believe that, in...
is important to establish first the backgro...
ness is conducted, including the key factors...
the company will explore its *long-term vision* a...
be only achieved over a number of years and wou...
new technologies and ideas. A *medium-term plan* ca...
two or three years, where the environment is sufficient...
and budgets consistent with the medium term are then...
see this process as not just happening in sequence but inv...
revisiting before each stage is finalised. Figure 17.7 illustrates th...

Sometimes such a cycle is repeated by the company every ye...
describes such a process at Nestlé. However, because of the potenti...
length of such investigations, it would be most unusual if *every* aspect...
was reviewed every year from a long-term perspective. Product groups, s...
core competencies, different group objectives are often chosen as starting...

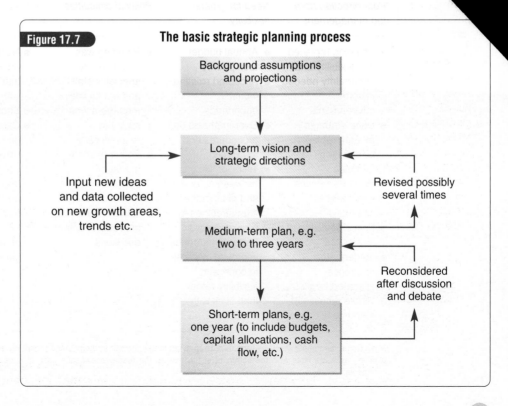

Figure 17.7 **The basic strategic planning process**

Background assumptions and projections

Long-term vision and strategic directions

Input new ideas and data collected on new growth areas, trends etc.

Revised possibly several times

Medium-term plan, e.g. two to three years

Reconsidered after discussion and debate

Short-term plans, e.g. one year (to include budgets, capital allocations, cash flow, etc.)

us, the former

the ... mental

erior financial
s the oil price
as we saw in
cording to its
plication.[23][24]
bit 17.5 sum-
e noted that
, confined to
on a broader
for the nar-

nning is no
, many com-

te culture

to develop
sation
that can cope
with uncertainty

alises the strategy process in some organisations. More specifically, the plan
he activities of the organisation and specify the *timetable* for the comple-

Day is right when he suggests[20] that strategic planning should not
hat culminates in a clear-cut decision. Instead, it should be an
onds simultaneously to the pressure of events and the dictates
organisational commitment, involvement in the planning
levels of the organisation – each with a distinct role in
ring the integration of corporate resource allocations,

undertaking the strategic planning process, it
nd assumptions and the basis on which busi-
for success (*see* Chapter 3). Following this,
d broad strategic direction: these might
ld be expected to include the input of
n then be developed for the next
ly stable. *Short-term annual plans*
developed. It is important to
lving much iteration and
basic process.
ar – Case study 17.3
al complexity and
of the business
ecial topics,
points for

in some environments	...ccepted existing industry boundaries	specialist staff and not by line managers who have the responsibility	that can cope with uncertainty
• Deep strategic thought replaced by planning formulae	• Overemphasis on procedures and form filling	• Power of some managers threatened by new procedures	• Short-termism
• Short-term focus and financial emphasis	• Tests for 'fit' between resources and plans rather than stretches for new resources	• Ability of entrenched interests to delay decisions	• Overemphasis on financial results
• Poor discussion of key issues	• Better to introduce improved systems to cope with flexibility rather than stick with rigid plan		• Lack of risk taking and entrepreneurial flair
• Inadequate resources allocated for plans			• Little toleration of the occasional failure
• Whole process of resource allocation			

Note: Some comments might be regarded as applying to any form of strategy development rather than strategic planning as such. Note also the comment in the text on the research evidence used to support some of the comments.

panies still need to look beyond the short term and to co-ordinate their main activities, especially where significant commitments have to be made over lengthy time spans. The two main case studies on Nestlé and Canon in this chapter have been chosen from successful companies which still use some form of strategic planning. Consequently, attitudes to strategic planning are beginning to change again. Even Mintzberg, who has been highly critical of strategic planning in the past, has now conceded that it does fulfil a useful function within certain limits.[27]

Comment

Mintzberg is right in his emphasis on the need for innovative thinking, which may not be best served by a strongly bureaucratic strategic planning process. Overall, this book takes the view that Mintzberg is correct in his identification of the role for strategic planning: it summarises the decisions taken elsewhere and is useful for making strategy operational. Strategic planning is no substitute for careful and innovative thinking on the main strategic issues.

17.5.3 Planning strategies and styles

Although a large number of companies undertake some form of strategic planning, it is important to understand that there are many variations in the way that it is conducted. The reasons for this include:

- *Environment.* Stable environments lend themselves to longer time-horizons. Stability also favours a more centralised approach to planning, because there is less need to respond to rapid variations in the market, e.g. Nestlé.

- *Product range.* As products become more diverse across a company, it becomes more difficult to develop coherent core competencies, synergies and linkages across the value chain. In these circumstances, the planning style may move from one seeking co-operation across divisions to one based on simple financial linkages, e.g. the more unrelated parts of General Motors in Chapter 16.

- *Leadership and management style.* Particularly in smaller companies, this will inevitably guide the approach to the development of strategy and its co-ordination across the company. It may also apply in some larger companies, e.g. Richard Branson at Virgin, Jürgen Schrempp of DaimlerChrysler and Rupert Murdoch of News Corporation.

There has been no wide-ranging international study on the range of management styles. However, Goold and Campbell conducted such a study during the 1980s on 16 diversified UK companies.[28] They distinguished several different styles for conducting strategic planning. The purpose of identifying the different approaches was to define the manner in which the *centre* added value to the company's separate businesses. The researchers suggested that there were two main ways in which value could be added:

1 The centre could help to shape the plans of each business – the *planning influence.*

2 The centre could control the process as the plans were being implemented – the *control influence.*

From the empirical research, three main styles of strategic planning were then identified as being most common:

1 *Strategic planning.* The centre is involved in formulating the *plans* of the various businesses. Then the emphasis is on long-term objectives during the *control* process. Canon

is an example that conforms approximately to this, although there is more collaborative effort at Canon than is perhaps implied by the definition. *See* Case study 17.2.

2 *Financial control.* The centre exercises strong short-term financial control but otherwise the businesses are highly decentralised and able to operate as they wish. The individual businesses are able to develop longer-term plans if they judge that it is useful. It should be noted that there is little attempt to co-ordinate across companies in such an arrangement. Synergies, value chain linkages and core competencies are largely absent. Relatively few companies operate rigidly this way in the new millennium. Cisco Systems' financial controls have some of these characteristics. *See* Case study 18.2.

3 *Strategic control.* This lies between strategic planning and financial control. In planning terms, the company is not as centralised as a strategic planning company, nor as decentralised as a financial control company. Greater initiative is given to the individual businesses. In *control* terms, long-term strategic objectives are used but short-term profits are also required. Nestlé is a possible example here, except that the centre is closely involved at various stages of the strategy development process. *See* Case study 17.3.

A further style was also identified but not analysed in depth in the research: *the centralised style.* In this style, all the major strategy decisions are held at the centre, with day-to-day implementation being delegated to the various businesses.

Within these broad types of planning, there were then further variations. The purpose of the research was not to choose between the styles but rather to explore how the resulting strategic process could be more successful. The researchers drew four conclusions:

1 Style should be matched to the circumstances of the business: technology, product range, speed of environmental change, leadership and so on.

2 Some styles demand greater understanding of the businesses than others: for example, the debate between the centre and its subsidiaries in the strategic control style is much more keen than that to be found in the distant monitoring of financial performance in a financial control style.

3 Successful styles benefit from openness and mutual respect between those involved across the company. Suspicion and lack of trust between the centre and the parts of the business will cause real problems.

4 Shared commitment to work together to implement the agreed strategies is vital. This may come from inspired leadership or it may derive from the clarity of the objectives.

Comment

This research presents a useful and unique insight into strategic planning, but its attempt to categorise planning into a few distinct types is based on a sample of only 16 companies. There are other possible styles, e.g. entrepreneurial, that were not part of the sample. Moreover, styles change as companies, their environments and leaders change.

Exhibit 17.6 speculates on some possible styles in the public and not-for-profit sectors, where strategic planning is also possible.

17.5.5 Strategic planning in small companies

By comparison with large diverse companies, there is a much narrower product range in smaller companies. By definition, the scope of the issues may also be narrower. Hence, there may be less need to go through a formal planning process and resource

---

Exhibit 17.6   **Possible styles of strategic planning in the public and not-for-profit sectors**

1 **Bureaucratic** (e.g. civil service)
- Clear goals
- Great reliance on rules
- Decisions follow standard operating procedures

2 **Organised anarchy** (e.g. some charitable trusts)
- Unclear goals, difficult to quantify
- Very decentralised organisation
- *Ad hoc* decisions
- Haphazard collection and use of information
- Decisions not linked to goals, but rather to the intersection of persons, solutions and problems

3 **Political power** (e.g. university)
- Goals consistent with social role but pluralistic in organisation
- Shifting coalitions of interests
- Disorderly decision making but becoming less so
- Information used strategically or withheld strategically
- Decisions bargained among interested parties

---

allocation procedure. Planning systems may also be simpler and shorter. Changes in the environment will be less of an issue in the planning sense: small companies should be able to react more quickly and responsively.

Nevertheless, the same basic planning process will apply: background assessment, vision for the future plus long-term aims, and then medium-term and short-term plans. The time-horizon may differ and the planning style is likely to be more informal. As soon as external finance is needed to support or expand the business, however, basic plans will be required. Such plans will need the same strategic logic, evidence and justification as apply to larger organisations.

Key strategic principles

- Strategic planning operationalises the strategy process in some organisations. It is no substitute for basic and innovative strategic thinking.
- The basic process may well cover background assumptions, long-term vision, medium-term plans and short-term plans. Importantly, new ideas are input into the process and revisions are a significant element of its development.
- Strategic planning has been heavily criticised by some researchers as being too bureaucratic and rigid in its approach, but attitudes are beginning to mellow as long as the process is narrowly defined.
- There are a number of different styles for conducting the strategic planning process: for example, strategic planning, strategic control and financial control. The selection of a style depends on the circumstances of the company.
- Formal strategic planning in small companies may also prove beneficial, especially where external finance is being sought.

17.6 Information, monitoring and control[29]

17.6.1 Why are monitoring and controls important?

Monitoring and control procedures are an important aspect of implementation because information can be used:

- to assess resource allocation choices;
- to monitor progress in implementation;
- to evaluate the performance of individual managers as they go about the achievement of their implementation tasks;
- to monitor the environment for significant changes from the planning assumptions and projections;
- to provide a feedback mechanism and the fine-tuning essential for emergent strategy implementation, especially in fast-changing markets.

More generally, monitoring becomes increasingly important as the *concept* of strategy moves from being an isolated event towards being an ongoing activity.

> *Strategy creation is seen as emerging from the way a company at various levels acquires, interprets and processes information about its environment.*[30]

For all these reasons, companies like Nestlé and Canon spend significant resources on monitoring their activities. Because of the vast range of potential information, they may concentrate on the *key factors for success* as a first step (*see* Chapter 6). Some major companies have complete departments whose sole task is to monitor competitors. It is also a characteristic of some small businesses that they are acutely aware of their immediate competitors and customers, the market prices and other forms of strategic activity.

17.6.2 What are the main elements of a strategic control system?

Strategic control systems monitor the main elements of the strategy and its objectives. The crucial point of this is to obtain information in time to be able to take action. Information for its own sake has limited value: the real test is whether it is useful and timely in revising the implementation process, where required. Strategic control systems will include some financial measures but will also involve:

- customer satisfaction;
- quality measures;
- market share.

It may also be necessary to apply such indicators externally to monitor competition in order to assess the *relative* performance of the organisation against others in the market place.

It is important to distinguish between *financial monitoring* (cash flow, earnings per share, etc.) and *strategic controls* which may include these financial elements but will also have a broader perspective.

17.6.3 How can strategic controls be improved?[31]

To some extent, this question cannot be fully answered unless the precise strategy style has been established. Nevertheless, there are some useful guidelines designed to obtain the best from such systems:

- *Concentrate on the key performance indicators and factors for success.* There is a real danger that too many elements will be monitored, with resulting information overload.

- *Distinguish between corporate, business and operating levels of information and only monitor where relevant.* For example, not everyone at the centre needs to know that a minor product has just achieved its sales target. Equally, a division may have limited interest in market share data from another division, even if this is important at the centre.

- *Avoid overreliance on quantitative data.* Numbers are usually easier to measure but may be misleading and simplistic. Qualitative data and information that is difficult to quantify in such areas as service may be far more relevant to strategy monitoring.

- *As controls become established, consider relaxing them.* Eventually, they may interfere with the most important task of clear and insightful strategic exploration. For example, it was for this reason that Jack Welch at GE reduced them, but he did not do so until the principles had been learnt. Every organisation may need to go through this stage of learning before controls are relaxed.

- *Create realistic expectations of what the control system can do as it is being introduced or upgraded.* Some managers may regard strategic controls as a waste of time. Their reasoning is that it is difficult to see early results because of the long time scales involved. Such an objection cannot be avoided but can be anticipated. It is better to acknowledge that the benefits in terms of improved strategy, resources and results will not be immediately obvious.

17.6.4 Strategy control, budgets and cost accounting

Bungay and Goold[32] state that it is 'vital' to link strategy monitoring into the budget process. They argue that, if the two processes are controlled by two different departments, there is a danger that short-term budget considerations will take precedence over longer-term important strategic decisions. This is a realistic but short-term Anglo-American view of the way that business operates. It is particularly associated with the financial control style described in Section 17.5. It holds the real danger that *strategy controls* and *budgeting variances* will be confused. Budgeting is concerned with the achievement of targets planned monthly or quarterly on the basis of revenue and costs. Strategy rarely concerns itself with such short-term matters.

> ### ▶ Key strategic principles
>
> - Monitoring and control systems are important for their contribution to assessing how strategies are being implemented and how the environment itself is changing.
>
> - The important point about information and control is the necessity of obtaining information in sufficient time to take action, where required.

> **Key strategic principles continued**
>
> - There are a number of ways in which strategic controls can be improved. All of them rely on the establishment of simple, cost-effective and useful information about the organisation and its environment.
>
> - It has been argued that strategy control and budgeting should be linked. This is not recommended because strategy monitoring is more concerned with exploration, while budgeting is more focused on achieving specific short-term targets.

17.7 Implementation of international strategy

International aspects of implementation are more complicated because of factors such as culture and geographical diversity. However, they essentially follow the principles already outlined in this chapter and the special comments elsewhere in this book.

KEY READING

Corporate planning: formality without bureaucracy[33]

In this extract from their book Strategic Control, *Michael Goold and John Quinn suggest ways of overcoming a major problem in strategic planning.*

A formal and explicit strategic control process helps to clarify the criteria of good strategic performance. But formal processes can easily become rigid and bureaucratic. How can the strategic control process be formal and explicit but not bureaucratic? Large departments and lengthy reports should be avoided. Line managers themselves should be in the best position to identify the sources of advantage in their businesses, and should not have to hire planners simply to fill in their corporate reports. Reports should focus on the few key targets that have been identified, and should not become glossy and extensive documents.

Most of the information should be readily available. If it is not, it should be specially gathered only if it is likely to help in running the business. Information on progress against key strategic objectives should, of course, be an important part of the data base of any business, whether or not it is called for as part of a corporate control process.

Face-to-face meetings and discussions help to prevent formal control reports from becoming simply a bureaucratic routine. Written reports that are greeted only with a resounding silence do not add value for the business, and should be avoided.

The existence of formal strategic control reviews should not preclude wider, less formal background reviews of progress that are not limited to the explicitly defined strategic objectives. These reviews, which should occur as part of the ongoing line management contacts between the businesses and the centre, are needed to allow the centre to gain an understanding of the sources of competitive advantage in the business and to determine what issues are most important for the business to address. They should also assist the centre in determining whether the agreed milestones are suitably stretching and in deciding on how to react to deviations from planned achievements.

A structured and systematic control process should not stop important decisions from being taken as and when issues arise. A formal strategic control process provides a safety net to prevent issues being missed, but it is not intended as a substitute for an effective and speedy line management decision process, and it should not interfere with the functioning of such a process.

Source: Goold, M and Quinn, J J (1991) *Strategic Control*, pp197–8. Pitman Publishing, London. Reprinted with permission.

Summary

- Implementation covers the activities required to put strategies into practice. The basic elements of this process are: general objectives; specific plans; the necessary finances; and a monitoring and control system to ensure compliance.

- There are three major approaches to implementation: comprehensive, incremental and selective. Implementation in small and medium-sized businesses may be less elaborate but should follow the same general principles.

- According to Pettigrew and Whipp, implementation is best seen as a *continuous* process, rather than as one following the formulation of the strategy. Hrebiniak and Joyce placed *boundaries* on implementation, depending on the ability of managers to consider every choice rationally and to evaluate the impact of implementation on the strategy itself. Emergent approaches to strategy imply that implementation needs to be considered not just as a single event but as a series of activities whose outcome may to some extent shape the strategy.

- Kaplan and Norton developed the *Balanced Scorecard*. It combines quantitative and qualitative measures of the selected strategy. It acknowledges the different expectations of the various stakeholders and it attempts to link scorecard performance measures to the chosen strategy.

- When setting objectives and tasks, first establish who *developed* the strategy that is to be implemented. This will influence the implementation process.

- Individual objectives and tasks will follow from the agreed overall objectives. It may be necessary to experiment to find the optimal combination of events. In fast-changing environments, rigid objectives may be made redundant by outside events.

- Communication and co-ordination are vital to satisfactory implementation, and are especially important to ensure understanding of the plan and its underlying assumptions.

- The resource allocation process provides the necessary funds for proposed strategies. Where resources are limited, allocation of funds is usually from the centre of the organisation, using various decision criteria. Criteria for allocation include the delivery of the organisation's mission and objectives, the support of key strategies and the organisation's risk-taking profile, together with special circumstances, such as unusual changes in the environment. There is a risk that the resource allocation process will ignore the need to use resources more effectively and strategically.

- Strategic planning makes the strategy process operational in some organisations, but it is no substitute for basic and innovative strategic thinking. The basic process of strategic planning may well cover background assumptions, long-term vision, medium-term plans and short-term plans. Importantly, the input of new ideas and revisions to the process are significant elements of its development. Strategic planning has been heavily criticised by some researchers as being too bureaucratic and rigid in its approach, but attitudes are beginning to mellow as long as the process is narrowly defined.

- There are a number of different styles of conducting the strategic planning process, including strategic planning, strategic control and financial control. The selection of a style depends on the circumstances of the company and formal strategic planning in small companies may help when external finance is being sought.

● Monitoring and control systems are important in assessing strategy implementation and how the environment is changing. The necessity of obtaining information in sufficient time to take the required action is crucial. There are a number of ways in which strategic controls can be improved. All rely on having simple, cost-effective and useful information about the organisation and its environment. It has been argued that strategy control and budgeting should be linked. This is not recommended because strategy monitoring is concerned with exploration, while budgeting is focused on achieving specific short-term targets.

● International aspects of strategy implementation follow the same principles but are complicated by culture, geographical diversity and other factors.

QUESTIONS

1 Compare the Canon and Nestlé styles of strategic planning and discuss why they are different. Is one better than the other and, if so, which?

2 Does a small company need a formal strategic plan?

3 Apply the basic implementation process outlined in Figure 17.2 to the current procedures of an organisation with which you are familiar. Where does it differ and where is it the same? What conclusions can you draw about the process?

4 'Nothing chastens the planner more than the knowledge that s/he will have to carry out the plan.' (General Gavin, quoted by Professor George Day)

Discuss this comment in the context of the implementation process.

5 What are the implications of bounded rationality and minimum intervention in developing the strategic process?

6 How can objectives and tasks be communicated from senior management while at the same time motivating those who have to implement them?

7 'If top management devotes more effort to assessing the strategic feasibility of projects in its allocational role than it does to the task of multiplying resource effectiveness, its value added will be modest indeed.' (Professors Gary Hamel and C K Prahalad)

Discuss.

8 Is strategic planning dead or does it have a role to play in most organisations?

9 Explain briefly why strategic controls are necessary and indicate how they might be improved. Consider an organisation with which you are familiar and assess its strategic controls with reference to your explanation.

STRATEGIC PROJECT

This chapter has explored some of the criticisms of strategic planning. You might like to follow up this subject by consulting texts from the 1970s and 1980s that placed heavy reliance on this process and making a comparison with modern practice.

FURTHER READING

Hrebiniak, L and Joyce, W (1984) *Implementing Strategy*, Macmillan, New York. An abridged paper based on this book appeared in the following: De Wit, B and Meyer, R (1994) *Strategy: Process, Content and Context*, West Publishing, MN, pp192–202.

Kaplan, D and Norton, R (1996) *The Balanced Scorecard*, Harvard Business School Press, Boston, MA.

The classic study of different types of strategic planning is that by Goold, M and Campbell, A (1987) *Strategies and Styles*, Blackwell, Oxford and is well worth reading.

Arie de Geus wrote a useful article on strategic planning: (1988) 'Planning as learning', *Harvard Business Review*, Mar–Apr.

Professor H Mintzberg has changed his views on strategic planning: (1994) 'The fall and rise of strategic planning', *Harvard Business Review*, Jan–Feb, pp107–14. *See* also his book, Mintzberg, H (1994) *The Rise and Fall of Strategic* *Planning*, Prentice Hall, New York. Note that Professor Colin Egan provides a logical and well-argued critique of Mintzberg's work in Egan, C (1995) *Creating Organisation Advantage*, Butterworth–Heinemann, Oxford, Ch 7.

NOTES & REFERENCES

1 Sources for this case are the author's life-long support for Portsmouth Football Club and *Financial Times*, 6 August 1998, p32; 11 March 1999, p25; 21 July 2001, p9; 22 July 2000, p13; 29 July 2000, p17; 18 August 2000, p13; 27 October 2000, p20; 29 March 2001, p14; 11 August 2001, p14; 24 August 2001, p9; 2 September 2001, p11; 6 October 2001, p16; 7 December 2001, p16; 23 February 2002, p13; 1 March 2002, p15; 9 March 2002, pp12, 14.

2 Day, G S (1984) *Strategic Market Planning*, West Publishing, MN, Ch8.

3 Yavitz, B and Newman, W (1982)*Strategy in Action: The Execution, Politics and Payoff of Business Planning*, The Free Press, New York. It should be noted that Hrebiniak and Joyce (1984) also describe similar distinctions in *Implementing Strategy*, Macmillan, New York.

4 Day, G S (1984) Op. cit., Ch8.

5 Author's experience based on strategy development in fast-moving consumer goods, telecommunications and consultancy.

6 For example: Wheelen and Hunger, Jauch and Glueck, Thompson and Strickland, Johnson and Scholes, Hofer and Schendel.

7 Pettigrew, A and Whipp, R (1991) *Managing Change for Competitive Success*, Blackwell, Oxford, pp26, 27.

8 Hrebiniak, L and Joyce, W (1984) Op. cit. An abridged paper based on this book appeared in: De Wit, B and Meyer, R (1994) *Strategy: Process, Content and Context*, West Publishing, MN, pp192–202.

9 Leadbeater, C. (1997) 'Flying with a clear view', *Financial Times*, 1 Apr, p17. Direct quote from David Norton.

10 Kaplan, D and Norton, R (1996) *The Balanced Scorecard*, Harvard Business School Press, Boston, MA, p77.

11 Kaplan, D and Norton, R (1996) Op. cit.

12 Pettigrew, A and Whipp, R (1991) Op. cit., p176.

13 Harvard Business School Case (1983) *Canon Inc (B)*, reference number 9-384-151, and *Note on the World Copier Industry in 1983*, reference 9-386-106; Kono T (1992) *Long Range Planning of Japanese Corporations*, de Gruyter, Berlin; *Financial Times*, 16 Feb 1996, p31; *Canon Inc.*, Annual Report and Accounts 1994 and 1998 (English version); Hamel G and Prahalad C K

(1994) *Competing for the Future*, Harvard Business School Press, Boston, MA.

14 Hunger, J and Wheelen, T (1993) *Strategic Management*, 4th edn, Addison-Wesley, Reading, MA, p238.

15 Day, G S (1984) Op. cit., p186.

16 Galbraith, J and Kazanjian, R (1986) *Strategy Implementation*, 2nd edn, West Publishing, MN, p98.

17 Goold, M and Campbell, A (1987) *Strategies and Styles*, Blackwell, Oxford, p21.

18 Hamel, G and Prahalad, C K (1994) *Competing for the Future*, Harvard Business School Press, Boston, MA, p159.

19 References for Nestlé case: *Financial Times*, 6 May 1992, p16; 15 May 1992, p13; 20 Apr 1994, p19. Goold, M and Quinn, J (1990) *Strategic Control*, Hutchinson Business Books, London, pp118–19.

20 Day, G S (1984) Op. cit., p189.

21 De Geus, A (1988) 'Planning as learning', *Harvard Business Review*, Mar–Apr.

22 Marx, T (1991) 'Removing the obstacles to effective planning', *Long Range Planning*, Aug, Pergamon Press, Oxford.

23 Loasby, B (1967) 'Long range formal planning in perspective', *Journal of Management Studies*, Oct.

24 Lenz, R and Lyles, M (1985) 'Is your planning becoming too rational?', *Long Range Planning*, Aug, Pergamon Press, Oxford.

25 Hamel, G and Prahalad, C K (1994) *Competing for the Future*, Harvard Business School Press, Boston, MA, p283.

26 Exhibit 17.5 is developed from references 22, 23 and 24.

27 Mintzberg, H (1994) 'The fall and rise of strategic planning', *Harvard Business Review*, Jan–Feb, pp107–14. *See* also his book (1994) *The Rise and Fall of Strategic Planning*, Prentice Hall, New York. Note that Egan provides a logical and well-argued critique of Mintzberg's work in Egan, C (1995) *Creating Organisation Advantage*, Butterworth–Heinemann, Oxford, Ch7.

28 Goold, M and Campbell, A (1987) Op. cit.

29 This section has benefited from Galbraith, J and Kazanjian, R (1986) Op. cit., pp85–7.

30 Pettigrew, A and Whipp, R (1991) Op. cit., p135.

31 This section has benefited from the paper by Bungay, S and Goold, M (1991) 'Creating a strategic control system', *Long Range Planning*, June, Pergamon Press, Oxford.

32 Bungay, S and Goold, M (1991) Op. cit.

33 Extracted from Goold, M and Quinn, J J (1991) *Strategic Control*, Hutchinson Business Books, London, pp197–8. © Copyright M Goold and J J Quinn and Pitman Publishing. Reproduced with permission.

Organisational structure and people issues

When you have worked through this chapter, you will be able to:

- understand the main principles involved in designing the structure of an organisation to meet its chosen strategy;
- outline the six main types of organisation structure and assess their advantages and disadvantages in relation to a particular strategy;
- develop the special organisation structures that are more likely to lead to innovative strategies;
- make recommendations on the most appropriate organisation structure;
- explore how senior managers can be selected and motivated to implement the chosen strategies;
- outline the additional considerations that apply when developing structures for international organisations.

Figure 18.1   **Organisation structure and people issues**

Basic considerations

↓

Six main types of organisational structure

↓

Organisational structures for innovation

↓

Building the most appropriate organisational structure

↓

Motivation and staffing in strategy implementation

↓

International strategy and structure

▰ Introduction

Whether strategy comes before or after structure, every organisation needs to build and maintain the optimal organisation structure to generate and develop its strategies. This chapter explores this process and has as its starting point the demands made on the organisation by its mission and objectives. Six general types of organisation structure are identified and then, given the importance of innovation in corporate strategy, particular emphasis is placed on the structures that are most likely to achieve this. We explore the role of effective reward structures and selection procedures in providing capable and well-motivated senior managers to implement strategy successfully. Finally, in the light of these considerations, an appropriate organisation structure can then be developed, as summarised in Figure 18.1.

CASE STUDY 18.1

PepsiCo: Organising to integrate its acquisitions

Over a three-year period from 1998 to 2001, the US food and drink company PepsiCo made two major acquisitions. Each purchase was bought for a price premium that could only be repaid by finding new synergies and economies of scale. This required PepsiCo to develop new organisation structures designed to deliver these benefits.

Background – the company itself

PepsiCo is probably best known for its carbonated cola drink, Pepsi Cola, which it sells in most countries around the world, often in second place to its great rival Coca-Cola. However, in terms of total sales, PepsiCo is actually much larger than Coca-Cola – sales of US$27 billion in 2001 compared with Coke's US$18 billion. The main reason for the greater size is that PepsiCo is also the world's largest snack and crisp manufacturer, with a series of brands in regions of the world – including Frito-Lays in North America and Walkers in the UK. However, the company also has some other famous brand names like Tropicana fruit juices and Quaker breakfast cereals. Table 18.1 sets out some of its leading products, including those that arrived through its acquisition strategy in the three years to 2001.

Company major acquisitions – Tropicana and Quaker

Both the Tropicana range of fresh fruit drinks and the Quaker range of products came from PepsiCo acquisitions in the period 1998 to 2001. Tropicana was bought from Seagram for US$3.3 billion in 1998 and Quaker for US$15 billion in 2001. In both cases, PepsiCo paid a significant premium over the asset book value of the companies. It took the view that there were significant synergies and economies of scale to be gained from these two acquisitions.

Table 18.1 PepsiCo's top ten products at retail prices

Brand	Worldwide sales – US$ bn	
Regular Pepsi	6.3	
Mountain Dew	2.8	
Diet Pepsi	2.2	
Lays Potato Chips	2.0	
Gatorade Sports Drink	1.8	Acquired 2001
Tropicana Juice Drink	1.4	Acquired 1998
Doritos Tortilla Chips	1.3	
Quaker Cereals	1.0	Acquired 2001
Cheetos Cheese Flavored Snacks	0.7	
Ruffles Potato Chips	0.6	

With regard to Quaker, PepsiCo was particularly interested in the sports drink Gatorade, which delivered the market leader in new and fast-growing segment of the beverage market. Unfortunately for PepsiCo, such an attractive purchase also came with the Quaker cereal range, which was under heavy competitive pressure from Kellogg and General Mills – *see* Case study 2.1. In spite of this, PepsiCo then set about organising the company to gain the benefits of its acquisitions.

PepsiCo company reorganisation to exploit the full acquisition potential

Building on its strong competitive resources was the prime starting point in developing the revised organisation structure for PepsiCo. Such resources included its major network of contacts with supermarkets across North America and, to a lesser extent, other countries. They also included its existing brand franchises in names like Pepsi and Frito-Lays, Quaker and Tropicana. The company also had a specialist distribution structure designed to deliver fresh and fragile snacks every week directly to 15 000 outlets across the US and indirectly to around 500 000 outlets. It also had a strong network of bottlers who were responsible for delivering Pepsi. The company also had a record of product and packaging innovation. This came from its Pepsi and Frito-Lay technical development units, the Gatorade Sports Science Institute and the Tropicana Nutrition Center. All were skilled at developing new products and packaging. Such units were kept centrally at headquarters on behalf of all operating companies.

Because PepsiCo was particularly strong in North America in virtually every product category, it was decided to set up North American divisions and separate these from its other, international operations. In addition, although the sports drink Gatorade and the Quaker cereal products were important in North America, they had a more limited franchise internationally – especially Gatorade, which was largely unknown outside the American continent. It was decided to combine these product areas internationally with some of its other product groups.

PepsiCo main organisation structure

PepsiCo therefore had the following organisational divisions, each reporting to headquarters:

- *Pepsi Cola North America* – responsible not only for the largest brand but also for building a new product range of non-carbonated drinks such as bottled water. The company was not expecting this area to yield major savings from its two acquisitions.

- *PepsiCo Beverages International* – contained the combined international operations of Pepsi Cola, Tropicana and Gatorade. It was planned to combine general and administrative functions and gain 'very substantial cost savings'. One of the problems here was that, although the Pepsi brand was strong in the US, its international brand share was weaker – especially in parts of Europe. It was therefore more cost-effective to combine it with Tropicana (Gatorade was too small to be important) and gain cost savings from shared overheads.

- *Frito-Lay North America* – had part of the Quaker range of sweet cereal bars, energy bars and similar products combined with its existing savoury crisps and snacks. The aim was to gain substantial cost savings and at the same time to offer the broader range of products to its existing outlets, thus increasing sales.

- *Frito-Lay International* – the snack and crisp products were sold across some 40 countries. The company already had some strong market positions, e.g. 80 per cent of the Mexican snack market and 40 per cent of the UK snack market with Walkers Crisps. The aim here was to add the Quaker food distribution and gain major cost savings on distribution. The Quaker international cereal product range was also included in this area – probably because it was convenient and PepsiCo had to buy this product range in order to obtain Gatorade, as mentioned above.

- *Gatorade/Tropicana North America* – These two major product areas – sports drinks and fruit juices – were combined as a separate area from cola drinks because they were used and sold in different ways and through different outlets. More specifically, there was a common 'hot-fill' manufacturing process that could be used to deliver substantial cost savings.

- *QuakerFoods North America* – PepsiCo decided to keep the Quaker cereals and related products, like Aunt Jemima syrup, separate from its other ranges in North America. Some commentators suspected that this separate division would also allow the product range to be sold more easily at some later stage – it simply did not fit in with the main strengths of PepsiCo and faced strong competition in both North America and internationally.

Sources: See reference 1.

CASE STUDY 18.1 continued

Case questions

1 *Why was PepsiCo essentially organised into North American and international divisions? Why were there some variations in this structure? Examining the organisation structures outlined in this chapter, in which category would you put PepsiCo?*

2 *What benefits was the company seeking from its acquisitions? How did the organisation structure*

contribute to such benefits? In order to achieve such benefits, what actions would have to be taken? Would they have any human consequences? If so, what?

3 *What lessons, if any, on strategy and organisation structure can be drawn from the approach of PepsiCo in developing its new organisation structure?*

18.1 Building the organisation's structure

18.1.1 Consistency with mission and objectives

The organisation's structure is essentially developed to deliver its mission and objectives. Building the organisation structure must therefore begin at this point. Before considering the possible structures in detail, it is useful to explore some basic questions in the context of the analysis and development undertaken in Chapter 12.

● *What kind of organisation are we?* Commercial? Non-profit making? Service-oriented? Government administration? (These questions are not an exhaustive list.)

● *Who are the major stakeholders?* Shareholders? Managers? Employees?

● *What is our purpose?*

● *What does our purpose tell us in broad terms about how we might be structured?*

There is no simple or 'right' answer to the last question; this deserves careful thought. Every organisation is unique in size, products or services, people, leadership and culture. Exhibit 18.1 shows some of the possible implications. It can be useful to think in this general unformed way before plunging into the detail of organisation design.

18.1.2 The main elements of organisation design

Before embarking on the design process, it is worth reviewing the analysis of the organisation undertaken in Chapter 7. We will be using the work and insights described in that earlier analysis. It is important to remember that many organisations have existing structures and that the primary task of organisation design is usually not to invent a totally new organisation but to adapt the existing one. These matters are reflected in the nine primary determinants of organisation design:

1 *Age.* Older organisations tend to be more formal: for example, *see* Greiner in Chapter 7.

2 *Size.* Essentially, as organisations grow, there is usually an increasing need for formal methods of communication and greater co-ordination, suggesting that more formal structures are required.

3 *Environment.* Rapid changes in any of the *Five Forces* acting on the organisation will need a structure that is capable of responding quickly (*see* Chapter 3). If the work undertaken by the organisation is complex, then this will make its ability to respond to the environment more difficult to organise and co-ordinate.[2]

Exhibit 18.1   **Examples of the connection betw**
organisation desig

Purpose	Implications for orga
'Ideas factory' such as an advertising or promotions agency	Loose, fluid structure relationships. As it gro structures are usually i
Multinational company in branded goods	Major linkage and resou co-ordinated structures, ...suppliers or common supermarket customers for separate product ranges
Government civil service	Strict controls on procedures and authorisations. Strong formal structures to handle major policy directions and legal issues
Non-profit-making charity with a strong sense of mission	Reliance on voluntary members and their voluntary contributions may require a flexible organisation with responsibility devolved to individuals
Major service company such as a retail bank or electricity generating company	Formal structures but supported by some flexibility so that variations in demand can be met quickly
Small business attempting to survive and grow	Informal willingness to undertake several business functions such as selling or production, depending on the short-term circumstances
Health service with strong professional service ethics, standards and quality	Formalised structure that reflects the seniority and professional status of those involved while delivering the crucial complex service provisions
Holding company with subsidiaries involved in diverse markets	Small centralised headquarters acting largely as a banker, with the main strategic management being undertaken in individual companies

4 *Centralisation/decentralisation decisions.* To some extent, most organisations have a choice over how much they wish to control from the centre. In summary, there are four main areas that need to be explored:

● the nature of the business, e.g. economies of scale will probably need to be centralised;

● the style of the chief executive: a dominant leader will probably centralise;

● the need for local responsiveness;

● the need for local service.

5 *Overall work to be undertaken.* Value chain linkages (*see* Chapter 6) across the organisation will clearly need to be co-ordinated and controlled. They may be especially important where an organisation has grown and become more diverse. Divisional or

atrix structures may be needed, with the precise details depending on the specific requirements and strategies of the organisation.

6 *Technical content of the work.* In standardised mass production, the work to be undertaken controls the workers and their actions.[3] However, Japanese production methods have recently shown that flexibility may be highly desirable in mass-production (*see* Chapter 9).

7 *Different tasks in different parts of the organisation.* It is clear that the tasks of production are not the same as those of the sales and marketing areas. Mintzberg's description of the main tasks was explored in Chapter 16.

8 *Culture.* The degree to which the organisation accepts change, the ambitions of the organisation and its desire for experimentation are all elements to be considered.[4]

9 *Leadership.* The style, background and beliefs of the leader may have an important effect on organisation design. This will be particularly true in *innovative* and *missionary* organisations which were explored in Chapter 16.

In bringing all the above elements together, there is a danger of overcomplicating the considerations and arguments. *Simplicity in design* should guide the proposals because the structure needs to be understood and operated after it has been agreed. We return to this area later in this chapter.

It is usual in undertaking such an analysis to consider the *responsibilities* and *powers* of the main individuals and groups involved, even if they are deliberately left vague in some structures. Responsibility and power need to be *controlled* and *monitored* and this needs to be built into the organisational structure. However, the control systems of the organisation can usually be considered after the proposed structure has been resolved (*see* Chapter 17).

18.1.3 Building the most appropriate structure

For most organisations, to have no structure is not an option; the choice lies between what the organisation has now and what it might have as its strategy changes (*see* Chapter 7 on Greiner's depiction of organisational change and its relationship to

---

Exhibit 18.2 **Nature of business activity and organisational structure**

Nature of business	*Likely organisational structure*
Single business	Functional
Range of products extending from a single business	Functional but monitor each range of products using separate profit and loss accounts
Separate businesses within group with limited links	Divisional
Separate businesses within group with strong links	Matrix (or divisional with co-ordination if matrix is difficult to manage)
Ideas factory	Innovative structure
Unrelated businesses	Holding company
Related businesses owned jointly or by minority shareholdings	Holding company

---

structure and Johnson's Cultural Web – a useful analytical tool with which to examine the organisation's culture).

In addition to these issues, there is a connection between the range of an organisation's business and the most appropriate organisational structure[5] (*see* Exhibit 18.2).

18.1.4 Environment

In Chapter 16, Mintzberg's configuration of six different types of organisation and their associated environments was set out. Although six were named, it is useful to concentrate on four main characteristics of the environment that influence structure (*see* Exhibit 18.3).

1 *Rate of change.* When the organisation operates in a more dynamic environment, it needs to be able to respond quickly to the rapid changes that occur. In static environments, change is slow and predictable and does not require great sensitivity on the part of the organisation. In dynamic environments, the organisation structure and its people need to be flexible, well co-ordinated and able to respond quickly to outside influences. The dynamic environment implies a more flexible, organic structure.

2 *Degree of complexity.* Some environments can be easily monitored from a few key data movements. Others are highly complex, with many influences that interact in complex ways. One method of simplifying the complexity is to decentralise decisions in that particular area. The complex environment will usually benefit from a decentralised structure.

3 *Market complexity.* Some organisations sell a single product or variations on one product. Others sell ranges of products that have only limited connections with each other and are essentially diverse. As markets become more complex, there is usually a need to divisionalise the organisation as long as synergy or economies of scale are unaffected.

4 *Competitive situation.* With friendly rivals, there is no great need to seek the protection of the centre. In deeply hostile environments, however, extra resources and even legal protection may be needed: these are usually more readily provided by central HQ. As markets become more hostile, the organisation usually needs to be more centralised.

Exhibit 18.3	Environmental types and their impact on organisational structure	
Type of environment	*Range*	*Consequences for organisational structure*
Rate of change	Static ←——→ Dynamic	As rate increases, the organisation needs to be kept more flexible
Degree of complexity	Simple ←——→ Complex	Greater complexity needs more formal co-ordination
Market complexity	Involved in ←——→ Involved in single market diversified markets	As markets become more diversified, divisionalisation becomes advisable
Competitive situation	Passive ←——→ Hostile	Greater hostility probably needs the protection of greater centralisation

18.1.5 The strategy to be implemented

Every organisation is to some extent unique – the result of its past, its resources and its situation. In addition, the key factors for success (*see* Chapter 6) and the major strategies chosen by whatever process will depend on the situation at that time. It is difficult to specify clear and unambiguous rules to translate strategy into organisational structures and people processes. Thompson and Strickland[6] recommend five useful steps that will assist this process but they caution against certainty:

1 Identify the tasks and people that are crucial to the strategy implementation.

2 Consider how such tasks and people relate to the existing activities and routines of the organisation.

3 Use key factors for success to identify the chief areas around which the organisation needs to be built.

4 Assess the levels of authority needed to action the identified strategies.

5 Agree the levels of co-ordination between the units in the organisation necessary to achieve the strategy.

The above are all rather generalised but this is inevitable in view of the unique nature of each organisation.

18.1.6 Consequences for employment and morale

People implement strategies, not plant machinery nor financial resources. New organisational structures can provide new and interesting opportunities for managers and employees. Alternatively, structures may deliver a threat to their scope for work and possibly even their employment. Developing new organisational structures without considering the consequences for those who will be affected is clearly unsatisfactory. This is a major task for any strategy and is considered separately in Chapter 21.

> ### ▶ Key strategic principles
>
> - In building the organisation's structure, it is essential to start by considering its purpose. This will often provide some basic guidance on the structure required.
>
> - There are eight main elements of organisational design: age, size, centralisation/decentralisation, overall work, technical content, tasks in different parts of the organisation, culture and leadership. All these elements will be interrelated with the organisation's strategy.
>
> - Environmental factors such as market change and complexity will impact on the proposed structure. In general, increased change and complexity suggest more flexible, less centralised structures.
>
> - Each organisation is unique and so it is difficult to develop unambiguous rules to implement strategy in terms of organisation structure and people issues.
>
> - The impact of strategic change on employees and managers is a major consideration that deserves separate and detailed work.

18.2 Types of organisational structure

From all the above considerations, it is possible to identify some basic types of organisational structure that can serve to implement the chosen strategy:

- small organisation structure;
- functional organisation structure;
- multidivisional structure (sometimes shortened to *M-form* structure);
- holding company structure (sometimes shortened to *H-form* structure);
- matrix organisation structure;
- innovative organisation structure.

18.2.1 Small organisation structure

In small organisations, there will often only be limited resources. Individuals will need to be flexible and undertake a variety of tasks. The informality of the structure will allow fast responses to market opportunities and customer service requirements. However, problems may be caused by the duplication of roles, confusion of responsibilities and muddled decision making, and it may not be realistic to draw up a clear organisational structure. Depending on the management style of the owner/leader, there may be many people or only the leader contributing to the organisation's strategy. Examples of such a company are a small family business or a specialist local computer service supplier.

18.2.2 Functional organisation[7]

As the organisation grows from being a small company, the functional organisation structure is often the first structure that is adopted (*see* Figure 18.2). It allows experts in a functional area to be grouped together and economies of scale to operate. For example, a single product range production or service company, such as a regional bus company, is likely to have a functional structure. Exhibit 18.4 lists some of the advantages and disadvantages of this type of organisation structure.

Figure 18.2   **The functional organisation structure**

Chief Executive Officer
(strategy decided here)

Operations   Finance   Personnel   Marketing

Exhibit 18.4	Advantages and disadvantages of the functional organisation structure

Advantages	Disadvantages
● Simple and clear responsibilities	● Co-ordination difficult
● Central strategic control	● Emphasis on parochial functional areas in strategy development rather than company-wide view
● Functional status recognised	● Encourages interfunctional rivalry
	● Strategic change may be slow

18.2.3 Multidivisional structure

This form of organisational structure was developed in the early 1920s by the future head of General Motors, Alfred Sloan, and was recorded by Alfred Chandler[8] (*see* Chapter 16).

As organisations grow, they may need to subdivide their activities in order to deal with the great diversity that can arise in products, geographical or other aspects of the business (*see* Figure 18.3). For example, there would be little to be gained by General Motors in Case study 16.2 by combining EDS, its separate computing networking subsidiary, with its Delphi Automotive Systems company, supplying car parts for the group. They have different customers, factories and methods of operation; the strategies of the two divisions are totally different. Chandler argued that strategy was decided at the centre, but in modern companies it is often partially determined by the divisions. However, the centre does influence strategy and allocate resources. *See* also Exhibit 18.5.

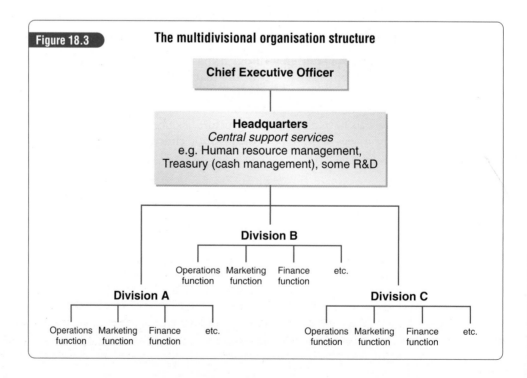

Figure 18.3 The multidivisional organisation structure

Exhibit 18.5 — **Advantages and disadvantages of the multidivisional organisation structure**

Advantages	Disadvantages
• Focuses on business area	• Expensive duplication of functions
• Eases functional co-ordination problems	• Divisions may compete against each other
• Allows measurement of divisional performance	• Decreased interchange between functional specialists
• Can train future senior managers	• Problems over relationships with central services

---

18.2.4 Holding company structure

Further growth in organisations may lead to more complex arrangements between different parts of the organisation and outside companies. For example, joint ventures with totally new companies outside the group, alliances, partnerships and other forms of co-operation may be agreed. As a result, the original company may take on the role of a central shareholder for the various arrangements that may be set up: it becomes a holding company (*see* Figure 18.4). Its role becomes one of allocating its funds to the most attractive profit opportunities. The holding company structure became more prominent in the period from 1970 onwards and was explored by Williamson (*see* Chapter 16). *See* also Exhibit 18.6.

Exhibit 18.6 — **Advantages and disadvantages of the holding company organisation structure**

Advantages	Disadvantages
• Allows for the complexity of modern ownership	• Little control at centre
• Taps expertise and gains new co-operations	• Little group contribution beyond 'shareholding/banking' role
• New market entry enhanced	• Problems if two partners cannot co-operate or one partner loses interest
• Spreads risk for conglomerate	• May have very limited synergy or economies of scale

---

Bouygues (France) (described in Case study 6.2) is an example of a larger company that is well known for such arrangements:[9] it has extended its involvement into new markets and products. Some small companies have also become increasingly involved in such strategies in order to develop rapidly and exploit new opportunities. This is also seen in some of the large Japanese, Hong Kong and South-East Asian conglomerates.

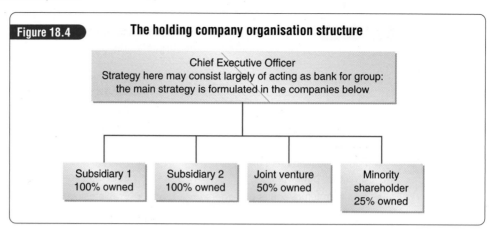

Figure 18.4 The holding company organisation structure

18.2.5 Matrix organisation structure

In some cases, it may be disadvantageous for a large company to set up separate divisions. This is most likely to arise where close co-operation is still required between the groups that would form the separate divisions. For example, an oil company such as Royal Dutch/Shell may need to take strategic decisions not only for its oil, gas and chemical products but also for countries such as the UK, Germany, the US and Singapore. It may be necessary to set up an organisation which has responsibilities along both product and geographical dimensions. Such dual-responsibility decision-making organisation structures are known as *matrix organisations*. The two dimensions do not necessarily have to be geography and product: any two relevant areas could be chosen (*see* Figure 18.5). Readers are referred to Case study 16.3 on Asea Brown Boveri for the problems in a matrix structure. *See* also Exhibit 18.7.

Exhibit 18.7 Advantages and disadvantages of the matrix organisation structure

Advantages	*Disadvantages*
● Close co-ordination where decisions may conflict	● Complex, slow decision making: needs agreement by all participants
● Adapts to specific strategic situations	● Unclear definition of responsibilities
● Bureaucracy replaced by direct discussion	● Can produce high tension between those involved if teamwork of some parts is poor
● Increased managerial involvement	

18.2.6 Innovative organisation structures

In some cases, large organisations need to lay special emphasis on their creativity and inventiveness – for example, advertising agencies, some service companies and innovative design companies. In these circumstances, there is a case for having strong teams that combine experts from different functional areas and have an open style of operation. The free-flowing nature of the group and its ideas may be important in the development of some aspects of strategy. In essence, strategy will be developed anywhere and everywhere. No simple organisation diagram can usefully be drawn.

Figure 18.5

The matrix organisation structure

Chief Executive Officer

	Product group 1	Product group 2	Product group 3
Geographical area 1			
Geographical area 2		*Strategy perhaps decided in each of the matrix groups and perhaps at the centre*	
Geographical area 3			

▶ Key strategic principles

- There are six main types of organisational structure, each having advantages and disadvantages.

- The small organisation has limited resources but an informal structure, allowing flexibility in response, but giving unclear lines of responsibility.

- The functional organisation has been used mainly in small to medium-sized organisations with one main product range.

- As organisations develop further ranges of products, it is often necessary to divisionalise them. Each division then has its own functional structure, with marketing, finance, production, etc.

- As organisations become even more diverse in their product ranges, the headquarters may just become a holding company.

- An alternative form of structure for companies with several ranges of products is the matrix organisation, where joint responsibility is held by two different structures, e.g. between product divisions and another organisational structure such as geographical or functional divisions. This type of organisation has some advantages but is difficult to manage successfully.

- Innovative organisations may have cross-functional teams.

- The place where strategy is developed depends on the organisational structure.

Cisco Systems: Benefits of a highly structured organisation

Cisco Systems, the international telecommunications company, operates a highly structured organisation that cuts bureaucracy and costs. But does it also have some disadvantages?

On the outskirts of San José, California, is a collection of 35 virtually identical brown office blocks that can be told apart only by the letters on the doorways. Inside each building, the floors are divided into cubicles and offices. The cubicles come in two sizes and the offices are all 10ft × 12ft. None have windows. The floor plans displayed on the walls look more like computer circuits than maps of where to find people.

These are the offices of Cisco Systems, one of the world's leading telecommunications equipment companies. The company has outperformed the competition and won new business with relentless efficiency.

How does the company work? How is it organised?

Mr Larry Carter is the company's chief financial officer and takes personal pride in the company's Spartan surroundings. Every chair at Cisco, he says with satisfaction, is the same. Mr Carter joined the company in 1995, having spent most of his life in the semiconductor industry. He has dedicated himself to building a system of computerised accounting and management controls that cuts out every dollar of unnecessary cost. But he insists he is not a bean-counting control freak. His main aim, he says, has been to create a system that operates with the minimum of bureaucracy and allows the greatest flexibility to employees.

Take expenses. At Cisco, any employee can travel anywhere without prior approval. The employee enters the travel request into the system and as long as it meets company policy – coach (tourist) class air tickets only – he or she will be automatically reimbursed within 48 hours. The point, Mr Carter says, is to ensure that employees are free to do whatever is necessary for the customer rather than wasting time on bureaucracy. 'There will always be some who will abuse it,' Mr Carter says, 'but we do not slow down the whole company because of that 1 or 2 per cent. I will catch those who abuse it.'

The result is a company that claims the highest level of revenues per employee in the industry and spends only 1 per cent of those revenues on its finance department. The cost control system has contributed, in large part, to Cisco's success. From his desk each morning, Mr Carter can track exactly how much money his company is making, how each division is doing around the world, and even how each salesperson is performing against his or her target. He calls up a page showing sales and margins for every region of the world: the information is no more than 24 hours old. He can review the figures by region, by product line, or by customer. He clicks on the US to get sales by state; then on Arizona for the figures for each salesperson. If anything looks amiss he can instantly fire off an e-mail to the individual concerned.

Working under such close scrutiny is not to everyone's liking. Those who are uncomfortable with the system generally do not last long at the company. 'We aim to take out the bottom 5 per cent constantly,' says Mr Carter. Cisco's modus operandi is unforgiving of people who are less than 100 per cent committed to their work and the company. But for those who are committed, the rewards are bountiful. The company's 17 000 employees get paid in part with options on Cisco stock which rose 10-fold in the four years 1996–99, making them extremely wealthy.

Mr Carter's system may be impersonal, but it is undoubtedly efficient. Purchasing, sales, marketing and even the hiring of staff are managed through a co-ordinated network. About 70 per cent of Cisco's US$11 billion sales arise from direct orders over the Internet, making it one of the largest e-commerce operations in the world. Mr Carter believes his system gives him an almost complete view of how the company is trading at the end of every day. This cuts down the likelihood of nasty surprises when company results are published and it means that the company can take action earlier if results are falling short of plan. The results have been so impressive that Mr Carter says that he has had calls from his peers at Dell and Texas Instruments who want to copy the Cisco system. Mr Carter believes that, one day, all companies will be run his way.

Case adapted by Richard Lynch from an article by Roger Taylor in the *Financial Times*, 12 April 1999, p13. © *Financial Times* 1999. Reproduced with permission.

CASE STUDY 18.2 continued

Case questions

1 What are the advantages and disadvantages of working in such an organisation?

2 To what extent, if at all, does the organisation allow room for personal initiative and innovation? Could it do

more to support innovation? If so, how? If not, would you change the organisation structure? If so, how?

3 Would you like to work in such a company? [We are all entitled to make choices about where we would like to work.]

18.3 Organisational structures for innovation

Innovative structures and processes were introduced in Section 18.2, but innovation is too important to the whole corporate strategic process for it to be described as only suitable for some specialist organisation types. *Every* organisation needs an element of innovation: hence, *every* organisation needs structures capable of producing this, even if these structures are only temporary, e.g. a team is formed for a particular project and disbanded once the work is completed.

18.3.1 Innovation needs to be commercially attractive

Before exploring how an organisation can best structure itself to be innovative, it is useful to examine what is required. In a competitive market place, it is not enough to be innovative: the new product or service has to be commercially attractive to potential customers, i.e. it must offer value for money compared with existing products and services. Gilbert and Strebel[10] call this the *complete competitive formula*.

It may be desirable to include a broader range of benefits in addition to the innovation itself. Often, the real breakthrough comes not with the technical development but with the extended package of promotion, distribution, support and customer service. All of these elements are geared towards making the innovation user-friendly and more commercially attractive. This requires an *integrated* organisation structure across all functions of the business. For example, one of the reasons that the World Wide Web has taken off on the Internet over the last few years has been the introduction of innovative user-friendly software such as Netscape. However, the real breakthrough for the company came when it arranged for free distribution through computer magazines of certain types of its software for evaluation by personal use. The result has been that, at the time of writing, Netscape has become the dominant software on this new, growing medium. From the organisational viewpoint, such developments need integration and co-ordination across all the functions if innovative solutions are to be obtained.

18.3.2 The nature of the innovative process

In Chapter 11, we examined Quinn's use of the concept of 'controlled chaos' to describe the innovative process. Innovation is flexible, open-ended and possibly without a clearly defined or fixed objective. The process needs to be free-wheeling and experimental. Within this, it is useful to distinguish between:[11]

● *simple innovation*, which might be possible in any organisation and relies on one person or a small group, and

- *complex innovation*, which may require experts drawn from a variety of business functions to form project teams. This is likely to involve larger resources and greater organisational complexity.

Mintzberg's comments on the innovative process (*see* Chapter 16) had complex innovation particularly in mind when outlining three guidelines for organising project teams, which are summarised in Exhibit 18.8.

Exhibit 18.8   **Guidelines for organising innovative project teams**

1 *Flexible structures* are needed that allow experts not just to exercise their skills but to break through conventional boundaries into *new* areas.

2 *Co-ordination* within the team needs to be undertaken by experts with a technical background in the area, rather than a superior with authority from outside.

3 *Power* in the team needs to be distributed among the experts, where appropriate. Much of the activity will consist of liaison and discussion among the experts as they progress their innovative ideas.

Ultimately, the strategy that emerges from the innovative process may remain vague and ill-defined. This has the advantages of being flexible, responsive and experimental. However, the disadvantages associated with a lack of definition may not satisfy the culture of organisations wanting quick and precise results.

18.3.3 Organisational structures and procedures for innovative companies

Kanter[12] surveyed a number of US companies in the 1970s and 1980s in an attempt to identify the organisation structures and processes that were most conducive to innovation. Among her conclusions were:

- *The importance of matrix structures.* These were more likely in innovative companies. They tended to break down barriers and lead to the more open reporting lines that were important to the innovative process. Decision making may have been slow and complex in matrix structures, but it provided the network for individuals to move outside their own positions and make the interconnections useful to innovation.

- *The need for a parallel organisation.* A separate group to run in tandem with the existing formal hierarchy was often highly valuable. It was specifically tasked with finding innovative solutions to problems, especially where a matrix structure was not in operation. It was able to act independently, without the day-to-day pressures and politics of the existing structure. It was then left to the existing organisation to define routine jobs, titles and reporting relationships. Instead of contacts and power flowing up and down the existing structure, the parallel organisation allowed new relationships and ideas to develop.

- *The work of a parallel organisation.* This had to be problem solving, possibly focused on a single business problem and structured around the team. The work was integrative, flexible and with little hierarchical division. The function of such a group was often to re-examine existing routines and systems, concentrating especially on areas that were partially unknown and needed challenging. It often provided a means of empowering people lower down in the organisation.[13]

- *Participative/collaborative management style.* This was often employed to encourage innovation. It involved persuading rather than ordering, seeking advice and comments and sharing the favourable results of successful initiatives.[14]

From her research, Kanter recommended five pointers to action that could be taken to encourage innovation in weaker organisations[15] (see Exhibit 18.9). The most successful global companies, such as Toyota and McDonald's, have been particularly successful at pursuing such policies.

Exhibit 18.9   **Five pointers to encourage innovation**

1 Publicise and take pride in existing achievements.

2 Provide support for innovative initiatives, perhaps through access to senior managers, perhaps through project teams.

3 Improve communication across the enterprise by creating cross-functional activities and by bringing people together.

4 Reduce layers in the hierarchy of the organisation and give more authority to those further down the chain.

5 Publicise more widely and frequently company plans on future activity, giving those lower down in the organisation a chance to contribute their ideas and become involved in the process.

Comment

All of Kanter's ideas were researched and proposed in the context of the North American corporation. Some may not work at all or may need to be substantially modified in other national cultures. Moreover, the problems that were observed in terms of innovation may not be the same in other countries. What they do illustrate is that, for strategic innovation at least, the flexible, *open structure* of the organisation may need to come before the *innovatory strategies* that subsequently emerge.

Key strategic principles

- All companies need to be able to innovate as part of the strategic process.

- Such innovation needs to be commercially attractive if it is to be viable. An organisation structure that integrates and co-ordinates all the functional areas of a business is desirable.

- Innovation is open-ended and flexible, so the process needs to be experimental, with flexible structures, close co-ordination and power distributed throughout the innovating group.

- In terms of structure, a matrix organisation may be more effective because it is more integrative. In some circumstances, a separate, parallel organisation tasked with developing innovative solutions can be usefully employed.

18.4 Motivation and staffing in strategy implementation

Capable and well-motivated people are essential to strategy implementation, especially at senior management level. This section explores the *formal organisation* needed to achieve this:

● reward systems that can increase motivation;

● staffing and selection procedures that are necessary for a successful strategy.

The *informal* aspects of this subject, associated with strategy implementation, such as leadership and culture, are left to Chapter 21.

18.4.1 Reward systems

The measurement of achievement and the reward for good performance against the organisation's objectives can be powerful motivators for the delivery of corporate strategy. The linkage between reward and motivation has been extensively researched over the last few years and the connection well established.[16] Rewards need to be seen more broadly than simple payment: they may involve other forms of direct remuneration but also promotion and career development opportunities.

In designing reward systems to achieve strategic objectives, several factors need to be considered:

● *Strategic objectives.* These tend to have a longer-term element, whereas managers may well need to have short-term rewards. Hence, there may be a conflict between rewarding achievement of strategic objectives and a personal desire for short-term recompense. Moreover, not all strategic objectives are easily measurable, thus making accurate assessment difficult. To some extent, these problems have been resolved by rewarding individuals with shares in the enterprise but this incentive may not be available to all organisations and is still subject to manipulation.

● *Rewards focusing on individual performance.* These may not be appropriate when group objectives have been identified as crucial to strategy. Careful consideration of the impact of reward systems may therefore be required.

● *Rewards encouraging innovation and risk taking.* These may need to move beyond quantitative measures of performance, such as an increase in return on capital or earnings per share, to qualitative assessments based on the number and quality of the initiatives undertaken. There may well be a greater element of judgement involved, which may in turn lead to accusations by others of unfairness unless handled carefully.

In recent years, reward systems have been given new emphasis by the introduction of *performance contracts.* Some companies have developed a system whereby strategy implementation is split into a series of measurable milestones. Individual directors and senior managers then sign contracts to deliver these targets and their performance is reviewed accordingly. Case study 21.1 describes the use of this procedure at the UK company BOC Group.

18.4.2 Formal organisation structures and staffing procedures

New strategies may well call for new business approaches, new skills and new knowledge. Existing members of staff will not necessarily have these. It may be necessary therefore to introduce formal structures and procedures to train existing staff or recruit new people in order to implement the strategy successfully.[17]

For motivational reasons, it is often appropriate to begin with existing staff members and assess their suitability for new positions. However, they may not possess the required knowledge and skill levels required, in which case outside recruitment becomes essential.

In corporate strategy, staffing issues primarily concern the most senior managers in the organisation. In cases of major strategic crisis, the chief executive officer may need to be replaced: there are countless cases during the 1990s of this one act being crucial to strategic change. However, it should be said that this may only be the *beginning* of a new strategy, rather than its implementation. When Lou Gerstner was recruited to head IBM after its spectacular profit problems in 1994 (*see* Chapter 1), he was hired on the basis that he had complete freedom to identify the main strategic problems, solutions and strategies. In this case, the first stage of the new IBM strategy was to hire an outsider to rescue the company. However, it should be pointed out that the previous chief executive was also aware of the difficulties and the need for change. It will be evident that, in general, recruiting senior talent to implement identified strategies can be a crucial element in an organisation's continued success or failure.

For the many companies that do not experience major crises, the provision of a sound *performance appraisal system* will be a major contribution to successful strategy implementation. This may be accompanied by *staff training* and broader *staff development programmes* to build up the people elements in corporate strategy. These are part of the area of human resource management strategy for the company. Coupled with recruitment and reward, they underline the crucial importance of this functional area at the highest levels of corporate strategy development.

▶ Key strategic principles

- Measurement of achievement and the subsequent reward for good performance can be powerful methods for directing corporate strategy.

- However, reward systems may be difficult to develop that fully coincide with the organisation's strategic objectives for a variety of reasons.

- Staffing issues, such as recruitment, appraisal and training, are essential to the implementation of strategy. Formal procedures need to be built into the consideration of new or revised human resource management procedures.

18.5 Strategy and structure in international organisations – the role of headquarters

As organisations become more international, their structures become more complex. Country and regional divisions join the product and functional interests in the organisation structure. Some aspects of international structure need to be considered in the context of international strategy development: these matters are explored in the next chapter. However, since the case studies in this chapter touch on the role of headquarters in directing subsidiary staff it is relevant to consider this matter now.

For reasons of history, leadership and national cultural attitudes, different companies have different approaches to their foreign operations. This can be characterised by examining the role of the headquarters of the organisation in relation to its various operations. In the late 1960s, Professor Howard Perlmutter identified four different types of relationship that have stood the test of time:[18]

1 *Ethnocentric*. In this case, the role of headquarters is to represent the parent company's approach to strategic development. Culture, style and strategy formulation are largely decided at the centre. The home country dominates and foreign operations are mainly run as they would be back home.

2 *Polycentric*. In this case, the role of headquarters is diminished, with each foreign operation running its own affairs and developing its own strategy. National cultures will therefore predominate and each country will largely decide its performance objectives within the purpose defined by headquarters.

3 *Regiocentric*. In this case, the headquarters seeks to negotiate with its foreign subsidiaries on mutually acceptable objectives. There are likely to be regional activities, i.e. for an area of the world such as Europe or South America.

4 *Geocentric*. In this case, the headquarters is the centre of a global web of activity. It will co-ordinate global production and markets but also encourage appropriate local product variations. We will explore this aspect further in the next chapter.

Although such characterisations may oversimplify reality, they are useful because they help to identify a key aspect of management in international operations. They also assist in the process of implementing strategy because they raise questions about the appropriate method of seeking change in international organisations.

▶ Key strategic principles

- The role of headquarters in relation to its subsidiaries can be classified into four main types: ethnocentric, polycentric, regiocentric and geocentric.

- Each involves a different working relationship between the HQ and its subsidiaries and different degrees of freedom for such subsidiaries.

CASE STUDY 18.3

Ford Motors – Reorganising back to basics[19]

In late 2001, the world's second-largest vehicle company, Ford Motors, took the decision to improve radically the profitability of its main volume car and truck business: it went 'back to basics'. The case traces the strategies and organisation structures the company has used in recent years and examines the organisational implications of the 'basics' strategy.

Global strategy and structure in the mid-1990s

In 1994, Ford had total sales of US$128 billion and a global workforce of 320 000. Its sales were more evenly spread geographically than those of its larger rival, General Motors. However, its profitability was below that of competitors and its quality ratings were lower than its Japanese rivals. The company decided that radical new strategies were required but it had to start from the constraints imposed by its existing multinational organisation. Essentially, up to that time, it had operated as a series of semi-autonomous units under the Ford brand.

After careful study, Ford decided to implement a new global strategy. This involved close co-operation between the various parts of the company around the world so that it could gain economies of scale from its various development and production activities. Ford estimated that such a strategy could make cost savings of US$3 billion per annum by 2000. But it would mean combining the elements of its semi-independent regional structure. The two largest regions, North America and Europe, would be combined from January 1995, with the other regions to follow later. The new organisation structure would involve new global *product development* responsibilities and a new *matrix management* organisation structure.

The emphasis was placed on five vehicle programme centres (VPCs) to develop new models globally. Four of the five VPCs would be based in the US but the one located in Europe, that for small cars, probably had the most potential for long-term growth at Ford and would account for 50 per cent of production by the year 2000. In addition to the VPCs, there would be functional management across all the main operations on a global basis. Figure 18.6 shows the agreed structure in outline.

To balance the matrix management structure, the Ford 2000 project also centralised its key strategic decision making, with one Automotive Strategy Office worldwide. The objective was to centralise the key strategic decision making by taking the widest possible view of global developments and opportunities. It was also to encourage the development of global cars, serving many markets, that would increase the profit from every dollar spent on investment.

After operating for two years, Ford decided to simplify its global matrix structure. Essentially, it had become too difficult and complex to operate with five different US and European product divisions. All the US divisions were therefore combined into one large car and truck division with global responsibilities. Europe was then made responsible for all small car developments.

Shift in strategy – the Premier Automotive Group
Then in September 1998, Jac Nasser was named as the new Ford chief executive. He supported the globalisation strategy but was also attracted by a new strategy that involved Ford developing its sales in the premium segment of the car market where

the profit margins were much higher. In early 1999, Ford purchased the Swedish Volvo Cars company for US$6.5 billion and later in the same year Ford bought the British specialist four-wheel drive vehicle company Land Rover for US$2.8 billion. These two companies were then combined with Ford's existing ownership of Jaguar cars, Lincoln cars (an up-market US car range) and Aston Martin sports cars into a new division called the Premier Automotive Group. It was planned to keep this group independent of Ford's volume car activities. This new group was expected to deliver one third of Ford's total profits by 2005.

Immediate problems in Europe – 2000
For all the claims about the new global strategy, the reality was that Ford's European market share was dropping alarmingly – down from 12 per cent in 1994 to 8.7 per cent in 2000. Coupled with plant inefficiencies, this caused the company to show a US$1 billion loss in Europe in 2000. Radical action was therefore taken to cut capacity, with plant closures in the UK, Portugal, Poland and Belarus and plant cutbacks in most of Ford's other European plants. The changes were assisted because the supposed 'global' matrix had a separate European section on which to focus. Global strategy did not appear to form a significant part of the European cutbacks.

Problems in North America – 2001
As Case 12.1 described, the Ford chief executive, Jac Nasser, was sacked in October 2001. A major cost-cutting exercise was then begun in North America to restore the profitability of this part of the company. Again, the 'global' structure, which had a separate section for North America, along with the worldwide Automotive Strategy Office, provided a focus for the required action. Essentially, it was decided to axe five plants and 22 000 jobs in North America. Ford would also downsize activities at another 11 plants. In addition, it would also cut four low-profit models and sell US$1 billion of non-core assets and cut the company dividend by one-third. The new chairman, Bill Ford, explained with the benefit of hindsight: 'We pursued strategies that were either poorly conceived or poorly timed. We strayed from what got us to the top of the mountain and it cost us dearly.'

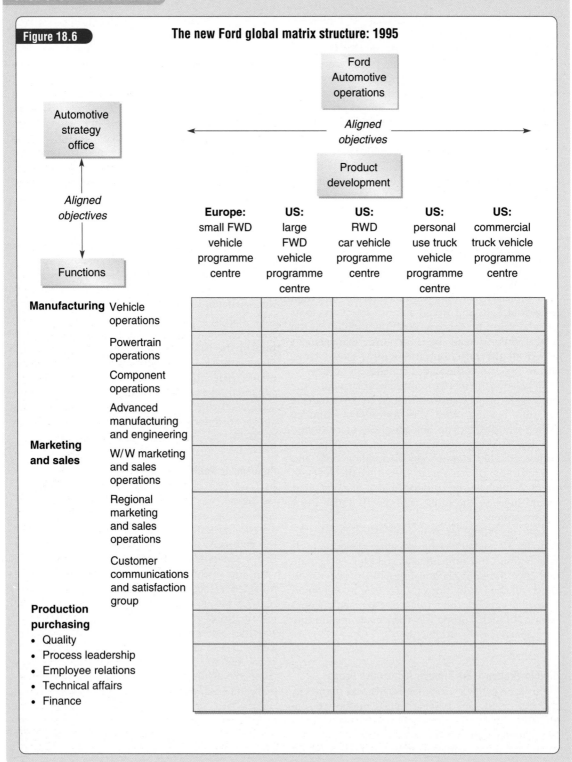

Figure 18.6 — The new Ford global matrix structure: 1995

Conclusion

It will be evident from all this that the Ford global strategy was not the driving force behind the new back to basics strategy. The organisation structures were essentially continent wide rather than world-wide. It was not clear whether the company would ever return to its global structure and strategy for its volume car business – certainly not until the ongoing problems were reversed around 2005. However, Ford's Premier Automotive Group was still firmly in existence and this was arguably global in its approach.

Case questions

1 *What were the arguments in favour of the new global strategy?*

2 *What are the advantages and problems of the matrix structure that was set up to manage global operations? How did Ford plan to overcome the difficulties that can arise? Are you convinced by Ford's arguments, especially given its later simplification?*

3 *Given that the global strategy and structure appears to be dead in Ford's volume car business, does this have any implications for global strategy and structure in other companies? Or are the problems unique to Ford?*

KEY READING

The importance of good structure[20]

In this extract from his book Management and Organisational Behaviour, *Laurie Mullins provides an organisational behaviour perspective on structure design. He emphasises the human and informal aspects of such a process.*

The structure of an organisation affects not only productivity and economic efficiency but also the morale and job satisfaction of the workforce. Structure should be designed therefore so as to encourage the willing participation of members of the organisation and effective organisational performance.

The functions of the formal structure, and the activities and defined relationships within it, exist independently of the members of the organisation who carry out the work. However, personalities are an important part of the working of the organisation. In practice, the actual operation of the organisation and success in meeting its objectives will depend upon the behaviour of people who work within the structure and who give shape and personality to the framework.

The overall effectiveness of the organisation will be affected both by sound structural design and by the individuals filling the various positions within the structure. Management will need to acknow-ledge the existence of the informal organisation which arises from the interactions of people working in the organisation. The organisation is a social system and people who work within it will estab-lish their own norms of behaviour, and social groupings and relationships, irrespective of those defined in the formal structure.

The human relations writers are critical of the emphasis on the formal organisation. They favour a structure in which there is increased participation from people at all levels of the organisation, greater freedom for the individual, and more meaningful work organisation and relationships. One of the strongest critics of the formal organisation is Argyris.[21] He claims that the formal, bureaucratic organisation restricts individual growth and self-fulfilment and, in the psychologically healthy person, causes a feeling of failure, frustration and conflict. Argyris argues that the organisation should provide a more 'authentic' relationship for its members.

The view of the human relations writers repre-sents more of an attitude towards organisation than specific proposals, but it reminds us of the importance of the human element in the design of structure. Managers need to consider how struc-tural design and methods of work organisation influence the behaviour and performance of mem-bers of the organisation.

The operation of the organisation and actual work-ing arrangements will be influenced by the style of

▶

management, the personalities of members and the informal organisation. These factors may lead to differences between the formal structure of the organisation and what happens in practice. Building an organisation involves more than concern for structure, methods of work and technical efficiency.

The hallmark of many successful business organisations is the attention given to the human element: to the development of a culture which helps to create a feeling of belonging, commitment and satisfaction.

Source: Mullins, L (1996) *Management and Organisational Behaviour*, Pitman Publishing. Reprinted with permission.

Summary

- In building the organisation's structure, it is essential to start by reconsidering its purpose. This will often provide some basic guidance on the structure required. In addition, there are eight main elements of organisational design: age, size, centralisation/decentralisation, overall work, technical content, tasks in different parts of the organisation, culture and leadership. All these elements will be interrelated with the organisation's strategy.

- There are six main types of organisational structure, each having advantages and disadvantages. The *small organisation* structure is self-explanatory. The *functional organisation* structure has been mainly used in small to medium-sized organisations with one main product range. As organisations develop further ranges of products, it is often necessary to *divisionalise*. Each division then has its own functional structure – marketing, finance, production, etc. As organisations become even more diverse in their product ranges, the headquarters may just become a *holding company*. An alternative form of structure for companies with several ranges of products is the *matrix organisation*, where joint responsibility is held between the products structure and another organisational format such as the functional structure. This type of organisation has some advantages but is difficult to manage successfully.

- In building the most appropriate organisation structure, it is important to keep in sight the need for simple, cost-effective structures. Environmental factors, such as market change and complexity, will also impact on the proposed structure. In general, increased change and complexity suggest more flexible, less centralised structures.

- All organisations must be able to innovate as part of the strategic process, but such innovation needs to be commercially attractive if it is to be viable. An organisation structure that integrates and co-ordinates all the functional areas of a business is desirable. Because innovation is open-ended and flexible, the process needs to be experimental, with flexible structures, close co-ordination and power distributed throughout the innovating group.

- In terms of innovative structures, a matrix organisation may be more effective because it is more integrative. In some circumstances, a separate, parallel organisation tasked with developing innovative solutions can be employed.

- Measurement of achievement and the subsequent reward for good performance can be powerful methods for directing corporate strategy. However, it may be difficult to develop reward systems that coincide fully with the organisation's strategic objectives. Staffing issues, such as recruitment, appraisal and training, are essential to the implementation of strategy. Formal procedures need to be built into the consideration of new or revised human resource management procedures.

● In international structures, the role of the headquarters in relation to its subsidiaries can be classified into four types: ethnocentric, polycentric, regiocentric and geocentric. Each involves a different working relationship and different degrees of freedom for foreign subsidiaries.

QUESTIONS

1 Explain the structure of an organisation with which you are familiar, using the elements outlined in Section 18.1 as your guide.

2 What structure would you expect the following organisations to have?

   (a) A small management consultancy company based in one country only.

   (b) A voluntary group providing volunteers to visit the elderly and house-bound.

   (c) A medium-sized company with 1500 employees, two factories and a separate headquarters.

   (d) A leisure park business owned and operated by a family company.

   (e) A medium-sized computer company with 80 employees which writes software for games machines.

3 'If structure does follow strategy, why should there be a delay in developing the new organisation needed to meet the administrative demands of the new strategy?' (Alfred Chandler)

How would you answer this question?

4 If you were asked to make Cisco Systems more innovative, what would you do? In answering this question, you should take into account the existing culture of the company.

5 'Every organisation needs an element of innovation' (see Section 18.3). Is this correct?

6 'All any company has to do to explore its own potential to become a more innovatory organisation is to see what happens when employees and managers are brought together and given a significant problem to tackle.' (Professor R M Kanter)

Discuss.

7 Why is it difficult to develop reward systems to deliver the organisation's objectives? How might such difficulties be overcome in a small entrepreneurial business venture?

8 The managing director of a large company making bicycles has become worried by the lack of growth in sales, believing the company has lost its earlier innovative spark, and has turned to you for advice. What would you recommend?

9 'The hallmark of many successful business organisations is the attention given to the human element.' (Laurie Mullins)

Is the human element more important than competitive strategy?

STRATEGIC PROJECT

Restaurants and catering establishments have traditionally been fragmented industries, then came McDonald's, Burger King, Pizza Hut and Kentucky Fried Chicken (see Case study 13.1). Branding and building up regional, national and international chains of restaurants was one of the major strategy successes of the 1980s and 1990s. Investigate how this was undertaken and the organisation structures used to achieve such development.

FURTHER READING

Professor Henry Mintzberg has a useful discussion on organisation structure and strategy in 'The structuring of organisations', p341 in Mintzberg, H and Quinn, J B (1991) *The Strategy Process*, 2nd edn, Prentice Hall, New York.

Laurie Mullins (1996) *Management and Organisational Behaviour*, 4th edn, Pitman Publishing, London, can be consulted for an extended discussion on organisational issues.

Professor Gerry Johnson's paper (1989) 'Rethinking incrementalism', *Strategic Management Journal*, Jan–Feb, is worth reading. It is reprinted in De Wit, B and Meyer, R (1994) *Strategy: Process, Content and Context*, West Publishing, St Paul, MN.

Professor Rosabeth Moss Kanter (1985) *The Changemasters*, Unwin, London, has a useful empirical study of innovative practice.

NOTES & REFERENCES

1 Sources for PepsiCo Case: Tropicana Website May 2002; PepsiCo Annual Report and Accounts 2001; *Financial Times* 22 July 1999, p2; 28 February 2000, p25; 15 March 2001, p20; 5 April 2002, p16.

2 Laurence, P R and Lorsch, J W (1967) *Organisation and the Environment*, Richard D Irwin, Burr Ridge, IL, contains a full discussion of this important area.

3 Mintzberg, H (1991) 'The structuring of organisations', p341 in Mintzberg, H and Quinn, J B (1991) *The Strategy Process*, 2nd edn, Prentice Hall, New York.

4 Johnson, G (1989) 'Rethinking incrementalism', *Strategic Management Journal*, Jan–Feb. Reprinted in De Wit, B and Meyer, R (1994) *Strategy: Process, Content and Context*, West Publishing, St Paul, MN.

5 Developed from Galbraith, J R (1987) 'Strategy and organisation planning', *Human Resource Management*, Spring–Summer. Republished in Mintzberg, H and Quinn, J B (1991) Op. cit., pp315–24.

6 Thompson, A and Strickland, A (1993) *Strategic Management*, 7th edn, Irwin, Homewood, IL, p220.

7 Mintzberg, H (1979) *The Structuring of Organisations*, Prentice Hall, New York.

8 Chandler, A (1962) *Strategy and Structure*, MIT Press, Cambridge, MA. *See* also Channon, D (1973) *The Strategy and Structure of British Enterprise*, Macmillan, London, for evidence in the UK.

9 Bouygues moved from construction into media and mobile telephones in the 1990s.

10 Gilbert, X and Strebel, P (1989) 'From innovation to outpacing', *Business Quarterly*, Summer, 54, pp19–22. Reprinted in De Wit, B and Meyer, R (1994) Op. cit.

11 Mintzberg, H (1991) 'The innovative organisation', Ch13 in Mintzberg, H and Quinn, J B (1991) Op. cit., pp731–46.

12 Kanter, R M (1985) *The Changemasters*, Unwin, London, p146.

13 Kanter, R M (1985) Ibid, p205.

14 Kanter, R M (1985) Ibid, p237.

15 Kanter, R M (1985) Ibid, pp361–2.

16 Galbraith, J and Kazanjian, R (1986) *Strategy Implementation*, 2nd edn, West Publishing, St Paul, MN. Chapter 6 contains a thoughtful review of the evidence.

17 Hunger, J and Wheelen, T (1993) *Strategic Management*, 4th edn, Addison Wesley, Reading, MA, Ch9.

18 Perlmutter, H V (1969) 'The tortuous evolution of the multinational corporation', *Columbia Journal of World Business*, 4(1), pp9–18.

19 References for this case study: *Financial Times*, 29 Mar 1994, p30; 11 Apr 1994, p20; 22 Apr 1994, p17; 23 Apr 1994, p11; 6 Jan 1995, p17; 3 Apr 1995, p11; 13 May 2000, p20; 7 June 2000, p38; 23 June 2000, p29; 17 May 2001, p14; 4 December 2001, p21; 12 January 2002, p14; 14 January 2002, p24; *Ford Annual Report and Accounts* 1994 and 2001.

20 Extracted from Mullins, L (1996) *Management and Organisational Behaviour*, 4th edn, Pitman Publishing, London, pp337–8.

21 Argyris, C (1964) *Integrating the Individual and the Organization*, Wiley, Chichester.

Chapter 19

International expansion and globalisation strategies

Learning outcomes

When you have worked through this chapter, you will be able to:

- explain what is meant by globalisation and distinguish it from international expansion;
- outline the main theories of international trade and explain their relevance to corporate strategy;
- identify the main institutions involved in international trade and investment and their influence on corporate strategy;
- explain the importance of trade blocks and their relationship with the development of corporate strategy;
- explore the main benefits and problems of globalisation strategies and comment critically on theories of globalisation;
- understand the main organisation structures needed to operate global strategy successfully;
- outline the main development routes and methods for global expansion;
- consider the implications of globalisation on both the companies operating it and the countries involved in its development.

Introduction

For some companies, international expansion and globalisation have become a vital aspect of strategy development and implementation. They present new opportunities to generate extra value added which deserve exploration. They may also entail increased competitive risk: international expansion may expose a company to new and sophisticated competitors. However, international strategy is not the same as global strategy, so the starting point is to explore what is meant by the two.

To understand international expansion, it needs to be viewed in the strategic context of international trade and investment development over a number of years. This involves the theories of international trade and the institutions that govern such activities.

Within the context of foreign trade and investment issues, international and globalisation strategies then need to be explored – the benefits and problems need to be understood if such strategies are to be successful. Because of the increased scope of international operations, issues of organisational structure are particularly important. In addition, the routes to international development also need careful exploration since they may vary, depending on the markets and the countries. Finally, the relationships between the companies seeking global strategies and the sovereign countries

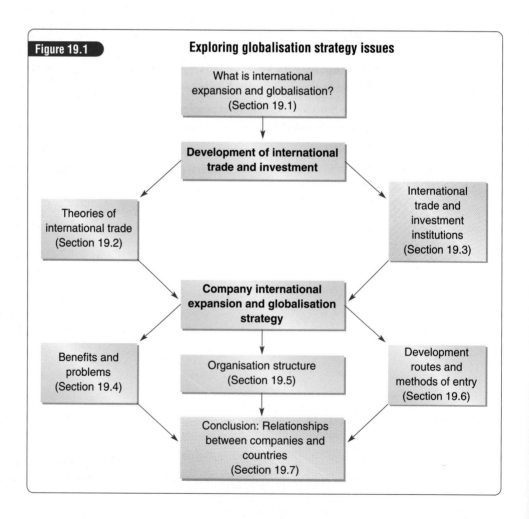

Figure 19.1   **Exploring globalisation strategy issues**

What is international expansion and globalisation? (Section 19.1)

Development of international trade and investment

Theories of international trade (Section 19.2)

International trade and investment institutions (Section 19.3)

Company international expansion and globalisation strategy

Benefits and problems (Section 19.4)

Organisation structure (Section 19.5)

Development routes and methods of entry (Section 19.6)

Conclusion: Relationships between companies and countries (Section 19.7)

providing the markets need to be investigated because they are mutually dependent. Figure 19.1 summarises the structure of this chapter.

International trade has its origins and theoretical foundation in the prescriptive topic of international economics. Thus some parts of international strategy seek prescriptive solutions. However, some of the more recent areas have taken more experimental routes which would fit more naturally within emergent strategic perspectives. Thus the early part of the chapter – on trade development – is more prescriptive, with emergent approaches being more appropriate later, in the section on company international expansion.

CASE STUDY 19.1

Globalisation at Giant Bicycles

Giant Bicycles are Taiwanese-owned, but designed in the US and made in the Netherlands – a global company. This case reports on an interview in 1997 with the chief executive, King Liu, about the company's global strategy.

The Giant Bicycles Company is based in Taiwan and is one of the world's biggest bicycle manufacturers with annual sales of around US$400 million – 93 per cent outside Taiwan. According to Mr Liu:

Because of the small market for bicycles in Taiwan, we don't have any choice – we have to be a global company. The biggest markets are in Europe and the US, which account for just over half our sales. We started manufacturing in the Netherlands because of the attractive market in Europe, where we expected to sell more than 400 000 bikes in 1997. That's out of a demand for bikes in Europe of about 15 million annually.

To start with, we will be making just 100 000 bikes a year from our European factory, but we envisage this climbing threefold by early next century. The main reason for transferring some production from the Far East to the Netherlands is to increase flexibility. Fashions are changing quickly and market trends must be followed closely. Having a production base next to the market means that we should be able to satisfy our customers better. Wage costs in the Netherlands are 60 per cent higher than in Taiwan but, because we should get better productivity in Europe, this will not affect overall costs too much.

We are considering opening another plant in the US – we expect to decide on this around year 2000. Our Taiwan plant makes about 1 million bikes a year out of a total 2.5 million bikes for our company – including bikes produced by a joint venture in China. I expect the proportion of Taiwanese bikes to decline over the next few years as we switch production away from Asia.

Developing new products is as important as manufacturing. Bicycles are as much a fashion item as a piece of machinery. We sell bikes in several thousand variations. In the early 1990s we introduced up to three new products every year. Today, however, that figure has grown to between five and ten, reflecting increased demands by customers. One of our strengths is the ability to introduce regional product lines, within the context of an international approach. About three-quarters of the products we sell around the world are the same – but for the remaining 25 per cent we give our regional people freedom to specify products they think will appeal locally.

Worldwide, we have 65 designers and development engineers. We spend 2 per cent of our annual sales on design. Forty-five of the designers are in Taiwan, the rest are based in China, Japan, the US and the Netherlands. Through the global design approach we aim to pool many different concepts – the people in China and Japan concentrate on commuting bikes, the designers in the Netherlands contribute ideas from the European racing bike tradition, while in the US they are more likely to be working on variants of mountain bikes. In Taiwan, we try to incorporate all of the ideas, working on new materials such as carbon fibre to reduce the weight of the frame. Our designers can talk on the phone and swop ideas using computer-aided design, but they get together twice a year in Taiwan to review their work. The common language we use is English.

Subsequently, the company has shifted some manufacturing from Taiwan to mainland China because the latter has lower costs for labour and land. China now accounts for over half the company's production. However, the company still believes that its

Taiwanese-based research and marketing teams are best placed to understand both the developed markets of the West and the developing markets of Asia.

© Copyright *Financial Times* 1997. Interview by Peter Marsh, 24 Oct 1997, p16. Update from *Financial Times*, 25 October 2001, Taiwan Supplement, p2.

Case questions

1 *What benefits does the company gain from its global strategy? And what have been the problems?*

2 *What, if anything, can other medium-sized companies learn from Giant Bicycles?*

19.1 International expansion and globalisation: their meaning and importance

For a series of structural reasons which we will explore later, international trading activities – *country exports and imports* – have increased substantially over the last 50 years. Moreover, in addition to trading, companies have also invested substantial capital sums in countries outside their home nation to set up factories and other facilities. The world is becoming more international and this has significant implications for corporate strategy. International expansion and globalisation issues are amongst the most important factors in the business environment influencing strategy development in the twenty-first century.

The Giant Bicycle Company shows that such expansion is not just an issue for the major multinational enterprises (often abbreviated to MNEs) like the Ford Motor Company (US) and Coca-Cola (US). It may also be a significant issue for many rather smaller companies involved in international trade. It has also become increasingly important in not-for-profit activities such as international aid agency work and international rescue. However, this chapter concentrates on commercial activities for reasons of space.

As background to our understanding of globalisation, this section begins by looking at recent trends in world trade activity. It then uses this strategic context to explore the meaning of globalisation. Words like 'globalisation' and 'internationalisation' are used interchangeably to explore the strategic issues but they are not the same. The distinction between them is important because it may lead to different strategic activities. Finally, the main strategic implications of globalisation are then examined in terms of the activities of both countries and companies.

19.1.1 The importance of world trade and investment: the strategic context

In 1994, world merchandise trade amounted to US$4000 billion and grew by over 9 per cent over the previous year:[1] *trade* means the exporting and importing activities of countries and companies around the world. At the same time, world output of goods increased by 3.5 per cent: *output* is the total production of goods by companies and public organisations aggregated together across the world. In fact, as shown in Table 19.1, world merchandise trade outstripped world output during the period 1970–90.[2] Countries are trading more with each other and faster than they are increasing their output. This should present continuing opportunities for the development of corporate strategy.

The reasons for the major increase in world trade are shown in Exhibit 19.1.

Table 19.1 Comparison of world exports and world manufacturing value added

	1960–70	1970–80	1980–90
Annual growth in world trade	9.2%	20.3%	6.0%
Annual growth in manufacturing value added (1990 US$)	n.a.	3.1%	2.1%

Source: UNIDO.[3]

Exhibit 19.1 **The reasons for the major increase in world trade**

- *New or enhanced trade blocks* have been agreed over the last 20 years, e.g. the Single Europe Act 1986 certainly encouraged and supported trade across the EU. The ASEAN pact has been extended because benefits have been identified. New trade agreements are expected to keep this momentum for the next few years. There are several recent examples:

  1 The Uruguay Round of the General Agreement on Tariffs and Trade (GATT) was signed in December 1993 and is expected to increase global welfare by between US$213 and 274 billion in 1992 dollars by the year 2002.[4]

  2 The Mercosur Treaty has brought together Brazil, Argentina, Paraguay and Uruguay in South America to form a new regional trade pact.

  3 The North American Free Trade Agreement (NAFTA) was signed in late 1994 and brought increased trade between USA, Mexico and Canada.

- *World and regional trade organisations* have themselves been strengthened and reformed: for example, the European Bank for Reconstruction and Development (EBRD) has been renewed following a difficult early period and has now begun to offer significant funds for development in Eastern Europe. The WTO, the World Bank and the IMF have also been strengthened. These institutions are explained in Section 19.3.

- *Multinationals* have become an important source of world sales and investment. According to UN estimates,[5] foreign sales by transnational corporations reached US$5500 billion in 1992. The same companies have accumulated US$2000 billion worth of foreign direct investment.

- *New technology* has made telecommunications, travel and media and all international communications much easier. This has brought countries together and influenced political and economic decision making.

In many respects, world merchandise trade has come to be an important *driver* of country economic growth around the world. Corporate strategy has played a significant part in achieving this and, equally, has benefited from it. We are concerned here with the way international markets and industry structure interact with international company activity. Some industries cannot survive without overseas trade: for example, aerospace and defence companies such as Boeing (US), Aerospatiale (France) and British Aerospace (UK) need sales beyond their home countries to make a profit. The Giant Bicycle Company featured in Case study 19.1 needs international sales since its national market in Taiwan is so small. Other industries simply benefit from being able to sell their products or services internationally.

19.1.2 The distinction between foreign trade and foreign direct investment

In addition to engaging in trading activities, companies may also engage in foreign direct investment (often abbreviated to FDI). It is important to distinguish between the two:

- *Trading activities*: the export and import-selling activities of an individual country or a nation state – for example, Giant Bicycle's exports from Taiwan.

- *Foreign direct investment*: the long-term investment by a company in the technology, management skills, brands and physical assets of a subsidiary in another country. Such investment is then used to generate sales in that country, quite possibly replacing exports from the home country – for example, the FDI by Giant in its factory in the Netherlands.

The role of overseas trade and foreign direct investment has changed significantly for many companies and has come to be a direct part of corporate strategy. But an increase in *international* activity is not the same as an increase in *globalisation*.

19.1.3 Defining and exploring different types of international expansion

In analysing international company activity, Bartlett and Ghoshal distinguished between three different types:[6]

1 *International* – when a significant proportion of an organisation's activities are outside the home country and they are managed as a separate area. For example, a small company engaged in exporting some of its product beyond its home country would be international according to this definition. The focus of such a business is its domestic operation, with international activity being an appendage to this.

2 *Multinational* – when a company operates in many countries, though it may still have a home base. One purpose of such operations is to respond to local demand. For example, the MTV music television company has at least three different operations to suit three different music traditions – Asian, North American and European – that are owned by its home-base operation in the US. The focus of the business is a series of semi-independent operations, perhaps under a global brand name like MTV.

3 *Global* – when a company treats the whole world as one market and one source of supply. There is only limited response to local demand – for example, Rolex watches or Disney's Mickey Mouse. The focus of the business is one world market, with each of the operations delivering contributions to that activity.

These distinctions are important because they have different strategic implications:

- With the international activity, the primary strategic driver is the home market and the competitive advantage that it delivers, with international sales being subsidiary to this.

- With the multinational business, the competitive advantage is separately determined for each of the various national or regional markets in which the organisation is engaged.

- With the global business strategy, competitive advantage usually comes from common global brands and from concentrated production activity that has been sited to deliver significant economies of scale and resource sourcing. There may be some adjustment of the product or service for local needs but essentially it is the same around the world. The whole world is treated as one market.

In addition to the above on *company* activity, the term 'globalisation' is also used to cover three other topic areas:[7]

1 *Globalisation of economies, trade activities and regulatory regimes.* World economies are slowly coming together, with barriers to trade being lowered. We will explore this in Sections 19.2 and 19.3 below.

2 *Globalisation of industries.* Whole industries like the car industry, the aerospace industry and the paper and pulp industry are beginning to trade as one market rather than as a series of regional markets. We will explore this in Sections 19.4 and 19.5 below.

3 *Morality of globalisation.* It is argued by some commentators that the globalisation process has led some companies to pillage the environment, destroy lives and fail to enrich poor people as promised.[8] These are important issues that are beyond the scope of this text. However, the underlying principle of this book is that companies will act responsibly and in the interests of the wider community, as well as those of the owners of the organisation. These issues deserve our serious attention.

Comment

Those organisations that fail to distinguish between international and global strategy miss important elements of strategic development. Many companies that claim to be 'global' are not global in the sense set out above – they are merely selling in many parts of the world. This means that such companies are international or multinational, but it does not mean that they are global. In practice, as we will see later, the distinctions between these areas are not as clear as set out above, but they serve as a useful starting point in exploring globalisation.

19.1.4 International expansion and globalisation: the C–C–B Paradigm

In order to explore the relationships between companies and the many countries within which they operate, it is useful to identify the essential elements. These are set out in the C–C–B Paradigm shown in Figure 19.2. It is developed from an earlier paradigm by the international economist Professor John Dunning, but has been substantially altered to concentrate on corporate strategy issues.[9] The main elements of the paradigm are:

- *C–C–B.* This refers to three essential components of the paradigm: the Company, the Country in which the company is operating and the Bargaining that will take place between the company and the country.

- *Underlying assumption of the paradigm.* Companies have different interests from countries. The conflict between these interests is resolved through bargaining between the two parties. The main areas of advantage can be identified by exploring the concept of competitive advantage – *see* Chapter 6 for companies and Section 19.2 below for countries.

- *Company.* Each company will have sustainable competitive advantages, based on its resources. For example, Giant Bicycles has expertise in bicycle design and manufacture as well as its brand names. These advantages will be used in selling its products in international markets.

- *Country.* Each country will have some competitive advantages, based on its resources. For example, these might include its physical location, such as Singapore's position on shipping routes between Europe and Asia. However, resources will also include the country's investment in education, such as Singapore's substantial investment in

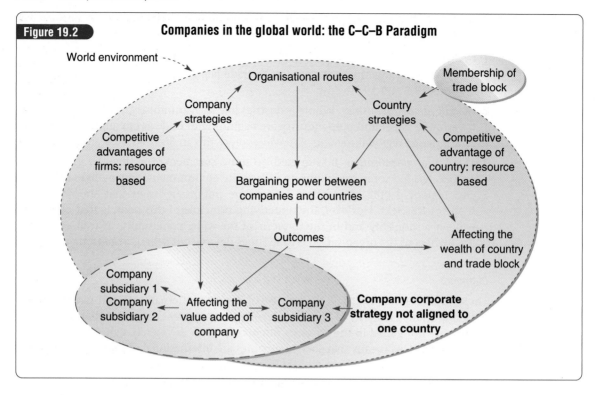

Figure 19.2 — **Companies in the global world: the C–C–B Paradigm**

this area over the last 20 years, and its technical knowledge, such as Singapore's financial and electronics expertise developed over this period.

- *Bargaining power.* Companies and countries will negotiate with each other on the basis of customer market size, investment required, availability of investment incentives, country infrastructure and so on.
- *Outcomes.* The results of such bargaining will deliver *wealth* to the country receiving the trade and the foreign direct investment and *value added* to the company.
- *Value added of the company.* There may be more than one subsidiary of the company involved. Moreover, some subsidiaries may have other relationships with each other, not always inside the country. In addition, the stakeholders of the company are unlikely to be located in the country. The result is that the company's corporate strategy will not necessarily be aligned to that of one country.

We will explore these elements further as we progress through the chapter.

19.1.5 Corporate strategy and international expansion – including globalisation

To deliver value added and sustainable competitive advantage, corporate strategy seeks two main opportunities from international expansion:

1 Market opportunities in many countries will deliver significant new sales, particularly as barriers to trade have been reduced over the last 50 years.

2 Production and resource opportunities will arise in some countries as a result of their special resources, such as the availability of low-cost labour, special skills and natural resources (like oil).

The result has been the creation of new international configurations of business that cover all the main elements of commerce: trade; services (such as advertising and technology); people (such as those needed to manage businesses locally); factor payments (such as profits, interest payments, licensing); and the foreign direct investment referred to above. In one sense, the principles of corporate strategy are just the same whether they are applied in one country or on a global scale. In another sense, there are some extra dimensions that arise from global competition and the interests of individual countries or groups of countries. We begin our exploration of these additional dimensions by exploring country issues in the next three sections of this chapter. We then turn to company issues in the following three sections of the chapter.

▶ Key strategic principles

- International expansion and globalisation are amongst the most important strategic influences in the business environment in the twenty-first century.

- International expansion has become an important driver of country economic growth. Companies have contributed to this and benefited from it.

- It is important to distinguish between foreign trade – exports and imports – and foreign direct investment – the investment in capital, factories and people in foreign locations.

- It is important also to distinguish between three types of international and global expansion: *international*, where a significant proportion of an organisation's activities take place outside its home market but it is still the domestic market that is the prime focus of strategy; *multinational*, where a company operates in many countries and varies its strategy country by country; *global*, where a company treats the world as one market.

- Significantly, each of the three areas above implies a different international expansion strategy.

- The *C–C–B Paradigm* explores the resource relationships between the **C**ompany, the **C**ountry in which it operates and the **B**argaining that takes place between the two. The twin purposes of such bargaining are to deliver increased value added to the company and increased wealth to the country.

CASE STUDY 19.2

International strategy in the world pulp and paper industry

This case study explores the background to this major international industry which is beginning to move from regional to global operations. In particular, it examines the links between company resource strategy and the trends towards global markets.

Products and companies: the five main sectors involve different markets and employ some different resources

Between them, the regions of North America and Scandinavia produce the bulk of the world's pulp and paper. Table 19.2 lists the leading companies. Profitability depends on two main factors: the price of wood pulp and the type of paper that is then made from it. Virtually all paper and carton board is made from trees. To develop strategy, it is useful to distinguish among five main markets in the industry:

▶

1 *Newsprint and other printing papers.* The majority of wood pulp goes into making types of newsprint for the world's newspapers and magazines. There are various different qualities, depending on the costs and the type of printing and presentation required.

2 *Other fine papers.* In addition to newsprint, there are other types of graphic paper which are used for copying, typing and other purposes.

3 *Hygiene products.* These are the products that absorb body and other fluids, such as those in incontinence pads and feminine hygiene products.

4 *Tissue.* That is, crêped soft paper used for napkins, toilet rolls and kitchen towels.

5 *Packaging.* This is the carton packaging used to contain and present products. It may be a simple carton that holds the final product or stronger packaging, such as corrugated board, that provides a higher degree of protection. Corrugated board contains two outer layers of paper with an intermediate layer of fluted/folded paper to give extra strength.

Table 19.2 Leading companies in the world pulp and paper industry in 1999

Company	Country	Capacity (megatonnes)
International Paper and Union Group	US	14.0
Stora Enso	Sweden/Finland	13.0
UPM-Kymmene	Finland	8.1
Smurfitt-Stone Consolidated	Ireland/US	7.7
Georgia-Pacific	US	6.7
Oji Paper	Japan	6.1
Nippon	Japan	6.0
SCA	Sweden	5.7
Metsä-Serla Group	Finland	5.0
Weyerhauser & MacMillan Bloedel	US	5.0
Sappi	Japan	5.0

Source: Author based on data from UPM-Kymmene and the *Financial Times*.

Because paper products use pulp made from trees, all the leading companies in the market are acutely aware of the potential impact that such activity will have on the earth's environment. Firms take the view that cutting down trees for pulp and paper can be done in a responsible way, but it is essential to employ good forest and production management practices.

Each of the above five product sectors has different customers and competitors – the strategic environment. Each area also requires specialist resources, skills and abilities – strategic resources. However, there is one core resource that is common to all companies, namely wood pulp. This resource deserves special attention because it is important for profitability in the industry.

Some companies make products in all areas, while other companies concentrate on some product areas only. For example, the Swedish company SCA makes products in *all* the main groups above, but the well-known US multinational Procter & Gamble specialises in only *one*: hygiene products for babies and for women. It is against this background that companies have had to devise their corporate strategy. The next section explores the environment and the following two sections then examine resources, starting with the core resource of wood pulp.

Trends leading to international expansion: mature markets, new international competitors, increased product specialisation and industry economic cycles

Mature markets and technology

Up to the late 1990s, the pulp and paper industry operated as a series of regional geographic markets – for example, the European market and the North American market. There were three basic reasons for this:

1 a reluctance by the leading companies to enter each other's markets and so increase competition;

2 substantial transport costs in distributing some types of paper, providing a barrier to entry unless a complete new plant was installed in an overseas location;

3 significant profit opportunities from expanding in the region itself, especially North America and Europe.

More fundamentally, the basic technology of the industry did not lend itself to global expansion.

Economies of scale were available but insufficient to justify one plant for a whole region of the world. Transport costs are high and paper does not travel well, due to moisture absorption and its bulky nature. The technology was relatively mature, meaning that old plant could still compete on costs on some applications. Even the supposed 'paperless office' did not result in lower paper usage, thus applying no pressure to upgrade the technology. International expansion during the 1980s and early 1990s therefore concentrated on consolidating market share in a region of the world (Case study 19.3 on the Swedish paper company SCA explores this).

However, the late 1990s have seen a change in attitudes to world expansion. Given the maturity of existing markets, foreign expansion through acquisition, merger or joint venture has represented a route to sales growth. The first reason is that the industry claims that global customers want global suppliers. In addition, such methods of expansion often represent the only way to gain growth and deliver pricing power in markets – larger size in a mature market may be associated with greater concentration of suppliers. Recent examples of consolidation include:

- Stora Enso (Sweden) acquired Consolidated Papers (US).
- International Paper (US) merged with Champion Paper (US).
- Abitibi-Consolidated (Canada) acquired Donohue (Canada).
- Stora (Sweden) acquired Avenor (Canada).
- Jefferson Smurfitt (Ireland) merged with Stone Container (US).
- UPM-Kymmene (Finland) acquired Blandin (US).
- SCA (Sweden) acquisitions are explored in Case 19.3.

Increased international competition

As a result of such activity, a related reason for international expansion has become the very presence of foreign competition itself. In other words, once competition has started, it may lead to a scramble for global position. Certainly, the industry still has a long way to go in terms of industrial concentration. Even the largest company, Stora Enso, still only controlled some 4 per cent of world capacity in 1999.

Increased product specialisation

Coupled with international expansion, there has also been an industry trend to increased specialisation in certain types of paper. For example, a company might concentrate its product strategy on fine papers or disposable hygiene products. The reasons for this trend are two-fold:

1 Specialist technology for certain types of packaging and certain end-uses, e.g. medical, has been changing faster than the general paper market. But this requires research and development coupled with more specialist marketing.

2 The prospect of dominating a specialist segment of the market with its consequent implications for market share and, possibly, profitability.

Such specialisation may then lead to a focused international expansion strategy in the latter area alone. The best example is possibly Procter & Gamble (US) above.

Industry economic cycles

The final reason for international expansion has been the desire of companies to avoid some of the effects of national and regional economic cycles. As economies turn down, the price of paper products is depressed. By operating in totally new markets, companies attempt to avoid the economic depression of their home markets.

Corporate strategies to cope with market maturity and demand cyclicality: grow larger or exit the industry

Pulp and paper companies around the world are well aware of the problems caused by the mature industry environment and the need for renewable resources. They are constantly examining the following corporate strategy options to overcome the difficulties:

- *Merge.* Ten major mergers have taken place in the last few years. The reasoning has been the need for companies to consolidate in a capital-intensive industry.

- *Invest in new plant with greater efficiency and lower costs.* This would reduce break-even. Importantly, it replaces existing capacity, so the costs of plant closure and redundancy would need to be included in the estimates. The problem is that it fails to deliver competitive advantage as it is a strategy that can be adopted by all companies.

- *Acquire companies and plant in growing world markets*. This was explored in the previous section.
- *Invest in higher-added-value production*. Fine papers, graphic papers, hygiene and tissue papers command higher prices than newsprint. They have higher added value through the need for specialist production skills, coatings and ingredients that are then reflected in higher prices. But it should be noted that such a strategy is well known and may bring basic paper companies into competition with other buyers of paper products.
- *Invest in plant to recycle newsprint*. It is estimated that about 50 per cent of paper from newspapers was recovered in 1994. By the new millennium, environmental legislation was expected in some countries to require this figure to rise to 65 per cent of all newsprint. New, specialised plant is better at recycling than some existing machinery. Competitive advantage here is difficult to estimate.

- *Exit the industry*. If it is no longer possible to generate real profits from the industry without massive investment, then some companies will choose to exit the industry.

Sources: See reference 10.

© Copyright Richard Lynch 2003. All rights reserved. This case was written by Richard Lynch from published information only.

Case questions

1 *Is the expansion strategy in the world pulp and paper industry one of 'international expansion' or 'global expansion'?*

2 *What are the benefits and costs of global strategy in pulp and paper? Do other industries like cars and the media have much the same benefits and costs? (See the Ford, DaimlerChrysler and News Corporation case studies for data on these areas.)*

3 *Should other mature industries expand internationally by acquisition? What are the benefits and problems?*

19.2 World trade and the international expansion strategies of companies

To understand the basis of company international expansion and globalisation, it is essential to explore why and how national markets have become increasingly global over the last 50 years. Between 1950 and 1996, world trade in merchandise goods increased by 1500 per cent. Virtually all of this increased activity has been channelled through companies engaged in international activities. Globalisation is therefore capable of delivering major company strategic opportunities.

However, globalisation is also dependent on national government strategy. For example, the world paper and pulp industry would be totally unable to operate without the willing permission of governments to allow the import and manufacture of such products from Scandinavia and North America to other countries that do not have forestry and paper-producing resources. We begin by exploring the theories of world trade, which have been mainly developed at the *country* rather than the *company* level. After setting the theories in historical context, we pick out some leading theories and then examine their strategic implications.

Until recently, world trade was mainly in commodities like agricultural products.[11] It turned down in the 1930s as countries attempted to protect their new industrial ventures. From the late 1940s, it has grown dramatically as countries have lowered barriers to trade and developed institutions to encourage international trade. The reasons for this growth are clearly relevant to corporate strategy but are complex and not easy to resolve.

Over the last 200 years, economists in particular have been developing theories to explain the growth and advantages of international trade. They have explored the benefits and problems in the context of empirical evidence that increased trade has generally been beneficial to those countries that have engaged in it.[12] The importance of such theories for corporate strategy is threefold:

1 They explain the way that nation states view their *bargaining position* with companies wanting to expand internationally.

2 They provide a *framework* in which to analyse the corporate strategy relating to international opportunities and threats.

3 They help to identify the *sustainable competitive advantages* of the nations that might be selected by companies to form part of an international corporate strategy.

Amongst the many theories of international economic growth, three can usefully be identified and contrasted for their impact on corporate strategy. They are explored in the sections that follow. There is no agreement amongst economists on the 'correct' theory: they all have some merit but all fail to capture the complexity of the full international strategic implications.

19.2.1 Theories of trade based on the resources of the country

In the theories of the nineteenth century to the present day, some economists have argued that free trade between nations will deliver increased wealth. Early theories to support this argument relied on simple views of comparative labour costs between nations. More recent theories have concentrated on the economies of scale that arise as companies inside nations produce on a larger scale and thus reduce their costs. In both cases, these theories will depend on the resources of the country – such as the availability of raw materials and energy – along with the resources of the individual companies and industries within the country. None of these theories provides a complete explanation of the complex reasons for the growth in world trade.[13]

Whatever the reasons, evidence of the effects of removing some trade barriers during the period 1965–95 came from the experience of Eastern Asia.[14] Singapore, Hong Kong and, later, South Korea and Taiwan lowered some trade barriers rather than protect their home industries. The four Asian newly industrialised nations raised their average real incomes per head from 20 per cent of those of the high-income countries (like the US and the EU) in 1965 to 70 per cent by 1995. Contrasts were drawn between North and South Korea, mainland China and Hong Kong, West and East Germany. From the mid-1980s, mainland China itself began to take a different path, with successful results, especially in Shanghai and Guandong Province. In the late 1990s, even countries like India that had feared the effects of trade liberalisation on their own national industries began to think again.

From a corporate strategy perspective, the significance of this theory is that it stresses the importance of identifying the resources of a country or region within a country as part of international strategy development.

19.2.2 'Diamond' theory of competitive advantage of nations – the contribution of Porter

In the late 1980s, Michael Porter embarked on a major empirical study of ten nations and four major world industries. His purpose was to identify those factors that contributed to national success in international markets. The countries surveyed were: Denmark, Italy, Japan, Singapore, South Korea, Sweden, Switzerland, the UK, the US and West Germany. The industries were German printing presses, US patient-monitoring equipment, Italian ceramic tiles and Japanese robotics. The result was a diamond formed from four interrelated factors, as shown in Figure 19.3. In addition, there were two other factors outside the diamond: government policy and chance events.

The four factors are as follows:

1 *Factor conditions.* Porter emphasised that competitiveness was not just a matter of comparative advantage. Resources can also be 'home grown' and specialised. Thus, the provision of education, universities, excellent telecommunications goes well beyond the natural resources but can assist in delivering national competitiveness. The success of countries like Singapore and Malaysia has depended, at least in part, on the national government's willingness to invest in these areas over long periods of time.

2 *Related and supporting industries.* Internationally competitive *suppliers* and other related industries represent a critical resource for international success. Clusters of such industries, each offering expertise and world-class service, can be vital. For example, Hollywood USA relies for its world success not just on film studios but on a range of other related companies in film recording, electronics, design and music.

3 *Firm strategy, structure and rivalry.* Fierce national *competition* will drive innovation, force down costs and develop new methods of competing that can then be used internationally by the same companies. For example, Porter argued that the global strength of the Japanese consumer electronics companies like Mitsubishi and Hitachi was directly related to the strength of the highly competitive home market for such goods.

4 *Demand conditions.* Highly sophisticated and demanding *customers* in a nation's home market will drive up innovation and quality. Porter pointed to the sophistication of Japanese cameras, like Canon, and the quality of German cars, like BMW, being the result of demanding national customers.

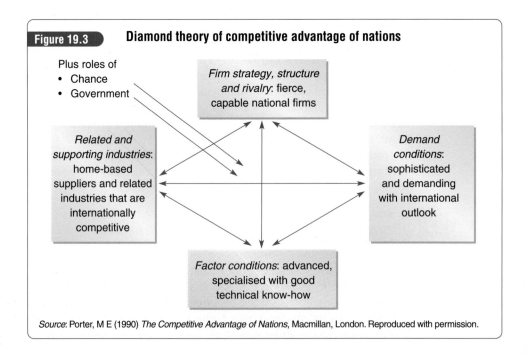

Figure 19.3 **Diamond theory of competitive advantage of nations**

Plus roles of
• Chance
• Government

Firm strategy, structure and rivalry: fierce, capable national firms

Related and supporting industries: home-based suppliers and related industries that are internationally competitive

Demand conditions: sophisticated and demanding with international outlook

Factor conditions: advanced, specialised with good technical know-how

Source: Porter, M E (1990) *The Competitive Advantage of Nations*, Macmillan, London. Reproduced with permission.

In addition, Porter identified two other factors that are important:

1 *the role of government*, which can influence any of the above by subsidies, regulation, investment in education and so on;

2 *the role of chance events*, which can shift competitive advantage in unpredictable ways: for example, war, inventions, oil price rises and so on.

From a corporate strategy perspective, this significant theory helps identify and select countries for production investment. It also provides evidence on the nature of customers and competitors in such countries. Importantly, it suggests that the size of a market matters less than its characteristics.

Comment

In spite of its clear relevance to the development of international and global strategy, Porter's theory has a number of difficulties:[15]

- *Sample*. Readers can work out which countries and industries were left out and what this might mean for the conclusions.

- *Government*. This is not included in the diamond but crucial to many elements of it, such as national competition policy.

- *Chance*. This appears to be the only explanation for many events that may be crucial.

- *Company, not country, competition*. Porter took as his starting point the concept that countries compete in international markets. This is misleading because it is companies that compete – for example, Sweden and Finland do not compete on paper and pulp but companies like SCA and Stora Enso do.

- *Multinational influence*. Porter totally ignores the major multinational companies, yet they are the main contributors to foreign trade and foreign direct investment. Dunning suggests that MNEs accounted for between 25 and 30 per cent of the GDP of the world's market economies in the mid-1980s. They were also responsible for around three-quarters of the world's commodity trade and four-fifths of the trade in technology and managerial skills.[16]

- *Home country advantage*. For some MNEs, the location of their home countries is largely irrelevant. The fact that ABB – *see* Case study 16.3 – is located in Switzerland and Sweden has almost no bearing on its global strategies. This means that the basis of the Porter thesis – the 'home country' advantage (of Japanese consumer electronics, for example) – is irrelevant for such companies.

These and other criticisms suggest that the theory is only a partial explanation of complex issues. However, it does alert companies to important country issues that need to be addressed.

19.2.3 Theory of limited state intervention – attributed to the World Bank

In its work in supporting investment in developing countries over the last few years, the World Bank has had the opportunity to examine the areas of investment that deliver real increases in the wealth of countries. It has never published the results as a 'theory' as such but its empirical findings can be found in its annual reports. It is these that have been summarised as the limited state intervention theory outlined in Figure 19.4.

Essentially, the theory suggests that companies gained from national government investment in the early years in such areas as telecommunications and roads, but that

---

Figure 19.4 **Theory of limited state intervention**

← →

Early stages of development
- Economic stability
- Low inflation
- Stable finances and currency
- Export support for selected areas
- Quality civil service and training
  institutions
- Agricultural development policies

Later stages of development
- Maintain openness to
  international trade
- Allow free markets to operate
- Continue to invest in
  infrastructure but privatise
  where possible
- Low tariff barriers

Company strategy should be seeking evidence of the above

---

as nations become more wealthy the state should withdraw its support and allow free market pressures to operate. This means that state support for home-grown industries should be reduced if companies are to compete internationally.

From a corporate strategy perspective, the findings indicate the attitudes that companies should have towards government intervention. They indicate that companies should be wary of governments that deny open market access. Governments should also be seeking to stabilise the economy of a country and its currency as a matter of policy and should invest in its infrastructure and education. This provides clear guidance to companies on country selection for market potential and for production plant location.

19.2.4 Implications of international trade theories for corporate strategy

Overall, they point to the important role of government policy in several areas:

- *Developing basic infrastructures.* These concern such areas as water supplies, telecommunications and roads. It is difficult for company corporate strategy to make much headway in a country if governments are unwilling to invest in these areas.

- *Training and the quality of education.* These too are also vital. The stock of human capital is an important element in the development of new investments because of the need to recruit and train nationals to work for the company. In selecting countries for international strategic development, this may be a major factor.

- *Economic stability and selected export stimuli.* Most organisations are able to work better if inflation is low and the economy is stable. In the early stages of development, there is also some evidence that governments can usefully support certain industries in terms of export assistance to stimulate early growth.

- *Competitive and open home market.* Although there is a risk that home industries may be swamped by large international companies entering the home market, this is not what has tended to happen in practice. When the home market is open, it has stimulated new entrants to open factories, created jobs and thus wealth. For example, India has for years had home markets that were partially closed to international trade. Singapore and Malaysia have opened up their markets and benefited accordingly. And so have companies like Sony (Japan) and Philips (Netherlands) that have invested in such countries.

More specifically from a company perspective, it is important to examine the extent and nature of the main barriers that might exist to the opportunities associated with free trade: these are shown in Exhibit 19.2. In the short term, some barriers may be small and outside the more fundamental scope of corporate strategy. However, at a deeper level, such barriers may be fundamental to company survival and development. For example, the production plant investment by the Japanese car companies Nissan, Toyota and Honda inside the EU in the 1980s and 1990s was a direct strategic response, at least in part, to trade barriers and EU sensitivities in this area.

Exhibit 19.2 **The main barriers to trade**

- *Tariffs*: taxes on imported goods. They do not stop imports but do make them less competitive.
- *Quotas*: a maximum number placed on the goods that can be imported in any one period.
- *Non-tariff or technical barriers*: local laws or other technical means imposed by governments to make it difficult for imports to enter the country.
- *Financial subsidies for home producers.*
- *Exchange controls*: government control of the access its citizens have to foreign currency so that it becomes difficult to pay for imports.

Key strategic principles

- Early theories of international trade concentrate on the *resources of the country*. They suggest that a reduction in trade barriers can be coupled with the economies of scale available to companies in explaining the growth of international trade over the last 50 years.

- Porter's *diamond theory of the competitive advantage of nations* identified four home country factors that explained why some countries were particularly successful internationally: factor conditions; related and supporting industries; firm strategy structure and rivalry; demand conditions. In addition, he identified two outside factors – government policy and chance – that were also significant.

- The *theory of limited state intervention* was attributed to the World Bank and identified the role of government in different stages of economic growth. As countries become more wealthy, governments should let free markets operate.

- Theories of international trade identify the role of government in encouraging international investment. They also help companies select which countries offer the best international prospects.

19.3 Influence of institutions involved in international trade

In any development of international and global strategy, it is useful to have some background knowledge of the main institutions involved and their roles in its development. Corporate strategists may meet them directly and will certainly encounter their policy decisions indirectly over time. It should be noted that the United Nations is not identified separately below. However, it has come to have an important policy role in a number of areas such as education, health and agriculture, which will have relevance to specific product strategy initiatives.

19.3.1 Three international trade institutions

In order to promote free trade after the mistakes of the 1930s, the major Western nations decided during the 1940s that they would need new bodies to oversee international trade. They attempted to establish three international institutions that would be directly relevant to companies involved in international trade:

1 *The International Monetary Fund* (IMF). Its purpose was to oversee international payments. It also provided a forum for the regulation of currencies up to 1973.

2 *The International Bank for Reconstruction and Development.* This is often called the World Bank. It was set up to provide long-term capital aid for the economic development of nations – roughly US$10 billion per annum. It still provides lending for infrastructure, tourism and other projects with the aim of long-term improvement in growth.

3 *The International Trade Organisation* (ITO). This was to be set up to regulate trade activity and sort out the trade disputes that had been so disastrous during the 1918–39 period. It was never allowed to operate but the World Trade Organisation, which was formed in 1995, was its direct successor.

The IMF and the World Bank were successfully inaugurated and continue to the present. Unfortunately, the US failed to ratify the treaty setting up the ITO in 1948. As an interim measure, the General Agreement on Tariffs and Trade (GATT) was signed by 23 signatory countries in 1947 and this then continued as the main mechanism to ensure free trade up to 1995. Exhibit 19.3 shows the main GATT principles. By the late 1990s, over 140 countries had signed the GATT because the results were seen to be beneficial.

Exhibit 19.3   **The main principles of the GATT**

There are three major principles:

1 *Non-discrimination.* Each country will give all other countries the same rates on import duties. Giving more to one country means giving more to all signatories [called *most favoured nation* status].

2 *Consultation.* When disputes arise, GATT brings the parties together and encourages compromise, rather than the squabbles of the 1930s.

3 *Sanctions for non-compliance.* Where no compromise is possible, then the WTO is empowered to adjudicate and impose a solution. It has semi-judicial status.

Over the period from 1947, GATT has sponsored eight major rounds of tariff and other trade barrier reductions to encourage world trade (barriers to trade are explored in the next section). Each negotiation round is named after the country or town where it was begun. The latest completed round was the Uruguay Round which started in 1986 and was signed in 1993.[17]

The World Trade Organisation (WTO) was set up in 1995 to administer the GATT and to undertake the functions originally envisaged as being part of the ITO.[18] It has become a prime mover in the continued development of international trade and highly beneficial to those companies developing international corporate strategy. For example, the 'Banana War' between the US and the EU in 1998–99 was eventually decided under the GATT rules. The WTO judged that the US was entitled to complete access for its banana exports and could apply sanctions against a range of EU companies if such entry was denied. The corporate strategy of a large number of firms, including many that had no involvement with bananas, was affected by this move.

19.3.2 Third World countries and the GATT

Although GATT gave important protection to poorer and smaller countries when they reduced their barriers to large and powerful partners, such countries still felt that it assisted industrialised countries. They pointed to the fact that their share of world trade was declining. They therefore encouraged the United Nations to form the United Nations Conference on Trade and Development (UNCTAD). This body has been concerned with highlighting the trade concerns of the developing nations. It has a more limited role in the development of corporate strategy.

19.3.3 Institutions involved in currency regulation

In addition to trade, another major area of concern in 1945 was *exchange rates for currency* between countries: there is little point in fixing a price, regardless of tariffs, if the unit in which it is quoted then collapses. This will clearly have an immediate impact on company profitability. There had been real problems in this area in international trade in the 1930s. A system of largely fixed exchange rates was agreed internationally in 1944: the 'Bretton Woods' Agreement. This lasted until 1973 but was then replaced by floating exchange rates around the world. The International Monetary Fund (IMF) was set up to oversee the fixed system but did not disappear when the fixed system was discontinued. Today, it has more of a background role. It lends funds to countries in balance of payments difficulties and helps to support international trade stability through co-operation and discussion.

19.3.4 Importance of trade blocks

To pursue international strategy, companies usually need to negotiate with national governments. At its most basic level, this means that the company will need to assess the political attitudes of the government – *see* Chapter 3. This section concentrates on the international dimensions only.

In addition to individual countries, various *trade blocks* have also developed around the world. A trade block is a group of countries that have agreed to give each other preferential international trading terms. The purpose of a trade block is to encourage trade between its members on the basis of the theories related to trade barriers and economies of scale. Because it is conducive to free trade, such a block may also help in stabilising a country's political and economic environment.

Some trade blocks have already been mentioned, one of the best known being the EU. Other well-known ones include ASEAN (Association of South East Asian Nations) and NAFTA (North American Free Trade Agreement). Each block is governed by its own rules: for example, the EU has a tight set of rules and relatively close degree of co-operation, while ASEAN is a looser grouping of countries, each having a stronger degree of independence.

For companies engaged in international expansion, the main tasks are to assess the opportunities in specific countries and the trade blocks to which such countries belong.

19.3.5 Conclusions for corporate strategy

At a senior level, there is increasing contact between the leading multinational companies and the main institutions outlined above. For smaller companies, there is always the possibility of *lobbying* to gain benefits and influence decisions that might be taken. For example, the world's leading banks are usually represented at the biannual conferences of the IMF and individual companies have made representations to the WTO. These are important areas of strategic influence for the senior officers of any company.

> ### ■ Key strategic principles
>
> - Three major international institutions have significant influence on international trade. The International Monetary Fund (IMF) oversees international payments. The World Bank provides long-term capital aid. The World Trade Organisation (WTO) regulates trade activity and resolves trade disputes between nations.
>
> - The General Agreement on Tariffs and Trade (GATT) is the general treaty covering trade between many nations of the world. Various rounds of tariff reductions have been sponsored under the GATT. They have opened up world markets over the last 50 years and significantly increased international trade.
>
> - The United Nations Conference on Trade and Development (UNCTAD) represents the interests of Third World countries in international negotiations.
>
> - Trade blocks consist of countries that agree to give each other preferential trading terms. Corporate strategy will need to consider such blocks and their impact on trade.

CASE STUDY 19.3

What strategy now for SCA?

SCA is one of Europe's largest pulp and paper companies. This case explores how the company has built its business and poses the question: does it have the best strategies for international expansion?

SCA: the company and its full product range

SCA has built its strong position over the last 20 years from a background in timber and forestry products in its home country of Sweden (its growth is examined in the next section). By the late 1990s, the company's business activities were centred around one basic core product area – wood pulp – and three main product areas:

1 hygiene products – including consumer paper tissues and hospital products;

2 packaging – including corrugated board for transporting products and finished packaging;

3 forest products – including paper for publications and basic timber for items like furniture.

Starting with a clear vision of its purpose, the company developed a focused approach to its core resources, with a programme of acquisitions and disposals. This resulted in the company's turnover rising almost threefold over the years 1988–96. This was achieved in the mature pulp and paper industry – *see* Case study 19.2 – which traditionally has poor and highly cyclical profit margins. SCA has attempted to outperform the industry by concentrating on profitable and growing product areas – like hospital products and specialist packaging – by organic growth and by acquisition.

Company purpose at SCA: solid profitability and limited in the context of a mature industry

In broad terms, the company is concerned to offer the market customised and value-added products. More specifically, the SCA Group states that its objective is to give SCA's shareholders satisfactory growth in value and dividend levels. The emphasis on growth is reflected in a programme of acquisition

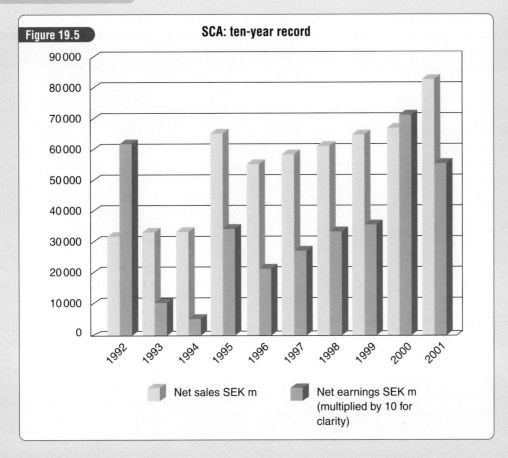

Figure 19.5 SCA: ten-year record

Net sales SEK m
Net earnings SEK m (multiplied by 10 for clarity)

activities undertaken by the company over the last few years.

In its 2001 annual report, the company defined its financial goals: 'SCA's overall goal is to provide shareholders with good growth in value and a rising dividend. Financial evaluation of both current operations and strategic development is measured based on cash flow.' In fact, the company has not always achieved these targets in the last few years. However, a significant part of the shares in the company were in the control of one of Sweden's most powerful and wealthy families – the Wallenbergs. Typically, such families were able to take a longer-term view than was the case in companies with more openly traded shares.

SCA main product areas

To gain an overall picture of the group, Table 19.3 has been assembled from published group data – it

should be noted that the consolidated figures in the published accounts are not always totally consistent with the three business areas. This is typical of many companies and is not material from a strategy perspective, though it has to be admitted that the figures do not always add up from an accounting perspective. Essentially, the data show that the SCA Group is particularly reliant for its absolute profits on its hygiene products and, to a lesser extent, its packaging products. These are the two areas that SCA believes have the greatest growth potential, because the market segments in which the company is involved are growing faster and the products have higher added value.

Hygiene product strategy

SCA sells products in two main areas within this category. It claims to be one of Europe's leading

Table 19.3 SCA: main product areas (SEK million)

	2000	2001
Net sales		
Hygiene products	31 040	40 797
Packaging products	24 636	29 230
Forest products	12 876	13 556
Operating profits		
Hygiene products	2 909	4 473
Packaging products	2 977	3 286
Forest products	2 720	2 976
Capital employed		
Hygiene products	18 066	26 374
Packaging products	14 237	16 288
Forest products	13 331	13 544

suppliers of tissue and fluff products – for example, boxed tissues for handkerchiefs. It is also world leader in incontinence products – especially those for specialist hospital use, the market leader in Europe and the third-largest supplier of tissue to the American away-from-home (AFH) market – hotels, hospitals and similar areas. It has built a position of market leadership in these selected segments largely by acquisition in the past. For example, it purchased the US-based Georgia-Pacific tissue business in the AFH segment for around US$800 million in 2001. It acquired the Serenity incontinence brand from the US company Johnson & Johnson in 2000. It is now developing its world-wide product range by using its technical expertise to develop new patented products and by developing its brand names. However, its major international competitors include the formidable US company Procter & Gamble and the well-known paper company Kimberley-Clark. For these reasons, it has been focusing on areas that are specialist, such as its specialist hospital products. It is also attempting to build strong brands, but the costs and time involved in such a process must make this more difficult to achieve.

Packaging product strategy

SCA claims to be Europe's leading producer of corrugated board and containerboard. These products are used for transporting and merchandising many products – everything from wine bottles to computers. The company's strategy is to focus on packaging solutions for individual large customers where possible – this means adapting its products to serve such customers, which is expensive but also has the benefit of locking a satisfied industrial customer into SCA. The company has therefore set up a range of production units in European countries that are able to respond locally to large customer demand – often at relatively short notice, perhaps even using just-in-time techniques – *see* Chapter 9.

The specialist packaging market has been growing steadily over the last few years and SCA has moved internationally by acquisition where possible. For example, it bought the American packaging specialist company Tuscarora in 2001 because it provided not just another opening into the large US market but also a company that was strong in a specialist product area – customised, interior, protective packaging – which will have higher profit margins and competitive advantage. SCA intends to extend the special products from this acquisition worldwide. The strategy therefore relies on finding specialist market segments, exploiting special technology and providing service to large customers at short notice.

Forest product strategy

There are two main subcategories within this group – paper for such end-products as newsprint and timber for use in finished timber products. In both cases, the market is declining across Europe and SCA is not a market leader. There is a contrast here with the two areas above, where the company does have market leadership, in some cases in specialist market segments. Both product markets are subject to changes in the national economy – printed paper demand reduces when advertising goes down and solid wood products also suffer from a slowdown in a national economy.

The company has therefore regarded this product area as being useful but not the main engine for growth. Its importance lies partly in providing the backbone of the SCA group's wood pulp and fibre-related expertise. The area is also a major generator of cash which has contributed to the funds used to make acquisitions and more general investments in the other areas outlined above.

Future growth

Some areas of the company – such as its specialist AFH products – show significant potential but they will require investment in both technical development and marketing funds. Other areas would seem to have less obvious competitive advantage and be open to heavy competition from rival companies. Yet the company feels able to take a long-term view of its future and allow acquisitions to develop over time.

Sources: See reference 19.

Case questions

1 *How should SCA develop its various business areas? Should it pursue global strategies? Consolidate further in Europe? Move further into branded products? Develop niche markets only? Or perhaps leave some businesses completely?*

2 *Are there any lessons that other companies in mature markets can learn from the SCA experience?*

19.4 International and global expansion strategies: the company perspective

We now move from issues concerning country competitive advantages to those relating to the company. This section explores basic issues surrounding international and global expansion strategies: the basic business case, the case for global strategy, the case for a global and local strategy, and some other international considerations. The following two sections explore organisational structures and specific entry routes and problems.

19.4.1 The basic business case for international expansion

In exploring international expansion, the starting point has to be the strategic business case and the impact on the company of any significant form of international expansion.

Strategic business case: combination of strategy development and implementation

The main elements of this have been covered in earlier chapters. In principle, the development of international strategy is no different from any other strategic process. The starting point is clarity on the objectives and reasons for international expansion. Within this guiding principle, the basic business case will then seek to establish the opportunities and costs of the available options. This may be by using a prescriptive route or it might be more experimental, using emergent approaches.

However, international expansion is likely to be complex and may involve additional uncertainties above those normally present in national markets – anything from currency uncertainty to limited market information on 'foreign' customers. It is therefore quite likely that international expansion will involve a *staged development process*. Thus this might easily involve developing experimental international strategies in some new geographic areas while implementing other, more established international strategies in other parts of the world. For example, the Gillette Mach 3 razor was launched successively in North America, then parts of Europe and other parts of the world. At the same time, Gillette was developing further new products for later launch. In this sense, there is likely to be a combination of strategy development and implementation in international strategy. Such a process is likely to be both prescriptive and emergent.

The history and culture of the organisation

The former head of the management consultants McKinsey in Japan, Kenichi Ohmae, has argued persuasively that company culture is also an important area.[20] The reading at the end of this chapter from Mr Ohmae gives more detail but, in summary, the organisation's culture may make it difficult or easy to expand internationally. For example:

- A company that has acquired another outside its home country may have to live with the need to continue to satisfy its newly purchased local management and therefore provide some local autonomy to its new subsidiary.

- By contrast, the company that has set up an overseas operation from the beginning may have taken longer over the process, but will have been able to recruit, train and develop its people in exactly the way that it wishes, without any previous history.

In some of the literature, there is little consideration of the real strategic difficulties faced by organisations as a result of company historical and cultural influences. These can have a significant effect on strategic choice. For example, even in international companies like Walt Disney pictures and Renault cars, the senior management is largely North American and French respectively. More recently, several authors[21] have produced useful analyses on this subject. The general conclusion seems to be that much of the key strategic decision making still remains centred on the home country, even if national responsiveness is needed. There is a need to consider these matters when international strategic development is being undertaken.

19.4.2 The case for global strategy

Global strategy means treating the world as one market and one interconnected source of supply. Some markets may be regional rather than global. For example, SCA tissue products were largely European in 1999 – *see* Case study 19.3. Companies need to explore the business case for extending this into operating a global market. As Chapter 5 explained, Professor Theodore Levitt argued that global strategy can deliver extra value added and sustainable competitive advantage. There were two main factors that needed to be present to justify a global strategy:[22]

1 *Resources.* These may be more economically manufactured and sourced on a global basis.[23] This was explored in Chapter 9. It is a factor commonly used in the consumer electronics industry, where there are both economies of scale and considerable cost savings by manufacturing labour-intensive items in countries with efficient production equipment and low labour costs, such as some Asian countries. Companies such as Sony (Japan) and Philips (Netherlands) now operate in this way.

2 *Customer demand.* This is essentially the same around the world for some products. Companies such as Coca-Cola (US) and Nike (US) make products that are essentially branded in the same way in all countries. In so far as there are any differences, then customers will be prepared to compromise as a result of the lower prices gained by the economies of scale from the global manufacturing operation outlined above. This was explored in Chapter 5.

Professor George Yip has further developed the arguments in favour of globalisation.[24] He suggests that some organisations may fear being left behind. Moreover, the adoption of 'Western' values and customs has also contributed to globalisation because it promotes common customer demand. He lays particular emphasis on the ability of global products to spread the considerable costs of research and development across more countries – for example, the costs of drug development explored in Chapter 6.

Fundamentally, Yip argues that globalisation may increase the competitive leverage of a company, i.e. it may increase its competitive advantage as a result of its global scope. This presents the clear opportunity of globalisation. But it also raises the question of the number of markets that are truly global: even McDonald's has had to adjust parts of its menu to suit local tastes and dispense with the Big Mac completely in India. Rolex Watches and Yves St Laurent clothing will arguably be global, but many other products may have to be significantly adapted to local needs.

19.4.3 The case for a global/local strategy

In arguing the case for a global strategy, Levitt's arguments largely stopped with the two considerations outlined above. However, for many organisations the global considerations have to be balanced by the need to respond to variations in local demand: the case for the global/local strategy. This is sometimes summarised in the phrase: 'Think global, act local.'

About three years after Levitt produced his paper in favour of globalisation, Professors Susan Douglas and Yoram Wind delivered a suitably robust response.[25] For most companies, there is likely to be a need for some local variation: even supposedly global companies like Nike – *see* Chapter 11 – need to have local variations simply because body sizes vary in different countries.

Local responsiveness clearly pulls in the opposite direction to the pressure for global activity. There are four main reasons behind this:

1 Customer tastes and conditions of usage may vary between countries. This was examined in Chapter 5.

2 National governments may be concerned that the interests of their countries are better served by some variation special to that country. This was explored earlier in this chapter.

3 Different technical standards, different legislation and other social issues may make it essential to produce products especially for a particular country. For example, it is still necessary for domestic electrical plugs and sockets to be produced for specific EU countries because of the different electrical connections (two- or three-pin) in each country.

4 Different national competitors may make it difficult to offer precisely the same competitive advantage in every market. For example, the UK chocolate company Cadbury has had difficulty selling some of its chocolate block products in France and Spain because it faces stronger competition from Kraft Jacobs Suchard (part of Philip Morris, US) in these markets than in its home UK market.

If local responsiveness is required, then this will dilute the value added that might be gained by the scale benefits of globalisation. However, many companies have found that such local issues can be accommodated within global expansion.

Table 19.4 The balance between global expansion and national responsiveness

Pressure for global strategy*	Pressure for international strategy but still responsive to national variations*
● Global or multinational customers	● Differing customers or customer segments by nation or region
● Global or multinational competitors	● Differing competitors or distributors by nation or region
● High levels of investment or technology that need large sales for recovery, e.g. in production, branding or R&D	● Need to adapt product extensively to meet national needs
● Economies of scale in production and purchasing	● Product life cycle at a different stage in local country
● High levels of investment in marketing and brand building	● High skill levels in local country that will permit product adaptation to that country
● Desire by customers for a global 'image'	● Differing conditions of usage, e.g. climate
● Need to cut costs by seeking low labour sources	● Pressure from governments for national activity, e.g. tariff or quota restrictions on global activity
● Global sourcing of raw materials or energy	● National purchasing of key supplies essential

* These are not mutually exclusive.

In practice, therefore, many supposedly global initiatives also need to accommodate significant national responsiveness. Even companies like Coca-Cola, Walt Disney and McDonald's provide some local variations in tastes, languages or national menu items respectively. The difficult strategic choice is often to find the *balance* between global expansion and local responsiveness. The global/national balance is summarised in Table 19.4.

19.4.4 Four prescriptive strategic options for international expansion

Considering the issues explored above, companies have at least four options for international expansion.[26] They are essentially prescriptive in their approach and arise from a consideration of the benefits to be obtained by the two main factors: global strategy and national (or regional) demand.

1 Some companies may decide to undertake purely global expansion, e.g. Gucci or Rolls-Royce cars.

2 Some companies opt for a global strategy *and* for national responsiveness, e.g. Toyota cars and Hewlett-Packard printers.

3 Some companies may need to be largely responsive to national demands and gain little from any form of global activity, e.g. Bata shoes.

4 Some companies may face *neither* of these pressures but still see opportunities to sell their products or services internationally, e.g. any domestic company that is willing to export some of its products.

The four options have been given names and are shown in Figure 19.6. However, it is important to note that the choice of one option does not preclude the choice of another at a later stage. For example, Yip argues that companies do not immediately choose the global option.[27] The global process will go through three stages that will take time and, arguably, some companies will not move beyond the first two stages. Yip's three-stage global process is:

- *Stage 1: Develop the core strategy* – the basis of competitive advantage. This is often developed for the home country first.
- *Stage 2: Internationalise the core strategy* – by launching it across a number of countries.
- *Stage 3: Globalise the strategy* – by seeking out the integration benefits that come from having one global market.

In practice, various other international strategy options have been identified. They are given various titles with the following being representative:

- *Multicountry strategy.* This targets individual countries or groups of countries according to their customer potential and competitor presence. International co-ordination is secondary to a country-by-country expansion programme. For example, Danone (France) has marketed biscuits across Europe according to the local expansion opportunities rather than using a pan-European brand.
- *Global low-cost strategy.* This sources production where production costs are lowest and then sells globally. For example, Philips (Netherlands) manufactures radios in Hong Kong and sells them in Europe.
- *Global niche strategy.* The same product is sold in the same market niche in all countries of the world. For example, Dunhill (UK) and Yves St Laurent (France) products are presented in the same upmarket fashion in all countries.
- *International regional strategy.* Regions of the world will have their own production and there will be some regional or national variation in the products made and marketed,

Figure 19.6 **Four prescriptive options for international expansion**

	Low	**High**
High	Global product company	Multinational company for global and nationally responsive products
Low	International subsidiary	Nationally responsive company of an international division

Benefits of global-scale opportunities

Need for national responsiveness

but the *global underpinning* of strategy is clear. For example, most car companies, such as Toyota (Japan) and General Motors (US), follow such a strategy.

There are many other strategy variations that may also be chosen. The final decision will be *specific* to the product group and the organisation but it may be assisted by the summary arguments presented in Table 19.4.

19.4.5 Some other considerations in international expansion and global strategy

The global/local debate is not the only one that will guide international expansion. Two major issues are explored in the sections that follow: organisation structures and entry methods. However, there are issues in three other areas that need to be explored: competition, channels of distribution and government matters. These are summarised in Figure 19.7. All the issues may be important:

● *Competition.* Global expansion must take into account the activities of rival companies, their resources and position in target markets.

● *Channels of distribution.* These may be vital to product or service success. They need to be considered as a fundamental part of strategy development, where relevant.

● *Government.* Policy may impose excessive tariffs or other barriers. Even if the company can make profits, there may be substantive taxes and it may not be possible to repatriate any remaining profits to the home country. There may also be restrictions on the transfer of technology and poor country infrastructure – *see* earlier in this chapter.

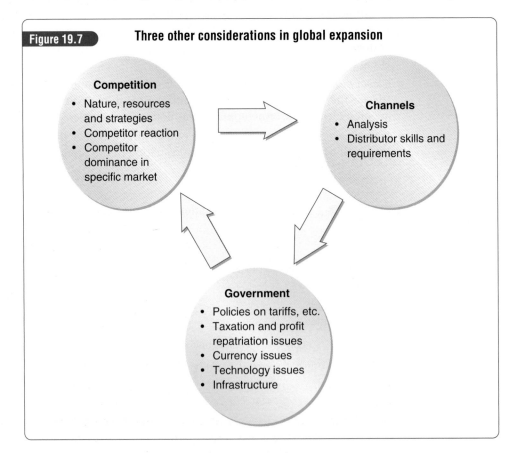

Figure 19.7 Three other considerations in global expansion

Competition
- Nature, resources and strategies
- Competitor reaction
- Competitor dominance in specific market

Channels
- Analysis
- Distributor skills and requirements

Government
- Policies on tariffs, etc.
- Taxation and profit repatriation issues
- Currency issues
- Technology issues
- Infrastructure

▶ Key strategic principles

- International strategy expansion will follow the basic principles of strategy development. However, its greater complexity and uncertainty may mean that a staged development process is employed and selection is more complex. The starting point is clarity on the objectives and reasons for international expansion.

- Organisational history and culture, often based on home country senior management, also need to be considered.

- The case for a global strategy rests on two major elements: resources may be more economically procured and manufactured on a global basis. In addition, customer demand may be essentially the same around the world, thus allowing the world to be treated as one market.

- The case for a strategy that is both global and local derives from the need to gain the benefits of a global market while responding to the needs of national market variations. Local variations may arise as a result of customer demand and conditions of usage, national governments, differing technical standards and different national competitors.

- In practice, there is often a need to balance both global and local issues in strategy development.

- At least four prescriptive options emerge from such considerations: global, international, multinational and nationally responsive. In practice, many other variations in international expansion strategies have been developed.

- Other considerations in international expansion include careful consideration of competitors, investigation of distribution channels and a full analysis of national government restrictions and requirements.

19.5 International and global expansion strategies: organisation structures

Much of the thinking so far in this chapter has taken a prescriptive approach. This is probably because the background and foundation lie in the prescriptive routes adopted by international economic analysis and marketing strategy development. However, we also know that some organisational theorists like Mintzberg and Quinn have approached strategy development from an emergent perspective. This is reflected in some of the more recent work on organisational structures for international expansion. This review begins by examining what is essentially a prescriptive route for developing international organisation structures. It then contrasts this with a more recent emergent approach.

19.5.1 Organisational development leading to a matrix structure

In the early 1970s, research was published by Stopford and Wells suggesting that organisational structures evolved over time as international expansion proceeded: their model is shown in Figure 19.8.[28] In the early period international expansion was handled by a separate international division which was often isolated from the main

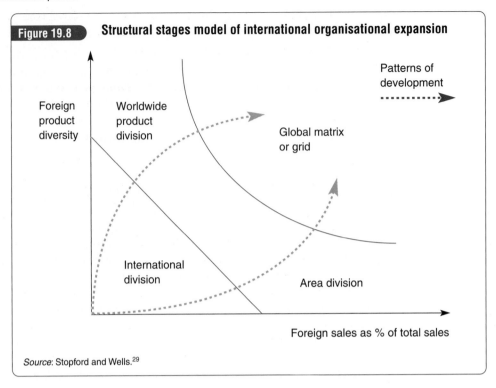

Figure 19.8 Structural stages model of international organisational expansion

Patterns of development

Foreign product diversity

Worldwide product division

Global matrix or grid

International division

Area division

Foreign sales as % of total sales

Source: Stopford and Wells.[29]

areas of strategic decision making. As international sales and business activity continued to grow, the organisational structure changed. The next stage depended on whether the dominant strategic problem was that of:

- organising across different geographic parts of the world, leading to the *area division* structure;
- or organising across increasingly diverse product groups, leading to a *worldwide product group* structure.

Subsequently in the 1980s, the globalisation/localisation debate explored in the previous section led to a new organisational structure: the *matrix structure* where both area divisions and product divisions were employed.[29] This form of organisational structure was explored in Chapter 18 – the criticisms made then also apply here:

- Dual responsibilities, e.g. area and product, are difficult to manage.
- The matrix amplified differences in perspectives and interests by forcing issues through a dual chain of command.
- Management became slower, more costly and possibly even acrimonious.

As a result, some larger companies, such as Unilever, tried and then abandoned the matrix organisation structure. At the end of the 1980s, along came a new organisational solution – the 'transnational structure'. It should be noted that this was *not* a new organisational form, but rather a way of conducting the business of a large international organisation.

19.5.2 Organisational structure: the transnational solution

In the late 1980s, Bartlett and Ghoshal published the results of a study of nine multinational companies that focused on the way that they organised their business and their ability to be both global and locally responsive. This placed considerable emphasis on the importance of innovation and technology development which was disseminated rapidly through the company.[30] The nine companies were grouped into three product areas:

1 branded packaged goods: Unilever (UK/Netherlands), Kao (Japan) and Procter & Gamble (US)

2 consumer electronics: Philips (Netherlands), Matsushita (Japan) and General Electric (US)

3 telecommunications switching: ITT (US), NEC (Japan) and Ericsson (Sweden).

From an extensive study of the strategic requirements of these businesses and the way that each handled its main resources, the two authors identified both existing problems and the methods that these companies had developed to overcome them.

According to Bartlett and Ghoshal, the basic problem with a matrix structure was that it focused on only one variable – the formal structure – that could not capture the complexity of the international strategic task. They defined this task as being to reshape the core decision-making systems and management processes of large MNEs: their administrative systems, their communications channels and their interpersonal relationships. The authors argued that, in the complex and fast-moving environment of global business, it was difficult to use a simple 'structural fit' between strategy and structure in the way suggested by Chandler – *see* Chapter 16. What was needed was to build in *strategic and organisational flexibility*. They therefore developed the Transnational Form, which would have the following characteristics:

● Assets and liabilities: dispersed, interdependent, with different parts of the organisation specialising in different areas. Thus, one country/company might take the lead on one product, another on another product, but all would co-ordinate and co-operate fully.

● Role of overseas operations: within an integrated worldwide structure, each country or product group would make a differentiated contribution.

● Development and diffusion of knowledge: this would be developed jointly and shared around the world. Chapter 11 explored this concept.

The two authors commented that the Transnational Form was 'not an organisational form but a management mentality.'[31] They suggested from their empirical evidence that the locus of decision making was likely to vary:

● across functions like finance and marketing (some might need to be more centralised than others);

● across different product categories (some might be more global than others).

Figure 19.9 is an attempt to capture the approach.

It was Kogut who later added an important word of caution: new organisational structures take longer to diffuse across MNEs than technological innovations.[32] This has the implication that the Transnational Form cannot simply be introduced overnight into a company. It will take some years to develop.

Comment

This research has been highly influential in many large, international companies in terms of their style of operation. Essentially, it is emergent in its approach and emphasises the knowledge and learning aspects of organisational development in a way that is

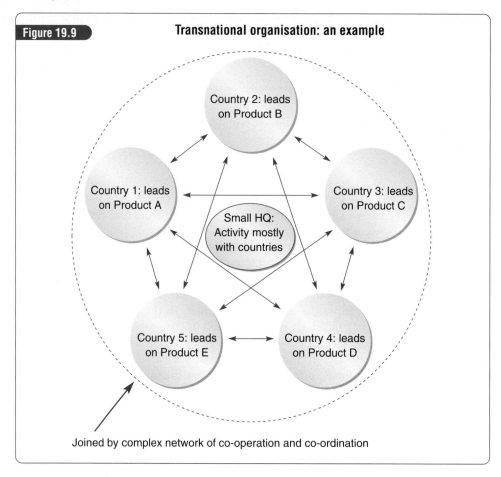

Figure 19.9 **Transnational organisation: an example**

Country 2: leads on Product B

Country 1: leads on Product A

Small HQ: Activity mostly with countries

Country 3: leads on Product C

Country 5: leads on Product E

Country 4: leads on Product D

Joined by complex network of co-operation and co-ordination

not captured in other models. Yet it was developed from observations on only nine companies. Moreover, its proposals remain essentially vague and without clear guidance on pressing issues like the relative roles of national companies and product groups. The reorganisation at Unilever in the late 1990s – *see* Case study 14.3 – clearly borrows something from the approach but it was not enough to show the company how to balance the individual elements of its far-flung interests.

▶ Key strategic principles

- Organisational structures for international expansion often start by creating a separate division for international activities. As they grow in importance, such activities may then be reorganised either into a geographical area structure or one based on product divisions. This may then lead to a matrix structure with all its difficulties.

- The transnational solution to international organisation structure has been used by some companies. It involves dispersed and interdependent subsidiaries that are integrated into a worldwide operation.

19.6 International and global expansion strategies: developing external relationships

Many companies involved in international expansion have been rethinking their relationships with other companies as customers, suppliers and associates. Many different outside relationships are possible – Chapter 13 outlined some of the major options. Two are explored in this section because they have particular relevance for international expansion: joint ventures and alliances. Exhibit 19.4 sets out some basic questions that need to be examined for both areas.

Exhibit 19.4 **Some basic questions on the nature of external relationships**

- *Nature*: who with?
- *Purpose*: what for?
- *Strategy*: how does it fit with the MNE's objectives and strategies?
- *Bargaining*: who gains what?
- *Verticality*: how are risks shared?
- *Behaviour*: what is expected of the venture by governments?

Source: Dunning, J H (1993) *Multinational Enterprises and the Global Economy*, Addison Wesley, Wokingham, p240.

19.6.1 Basic forms of external relationships

In many circumstances, companies will decide that international expansion is best served by some form of external relationship with other companies. An external relationship means a contractual relationship between the *home* company and a *host* company in a foreign location. Essentially, the home company no longer has complete ownership of some aspect of its international strategy. There are three main reasons for developing external relationships:

1 *learning* – about the country and its culture, about the technologies contributed by the home and host companies and about the organisation and resources of its new host company;

2 *cost minimisation and risk reduction* – for example, lower-cost production sources, research, different regulatory systems and project economies;

3 *market factors* – international market access and distribution, competitive positioning, customer service.

The nature of the relationship is clearly important in determining the success of a new venture: *ownership* is an important starting point. Should the new venture be *wholly owned*, with the external relationships then applying to other elements of the value chain, such as suppliers and distributors? Or should it be a *joint venture*, in which both the home and host companies have shares? Or should it be simply an *alliance* with no shareholding involved and some rather weaker form of co-operation? The answers to these questions will vary with each company and its strategic situation. However, it is possible to provide some general guidelines on the factors that will determine the likely success of external relationships – *see* Exhibit 19.5.

> **Exhibit 19.5** **Factors determining success of external relationships**
>
> - *Complementarity.* The partners should bring different resources to the relationship.
> - *Agreement on objectives.* If this cannot be achieved, then the relationship will be difficult.
> - *Compatible strategies and cultures.* They do not have to be the same but there should be some degree of empathy.
> - *No surrender of key resources or core competencies.* The home partner must keep control of important strategic elements.
> - *Stakeholder agreement.* There must be no conflict here.
> - *Low risk of the host becoming a competitor.* It has occasionally been the case that a strong position has been established only for the host to set up in competition with the home partner.

19.6.2 Joint ventures[33]

Joint ventures can take many forms, the most obvious one being a 50/50 shareholding in a joint company. An example of a recent successful operation has been that of the Cereal Partners joint venture. This is a joint company set up by the multinational food companies Nestlé (Switzerland) and General Mills (US) – *see* Chapter 2 – with 50 per cent of the joint venture being owned by each of the two parents. It was formed to attack the breakfast cereal market around the world outside North America and has had some significant success. Such a share arrangement may not be appropriate in a different strategic context and with different strategic resources and competitors. It is essential to research well both the market and the chosen partner.

The main benefits that can arise from joint ventures between a large multinational and a local company are:

- risk reduction through sharing the project;
- rapid market access and speedy profits;
- the local firm's involvement and contacts, which may make the multinational more acceptable in the local community.

However, problems can arise from such joint venture activity:

- domination of the local market by the local partner so that the multinational remains insulated from direct customer contact;
- inability to work with the local partner for reasons of organisational culture, trust and national culture;
- the global objectives of the multinational may be in conflict with those of the national objectives of the local partner.

There is no simple way to determine the long-term success of joint ventures. Dunning is cautious, pointing to the difficulties of researching a topic with so many different variables.[34] Kogut is more pessimistic, commenting that they may succeed in mature markets but success is less likely in fast-growing markets. The reason for the problem is that high growth is usually accompanied by the need for a rapid extra cash injection and at least one partner often has a problem with such demands.[35] Tomlinson is probably right to emphasise the *partnership nature* of a joint venture.[36] He argues that the joint venture must involve an opportunity for reciprocal benefits to both parties. Moreover, there needs to be mutual trust and forbearance to make the association work. This will ultimately mean compatible goals. It is also likely to imply a clear definition of asset ownership and specific areas of contribution so that the partners are clear on their respective resource contributions.

19.6.3 Strategic business alliances[37]

A business alliance is some form of contractual relationship designed to secure an international venture without involving a shareholding. A strategic business alliance (SBA) goes beyond this. Dunning concludes that: 'SBAs are deliberately designed to advance the sustainable competitive advantage of the participating firms.'[38] From a corporate strategy perspective, it is this latter form of activity that is of interest. The 1990s saw a substantial growth in SBAs because of the increasing cost of R&D and because forms of collaboration bring economies of scale and scope. Moreover, SBAs may bring other cost benefits if the partners are able to specialise or rationalise their operations. For example:

- European and North American pharmaceutical companies have been operating SBAs to distribute new drugs without the expense of setting up totally new marketing networks.

- Telecommunications companies have been setting up world SBAs to deliver seamless telephone services to their major multinational customers around the world without being present in every country – *see* Case study 15.2.

- National airline carriers have agreed SBAs to offer seamless ticketing across continents to their customers without opening offices in every airport.

In practice, the broad nature of such relationships suggests that there will be many reasons for SBAs. Exhibit 19.6 summarises the main reasons.

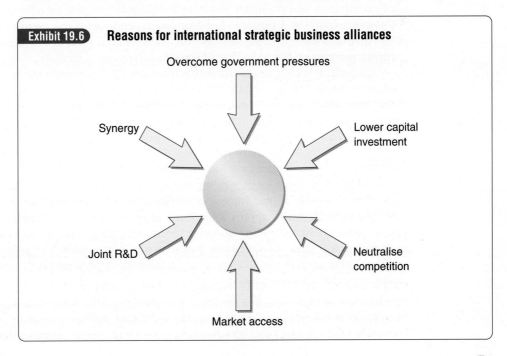

Exhibit 19.6 **Reasons for international strategic business alliances**

Overcome government pressures

Synergy

Lower capital investment

Joint R&D

Neutralise competition

Market access

Professors Yves Doz of INSEAD and Gary Hamel of the London Business School investigated alliance relationships in the early 1990s.[39] They concluded that they were more likely to be successful when each partner was clear about the intent of the other and accepted that such relationships were likely to evolve over time. They also suggested that it was preferable for the governance relationships of the two parties in such alliances to be similar. The reason was that this would avoid conflicting objectives. It was also important that any national or organisational differences in culture were respected as part of the SBA. They also found that it was better if the participants were able to balance their needs inside the SBA with their other interests outside the partnership.

Although the above conclusions are useful, SBAs are difficult to research because they can take so many forms. It is therefore appropriate to be cautious about the long-term success of SBAs in international strategy development.

> ### ▶ Key strategic principles
>
> - In developing international relationships with other companies, ownership issues need to be investigated. Joint ventures and alliances represent differing degrees of closeness in international co-operation.
>
> - A joint venture between a multinational and a local company can provide rapid market access and local market involvement. But the differing objectives of the two partners may lead to problems.
>
> - Strategic business alliances cover relationships that do not involve a cross-shareholding. Benefits include cost savings and market access, but the nature of the linkage is essentially weak and it may not survive in the long term.

19.7 Relationships between companies and countries[40]

Both companies and countries will have sustainable competitive advantages. They will be resource-based and capable of evolution, depending on the nature of the relationship. International corporate strategy will examine both parts of the relationship but its primary perspective has to be that of the company.

Ultimately, it is companies rather than countries that represent the focus of commercial competition internationally. Nevertheless, companies can often gain useful support from their home governments in the development of competitive advantage. Many international trade theories support this perspective on the role of governments. It is likely therefore that companies will seek to negotiate with their home governments in the development of international strategy. Such negotiation is often best conducted through professional industry associations and lobby companies.

In addition, companies expanding outside their home countries will often need to gain the agreement of host foreign governments if they are to be successful. This may take the form of simple approvals or some more substantive assistance, perhaps based on employment or technology supplied to the foreign host nation. The extent to which companies will gain such facilities will depend on the *balance of power* between the parties. There are two possible areas of negotiation, depending on the requirements of company international strategy:

1 *International foreign trade discussions.* The company may wish to import products or services from other countries, possibly including the home country. Governments may impose various forms of barriers to entry, as discussed earlier in this chapter.

2 *International foreign direct investment discussions.* The company may wish to set up a plant or other permanent structures in a company that will involve employment, investment and possibly technology transfer. Governments often express a keen interest in this for understandable reasons.

The negotiation process between the company and the foreign government may be simple or complex. It is also likely to involve some form of strategy development and experimentation in order to arrive at a mutually agreeable solution. Such an approach is essentially emergent beyond the initial considerations that prompt an initial approach. In order to structure the main elements of such negotiations, it is relevant to return to the C–C–B Paradigm outlined earlier in this chapter. Figure 19.10 shows how this can be adapted to highlight the main elements:[41]

● *Company.* The basis of its bargaining position will be its *resource-based* competitive advantages, explored earlier in this text. The company usually has other countries in which it can invest, besides the country in question. The threat of a move elsewhere may enhance its bargaining position.

● *Country.* The basis of its bargaining position will also be its resource-based competitive advantages but the *sheer size* of its markets may also be an attraction, as in China and India. The country may also be negotiating with other companies besides the one engaged in the current discussion. This will enhance the bargaining position of the country.

● *Bargaining.* The negotiations between the two parties will seek to find a mutually attractive deal – expressed by the overlap in the two circles of interest in Figure 19.9. Both parties will have reserve positions beyond which they will not be willing to compromise. The conduct of negotiations will broadly follow the paths laid out under game theory in Chapter 15.

Although the two parties – the company and the country – are bargaining, the best outcome is that the game is played as a *win–win game*, with both parties making gains.

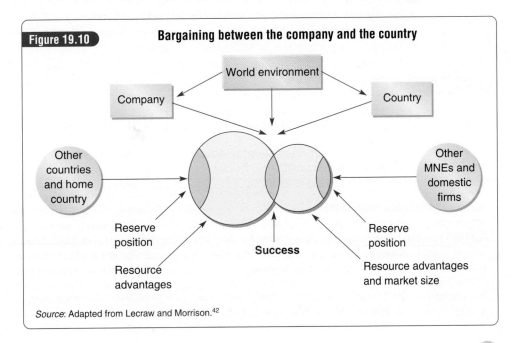

Figure 19.10 **Bargaining between the company and the country**

Source: Adapted from Lecraw and Morrison.[42]

The reason for this is that it is the best basis for a long-term relationship: most international strategy development takes so long to develop that lengthy relationships are more likely to produce added value. Exhibit 19.7 illustrates some of the policy areas that may need to be negotiated beyond the strategy itself.

Exhibit 19.7 **Policy areas that may need to be negotiated between company and country**

Countries may impose conditions on entry:

- Degree of foreign ownership
- Kind of goods where companies are allowed to participate
- Financing of inbound investments – relates to capital availability in country
- Location within country
- Investment incentives for entry

Countries may also insist on operating requirements after entry:

- Range of instruments, e.g. proportion of output exported, recruitment and training, percentage of supplies purchased inside country, local purchases of capital goods, etc.
- Commitment to local content and restraint where company has dominant product
- Some governments use controls on companies to substitute for appropriate macroeconomic policies – this use is unwise and inappropriate.

▶ Key strategic principles

- **Relationships between companies and countries will develop from both partners exploiting their respective resource-based strategic advantages.**
- **Such relationships can be modelled using the C–C–B Paradigm, with the balance of power being the deciding factor in how they develop. Game theory can be used to explore the factors involved.**

CASE STUDY 19.4

Tate & Lyle plc: globalisation to sweeten the profit line

As one of the world's largest producers of sweeteners and starches, the UK-based company Tate & Lyle should be well placed to generate profits from its global operations. Yet its profitability declined as it became more global. This case explores some of the problems of international expansion.

Greater globalisation, lower profits

Over the period 1988–97, Tate & Lyle grew from a UK/European food company into one of the largest producers of sweeteners and starches in the world. Expansion came from two large acquisitions – Staley Industries in the US in 1988 and Bundaberg in Australia in 1991 – and a series of smaller purchases, joint ventures and other co-operative deals in many parts of the world. For example, in May 1998 the company purchased the well-known citric acid company Haarman and Reimer from the German chemical giant Bayer for US$219 million (£130 million).

In spite of this major expansion programme, Tate & Lyle has not been able to generate a similar increase in profits. Table 19.5 compares its turnover and profits in 1991, 1994 and 1997. Over the

Table 19.5 Tate & Lyle: higher turnover... pity about the profits

Turnover £m	1991	1994	1997
UK	790	828	772
Rest of Europe	690	905	931
US	1358	1648	1863
Rest of world	424	840	1085
Total	3262	4221	4651

Profit before interest £m			
UK	48	71	24
Rest of Europe	58	64	30
US	154	147	127
Rest of world	20	31	39
Total	280	313	220

Source: Annual accounts for various years.

period, the company generated £1.4 billion extra turnover, largely outside Europe, but profits were down £60 million.

Products: global reach but low value added

Tate & Lyle's operations are mainly involved in two world markets:

1 *The world market for nutritive sweeteners.* This covers agricultural crops such as sugar cane and sugar beet, but also includes sweeteners made from cereals such as maize and wheat. The sweeteners are used in a wide variety of food products, including drinks, cakes and cooking ingredients. Europe and the US account for nearly 20 per cent of world consumption of these basic food products. The market is mature, with annual growth being only around 2 per cent.

2 *The world market for starch products.* This is derived mainly from cereals but also from potatoes. The products form a staple and versatile ingredient of many processed foods. Europe and the US account for around 40 per cent of world consumption: this is higher than for sugar because starch-type products are more suited to Western tastes and also because they are used in the greater amount of processed

food that is sold in Western countries. The market is mature in Europe and the US, with annual growth of around 3 per cent, but growth is higher in other areas of the world of around 5 per cent.

Essentially, Tate & Lyle's companies take agricultural crops and process them into the sweeteners and starches outlined above. This means that the company is involved in adding value to commodity agricultural products that are subject to price fluctuation, natural disasters and the many currency problems that are outside the company's control. For example, the company reported in 1997 that its profits were reduced in the UK by £16 million as a result of EU/Green Pound changes and another £25 million from currency translation changes elsewhere in the world. In addition, there were unquantified competitive pressures on profit margins for some products in the US. They were also reduced by poor cane sugar prices in Australia and several other difficulties.

Global strategy: spread the risk of downturn and move to higher-added-value products

The company's strategy has been to extend its operations worldwide. The purpose has been twofold:

1 to reduce the impact of individual geographic markets;

2 to balance downturns in some markets with favourable movements in both prices and growth in other world markets.

The result has been major global expansion over the last ten years, the results of which are shown in Table 19.6.

In spite of the wider geographic spread, most of these activities remain in product categories that have low profit margins. For these reasons, the company has also been investing in new products with higher value added, such as its recent development of a new low-calorie sweetener, sucralose. This gained US Food and Drug Administration approval for use in 15 food and drink categories in early 1998. The product is more stable than other sweeteners, which lose their sweet properties with time or when used at high temperatures. In previous years, Tate & Lyle has developed other new products that can also command higher prices and therefore contribute to the company's competitive

Table 19.6 Globalisation at Tate & Lyle: some examples of its far-reaching spread of activities

Europe	● UK: Tate & Lyle
	● Belgium, Holland, France: Amylum
	● Spain: Alcântara
	● Russia: T&L International
	● Hungary: Kaba
	● Slovakia: Juhocukor
North and Central America	● US: Staley
	● US: Domino
	● Canada: Redpath
	● Mexico: Occidente
Africa and Middle East	● Zambia: ZSR
	● South Africa: Booker Tate
	● Saudi Arabia: United Sugar
Australasia and Pacific	● Australia: Bundaberg
	● Vietnam: Nghe T&L
	● Thailand: UFIC Group
	● China: T&L Swire

Note: Some of the above are joint ventures with local or regional companies. The information is sourced from various annual reports of the company.

advantage. The difficulties with such a specialist strategy are the length of time and considerable investment needed to achieve success. Moreover, such activities often have only a limited impact on the basic commodity nature of much of the company's volume production. Low-cost strategies are also required.

Global strategy: drive down manufacturing costs and compete on price

Because of its involvement in the wayward shifts of agricultural commodity markets, Tate & Lyle, like many companies, has little control over its raw material costs. In addition, such companies can develop little competitive advantage and the rates of growth in the market are low. All this means that the only way to increase profits is to drive down the costs of processing the basic commodity prod-

ucts and compete on price. This strategy has been pursued relentlessly by Tate & Lyle over the last few years. Examples of its 1997 activities include the following:

● continued investment programme of over £500 million in totally new plant at its Belgian operation, Amylum (66 per cent owned);

● North American Business Improvement Project pursued at a cost of £82 million. This will bring together five separate businesses and save on overheads;

● £45 million investment in new projects in India, Hungary and the Czech Republic;

● construction of the first new sugar cane mill for 70 years in Queensland, Australia.

The difficulty with such developments is that competitors are also making similar investments. At the same time, new entrants are coming into the market. In addition, the new production capacity is only truly effective when it drives out older, less efficient companies. This takes time and means that there is often excess production capacity in the market in the interim period, which in itself will push down prices. Moreover, there are uncertainties in the commissioning process for new plant that often mean that it takes time for the new lower costs to be realised: this has had a significant impact on Tate & Lyle in recent years. A related difficulty is that production needs to be sited close to the crop. Hence, it is not possible to obtain the centralised economies of scale and the close co-ordination of product sourcing that can reduce costs in other global industries. All this means that it is tough for a company like Tate & Lyle to drive down manufacturing costs.

In addition to the production problems, there are difficulties with customers in the food industry. They are often sophisticated and aggressive, global, branded food and soft drink manufacturers. These customers are able to drive prices down and attempt to ensure that such prices never fully recover. For example, in 1997 Tate & Lyle reported that customer pressures had hit its HFCS business in the US. In the early 1990s, HFCS products used to contribute 75 per cent of the total profits at its US subsidiary, Staley Industries. However, by 1997, customer pressures had driven down prices to the

Table 19.7 Decline in profitability at Tate & Lyle

Return on capital before interest (%)	1993	1994	1995	1996	1997
Sweeteners and starches					
● North America	14.9	20.3	20.7	12.9	14.5
● Europe	25.8	23.5	24.5	20.9	9.3
● Rest of world	15.2	14.8	11.3	11.7	(0.8)
Animal feed and bulk storage	27.4	26.0	23.6	22.0	6.9
Total for group	18.1	20.1	20.5	16.1	10.5

Source: Author, calculated from annual report and accounts.

extent that the HFCS business contributed under 10 per cent of profits.

In the context of global strategy, low-cost manufacturing and pricing therefore have significant problems. The overall result of such a cycle of investment, competitive pressure and erratic commodity prices is the decline in profitability at Tate & Lyle, as shown in Table 19.7.

Conclusion: Tate & Lyle is now unscrambling its global activities

For several years after the above activities, the group's profitability continued to decline due to unexpected events. For example, Staley's starch profits had improved in 1998 but the US business was hit by disease in the sugar beet harvest. The American operations were sold to a local farmers' group in 2002 and Tate & Lyle largely pulled out of North America. There were also extra costs in commissioning the massive new plant at Amylum, Belgium, and for other plants around the world. All this led the company to abandon its global strategy when new management took over in 2000 – many activities outside Europe are now being sold or closed. For example, the Australian venture Bundaberg was sold in 2001.

Case questions

1 *How do Tate & Lyle's globalisation strategies fit with the globalisation advantages outlined by Levitt?*

2 *To what extent are the company's difficulties specific to commodity markets like sugar and starch? Will companies in other industries also experience such problems? What, if any, are the implications for a strategy of globalisation?*

3 *What strategies would you now recommend for the company? Should it continue along its current trajectory or rethink its whole position?*

Globalisation: getting rid of the headquarters mentality

Kenichi Ohmae is the former head of the Japanese operation of the global management consultants McKinsey. Here he comments on the need for companies to think beyond the home country if they want to develop a global strategy.

A cosmetics company with a once-enviable position in Japan went through a series of management shake-ups in its American home country. As a result, the Japanese operation, which had grown progressively more important, was no longer able to enjoy the rough autonomy that made its success possible. Several times eager American hands reached in to change the head of activities in Japan, and memos and phone calls kept up a steady barrage of challenges to the unlucky man who happened to be in the hot seat at the moment. Relations became antagonistic, profits fell, the intervention grew worse, the whole thing just fell apart. Overeager and overanxious managers back at headquarters did not have the patience to learn what really worked in the Japanese market. By trying to supervise things in the regular 'corporate' fashion, they destroyed a very profitable business.

This is the familiar pattern. The local top manager regularly changes from a Japanese national to a foreigner, to a Japanese, to a foreigner. Impatient, headquarters keeps fitfully searching for a never-never ideal 'person on the spot'. Persistence and perserverance are the keys to long-term survival and success. But headquarters is just not able to wait for a few years until local managers – of whatever nationality – build up the needed rapport with the vendors, employees, distributors, and customers. And if, by a miracle, they do, then headquarters is likely to see them as having become too 'nationalized' to represent their interests abroad. They are no longer 'one of us'. And if they do not build up this rapport, then obviously they have failed to win local acceptance.

This headquarters mentality is not just a problem of bad attitude or misguided enthusiasm. These would be relatively easy to fix. Instead, it rests on – and is reinforced by – a company's entrenched systems, structures, and behaviours. Dividend payout ratios, for example, vary from country to country. But most global companies find it hard to accept low or no payout from investment in Japan, medium returns from Germany, and larger returns from the United States. The usual wish is to get comparable levels of returns from all activities, and internal benchmarks of performance reflect that wish. Looking for a 15 per cent return on investment a year from new commitments in Japan is going to sour the company on the country very quickly. The companies that have done best there – the Coca-Colas and IBMs – were willing to adjust their conventional expectations and settle for the long term.

Source: Ohmae, K (1990) *The Borderless World*, Collins, London, pp83–84. © Copyright McKinsey & Co 1990. Reproduced with permission.

Summary

● International expansion and globalisation are amongst the most important strategic influences in the business environment in the twenty-first century. International expansion has become an important driver of country economic growth. Companies have contributed to this and benefited from it.

● It is important also to distinguish between three types of international and global expansion: *international*, where a significant proportion of an organisation's activities take place outside its home market but it is still the domestic market that is the prime focus of strategy; *multinational*, where a company operates in many countries and varies its strategy country by country; *global*, where a company treats the world as one market. Significantly, each of the three areas above implies a different international expansion strategy.

● The *C–C–B Paradigm* explores the resource relationships between the Company, the Country in which it operates and the Bargaining that takes place between the two. The twin purposes of such bargaining are to deliver increased value added to the company and increased wealth to the country.

● Theories of international trade identify the role of government in encouraging international investment. They also help companies select which countries offer the best international prospects. A number of theories can usefully be identified: some theories concentrate on trade barrier reduction and company economies of scale. Two theories are particularly useful: Porter's *diamond of national competitive advantage* and the *theory of limited state intervention* attributed to the World Bank.

● Three major international institutions have significant influence on international trade. The International Monetary Fund (IMF) oversees international payments. The World Bank provides long-term capital aid. The World Trade Organisation (WTO) regulates trade activity and resolves trade disputes between nations.

● A trade block is a group of countries that have agreed to give each other preferential trading terms. Some blocks have stronger ties than others. All influence trade development.

● The case for a global strategy rests on two major elements: resources may be more economically procured and manufactured on a global basis. In addition, customer demand may be essentially the same around the world, thus allowing the world to be treated as one market. The case for a strategy that is both global and local derives from the need to gain the benefits of a global market while responding to the needs of national market variations. Local variations may arise as a result of customer demand and conditions of usage; national goverments; differing technical standards; and different national competitors. In practice, there is often a need to balance both global and local issues in strategy development.

● Organisational structures for international expansion often start by establishing a separate division for international activities. As they grow in importance, such activities may then be reorganised either into a geographical area structure or one based on product divisions. This may then lead to a matrix structure with all its difficulties. The *transnational solution* to international organisation structure has been used by some companies. It involves dispersed and interdependent subsidiaries that are integrated into a worldwide operation.

● In developing international relationships with other companies, ownership issues need to be investigated. Joint ventures and alliances represent differing degrees of closeness in international co-operation.

● Relationships between companies and countries will develop from both partners exploiting their respective resource-based strategic advantages. Such relationships can be modelled using the C–C–B Paradigm, with the balance of power being the deciding factor in how they develop. Game theory can be used to explore the factors involved.

QUESTIONS

1 If international expansion is the most important strategic trend of the twenty-first century, should every organisation, even the smallest, develop international strategies? If so, what strategies might be adopted by (a) a medium-sized engineering company based primarily in one part of the world, such as Europe, and (b) a major grocery retailer whose sales are mainly in one country?

2 What different international expansion strategies are implied by international, multinational and global approaches to strategy development? Give examples to support your explanation.

QUESTIONS continued

3 Do theories of international trade help to explain why and how companies like Giant Bicycles, SCA and Tate & Lyle have developed internationally?

4 How do the major institutions of world trade influence strategy development?

5 Name two trade blocks and show how each of them influences the development of international strategy. In particular, identify any factors that are unique to each trade block.

6 How useful is Porter's diamond of national competitive advantage in the development of a company's business strategy?

7 'Whether to globalize and how to globalize have become two of the most burning strategy issues for managers around the world.' (Professor George Yip)

Comment critically on the usefulness of such generalisations in the development of international business strategy.

8 Does the 'transnational organisation' offer a solution to the difficulties facing major companies when they organise their international operations? Could this be used by Ford Motors in restructuring its international operations – *see* Case study 18.3?

9 What are the problems with using alliances and joint ventures in international strategy development? How might they be overcome?

10 'The adoption of a global perspective should not be viewed as the same as a strategy of global products and brands. Rather, for most companies, such a perspective implies consideration of a broad range of strategic options of which standardisation is merely one.' (Professors Susan Douglas and Yoram Wind)

Do you agree with this comment? What, if any, are the implications for international business strategy?

STRATEGIC PROJECT

Take the two other major agricultural commodity companies that are the leading competitors of Tate & Lyle – Cargill (US) and Eridiana Beghin-Say (France) – and explore how the competitors have expanded internationally. Make a comparison with Tate & Lyle and then draw some conclusions on global expansion in that particular industry. Is globalisation possible? Is it profitable? If so, how might it be achieved?

FURTHER READING

Daniels, J D and Radebaugh, L H (1995) *International Business*, 7th edition, Addison Wesley, Reading, MA. Useful basic background in international expansion.

Dunning, J (1993) *Multinational Enterprises and the Global Economy*, Addison Wesley, Wokingham. Very strong academic foundation – top-quality text if you are an economist.

Robock, S H and Simmonds, K (1989) *International Business and Multinational Enterprises*, Irwin, Homewood, IL. Now out of print but strong readable account of main issues.

Jones, G (1996) *Evolution of International Business*, Routledge/International Thompson, London. Excellent text for providing a historical context.

NOTES & REFERENCES

1 United Nations Industrial Development Organisation (UNIDO) (1993) *Industry and Development Global Report 1993/94*, Vienna, p81. Interesting and thoughtful material with additional references useful for essays and assignments.

2 Williams, F (1995) *Financial Times*, 4 Apr, p3.

3 UNIDO (1993) Op. cit., pp88, 89.

4 Woolf, M (1993) *Financial Times*, 16 Dec, p19.

5 UNIDO (1993) Op. cit., p81.

6 These are based on Bartlett, C A and Ghoshal, S (1989) *Managing Across Borders: The Transnational Solution*, Century Business, London, Ch3.

7 I am grateful to one of the anonymous reviewers of the second edition of this text for prompting these important distinctions.

8 Harding, J (2001) 'Globalisation's children strike back', *Financial Times*, 11 September, p14.

9 Dunning, J H (1993) *Multinational Enterprises and the Global Economy*, Addison Wesley, Wokingham. *See* also: Dunning, J H (1995) 'Re-appraising the electic paradigm in an age of alliance capitalism', *Journal of International Business*, 3rd Quarter, pp461–91.

10 Sources for global paper and pulp Case: *The Economist*: 20 May 2000, p117; *Financial Times*: 18 September 1998, p32; 28 January 1999, p17; 1 September 1999, p20; 8 September 1999, p42; 18 February 2000, p26; 23 February 2000, p25 (facts not fully accurate); 4 April 2000, p32; 1 March 2001, p36; 12 October 2001, p29; 21 December 2001, p23; 30 January 2002, p22.

11 One of the best books at tracking these developments is Kennedy, P (1992) *The Rise and Fall of the Great Powers*, Fontana Press, London.

12 Kennedy, P (1992) Op. cit., Ch7.

13 Jepma, C J, Jager, H and Kamphnis, E (1996) *Introduction to International Economics*, Netherlands Open University/Longman, London, Ch3.

14 World Bank (1993) *The East Asian Miracle*, Oxford University Press, New York.

15 Useful critiques are contained in Rugman, A and Hodgetts, R (1995) *International Business*, McGraw-Hill, New York, Ch10; Dunning, J H (1995) *The Globalization of Business*, Routledge, London, Ch5.

16 Dunning, J H (1993) Op. cit., p14.

17 *See Financial Times*, 16 Dec 1993, for a summary of the new Uruguay Round deal that had been negotiated over many months.

18 A useful short history of the WTO was published by the *Financial Times* as a supplement on the WTO's 50th birthday in 1998: 'The World Trade System at 50', *Financial Times*, 18 May 1998.

19 Sources for SCA Case: SCA Report and Accounts for 2001, *Financial Times*: 30 June 1999, Engineering Supplement pVI; 1 September 1999, p17; 2 November 1999; 8 December 1999, special supplement. *See* also references for Case study 19.2.

20 Ohmae, K (1990) *The Borderless World: Power and Strategy in the Interlinked Economy*, Collins, London, Ch6.

21 *See* Bartlett, C and Ghoshal, S (1989) *Managing across Borders: The Transnational Corporation*, Harvard Business School Press, Boston, MA. *See* also Turner, I and Henry, I (1994) 'Managing international organisations: Lessons from the field', *European Management Journal*, 12(4), p417.

22 Levitt, T (1983) 'The globalization of markets', *Harvard Business Review*, May–June.

23 This argument is also supported by Hout, T, Porter, M E and Rudden, E (1982) 'How global companies win out', *Harvard Business Review*, Sept–Oct, p98; Hamel, G and Prahalad, C K (1985) 'Do you really have a global strategy?', *Harvard Business Review* July–Aug, p139.

24 Yip, G S (1989) 'Global strategy – In a world of nations?', *Sloan Management Review*, Fall, pp29–41. This article represents the clearest exposition of globalisation.

25 Douglas, S and Wind, Y (1987) 'The myth of globalization', *Columbia Journal of World Business*, Winter.

26 Prahalad, C K and Doz, Y (1986) *The Multinational Mission: Balancing Local Demands and Global Vision*, The Free Press, New York.

27 Yip, G S (1989) Op. cit., p29.

28 Stopford, J M and Wells, L M (1972) *Managing the Multinational Enterprise: Organization of the Firm and Ownership of Subsidiaries*, Basic Books, New York.

29 For an extended discussion of this trend, *see* Turner, I and Henry, I (1994) Op. cit., pp417–31.

30 Bartlett, C A and Ghoshal, S (1989) *Managing Across Borders: The Transnational Solution*, Century Business, London.

31 Bartlett, C A and Ghoshal, S (1989) Op. cit., p17.

32 Kogut, B (1990) 'The permeability of borders and the speed of learning amongst countries', *Globalization of Firms and the Competitiveness of Nations, Crafoord Lectures, University of Lund, Lund*. Quoted in Dunning, J H (1993) Op. cit., Ch8.

33 Dunning, J H (1993) Op. cit., Ch9, has a comprehensive survey of joint venture research. *See* also Kogut, B (1997) 'Globalization and alliances in high technology industries', *Financial Times Mastering Management*, Pitman Publishing, London, pp491–4.

34 Dunning, J H (1993) Op. cit., p245.

35 Kogut, B (1997) Op. cit., p493.

36 Tomlinson, J W L (1970) *The Joint Venture Process in International Business*, MIT Press, Cambridge, MA.

37 Dunning, J H (1993) Op. cit., Ch9, also has a useful survey of alliances.

38 Dunning, J H (1993) Op. cit., p250.

39 Doz, Y and Hamel, G (1993) *The Competitive Logics of Strategic Alliances*, The Free Press, New York.

40 This section of the text has benefited significantly from the work of Dunning, J H (1993) Op. cit., Chs 20 and 21.

41 Lecraw, D J and Morrison, A J (1991) 'Transnational corporations–host country relations: A framework for analysis', *South Carolina Essays in International Business*, No. 9. Quoted in Dunning, J H (1993) Op. cit., p552.

Chapter 20

The dynamics of strategy development

Learning outcomes

When you have worked through this chapter, you will be able to:

- outline the relationship of the organisation's purpose with the dynamics of its development;
- explain the dynamics of resource development and comment upon the quality of its insights;
- identify the dynamics of environmental development and comment critically on the main elements;
- explore the dynamics of fast-moving environments, especially in the context of innovation and the opportunities available for small and medium-sized enterprises;
- outline the environmental dynamics of slow-moving markets, especially those involving small and medium-sized enterprises;
- explain the dynamics of the relationship between strategy development and strategy implementation.

Introduction

Both organisations and the strategies that they pursue change continuously over time. They alter as the environment shifts and they may change as the organisation's own resources grow or decline. The mechanisms by which these processes occur are not fully understood because they are complex and our knowledge of the various elements requires further development. This chapter on the dynamics of strategy development explores the current state of knowledge.

In particular, it seeks to examine how an organisation can enhance its value added and its competitive advantage in the context of the dynamics of strategic change. It also seeks to address the implications for small and medium-sized enterprises (often abbreviated to SMEs) because fast-moving dynamics may present such organisations with particular opportunities and threats. We begin our exploration of the topic by considering the purpose of the organisation, We then examine the dynamics of change

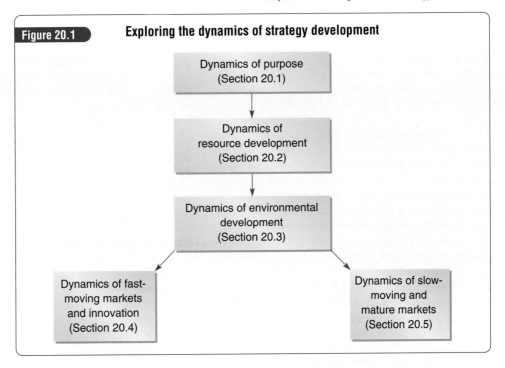

Figure 20.1 **Exploring the dynamics of strategy development**

Dynamics of purpose
(Section 20.1)

Dynamics of
resource development
(Section 20.2)

Dynamics of environmental
development
(Section 20.3)

Dynamics of fast-
moving markets
and innovation
(Section 20.4)

Dynamics of slow-
moving and
mature markets
(Section 20.5)

inside the organisation. Specifically, we examine the dynamic relationship between competitive advantage and the changing resources of the organisation.

In addition to resource-based change, the environment of the organisation is also changing, sometimes in ways that are turbulent and unpredictable. Such *outside* pressures in the environment will also influence strategy development, perhaps in unpredictable ways. These need to be assessed and techniques developed for monitoring and coping with the dynamic changes arising from them. To consider the strategic consequences in more depth, we explore two environmental situations in more depth: slower-moving markets and fast-moving markets. The dynamic opportunities for SMEs are highlighted in these two areas. These areas are summarised in Figure 20.1.

CASE STUDY 20.1

eBay – the auction market that spans the world

In spite of the 'dot.com disaster' suffered by many companies, there is at least one Internet site that is actually making a profit. It is eBay – the site where it is possible to buy products and services both by auction and by paying a fixed price. This case explores the strategy of the company, including its ability to deliver business opportunities to small and medium-sized companies.

eBay began back in 1997 as a small Internet start-up in California. While its peers burned their start-up cash, eBay became a phenomenon – a Silicon Valley company that has always made a profit. It is the world's most successful Internet group, with 38 million customers making deals at the rate of US$9.4 billion in 2001, of which eBay takes just under 10 per cent net. The profit potential is huge

▶

because eBay has almost no cost of goods, no inventories, few marketing costs and no large capital expenditure. Basically, the company simply acts as a computer Internet medium between buyer and seller.

The figure of US$9.4 billion, according to Meg Whitman, chief executive since 1998, is just the start. She has promised that by 2005 deals will have more than tripled to US$35 billion and eBay revenue will also have tripled to around US$3 billion. To put this into perspective, this would mean that eBay was handling the same revenue as the big US retailers JC Penney and Kmart, which achieved turnover of US$33 billion and US$37 billion in 2001 respectively .

But she will face a massive challenge. To achieve her targets, she must transform eBay. She must expand the number of different audiences the company serves, and move into sectors with higher average selling prices, such as cars. She must increase the range of formats, shifting increasingly from auctions to fixed-price sales – without alienating traditional customers. She also needs to attract more large sellers, particularly corporations. And she must do this without giving her competitors – like Yahoo and Amazon – an opportunity to expand market share. Finally, she must reinforce eBay's international sales. eBay started as a small Internet site that allowed people in California to exchange and sell unwanted items. Thus the culture of eBay has been one of trust. This was reinforced by the company setting up a system of feedback: the aim was to give buyers and sellers an idea of each other's good faith and reliability. Each seller has a scorecard showing positive, neutral and negative feedback for each transaction, as well as detailed comments. 'That is very powerful. If you saw the comments of everyone who shopped in a store, it would completely change the way you shopped,' explains Rajiv Dutta, the chief financial officer of eBay.

Alternative sites do not have the right format or sense of community, explains Geoff Giglio, who has a small company selling computers and IT equipment on eBay. 'Other companies just can't figure it out. I have tried Yahoo and Amazon and didn't sell a thing.' In fact, eBay has rapidly grown into an important channel for SMEs to sell their goods – anything from painted furniture to baby clothes.

But this is both the strength and the weakness of the site – it will be difficult to move from the local relationships that characterised the old eBay to its new more sophisticated self. Patti Waldmeir, a devotee of the site, commented in May 2002:

For the past year, eBay has been increasingly acting the part of Big Brother, closely monitoring auctions for fraud. Now citizens of eBay will also have to carry what amounts to a national identification card... I write to mourn the demise of the civilisation called eBay.

There is no doubt that eBay has been transformed over the last few years from a site that held auctions in 300 categories to a global enterprise, operating in 18 countries and offering 16,000 categories. The journey has not been easy – possibly the worst moment was when the Internet site went down for 22 hours in June 1999 – no site, no income. But the proposed drive to expand the business will run two significant risks:

1 The strategy of attracting large corporate sellers – such as IBM, now its biggest supplier – has raised fears among smaller, traditional clients. Such a move risks antagonising the 'power sellers' – the army of entrepreneurs that have formed the bedrock of eBay's sellers and make their living trading on its site.

2 The possibility that competitors such as Yahoo and Amazon can take advantage of the disquiet amongst such sellers. Yahoo is particularly aggressive. It makes no secret of going after eBay and its 23 per cent operating margins. The group claims to be listening harder to its sellers and is undercutting eBay heavily on price. Amazon is also trying to convert its 23-million-strong active customer base to the lucrative area of person-to-person selling.

For the moment, the competitive threat is remote. Neither company can match the number of buyers on eBay. 'I'm not concerned about competitors trying to undercut eBay transaction prices,' says one outside commentator. 'Buyers want to be where the most sellers are. The economies of scale ensure more transaction completions and higher average selling prices, so, even though the fees might be a bit higher, they are more than compensated.' Thus, if the eBay CEO Meg Whitman can keep her user base, she could conceivably achieve the ambitious goals she has set for 2005.

© Copyright *Financial Times*. Case heavily adapted, reorganised and supplemented by Richard Lynch from an article by Paul Abrahams and Thorold Barker, 11 January 2002, p24. Quote from an eBay article by Patti Waldmeir in the same paper on 16 May 2002, p15. Both used with permission. You might like to look at the website – www.eBay.com ... and the rivals ... Amazon.com and Yahoo.com.

Case questions

1 *What delivers profits in this company and how is the situation changing?*

2 *To what extent are the competitive and supplier threats real? Would they alter your view of the future goal of this company? Do you believe that the goal will be achieved?*

3 *Are there any lessons for other companies with regard to developing successful Internet sites?*

20.1 The dynamics of purpose

The purpose of an organisation can and probably will change over time – eBay is an example of how companies can start with a simple objective and then expand.[1] Purpose is subject to the judgement and priority setting of senior management, which may also vary over lengthy periods. The balance of influences that will be taken into account in arriving at the purpose of the organisation was outlined in the *polygon of purpose – see* Figure 12.3. This represents a shifting coalition that will alter depending on two factors:

1 *The choice and activities of the organisation.* For example, the recruitment of a new chief executive at eBay in 1998 was crucial to its present success – *see* Case 20.1.

2 *The activities and choices of others outside the organisation.* For example, the increased competitive activity of Yahoo in the Internet auction market is already having some influence on the purpose of eBay.

More generally, some of the dynamic factors influencing the purpose of an organisation are shown in Exhibit 20.1. Their relationships with each other and their influence on the overall direction of the organisation remain largely uncharted. This means that their dynamics at this stage of our knowledge remain essentially unknown.

Importantly, although purpose may be a shifting coalition, the dynamics of purpose are, at least partially, in the control of the organisation itself. In principle at least, every organisation has the *choice* to change its purpose. For example, it may wish to reconsider its attitude to the key topics of added value and sustainable competitive advantage. These are matters of judgement that will influence the purpose and therefore the dynamics of purpose. For example, entrepreneurs may reach different conclusions on the direction of purpose from senior managers of large, stable multinationals like Unilever in Chapter 14.

Equally, it is sometimes claimed that every organisation should make growth part of its purpose. The management writer Tom Peters says: 'A firm is never static – it is either growing or stagnating.'[2] However, it should be noted that such generalisations are not necessarily true of every organisation: they involve a normative judgement about the importance of growth that some will not share. Thus every organisation will develop its own response to the concept of growth as part of purpose and there are no absolute rules.

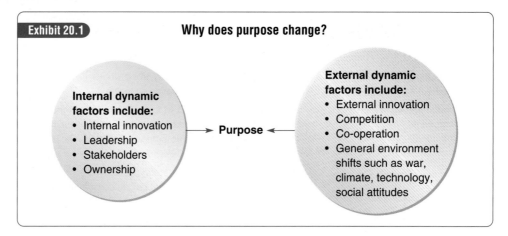

Exhibit 20.1   **Why does purpose change?**

Internal dynamic factors include:
- Internal innovation
- Leadership
- Stakeholders
- Ownership

Purpose

External dynamic factors include:
- External innovation
- Competition
- Co-operation
- General environment shifts such as war, climate, technology, social attitudes

More generally, every organisation will bring judgement, values and ambitions to its definition of purpose. Small businesses without public shareholdings may have more scope for flexibility in purpose. Medium-sized enterprises like eBay with public share quotations may find that this reduces their room for manoeuvre.

Given the complexity of purpose, this book has chosen to concentrate on two aspects – value added and sustainable competitive advantage – in the development of strategy. This is important because if purpose cannot be made explicit then it is difficult to explore its dynamics. However, it needs to be acknowledged that this is a simplifying assumption, with all the weaknesses that this implies.

Key strategic principles

- The purpose of an organisation can and will change over time. The coalition of interests that defines and develops purpose will be influenced by factors both inside and outside the organisation.

- Importantly, the purpose of the organisation is at least partially in the control of the organisation itself

- Although purpose is complex, it is usual in strategy to concentrate on two common elements: value added and sustainable competitive advantage.

20.2 The dynamics of resource development

In Chapter 6, the resources of the organisation were classified into four main areas and the concept of the *hierarchy of resources* was explored. However, the balance between the four areas does not stay static over time.[3] Figure 20.2 illustrates how resources might be expected to alter dynamically over time. This section explores how and why such changes might occur.

Resources will change as the organisation's purpose changes. In addition, they will also be influenced by what is happening outside in the environment. For example, even if the eBay Internet auction house had made no decision to expand its resources by including larger suppliers like IBM, it would still face resource decisions on its Internet sites as a result of the aggressive actions of its competitors like Yahoo and Amazon. Thus competitive resources will also be influenced by the outside activities of competitors and by the

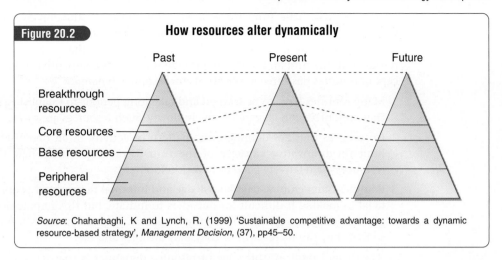

Figure 20.2 **How resources alter dynamically**

Source: Chaharbaghi, K and Lynch, R. (1999) 'Sustainable competitive advantage: towards a dynamic resource-based strategy', *Management Decision*, (37), pp45–50.

Internet expanding over time. However, as a starting point, this section will concentrate primarily on resource dynamics, with the next section exploring the environment.

Given that an organisation has made the normative and reasonable choice to increase its value added, the dynamics of resource development can be considered as having three main dimensions:[4]

1 *time* – resource configurations developed and destroyed over time;

2 *early-mover advantages* – resource developments when moving into a new market place;

3 *imitation pressures* – resource changes related to the existing resources.

20.2.1 Resource configurations developed and destroyed over time: the contributions of four leading economists

Four leading economists have explored aspects of resource dynamics, each making their own contribution:

● Penrose: the two sources of new resource growth;

● Nelson and Winter: the delaying effect of routines in companies;

● Schumpeter: the mechanism that destroys resources over time.

In exploring the future growth of the firm, Professor Edith Penrose was very clear. It would partially come from the resources already present in the company: 'In planning expansion, a firm considers two groups of resources – its own previously acquired or "inherited" resources, and those it must obtain from the market in order to carry out its production and expansion programmes.'[5] The clear implication of this statement is that the starting point of resource dynamics will be these two aspects, which we can extend to any organisation rather than just the firm. It also follows that organisations may be constrained by their previous resources: this is an example of *strategy as history* as explored in Chapter 2.

Writing originally in the 1950s, Penrose considered the dynamics of the resources only in the context of the growth of the firm. Some 20 years later, Professors Richard Nelson and Sidney Winter developed a view of evolutionary economics that examined how firms changed over time, possibly but not necessarily with growth as the objective. They identified the *routines* of the firm as being the basis of its resources and its strategic decision making.[6] They defined such routines as the well-practised patterns of activity inside the firm: for example, the Toyota Production System described in Chapter 9 and the European branding policy introduced by Unilever on its ice cream products explored in Chapter 5. It is these routines that deliver some distinctive resources to the firm and therefore provide some of its competitive advantage. The concept of routines has three implications for resource dynamics:

1 Many routines have to be learned and take long periods to establish. This means that these resources will change relatively slowly. Such resources are *sticky*.

2 In so far as routines dominate the pattern of activity in an organisation, they may limit the innovative capacity of the firm to develop totally new resources. Such resources are relatively *blind* to new developments.

3 Routines often employ tacit knowledge and informal networks of people. This is beneficial in making it difficult for outsiders to imitate, but this imprecision will make it more difficult to replicate inside the company. Such resources will *require investment* so that they can be relearnt or they may atrophy and die.

The overall result of this view of resource dynamics is that resource configurations develop over time, they are constrained by what has gone before and they require investment if they are to continue. Now it might be thought that resource development could continue in this way for ever. It was Professor Joseph Schumpeter who argued that such a pattern was inherently unlikely over long time periods.

Schumpeter explored the dynamics of resource development.[7] In particular, he identified the way that innovation and entrepreneurship operate over lengthy time periods. He said that there were patterns of development in all markets, with periods of comparative calm, during which firms develop superior products and reduce costs, followed by periods of shock or discontinuities. It was during these latter times that new technologies, new services and totally new ways of operating were introduced. He was writing in the early 1940s during the upheaval of the Second World War and was also able to look back to the First World War and the relatively calmer period in between. He had no knowledge of the 'dot.com' boom-and-bust scenario of the period 1999–2000, but this is a more recent example of his concept. He argued that entrepreneurs who were able to exploit the market opportunities during such periods of shock would benefit during the subsequent periods of calm. At the time of writing, it is not clear who the 'dot.com' winners will be – perhaps eBay in Case 20.1. Schumpeter called this process *creative destruction*.

From the perspective of resource dynamics, the significance of creative destruction is that all resources should have a limited shelf-life. They cannot go on for ever and will be superseded by innovatory new products. Thus Schumpeter would argue that Bill Gates and his colleagues at Microsoft may have made a fortune with the Windows computer operating system, but it will ultimately be overtaken by some new development. Competitive resources will become uncompetitive over time as a result of innovation and new organisational knowledge.

If Schumpeter's argument is correct, then the strategic problem is that competitive resources never stand still. The strategic solution is to develop new resources before the competition. We examine this in the next section.

Comment

It is interesting to note that it took Microsoft several years to see the potential threat of Netscape's Internet Browser as an alternative means of delivering computer software services. No wonder Microsoft reacted so vigorously to the opportunities presented by the Internet.[8] On this evidence, Schumpeter's view of *creative destruction* is useful in high-technology markets.

However, creative destruction may have less relevance as a resource dynamic in relation to more traditional markets. For example, the substantial worldwide market for chocolate products like Nestlé's KitKat or Mars' Milky Way does not seem, so far, to have been subject to creative destruction. In some product categories, evolutionary resources may continue for substantial periods without destruction.

20.2.2 The early-mover advantage: resource developments when moving into a new market place

In some markets, the firm that acquires a competitive advantage early in the life of a market may find that this sets in motion a resource dynamic that preserves the advantage during the life of the market: *the early-mover advantage*. For example, by being one of the early companies into the market for computer operating systems and by co-operating with the market leader at the time, IBM, Microsoft was able to establish a user base for its Windows system that other companies have been unable to match – *see* Case study 1.2. Equally, by being one of the early companies into producing mobile telephones on a global scale, Nokia has established itself as one of the leaders in that market and delivered sustainable competitive advantages based on economies of scale and product design – *see* Case study 14.1.

Importantly, being the early mover does not necessarily mean being *first* into a new market. The very first companies can make mistakes from which they never recover – perhaps from poor technical performance, perhaps in marketing. Learning from what others have already done may be useful, while still being one of the early-but-not-first movers may be all that is required.

There are at least five resource advantages delivered by an early move into a market:

1 *Establishment of the benchmark technical format.* Innovation may introduce a basic technology that will set the standard for the market. It may not even be the most efficient technology but it may still deliver useful advantage. The example usually quoted is the QWERTY typewriter layout which was introduced in 1899 and is still used in keyboards today. Although this configuration of letters on the keyboard is technically not as fast as some others, it has become the dominant design.[9]

2 *Building networks of complementors.* For some products, such as computers, computer games and sound systems, it is not just the product itself that matters but the complementors who supply the software, the new games and the recording artists. These networks take time to establish and early movers have an advantage in terms of an installed base of suppliers and users that becomes difficult to shift. For example, in the early 1990s, both Sega and Nintendo video games companies placed considerable emphasis on gaining and keeping their installed base of games users. Nintendo made a major strategic mistake when it introduced its 16-bit machine in the 1990s and made no attempt to build on its previous users of its 8-bit machine.[10]

3 *Early move down the learning curve.* Early production experience should allow a company to learn before its competitors and move down the learning curve – *see* Chapter 13.

4 *Usefulness of reputation when buyers are uncertain.* When new products cannot be assessed fully by customers before they are purchased, the reputation of the company launching such product becomes a useful customer guide to subsequent performance. For example, a new format video camera from Sony is more likely to carry conviction than the same product from an obscure brand name.

5 *Costs to the buyer from switching products.* When new products are launched, buyers may be reluctant to switch to them if the costs involved are high. For example, switching retail bank accounts used to be an immense administrative task with high costs. In the era of telephone banking, rivals have attempted to reduce such costs by using new technology, but there is still a resource advantage for those banks with an established customer base.

Thus the dynamics of resources are conditioned by the early-mover advantages. However, there are also obvious problems with being the early mover: most companies have to make a bet on the new technology and this may turn out to be incorrect. They may *choose the wrong technology.* For example, Sony took the view that its Betamax technology would become the dominant tape format for television videotape machines, but JVC ended up with the more widely accepted format and Sony was eventually forced to withdraw its system.[11]

Moreover, companies may be unable to understand or afford the organisational and administrative back-up that is necessary to support the introduction of a totally new technology: they may lack the *complementary assets.* For example, when it was first introduced, the EMI scanner was technically the most advanced machine of its kind for scanning human bodies. But the company's resources were primarily engaged in recorded music and television rental and it simply lacked the resources to develop the market.[12] EMI was forced to withdraw and sell out to General Electric (US) which had the relevant resources.

20.2.3 Imitation pressures: resource changes related to existing resources

For existing products and services, the luxury of being an early mover does not apply. Resource dynamics are driven by the need to deter rivals from imitation. The dynamics of gaining and improving resources that cannot be imitated lie in five main areas:

1 *Incremental improvements in the product or service.* Probably the most widely used way of preventing resources being imitated is a regular programme of product improvement. Consumer companies like Procter & Gamble (US) in household detergents like Ariel, and PepsiCo (US) in its Walkers and Frito-Lay snack products have ongoing activities designed to keep their products one step ahead of the competition. None of the resource changes is radical in itself but all represent genuine improvements that allow these companies to maintain their competitive advantage. The dynamic is slow, steady resource change.

2 *Legal barriers to imitation.* Patents, copyrights and trademarks all represent means of reducing the ability of competitors to imitate products. For example, The Disney Corporation (US) not only owns the exclusive rights to the Disney characters like Mickey Mouse but has also acquired rights to other characters such as Winnie the Pooh. The resource dynamic is powerful and one-way, as long as the resources remain relevant to the customer.

3 *Developing superior relationships with suppliers and customers.* Networks that involve customers and suppliers have been explored extensively in this text – *see* Chapters 3, 9 and 15. Good supply networks can provide lower costs and higher quality from suppliers. Equally, strong and loyal customer networks can provide larger sales and greater profitability over time. The resource dynamic here is most likely to be broken if technology changes or the balance of power alters.

4 *Exploiting market size and scale economies.* Imitation will clearly be more difficult when profits are derived, at least in part, from a minimum size and economies of

scale. Thus Asian car companies like Daewoo (Korea) and Proton (Malaysia) have had difficulty moving into European markets because of the need to provide adequate levels of service support. There are ways around this problem, so the resource dynamic tends to slow the rate of change rather than stop it completely.

5 *Developing intangible barriers to imitation*. There are a whole series of barriers here that have been explored in Chapters 6 and 11. They include *tacit knowledge*, which is difficult for the company to codify, let alone for competitors to imitate; *innovative ability*, which is difficult to define but represents a real resource in companies like 3M; *causal ambiguity*, which makes it difficult for competitors to understand how a firm has developed a competitive advantage. The resource dynamics here can present real and practical barriers to imitation.

Conclusion

The purpose of much of the investigation of resource dynamics has been to identify those areas that provide sustainable competitive advantage and increase added value. The above areas provide some important guidance on this task. However, their weakness is that they remain lists of possible areas rather than providing more specific strategic conclusions. They also clearly need to be related to the changing environment within which the organisation is operating. We tackle this topic next.

▶ Key strategic principles

- From a dynamic perspective, resources in organisations are developed and destroyed over time. There are three main dimensions: time, early-mover advantages and imitation pressures.

- When exploring the time dimension, there are three main considerations: the two sources of new resource growth; the delaying effect of routines in companies; the mechanism that destroys resources over time.

- In terms of early-mover advantages, there are five main areas: the establishment of the benchmark technical format; the building of networks of contacts; the early movement down the learning curve; the usefulness of reputation; the subsequent costs to the buyer when switching from the early mover.

- The pressures that arise from imitating an existing product or service can be countered by five resource activities: incremental improvements in the product or service; legal barriers to imitation, such as patenting; developing superior relationships with customers and suppliers; exploiting market size and scale economies; developing intangible barriers to imitation.

20.3 The dynamics of environmental development

Throughout this book, we have analysed the main environmental factors that influence strategy, including general policies and events, competitors, customers and suppliers. All such factors are continuously changing, both in relation to each other and to their influence on the organisation. This section explores the dynamics of such continuous change on the strategy of the organisation. The two sections that follow select some particular circumstances for further consideration.

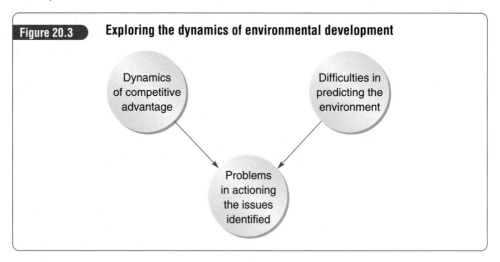

Figure 20.3 Exploring the dynamics of environmental development

Dynamics of competitive advantage

Difficulties in predicting the environment

Problems in actioning the issues identified

Although there are many dimensions to the environment, it is useful to divide our consideration of the dynamics into three related areas (*see* Figure 20.3):

1 *The dynamics of competitive advantage.* Although it is generally accepted that this concept is important in strategy development, it is often treated as if it is fixed at a point in time. In reality, it will be changing continuously.

2 *The predictability of the environment.* When the environment is growing or declining steadily, the dynamics may be easy to predict. However, not all environments are predictable, so the issue needs to be explored.

3 *Resource responsiveness to environmental change.* Even though the dynamics of the environment may be *understood*, this does not necessarily mean that the organisation is able to *act* on that understanding. The relationship between the two areas needs to be investigated.

20.3.1 The dynamics of competitive advantage

Amongst strategists, there is a widely held view that the search for competitive advantage is fundamental to strategic success. To quote Professor Michael Porter:

> *Competitive strategy is the search for a favourable competitive position in an industry . . . Competitive strategy aims to establish a profitable and sustainable position against the forces that determine industry competition.*[13]

There are two difficulties acknowledged by Porter in this statement:

1 The forces determining industry competition are changing all the time.

2 The firm itself will not only respond to such forces but will also attempt to '*shape* that environment in a firm's favour [my italics].'[14]

In other words, Porter argues that the dynamics of competitive advantage have at least two dimensions:

1 the nature of the competitive advantage operating in an industry;

2 the degree to which a firm is able or willing to shift the balance of competitive advantage towards itself by its new strategies in that industry.

However, according to Professors Gary Hamel and C K Prahalad, this misses an important element in the dynamics because it concentrates on the *current* industry boundaries:

Strategy is as much about competing for tomorrow's industry as it is about competing within today's industry structure. Competition within today's industry structure raises such issues as: What new features should be added to a product? How can we get better channel coverage? Should we price for maximum market share or maximum profits? Competition for tomorrow's industry structure raises deeper questions such as: Whose product concepts will ultimately win out? How will coalitions form and what will determine each member's share of power? And, most critically, how do we increase our ability to influence the emerging shape of a nascent industry?[15]

Although Hamel and Prahalad were addressing their remarks primarily to new industry opportunities like satellite television and Internet record distribution, the same logic can be applied to existing and more mature markets. To quote Baden-Fuller and Stopford on mature market strategy: 'The real battles are fought among firms taking different approaches, especially those that counter yesterday's ideas.'[16] In other words, the dynamics of competitive advantage need to be viewed not just as a battle between the existing firms but also as an attempt to break out of the existing competitive framework. This carries the significant difficulty of shaping such a dynamic so that it is still manageable within the resources of an organisation. Exhibit 20.2 shows a three-stage process that might elucidate the dynamics and identify the opportunity.[17]

Exhibit 20.2   **Investigating the dynamics of competitive advantage**

Three possible steps:

1 *Develop a vision about the future direction of an industry and related areas.* For example, the Ford Motor Company has taken the view that strategy in the global car industry will involve control of distributors, second-hand cars and servicing in addition to car manufacturing. This is the organisation identifying the opportunity.

2 *Manage the paths that will service this vision.* This will involve building before rivals such areas as the key resources, the new products and services, the relevant networks and alliances. For example, the UK retailer Tesco was amongst the first to establish a home shopping service using the Internet which required both a website and a well-organised home delivery service. This is the organisation shaping the strategy.

3 *Compete within the chosen market for market share.* This will involve such areas as the level of service, the marketing mix and the reduction in costs through operations strategies.

   Keypoint: it is this last stage that is often portrayed as the conventional battleground of sustainable competitive advantage, whereas it may be the two earlier areas that contain the most useful dynamic opportunities.

20.3.2 The predictability of the environment

From a strategic management perspective, the dynamics of the environment can be managed better if the environment can be predicted. The changes are known in these circumstances and the strategic implications can therefore be actioned. We examine this issue by first exploring some of the types of prediction that can be and have been undertaken. We then explore the argument of Mintzberg that much of this activity is a waste of time.

The purpose of prediction

The objective of undertaking prediction is to cope better with uncertainty in the environment. There will always be some residual risk but prediction should help to reduce this and increase the chance of success. In other words, the dynamics of the environment may be at least partially controlled, if they can be predicted.

According to some strategists,[18] the key to tackling strategic prediction is to understand that some environments are more predictable than others. For example, the market for ice cream – *see* Case studies 4.1 and 4.3 – can be predicted with some certainty. Some revolutionary new technology might invalidate this prediction, but this is unlikely. By contrast, the Internet recording market – *see* Case study 20.2 – cannot be so easily predicted, because the future direction is highly uncertain. However, although the second is more open, there are some techniques that will reduce the uncertainty and make the environment partially predictable.

For our purposes, it is useful to identify three types of environment and the techniques that might be employed in their prediction: these are shown in Exhibit 20.3. This book has explored the main techniques elsewhere so they are not repeated here. The main point is that, even where there is strong residual uncertainty, some prediction of the environment may be possible within broad limits.

Exhibit 20.3 **Coping with different levels of environmental uncertainty**

Environment 1	*Environment 2*	*Environment 3*
Reasonably predictable, barring catastrophe	**Alternatives clear, but precise outcome remains unknown**	**Many possible outcomes with no clear idea of way ahead**

Environment 1	*Environment 2*	*Environment 3*
Techniques: market and competitor projections – *see* Chapters 3 and 14	*Techniques*: market projections, decision analysis plus options from game theory – *see* Chapters 3, 14 and 15	*Techniques*: market outlook, technology forecasting and scenario planning – *see* Chapters 3, 14 and 15
Prediction: single outcome with upside and downside	*Prediction*: series of discrete outcomes that will encompass the main future possibilities	*Prediction*: some possible outcomes that provide a general sense of direction only; even this may be of only limited value
Example: Nestlé's food markets – *see* Case study 17.3	*Example*: Prediction of the likely outcomes to the consolidation of the European defence industry – *see* Case study 15.3	*Example*: The outcomes of the opportunities that will arise from the Internet Record industry – *see* Case study 20.2

The fallacy of prediction?

Within the context of this conclusion, we now turn to the comments of Professor Henry Mintzberg. He has argued that prediction is often a complete waste of time.[19] He describes how traditional prescriptive strategic planning will make a prediction about the environment and then expect the world to stay on this predicted course while the strategy is developed and implemented.

As an example of what he regards as the fallacy of prediction, Mintzberg quotes from one of the early pioneers of corporate strategy, Professor Igor Ansoff, who wrote in his book on *Corporate Strategy*: 'We shall refer to the period for which the firm is able to construct forecasts with an accuracy of, say, plus or minus 20 per cent as the planning horizon.' Mintzberg comments:

> *What an extraordinary statement! How in the world can any company know the period for which it can forecast with any accuracy?...While certain repetitive patterns, such as seasons, may be predictable, the forecasting of discontinuities, such as technological innovation or a price increase, is virtually impossible.*

Thus Mintzberg argues that, where environmental prediction really matters, for example in predicting innovations, it is largely worthless. He dismisses the value of future visions of markets, explaining that they arise from essentially personal and intuitive approaches.

Comment

What does this mean for environmental dynamics? Mintzberg is right to dismiss the value of precise predictions in areas of great uncertainty. Thus financial DCF calculations based on predictions about the size of the Internet record industry in ten years' time – *see* Case study 20.2 – have little value, beyond the general implication that considerable growth is likely. However, Mintzberg takes his argument too far when he suggests that nothing can be done: scenarios, options and general forecasts may prove beneficial, as outlined in Exhibit 20.3. Moreover, where the environment is more stable, environmental dynamics can benefit from prediction.

20.3.3 Acting on the dynamics of the environment

Even though organisations are able to see and understand changes in the environment, they are not always able to act upon them. There is an inertia in organisations that arises from the difficulties, costs and risks implied by such change. The result is that the dynamics of the environment will not necessarily be translated immediately into actions inside the organisation, especially in terms of resource-based change. The economist Professor Richard Rumelt has suggested that there are five reasons for this:[20]

1 *Distorted perception.* Although individuals in organisations may be able to see the environment clearly, the organisation taken as a whole may have more difficulty. The reasons may include a desire to stay with short-term certainties, a fear of what the future might bring or a selective desire to stay with current habits.

2 *Dulled motivation.* Even though organisations understand the environment, they may not perceive with sufficient clarity the threat that it poses. Thus they will not be sufficiently motivated to act on the information.

3 *Failed creative response.* The organisation may be unable to find a creative way out of the threat posed, even though it perceives it accurately.

4 *Political deadlocks*. Organisational politics may make it impossible to develop the best strategy to cope with the perceived opportunity or threat.

5 *Action disconnects*. Leadership, organisational routines and stakeholder interest groups may all make it impossible to react to environmental change.

We explore some of these areas in more depth in Chapter 21, but it is appropriate here that we acknowledge the difficulty of connecting the environment with the resources of the organisation.

▶ Key strategic principles

- The dynamics of environmental development have many dimensions but can usefully be considered from three perspectives: the maintenance of competitive advantage; the predictability of the environment; the ability of the organisation's resources to respond to changes in the environment.

- The maintenance of competitive advantage will depend on the nature of the advantages operating in an industry. It will also involve the willingness of a firm to shape new advantages and the nature of the future advantages that might operate in an industry.

- If the environment is predictable then it allows the dynamics of the environment to be managed more easily. Although no environment is entirely predictable, some strategists argue that the process is largely a waste of time, with no meaningful results where it matters.

- Although an organisation may have understood the nature of environmental change, it may not be able to act upon it. Five major reasons have been identified for this: distorted perception; dulled motivation; failed creative response; political deadlocks; action disconnects.

CASE STUDY 20.2

Recorded music on the Internet: only the beginning of the broadband revolution?

Over the seven-year period 1999 to 2006, recorded music sales through the Internet are predicted to grow from US$50 million to US$4 billion. And there are expectations that the spread of broadband technology will extend this to computer games and films.

Recorded music sales in the year 2000: the Big Five dominate

Around the time of the new millennium, five leading record producers dominated the global record industry: they accounted for nearly 90 per cent of the total sales of US$38 billion – *see* Table 20.1. Although the main area of market demand was pop music, there were also substantial segments in such areas as classical and country and western music. Pop music itself also had many sub-segments, with the main record companies being represented in most of the leading areas.

The competitive advantages of the Big Five come from three related areas:

1 *Recording contracts*. Most of the world's top artists are signed up to one of the leading record producers. For example, Elton John, Cher, Michael Jackson and Madonna all have exclusive contracts that provide sustainable competitive

Table 20.1 The leading global record producers 2000

Company	Market share	Comment
Universal	30%	Owned by Vivendi. Also includes the market share of Polygram acquired in 1998
Sony	17%	Part of Sony multimedia empire
Warner	15%	Part of AOL Time Warner
BMG	14%	Owned by German media parent Bertelsmann
EMI	11%	UK-based group
Others	13%	Many specialist smaller groups

Source: Author from trade sources.

advantage for their record companies. George Michael's very public dispute with his record company only highlighted the control that generally exists in the industry.

2 *High promotional barriers*. Entry barriers for new artists are high because of the marketing funds needed to promote international stars. In addition, considerable expertise and networks are employed to promote and distribute records.

3 *Record sales through retail stores*. The majority of sales are through the leading recorded music stores. These prove a barrier for the smaller companies and an opportunity for the large record producers because the latter have the bargaining power to handle such important customers.

Competitive threat from the Internet: new and growing fast

Although existing record companies dominate traditional distribution, the Internet is beginning to change this. Already thousands of teenagers routinely download music from Internet sites through MP3 computer files. On-line music delivery can take place in a number of ways, including:

- Legitimate Internet sites selling CDs and cassettes in competition with the high-street retail outlets. These sites will be supplied by the Big Five above; indeed, several either own or are in the process of setting up their own sites. The danger is that they upset their traditional retail outlets.

- Digital juke boxes run by small, independent music companies like IUMA and MP3.com. These have been specially set up to distribute the music of new groups unable to get contracts from the Big Five. Each music group pays only US$250 to put a recording on the site. Consumers can listen for free and download for only 99 cents. By 2000, IUMA had extended this activity from its base in the US to Europe and Asia.

- Underground Internet sites playing music illegally from the Big Five without paying royalties, thus allowing others to download without buying the recordings. Napster is probably the most famous but is only one of many. One estimate claims that 150 000 songs were available on MP3 files by the end of 1998 and 3 million by 2002. Portable MP3 recorders, like the Rio introduced in 1998 for only US$199, have only underlined the problem.

It is this last route that has, so far, alarmed the Big Five recording companies. They have been developing a new pirate-proof Internet system to distribute their own music in response. But after five years of development, the joint technical standard was still not finalised between the leading producers and the developer, the world's largest computer company IBM.

Extension via broadband to film and computer games

In the longer term, the Internet has made it much easier for individuals and small groups to bypass the traditional record companies and gain distribution for their music. The widespread introduction of broadband technology (*see* Case study 15.2) will increase the speed of transfer – 3 minutes to download a complete CD. Importantly, the spread of broadband at home is already having broader effects in some countries – for example, Korea already has wider use of broadband than much of Europe and it is being used to transmit computer games, which were previously too slow on the older Internet technology. It cannot be long before films are exchanged over the Internet using broadband technology – just as illegal as distributing copyright recorded music, but just as much a threat to the leading film companies. However, some companies see broadband as a business *opportunity*: for example, Microsoft is developing applications for its new X-box games player. All companies recognise that the technology presents new opportunities, especially for the smaller companies. The real issue is how to exploit them.

Sources: See reference 21.

Case questions

1 *What characteristics of the Internet threaten the Big Five record companies? What are the advantages for small companies of using the Internet? And what are the problems?*

2 *One estimate of the Internet record market puts the size at US$4 billion in 2006. What reliance would you place on this figure? What implications does this have for any strategy proposals that you might have for the industry? And for other industries like computer games and films?*

3 *What lessons can be drawn from the case on the opportunities presented by new technology in the dynamics of strategy development?*

20.4 The dynamics of fast-moving markets

Fast-moving markets present real opportunities and challenges for strategists. The dynamics of the Internet record industry above show just what scope there is for strategic development, including real opportunities for small and medium-sized enterprises (SMEs). The dynamics of such fast-moving markets are mainly governed by the pace and change of innovation.

By its nature, innovation is difficult to define. Thus some innovations are relatively small, while others revolutionise whole industries. For example, the compact disc method of recording was innovative in producing increased sound quality in the record industry but was hardly revolutionary, whereas the possible distribution of music by the totally new technology of the Internet may cause the market to open up significantly. This latter development will be both innovative and revolutionary. In exploring innovation dynamics, there are several interrelated areas that need to be explored: these are shown in Figure 20.4.

20.4.1 Innovation dynamics: market dominance issues

Where an industry is subject to rapid technological change, then there are two problems facing a company that dominates an industry and has *already* committed its resources to a specific technology:

1 *Sunk cost effect.* Firms that have already committed substantial resources to a specific technology may be reluctant to change. Resources and organisational abilities will have been developed for that technology and will be less valuable in any new technology. Such resources represent costs sunk into that technology: for example, the massive investment in record promotion networks to retail shops by the Big Five would be largely useless on the Internet. In deciding whether to switch to new technology, the sunk costs should be ignored because they have been spent. But inevitably such costs may bias firms like the Big Five against making the innovative change.[22]

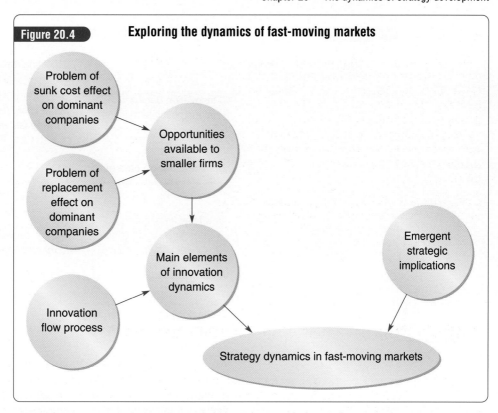

Figure 20.4   **Exploring the dynamics of fast-moving markets**

- Problem of sunk cost effect on dominant companies
- Problem of replacement effect on dominant companies
- Innovation flow process
- Opportunities available to smaller firms
- Main elements of innovation dynamics
- Emergent strategic implications
- Strategy dynamics in fast-moving markets

2 *Replacement effect.* Existing large firms have less incentive to innovate than new companies. The reason is that new companies might expect to gain market dominance by innovation, whereas existing large firms gain no further dominance by such a process. For existing large firms, their market dominance by one technology is simply replaced by that of a new technology – the replacement effect.[23]

20.4.2 Innovation dynamics: the opportunities available to smaller companies

In fast-moving markets, SMEs that do not dominate the market should have significant opportunities. They should be faster and more flexible. Their cultures should be more entrepreneurial and seek out the opportunities presented by the market dynamics. For example, it is the smaller, independent record companies that have developed new artists over the years: as they have benefited from their growth, so they have been acquired in many cases by the Big Five.

Innovation is about process as well as product. For example, in the record industry it is not only about new artists and music (product) but also about new forms of Internet distribution (process). Small companies that do not have vested interests in existing processes will also gain by new process methods, such as using the Internet.

20.4.3 Innovation dynamics: the innovation flow process

Clearly, it is the substantive, major innovation that will provide important opportunities for SMEs to transform an industry and gain substantial new added value. Professor James Utterback of the Massachusetts Institute of Technology has explored innovation

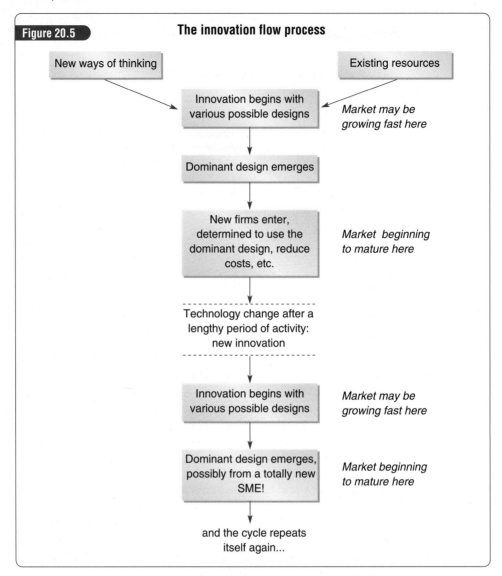

Figure 20.5 **The innovation flow process**

New ways of thinking

Existing resources

Innovation begins with various possible designs

Market may be growing fast here

Dominant design emerges

New firms enter, determined to use the dominant design, reduce costs, etc.

Market beginning to mature here

Technology change after a lengthy period of activity: new innovation

Innovation begins with various possible designs

Market may be growing fast here

Dominant design emerges, possibly from a totally new SME!

Market beginning to mature here

and the cycle repeats itself again...

and its dynamics. In particular, he studied how substantial innovation has revolutionised a number of industries.[24] Other writers have also investigated the importance of innovation in revolutionising the structure of industries, especially the way that new firms come to dominate industries.[25]

From the various empirical studies, it is possible to identify the elements of the way that innovation changes whole industries over time: this is shown in Figure 20.5. Essentially, innovation starts with the existing resources of an organisation and an influx of new ideas from outside. In the early stages, there is often no dominant technology or design. This has the advantage of allowing many companies to participate but the disadvantage of making cost reduction of such a design difficult. Once a dominant design has emerged, then a small group of firms may come to dominate that market and cost reduction begins. After a period of time, a totally new technology emerges and the process begins all over again. The significance of this is that it highlights the opportunities for small, new companies to come to dominate an industry as a result of innovative change: the classic example is the Microsoft dominance of personal computers with its Windows operating system – *see* Case study 1.2.

20.4.4 The emergent strategic implications of fast-moving dynamics

When a market is new and fast growing, it is not clear how it will develop. Technology may still be in its early stages, with little agreement on industry standards. Companies will still be low on the experience curve (*see* Chapter 13, Section 13.7.2) and will be operating emergent strategies to find the best route forward.

Dominant market shares will have less meaning because the market is changing fast. New customers will still be entering the market and will need to be introduced to the products. Competitors should all be experiencing significant sales growth, with the problem being to provide adequate finance for this and for further research at the same time. For example, some of the small record companies mentioned in Case study 20.2 were swallowed up by the Big Five because they were unable to generate sufficient cash: that was how the group U2 came to Universal and Oasis ended up at Sony. Exhibit 20.4 summarises some of the strategic implications of the strategy dynamics of fast-moving markets.

Exhibit 20.4 **Strategy dynamics in fast-moving industries**

- *Bold initiatives* to capture market share and build on cost experience effects.
- Significant investment to develop the *basic technology* and adapt it to customer tastes.
- Search for a viable *customer base* beyond the initial trialists, e.g. a market segment.

Examples of such markets in the new millennium include the new 3G technology for mobile telephones and some new uses for the Internet.

▶ Key strategic principles

- In fast-moving markets, the dynamic process is dominated by innovation.
- Companies that already dominate their markets and have committed resources to a specific technology are less likely to innovate for two reasons: the sunk cost effect and the replacement effect.
- Small and medium-sized companies should have more opportunities in such markets if they are faster, more flexible and entrepreneurial.
- The dynamics of innovation go through a series of phases that depend on one technical design becoming dominant.
- Emergent strategic processes are more appropriate in fast-moving markets.

20.5 The dynamics of slow-moving and mature markets

In slow-moving and mature markets, the dynamics are essentially slower and less likely to be subject to significant technological change. However, this does not mean that such companies should ignore innovation. Indeed, Baden-Fuller and Stopford have argued that there are no slow-moving and mature markets.[26] However, for our purposes, it is useful to distinguish between three areas of slower-moving activity:

1 *Fragmented markets*: these are markets where many companies are present, each with a relatively small market share. Often these markets are relatively mature and unlikely to produce dominant companies. Where each company has a small market share, it may be possible to devise a business formula that will allow replication. Franchising is an example here. Specialisation is another strategy that may work.

2 *Mature markets*: Maturing markets are characterised by fewer opportunities for natural sales expansion. Thus, companies seeking growth are forced to take share from their competitors, which is often expensive and difficult. In such markets, it is important to distinguish between the strategies of the market leader and those of a rather smaller company. The leader is likely to follow aggressive strategies designed to deter others, whereas the smaller company will seek market niches and other forms of specialisation.

3 *Declining markets*: The starting point is to determine the rate of decline: if it is fast, e.g. the markets for Hula-Hoops, straw hats, LP records, then all companies will have to consider leaving those markets. More often than not, decline is slow and this will provide the opportunity to develop a survival strategy. A return to distinctive competencies and innovation may be the only strategies with any chance of success.

▶ Key strategic principles

- In slow-moving and mature markets, the dynamics are likely to be slower and less subject to significant technological change. However, this does not mean that companies in such markets should ignore innovation.

- In fragmented markets, where each company has a small market share, it may be possible to devise a business formula that will allow replication. Specialisation is another strategy that may work.

- In mature markets, it is useful to distinguish between the strategies of the market leader and those of a rather smaller company. The leader is likely to follow aggressive strategies designed to deter others, whereas the smaller company will seek market niches and other forms of specialisation.

- In declining markets, a return to core competencies and innovation may be the only strategies with any chance of success.

CASE STUDY 20.3

Making an impact in only 100 days

Dynamic change may require new people and organisational structures. This case describes how Mr Glenn Cooper went about this process at the medium-sized manufacturing company ICS.

Glenn Cooper made quite an impact on the day he took up his post as managing director at ICS, safety and control systems manufacturers, in Malden, Essex, UK, some six years ago. 'I arrived at 10 am and at 11 am I sacked the manufacturing director. At 12 am I sacked the technical director, so by lunchtime everybody knew I had arrived', he says. 'I think it was very clear to everybody that I was going to start at the top and not at the bottom. I suppose it was the classic 100 days to make an impact.'

It was a difficult time for manufacturing, he says, not only because of the recession but because business process re-engineering, which offered lower-cost production, required fundamentally different approaches from the way that work was managed and organised. Flatter structures, total quality management, team working and empowerment presented new challenges for managements steeped in the traditions of command and control. Some managers understood the language of change. Across industry many who did not found themselves out of a job.

Mr Cooper: agent for change

Mr Cooper made such an impression that he has now been made president of ICS Triplex, the biggest company in the 30-year-old quoted Industrial and Control Systems Group, which is also headquartered in Malden with plans to move the head office to London. This also makes him head of the ICS operations in Houston in the US.

Mr Cooper first proved himself while running one of the group's subsidiaries, EDMS, a contract assembly business making printed circuit boards. The business grew from a turnover of £2 million (US$3 million) in 1986 to £17 million in 1993 when it was sold after Mr Cooper had been moved to run the ICS core business. This has been brought together with its sister operations in the US under ICS Triplex.

The control systems, built in Malden, were originally made for North Sea offshore oil and gas extraction, but they are now also applied to other sectors such as petrochemicals, power distribution, waste and rail transit. A reduction in investment in the North Sea offshore industry over the past few years has led to a greater concentration on reducing costs.

Changing customer relationships

'It was all about bringing down our clients' costs and to do that there was a need for a change of culture and attitude within the industry. Part of this involved putting our engineers in clients' offices,' says Mr Cooper.

This does not mean that we were suddenly going to become servile but the contractual relationship which used to be the equivalent of man-to-man marking,

with everybody watching each other, had to change. We had to move from being aggressive to being assertive.

Today the relationship with customers is more co-operative. In fact, ICS has begun to run training days and quality training seminars for important customers. 'This not only allows companies to find out how the systems, which are vital for the safe running of their plants, are put together but it helps them keep abreast with new standards coming into the industry,' says Mr Cooper.

Internal resource changes: communication vital

Two areas in which ICS at Malden has made its biggest strides are quality management and workforce communications. Quality control has been built into the working process, with staff given responsibility for checking their own work. Job timings are arrived at through a process of discussion and negotiation between manager and employee. 'We say here that ICS stands for implementing common sense because that's the way we look at quality,' explains Mr Cooper.

Some improvements come from suggestions posted in a quality improvements box. A team of employees called a quality communications group ensures that all ideas are considered. But it is the way that the company disseminates information from the top that brought the greatest praise in an independent external study of the company. Each director at the monthly board meetings has a responsibility to pass on the decisions of the meetings to managers, who must then relay the information to their teams. Any plans for the installation of new equipment are posted up on a noticeboard, with the full schedule and dates attached. 'This allows anyone to question the schedule if they think it is unrealistic and to prepare for it happening,' says Mr Cooper.

ICS's staff communications system was tested to the full during one incident in 1998 when the group was forced to put together a refinancing package because of poor investments in other parts of the group. Now, with board changes at group level, the company believes it is well placed to build on its success.

Change and strategic planning

All employees work to a yearly business plan, drawn up over three months and distilled into six priorities by senior managers working with Mr Cooper, who are then asked to put their names to it. 'Initially they were reluctant to sign the document but not now. It means they have read it, understood it and contributed to it,' says Mr Cooper. The plan is then posted up so everyone can see it. 'We have been developing this process with Essex Business Link, an arm of the UK government's Department of Trade and Industry, with plans to roll it out throughout the division,' he says.

Managers are also being asked to undergo personality tests – the company uses one published by Thomas International. 'Before asking them to go ahead I showed them one that had been completed about me. The idea is to point up strengths and weaknesses and see if we are fitted to the job,' explains Mr Cooper. One senior technician, he said, was one of the best people technically in the

company but had no interest in managing people. 'We need to have people working where they are most effective,' he says.

Case questions

1 *What do the dynamics of purpose, resources and the environment suggest about the strategic issues facing the company?*

2 *The company seems to have been involved mainly in working within its existing resource base over the last few years. Where does such an approach fit into the dynamics explored in this chapter? Is there any real scope for a different approach?*

3 *Should small and medium-sized companies rely mainly on the strategic approach developed at ICS or is there room for more innovation?*

Entrepreneurship in a dynamic world

Continuing the theme of small and medium-sized enterprises, Philip Wickham of Teesside School of Business and Management in Northern England argues the case for a more entreprenurial strategy in a dynamic and changing world.

Of all the players who feature in the management of the modern world economy, it is entrepreneurs who most attract our attention. We all have some view of them. We may see entrepreneurs as heroes: as self-starting individuals who take great personal risk in order to bring the benefits of new products to wider world markets. We may express concern at the pace of economic and social change entrepreneurs bring and at the uncertainty they create. We may admire their talents, or we may question the rewards they get for their efforts. Whatever our instinctive reaction to them, we cannot ignore the impact of entrepreneurs.

The modern world is characterised by change. Every day we hear of shifts in political orders, developments in economic relationships and new technological advancements. These changes feed off each other and they are global. Developments in information technology allow capital to seek new business investment opportunities ever more

efficiently. Success is sought out more quickly; failure punished more ruthlessly. Customers expect continuous improvement in the products and services they consume. As a result, businesses are having to become more responsive. In order to keep their place in their markets they are having to innovate more quickly. In order to compete, they are having to become more agile. This is not just an issue for profit-making organisations but for all corporate bodies. The boundary between the world of the 'market' and the public domain is being pushed back and blurred.

Consequently, the world is demanding both more entrepreneurs and more *of* entrepreneurs. In the mature economies of the Western world they provide economic dynamism. The fast-growing businesses they create are now the main source of new job opportunities. The vibrant economies of the Pacific rim are driven by the successes of thousands of new ventures. It is individual entrepreneurs who must restructure the post-Communist countries of eastern and central Europe and provide them with vibrant market economies. In the developing world entrepreneurs are increasingly responsible for the creation of new wealth and for making its distribution more equitable.

Change presents both opportunities and challenges. The opportunities come in the shape of new possibilities, and the chance for a better future. The challenges lie in managing the uncertainty these possibilities create. By way of a response to this challenge, we must aim to take advantage of the opportunities while controlling and responding to the uncertainties. This response must be reflected in the way we manage our organisations. In short: we must become more entrepreneurial.

Source: Wickham P (1998) *Stragetic Entrepreneurship*, Pitman Publishing, London, pp2–3.

◼ Summary

- The purpose of an organisation can and will change over time. The coalition of interests that defines and develops purpose will be influenced by factors both inside and outside the organisation. Importantly, the purpose of the organisation is at least partially in the control of the organisation itself. Although purpose is complex, it is usual in strategy to concentrate on two common elements: value added and sustainable competitive advantage.

- From a dynamic perspective, resources in organisations are developed and destroyed over time. There are three main dimensions: time, early-mover advantages and imitation pressures. When exploring the way that resources change over *time*, there are three main considerations: the two sources of new resource growth, the delaying effect of routines in companies and the mechanism that destroys resources over time.

- Some strategists argue that moving early into a market will help to establish a particular type of sustainable competitive advantage: it is called the *early-mover* advantage. There are five main benefits associated with this, many of them being built on the assumption that such a move will be accompanied by a technical breakthrough that competitors will find difficult to match. The *imitation pressures* that arise from competitors attempting to match an existing product or service can be countered by five resource activities: incremental improvements in the product or service; legal barriers to imitation, such as patenting; developing superior relationships with customers and suppliers; exploiting market size and scale economies; developing intangible barriers to imitation.

- The dynamics of environmental development have many dimensions but can usefully be considered from three perspectives: the maintenance of competitive advantage; the predictability of the environment; and the ability of the organisation's resources to respond to changes in the environment. The maintenance of competitive advantage will depend on the nature of the advantages operating in an industry. It will also involve the willingness of a firm to shape new advantages and the nature of the future advantages that might operate in an industry.

- If the environment is predictable then it allows the dynamics of the environment to be managed more easily. Although no environment is entirely predictable, some strategists argue that the process is largely a waste of time, with no meaningful results where it matters. Although an organisation may have understood the nature of environmental change, it may not be able to act upon it. There are five major reasons that have been identified for this. They are based on the difficulties that organisations and individual managers have in perceiving and acting upon the changes in the environment.

● In fast-moving markets, the dynamic process is dominated by innovation. Companies that already dominate their markets and have committed resources to a specific technology are less likely to innovate for two reasons: the sunk cost effect and the replacement effect. Small and medium-sized companies should have more opportunities in such markets if they are faster, more flexible and entrepreneurial.

● The dynamics of innovation itself go through a series of phases that depend on one technical design becoming dominant. At a time of rapid change in the early stages of the dynamics, emergent strategic processes are more appropriate.

● In slow-moving and mature markets, the dynamics are likely to be slower and less subject to significant technological change. However, this does not mean that companies in such markets should ignore innovation. In *fragmented markets*, where each company has a small market share, it may be possible to devise a business formula that will allow replication. Specialisation is another strategy that may work. In *mature markets*, it is useful to distinguish between the strategies of the market leader and those of a rather smaller company. The leader is likely to follow aggressive strategies designed to deter others, whereas the smaller company will seek market niches and other forms of specialisation. In *declining markets*, a return to core competencies and innovation may be the only strategies with any chance of success.

QUESTIONS

1 Using Exhibit 20.1, identify how purpose has changed in an organisation of your choice and explain why these changes occurred. What have been the implications for the strategy of the organisation?

2 What are the main reasons for resource changes in an organisation? How do they affect sustainable competitive advantage and value added? Give examples to support your explanation.

3 Does the 'early-mover advantage' have any relevance from the perspective of strategy development in more mature markets, like those for chocolate and beer?

4 If you were attempting to defend an existing pharmaceutical product against the announcement by a rival of a similar new drug, which of the five resource-based imitation strategies would you employ? Use Section 20.2.3 to assist you. Give reasons for your approach.

5 Why is it sometimes difficult for an organisation to act upon the changes that it sees taking place in the environment? What can it do to overcome such problems? Give examples to support your views.

6 '*A successful business strategy is affected by many amplifying feedback processes that are outside the control of its managers and produce effects that they did not intend.*' (Professor Ralph Stacey)

Discuss this comment in the context of the dynamics of the environment.

7 Take a fast-moving market with which you are familiar – such as the provision of services on the World Wide Web – and investigate the strategies that might be available for entering such a market. Identify those strategies, if any, that are more likely to deliver sustainable competitive advantage.

8 In the mature market for world steel, what strategies are available for the smaller business to gain market share and value added (*see* Case study 3.3)? You should consider whether such companies are exploiting all the available strategic opportunities.

9 Why are there difficulties in splitting strategy choice from strategy implementation? What are the implications for the development of strategy in the Internet record industry of Case study 20.2?

STRATEGIC PROJECT

Explosive growth in the Internet will provide major strategic opportunities over the next few years for small and medium-sized enterprises (SMEs); Case study 20.2 describes one example for the record industry. Identify further Internet opportunities and use the concepts explored in this chapter and other parts of this book to develop strategies for SMEs to exploit them.

NOTES & REFERENCES

1 Drucker, P (1961) *The Practice of Management*, Mercury Books, London, p74.
2 Peters, T (1989) *Thriving on Chaos*, Pan Books, London.
3 Chaharbaghi, K and Lynch, R (1999) 'Sustainable competitive advantage: towards a dynamic resource-based strategy', *Management Decision*, 37(1), pp45–50.
4 Parts of this section have benefited from Chs14 and 15 of Besanko, D, Dranove, D and Shanley, M (1996) *The Economics of Strategy*, Wiley, New York.
5 Penrose, E (1995) *The Theory of the Growth of the Firm*, Oxford University Press, Oxford, p85.
6 Nelson, R R and Winter, S G (1982) *An Evolutionary Theory of Economic Change*, Belknap Press, Cambridge, MA.
7 Schumpeter, J (1942) *Capitalism, Socialism and Democracy*, Harper & Row, New York.
8 At the time of writing, Microsoft is the subject of a US Federal and State Government investigation into its competitive reaction against Netscape's browser success.
9 Utterback, J M (1996) *Mastering the Dynamics of Innovation*, Harvard Business School Press, Boston, MA, pp10, 30.
10 Nalebuff, B J and Brandenburger, A M (1997) *Co-opetition*, HarperCollins Business, London, p241.
11 Utterback, J M (1996) Op. cit., p28.
12 There is a Harvard Business School case that explores this well.
13 Porter, M E (1985) *Competitive Advantage: Creating and Sustaining Superior Performance*, The Free Press, New York, p1.
14 Porter, M E (1985) Op. cit., p2.
15 Hamel, G and Prahalad, C K (1994) *Competing for the Future*, Harvard Business School Press, Boston, MA, p42.
16 Baden-Fuller, C and Stopford, J (1992) *Rejuvenating the Mature Business*, Routledge, London, Ch2.

17 Based loosely on Hamel, G and Prahalad, C K (1994) Op. cit., p47.
18 Courtney, H, Kirkland, J and Viguerie, M (1997) 'Strategy under uncertainty', *Harvard Business Review*, Nov–Dec, pp67–79.
19 Mintzberg, H (1994) 'The fall and rise of strategic planning', *Harvard Business Review*, Jan–Feb, pp107–14.
20 Rumelt, R (1995) 'Inertia and transformation', in Montgomery, C A (ed) *Resource-based and Evolutionary Theories of the Firm: Towards a Synthesis*, Kluwer Academic, Boston, MA, pp101–32.
21 References for the record industry case: Ghosh, S (1998) 'Making business sense of the Internet', *Harvard Business Review*, Mar–Apr, p180. Also *Financial Times*, 25 June 1996, p17; 24 May 1997, p7; 23 Aug 1997, p2; 15 May 1998, p28; 2 June 1998, p22; 19 Nov 1998, p8; 27 Nov 1998, p6; 13 Jan 1999, p18; 8 Apr 1999, p34.
22 Besanko, D, Dranove, D and Shanley, M (1996) *The Economics of Strategy*, Wiley, New York, p581.
23 Concept originally developed by Professor Kenneth Arrow: Arrow, K (1962) 'Economic welfare and the allocation of resources for inventions', in Nelson, R (ed) *The Rate and Direction of Inventive Activity*, Princeton University Press, Princeton, NJ. Concept outlined in Besanko, D, Dranove, D and Shanley, M (1996) Op. cit., p584.
24 Utterback, J M (1996) Op. cit.
25 For example, see the references in the discussion on innovation in Chapter 11.
26 Baden-Fuller, C and Stopford, J (1992) Op. cit., Ch2. Republished in De Wit, B and Meyer, R (1994) *Strategy: Process, Content and Context*, West Publishing, St Paul, MN, p405.

Managing strategic change

Introduction

Corporate strategy invariably involves change for people working in organisations. Sometimes they resist such proposals and make strategy difficult to implement; sometimes they are enthusiastic and make a significant contribution to the proposed developments. Understanding and exploring the impact of change on people is therefore important for strategy implementation.

As a starting point, it is useful to analyse the causes of strategic change. It is also important to understand the dynamics of the change process in the context of the strategies proposed. These can be used to suggest how such a change process can be managed in principle. Finally, a strategic change programme can be developed either on a one-off or permanent basis. The main areas to be explored are summarised in Figure 21.1.

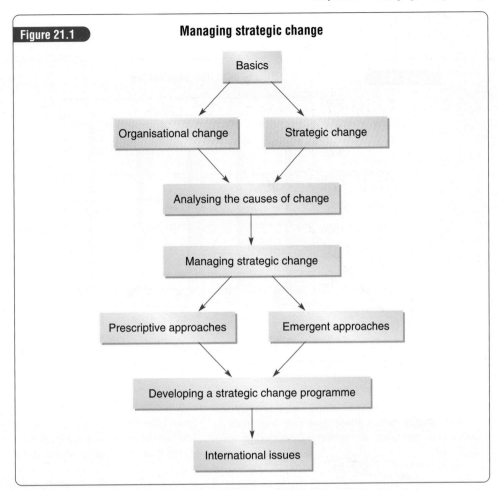

Figure 21.1

Managing strategic change

- Basics
  - Organisational change
  - Strategic change
- Analysing the causes of change
- Managing strategic change
  - Prescriptive approaches
  - Emergent approaches
- Developing a strategic change programme
- International issues

CASE STUDY 21.1

Shock tactics at BOC

After years of underperforming, the company that dominates the market for industrial gases in the UK and has extensive worldwide interests, BOC, is being forced into strategic change by its new managing director.

BOC's attempt to end years of lacklustre performance began by shocking the top management into silence. It was May 1998 and the UK industrial gases group's most senior executives had gathered in Chantilly, Virginia, for their annual get-together. 'There was none of the usual cosies: "Did you have a nice flight?" and all that,' recalls Danny Rosenkranz, the chief executive. 'It was right between the eyes. I really rattled them.'

The process, known as Project Renew, culminated in March 1999 when the final parts of the group's new structure were put into place. A few weeks earlier Mr Rosenkranz had signed performance contracts with the 19 managers chosen to head the business units that are key to the new BOC. In the intervening ten months, the group had begun a £120 million (US$180 million) cost-cutting plan involving 5000 redundancies at group and associate

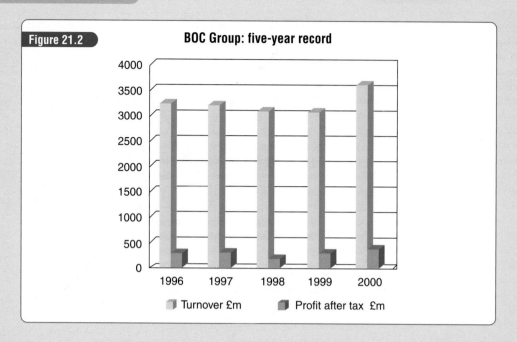

Figure 21.2
BOC Group: five-year record

Turnover £m   Profit after tax £m

companies; reorganised along global business rather than regional lines; and put hundreds of managers through an arduous reselection programme.

Mr Rosenkranz opted for 'shock tactics' – his opening speech in Chantilly was accompanied by a video where critical City analysts berated BOC's performance – after concluding that he had failed to drive home his message on the same occasion the previous year. 'We had had a good debate but then everyone went home and forgot about it. No one really heard me,' he says. 'We were a FTSE 100 company 20 years ago and still are now. A lot of people had a "we're there" mentality. We were the typical type of company that could lose the plot.'

Mr Rosenkranz, who became chief executive in 1996, had measured the group against its competitors and found its results in the bottom half. He believed the core gases business – BOC is also in distribution – was not performing as well as it should. Central to the project, which also aims to generate sales growth and lay the foundations for improvements in profitability, has been the creation of a transparent group organisation.

After working with McKinsey, the management consultants, BOC has abandoned its traditional regional organisation where top executives were

responsible for continents, with all operations in a given country reporting to a locally based manager. Instead there are four main global lines of business (LOB) that comprise business units, most of which cover a geographic area. In a break with the past, it is the heads of these 19 units, rather than the LOB chiefs, who are primarily responsible for day-to-day operations and profitability.

The group as a whole committed itself to achieving a return on assets of 16 per cent by 2000 and to increasing turnover to £5 billion in five years, up from £3.33 billion in 1998 – targets that have been met with some scepticism in the city. Unit heads have individual goals laid out in their performance contracts, to be reviewed quarterly by Mr Rosenkranz. 'The idea was to push responsibility lower down the company,' he says, adding that group incentive schemes are being widened to reflect this.

Barry Beecroft, one of the architects of Project Renew and an LOB head, adds: 'Before we had a vertical, top-down approach, with the division boss deliberately interventionist and sometimes quite autocratic. LOB chiefs can't do that any more, they don't have the staff.'

Previously, regional divisions, and country managers, had their own support service teams, ranging from information technology and finance to health and safety. Now LOB heads have just a handful of staff and share enabling functions grouped in service centres. Many of the redundancies are being made among support staff. A uniform IT system, for example, is replacing the differing systems used in the group. 'The regional chiefs have been used to having their own army of staff,' says Mr Beecroft, who was formerly head of BOC's European gas operations. 'Some anxieties have been working through that resources are further away and less directly controlled.' His new role, he says, is about setting strategy and coaching the heads of his LOB's four business units: 'We have to bring on tomorrow's management stock.'

While LOB chiefs have to adjust to a less hands-on approach, some of the unit heads find the new structure liberating. 'We have greater responsibility and more autonomy and influence than before,' says John Bevan, an Australian who leads a unit in Beecroft's LOB and was previously head of BOC's Thai operations. 'Having the enabling functions taken away has freed up quite a lot of time. This way you are closer to the customer and able to adjust and compete more quickly.'

Despite having worked for BOC for more than two decades, Mr Bevan, like the other unit heads, had to go through a rigorous reselection process. BOC brought in Egon Zender, the headhunter and management appraisal firm, to interview the 45 staff who had applied to be unit heads and the 25 hoping for the top positions in support services. Other consultants carried out a less intensive process with more than 300 staff seeking positions in the next two levels of management.

'No job was sacrosanct. There were no sitting tenancies,' says Mr Rosenkranz, adding that BOC followed most, but not all, of the consultants' recommendations. 'The new structure will also help us see the next group who will lead the company. On the management board, we are all around the same age.'

The new divisions are organised on similar lines, making it easier to compare performance. 'Before there were different structures in the different geographies. This made it hard to get people with similar concerns and responsibilities around the table,' says Jim Ford, another of the new unit heads. 'Looking on a global basis now, it's also easier to see which the important contracts are, to make sure the prize is big enough.'

Playing to the organisation's increased transparency, Mr Rosenkranz has also developed what he calls a 'peer process'. The unit heads have been divided into small groups, across divisions and around the world, that meet and talk (via video link) regularly to share ideas, evaluate each other and swap best practice. Mr Rosenkranz expects the process to take up 20–25 per cent of the time of those involved. 'In time, once we've got to know each other, this process could be quite powerful,' says Mr Ford. 'I've been looking at an acquisition and my peer group is involved in reviewing the decision. There's an element of challenging each other.'

Case adapted by Richard Lynch from an article by Virginia Marsh in the *Financial Times*, 29 Apr 1999, p22. © Copyright the *Financial Times*.

Case questions

1 *Why were shock tactics necessary at BOC? What are the problems with this approach?*

2 *What were the main elements of the BOC change programme? Are they consistent with any of the models outlined in this chapter?*

3 *Are there lessons for other companies from this approach to change? Would you recommend other companies to adopt the same process?*

21.1 The basic concept of strategic change

In this section, the concept of strategic change is explored and its importance for strategy implementation is explained. A distinction needs to be made between *organisational change*, which happens in every organisation and is inevitable, and *strategic change*, which can be managed.

21.1.1 Organisational change

Change takes place continuously within organisations. The pace of change can be represented by two extremes:

1 *Slow organisational change.* This is introduced gradually, and is likely to meet with less resistance, progress more smoothly and have a higher commitment from the people involved.

2 *Fast organisational change.* This is introduced suddenly, usually as part of a major strategic initiative, and is likely to encounter significant resistance even if it is handled carefully. However, some prescriptive change may be unavoidable, e.g. factory closure as part of a cost-cutting project.

Organisations usually prefer to choose slow change, where possible, because the costs are likely to be lower. In fact, much change follows this route, otherwise organisations would be in perpetual turmoil. Where there is a faster *pace* of change, it may be associated with strategic change, which is *proactive* in its approach.

21.1.2 What is strategic change?

Strategic change is the *proactive management of change* in organisations to achieve clearly identified strategic objectives. It may be undertaken using either prescriptive or emergent strategic approaches.

Because strategy is fundamentally concerned with moving organisations forward, there will inevitably be change for some people inside the organisation. However, strategic change is not just a casual drift through time but a *proactive search* for new ways of working which everyone will be required to adopt. Thus strategic change involves the implementation of new strategies that involve substantive changes *beyond the normal routines* of the organisation. Such activities involve:

> the induction of new patterns of action, belief and attitudes among substantial segments of the population.[1]

Thus the chief executive of BOC altered the responsibilities and activities of his senior managers.

Many researchers and writers have explored the important topic of *organisational change.*[2] This text concentrates on those who have examined such concepts from a *strategic* perspective. Within this subject area, some researchers have seen the management of change as clear and largely predictable: the *prescriptive* approach (the actions of BOC would probably fall into this category). Other researchers have formed the view that change takes on a momentum of its own and the consequences are less predictable: the *emergent* approach. (Emergent strategists might argue that in the BOC case, although the initial consequences were well known, the longer-term results were more difficult to predict and were taking time to emerge.) In the emergent sense, change is not managed, but 'cultivated' (*see* Handy).[3]

It should be noted that emergent theorists may use the word *change* in a different way from prescriptive theorists:

- In prescriptive theories, change means the *implementation actions that result* from the decision to pursue a chosen strategy. In extreme cases, it is probable that the changes will be imposed on those who then have to implement them (such as the managers being forced to reapply for their jobs at BOC).

- In emergent theories, change can sometimes mean the *whole process of developing the strategy*, as well as the actions that result after it has been developed. This may involve experimentation, learning and consultation for those involved in the change.

We will return to this distinction in Sections 21.3 and 21.4.

21.1.3 Pressure points for strategic change

Strategic change is primarily concerned with *people* and the *tasks* that they perform in the organisation. They undertake their work through *formal organisation structures*, explored in Chapter 18. Groups of like-minded people also form *informal organisation structures* to pursue particular common interests: sometimes social groups, such as the company sports club, sometimes commercial groupings, such as a group seeking a minor change in working practices. All such groups inevitably discuss, formally or informally, any new developments that affect their lives, such as the announcement or the rumours of strategic change. Importantly, such informal groups can abide by, interpret or change any element of the strategy implementation process: this can be advantageous but it can also be a focus for problems if the group does not like the proposed strategies.

Whether the groups are formal or informal, they provide a channel of opportunities for senior management to influence strategic change and to be influenced by the comments of those affected by such changes. In the BOC case, Mr Rosenkranz was engaged in this task when he introduced the 'peer process'. This used video conferencing to encourage senior managers to exchange views around the world and share best practice.

Identification of such groups and individuals constitutes an analysis of the *pressure points for influence* in the organisation (*see* Figure 21.3). The pressure points provide important links between the basic strategic change process and the people involved.

In more general terms, strategic change borrows from a number of academic disciplines and does not have a clearly defined set of boundaries.[4] The basic issues were outlined in Chapter 7 and the main themes will be explored during the course of this chapter.

21.1.4 Why is strategic change important?

In many cases, strategic change is accompanied by a degree of risk and uncertainty. Although risk assessment can be undertaken in an impersonal way at the corporate level,[5] uncertainty cannot be assessed in the same way at the *personal* level in an organisation.

In some organisational cultures, individuals do not like the consequences of strategic change and seek to resist the proposals that are the cause of their problems. Strategic change may spark objections, thus making it difficult to implement. For example, initial indifference at BOC to the call for action was a typical response of those unconvinced of the need for strategic change.

In other organisational cultures, where learning and open debate have been part of the management process, change may be welcomed. However, even here, change will take time and will involve careful thought. Moreover, it will also be recalled from Chapter 16 that, even in a classic learning organisation such as ABB, there may still be some managers who do not like change.

To overcome problems associated with resistance to change, strategic change is therefore often taken at a slower pace – 'strategy is the art of the possible', to quote

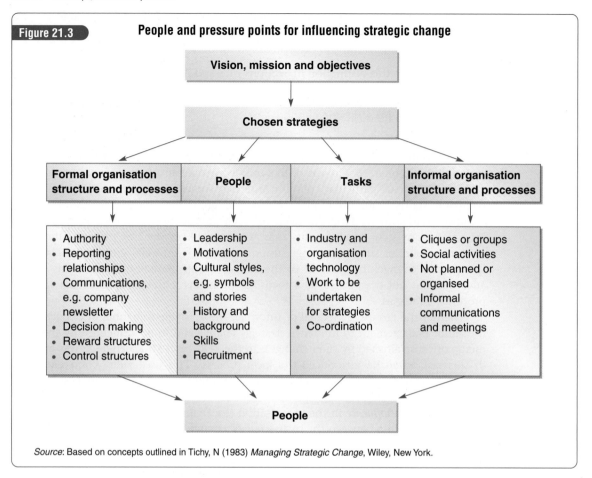

Figure 21.3 **People and pressure points for influencing strategic change**

Vision, mission and objectives

Chosen strategies

Formal organisation structure and processes	People	Tasks	Informal organisation structure and processes
• Authority • Reporting relationships • Communications, e.g. company newsletter • Decision making • Reward structures • Control structures	• Leadership • Motivations • Cultural styles, e.g. symbols and stories • History and background • Skills • Recruitment	• Industry and organisation technology • Work to be undertaken for strategies • Co-ordination	• Cliques or groups • Social activities • Not planned or organised • Informal communications and meetings

People

Source: Based on concepts outlined in Tichy, N (1983) *Managing Strategic Change*, Wiley, New York.

from Chapter 7. More consultation, more explanation and more monitoring of reactions are therefore involved in these circumstances. Figure 21.4 illustrates how the apparently simple process of strategic action is complicated by the reality of the many factors involved in successful strategic implementation.

All such discussion takes time and resources. For example, the cost at BOC can be measured by the length of time – two years – it took to implement the new style of working. Hence, strategic change is important because even successful change has an *implementation* cost for the organisation to set against the *direct benefits* identified from the new strategies. Although there are costs involved in strategic change, it may be possible to reduce them. A partial test of a successful strategic change programme is the extent to which such implementation costs can be minimised.

However, it is important not to exaggerate the negative effects of strategic change on people. Strategic change can also be positive: people may feel enthused by the new strategies. Their contribution may be more than a passive acceptance of the proposed strategies, resulting in even lower costs. Hence, another test of a successful strategic change programme might be the extent to which such costs are *reduced* beyond those identified in the strategy itself. All this will depend on the context of the change – the culture of the organisation, the way in which strategic change is introduced and the nature of the changes proposed. In brief, strategic change is context-sensitive.

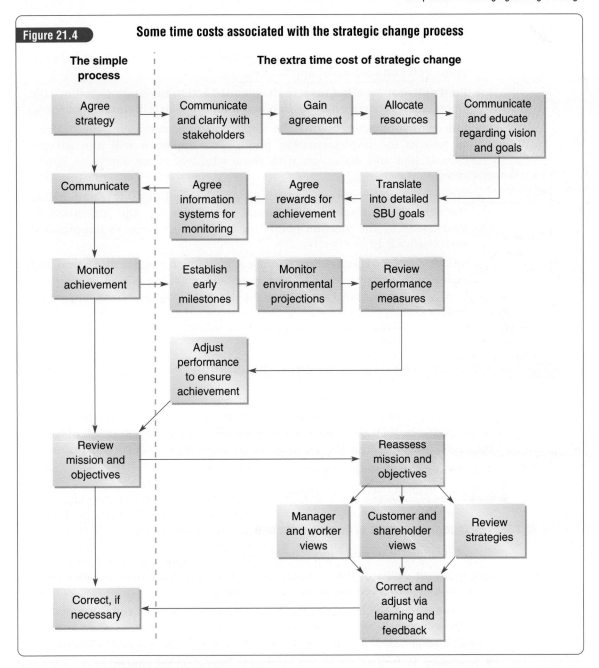

Figure 21.4 — Some time costs associated with the strategic change process

Key strategic principles

● A distinction needs to be made between the pace of change, which may be fast or slow, and strategic change, which is the proactive management of change in an organisation.

● Strategic change is the implementation of new strategies that involve substantive changes to the normal routines of the organisation.

> ▶ *Key strategic principles continued*
>
> - In managing strategic change, it is useful to draw a distinction between prescriptive and emergent approaches.
> - Prescriptive approaches involve the planned action necessary to achieve the changes. The changes may be imposed on those who will implement them.
> - Emergent approaches involve the whole process of developing the strategy, as well as the implementation phase. This approach will also involve consultation and discussion with those who will subsequently be implementing the change.
> - Strategic change is concerned with people and their tasks. It is undertaken through the formal and informal structures of the organisation. Understanding the pressure points for influencing change is important if such change is to be effective.
> - Strategic change is important because it may involve major disruption and people may resist its consequences. Even where change is readily accepted, it will take time and careful thought. Strategic change carries important hidden costs.

21.2 Analysing the causes of strategic change

In order to manage strategic change effectively, it is important to understand its causes. Strategic change can arise for all the reasons explored in Parts 2 and 3 of this book. Analysis of the specific causes is useful because it may provide clues to the best means of handling the change issues that arise. The two main classifications of the causes of change are:

1 Tichy's four main causes of strategic change;

2 Kanter, Stein and Jick's three dynamics for strategic change.

21.2.1 The four main causes of strategic change

Tichy[6] identified four main triggers for change:

1 *Environment.* Shifts in the economy, competitive pressures and legislative changes can all lead to demands for major strategic change.

2 *Business relationships.* New alliances, acquisitions, partnerships and other significant developments may require substantial changes in the organisation structure in order to take advantage of new synergies, value chain linkages or core competencies.

3 *Technology.* Shifts here can have a substantial impact on the content of the work and even the survival of companies.

4 *People.* New entrants to organisations may have different educational or cultural backgrounds or expectations that require change. This is especially important when the *leadership* of the organisation changes.

 The implications of the above need to be considered in the context of the organisation's dynamic and complex structure. Tichy suggests that change is not only inevitable in such circumstances but can be managed to produce effective strategic results. This is explored later in the chapter.

21.2.2 Three dynamics for strategic change

Kanter, Stein and Jick[7] identified three causes of strategic change, one of which is the same as in the Tichy classification:

1 *Environment.* Changes in the environment compared with the situation in the organisation can lead to demands for strategic change.

2 *Life cycle differences.* Changes in one division or part of an organisation as it moves into a phase of its life cycle that is different from another division may necessitate change. For example, in a telecommunications manufacturer such as Nokia, mobile telecommunications would still be growing while network telecommunications might be in a more mature market phase. Typically, change issues relate to the size, shape and influence of such parts and involve co-ordination and resource allocation issues between them.

3 *Political power changes inside the organisation.* Individuals, groups and other stakeholders may struggle for power to make decisions or enjoy the benefits associated with the organisation. For example, a shift in strategy from being production-oriented to customer-oriented would be accompanied by a shift in the power balance between those two functions.

The description of such changes suggests that they relate not only to strategic change but also to other complex factors, such as the interplay between people and groups. The researchers suggested that the causes were constantly shifting, sometimes slowly and at other times faster. Essentially, such causal effects prompted the need at various points for substantive strategic change.

21.2.3 Analysis of causality

In practice, there is a need to define more *precisely* the causes that apply to a particular organisation. The above interpretations may supply some general pointers but precision will prove more useful when it comes to managing strategic change. Equally, the causes described above raise important issues regarding how strategic change then takes place. This is examined in Sections 21.3 and 21.4 from the prescriptive and emergent change perspectives.

▶ Key strategic principles

- To manage strategic change, it is important to understand what is driving the process. There are numerous classifications of the causes, two of which are explored in this text.

- Tichy identifies four main causes of strategic change: environment, business relationships, technology and new entrants to the organisation, especially a new leader.

- Kanter, Stein and Jick identify three dynamics for strategic change: environment, life cycle differences across divisions of an organisation and political power changes.

- Precision regarding the causes of change is important in order to manage the change process effectively.

Owens-Corning reveals its strategies for change[8]

The US company Owens-Corning describes the strategy change procedures it used after the acquisition of the UK company Pilkington Insulation. The company was purchased from the Pilkington Glass group for US$113 million in June 1994. If its 20 per cent increase in sales after takeover is taken as a guide, the change processes were successful.

The Owens-Corning executive in charge of the takeover was Mr Warren Knowles, president of the European building products division of the company. The lessons learnt were such that Mr Knowles now gives talks to senior Owens-Corning management on the experience gained in making the acquisition. According to Mr Knowles, a takeover is more about the aftermath than the deal itself. 'You have to think about integration before closing the deal,' he comments, quoting research that found that between 80 per cent and 90 per cent of acquisitions by US companies outside the US fail.

The deal, he stresses, is only the tip of an iceberg – making it work is the important bit. Furthermore, of all the elements making it work, communicating core messages and strategies to the workforce is perhaps the most crucial. Indeed, one of the goals Mr Knowles set for the acquisition was that employees should know both what was going on and what was in it for them.

He faced very worried employees in 1994: worried about the invasion of Americans, worried about the security of their jobs, and worried about their future. Mr Knowles explains: 'People had an emotional reaction and there was a tendency to deny the evil day. Productivity drains away in this situation and people lose sight of the customer. You have to get people refocused on the customer.' He also faced a workforce used to being a non-core division, with a consequent lack of interest on the part of senior management. Investment of about US$15 million helped persuade people that Owens-Corning was serious, followed up with constant repetition of the message of individual responsibility: 'I had to say: I cannot guarantee your jobs. Only you can do that.'

The introduction of gain-sharing and pay for performance hammered home the same message. According to Mr Knowles, 'People have to under-

stand the drivers of the business and we learnt pretty quickly that if it affects their pay, people understand it.' Making clear the link between the factory line down-time and profitability brought the customer closer to the shop floor. 'Customer satisfaction is measured by market share. You have to focus on repeat business,' he says.

The other problem Mr Knowles had to tackle was integrating the European division. Having lived in Belgium for some time, he was not surprised by the lack of common European perspective, but he wanted to create a common set of values. 'There has to be a common set of expectations about how to behave so that, for example, everyone is trying to reduce cycle times. You have to speak a common language.'

One of the lessons of the acquisition that he feels companies ignore at their peril is that of 'soft' due diligence – relating to employees' needs and expectations, and their emotional response to the takeover. It is important, he believes, for senior managers to be accessible – but not only during official office hours. Being seen in the social club, going to sporting events or dances are just as important; being around when people are at their most relaxed can make a significant difference to the feel-good factor.

Source: Financial Times, 23 Feb 1996. © Copyright Financial Times 1996.

Case questions

1 *What were the main problems at the acquired company?*

2 *How would you categorise the strategic change analysis here?*

3 *Do you think the approach would have been the same if a substantial number of employees were to be made redundant as part of the takeover?*

21.3 Prescriptive approaches to managing strategic change

In developing and implementing strategy, managers will need to consider how to *manage* the change process. For example, in the Owens-Corning case, the acquiring company clearly set out to manage its takeover of its new UK subsidiary. Specifically, it undertook the following actions:

● It reassured its new employees by signalling new investment.

● It insisted that its new workers followed the Owens-Corning definition of best practice.

● It instituted new reward procedures to encourage new performance levels.

Two *prescriptive* routes for the management of change are examined in this section and then two *emergent* routes are examined in Section 21.4. The overall argument from the two sections is that the choice of prescriptive or emergent change is context-sensitive.

21.3.1 The three-stage prescriptive approach

During the late 1980s and early 1990s, research into change management by Kanter and her colleagues identified three major *forms* taken by the change process.[9] They linked these three forms with three *categories of people* involved in the change process, to produce a *three-stage process for managing change*. Their three forms were:

1 *The changing identity of the organisation.* As its environment changes, the organisation itself will respond. For example, it may need to react to a shift in the political stance of a national government. The dynamic is likely to be slow rather than fast, unless a political or other major revolution occurs.

2 *Co-ordination and transition issues as an organisation moves through its life cycle.* Relationships inside an organisation change as it grows in size and becomes older. Chapter 7 examined Greiner's depiction of the four stages of organisation development, with each being associated with a 'crisis'. Whether such a precise event occurs or not, the dynamic shifts associated with such change are predictable with regard to their pressures on groups and individuals. For example, the decision to create a separate division for a product range that is growing increasingly wide will give rise to change issues that are well known, but need management.

3 *Controlling the political aspects of organisations.* This results directly from the political pressures outlined in Section 21.2.2. Sometimes an orderly shift in power can be made but, occasionally, a more radical move is required – for example, the sudden departure of a chief executive 'after a clash over strategy and structure'.[10]

The three major categories of people involved in the change process were also identified:

1 *Change strategists.* Those responsible for leading strategic change in the organisation. They may not be responsible for the detailed implementation.

2 *Change implementers.* Those who have direct responsibility for change management (the programmes and processes that are explored later in this chapter).

3 *Change recipients.* Those who receive the change programme with varying degrees of anxiety depending on the nature of the change and how it is presented. They often perceive themselves to be powerless in the face of decisions made higher up the

organisation. In extreme cases they may object strongly, as was seen at Pilkington Insulation after the Owens-Corning takeover.

Essentially, the researchers observed that, in their sample, managing change was a top-down, prescriptive process. Emergent strategists would point to the obvious weakness in such an approach: the lack of knowledge and co-operation in advance is quite likely to cause anxiety and resistance. Prescriptive strategists would counter this by pointing to the difficulty of exploring a hostile acquisition with the change recipients before the acquisition takes place. Prescriptive strategists might cite a famous case from 1993, in which contact was made with future employees prior to acquisition, resulting in the workers eventually rejecting the offer. Volvo Car workers joined its Swedish management and a majority of shareholders in repudiating the proposed joint venture with the French car company, Renault.[11]

Comment

Kanter, Stein and Jick offer one way of structuring and managing aspects of the change process. However, their categories of people only give limited indicators of how to manage the process. Their model may also be more suited to major changes than the more common ongoing strategic process.

21.3.2 Unfreezing and freezing attitudes

In the 1950s, Lewin developed a three-step model to explain the change process:[12]

1 *Unfreezing current attitudes.* For change to take place, the old behaviour must be seen to be unsatisfactory and therefore stopped. Importantly, this need for change must be felt by the person or group themselves: it is a *felt need* and cannot be imposed. This process might be undertaken by leaking relevant information or openly confronting those involved.

2 *Moving to a new level.* A period of search for new solutions then takes place. This is characterised by the examination of alternatives, the exploration of new values, the changing of organisational structure and so on. Information continues to be made available to confirm the new position.

3 *Refreezing attitudes at the new level.* Finally, once a satisfactory situation has been found, refreezing takes place at the new level. This may well involve positive reinforcement and support for the decisions taken. For example, good news about the new position might be circulated along with information about changes in status, changes in culture, reorganisation and reconfirmation of investment decisions.

Comment

This apparently simple model has been widely used to analyse and manage change. It tends to treat people as the objects of manipulation and does not involve them in the change process at all. However, it can be useful on occasions (*see*, for example, Figure 21.5 where the Owens-Corning case has been interpreted using the Lewin model).

21.3.3 Comment on prescriptive models of change

There are other similar models that take a prescriptive approach to organisational change.[13] We have explored the criticisms of the prescriptive approach elsewhere in this book and can summarise the issues here with regard to change models.

Figure 21.5	Owens-Corning takeover using the Lewin model	
Typical activities in the organisation	*Lewin model*	*Owens-Corning case study example*
• Realisation among group of need for change • Signals from top management that 'all is not well' (perhaps even exaggerated news circulated) • Data on nature of the problem made known throughout the organisation	**Unfreezing current attitudes**	• Information about the current situation given to all employees after takeover • News that productivity and performance have fallen to unacceptable levels
• Specific call for change coupled with discussion of what is required • Views gathered on possible solutions • Information built on preferred solution • Experiment	**Moving to a new level** (State of flux: reactions tested to proposed solutions; organised debate and discussion)	• Emotional reactions • Productivity losses • Use of 'soft' management contacts to probe feelings • Senior managers present at social activities • Factory down-time linked to profits
• Make announcement • Reassure those affected • News circulated to show that new solution is working	**Refreezing attitudes at the new level**	• Introduction of gain-sharing and performance pay • US$15 million investment • Common set of values across Europe

● The assumption is made in prescriptive models that it is possible to move clearly from one state to another. This may not be possible if the environment itself is turbulent and the new destination state therefore unclear.

● Where major learning of new methods or substantial long-term investment is needed for the new situation, it may not even be clear when the new refrozen state has been reached – the situation may be soft-frozen.

● The assumption is also made that agreement on the new refrozen state is possible. This may be unrealistic if the politics within the organisation remain in flux. Given that prescriptive models involve only limited consultation, this assumption can be shown to have real weaknesses in some cultural styles characterised by competition and power building.

● Such models rely on the *imposition* of change on the employees concerned. This may be essential in some circumstances, e.g. factory closure, but, where the co-operation of those involved is needed or the culture works on a co-operative style, the prescriptive models may be totally inappropriate.

▶ Key strategic principles

- There are a number of prescriptive routes for the management of change: two were examined in this section.

- Kanter, Stein and Jick recommend a three-stage approach involving three forms of change and three categories of people involved in the change. Essentially, the route is a top-down guide to managing planned change and its consequences throughout the organisation.

- Lewin developed a three-stage model for the prescriptive change process: unfreezing current attitudes, moving to a new level and refreezing attitudes at the new level. This model has been widely used to analyse and manage change.

- Prescriptive models of change work best where it is possible to move clearly from one state to another: in times of rapid change, such clarity may be difficult to find and such models may be inappropriate.

CASE STUDY 21.3

United Biscuits – a shadow of its former self[14]

In the early 1990s, United Biscuits was one of the world's leading biscuit and snack companies. By 2001, many of its leading operations had been sold and the company was no longer a major player in food markets. This case study explores the reasons and questions the implications for managing the strategic change.

Background – early 1990s

With 1994 sales of US$5.2 billion, the UK-based company United Biscuits (UB) was the third-largest biscuit manufacturer in the world. It was also joint equal market leader across Europe in crisps and nut snacks with PepsiCo – *see* Case study 18.1. European brands included McVities biscuits (UK), KP snacks (UK), Verkade biscuits (Holland and France), Fazer biscuits (Finland), Oxford biscuits (Nordic region). Asia–Pacific operations were centred on its 1993 Australian acquisition of the Smith's Snackfood company.

US brands were centred around the Keebler biscuits and snacks company which UB had purchased in 1979. It was second in the US market but a distant second to the market leader, Nabisco. The UB operation had moved into losses in 1993 and 1994 but the company was confident of turning events around. It added to its US interests in 1993 by acquiring the US's foremost private label cookie company, Bake-Line. It announced an investment programme in 1994 amounting to US$160 million in the Keebler company. However, it later announced that it was withdrawing from some geographical areas of the US in order to consolidate its strengths in its main areas.

New global strategy: February 1995

In February 1995, UB was so confident of its trading future that it announced a new strategy and reorganisation aimed at producing:

- worldwide co-ordination of its biscuits and snacks activities in order to develop synergies, share experience, best practice and innovation;

- three new geographic areas – Europe, Asia–Pacific, US – each with its own director;

- increased worldwide co-ordination of R&D in order to 'champion' new product innovation around the world.

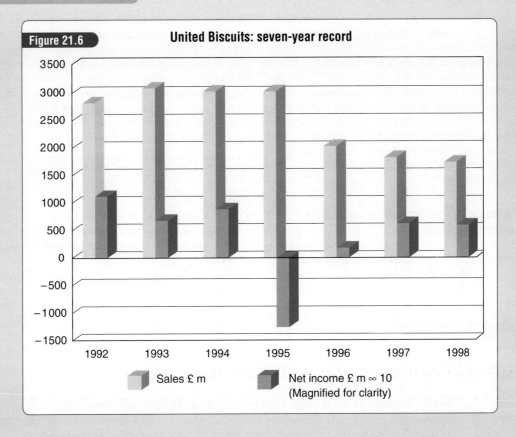

Figure 21.6

United Biscuits: seven-year record

Sales £ m

Net income £ m ∞ 10
(Magnified for clarity)

The statement was accompanied by a new detailed chart that identified senior members of the company and their new worldwide responsibilities. It also showed how the company's efforts would be increasingly co-ordinated to produce enhanced synergies in product development and innovation.

Withdrawal from the US: July 1995

In July 1995, UB announced that it was pulling out of the US completely and selling its Keebler and salty snack businesses for the best possible price. The managing director said: 'It's never easy to make statements like this, but this is decisive action that's right for the company.'

Keebler was finally sold in November 1995 for just under US$600 million, barely covering the asset valuation in its accounts. Since UB had invested another US$150 million in the previous two years in the US, its exit had some additional financial consequences. The reason for the withdrawal was that the company had concluded that competition

and market conditions were too tough – it was simply not possible to operate profitably.

Further pressures on UB in 1995

The overall reasons for the sudden shift in UB strategy were also influenced by three major strategic problems elsewhere in the world:

1 Downturn in its most profitable market, the UK – supermarkets were squeezing its leading brands.

2 Fierce European competition in snackfoods from a powerful and increasingly aggressive rival – PepsiCo, trading as Walkers in the UK and Frito in the rest of Europe. Pepsi was the biggest snackfood maker in the world and had decided to build its European brands aggressively.

3 Net debt at US$700 million was 64 per cent of shareholders' funds in December 1994.

Some observers regarded it as no coincidence that a new chairman, Mr Colin Short, was appointed to

▶

UB in spring 1995 from outside the food industry. He had a reputation for facing unpleasant facts and taking hard decisions. By the end of 1995, the sale of its US interests had made UB more vulnerable to a hostile takeover bid than at any time in its history: it had a poor profit record and was unable to show the benefits of its US disposal. The trading difficulties of the company began to have an impact on the morale of employees and managers – for example, there were only limited funds to develop new product ranges and there were cutbacks in other areas.

All change at UB – not necessarily bad news for employees and managers

In 1997, UB sold its remaining snack operations in Australia and Europe to PepsiCo. It said that the new, slimmed-down company was seeking to concentrate on its European biscuit operations. Over the next two years, the company began to reinvigorate and support its UK market leadership.

However, the main UK biscuit operations were sold to the French multinational, Danone, in 2001. Arguably, the uncertainty and change of being part of a failed operation were now finally ended – employees and managers were now part of companies that were committed to developing major international businesses. Admittedly, there were some redundancies but, for the majority that remained, the future was more secure.

Case questions

1 *What would be the effect on employees of the major strategic switch between February and July 1995? What actions would you have taken in July/August 1995 in these circumstances, if any?*

2 *Given the successful acquisitions of parts of UB by PepsiCo and Danone in the late 1990s, what strategic change programmes should be set up by these companies?*

21.4 Emergent approaches to managing change

From Section 21.3, it will be clear that there are occasions when prescriptive approaches to strategic change are essential, usually where some major shift in strategy is undertaken, such as in the United Biscuits case. However, the human cost may be high in terms of resistance to the changes and the consequences that follow from this. Emergent approaches therefore deserve to be investigated.

Within emergent theories, there is no one single approach. Some emphasise the need for responsiveness in an increasingly turbulent world. Others concentrate on the longer-term need to change an organisation's skills, style and operating culture fundamentally and over long time periods. It is these latter theories that are explored in this chapter, since they are more closely related to issues of strategic change. The two emergent areas chosen for examination have already been explored:

1 learning theory, as developed by Senge and others;[15]

2 the Five Factors theory of strategic change, as developed by Pettigrew and Whipp.

21.4.1 Learning theory

According to Senge,[16] the learning organisation does not *suddenly* adopt strategic change but is *perpetually* seeking it. The process of learning is continuous: as one area is 'learnt', so new avenues of experimentation and communication open up. In addition, the learning approach emphasises the following areas:

● team learning;

● the sharing of views and visions for the future;

- the exploration of ingrained company habits, generalisations and corporate interpretations that may no longer be relevant;
- people skills as the most important asset of the organisation; and, most importantly,
- systems thinking – the integrative area that supports the four above and provides a basis for viewing the environment.

It will be evident that the learning approach can work well where the company has the time and resources to invest in these areas. The objective is for the people in the organisation to shape its future over time. (The Owens-Corning acquisition included elements of this in the comment, 'I cannot guarantee your jobs. Only you can do that.')

Arguably, learning would not be so applicable where there was a sudden change in strategic direction – for example, the UB move out of the US. The gradual assimilation of change and the ability of employees to guide their own destiny is limited, if rapid change is imposed for outside commercial reasons. The learning approach appeared to offer little in the short term for UB's 1995 predicament, for example.

Comment

The principle of the learning organisation appears to have a significant difficulty: precisely how and when companies should be developed into 'learning' organisations.[17] The outline concept is clear enough but the practicalities of how this is achieved are vague and lacking in operational detail. Egan has commented on the definitional and conceptual ambiguity in the learning concept 'which has stifled the practical adoption of what could otherwise be an extremely powerful idea'.[18] Garvin has attempted to answer these difficulties by exploring the management and measurement of such new processes.[19] He suggests some first useful steps that might be adopted to begin the process, e.g. *learning forums* or discussion groups in the organisation to tackle specific change issues.

21.4.2 The Five Factors theory of strategic change

Pettigrew and Whipp[20] (*see* Chapter 17) undertook an in-depth empirical study of strategic change at four companies: Jaguar cars, Longman publishing, Hill Samuel merchant bank and Prudential life assurance. They also undertook a more general examination of the industries in which the four companies were operating. Their conclusions were that there were five interrelated factors in the successful management of strategic change (*see* Figure 21.7):

1 *Environmental assessment.* This should not be regarded as a separate study but a separate function. All parts of the organisation should be constantly assessing the competition. Strategy creation emerges constantly from this process.

2 *Leading change.* The type of leadership can only be assessed by reference to the particular circumstances of the organisation. There are no universal 'good leaders'. The best leaders are always constrained by the actual situation of the firm. They are often most effective when they move the organisation forward at a comfortable, if challenging, pace: bold actions may be counterproductive.

3 *Linking strategic and operational change.* This may be partly prescriptive in the sense of a specific strategy for the organisation – 'This is my decision.' It may also be partly

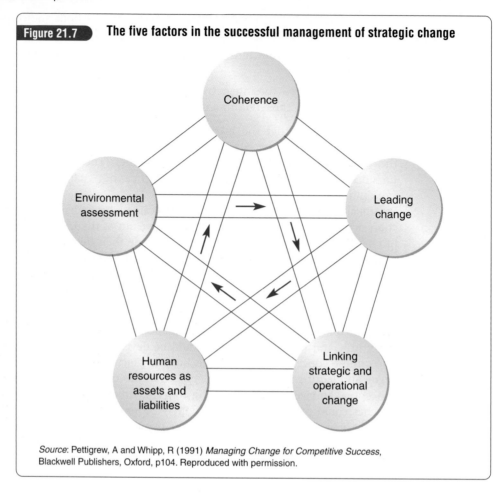

Figure 21.7 **The five factors in the successful management of strategic change**

Coherence

Environmental assessment

Leading change

Human resources as assets and liabilities

Linking strategic and operational change

Source: Pettigrew, A and Whipp, R (1991) *Managing Change for Competitive Success*, Blackwell Publishers, Oxford, p104. Reproduced with permission.

emergent in that the strategy may allow for evolution over time – 'But naturally our new strategy will evolve as we implement it.'

4 *Strategic human resource management – human resources as assets and liabilities*. These resources constitute the knowledge, skills and attitudes of the organisation in total. Crucially, some people are better than others at managing people. It is a skill acquired over time and needing a learning approach (*see* Section 21.3.1). Long-term learning is essential for the organisation to develop its full potential.

5 *Coherence in the management of change*. This is the most complex of the five factors. It attempts to combine the four above into a consistent whole and reinforce it by a set of four complementary support mechanisms:

- *consistency* – the goals of the organisation must not conflict with each other;
- *consonance* – the whole process must respond well to its environment;
- *competitive advantage* – the coherence must deliver in this area;
- *feasibility* – the strategy must not present unsolvable problems.

Note that the five factors relate to the whole strategy development process, not just to the implementation process.

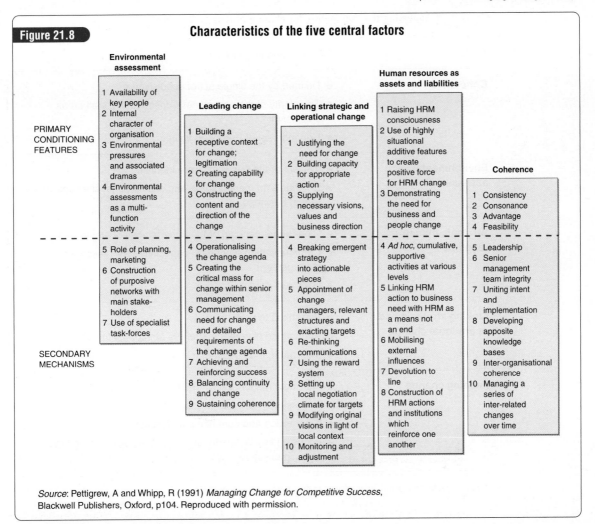

Figure 21.8

Characteristics of the five central factors

Source: Pettigrew, A and Whipp, R (1991) *Managing Change for Competitive Success*, Blackwell Publishers, Oxford, p104. Reproduced with permission.

Overall, the organisation needs to be able to develop a *balanced approach* to change that is both focused and efficient internally, while adapting successfully to external changes. To assist this process, the researchers included two additional components for each factor:

1 *the primary conditioning features;*

2 *the secondary actions and mechanisms* which can only come into effect once the primary conditioning features are present.

These additional components are shown in Figure 21.8.

To illustrate how the five factors might be used, the Owens-Corning takeover of Pilkington Insulation (*see* Case study 21.2) has been analysed using this approach. The results are shown in Table 21.1. The model provides a useful way of taking the facts from a strategic change situation and structuring them to highlight the important items. Where data have not been gathered on one of the five elements of change, it

Table 21.1 Analysing the five factors for change at Owens-Corning

Factor	Owens-Corning analysis
Coherence	• Defined by the single act of acquisition • The clarity of the new owner's desire to make all areas successful • Common set of European values
Environmental assessment	• 'Drivers of the business' were identified • Emphasis on market share and customer satisfaction through repeat business
Strategic human resource management	• Clear understanding of the uncertainties of employees • Communication emphasis, especially core messages • 'Soft' due diligence
Linking strategic and operational change	• Pay linked to performance • Attendance of senior managers at informal functions • Motivation and customer focus
Leading change	• Individual responsibility: the role of Mr Knowles • Accessibility of senior managers • Clear vision and common set of values • Focus on key factors for success: customer, reduced cycle times, motivation

Note: The factors are in the order relevant to the Owens-Corning takeover.

highlights this area. The model may also suggest additional areas that need to be explored in the organisation in order to understand the dynamic of change, especially in the area of coherence.

Comment

Although the comprehensiveness of the model is its greatest strength,[21] it is also its most significant weakness. Some of the factors represent truths that most would agree with, but contain areas that are so generalised that they may provide only limited guidance on the difficult issues involved in strategic change. Thus, some of the five factors needed to be treated with caution.

- *Environmental assessment* is a well-known factor requiring constant monitoring. However, the more detailed comments against this heading in the model provide more limited guidance than those in Part 2 of this book.
- *Linking of strategic and operational change* is an important area of study, but many would regard this as being the same as the 'implementation' process discussed by other writers and explored in this book.

- *Leading change* and its complexity has been recognised as a change factor for many years.[22]

However, the emphasis on *human resource assets and liabilities* is a welcome emphasis not present in some other analyses, such as Porter's generic strategies or portfolio matrices. Moreover, the identification, definition and logic of *coherence* as a major factor is also useful.

21.4.3 Comment on emergent models of change

The UB case illustrates the difficulties of using emergent models of strategic change. For whatever reasons, between February and July 1995 the company found itself being forced to undertake a completely different approach to its strategy:

- Worldwide and US activities were dropped in favour of a more modest European and Asia–Pacific programme.
- Its major US subsidiary, Keebler, was sold off.

It could certainly be argued that the company had signalled the difficulties it was facing in North American markets during 1993–94, both to the Stock Exchange and to employees. However, the *emergent* models of strategic change, with their long-term approach to learning, provide only limited clues to interpreting the difficulties and suggesting how they might be tackled over this period. The subsequent sale of many of the remaining UB assets between 1997 and 2001 is also not handled well by emergent models of change – such disposals are sudden by their nature. By contrast, the three-phase Lewin *prescriptive* model does provide a means of interpreting the events and their meaning for change (*see* Figure 21.9).

Emergent models of strategic change have a number of weaknesses that may make them difficult to employ:[23]

- The 'long-term learning' approach of Pettigrew and Whipp[24] necessary to achieve emergent strategies may have little practical value where an organisation faces a short-term unforeseen crisis. There is no guarantee that the 'learning' that has already taken place will be relevant to the crisis. Arguably, the crisis may partly have arisen because the learning was incorrect.
- In some emergent models, increased turbulence of the environment is assumed as a justification for the emergent strategies. Such generalisations about the environment need empirical evidence. There are a number of environments that are generally predictable.
- A reliance on a learning culture may be counterproductive for some managers and employees. Some managers may refuse to learn because they will realise that such a process will reduce their power.[25] Empowerment of some employees will certainly mean that others will have less power and may react accordingly.

Overall, the way forward proposed by some emergent strategists often amounts to the need to start earlier so that the organisation is able to adapt when the change comes. This may not be sufficient at the time when a sudden change hits the organisation.

Figure 21.9   **Unfreezing and freezing attitudes at UB in 1995**

Typical activities in the organisation	Lewin model	UB case study example
• Realisation among group of need for change • Signals from top management that 'all is not well' (perhaps even exaggerated news circulated) • Data on nature of the problem made known throughout the organisation	**Unfreezing current attitudes**	• Aggressive rival attacks market share across US and Europe: 1994–95 • US subsidiary continues to make substantive losses after three years of investment: 1993–95
• Specific call for change coupled with discussion of what is required • Views gathered on possible solutions • Information built on preferred solution • Experiment	**Moving to a new level** (State of flux: reactions tested to proposed solutions; debate and discussion organised)	• Announce job losses in Europe and US in 1994 • Executives undertake studies of UK and US markets: 1994–95 • Conclude that US position cannot be maintained • Announce withdrawal from part of US in 1994 • No real experimentation at this time: arguably took place in 1994
• Make announcement • Reassure those affected • News circulated to show that new solution is working	**Refreezing attitudes at the new level**	• Announce sale of all US interests: 1995 • 'It's never easy...' statement from managing director • Reorganise the remainder of the company • Reassure the remaining employees

---

21.4.4 The choice between emergent and prescriptive strategic change

The choice between the prescriptive and emergent routes is context-sensitive. Potentially, organisations may wish to choose emergent strategic change management because it is less disruptive and therefore has a lower cost. However, there may be occasions when the strategic circumstances force prescriptive change. The choice depends on the situation facing the organisation at the time.

> ## ▶ Key strategic principles
>
> - There are a number of emergent approaches to strategic change. The two explored in this section concentrate on the longer-term, learning culture routes to change.
>
> - According to Senge, the learning organisation does not suddenly adopt strategic change but is perpetually seeking it. Hence, the organisation is using its learning, experimentation and communication to renew itself constantly. Strategic change is a constant process.
>
> - According to Pettigrew and Whipp, their empirical study of strategic change identified five factors in the successful management of the process. They were environmental assessment, leadership of change, the link between strategic and operational change, human resource aspects, and coherence in the management of the process.
>
> - Emergent models of strategic change take a long-term approach and may have limited usefulness when the organisation faces short-term strategic crisis.
>
> - The choice between prescriptive and emergent strategic change processes will depend on the situation at the time: ideally, emergent change should be chosen because it is less disruptive and cheaper. In reality, a prescriptive approach may be necessary.

21.5 Developing a strategic change programme

The starting point for any programme of strategic change is *clarity* regarding the changes required. These will relate back to the organisation's objectives explored in Chapter 12 but may also include a more experimental element. They may also need to be modified by some aspects of the implementation programme – 'the art of the possible' from Chapter 7. A strategic change programme might also include the introduction of a 'learning culture' as part of its way forward.

Furthermore, most programmes of strategic change concentrate on certain key tasks: for example, they may identify individuals or groups with particular power to make or break a proposed change. In this context, the organisation has the ability to make changes among many variables and would be well advised to consider all of these before making its selection. Since one of the main problems may be the resistance to changes that are proposed and another will be the need to persuade people to support the proposals, it is also important to give these matters serious consideration at the commencement of the programme. The change programme needs to address four questions:

1 What areas of change are available?

2 What areas will we select and why?

3 Will people resist change? If so, how can this be overcome?

4 How will people use the politics of an organisation?

21.5.1 What areas of change are available?

In Section 21.1, four general areas of activity associated with people, referred to as pressure points for influence, were identified – formal organisation structure, people, tasks

Figure 21.10

Change options matrix

	Areas of people activity			
	Formal organisation structure	**People**	**Tasks**	**Informal organisation structure**
Technical and work changes from the strategy to be undertaken	• Organisation of work and reporting • Strategy and structure	• Selection, training • Matching of management style with skills • Routines	• Consider environment, technology, learning, competitor activity • Learn and carry out new tasks	• Understand and monitor • Feed with 'good news'
Cultural changes Style of company, history, age, etc.	• Managerial style • Mintzberg's subcultures *(Chapter 15)* • Handy's cultures *(Chapter 7)*	• Individual and corporate values matched • Management of groups and teams • Leadership choice	• Symbols, stories • Unfreezing • Make role models of key people • Clarify values • New recipes	• Awards, symbols • Develop networks • Encourage useful groups • Develop social activities
Political changes Interactions and power inside the organisation	• Formal distribution of power • Balance of power between departments	• Use available skills and networks • Match with new strategies • Incentives and rewards	• Lobbying • Develop structures • Influence formal and informal groups	• Attempt to manage • Make contacts • Network and circulate

Three main areas of strategic change

and informal organisation structure. These can be coupled with three main areas of strategic change activity[26] to produce the *change options matrix* shown in Figure 21.10. In practice, every organisation undertaking change will need to develop activities in most of these options. However, for most organisations, there will be a need to concentrate effort and monitor results. Hence, it will be useful to *focus and direct activities more tightly*: selection among the options will be a priority.

21.5.2 What areas will we select from the change options matrix and why?

The response to these questions will depend on the organisation, its culture and leadership. For example, organisations that have a history of top-down management might select items from the change options matrix that match this style of operating – that is, organisation of work and formal distribution of power.

However, organisations that have selected an open-learning, co-operative style of operating might select as their starting point team building and training and education.

The clear implication is that it is essential to review the organisation's culture analysis: Johnson's *Cultural Web* from Chapter 7 should provide a useful guide here.

There are no universal answers. As we have seen, some researchers have recently tended to favour the more co-operative, learning organisation approach. However, it should be recognised that this may be a fashion of the turn of the century: only time will tell.

Whatever route is chosen, a more detailed answer to the question then needs to be followed through. As an illustration of the issues that can then arise, the *assumption* is made here that the co-operative, learning approach has been chosen. Within this route, Beer, Eisenhort and Spector[27] provide a detailed six-point plan on how to proceed, beginning by stressing that the areas to be selected for change should be chosen not by top management but by *those involved in the implementation process*. The six overlapping areas are:

1 *Mobilise commitment to change through joint diagnosis of business problems arising from the change objective.* One or more task forces might be employed here. They should represent all stakeholders in the organisation and be directed at specific aspects of the change objective.

2 *Develop a shared vision of how to organise and manage for competitiveness.* Senior management may lead the process but the identification of the new roles and responsibilities is undertaken by those involved in implementation. Typically, this will be through the task forces.

3 *Foster consensus for the new vision, competence to enact it and cohesion to move it along.* This book has already explored vision, competencies and cohesion. The key new word is *consensus*, which the researchers suggest needs to come from strong leadership at the top. New competencies may be required, resistance may build and some individuals may turn out to be more reluctant than others. Difficulties may be overcome by teamwork coupled with training to provide support. However, it is likely that leadership will also be needed.

4 *Spread revitalisation to all departments, pushing it from the top.* Change is spread to the departments that supplied the members of the task force. However, such change cannot be forced onto departments. They must be allowed some freedom, but they can be guided and revitalised by top management.

5 *Institute revitalisation through formal policies, systems and structures.* Up to this stage, the process has contained a degree of freedom of choice, experimentation and action. Now the time has come to 'refreeze' the procedures, both to ensure commitment and understanding and to provide the basis for future monitoring and controls.

6 *Monitor and adjust strategies in response to problems in the revitalisation process.* Having 'learnt' an area, the organisation should be able to repeat the process as the environment continues to change and more is understood about the changes already introduced.

With the emphasis on joint task forces and learning through doing, it might well be asked what role senior management can perform. The researchers suggested they had three prime tasks:

1 *To create the prime conditions for change* – forcing recognition of the need, setting the standards and monitoring performance. Owens-Corning senior management is a good example here.

2 *To identify those teams and organisation units that had achieved successful change and then praise them as role models for the rest.* Educational visits to them and training by them can then be helpful in spreading best practice.

3 *To identify individuals and promote them on the basis of their success in leading change.*

Finally, it should be emphasised again that this approach is suitable for one type of organisation but may not be appropriate for other types.

21.5.3 Will people resist change and how can this be overcome?

In practical terms, the issue of resistance to change is probably the chief obstacle to the successful implementation of strategic change. The reasons are many and the ways of overcoming them will depend on the circumstances. Exhibit 21.1 presents a list of some of the more common areas of resistance and suggests ways of overcoming them.

Exhibit 21.1   **Resistance to change**

Why people resist change

- Anxiety, e.g. weaknesses revealed or loss of power or position
- Pessimism
- Irritation
- Lack of interest
- Opposition strategy proposals
- Different personal ambitions

Overcoming resistance

- Involving those who resist in the change process itself
- Building support networks
- Communications and discussion
- Use of managerial authority and status
- Offering assistance
- Extra incentives
- Encouraging and supporting those involved
- Use of symbols to signal the new era

More positively, resistance will be less if the change is not imposed from outside but developed by those involved in the change procedures. Change will be more welcome if it is seen to reduce, rather than increase, the task of those involved and to be consistent with the values that they hold. Change is also more likely to be accepted if it offers an interesting challenge and a change from existing routine. Importantly, change is more likely to be appreciated if the outcome is genuinely valued by senior management, who have wholeheartedly supported the process as it has developed.

21.5.4 How will people use the politics of an organisation?

In the context of strategic change, politics starts by *persuading* people to adopt a new strategy. It may not be a question of meeting open resistance but rather one of different priorities, different power blocks or differences of opinion on the way forward. The first step is usually to establish the organisation's 'ground rules': that is, any criteria that it has for the acceptance of projects, such as minimum levels of profitability and so on.

The more difficult aspects of politics usually begin when these criteria have been met but there is still resistance. Politics then becomes *discussion*, *negotiation* and even *cunning* and *intrigue*. The Florentine diplomat and writer Nicolo Machiavelli (1469–1527) remains well known to this day for his insights into the ways that people use the politics of the organisations to which they belong.[28] His writing appears cynical, devious and self-serving but he certainly understood management politics at its worst:

> *It is unnecessary for a good prince to have all the qualities I have enumerated but it is very necessary to appear to have them.*

On the subject of change:

> *There is nothing more difficult to take in hand, more perilous to conduct, or more uncertain in its success, than to take the lead in the introduction of a new order of things.*

Machiavelli saw little benefit in persuasion, except as a means of avoiding the alternative, which was to use direct force and possibly end up making enemies. His attitude was that reason mattered less than power, and human nature was best considered as acting for the worst possible motives. He would have chuckled cynically at such strategic change concepts as communication, discussion and empowerment.

In some organisations, Machiavelli still remains relevant today. Certainly, it is highly unlikely that major strategic change can be implemented if it meets strong political barriers. Strategists therefore have to be skilled not only at devising their proposals but also at building support for them through the organisation's political structure. Hence, it is important to understand how the *decision-making system* works in the organisation: this will include not only any final presentation but also the preceding discussions, consultations and lobbying. It may be useful to call for advice from those who have had previous experience of its processes.

Inevitably, the politics of an organisation will take time to understand. It will include the activities of other people and their interaction with strategy across a whole range of activities. People will have many motives: some good and some less attractive. They may employ many different types of activity that could loosely be described as political. Table 21.2 lists some that have been shown by empirical research to be important.

By definition, change involves moving from a previous strategy and therefore the starting point for the persuasion process might appear to be an attack on the existing strategy. However, politically this may be a mistake. It may force those who introduced

Table 21.2 Politics in organisations[29]

Objective	Activities undertaken to achieve the objective	Reaction by superiors or rivals to the activities
Resist change or resist authority	• Sabotage • Rebellion	• Fight back • Institute new rules and regulations
Build power	• Flaunt or feign expertise • Attach oneself to superior • Build alliances with colleagues • Collect subordinates: empire build • Control resources	• Call bluff • Find heir • Reorganise department • Reclaim control of resources
Defeat rival	• Battles between units • Battles between staff and line • Expose mistakes (we all make them)	• Good leadership should provide balance
Achieve fundamental change in strategy, authority and leadership	• Form power group of key executives • Combine with other areas above • Inform on opponent • Leak damaging material to public media	• Intelligence essential • Recognise and cultivate those who are particularly influential • Seek out rival power groups • Respond with own leaks

the previous strategy to defend their decisions and therefore raise barriers to the new proposals. The people who are antagonised by the new strategies may be the very individuals whose support is vital for them.

Beyond these considerations, the person(s) responsible for seeking agreement to a new strategy will need to undertake several important tasks:

- identify potential and influential supporters and persuade them to support the new strategy;
- seek out potential opposition and attempt to change opinions or, at least, to neutralise them;
- build the maximum consensus for the new proposals, preferably *prior* to any formal decision meeting.

Finally, it is important to keep political matters in perspective. They are important but this book has hopefully shown that strategy does not deal in certainties. It is an art as well as a science. This means that there is room for differing views and the use of judgement and debate in arriving at decisions. Strategy is the art of the possible.

▶ Key strategic principles

- The change options matrix sets out the main areas where change is possible: it is important within this to focus and select options.
- Selection from the matrix needs to be undertaken. This can best be undertaken by an understanding of the culture of the organisation: the Cultural Web can be useful here. A more detailed process to achieve change can then be planned out, with six overlapping areas providing a starting point.
- Resistance to change is probably one of the chief obstacles to successful strategy implementation. It is likely to be lower if strategies are not imposed from the outside.
- The politics of strategic change needs to begin by attempting to persuade those involved to adopt the new strategy recommendations. Beyond this, a Machiavellian approach may be necessary to ensure the desired changes are achieved. More generally, strategic change activities may include identifying supporters, attempting to change opposition views and building the maximum consensus for the new proposals. Preferably, this should be undertaken prior to any decision meeting.

CASE STUDY 21.4

StanChart chief swept out by culture clash

Tensions within Standard Chartered Bank came out into the open in late 2001 when chief executive Rana Talwar was ousted and the bank became a takeover target.

Rudyard Kipling once wrote: 'East is East and West is West and never the twain shall meet.' The ousting in December 2001 of Rana Talwar, the Indian-born chief executive of Standard Chartered Bank (or StanChart as it is known), may have proved the colonial author's insight right. Those who know the history of StanChart might have seen it coming: it has always been the bank where cultures have clashed.

When it was created in 1968 after the merger of Standard Bank, one of the leading banks in Africa, with Chartered Bank, its rival in India and East Asia, the two halves failed to integrate on the most basic levels. The Standard Chartered executives would eat lunch in the Eastern canteen, while their Chartered counterparts ate in the Western canteen. In recent years, the collision of the cultures is between the old and the new. The City of London was surprised, but insiders at the bank were not. Tensions between Sir Patrick Gillam, the StanChart chairman, and Mr Rana Talwar had been simmering for most of 2001 and had come to the boil in April 2001 at a remuneration committee meeting. The two men found themselves engaged in a shouting match over incentives, which left their fellow directors in no doubt that the relationship would not last.

StanChart, however, continued to maintain its British reserve. At the beginning of November 2001, rumours started to surface about Barclays Bank, one of the leading UK banks, considering a takeover bid for StanChart. As expected, StanChart insisted: 'We have a great future as an independent bank.' But behind the scenes, it was nervous. At the same time, tensions were growing between Sir Patrick and Mr Talwar. On a Tuesday evening in late November 2001, Mr Talwar was hosting a cocktail party for business analysts, accompanied by Nigel Kenny, the finance director, and Christopher Keljik, an executive board member. Meanwhile, a select group of board members had gathered in StanChart's cheerless City of London headquarters to decide Mr Talwar's fate. The meeting lasted one and a half hours. 'There was a clear divide between the executives who believed Patrick should step down and the non-executives who complained about Rana's management style,' said one board member present. However, Sir Patrick, who was not present at the board meeting, denied this. 'The non-executives were unanimous,' he said. Furthermore, he refuted suggestions that the tension was between himself and his chief executive: 'There was a culture clash between Mr Talwar and his bank colleagues.'

Mr Talwar's departure both surprised and angered some of StanChart's biggest shareholders. He was the second chief executive to leave in less than three years at a time of stiff competition from rival banks. His predecessor, Malcolm Williamson, left abruptly after it emerged that he had held informal discussions with Martin Taylor, chief executive of Barclays, over a merger that Sir Patrick strongly opposed. 'Malcolm was not ousted,' Sir Patrick said. 'He had reached retirement age and had agreed to go to Visa.' The City, aware of Sir Patrick's domineering management techniques, found it difficult to understand why it was Mr Talwar who was asked to leave. Sir Patrick, aged 69, had already announced his retirement for 2003. Not known for his modesty, he claimed that his management style had never been questioned: 'I may be old, but I'm not old-fashioned. I am a dynamic, modern manager, even if I say so myself.'

But investors and analysts did also express concern over the board's choice of successor, Mr Mervyn Davies. First, they argued, was it right to hire from inside the bank? Second, if Sir Patrick disliked Mr Talwar's abrasive US-style of management, why had he chosen yet another executive who learnt his trade at Citigroup, the US financial giant where Mr Talwar had spent more than 30 years? 'This would not have happened in a world of true corporate governance,' said one large institutional shareholder in StanChart. 'What Patrick has done is appoint a chief executive who will toe the party line,' he added. Indeed, this is a view shared by many in the City of London. Mr Talwar was clearly ready to take on his chairman. One advisor said he had clashed with Sir Patrick and other old StanChart hands over his determination to promote locals to run the Asian and Asia–Pacific operations. This was not liked by the old guard, who wanted to deploy head office executives abroad.

Analysts were also familiar with these tensions. 'Rana used to tell them that they could not succeed in Asia if they had so many middle-aged white faces running the bank. He was right – how could he compete against HSBC or Citigroup in Asia with English bank executives? Times have changed,' one said. Sir Patrick refuted this, citing the cultural diversity of the bank: 'We have a Greek-American running the Emirates, Pakistan and Sri Lanka, an Indian running India, and Singapore run by a Singaporean, to name a few.' The cultural clash between Sir Patrick and Mr Talwar also started to concern the bank's financial advisers, Dresdner Kleinwort Wasserstein and Goldman Sachs, as well as their brokers, Cazenove and UBS Warburg.

▶

Some directors were not convinced about a move to acquire Grindlay's Bank for US$1.3 billion, which had been initiated by Mr Talwar. However, given the lacklustre Asian markets on which StanChart had come to depend expansion was necessary to find new growth opportunities. Others took a more measured view, suggesting that Mr Talwar was unlucky to be hit by a second economic recession in five years. But if economic conditions were to worsen and shareholders felt the impact, their patience was unlikely to stretch much further. In those circumstances, Mr Talwar's departure would force StanChart at least to consider a takeover approach. StanChart was now considered to be vulnerable to takeover, despite Sir Patrick's mission to keep it independent.

© Copyright *Financial Times*. Article slightly shortened by Richard Lynch from 'StanChart chief swept out by culture clash' *Financial Times*, 1 December 2001, p 14 by Lina Saigol. All opinions and conclusions expressed in the case study are those of the *Financial Times* and its editorial team.

Case questions

1 *Undertake an analysis of the changes that have taken place in the culture and power balance across the company. What conclusions can you draw for employees and management?*

2 *With hindsight, would you have managed the essential changes at the merchant bank differently from the senior managers who undertook them at the time?*

3 *Is the company likely to come through the change period with success or will there be permanent problems?*

Mobilising middle managers[30]

In this extract from their book Rejuvenating the Mature Business, *Charles Baden-Fuller and John Stopford explain how middle managers are the key to the successful implementation of corporate strategy.*

Middle managers are the people who will make or break the organisation. Not only are they the key to 'the doing of management' but also they are vital to new thinking. The ideas that informed the choice of strategy in the first place can come from many sources in the firm, not just the top. Thus it is that those in the middle have to take the ideas from all quarters and make them work in daily operations. The common distinctions made among top-down, bottom-up and lateral processes of communication blur when considering what happens in practice: all have to be operative in entrepreneurial organisations. Unless middle managers are clear about their central role in company-wide affairs, they will inhibit progress.

Sometimes the difficulty of starting the process of mobilising the middle is that the chief executive may personally be unwilling or unable to provide the leadership needed to legitimise the effort. One of the less successful rejuvenators confessed to our survey that he had so far worked only with his top team of six people and had not 'got much further down'. He, like many others, once believed that the strategy was so commercially sensitive that it could not be shared. Like others he saw his mistake: 'We were initially afraid our competitors would get hold of the plan. But we then discovered they had it already and our employees were the only ones in the dark before our presentations.'

All too often middle managers wait until the corporate plan has been unveiled before they act. Top management must mobilise middle managers to look upwards, sideways and downwards as an essential part of their role in a complex network of relationships. Only then will they espouse the values of becoming more proactive, more questioning and will not wait either for external events or instructions from above to trigger change. But to get to that state, considerable resistance must be overcome.

One common source of resistance is that initial enthusiasm may give way to fear. In pyramidal organisations whole layers of middle managers can exist merely to pass on – and often distort – information. They make no decisions of any competitive consequence. In the pre-information age they had a purpose in the control structure, but today they can become an endangered species. An example from one of our research sample shows the way forward. Reflecting on a controversial proposal to cut jobs at a time of business expansion, one chief executive recalled:

I set a man on the task of finding out what could be done. His evidence was so overwhelming that now everyone agrees that the cuts were necessary and obvious. Even the workforce agrees, though not the unions. Putting people on such projects releases ideas and adds further information and options. We aim to build consensus by discussion, where parochial feelings are eroded. Even where the functions of several directors were threatened, I heard no cries of 'it can't be done'.

In other words, he had been careful to co-opt middle management in the process of seeking a solution. But he had done more. He had earlier built a climate in which it was possible for the evidence to be credible and become a force for action. He had set the target but he had not imposed a solution. As he added, 'The solution we finally adopted went far beyond what I had originally in mind.'

Perhaps even more importantly, he had reduced the personal risks to acceptable proportions for all involved. In another company we heard, 'You don't get fired for making mistakes; not learning from them is a sin.' Even when individuals fall by the wayside, the climate of progress can be retained. One chief executive commented, 'My dilemma is that too many of the team have fixed "achievement ceilings". We have to find homes for these people somewhere in the firm, for I do not believe in hire-and-fire.'

Such approaches place a high premium on frank and honest communications. The necessary climate for progress cannot be created when managers obfuscate. All too often, 'managers who are skilled communicators may also be good at covering up real problems'. Defensive routines and perhaps reluctance to risk personal friendships that grew up during earlier, less stressful periods can undermine the drive for progress and continuous change.

Learning organisations have to confront the persistent problem that many middle managers feel their status rests heavily on their power to tell others what to do. This is especially so in large organisations with long traditions of powerful specialist functions, such as engineering. Comfortable in a world of specific plans and actions, managers can find it acutely uncomfortable to ask themselves or their juniors to think through what the goals ought to be. This problem has been tackled head-on in Exxon Chemicals. Though progress has been rated as 'painfully slow', one corporate vice-president stated:

We're steadily improving performance. What we have done...is to drop plan reviews at the company level and replace them with strategy discussions. After all, if the top of the organisation isn't thinking in strategic terms, who is?...When objectives and strategies are clear and understood, planning is no problem and the reviews of plans at lower levels assume a different and more positive character.

Source: Baden-Fuller, C and Stopford, J (1992). Reprinted with permission from International Thomson Publishing Services Limited. Copyright © Charles Baden-Fuller and John Stopford 1992.

◼ Summary

● In the management of strategic change, a distinction needs to be made between the *pace of change*, which can be fast or slow, and *strategic change*, which is the proactive management of change in an organisation. Strategic change is the implementation of new strategies that involve substantive changes beyond the normal routines of the organisation.

● In managing strategic change, it is useful to draw a distinction between prescriptive and emergent approaches. Prescriptive approaches involve the planned action necessary to achieve the changes. The changes may be imposed on those who will implement them. Emergent approaches involve the whole process of developing the strategy, as well as the implementation phase. This approach will also involve consultation and discussion with those who will subsequently be implementing the change.

● Strategic change is concerned with people and their tasks. It is undertaken through the formal and informal structures of the organisation. Understanding the *pressure points* for influencing change is important if such change is to be effective. Strategic change is important because it may involve major disruption and people may resist its consequences. Even where change is readily accepted, the changes will take time and careful thought. Strategic change carries important hidden costs.

● To manage strategic change, it is important to understand what is driving the process. There are numerous classifications of the causes, two of which are explored in this text, those of Tichy and Kanter, Stein and Jick.

1 Tichy identifies four main causes of strategic change: environment, business relationships, technology and new entrants to the organisation, especially a new leader.

2 Kanter, Stein and Jick identify three dynamics for strategic change: environment, life cycle differences across divisions of an organisation and political power changes. Precision regarding the causes of change is important in order to manage the change process effectively.

● There are a number of *prescriptive routes* for the management of change, two of which are examined.

1 Kanter, Stein and Jick recommend a three-stage approach involving three *forms* of change and three *categories of people* involved in the change. Essentially, the route is a top-down guide to managing planned change and its consequences throughout the organisation.

2 Lewin developed a three-stage model for the prescriptive change process: unfreezing current attitudes, moving to a new level and refreezing attitudes at the new level. This model has been widely used to analyse and manage change.

● *Prescriptive models* of change work best where it is possible to move clearly from one state to another: in times of rapid change, such clarity may be difficult to find and such models may be inappropriate.

● There are a number of *emergent* approaches to strategic change. The two explored in this chapter concentrate on the longer-term, learning culture routes to change. According to Senge, the learning organisation does not suddenly adopt strategic change but is perpetually seeking it. Therefore, the organisation is using its learning, experimentation and communication to renew itself constantly. Strategic change is a constant process.

● According to Pettigrew and Whipp, their empirical study of strategic change identified five factors in the successful management of the process. These were environmental assessment; leadership of change; the link between strategic and operational change; human resource aspects; and coherence in the management of the process. Emergent models of strategic change take a long-term approach and may have limited usefulness when the organisation faces a short-term strategic crisis.

● The choice between prescriptive and emergent strategic change processes will depend on the situation at the time: ideally, emergent change should be chosen because it is less disruptive and cheaper. In reality, circumstances may make a prescriptive approach necessary.

● In developing a change programme, the *change options matrix* sets out the main areas where change is possible: it is important to focus and select options from the matrix. This can best be undertaken by an understanding of the culture of the organisation: the *Cultural Web* can be useful here.

● A more detailed process to achieve change can then be planned out, with six overlapping areas as a starting point. Resistance to change is probably one of the chief obstacles to successful strategy implementation. It is likely to be lower if strategies are not imposed from the outside.

● The politics of strategic change first require the persuasion of those involved to adopt the new strategy recommendations. Additionally, a Machiavellian approach may be necessary to ensure the desired changes are achieved. More generally, strategic change activities may include identifying supporters, attempting to change opposition views and building the maximum consensus for the new proposals. Preferably, this should be undertaken prior to any decision meeting.

QUESTIONS

1 How would you characterise the strategic changes at the four companies in this chapter – fast or slow? How would you describe their strategic management process – as prescriptive or emergent?

2 '*The twin tasks for senior executives are to challenge misconceptions among managers and to foster a working environment which facilitates rather than constrains change.*' (Professor Colin Egan)

Discuss.

3 Identify the pressure points for influencing strategic change in an organisation with which you are familiar.

4 If strategic change is important, why do some people find it difficult to accept and what are the consequences of this for the change process? How can these difficulties be overcome?

5 '*The sad fact is that, almost universally, organisations change as little as they must, rather than as much as they should.*' (Professor Rosabeth Moss Kanter)

Why is this and what can be done about it?

6 Given the problems associated with prescriptive change, why is it important and what can be done to ease the process?

7 Does the comment in this chapter that the way forward proposed by some emergent strategists often amounts to the need to start earlier mean that emergent approaches have little useful role?

8 Examining United Biscuits in July 1995 (*see* Case study 21.3), use the change options matrix to determine what areas of change were available. What areas would you select to enact the proposed changes and why?

9 Analyse the politics of an organisation with which you are familiar. If you were seeking significant strategic change in the organisation, how would you approach this?

10 Leadership may be important for strategic change, but is it essential?

STRATEGIC PROJECT

Follow up one or more of the cases of strategic change outlined in this chapter. What has happened since and with what results? Has there been any fundamental change in the management and its style?

FURTHER READING

Bernard Burnes (1996) *Managing Change*, 2nd edn, Pitman Publishing, London, has a most useful broad survey of the areas covered in this chapter.

Professor Charles Handy (1993) *Understanding Organisations*, Penguin, Harmondsworth, is still one of the best available reviews of organisational change.

Kanter, R M, Stein, B and Jick, T (1992) *The Challenge of Organisational Change: How Companies Experience it and Leaders Guide it*, The Free Press, New York, has some thoughtful guidance on strategic change.

A most useful article is that by Garvin, D (1993) 'Building a learning organisation', *Harvard Business Review*, July–Aug, pp78–91.

Professors A Pettigrew and R Whipp (1991) *Managing Change for Competitive Success*, Blackwell, Oxford, has some important strategic evidence and insights.

NOTES & REFERENCES

1 Schein, E H (1990) *Organisational Psychology*, 2nd edn, Prentice Hall, New York.

2 Burnes, B (1996) *Managing Change*, 2nd edn, Pitman Publishing, London. Part 1 of this book presents a useful broad survey of this area.

3 Handy, C (1993) *Understanding Organisations*, Penguin, Harmondsworth, p292 (see Chapter 7 for further discussion of Handy and note that his view is emergent rather than prescriptive).

4 Burnes, B (1996) Op. cit., p173.

5 Ansoff, I (1987) *Corporate Strategy*, 2nd edn, Penguin, Harmondsworth.

6 Tichy, N (1983) *Managing Strategic Change*, Wiley, New York, pp18–19.

7 Kanter, R M, Stein, B, Jick, T (1992) *The Challenge of Organizational Change: How Companies Experience it and Leaders Guide it*, The Free Press, New York.

8 Adapted from an article by Clare Gascoigne (1996) *Financial Times*, 23 Feb, p23.

9 Kanter, R M, Stein, B and Jick, T (1992) Op. cit.

10 *Financial Times* (1996) 24 Apr, p1.

11 *Financial Times* (1993) 1 Nov, p19; 6 Dec, p17.

12 Lewin, K (1952) *Field Theory in Social Science*, Tavistock, London.

13 Burnes, B (1996) Op. cit., pp179–86 has a useful summary.

14 References for UB case: UB press release dated 3 Feb 1995, *Financial Times*: 22 Nov 1995, p30; 7 Nov 1995, p21; 15 Sept 1995, p18; 19 July 1995, p17; 18 July 1995, pp1, 20; 23 June 1995, p20; 25 Feb 1995, p8; 18 Mar 1994, p21; 16 Feb 1993, p23; 28 Jan 1993, p23; 16 August 1999, p18; 10 September 1999, p33; 6 October 1999, p30; 9 October 1999, p18.

15 For other writers and a wider review of the research, see Burnes, B (1996) Op. cit., pp161–3.

16 Senge, P (1990) *The Fifth Discipline: the Art and Practice of the Learning Organization*, Doubleday, New York.

17 Jones, A and Hendry, C (1994) 'The learning organisation', *British Journal of Management*, 5, pp153–62. Egan, C (1995) *Creating Organizational Advantage*, Butterworth–Heinemann, Oxford, pp131–8, also has a useful critical discussion.

18 Egan, C (1995) Ibid, p135.

19 Garvin, D (1993) 'Building a learning organization', *Harvard Business Review*, July–Aug, pp78–91.

20 Pettigrew, A and Whipp, R (1991) *Managing Change for Competitive Success*, Blackwell, Oxford.

21 Egan, C (1995) Op. cit., p178.

22 *See*, for example, Handy, C (1993) Op. cit., Ch4.

23 Burns, B (1996) Op. cit., pp194–5.

24 Pettigrew, A and Whipp, R (1991) Op. cit., p237.

25 Whittington, R (1993) *What is Strategy and Does it Matter?*, Routledge, London, p30.

26 Tichy, N (1983) Op. cit., pp126, 135, 131.

27 Beer, M, Eisenhart, R and Spector, B (1990) 'Why change management programs don't produce change', *Harvard Business Review*, Nov–Dec, pp158–66.

28 Machiavelli, N (1961) *The Prince*, Penguin, Harmondsworth. There is a short article that summarises his work: Crainer, S (1994) *Financial Times*.

29 There are four sources for this table: Machiavelli, N (1961) Op. cit.; Mintzberg, H (1991) 'Politics and the political organisation', Ch8 in Mintzberg, H and Quinn, J B (1991) *The Strategy Process*, 2nd edn, Prentice Hall, New York; Handy, C (1993) Op. cit., Ch10; and the author's own experience.

30 Baden-Fuller, C and Stopford, J (1992) *Rejuvenating the Mature Business*, Routledge, London, pp186–8.

Building a cohesive corporate strategy

When you have worked through this chapter, you will be able to:

● explain how emergent and prescriptive approaches are part of one cohesive strategy process;

● understand how the organisation's various elements can combine to form the organisation's corporate strategy;

● evaluate critically whether there is one standard of excellence for all corporate strategy situations;

● examine the contention that contradictions and tensions assist the corporate strategy process;

● focus on longer-term strategy issues including purpose, value added and sustainable competitive advantage.

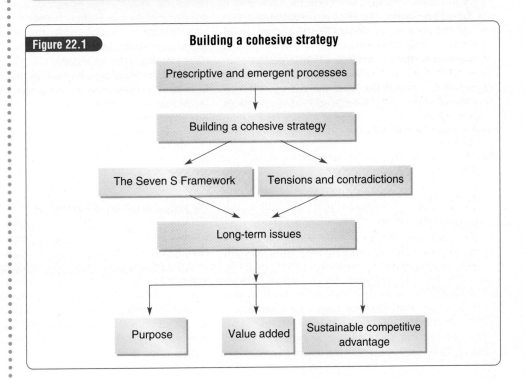

Figure 22.1

Building a cohesive strategy

▬ Introduction

Although corporate strategy has been explored as a series of separate elements – such as the resource-based view of strategy development and the consideration of learning-based strategy routes – the topic needs also to be considered as a whole. The purpose of this chapter is to bring these elements together in order to build a cohesive strategy.

One of the key distinctions running through the text has been that of prescriptive and emergent strategic processes: we need to explore whether these two areas can be combined.

One way of bringing the various strategy elements together is the *Seven S Framework*. This will lead us to consider the contention of some strategists that there is standard of excellence – 'one best way' – to develop and implement corporate strategy: this deserves critical evaluation. Finally, there is a need to focus on some longer-term strategic issues such as purpose, value added and sustainable competitive advantage. The structure of the chapter is summarised in Figure 22.1.

CASE STUDY 22.1

Next steps for Novartis

In March 1996, two major Swiss companies, Ciba and Sandoz, agreed to merge their worldwide operations under the new company name Novartis. The immediate merger was successful but the company then faced the challenge of developing the next stage of its strategy.

Background

With 1995 sales of US$26 billion, Ciba was a medium-sized competitor in the global markets for pharmaceuticals and agricultural chemicals. In the same year, Sandoz had sales of US$18 billion and was more heavily involved in pharmaceutical markets with a range of products that complemented those of Ciba. Together, after the merger, the two companies formed the world's second-largest drugs company, with a market share of 4.4 per cent: at the time, only Glaxo Wellcome was larger, at 4.7 per cent. Subsequently, other mergers have taken place and Novartis has dropped down the list to number six, with a 3.9 per cent share. Both Ciba and Sandoz also had non-drug businesses that were subsequently demerged so that Novartis became essentially a drug and agribusiness company.

In their merger, the two companies were following recent trends in the pharmaceutical industry, which had seen some global consolidations over the previous five years: for example, Smith Kline (US) with Beecham (UK), Glaxo (UK) with Wellcome (UK) and subsequently SmithKleinBeecham – *see* Chapter 6 – and Pharmacia (Sweden) with Upjohn (US). The strategy was to build size in order to spread heavy R&D costs and marketing expenditures across a wider range of products. It was also to counter the increasing negotiating power of distributors and government health bodies. However, some leading industrialists disagreed with this approach and regarded dominance in specific drugs and critical mass as being more important.

Not all previous mergers had been successful: the GlaxoSmithKline merger went smoothly at the second attempt, but the Pharmacia Upjohn merger was generally regarded as a disaster because the organisational cultures of the two companies were so different and there was no dominant partner to put its stamp on the other.

The merger operation at Novartis

The newly merged company was located, like its two parents, in the Swiss city of Basle. Some 10 000 jobs were lost out of a combined workforce of 130 000 over the following two years. These occurred mainly in Basle but also in New Jersey, where both companies had their US headquarters. The restructuring cost around US$2.5 billion but was expected eventually to save US$2.2 billion annually. In subsequent years, this proved to be the case, with significant savings being made.

Ciba and Sandoz arranged the deal through an exchange of shares and so avoided the need to raise heavy debt to finance the merger. They then faced the problem of making the deal work in human terms. Although they were both Swiss companies headquartered in the same city, their backgrounds were very different. Sandoz was the faster-growing of the two, with a greater product concentration in drugs. Ciba had slower sales growth and had a stronger portfolio in some lower-growth chemical products. In the past, the two companies had not been direct competitors but they had been rivals in terms of culture and local civic pride.

However, the merger turned out to be a success. According to the chief executive of the new Novartis, Dr Daniel Vasella, the secret was speed and focus. Negotiations took place swiftly and quietly in 'shabby hotels' so that even the company's chief pharmaceutical Swiss competitor, Roche, was left wondering how the deal was completed. 'We knew the deal would fall apart if there were market rumours,' said Dr Vasella. So the two companies went ahead and sorted out every major detail before making an announcement. They were fortunate because they were able to agree on what is often the real problem area: the purpose and objectives of the newly merged venture. 'There was total agreement achieved during the merger on common objectives

and common strategies. If you had to start to battle at a later stage, it becomes extremely difficult.'

The new strategic task: growth

After the immediate period of the merger, sales held up strongly in the new company. But in subsequent years, there have been problems. The company needs new drugs to reinvigorate its portfolio of products. It is investing around Sfr 2.3 billion (US$1.6 billion) each year in research and development, which is amongst the largest budgets in the pharmaceutical industry. The company had a wide range of drug products but no real blockbuster that would set it apart for some years. For example, the company launched five new medicines in February 2001, but some did not live up to expectations. However, further drug approvals were gained in August 2001 so that the double-digit sales growth was still possible for at least another year.

Organisation and purpose

According to Dr Vasella, there is another important aspect to growth: organisation and purpose. He believes that drug companies conducting research in a number of countries and subsidiaries often lack the knowledge-sharing necessary for the new breakthrough. A small advance in one subsidiary might be

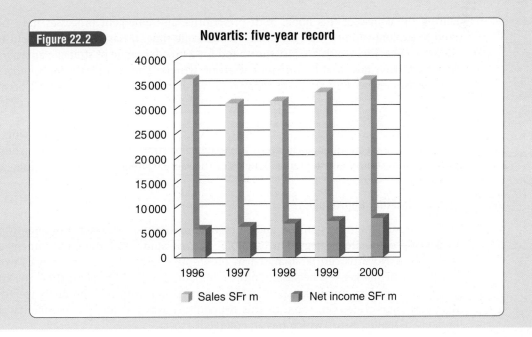

Figure 22.2

Novartis: five-year record

Sales SFr m   Net income SFr m

ignored by that company. Yet, if the same development was shared around the group, it might represent the final element in a major drug development for another part of the company. 'That is why I hate fiefdoms,' says Dr Vasella. 'They are extremely bad for companies like ours. With decentralisation and strong local managers, there is always that danger...and there are small pockets of resistance.' However, this approach to central co-operation and knowledge sharing has upset some senior managers who feel that there may be too much centralisation: 'He's sometimes a bit too controlling,' commented one of his boardroom colleagues.

Dr Vasella responded by pointing to the importance of developing the purpose of Novartis. 'Being a good manager is to formulate a purpose of the company, to picture a future [that] people can imagine and embrace.' He saw purpose not only in sales and profit terms but also as a means of communicating the good things about working for the new company. But that still left him and his colleagues with the task of developing a viable strategy that would go beyond the immediate cost savings of the merged company. He needed to develop a growth strategy.

Note: The case of Novartis's Swiss competitor, Roche, is considered later in this chapter.

Source: See reference 1.

Case questions

1 *Dr Vasella defined the company's purpose in a way that went beyond the delivery of profits. Do you agree with this approach? Or are profits the most important element by far?*

2 *He also saw the way that the company was organised as being at the core of the company's new strategy. Are there any problems with this approach? And, if so, are there any solutions?*

3 *Will a strong R&D programme be enough to provide growth? Or does the company need to consider other aspects of strategy like knowledge, the resource-based view and learning-based strategy development? If so, how?*

4 *Can other companies learn from the experience of Novartis in the search for growth?*

22.1 Cohesion in prescriptive and emergent processes

During the course of this book, both prescriptive and emergent processes have been used to explore various strategic issues. At the same time, it has been pointed out that these two headline words are just shorthand for a broader range of strategic approaches that have been favoured by different strategic writers. The two particular approaches were identified because they are representative of those broader routes and because they provided a convenient contrast in the treatment of the issues of strategic content, process and context.

Having reached this stage in the text, it is now appropriate to consider whether there really are a number of different approaches to strategy development or whether they would be better considered as aspects of the same strategic development task.

22.1.1 Two contrasting approaches?

In Parts 2 and 3 both prescriptive and emergent approaches were used at different times to develop corporate strategy. For example, in Case study 22.1 the environment and resources at Novartis can be analysed in prescriptive terms – such an analysis would show that the market was becoming more competitive and, at the same time, the company was forced to invest substantial funds on research into new products to attract new customers. However, some of this expenditure was inevitably experimental and unlikely to be successful, which has an emergent aspect.

In Part 4, the purpose of the organisation included prescriptive elements – such as the definition of the mission and objectives – and emergent elements such as the exploration of knowledge and innovation. This contrast can be seen in a company like Novartis, which chose not only to define its purpose in terms of profit but also to acknowledge other aspects of the purpose that involved sharing knowledge amongst its subsidiaries.

In Part 5, the process of developing strategy first considered the prescriptive route of options and choice and then considered the emergent process in Chapters 15 and 16. Part 6 has used both approaches, where appropriate. Thus at Novartis, it was possible to identify the prescriptive solutions that were used for the cost-cutting task essential to gain the benefits of the merger. However, it was also possible to identify broader, emergent strategies related to new drug developments that were also being pursued and were more experimental in their results.

In strategic terms, it is possible to develop prescriptive and emergent approaches to strategy development. While acknowledging the reality of a broader range of strategic routes, this book has chosen to concentrate on these two generic approaches as a device to explore the main issues. This is useful in highlighting various important issues that arise in the development of strategy, especially those contrasting the analytical – *prescriptive* – with the more entrepreneurial – *emergent*.

22.1.2 Better combined: one approach with a number of facets

Some strategists might recommend that corporate strategy concentrates on one approach rather than another: many strategy texts only explore one route – the prescriptive – in any depth. However, this book has demonstrated that an eclectic approach is more productive. Both prescriptive and emergent routes have their contributions to make: one is logical and follows from the evidence of markets, financial criteria and specific targets; the other is more creative, open-ended and experimental. In many respects, these two routes reflect the modern trend in scientific development to consider both rational and post-modern approaches.

To concentrate on just one approach would be to miss important elements of the other. This book takes the view that there is one corporate strategy process but it has *at least* two facets: prescriptive and emergent.

In reality, strategic content, process and context have a number of facets: knowledge-based, learning-based, negotiation-based and so on – *see* Chapters 14 and 15 for some of the routes. In essence, the development of corporate strategy is better aided by combining the various strategic processes, rather than concentrating on one of them.

▶ Key strategic principles

- Although prescriptive and emergent processes have been one of the themes of this text, they have been used as shorthand for a number of approaches to strategy development.

- It is possible to analyse many strategic tasks from prescriptive and emergent perspectives. This is useful in highlighting various important issues that arise in the development of strategy, especially those contrasting the analytical with the entrepreneurial.

> **Key strategic principles continued**
>
> ● This book has demonstrated that an eclectic approach is preferable. The combination of a number of strategic approaches allows different aspects of the strategic problem to be explored.
>
> ● The strategic process has a number of facets which go beyond prescriptive and emergent approaches. All of them provide insights and guidance in the development of corporate strategy.

22.2 Combining the elements of corporate strategy: the 'Seven S Framework'

One way of building a cohesive strategy is to use the 'Seven S Framework'. This is explored in the early parts of this section. The concept led to the proposition that there was 'one best way' of developing corporate strategy. Such an approach deserves to be evaluated critically. Finally, an alternative to the 'Seven S Framework' is explored; this examines the contradictions in strategy development and attempts to bring them together. Again, this approach to cohesive strategy deserves to be examined critically.

22.2.1 Background

Back in the 1970s, the well-known US consultancy company Boston Consulting Group was highly successful with its launch of the product portfolio matrix of problem children, cash cows, dogs and stars. One of its chief rivals, McKinsey & Co, charged four of its consultants with the task of finding a rival model to analyse organisations. The result was the *Seven S Framework*. The four consultants were Richard Pascale and Tony Athos (who published the diagram in their book *The Art of Japanese Management*), and Tom Peters and Bob Waterman (who published the same diagram in their book *In Search of Excellence*).[2]

The purpose of the model was to show the *interrelationships* between different aspects of corporate strategy. It was developed out of a realisation that the effective corporate strategy was more than merely a group of analytical tools, organisation structures and strategies: this is the disadvantage of the dissecting approach that has been adopted throughout this book. The elements need to be brought together. For example, the way that Novartis is now being combined into one company will involve a large number of elements, all of which are important in themselves but together will forge a totally new company.

22.2.2 The 'Seven S Framework'

The framework has no obvious starting point: *all the elements are equally important.* Moreover, all the elements are interconnected, so that altering one element may well impact on others. Fundamentally, the framework makes the point that effective strategy is more than individual subjects such as strategy development or organisational change – it is the relationship between strategy, structure and systems, coupled with skills, style, staff and superordinate goals.[3]

● *Strategy* – the route that the company has chosen to achieve competitive success (*see* Chapters 14 and 15).

- *Structure* – the organisational structure of the company (*see* Chapters 16 and 18).
- *Systems* – the procedures that make the organisation work: everything from capital budgeting to customer handling (*see* Chapter 17).
- *Style* – the way the company conducts its business, epitomised especially by those at the top (*see* Chapters 10 and 16).
- *Staff* – the pool of people who need to be developed, challenged and encouraged (*see* Chapters 7 and 18).
- *Skills* – not just the collection of skills that the organisation has but the particular combinations that help it to excel. The resource-based view was a concept invented after the framework but may at least partially capture the special nature of skills (*see* Chapters 6 and 13).
- *Superordinate goals*. This means goals 'of a higher order' and expresses the values, concepts and vision that senior management brings to the organisation (*see* Chapters 10, 11 and 12).

The framework is shown in Figure 22.3.

As a minimum, the framework provides a checklist of important variables for evaluation of proposed strategy developments. More fundamentally, it provides a structure for the network of interrelationships that exist between the various elements, especially when an organisation is ensuring that they are all *coherent* during the strategy process. For example, its application to the Novartis merger would show the many varied links that need to be developed in the new combined organisation.

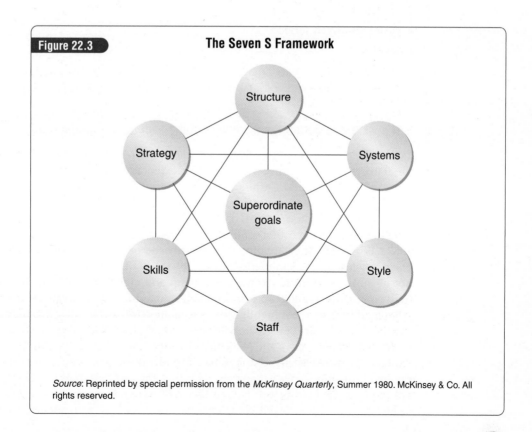

| Figure 22.3 | **The Seven S Framework** |

Source: Reprinted by special permission from the *McKinsey Quarterly*, Summer 1980. McKinsey & Co. All rights reserved.

A particularly useful distinction is drawn by the developers of the framework between its *hard* elements – strategy, structure and systems – and its *soft* elements – style, skills, staff and superordinate goals. The hard elements are more tangible and definite, and so they are often the ones that gain the greater attention, even in some books. However, the soft elements are equally important, even if they are less easy to measure, assess and plan. The comments of some Novartis workers on not wishing to wait and see if they had jobs in the new, merged company is a good example of soft issues at work: certainly Novartis fully accepted that the way the company treated its workers was just as important as its merger strategy.

Comment

The framework provides a way of examining the organisation and what contributes to its success. It is good at capturing the importance of the *links between the various elements* and, for this reason, it appears at this point in the text. However, Peters and Waterman used it only as the *starting point* for their search for more detailed interconnections. The framework shows that relationships exist and it provides some limited clues as to what constitutes more effective strategy and implementation. Beyond this, however, it is not precise: for example, *strategy* is just that and nothing more. Essentially, the framework says little about the *how* and the *why* of interrelationships. The model is therefore weak in explaining the logic and the methodology in developing the links between the elements.

Moreover, the model does not highlight or emphasise other areas that have subsequently been identified as being important for corporate strategy, such as:

- innovation;
- knowledge;
- customer-driven service;
- quality.

At least three of the four originators of the framework were not entirely satisfied with its usefulness and decided to develop it further, addressing its weaknesses.

22.2.3 Is it possible to define the attributes of the excellent organisation?

Two of the developers of the 'Seven S Framework', Tom Peters and Bob Waterman, used the framework as a starting point for their exploration of the lessons to be learnt from the US's best companies. During the late 1970s and early 1980s, they interviewed many senior executives in 43 major US companies on the reasons behind their success. They also tracked the history of the companies for the previous 25 years. The conclusions were presented in their best-selling book *In Search of Excellence*, which was published in 1982.[4] Essentially, they attempted to identify the best US practice of strategy in action. Their conclusions are summarised in Exhibit 22.1, although it should be noted that it is not possible to do justice to the enthusiasm and vigour with which the authors made their comments. Exhibit 22.1 also includes three further observations from Peters and Waterman that were not highlighted as separate attributes in their list: they are included here because they are consistent with other conclusions reached throughout this text.

Without doubt, Peters and Waterman took the view that it *was* possible to define the attributes of the excellent organisation. They identified eight attributes that characterised the excellent, innovative companies. 'Most of the attributes are not startling. Some, if not most, are motherhoods.'[5] Not all the eight were present or conspicuous to the same degree in all of the excellent companies, but in every case a preponderance was present.

The authors noted that, when they presented the material to students who had no business experience, the response was occasionally boredom[6] because students felt that some of the conclusions were self-evident. In such cases, the authors pointed out that their empirical evidence showed that many US companies *did not follow* such 'self-evident' best practice.

Comment

Unfortunately, as Tom Peters himself pointed out in 1992,[7] many of the excellent companies described in this book, *In Search of Excellence*, went through major strategic difficulties during the 1980s. For example, the original sample included extensive and enthusiastic endorsement of IBM's strategies: Chapter 1 showed what happened to that company in the 1980s and 1990s. The overall result has been to cast doubt on the evidence and conclusions of the original research. This has not stopped Mr Peters pursuing some of the major conclusions in his later research and writings. He remains one of the major *gurus* of the early twenty-first century (*see* the Key Reading later in this chapter). Essentially, he has focused even more on empowerment, innovation and the use of local initiatives rather than central direction in strategy.

Exhibit 22.1   **Qualities of excellent companies: Peters and Waterman**

- *Operate on loose–tight principles.* The best companies were both tightly controlled from the centre and yet, at the same time, encouraged entrepreneurship.

- *Incline towards taking action.* There may be analysis, but there is always a bias towards practical and fast solutions where possible.

- *Close to the customer.* The best companies offered customers quality, reliability and service.

- *Innovative autonomy.* Responsibility is moved to individuals, who are encouraged to be as innovative as possible.

- *Simplicity of organisational form.* Organisation structures work better when they are clear and simple and have well-defined lines of authority and responsibility. Matrix management structures were not to be encouraged because they were too complex. When organisations were organised simply, they were more able to combine quickly into effective teams, task forces and project groups.

- *The importance of the people resource, not just as an abstract concept but as individuals to be respected.* The better companies not only made tough demands on employees but also treated them as individuals to be trained, developed and given new and interesting challenges.

- *Clarity regarding the organisation's values and mission.* In the best companies, many employees were clear both about the company's values and about why such values had been chosen. Better companies made a significant attempt to communicate, debate and seek to inspire all within the organisation.

- *Stick to the knitting.* Organisations may diversify into other related areas but the companies that do best are the ones that concentrate on their core skills. Companies should not move into unrelated areas.

  In addition, three other elements of excellent companies can be identified from the Peters and Waterman research that are consistent with other areas of this book:

- *Excellent companies have flexible organisation structures.* This flexibility enables them to respond quickly to changes in the environment.

- *Excellent companies have quite distinctive cultures.* The company culture integrates the organisation's desire to meet its defined mission and objectives with two other important areas: serving customers and providing satisfying work for its employees.

- *Successful strategy emerges through purposeful, but essentially unpredictable, evolution.* Excellent companies are learning organisations that adapt their strategy as the environment changes through experimentation, challenge and permitting failure.

Source: See reference 8.

One of Peters' original co-developers of the 'Seven S Framework', Richard Pascale,[9] pointed out that, within five years of publication, two-thirds of the 'excellent' companies had slipped from their pinnacle, with some in serious trouble, e.g. Atari Computers and Wang Office Systems. He also criticised the *methodology* of the research:

Simply identifying attributes of success is like identifying attributes of people in excellent health during the age of the bubonic plague... The true path to insight required a study of both the sick and the healthy.

Two issues arise from the above:

1 *How reliable are the conclusions of Peters and Waterman?* Pascale is correct: the methodology is flawed. However, the conclusions are not inconsistent with other areas covered in this book. For example, it was Lawrence and Lorsch who first produced empirical evidence of the *loose–tight* principle.[10] The conclusions are largely reliable because, as Peters and Waterman said, the recommendations are 'not startling'. In truth, they support some important areas of strategy development and perhaps oversimplify others. Moreover, their research is being assessed with hindsight. In fairness, it is easier to be wise after the events have taken place.

2 *Is it possible to identify universal recipes for excellence?* This is one of the essential questions that we have been exploring throughout this book. Much of strategy development is context-sensitive, resource-sensitive and environment-sensitive. At best, this makes it difficult to derive universal solutions such as *recipes for excellence*; at worst, it is most unlikely.

Importantly, the *excellence* research was widely praised in the 1980s. Part of the reason for its inclusion here is to encourage the reader to review *critically* new evidence and theories in strategy development. A number of corporate strategy texts claim to offer the universal recipe. We examine another in Section 22.2.4.

22.2.4 Building a cohesive strategy through contradictions and tensions

One of Peters' colleagues in the development of the 'Seven S Framework', Richard Pascale, worked independently of the others to produce his own insights in 1990 into the development of corporate strategy, *Managing on the Edge*. He reviewed the main areas of strategy research and development in a similar way to that of Chapter 2 of this book. He concluded that:

A common thread runs through almost all... organisational theories: each is predicated on seeking or maintaining order. Weber, Taylor and Chandler clearly belong to this school. The same is true of the writings of... Herbert Simon and the Hawthorne Experiments as reported by... Mayo. The contingency theorists, such as Lawrence and Lorsch, while acknowledging fluctuations in the environment, propose multiple strategies to retain coherence in the face of environmental uncertainty.

Readers will also recall the theory of Pettigrew and Whipp in Chapter 21 that laid great emphasis on *coherence*.

Pascale did not agree that organisations should seek stability. He argued that every organisation had inherent tensions and contradictions that needed to be recognised in the development of corporate strategy, especially where change was the main objective. Strategy must *contend* with these contradictions and not try to reduce them. Thus coherence or the maintenance of order was not always appropriate.

Pascale highlighted what he described as 'compelling and surprising' research from Miller and Friesen.[11] They had established from empirical research into 26 companies over a prolonged period that *significant* change occurs in *revolutionary* ways. It does not just evolve and there is no question of 'seeking or maintaining order'. There is a wall of inertia that naturally blocks important new strategic initiatives. Pascale concluded from this that the way to encourage major strategic change was to seek a major disturbance of the existing state in an organisation, i.e. to seek to destabilise it by *managing on the edge*. It takes 'a concerted frontal assault to break through the wall'.[12] He then proceeded to produce his own evidence to support this contention with a study of six major US companies: Ford, General Motors, General Electric, Citicorp, Hewlett-Packard and Honda, US.

Overall, Pascale concluded that strategy must *transcend* these difficulties and create opportunities with a *new vision* that will transform the organisation (*see* Chapter 10). Importantly, the outcome is not entirely predictable. There will always be uncertainties that have to be taken as they come. The management itself will have to change as it enacts its new strategies. It will have to learn, experiment and adapt along the way.

To manage strategic transformation, Pascale suggested that there were four factors that influenced stagnation and renewal in organisations: *fit, split, contend* and *transcend*. All four are summarised in Exhibit 22.2.

Exhibit 22.2   **Factors that drive strategic stagnation and renewal (Pascale)**

Fit – *the consistencies,coherence and congruence of the organisation.* Specifically, this is the fit between objectives, strategies and identified elements of change. For example, a strategy of increased customer service will not 'fit' if funds are withdrawn from the customer service department and reward systems are defined simply by short-term profits. This is similar to the concept of *coherence* explored in Chapter 21.

Split – *the variety of techniques that can be employed to develop and sustain the autonomy and diversity of large organisations.* An example would be setting up profit-accountable subsidiaries or profit centres. This concept includes both divisionalisation and the multifunctional task forces to encourage innovation, as described in Chapter 18.

Contend – *the constructive conflict that every organisation needs.* For example, conflict generated between different functional areas needs to be channelled productively, not suppressed. Resolution of such conflicts is an ongoing management task.

Transcend – *given the inevitable complexities of the above three areas, organisations need an approach to management that will cope with the difficulties.* This cannot be achieved by compromise but needs a totally different mindset (or paradigm) that copes with conflict and uses it to move the organisation forward.

Source: Adapted from Pascale, R (1990).[14]

Comment

Having criticised Peters and Waterman for the inadequacy of their research, Pascale then proceeded to base his main conclusions on a sample of six companies that are not representative of the whole of US industry. It is possible that a wider sample would have produced some different evidence on the strategy development process.

Pascale argued that a totally new mindset or paradigm is needed to cope with the inevitable complexities and tensions of strategy development. He described this as *transcending* the existing difficulties and opportunities. However, it might be argued that this recipe for transformation is vague and unconvincing in terms of its usefulness. He describes no tests, gives no clear guidance and develops a concept that is difficult to define clearly, let alone manage.

▶ Key strategic principles

- The 'Seven S Framework' can be used to bring the elements of strategy together. Each element is equally important and all need to be considered in the development of corporate strategy: strategy, structure, systems, style, staff, skills, superordinate goals. However, the model does little to explain the logic and the methodology of developing the links between the elements.

- Peters and Waterman used the 'Seven S Framework' as the basis for an empirical study on the attributes of the excellent US companies in the 1980s. They emerged with eight qualities, some of which were very basic and some more demanding. Included among the latter was an emphasis on innovation and on the devolution of power to individuals and groups.

- Pascale also used the 'Seven S Framework' when he investigated apparent tensions and conflicts between the various elements. His research established what he described as four factors that would drive stagnation or renewal in the strategic process: fit, split, contend and transcend.

- *Fit* relates to the coherence of strategy. *Split* describes the need to devolve responsibility in large organisations. More controversially, Pascale concluded that there would always be some tensions and contradictions in strategic development: he called this the *contend* factor. His research also suggested that the strategic challenge was to attempt to manage such difficulties: he called this the *transcend* factor. Some parts of the theory appear to suffer from a lack of operational usefulness.

22.3 Longer-term strategy issues

22.3.1 Implementation

As Chapter 1 pointed out, the separation in prescriptive strategy between analysis, options and choice and implementation is useful but does not really capture much of the ongoing strategy work that occupies organisations on a regular basis. Even where major upheaval occurs, such as the creation of Novartis, the success of the venture will depend on how it is implemented over a relatively short space of time. Such issues will remain part of the longer-term strategic task of the organisation.

In general terms, *milestones* and *controls* need to be set up to oversee implementation issues:

- *Milestones* are used to measure precisely what progress of the strategy towards a final implementation goal has been made at some intermediate point. They are important because it is only by assessing activity while it is still in progress that useful corrective actions can be taken.

- *Controls* are employed to ensure that financial, human resource and other guidelines are not breached during the implementation process. For example, they might include cash flow, cost expenditures against budget, training programme achievement, plant installation procedures and many other tasks. They differ from milestones in that they are more detailed, ongoing and function specific.

Some further guidelines on implementation issues are shown in Exhibit 22.3.

Exhibit 22.3   **Some key guidelines on strategy implementation and control**

Problems of successful implementation tend to focus on how well or badly the organisation's reporting proves to be.

Problems arise:

- where implementation cuts across traditional organisational units;
- when information monitoring is poor;
- when an organisation resists change;
- when rewards for performance are geared to past performance rather than future action.

For successful implementation:

- allocate clear responsibility and accountability;
- pursue a limited number of strategies;
- identify the required actions and gain agreement from those who will implement them;
- produce 'milestones' so that it is clear earlier rather than later if implementation is off-course;
- above all, secure the active support of the chief executive.

22.3.2 Re-examining the future environment

In developing a coherent strategy, organisations may take the view that it is useful to identify the main trends that are likely to affect them over the next few years. Both Novartis and other pharmaceutical companies have clearly found the need to re-examine the future pharmaceutical market as part of their development of strategy.

However, one of the most respected management writers, Peter Drucker, cautions against such predictions:

> *It is not very difficult to predict the future. It is only pointless. Many futurologists have high batting averages – the way they measure themselves and are commonly measured. They do a good job foretelling some things. But what are always far more important are fundamental changes that happened though no one predicted them or could possibly have predicted them.*[15]

In general, there are real problems with predicting the future. Yet there is no denying its importance. It has even been argued that strategy should attempt to shape the future.[16] Some emergent strategists believe the process of prediction to be largely a waste of time (*see* Chapter 2). Possibly a useful route forward for those who believe in prediction is to adopt the scenario-building approach of companies such as Royal Dutch/Shell (*see* Chapter 16). However, it will be recalled that part of the reasoning for scenario building was not *prediction* but rather *preparation* in the event of the unpredictable happening.

22.3.3 Re-examining the organisation and its purpose

As well as examining their environment, organisations will need to reconsider their vision, purpose and mission. Organisations rarely stand still: some grow fast like the producers of Xbox and other computer games. Some grow more slowly, such as major multinationals, unless they make a major strategic shift, like Novartis. Some decline for a whole variety of reasons. Some are changing beyond all recognition: the case of Novartis is an example.

The changes that take place raise fundamental questions about the purpose of the organisation. These were explored in Chapters 10 to 12 but deserve to be raised again here because they are part of the longer-term implementation programme, which becomes the *starting point* for the next round of corporate strategy. The four areas that deserve re-examination are:

1 *The purpose of the organisation.* Does it actually matter if we decline? How important is it that we achieve our stated growth targets? The answers to these questions will relate to the values of the organisation and those of its management, employees and shareholders.

2 *Sustainable competitive advantage.* How and where will we retain or develop this? What are the implications for the resources of the organisation?

3 *The culture and style of the organisation.* How do we undertake our work? What style do we wish to adopt? Again, these are fundamental questions that go beyond immediate implementation issues to the underlying philosophy of the business.

4 *The values and ethical standards.* What values do we hold? Why? How do we wish to conduct ourselves? How do we measure up to these ideals? As organisations move into the new millennium, some have questioned previously held views on sustaining the environment, equal treatment for minorities, political affiliations and so on. These are legitimate matters of corporate strategy and deserve to be revisited.

This book has argued in favour of customer-driven quality, innovation and the learning organisation. It has also simplified purpose down to value added and strategy down to the search for sustainable competitive advantage. Such considerations will not necessarily be appropriate for all organisations, but all will need to determine their long-term perspectives, whatever they are.

22.3.4 Conclusions on corporate strategy issues

Coupled with changes in the environment and in the organisation, new issues are constantly emerging in corporate strategy itself. The research papers, journals, books and magazines quoted throughout this book will provide guidance on the subjects that are currently under study[17] – the subjects that make corporate strategy dynamic, stimulating, controversial and relevant to our future.

Finally, it should not be forgotten that, in spite of all the corporate strategy attempts to guide and cope with the future, there are always the *unpredictable* elements that are beyond strategic theory, In the words of the German chemical company, Henkel, 'To succeed in business, you need skill, patience, money...and a bit of luck.'[18]

▶ Key strategic principles

- When implementing corporate strategy, it is useful to identify the tasks that need to be undertaken. These will include setting *milestones* to measure the progress along the way and setting up *controls* to ensure that overall guidelines on finance and other resources are not breached as the implementation proceeds.

- Many organisations attempt to re-examine the future environment. However, the most important elements may be difficult to predict. A useful route forward may be to adopt the scenario-building approach. Part of the reasoning for scenario building is not *prediction* but rather *preparation* in the event of the unpredictable happening.

- Organisations rarely stand still: it may also therefore be appropriate to re-examine the vision, purpose and mission of the organisation and also its culture and style. The values and ethical standards also deserve to be reappraised, along with an examination of stakeholder relationships.

- There will always be an element of chance in corporate strategy. Luck will make a contribution to the development of workable proposals.

CASE STUDY 22.2

Side-effects of age leave Roche reeling

When the 105-year-old Swiss pharmaceutical group discovered Novartis had bought one-fifth of its voting stock, it was one more on a growing list of problems that had seen the decline of a once great company.

Franz Humer replaced the handset slowly. The Roche chairman was still in a state of shock as he tried to make sense of what he had heard. Mr Humer, 54, had just taken a call from Daniel Vasella, his younger, more suave counterpart at Novartis, the drugs group that faces Roche across the Rhine in Basel, Switzerland. Mr Vasella had told him that Novartis – a company with a five-year history compared with Roche's 105-year one had just put the finishing touches to a transaction: buying one-fifth of Roche's voting shares. A chunk of Roche had somehow slipped into the hands of its arch-rival.

Mr Vasella's call could not have come at a worse time. Roche was in turmoil. Two of Mr Humer's senior lieutenants, including the head of the vital US operations, had quit. Fritz Gerber, whom

Mr Humer had replaced as chairman only days before, still loomed large – both as a board member and the spokesman for the Hoffmann families that controlled Roche. Mr Humer was having blazing rows with another senior executive, Anton Affentrager, his recently appointed finance director. Mr Affentrager was to be fired within a week. And that was the good news.

Deeper malaise

The personnel problems were symptomatic of a much deeper malaise. Martin Ebner, the Swiss corporate raider who sold his stake to Novartis, had been complaining for years about Roche's archaic share structure. Senior executives warned that the pharma (short for pharmaceutical) division lacked a clear

▶

strategy and that swift, decisive action was needed. In March 2001, Roche had released a dreadful set of results. Although diagnostics was performing well, the flagship pharmaceuticals division was a disaster. Sales of prescription drugs had fallen 2 per cent – quite a feat in an industry where double-digit growth was the norm. No fewer than three of Roche's biggest-selling drugs were nearly two decades old, rapidly nearing the end of their life. More alarming still, sales of Xenical, the slimming pill on which Mr Humer had staked much of his reputation, had stalled in only in its third year on the market.

At about the time of Mr Vasella's call, Mr Humer had been finalising a cost-cutting exercise that would see 3,000 pharma jobs go. Losses would be heavy in Roche's US subsidiary, where most drug companies were frantically expanding. But facts had to be faced. Roche was no longer the company of a mere five years earlier, when it was vying with Merck of the US for the industry's top slot – it had fallen to eleventh place. What had gone wrong? As with most corporate stories – especially in pharmaceuticals where it takes at least a decade to invent a medicine – there was a long- and a short-term answer.

Long-term strategic problems

Back in 1985, Roche faced a major problem: the 1985 patent expiry of Valium. This drug and its precursor, Librium, were the medicines that made Roche great. Librium was a sensation from the moment of its launch in the early 1960s as the drug that could tame lions and tigers. Valium quickly became the biggest-selling medicine of all time. As the patent expiry loomed, the company began to revamp its strategy, shedding non-core assets and regrouping into four divisions. In 1985, under its then celebrated R&D director Jurgen Drews, it started pouring billions into research towards the next block-buster. Fifteen years later, nothing – certainly nothing that remotely compared with Valium.

Instead, the company embarked on a decade-long acquisition spree that saw it buy, among other things, Genentech, a San Francisco-based biotechnology pioneer, and Syntex, another Californian start-up. In 1997, it splashed out a further US$10.2 billion for a diagnostics group, Boehringer Mannheim. Without these acquisitions, Roche's portfolio would be practically empty in 2001. But, astute as these deals were, the company was substituting for self-generated growth. 'Once you start going down the track of buying, maybe you lose your soul as a company,'

says a chief executive of a rival group. 'You just buy something, strip out the costs and then buy the next one. Ultimately, you run out of steam.'

Most of the acquisitions were engineered by Henri Meier, the brilliant finance director who had another means of compensating for the pharma division's shortcomings. He seemed to be able to produce cash from thin air. Under his stewardship, Roche made such fabulous returns that it became known as a bank with a pharma business attached – in 2000 for example, financial income was nearly 30 per cent of group profits.

One of the reasons Roche became so reliant on acquisition and financial conjuring tricks stemmed from its archaic share structure. This prevented it from participating fully in the consolidation that was transforming the industry in the 1990s. Founded by Fritz Hoffmann in 1896, the company was still controlled by his descendants, who had 50.1 per cent of the voting shares with only 10 per cent of the capital. Thus, while companies like Novartis were being formed by smaller rivals, Roche shareholders were reluctant to take part because they might lose control of the combined group.

Roche's short-term strategy in the late 1990s

Mr Humer had become chief executive in 1996. He had arrived in 1995 from Glaxo and had observed how such companies had grown fat by exploiting the primary care market: selling drugs for asthma, blood pressure and other chronic conditions to doctors directly. He decided that Roche needed to join this gravy train. Mr Humer's team scoured Roche's labs for drugs that could be turned into blockbusters. They found two.

One was Posicor, a molecule for high blood pressure intended as a specialist drug. The new Roche team thought it could become a medicine for medical general practice. The only problem, as some employees pointed out, was that Posicor could cause dangerous side-effects if taken with other medications. That was a big drawback for a mass-market drug and, sure enough, Posicor was withdrawn in June 1998 less than a year after launch.

The second possible blockbuster was Xenical. Mr Humer's team rescued the obesity pill after it had languished in the laboratory for several years. Obesity was a huge problem. Surely this was the drug on which to build Roche's future? After a few teething problems, Xenical was launched with great excitement in 1999, a few months after Viagra, Pfizer's impotence pill, had created a craze for life-style drugs. Xenical got off to a flying start, garnering sales of SF940 million in its first year. But then it stalled. The main problem was a side-effect delicately referred to as 'rectal leakage' by the company. People were trying Xenical for a few months and then giving up. In addition, Roche's marketing strategy was not clear. On the one hand, Roche said that Xenical should be positioned as a serious drug with real health benefits, not a casual slimming drug. On the other, it piled millions of dollars into a huge American TV campaign that played down the unpleasant side-effects.

Additional problems at Roche

As Xenical's problems were becoming clear, Roche was hit again. In May 1999, US trust-busters fined the Roche vitamins division a record US$500 million for organising a price-fixing cartel. A former Roche executive was jailed and the company took SF2.4 billion in charges to cover law suits. It was an episode unlikely to boost morale at a time when the pharma division was drifting. No fewer than nine drugs had fallen at the last hurdle – a failure rate that raised eyebrows throughout the industry. Given Xenical's disappointing performance, there were simply not enough new drugs to replace the

cash cows. That left Mr Humer with little option but to scale back costs – which he did in 2001.

But some fellow executives, including the departed Mr Affentrager, thought that more drastic action was needed. Any further move, such as an acquisition or even a merger, would almost certainly be tougher with the Novartis shareholding in place. Importantly, power ultimately rested with the secretive descendants of Fritz Hoffmann, Swiss billionaires who have stuck with Roche through 100 years of ups and downs. Mr Humer needed at all costs to retain their support.

Case adapted by Richard Lynch from an article by David Pilling, with additional reporting by William Hall, in the *Financial Times*, 1 June 2001, p25. © Copyright *Financial Times* 2001. Reproduced with permission.

Case questions

1 *What are the main strategic problems at Roche? How would you overcome them?*

2 *Is another acquisition the answer? Or do you accept the arguments of the commentator quoted in the case?*

3 *What lessons, if any, can other companies learn from Roche's difficulties?*

Tom Peters: performance artist

The first book by Tom Peters, co-written with Robert Waterman, became the original management blockbuster. *In Search of Excellence* sold 1 million copies on its first printing in 1982 and turned both of its authors into millionaires. Since then Mr Peters has become a fixture on the international lecture circuit, outlasting and outearning such shooting stars as Ronald Reagan and Oliver North. Every year thousands of middle managers gape in awe as Mr Peters, arms flailing, brow sweating, voice hoarse, urges them to nuke hierarchy and thrive on chaos.

Mr Peters's prominence is not an unmixed blessing for his profession. Many people only have to watch him on television or read one of his many newspaper columns (which cover everything from 'power walking' to Zen Buddhism) to have their prejudices about management theory redoubled.

How can a 51-year-old parade around like that? How can he litter his books with phrases like 'Yikes', 'Wow' and 'Ho Hum'? As if to taunt his critics, his 1994 book, *The Tom Peters Seminar: Crazy Times call for Crazy Organisations*, has a cover picture of him dressed in his underpants.

There is a lot more to Mr Peters than that. True, he has contradicted himself spectacularly over the past decade; but then the business world has changed spectacularly, too. True, he has a penchant for dashing off fairly flimsy newspaper columns; but he also wrote an admirably obscure doctoral thesis, and churns out heavyweight articles for the *California Management Review* and the like. True, he is willing to rant to get his point over; but he has persuaded more managers to reflect on what they are doing than almost anyone else alive.

In addition, even Mr Peters's detractors have to grant him two talents. The first is an intimate knowledge of corporate life around the world, in Europe and Asia as well as the United States. Having started his career as a consultant with McKinsey, he continues to inveigle his way into hundreds of companies. Mr Peters cannot book into a hotel or park his car without finding an interesting management angle.

The second talent is an unfailing nose for business trends. Mr Peters senses where the corporate world is heading, usually correctly, and then shouts it from the rooftops. He was one of the first people to predict the fashion for 'downsizing', sensing that global competition would force firms to reduce labour costs, and that information technology would allow them to get rid of layers of middle managers. His 800-page tome, *Liberation Management* (1992), may ramble – Mr Peters has not extended his passion for downsizing to his own prose – but it is also a well-illustrated guide to the latest management fads, such as 'the fashionisation of everything' (Sony invents a new variant on the Walkman once every three weeks) and 'necessary disorganisation' (Asea Brown Boveri has subdivided itself into 5000 largely independent profit centres).

Mr Peters has the knack of saying the right thing at the right time. *In Search of Excellence*, which appeared in the week that American unemployment rose to 10 per cent, its highest level since the Depression, appealed to an America worried about declining competitiveness but sick of being told about the Japanese miracle. Sounding the 'morning in America' theme before Ronald Reagan, the book insisted that America had its own models of excellence. Five years later, *Thriving on Chaos* appeared on Black Monday, as Wall Street fell 20 per cent: it articulated a widespread feeling that, in a world running out of control, businesses needed to reinvent themselves or die.

Add to his nose for the zeitgeist a genius for marketing – the Tom Peters Group churns out seminars, video cassettes and newsletters – and you begin to understand why Mr Peters is a multi-millionaire, with a house in Palo Alto, California, and a 1300-acre farm in Vermont, complete with cattle and llamas. But is he anything more than a shrewd trend-watcher with a talent for self-publicity?

Guru, guru on the wall

Two common criticisms are levelled at Mr Peters. One, which is hard to refute, is that he has often got it wrong: famously, two-thirds of the companies singled out as excellent in 1982 have now fallen from grace. Another is that he contradicts himself as frequently as the average politician. Having started his career genuflecting before big companies, he now preaches that small is beautiful. Having launched the 'excellence movement' with his first book, he opened his third book, *Thriving on Chaos*, with the flat assertion that 'Excellence isn't. There are no excellent companies.'

And yet, given such flagrant self-contradictions, there is a surprising amount of consistency in his work. Everything Mr Peters writes can be read as an extended critique of the ultra-rationalist school of management thinking, invented by Frederick Winslow Taylor (the father of stopwatch management) in the 1900s and embodied in the assembly line. Mr Peters learned to hate the rationalist model in the Pentagon, where he was posted for two years when he was a young naval officer, and at McKinsey, where he worked for eight years. He felt that it put too much emphasis on financial controls, too little on motivating workers or satisfying customers; that it worshipped size for its own sake; and that it rested on a simplistic reading of human nature.

It is as an antidote to all this that Mr Peters's intellectual contribution lies. For the past decade he has enjoyed the rare privilege of preaching from the heart and getting paid handsomely for it. The only thing he needed to do to sell more books was to get more radical. Lately, however, the corporate mood has started to change. Managers are wondering whether it has all gone too far: slimming, it seems, is turning into anorexia, delayering into disorganisation, anti-rationalism into insanity. Mr Peters may soon have to face a wrenching choice, between staying crazy and staying fashionable.

Source: ©*The Economist*, London, 24 Sept 1994. Reproduced with permission.

Question

Choose one of Tom Peters' books, such as Liberation Management *or* In Search of Excellence, *and critically appraise it. You should take into account that his books are targeted at practising managers rather than students.*

▄ Summary

- Although prescriptive and emergent processes have been one of the themes of this text, they have been used as shorthand for a number of approaches to strategy development. It is possible to analyse many strategic tasks from these two perspectives. However, this book has demonstrated that an eclectic approach is preferable. In reality, the strategic process has a number of facets which go beyond prescriptive and emergent approaches. All of them provide insights and guidance in the development of corporate strategy.

- The 'Seven S Framework' can be used to bring the elements of strategy together. Each element is equally important and all need to be considered in the development of corporate strategy: strategy, structure, systems, style, staff, skills and superordinate goals. However, the model does little to explain the logic and the methodology of developing the links between the elements.

- Peters and Waterman used the 'Seven S Framework' as the basis for an empirical study on the attributes of the excellent US companies in the 1980s. They emerged with eight qualities, some of which were very basic and some more demanding – the latter including an emphasis on innovation and on the devolution of power to individuals and groups.

- Pascale also used the 'Seven S Framework' when he investigated apparent tensions and conflicts between the various elements. His research established what he described as four factors that would drive stagnation or renewal in the strategic process: fit, split, contend and transcend. *Fit* relates to the coherence of strategy. *Split* describes the need to devolve responsibility in large organisations. More controversially, Pascale concluded that there would always be some tensions and contradictions in strategic development: he called this the *contend* factor. His research also suggested that the strategic challenge was to attempt to manage such difficulties: he called this the *transcend* factor.

- In implementing corporate strategy, it is useful to identify the immediate tasks that need to be undertaken: they will include setting *milestones* to measure the progress along the way and setting up *controls* to ensure that overall guidelines on finance and other resources are not breached as the implementation proceeds.

- Many organisations attempt to re-examine the future environment, but the most important elements may be difficult to predict. A useful route forward may be to adopt the scenario-building approach. However, part of the reasoning for scenario building is not *prediction* but rather *preparation* in the event of the unpredictable happening.

- Organisations rarely stand still: it may also, therefore, be appropriate to re-examine the vision, purpose and competitive advantages of the organisation and also its culture and style. The values and ethical standards also deserve to be reappraised, along with an examination of stakeholder relationships. There will always be an element of chance in corporate strategy. Luck will make a contribution to the development of workable proposals. Finally, it is the conclusion of this book that both prescriptive and emergent approaches should be used in the development of corporate strategy.

QUESTIONS

1 Use the 'Seven S Framework' to analyse the proposed changes at Novartis.

2 Is it possible to have excellent companies against which to compare performance?

3 What is your assessment of Pascale's theory of strategic change? Will there always be tension and is this intrinsic to change?

4 Examine a strategic decision with which you are familiar and use the various strategic processes explored in this

text – prescriptive, learning-based, knowledge, etc. – to plot the way the decision was derived and comment on the usefulness of each process.

5 This book has highlighted 'customer-driven quality, innovation and the learning mechanism' as being particularly important in the development of corporate strategy. Are there other areas that you would wish to select and, if so, what are they and why would you select them?

STRATEGIC PROJECT

Follow up the changes in the pharmaceutical industry. The cases in this chapter indicate the scope for strategic development. The *Corporate Strategy* website has an article with basic data on companies in the industry.

FURTHER READING

It is worth examining Peters, T and Waterman, R (1982) *In Search of Excellence*, Harper Collins, New York. The main argument was reprinted in De Wit, R and Meyer, B (1994) *Strategy: Process, Content and Context*, West Publishing, St Paul, MN, pp176–82. Any of Tom Peters' books is also worth examining. Try Peters, T (1992) *Liberation Management*, Macmillan, London.

Richard Pascale's book (1990) *Managing on the Edge*, Viking Penguin, London, is also worth exploring.

To look into the strategic future, it is certainly worth reading Hamel, G and Prahalad, C K (1994) 'Strategy as a field of study: why search for new paradigms?', *Strategic Management Journal*, Special Issue, 15, pp5–16. The 'Special Issue' of *Long Range Planning*, Apr 1996, also has a most interesting review of this area.

NOTES & REFERENCES

1 References for Novartis case: *Financial Times*, 8 Mar 1996, pp1, 17, 28; 19 Mar 1996, p25; 11 Apr 1996, p18 (Dr Håken Mogren's comments); 12 Oct 1998, p15; 16 July 1999, p27; 18 February 2000, p26; 11 July 2000, p34; 16 February 2001, p25; 8 May 2001, p19; 14 May 2001, p27; 22 August 2001, p20; 28 November 2001, p23; *See* also Lynch, R (1994) *European Business Strategies*, 2nd edn, Kogan Page, London, pp31–2, for an earlier exploration of global strategies in the drugs industry.

2 Handy, C (1993) *Understanding Organisations*, 4th edn, Penguin, Harmondsworth, p187. *See* also: Pascale, R and Athos, A (1982) *The Art of Japanese Management*, Allen Lane, London, and Peters, T and Waterman, R (1982) *In Search of Excellence*, HarperCollins, New York.

3 In the original publication by McKinsey & Co, the central 'S' was for 'Superordinate goals'. This was

later changed by Peters and Waterman to 'shared values', which they interpreted as meaning culture when they repeated the diagram in their book *In Search of Excellence*. This appears to have been not just a semantic change but to alter the fundamental meaning of the model. In the original publication, the authors coupled the word 'style' with culture and left 'superordinate goals' to mean the mission and purpose of the organisation. To avoid confusion, the original wording has been adopted in this book. *Original reference*: article reprinted in De Wit, R and Meyer, B (1994) *Strategy: Process, Content and Context*, West Publishing, St Paul MN, pp176–82. *Revised reference*: Peters, T and Waterman, R (1982) *In Search of Excellence*, HarperCollins, New York, p9.

4 Peters, T and Waterman, R (1982) Ibid.

5 Peters, T and Waterman, R (1982) Ibid, p16.

6 Peters, T and Waterman, R (1982) Ibid, p17.

7 Peters, T (1992) *Liberation Management*, Macmillan, London.

8 *Source*: Adapted by the author from Peters, T and Waterman, R (1982) Ibid, pp13–15. The last three areas have been summarised from pp308, 103 and 110 respectively.

9 Pascale, R (1990) *Managing on the Edge*, Viking Penguin, London, pp16, 17.

10 Lawrence, P R and Lorsch, J W (1967) *Organisation and Environment*, Harvard University Press, Cambridge, MA.

11 Miller, D and Friesen, P (1982) 'Structural change and performance: Quantum versus Piecemeal-incremental approaches', *Academy of Management Journal*, pp867–92. Quoted in Pascale, R (1990) Op. cit., pp113, 295.

12 Pascale, R (1990) Op. cit., p115.

13 Adapted by the author from Pascale, R (1990) Op. cit., Ch3.

14 Adapted by the author from Pascale, R (1990) Op. cit., p24.

15 Drucker, P (1995) *Managing in a Time of Great Change*, Butterworth–Heinemann, Oxford, pvii.

16 Whitehill, M (1996) 'Introduction to foresight: Exploring and creating the future', *Long Range Planning*, Apr, p146. This issue has a range of articles that tackle this subject from a number of perspectives, including those that believe it is a waste of time.

17 *See*, for example, Hamel, G and Prahalad, C K (1994) 'Strategy as a field of study: why search for new paradigms?', *Strategic Management Journal*, Special Issue, 15, pp5–16. *See* also *Long Range Planning*, Apr 1996.

18 Henkel, A G, *Annual Report and Accounts: 1987*.

Glossary

Added value The difference between the market value of the output and the cost of the inputs to the organisation.

Architecture The network of relationships and contracts both within and around the organisation.

Backward integration The process whereby an organisation acquires the activities of its inputs, e.g. manufacturer into raw material supplier.

Benchmarking The comparison of practice in other organisations in order to identify areas for improvement. Note that the comparison does *not* have to be with another organisation within the same industry, simply one whose practices are better at a particular *aspect* of the task or function.

Bounded rationality The principle that managers reduce tasks, including implementation, to a series of small steps, even though this may grossly over-simplify the situation and may not be the optimal way to proceed.

Branding The additional reassurance provided to the customer by the brand name and reputation beyond the intrinsic value of the assets purchased by the customer.

Break-even The point at which the total costs of undertaking a new strategy are equal to the total revenue from the strategy.

Bretton Woods Agreement System of largely fixed currency exchange rates between the leading industrialised nations of the world. In operation from 1944 to 1973.

Business ethics *See Ethics.*

Business process re-engineering The replacement of people in administrative tasks by technology, often accompanied by delayering and other organisational change.

Capability-based resources Covers the resources across the entire value chain and goes beyond key resources and core competencies.

Change options matrix This links the areas of human resource activity with the three main areas of strategic change: work, cultural and political change.

Changeability of the environment The degree to which the environment is likely to change.

Competitive advantage The *significant* advantages that an organisation has over its competitors. Such advantages allow the organisation to add more value than its competitors in the same market.

Competitor profiling Explores one or two leading competitors by analysing their resources, past performance, current products and strategies.

Complete competitive formula The business formula that offers both value for money to customers and competitive advantage against competitors.

Complementors The companies whose products add more value to the products of the base organisation than they would derive from their own products by themselves – for example, Microsoft software adds significantly to the value of a Hewlett-Packard Personal Computer.

Concentration ratio The degree to which value added or turnover is concentrated in the hands of a few firms in an industry. Measures the dominance of firms in an industry.

Contend The constructive conflict that some strategists argue is needed by every organisation.

Content of corporate strategy The main actions of the proposed strategy.

Context of corporate strategy The environment within which the strategy operates and is developed.

Contingency theory of leadership Argues that leaders should be promoted or recruited according to the needs of the organisation at a particular point in time. *See also Style theory* and *Trait theory.*

Controls Employed to ensure that strategic objectives are achieved and financial, human resource and other guidelines are not breached during the implementation process or the ongoing phase of strategic activity. The process of monitoring the proposed plans as they are implemented and adjusting for any variances where necessary.

Co-operation The links that bring organisations together, thereby enhancing their ability to compete in the market place. *See also Complementors.*

Co-operative game Has positive pay-off for all participants.

Core competencies The distinctive group of skills and technologies that enable an organisation to provide particular benefits to customers and deliver competitive advantage. Together, they form key resources of the organisation that assist it in being distinct from its competitors.

Core resources The important strategic resources of the organisation, usually summarised as architecture, reputation and innovation.

Corporate governance The selection of the senior officers of the organisation and their conduct and relationships with owners, employees and other stakeholders.

Corporate strategy The pattern of major objectives, purposes or goals and the essential policies or plans for achieving those goals. Note that this is not the only definition.

Cost/benefit analysis Evaluates strategic projects especially in the public sector where an element of unquantified public service beyond commercial profit may be involved. It attempts to quantify the broader social benefits to be derived from particular strategic initiatives.

Cost of capital The cost of the capital employed in an organisation, often measured by the cost of investing outside in a risk-free bond coupled with some element for the extra risks, if any, of investing in the organisation itself. *See also Weighted average cost of capital.*

Cost-plus pricing Sets the price of goods and services primarily by totalling the costs and adding a percentage profit margin. *See also Target pricing.*

Cultural Web The factors that can be used to characterise the culture of an organisation. Usually summarised as stories, symbols, power structures, organisational structure, control systems, routines and rituals.

Culture *See Organisational culture* and *International culture.* It is important to distinguish between these two quite distinct areas of the subject.

Customer–competitor matrix Links together the extent to which customers have common needs and competitors can gain competitive advantage through areas such as differentiation and economies of scale.

Customer-driven strategy The strategy of an organisation where every function is directed towards customer satisfaction. It goes beyond those functions, such as sales and marketing, that have traditionally had direct contact with the customer.

Customer profiling Describes the main characteristics of the customer and how customers make their purchase decisions.

Cyclicality The periodic rise and fall of a mature market.

Delayering The removal of layers of management and administration in an organisation's structure.

Demerger The split of an organisation into its constituent parts with some parts possibly being sold to outside investors.

Derived demand Demand for goods and services that is derived from the economic performance of the customers. *See also Primary demand.*

Differentiation The development of unique benefits or attributes in a product or service that positions it to appeal especially to a part (segment) of the total market.

Dirigiste policy Describes the policies of a government relying on an approach of centrally directed government actions to manage the economy. *See also Laissez-faire policy.*

Discontinuity Radical, sudden and largely unpredicted change in the environment.

Discounted cash flow (DCF) The sum of the projected cash flows from a future strategy, after revaluing each individual element of the cash flow in terms of its present worth.

Division A separate part of a multi-product company with profit responsibility for its range of products. Each division usually has a complete range of the main functions such as finance, operations and marketing.

Double loop learning The first loop of learning checks performance against expected norms and adjusts where necessary. The second, more fundamental loop re-appraises whether the expected norms were appropriate in the first place.

Economic rent Any excess that a factor earns over the minimum amount needed to keep that factor in its present use.

Economies of scale The extra cost savings that occur when higher volume production allows unit costs to be reduced.

Economies of scope The extra cost savings that are available as a result of separate products sharing some facilities.

Emergent change The whole process of developing a strategy whose outcome only emerges as the strategy proceeds. There is no defined list of implementation actions in advance of the strategy emerging. *See also Prescriptive change.*

Emergent corporate strategy A strategy whose final objective is unclear and whose elements are developed during the course of its life, as the strategy proceeds. *See also Prescriptive corporate strategy.*

Empowerment The devolution of power and decision-making responsibility to those lower in the organisation.

Environment Everything and everyone outside the organisation: competitors, customers, government, etc. Note that 'green' environmental issues are only one part of the overall definition. *See also Changeability of the environment* and *Predictability of the environment.*

E–S–P Paradigm This analyses the role of government in strategy development along three dimensions: Environment, System and Policies.

Ethics The principles that encompass the standards and conduct that an organisation sets itself in its dealings within the organisation and with its external environment.

Expansion method matrix Explores in a structured way the methods by which the market opportunities associated with strategy options might be achieved.

Experience curve The relationship between the unit costs of a product and the total units *ever produced* of that product, plotted in graphical form. Note that the units are cumulative from the first day of production.

Fit The consistencies, coherence and congruence of the organisation.

Floating and fixed exchange rates Currency exchange rates, such as the rate of exchange between the US$ and the German DM, are said to *float* when market forces determine the rate depending on market demand. They are *fixed* when national governments (or their associated national banks) fix the rates by international agreement and intervene in international markets to hold those rates.

Focus strategy *See Niche marketing.*

Formal organisation structures Those structures formally defined by the organisation in terms of reporting relationships, responsibilities and tasks. *See also Informal organisation structures.*

Forward integration When an organisation acquires the activities of its outputs, e.g. manufacturer into distribution and transport.

Functional organisation structure A structure in which the different functions of the organisation, such as finance and operations, report to the chief executive. Used in organisations with a limited product range.

Game-based theories of strategy Focus on the decisions of the organisation and its competitors as strategy is developed – the *game* – and the interactions between the two as strategic decisions are taken.

Game theory Structured methods of bargaining with and between customers, suppliers and others, both inside and outside the organisation.

Gearing ratio The ratio of debt finance to the total shareholders' funds.

General Agreement on Tariffs and Trade (GATT) International agreement designed to encourage and support world trade.

Generic strategies The three basic strategies of cost leadership, differentiation and focus (sometimes called niche) which are open to any business.

Global and national responsiveness matrix This links together the extent of the need for global activity with the need for an organisation to be responsive to national and regional variations. These two areas are not mutually exclusive.

Global product company This will often involve the global integration of manufacturing and one common global brand. There is only *limited* national variation. *See also Transnational product company.*

Growth-share matrix *See Portfolio matrix.*

Hierarchy of resources The four levels of resource that are the full resources of the organisation. The distinguishing feature of the higher levels is an increased likelihood of sustainable competitive advantage.

History *See Strategy as history.*

Holding company organisation structure Used for organisations with very diverse product ranges and share relationships. The headquarters acts only as a banker, with strategy largely decided by the individual companies. Sometimes shortened to *H-Form* structure.

Horizontal integration When an organisation moves to acquire its competitors or make some other form of close association.

Human resource audit An examination of the organisation's people and their skills, backgrounds and relationships with each other.

Human resource-based theories of strategy Emphasise the importance of the people element in strategy development. *See also Emergent corporate strategy, Negotiation-based* and *Learning-based strategic routes forward.*

Implementation The process by which the organisation's chosen strategies are put into operation.

Informal organisation structures Those structures, often unwritten, that have been developed by the history, culture and individuals in an organisation to facilitate the flow of information and allocate power within the structure. *See also Formal organisation structures.*

Innovation The generation and exploitation of new ideas. The process moves products and services, human and capital resources, markets and production processes beyond their current boundaries and capabilities.

Intangible resources The organisation's resources that have no physical presence but represent real benefit to the organisation, like reputation and technical knowledge. *See also Tangible resources* and *Organisational capability.*

Intellectual capital of an organisation The future earnings capacity that derives from a deeper, broader and more human perspective than that described in the organisation's financial reports.

International culture Collective programming of the mind that distinguishes one human group from another.

International Monetary Fund (IMF) International body designed to lend funds to countries in international difficulty and to promote trade stability through co-operation and discussion.

Just-in-time System that ensures that stock is delivered from suppliers only when it is required, with none being held in reserve.

Kaizen The process of continuous improvement in production and every aspect of value added (Japanese).

Kanban Control system on the factory floor to keep production moving (Japanese).

Key factors for success Those resources, skills and attributes of the organisations in an industry that are essential to deliver success in the market place. Sometimes called *critical success factors.*

Knowledge A fluid mix of framed experience, values, contextual information and expert insight. Note that knowledge is *not* 'data' or 'information'.

Knowledge management The retention, exploitation and sharing of knowledge in an organisation that will deliver sustainable competitive advantage.

Laissez-faire policy Describes the policies of a government relying on an approach of non-interference and free-market forces to manage the economy of a country. *See also Dirigiste policy.*

Leadership The art or process of influencing people so that they will strive willingly and enthusiastically towards the achievement of the group's mission.

Learning The strategic process of developing strategy by crafting, experimentation and feedback. Note that learning in this context does *not* mean rote or memory learning.

Learning-based strategic route forward Emphasises learning and crafting as aspects of the development of successful corporate strategy. *See also Human resource-based theories of strategy.*

Leveraging The exploitation by an organisation of its existing resources to their fullest extent.

Life cycle Plots the evolution of industry annual sales over time. Often divided into distinct phases – introduction, growth, maturity and decline – with specific strategies for each phase.

Logical incrementalism The process of developing a strategy by small, incremental and logical steps. The term was first used by Professor J B Quinn.

Logistics The science of stockholding, delivery and customer service.

Loose–tight principle The concept of the need for tight central control by headquarters, while allowing individuals or operating subsidiaries loose autonomy and initiative within defined managerial limits.

Macroeconomic conditions Economic activity at the general level of the national or international economy.

Market equilibrium The state that allows competitors a viable and stable market share accompanied by adequate profits.

Market options matrix Identifies the product and the market options available to the organisation, including the possibility of withdrawal and movement into unrelated markets.

Market segmentation The identification of specific groups (or segments) of customers who respond to competitive strategies differently from other groups. *See also Market positioning*.

Market positioning The choice of differential advantage possessed by an organisation that allows it to compete and survive in a market place. Often associated with competition and survival in a segment of a market. *See Market segmentation*.

Mass marketing One product is sold to all types of customer.

Matrix organisation structure Instead of the product-based multi-divisional structure, some organisations have chosen to operate with two overlapping structures. One structure might typically be product-based, with another parallel structure being based on some other element such as geographic region. The two elements form a *matrix* of responsibilities. Strategy needs to be agreed by both parts of the matrix. *See also Multi-divisional organisation structure*.

Milestones Interim indicators of progress during the implementation phase of strategy.

Minimum intervention The principle that managers implementing strategy should only make changes where they are absolutely necessary.

Mission statement Defines the business that the organisation is in or should be in against the values and expectations of the stakeholders.

Monopoly rents Economic rent deriving from the markets in which the organisation operates. *See also Economic rent*.

Multi-divisional organisation structure As the product range of the organisation becomes larger and more diverse, similar parts of the product range are grouped together into divisions, each having its own functional management team. Each division has some degree of profit responsibility and reports to the headquarters, which usually retains a significant role in the development of business strategy. Sometimes this is shortened to *M-Form* structure. *See also Matrix organisation structure*.

Multinational enterprise (MNE) One of the global companies that operate in many countries around the world, for example, Ford, McDonald's and Unilever.

Negative-sum game Actions of each party undermine both themselves and their opponents.

Negotiation-based strategic route forward Has both human resource and game theory elements. Human resource aspects emphasise the importance of negotiating with colleagues in order to establish the optimal strategy. Game theory aspects explore the consequences of the balance of power in the negotiation situation.

Net cash flow Approximately, the sum of pre-tax profits plus depreciation, less the capital to be invested in a strategy.

Niche marketing Concentration on a small market segment with the objective of achieving dominance of that segment.

Objectives or goals State more precisely than a mission statement what is to be achieved and when the results are to be accomplished. They may be quantified.

Oligopoly A market dominated by a small number of firms.

Organisational capability The skills, routines, management and leadership of its organisation. *See also Tangible resources* and *Intangible resources*.

Organisational culture The style and learned ways that govern and shape the organisation's people relationships.

Outsourcing The decision by an organisation to buy in products or services from outside, rather than make them inside the organisation.

Paradigm The recipe or model that links the elements of a theory together and shows, where possible, the nature of the relationships.

Parenting The special relationships and strategies pursued at the headquarters of a diversified group of companies.

Payoffs The results of particular game-plays. *See also Game theory, Zero-sum game, Co-operative game, Negative-sum game.*

PESTEL analysis Checklist of the political, economic, socio-cultural, technological, environment and legal aspects of the environment.

Plans or programmes The specific actions that follow from the strategies. Often a step-by-step sequence and timetable.

Portfolio matrix Analyses the range of products possessed by an organisation (its portfolio) against two criteria: relative market share and market growth. It is sometimes called the growth-share matrix.

Predictability of the environment The degree to which changes in the environment can be predicted.

Prescriptive change The implementation actions that result from the selected strategy option. A defined list of actions is identified once the strategy has been chosen. *See also Emergent change.*

Prescriptive corporate strategy A strategy whose objective has been defined in advance and whose main elements have been developed before the strategy commences. *See also Emergent corporate strategy*, where such elements are crafted during the development of the strategy and not defined in advance.

Pressure points for influence The groups or individuals that significantly influence the direction of the organisation, especially in the context of strategic change. Note that they may have no *formal* power or responsibility.

Primary demand Demand from customers for themselves or their families. *See also Derived demand.*

Process of corporate strategy How the actions of corporate strategy are linked together or interact with each other as strategy unfolds.

Profit-maximising theories of strategy Emphasise the importance of the market place and the generation of profit. *See also Prescriptive corporate strategy.*

Profitability The ratio of profits from a strategy divided by the capital employed in that strategy. It is important to define clearly the elements in the equation, e.g. whether the profits are calculated

before or after tax and before or after interest payments. This is often called the *Return on capital employed*, shortened to ROCE.

Quota A maximum number placed by a nation state on the goods that can be imported into the country in any one period. The quota is defined for a particular product category.

Reputation The strategic standing of the organisation in the eyes of its customers.

Resource allocation The process of allocating the resources of the organisation selectively between competing strategies according to their merit.

Resource-based view Stresses the importance of resources in delivering the competitive advantage of the organisation. *See also Prescriptive corporate strategy.*

Retained profits The profits that are retained in an organisation rather than distributed to shareholders. These can be used to fund new strategies.

Reward The result of successful strategy, adding value to the organisation and the individual.

Ricardian rents Economic rent deriving from the resources of the organisation. *See also Economic rent.*

ROCE *See Profitability.*

Scenario Model of a possible future environment for the organisation, whose strategic implications can then be investigated.

Schumpeterian rents Economic rent deriving from new and innovatory products and services that allow the organisation to charge significantly above the costs of production. *See also Economic rent.*

Seven S Framework The seven elements of super-ordinate goals: strategy, structure, systems, skills, style and staff. In some later versions, the first item was replaced by share values.

Share issues New shares in an organisation can be issued to current or new shareholders to raise finance for new strategy initiatives.

Shareholder value added The difference between the return on capital and the cost of capital multiplied by the investment made by the shareholders in the business.

Socio-cultural theories of strategy Focus on the social and cultural dimensions of the organisation in developing corporate strategy. *See also Prescriptive corporate strategy.*

Split The variety of techniques that can be employed to develop and sustain the autonomy and diversity of large organisations.

Stakeholders The individuals and groups who have an interest in the organisation and, therefore, may wish to influence aspects of its mission, objectives and strategies.

Strategic business unit (SBU) The level of a multi-business unit at which the strategy needs to be developed. The unit has the responsibility for determining the strategy of that unit. Not necessarily the same as a division of the company: there may be more than one SBU within a division and SBUs may combine elements from more than one division.

Strategic change The proactive management of change in organisations in order to achieve clearly defined strategic objectives. *See also Prescriptive change* and *Emergent change*.

Strategic fit The matching process between strategy and organisational structure.

Strategic groups Groups of firms within an industry that follow the same strategies or ones that have similar dimensions and which compete closely.

Strategic planning A formal planning system for the development and implementation of the strategies related to the mission and objectives of the organisation. It is no substitute for strategic thinking.

Strategic space The identification of gaps in an industry representing strategic marketing opportunities.

Strategies The principles that show how an organisation's major objectives or goals are to be achieved over a defined time period. Usually confined only to the *general logic* for achieving the objectives.

Strategy as history The view that strategy must, at least in part, be seen as a result of the organisation's present resources, its past history and its evolution over time.

Style theory of leadership Suggests that individuals can be identified who possess a general style of leadership that is appropriate to the organisation. *See also Contingency theory of leadership* and *Trait theory of leadership*.

Survival-based theories of strategy Regard the survival of the fittest in the market place as being the prime determinant of corporate strategy. *See also Emergent corporate strategy*.

Sustainable competitive advantage An advantage over competitors that cannot be easily imitated. Such advantages will generate more value than competitors have.

SWOT analysis An analysis of the strengths and weaknesses present internally in the organisation, coupled with the opportunities and threats that the organisation faces externally.

Synergy The combination of parts of a business such that the sum is worth more than the individual parts – often remembered as '2 + 2 = 5'.

Tangible resources The physical resources of the organisation like plant and equipment. *See also Intangible resources* and *Organisational capability*.

Target pricing Sets the price of goods and services primarily on the basis of the competitive position of the organisation, the profit margin required and, therefore, the target costs that need to be achieved. *See also Cost-plus pricing*.

Targeted marketing *See Market segmentation*.

Tariffs Taxes on imported goods imposed by a nation state. They do not stop imports into the country but make them more expensive.

Taylorism Named after F W Taylor (1856–1915). The division of work into measurable parts, such that new standards of work performance could be defined, coupled with a willingness by management and workers to achieve these. It fell into disrepute when it was used to exploit workers in the early twentieth century. Taylor always denied that this had been his intention.

Tiger economies Countries of South-East Asia exhibiting exceptionally strong economic growth over the last 20 years, including Singapore, Malaysia, Hong Kong, Thailand and Korea.

Trade barriers The barriers set up by governments to protect industries in their own countries.

Trade block Agreement between a group (or block) of countries designed to encourage trade between those countries and keep out other countries.

Trait theory of leadership Argues that individuals with certain characteristics (traits) can be identified who will provide leadership in virtually any situation. *See also Contingency theory of leadership* and *Style theory of leadership*.

Transcend Given the inevitable complexities of corporate strategy, some strategists argue that every organisation needs an approach to management that *transcends* these problems and copes with such difficulties.

Transfer price The price for which one part of an organisation will sell its goods to another part in a multi-divisional organisation.

Transnational product company This usually involves some global integration of manufacturing coupled with *significant* national responsiveness to national or regional variations in customer demand. *See also Global product company.*

Uncertainty-based theories of strategy Regard prediction of the environment as being of little value and therefore long-term planning as having little value. *See also Emergent corporate strategy.*

United Nations Conference on Trade and Development (UNCTAD) A trade body set up to highlight the trading concerns of the developing nations of the world and promote their interests.

Value chain Identifies where the value is added in an organisation and links the process with the main functional parts of the organisation. It is used for developing competitive advantage because such chains tend to be unique to an organisation.

Value system The wider routes in an industry that add value to incoming supplies and outgoing distributors and customers. It links the industry value chain to that of other industries. It is used for developing competitive advantage.

Vertical integration The backward acquisition of raw material suppliers and/or the forward purchase of distributors.

Vision A challenging and imaginative picture of the future role and objectives of an organisation, significantly going beyond its current environment and competitive position. It is often associated with an outstanding leader of the organisation.

Weighted average cost of capital The combination of the costs of debt and equity capital in proportion to the capital structure of the organisation. *See also Cost of capital.*

Zero-sum game Has no pay-off because the gains of one player are negated by the losses of another.

Name index

Aaker, D. 95, 108, 144
Adcock, D. 191
Alborg, Al 191
Amit, R. 205
Andrews, K. 44, 464
Ansoff, I. 7, 41, 43, 44, 54, 478, 747
Argenti, J. 19
Argyris, C. 49, 395, 579
Athos, A. 800

Baden-Fuller, C. 470, 753, 790, 791
Baker, M. 108
Banbury, C. 617
Bapista, J. P. 360
Bartlett, C. 718, 719
Beer, M. 785
Bennis, W. 364, 371
Bradfield, R. 191
Brown, A. 130, 262, 279
Buddn, R. 586
Bungay, S. 657
Burt, T. 367
Butler, S. 270
Buzzell, R. 140

Campbell, A. 8, 448, 653
Cannon, T. 430
Chaharbaghi, K. 427, 739
Chakravarthy, B. 44
Chandler, A. 54, 68, 253, 535, 596, 597, 598, 599, 606, 614, 672, 719
Christoper, M. 338
Coase, R. 208
Collis, D. 228
Cool, K. 56
Cyert, R. 19, 41, 49, 54, 64, 635

Darwin, Charles 560
Davenport, T. H. 390, 396
Day, G. S. 144, 478, 651
Dean, J. 297
De Geus, A. 652
Dierickx, I. 56
Douglas, S. 187, 713
Doyle, P. 163
Doz, Y. 724
Drucker, P. 7, 56, 390, 442, 451, 615, 807
Dunning, J. 723

Egan, C. 116, 777
Eisenhardt, K. M. 130
Eisenhort, R. 785

Fayol, Henri 39, 40, 598
Friesen, B. 62, 63, 805

Galbraith, J. R. 606, 610
Gale, B. 140
Garvin, D. 297, 777
Gertz, D. 360
Ghoshal, S. 718–19
Gilbreth, F. 598
Gilbreth, L. 598
Glautier, M. W. W. 311–12
Gleuck, W. 19
Gluck, F. 413
Goold, M. 653, 657
Granovetter, M. 59
Grant, R. M. 297
Greiner, L. 268, 668, 771

Hall, R. C. 61
Hamel, G. 55, 167, 228, 235, 364, 391, 490, 647, 724, 745
Handy, C. 261, 262, 271, 609, 615
Hart, S. 616, 617
Harvey-Jones, J. 108
Hayes, R. 297
Hendry, C. 471
Hill, T. 333, 346, 348
Hitch, C. J. 61
Hofstede, G. 274, 610
Hrebiniak, L. 635, 638
Hunt, J. 365

Jarillo, C. 573
Jauch, L. R. 193
Jick, T. 769, 772, 792
Johnson, G. 49, 784
Joyce, W. 635, 638

Kanter, M. 571, 606, 678, 679, 769, 772, 792
Kaplan, R. 635–6, 659
Kay, J. 11, 55, 56, 128, 179, 212–13, 228, 233, 235, 403, 470, 498, 503, 529
Kazanjian, R. K. 610
Kluckhohn, C. 273
Kogut, B. 722
Kotler, P. 134

Lao Tsu 370
Lawrence, P. R. 804
Lecraw, D. J. 725
Leonard-Barton, D. 398

Levicki, C. 381–2
Levitt, T. 162, 186, 344, 712, 713
Lewin, K. 772, 792
Liddell-Hart, B. H. 44, 135
Little, Arthur D. 525–7
Lorange, P. 44
Lorsch, J. W. 804
Lynch, R. 125, 132, 145, 147, 176, 213, 275, 279, 291, 367, 374, 389, 400, 411, 426, 427, 440, 485, 518, 532, 543, 553, 560, 570, 586, 739

Machiavelli, N. 786, 787, 788, 793
Mansfield, 412
March, J. 19, 41, 49, 54, 64, 635
Marris, R. 59
Marsh, P. 411
Marx, Karl 149
Marx, T. 536
Mayo, E. 49, 804
Meade, R. 274
Merrett, A. J. 297
Miles, R. E. 266
Miller, D. 62–3, 470, 805
Mintzberg, H. 9, 19, 45, 49, 55, 64, 271, 578, 609, 610, 611, 614, 653, 669, 678, 745, 747
Montgomery, C. 228
Morgan, G. 361
Morison, A. J. 725
Morris, H. 416
Mullins, L. 685, 686

Nanus, B. 364, 371
Nelson, R. 64, 739
Nonaka, I. 418
Nonaki, I. 391
Norton, D. 635–7, 659

Ohmae, K. 9, 55, 174, 191, 204, 205, 500, 514, 712, 729
Olie, R. 276

Pascale, R. 553, 800, 804, 805, 806
Penrose, E. 41, 68, 208, 360, 490, 739
Peteraf, M. 56, 228
Peters, T. 606, 615, 800, 802, 803, 804, 806, 811–12, 813
Pettigrew, A. 18, 49, 634, 638, 659, 776, 777, 779, 783, 792, 804

Name index

Porter, M. E. 8, 43, 44, 56, 94, 103, 108, 109, 126, 132, 134, 153, 174, 204, 208, 216, 219, 226, 253, 357, 403, 415, 466, 468, 471–2, 497, 502, 573, 701, 702, 703, 705, 744
Prahalad, C. K. 55, 167, 228, 235, 364, 490, 647, 745
Prusack, L. 390, 396

Quinn, J. B. 413, 448, 607, 613, 638, 677

Ricardo, D. 222, 223
Rosen, R. 118, 391
Ross, C. 191
Rumelt, R. 54

Schendel, D. 54
Schumpeter, J. 739, 740
Senge, P. 49, 578, 579, 580, 603, 607, 609, 614, 638, 776, 783

Shoemaker, 205
Simon, H. 49, 64, 93, 804
Singh, R. 134
Skinner, W. 337
Sloan, A. 41, 54, 535, 598, 601, 607, 672
Smith, Adam 54, 149
Snow, C. C. 266
Spector, B. 785
Stein, B. 769, 772, 792
Stopford, J. 470, 717, 753, 790, 791
Strebel, P. 62, 325
Strickland, A. 307, 670
Strodtbeck, F. 273
Sykes, A. 297

Takeuchi, A. 391
Taylor, F. W. 39–40, 598
Teece, D. 54
Thompson, A. 307, 670
Tichy, N. 792

Underdown, B. 311, 312
Utterback, J. M. 412, 751

Waterman, R. 615, 800, 802, 803, 804, 806, 813
Welch, J. 657
Wells, L. M. 717
Wernerfelt, B. 56
Whipp, R. 18, 634, 638, 659, 776, 777, 779, 783, 792, 804
Whittington, R. 59, 255, 583
Wickham, P. 756, 757
Willey, B. 416
Williamson, O. 208, 357, 596
Wind, Y. 187, 713
Winter, S. 64, 739

Yeung, S. 448
Yip, G. 713

Subject index

accounting profit 224, 225
  see also economic rent
Acer computers 228
acquisitions
  in computer industry 71
  evidence on 284
  as means of expansion 482–3,
    485
  in pharmaceuticals 202–3
  strategy 228–9
adding value 8, 9–11, 212–14
  see also value
ADL matrix 525–6
aerospace industry 166, 190
Aerospatiale 568
Agusta 568
Airbus 166, 180, 183, 187–91
aircraft market 187, 194, 567
Air France 28
Air Lib 31
airlines, Europe's budget 27–32
Aldi retailing 136, 206
Alenia defence 568
Alitalia airline 28–9
alliances *see* co-operation in strategy
    development; strategic
    business alliances
Ambev brewing 285
America *see* USA
Anheuser Busch brewing 285, 314
Apple computers 13, 228
appropriability of resources 229
Arbed steel 87, 100, 128, 206
architecture resources 233–5
Asea Brown Boveri (ABB) 206, 606,
    617–19, 622
Asia 41, 476, 593
Asia-Pacific 42, 474, 781
Association of South East Asian
    Nations 707
attack strategies 136–7, 139
Australia 206
Austrian airlines 29

Bajaj Motorcycles 341–2
Balanced Scorecard
  comment 637, 659
  elements 635
  rationale 636, 639
barriers to entry 105–6
barriers to trade 705
Bass brewing 285
Bayer chemicals 233

BCG Matrix 139, 140–2, 144, 155
  see also product portfolio matrix
Ben & Jerry's ice cream 97, 156
benchmarking 239–40, 241, 278
Benetton Clothing 208–9
Bertelsmann media 487
Bethlehem Steel 100
biotechnology companies 796, 809
Boashan steel 100
BOC industrial gases company
    761–3
Boeing defence 567
bounded rationality 635
Bouygues construction and media
    211, 214, 236
branding 127, 166, 176–8, 180,
    205, 225, 719
breakeven analysis 514, 520, 522
breakfast cereal market 38
breakpoints 62
brewing industry 290–1
British Aerospace 568–70
British Airways (BA) 27–8, 166
British Petroleum (BP) 263–5,
    380
British Steel 87, 104
British Telecom 559
bureaucracy 26, 599
  see also planning
Burton retailing 310
business judgement *see* judgement
    in strategy
business process re-engineering
    269, 278
buyers *see* customers
buyers bargaining power 103,
    104–5, 167
Buzz (Netherlands) airline 27, 31

Cadbury Schweppes 76, 176
Call of Africa grows louder 151–2
Canon electronics 9, 206, 223, 413,
    639–42, 656
capacity utilisation 499
capital asset pricing model 312
capital investment 105, 528–9
Carlsberg brewries 285, 290
car market 107
Carrefour 177
Casa aerospace 568
cash flow 514
C–C–B Paradigm 695, 730–1
centralisation 600, 620

Cereal Partners 38, 49
change *see* strategic change
chaos theory 563
chaotic systems 62
charities *see* non-profit organisations
China 39, 148, 325
China steel 100
Ciba pharmaceuticals and chemicals
    796
Cisco Systems 676
Coca-Cola 439–40, 692, 730
coherence in strategy 778, 804–5
communications 643
Compaq 7, 117
competition
  analysis 89, 103–4
  extent 107
  free market 42
  good competitors and 153–4
  intensity 132–4, 138
  international 152–3, 155
  key success factors 205
  life cycle and 95
  objectives of 135–6
  operations and 322–3
  perfect 133
  profiling 113–14
competition and customer matrix
    168
competitive advantage 7, 9, 10
  customers and 179–81
  dynamics of 129–30, 154–5, 745
  'good' strategy and 23
  human resources and 253
  importance of 125
  knowledge management and 237
  of nations 701–3
  operations and 331–2
  prescriptive and emergent 127
  in public services 126
  and purpose of 377–80
  resource options 228–31
  sources of 109, 228
  stability and 128
  technology and 402
  tests for 129
  see also competition
competitive positioning 69,
    174–6
  see also market segmentation
Competitive rivalry 107, 188
competitive strategies 134
complementors 110, 111

computer industry 34
concentration ratio 155
consistency with strategy 511, 516, 544
content *see* strategy content
context *see* strategy context
contingency theories of leadership 368–9
controls
    budgeting and 657
    definition of 16
    elements of 21, 656
    financial 654
    implementation and 657, 807
    planning and 650–3
control systems 660
co-operation in strategy development 110–11, 138
    see also Four Links Model
core competencies 235–7
    at Canon electronics 640
    definition 235, 493–4
    hierarchy 494
    limits of 494
    link with vision and 487
    options and 494
    skills and 235
    see also resource-based theories of strategy
corporate governance
    corporate conduct 380
    information flows 378
    power of 378
    stakeholders and 376–7, 379
corporate planning *see* strategic planning
corporate strategy
    core areas 4, 6–8, 15–17
    definition 5, 6
    emergent approach 19–20, 33
    globalisation and 401
    importance of 4
    information technology 401
    innovation 407
    objectives and 440–1
        see also strategy
    operations and 322
    overcoming problems in 536
    parenting 443
    prescriptive approach 19–20, 33
    purpose of 10
    quality 445–7
    resource-based view and 207
    technology 400
Corus steel 100–1, 121
cost/benefit analysis 524, 544
cost of finance *see* financial resources
cost focus strategy 470
cost leadership 467, 473, 502

cost reduction 325–7
    options 499, 500
costs
    of competitors 499
    global 325–6
creative destruction 740
CSI steel 86, 93
cultural web 259–60
culture
    change options and 621
    elements 128
    environmental influencs 257–8
    feasibility and 512–14
    guidelines for analysing 262
    international 27, 272–4
    mission and 435
    of organisation 154, 257, 261–2, 279, 422
    strategic change and 788
    strategic implications of 258
    structures and 670
    values and style 261
currency 707
customer competitor matrix 168
customer-driven strategy 96, 162–4
customer profiling
    breakthrough strategies and 167
    competitive advantage and 165
    customer/competitor matrix 168–9
    see also competitive positioning; market segmentation
customers
    analysis 115, 120, 158–9, 236
    branding and 166
    communication and 166, 179–81
    company relationship and 164, 195
    defining 162–3
    demand measure 189
    international 186–7
    key factors for success and 205
    market positioning and 170
    pricing and 181
    profiling *see* customer profiling
    segmentation and 115, 173
    service and 283
    strategy 163–5
    types of 166
    unmet needs of 167
    see also market segmentation
customer switching 167

Daimler Benz cars and aerospace 225
DaimlerChrysler 355–7
Dalgety foods 47, 66–8, 76
Danone foods and brewing 76, 290, 292
DASA aerospace 568
Dassault Aerospace 568

debt finance 292
    see also long-term debt; short-term debt
decentralisation *see* centralisation
declining markets 754
defence industry 567–70
delayering 269
Dell computers 34, 228, 320–1
designing-in-cost reduction 128, 337–8, 496
Deutsche Bank 449
Deutsche Telekom 558
Diageo spirits, brewing and food 310–11
diamond theory of world trade 701–3
differentiation 105, 107, 127–8, 154, 236, 468–9, 472
    focus strategy 469, 502
Directional Policy Matrix 139, 142–4, 155
    see also Product Portfolio Matrix
dirigiste policy 149, 151, 155
discounted cash flow (DCF) 520, 521–2
distinctive capabilities *see* resource-based theories of strategy distribution
distribution
    analysis 145–6
    in ice-cream 146–7
diversification 480–1
dividend payout 293
divisional structures 671
durability of resources 230
dynamics of strategy
    acting on dynamics 747–8
    entrepreneurship 756
    environmental development 743–8
    fast-moving markets 735, 750–3
    implementation 753
    purpose 735, 737–8
    resource development 738–43
    slow moving markets 735, 753–4
Dyson vacuum cleaners 159–61, 171

early entrants 95
Easyjet airline 27, 29, 31–2
eBay auction market 735–7
economic rent 222–6
    see also accounting profit
economies of scale 105, 496–7
    world trade and 27, 701
economies of scope 496–7
emergent strategy 49, 74, 204, 448
    advantages 50–1
    cohesion and 798–9
    concept 59
    difficulties 51

implementation and 50
process 596
theories of 59–65
see also human resource-based
theories of strategy;
learning-based strategy
EMI records 749
employees 7, 42, 325
empowerment 605, 620
entrepreneurship 756
entry
barriers to 149
early 95
environment 8
analysis 20–1, 82, 88, 109–10
culture and 257–60
definition of 8–9
dynamics of 91
exploration of 751
history and 40
importance of 87–8, 90, 118–19
operations and 323
organisation structure and 85
prediction of 15, 18
prescriptive process and 88
strategic change and 17
strategy and 9
see also dynamics of strategy
environmental turbulence 65
see also prediction
Epson 9, 206, 413
Ericsson telecommunications 719
ESP Paradigm 147–8
ethics
basic issues 374–7
shareholders and stakeholders
376–7
Eurofreeze 516–18, 538–43, 547
European bank for Reconstruction
and Development (EBRD) 149
European Commission 28, 30
European football 630–1
European ice cream market 172–3,
175, 205, 470
European single market 340
European steel industry 107
European telecommunication
companies 557–60
European Union 147, 707
evaluation criteria
attractiveness to shareholders 515,
544
business risk 514–15
in commercial organisations 518–19
consistency 544
feasibility 512, 513, 544
international variations 545
non-profit organisations 519
suitability 511, 544
validity 511–12, 544

excellent organisations 802–4
exit from industry
paper industry 698–9
strategies for 477–8
Expansion Method Matrix 482–6
experience curve 497–8
explicit knowledge 391–2
exporting 483, 484

fast-moving markets
dynamics of 473, 750–1
innovation flow 751–2
market dominance of 750–1
feasibility criterion 512–13, 544
financial appraisal of strategy 296–7,
520–2
assessment 297
assumptions 298
basic cash flow analysis 299–300
country approaches 309
general concepts 297
prediction 297–8
ratios 317
risk and 309, 522
financial controls 654
financial objectives 307
corporate objectives and 306–7
financial resources
analysis of 283
constraints 291–2
cost of capital 294–5
cost of equity 294
cost of funds 294, 296
cost of long-term debt 295
international issues 308–9
optimal capital structure 295–6
relationship with corporate
strategy 306, 311
sources of finance 287–8
financial risk analysis 514–15
Finnair airline 29
Five Forces model 89, 103, 108–9,
120, 132
focus strategy 469–70
food industry 78
Ford, Henry 39, 41, 369, 597
Ford Motor Company 149, 225, 228,
239, 423–6, 437, 682–5, 692
forecasting 296
see also prediction
Four Links Model 89, 109–10, 112, 120
fragmented markets 754
France 449, 567
France Telecom 212
franchising 209, 484–5
functional organisation structure 686

game-based theories of strategy
checklist 57–8
comment 59

main elements 138, 578
rules of game 575
see also complementors;
negotiation-based strategy
GameCube 243
gearing 292–3
GEC Marconi defence 567–9
GEC (UK) 567
Genentech pharmaceuticals 324
General Agreement on Tariffs and
Trade (GATT) 26, 326, 706–7
General Dynamics defence 567
General Electric (US) 358, 475,
481, 719
General Mills food products 38, 228
General Motors 41, 228, 327, 535,
600–3
generic strategies 525–9
Georgia-Pacific Paper 698
Germania airline 27
Germany 28, 449
Giant Bicycles 691–2
Glaxo SmithKline pharmaceuticals
201–3, 210–11, 219, 228,
236–7, 412
Glaxo Wellcome pharmaceuticals
106, 202, 213, 796
globalisation
business case 152–3, 712–13
company perspectives 711–16
definition 712
international expansion 537,
692–7, 721–4
matrix structures 717–18
organisation structures 717–20
transnational solution 718–20
global services network 326
global strategy
in biscuits 774
branding and 156
in brewing 285
in cars 225, 329, 423–6, 682–5
competition and 716
cost reduction and 325–6
customers and 86
economies of scale and 105
headquarters role 729
international trade and 697
market forces and 40, 42
operations and 326
politics and 716
prescriptive options 715–16
in pulp and paper market 697
in steel 85
strategy and 42
in telecommunications 11,
557–60
in television 474–6
theories of 700–1
good strategy, tests of 23–6

government
    ESP Paradigm 147–8
    growth and purpose 426
    history 148
    industry relations 149
    influence on strategy and 147–51, 155
    international 724–5
    national economy 150–1
    national policy 148, 150
    role of state 149, 155
    strategic choice 150–1, 515
    trade issues 502–3
Great Future Textiles Ltd 325
growth
    lifecycle and 94
    in national economies 150–1
    rate of 94–7
    share matrix 140–2
    strategy issues 797
Guiness brewing 285

Häagen-Dazs ice cream 173
Hanson group 481
headquarters role 7, 681–2, 729
    see also parenting
Heineken brewing 284–7, 290–1, 292–3, 315–16
Hewlett-Packard computers 5–6, 7, 9–10, 117, 639
hierarchy of resources 230–1
history, strategy as 68–9, 531, 561
holding companies 475, 673, 686
Honda cars and motorcycles 225, 228, 413, 552–3
Hong Kong 274–5
Hoogevens steel 87
human resource-based theories of strategy 9, 63–4, 66, 75
human resources
    analysis of 9, 253–4
    audit 249, 255–6
    change programme 339
    competitive advantage and 254
    corporate strategy and 260
    culture and style 617
    international culture and 274
    morale and 679
    operations and 333, 335, 339
    organisational culture and 249
    power and politics 249, 270–2
    strategic change and 249
    strategic issues and 249, 254–5, 256
    see also motivation; politics of organisation

Iberia airline 28–9
IBM computers 12–14, 17, 69–72, 116, 228, 730
ice cream market 97–8

ICI chemicals 382
ICS manufacturing company 754–6
implementation 659
    elements 631–3
    guidlines 631–3
    strategic development and 634–8
India 39
Indonesia 284, 325
industry characteristcs 274–5
    concentration 133
    criticisms of life cycle 98
    key factors for success 102–3, 205–7
    life cycle and 89, 94–5, 119
information technology strategy 402
    competitive advantage and 403
    globalisation and 402
innovation 11
    capability 233–5
    controlled chaos 413
    corporate strategy and 137
    definition 418
    dynamics 750–3
    flow process 411–12, 751–2
    international 415
    knowledge-based theories of strategy 64–5, 66
    market pull 408
    organisation structure and 565, 677–9
    process 411–12
    purpose and 407, 415–16
    routes to 413–15
    strategic role of 137, 407–8, 753
    technology push 138, 409
Intel computer chips 13, 70
Interbrew brewing 285
International Bank for Reconstruction and Development (World Bank) 706
International markets see world trade
International Monetary Fund (IMF) 149, 707, 731
International Paper 698
International strategy development
    brewing industry and 290–1
    company and country relationships 724–6
    coporate strategy and 26–7, 537–8
    cost of capital 309
    country strategy and 696
    definitions 694–5
    dimensions and types 634
    external relationships 721–4
    operations and 325–7, 340
    organisation and 711–14
    steel industry and 99–101
    strategic options 714–16

sugar industry 726–9
telecommunications and 559, 584, 588
trade theories 704–5
    see also globalisation; global strategy
international trade institutions 705–8
International Trade Organisation 706
Internet
    record retailing and 138, 748–50
    retail banking and 399–400
    strategy 399
Iran 39
Iraq 39
Ispat steel 100
Italy 274–5, 325, 449
ITT defence 567

Japan 9, 274–5, 484
Jefferson Smurfitt pulp and paper 699
Johnson & Johnson 228
joint ventures 112, 138, 283, 483–5, 722–3
Jubilee Line Extension 433–4
judgement in strategy 10, 15, 530, 544
just-in-time systems 329

Kaizen 327–8
Kanban system 328
Kelloggs breakfast cereals 38, 44, 228, 484
key factors for success 89, 102–3, 204–7, 255
    definition 204
    examples 205–6
    in global TV 475
    government and 148
    importance of 204
    mission and 210
    planning and 205
Kirin brewing 285
KLM airline 28, 31
KLM Royal Dutch 28
knowledge
    acquisition 396
    audit 392–4
    creation process 395, 396–7, 418
    creation and purpose 390
    definition 390–1
    diffusion of 398
    management 394
    purpose and 397–8
    as a resource 237
    tacit and explicit 391–2, 418
    transfer 397
Korea 39, 274–5, 450

KPN telecommunications and
    post 558
Kronenburg beer 285, 290

Lagardère group defence 568
laissez-faire policy 149, 151, 155
layout of plant 329
leadership
    analysing types of 128, 368–9
    best fit approach 369
    influence of 139, 154, 283,
        367–71
    prescriptive and emergent
        approaches 371–2
    purpose and 233, 367
    strategic change and 607, 609
    style choice 365–7, 370–1,
        383, 607
    trust and enthusiasm in 371
lean thinking 233, 335, 338–9
learning-based strategy
    change and 586
    comment 65
    consequences 580–1, 587
    leadership and 607–8
    organisation structure 605
    rationale 578–9
learning disciplines 395, 580
learning mechanisms 395
learning organisation 605–6
leasing 283, 289, 291
leveraging resources 240, 241
life cycle 89, 94–7
life cycle matrix 527
limited state intervention theory
        703–4
Litton Industries 567
loans 288–9
lobbying 707
Lockheed Martin defence 567
logical incrementalism 73, 608
logistics 338
long-term debt 283, 287, 291
loose–tight principle see
        centralisation
Lord of the Rings 117–18
low-cost production 424, 467
LucasVarity car components 310
Lufthansa airline 27–8, 166
3M company 130, 404–6, 419,
        443, 743

McDonalds restaurants 128, 149,
        166, 180, 183, 206, 233, 484
    new strategy options 462–4
macroeconomic analysis 151
Maersk 31
make-or-buy decision 209, 335
Malaysia 39, 206, 284, 450
management 615–16

manufacturing strategy 336–7, 340
    see also operations
market
    centrally directed policy 149
    free market policy 149
market dominance 750–1
market growth 94–7, 140
    product portfolio and 155
market intelligence 134–5
market maturity 530
Market Options Matrix 477–81, 503
market penetration 479
market segmentation 89, 115–16,
        170–2, 189
    see also competitive positioning
market share 528
    evidence on 528
    fragmentation and 96–7, 573
    relative share and 140
    strength 285, 527
Marks & Spencer retailing 220, 239
Mars confectionery and ice cream
        98, 146–7, 174, 176, 233
Matra Aerospace 568
matrix organisation structure 686
    see also globalisation
Matsuhita electronics 326
mature markets 698, 754
maturing industries 95–6
media companies 474–6, 486–9, 504
mergers 483, 529–30, 544
Metsa-Serla pulp and paper 698
Michelin rubber 367
Microsoft computer software 10–11,
        70, 206, 223, 237, 513
milestones 644, 807
Miller brewing 285
Minnesota Mining and
        Manufacturing Company
        see 3M company
mission
    competitive advantage and 436
    criteria 437
    definition 6, 436, 451
    developing 435–8
    key factors for success and 204
    leadership and 428
    in non-profit organisations
        449–50
    objectives and 583
    organisation structure and 438
    selection of 437
mission statement 16
    at Ford Motor Company 437
Mitsubishi 275
Mitsui 275
mobile telephones 151–2
monitoring see controls
monopolies 557
monopoly rent 223–4, 226

motivation 680–1
motorcycle industry 552–3
Motorola telecommunications
        equipment 546
multidivisional organisation
        structure 672

National health Service (NHS) 48
Nederlandse Spoorwegen (Dutch
        Railways) 210, 211, 214,
        234, 236
negotiation-based strategy
    checklist 589
    elements of 570–1, 576–8
    nature of 74, 587
    rationale 571–4
    see also complementors;
        game-based theories of
        strategy; human resource-based
        theories of strategy
Nestlé foods 38, 174, 176, 206,
        648–50, 656
net cash flow 520, 521
network-based theories of strategy
        688–9
News Corporation 475, 482, 486–90,
        504
niche strategy 127, 154
    see also focus strategy
Nigeria 39
Nike shoes and clothing 208, 387–9
Nippon Paper 698
Nippon Steel 100
Nissan cars 107
NKK/Kawasaki steel 100
Nokia telecommunications 509–10,
        546
non-profit organisations 25–6,
        126–7, 166–7, 180, 183, 214,
        501, 519–20, 525
North American Free Trade
        Association (NAFTA) 26, 707
North Grumman defence 567
Novartis pharmaceuticals and
        chemicals 796–8
Nucor steel 100

objectives
    balancing 16, 441, 451
    coherence and 441
    communicating 642, 645
    corporate 7, 442
    definition 16, 440, 445–6
    development 440–3
    fast changing markets and 645
    implementation and 433–4, 598,
        642–6
    international 537
    setting 642–5
    strategic and financial 307

Oetker foods 125
oil companies 281
Oji Paper 698
operations
    corporate strategy and 322–3,
        334–5
    definition 319–20
    environment and 323–7
    guidelines for 340
    human resources and 333, 335,
        339
    international considerations 582,
        584, 587
    manufacturing and 340
    in service markets 343–5
    technology and 323
    value added and 333
    see also manufacturing
options
    development 21, 175
    environment-based 461,
        466–86
    resource-based 461, 496–500
Orange telephone services 558
organisational culture see culture
organisation change 768
    see also strategic change
organisation structure
    age and 262
    building 666–70
    centralisation 275–6, 599, 600
    co-ordination and 599, 610
    definition 21, 595
    elements of 611–12
    environment and 360–1
    innovation and 612–13, 677–9
    in international companies
        681–2
    leadership and 609
    learning and 605
    motivation and 680–1
    purpose and 352, 354, 357–9,
        426–8, 808
    size and 360
    strategy and 352, 596, 603–7, 611
    types of 671–5
    vaue chain and 606
Owens-Corning glass 770, 773, 780

Pan Am airline 72
Pan-European steel companies 85–6
parenting 443–5, 452
payback period 520, 521
payoffs 574
PepsiCo 664–5
PESTEL analysis 89, 92–3, 94
pharmaceutical industry 201, 247,
    796, 809
Philip Morris tobacco 368, 483
Philippines 39

Philips electronics 206, 409–11,
    412, 719
PIMS Databank 526, 528, 530, 544
planning 16, 535, 536, 659
    see also strategic planning
plans, definition 16
plant capacity 283
PlayStation 243
politics of nation
    attitudes to free trade 851
    global companies and 853
    industry analysis and 850
    macroeconomic analysis and 161
    macro and micro level 852
    role of state and 526, 852
politics of organisation 786–8
    change and 786
polygon of purpose 422, 427, 451
portfolio matrices 140, 142–4
Portsmouth's Millennium Tower
    372–4
Posco steel 100
positioning see competitive
    positioning
prediction
    different levels of 746
    fallacy of 747, 807–8
    purpose of 746
prescriptive strategy 43–5, 74, 204,
    518–24
    advantages 44
    change and 771
    cohesion and 798–9
    concept of 42–3, 46, 53
    evaluation 510–15
    learning and 566
    negotiation and 577
    problems with 45, 535–6
    process 533–5
    survival and 560
    theories of 53–7
    uncertainty and 566
pricing
    basic considerations 182, 185–6
    negotiated deals 183
    target pricing 184–5
    value for money and 181, 183
privatisation 478, 479
process see strategy process
Proctor & Gamble consumer
    products 719
product development 480
Product Portfolio Matrix 142, 155
    see also BCG Matrix; Directional
    policy Matrix
profitability, business units and
    227–8, 526
profit-maximising theories 43, 53–5
public organisations 25, 126
public relations 167

pulp and paper industry 697–700
purpose
    areas of activity and 358
    in conglomerates 422–3
    corporate governance and 377–80
    ethics and 375
    general issues 23, 357–62, 426–8,
        667
    growth and 360
    innovation and 386, 402–9
    knowledge creation and 396
    leadership and 367–72
    polygon of 422, 427
    P–P–O paradigm and 361–2
    re-examination of 808–9
    stakeholders and 360
    strategy dynamics and 737–8
    technology development and 386
    value added and 386
    vision and 363–5
    see also leadership; mission;
        objectives; parenting

quality 128, 205–6, 452
    profit and 447
    strategy 422
    total quality management and
        446, 448, 528
quotas 705

Rank Hovis McDougall (RHM) 52
Raytheon defence equipment 567
RCA electronics 72
Refrigor 538–40, 543, 547
reputation resource 178, 179, 232,
    233–5, 283
research and development strategy
    96, 225, 283
resource-based options
    checklist 495
    cost reduction 496–500
    the resource-based view and 333,
        493–5
    special types of 501–2
    value chain 490–2
    see also financial resources; human
        resources
resource-based theories of strategy
    59, 74
    reasons for development 226–7
resource-based view 226–30, 237–8
    see also resource-based theories
        of strategy
resource change
    early mover advantage 741–2
    imitation pressures 742–3
    over time 739–40
resources
    adding value 8, 212–14
    allocation of 207–8, 646–7

alternative uses for 223
analysis of 20–1, 65, 201, 239
appropriability of 229–30
competitive advantage and
    228–30
different types of 207–8
durability 230
economic rent 222–3
hierarchy of 201, 231
improving resource base 239–41
make-or-buy decision 208–9
prescriptive and emergent issues
    203–4
small and medium-sized
    enterprises 237–8
sustainable competitive advantage
    232–5
upgrading 241
restaurant industry 687
retailers, European 75
retained profits 283, 287–8, 291
return on capital employed (ROCE)
    520, 521
return on investment 528–9
reward
    definition 16
    systems 860
Ricardian rent 223, 225
risk
    evaluation criteria 24, 514–15
    financial issues and 303
    in global TV 475
    resource allocation and 647
Riva steel 87, 100
Roche pharmaceuticals 324, 483,
    809–11
Rolls Royce cars 225
Royal Dutch Shell oil 206, 250–3,
    579
rules of the game see game-based
    theories of strategy
Ryanair airline 27, 29, 31–2

Saab defence equipment 568
Sabena airline 27, 29
Sail steel 100
Sainsbury retailing 177, 236
sale of assets 289, 291, 312
Sandoz pharmaceuticals and
    chemicals 796
Sappi paper 698
SAS airline 27–8, 31
Saudi Arabia 39
Scandinavian Airlines 31
SCA pulp and paper 127, 304–5,
    698–9, 708–11
scenario analysis 93–4
Schoeller foods 173
Schumpeterian rents 223
scientific management 323

Scottish & Newcastle brewing 285
sensitivity analysis 515
service operations 326, 333, 343–5
service strategy 128, 138, 344
Seven S framework 795, 800–6, 813
Severstal (Cherepovets) steel 100
shareholders 283, 287, 360, 376–7
    see also stakeholders
shareholder value added
    calculation of 302–3, 523
    concept 301
    future strategy for 303
    problems with 303–4
share issues 288, 291
Sharp electronics 233, 235
Shell Oil see Royal Dutch Shell oil
short-term debt 283, 287, 289, 291
Singapore 39, 149, 206, 450, 567
Skandia insurance company 392–3
Skyways (Sweden) 31
slow-moving markets dynamics
    753–4
small business
    objectives of 686
    resources and 501, 503
SmithKline Beecham pharmaceuticals
    106, 202, 796
Smurfitt Stone Paper 698
socio-cultural theories of strategy
    58–9
Sony electronics and media 10, 242,
    475, 593–5
South Africa 39, 149
South African breweries 285
Spain 449
Spillers foods 45, 46–7, 52–3
staff 680–1
    see also human resource-based
    theories of strategy
stakeholder options evaluation
    criteria 515
stakeholders 306, 360, 376, 422,
    515–16, 582
    analysis 429–32
    co-operatives and 449–50
    international 449–50
Stanard Chartered Bank (StanChart)
    788–90
steel industry 99–101, 107, 121
stock control 338
Stora Enso pulp and paper 698–9
strategic business alliances 483–5,
    723–4
strategic business units (SBUs) 524,
    533, 535
strategic change
    in British Petroleum 263–5
    causes of 768–9
    concepts of 763–7
    definition 265, 763, 764–5

emergent 776–82
five factors theory of 777–9
managing the process 607, 761
in merchant banking 788
organisation structure and 267–9
politics and 250, 786–8
prescriptive 771–4
pressure points for 266, 269, 765–6
programme 783–8
resistance to 786
time costs of 767
strategic decisions, key elements
    10–11
strategic fit 610, 614, 621
strategic options see options
strategic planning 46, 650–6
    at Canon 639–42
    reasons for failure 652
    in small companies 654–5
    status of 652–3
    styles of 653–4
Strategic Planning Institute 526
strategy
    analysis of 15–16
    attack 137
    coherence in 778, 804, 805
    core areas 15–17
    definition 6, 17
    designing structures to fit 598–9,
        806
    development 15, 22, 65, 461
    dynamics see dynamics of strategy
    evaluation 520
    historical foundations 39
    as history 68–9, 554
    relationship of elements 554–5
    tests of good strategy 24–5, 32–3
strategy content 17
    context and process relationship
        553–5
    criteria on 510–15
        see also financial appraisal of
        strategy
    empirical evidence for 525
    procedures 518–24
strategy context 17, 553, 586
    importance of 553–6
    problems with 555
strategy process 18–20, 553, 608
    chaos-based 556
    coherence and contention 80,
        778, 804
    combining elements 18–21
    definition 508
    implementation 65, 634–8
    learning-based 556, 578–81
    negotiation-based 556, 570–7
    prescriptive 533–7
    survival-based 556, 560–3
    uncertainty-based 563–6

structure *see* organisation structure
stuck in the middle 470
style
    of organisation 21–2, 27, 128, 621
    theories of leadership 368
substitutes 104, 106–7, 229
suitability criterion 511, 516, 544
Sumitomo Metal 100
superordinate goals *see* vision
suppliers
    bargaining power of 103, 104
    relationships with 336
survival, purpose and 427–8
survival-based theories of strategy
        60–1, 65, 560–1, 586
    consequences of 74, 562–3
sustainable competitive advantage
        see competitive advantage
Swiss Air 27–8
SWOT analysis 114, 461, 464–6,
        494, 511, 534
synergy 128, 154

tacit knowledge 391–2, 743
tariffs 705
Tate & Lyle sugar and starch 726–9
team working 139, 776
technology strategy 127, 138,
        323–7, 400–3
    change and 768, 770
    competitive advantage and 400–2
    development 409
    discontinuities 324–5
    innovation 416
    new technologies and 399–400
    operations and 323–4
    see also information technology
        strategy
Telecom Italia 558
telecommunications 557–60
Telefonica de Espagna 558
television companies 474–6
Tesco retailing 206
tests of 'good' strategy 23–5
Thailand 326

Thyssen Krupp Stahl steel company
        87, 100
'tiger' economies 149
time and purpose 475
Time Warner media 475
Toshiba electronics 235
total quality management (TQM)
        446–7, 448, 453
tourism industry 372–4
Toyota cars 107, 206, 225, 228, 233,
        327–30, 333, 338
trade *see* world trade
trade blocks 707, 731
trait theories of leadership 368
transnational organisation structures
        718–20
turbulence of environment 91

UK 449, 486, 567, 573
uncertainty-based theories of
        strategy
    consequences 61, 564–6
    nature of 62, 65, 244–5, 563–4,
        586
Unilever 124–5, 130, 150, 166, 175,
        180, 183, 719
    strategic leadership at 530–2
United Biscuits 774–6, 782
United Technologies defence 567
Universal media and records 475,
        749
upgrading resources 241
UPM/Kymmene paper and pulp
        698–9
USA 28, 39, 449, 707
Usinor steel 87, 90, 100, 104,
        128, 206
US steel 100

validity criterion 511, 516
value added
    improving 221
    international 696
    purpose and 427
    resource analysis and 212–15

resource options and 490–2
    strategic implications 15, 215
    upstream and downstream 490–2
value chain
    definition 216–18, 222
    linkages 11, 218, 220–2
    operations and 503, 606
    resources and 201, 490–2
value system 216, 218–19
vertical integration 128, 154
Viacom media 475
Virgin airline 29
vision 11, 21, 22, 65
    core competences 363
    criteria for 364
    link with market opportunities
        and 488
    superordinate goals 364
Viveni Universal 475
Vodaphone mobile telephones
        584–6

warfare strategies 134–9
Web strategy at Boo.com 131–2
weighted average cost of capital
        (WACC) 295, 312
Weyerhauser & MacMillan Bloedel
        paper 698
World Bank 149, 703, 731
world trade
    analysis 152–3
    barriers to 705
    C–C–B Paradigm 695–7
    definitions 700–1
    development of 41, 700–5
    institutions 705–8
    theories of 701–5, 730–1
World Trade Organisation (WTO)
        706

Xbox (Microsoft) 11, 242–3
Xerox (Europe) 276–9
Xerox (US) 223, 407, 639

Zantac 106, 214, 412, 480